THE ACTS OF THE APOSTLES

VOLUME III

The Text of Acts

F. J. Foakes Jackson and Kirsopp Lake

THE BEGINNINGS OF CHRISTIANITY

THE BEGINNINGS
OF CHRISTIANITY

PART I
THE ACTS OF THE APOSTLES

EDITED BY

F. J. FOAKES JACKSON, D.D.

AND

KIRSOPP LAKE, D.D.

VOL. III

THE TEXT OF ACTS

BY

JAMES HARDY ROPES

BAKER BOOK HOUSE
Grand Rapids, Michigan

Paperback edition issued 1979
by Baker Book House Company

ISBN: 0-8010-5084-7 (set)

PHOTOLITHOPRINTED BY CUSHING - MALLOY, INC.
ANN ARBOR, MICHIGAN, UNITED STATES OF AMERICA
1 9 7 9

TO

MY WIFE

FIERI autem omnino non potest ut unius hominis industria editio novi testamenti historiae ut ita dicam fide adornata perficiatur. nam etiam libris edendis eam legem scriptam esse didici ut lente festinetur, ne dum omnia simul assequi velis nihil assequaris.

Id ago ut theologis apparatum non quidem locupletem sed pro humanarum virium infirmitate certissimum congeram.

PAUL DE LAGARDE (1857).

PREFACE

THE study of the textual criticism of the New Testament, like that of the kindred science of palaeontology, rests on morphology, but necessarily expands into an historical inquiry. Without an adequate history of the text the determination of that text remains insecure. But textual history has also intrinsic value, for it is a true, though minor, branch of Church history. As an account of the development of one phase of the life and activity of the Church it is significant for its own sake, and not unworthy to take a place beside the history of liturgies or creeds or vestments. Not only does it abundantly illustrate the history of biblical exegesis, but in it many characteristic traits of the thought and aspiration of successive ages may be studied from original sources.

These considerations have been in mind in preparing the present volume, and especially in the Introductory Essay ; and a summary sketch of the textual history of the Book of Acts, so far as present knowledge permits, has been offered on pp. ccxc-ccxcvii. Every part of the section on the Sources of Knowledge for the text will reveal how wide is the range of general history, both sacred and secular, into contact with which the student of textual history is brought. Some of the specific tasks as yet unperformed which are requisite to a completer knowledge of textual history and a securer confidence in the results of textual criticism are mentioned at the close of the Essay.

The large space occupied in this volume by the discussion of the text called ' Western ' (for which it is unfortunate that no better name should be at hand) might seem excessive in view of

the conclusion here presented that that text is inferior to the
text found in the Old Uncials, or even in the mass of later manuscripts.   But in fact the creation of the 'Western' text was the
most important event in the history of the text of Acts, and the
recovery of it, so far as that is practicable, from the many corrupt
documents in which its fragments now repose is an essential
preliminary to a sound judgment on the textual criticism of the
book.   That the 'Western' text, if, as I hold, not the work of
the original author of Acts, was a definite rewriting, rather than
an accumulation of miscellaneous variants, ought not to have
been doubted, and that for two reasons.   In the first place, it has
an unmistakably homogeneous internal character.   Secondly, its
hundreds or thousands of variants are now known to have arisen
in a brief period, scarcely, if at all, longer than the fifty years
after the book first passed into circulation.   In that period a
pedigree of successive copies was short, and to produce so many
variants the mere natural licence of copyists would be insufficient.
And since one rewriting would suffice, any theory that more than
one took place in those years would seem to fall under the con-
demnation of Occam's razor.   Of course the 'Western' text,
once produced, was liable to modification and enlargement, and
the Bezan form, in which it is most commonly read, while invaluable, is full of corruptions, but a full study of the evidence
contained in this volume and elsewhere is likely to bring conviction that a definite 'Western' text, whether completely
recoverable in its original form or not, once actually existed.

If the 'Western' text had never been created, the problem
of the textual criticism of the New Testament would have been
relatively easy, and the variants not unduly numerous.   Textual
history, in nearly all its more difficult phases, is the story of a
long series of combinations of the 'Western' text with its rival,
the text best known to us from the Old Uncials and the Bohairic
version.   One of these combinations, for which I have used the
name 'Antiochian,' became the text most widely employed
throughout the later Christian centuries.   Nevertheless, if the

' Western ' text had not been created, although the critic's task
would be easier, we should be the poorer, for those fragments of
its base, which it enshrines like fossils in an enveloping rock-mass,
would probably have perished, and we should have lost these
evidences of a good. text of extreme antiquity, vastly nearer
in date to the original autographs than any of our Greek
manuscripts.

With regard to the ' Western ' text itself the most interesting
idea that I have been able to bring forward seems to me one
worthy of further discussion, but hardly susceptible of direct
proof, although it may be possible to show that as an hypothesis
it fits well all the known facts, and would elucidate some otherwise perplexing problems.   I refer to the suggestion that the
preparation of the ' Western ' text, which took place early in the
second century, perhaps at Antioch, was incidental to the work
of forming the collection of Christian writings for general Church
use which ultimately, somewhat enlarged, became the New Testament ; in a word, that the ' Western ' text was the text of the
primitive ' canon ' (if the term may be pardoned in referring to
so early a date), and was expressly created for that purpose.
Such a theory is recommended by its aptness to explain both the
wide spread of the ' Western ' text in the second century, as if
issued from some authoritative centre, and its gradual disappearance from general use thereafter, as well as its inferiority, when
judged by internal evidence.   That this conception would throw
a direct light on certain dark places in the history of the New
Testament canon is at once manifest.   It is probably inconsistent
with some current hypotheses and conclusions in that field, since
it would require the admission that at the date of the rewriting
those rewritten books already formed a collection ; but it may
be remarked that in any case the very act of making a rewritten
text of these books must of itself have produced a kind of
collection.   On the side, however, of the history of the canon
by virtue of which it appears as a topic in the history of Christian
dogma rather than of Christian antiquities and usages, the theory

here proposed does not seem to run counter to any views commonly held by scholars.

If the 'Western' text was a revision made in the first half of the second century, it is a monument of the life and thought of that period, an historical source, although one not easily reconstructed with completeness and accuracy. It is more difficult to study than the contemporary Apostolic Fathers, but not less worthy of attention than they are.

The plan of the text and apparatus of this volume is set forth fully in the Explanatory Note following the Introductory Essay. What is offered is neither a fresh text nor a complete apparatus, but rather a selection of important material and a series of investigations in the form partly of apparatus, partly of textual notes. The time for making a satisfactory new critical text does not appear to me to have yet arrived, and although—often with reasons given—I have fully stated the readings in which, with varying degrees of confidence, I am disposed to believe Codex Vaticanus wrong, that is a very different thing from propounding a complete new text, with the necessary decision of innumerable questions of orthography, punctuation, and typography, as well as of the body of words to be included. In the nature of the case a new text could not at present lay claim to finality, and the only certainty about it would seem to be that it never existed until its author, the critic, created it.

In the several apparatus the aim has been clearness and simplicity, and with that in view much has been omitted that finds appropriate place in a complete thesaurus of readings. Even so, the apparatus are complicated enough. They are intended to afford a knowledge of the variation within limited range manifested by the chief Greek 'Old Uncial' authorities, and a definite notion of the oldest form of the 'Antiochian' text, preserved as it is with singular exactness in the manuscripts. For the 'Western' text, in consequence of the highly mixed character of nearly all the witnesses, equal completeness in the apparatus of these pages is impracticable. Whether there ever was an ' Alexandrian ' revision of the text of Acts is uncertain, but that question also can be studied in the Old Uncial apparatus and in the exhibition of the Bohairic version given in Appendix V.

To the Appendices, in which the ingredient readings of the four chief versions are set forth in full, special attention is asked. These tables give in a different arrangement, and with careful analysis of relevant attestation, most of the information about the four versions which is usually included in a textual apparatus to Acts, and they will serve some purposes of study better than the ordinary plan. It is a pity that the Armenian and Georgian and Ethiopic versions could not also have been analysed.

The concluding portion of the volume consists of a translation of the full Commentary of Ephrem Syrus on the Book of Acts, made for the present use by the late Dr. Frederick C. Conybeare, whose acuteness and learning detected the existence of this work in an Armenian MS. at Vienna. The lamented death of this eminent and beloved scholar prevented him from seeing his work in its final printed form, but the first proof had been revised by him, and I am confident that what is here offered is not unworthy of the memory of the generous friend who so often, as here, put other scholars under obligation. The translation both of the Commentary and of the accompanying Catena-extracts has been compared with the original Armenian by the self-denying labour of my colleague, Professor Robert P. Blake of Harvard University.

It remains to express gratitude to many who have helped me. The Editors of *The Beginnings of Christianity* have followed the preparation of the work with constant and sympathetic aid, and I am indebted to my colleague, Professor Lake, not only for the original proposal and for a large share in the development of the plan, but for innumerable valuable suggestions, incisive criticisms, wise counsels, and cheerful encouragement. Sir Herbert Thompson's characteristic kindness and accurate scholarship have supplied, through his collations of the Sahidic and Bohairic versions, knowledge which was not otherwise accessible, and the Appendices drawn from his work make it possible to approach the Egyptian versions with confidence in a way which has not hitherto been open to New Testament scholars. My colleague, Professor Henry J. Cadbury, has rendered admirable service in the laborious task of collating the Vulgate and the Peshitto.   From Professor F. C. Burkitt, Professor Alexander Souter, and Professor Charles C. Torrey I have received much valuable aid, and likewise from Professor Paul Diels of Breslau, Professor James A. Montgomery and Professor Max L. Margolis of Philadelphia, and Professor J. E. Frame of New York.   To the great courtesy of Mgr. G. Mercati I owe information which he alone could give.   For wise advice, which contributed fundamentally to better the general plan of the volume, I have to thank honoured friends—Professor von Dobschütz, Professor Jülicher, Dean H. J. White of Christ Church, Dean J. Armitage Robinson of Wells, Professor George Foot Moore ; and to Professor C. H. Turner and the Oxford University Press I owe the kind permission to use the text of *Novum Testamentum Sancti Irenaei.*

To the devoted and efficient aid of Miss Edith M. Coe, who has assisted in the work through its whole progress, every reader will be indebted as long as the book is used ; and it would be ungrateful indeed not to express appreciation of the remarkable skill and large knowledge which have enabled the printers to solve the complicated problem of clear arrangement of the pages of text and apparatus.

In spite of the accurate work of the printers and of much pains taken to secure correctness of statement and of citation, it is inevitable that a work like this should contain errors. I shall be much obliged to any reader who may find such and will take the trouble to send them to me.

JAMES HARDY ROPES.

HARVARD UNIVERSITY,
  May 25, 1925.

CONTENTS

xiii

CONTENTS

THE TEXT OF ACTS

I. THE SOURCES OF KNOWLEDGE FOR THE TEXT

1. GREEK MANUSCRIPTS [1]

§ 1. LISTS

(a) UNCIALS [2]

Century III. or IV.

Pap 29. Oxyrhynch. 1597.
  Acts xxvi. 7-8, 20. Text in *Oxyrhynchus Papyri*, vol. XIII.,
  1919.

Century IV.

B (δ 1). Codex Vaticanus. Rome, Vatican Library, gr. 1209.
Pap 8 (*a* 8). Berlin, Altes und Neues Museum, Aegypt. Abth., P
  8683.

---

[1] In the account of the Greek manuscripts of Acts here given it is not intended in general to repeat the information given in Gregory's ' Prolegomena ' to Tischendorf, *Novum Testamentum Graece, editio octava*, Leipzig, 1894, and in the same writer's *Textkritik des Neuen Testamentes*, Leipzig, 1900–1909. In referring to minuscule codices, and to the less familiar uncials, the later numbering of Gregory will be followed, as found in his *Griechische Handschriften des Neuen Testaments*, Leipzig, 1908, and (less conveniently) in his *Textkritik*, vol. iii., 1909. The earlier numbering, from the list in the Prolegomena, will sometimes be indicated, with the word ' formerly.' The numbers of von Soden's list, when referred to, are recognizable by the prefixed Greek letter δ or *a*, or the symbol O or A$^{\pi\rho}$ with a superior figure.

[2] The determination of the century is in some cases open to doubt. For instance, V. Gardthausen, *Griechische Paläographie*, 2nd ed., vol. ii., 1913, pp. 122-134, holds confidently, against many other scholars, that Codex Sinaiticus was written in the fifth, not in the fourth century.

Acts iv. 31-37 ; v. 2-9 ; vi. 1-6, 8-15. Text in Gregory, *Textkritik*, pp. 1087-1090.

057. Berlin, Altes und Neues Museum, Aegypt. Abth., P 9808. Acts iii. 5, 6, 10-12.

Century IV. or V.

א (δ 2). Codex Sinaiticus, Petrograd, Public Library, 259.

0165. Berlin, Altes und Neues Museum, Aegypt. Abth., P 271. Acts iii. 24-iv. 13, 17-20. Text in Gregory, *Textkritik*, pp. 1369 f.

Century V.

048 (ב ; *a* 1). Rome, Vatican Library, gr. 2061. Acts xxvi. 4-xxvii. 10; xxviii. 2-31. Palimpsest. Written in three columns.

066 (I^2 ; *a* 1000). Petrograd, Public Library, gr. VI. II. 4. Acts xxviii. 8 νος—ιεροσολυμων 17. Palimpsest. Text in Tischendorf, *Monumenta sacra inedita*, vol. i. pp. 43 f.

077. Sinai, Monastery of St. Catherine. (Harris, No. 5.) Acts xiii. 28-29. Text in *Studia Sinaitica*, ɪ., 1894, p. 98, No. 5.

0166 (*a* 1017). Heidelberg, Papyrus-Sammlung, 1357. Acts xxviii. 30-31. Text in A. Deissmann, *Die Septuaginta-papyri und andere altchristliche Texte der Heidelberger Papyrus-sammlung*, 1905, p. 85.

0175. Florence, Società Italiana. Oxyrhynchus fragment. Acts vi. 7-15. Text in *Papiri greci e latini*, vol. ɪɪ., 1913, No. 125.

Century V. or VI.

A (δ 4). Codex Alexandrinus, London, British Museum, Royal Library I. D. V-VIII.

C (δ 3). Codex Ephraemi, Paris, Bibliothèque Nationale, gr. 9. Acts i. 2 πνευματος—εις την iv. 3 ; v. 35 ειπεν—και νεκρων x. 42 ; xiii. 1 ος μαναην—εν ειρηνη xvi. 36 ; xx. 10 λων αυτου—αι θυραι xxi. 30 ; xxii. 21 και ειπεν—προς τον

χιλιαρ ; xxiv. 15 πιδα εχων—απειθης τη xxvi. 19 ; xxvii.
16 φης ην αραντες—ουκ ειασεν xxviii. 4. Not quite two-
thirds of Acts extant. Palimpsest. Text in Tischendorf,
Codex Ephraemi Syri, Leipzig, 1843.

D (δ 5). Codex Bezae. Cambridge, University Library, 2. 41.
Graeco-Latin. Acts i. 1-viii. 29 ; x. 14-xxi. 2 ; xxi. 10-16 ;
xxi. 18-xxii. 10 ; xxii. 20-29. Reconstruction from trustworthy sources of xxi. 16-18 (and the Latin of the obverse)
in J. H. Ropes, ' Three Papers on the Text of Acts,' *Harvard
Theological Review*, vol. xvi., 1923, pp. 163-168, see also pp.
392-394.

076. Norfolk, England, Collection of Lord Amherst of Hackney.
Acts ii. 11-12. Text in Grenfell and Hunt, *The Amherst
Papyri*, i. No. VIII.

Century VI.

093 (a 1013). Cambridge, University Library, Taylor-Schechter
Collection.
Acts xxiv. 22-26, 27. Palimpsest. Text in C. Taylor,
*Hebrew-Greek Cairo Genizah Palimpsests from the Taylor-
Schechter Collection*, 1900, pp. 94 f.

Wess[59 c]. Vienna, parchment fragment, partly Sahidic, partly
Greek.
Acts ii. 1-5. Text in C. Wessely, *Griechische und koptische
Texte theologischen Inhalts* ii. (Studien zur Paläographie
und Papyruskunde; Heft 11), 1911, No. 59 c.

Century VI. or VII.

E (a 1001). Codex Laudianus. Oxford, Bodleian Library,
laud. 35.
Acts i. 1 τον μεν—παυλος xxvi. 29 ; xxviii. 26 πορευθητι—
ακωλυτως xxviii. 31. Contains Acts alone (Greek and Latin).
Text in Tischendorf, *Monumenta sacra inedita*, vol. ix., 1870.

Pap 33 (Pap Wess[190]). Vienna, leaf from papyrus codex.
Acts xv. 22-24, 27-32. Text in C. Wessely, *Griechische und*

koptische Texte theologischen Inhalts iii. (Studien zur Paläographie und Papyruskunde, Heft 12), 1912, No. 190 (Litterarischer theologischer Text No. 25).

Century VII.

095 (G ; *a* 1002). Petrograd, Public Library, gr. 17.

Acts ii. 45-iii. 8. See Tischendorf, *Notitia editionis codicis Sinaitici*, 1869, p. 50, and Tischendorf, *Novum Testamentum graece*, ed. octava, apparatus, *ad loc.*

096 (I⁵ ; *a* 1004). Petrograd, Public Library, gr. 19.

Acts ii. 6-17 ; xxvi. 7-18. Palimpsest. Text in Tischendorf, *Monumenta sacra inedita*, vol. i. pp. 37 f., 41 f.

097 (I⁶ ; *a* 1003). Petrograd, Public Library, gr. 18.

Acts xiii. 39-46. Palimpsest. Text in Tischendorf, *Monumenta sacra inedita*, vol. i. pp. 39 f.

Century VIII.

0123 (formerly Apl 70 b ; *a* 1014). Petrograd, Public Library, gr. 49.

Acts ii. 22, 26-28, 45-47 ; iii. 1-2.

Century VIII. or IX.

S (049 ; *a* 2). Athos, Laura, A 88.

Mutilated in Acts i. 11-14, xii. 15-19, xiii. 1-3. Photograph in the J. Pierpont Morgan Collection, Harvard College Library.

Ψ (044 ; δ 6). Athos, Laura, B 52 (earlier, 172).[1]

Photograph in the J. Pierpont Morgan Collection, Harvard College Library.

Century IX.

H (014 ; *a* 6). Modena, Biblioteca Estense, [CXCVI] II. G. 3.

Acts v. 28 και βουλεσθε—πασαι ix. 39 ; x. 19 ανδρες—μεν

---

[1] On Codex Ψ see K. Lake, *Journal of Theological Studies*, vol. i., 1899-1900, pp. 290-292 ; *Texts from Mt. Athos* (also in *Studia Biblica et Ecclesiastica*, v., 1902, pp. 89-185).

γαρ xiii. 36 ; xiv. 3 γινεσθαι—τυχειν xxvii. 3. Contained
Acts alone, without Catholic Epistles, which have been
supplied in hand of fifteenth or sixteenth century. Readings
in Tregelles' apparatus.

L (020 ; a 5). Rome, Biblioteca Angelica, A. 2. 15.
Acts viii. 10 μις του θεου—ακωλυτως xxviii. 31. Readings
in Tregelles' apparatus.

P (025 ; a 3). Petrograd, Public Library, 225.
Palimpsest. Acts ii. 13 εισι—ακωλυτως xxviii. 31. Text
in Tischendorf, *Monumenta sacra inedita*, vol. vi. pp. 89-248.

0120 (G[b] ; a 1005). Rome, Vatican Library, gr. 2302.
Acts xvi. 30-xvii. 17 ; xvii. 27-29, 31-34 ; xviii. 8-26.
Palimpsest. Text in J. Cozza, *Sacrorum bibliorum vetustis-
sima fragmenta Graeca et Latina e codicibus Cryptoferratensi-
bus eruta*, iii. Rome, 1877, pp. cxxi-cxxxiv ; and Gregory,
Textkritik, p. 1078.

1874 (formerly Apl 261 ; a 7). Sinai, Monastery of St. Catherine,
273.

Century X.

056 (formerly 16 ; O[7]). Paris, Bibliothèque Nationale, coisl. gr.
26.

0140. Sinai, Monastery of St. Catherine. (Harris, No. 41.)
Fragment. See *Studia Sinaitica*, i., London, 1894, p. 116.

0142 (formerly 46 ; O[6]). Munich, Staatsbibliothek, gr. 375.

Century XI. or XII. (?)

Pap Wess[237]. Vienna, K 7541-7548.
Acts xvii. 28-xviii. 2 ; xviii. 24-27 ; xix. 1-8, 13-19 ; xx.
9-16, 22-28 ; xx. 35-xxi. 4 ; xxii. 11-14, 16-17. Eight
leaves of Greek and Sahidic bilingual papyrus codex. Text
in C. Wessely, *Griechische und koptische Texte theologischen
Inhalts* iv. (Studien zur Paläographie und Papyruskunde,
Heft 15), 1914, No. 237 ; also below in Appendix I., pp.
271-275.

(b) Minuscules

The above-named MSS. of Acts are all uncials. Four are papyri. In addition, the following minuscules may be specially mentioned :

33 (formerly 13^{ac} ; δ 48). Paris, Bibliothèque Nationale, gr. 14 (formerly colbert. 2844).

Ninth or tenth century. "The queen of the cursives." Readings in Tregelles' apparatus.

81 (formerly 61^{ac} ; a 162 ; p^{scr}). London, British Museum, add. 20,003.

A.D. 1044. Acts i. 1-4, 8 ; vii. 17-xvii. 28 ; xxiii. 9-28, 31. About three-quarters of Acts extant. Another portion of this codex, containing the Catholic and Pauline epistles, is 1288 (formerly 241^{ac} 285^{paul} ; a 162), Cairo, Patriarchal Library, 59 (formerly 351). Readings of Acts in Tregelles' apparatus, and in Scrivener, *Codex Augiensis*.

462 (formerly 101^{ac} ; a 359). Moscow, Synodal Library, Wladimir 24, Sabbas 348, Matthäi 333.

Thirteenth century. Readings in Matthäi, *S. Lucae Actus Apostolorum graece et latine*, Riga, 1782, with the symbol ' f.'

614 (formerly 137^{ac} ; a 364). Milan, Biblioteca Ambrosiana, E. 97 sup.

Thirteenth century (eleventh century ?). Photograph in the J. Pierpont Morgan Collection, Harvard College Library.

383 (formerly 58^{ac} ; a 353). Oxford, Bodleian Library, clark. 9.

Thirteenth century. Readings of Acts in A. Pott, *Der abendländische Text der Apostelgeschichte und die Wir-quelle*, 1900, pp. 78-88.

102 (formerly 99^{ac} ; a 499). Moscow, Synodal Library, Wladimir 412, Sabbas 5, Matthäi 5.

A.D. 1345 (1445 ?). Collation in Matthäi, *S. Lucae Actus Apostolorum graece et latine*, Riga, 1782, with the symbol ' c.'

69 (formerly 31^{ac}; δ **505**; m^{scr}). Leicester, England, Library of Town Council.

Fifteenth century. Readings in Tregelles' apparatus.

The minuscule Greek manuscripts which contain Acts number upwards of 500 copies. The following tables (which include also most of the uncial codices and fragments) are drawn from the classification reached by Hermann von Soden, *Die Schriften des Neuen Testaments, I. Teil: Untersuchungen*, 1902–1910, pp. 1653 f., 1686-1688, 1760, 2162 f., 2172-2174. From this classification must proceed all future investigation of the text found in the minuscules. In the enumeration the numbers preceded by the Greek letter δ (for διαθήκη) refer to manuscripts containing the Gospels, Acts, and Epistles (with or without the Apocalypse). Numbers without preceding Greek letter do not contain the Gospels, and are those to which in von Soden's catalogue (pp. 215-248) the Greek letter *a* is prefixed. The designation A^{πρ} refers to manuscripts in which the text of Acts is accompanied by the catena of 'Andreas.' O^{πρ} designates a manuscript containing with the text the commentary ascribed to 'Oecumenius.'

In the columns headed 'Formerly' are given the numbers (in the list of MSS. of Acts and Catholic Epistles) of Gregory's 'Prolegomena' to Tischendorf, *Novum Testamentum graece*, editio octava, 1890, pp. 617-652, and Gregory's *Textkritik des Neuen Testamentes*, vol. i., 1900, pp. 263-294; in the columns headed 'Gregory' the numbers of Gregory's final list, to be found in his *Griechische Handschriften des Neuen Testaments*, 1908, as well as in the 'Nachtrag' which constitutes *Textkritik*, volume iii., 1909. These last-mentioned numbers are employed consistently in the present volume to designate the minuscules and all except the better known of the uncials.

Brackets are here used to connect the numbers of manuscripts said by von Soden to be closely akin to one another, or even in some cases to constitute pairs of sister manuscripts.

It will be remembered that von Soden's system of enumeration is as follows :

δ 1–49	} before end of ninth century
a 1–49	
a 1000–1019	before end of tenth century
δ 50–99	} tenth century
a 50–99	
δ 100–199	
a 100–199	} eleventh century
a 1100–1119	
δ 200–299	
a 200–299	} twelfth century
a 1200–1219	
δ 300–399	
a 300–399	} thirteenth century
a 1300–1319	

and similarly for later centuries.

Von Soden's Classification

H (Hesychius)

(arranged approximately in order of date)

von Soden.	Formerly.	Gregory.
δ 1	B	03
δ 2	ℵ	01
δ 3	C	04
δ 4	A	02
δ 6	Ψ	044
8	ʼ	Pap 8
δ 48	13	33
1002	G	095
1004	I⁵	096
74	389	1175
103 }	25	104
104 }	89	459
162	61	81
257	33	326
δ 371	290	1241

I (Ierosolyma)

Von Soden's designation of I^a forms the largest division of the I-group; I^{b1} and I^{b2} are two sections of a distinct sub-group I^b; likewise I^{c1} and I^{c2} are sections of an equally distinct sub-group I^c. In each list the MSS. are arranged approximately in the order of their value as preserving in von Soden's opinion the original type of their section.

$$I^a$$

von Soden.	Formerly.	Gregory.
δ 5	D	05
7 ⎫	apl 261	1874
264 ⎬	233	917
200 ⎫	83	88
382 ⎬	231	915
70 ⎫	505	1898
101 ⎬	40	181
1001	E	08
252 ⎫	391	1873
δ 251 ⎬	271	927
δ 459 ⎭	195	489
δ 203 ⎫	265	808
δ 300 ⎬	65	218
δ 157 ⎫	202	547
δ 507 ⎬	104	241
397 ⎫	96	460
106 ⎬	179	177
158 ⎭	395	1245
184	..	2143
193	239	1270
261	142	618
205	51	337
δ 453 ⎫	5	5
367 ⎬	308	1827
173 ⎭	156	623
δ 254[1] ⎫	1	1
δ 457 ⎬	95	209
δ 500 ⎭	93	205

[1] Codex δ 254 is the one described by von Soden, p. 104, under the designation δ 50; see his volume i., ' Ergänzungen und Verbesserungen,' p. xi.

von Soden.	Formerly.	Gregory.
554	238	2288
1100 ⎫	310	1829
55 ⎭	236	920
δ 180 ⎫	1319	1319
δ 355 ⎭	19	38
δ 505	31	69
502	116	467
552	217	642
251	326	1843
175	319	1838
192	318	1837
170	303	1311
464	218	1522
δ 454	262	794
172	73	436
δ 156	108	226
1202	249	1526
56	316	1835
64	328	1845
152	388	1162
168	226	910
202	309	1828
361	248	1525
δ 268	180	431
$A^{\pi\rho}$ 10	502	1895
$A^{\pi\rho}$ 11 ⎫	15	307
$A^{\pi\rho}$ 20 ⎭	36	36[a]
$A^{\pi\rho}$ 12	74	437
$A^{\pi\rho}$ 21	130	610
$A^{\pi\rho}$ 40	81	453
$A^{\pi\rho}$ 41	..	1678

I^{b1}

62	498	1891
δ 602	200	522
365	214	206
396 ⎫	..	1758
472 ⎭	312	1831

von Soden.	Formerly.	Gregory.
398	69	429
δ 206 ⎱	105	242
δ 264 ⎰	201	536
δ 414	..	2200
δ 152 ⎱	196	491
δ 368 ⎰	266	823
270 ⎱	54	43
306 ⎰	119	469
253 ⎱	2	2
δ 600 ⎰	124	296
161	173	635
δ 360	197	496
368	344	1099
490	382	1868
461	163	630
275	..	2194
567	207	592

$$I^{b2}$$

78 ⎱	..	1739
171 ⎰	7	2298
157	29	323
δ 260 ⎱	111	440
469 ⎰	215	216
δ 356	6	6
209 ⎱	386	1872
δ 370 ⎰	288	1149
76	403	1880
δ 309	14	35
550	27	322

$$I^{b} \text{ (not identifiable as } I^{b1} \text{ or } I^{b2})$$

1000	I^2	066
1003	I^6	097

$$I^{c1}$$

208	307	1611
370	353	1108

von Soden.	Formerly.	Gregory.
116	..	2138
551	216	1518

I^{c2}

364	137	614
353	58	383
δ 299	..	2147
466	302	257
470	229	913
486	..	1765
258	56	378
487	..	1717
506	60	385
69	221	221
169	192	639
114	335	1852
174	252	255
δ 101	199	506
154	381	1867
471 }	313	1832
356 }	224	876
503 }	139	616
δ 298 }	43	76

I^c (not identifiable as I^{c1} or I^{c2})

$O^{\pi\rho}$ 20	232	916

K (koinē)

Virtually all the Greek MSS. of Acts not comprised in the above lists (types H and I) are known, or believed, to present in greater or less purity the K-text. Some of these contain in varying degrees a weak infusion of I-readings. Two groups, distinguished by special selections of such readings as well as in other ways, are designated K^c ('complutensis') and K^r ('revidierte'). The following lists, arranged approximately in order of date, include the oldest codices of the K-type and the K^r-type, and all those assigned by von Soden to the K^c-type. Mention of many others will be found in von Soden, *Die Schriften des Neuen Testaments*, pp. 1760 f., 2162 f., 2172-2174.

K

von Soden.	Formerly.	Gregory.
. .	Ϛ	093
2	S	049
3	P	025
5	L	020
6	H	014
47	323	1841
48	112	2125
50	. .	1760
51	17	93
52	86	456
53	160	627
54	384	1870
61	122	602
67	87	457
72	334	1851
75	394	1244
δ 95	41	175
δ 97	285	1073

and upwards of 250 other codices of the eleventh and later centuries.

K^c

107	42	42
186	223	223
δ 255	35	57
271	. .	2115
δ 359	193	479
δ 364	32	51
δ 365 ⎫	57	234
δ 375 ⎬	. .	1594
δ 376 ⎭	194	483

von Soden.	Formerly.	Gregory.
δ 366	164	390
366	228	912
395	..	1753
δ 410	206	582
450	..	1766
555	305	1405
557	331	1848

The above list includes all the codices assigned by von Soden to the group K^c.

$$K^r$$

δ 269	300	1251
δ 304	260	757
δ 357	92	204
δ 378	1400	1400
δ 390	..	1622
δ 393	..	1490
358	38	328
362	..	1752
371	356	1140
372	360	1855
373	361	1856
380	378	1865
385	..	1725

and many other codices of the fourteenth and later centuries.

(c) LECTIONARIES

Many lectionaries containing lessons from Acts are known, and are catalogued in Gregory's lists. Of these l^{a}171 is of the ninth century, l^{a}59 and l^{a}173 of the ninth or tenth; l^{a}156 is of the tenth century, and l^{a}597 and l^{a}1316 of the tenth or eleventh. From the eleventh century on many extant lectionaries are assigned to each century. The text of the lectionaries has never been investigated.

§ 2. CODICES BℵACDE

A discussion of the history and peculiarities of some of the
chief manuscripts named above is more conveniently placed
here ; the character of the New Testament text in the several
documents will be treated later in connexion with the history
and criticism of the text of Acts.

B. CODEX VATICANUS

Codex Vaticanus is mentioned in the catalogue of the Vatican History.
library of the year 1475.[1] Whence it came into the library is

[1] The catalogue of 1475 (Vat. cod. lat. 3954) made by Platina, the librarian,
is printed in full by E. Müntz and P. Fabre, *La Bibliothèque du Vatican au XV*
siècle, Paris, 1887.   It is arranged in two parts (Latin and Greek) and by subjects
in each part.   At that date the books had no fixed places (P. Fabre, *La Vaticane
de Sixte IV* [Mélanges d'Archéologie et d'Histoire, xv.], 1898, p. 473).   In the
list of Greek MSS. is included under the heading ' *Testamentum antiquum et
novum* ' (Müntz and Fabre, p. 244) the entry ' *Biblia. Ex membr. in rubeo.*'
This is the only Greek MS. mentioned which purports to contain the whole
Bible.   This entry can hardly refer to any other than our Codex Vaticanus
1209, for in a shelf-list, or catalogue arranged by the book-cases of the several
rooms of the Library, made by Platina with the aid of his subordinate Demetrius
Lucensis in 1481 (Vat. codd. lat. 3952 and 3947, the latter MS. being a copy of
the former ; see Müntz and Fabre, pp. 142 f., 250 f.), the statement is found,
relating to the left side of the library, as you enter : ' *In primo banco bibliothecae
grecae.   Biblia in tribus columnis ex membranis in rubeo* ' (I. Carini, *Centralblatt
für Bibliothekswesen*, vol. x., 1893, pp. 541 ff.).   This unmistakably refers to
Codex B; and that it is a fuller description of the same Bible which the catalogue
of 1475 designated more summarily is not only made probable by the identity
of the binding in both notices (*in rubeo*), but is clearly shown by the fact that
no other book mentioned in this later inventory can be the same as the Bible
of the earlier one.   In the inventory of 1481 the only other Bible mentioned is
described as ' bound in black ' (*in nigro*) ;   this was in fact a copy of part of
the Old Testament (Vat. gr. 330), afterward lent to Cardinal Ximenes for the
Complutensian Polyglot.   The information with regard to the inventory of
1481 I owe to the kindness of Mgr. G. Mercati, of the Vatican Library.   For
the former controversy on this subject see *The Academy*, May 30 and June 13,
1891 ;   *Centralblatt für Bibliothekswesen*, vol. x., 1893, pp. 537-547 ;   F. G.
Kenyon, *Handbook to the Textual Criticism of the N.T.*, 2nd ed., 1912, p. 77.
The position of B as Cod. graec. 1209 in the enumeration of the Vatican MSS.
throws no light on the source from which it came into the Vatican library
(founded about 1450).   The present numbering is due to the brothers Rainaldi
about 1620, and in the list Codex B is preceded by codices known to have been
acquired as late as the years 1594 and 1612 ; see P. Batiffol, *La Vaticane de
Paul III à Paul V*, pp. 82 f. ;   J. B. De Rossi, ' De origine, historia, indicibus

not known, but it has been observed that the hand which has written extended scholia on fol. 1205^v, 1206, 1239, and elsewhere in Codex B, resembles a Greek hand of the thirteenth century, "easily recognizable by its ligatures as well as by the greenish ink which it employs," which annotated two codices formerly belonging to the library of the abbey of Rossano, one containing Chrysostom on 1 Corinthians (Vaticanus, gr. 1648, tenth century) and one Gregory Nazianzen (Vaticanus, gr. 1994, eleventh century).[1] That Codex B had previously been in the possession of Cardinal Bessarion († 1472) has sometimes been suggested in view of the fact that in Codex Venetus, Marc. graec. 6, which was probably written for the Cardinal, several Old Testament books are copied from it,[2] and it would not be unnatural to suspect that the MS. was found by him in one of the Greek monasteries of South Italy, oversight of which was entrusted to him by the Pope in 1446, and from which many of his manuscripts are said to have come.[3] But it is hard to believe that so eager

scriniae et bibliothecae sedis apostolicae,' in *Codices palatini latini bibliothecae Vaticanae*, vol. i., Rome, 1886, pp. cxiii-cxvii.

[1] This observation was made by P. Batiffol, *L'Abbaye de Rossano*, 1891, p. 49 note 1. Codex Vat. gr. 1648 was at Rossano in the fifteenth century, later at Grotta Ferrata. For the statement found, for instance, in P. Batiffol, *La Vaticane de Paul III à Paul V*, Paris, 1890, p. 82, that Codex B was in South Italy in the tenth and eleventh centuries, positive grounds are not given. The restoration of the codex by retracing the letters, etc., is commonly associated with the work of a certain corrector who occasionally lapsed into minuscules that betray his date as the tenth or eleventh century (Tischendorf, *Novum Testamentum Vaticanum*, p. xxvii) ; but as to the locality where these corrections were made there seems to be no evidence. The Roman editors, ' Prolegomena,' 1881, p. xvii, hold the re-inking and the addition of breathings and accents to be the work of the scribe (Clemens monachus) who, they think, supplied the missing portions of the codex in the early fifteenth century.

[2] Bessarion's manuscripts as a whole, however, were given by him in 1468 or 1469 to the Library of San Marco in Venice. The source from which a fifteenth-century hand supplied Gen. i. 1-xlvi. 28 in B is said by Nestle (*Septuagintastudien* [i.], Ulm, 1886, p. 9) to be the Roman twelfth-century Codex Chisianus R. VI. 38 (Rahlfs 19). No one seems to have discovered the source of the addition by the same hand which now fills the second lacuna, Ps. cv. 27-cxxxvii. 6. Gregory, *Prolegomena*, p. 359, states that the source from which the later part of Hebrews and Revelation were added was a manuscript belonging to Bessarion.

[3] G. Voigt, *Die Wiederbelebung des classischen Altertums*, 3rd ed. vol. ii., 1893, pp. 123 ff., esp. pp. 130 f. ; Batiffol, *La Vaticane de Paul III à Paul V*, p. 82.

a collector as the Cardinal would have given up voluntarily his greatest treasure. In any case he would not have given it to the Vatican Library at any period after the date at which he fell out of favour at Rome.

If it is proper to hazard a conjecture as to the earlier history of Codex B, it would be that the codex was brought from Alexandria to Sicily by fugitives from the conquering Arabs, in the seventh century, and thence to Calabria.[1] Nothing is known which suggests that it remained in the East until the fifteenth century and was then brought to Rome under the influence of the revival of letters.[2]

The date of the Codex Vaticanus is admitted to be the fourth century. From the peculiar selection and order of the books included in the Old Testament and the order in the New Testament it is evident that the manuscript is to be associated with the influence of Athanasius ;[3] but it is not certain that it need have been written after his 39th Festal Letter of 367, for the Patriarch's views on the canon there stated, although perhaps original with him, were doubtless formulated before that date.

Date.

[1] The ancient Hellenistic character of the civilization of Magna Graecia had substantially disappeared by the time of Procopius († ca. 562) and Gregory the Great († 604). On the movement from Alexandria to Sicily in the seventh century, and from Sicily to Calabria in the ninth and tenth centuries, and on the fresh hellenization of South Italy in the seventh and subsequent centuries, see below, pp. lxiv-lxvii.

[2] A partial parallel to the history here suggested may be seen in the history of the Codex Marchalianus of the prophetic books of the Old Testament (Vatican, gr. 2125), which was written in Egypt in the sixth century, shows annotations made there at some time not later than the ninth century, was then brought to South Italy, perhaps before the twelfth century, and there received further annotations. As in the case of B, but in much less degree, Codex Marchalianus has suffered re-inking. It came later to Paris, and was bought for the Vatican Library in 1785. A. Ceriani, *De codice Marchaliano*, Rome, 1890, pp. 34-47.

[3] This was first fully shown by A. Rahlfs, ' Alter und Heimat der vatikanischen Bibelhandschrift,' *Nachrichten von der Gesellschaft der Wissenschaften zu Göttingen, Phil.-hist. Klasse*, 1899, pp. 72-79. Hug, *Einleitung in die Schriften des Neuen Testaments*, 1808, § 50, had observed that Athanasius and B agree in the position of Hebrews ; and Grabe, *Epistola ad Millium*, 1705, pp. 41 f., thought himself to have proved that the translation of Judges found in B was the same as that used by Athanasius, *Ep. I. ad Serap.* p. 651, as well as by Cyril.

The place of origin of B has now been established as Egypt in spite of the contention of some earlier scholars (R. Simon, Wetstein, Ceriani, Corssen, Hort) that it was written in Rome or in southern Italy.[1] Even under the dubious guess which attempts to identify B with the copy (or, possibly, one of several copies) prepared for the Emperor Constans by Athanasius in the earlier years (339–342 or 340–343) of his exile at Rome,[2] it would have to be admitted that the scribes, the composition, and the text of B were Egyptian, so that the manuscript could in no way claim to be a product of the West or to show Western practice.[3]

Among the reasons which have led to the conclusion that B is Egyptian are the following. They depend in part on the assumption that a codex of that period giving the characteristic text of a locality was written in the locality.

1. Its relation to Athanasius.

2. The fact that in the exemplar from which the Pauline

[1] The chief reasons given by Hort (' Introduction,' pp. 265 f.) for suggesting such a conclusion are these : (1) The spellings ισακ and ιστραηλ[ειτης] or ισδραηλ[ειτης]. On the former word see Thackeray, *Grammar of O.T. in Greek*, vol. i. p. 100 ; on the latter J. H. Moulton and W. F. Howard, *Grammar of N.T. Greek*, vol. ii. part i., 1919, p. 103, and Lake, *Codex Sinaiticus Petropolitanus*, p. xi. The spelling ισακ is found in the early fourth - century Oxyrhynchus papyrus 675 of the Epistle to the Hebrews ; see *Oxyrhynchus Papyri*, iv. pp. 36 ff. (2) The wrong substitution in B, especially in the Pauline epistles, of χριστος ιησους for ιησους χριστος. (3) The chapter-enumeration of 69 chapters in Acts ; on this see below pp. xli, xliv. No one of these reasons remains even partially convincing. For Ceriani's judgment see his *Monumenta sacra et profana*, iii. 1, 1864, p. xxi, and the utterance reported in *Epistularum Paulinarum codices . . . Augiensem, Boernerianum, Claromontanum examinavit . . . P. Corssen*, ii. (Jever programme), Kiel, 1889, p. 3 note, together with Ceriani's reaffirmation in *Rendiconti, Reale Istituto Lombardo*, Series II. vol. xix., 1886, pp. 212 f. ; cf. vol. xxi., 1888, pp. 540-549.

[2] Athanasius, *Apol. ad Constantium* 4 (i. p. 297) τῷ ἀδελφῷ σου οὐκ ἔγραψα ἢ μόνον ὅτε οἱ περὶ Εὐσέβιον ἔγραψαν αὐτῷ κατ' ἐμοῦ καὶ ἀνάγκην ἔσχον ἔτι ὢν ἐν τῇ Ἀλεξανδρείᾳ ἀπολογήσασθαι, καὶ ὅτε πυκτία τῶν θείων γραφῶν κελεύσαντος αὐτοῦ μοι κατασκευάσαι ταῦτα ποιήσας ἀπέστειλα. As Zahn points out (*Gesch. d. Neutest. Kanons*, i., 1888, p. 73, note 1; *Athanasius und der Bibelkanon*, 1901, p. 31 note 56), the context shows that the Bible (or Bibles) must have been dispatched within the first three years of Athanasius's exile.

[3] The old uncial numeration on the verso of each leaf, perhaps inserted before the issuance of the codex, was believed by Gregory to be by an oriental hand ; *Prolegomena*, p. 450.

epistles were drawn Hebrews immediately followed Galatians, a singular order strikingly like that of the Sahidic version, in which Hebrews is found between 2 Corinthians and Galatians.

3. The close relation of the text to the Bohairic version, and in a less degree to the Sahidic.

4. The type of text to which B belongs was current in Egypt, being that employed by Athanasius and Cyril. The Egyptian fragments of the Gospels designated as T show a text closely related to B, though not perfectly identical with it, and the same is true of most of the papyri.[1]

5. The occurrence in Heb. i. 3 of the singular reading φανερων for φερων, elsewhere found only in the Egyptian monk, Serapion ; together with the singular readings in Heb. iii. 2, 6 found only in papyri.[2]

6. The presence in B of a translation of the Book of Judges which is of Egyptian origin.

7. A more doubtful line of evidence is the occasional, but rare, occurrence in B of spellings which are believed to proceed from peculiar Egyptian pronunciation. Thus κραυη for κραυγη, Is. xxx. 19, Ez. xxi. 22, and a few cases of the omission of χ, τ, λ, and σ between vowels, together with the confusion of κ and γ and of the dental mutes.[3] But these phenomena are notably less frequent in B than in other old uncials.

8. The close resemblance of the text of B, at least in 1-4 Kingdoms, to the non-hexaplaric text found in some of Origen's quotations, and to the text underlying the Ethiopic.[4] The

---

[1] Bousset, *Textkritische Studien zum Neuen Testament* (Texte und Unter-suchungen, xi.), 1894, ' Die Recension des Hesychius,' pp. 74-110 ; Burkitt, in P. M. Barnard, *The Biblical Text of Clement of Alexandria* (Texts and Studies, v.), 1899, pp. viii f., x f. The Egyptian LXX - fragment (fifth or sixth century) designated Z^III also shows striking agreement with B ; see Rahlfs, *Lucians Rezension der Königsbücher*, 1911, p. 193 note 2. See also below, p. xxxvi note 1.

[2] J. Armitage Robinson, in P. M. Barnard, *op. cit.* p. x ; G. Wobbermin, *Altchristliche liturgische Stücke aus der Kirche Ägyptens* (Texte und Unter-suchungen, xvii.), 1899, p. 23.

[3] Thackeray, *Grammar of the O.T. in Greek*, vol. i. pp. 101, 103 f., 111-114.

[4] Rahlfs, ' Origenes' Zitate aus den Königsbüchern,' *Septuaginta-Studien*, i., 1904, pp. 82-87.

Ethiopian Church was dependent on Egypt, and would naturally acquire thence its text of the Bible.

These indications all point to Egypt, and the palaeographic [1] and linguistic characteristics of the manuscript include nothing which is not consistent with this conclusion.[2] No evidence which in the light of present knowledge continues to be valid tends to indicate an origin in the West. If the codex had its home in Egypt, it was probably written in Alexandria.

Constan-
tine's fifty
copies.

The suggestion has, however, often been made that Codex Vaticanus and Codex Sinaiticus formed two of the fifty copies of the Bible [3] prepared by Eusebius, doubtless in Caesarea, by order of the Emperor Constantine about the year 332 (Eusebius, *Vita Constantini*, iv. 35-37), which Eusebius describes as [ἀντί-γραφα] τρισσὰ καὶ τετρασσά. But this theory has no inherent strength sufficient to overthrow the positive reasons for assigning an Egyptian origin to B. On this point some further discussion is necessary.

τρισσὰ καὶ
τετρασσά.

The expression τρισσὰ καὶ τετρασσά has received many interpretations.[4] (1) The rendering *terniones et quaterniones*, found in the Latin translation of Valesius' edition and accepted by Montfaucon (*Palaeographia Graeca*, p. 26) is probably impossible in itself, and is not well suited to the context, as, indeed, Valesius observed—to say nothing of the fact that ternions seem never to have been a usual form of gatherings. (2) The meaning

---

[1] On the resemblance of the uncial writing of both B and ℵ to Papyrus Rylands 28 see Lake, *Codex Sinaiticus Petropolitanus*, p. xi. The Greek hand of B is extraordinarily like the Coptic hand of a papyrus MS. of the Gospel of John ; see H. Thompson, *The Gospel of St. John according to the Earliest Coptic Manuscript*, London, 1924, p. xiii.

[2] V. Gardthausen, *Griechische Paläographie*, ii. pp. 248 ff., has, however, shown that the so-called ' Coptic ' form of M cannot be used as positive evidence of Egyptian origin.

[3] That the books ordered by Constantine were copies of the whole Bible is not certain, although the language of Eusebius makes it probable. E. Schwartz (art. ' Eusebios,' in Pauly-Wissowa, *Real-Encyclopädie*, vi., 1909, col. 1437) thinks that they were copies of the Gospels only, some containing three, others all four. The meaning of τρισσὰ καὶ τετρασσά required by this theory makes it impossible. See also John Lightfoot, *Horae hebraicae*, on John viii.

[4] K. Lake, ' The Sinaitic and Vatican Manuscripts and the Copies sent by Eusebius to Constantine,' *Harvard Theological Review*, xi., 1918, pp. 32-35.

'three and four at a time' would suit the verb διαπεμψάντων, but not the proper sense of the adjectives themselves, for these latter are virtually synonymous with τριπλᾶ and τετραπλᾶ, and mean that the copies themselves had 'three and four' of something. (3) 'Having three and four *volumes*' in each copy would make sense, but nothing in particular tends to confirm this interpretation. (4) The meaning 'having three *columns* and four *columns*' is said to have been a conjecture of Tischendorf,[1] and is probably to be accepted.[2] It suits the natural meaning of the terms, and can be accounted for in the context from the author's manifest desire to emphasize the splendour of these copies.[3] Manuscripts in three or four columns would certainly be large and costly. A similar desire to emphasize the large size and dignity of the book seems to be present in the following interesting passage (*Menaea*, October 15), where τρισσός is used in describing a fourth-century codex of the whole Bible, written with three columns to the page by the famous martyr, Lucian of Antioch :

εἰς κάλλος δὲ γράφειν ἐπιστάμενος, βιβλίον κατέλιπε τῇ Νικομηδέων ἐκκλησίᾳ, γεγραμμένον σελίσι τρισσαῖς (εἰς τρεῖς στήλας διῃρημένης τῆς σελίδος), περιέχον πᾶσαν τὴν παλαιάν τε καὶ τὴν νέαν διαθήκην.[4]

The word τετρασσός is used in Eusebius, *H.e.* vi. 16, 4 (Schwartz's text ; *v.l.* τετραπλοῖς) to refer to the Tetrapla of

---

[1] Gregory, *Prolegomena* [1884], p. 348 ; but in *Novum Testamentum Vaticanum*, 1867, p. xviii, Tischendorf still followed the explanation of Valesius. The earliest mention which I have met with of the interpretation 'in three and four columns' is by W. Wattenbach, *Das Schriftwesen im Mittelalter*, 1871, p. 114. C. Vercellone, in a paper read before the Pontifical Academy, July 14, 1859, and published in his *Dissertazioni accademiche*, Rome, 1864, pp. 115 ff., connects Codex Vaticanus with the fifty manuscripts of Eusebius, but does not seem to have thought of the aptness of the word τρισσά to describe the three columns of that codex. So also Scrivener, *A Full Collation of the Codex Sinaiticus*, 2nd ed., 1867, p. xxxvii, with reference to ℵ.

[2] For a good, but exaggerated, statement see F. C. Cook, *The Revised Version of the First Three Gospels*, 1882, pp. 162 f. note.

[3] So Wattenbach, *op. cit.* p. 114, 3rd ed., 1896, p. 181.

[4] This is found in a somewhat different form, containing, however, the word in question, in 'Synaxarium ecclesiae Constantinopolitanae,' *Propylaeum ad Acta Sanctorum, Novembris* [vol. lxi. bis], 1902, p. 139.

Origen ; but no other occurrence of the word, except the one under examination, has been produced. $\tau\rho\iota\sigma\sigma\acute{o}s$ is a not uncommon word.

The notion, often brought forward, that the three columns of Codex B and the four columns of Codex ℵ show that one or both of these splendid manuscripts made a part of the shipment with which Eusebius filled Constantine's order, would only be justified if confirmed by the resemblance of their text to that used by Eusebius.[1] This is not the case in the New Testament, and still less in the Old.   There were rich patrons of churches in the fourth century in other places besides Constantinople, and no trait of the text of either B or ℵ, or known fact of their history, serves to connect either of these codices with that city.[2]

Scribes.   Codex B was written[3] by either three or four scribes : B[1] (pp. 1-334, Gen. to 1 Kingds. xix. 11), B[2] (pp. 335-674, 1 Kingds. xix. 11-Ps. lxxvii. 71), B[3] (pp. 675-1244 [?], Ps. lxxvii. 72-Matt. ix. 5), B[4] (pp. 1245-fin., Matt. ix. 5-fin.).   Of these B[2] and B[4] may be the same.   The frequently repeated opinion of Tischendorf that the scribe (now believed to be two scribes) who wrote the New Testament of B was also one of the scribes of ℵ has been shown by Lake to be an error.

Ortho-graphy.   B was very carefully written, and its orthography is more correct than that of most other uncials.[4]   The common confusion of vowels is relatively infrequent.   The most noteworthy peculiarity is the strong preference for $\epsilon\iota$ where earlier usage and the practice of the later grammarians wrote ι.   This was not by

[1] On the text probably used for Eusebius's fifty copies see Streeter, *The Four Gospels*, 1924, pp. 91 f., 102-105.

[2] Hort, 'Introduction,' pp. 74 f. : " The four extant copies [BℵAC] are doubtless casual examples of a numerous class of MSS.; derived from various origins, though brought into existence in the first instance by similar circumstances."   The fifth-century palimpsest ' Codex Patiriensis ' (ℶ; 048) was written in three columns.

[3] L. Traube, *Nomina sacra*, 1907, pp. 66 f.

[4] Thackeray, *Grammar of the O.T in Greek*, vol. i., 1909, p. 72 : " The generalization suggested by the available evidence is that B is on the whole nearer [than A and ℵ] to the originals in orthography as in text," cf. pp. 78, 86 ; H. von Soden, *Schriften des N.T.* p. 909.

inadvertence, but represents a deliberate attempt to convey the sound of long $\bar{\iota}$ by $\epsilon\iota$.[1] Perfect consistency, however, was not attained, and some mistakes can be pointed out.[2] The confusion of $\alpha\iota$ and ϵ occurs only occasionally, and testifies to the absence in the fourth century of a fixed standard of spelling.[3] Letters are occasionally omitted (sometimes perhaps in consequence of dialectal pronunciation). In the present edition of B the spelling of the manuscript has been followed, except where it is manifestly a case of clerical error and in a few places where the strange spelling causes undue difficulty to the modern reader. In all cases where a change has been made, the spelling of the manuscript has been indicated in the line next below the text. The aim has been to leave in the text (with a very few exceptions) all those spellings which the scribe himself would probably have been disposed to defend as tolerable. The notion that B is full of bad spellings is unjust.

Although the general correctness of B is thus very great, yet, as will appear below in the discussion of the criticism of the text, it shows in Acts a considerable series of 'singular,' or virtually 'singular,' readings. Of these hardly any can be accepted as superior to the rival readings of the Old Uncial group, so that the great body of those others which are not susceptible of judgment on transcriptional grounds (as well as those judged to be transcriptionally inferior) are to be rejected. Striking peculiar readings (like $\kappa\eta\rho\nu\gamma\mu\alpha$ for $\beta\alpha\pi\tau\iota\sigma\mu\alpha$ Acts x. 37) are rare among these; there are some omissions of necessary words (such as $\kappa\lambda\alpha\nu\delta\iota\sigma\nu$, xviii. 2 ; $\zeta\eta\nu$, xxv. 24), a few repetitions (like $\mu\epsilon\gamma\alpha\lambda\eta\ \eta$ $\alpha\rho\tau\epsilon\mu\iota\varsigma\ \epsilon\phi\epsilon\sigma\iota\omega\nu$, xix. 34). Stupid blunders, yielding no intelligible sense, are extremely rare, apart from a moderate number of cases where letters or syllables are omitted (as $\epsilon\beta\alpha\sigma\tau\alpha\zeta\epsilon$ for $\epsilon\beta\alpha\sigma\tau\alpha\zeta\epsilon\tau\sigma$, iii. 2 ; $\gamma\epsilon\nu\sigma\varsigma$ for $\gamma\epsilon\nu\sigma\mu\epsilon\nu\sigma\varsigma$, vii. 32 ; $\epsilon\iota\rho\eta\nu$ for

(margin: Errors.)

---

[1] On the systematic use of $\epsilon\iota$ to represent long $\bar{\iota}$ in the Michigan papyrus of the Shepherd of Hermas, probably written not later than A.D. 250, see C. Bonner, in *Harvard Theological Review*, vol. xviii., 1925, p. 122.

[2] Thackeray, pp. 85-87.

[3] F. Blass, *Grammatik des neutestamentlichen Griechisch*, 1896, pp. 6 f.

ειρηνην, x. 36 ; κεκρει for κεκρικει, xx. 16). An instructive classification of such individual errors of B is given by von Soden.[1]

Correctors. Codex B has been corrected at more than one date, but the discrimination of the several correctors by Fabiani (Roman edition, vol. vi. 1881) is unsatisfactory, and a critical investigation of the corrections throughout the manuscript is much to be desired.[2] Some revision of the Roman editors' results is to be found in Tischendorf's apparatus. The designations are to be regarded as referring to groups of correctors, rather than to individuals. The earliest corrections (B[1] and in part B[2]) are doubtless those of the diorthotes, added before the codex was sent out from the scriptorium.[3] Others (B[3]) are commonly ascribed to a hand of the tenth or eleventh century,[4] who added the breathings

---

[1] Pp. 907-914, 1655-1657. Von Soden's combination of this list of individual errors with groups of readings which he ascribes to the influence of the K-text, the I-text, and the Egyptian versions, tends to blur the important distinction between the 'singular' readings of B and those which B shares with other authorities. His description of the scribe of B is interesting (p. 907) : " Der Schreiber von δ1 scheint ein Schönschreiber von Beruf gewesen zu sein, der mechanisch abschrieb, obgleich er gut verstand, was er schrieb." Gregory's statement (*Prolegomena*, p. 359), " erroribus scribae scatet," can only be pronounced obsolete. One interesting piece of evidence is the fact that the spelling ουθεις, which was already expiring in the first century after Christ, and was wholly extinct after about A.D. 200, is found seven times ; cf. Thackeray, pp. 62, 104 f., Moulton and Howard, *Grammar of N.T. Greek*, vol. ii. p. 111. In Acts xv. 9, ουθεν, as found in B, has passed into the Antiochian text, against ουδεν in אACD 81.

[2] See A. Ceriani, *Rendiconti, Reale Istituto Lombardo*, Series II. vol. xxi., 1888, pp. 545 f.

[3] Hort, ' Introduction,' p. 270, says of B[2], the corrector : " Among his corrections of clerical errors are scattered some textual changes, clearly marked as such by the existence of very early authority for both readings : the readings which he thus introduces imply the use of a second exemplar, having a text less pure than that of the primary exemplar, but free from clear traces of Syrian influence. The occurrence of these definite diversities of text renders it unsafe to assume that all singular readings which he alters were individualisms of the first hand, though doubtless many of them had no other origin." Many scholars would now hold that more of these ' singular' readings are " individualisms of the first hand " than Westcott and Hort allowed, and that too many of them were admitted into the text of those editors.

[4] The date (tenth to eleventh century) is assigned to B[3] chiefly because of the character of the minuscules into which he occasionally lapses. On the correctors see especially Tischendorf, *Novum Testamentum Vaticanum*, 1867, pp. xxiii-xxviii.

and accents, and re-inked the already faded letters of the text, leaving untouched letters and words which he disapproved. It is only in these latter (for instance, 2 Cor. iii. 15, where nearly the whole of four lines had inadvertently been written twice) that the fineness and beauty of the original work can now be observed. This work of B[3], it should be noticed, in all its branches is held by Fabiani to have been done in the early fifteenth century, and to have included long Greek interpretative scholia, Latin notes in Greek letters, and the sixty-two supplementary pages, but this is doubtful.[1] A hand later than the tenth or eleventh century added liturgical notes, which do not seem to have been carefully studied by any scholars in recent times.

As B in the Gospels has peculiar chapter divisions (Matt., 170 chapters; Mark, 62; Luke, 152; John, 80), marked on a system elsewhere used only (and but in part) in Codex Ξ (eighth century), so in the Book of Acts two noteworthy sets of chapters are indicated. One of these divides the book into 36 chapters, the other into 69. *Chapter divisions.*

The former (36 chapters) is by a hand of early, but uncertain, date, possibly as old as the codex itself but quite as possibly later,[2] and is also found for substance (von Soden, p. 440) in connexion with the 'Euthalian' material in codices 1874, 1898, 1175, 1244, 181, 1162, 917 (?), 1248 (?), ranging from the ninth to the fourteenth century and representing many types of text. Von Soden has shown (pp. 442 ff.) that this system is closely related to the division into 40 chapters, which constitute the κεφάλαια, or main sections, of the 'Euthalian' system. Whether the 36 chapters or the 40 chapters represent the original system which was altered so as to create the other, has not been determined.

The other system (69 chapters) was inserted in B by a somewhat later hand, and also in ℵ, chapters i.-xv., it is found for substance, introduced by a hand described by both Tischendorf

---

[1] Note Batiffol's observation, mentioned above, p. xxxii.
[2] J. A. Robinson, *Euthaliana* (Texts and Studies, iii.), 1895, p. 36.

and Lake as " very early." [1] By Lake (and apparently by
Tischendorf also) the ' tituli,' or chapter-headings, are attributed
to the same hand. Tischendorf held that this was not the same
as any of the correctors designated by him by the symbols ℵ[a]
and ℵ[b], but Lake is disposed to identify it with ℵ[a.2] and to think
that the ' tituli ' and chapter-numbers were introduced before
the manuscript left the scriptorium. In ℵ the system is only
incompletely entered, and in B there are some manifest errors, [2]
but the origin of this chapter-division can be made out with
reasonable certainty. It is a slightly altered, probably corrupt,
form of a combination of the 40 sections (κεφάλαια) and 48 subsections (ὑποδιαιρέσεις) of the system attributed to Euthalius,
belonging to the earliest stratum of the ' Euthalian ' material, [3]
and found in many manuscripts of Acts. The 40 sections and 48
subsections (probably the latter were originally designated by
asterisks, not by numbers) were counted in one series, making 88
in all, but in the corrupt (perhaps altered) form found in B
omissions (chiefly of very brief subsections) have reduced the total
to 69. That the division into 69 and that into 88 chapters are
not independent of one another is demonstrated by the nature
of their distinctive and complicated agreement, which cannot be
accidental. [4]

[1] Tischendorf, *Nov. Test. graece ex Sinaitico codice*, Leipzig, 1863, p. xxiv ;
Lake, *Codex Sinaiticus Petropolitanus*, 1911, p. xxi.

[2] Notably the omission of a division at xv. 1, which causes a difference of one
number between B and ℵ in the numbering of the subsequent chapters, as far
as the end of the enumeration in ℵ. Other differences between B and ℵ are
unimportant.

[3] Robinson, *op. cit.* pp. 21-24, 36-43. The Euthalian problem cannot be
discussed here, and, indeed, cannot be satisfactorily treated at all without a
much larger collection of data than has yet been published. See von Soden,
pp. 637-682 ; E. von Dobschütz, art. ' Euthalius ' in *Protestantische Realencyklopädie*, vol. xxiii., ' Ergänzungen und Nachträge,' pp. 437 f. The ' Euthalian '
sections and subsections, and the full τίτλοι in which the contents of Acts are
summarized, will be found in von Soden, pp. 448-454.

[4] See von Soden, pp. 444-448 ; Robinson, *op. cit.* p. 42. The " surmise "
put forward by Hort (' Introduction,' p. 266) that the resemblance between the
system of division in Codex Amiatinus of the Vulgate (and other Latin codices)
and the system of 69 chapters of B and ℵ tends to indicate that the two latter
codices were both written in the West, may, in the light of the knowledge now
available, be left out of account.

B and (for chapters i.-xv.) א agree in omitting certain of the
' Euthalian ' subsections, and so betray the fact that while their
independence of one another is shown by certain differences
between them, they are both derived from the same corrupt, or
altered, form of the system. Now some codices which have the
' Euthalian ' material (notably H[paul], 88 [formerly 83 ; Neapol.
II. Aa. 7], and Armenian codices) also contain colophons, both
to the Pauline epistles and to the Acts and Catholic epistles,
stating that the manuscript in question (that is, probably, in
many or all cases one of its ancestors) has been compared with
the copy at Caesarea written by Pamphilus. In consequence of
this some scholars have suggested that B and א each lay during
some period of its history at Caesarea, and there received the
numbers of the 69-fold system of chapters in Acts.[1] But it is
difficult to follow this inference. If the 88-fold system of
' Euthalius ' was contained in a standard manuscript at Caesarea,
it would seem unlikely that the corrupt form of it with only 69
chapters, now found in these two costly manuscripts, was drawn
from a codex of that library. It is much more likely that the
corrupt form was that current in some other locality, for instance
Alexandria, and that B and א received it in such a locality.
Moreover, the two colophons which mention Caesarea are probably not an integral part of the work of ' Euthalius,' and in fact
nothing at present known seems to connect the author of the
' Euthalian ' material with Caesarea.[2]

In the present edition of B the chapter divisions of the codex

---

[1] Robinson, *op. cit.* p. 37. J. R. Harris, *Johns Hopkins University Circulars*,
vol. iii., March-April 1884, pp. 40 f., and *Stichometry*, 1893, pp. 71-89 (' The
Origin of Codices א and B '), urged a similar conclusion as to the common
relation of B and א to Caesarea on the ground that the other division, that into
36 chapters, is found both in B and in the ' Euthalian ' material, and further
that there is a connexion between B and א and between a corrector of א and
Caesarea. But Robinson, p. 24, pointed out that the 36 chapters in the
' Euthalian ' material are a later addition in the apparatus ascribed to
Euthalius. He states : " There is no ground at all for connecting it with the
original edition of Euthalius " ; and it may be added that in fact there seems
no particular reason for associating with Caesarea in any way the ' Euthalian '
testimony to the 36 chapters.   [2] See Robinson, *op. cit.* pp. 34 f.

have not been printed, because the division into 69 chapters represents neither the original form nor the full later development of any system ; while the division into 36 chapters is very likely not the original form of its own system, but rather a corruption, and in any case is not unique but is abundantly found elsewhere. The study of the relations, history, and origin of these divisions would be instructive, but it requires a special and comprehensive apparatus in tabular form. The facts relating to B are elsewhere easily accessible,[1] and by themselves are incapable of yielding much fruit.

Character of text.   The pre-eminence of B among the manuscripts of Acts is due to the current acceptance by scholars of the type of text to which it belongs as generally superior both to the ' Western ' and to the Antiochian recension, and also to the absence in B, at least as compared with other codices of its type, of influence from these divergent and inferior types. Apart from this superiority B, while a good manuscript, carefully written, has its own due proportion of individual errors. This general character of B for Acts applies also to the Gospels and to the Catholic epistles, but not wholly to the epistles of Paul. In many books of the Old Testament a corresponding character has been determined for B by recent study of the text of the Septuagint.

ℵ. CODEX SINAITICUS

History.   Codex Sinaiticus is the only one of the four great Bibles of which we know with certainty the locality in the East where it lay in the period immediately preceding its emergence into the light of Western knowledge. But whence it was brought to Mount Sinai, and how long it had been there when in 1844 Tischendorf first saw some leaves of it, we do not know. Tischendorf's own elaborate and protracted study has now been supplemented by the investigations of Lake, as reported in his Introductions to

---

[1] For instance, in the convenient table printed by Robinson, *Euthaliana*, pp. 39 f. Both systems are entered on the inner margin of Nestle's text, 7th edition, 1908.

the photographic facsimiles published .in 1911 and 1922.[1] The most important contribution there made is the demonstration that Tischendorf was wrong in supposing that the scribe D of ℵ was the same hand that wrote the whole (or, rather, nearly the whole) New Testament of Codex Vaticanus.[2] This mistaken theory has had such far-reaching consequences in critical discussion that any treatment of these two codices in which it is even mentioned as probably correct needs to be carefully scrutinized to make sure that the supposed connexion in origin of the two manuscripts has not somewhere affected or warped the judgment of the critic. Even Lake's opinion (p. xii) that the two codices probably came from the same scriptorium, in support of which he adduces the similar character of the subscriptions to Acts, ought not to be used as the foundation of any inferences, for such resemblances may well be due merely to a tradition persisting for a long period among Alexandrian calligraphers of different workshops. The writing of ℵ is much less elegant than that of B.

On the history of the codex light is thrown chiefly by the corrections made at some time in the period from the fifth to the early seventh century to make the text agree with the codex at Caesarea corrected by the hand of Pamphilus the Martyr. The notes appended to Nehemiah (2 Esdras) and Esther [3] seem to indicate (although not quite indubitably) that the codex was actually taken to Caesarea and the corrections made on the spot from the original Codex Pamphili, not merely introduced in some other locality from a copy of that codex. The hand by which these notes are written is, according to Lake, probably not the corrector known as ℵ[c.a] but another of the group that Tischendorf designated as ℵ[c]. In the Old Testament prophets the corrector ℵ[c.b] seems actually to have followed a standard which

[1] K. Lake, *Codex Sinaiticus Petropolitanus*, Oxford, 1911 ; *Codex Sinaiticus Petropolitanus et Frederico-Augustanus Lipsiensis*, Oxford, 1922.

[2] Lake, *Codex Sinaiticus Petropolitanus*, 1911, pp. xii-xiii, xix, Illustrative Plate III.

[3] For the text of these notes see below, p. c note 6.

corresponded to what we should expect Pamphilus's copy of the fifth column of the Hexapla to contain. The significance of the corrections of ℵ is a complicated question which has not been fully elucidated for either Testament. In the New Testament we do not know what was the text of Pamphilus.

Scribes. Codex Sinaiticus was written by several hands,[1] but the New Testament is all by the same scribe except for seven leaves (three and one half sheets, not including any portion of Acts) written by a different scribe, who was also employed in the correction of the New Testament. These seven leaves were probably substituted for the corresponding cancelled pages of the work of the original writer. A good deal of work was evidently done on the manuscript before it was regarded as complete, and several persons employed in perfecting it for issuance from the scriptorium.

Date. The date of ℵ is ordinarily given as the fourth century,[2] but palaeographical reasons make it wholly probable that it represents a later style than that of B. In the Gospels the Eusebian sections and canons have been entered, not by the original hand but apparently by one of the same date, so that Lake believes this to have taken place before the codex was issued. But the earliest date at which this could have taken place is uncertain ; Eusebius died in 339–340. A later date for ℵ has been urged by Viktor Gardthausen, who in an elaborate discussion confidently assigns it to the early part of the fifth century.[3]

Egyptian origin. For determining the place of origin of ℵ less evidence is available than in the case of B. Hort, relying on a part of the same grounds as in the case of B (see above, p. xxxiv note 1), argued for the West, probably Rome. Ceriani, who had previously thought of Palestine or Syria,[4] later decided for South Italy on the ground both of the palaeographical and the textual character

---

[1] See Traube, *Nomina sacra*, pp. 66-71 ; Lake, *op. cit.* pp. xviii f.

[2] F. G. Kenyon, *Handbook to the Textual Criticism of the N.T.*, 2nd ed., 1912, p. 67 ; Lake, *op. cit.* pp. ix f.

[3] *Griechische Paläographie*, 2nd ed. vol. ii., 1913, pp. 122-134.

[4] *Monumenta sacra et profana*, iii. 1, 1864, p. xxi.

of ℵ.[1] For the suggestion of Caesarea, urged by J. R. Harris, no convincing arguments have been presented.[2] For an origin in Egypt (doubtless Alexandria) speaks the fact that in spite of noteworthy differences ℵ exhibits beyond question, in a large part of those books of the Old Testament which it contains (see below, pp. xcviii f.), and in the New Testament, the same type of text as B, and one closely related to the Egyptian and Ethiopic versions, which were derived from Egyptian sources.[3] To this is to be added the evidence that the writing of ℵ is "closely akin to that of the older Coptic hands," and that certain peculiarities of spelling are regarded as characteristic of Egypt.[4] The force of these technical arguments is less than that drawn from a consideration of the text itself, since we have little parallel knowledge of what scribes in other centres of book-manufacturing were capable of producing, but, as in the case of B, the palaeographical and linguistic phenomena present, at any rate, no

---

[1] *Rendiconti, Reale Istituto Lombardo*, Series II. vol. xxi., 1888, p. 547.

[2] J. R. Harris, *Johns Hopkins University Circulars*, vol. iii., March-April 1884, pp. 40 f., and *Stichometry*, 1893, pp. 74 f. Harris's often-quoted geographical argument from the reading αντιπατριδα for πατριδα, in Matt. xiii. 54, which he thinks shows that the scribe lived somewhere in the region of Antipatris, has enlivened criticism but cannot be accepted. The motive for the reading, as Hilgenfeld suggested (*Zeitschr. f. wiss. Theol.* vol. vii., 1864, p. 80), is plain. The scribe, in order to avoid calling Nazareth the 'native place' of Jesus, coined a word (or else used a very rare one) to mean 'foster-native-place.' Cf. ἀντίπολις, 'rival city'; ἀντίμαντις, 'rival prophet'; ἀνθύπατος, 'pro-consul,' etc. etc. ἀντίπατρος itself seems to mean 'foster-father,' or 'one like a father.' As Kenyon points out (*Handbook to the Textual Criticism of the N.T.*, 2nd ed. p. 83), " The fact that ℵ was collated with the MS. of Pamphilus so late as the sixth century seems to show that it was not originally written at Caesarea ; otherwise it would surely have been collated earlier with so excellent an authority." Indeed, if written at Caesarea, ℵ ought to show the text of Pamphilus. To the reasons for Caesarea given by Lake, *The Text of the New Testament*, Oxford, 1900, pp. 14 f., was later added the point that the Eusebian canons might have been inserted in Caesarea, but no one of the arguments holds, nor do all of them together constitute a cumulative body of even slight probabilities. For Lake's statement of his change of view in favour of Egypt see his Introduction to the facsimile of Codex Sinaiticus, pp. x-xv.

[3] The resemblance of the text of the Psalms in ℵ to that which underlies the Coptic *Pistis Sophia* is one piece of evidence ; cf. Harnack, *Ein jüdisch-christliches Psalmbuch* (T.U. xxxv.), p. 13.

[4] Thackeray, *Grammar of the Old Testament in Greek*, vol. i. pp. 72, 112-115, 147. See also above, p. xxxv note 3.

obstacle to the conclusion to which the textual relations clearly point, namely, that ℵ was written in Egypt.[1] Nevertheless the inclusion of Barnabas with Hermas as the books to be added to the New Testament seems to show that ℵ was not written, as B has been thought to have been, under substantial control of the views of Athanasius, expressed in his Festal Letter of 367.[2]

Errors.   Codex Sinaiticus is carelessly written, with many lapses of spelling due to the influence of dialectal and vulgar speech,[3] and many plain errors and crude vagaries.[4] Omissions by homoeo-teleuton abound,[5] and there are many other careless omissions. All these gave a large field for the work of correctors, and the manuscript does not stand by any means on the same high level of workmanship as B. 'Singular' readings of ℵ hardly ever commend themselves. On the other hand, readings of ℵ which

[1] V. Gardthausen, *Griechische Paläographie*, 2nd ed., 1913, vol. ii. pp. 122-134, holds strongly to the Egyptian origin of ℵ.

[2] Zahn, *Die Offenbarung des Johannes*, 1924, pp. 129 f.   Athanasius expressly names the Didache and the Shepherd, with certain of the Old Testament apocrypha, as books not included in the canon but ancient and suitable to be read by catechumens.

[3] Thackeray, *passim* (cf. above, p. xxxv note 3).

[4] For instance, i. 9 ειπορτων for ειπων ; iii. 13 πρα for παιδα, απολλυειν for απολυειν ; v. 1 παμφιρη for σαπφειρη ; vii. 35 δικαστην for λυτρωτην ; viii. 5 καισαριας for σαμαριας ; viii. 26 την καλουμενην καταβαινουσαν ; xi. 20 ευαγγε-λιστας for ελληνιστας ; xiv. 9 ουκ ηκουσεν for ηκουσεν ; xv. 1 εθνει for εθει ; xv. 33 εαυτους for αυτους ; xvi. 23 παραγγειλας τε for παραγγειλαντες ; xviii. 24 απελλης for απολλως ; xxi. 16 ιασονι for μνασονι ; xxvii. 43 βηματος for βουλημaτος ; xxviii. 25 περι for δια ; xxviii. 27 εβαρυνθη for επαχυνθη, etc. etc.   Whether the preference shown by ℵ for εις as against εν is to be reckoned here or shows fidelity to the archetype, is a question ; cf. ii. 5, iv. 5, ix. 21, xvi. 36.   For a summary of the tendencies to error in ℵ and lists of errors see H. von Soden, *Schriften des N.T.* pp. 917-921, 1657-1659 ; also P. Buttmann, ' Bemer-kungen über einige Eigenthümlichkeiten des Cod. Sinaiticus im N.T.,' *Zeitschrift für wissenschaftliche Theologie*, vol. vii., 1864, pp. 367-395 ; vol. ix., 1866, pp. 219-238 ; Hort, ' Introduction,' pp. 246 f.   That the vagaries are not the mere ineptitudes of an ignorant monk may be seen, for instance, from James v. 10, καλοκαγαθιας for κακοπαθειας.   In the Epistle of Barnabas, Gebhardt concluded that ℵ unsupported by other witnesses is nearly always wrong ; Gebhardt, Harnack, and Zahn, *Patrum apostolicorum opera*, i. 2, 1878, p. xxxvii.

[5] Especially in John, but not there alone.   There are said to be sixty such omissions in the Gospels.   See H. S. Cronin, ' An Examination of some Omis-sions of the Codex Sinaiticus in St. John's Gospel,' *Journal of Theological Studies*, vol. xiii., 1912, pp. 563-571 ; von Soden, p. 920.

at first sight look like errors are sometimes confirmed by other and better witnesses, and prove to be right. But ℵ does not seem to preserve earlier and perhaps original spelling so faithfully as B.[1]

In the text of Revelation it is recognized that ℵ is perhaps the least trustworthy of all the chief manuscripts.[2] In the Gospels the text has suffered much from harmonization, both in passages where other manuscripts share the defect and in other cases where the harmonization is peculiar to ℵ.

The correctors of ℵ are numerous, and deserve more com- Correctors. plete study than they have received hitherto. They are classified by Lake (on the basis of Tischendorf [3]) as follows :

Fourth century. ℵ^a. Various hands employed in the scriptorium, together with others of about the same time, all of whom probably worked in the locality where the codex was written. ℵ$^{a.1}$ and ℵ$^{a.2}$ are probably the same hand, and denote the diorthotes (Tischendorf's scribe D), who was likewise the writer of the substituted leaves, or cancel-leaves, referred to above (p. xlvi).

Fourth and fifth centuries. ℵ^b, ℵ$^{b.a}$, and possibly others. Locality unknown.

Fifth to seventh century. ℵ^c, together with ℵ$^{c.a}$, ℵ$^{c.b}$, and a number of others. The view that one set of these corrections was made in Caesarea has led Lake to connect the whole group with that place, but in the LXX prophets the standards followed by ℵ$^{c.a}$ and ℵ$^{c.b}$ are said to be opposed to each other. On the work of this group in the Old Testament see below, pp. xcix-c. From one or more of this group (designated merely as ℵ^c by Tischendorf) proceed many corrections in the New Testament, often such as to bring the manuscript into harmony with the Antiochian revised text. In Hermas, ℵ$^{c.a}$ introduced

---

[1] Thackeray, *Grammar*, vol. i. pp. 72, 86.

[2] See R. H. Charles, *Critical and Exegetical Commentary on the Revelation of St. John*, vol. i. pp. clx-clxxxiii, especially the tables on pp. clxiv and clxxxi.

[3] Tischendorf's mature views on the several hands and correctors are most conveniently learned from his *Novum Testamentum graece ex Sinaitico codice*, Leipzig, 1865, pp. xxvi, xxx-xl, lxxxiii.

corrections from another copy of the book.[1] So also ℵ^{c.c} in Barnabas.[2]

Eighth to twelfth century. ℵ^d ℵ^e. At least two unimportant correctors, who were perhaps monks on Mount Sinai. ℵ^d did not touch the New Testament.

In Acts corrections are found from ℵ^a and ℵ^{c.a}.

ℵ and B.   The text of ℵ, as has already been said, is much like that of B, and the two manuscripts in both Old and New Testaments largely represent in different examples the same general type, a type current in the fourth century in Egypt. Not only do they often agree (a circumstance which might merely indicate that both are often true representatives of the remote original), but they seem to rest on a common base, containing a definite selection of readings. This base was subjected to different treatment in the ancestors of the two manuscripts respectively, and has suffered deterioration in both. But it was in most books a good text ; in the New Testament (apart from Revelation) it was an excellent one and ℵ and B rarely agree in detectable error. The one striking instance which Westcott and Hort thought to be a manifest blunder found in ℵ and B, and not due to coincidence (James i. 17), has in recent years received confirmation from a papyrus, and can be confidently accepted as giving the true reading of the author.[3] But ℵ and B also show great differences in every part, and Hort's elaborate argument [4] to prove that they are not descended from a common proximate ancestor is substantiated by later criticism. Apart from their text itself, the difference of origin of the two codices may be inferred from their difference in the contents and arrangement of the Old Testament, and in the order of books in the New Testament (in ℵ the Pauline

---

[1] O. von Gebhardt, in Gebhardt, Harnack, and Zahn, *Patrum apostolicorum opera*, iii., 1877, pp. vi f.

[2] *Ibid.* i. 2, 1875, p. xxxiii.

[3] The difficulty disappears with the correct interpretation of the unaccented text; not παραλλαγὴ ἢ τροπῆς ἀποσκιάσματος, but παραλλαγὴ ἢ τροπῆς ἀποσκιάσματος (Bℵ Pap. Oxyrh. 1229). See J. H. Ropes, *Commentary on the Epistle of St. James*, 1916, pp. 162-164 ; Hort, ' Introduction,' pp. 217 f.

[4] Hort, ' Introduction,' pp. 212-224.

epistles immediately follow the Gospels ; in B they follow the
Catholic epistles).

A. CODEX ALEXANDRINUS

Codex Alexandrinus seems to have borne that name from History.
about the time of its arrival in England (1628) ; [1] it gained
it, however, not from any certainty as to its place of origin, but
only because it had lain in Alexandria while in the possession of
the Patriarch Cyril Lucar, who presided over that see from 1602
to 1621, and by whom, while Patriarch of Constantinople, it was
offered to King James I. in 1624–1625, and actually given to
King Charles I. in 1627. A series of notes in the codex, two in
Arabic, two in Latin, make the following statements : (1) An
Arabic note of wholly uncertain date affirms that the manuscript
was written by Thecla the martyr.[2]   (2) A Latin note in the hand
of Cyril Lucar himself says that current tradition declares the
codex to have been written by Thecla, a noble lady of Egypt in
the fourth century, whose name the tradition also declares to
have stood formerly at the end of the book on a page torn away
by the Mohammedans.[3]   (3) An Arabic note says that it belonged
to the Patriarchal cell (*i.e.* residence) in Alexandria.[4]   This is
signed by ' Athanasius,' who has commonly been identified
with the Patriarch of Alexandria, Athanasius III. († *ca.* 1308),

---

[1] The name ' Alexandrinus ' and the designation ' A ' are used in Walton's
Polyglot, 1657.

[2] This Arabic note reads : " They relate that this book is in the handwriting of Thecla the martyr."

[3] " Liber iste script^{ae} sacrae N. et V. Testam^{ti}, prout ex traditione habemus,
est scriptus manu Theclae, nobilis feminae Agyptiae, ante mile et trecentos
annos circiter, paulo post concilium Nicenum. Nomen Theclae in fine libri
erat exaratum, sed extincto Christianismo in Agypto a Mahometanis et libri
una Christianorum in similem sunt reducti conditionem. Extinctum ergo et
Theclae nomen et laceratum sed memoria et traditio recens observat. ✠ Cyrillus
Patriarcha Constantin."

[4] The note reads : " Bound to the patriarchal cell in the fortress of
Alexandria. He that lets it go out shall be cursed and ruined. The humble
Athanasius wrote (this)." A cross (of a shape found elsewhere as late as
about 1600) is added at the right of this note. Both Arabic notes may well be
by the same hand, according to Burkitt.

but may at least equally well have been some otherwise
unknown librarian of Cyril Lucar, bearing the same distinguished
name. (4) A Latin note on a fly-leaf, in a hand of the late
seventeenth century, states that the codex was given to the
Patriarchal cell in the year of the Martyrs 814 (A.D. 1098).[1]
The source of this information (or conjecture) is not known.

It thus appears that the evidence from tradition for any
Alexandrian connexion for Codex Alexandrinus cannot be traced
with certainty farther back than Cyril Lucar.[2]

On the other hand, Wetstein (*Novum Testamentum Graecum*,
vol. i., 1751, p. 10) quotes two letters of his great-uncle, J. R.
Wetstein, dated January 14 and March 11, 1664, both stating
on the authority of his Greek teacher, one Matthew Muttis of
Cyprus, a deacon attached to Cyril Lucar, that Cyril procured
the codex from Mount Athos, where he was in 1612–13. In
that case it would be not unnatural to suppose it to have come
from Constantinople.

Place of
origin.

Palaeographical and orthographical evidence has generally
assigned A to Egypt,[3] but it is doubtful whether our knowledge
of the difference between the uncial hands of Alexandria and of
Constantinople in the fifth or sixth century is sufficient to justify
confident assertion here.[4]

The very mixed character of the text of A in both Old and
New Testaments (see below, pages ci-ciii); its use in many

---

[1] " Donum datum cubiculo Patriarchali anno 814 Martyrum."

[2] F. C. Burkitt, ' Codex " Alexandrinus," ' *Journal of Theological Studies*,
vol. XI., 1909–10, pp. 603-606.

[3] Thackeray, *Grammar*, vol. i. p. 72 (kinship to older Coptic hands), pp. 100-
105 (interchange of consonants), p. 110 ; Kenyon, *Handbook to the Textual
Criticism of the N.T.*, 2nd ed. p. 76, on the forms of Δ and M in a few instances
in titles and colophons (but not in the text itself), but see Gardthausen, *Griechische Paläographie*, 2nd ed. pp. 248 ff., on the widespread use of the ' Coptic '
M, also H. Curtius, in *Monatsbericht* of Berlin Academy, 1880, p. 646.

[4] For palaeographical and historical discussion see the introductions to the
facsimile editions, by E. Maunde Thompson (1881) and F. G. Kenyon (1909).
G. Mercati, ' Un' oscura nota del codice Alessandro,' in *Mélanges offerts à M.
Émile Châtelain*, Paris, 1910, shows that a note on fol. 142b (417b) together
with the form of the table of contents make it plain that the codex originally
consisted of two volumes, the second of which began with the Psalms.

parts of the Septuagint of a text distinctly different from, and
sometimes, though not always, superior to, the special type of
B and ℵ ; the presence in the Apocalypse of a text different
from, and far superior to, that of ℵ ; the large amount of hexaplaric influence in the Old Testament, and of influence in both
Testaments from the Antiochian recension (to which in the
Psalter and the Gospels, though somewhat mixed, it is the oldest,
or one of the two oldest, of extant Greek witnesses)—all these
facts would probably be more easily accounted for if A could be
referred to Constantinople rather than to Alexandria.

The date assigned to A is the first half, the middle, or the Date.
close of the fifth century ; but no strong reason seems to be
given why it could not have been written as late as the first
half of the sixth century.

Two hands are distinguished in A in the Old Testament, and Scribes.
three in the New, writing as follows : (1) Matthew, Mark, and
the Pauline epistles from 1 Cor. x. 8 on ; (2) Luke, John, Acts,
the Catholic epistles, and Rom. i. 1-1 Cor. x. 8 ; (3) Apocalypse.
The Clementine epistles were written by the same scribe who
wrote the earlier historical and some other books of the Old
Testament.[1] The codex has received various corrections ; A[1]
was probably the original scribe, A[a] perhaps a diorthotes of the
scriptorium. In the New Testament " other corrections are
very much fewer and less important." [2]

Codex Alexandrinus is written with a fair standard of accuracy, Ortho-
as may be seen in Chronicles–Ezra–Nehemiah and 1 Esdras, graphy.
where the proper names are usually given without monstrous
distortion, and where ancient errors, which might easily have
been corrected, have generally been allowed to stand.[3] It
contains in the New Testament relatively few readings peculiar

---

[1] Kenyon, *Handbook to the Textual Criticism of the N.T.*, 2nd ed., 1912, p. 74 ;
but cf. Traube, *Nomina sacra*, pp. 72 f.
[2] Kenyon, *op. cit.* p. 74 ; cf. Kenyon, Introduction to facsimile (1909),
Swete, *Introduction to the O.T. in Greek*, p. 126, and especially Rahlfs, *Der Text
des Septuaginta-Psalters*, pp. 58 f.
[3] Torrey, *Ezra Studies*, 1910, pp. 91-96.

to itself, and those which it does have are mostly unimportant.[1] Its orthography in the LXX is probably largely that of later copyists and not of the date of the autographs ; even where ancient forms are found they are in many cases to be referred to literary correction ; skilful conjectural emendations of the Greek are sometimes detected.[2]

Mixed character of text.

The most striking characteristic of A among the chief uncials is its plainly heterogeneous composition, which has been referred to above (p. lii), and which marks both Testaments in ways partly different, partly parallel (see below, pp. ci-ciii). In the New Testament the Gospels show a mixture of the Antiochian revision with an earlier (chiefly ' Western ' [3]) text, in which the former strongly predominates. Its ancestor here was probably a text of ancient type which was systematically, but not quite completely, corrected in conformity with the Antiochian type which later became current.[4] In Acts and the Pauline epistles the ' Western ' element is smaller ; and in Acts, at least, correction from the Antiochian cannot be affirmed. For the

[1] Von Soden, *Schriften des N.T.*, vol. i. pp. 877, 1662-1664, 1928.

[2] Thackeray, *Grammar*, vol. i. pp. 65, 72, 98, note 3.

[3] Hort, ' Introduction,' p. 152.

[4] Von Soden, p. 877. Von Soden, pp. 878 f., 1662, gives some interesting instances where the reading of A seems to be due to the misunderstanding of corrections in the archetype, in which an Antiochian reading (as he thinks, of the type K^a) was intended to be substituted for an earlier one. For instance, Luke xi. 42 (I follow von Soden's notation) H παρειναι, K αφιεναι, δ4 (*i.e.* Codex A) παραφιεναι ; xix. 23 H αν αυτο επραξα, KK^a αν επραξα αυτο, δ4 αν αυτο ανεπραξα ; xxiv. 53 KK^a add αινουντες και after εν τω ιερω, δ4 αινουντες και instead of εν τω ιερω ; Acts iii. 18 παθειν τον χριστον αυτου, K αυτου παθειν τον χριστον, δ4 omits παθειν τον χριστον ; and many others. The view of von Soden that an older text has been corrected by the Antiochian rather than *vice versa* receives strong support from some of the cases noted in the pages referred to, and is inherently more probable than Hort's idea (if he meant it in an historical and not merely a logical sense) of " a fundamentally Syrian text, mixed occasionally with pre-Syrian readings, chiefly Western " (' Introduction,' p. 152). Hort called attention to the striking agreement of A and the Latin Vulgate in some books. Von Soden, in his ' Erster Theil : Untersuchungen,' §§ 172-182, designated the Gospel text of A (together with about one hundred other codices) as K^a. Later in the same volume, §§ 235-237, in consequence, it would appear, of some alteration of judgment as to the significance of the older element in the text, he includes it under the ' I-form,' and in the text-volume the group appears as I^k.

Apocalypse, as in some parts of the Old Testament, it is the best of all extant manuscripts. The usefulness of A for the reconstruction of the text of the New Testament is considerably limited by the circumstances here mentioned.

C. CODEX EPHRAEMI

Of the earlier history of this codex before it came into the possession of Cardinal Ridolfi of Florence († 1550) nothing is known. It was broken up and the parchment rewritten with Greek tracts of Ephraem Syrus in the twelfth century, perhaps at Constantinople.[1] The manuscript is written carefully and accurately, by a different hand in the New Testament from that which appears in the Septuagint fragments; and possibly a third hand appears in Acts.[2] There seems to be no sufficient reason for any confident assertion that it is of Egyptian origin. *History.*

The chief ground adduced for ascribing C to the fifth century is its resemblance in writing (and to some degree in text) to Codex Alexandrinus (see above, p. lii). It has been corrected by a hand C², assigned to a date perhaps one century later than the original, and again by a later hand, C³ or C^c, deemed to be not later than the ninth century. *Date.*

The text of the Gospels in C is fundamentally of the type of B and ℵ, but has probably been affected by the influence of the Antiochian revision, and contains some ' Western ' readings. There are but few individual peculiarities. In the Pauline epistles the character of the text is the same, but with less influence from the Antiochian; and the same may be said of the text of Acts, as more fully discussed below, although in Acts von Soden estimates the Antiochian and ' Western ' influences as about equal. In some cases in Acts the same Antiochian reading *Character of text.*

[1] Tischendorf, *Codex Ephraemi Syri rescriptus sive fragmenta Novi Testamenti*, 1843, p. 16. Ceriani, *Rendiconti, Reale Istituto Lombardo*, Series II. vol. xxi., 1888, p. 547, expresses doubts as to the accuracy of Tischendorf's edition of C.

[2] Traube, *Nomina sacra*, pp. 70-73.

has been adopted by A and C, but the two manuscripts do not seem to be derived from any common mixed original.[1]

D. CODEX BEZAE

History.   Codex Bezae (graeco-latin [2]) was obtained by Théodore de Bèze, the French reformer of Geneva, from the monastery of St. Irenaeus at Lyons, where it was found during the civil commotions of 1562, doubtless at the sack of the city by Huguenot troops in that year.[3] A few years earlier it had been taken to the Council of Trent by William à Prato (Guillaume du Prat), Bishop of Clermont in Auvergne, and used there in 1546 as evidence for several unique or unusual Greek readings relating to matters under debate by the members of the council.[4] While it was in Italy a friend communicated many

---

[1] Von Soden, pp. 935-943, 1659-1662, 1928.

[2] Codex Bezae appears to be the oldest known graeco-latin MS. of any part of the New Testament.   Other early graeco-latin codices are the Verona Psalter (R, sixth cent.), Codex Claromontanus (D^{paul}, fifth or sixth cent.), Codex Laudianus (E^{ac}, sixth cent.); many graeco-latin Psalters and New Testament MSS. were written in the ninth and following centuries until the invention of printing. See E. von Dobschütz, *Eberhard Nestle's Einführung in das griechische Neue Testament*, 4th ed., 1923, pp. 58 f.

[3] For Beza's letter of gift to the University of Cambridge, containing his statements as to the source from which he acquired it, see Scrivener, *Bezae Codex Cantabrigiensis*, 1864, p. vi.   In the annotations to Beza's edition of the New Testament, 1598 (notes on Luke xix. 26 ; Acts xx. 3), the editor refers to the codex as 'Claromontanus.' This may be due to some knowledge on his part, not now to be recovered, or perhaps to a mere confusion between the Lyons MS. and the similar, but Pauline, Codex Claromontanus (D^{paul}), then at Beauvais, the readings of which he had been able to adduce as early as his second (third) edition, 1582.   Beza was not aware that the MS. from which the readings designated β^1 in Stephen's apparatus were drawn was the same as his codex ; J. R. Harris, *Codex Bezae : A Study of the So-called Western Text of the New Testament* (Texts and Studies, ii.), 1891, pp. 3-6.

[4] Our knowledge here comes from the statements of Marianus Victorius, Bishop of Amelia and later of Rieti († 1572), in the notes to his edition of the works of St. Jerome, first published at Rome, 1566.   They are as follows :

(1) Note on *Adv. Jovinianum*, i. 14, with reference to John xxi. 22 (ουτως), Antwerp ed., 1578, p. 570, col. 1 ; Paris ed., 1609, p. 509 F ; Cologne ed., 1616, vol. iii., Scholia, p. 33, note 32 : *sicut habet antiquissimus quidam Graecus codex, quem Tridentum attulit Claramontanensis episcopus anno domini 1549* [so Cologne ed. ; apparently mistake for 1546].

(2) Note on *Adv. Jov.* i. 18, with reference to Matt. i. 23 (καλεσεις); Cologne

readings of D to Robert Stephen, the Paris printer and editor, and they were included (to the number of over 350, with some inaccuracies) in the apparatus to his first folio edition of 1550.[1] The Bishop of Clermont evidently returned the manuscript to its owners at Lyons. In 1581 Beza presented it to the University of Cambridge, as he says, ' *asservandum potius quam publicandum.*' [2]

Codex Bezae has commonly been assigned to the sixth century, Date. but there seems no good reason for refusing it a place in the preceding one,[3] and a date even at the beginning of the fifth

---

ed., 1616, vol. iii., Scholia p. 34, note 40 : *et ita etiam scriptus est in antiquissimo codice Lugdunensi.*

(3) Note on *Epist.* 146, *ad Damasum,* with reference to Matt. ix. 13 (εἰς μετάνοιαν); Cologne ed., 1616, vol. iii., Scholia, p. 89, note 4: *desunt [haec verba] etiam apud Graecum codicem Vaticanum qui scriptus est iam sunt anni mille et ultra, et apud alterum antiquissimum librum Graecum Claremontensem.*

The first of these notes has been well known since the seventeenth century ; the other two were noticed by H. Quentin, ' Note additionnelle ' to ' Le Codex Bezae à Lyon au IXᵉ siècle ? ' (*Revue Bénédictine,* vol. xxiii., 1906, pp. 24 f.). As Quentin observes, all doubt as to the accuracy of Beza's statement about Lyons is removed by the second of these notes. See also J. R. Harris, *Codex Bezae,* pp. 36-39. It was natural that Marianus Victorius, who was present at the council, should have described a codex brought from Lyons by the Bishop of Clermont, now as ' Lugdunensis ' now as ' Claremontensis ' ; his variation throws no light on Beza's above-mentioned references to its readings as from a ' Claromontanus.'

[1] For the evidence that the authority designated β¹ in Stephen's ' editio regia,' 1550, was actually our Codex Bezae see Scrivener, *Bezae Codex Cantabrigiensis,* pp. ix-x. Stephen's statement in his ' Epistle to the Reader ' is τὸ δὲ β′ ἐστὶ τὸ ἐν Ἰταλίᾳ ὑπὸ τῶν ἡμετέρων ἀντιβληθὲν φίλων. The identification with D was made as early as Wetstein.

[2] Since the arrival of the codex at Cambridge, it has suffered at least twice by mutilations of the bottom of folio 504, succeeding an earlier cut or tear which may have taken place before 1581. The missing text, however, both Greek and Latin, can be securely reconstructed, mainly from early collations ; see below, pp. 202-5, and J. H. Ropes, ' The Reconstruction of the Torn Leaf of Codex Bezae,' *Harvard Theological Review,* vol. xvi., 1923, pp. 162-168. It may be fitting here to call attention to F. Blass, ' Zu Codex D in der Apostelgeschichte,' *Theol. Studien und Kritiken,* vol. lxxi., 1898, pp. 539-542, where will be found some corrections of Scrivener's edition of the manuscript in *Bezae Codex Cantabrigiensis,* 1864, in difficult places which Blass personally examined.

[3] F. C. Burkitt, ' The Date of Codex Bezae,' *Journal of Theological Studies,* vol. iii., 1901-2, pp. 501-513, partly in reply to Scrivener, who had presented as the chief argument against the fifth century " the debased dialect of the Latin version "—surely an unconvincing reason.

century has been urged.[1] Palaeography, whether Latin or Greek, has so far given little aid toward a definite solution of the problem of its date and origin.[2] Various characteristics, such as the ornamentation, subscriptions, titles, the numbering of the quires, and the form of the letters betray the training of the scribe in Latin methods,[3] and the presence, by inadvertence, of occasional Greek words and letters on the Latin side is no proof to the contrary.[4] It cannot be maintained that the codex originated in a centre of strictly Greek writing, where Latin was a wholly foreign language. On the other hand, it certainly did not

---

[1] J. Chapman, *Zeitschrift für die neutestamentliche Wissenschaft*, vol. vi., 1905, pp. 345 f.

[2] The writing of Codex Bezae shows marked resemblances to that of Codex Claromontanus of Paul, but the hand of Codex Bezae is less skilful and regular. The many points of contact of the two MSS. make it hard to believe that they are not to be associated in origin. The peculiar Latin text of the Pauline epistles in Codex Claromontanus is practically the same as that of Lucifer of Cagliari, a fact which has led Souter to suggest that Codex Claromontanus (and consequently also Codex Bezae) was written in Sardinia ; see A. Souter, ' The Original Home of Codex Claromontanus (Dpaul),' *Journal of Theological Studies*, vol. vi., 1904–5, pp. 240-243. The remarkable list (Canon Claromontanus) of the books of the Old and New Testaments which in Dpaul follows the thirteen Pauline epistles, as if the exemplar had lacked Hebrews, must be taken into account in any theory of the origin of both Codex Bezae and Codex Claromontanus.

[3] G. Mercati, ' On the Non-Greek Origin of the Codex Bezae,' *Journal of Theological Studies*, vol. xv., 1913–14, pp. 448-451. This article was in reply to E. A. Lowe, *Journal of Theological Studies*, vol. xiv., 1912–13, pp. 385-388, who had urged that the Latin uncials employed in D are of a grecizing type, used in Egypt, Asia Minor, Greece, and North Africa, and such as would probably have been used in Latin law-books written in Byzantium, and further that sundry Greek practices are exhibited by the manuscript, so that all these facts together would suggest an origin in a non-italian centre. But in a later article, ' The Codex Bezae and Lyons,' *Journal of Theological Studies*, vol. xxv., 1924, pp. 270-274, Lowe admits the conclusive force of Mercati's rejoinder, and withdraws his theory.

[4] Against the suggestion of South Italy, Kenyon, *Handbook to the Textual Criticism of the N.T.*, 2nd ed. p. 92, remarks, " The chief objection to this theory is that Greek was so well known in that region that we should have expected the Greek part of the ms. to be better written than it is. In point of fact, the Greek has the appearance of having been written by a scribe whose native language was Latin ; and some of the mistakes which he makes (*e.g.* writing *l* for λ or *c* for κ) point in the same direction. We want a locality where Latin was the prevalent tongue, but Greek was still in use for ecclesiastical purposes, for the liturgical notes are all on the Greek side."

proceed from any centre of the trained Latin calligraphy of the period.

Of the earlier history of the codex the work of the successive Correctors and annotators. correctors and annotators has left a partial record—if we could only interpret correctly the lessons to be drawn ! Some twenty successive hands can be distinguished, but their approximate dates are disputed, with a tendency on the part of palaeographical experts to assign them to more and more early periods.[1] No one of the correctors was probably the regular diorthotes of the manuscript. Nearly all were much more interested in the Greek text, and touched the Latin pages but little ; but one corrector (G, assigned to the seventh century, or even to about the same time as the original scribe [2]) concerned himself mainly with the Latin. The annotators include more than half of the improving hands ; in two cases the same hand undertook both kinds of addition. The Greek annotators were formerly thought to have begun with the ninth century, but recently have all been assigned to the period before 800.[3] Their work includes the marginal indication of lessons both in the Gospels and in Acts, drawn from the usual Byzantine system,[4] with modifications by other correctors ; titloi in Matthew, Luke, and John, in a form somewhat divergent from that commonly found ;[5] the numbers of the

---

[1] On the correctors and annotators see Scrivener, *op. cit.*, 1864, pp. xx, xxiv-xxix ; F. E. Brightman, ' On the Italian Origin of Codex Bezae. The Marginal Notes of Lections,' in *Journal of Theological Studies*, vol. i., 1899-1900, pp. 446-454 ; F. G. Kenyon, *ibid.* pp. 293-299 ; J. R. Harris, *The Annotators of the Codex Bezae (with some Notes on Sortes Sanctorum)*, 1901 ; F. C. Burkitt, ' The Date of Codex Bezae,' *Journal of Theological Studies*, vol. iii., 1901-2, pp. 501-513 ; E. A. Lowe, ' The Codex Bezae,' *ibid.* vol. xiv., 1912-13, pp. 385-388. It is surprising that the perfect accessibility of the codex, now available also in facsimile, the valuable foundation laid by Scrivener sixty years since, and the highly stimulating inquiries of Harris more than twenty years ago should not yet have led to the production of an adequate account of the facts as to these matters.

[2] E. A. Lowe, *l.c.* p. 387. So also F. C. Burkitt, *l.c.* pp. 511 f., who suggests that " G is the handwriting of the Bishop of the church for which Codex Bezae was originally prepared," and that the corrections were made before the manuscript was considered to be issued for use.

[3] So A. S. Hunt, as quoted by Lowe, *l.c.* p. 388.

[4] Brightman, *l.c.*   [5] Harris, *Annotators of the Codex Bezae*, p. 41.

Ammonian sections ; and in the margin of the Gospel of Mark, by a hand formerly assigned to the tenth century, but perhaps earlier, a set of seventy-one ' sortes sanctorum,' or soothsaying sentences in Greek. These last are closely like the more complete Latin series in the (Vulgate and Old Latin) Codex Sangermanensis (G) of the eighth or ninth century, probably written in the neighbourhood of Lyons.

No one of the annotators appears to have been a scholar.[1] The holy days for which lessons are marked include the Assumption of the Blessed Virgin, and the feasts of St. George and St. Dionysius the Areopagite, all of these by relatively late annotators.[2]

In the eighth or early ninth century [3] a single Latin scribe supplied the missing portions of both the Greek and Latin text of the Gospels, adding to the codex leaves of which nine are still extant. His Latin text was derived from the Vulgate.[4]

Use by Ado.

One other highly instructive piece of possible evidence as to the history of the codex before the sixteenth century remains to be mentioned, and is due to the critical acumen and the learning of H. Quentin.[5] It is drawn from the Martyrology of Ado of Lyons (later Bishop of Vienne), written in 850–860. In his summary accounts of the several martyrs Ado both makes allusions to the New Testament and draws quotations from it in abundance. These are ordinarily taken from the Old Latin

[1] Harris, *Annotators,* p. 75.

[2] *Ibid.* p. 105.

[3] Lowe, *l.c.* p. 388. Lowe describes the Greek of this hand as Western ' imitation uncials.' Scrivener, p. xxi, had assigned the supplementary leaves to the hand " of a Latin of about the tenth century." Harris, *Annotators,* pp. 106-109, observes that the hand is not Calabrian, and argues that it is that of a scribe unacquainted with spoken Greek.

[4] A parallel to the succession first of Greek and then of Latin annotators and correctors of Codex Bezae may be seen in Codex Marchalianus (Q) of the LXX, where the Greek correctors end in the ninth century, and later corrections are Latin (see above, p. xxxiii note 2).

[5] ' Le Codex Bezae à Lyon au IXe siècle ? ' in *Revue Bénédictine,* vol. xxiii., 1906, pp. 1-23. On Lyons in the ninth century, see S. Tafel, ' The Lyons Scriptorium,' in *Palaeographia Latina,* edited by W. M. Lindsay, Part II., London, 1923, p. 68.

fourth-century recension known to us from Codex Gigas and other sources, which was evidently the most widely used form of the Latin translation in the period just before the introduction of the Vulgate, and continued to be employed in various parts of the West for centuries after that date. But in seven instances he departs from the recension of gigas. Three of these [1] are cases where the gigas-recension lacked the reading, and in all of these unique or extremely rare readings Codex Bezae is a source from which the reading of Ado could be drawn. In one of the three the Greek of D is the only possible source known to us ; in the second the only other Latin witness is the African text of h, which Ado is hardly likely to have known ; in the third the only other Latin is the mysterious margin of the Bible de Rosas. In three other cases [2] Ado has twice combined renderings from the gigas-recension and the Vulgate with a third rendering found only in d, while for the third, and similar, case of this group he has taken one rendering from the gigas-recension and combined with it another found in both the Vulgate and d. In the seventh passage [3]

---

[1] (1) Acts xi. 28 *conversantibus autem nobis* (no Latin evidence) for συνεστραμμενων δε ημων D, apparently a direct translation, skilful, very apt, and not naturally suggested by the parallel Latin rendering (*congregatis*) otherwise known to us ; d has the erroneous rendering *revertentibus autem nobis*.

(2) Acts xviii. 2 *in Achaiam*, d h only among Latin MSS. ; so D hcl.*mg*.

(3) Acts xix. 1 *cum vellet ire Hierosolimam, dixit ei spiritus sanctus ut reverteretur in Asiam*, only d and second hand in margin of Bible de Rosas (eastern Spain, tenth cent.), with slight variations in both ; so D hcl.*mg*. It will be observed that in Acts xviii. 2 the addition, omitted in the gigas-recension, is African (codex h), and the same origin may be assumed for a reading of the Bible de Rosas.

[2] (1) Acts vi. 9, for συνζητουντες, *disputantibus* (vg e t p^mg) *et conquirentibus* (gig g₂ p) *atque altercantibus* (d only).

(2) Acts xviii. 3, for δια το ομοτεχνον ειναι (D δια το ομοτεχνον without ειναι), *propter artificium* (d only, incomplete to correspond with the number of words in D) *erant enim ejusdem artis* (gig vg *quia ejusdem erat artis*), *id est scenophegiae* (vg *erat autem scenofactoriae artis* ; so e, with variations). The strange error *scenophegiae* is an obvious reminiscence of John vii. 2.

(3) Acts vi. 12, for συνεκινησαν, *concitato* (cf. gig g₂ h) *populo ac senioribus scribisque adversus eum commotis* (cf. vg e p t ; d).

[3] Acts vi. 9 *qui erant* (d only) *de synagoga quae dicitur Libertinorum. Qui erant*, to which nothing corresponds in any known Latin text, is the characteristically exact rendering in d of των (εκ της συναγωγης) found in D and nearly all Greek MSS. (except א). For *quae dicitur* (d h p ; της λεγομενης D B C

Ado's text gives the exact reading of d. He seems to have brought it in in part (*quae dicitur*) in order to make the language conform to the usual Greek text, but in effecting this has not followed the Vulgate rendering, though equally available for the purpose. Another phrase (*qui erant*) common to d and Ado is unique in d among Latin texts, and may well be one of the cases where the Latin of Codex Bezae (possibly without any predecessor) has been brought into agreement with the Greek opposite page.

The inference drawn from these intricate facts is that the text of Codex Bezae has influenced the language of Ado's Martyrology. Quentin finds reason to think that an intermediate stage was a copy of the gigas-recension, which Ado used, equipped with marginal notes drawn from Codex Bezae. And he attributes the learning and critical interest here displayed not primarily to Ado, but to Florus, Bishop of Lyons († *ca.* 860), of whom it is known that he cherished these interests and that he had correspondents, also interested in the text of the Bible, in Italy. A further, and natural, step is the suggestion that to the instigation of Florus may be due the coming of Codex Bezae to Lyons. That event naturally brought to an end the long line of Greek correctors and annotators of the codex, of which it is now held (see above, p. lix, note 3) that all were, or may have been, earlier than Florus, although formerly scholars ascribed some of them to later centuries.

The subtle and carefully considered theory thus put forward by Quentin may well be correct, provided the dates of the Greek correctors do not stand in the way.[1]

Antiochian), the Vulgate (with e t) has *quae appellatur* (*appellabatur*) ; while the gigas-recension (gig g₂), alone among Latin texts, has *qui dicuntur* (for των λεγομενων אA minn). Ado has here deserted the gigas-recension, not for the Vulgate, but to adopt a reading conforming to the Greek text with the singular, and he has used for this purpose the Latin form found in d (and in h p, to neither of which does Ado's text show specific kinship).

[1] E. A. Lowe, ' The Codex Bezae and Lyons,' *Journal of Theological Studies*, vol. xxv., 1924, pp. 270-274, accepts as convincing Quentin's arguments, and adds striking confirmation from two observations : (1) Blue ink occurs in the colophon to the added pages of Mark in Codex Bezae (ninth century). The use of this ink in Latin MSS. has been observed elsewhere only in a ninth-

From the whole body of facts here summarized it is a fair inference that at an early time, certainly as early as the seventh century, and for a long period, the codex lay in a place or places where Greek was both the ecclesiastical language and was also (for long, at least) understood and used by the people, but where Latin was also familiarly known to a greater or less extent, a place that is, which was distinctly " not a Latin centre where Greek was merely read and written." [1] Where such a place is to be sought will be considered presently. Soon after the beginning of the ninth century the MS. lay in a strictly Latin environment.

On the question of where Codex Bezae was written the character of its Latin pages, and of their dialectal and vulgar peculiarities, whether as respects pervading linguistic traits or isolated phenomena, has hitherto thrown no light. Since it was found at Lyons in the sixteenth century, the suggestion has often been made that it was written and had always remained in the south of France, where in the second century the Christians of Lyons and certain other towns of the Rhone valley were Greeks. But this Greek life continued for only a limited period, and it is wholly improbable that Greek was the common language of this population or of these churches in the fifth, still less in the sixth, century. In Gaul of that period Greek was the cultivated art of the few.[2] Moreover, the place of origin of the codex would naturally bear a close relation to the scene of work of the early correctors and annotators of the seventh and eighth centuries, who clearly belong in Greek surroundings, to be found nowhere

Theory of origin in France.

---

century Lyons MS. (Lugd. 484), which is perhaps in Florus's own hand, and in one other MS., probably written at Luxeuil. (2) A peculiar interrogation mark, found in these added pages, is found also (and hitherto only) in five MSS., all of the ninth century, and all perhaps written or annotated by Florus himself. See also E. A. Lowe, *Codices lugdunenses antiquissimi*, Lyons, 1924.

[1] Harris, *Annotators*, p. 75.

[2] On the very limited amount of Greek ecclesiastical life in Gaul see Brightman, *Journal of Theological Studies*, vol. I., 1899–1900, pp. 451-454 ; C. P. Caspari, *Ungedruckte, unbeachtete und wenig beachtete Quellen zur Geschichte des Taufsymbols und der Glaubensregel*, iii., Christiania, 1875, pp. 228-231.

in Gaul. The ninth-century revival of letters in Lyons, under Bishop Agobard (814–840) and his successors of the days of Florus and Ado, would explain the addition by an undoubtedly Latin hand of the supplementary pages already referred to, but the predecessors of these men in the two preceding centuries were far removed from the attainments, capacity, and interests of the earlier annotators of the codex. And fatal to the whole theory of Southern France is the insertion of the Byzantine lesson-system, which was not used in Gaul.[1]

South Italy.

The other suggestion most often made is that Codex Bezae was written in South Italy, which in ancient times, as Magna Graecia, had been a recognized part of the Greek world. Here, it is true, in Reggio and the district nearest to Sicily, Greek seems to have been dominant at the beginning of the eighth century ; and in that and the following centuries Greek customs and the use of the Greek language made steady progress in all Calabria, in consequence of the incoming of immigrants—religious and secular—from Sicily and from the East. But in fact the origin of the codex in the fifth or sixth century, and its earliest use, fall in the intervening time between the ancient and the mediaeval Greek periods of Southern Italy.

Hellenism in South Italy.

At the end of the fifth century what Greek civilization and ecclesiastical life had survived there from a happier period disappeared, largely in consequence of the barbarian invasions. Even the remotest part of Bruttium, close to Sicily, seems to have become Latin in institutions and language, save for the cosmopolitan meeting-place of Reggio. In the middle of the sixth century the implications and explicit statements of Procopius, and at the end of that century the letters of Gregory the Great, make clear the same state of things in spite of the reconquest of Italy under Justinian, and it is likewise revealed by the evidence of the South Italian inscriptions of the fifth and sixth centuries. Cassiodorus himself († 562), with his native Calabrian aristocratic origin, and as well the Latin monastery

---

[1] F. E. Brightman, *op. cit.* pp. 446-454.

which he founded, are characteristic for his time. The Roman ecclesiastical system and Latin monasteries seem to have supplied substantially all there was of higher intellectual and moral forces.

The second hellenization of Southern Italy, which issued in the flourishing Greek civilization of the eleventh century, was due to a variety of causes. In the seventh century the advancing victories in Syria and Egypt, first of the Persians, then of the Mohammedans, led to the migration of oriental Christians to Italy and still more to Sicily. Toward the end of that century, and increasingly thereafter, measures were taken by Byzantium to consolidate its power in Southern Italy and to defend Sicily against Mohammedan invaders from Africa, and these steps must have caused a growth of the Greek population of Southern Italy, as they certainly enlarged the channels of Greek influence, both ecclesiastical and secular. In the eighth century Greek clergy and monks fleeing from the persecuting rigor of the imperial iconoclastic policy may have come in considerable numbers to Italy, where they were able to find a friendly theological environment ; while at the same time the administrative connexion of these South Italian dioceses with Constantinople was knit closer. In the early ninth century, when the Saracens conquered most of Sicily (taking Palermo in 831), many Sicilians fled to Italy, and Greek Sicilian monks began to wander through the wilderness and to be seen in the towns of Calabria. Before the middle of the tenth century St. Nilus appears, Greek monasteries are numerous, and the copying of Greek manuscripts is common. With the Norman rule great monastic centres of Greek intellectual life were constructed, and prospered, until, two centuries later, they shared in the general decay of civilization consequent upon the overthrow of the Normans, and at last fell into the wretched state in which the humanistic ecclesiastics of the fifteenth century found them. Fortunately these houses still had Greek books, many of which were brought at different periods to securer centres and incorporated in the great collections to which modern scholars resort.

In considering the origin of Codex Bezae this sketch of the progressive re-hellenization of Southern Italy from the seventh century on is necessary, because the abundant Greek life of Calabria in later ages is often assumed to have been present in the earlier period in which the codex was written and in which it had its home in a community using Greek as well as Latin. While, under the limitations of our knowledge, there is a bare possibility that in the fifth or sixth century some place existed in Southern Italy where it could have been written, nevertheless, no such place is known, and the general conditions which we do know make such an origin unlikely. This unlikelihood is raised to a very strong improbability by the difficulty of supposing that, even if the codex was written in South Italy, any locality there in the sixth or seventh century (and with some restrictions conditions were similar for a great part of the eighth) would have provided the background of church life implied by the extraordinarily numerous correctors and annotators.[1] South Italy certainly does not seem to offer a probable birthplace and still less a probable early home for this codex.[2]

[1] The suggestion that the writing of the annotator M resembles a Ravenna hand of the year 756 (Burkitt, *Journal of Theological Studies*, vol. III., 1901-2, p. 505 note) rests on a confusion. The hand in question (shown in E. M. Thompson, *Handbook of Greek and Latin Palaeography*, p. 144 ; *Introduction to Greek and Latin Palaeography*, pp. 26, 184) is, in fact, from the imperial chancery in Constantinople. The document is part of the original of a letter from the emperor to a French king, probably from Michael II. or Theophilus to Louis the Débonnaire, and brought by one of the embassies known to have been sent in the period 824–839 ; see H. Omont, *Revue Archéologique*, vol. XIX., 1892, pp. 384-393, with facsimile.

[2] The disappearance of the ancient hellenism of Magna Graecia and the fact that the mediaeval Greek civilization of Calabria was due to a fresh rehellenization several centuries later was brought out in the 'Ιταλοελληνικά of Spyridion Zampelios (Athens, 1864), and emphatically presented by F. Lenormant in *La Grande-Grèce*, 1881, vol. i. p. vii; vol. ii. pp. 371-382, 395. An illuminating sketch of the history is given by P. Batiffol, *L'Abbaye de Rossano*, 1891, pp. i-xxxix. See also Jules Gay, *L'Italie méridionale et l'empire byzantin*, 1904, pp. 5-24, 184-200, 254-286, 350-365, 376-386 ; Charles Diehl, *Études sur l'administration byzantine dans l'exarchat de Ravenne (568-751)*, 1888, pp. 241-288 ; K. Lake, ' The Greek Monasteries in Southern Italy,' in *Journal of Theological Studies*, vol. IV., 1902-3, pp. 345 ff., 517 ff. ; v., 1903-4, pp. 22 ff., 189 ff.

On the other hand, what is known of Sicily corresponds very well with the requirements for Codex Bezae. Greek was the language of Sicily under the Roman emperors, and never succumbed to the Latin influences which Roman rule brought in. In Sicily, unlike Magna Graecia, the landowners were a Roman aristocracy residing in a country with which they did not fully identify themselves. Latin was the official language, but the mass of the people, although affected by Latin culture, continued to speak Greek. At the end of the sixth century, under Gregory the Great, the clergy were largely Latin, but included Greeks, and from the beginning of the seventh century Greek language and culture made rapid progress among the Sicilian clergy, and there were strong personal relations with the churches of the Orient. By the middle of the century Greek was preponderant, and in the eighth century the clergy were firmly attached to the Eastern Church. By this time the same had become true of Calabria. During these centuries there seems to have been a steady influx of Greeks, especially in consequence of Persian and Saracen attacks on various centres of Christian life in the Greek world. In the early years of the ninth century came acute and persistent disturbance from Arab invasion.[1]

All this would well account for the origin of Codex Bezae and for its use for centuries in a locality or localities where the Greek language and Greek customs were continuously in vogue, but where Latin was also known. The disturbed condition of the country early in the ninth century would likewise explain the acquisition of the manuscript by scholars of Lyons at about that date.

Nothing, indeed, forbids the suggestion that emigrants or refugees from Sicily carried Codex Bezae with them to Calabria

---

[1] On the history of conditions in Sicily and the relation of Sicily to Calabria, see, besides the works of Batiffol, Gay, and Lake, mentioned in the preceding note, Adolf Holm, *Geschichte Siciliens im Altertum*, vol. iii., 1898, Buch ix. pp. 220-337 ; Josef Führer, *Forschungen zur Sicilia sotteranea* (Abhandlungen, Munich Academy, vol. xx.), 1897. On early monastic life in Sicily see D. G. Lancia di Brolo, *Storia della Chiesa in Sicilia nei dieci primi secoli del cristianesimo*, vol. i., Palermo, 1880, chapter xx.

in the eighth century, but no fact as yet known requires this assumption.

It thus seems likely that Sicily was the place of origin of Codex Bezae and of its mate Codex Claromontanus (D^{paul}), and that the correctors and annotators of the earlier period, who were chiefly concerned with the Greek pages, were Sicilians. Yet some of these latter may, for aught we know to the contrary, have been Calabrians. Somewhere about the year 800 the codex was probably sent to Lyons. Its history, partly conjectural, partly known, presents a remarkable parallel to that of the Codex Laudianus, written in Sardinia in the sixth or seventh century, brought (by way doubtless of Italy) to England in the seventh, to be used in the eighth by the Venerable Bede, and finally destined, like Codex Bezae, to pass into the hands of modern scholars in consequence of the looting of a monastery by Protestant soldiers in a war of religion.

Contents.

But we must turn from the history of Codex Bezae to its internal character. The four Gospels stand in the order, Matthew, John, Luke, Mark. This is the order of many Old Latin MSS., and is often called 'Western,' but it is also followed in W (Egyptian), X, the Apostolic Constitutions, and other Greek witnesses, and does not imply anything as to the place of origin of D.[1] Between the Gospels and Acts three leaves and eight quires are missing, to judge by the numbering of the quires. Since all quires contain eight leaves (except one which has six), the lost leaves must have numbered sixty-seven, of which perhaps the whole of one was filled by the close of the Gospel of Mark. The remaining sixty-six included at least some of the Catholic Epistles, for one page containing the closing verses of 3 John still immediately precedes the first page of Acts. Even all the seven Catholic Epistles, however, would not suffice to fill sixty-six

---

[1] J. Chapman, *Zeitschrift für die neutest. Wissenschaft*, vol. vi., 1905, pp. 339-346, argues from various indications that the order of the Gospels in the parent MS. of D was Matthew, Mark, John, Luke, as in Mommsen's Canon and the Curetonian Syriac. This he holds to have been the original ' Western ' order, for which is substituted in Codex Bezae the characteristic Latin order.

leaves, and what these pages contained has been the subject of much conjecture. The space would about suffice for the Apocalypse and the three Epistles of John.[1] Such a *corpus johanneum* would account for the unusual position of the Epistles of John, at the end of the collection of Catholic Epistles, which is, however, found in Codex 326, in the Muratorian fragment, and in Rufinus, and perhaps was the order of the Old Latin translation of Cassiodorus. The arrangement by which the Catholic Epistles preceded Acts is that of the Egyptian translations, and seems to have been not uncommon in the Latin world.

The codex seems to be the work of one scribe, and the Greek Errors. and Latin pages have a general aspect of deceptive similarity to one another.[2] It is badly written. On the Greek side the scribe is guilty of many obvious blunders and misspellings on nearly every page. Such are, for instance, Matt. vi. 7 βλαττολογησεται, Mark xii. 17 εθαυμαζοντο, Luke xii. 35 λυχλοι for λυχνοι, xxiii. 26 οπεισοθεν, John i. 3 ενεγετο, xvii. 25 ο κοσμος τουτος (for ουτος, itself probably due to imitation of the Latin rendering of ο κοσμος by *mundus hic*), Acts i. 4 συναλισκομενος, iii. 10 εκτασεως for εκστασεως, viii. 5 καλελθων for κατελθων, and many others. Many of these can be seen in the plain and troublesome errors which have been excluded from the text as printed in the present volume, but are given in the lines immediately below the text. In innumerable instances the endings are wrong, so that nonsense results, or, for instance, a pronoun does not agree in gender with the noun to which it refers. This is sometimes due to thoughtless assimilation to the ending of a neighbouring word (for instance, Matt. iv. 18 βαλλοντας αμφιβληστρος, Acts i. 3 οπτανομενοις αυτοις), sometimes it may be attributed

---

[1] F. C. Burkitt, *Encyclopaedia Biblica*, 1903, col. 4997 ; J. Chapman, ' The Original Contents of Codex Bezae,' *Expositor*, 6th series, vol. XII., 1905, pp. 46-53.

[2] The Latin page has at first glance a likeness to Greek writing somewhat like that which is found in a page of ancient Coptic, and rather greater than that of modern Russian. But see the articles of Lowe and Mercati referred to above. Such resemblance of the two sides in a graeco-latin MS. is not without parallels ; the Coislin Psalter of the seventh century (Paris, Bibl. nat., coisl. 186) is an example.

to the influence of the corresponding Latin word (thus, Acts xviii. 2 κλανδιος for κλανδιον, cf. d *Claudius*). It has been suggested that many of these errors may be due to some stage in the ancestry of the codex in which a copy was made from a papyrus text with easily misunderstood abbreviations for terminations (τ᾽ for την, etc.).[1] Nothing forbids this suggestion, but it likewise implies an ignorant, if not a careless, scribe, and many mistakes thus made ought subsequently to have been corrected by any competent later copyist. Mistakes in gender, as Matt. iv. 16 φως μεγαν, Luke ix. 1 πασαν δαιμονιον, are not infrequent, especially in pronouns. Semitic proper names receive strange forms. Good examples of some of these classes of error occur in Acts iii. 26, where D reads ευλογουντας for ευλογουντα, τ αποστρεφειν for τω αποστρεφειν, εκαστος for εκαστον ; xiv. 20, κυκλωσαντες for κυκλωσαντων, αυτου for αυτον, την επαυριον for τη επαυριον. Blunders such as these sometimes give the impression of a writer who understood Greek imperfectly, and some of them suggest that the *look* of a Greek word did not infallibly present to him a combination of sounds with which he was familiar.[2] Nevertheless his ignorance of Latin is also extraordinary.

In view of this character of the codex the frequent departure which it shows from other manuscripts in the omission, or (what is more common) the addition, of the Greek article will in many cases have to be attributed to eccentricity, not to a sound or ancient tradition.

---

[1] Kenyon, *Handbook to the Textual Criticism of the N.T.*, 2nd ed., pp. 96 f.

[2] The most complete account of these blunders (and the other peculiarities) of D will be found in von Soden, *Schriften des Neuen Testaments*, pp. 1305-1340, 1720-1727, 1814-1836. But even in the paragraphs devoted to ' unintentional errors ' von Soden has too little distinguished between actual errors and what may be called antiquated irregularities, such as would have been deemed tolerable, or even respectable, in a manuscript of the third or fourth century, before the reforming efforts of the grammarians had come to dominate the copying of books. Singularities of this latter type should be treated separately ; they may well have been derived from an exemplar of a remote antiquity, several stages back, and so testify only to the fidelity, not to the debased condition, of the copy which we have.

Besides these disfiguring blunders, the usual confusions of
vowels and consonants, due to itacism and the like, occur in
abundance, as well as the miscellaneous omissions and errors to
which scribal frailty is prone ; and the well-known grammatical
peculiarities of the older codices, especially in the forms of verbs,
are constantly encountered. Peculiar, or antiquated, spellings,
such as Matt. ii. 11 ζμυρναν for σμυρναν ; xii. 20, xxv. 8 ζβεν-
νυμι for σβεννυμι ; Luke xiii. 34 ορνιξ for ορνις, frequently
attract the attention of the reader. All these singularities are
found in greater abundance than in perhaps any other New
Testament manuscript.[1]

Harmonization of parallel passages as between the several
Gospels, and in the parts of Acts which strongly resemble one
another, are numerous, and often do not agree with the similar
harmonizations of the Antiochian text.[2] Omissions, by homoeoteleuton and otherwise, are relatively abundant, much more so
in the Gospels than in the Acts. A considerable group of these
omissions consists of the evident omission of whole lines, for
instance Acts ii. 31, where προιδων ελαλησεν περι της has fallen
out in both D and d ; more complicated cases are Luke viii. 41,
Acts v. 29. In some instances the misplacement or omission of

[1] For classified lists of these see Scrivener, *Bezae Codex Cantabrigiensis*,
pp. xlvi-xlviii. An adequate linguistic investigation of Codex Bezae (or indeed
of the other oldest New Testament manuscripts) seems never to have been
attempted. G. Rudberg, *Neutestamentlicher Text und Nomina Sacra*, Upsala,
1915, has a valuable discussion of the errors and confusions of spelling in D,
and is led to emphasize the conservative character of the copying. On the
peculiar variation in spelling, ιωαννης almost always in Matt., Mark, John i.-v. 33,
but ιωανης (with negligible exceptions) in Luke, Acts, see von Soden, pp. 2100 f. ;
J. Chapman, *Zeitschrift für die neutest. Wissenschaft*, vi., 1905, pp. 342-345 ;
Rudberg, pp. 13 f. The phenomenon can be accounted for in more than one way,
and does not necessarily indicate (as sometimes supposed, see Nestle, *Einführung
in das griech. N.T.*, 3rd ed., pp. 175 f.) that we have here a survival from the
period when Luke and Acts circulated together as two ' books ' of a single
history. The regular use of nomina sacra in D (ΘΣ, ΚΣ, ΙΗΣ, ΧΡΣ, ΠΝΑ) is
about as in B, while ℵ, A, and C show a much more fully developed system ;
see Rudberg, pp. 49-52.

[2] For some examples of such assimilation see E. von Dobschütz, *E. Nestle's
Einführung in das Neue Testament*, 4. Aufl. p. 29 ; see also H. J. Vogels, *Die
Harmonistik im Evangelientext des Codex Cantabrigiensis* (T.U. xxxvi.), 1910.

lines on one side or the other was either corrected by the original scribe or noted by him in the margin by numeral letters. Scrivener has been able to show from such cases that the exemplar had lines like those of Codex Bezae, but was not identical with it in the contents of the pages.[1]

Influence of Latin on Greek. Reference has already been made to the influence of the Latin page in causing errors, for instance in endings, in the Greek text. This latinizing influence has produced a far-reaching effect on the Greek text, the precise range of which is difficult to determine. The Latin rendering (due to the poverty of Latin in participial forms) of a Greek participle and finite verb by two finite verbs connected by 'and' is probably the cause of the unusual number of corresponding variants in the Greek D. In some cases και alone has been introduced from the Latin, without change in the Greek participle. Thus Mark vii. 25 ελθουσα και προσεπεσεν (*intravit et procidit*), xi. 2 λυσαντες αυτον και αγαγετε (*solvite illum et adducite*), xiv. 63 διαρρηξας τους χειτωνας αυτου και λεγει (*scidit vestimenta sua et ait*), Acts xiv. 6 συνιδοντες και κατεφυγον (*intellexerunt et fugerunt*). The necessary addition of a copula in rendering into Latin by a relative sentence has produced an inept imitation in the Greek, *e.g.* Matt. xi. 28 παντες οι κοπιωντες και πεφορτισμενοι εσται [for εστε] (*omnes qui lavoratis* [. . . . .] *estis*) ; Acts xiii. 29 παντα τα περι αυτου γεγραμμενα εισιν (*omnia quae de illo scripta sunt*) ; xvii. 27 ζητειν το θειον εστιν (*quaerere quod divinum est*) ; xxi. 21 τους κατα εθνη εισιν ιουδαιους (*qui in gentibus sunt judaeos*) ; so also xi. 1 οι (*qui*) added before εν τη ιουδαια. Not so grotesque, but probably due to adjustment to the Latin, are cases where an otiose but not incorrect participle is added ; so in Mark v. 40 τους μετ αυτου is expanded by the addition of οντας to correspond with *qui cum illo erant*, and similarly Mark ii. 25 ; and with these may be mentioned the frequent supplying of the copula, as in Mark x. 27 τουτο αδυνατον εστιν (*hoc impossibile est*). In a smaller number of cases the attempt to equalize the Greek and

---

[1] *Bezae Codex Cantabrigiensis*, p. **xxiii.**

Latin lines has caused not the addition but the omission of a word. These attempts at assimilation have sometimes led to secondary complicated, but plainly detectable, corruptions of the Greek. A few other instances out of many that have been collected [1] will serve to suggest the great variety of ways in which latinizing assimilation may reasonably be accepted as the corrupting force at work : Matt. xi. 22, 24 ανεκτοτερον εστε (for εσται) εν ημερα κρισεως ην υμειν, for η υμιν (*quam vobis*, misunderstood as if a relative) ; Matt. v. 24 προσφερεις, for προσφερε (*offeres*, itself probably corrupted from *offers*) ; Acts xiii. 10 υιοι (*fili*) for υιος ; Matt. xv. 11, 18, 20, Acts xxi. 28 κοινωνειν for κοινουν (*communicare*, which means not only ' share,' but also, in Tertullian, ' pollute ').[2] Examples, taken from countless others, of words which owe to the Latin either their presence in the text or their form are Matt. xxvi. 6 λεπρωσου for λεπρου, Acts ii. 11 αραβοι for αραβες, v. 32 ον (referring to πνευμα) for ο, vii. 43 ρεμφαμ for ρεμφαν, xvi. 12 κεφαλη (*caput*) for πρωτη, xvi. 13 εδοκει (*bidebatur*, i.e. *videbatur*) for ενομιζετο, xix. 14 ιερευς (*sacerdos*, a common Latin rendering of αρχιερευς) for αρχιερευς. In many cases there will obviously be great difficulty in deciding whether the corrupting force lay in the Latin or in a similar motive, independent and earlier, within the Greek text itself, but the presence of some degree of latinizing must be admitted in many expressions, and of the great range in which this can be surely assumed the above examples can give but an imperfect notion.

The types of latinizing described above have almost all been such as can be detected from traits present in Codex Bezae. But it is also probable that sometimes the striking omission from D of words and clauses found in other well-known, but less

Omissions due to Latin.

---

[1] See J. R. Harris, *Codex Bezae*, 1891, esp. chaps. viii., ix., and x. ; von Soden, *Schriften des Neuen Testaments*, pp. 1323-1337 and pp. 1815-1821, cf. also pp. 1802-1810. For Harris's later view see his *Four Lectures on the Western Text*, 1894, p. viii.

[2] In Codex D κοινωνειν for κοινουν is found uniformly in Matthew, never in Mark, and in one case out of three in Acts.

continuous, witnesses to the ' Western ' text is to be associated with the fact that these ' glosses ' are not found in all or most of the Old Latin witnesses known to us.   Thus in the complicated passage Acts xviii. 21, 22, the important sentences τὸν δὲ Ἀκύλαν εἴασεν ἐν Ἐφέσῳ, αὐτὸς δὲ ἀναχθεὶς ἦλθεν are found in 614, hcl.*mg*, and in part in other Greek minuscules and in the Peshitto, but not in D d, nor in any Latin text whatever.   It is natural to suppose that the words belonged to the fundamental Greek text from which D is drawn, but were omitted because nothing in the Latin version corresponded to them.   The alternative supposition of an excision in order to conform to the Antiochian text is rendered unlikely by the number of ' Western ' readings remaining in the immediate context of D d.   Similarly, at the close of Acts xiv. 18 the words ἀλλὰ πορεύεσθαι ἕκαστον εἰς τὰ ἴδια are found translated in hcl.*mg*, and have survived in Greek in C 81 614 and many minuscules ; but they are lacking in D d and all Latin texts (except that h contains a clause vaguely resembling the Greek, perhaps a loose paraphrase of it). Other examples of the same phenomenon could be collected (cf. some of the omissions mentioned below, pp. ccxxxvi-viii).

Theory of influence of Syriac.

That the Greek text of Codex Bezae has been influenced from the Syriac has also been strongly urged,[1] and some of the facts can be explained thereby, just as they can from the Latin, and in some instances ingenuity can point out with considerable plausibility that a possible confusion in the Syriac text would account for the variant in the Greek.   But whereas influence from Latin is naturally indicated as likely to take place in a graeco-latin codex, the theory of Syriac influence has no such

---

[1] F. H. Chase, *The Old Syriac Element in the Text of Codex Bezae*, 1893 ; *The Syro-Latin Text of the Gospels*, 1895 ; cf. J. R. Harris, *Codex Bezae*, pp. 178-188.   A similar view was favoured many years earlier by J. D. Michaelis, *Einleitung in die göttlichen Schriften des Neuen Bundes*, 3rd ed., 1777, pp. 503 f. (but cf. pp. 336-340), and David Schulz, *Disputatio de Cod. D Cantabrigiensi*, Breslau, 1827, p. 16 ; but Chase was the first to undertake to explain completely and in detail the ' Western ' text as the product of influence from the Syriac version.   For criticism of Chase's theory see J. R. Harris, *Four Lectures on the Western Text of the New Testament*, 1894, pp. 14-34, 68-81.

prima facie probability, and in order to be accepted requires telling instances of demonstrative force, such as are actually found in some of the instances of latinizing cited above. This proof, however, is not forthcoming, and the point is well taken that for some of the frequently occurring characteristics of D the Syriac offers no explanation whatever. Thus the addition of the copula is against Syriac idiom, and such a variant as the addition in Acts xiv. 2 ο δε κυριος εδωκεν ταχυ ειρηνην cannot have been drawn from a Syriac expansion, for the corresponding Syriac would mean, not 'give peace,' but 'say farewell.'[1] There are in D some Semitic traits, such as the use of Hebrew, instead of Aramaic, in the words from the Cross in Matt. xxvii. 46, Mark xv. 34; the readings απο καρνωτου John xii. 4, xiii. 2, 26, xiv. 22 (also in ℵ John vi. 71), σαμφουρειν for εφραιμ, John xi. 54, and perhaps ουλαμμαους for εμμαους, Luke xxiv. 13.[2] Also the otiose αυτοις Acts xiv. 2 might be Semitic ; μετα των ψυχων αυτων Acts xiv. 27 sounds more Semitic than Greek. But these are isolated phenomena, and a better explanation of some of them will be found below (pp. ccxlii-iv). The theory of systematic or continuous Syriac influence does not furnish a satisfactory solution of the problem of Codex Bezae.

It is not to be supposed that all the peculiarities and errors of Codex Bezae were introduced at the latest, or at any single earlier stage. Much of the orthography is doubtless very ancient, or possibly original. Scribal errors of the various usual types may have been introduced at each copying, including that which produced the codex itself. The adjustment of the Greek to the Latin and the converse (of which something will be said later) may well have taken place, in part at least, in different periods. An interesting illustration of a succession of corruptions which must have preceded the present text is the unique reading

Successive corruptions.

---

[1] Harris, *Four Lectures*, pp. 69 f. It is to be observed that Chase's theory was quite as much intended to explain the variants of the ' Western ' text as the eccentricities of Codex Bezae.

[2] Cf. E. von Dobschütz, *E. Nestle's Einführung in das griechische N.T.*, 1923, p. 5.

Luke xxii. 52 στρατηγους του λαου (for ιερου, d *praepositos populi*).   Here λαου seems clearly a corruption for ναου, and that again a substitute (intelligible, but incorrect in point of technical usage) for ιερου of all other witnesses.   In general, if at first the Latin was made approximately to correspond with the Greek, the widespread assimilation of the Greek to the Latin may have been due to the pains of a later scribe ; or both assimilations may have been made concurrently—now from one side, now from the other—when this bilingual edition was first constructed.   One stage in the ancestry of our codex may have been an interlinear graeco-latin text, like the Codex Boernerianus (G^paul).

Opinions on Latin influence.   The general relation of the Greek text of Codex Bezae and the Latin version associated with it has long been the subject of discussion.[1]   The two texts, as they stand, bear intricate relations of likeness ; yet they are by no means identical,[2] and the difference between them cannot as a whole be accounted for by later correction of one side or the other from the Antiochian text.[3] The older debate revolved about too simple a formulation of the question, and was too much interested in proving or disproving the worthlessness of the codex for the practical uses of textual critics.   The seventeenth-century scholars, from Erasmus to Grotius (except Morinus [4]), seem to have held that the Greek text of D had been so adapted to the Latin version as to be practically worthless.   A more moderate view was that of Mill (1707), who deemed the Greek text to have been copied from a

[1] See Harris, *Codex Bezae*, pp. 41-46.

[2] Scrivener, *Bezae Codex Cantabrigiensis*, pp. xxxix f., states that nearly 2000 divergencies are found between the Greek and the Latin.   Of these Acts contains 631, of which 285 are " real various readings " of some consequence, on the Latin side not infrequently showing agreement with the Vulgate.

[3] See, for instance, how the Antiochian (or Old Uncial) correction in chap. xviii. has affected both Greek and Latin equally.   But some cases of one-sided correction can be pointed out ; thus Acts xix. 39 περι ετερων seems to be a correction in accord with ℵA Antiochian, while the corresponding Latin *ulterius* has retained the ' Western ' reading, as found also in gig.

[4] J. Morinus, *Exercitationes biblicae de hebraei graecique textus sinceritate*, Paris, 1660, lib. i., exerc. ii., c. iii., pp. 47-54.   Morinus, convinced of the superiority of the Latin Vulgate, rejoiced to find Vulgate readings confirmed by Codex Bezae and Codex Claromontanus.

Greek original, similar to that from which the Latin version was made, but later to have been altered in conformity to the Latin at a few points here and there (" *paucula hinc inde* "), and who gives well-chosen examples of such readings.[1] Wetstein (*Prolegomena*, 1751) agreed with Mill; and Middleton (1808) [2] urged with much vigour the latinizing tendency of D as evidence (and as one cause) of its worthlessness. Meanwhile, however, J. D. Michaelis [3] had pointed out that this tendency, if it existed, explained but a small part of the peculiarities of D, and Griesbach [4] protested that the conformation to the Latin was negligible, and that the Greek text itself was of Greek origin and a witness to a very ancient stage of the text of the Gospels and Acts. With Griesbach agreed Marsh in his notes to the translation of Michaelis's Introduction (1793), and this general view appears to have held the ground through the greater part of the nineteenth century. Hort (' Introduction,' 1881, pp. 82 f.) regarded d as of little practical value for Old Latin evidence, because it had been " altered throughout into verbal conformity with the Greek text by the side of which it had been intended to stand " ; again (p. 120), he refers with contempt to the " whimsical theory " that " the Western Greek text owed its peculiarities to translation from the Latin " ; in his account of Codex Bezae (pp. 148 f.) he makes no reference whatever to any latinizing tendency in the MS. Similarly Burkitt regards Codex Bezae as a Greek book with a Latin version.[5] But in the meantime J. R. Harris, in his *Codex Bezae*, 1891, presented at length the opposing theory that " the major part," or (p. 203) nine-tenths, of the variants in the Acts of D are due to the attempt to make the Greek text conform to the Latin, and drew attention to a great body of

---

[1] *Prolegomena*, par. 1282.

[2] T. F. Middleton, *The Doctrine of the Greek Article*, 1808, Appendix, pp. 677-698.

[3] *Einleitung*, 4th ed., 1788, pp. 582 f.

[4] *Symbolae criticae*, vol. i., 1785, pp. cx-cxvii.

[5] *Journal of Theological Studies*, vol. III., 1901–2, p. 505. Scrivener, *Bezae Codex Cantabrigiensis*, p. xxxii: " The Latin version is little better than a close and often servile rendering of the actually existing Greek."

evidence in support of this claim.[1]   Von Soden assigns a large place to latinization.

Relation of Greek and Latin sides.   The result of this debate has been to establish that D can neither be rejected as worthless, on the ground that it is secondary and dependent throughout on the Latin, nor yet used, in a fashion which has been all too common, as in every respect a trustworthy witness, as it stands, to the ' Western ' text.   The Latin d, while it has no doubt been affected in countless readings by its Greek partner, is yet by no means a mere literal translation of the Greek D, but neither is D a mere late construction designed to give Greek support to d.   Both sides are mixed texts, and this is exactly what our knowledge of other manuscripts written with parallel columns would lead us to expect.   Indeed, the interaction is probably less marked in Codex Bezae than in cases where the single lines are shorter.   In the very short lines (one to three words each, on the average) of Origen's Hexapla the order of words in the LXX column is believed to have been altered to match the others.[2]   In many graeco-latin Psalters from the sixth to the tenth century the Greek text has been altered to conform to the Latin.[3]   Codex Boernerianus (G^{paul}) is said to show conformation in both directions.[4]   Codex Claromontanus (D^{paul}) probably shows correction of the Latin to agree with the Greek.[5]   The case of Codex Laudianus (E^{ac}) is discussed below.[6]   From a much later date (fourteenth or fifteenth century)

---

[1] Searching criticism of Harris's views were contained in two excellent articles by A. S. Wilkins, ' The Western Text of the Greek Testament,' *Expositor*, 4th series, vol. x., 1894, pp. 386-400, 409-428.   Wilkins admits the existence of latinizing influence, but points out that many of Harris's examples are not convincing, and that in many cases variation common to D and d " may have originated in either."

[2] A. Rahlfs, *Studie über den griechischen Text des Buches Ruth*, 1922, pp. 69 f., n. 3.

[3] Rahlfs, *Der Text des Septuaginta-Psalters*, 1907, pp. 94-101.

[4] E. Diehl, *Zeitschrift für die neutestamentliche Wissenschaft*, vol. xx., 1921, p. 107 ; Hort, ' Introduction,' p. 82.   [5] Hort, ' Introduction,' p. 82.

[6] Jülicher, *Zeitschrift für die neutest. Wissenschaft*, vol. xv., 1914, p. 182, speaks of the " Unmöglichkeit," that D and E should have been conformed to d and e, but the author informs me that the word is a mistake of the press, or the pen, for ' Möglichkeit.'

Codex 629 (Vat. ottobon. 298, see Gregory, *Prolegomena*, p. 635) has a Greek text extensively accommodated to its parallel Vulgate columns. The Latin codex f of the Gospels is thought to be drawn from a bilingual Gothic-Latin codex in which the Latin had been altered to correspond with the Gothic.[1] Even the editors of the Complutensian Polyglot transposed the Greek to make it agree in order of words with their Hebrew column.[2] Apart from the other kinds of corruption, the latinized element in D must always be kept in mind in using Codex Bezae. In such cases the only safe or possible method is by comparison with other witnesses to the same type of text. It cannot be admitted that a Latin influence is accountable for the ' Western ' variants found equally in other Greek, Syriac, and Sahidic sources.[3] Where such evidence is at hand, we may accept the text of D as free from influence from d. Contrariwise, the renderings of d can be supposed to be directly translated from D only where no other Old Latin witness attests them. Within the field thus narrowed, where either D or d can be a direct translation from the other, many cases will be so related to Latin or to Greek idiom, or to the recognizable characteristics of the Greek ' Western' reviser, as to point convincingly to a conclusion ; many others will not. Often doubt will remain. In considering this question it must never be forgotten that the process of mind of a scribe improving the text is in many respects essentially the same as

[1] Burkitt, *Journal of Theological Studies*, vol. i., 1899–1900, p. 131 ; vol. xi., 1909–10, p. 613 ; Wordsworth and White, *Novum Testamentum Latine*, Evangelia, 1889, pp. 653 f., held f to represent substantially the Old Latin text on which the Vulgate revision was founded.

[2] Flaminius Nobilius, in *Vetus Testamentum secundum LXX latine redditum*, 1588 (fourth page of ' Praefatio ad lectorem '), cited by G. F. Moore, ' The Antiochian Recension of the Septuagint,' *American Journal of Semitic Languages and Literatures*, vol. xxix., 1912, pp. 57 f.

[3] It is for this reason that the striking contentions of Harris with regard to the reading, Luke xxiii. 53, και θεντος αυτου επεθηκεν τω μνημειω λειθον ον μογις εικοσι εκυλιον, remain unconvincing. Since the Sahidic, and not merely some Old Latin texts, bears witness to it, it must be supposed to have arisen in Greek, and the imperfect Latin hexameter, *imposuit lapidem quem vix viginti movebant*, must be accounted for, as it can be, by assuming it to be the work of an ingenious Latin translator from the Greek.

that of a translator into another language. That d has affected
D seems beyond doubt in view of such facts as those adduced
above (pp. lxxii-lxxiv) ; but the proof is in most cases demonstrative only for details, many cases must remain doubtful, and
in a great mass of instances, including most of the larger and
more interesting readings, Codex Bezae has certainly preserved
approximately the Greek text of the ' Western ' recension.[1]

Latin text
of Codex
Bezae. The Latin text of d is not carefully written, but offers to the
student of late and dialectal Latin a great storehouse of facts
which seem to have been but little used by philologists.[2] The
obstacles to the use of it for the Old Latin have already been
sufficiently indicated. That it has been extensively corrected
to correspond to the Greek text would be expected, and is
altogether probable.[3] Undoubtedly the Greek text from which
was made the Latin version on which d rests was a ' Western '
text closely akin to the fundamental text which appears in
corrupt form in D. Of the character of the Latin rendering
found in Codex Bezae more will be said below in connexion with
the Old Latin version in general (p. cxi).

Contamina-
tion from
non-
western
Text. An extensive influence of capital importance which came in
after the fundamental text of Codex Bezae was formed, but early
enough to control also the Latin side, was the introduction,
sometimes by conflation, sometimes by substitution, of readings
not ' Western,' but drawn from the rival type of text.[4] Whether

---

[1] With Codex Laudianus (E) the situation is different, as will be shown
below.

[2] The chief study of these is to be found in Harris, *Codex Bezae*, chaps. iv.,
v., xii., xix., xxvi. Cf. K. S. de Vogel, *Bulletin Rylands Library*, viii., 1924,
pp. 398-403. On nomina sacra in d see Traube, *Nomina sacra*, pp. 178 f.

[3] So Hort, 'Introduction,' p. 82; but the arguments and illustrations put
forward by Scrivener, *Bezae Codex Cantabrigiensis*, pp. xxxi-xxxiv, do not
prove this, as is shown by Wilkins, *Expositor*, 4th series, vol. x., 1894, pp. 390-
392. The proof can be brought by a collection of instances where readings of
d not attested elsewhere in Latin correspond to readings of D that are shown by
other evidence to be genuine Greek variants.

[4] Especial attention was called to this phenomenon by the memorable essay
of P. Corssen, *Der Cyprianische Text der Acta apostolorum*, Berlin, 1892 ; see
also *Göttingische gelehrte Anzeigen*, 1901, pp. 9 f. Blass, *Acta apostolorum*,
editio philologica, 1895, p. 25, admits this contamination ; as does B. Weiss, *Der*

these came from the Old Uncial text of B and its associates or
from the Antiochian text has not been fully determined, although
an answer to that question could probably be found.[1] In some
cases the source seems to be the Antiochian text,[2] and this would
be what the general history of textual succession and contamination would lead us to expect. As a striking and representative
example of such conflation reference may be made to Acts xviii.
3-6 (see Textual Note), where the original ' Western ' text without
conflation is found in the Syriac hcl.*mg* and the African Latin h.
A remarkable instance of the contamination is Acts iv. 13-15,
where in D one small addition is almost the only indication that
its fundamental text once possessed widely different readings
which are still in large measure recoverable from the Latin h and
the Peshitto. Sometimes in the process of such conflation a
necessary word was accidentally omitted (so η $\sigma\omega\tau\eta\rho\iota\alpha$ in Acts
iv. 12 ; see Textual Note), but the student has no right to assume
this except where other reasons show that such a process of
substitution or insertion has taken place. In some cases the
omission in D of words still found in other witnesses to the
' Western ' text is doubtless due to deliberate conformation to
the rival text.[3]

Codex D in der Apostelgeschichte (Texte und Untersuchungen, xvii.), 1897, pp.
15 f., albeit on a small scale. The latter gives some examples ; he assumes that
the source of the mixture was the Old Uncial text.

[1] In the Textual Notes below, when such conflations are discussed, the term
' B-text ' has often been used for convenience of brevity without regard to the
distinction pointed out here, and without prejudice to the question of whether
the contamination came from the Old Uncial text or from the Antiochian text
which had been developed from it.

[2] See von Soden, pp. 1309-11, 1722 f.   For Acts he adduces the Antiochian
readings in x. 46-xi. 2, xi. 3-20, and finds instances here, as in the Gospels, of
the misunderstanding of corrections from the Antiochian text on the part of the
scribe of D or its ancestor.   Von Soden (p. 1310) is of opinion that these intru-
sions in the Gospels are the work of more than one of the successive owners and
copyists.

[3] Von Soden, p. 1723.   In such cases as xvii. 17, where a misplacement of
lines occurs only in d, this is probably due to the misplaced substitution of the
non-western text for the original ' Western.'   The observation is confirmed
both by the fact that $\tau o\iota s$ (before $\epsilon\nu$ $\tau\eta$ $\alpha\gamma o\rho\alpha$) added to the usual text in
D hcl.*mg* sah seems to imply an original $\pi\alpha\rho\alpha\tau\nu\chi o\nu\sigma\iota\nu$ instead of $\pi\rho o s$ $\tau o\nu s$
$\pi\alpha\rho\alpha\tau\nu\chi o\nu\tau\alpha s$ and by the form *his* in company with (twice) *hiis* in d.

It would be tedious to multiply illustrations of this characteristic of Codex Bezae. The facts can be properly weighed only after a careful study of the instances themselves and of the outside evidence bearing on them ; many of them are touched on in the Textual Notes. But the fact plainly advises wariness to every student of the ' Western ' text, and the following list of passages (but a small part of the whole number) where contamination of this sort is probably present in D may be useful, and is certainly instructive : i. 2, 9 ; ii. 14 ; iii. 8, 11, 13 ; iv. 5, 10, 12, 34 ; v. 26, 27, 28, 29 ; vii. 26, 43, 55 ; xii. 5 ; xiii. 3, 4, 27-29, 44 ; xiv. 5, 15, 18, 19, 21 ; xv. 5, 18 ; xvi. 4, 38, 39 ; xvii. 1 ; xviii. 2, 3, 5, 6, 8, 12, 19, 21, 22 ; xix. 8, 20, 29 ; xx. 7, 18, 35 ; xxii. 6. In the study of such cases as these it must be borne in mind that agreement between the text of D and the Antiochian may be due to the adoption of ' Western ' readings by the Antiochian, not to contamination of D from the latter. A decision will have to be reached in each case partly by considering the outside evidence for the reading, but partly also from the intrinsic character of the reading itself. The two texts have each its own distinctive character, which the student learns in a measure to recognize. It is likewise to be observed that the agreement of D and one or more of the Old Uncials may either have arisen from contamination or be due to participation in the same ancient, perhaps original, text. No mechanical rule, such as critics have often attempted to frame, can be applied in these cases.

Use of D.   The proper mode of using Codex Bezae is determined by the characteristics which have been described. Its Greek side is unique in furnishing a continuous ' Western ' text of Acts. But that ' Western ' text was copied with many scribal errors, has been conformed to the parallel Latin in details on a large scale, has probably suffered the excision of clauses not found in the Latin used to make the bilingual, while in many striking instances, and doubtless in many others not so easy to recognize, it has been altered, at some time before the present copy was made, so as to agree either with the Antiochian text or with the text of B and its associates. All these various sources of corruption must be constantly borne in mind, and only when their distorting effects have been recognized in every case can the fundamental Greek text be discovered of which D is a broken light. In other words, D, although the oldest Greek text of Acts containing many 'Western' readings, and the only one possessing anything like continuity, is, like the other witnesses, but mixed after all.[1] Nevertheless, the antiquated character of some of the spelling,[2] as well as other traits, give confidence that where the well-known sources of corruption have not been at work, the copying has been highly faithful, in the sense that the form of the 'Western' text, so far as it has been preserved at all, has not been ' modernized.' [3] Another aspect of this consideration is the warning that extra-ordinary readings of D ought never to be neglected as insignificant. Senseless as they seem, they sometimes prove to be not mere blunders of a thoughtless scribe, but genuine survivals of an ancient text. For instance, in Acts xiii. 29 the meaningless μεν probably represents μετα of the fundamental 'Western' text, as discoverable from a comparison of D with the astericized and marginal readings of the Harclean Syriac; in Acts iv. 18 παρ-ηγγειλαντο κατα το represents the reading παρηγγειλαν το καθολου found also in A and the Antiochian text. The text of Codex Bezae is far more than an accumulation of scribal errors combined with the influence of the Latin version.

What has been said will have already made abundantly clear the important distinction, not generally sufficiently noticed, between the text of D and the 'Western' text. Each of these constitutes a problem for itself, and these two problems must, so

---

[1] The large number of agreements, often small but nevertheless significant, of pesh and h, and of pesh and gigas, against D also seem to show that the text of D has been corrected, and true 'Western' readings eliminated, to a greater extent than would otherwise be suspected.

[2] Cf. what is said on the use of ϛμ and ϛβ for σμ and σβ in J. H. Moulton and W. F. Howard, *Grammar of New Testament Greek*, vol. ii., 1919, p. 107; Thackeray, *Grammar*, p. 108; and Rudberg (above, p. lxxi note 1).

[3] On the nomina sacra in D see Traube, *Nomina sacra*, pp. 78 f.

far as possible, be kept separate.[1] The discussion at the present
point of this Essay is intended to relate to the problems of Codex
Bezae ; the questions relating to the ' Western ' text (to which
it is only one, although the most important, witness) will find
their place at a later stage of the discussion.[2]

Of a different nature from the excellent edition of Codex
Bezae by Scrivener (1864) are a succession of New Testament
texts mainly or largely founded on this MS. : Bornemann, *Acta
apostolorum ad Codicis Cantabrigiensis fidem recensuit*, 1848 ;
Blass, ' editio philologica,' 1895, and in smaller form with a somewhat different text, 1896 ; Hilgenfeld, *Acta apostolorum*, 1899.
Whiston published an English translation in 1745 ; J. M. Wilson
another in 1923.   Zahn's reconstruction of the Greek ' Western '
text in his *Die Urausgabe der Apostelgeschichte des Lucas* (Forschungen zur Geschichte des neutestamentlichen Kanons und der
altkirchlichen Literatur, ix.), 1916, uses all the available evidence,
and is a work of permanent importance.   Nestle's collation of D
in his *Novi Testamenti graeci supplementum*, 1896, will be valuable
to the student for some purposes, but no presentation of the
variants, however complete, can take the place of the use of
the continuous text of D.

E. Codex Laudianus [3]

History.   Codex Laudianus (graeco-latin, containing Acts only) was in
Sardinia at some date after the year 534, as is shown by a note

[1] The theories of Blass, von Soden, Harris (Montanistic), and A. C. Clark
pertain to the ' Western ' text in general rather than to Codex Bezae in particular, and are accordingly reserved for later mention.   On the theory of Credner,
adopted by Alfred Resch, that the text of Codex Bezae was of Jewish-Christian
(Ebionite) origin, it is sufficient to refer to the crushing criticism of J. R. Harris,
' Credner and the Codex Bezae,' in *Four Lectures on the Western Text*, pp. 1-13.

[2] The term ' Bezan text,' by which it was sought to avoid the fallacy (or at
least the *petitio principii*) implied in the name ' Western text,' has done more
positive harm than the latter.

[3] For a more extended discussion of E see J. H. Ropes, ' The Greek Text of
Codex Laudianus,' *Harvard Theological Review*, vol. XVI., 1923, pp. 175-186,
from which some paragraphs and sentences are here used without substantial
change.   Much additional material is also to be found in von Soden, pp. 1717-
1720, 1811-1814.

in the volume, and may well have been written in that island in the late sixth or early seventh century. The opening years of the eighth century found it in England at Jarrow, for it is the Greek codex abundantly referred to by the Venerable Bede in his commentary on Acts. It is likely that it was brought to England from Italy by Benedict Biscop and Ceolfrid not long after 650 (rather than by Theodore of Tarsus in 668, for the latter is not recorded to have brought any books).[1] The scribe of Codex Amiatinus (shortly before 716) seems here and there to have drawn readings from its Latin side.

At a later date the codex was in Germany, doubtless transported thither by one of the English missionaries, Willibrord or Boniface, or some one of the latter's disciples.[2] Its home may have been the monastery of Würzburg, and it may have come to that house, like many other manuscripts, through Burchard, whom Boniface consecrated bishop of Würzburg in 741 or earlier.[3] In 1631, during the Thirty Years' War, Würzburg was sacked by the Swedish army, and Codex E was somewhere obtained by the agents employed in Germany by Archbishop Laud to purchase manuscripts which became available through the disorders of the time. Laud gave it to the Bodleian Library in 1636.

The scribe of E was a Greek, who knew his own language better than Latin, although he wrote both with reasonable accuracy. The manuscript was copied from a similar bilingual predecessor.[4]

As between the Latin and Greek columns there are some differences, enough to show that the Latin is not a mere rendering *Dependence of Greek on Latin text.*

[1] J. Chapman, *Notes on the Early History of the Vulgate Gospels*, 1908, pp. 158, 160.

[2] The proof that the codex was in Germany before it fell into the hands of Laud was, it would appear, first observed by E. W. B. Nicholson, Librarian of the Bodleian Library.

[3] C. H. Turner, art. ' New Testament, Text of,' in Murray's *Illustrated Bible Dictionary* (ed. W. C. Piercy), 1908, p. 586 ; A. Souter, *The Text and Canon of the New Testament*, 1913, p. 29.

[4] A. Jülicher, *Zeitschrift für die neutestamentliche Wissenschaft*, vol. xv., 1914, pp. 182 f.

of this Greek text; but they consist in most cases of trifling variations in a single word, while agreement has been secured by systematic adjustment of the two columns to one another. The Latin text shows many instances of Latin solecisms, and strange expressions, plainly due to imitation of the Greek, and not drawn from the Latin 'gigas-recension,' which was used as the foundation of the text.[1]   The Greek, on the other hand, has been modified to make it agree with the Latin. Thus, Acts vi. 7, the old Latin translation *discentium* for των μαθητων has evidently given rise to the Greek των μανθανοντων, which is quite as impossible Greek as 'the learners' for 'the disciples' would be in an English translation; so also, xii. 14, the Latin *januam* for τον πυλωνα, evidently the cause of the unique Greek reading την θυραν; xxiv. 25, καιρω δε επιτηδιω for καιρον δε μεταλαβων, and other cases.

In a considerable series of instances where even the partly expurgated Latin version used for this codex had retained 'Western' enlargements, it was necessary to translate these into Greek in order to equalize the two columns, and that this took place is made certain by the difference in the Greek form from the corresponding 'Western' reading in D.   Thus, to cite a few of the instances :

e	E	D
iii. 13. in judicium	εις κριτηριον	εις κρισιν
iv. 32. et non erat separatio in eis ulla	και ουκ ην χωρισμος εν αυτοις τις	και ουκ ην διακρισις εν αυτοις ουδεμια
v. 15. et liberarentur ab omni valitudine quam habebant	και ρυσθωσιν απο πασης ασχθενιας ης ειχον	απηλλασσοντο γαρ απο πασης ασθενιας ως ειχεν εκαστος αυτων
vi. 10. propter quod redarguerentur ab eo cum omni fiducia : cum ergo non possent contradicere veritati	διοτι ηλεγχοντο υπ αυτου μετα πασης παρρησιας· επιδη ουκ ηδυναντο αντιλεγιν τη αληθεια	δια το ελεγχεσθαι αυτους επ αυτου μετα πασης παρρησιας· μη δυναμενοι ου⟨ν⟩ αντοφθαλμειν τη αληθεια

---

[1] Tischendorf, *Monumenta sacra inedita, Nova collectio,* vol. ix. pp. xvi f. ; Jülicher, *op. cit.* pp. 183-185.

	e	E	D
xiii. 43.	factum est autem per universam civitatem diffamari verbum	εγενετο δε κατα πασαν πολιν φημισθηναι τον λογον	εγενετο δε καθ ολης της πολεως διελθειν τον λογον του θυ
xiv. 7.	et commota est omnis multitudo in doctrina eorum. paulum autem et barnabas morabantur in lystris	και εξεπλησσετο πασα η πολυπληθια επι τη διδαχη αυτων. ο δε παυλος και βαρναβας διετριβον εν λυστροις	και εκινηθη ολον το πληθος επι τη διδαχη. ο δε παυλος και βαρναβας διετριβον εν λυστροις

In many. of the simple phrases and words the appropriate Greek rendering was inevitable, and could not fail to agree with the original, as found in D or elsewhere, but in the more complicated instances (a few of which are given above) the well-educated Greek to whom we owe the retranslation was forced to go his own way, and produced a different text from the parallel in the Greek authorities, with which he would seem not to have been acquainted. In some few cases the readings of E may possibly be due to sporadic ' Western ' readings in the Greek codex from which it is derived, but the observed facts cause the presumption in any single case to be against such an origin. The text itself bears hardly any, if any, resemblance to D, except in readings which are probably the result of retranslation from the Latin. It is not to be regarded as in any sense a witness to a Greek ' Western ' text, although of course its Latin column (e) rests in part on such a text. The Greek text properly so called from which E (or, rather, its ancestor [1]) was taken was one of the Old Uncial type which had been extensively corrected to the Antiochian type. To judge by an incomplete examination, perhaps in somewhat more than two-thirds of the cases where an Antiochian variant might have been introduced, the corrector who effected that ancient mixture has actually introduced it. Codex Laudianus, apart from Latinisms, thus gives substantially an Antiochian text of Acts, and is the oldest extant codex of any degree of completeness which does so. Its ' Western ' readings on the Greek

[1] Jülicher, *Zeitschr. f. d. neutest. Wissenschaft*, vol. xv., 1914, pp. 182 f.

side can teach us nothing, and may rightly, as mere curiosities, disappear from the apparatus to Acts.   The Greek of Codex Laudianus is therefore not included in any apparatus of the present volume, although its readings are sometimes adduced, for the sake of completeness, in the Textual Notes.[1]

§ 3. THE TEXT OF CODICES BℵAC IN THE OLD TESTAMENT

Bearing of LXX on New Testament textual criticism.
From the beginning the Greek-speaking Christian Church read the Old Testament in Greek translations, and from these were made the early versions of the Old Testament into Latin, the Egyptian vernacular dialects, and Ethiopic.   The text of the Greek Old Testament was consequently subjected to some of the same influences, and underwent in part the same history, as the text of the New Testament.   The four oldest extant New Testament manuscripts (Vaticanus, Sinaiticus, Alexandrinus, and Ephraemi) are pandects which originally contained the whole Bible in Greek ; and other manuscripts contain, in whole or in part, both the Old and New Testaments.   Especially the Psalter was in ancient times, as to-day, included in the same volume with the New Testament.   Not only do the results of textual criticism of the Greek Old Testament reveal a parallel to the process of New Testament textual development, but they throw light on the specific character and value of the New Testament part of the four great Bibles.   The use of these results, however, calls for discriminating judgment : for the history of the Septuagint contains elements wholly lacking in that of the New Testament ; the character of any great Bible is likely to vary in different parts ; and it would be easy to draw utterly wrong conclusions by making direct inferences, not independently supported, from one field to the adjacent one.   Nevertheless, both the guidance

---

[1] For substantially the same conclusion with regard to Codex E see H. Coppieters, *De historia textus Actorum Apostolorum*, Louvain, 1902, pp. 68-71 ; F. C. Burkitt, *Encyclopaedia Biblica*, col. 4996 ; F. Blass, *Acta apostolorum*, 1895, pp. 28 f.

and the confirmation furnished by Septuagint criticism are to be highly prized. With these considerations in view it has seemed worth while at this point to interrupt the account of the sources for the text of Acts with a summary of the main results thus far reached in the investigation of the four great Bibles which originally contained both the Old and New Testaments in Greek.

Of the Septuagint the two great editions by which a wide influence was exerted were the fifth column of Origen's Hexapla (completed A.D. 240–245) and the edition of Lucian of Antioch (died at Nicomedia in 311 or 312). In Origen's edition stood a text drawn by him from some previous copy, which he approved but modified in three ways : (1) by slight tacit improvements, and by occasional rearrangements (in detail or on a larger scale) for the sake of agreement with the other columns ; (2) by prefixing obeli, and appending metobeli, to Greek words to which nothing in the original Hebrew corresponded ; (3) by the interjection of Greek words, phrases, and passages, not found in the LXX-text on which in the main he drew, but required in order to supply the *plus* of the Hebrew. These intruded words and portions were marked by asterisks and metobeli, and were themselves usually drawn from the version (made from the Hebrew) of Theodotion or of Aquila.[1] From the huge series of codices which were part of Origen's legacy to the library at Caesarea, his fifth column was copied, with the critical marks, in the early fourth century, under the supervision, partly perhaps by the hand, of Pamphilus († 309) and his venerator Eusebius the church historian, and was doubtless used in various ways in the formation and correction of other copies, so that it produced a definite edition, large knowledge of which is still recoverable in greater or less accuracy and completeness from many manuscripts.

Hexapla of Origen.

The edition of Lucian of Antioch had in part the same purpose as that of Origen, to bring the current Greek translation

Lucian.

---

[1] H. B. Swete, *Introduction to the Old Testament in Greek*, 2nd ed., Cambridge, 1914, pp. 59–78.

of the Old Testament into closer harmony with the Hebrew original ; in part his aim was to produce a more polished, and otherwise improved, translation. But Origen mainly limited himself to creating an instrument for the use of scholars ; while Lucian's edition was merely a new text, not provided with critical apparatus. A fair number of extant MSS. can be identified as giving, often in corrupt form, this edition. The shadowy figure of Hesychius, whose text, we are told by Jerome, was used in the fourth century in Egypt, must also be mentioned here, but it constitutes a problem of critical inquiry, not a starting-point of further investigation. He has been thought to be a contemporary of Lucian, but all that is known of his work is that it can have affected but little the previously existing text.[1]

Hesychius.

The first task of Septuagint textual criticism is thus to determine as perfectly as possible from MSS., versions, and patristic evidence the exact form of the 'hexaplaric' and of the 'Lucianic' texts, and then to inquire how far either or both of these two great sources of influence have affected the several copies of the Septuagint which we possess. In the MSS. which include several groups of Old Testament books, the inquiry has to be made for each group separately, and sometimes different books of the same group are found to vary in their type of text within a single manuscript. Recent critical investigations cover a part of the Old Testament. The most elaborate and instructive so far published are those by Alfred Rahlfs and the scholars who, under his incentive and supervision, and following the traditions of Lagarde, have issued preliminary studies for the edition of the Septuagint planned by the Göttingen Academy. But other scholars in their measure have made important contributions.[2]

Codex
Vaticanus.

For a series of books it has been shown that Codex Vaticanus

---

[1] A. Rahlfs, *Der Text des Septuaginta-Psalters*, 1907, pp. 226 f.

[2] See F. C. Burkitt, *Fragments of the Books of Kings according to the Translation of Aquila*, 1897, pp. 18-20 ; L. Dieu, ' Les Manuscrits grecs des livres de Samuel,' *Le Muséon*, xxxiv., 1921, pp. 17-60. Other studies are mentioned in the notes below.

gives a text nearly akin to that which Origen found in existence and adopted as the basis of the fifth column of the Hexapla,[1] and that B itself has been influenced by the Hexapla in but small degree, in some books perhaps not at all. This is the case in Joshua, Ruth, 1-4 Kingdoms, Psalms, Ezekiel, and apparently Esther.[2] In probably all of these books B (with, or more often without, support from its closest adherents) shows some peculiar readings, which are usually to be rejected.[3] Of the influence of the Lucianic recension B shows no trace in these books.

In these instances, with which could doubtless be associated other books of which no thorough investigations have yet been produced, B represents a very old LXX-text, which can sometimes be distinguished from other extant strains of pre-origenian text. It contains, however, errors, as compared with these, and

---

[1] The idea apparently intended by Lagarde, *Anmerkungen zur griechischen Übersetzung der Proverbien*, 1863, p. 3, that Codex B was drawn from an edition of the fifth column of the Hexapla with the astericized portions omitted (a view followed by Burkitt, *Encyclopaedia Biblica*, col. 5022, cf. Torrey, *Ezra Studies*, pp. 96 f.) has been abandoned by Rahlfs in the books treated in his monographs in favour of the conclusion stated in the text. Rahlfs' scrupulously formed judgment may be received with the more confidence in that his work has all been conceived and executed in pursuance of the plans marked out by the master, to whose memory the first instalment of Rahlfs' Septuagint Studies is dedicated. For Ezekiel the view suggested by Lagarde was strongly maintained by C. H. Cornill, *Das Buch des Propheten Ezechiel*, 1886, pp. 80 f., 94 f., but after criticism by Lagarde himself (*Göttingische gelehrte Anzeigen*, 1886; reprinted in *Mittheilungen*, ii. pp. 49 ff.) and by Hort (*The Academy*, December 24, 1887) it was withdrawn by Cornill (*Nachrichten*, Göttingen Academy, vol. xxx., 1888, pp. 194 ff.).

[2] For Joshua I owe this information to Professor Max L. Margolis. For Ruth see Rahlfs, *Studie über den griechischen Text des Buches Ruth* (Mittheilungen des Septuaginta-Unternehmens, vol. iii., Heft 2), 1922, pp. 60, 119; for 1-4 Kingdoms, Rahlfs, *Studien zu den Königsbüchern* (Septuaginta-Studien i.), pp. 85-87; for the Psalter, Rahlfs, *Der Text des Septuaginta-Psalters*, p. 228; for Ezekiel, O. Procksch (cited below); for Esther, L. B. Paton, *Critical and Exegetical Commentary on the Book of Esther* (International Critical Commentary), 1908, p. 31.

[3] So, for instance, Ruth, Rahlfs, *Studie über den griechischen Text des Buches Ruth*, pp. 120 f.; Kingdoms, Rahlfs, *Studien zu den Königsbüchern*, 1904, pp. 83 f.; in Kingdoms the Ethiopic text sometimes gives the means of restoring the true reading of the type, when B has departed from it (Rahlfs, p. 84).

may be the result of a recension. Rahlfs is disposed to regard the text of B and its congeners as due to the recension of Hesychius. This may be a sagacious conjecture, but seems to furnish no aid to the actual investigation, and there is danger of proceeding as if the conjecture were a ground for inferring the date and Egyptian origin of the text, instead of being itself an inference from the conclusions reached by study of the text itself. Nothing points to influence from any locality outside of Egypt. The great significance of B lies in the general soberness of its text (except in the proper names) and its relative freedom from deliberate revision.

Daniel.   The text of Daniel in B, as in all Septuagint manuscripts with the exception of the hexaplaric Codex Chisianus, gives the version of Theodotion, and is the best extant copy of that text, with valuable support from the Old Latin and Sahidic, which occasionally provide means for the correction of the text found in B. B shows in Daniel but few mistakes or interpolations, but displays some tendency to abbreviation.[1]

Psalms.   In the Psalms the situation is in some respects peculiar, and is full of interest for the New Testament critic. The relation, indeed, of the Psalter to the New Testament is unique among Old Testament books, for the liturgical use of the Psalms by Christians, and perhaps also the occasional practice of combining the Psalms with a part or the whole of the New Testament, has led to an agreement in the textual history of the two not found elsewhere.[2] More than one striking illustration of this can be pointed out.[3] Thus the Antiochian (Lucianic) recension of the Psalms, like the corresponding Antiochian recension of the New Testament, became the prevalent form in the Greek-speaking

---

[1] This statement about Daniel I owe to Professor James A. Montgomery.

[2] Rahlfs, *Der Text des Septuaginta-Psalters*, p. 237.

[3] Somewhat similar is the preservation of Coverdale's English Psalter in the later editions of the Great Bible and in the Prayer Book ; also the fact that the Latin text used for the Psalter of the French translation of the thirteenth century was a compilation, not the University of Paris text from which all the rest of the translation was made (S. Berger, *La Bible française au moyen âge*, 1884, p. 155).

world, while in the rest of the Old Testament the prevalent later Greek text was of a different type.[1] Again, in the Psalter the Syrian translator Paul of Tella deliberately deserts the hexaplaric Greek which he elsewhere translates, and follows an entirely different type of text,[2] while similarly Codex Alexandrinus, which in most of the other important books is strongly, and sometimes almost completely, under hexaplaric influence, is not reported as showing any trace of this in the Psalms, but seems to be wholly a combination of pre-origenian and Lucianic elements. It is no accident that both in the Psalms and in the New Testament Codex Alexandrinus is one of the two oldest extant witnesses to the revised Antiochian text, although in both cases in a mixed form.

To return to the matter under discussion, the various extant documents for the Psalter not only exhibit the Lucianic revision, the Hexaplaric text, and the pre-hexaplaric text found in B, the Ethiopic, the Bohairic, and the non-hexaplaric citations of Origen, but also reveal the existence of two other divergent pre-origenian types of text. One of these is found in the Leipzig papyrus L (Universitätsbibliothek, pap. 39) from the southern border of Middle Egypt, in the London papyrus U (Brit. Mus. pap. 37) from Thebes, and in the Sahidic version.[3] It receives some support from Clement of Alexandria, as well as from Clement of Rome, Barnabas, Justin, and Irenaeus. It is not a text of great correctness, but shows a tendency to unrestrained variation, to careless errors due to resemblance of sound and form, to influence from neighbouring and parallel passages, and to licence in making additions, in part prompted by Christian motives (*e.g.* Ps. l. 9 απο του αιματος του ξυλου added after νσσωπω ; Ps. xcv. 10 απο του ξυλου added after ο κυριος εβασιλευσεν).

---

[1] On the reasons why the Lucianic Old Testament failed to gain the same acceptance as the corresponding Antiochian text of the New Testament, see B. H. Streeter, *The Four Gospels*, 1924, pp. 42 f.

[2] Rahlfs, *op. cit.* pp. 122-124.

[3] Rahlfs, *op. cit.*, *passim*, esp. pp. 5, 141-164, 209, 211 f., 219-225.

The other noteworthy divergent text of the Greek Psalms is that underlying the Old Latin.[1] Many manuscripts of one or another form of this are known, including those of the so-called Roman Psalter of Jerome, and it was used by certain Latin church fathers. This Latin translation in a modified form has continued in liturgical use until modern times in Rome (until nearly 1600), Milan, Venice (to 1808), and Spain. It bears some slight relation to the text just mentioned from Upper Egypt (L U Sahidic), and like that text is to be distinguished from the text of B (with Bohairic and Ethiopic), but it is more restrained in character than the Upper Egyptian, and sometimes stands quite alone in offering the original Septuagint reading.

The parallel in some respects to the 'Western Text' of the New Testament offered by these two types is at once apparent, and does not need to be set forth in detail. The two types of the Psalter are alike ancient and both diverge from the text commonly used in the third and later centuries in Lower Egypt (B) ; one of them was the text from which the early Latin version was made, while the other appears in Upper Egypt, and was an ingredient of the text used by Clement of Alexandria. In the nature of the case, the completeness of the parallel to the New Testament is limited by the fact that the old Syriac fathers used in their Peshitto a version of the Psalms translated directly from the Hebrew, not drawn from the Greek rendering.[2]

The text of the Psalms in B (with which the Bohairic is almost, though not quite, identical, and to which the Ethiopic is only a little less similar) is clearly pre-origenian, being not at all affected by the Hexapla ; and probably it is substantially the

---

[1] Rahlfs, *op. cit.* esp. pp. 25-31, 61-101, 225 f. ; Capelle, *Le Texte du psautier latin en Afrique*, pp. 195-211.

[2] A similar parallel to the 'Western Text' of the New Testament, at least in the branch of that text found in the Old Latin version, seems to be indicated by the fact that the Greek text of the Books of Kingdoms on which rest the Latin translations given by Tertullian and by Cyprian (whom Lactantius followed) is unlike any type of Greek text known to us, and in at least one case a Greek reading is implied of which we have otherwise no knowledge whatever ; cf. Rahlfs, *Lucians Rezension der Königsbücher*, 1911, pp. 138-143.

text used by Origen as the basis of his fifth column.[1] In the
text of B here (as in all other books) are included a number of
peculiar readings, which may well be due to later revision and
consequently be wrong.[2] In a few instances we find the distinctive reading of the Upper Egyptian (L U Sah) text.[3] It does
not appear that B has anywhere been influenced by the Lucianic
text.

In certain other books of the Old Testament the relation of
texts seems to be quite different. In 1 Esdras, and Chronicles–
Ezra–Nehemiah, Torrey has shown that B, whose text in these
books he finds to be very corrupt, is similar to Origen's fifth
column, but without the astericized portions and with badly
damaged forms of the proper names. But the evidence which
he presents does not seem to justify his conclusion that B is
derived from the Hexapla column, and the facts, so far as given,
especially the considerable divergence of B from the Syro-
hexaplaric text, suggest rather that here, as in the books referred
to in preceding paragraphs, B's text is pre-origenian, and closely
similar to that which Origen took as the basis of his LXX-
column. The fact that the Hebrew–Aramaic counterpart of
1 Esdras seems to have perished before the later Greek versions were made, and that the Greek version of Chronicles–
Ezra–Nehemiah appears to be Theodotion,[4] necessarily restricts
the field from which evidence on this point can be drawn.

1 Esdras, Chronicles– Ezra– Nehemiah.

---

[1] Rahlfs, *Der Text des Septuaginta-Psalters*, p. 228. The determination of
the exact character of Origen's text in the Psalter is made difficult through the
defection of the Syriac translation of Paul of Tella, which here did not follow
the Hexapla but took a wholly different text. This procedure is itself instructive. The Greek hexaplaric fragments are important but meagre. Rahlfs, *op.
cit.* pp. 122-124, 109-111.

[2] Rahlfs, *Der Text des Septuaginta-Psalters*, pp. 228 f., regards these as
probably the work of Hesychius. Rahlfs' conclusion that the text of B gives
the Hesychian recension is drawn from the agreement of B with Cyril of Alexandria and the Bohairic version (*op. cit.* pp. 183 f., 197, 226-229, 235 f.). See
also Rahlfs, *Studie über den griechischen Text des Buches Ruth*, p. 148.

[3] Rahlfs, *Der Text des Septuaginta-Psalters*, p. 163.

[4] Charles C. Torrey, *Ezra Studies*, Chicago, 1910, pp. 66-82 ; cf. Thackeray,
Grammar, vol. i. pp. xx, 13 ; F. C. Burkitt, *Encyclopaedia Biblica*, col. 5019 ;
but see also Rahlfs, *Lucians Rezension der Königsbücher*, p. 85, note 2.

The monstrous corruption of the proper names may have taken place at any period, and need not have been limited to the years between Origen and Athanasius ; while the supposition that a copy of Origen's column was ever made with the astericized portions (not merely the asterisks themselves) accurately excised, lacks support, so far as appears, from any extant manuscript or text, and is improbable in view of the practice that we do know.[1]   Important observations of Torrey are that B and the others of its group were copied from their archetype with extraordinary fidelity, as is shown by the numerous " glaring blunders " which they have preserved in common ; that deliberate revision is rarely to be detected in their text ; and that B itself is frequently disfigured by omissions due to carelessness.   Torrey connects the text of B with Egypt.

Judges.   In the Book of Judges, B gives not the Septuagint proper but a different translation, found in a number of other MSS. and made with the aid of an Egyptian form of the LXX-text.   This version was used by Cyril of Alexandria († 444), and is that rendered by the Sahidic version but by no other.[2]

[1] Torrey, *op. cit.* chap. iv. pp. 62-114 (first published in *Studies in Memory of William Rainey Harper*, vol. ii., Chicago, 1908).   Torrey's conclusions as to the hexaplaric character of B were probably affected by his understanding that the subscription to Nehemiah in ℵ is from the original scribe of the MS.   On this point we must take the judgement of the only two scholars who have studied the original codex itself, Tischendorf and Lake, both of whom hold the subscription to be the work of one of the correctors known as ℵᶜ.   It is to be noted that one of these correctors, ℵᶜ·ᵇ (from whom this subscription may come), perhaps followed in general in his corrections a hexaplar text ; cf. O. Procksch, *Studien zur Geschichte der Septuaginta : Die Propheten*, 1910, p. 85 ; also G. Bardy, ' Notes sur les recensions hésychienne et hexaplaire du livre de Néhémie (II. Esdras),' in *Revue Biblique*, vol. v., 1918, pp. 192-199.   But the practical difference between Torrey's view of the relation of B to the Hexapla and that suggested above is in most respects not so great as might at first appear.

[2] G. F. Moore, *Critical and Exegetical Commentary on Judges*, 1895, pp. xliv-xlvi, and ' The Antiochian Recension of the Septuagint,' in *American Journal of Semitic Languages*, vol. XXIX., 1912, pp. 41 f.   The discovery of a sixth-century papyrus of Cyril shows that his Old Testament text was even closer to B than could be known from the altered form of the later MSS. of Cyril's works, in which the Old Testament text quoted resembles rather that of codices F (fifth cent.) and A ; see D. Serruys, ' Un " codex " sur papyrus de Saint Cyrille d'Alexandrie,' in *Revue de Philologie*, vol. XXXIV., 1910, pp. 110-117.

Of the prophetic books apart from Ezekiel (of which mention Prophets. has already been made) it is to be said that in Isaiah, Jeremiah, and the Twelve, the text of B is more affected by hexaplaric influence, although not a direct copy of the fifth column of the Hexapla, and is less valuable.[1] Nevertheless the basis of B seems to have been, as in so many books, the same text as that chosen by Origen for his textual work.[2] The tendency of B is not so much to expand the Greek text by large additions of a translation of the *plus* of the Hebrew, as to improve it in detail by the aid of the Hexapla, and especially to omit words and phrases not found in the Hebrew and therefore usually marked by Origen with the obelus. The text of B shows many peculiar readings, not shared by other uncials, and these are usually wrong wherever a decision is possible ;[3] on the other hand, B is at least nearly free from any influence of Lucian.[4] In the Minor Prophets B (with ℵ) is not the text followed by Cyril, so far as our manuscripts of Cyril can be depended on.[5] Daniel has already been mentioned above.

In Job, B follows the Hexapla, with its supplementary addi- Job. tions from Theodotion, as against the abridged text of the Septuagint, which can be reconstructed with the aid of the Sahidic version and those hexaplaric manuscripts which have retained Origen's diacritical marks.[6]

---

[1] O. Procksch, *Studien zur Geschichte der Septuaginta : Die Propheten* (Beiträge zur Wissenschaft vom Alten Testament, edited by R. Kittel, 7), 1910. For the character of B𝕸A in the prophetic books other than Ezekiel, I am mainly dependent on the monograph of Procksch, with reference to which see the review by Rahlfs, *Göttingische gelehrte Anzeigen*, vol. CLXXII., 1910, pp. 694-705. Compare the remarks of F. C. Burkitt, *The Book of Rules of Tyconius* (Texts and Studies, iii.), 1894, p. cxvii, who finds that in most cases B is free from the hexaplaric insertions, but occasionally contains them, especially in Isaiah. See also P. Volz, *Studien zum Text des Jeremia*, Leipzig, 1920, p. xiv.

[2] Procksch, pp. 68, 112 ff.

[3] Procksch, pp. 52-54, 113.

[4] Procksch, p. 85.

[5] Procksch, pp. 100 f. ; but cf. the article of Serruys mentioned in a previous note.

[6] A. Ceriani, *Rendiconti, Reale Istituto Lombardo*, Series II., vol. XXI., 1888, p. 543 ; Edwin Hatch, *Essays on Biblical Greek*, 1889 ; Dillmann, *Textkritisches zum Buch Ijob* (Sitzungsberichte, Berlin Academy), 1890 ; Burkitt, *Encyclo-*

Ecclesi-
astes ;
Lamenta-
tions.

In Ecclesiastes, B is like all the other MSS. in having a text which shows many of the characteristic traits of Aquila's version ; B's text is better than that of any other uncial, but is inferior to the closely kindred Codex 68 (fifteenth century ; copy probably made for Bessarion), which " has the excellencies of B without some of its defects." In Lamentationᵉ the text of B is non-hexaplaric ; it shows peculiarities not found elsewhere and perhaps ultimately due to Aquila.[1]

Apocrypha.

In the books of the Old Testament to which no Hebrew corresponds, the texts of the different Greek manuscripts sometimes show strong divergences. In the absence of probability that these books (except 1 Esdras and Baruch) were included in Origen's Hexapla, one of the chief instruments of criticism elsewhere used is lacking. Also the question of the Lucianic text does not seem to have been worked out here. In Wisdom the text of B is often inferior to that of A ; in Ecclesiasticus it differs widely from most others, and is inferior ; in Tobit, although the form of the book given in ℵ may be nearer to the Semitic original, yet it is held that the text of B (with A and the Syriac of Paul of Tella) is probably a more correct form of the Alexandrian version.[2]

Codex
Sinaiticus.

Of Codex Sinaiticus in the Old Testament only great fragments remain. The Octateuch (except for a few scraps), the books of Kingdoms, 1 Esdras, 2 Chronicles, Ezekiel, Hosea, Amos, Micah, are all lacking, not to mention minor defects. Of what remains, the text is in large measure akin to that of B, but

---

paedia Biblica, 1903, cols. 5027 f. (Burkitt, *Ency. Bibl.*, cols. 5022, 5027 f., withdraws the view stated in his *The Old Latin and the Itala*, 1896, p. 8, that the *original* state of the Greek translation survives in the Sahidic.)

[1] On Ecclesiastes see A. H. McNeile, *An Introduction to Ecclesiastes*, Cambridge, 1904, pp. 135-168 ; on Lamentations, F. C. Burkitt, *Encyclopaedia Biblica*, cols. 5018, 5022.

[2] J. R. Harris, ' The Double Text of Tobit,' in *American Journal of Theology*, vol. III., 1899, pp. 541-554. That the text of B in Tobit is certainly an abridgment, is maintained by C. C. Torrey, *Journal of Biblical Literature*, vol. XLI., 1922, pp. 237 f., 239, 241 f.

nowhere without marked differences from that manuscript. In Chronicles–Ezra–Nehemiah, ℵ belongs to the same group with B, and gives a better text than that or than other of the witnesses to the group.[1] In Esther, ℵ is much like B, but shows some hexaplaric influence.[2] In the Psalter also its text is much like that of B (but less so than is the Bohairic version) ; it often shows hexaplaric influence, and has in some cases readings drawn from the Lucianic revision.[3] In the Prophets (Ezekiel is lacking) it forms part of a group with B, and shows as its base a pre-origenian text, similar to that used by Origen for the construction of his fifth column;[4] in common with B it has been sporadically subjected to hexaplaric influence, but reveals on the whole less of this than B and is in general better than B,[5] although it shows Lucianic influence, as B hardly does.[6] Of the revision, whatever it be, that has given B in a series of readings in the Prophets an isolated position ℵ of course shows no sign ;[7] and it stands alone among the uncials far less often than does B, although it contains many orthographic errors.[8]

In Tobit, ℵ (with the Old Latin) gives a different recension from B.

The extensive corrections of ℵ known as ℵ[c.a] and ℵ[c.b] and Correctors. ℵ[c], made in the fifth, sixth, or seventh century, are important. For the individual discrimination of them, scholars are mainly dependent on Tischendorf's minute study of the codex, supplemented by Lake's observations. First, as to ℵ[c.a]. This corrector in Nehemiah has introduced the *plus* of the Hebrew, and made extensive insertions from the Lucianic text (of the doublets), as well as other corrections.[9] In the Psalter he has systematically tried to make the text conform to the Lucianic standard, although

---

[1] Torrey, *Ezra Studies*, pp. 91 f.

[2] L. B. Paton, *Commentary on Esther*, p. 32.

[3] Rahlfs, *Der Text des Septuaginta-Psalters*, pp. 54, 134 note, 137 note, 217, 235.

[4] Procksch, *Studien zur Geschichte der Septuaginta : Die Propheten*, pp. 49 ff., 68.

[5] Procksch, pp. 51, 59.   [6] Procksch, p. 85.

[7] Procksch, pp. 46, 54 (cf. pp. 52-54).

[8] Procksch, p. 49.   [9] Torrey, pp. 96, 97, notes.

he overlooked some readings.[1]   In the Prophets also his standard is close to Lucian,[2] as appears to be the case in Job to a large extent,[3] but in Esther it is hexaplaric.[4]   A (probably) different corrector of the same period [5] has added notes at the close of Nehemiah and of Esther stating in each case that it (that is, apparently, Codex א) has been compared with "a very old copy" which had been corrected by the hand of Pamphilus the Martyr.[6] The note to Esther states that the copy used as a standard for correction began with 1 Kingds. and ended with Esther. The natural understanding of this is that the corrector himself made the comparison ; although conceivably he might have copied the note from an exemplar which he used for correcting א and which had itself been compared with the codex of Pamphilus.   With regard to א[c.b] in the Prophets, the standard by which he worked may be hexaplaric.[7]

---

[1] Rahlfs, *Der Text des Septuaginta-Psalters*, p. 57.   [2] Procksch, p. 84.
[3] L. Dieu, as cited below, pp. 272 f.   [4] Paton, *op. cit.* p. 35.
[5] It appears to be impossible to determine which of the correctors known collectively as א[c] wrote these notes ; but in any case they are probably not from א[c.a] ; see Lake, *Codex Sinaiticus*, New Testament, pp. vii f., Old Testament, pp. x f.   Tischendorf, *Bibliorum codex Sinaiticus Petropolitanus*, vol. i., 1862, p. 13*, seems to ascribe them to either א[c.a] or א[c.b] ; cf. *N.T. graece ex Sinaitico codice*, 1867, pp. lxii f.

[6] Note at the end of Nehemiah :

ἀντεβλήθη πρὸς παλαιώτατον λίαν ἀντίγραφον δεδιορθωμένον χειρὶ τοῦ ἁγίου μάρτυρος Παμφίλου, ὅπερ ἀντίγραφον πρὸς τῷ τέλει ὑποσημειώσίς τις ἰδιόχειρος αὐτοῦ ὑπέκειτο ἔχουσα οὕτως·

μετελήμφθη καὶ διορθώθη πρὸς τὰ Ἑξαπλᾶ Ὡριγένους.
Ἀντωνῖνος ἀντέβαλεν.   Πάμφιλος διόρθωσα.

Note at the end of Esther :

ἀντεβλήθη πρὸς παλαιώτατον λίαν ἀντίγραφον δεδιορθωμένον χειρὶ τοῦ ἁγίου μάρτυρος Παμφίλου· πρὸς δὲ τῷ τέλει τοῦ αὐτοῦ παλαιωτάτου βιβλίου, ὅπερ ἀρχὴν μὲν εἶχεν ἀπὸ τῆς πρώτης τῶν Βασιλειῶν εἰς δὲ τὴν Ἐσθὴρ ἔληγεν, τοιαύτη τις ἐν πλάτει ἰδιόχειρος ὑποσημειώσις τοῦ αὐτοῦ μάρτυρος ὑπέκειτο ἔχουσα οὕτως·

μετελήμφθη καὶ διορθώθη πρὸς τὰ Ἑξαπλᾶ Ὡριγένους ὑπ' αὐτοῦ διορθωμένα.
Ἀντωνῖνος ὁμολογητὴς ἀντέβαλεν.   Πάμφιλος διορθώσατο τεῦχος ἐν τῇ φυλακῇ.
διὰ τὴν τοῦ θεοῦ πολλὴν καὶ χάριν καὶ πλατυσμὸν καὶ εἴγε μὴ βαρὺ εἰπεῖν τούτῳ τῷ ἀντιγράφῳ παραπλησίον εὑρεῖν ἀντίγραφον οὐ ῥάδιον.
διεφώνη δὲ τὸ αὐτὸ παλαιώτατον βιβλίον πρὸς τόδε τὸ τεῦχος εἰς τὰ κύρια ὀνόματα.

[7] Procksch, p. 85.   But is the remark of Procksch more than an inference from the subscriptions to Nehemiah and Esther ?

Codex Alexandrinus contains the whole Old Testament, with Codex Alexandrinus.
but a few leaves lacking. Its text, as in the New Testament,
is not homogeneous, and shows remarkable phenomena of
mixture from widely divergent sources. In Joshua it combines
hexaplaric elements with others from " the common text and a
residue of readings which seem to rest upon the Palestinian *Koinē*
which served as a basis for Theodotion." [1] In Judges it gives
the older Greek translation, in a form similar to that which
Origen adopted for his fifth column.[2] In Ruth the basis of its
text is pre-origenian, but corrected unsystematically from the
Hexapla and influenced by other texts.[3] Esther is similar.[4] In
1-4 Kingdoms A is purely hexaplaric.[5] In 1 Esdras and
Chronicles–Ezra–Nehemiah (Theodotion) the text of A is pre-
origenian, and here, although somewhat corrupted in transmission and (in the latter group) with the transliterations of
Theodotion occasionally altered to translations, it gives a text
distinctly better than that of any one of its own group of accompanying minuscules, as well as much better than that shown in
B and others and adopted by Origen for his Hexapla. In these
books it represents a text, probably Alexandrian, different from
that used as the basis of the Lucianic recension.[6] In Job the
text of A, which has not hitherto been found attested in any
minuscule,[7] is probably Lucianic.[8]

[1] This statement I owe to Professor Max L. Margolis.

[2] G. F. Moore, *Commentary on Judges*, p. xliv ; Rahlfs, *Studie über den griechischen Text des Buches Ruth*, p. 122.

[3] Rahlfs, *op. cit.* pp. 122 f.   [4] Paton, *op. cit.* p. 32.

[5] Rahlfs, *Studie über den griechischen Text des Buches Ruth*, p. 122 ; *Lucians Rezension der Königsbücher*, p. 6 ; *Studien zu den Königsbüchern* (' Origenes' Zitate aus den Königsbüchern'), p. 48 ; S. Silberstein, ' Über den Ursprung der im Codex Alexandrinus und Vaticanus des dritten Königsbuches der alexandrinischen Übersetzung überlieferten Textgestalt,' in *Zeitschrift für alttestamentliche Wissenschaft*, vol. XIII., 1893, pp. 1-75 ; XIV., 1894, pp. 1-30.

[6] Torrey, pp. 79, 92-96, 101.

[7] A Jerusalem palimpsest fragment, published by E. Tisserant, *Revue Biblique*, vol. IX., 1912, pp. 481-503, has a similar text to that of A, but less fully Lucianic ; the corrections of א[c.a] in Job largely follow the same text as A.

[8] L. Dieu, ' Le Texte de Job du Codex Alexandrinus,' *Le Muséon*, vol. XIII., 1912, pp. 223-274.

Psalter.

In the Psalter the case is quite another. The text of A proves to be a clean mixture of the B-type with Lucian, in about equal proportions, but irregularly distributed. No hexaplaric influence or kinship appears to be present (on this striking circumstance see above, p. xciii). A is here the earliest extant Greek witness to the Antiochian revision.[1]

Prophets.

In the Prophets, Ezekiel stands somewhat by itself. Here the base of the text of A is pre-origenian, of a type different from that of B, but has been very strongly influenced by the Hexapla, more so than B.[2] In this book the Old Latin, Bohairic, Ethiopic (older form), and Arabic (older form as found in the Paris Polyglot) follow A closely, and especially the Bohairic sometimes provides the means of recovering the text of this type where A (which contains not a few wrong 'singular' readings) is in error.[3] In Jeremiah, likewise, A often shows a different type of pre-origenian text from that of B (and ℵ), but here, too, it has often suffered through correction from the Hexapla, although less severely than in Ezekiel.[4] In Isaiah and the Twelve Prophets we find a similar condition, but in these books it is B and ℵ which have been most corrected, and the text of A is less hexaplarized than is theirs;[5] the text of A is not the basis used by Lucian, who employed rather a text akin to Bℵ.[6] On the other hand, the text of A seems itself to have been somewhat affected here by Lucian's recension.[7]

Daniel.

In Daniel, A is said to give a revision of the hexaplaric text, made with the use of the pre-origenian text, but is an inferior representative of this revision, being itself full of gross errors. It is suggested that the revision was that issued by Eusebius, and

[1] Rahlfs, *Der Text des Septuaginta-Psalters*, pp. 54, 56 f., 235, 236 ; *Studie über den griechischen Text des Buches Ruth*, p. 122.

[2] Procksch, pp. 46 f., 48, 57 ; C. H. Cornill, *Das Buch des Propheten Ezechiel*, pp. 67, 71, 73, 76.

[3] Cornill, pp. 32-35, 36, 42, 55, 67 ; Procksch, p. 59.

[4] Procksch, pp. 56 f.

[5] *Ibid.* ; Burkitt, *The Book of Rules of Tyconius*, 1894, p. cx note 1, says that B has " a worse text in Isaiah than in the rest of the Prophets."

[6] Procksch, p. 79.

[7] *Ibid.* p. 86.

that it constituted a kind of received text of Constantinople. It appears to be the basis of the Bohairic and of the Arabic (Melchite) version.[1]

Of the other books it is possible to say that in Wisdom A is sometimes better than B,[2] and that in 1 Maccabees it is generally not so good as ℵ.[3]   *Wisdom; 1 Maccabees.*

The relation of the LXX-text of A to the New Testament has not been fully elucidated. The New Testament quotations from the Old Testament tend to agree with the text of A, especially in the Gospels, where, however, the question is complicated by the possibility of fresh translation from the Hebrew, with or without LXX influence. Yet in certain cases the text of A seems unmistakably conformed to the New Testament standard, for instance, in Isaiah xl. 14, where A (with ℵ minn) has inserted Job xli. 3, evidently because the two verses are combined in Rom. xi. 35.[4]   *Relation to New Testament.*

Of the text of Codex Ephraemi (C) in the Old Testament nothing can be said; only sixty-four leaves have been preserved, scattered through Proverbs, Ecclesiastes, Canticles, Job (nineteen leaves), Wisdom, Ecclesiasticus (twenty-three leaves).   *Codex Ephraemi.*

When the forms of the two recensions (the Hexapla and Lucian) which chiefly influenced our Old Testament text have been determined,[5] and their relation to the extant individual   *Principles of Septuagint criticism.*

[1] This statement I owe to Professor James A. Montgomery.

[2] C. H. Toy, *Encyclopaedia Biblica*, art. ' Wisdom (Book),' col. 5348.

[3] C. C. Torrey, *Encyclopaedia Biblica*, art. ' Maccabees (Books),' col. 2867.

[4] Procksch, pp. 56, 89-98, 133 ; W. Staerk, in *Zeitschrift für wissenschaftliche Theologie*, vol. xxxvi., 1893, p. 98 ; Swete, *Introduction*, pp. 395 f., 403, 413, 422, 489.   Rahlfs, *Der Text des Septuaginta-Psalters*, p. 198, refuses to use the New Testament quotations at all as evidence for the text of the Septuagint, because of the doubt which he thinks is everywhere present as to whether the New Testament was the receiver or the giver.   Torrey holds that in the passages quoted in the Gospels the Old Testament text of A has been systematically made to agree with the text of the New Testament.

[5] The recension of Hesychius was a *vera causa*, and it is not unlikely that the Bohairic version was largely, if not wholly, made from it.   Perhaps to some extent his recension can be identified among the forms of the Greek text known to us.   But Hesychius, as has been pointed out above, does not seem to have

manuscripts discovered and worked out in detail, a body of readings remain, most of which are pre-origenian in date, and which can be grouped as belonging to different types by studying the groups of the uncial and minuscule manuscripts which contain them. One of the chief problems concerns the basis of the Lucianic recension, and the extent to which readings of that recension can be accepted as probably inherited, not produced, by Lucian and his fellow-workers. That some ancient readings otherwise unknown can be recovered from Lucianic manuscripts seems to be admitted, and Lucianic evidence is sometimes valuable in supporting the testimony of the non-lucianic manuscripts. Finally, with the pre-origenian readings from all sources before him, the critic will determine the relative value of such pre-origenian types as can be elicited, and choose among the readings they offer. Hort's statement,[1] that B " on the whole presents the version of the Septuagint in its relatively oldest form," has been substantiated for many books, but in others A will have to be preferred ; and not infrequently, in those parts where א represents the same type of text as B, the better reading is found in א rather than in B. The groups of minuscules, too, are held to constitute the most trustworthy sources of knowledge for some parts of the Old Testament.[2] The rules for the criticism of the LXX were formulated by Lagarde ; [3] they are governed by the character of the Septuagint

---

made far-reaching alteration in the Egyptian text on which he worked, and the precise text which left his hands is so tenuous and uncertain a magnitude that to operate with any theory of what it was is an embarrassment rather than an aid to the investigation, and does not tend to clarity of thought on the subject in general. See Rahlfs, as cited above on p. xc note 1.

[1] Quoted in Swete, *Old Testament in Greek*, vol. i. pp. xi f.; *Introduction to the Old Testament in Greek*, pp. 486 f.   [2] Procksch, pp. 102 f.

[3] *Anmerkungen zur griechischen Übersetzung der Proverbien*, 1863, p. 3 ; *Librorum Veteris Testamenti canonicorum pars prior*, 1883, p. xvi. Lagarde's statement of principles is cited in full by Swete, *Introduction*, pp. 485 f., and more briefly given by Burkitt, *Encyclopaedia Biblica*, art. ' Text and Versions,' col. 5021. For qualification of Lagarde's third axiom, that the Greek reading which departs from the Masoretic text of the Hebrew is to be accepted as original, see Torrey, *Ezra Studies*, p. 109 note 56 ; Rahlfs, *Der Text des Septuaginta-Psalters*, p. 231.

as a translation, and are consequently of a different nature from those by which the New Testament critic must be guided, although they ultimately rest on the same simple notion, namely, the inquiry as to how alteration of text will betray itself.   What is most instructive for the New Testament critic is the determination of the principles which controlled the formation of the text of those copies which contain both Old and New Testament. But, as has been said above, only with the aid of insight, and never by mechanical transference of conclusions from one field to the other, can the knowledge so gained be successfully used.

2. VERSIONS

§ 1. LATIN

(a) OLD LATIN TEXTS

Codices. UNDER the Old Latin are included all Latin texts which are not mainly composed of Vulgate renderings. Latin codices which contain the whole, or fragments, of a text of Acts substantially non-vulgate are known as follows :

h. Paris, Bibl. nat., 6400 G, formerly 5367. The Fleury palimpsest (Codex Floriacensis). Sixth century.[1] The fragments (printed in the present volume) contain about one quarter of Acts.[2] For a table of the more important differences of scholars in deciphering this palimpsest see below, pp. cccxiv-xv.

---

[1] The over-writing (eighth century) is Isidore of Seville, *De mundo.* On the date and origin of h see *Novum Testamentum Sancti Irenaei*, 1923, p. clxxxv ; E. Châtelain, *Uncialis scriptura*, Paris, 1901, tab. xv., and p. 28 ; D. de Bruyne, *Les Fragments de Freising* (Collectanea Biblica Latina v), 1921, p. xxiii note 1 ; L. Traube, *Nomina sacra*, pp. 191, 200 f. ; also S. Berger (see following note). It is believed that h was copied, possibly in Africa (so also k), from an exemplar giving the text of Acts, Catholic epistles, and Apocalypse, as used in some African church in the fifth century. This text was Cyprianic for Acts and (according to de Bruyne) the Apocalypse, but the Catholic epistles had been revised at some time subsequent to the date of Cyprian. The text of the Apocalypse is discussed by H. J. Vogels, *Untersuchungen zur Geschichte der lateinischen Apokalypse-übersetzung*, Düsseldorf, 1920, pp. 93-98. Vogels holds that in the Apocalypse the text of h probably shows some influence from the Vulgate.

[2] S. Berger, *Le palimpseste de Fleury*, Paris, 1889 ; E. S. Buchanan, *Old-Latin Biblical Texts*, No. V., Oxford, 1907. Wordsworth and White's citation of h is dependent on Berger alone. For further discussion of the readings, with corrections and conjectures, see P. Corssen, *Der Cyprianische Text der Acta apostolorum*, 1892, p. 20 ; S. Berger, ' Un ancien texte des Actes des Apôtres,' *Notices et extraits*, vol. xxxv., 1896–97, p. 181 note 3 ; E. S. Buchanan, *Journal of Theological Studies*, vol. viii., 1906-7, pp. 96, 100; vol. ix., 1907-8, pp. 98-100;

The text of h is shown by comparison with the *Testimonia* of Cyprian,[1] as well as by internal characteristics, to be of African origin.   In the passages where comparison is possible, it differs hardly at all from Cyprian and represents the African translation current in the early third century with but little variation in Latin expression and virtually none in underlying Greek text.[2]   The manuscript is written with many errors.[3]   The rendering into Latin is often very free, although the Greek text followed can usually be discerned.   In particular the omissions of words and phrases are not wholly due to the underlying Greek text, so that inferences have to be drawn with caution; thus in the narrative of Paul's voyage, Acts xxviii. 1-13, we seem to have a corrupt form of an abridgement made by the translator.[4]   In Acts iii. 11 the words *et concurrit omnis populus ad eos [in porti]cu quae vocatur solomonis stupentes* agree substantially with the usual Greek text against D d, and are apparently due to a later correction based on that text ; in vss. 12,

---

vol. x., 1908–9, p. 126 ; *Old-Latin Biblical Texts*, No. VI., 1911, ' Addenda et corrigenda,' p. 197 ; F. C. Burkitt, *Journal of Theological Studies*, vol. IX., 1907–8, p. 305 ; A. Souter, *ibid.* vol. XI., 1909–10, pp. 563 ff. ; Th. Zahn, *Urausgabe*, 1916, pp. 114, 138, 172.   These have all been considered in preparing the text of h printed in the present volume.   References to the earlier scholars who deciphered and published portions of the MS. are given by Buchanan, *Old-Latin Biblical Texts*, No. V., p. 97.

[1] The resemblance of the two texts was apparent to Sabatier from the small fragments of h (Acts iii. 2-12, iv. 2-18) known to him, but the comparison was first made with thoroughness by P. Corssen, *Der Cyprianische Text der Acta apostolorum*, Berlin, 1892.

[2] About 203 verses of Acts are extant in h, and in these but 10 differences from the Cyprianic text of the *Testimonia* appear ; see Hans von Soden, *Das lateinische Neue Testament in Afrika zur Zeit Cyprians* (Texte und Untersuchungen, vol. XXXIII.), 1909, esp. pp. 221-242, 323-363, 550-567.   That at least some parts of the African Bible existed from an early time in varying forms and that the text underwent natural modification and development (apart from certain definite recensions) is shown by P. Capelle, *Le texte du psautier latin en Afrique*, Rome, 1913.   Von Soden, pp. 238 f., gives examples of ' Degeneration der Africitas ' in h ; but these changes of Latin phraseology do not pertain to the Greek text underlying the codex.

[3] Hans von Soden, *op. cit.* pp. 234-236.

[4] Instances of omission in h are the following : ix. 12 (the whole verse) ; xxvi. 22 αχρι της ημερας ταυτης ; xxvi. 26 παρρησιαζομενος, ου πειθομαι, ου γαρ εστιν εν γωνια πεπραγμενον τουτο ; for many others see below, pp. ccxxxvi-viii.

13, and 14 further readings occur in which h agrees with B against D. In several of these latter Irenaeus agrees with h. Other cases of agreement of h with B against D are iv. 6, where h reads 'Johannes,' not, like other 'Western' witnesses, 'Jonathan'; v. 36 διελύθησαν; xi. 6 *hos* (cf. *quos* d). But such instances are extremely rare. In iii. 4 *aspice et contemplari* might be a conflation due to the rival Greek readings βλεψον and ατενισον,[1] but may equally well be accounted for from ατενισον alone by the African tendency to translation by two words.[2]

The Old African Latin text gives the 'Western' recension in the purest form known to us in continuous sections, and constitutes a source of knowledge for that recension of equal value, so far as it is available, with Codex Bezae and the Harclean apparatus. In not a few instances h provides conclusive evidence of the conflate character of the text of D (so, for instance, v. 29, xviii. 5).

perp or **p.** Paris, Bibl. nat., lat. 321. Thirteenth century. A manuscript from Perpignan, near the Spanish border, and probably written there.[3] In Acts i. 1-xiii. 6, xxviii. 16-31, the text is Old Latin. The corrections of perp come from a pure Languedocian Vulgate text, and this is also the source of the part of Acts which is drawn from the Vulgate. This type of Vulgate text is characterized by the inclusion of many isolated Old Latin survivals; but the line is perfectly distinct between the Vulgate section and the Old Latin sections of the ms., which is properly described as containing not a mixed, but a divided, text.[4]

---

[1] So Jülicher, in *Zeitschrift für die neutestamentliche Wissenschaft*, vol. xv., 1914, p. 168.

[2] Harris, *Codex Bezae*, p. 254; cf. h, Acts iii. 14 *vivere et donari*, xiv. 9 *clamans dixit*. This tendency is also found in the Peshitto.

[3] S. Berger, 'Un ancien texte latin des Actes des Apôtres retrouvé dans un manuscrit provenant de Perpignan,' *Notices et extraits des mss. de la bibliothèque nationale*, xxxv., Paris, 1896, pp. 169-208, prints the two Old Latin sections in full; F. Blass, 'Neue Texteszeugen für die Apostelgeschichte,' *Theol. Studien und Kritiken*, lxix., 1896, pp. 436-471.

[4] Zahn, *Urausgabe*, p. 15; Berger, *op. cit.* p. 187.

Jülicher's analysis of perp is of much interest.[1] The text in the Old Latin chapters is related to nearly all the known types, to the Cyprianic text, to gig d e m t (but not to s), and to the Vulgate. Carefully formed as a recension, not a mere conglomeration of readings, and bearing a uniform character, with a distinct standard both of lucidity and of taste, it is punctiliously literal, strives to omit nothing (hence its many ' Western ' additions, besides which it has others of Latin origin), strictly eliminates foreign expressions (an African trait),[2] is old-fashioned in the choice of words. Comparison with gigas and the Vulgate leads on the whole to the conclusion that the editor was not acquainted with those ancient texts, although perp and gig may well be thought to show common dependence on an earlier recension. The late date of the actual manuscript need not lead us to assume that many readings have intruded themselves into the text of these chapters at a period more recent than the fourth century.

To this Souter [3] adds that perp " has points of contact with the quotations in the homilies of Gregory of Elvira " (that is, the fourth-century pseudo-origenian tracts, *De libris sacrarum scripturarum*, see below, p. cxvii), and that Augustine's readings so often agree with perp as to suggest that perp is a Spanish revision of the Old African text.

gig or **g.** Codex Gigas. Thirteenth century, not earlier than 1239. Complete.[4] Brought in 1648 from Bohemia to Stockholm (hence called Codex Holmiensis ; now in the Royal Library).

---

[1] Jülicher, *op. cit.* pp. 180-182.

[2] Thus εὐαγγελίζεσθαι is rendered *bene* (*ad*)*nunciare* ; συναγωγή *conventio* ; ἐλεημοσύναι *misericordiae* ; ἔκστασις *mentis alienatio, stupor mentis* ; εὐνοῦχος *spado, Eunicus* (!) ; γάζα, *diviciae*.

[3] *Text and Canon of the New Testament*, 1912, p. 45.

[4] Continuous text, J. Belsheim, *Die Apostelgeschichte und die Offenbarung Johannis in einer alten lateinischen Übersetzung*, Christiania, 1879 ; for certainty as to readings use must be made of the apparatus of Wordsworth and White's Vulgate, for which a fresh collation was made. On the date see Belsheim, p. vii, and especially B. Dudik, *Forschung in Schweden für Mährens Geschichte*, Brünn, 1852, where a detailed history of this extraordinary codex will be found (pp. 207-235).

The text of gig in Acts can be used with confidence as representing a Latin text widely current in the fourth century, as is shown by its close agreement with the abundant quotations (more than one-eighth of Acts) of Lucifer of Cagliari in Sardinia, who wrote in exile in the East in 355–362, and must have brought his Latin Bible with him from the West. Lucifer's text is as yet known through a single MS., of the ninth or tenth century.[1] Where gig and Lucifer differ, comparison shows that they are about equally liable to go wrong. Lucifer shows no trace of the use of any Greek text with different readings from those of gig. Both he and gig are very rarely affected by the Vulgate.[2]

g_2. A fragment of a lectionary, now at Milan, containing Acts vi. 8-vii. 2 ; vii. 51-viii. 4, in a text substantially identical with that of gig. Tenth or eleventh century.[3]

t. Liber comicus. Paris, Bibl. nat., nouv. acq. lat. 2171. Eleventh century. Lectionarius missae, as used in the church of Toledo in the seventh century.[4] Of the fourteen lessons from Acts, seven contain an Old Latin text, freely handled and corrupt but similar to gig.[5] The Old Latin lessons comprise Acts i. 1-11, 15-26 ; ii. 1-21, 22-41 ; iv. 32-v. 11 ; vi. 1-vii. 2 with vii. 51-viii. 4 (partly Vulgate) ; x. 25-43. Occasional Old Latin readings are also found in the Vulgate lessons.

s. Codex Bobiensis. Vienna, Imperial Library, 16. Fifth or sixth century. Palimpsest, formerly at Bobbio.[6] Acts xxiii. 15-23 ; xxiv. 6, 8, 13-xxv. 2 ; xxv. 23-xxvi. 2 ; xxvi. 22-24, 26-xxvii. 32 ; xxviii. 4-9, 16-31.

d. Codex Bezae (see above, p. lxxx). Fifth or sixth century.

---

[1] The agreement of Lucifer with gig was mentioned by Hort, 'Introduction,' 1881, p. 83. A second MS. of Lucifer has been found in the Library of Ste. Geneviève, Paris ; see A. Wilmart, ' Un Manuscrit de De Cibis et des œuvres de Lucifer,' Revue Bénédictine, vol. xxxiii., 1921, pp. 124-135.

[2] Jülicher, pp. 169-171.

[3] Text in Ceriani, Monumenta sacra et profana, i. 2 (1865), p. 127.

[4] Text in G. Morin, Anecdota Maredsolana, i., 1893.

[5] The significant variations of t from gig seem to be due in part to the Vulgate, in part to ancient survivals ; cf. Jülicher, pp. 172 f.

[6] H. J. White, Old-Latin Biblical Texts, No. IV., Oxford, 1897.

The Latin side of Codex Bezae has been so extensively altered to make it agree with its Greek partner that it can seldom be used as a witness to the Old Latin text except where that text is known from other sources. It seems, however, that a text akin to, but not perfectly identical with, that of gig was used as the basis of d ; the text of d is farther removed from the African Latin than is that of e, gig, perp, or the Vulgate ; [1] in the Gospels d has sometimes preserved readings found elsewhere only in k and a, which are the chief sources respectively for the African and ' European ' Gospel text. [2]

e. Codex Laudianus (see above, pp. lxxxiv-viii). Sixth or seventh century.

The Latin of Codex Laudianus, like that of Codex Bezae, has been brought into conformity with the Greek text, but it seems to have retained its own character much more fully than d, and was often the dominant member of the partnership. The editor of this bilingual text, evidently a Greek of good education, seems to have understood Latin, but hardly to have mastered it for the purposes of composition. The Latin text which he took as a basis for his work had a resemblance to gig and also to the Vulgate, and may have been the common precursor of both of these, but shows a less close resemblance to d. The suggestion has been made that it may be the nearest extant representative of the text which Jerome used as the basis of the Vulgate. But few survivals of distinctively African renderings occur in e. [3]

Many other Latin codices contain Old Latin readings mixed with a prevailing Vulgate text, and these readings are valuable as evidence of the Greek text from which the Old Latin was drawn. The mixture in most cases was made from either Spanish (whence the characteristic Languedocian mixed Vulgate text) or Irish Old Latin sources. Of these codices the following are notable, but not the only, examples, and are sometimes counted as Old Latin :

---

[1] Jülicher, pp. 182, 185.   [2] Souter, *op. cit.* p. 42.
[3] Jülicher, pp. 182-185.

c. Paris, Bibl. nat., lat. 254. Codex Colbertinus. Twelfth century (second half). Believed to have been written in Languedoc.

dem. Codex Demidovianus (now lost). Twelfth or thirteenth century.[1] Formerly at Lyons.

r. Schlettstadt, Stadtbibliothek, 1093. Seventh or eighth century. Lectionary.[2] The Old Testament lessons are from the Vulgate ; but the New Testament lessons, fourteen in number, all from Acts, are Old Latin, with a text much like that of gig but also showing some resemblance to perp.

w. Wernigerode, Library of Graf Stolberg, Z.a.81. Fifteenth century. Contains a partial interlinear version in Bohemian.[3]

R. Paris, Bibl. nat., lat. 16. Bible de Rosas. Tenth or eleventh century. Written in eastern Spain. In Acts xi. and xii. another text has been written in the margin, and Old Latin readings, often agreeing with perp, are found in these chapters, sometimes in the main text, sometimes in the margin.[4]

D. Dublin, Library of Trinity College. The Book of Armagh.[5] First half of ninth century.

lux. Paris, Bibl. nat., lat. 9427. The Luxeuil lectionary. Eighth century.[6]

Latin Fathers. Of Latin ecclesiastical writers significant for the Old Latin text mention may be made as follows :

TERTULLIAN of Carthage (*ca.* 160–*ca.* 240). The chief cita-

---

[1] The text was edited by Matthäi, *Novum Testamentum XII. tomis distinctum Graece et Latine*, vol. ix., Riga, 1782.

[2] Text in G. Morin, *Études, textes, découvertes*, vol. i. (Anecdota Maredsolana, ii.), 1913, pp. 440-456, cf. p. 49. Readings from this lectionary will be found in the apparatus of Zahn, *Urausgabe*, but not in that of Wordsworth and White.

[3] F. Blass, *Theol. Studien und Kritiken*, LXIX., 1896, pp. 436-471 ; for further remarks on this MS. see below, pp. cxxxv-cxxxvi.

[4] For the readings of R see Wordsworth and White ; on the codex and its illustrations see W. Neuss, *Die katalanische Bibelillustration um die Wende des ersten Jahrtausends und die altspanische Buchmalerei*, 1922. The Bible de Rosas was probably written at the monastery of Santa Maria de Ripoll, which had a famous library and scriptorium.

[5] J. Gwynn, *Liber Ardmachanus, The Book of Armagh*, Dublin, 1913.

[6] Readings of lux are given by Sabatier, *Bibliorum sacrorum Latinae versiones antiquae*, vol. iii., Paris, 1751.

tions from the Acts found in the writings of Tertullian are
printed in full in the apparatus of the present volume.[1] His
text was of the ' Western ' type.[2] That at least one Latin translation of the Bible existed in his time in Africa is clear.[3] In
Tertullian's use of 1-4 Kingdoms the Greek text on which his
Latin version rests is different from any known to us, and in
particular shows no close relation to the Antiochian (Lucianic)
text.[4] In the Psalms the Greek text underlying the Old African
Latin was Old Antiochian mingled with Egyptian elements and
others more primitive (see below, p. cxxvi). The *Acts of Perpetua
and Felicitas* may have been written by Tertullian ; in them
several passages seem to show dependence on ' Western ' readings in Acts (notably Acts ii. 17 αυτων for υμων, twice ; iv. 24,
xvi. 10).[5]

CYPRIAN († 258 ; literary activity chiefly after 249). The
citations of Cyprian from Acts are chiefly contained in the collection of Biblical texts arranged by topics, *Ad Quirinum testimonia,*
for which Codex L (Laureshamensis, formerly at Lorsch) must
be used.[6] These and other scattered quotations are printed in

---

[1] The text followed is that of the Vienna edition so far as the latter is
available, elsewhere that of Oehler. Mere allusions of Tertullian are generally
not reproduced in the present volume.

[2] F. H. Chase, *The Syriac Element in Codex Bezae,* 1893, pp. 103-105, has
collected some good illustrations of this fact, which are supplemented with
examples elicited by characteristically subtle reasoning in J. R. Harris, *Four
Lectures on the Western Text of the New Testament,* 1894, pp. 55-59. The most
striking cases are the text of the Apostolic Decree (Acts xv. 28 f. ; see below,
pp. 265-269) and of Acts xiii. 33 ' *in primo psalmo* ' (see below, pp. 264 f.).

[3] This is convincingly argued afresh (against Zahn's view), and illustrated
from the Psalter, by P. Capelle, *Le Texte du psautier latin en Afrique,* 1913,
pp. 1-21. See also P. Monceaux, *Histoire littéraire de l'Afrique chrétienne,* vol. i.,
1901, pp. 105 f. ; Harnack, *Die Chronologie der altchristlichen Litteratur,* vol. ii.
pp. 296-302 ; *Die Mission und Ausbreitung des Christentums in den ersten drei
Jahrhunderten,* 4th ed., 1924, p. 800. Of Marcion's Bible also it is clear that
Tertullian had a Latin text ; Harnack, *Marcion,* 1921, pp. 46*-54*, 160*-163*.

[4] Rahlfs, *Lucians Rezension der Königsbücher,* pp. 141-143.

[5] Harris, *Codex Bezae,* pp. 148-153 ; J. A. Robinson, *The Passion of S.
Perpetua* (Texts and Studies, i.), pp. 48-50.

[6] Unfortunately the collation of Codex L in Hartel's edition (Vienna corpus,
1868) is not perfectly accurate ; see P. Capelle, *op. cit.* p. 24 ; H. L. Ramsay,
Journal of Theological Studies, vol. III., 1901-2, pp. 585 f. ; C. H. Turner, *ibid.*
vol. VI., 1904-5, pp. 264-268.

the apparatus below, and from them a considerable part of the
Old African text of Acts can be recovered in substantially trustworthy form.[1] It was an almost pure ' Western ' text. On
the Old Testament text of Cyprian the same statements can
be made as in the case of Tertullian.

SPECULUM, or *Liber de divinis scripturis* (cited as ' m ').
This collection of Biblical passages arranged by topics is known
from a number of MSS., of which the oldest is of the eighth or
ninth century. Formerly ascribed to Augustine, it has been
included in the edition of Augustine's works in the Vienna Corpus
(ed. F. Weihrich, 1887). The text of Acts (the longest quotation
being Acts ix. 36-42) shows kinship to perp. It appears to be a
Spanish form of the African text, probably dating from the
fifth century.[2]

LUCIFER OF CAGLIARI, who wrote in 355-362, used in Acts,
as has been pointed out above, the same Latin version which
we find in gig. It is worth noting that Lucifer's text [3] in Luke
is substantially (perhaps in an earlier stage) that of b (Codex
Veronensis, fifth century) ; in John that of a (Codex Vercellensis,
fourth century) and e (Codex Palatinus, fifth century) ; in Paul
that of d[paul] (Codex Claromontanus, fifth-sixth century), except,
of course, in those epistles where this MS. on its Latin side is
conformed to the Vulgate ; and that in the Old Testament it
agrees with the Vienna palimpsest fragments (fifth century ;
Genesis and 1 and 2 Kingdoms). In 1-4 Kingdoms Lucifer's
quotations have been shown to come from a text corresponding
partly to the Lucianic Greek, partly to the (older) non-lucianic.[4]

---

[1] Hans von Soden, *Das lateinische Neue Testament in Afrika zur Zeit Cyprians*
(Texte und Untersuchungen, XXXIII.), 1909, pp. 550-567.

[2] P. Capelle, *op. cit.* pp. 47-50. Jülicher, *op. cit.* p. 180, thinks the text of
m to be a true recension, with a mixture of the textual types represented by h
and gig.

[3] Burkitt, *Encyclopaedia Biblica*, cols. 4994 f., 5023 ; Sanday, *Old-Latin
Biblical Texts*, No. II., 1886, p. 140. On the quotations of Lucifer from Luke
and John, see Sanday, *Old-Latin Biblical Texts*, No. II., 1886, p. 140 ; H. J.
Vogels, *Theologische Quartalschrift*, vol. CIII., 1922, pp. 23-37, 183-200.

[4] Rahlfs, *Lucians Rezension der Königsbücher*, p. 161 ; Burkitt, *Fragments
of the Books of Kings according to the Translation of Aquila*, 1897, pp. 19 f. ;

In Lucifer's quotations from the Bible, however, attention must always be paid to the fact that he, like Lactantius and others, often derived them from the writings of Cyprian and not from his own reading of the biblical text.[1]

AMBROSE († 397). Ambrose must have used an Old Latin text of Acts, but his works are so largely founded on Greek sources that its nature can hardly be determined.

AMBROSIASTER (fl. 375–385) used in Acts the ' gigas-recension,' and his text is " almost to a letter identical with that of gig itself." In the Gospels the text of Ambrosiaster is to a considerable extent that of b (Veronensis), but sometimes departs from b and agrees with some other of the 'European' witnesses, especially ff$_2$. In the Pauline epistles Ambrosiaster used a text " closely related " to that of Lucifer, but apparently more polished.[2]

AUGUSTINE (baptized 387 ; † 430). Augustine knew and used for certain purposes the Vulgate of Acts, for instance in the Speculum [3] and in debate with Jerome (Ep. 82, 9, Acts xxi. 20-25). The text of Acts, however, used in the church of Hippo was Cyprianic, and Augustine quotes from this at length in De actis cum Felice Manichaeo, i. 4-5 (A.D. 404), in Contra epistulam Manichaei quam vocant Fundamenti (397 ?). In these his text is almost identical with that of Cyprian's Testimonia. In De consensu evangelistarum (A.D. 399) the influence of the African text of Acts is plain, but the quotations show traces of the Vulgate rendering, and were perhaps made from memory. The most important of these Old Latin quotations are printed in this volume ; but others will be found in the apparatus to the Latin

---

see also L. Dieu, ' Retouches Lucianiques sur quelques textes de la vieille version latine (I et II Samuel),' Revue Biblique, vol. xxviii., 1919, pp. 372-403.

[1] Dombart, Berliner Philologische Wochenschrift, vol. viii., 1888, cols. 171-176.

[2] A. Souter, A Study of Ambrosiaster (Texts and Studies, vii.), 1905, pp. 205-214.

[3] That the use of the Vulgate in the texts from both Testaments formally quoted in the body of the Speculum (A.D. 427) was in accordance with the purpose of Augustine himself has been made plain by Burkitt (against Weihrich), ' Saint Augustine's Bible and the Itala,' in Journal of Theological Studies, vol. xi., 1909–10, pp. 258-268.

text of Zahn's *Urausgabe*. A complete investigation of all
Augustine's quotations from Acts has never been made. The
agreement which he shows with perp is probably due to the Old
African element in that manuscript.[1] In some cases Augustine's
text of Acts seems due to dependence on Ambrosiaster.[2]

This use of the Vulgate for learned and critical purposes and
of the African version on other occasions accords with Augustine's
practice as seen in his use of the Psalms (see below, pp. cxxiv f.)
and of the Gospels,[3] although in the Gospels he appears to have
adopted the Vulgate for habitual use about the year 398.[4] In
the Apocalypse Augustine uses the African text, closely resembling
that of Cyprian, cited in the Commentary of Primasius (sixth
century) and found in the fragments of h, while in the Catholic
epistles his text is a late African revision, also found in h and in
r.[5] For the Pauline epistles, likewise, the revised African text
of r (the Freising fragments, probably Spanish) is that employed
by Augustine in Africa from 389 on. He may, indeed, himself
have made this revised text ; and it is not improbable that the
Epistle to the Hebrews as found in r was Augustine's own rendering from the Greek. While still in Italy (early in 388) he had
used a different text, similar to, and probably a precursor of,
the Vulgate.[6]

Other writers who used an Old Latin text must be briefly

---

[1] Souter, *Text and Canon of the N.T.* p. 45.

[2] So in Acts xv. 29, see below, p. 266 ; A. J. Smith, *Journal of Theological
Studies*, vol. xix., 1917–18, pp. 170, 176 ; vol. xx., 1918–19, p. 64.

[3] The Old Latin text of the Gospels used by Augustine in his earlier period
is substantially the revised African type found in e (Codex Palatinus, fifth
century) ; Souter, *op. cit.* p. 89.

[4] Burkitt, ' Saint Augustine's Bible and the *Itala* ; II. The Gospel Quotations in the De Consensu,' *Journal of Theological Studies*, vol. xi., 1909–10,
pp. 447-466, esp. p. 449.

[5] Souter, *Text and Canon of the New Testament*, p. 89 ; Burkitt, *Encyclopaedia Biblica*, col. 4997. De Bruyne, *Les Fragments de Freising*, 1921, p.
xxxviii, says : " Il ne serait pas difficile de montrer qu'Augustin cite pour les
Cath. un texte revisé qu'on ne trouve pas avant lui et dont il est sans doute
l'auteur."

[6] D. de Bruyne, *Les Fragments de Freising* (Collectanea Biblica Latina v.),
1921, pp. xviii-xlviii. On Augustine see also P. Corssen, *Der Cyprianische
Text der Acta apostolorum*, pp. 24 f.

mentioned.[1]   The anonymous (pseudo-origenian) tracts *De libris sacrarum scripturarum* (edited by P. Batiffol and A. Wilmart, 1900) of the fourth century, perhaps from Spain (? Gregory of Elvira † 392) ;   the anonymous *Prophetiae ex omnibus libris collectae* of the ninth-century St. Gall Codex 133,[2] probably African from the years 305-325 (the text is surely corrupt) ;   the third-century pseudo-cyprianic tract *De rebaptismate*, with a remarkable text of Acts, " a third-century African text as far as regards renderings, but without the ' Western ' glosses " ;[3] the tract *Contra Varimadum*, formerly attributed to Vigilius of Thapsus ;[4] the *Liber promissionum et praedictorum dei*, formerly attributed to Prosper of Aquitaine, but now known to be by an African, possibly Quodvultdeus, Bishop of Carthage, and to have been written in 440–450.[5]

The following names may be added.   From Africa : Optatus of Mileve (fl. *ca.* 368) ; Petilianus, Cresconius, and Tyconius the Donatists (at the close of the fourth century) ; Fulgentius of Ruspe († 533).   From Spain : Pacianus of Barcelona (fl. *ca.* 370), ' Priscillian ' (later fourth century), and the Priscillianist tract *De trinitate*.[6] From Italy : Gaudentius of Brescia, Jerome,[7] Philastrius of Brescia, Zeno of Verona (all these are of the middle or late fourth, or early fifth, century), with Paulinus

---

[1] On their significance for the text of Acts see Zahn, *Urausgabe*, pp. 17-25.

[2] A. Amelli, *Miscellanea Cassinese*, ii. vi., 1897, pp. 17 ff. ; Zahn in *Geschichtliche Studien Albert Hauck zum 70. Geburtstage dargebracht*, 1916, pp. 52-63.

[3] F. C. Burkitt, *Encyclopaedia Biblica*, art. ' Text and Versions,' col. 4996 ; Burkitt is inclined to the view " that it was not originally composed in Latin, and that we possess only the Latin translation."

[4] Perhaps Spanish in origin.   See G. Ficker, *Studien zu Vigilius von Thapsus*, 1897, pp. 42-50 ; Capelle, *op. cit.* p. 111 note 2.

[5] Capelle, *op. cit.* p. 87.   The text of the Psalter used by the *Liber promissionum* was substantially that of the Verona Psalter (R) and of the Old Latin Psalter of Carthage, as quoted by Augustine ; Capelle, pp. 87-169, 227-233.   On the attribution to Quodvultdeus see P. Schepens, *Recherches de science religieuse*, vol. x., 1919, pp. 230-243 ; D. Franses, *Die Werke des hl. Quodvultdeus* (Veröffentlichungen aus dem Kirchenhistorischen Seminar München, iv. Reihe, Nr. 9), Munich, 1920 ; *Theologische Quartalschrift*, vol. ciii., 1922, p. 129.

[6] G. Morin, *Études, textes, découvertes*, vol. i. pp. 151-205.

[7] Souter, *Text and Canon of the New Testament*, p. 89.   In at least one instance, Ep. 41, 1, § 2, Jerome quotes Acts (ii. 14-18) from a text " related to gig and p."

of Nola († 431), Valerian of Cimiez (near Nice ; middle of fifth century), and Cassiodorus († 575). From Gaul : Hilary of Poitiers († 367), Gregory of Tours († 593), and Ado of Lyons and Vienne († 875) ; from the British Isles, Pelagius (*ca.* 409) ; [1] from Dacia, Niceta of Remesiana (fl. 400). To these should be added the tract *De trinitate* ascribed to Vigilius of Thapsus, the *Acta Archelai* of Hegemonius, and the Latin version [2] of Irenaeus.[3] The quotations from Acts of nearly all these writers are few, and sometimes brief, but the list, which is not exhaustive, shows the abundance of available material for illustration of the history which awaits the student who will approach the Latin text of Acts with sound method, adequate knowledge, and historical sense.

History of Old Latin version.

On the complicated history of the Old Latin text of Acts two recent studies, one by Jülicher, the other by Capelle, have thrown fresh light, the one by direct approach, the other indirectly.[4] Jülicher, in an essay resting on thorough study of the documents considered, and no less full of learning and insight than it is delightful and sympathetic, has investigated the character of the six chief witnesses, and traced in this way the history of the text.[5] On his guidance the following account is largely, but not wholly, dependent.

[1] On Pelagius's text of Acts see A. Souter, *Pelagius's Expositions of Thirteen Epistles of St. Paul* : I. *Introduction* (Texts and Studies, ix.), 1922, pp. 169-171 ; " the evidence suggests that the British text was related to those used in Africa and Spain rather than any others " (p. 169).

[2] The biblical quotations in the Latin version of Irenaeus generally follow Irenaeus's Greek text, but in the form of language adopted for this purpose a fourth-century revised African text seems to have been in the translator's mind ; see A. Souter in *Novum Testamentum S. Irenaei*, pp. clxiii, clxv ; cf. pp. xvii f. ; see below, pp. clxxxvii-clxxxviii.

[3] These Latin writers are nearly all used in the apparatus of Zahn, *Urausgabe* ; most of the quotations are given by Sabatier.

[4] In addition to the investigations of Jülicher and Capelle here referred to see Paul Monceaux, *Histoire littéraire de l'Afrique chrétienne depuis les origines jusqu'à l'invasion arabe*, vol. i., 1901, chap. iii., ' La Bible latine en Afrique.' This comprehensive exposition by Monceaux is of great value, in spite of some misapprehensions with regard to the textual criticism and history of the Greek Bible, and although some matters would require restatement in the light of more recent studies.

[5] Adolf Jülicher, ' Kritische Analyse der lateinischen Übersetzungen der

The earliest evidence of the translation, or translations, of parts of the Bible into Latin comes from Africa through Tertullian, whose text, so far as we can learn it, was ' Western.' The text of Cyprian and Codex h was that of the church of Carthage,[1] for we find it in that church, with virtually no change, cited at length by Augustine in the report of the debate with Felix the Manichee in 404, as well as elsewhere in Augustine's writings. That the earliest form of this version was native to Africa, not brought from Europe or the East, is altogether probable, although the other view has been held. What was its further history has not been determined.[2] The analogy of the African text of the Psalter suggests some development of the text of Acts in the later centuries, both in Africa and when it was transplanted to Spain, but of the course of this nothing definite can at present be affirmed. Such a development would doubtless show the softening of African crudities under foreign influences from Italian texts and then from the Vulgate ; it would probably in certain types include the elimination of ' Western ' traits and some degree of approximation to the Greek texts later current. One example of such a later Spanish-African text, retaining a strong ' Western ' character, is probably what we find in the Old Latin portions of the Perpignan codex (thirteenth century) from South-western France (see above, pp. cviii-cix).

The few fragments of Donatist quotations, chiefly in passages which we are unable to compare with an earlier African text, are insufficient to show the nature of the Donatist text (after 330). They exhibit a certain contact with gig d e and the Vulgate,[3] and doubtless represent a type marked by similar

---

Apostelgeschichte,' *Zeitschrift für die neutestamentliche Wissenschaft,* vol. xv., 1914, pp. 163-188.

[1] The translation in h, Acts xviii. 2, of ἀπὸ τῆς 'Ρώμης by *ab urbe* (so also d *ex urbem*) does not imply Roman origin. See Zahn, *Geschichte des neutestamentlichen Kanons,* vol. ii. p. 132 note 1, for evidence from many parts of the empire.

[2] The uncertainty as to the origin of *De rebaptismate* (see above, p. cxvii) makes it impossible to draw inferences therefrom with regard to a later form of the African version.   [3] Jülicher, p. 180.

qualities to those found in Donatist texts from the Psalms, namely a high degree of conservatism together with some innovations.

Whether versions of the Latin Bible were made in Italy in independence of the African version is not known, but there is clear evidence that texts early used in Italy were strongly influenced by the labours of the African church in translating the Bible.[1] Intercourse between Italian and African Christians was active at all times ; the need of a translation into Latin would be felt less early in the Greek-speaking church of Rome than in Africa ; a new translator is commonly wise enough to avail himself of the aid of his predecessors' renderings, and the line between an independent translation in which such aid has been used and the revision of an earlier translation is hard, indeed impossible, to draw. Even if the line could be drawn in theory, it would be hard from any actual facts to gather which of two so nearly related processes had been employed. As time went on, however, Italian Christianity gained pre-eminence, and, moreover, the biblical text current in Italy, whatever its ultimate origin, came to present a better and more modern literary form than the African Bible, which must have sounded odd and archaic to the educated Christian in either land. Meantime Spain seems to have drawn its earliest text of the Bible, as it did its liturgy, from African sources.[2] This interplay of influences proceeding in the earliest period from Africa to affect Spanish and Italian Bibles (followed by a development in Italy), and then, at a later time, of counter-influences proceeding from Italy to affect the text of Africa [3] and Spain, goes far to account for the mingled elements which we actually find in most of the extant witnesses to the Old Latin text.

[1] Cf. Sanday and Turner, *Novum Testamentum Sancti Irenaei*, pp. xvii f.

[2] Capelle, *op. cit.* pp. 44 f., 118 f. note, 222 ; Cabrol, art. ' Afrique (Liturgie),' in *Dictionnaire d'archéologie chrétienne*, col. 613 note 1. On the service rendered by Spain in preserving and transmitting something of the secular literature current in Africa, see L. Traube, *Einleitung in die lateinische Philologie des Mittelalters* (Vorlesungen und Abhandlungen, ii.), Munich, 1911, p. 126.

[3] Capelle, p. 45.

The great event in the history of the Old Latin Acts was a revision which must have taken place as early as the year 350, and which speedily became widely influential. Well preserved in Codex Gigas and the ample citations of Lucifer, this revised text also appears in a fragment for liturgical use known as g₂ (tenth or eleventh century) ; it was used in s, perhaps as the basis of the editor's work ; and its influence appears in the lectionary of Toledo (t) in the seventh century, as well as probably in perp. Further, we find it employed by ' Ambrosiaster ' (fl. 375), by Niceta of Remesiana in Dacia (fl. 400),[1] and by Jerome himself.[2] Even in the ninth century it was the chief text relied on by Ado of Lyons. Where it was made is not known,[3] but it was intended to provide the educated reader with a text suited to his needs, conformed to Latin idiom, and clearly intelligible. African peculiarities are largely avoided ; Greek barbarisms have been dropped ; and its Latin is sometimes, because a less literal rendering, better than that of the Vulgate. It was plainly made with the use of a Greek text of non-western type,[4] and has been partly freed from ' Western ' readings, especially ' Western ' additions. Earlier revisions in the same direction may have preceded it ; on such perhaps e and the Vulgate were founded ; but this revision, made before 350, is the source of what has come in modern times to be called the ' European ' Latin text of Acts. Its publication meant a much closer approximation than heretofore of the most widely used Latin text to the current

[1] Burkitt in A. E. Burn, *Niceta of Remesiana*, pp. cxliv-cliv.

[2] Souter, *The Text and Canon of the New Testament*, pp. 44, 89, who cites Jerome, Ep. 41. 1, § 2 (p. 312, Hilberg), a letter believed to be from the year 384,

[3] Jülicher, p. 188, speaks of the recension as made neither in Africa nor in Rome. Africanisms have been eliminated more thoroughly than in the African revision of the Psalms of about the same date which produced the version of the Psalter used by Augustine. Doubtless the ground for supposing it to have originated outside of Rome lies in the fact that the text used as the basis of the Vulgate differed from the gigas-text.

[4] Jülicher, pp. 177-180, 185 f., from which has been learned most of what is said above about the gigas-recension. On Lucianic elements in later Old Latin texts of the Old Testament, see Berger, *Histoire de la Vulgate*, p. 6 ; Swete, *Introduction to the Old Testament in Greek*, p. 93.

Greek manuscripts of the period. In considering this recension of the Latin Acts, we may recall that the fourth century was a period of increasing contact of Western and Eastern Christian leaders, and that Athanasius resided at Rome from 339 to 342 (or 340 to 343).[1]

Among the Old Latin texts that of the fragments of the last chapters known as s (Codex Bobiensis, fifth or sixth century) occupies a place somewhat apart. It is allied to gig, and perhaps based on a slightly different form of that recension, and is related to the Vulgate in such a way as to suggest that its editor has also used an older text on which the Vulgate rests. Yet that it was directly influenced by the Vulgate is not impossible, although it does not seem to have been proved. It is the work of a competent scholar, who has tried to produce a text in good Latin idiom which should be wholly conformed to the Old Uncial Greek text, both in omitting longer ' Western ' additions and in details. The date of this work must lie in the fourth or fifth century.[2]

It thus appears that the two well-established landmarks (at least in the Book of Acts) for finding our way in the wilderness of the Old Latin version are the Cyprianic text, current by 240, and the gigas-revision, made before 350.[3]

[1] Abundant evidence (Hilary, Ambrose, Jerome, Augustine) shows that in the fourth century Greek texts of the Old Testament were used in the West ; Rahlfs, *Lucians Rezension der Königsbücher*, p. 153 ; *Der Text des Septuaginta-Psalters*, pp. 75-79 ; Burkitt, *The Old Latin and the Itala*, p. 8.

[2] For the above account of s, I am wholly dependent on Jülicher, *op. cit.* pp. 173-177.

[3] The Gigas-revision, as I have ventured to call it, produced much of the text which appears in the ' European ' representatives of the Old Latin. I have, however, ordinarily refrained from applying to it directly the term ' European,' because the latter covers so many different forms of text, and is in itself likely to mislead by reason of its direct parallelism to the term ' African.' The term ' Italian ' is also to be avoided. It was used by Augustine only with relation to the Old Testament. That he used it there to denote Jerome's translation must be accepted, especially since the remaining difficulties left by Burkitt's fundamental discussion in *The Old Latin and the Itala* (Texts and Studies, iv.), 1896, and Corssen's clear and instructive review in *Göttingische gelehrte Anzeigen*, 1897, pp. 416-424, seem to have been once and for all removed by the acute study of De Bruyne, ' L'Itala de Saint Augustin,' in *Revue Bénédictine*, vol. **xxx.**, 1913, pp. 294-314, where it is conclusively shown that these difficulties were due to the fact that the final edition of Augustine's *De doctrina christiana* differed sub-

The other study mentioned above is that of Capelle on the
Latin text of the Psalter in Africa, already often referred to,[1] a
treatise distinguished by a great elegance of method, a striking
sense of the concrete reality of events and circumstances, and a
comprehensive grasp of all the facts bearing on the author's field.

The history of the African Psalter is made out as follows.
By the time of Tertullian, or earlier, various local translations of
the Psalms were current in Africa in written form. From one
of these, not identical with that of Tertullian himself, grew up
the Psalter of Cyprian, of which we have much knowledge from
the *Testimonia* (Codex L). From one of the MSS. of the *Testimonia* (Codex V, known only from the collation of Latini), and
from the African writings prior to and contemporary with
Cyprian, it appears certain that the African Psalter was by no
means uniform in the time of Cyprian, and that a variety of
kindred but varying texts were in use. Later in the same
century the text of the *Testimonia* followed in the quotations of
Lactantius (who had probably lived only in Africa up to the date
of the composition of his *Divinae institutiones*, about 290) shows
some modification of the original African (for instance λόγος is
verbum, no longer *sermo*). If one MS. of Lactantius (Codex H)
gives a text which seems even more archaic than that of the
original *Testimonia*, that fact bears witness to the persistent
vitality of the Latin text in Africa, which had by no means
stiffened into uniformity at the end of the third century or even
later.

In the fourth century, about 330, the Donatist party became
organized, and the controversies of that period, resting on
biblical proofs, stimulated attention to the biblical text. In
accordance with their theological character, the Donatists used

---

stantially from the form in which it was first published. An earlier suggestion
of the explanation now convincingly elaborated by De Bruyne was made by
Paul Wendland, ' Zur ältesten Geschichte der Bibel in der Kirche,' *Zeitschrift
für die neutestamentliche Wissenschaft,* vol. i., 1900, p. 289 footnote.

[1] Paul Capelle, *Le Texte du psautier latin en Afrique* (Collectanea Biblica
Latina cura et studio monachorum S. Benedicti, vol. IV.), Rome, 1913.

a Psalter of a generally archaic type but yet containing some innovations as compared with Cyprianic standards.   About 350, perhaps partly in consequence of the Donatist controversy, there was made in the orthodox African church a revision of the Psalter in which European influences and a more culti-vated Latinity were brought into the African text.   This was a revolutionary, and must have been a sudden, departure from the Cyprianic text, even in the modified forms in which the first half of the fourth century had known that text.   It may have been called out by the desire to unify the varying texts current among the orthodox.   In a form which had been subjected to a further special revision (of but limited range) this text was that which Augustine found in use when he came to Africa in 388, and which was employed by the churches of Carthage and Hippo.   It was the text of the Psalter which Augustine always continued to quote, except when for certain more learned purposes he used the translation of Jerome.

A little earlier than Augustine's arrival in Africa, Optatus of Mileve's quotations (about 370) show that he had entirely broken with the Cyprianic Psalter.   The change was due to the same revision of which we see the later results in the text of Augustine.   Closely related to the transformed African Psalter used by Augustine is the text of the Psalms in the African *Liber promissionum et praedictorum dei* (440–450).[1]   It passed over to Italy also, and was long used there, for a continuous Psalter, a sister type of the same special revision used by Augustine, appears as the Latin side of the bilingual Verona Psalter (R) of the sixth century, where it has perhaps even had its effect on the Greek text opposite.

The text of Augustine and the Verona Psalter is in its whole fabric a thoroughly African text, well mixed from various African sources, " not merely a text with an African base, still

---

[1] A similar relation is found to subsist between Augustine's text of the Pauline epistles (extant in Codex r) and the text of the *Liber promissionum et praedictorum* ; De Bruyne, *Les Fragments de Freising*, 1921, pp. xxxv f.

less a foreign text africanized," [1] but the revision was made with the aid of European texts, although the precise type of these latter is impossible to determine. Vigorous and skilful African hands succeeded in producing a revision of the Psalter distinguished by homogeneity, by a certain purity and uniformity, by originality of apt rendering as compared with the European texts, and by great fidelity to the Greek text.[2] Perhaps St. Augustine himself had a share in perfecting the work.[3]

In addition to his use of this fourth-century African revised Old Latin, Augustine also used, especially for purposes of learning and criticism, a copy of Jerome's Gallican Psalter (made from a hexaplaric Greek text ; now included in the Vulgate). He seems to have drawn this not directly from a manuscript of the true Gallican version but from a gallicanized African Psalter.

Meantime the African text had been carried to Spain. Pacian of Barcelona (360–390) used a Psalter closely akin to that of Cyprian.[4] The pseudo-augustinian *Speculum* (' m ' in the New Testament) and the text of Cyprian's *Testimonia* (Codex A) found with it in the same MS. (Sessorianus) show kindred, but not identical, mixed texts of the Psalter, in which the Old African type current in Spain has been nearly, but not quite, supplanted by the text of the Mozarabic liturgy. This mixture of texts in Spain probably took place in the fifth century. The Mozarabic Psalter itself was not devoid of survivals of the Old African text, foreign to its main sources (which were the Roman Psalter and in less degree the Hebrew Psalter of Jerome).

For the rest of the fifth century and the first half of the sixth, the evidence of Victor of Vita (486), Vigilius of Thapsus (fl. 484), and Fulgentius of Ruspe (468-533) gives a just notion of what was taking place in Africa. Various texts were in use, but the Gallican Psalter was extending its sway. Yet it did not succeed in completely eliminating all Old African readings from the text

[1] Capelle, p. 116.
[2] Capelle, pp. 120, 129-131. On all these points Capelle furnishes illustrations.
[3] De Bruyne, *op. cit.* p. xxxviii.   [4] Capelle, pp. 44 f., 111 note.

of these writers, while Fulgentius perhaps shows some traces of the influence of Jerome's Roman Psalter. But Christian Africa was already decadent, and by 700 was in the hands of the Saracens.

It has seemed worth while to give at some length this sketch of the history of the Psalter in Africa, as worked out in the admirable book of Capelle, for although no direct application of his results to the text of the New Testament can at present be made, it is highly suggestive for New Testament textual history, both in method and conclusions. As, in the case of Acts, Cyprian and the gigas-recension form two trustworthy landmarks, so in the Psalter two fixed points stand out to our view, the one again the text of Cyprian, the other an African revision of about 350 which strongly reminds us of the gigas-revision of not far from the same date. These two fourth-century revisions, however, can probably not be brought into close relation, for so far as we know the gigas-revision was European, not African. Likewise, both in the Psalter and in Acts, texts passed from Africa to Spain and in that land mingled their readings with others coming from Italian or Gallic sources. And finally the work of Jerome, although only after a plainly discernible struggle, won virtually the whole ground.

Greek text ef the Psalter.   As to the Greek text which underlay the African Psalter, that of Tertullian's and Cyprian's Latin versions seems to have been an Old Antiochian text (hence it sometimes agrees with the late Antiochian revision of Lucian, but never where the hand of Lucian himself is apparent), combined with readings derived from Egyptian texts, especially that of Upper Egypt, and some other ancient elements.[1] The respective relations of Tertullian and of Cyprian to these several constituent elements were in part, but only in part, the same.[2] The revised African Psalter

---

[1] A similar conclusion as to the African Latin text of the Prophets is stated by Burkitt, *The Book of Rules of Tyconius* (Texts and Studies, vol. iii.), pp. cxvi f.

[2] Capelle, pp. 200-207. Capelle (p. 203 note 1) adds a discreet warning against the too confident assumption that these Antiochian and Egyptian readings originated in those regions, or that the text containing them was derived from those regions by the Christians of North Africa.

of 350 seems to show no large influence from any other type of
Greek text than that observable in the Old African.

(b) VULGATE

The Vulgate translation of the Gospels was presented to Character
Pope Damasus by St. Jerome in 384 ; the rest of the New Testa- of the
ment followed, but perhaps only after several years. In Acts Vulgate.
Jerome's revision rested on an Old Latin basis, which may have
been an ancestor of gig. In some cases he preserved African
renderings foreign to gig (for instance xx. 17 *majores natu* for
προσβυτεροι, where d gig have *presbyteri* ; or xxvii. 3, where the
peculiar reading of vg *ad amicos ire et curam sui agere* recalls
h *amicis qui veniebant [ad eum] uti curam ejus agerent*, while gig
reads *ire ad amicos et curam sui habere*), and he may well have had
at his disposal a variety of manuscripts. At any rate he has
retained a very large measure of Old Latin readings. But he
brought in some renderings of his own, and he purged the text
by the aid of a Greek text like that of the Old Uncials,[1] although
peculiarities of no single one of the extant uncials are reflected
in his translation.[2] Jerome's skill in departing as little as
possible from Old Latin renderings, while by slight changes and
rearrangement of words he yet attained, even in order, extraordinary exactness of agreement with his Greek standard, and
produced an excellent translation, is worthy of the greatest
admiration. Wordsworth and White believe that a series of
renderings which they collect show that his Greek text differed
somewhat from any known to us,[3] but on a close scrutiny these
instances, with hardly an exception, do not seem to require this
supposition.

The text of the Vulgate became mixed with the Old Latin
at an early date, and suffered from other corruption, as it was

[1] Jülicher, *op. cit.* pp. 167 f., 185-188 ; Wordsworth and White, *Actus Apostolorum*, pp. x-xiii.
[2] Wordsworth and White, pp. xii f.
[3] *Ibid.* p. xi.

copied and when it was carried to distant lands. Important events in its history were the attempts of Alcuin (801) and of the Spaniard Theodulf (early ninth century) to establish a corrected text.

Codices.   The primary codices of the Vulgate which Wordsworth and White have selected as the basis of their text are G C A F D, named in order of excellence, and chosen as independent representatives from five distinct types and from widely distant localities. The agreement of these five, when it presents itself, is taken as decisive ; when they differ, the internal probability of readings is invoked. The chief rules followed by the editors are that that reading is to be accepted which (1) agrees with the Greek, especially with the Old Uncials ; or (2) renders the Greek best ; or (3) is not found in the Old Latin ; or (4) is supported by a family of codices whose readings are approved as right in the immediate context ; or (5) is shorter. Attention must also be paid to obvious scribal errors. The five primary MSS. are the following :

GCAFD   G. Paris, Bibl. nat., lat. 11,553.   Codex Sangermanensis. Ninth century (first half). This MS. came from Southern Gaul, perhaps from Lyons.[1]

C. La Cava 14. Codex Cavensis. Ninth century. Probably written in Castile or Leon. C is the best representative of the Spanish family, and probably represents the edition of Peregrinus (450–500); it is superior to T (Codex Toletanus, eighth [tenth] century), which seems to give the text of Isidore of Seville (560–636).[2]

A. Florence, Bibl. laur. 1. Codex Amiatinus. *Ca.* 700 A.D. Written in Northumbria ; shows traces in Acts of influence

---

[1] G is distinguished not only by the singular excellence of its text in some parts of the New Testament, but by containing (in expanded form) at the close of the Old Testament a colophon, elsewhere known only in the Bible de Rosas (R), which claims to be by Jerome, and may be genuine ; see D. de Bruyne, ' Un nouveau document sur les origines de la Vulgate,' *Revue Biblique*, vol. x., 1913, pp. 5-14.

[2] D. de Bruyne, ' Étude sur les origines de la Vulgate en Espagne,' *Revue Bénédictine*, vol. xxxi., 1914–19, pp. 373-401.

from the Latin (e) of Codex Laudianus (E). The text is of Neapolitan origin, and probably drawn from that of Cassiodorus.[1]

F. Fulda. Codex Fuldensis. *Ca.* 545 A.D. Written at Capua. On the text of F, which lay in Northumbria in the late years of the seventh and early years of the eighth century, is closely dependent the revision of Alcuin.

D. Dublin, Library of Trinity College. The Book of Armagh. First half of ninth century. D contains many Old Latin readings which survived from the text earlier current in Ireland.[2]

The other codices used by Wordsworth and White fall into groups :

(1) Codex I (Iuveniani ; Rome, Santa Maria in Vallicella, I M B 25[2] ; now in Biblioteca Vittorio-Emanuele ; eighth or ninth century) and Codex M (Monacensis ; ninth or tenth century) represent the same type as Codex A.

(2) Codex S (Sangallensis ; eighth century) and Codex U S U (Ulmensis ; ninth century), both Iro-gallic and written at St. Gall, largely agree with Codex F, but contain some of the additions current in the work of Celtic scribes.

(3) Codex T (Toletanus ; originally from Seville ; now at T Madrid, Bibl. nac. ; eighth [tenth] century) [3] belongs with Codex C, but shows a later form of the Spanish text, probably that of Isidore of Seville (560–636).

(4) Codex O (Oxoniensis-Seldenianus ; sometimes designated O x of the Old Latin ; seventh or eighth century, written in the Isle of Thanet, Kent, England) has a peculiar text related both to the Irish and to the Northumbrian forms.

(5) Codex Θ (Theodulfianus ; early ninth century, probably θ copied at Fleury under the direction of Theodulf himself) best

---

[1] J. Chapman, *Notes on the Early History of the Vulgate Gospels*, 1908, chap. ii. ; and his article, 'Cassiodorus and the Echternach Gospels,' *Revue Bénédictine*, vol. xxviii., 1911, pp. 283-295.

[2] John Gwynn, *Liber Ardmachanus, The Book of Armagh*, Dublin, 1913.

[3] E. A. Lowe, 'On the Date of Codex Toletanus,' *Revue Bénédictine*, vol. xxxv., 1923, pp. 267-271.

represents the Theodulfian recension, which rested on a Spanish (or, rather, Languedocian) text akin to that of C T.

K B V R   (6) Codices K (Karolinus, British Museum, add. 10,546; ninth century, script of Tours), B (Bambergensis, ninth century, script of Tours), V (Vallicellanus, B. vi., ninth century), R (Bible de Rosas, tenth century) ; written in eastern Tarragonian Spain ; named in order of excellence, are the best representatives of the recension of Alcuin,[1] and are consequently closely related to F and, less nearly, to S U.

W   (7) Codex W (William of Hales, A.D. 1254) is taken as a good representative of the text current among scholars in the later Middle Ages.

History of the Vulgate.   The relation of these MSS. and groups is to be accounted for by the history of the Vulgate, in so far as that has been made out by the researches of scholars.[2]

Naples.   Good copies of St. Jerome's translation, or of large parts of it, were early in use in Italy and Southern Spain. At Squillace in South Italy in the sixth century Cassiodorus obtained from Naples an excellent text of the Gospels and a less good one of other parts of the Bible. He seems to have used these to correct an Old Latin text, from which some, though few and unimportant, survivals remained in his text.[3] From this text proceeded that brought to Northumbria, probably by Ceolfrid or Benedict Biscop about 680. Among many copies of this Northumbrian text Codex Amiatinus (A) is the best.

Also in the neighbourhood of Naples at Capua, in 541–546

---

[1] Codex V in Acts i.-ii. follows the family of Codex Amiatinus rather than the Alcuinian text ; Wordsworth and White, pp. viii, xv ; cf. Berger, *Histoire de la Vulgate pendant les premiers siècles du moyen âge.* pp. 197-204, 242. On this MS. see also P. Corssen, *Göttingische gelehrte Anzeigen,* 1894, pp. 855-875 ; H. Quentin, *Mémoire sur l'établissement du texte de la Vulgate,* Ière partie, Octateuque (Collectanea Biblica Latina, VI.), 1922, pp. 266 ff.

[2] S. Berger, *Histoire de la Vulgate,* 1893 ; H. J. White, art. ' Vulgate ' in Hastings's *Dictionary of the Bible,* vol. iv., 1902 ; John Chapman, *Notes on the Early History of the Vulgate Gospels,* 1908 ; *id.* ' Cassiodorus and the Echternach Gospels,' *Revue Bénédictine,* vol. XXVIII., 1911, pp. 283-295; H. Quentin, *op. cit.,* 1922.

[3] Chapman, *Revue Bénédictine,* vol. XXVIII., 1911, pp. 286-288.

was written Codex Fuldensis (F), which was brought to England, perhaps by the same hands as A, given to Boniface, and by him to the monastery of Fulda in Germany.[1] The resemblance of the text of A and F in the Gospels is thus easily accounted for by their common dependence on the text of Naples ; the divergence of the two texts in other parts of the New Testament has not been definitely explained.

From Italy also, and perhaps from Rome, copies of the Vulgate, which were independent of the Northumbrian text, came to England with the mission of Augustine of Canterbury (596) and with his successors in the following century. Roman Christianity, advancing from England into Ireland, gained dominance over the earlier Irish Christianity, introduced probably in the fourth century, which had maintained itself during the centuries of heathen aggression. But this Irish church of earlier foundation had used the Old Latin version of the Bible, and was strongly attached to it, so that one product of the new Roman mission in Ireland was a combination of the Old Latin with the new Italian Vulgate text brought by the new leaders. The Irish text which thus resulted was distinct from the Northumbrian ; in the great series of superb products of Irish scribes in Ireland and on the continent it had a long history and far-reaching influence, and in one of its forms it is found in the Book of Armagh (D). *England and Ireland.*

On the history of the Vulgate text in Italy recent researches have thrown but little light. A Roman type must have existed, and one stage of it may be represented by the English manuscripts of the Gospels traditionally connected with Canterbury and Gregory the Great ; of Acts nothing can be said. The difficulty of the problem and meagreness of the evidence are perhaps due to the long-continued use in Rome [2] and North Italy *Italy.*

---

[1] J. Chapman, *Notes on the Early History of the Vulgate Gospels*, pp. 157 f., 160 f., 188.

[2] Gregory the Great († 604) says that both the Old Latin and the Vulgate were alike in use at Rome in his time, *Expositio in librum B. Job* (*Moralium libri*), *Epistola ad Leandrum*, 5, Migne, vol. lxxv. p. 516 : *Novam vero trans-*

of the good revised form of the Old Latin (the so-called ' European '), as well as to the successive and terrible disasters which befell the city of Rome.[1]   In Northern Italy, in the province of Milan, a definite type of text established itself as early as the eleventh century, based on texts immediately or more remotely of Spanish origin but with combination of the text of Alcuin. It appears in MSS. of the eleventh and twelfth centuries, and may have had its origin at Rome.[2]   Another group in the Octateuch comprises chiefly MSS. written at Monte Cassino in the tenth, eleventh, and twelfth centuries, which have a text derived from Spain.[3]

Africa.

Of the history of the Vulgate text of the New Testament in North Africa very little is known.   The Vulgate Gospels and St. Jerome's Gallican Psalter (in a slightly modified form) were in use there in the time of St. Augustine.[4]

Spain.

In Spain the text of the Vulgate had its own development. As in Ireland, it came into rivalry, and then entered a combination, with the African Latin texts of earlier and of later type which had come across the Mediterranean from Africa, and with the revised ' European ' text which reached the peninsula from Italy and perhaps from Gaul.   At first in southern Spain, then, at the coming of the Mohammedan Moors in the eighth century (battle of Xeres de la Frontera, 711), driven to the north

---

lationem dissero, sed cum probationis causa exigit, nunc novam, nunc veterem, per testimonia assumo ; ut quia sedes apostolica, cui deo auctore praesideo, utraque utitur, mei quoque labor studii ex utraque fulciatur.

[1] Codex Iuveniani (I) and Codex Monacensis (M) may represent an Italian text akin to that of Codex Amiatinus.   It does not seem to be suggested that either of them is dependent on the text of Northumbria.   The participation of the text of Codex Fuldensis in the composition of Codex Sangallensis and Codex Ulmensis may be due to an Italian strain in these latter manuscripts.   But in the case of Alcuin's revision the close connexion with the Italian Codex F would seem more probably due to the relation of the two, each in its own way, to Northumbria.

[2] H. Quentin, *Mémoire sur l'établissement du texte de la Vulgate*, Ière partie, pp. 361-384.

[3] H. Quentin, *op. cit.* pp. 352-360.

[4] On Augustine's use of the Gallican Psalter see above, p. cxxv ; cf. also P. Monceaux, *Histoire littéraire de l'Afrique chrétienne*, vol. i., 1901, pp. 150 f.

and maintaining themselves in the kingdoms of Leon and Castile, the Visigothic Christians produced many copies of the Latin Bible, of which some, from the seventh century on, have come down to us. Some of these show that the Vulgate element in these mixed and interpolated texts was of excellent quality, faithful to the original which had earlier reached Spain. Codex Cavensis (C ; ninth century) seems to represent the edition of Peregrinus (probably northern Spain, 450–500), Codex Toletanus (T ; eighth century, perhaps completed in the tenth century) that of Isidore of Seville (560–636). From Leon and Castile (especially Toledo), and Catalonia, these texts made their way into Languedoc and up the Rhone valley to Vienne and Lyons, ancient seats of second-century Christianity which in the intervening centuries had, like Rome, exchanged Greek for Latin as the language of the Church. Spanish texts were carried even farther, to North Italy (Bobbio and the province of Milan) and so to Switzerland.

Corresponding on the other side to the entrance of the France Spanish text of the Vulgate into France was the bringing in of Irish and Northumbrian texts by innumerable missionaries who, from the seventh century on, worked in to a cordon of stations on the north and east and south-east, some of them following up the Rhine. From these centres Irish scribes and Irish texts penetrated into the very heart of the country. To name only points where the scribes or the texts are actually known, we find them at Tours and Angers, perhaps coming by way of Brittany, and in the neighbourhood of Lyons ; in Normandy, at Fécamp and St. Evroult ; on the east at Echternach, Würzburg, Metz ; in Switzerland, at St. Gall, the neighbouring Reichenau, and Pfäfers ; in Northern Italy, at Bobbio, founded by St. Columban.

In France itself no earlier type of Vulgate text had been current—indeed the Vulgate itself, especially for the New Testament, had but slowly and gradually superseded the Old Latin in the course of the fifth and sixth centuries ; but endless varieties of French text resulted from the conflict of Spanish

and British (Irish and English) influences. The most distinguished example of this mixture is the Codex Sangermanensis
(G ; ninth century ; probably from near Lyons), in which a text
largely, in the Old Testament almost wholly, of Spanish origin
has been mixed with an Irish strain and with a ' European '
Old Latin text (especially in the Gospel of Matthew). The
Acts of Codex G present a text of which neither its composition
nor the ground of its excellence is fully explained, but which,
on internal grounds, is accounted the best extant representative
of the Vulgate of St. Jerome.   Even in the Gospels those readings
of Codex G which are not otherwise accounted for often possess
almost unique value as survivals of the original Vulgate text.
In Acts G agrees more often with A than with F.[1]

Theodulf ;
Alcuin.

Toward a better text two attempts were made about the
year 800.   That of Theodulf († ca. 821), himself a Visigoth, was
mingled of various elements, Spanish and British, but in Acts
substantially reproduced the text of Languedoc.   Far more
powerful in its effects was the text of Alcuin, presented to Charle-
magne in 801.   For the formation of this, copies were brought
from York, where he had been brought up from infancy.   In
the ninth century this text was multiplied in a great number of
copies, but in these was immediately and progressively modified
and depraved.   Attempts to secure uniformity of use by a fresh
revision of the text of the Bible often produce at first a new
confusion, but they often mark an epoch.   It was so here ;
Alcuin's text, in the main of Northumbrian origin, was the
signal for the final disappearance of any considerable Old Latin
influence in the French text.

University
of Paris
text.

In succeeding centuries a succession of scholars endeavoured
to establish more correct texts than those current, until the
thirteenth century witnessed the rise into leadership of the
University of Paris, and with it, centring in Paris, an activity
never before equalled in the production of Bibles, many of them

---

[1] Wordsworth and White, *Actus Apostolorum*, pp. vi, xiii f., xvi ; *Quattuor
Evangelia*, ' Epilogus,' p. 717.

characterised by their handy form and beautiful execution. The text of the later Middle Ages was this Paris text, and from some of its forms was drawn the chief part of the modern printed text of which the Clementine edition of 1592 constitutes the standard.

From this sketch it will be apparent that the grouping of Wordsworth and White's classification is due to the real working of comprehensible historical forces, although not all of these can be traced in detail.

(c) VERSIONS MADE FROM THE LATIN

Interest and some importance attaches in Acts to certain daughter-versions of the Latin Vulgate, because they contain many 'Western' readings. These are the two Provençal versions (of Provence and of the Waldensian valleys), the German version made from the Provençal, the Waldensian Italian version, and the Bohemian version.[1] Their origin is but imperfectly known, but they are bound together by the heretical or sectarian character of the Christians (except the Italians) among whom they severally circulated and whose need of a translation of the Bible into the vernacular they served. In particular they illustrate the wide range of Waldensian activity in all southern Germany before the period of John Hus.[2]

1. *Provençal* [3]

In Languedoc a Latin text was current throughout the Middle Ages in which an important element containing many Latin text of Languedoc.

[1] The translation into the Catalan dialect of north-eastern Spain is in some of its forms partly based on a text containing ' Western ' readings (*e.g.* Acts xi. 1-2), as would be expected, but its complicated history is not well understood ; see S. Berger, ' Nouvelles recherches sur les Bibles provençales et catalanes,' *Romania*, vol. xix., 1890, pp. 505-561, especially pp. 514 f.

[2] S. Berger, *Histoire de la Vulgate*, p. 74 : " Deux pays seulement, à notre connaissance, montrent, en plein moyen âge, un attachement obstiné aux textes antérieurs à saint Jérôme : ce sont les pays albigeois et la Bohème, terres d'hérésie et d'indépendance religieuse autant que de particularisme fier et jaloux."

[3] S. Berger, ' Les Bibles provençales et vaudoises,' *Romania*, vol. xviii., 1889, pp. 353-422.

Old Latin readings had been drawn from Spain.[1] A noteworthy example of such a MS. is the Codex Colbertinus from Languedoc (Paris, Bibl. nat., lat. 254, twelfth century). In this the Gospels are mostly Old Latin (c), with some African readings. Another MS. showing considerable resemblance to Codex Colbertinus in the mixed Vulgate part of the latter, was the Codex Demidovianus (twelfth or thirteenth century), now lost, but published by Matthäi, 1782–1788, which came from the Jesuit house at Lyons. Still another pure copy of this text (but not from this region) is the Codex Wernigerodensis (Library of Graf Stolberg, Z.a.81), containing interlinear Bohemian glosses, and written in Bohemia very early in the fifteenth century.[2] Other manuscripts from Languedoc date from the tenth to the fourteenth century,[3] when this text disappears in fusion with the ordinary text of Paris. The revision of Theodulf (ninth century) probably rests in part on the Latin text of Languedoc.

Provençal versions.

From this Latin are derived two types of translation into Provençal.[4] (1) The first is a version found in two MSS. : one now at Lyons (Bibliothèque du Palais des Arts, No. 36), of the thirteenth century,[5] probably written in the modern Department of the Aude, not far from Carcassonne ; the other an inferior

---

[1] S. Berger, *Hist. de la Vulgate*, pp. 72-82 ; *Romania*, vol. xviii., 1889, pp. 354-356. It is necessary to remark that the Latin text so used was Catholic, not heretical or schismatic, although its wide spread in southern and eastern Europe was due to the fact that Languedoc was a centre from which pioneer movements spread. It is an error, although a natural one, to say that " only *among heretics* isolated from the rest of Western Christianity could an Old Latin text have been written at so late a period " (*sc.* the twelfth century).

[2] Berger, *Revue historique*, vol. xlv., 1891, p. 148 ; *Histoire de la Vulgate*, 1893, p. 80 ; W. Walther, *Die deutsche Bibelübersetzung des Mittelalters*, Braunschweig, 1889–1892, p. 190 ; readings given by Blass, *Studien und Kritiken*, vol. lxix., 1896, pp. 436-471, and in Wordsworth and White. The Latin Bible of the abbey of Werden (Rhenish Prussia) referred to by Berger, *Revue historique*, 1886, p. 467, may be another similar copy.

[3] " Un texte ancien dispersé dans des manuscrits récents," Berger, *Histoire de la Vulgate*, p. 82.

[4] Besides the references given in the following notes see E. Reuss, art. ' Bibelübersetzungen, romanische,' in *Protestantische Realencykl.*, vol. iii., pp. 139 f.

[5] According to Paul Meyer, between 1250 and 1280.

MS. at Paris (Bibl. nat., fr. 2425), of the first half of the fourteenth century, written somewhere in southern Provence. The Lyons codex [1] appears to have been copied directly from the interlinear Provençal gloss of a Latin MS., probably itself not much older than this extant copy. By the Catharist (Albigensian) liturgy which forms a part of it, appended to the New Testament, it is shown to have been written for the use of that sect. The Paris MS. gives a free and abridged version, by descent akin to the better translation of the Lyons MS. The margin is full of marks calling attention to the passages of Scripture especially valued by the Waldensians, and it seems to have been used by a Waldensian colporteur.[2] These Provençal texts both represent the same dialect. Of the origin of the translation nothing is positively known ; no taint of heresy has been discovered at any point in it.

(2) The second Provençal version is in the dialect of the Vaudois valleys of Piedmont, and is found in copies used by the Waldensians who dwelt there. The oldest and best MS. is that of Carpentras (Bibl. municipale, 22), in a southern French hand of the fourteenth century. Other important copies are at Dublin (A.4.13, written in 1522, but almost identical with the Carpentras MS.), Grenoble (about 1400), Cambridge (University Library, Dd 15.34 ; early fifteenth century), and Zürich (sixteenth century). Many other late copies are also known.

These two Provençal versions [3] are probably, though not certainly, derived from a common original translation into

---

[1] Facsimile in L. Clédat, *Le Nouveau Testament, traduit au XIIIe siècle en langue provençale suivi d'un rituel cathare*, Paris, 1887. See E. Reuss, ' Les versions vaudoises existantes et la traduction des Albigeois ou Cathares,' *Revue de Théologie* (Strasbourg), vol. v., 1852, pp. 321-349 ; ' Versions cathares et vaudoises,' *ibid.* vol. vi., 1853, pp. 65-96 ; S. Berger, *Romania*, vol. xviii., 1889, pp. 357-364 ; Paul Meyer, ' Recherches linguistiques sur l'origine des versions provençales du N.T.,' *Romania*, vol. xviii., 1889, pp. 423-429. Readings in Acts are collected by Blass, *Studien und Kritiken*, 1896, pp. 436-471.

[2] Berger, *Revue historique*, vol. xxx., 1886, p. 168.

[3] See the clear brief statement of the process of events in Berger, ' Nouvelles recherches sur les Bibles provençales et catalanes,' *Romania*, vol. xix., 1890, pp. 559-561.

Provençal. At any rate, although their readings are not everywhere identical, both are derived from the Latin text of Languedoc of the thirteenth century, and hence in Acts contain many ' Western ' readings of Old Latin origin. Indeed, " the Provençal versions form the best witness to the [mixed Vulgate] text of Languedoc," which " goes back directly to the ancient text of the Visigoths." [1] It is not to be supposed that the Waldensians, Catharists, and Bohemians deliberately adopted a text of Acts because they knew it to be different from that used by the orthodox Catholics. On the contrary, the translators of these texts merely used the text of Languedoc current in their own day and locality, which happened (through contiguity to Spain) to be widely mixed with Old Latin readings ; [2] the translators themselves may or may not have been sectaries. Nevertheless, it is for the most part because these translations were used by sectaries that they have been preserved for us.

2. *German* [3]

The German translation of the New Testament which was printed, with some variations, in many editions from 1466 to 1518, was probably translated in the fourteenth century in southern Bohemia from a Provençal text [4] brought to Bohemia

---

[1] Berger, *Histoire de la Vulgate*, p. 73.

[2] This fact is in itself an interesting illustration of the peculiar persistence in Africa and Spain of the ' Western ' African text of Acts side by side with later renderings of other books (thus in the *Liber promissionum et praedictorum dei*, about 450 ; codex h of the sixth century).

[3] S. Berger, *Revue historique*, vol. xxx., 1886, pp. 164-169 ; vol. xxxii., 1886, pp. 184-190 ; vol. xlv., 1891, pp. 147-149 ; *Romania*, vol. xviii., 1889, pp. 407 f. ; W. Walther, *Die deutsche Bibelübersetzung des Mittelalters* ; O. F. Fritzsche and E. Nestle, art. ' Bibelübersetzungen, deutsche,' in *Protestantische Realencyklopädie*, vol. iii., 1897, pp. 64-69 ; Karl Müller, *Studien und Kritiken*, vol. lx., 1887, pp. 571-594 ; and, on Müller's article, Berger's comments in *Bulletin de la Société d'Histoire vaudoise*, No. 3, Torre Pellice, December 1887, pp. 37-41.

[4] Th. Zahn, *Die Urausgabe der Apostelgeschichte des Lucas*, 1916, p. 16 ; Berger, *Revue historique*, 1891, pp. 448 f. The translator may have had the aid of a Vulgate text and of another German translation, but the instances adduced by Berger and Zahn seem to leave no doubt as to the fundamental

perhaps by Waldensians or Cathari. In any case it represents a Latin text of the type current in Languedoc in the thirteenth and fourteenth centuries, containing many ' Western ' readings in Acts. It is found in several MSS., of which two, the Codex Teplensis and the Freiberg MS., contain Acts.

The Codex Teplensis [1] (Library of the Praemonstratensian monastery, Tepl, in Bohemia, Ψ. VI. 139) is a little copy, with pages hardly more than two inches by three. It was evidently meant to be carried in the pocket of a Waldensian missionary, for whose use a great number of marks in the margin direct attention to useful passages, while other appropriate matter is added at the end, including a German translation of a Waldensian catechism. It was written, probably, toward the end of the fourteenth century.

The Freiberg manuscript [2] (Library of the gymnasium, Freiberg in Saxony, I. Cl. MS. 18) closely resembles the Codex Teplensis in size and hand, as well as in text, and is to be assigned to a date not far removed from that MS. It is not, however, derived from the same immediate exemplar, and its history seems to have been different, for soon after it was written it was in the possession of a Catholic pastor, who gave it in 1414 to a monastery, probably one of those from whose books the Freiberg Library was brought together.[3]

With these two MSS. is to be associated the text of the first German Bible (Strassburg, Joh. Mentel, 1466), which is drawn from a different, but similar, German MS.

The peculiar readings of all these texts in Acts, often

(margin notes: Codex Teplensis. / Freiberg MS.)

---

relation to the Provençal. That Latin MSS. containing this text were actually brought to Bohemia from Provence may be inferred from the Codex Wernigerodensis (see p. cxxxvi). Codex Gigas and the Bohemian version make it clear that the Latin copies which the Bohemians had were of various types.

[1] [Klimesch], *Der Codex Teplensis, enthaltend ' die Schrift des newen Gezeuges,'* Munich and Augsburg, 1884 ; readings are given by Wordsworth and White.

[2] M. Rachel, *Die Freiberger Bibelhandschrift* (programme), Freiberg, 1886 ; facsimile and comparison with Codex Teplensis in W. Walther, *Die deutsche Bibelübersetzung des Mittelalters,* 1889–1892, cols. 154 ff.

[3] K. Müller, *Studien und Kritiken,* vol. LX., 1887, p. 517.

'Western,' go back (partly at least through a Provençal version) to the mixed Vulgate text of Languedoc of the thirteenth century, which is adequately known from Latin MSS. The text of the German New Testament is closely related to that of the Lyons Provençal MS., but also shows relations to the Paris MS. and to the Vaudois MSS., especially that of Grenoble. These German texts are historically interesting, and throw light on the presence in Bohemia [1] of Old Latin texts and readings (for instance, Codex Gigas, Codex Wernigerodensis); but, since their Latin sources are adequately known, their direct contribution to textual criticism is but small.

3. Bohemian [2]

The New Testament was translated into Bohemian, the several books by different hands, in the course of the fourteenth century. As might be expected from the circumstances mentioned in the preceding paragraphs, the text of Acts in at least some forms of the version shows ' Western ' readings,[3] but the version has not been sufficiently studied to permit confident statements as to the channel through which these readings came to Bohemia, or even as to the particular form of Old Latin which they represent.

Readings. Some noteworthy readings from the Old Bohemian were communicated to Griesbach by Joseph Dobrowsky, the founder of Slavic philology (1753–1829),[4] and from Griesbach's New Testament (2nd ed., 1796, 1806) Tischendorf introduced them into his

[1] Yet the earlier Bohemian version (fourteenth century) does not seem to be founded on the text of Languedoc (see pp. cxxxv-vi).
[2] Leskien, art. ' Bibelübersetzungen, slavische,' in *Protestantische Real-encyklopädie*, vol. III., 1897, pp. 161 f. ; Gregory, *Prolegomena*, 1894, pp. 1127 f.
[3] Bohemia, "la patrie de la diversité religieuse et des textes bibliques les plus incohérents," S. Berger, *Revue historique,* vol. XLV., 1891, p. 148.
[4] J. Dobrowsky, ' Über den ersten Text der böhmischen Bibelübersetzung, nach den ältesten Handschriften derselben, besonders nach der Dresdener,' *Neuere Abhandlungen der königlichen böhmischen Gesellschaft der Wissenschaften*, diplomatisch-historisch-litterarischer Theil, vol. III., 1798, p. 260 : Griesbach, *Novum Testamentum Graece*, 2nd ed.. vol. I., 1796, pp. xci, xcvii.

apparatus. The readings in Acts xxiv. 24, xxv. 24, xxviii. 31 are striking 'Western' readings, all having parallels in the margin of the Harclean Syriac. The first is otherwise not attested (unless perhaps by Cassiodorus), the second only by the Book of Armagh (Codex D), the third (imperfectly, however) by Spanish MSS. For other Bohemian readings see Acts xi. 17 (cf. D hcl ✳ p Aug vg.*cod.ardm.* etc.) ; xxii. 28 (only in vg.*cod.ardm.*, *paris.* 17250² Bede). The readings of the Bohemian do not seem to be drawn from the usual text of Languedoc, but from some other 'Western' source. Since they come from chapters of Acts where Codex Bezae is lacking, they are of importance in themselves, and they create the expectation that a complete knowledge of the Old Bohemian Acts might yield results of much importance for the ' Western ' text of Acts.

Such a knowledge would not be difficult to secure, and it is Codices. not to the credit of New Testament scholarship that nearly a century and a half has passed without any use being made of sources easily accessible in Germany and Bohemia. The most important MSS. are the following : [1]

1. Dresden, Staatliche (formerly ' Königliche ') Bibliothek. *Ca.* 1410. From this copy Dobrowsky probably drew the readings which appear in Griesbach and Tischendorf. The MS. has been injured by fire, but not destroyed.

2. Leitmeritz, Czecho-Slovakia (Bohemia), Episcopal library ; and in collection of Prince Schwarzenberg, Wittingau, Třeboň, Czecho-Slovakia. 1411–1416.

3. Prague, University library. 1416. Written in Glagolitic script by the Benedictines of the Emmaus Monastery in Prague. Only preserved in part.

---

[1] For information with regard to these MSS. I am indebted to Professor Paul Diels of Breslau ; see also Dobrowsky in the article (1798) referred to above, pp. 242 f. J. Schindler, professor at Leitmeritz, examined certain Bohemian MSS. of Acts from the first half of the fifteenth century with a view to ' Western ' readings, but reported that he found but little. One interesting ' Western ' reading from a MS. of the year 1429 is cited by him, and will be found below in the Textual Note to Acts xvi. 40 ; see *Österreichisches Litteraturblatt*, vol. VI., 1897, cols. 163 f.

4. Olmütz, Czecho-Slovakia (Moravia), Studienbibliothek. 1417.

These MSS. are all believed to give the oldest recension of the Bohemian text. Still older is :

5. Nikolsburg, Czecho-Slovakia (Moravia), Chapter library of the Collegiate Church of St. Wenzel. 1406. But this is said to give a revised form of the version.[1] Whether the underlying Latin text may be the same is not known.

In the fifteenth century further revisions were made, of which many MSS. are known.

4. *Italian* [2]

A translation of the New Testament into Italian was made, probably in the thirteenth century, from a Latin text like that of Languedoc, and under the influence of the Provençal New Testament. It includes, like those texts, some ' Western ' readings in Acts. That it was made by a Waldensian is not improbable, but it circulated among Catholics and was revised with glosses by Domenica Cavalca, a Dominican of Pisa († 1342), as well as by others. From the translation of Cavalca the Waldenses took over the Book of Acts and rendered it into their own dialect, and in this guise it is still found for the second half of Acts (from the middle of chapter xvi.) in the Grenoble and Cambridge Vaudois MSS. mentioned above. Truly a strange piece of history, and instructive in more than one aspect !

§ 2. EGYPTIAN

The complicated textual history of the Sahidic and Bohairic versions has never been investigated. The material at hand, however, makes it possible to know with tolerable certainty what forms these translations respectively had at relatively very

---

[1] Leskien, *l.c.* p. 162.

[2] S. Berger, ' La Bible italienne au moyen âge,' *Romania*, vol. XXIII., 1894, pp. 358-431, cf. especially pp. 387, 390-395, 418.

early dates, forms not much altered from that of the original rendering.

(a) SAHIDIC [1]

The Sahidic version of Acts is found in a large number of MSS. and fragments, from which substantially the whole book is known. A full list will be found below, pp. 322 ff. The most important MSS. are the following : Codices.

B. London, British Museum, 7954. A.D. 350. Papyrus.

V. Vienna. A.D. 400. Parchment.

W. Oxford, Bodleian Library, MS. huntington. 394. Twelfth-thirteenth century. Paper.

The other MSS. are to be dated in the seventh (?)-thirteenth centuries.

The analysis of the collation of the Sahidic with the Greek of Codex B given below (pp. 325 ff.) shows that the Greek text on which it rested consisted largely of the readings of the Old Uncials, but also contained, besides some other elements, a distinct ' Western ' strand.[2] Since the ' Western ' readings with but few exceptions are small unimportant variants, it seems likely that the Greek from which the Sahidic of Acts was translated was a copy of a MS. in which a ' Western ' text had been almost completely corrected by a standard of the B-type. It is hardly conceivable that these trifling ' Western ' variants should have been specially selected for introduction into a non-western text and the great mass of interesting and important variants passed by. And indeed this current from ' Western ' to B text must Underlying Greek text.

---

[1] [G. Horner], *The Coptic Version of the New Testament in the Southern Dialect, otherwise called Sahidic and Thebaic*, vol. vi., Oxford, 1922; with list of MSS., pp. 666-672.

[2] Cf. Burkitt, *Encyclopaedia Biblica*, col. 5010. A peculiarly instructive case is to be found in Acts x. 33, where the Sahidic (Codex V)reads ' to us ' for προς σε. This is evidently a fragmentary survival from παρακαλων ελθειν προς ημας, which the ' Western ' text (Codex Bezae perp hcl ⁒) added to the sentence. In the process of correcting the Greek MS., or of using it after the correction, the wrong prepositional phrase was taken over ; and so this passed into the Sahidic without the accompanying verbs, which were necessary in order to justify its presence.

have characterized the adaptation and production of Greek MSS. in Egypt and elsewhere from the third century on. The Sahidic gives perhaps the most striking exhibition of it to be found in the New Testament.

Date.   Nothing seems to prevent the assumption that the Sahidic version of Acts was made in the third century,[1] but a date earlier than 300 is not indicated by any decisive positive evidence. The fact that the "White Monastery" (*dêr el-abjad*) was founded about 350 is perhaps not without significance in this connexion.

Character-istics.   The Sahidic translator frequently added personal pronouns not found in Greek, often made small omissions, and had a curious habit of reversing the order of two words in a composite phrase (for instance, Acts i. 7, 'seasons and times'; xxviii. 2, 'cold and rain,' for 'rain and cold'). As for the order of words in general, " Coptic grammar requires a word-position of its own, and the translation is rarely of any use in such a case." In the use of the collation printed below, it is to be borne in mind that it is made with Codex Vaticanus, but that no distinction is made between the renderings which positively imply the text of that codex and a certain number of neutral readings which might have proceeded equally well from that Greek text or from one of the known Greek variants. Thus, the Sahidic always writes the name ' Jesus ' with the definite article, so that in Acts i. 1 no inference can be drawn as to whether the Greek text before the translator read $\iota\eta\sigma\sigma\nu\varsigma$ (BD) or $o\ \iota\eta\sigma\sigma\nu\varsigma$ (אA 81). Similarly, in Acts the Sahidic " never uses any form but $\iota\epsilon\rho\sigma\nu\sigma\alpha\lambda\eta\mu$ (other-wise in the Gospels)." Again, " Coptic has no word for $\tau\epsilon$ when used with following $\kappa\alpha\iota$, and does not reproduce $\tau\epsilon$ itself except very rarely ; it is merely omitted." [2]   Other remarks and warn-

---

[1] So J. Leipoldt, according to Zahn, *Die Offenbarung des Johannes*, 1924, pp. 63 f. note 14, on the ground of the old-fashioned linguistic forms employed ; but in *Church Quarterly Review*, 1923, p. 352, Leipoldt refers the Sahidic trans-lation of Acts to " the time about A.D. 300."

[2] The statements about Coptic idiom here made are from Sir Herbert Thompson.

ings with regard to the use of the Sahidic for textual criticism
will be found in the paragraphs introductory to the Tables.

(b) Bohairic [1]

The Bohairic version of Acts is known from eleven MSS. *Codices.*
(besides some others), of which six are from the twelfth, thirteenth,
and fourteenth centuries, and five from the seventeenth and
eighteenth centuries (see below, pp. 357 f.).

The MSS. of chief importance for the text are :

A. London, British Museum, or. 424, A.D. 1307, said to be
copied from a text written *ca.* 1250. From this codex Horner's
text is printed and translated.

B. Milan, Bibl. Ambrosiana. Fourteenth century.

Γ. Deir el Muharrak, Egypt. Twelfth century.

" A is an eccentric MS., with many peculiar and often corrupt
readings " ; " B is a very close follower of the Greek Codex
Vaticanus." The text of Γ belongs to a different family, which
" seems to be somewhat influenced by the Sahidic version." [2]

A digest of the collation is given below (pp. 360 ff.). It *Character*
will show the extraordinary fidelity of this version to the text *and date.*
of the Old Greek Uncials, which extends in some cases to Codex
Vaticanus in particular. The date of the version is variously
estimated by different scholars. It was made later than the
Sahidic, and a date as late as 700 is possible, although a date
earlier in the seventh century, not too long after the Mohammedan
conquest, is not unlikely.[3] The earliest Bohairic MSS. (fragment-

---

[1] [G. Horner], *The Coptic Version of the New Testament in the Northern Dialect
otherwise called Memphitic and Bohairic*, vol. iv., Oxford, 1905 ; for the list of
MSS. see vol. iii. pp. x-lxviii.

[2] H. Thompson.

[3] " Erst als sich Ägypten von dem grossen Reichsverbande loszulösen
begann, waren die Bedingungen gegeben, unter denen eine volkstümliche
Litteratur auch im Delta entstehen konnte," Johannes Leipoldt, ' Geschichte
der koptischen Litteratur,' in Brockelmann, Finck, Leipoldt, and Littmann,
Geschichte der christlichen Litteraturen des Orients (Die Litteraturen des Ostens
in Einzeldarstellungen, vol. VII. 2), 2nd ed., 1909, p. 179.

ary) of any part of the New Testament date from the ninth
century. Certain counsels of prudence, in view of the nature of
Bohairic idiom, with regard to the use of the Bohairic for textual
criticism, are given in connexion with the Tables.

§ 3. ETHIOPIC

Codices. Of manuscripts containing the Ethiopic version of Acts
thirteen are mentioned in Gregory's list. No date is assigned
to four of these ; of the others, one (Paris, Bibl. nat., aeth. 26
[Zotenberg 42]) is of the fifteenth, one of the sixteenth, four of
the seventeenth, and three of the eighteenth century.

Editions. The Ethiopic New Testament was published at Rome, 1548–
1549 (reprinted in Walton's Polyglot, vol. v., London, 1657),
and by the British and Foreign Bible Society, London, 1830
(edited by Thomas Pell Platt). The manuscript of Acts used
for the Roman edition was defective, and the editors were com-
pelled to translate from Latin into Ethiopic considerable parts
of the book. The edition of Platt was made, doubtless from
the manuscripts in London, for missionary rather than critical
purposes.

History. The Ethiopic version was made from the Greek (both in the
Old and New Testaments) in the period from the fourth to the
seventh century. In more recent times (perhaps in the fourteenth
century) it was revised by the aid of the Arabic (the ' Alexandrian
Vulgate '), through which a Syriac influence recognizable in the
later text may have been introduced.[1] Most MSS. are of very
late date, and give a revised form of the text, in various types
of combination with the earlier form.

Character. An analysis of the Ethiopic version of Matt. i.-x., as found in
the oldest and best MS. (Paris, Bibl. nat., aeth. 22 [Zotenberg
32], thirteenth century), shows that it contains a combination of
' Western ' and Antiochian readings.[2] The Old Testament text

---

[1] J. Schäfers, *Die äthiopische Übersetzung des Propheten Jeremias* (Breslau
dissertation), 1912, p. 14.

[2] L. Hackspill, *Zeitschrift für Assyriologie*, xi., 1897, pp. 117-196, 367-388.

in Genesis agrees largely with the Sahidic and Bohairic ; [1] in Joshua it has a text like Codex Vaticanus for its basis (as does the Coptic) ; [2] in Judges it follows the older Greek version, not that found in Codex Vaticanus ; [3] in Ruth it is in the main pre-hexaplaric, and resembles Codex B, but has been subjected to hexaplaric and other later influences.[4] In the four Books of Kingdoms, the Ethiopic text is specially valuable, for it forms a compact group with B and the non-hexaplaric quotations of Origen ; in cases where B and Origen differ, the Ethiopic stands almost always on the side of Origen, and it gives in some respects a better text than does B.[5] In 1 Esdras the Ethiopic generally agrees with B, the Syro-hexaplaric version, and Codex 55, as against A and the minuscule text.[6] In the Psalter the Ethiopic stands closer to B than any other witness except the Bohairic and Codex ℵ ; in its original form it may have been even nearer.[7] In Jeremiah the oldest form of the Ethiopic belongs to the type of Codex ℵ.[8] In Ezekiel it largely agrees with the oldest and best MSS. of the Septuagint.[9]

The excellence and usefulness of at least many parts of the Ethiopic text of the Old Testament and the character of its New Testament readings in Matthew i.-x. justify the expectation that an investigation of this version in Acts and in other parts of the New Testament would produce interesting and valuable results.

[1] A. T. Olmstead, 'The Greek Genesis,' *American Journal of Semitic Languages*, vol. xxxiv., 1918, p. 153 ; O. Procksch, *Die Genesis* (Sellin's Kommentar zum A.T.), 1913, p. 14. Codex Vaticanus is lacking for nearly the whole of Genesis ; the Ethiopic closely agrees with the group f (53), i (56), r (129).

[2] Professor Max L. Margolis.

[3] G. F. Moore, *Commentary on Judges*, 1895, p. xlv.

[4] Rahlfs, *Studie über den griechischen Text des Buches Ruth*, 1922, pp. 134 f.

[5] Rahlfs, *Studien zu den Königsbüchern*, 1904, pp. 79, 84 f.

[6] Torrey, *Ezra Studies*, 1910, pp. 100 f.

[7] Rahlfs, *Der Text des Septuaginta-Psalters*, 1907, pp. 37, 56.

[8] Joseph Schäfers, *op. cit.* p. viii.

[9] Cornill, *Das Buch des Propheten Ezechiel*, p. 42.

§ 4. SYRIAC [1]

(a) OLD SYRIAC

The existence of an early translation of Acts into Syriac is known from the Armenian translations of two works of Ephrem Syrus (Nisibis and Edessa ; † 373), namely, his Commentary on the Acts, of which a translation is printed below, pp. 380 ff., and his Commentary on the Epistles of Paul.[2] These have to be employed with caution, since the Armenian translator may have made Ephrem's quotations conform to the Armenian Vulgate ; nevertheless it is clear that the Syriac text used by Ephrem was distinctly, and doubtless thoroughly, ' Western.' The few slight allusions to Acts found in the Homilies of Aphraates do not permit any inference as to the character of the Syriac text which he used. There seems nothing to show that the Syriac translation may not have been made before the end of the second century. The most natural source from which the Syrians could draw the Greek manuscripts they used would perhaps be Antioch, but it might have been Palestine, or possibly Rome.[3]

(b) PESHITTO

Under Rabbula, bishop of Edessa (411–435), a great reorganizing churchman, the Syrian New Testament was made more complete, and the translation thoroughly revised, both

[1] For detailed information of every sort relating to Syriac literary history reference can now be made to an invaluable thesaurus, A. Baumstark, *Geschichte der syrischen Literatur, mit Ausschluss der christlichpalästinensischen Texte,* Bonn, 1922.

[2] *Ephraem Syri Commentarii in epistolas Pauli ex Armenio in Latinum sermonem a Mekitharistis translati,* Venice, 1893.

[3] On the evidence of the use of Acts in the Syrian church, see Zahn, *Die Urausgabe der Apostelgeschichte des Lucas* (Forschungen zur Geschichte des neutest. Kanons, IX), 1916, pp. 203-220. Zahn's view (p. 205) is that Tatian brought from Rome not only the Gospels, but also the Acts and the Epistles of Paul. The *Doctrina Addaei* (ed. Phillips, p. 44) refers to " the Acts of the Twelve Apostles, which John, the son of Zebedee, sent us from Ephesus " ; this would seem to indicate that in circles which still knew the Diatessaron (p. 34) Acts was believed to have been in the possession of the Syrian church from the earliest times.

with reference to the Syriac form and by the aid of Greek MSS.,
the latter probably being drawn from Antioch. The resulting
Peshitto text of the Acts is analysed below (pp. 292 ff.), and
shows considerable survivals of a more primitive ' Western ' Old
Syriac, in the midst of a text substantially like that of the Old
Uncials. The rendering is often very free, somewhat after the
manner of the ' Western ' text (cf. for instance Acts xii. 6 in the
Peshitto) ; the translator has a habit of expressing one Greek
word by two Syriac ones. He but rarely omits anything that
was in his Greek text. The readings which depart from the Old
Uncial text and follow the Antiochian are usually also found in
' Western ' witnesses, and there seems no trace of the peculiar
and distinctive selection of readings which is the chief recognizable
characteristic of the Antiochian text.

The text of the Peshitto itself has been preserved with extraordinary fidelity from the earliest times ; moreover, at least one
MS. of Acts is extant, and used for Gwilliam's text (1920), which
may have been written in the very century in which the version
was made.

(c) PHILOXENIAN

As the influence of a great Syrian ecclesiastic of the first half Origin.
of the fifth century, Rabbula of Edessa, had produced the
Peshitto in Edessa, so, a little less than a century later, the next
important revision of the Syriac New Testament was due to the
instance of a great and militant leader of the Eastern monophysite Christians, Philoxenus (Mar Xenaia, † 523), bishop of
Hierapolis (Mabog, Bambyce), who, with his contemporary,
Severus of Antioch, founded Jacobite Monophysitism. The
work of translation was performed in 508, in the period when
the prestige of Philoxenus was at its height, by Polycarp, chorepiscopus in the diocese of Mabog ; it included, apparently for
the first time in Syriac, the four minor Catholic epistles (2 Peter,
2 and 3 John, Jude) and the Book of Revelation.[1] These the

---

[1] John Gwynn, art. ' Polycarpus Chorepiscopus,' and Edmund Venables,
art. ' Philoxenus,' in *Dictionary of Christian Biography* ; Gwynn, *Remnants of*

church of Edessa in the days of Rabbula, following its Greek authorities, had not accepted, and they had accordingly not formed a part of the Peshitto. This enlargement of the canon was in itself an indication of monophysite accessibility to Greek influence and of alienation from the old-fashioned Syrian ways of the Nestorians. It is instructive to observe that Philoxenus himself did not know Greek,[1] while Severus of Antioch, who was in manifold communication with the Alexandrian monophysites, was a Greek. What parts of the Old Testament were comprised in the revision is uncertain, although certain fragments of Isaiah found in a British Museum MS. (Add. 17,106) have been somewhat doubtfully supposed to be from this version, partly on the ground of a scholion in the Milan Syro-hexaplar codex. Even of the New Testament the only books which seem to have come down to us in the Philoxenian version are the five which it added to the Syriac Bible.[2]

The four minor Catholic epistles (2 Peter, 2 and 3 John, Jude) in Syriac were first published by E. Pococke in 1630, from a MS. now in the Bodleian Library (Or. 119, Catal. 35), were inserted in the Paris Polyglot of 1645, and have since appeared in all editions of the Peshitto. They were recognized by John Gwynn

---

the *Later Syriac Versions of the Bible*, London, 1909 ; Gwynn, *The Apocalypse of St. John, in a Syriac Version hitherto Unknown*, Dublin, 1897. The arguments of Gwynn must be accepted in spite of the contentions of J. Lebon, *Revue d'histoire ecclésiastique*, vol. XII., Louvain, 1911, pp. 412-436. Lebon's view rests on the articles by H. Gressmann, *Zeitschrift für die neutestamentliche Wissenschaft*, vol. v., 1904, pp. 248-252 ; vol. VI., 1905, pp. 135-152, who tried to draw from the Syriac (Karkaphensian) masora evidence that the express ascription of the version in the MSS. to Thomas of Harkel is a mistake. Adequate replies to this view are given in the criticism of Lebon (by Lagrange ?) in *Revue Biblique*, vol. IX., 1912, pp. 141-143, and the article of L. J. Delaporte, ' L'Évangélaire héracléen et la tradition karkaphienne,' *ibid.* pp. 390-402.

[1] J. Lebon, *Revue d'histoire ecclésiastique*, vol. xii., 1911, p. 417 note 1 (with references).

[2] N. Wiseman, *Horae Syriacae*, Rome, 1828, pp. 178 f. note, cites five brief passages from Romans, Corinthians, and Ephesians, which are ascribed to the Philoxenian in a MS. of the Karkaphensian material. The renderings closely resemble those of the Harclean, but are not identical with the text of our Harclean MSS.

as drawn from the Philoxenian.[1] The Apocalypse in the Philoxenian was discovered by Gwynn in the Crawford MS. now in the John Rylands Library, Manchester.[2]

The earliest extant notice of the Philoxenian version of the New Testament is that of Moses of Aghel [3] in a letter prefixed to his translation of the *Glaphyra* of Cyril of Alexandria, a work containing interpretations of passages in the Pentateuch :

Moses of Aghel.

And I ask the reader to attend to the words of this book, for they are deep. And when he finds quotations from the Holy Bible which are cited in this translation, let him not be troubled if they do not agree with the copies of the Syrians, for the versions and traditions [4] of the Bible vary greatly. And if he wishes to find the truth, let him take the translation of the New Testament which [and of David] [5] Polycarp the chorepiscopus made into Syriac (rest his soul !) for the worthy and for good works ever memorable ' Faithful ' man and teacher, Xenaias of Mabog. He will be astonished at the differences which exist in the translation of the Syriac from the Greek language. But as for us, inasmuch as we are now translating from the Greek language into Syriac (with the aid of Christ), we here indicate the word as it is in the Greek, by the hands of the brethren, our young pupils ; and when they make mistakes in the syllables or the points, and are observed, well-instructed readers will correct as the text ought to read.

[1] *Dictionary of Christian Biography*, vol. iv., 1887, pp. 432 f. ; *Hermathena*, vol. vii., 1890, pp. 281-314.

[2] Gwynn, *The Academy*, June 18, 1892, p. 592 ; *Transactions of the Royal Irish Academy*, vol. xxx., 1893 ; *Apocalypse of St. John*, 1897.

[3] Assemani, *Bibliotheca orientalis*, ii. p. 83. The Syriac text is printed by I. Guidi, in the *Rendiconti* of the Accademia dei Lincei, ser. 4, vol. ii., Rome, 1886, p. 404. The sole MS. known (divided between the Vatican and the British Museum) is of the sixth or seventh century. Evidence for dates in the life of Moses of Aghel is meagre. His prefatory letter above mentioned was written after the death of Philoxenus in 523. One of his other works was probably already current in 570, since it is included in a collection made at about that date.

[4] Translated by Merx : ' Ausgaben und Recensionen.'

[5] The words ' and of David ' (*we-dauid*), here put in brackets, are to be regarded either as an interpolation or as a corruption of some other word. Not only do they stand in a wholly unnatural position, but it is doubtful whether in any case the Psalms could be called ' David ' in such a context as this. They constitute, it may be noted, the only known ground for supposing that the Philoxenian version included the Psalms except for an allusion in a Syriac Psalter belonging to the Harvard Semitic Museum (No. 133).

The ' differences' here referred to seem plainly to be those readily observable between the Philoxenian version, conformed to a different Greek text, and the Peshitto.   But the statement of Moses throws no direct light on the reason why Philoxenus instituted a new translation.[1] We may assume that, incidentally to his general labours in consolidating the monophysite Syrians, he wished to provide them with a translation according both in text and in contents with approved Greek copies. But the meagre evidence does not point to an agreement in the Greek text used with that employed by Cyril of Alexandria.

Harclean subscriptions.The other chief evidence relating to the Philoxenian version is found in the subscriptions to the Gospels, Acts and Catholic epistles, and Pauline epistles, of the later revision by Thomas of Harkel (616).   Reference is there made to the version (on which that of Thomas is founded) made from the Greek at Mabog in the year 508 in the days of Philoxenus, bishop of that city.   In the subscription to the Pauline epistles it seems to be stated that the Philoxenian version of that portion rested on a Caesarean MS. written by Pamphilus with his own hand.[2]   The subscription to the Gospels directly states, and that to the Pauline Epistles implies, that the Philoxenian version was made from the Greek.

Later Syriac writers, Bar Salibi († ca. 1171), Bar Hebraeus

---

[1] The view of Gwynn, *Apocalypse of St. John*, p. lxxi note (cf. *Dict. of Christian Biography*, iv. p. 432), that Philoxenus was led to have the new version made because he observed " discrepancies between the Peshitto text and that of the citations of Cyril of Alexandria from LXX and N.T.," rests on a different understanding of the participle translated above ' he will be surprised.'   Gwynn took this as a causal participle referring to Polycarp, but the interpretation followed above is better.   The latter interpretation is also followed by A. Merx, *Zeitschrift für Assyriologie*, vol. XII., 1898, p. 350 note.

[2] In view, however, of the details of the form of statement employed in the colophon, it is probable that here, as in Codex H[paul], the reference to the codex written by Pamphilus was drawn from the well-known statement to the same effect in the ' Euthalian ' material, and cannot be taken as evidence for the actual Greek text used by Polycarp ; cf. Corssen, *Göttingische gelehrte Anzeigen*, 1899, pp. 670 ff.   That the Philoxenian of the Pauline epistles was supplied with ' Euthalian ' apparatus is shown by E. von Dobschütz, ' Euthaliusstudien,' *Zeitschrift für Kirchengeschichte*, vol. XIX., 1899, pp. 115-154.   See also F. C. Conybeare, ' On the Codex Pamphili and Date of Euthalius,' *Journal of Philology*, London and Cambridge, vol. XXIII., 1895, pp. 241-259.

(† 1286), and an anonymous life of Thomas of Harkel of uncertain date, make similar statements about the Philoxenian version, but seem to have had no further knowledge than could be drawn from the Harclean subscriptions.

Of the greater part of the Philoxenian New Testament, that, namely, in which it was possible for the reviser to use the Peshitto, nothing has been surely recognized in existing Syriac texts. It would be possible, however, to draw some safe inferences from the character of the four smaller Catholic epistles and the Apocalypse, of which a fresh translation had to be made. The style of these books is a free and fluent Syriac idiom, not slavishly conformed to the Greek, and clearly showing the influence of the style and diction of the Peshitto.[1] With regard to text, in the four epistles the Philoxenian does not seem to belong with B or with KLP (Antiochian).[2] But an adequate study of the Philoxenian text of these epistles remains to be made. In the Apocalypse the Philoxenian text contains a considerable Antiochian element in agreement with Q (046 ; formerly B) and the minuscules, but apart from that it gives an ancient text of mixed character, in part agreeing with the best uncials, not infrequently in accord with peculiar readings of ℵ, and showing a striking measure of agreement with the distinctive readings of the African Latin of Primasius.

Since the version was made at Mabog, a place of Syrian speech, and for practical ecclesiastical use, not for learned purposes, it is more likely that an existing Greek text was obtained and translated than that a new one was constructed out of varied

Style and text.

---

[1] Gwynn, *Apocalypse*, p. cv: "We justly claim [for the Philoxenian], as regards its general tone and manner, that it approaches the excellence of the Peshitto ; and in point of force, directness, and dignity, that it gives worthy expression to the sublime imagery of the Apocalyptist. It has strength and freedom such as few translations attain." Cf. also the interesting general descriptions in Gwynn, *Remnants*, Part I., pp. xxxii f. ; *Apocalypse*, pp. xvii-xxxviii. Philoxenus himself is said to be " one of the best and most elegant writers in the Syrian tongue " (Gwynn, *Dict. of Christian Biography*, iv. p. 393, citing Assemani).

[2] Gwynn, *Remnants of the Later Syriac Versions*, Part I., p. lxx. Merx's idea, *Zeitschrift für Assyriologie*, vol. XII., 1898, p. 358, that the true Philoxenian text gives the text of Lucian, is not well founded.

materials assembled for the purpose. Consequently it may well
be that the text of the four epistles and the Apocalypse, the
latter evidently containing a remarkable ' Western ' element,
would, if studied in the light of the knowledge now available,
acquaint us with a highly archaic Greek text,[1] and throw important light on the history of the text.

For the rest of the New Testament there is no means of
reconstructing the lost Philoxenian version. It must have shown
an affinity to the Peshitto at least as great as that to be observed
in the choice of language found in the books not previously
translated.[2] It would be natural to expect it to stand somewhere
between the Peshitto and the final Harclean revision.

One circumstance is noteworthy. Wholly unlike the Peshitto,
the Philoxenian, like the Greek texts, was subject to much scribal
modification and corruption. For the four epistles Gwynn used
twenty different MSS., the oldest being dated 823. They fall into
two groups, an older (ninth-twelfth century), and a later (fifteenth-
seventeenth century ; from this the usual printed editions have
been taken), besides several of intermediate character. There
is also an Arabic version of the Philoxenian, contained in a ninth-
century MS. from Mt. Sinai (Catalogue, No. 154), which mainly,
but not exclusively, agrees with the later group of Syriac MSS.[3]

[1] On the suggestion that the Philoxenian derived archaic elements from the
Old Syriac, see below, p. clxxvii note 1.

[2] Gwynn, *Apocalypse*, pp. xix-xx. Burkitt is disposed to think that the
Philoxenian version made very few changes in the Peshitto, and that Polycarp's
work consisted almost wholly in adding ' kephalaia ' to the Gospels and
equipping the Acts and Epistles with ' Euthalian ' apparatus. Such a substantial identity of text with the Peshitto is believed to account for the remarkable disappearance of all MSS. of the Philoxenian except for the five freshly
translated books. This theory makes it necessary to suppose that Moses of
Aghel, in referring to the translation made by Polycarp for Philoxenus, really
had in mind the Harclean version of 616. But in view of what is known of
the period of Moses' activity, it is difficult to believe that his letter prefatory to
the *Glaphyra* could have been written at so late a date.

[3] As between the two families, Gwynn has argued for the older, while A.
Merx, *Zeitschrift für Assyriologie*, vol. XII., 1897-98, pp. 240-252, 348-381 ;
vol. XIII., 1898-99, pp. 1-28, relying especially on the evidence of the Arabic
version, thinks that the later family (which is in less close agreement with the
Harclean version) better represents the original Philoxenian.

No reason exists for supposing that the Philoxenian version was supplied with marginal readings, or other critical apparatus except the ' Euthalian ' material.[1]

(d) HARCLEAN

In the period following Philoxenus of Mabog and Severus of Origin. Antioch the monophysite churches of Syria were subjected to stern imperial persecution and were rent by internal theological faction. From the state of weakness and disintegration which resulted they were rescued by the untiring apostolic labours of Jacob Baradaeus (b. before 500, † 578), honoured from that day to this by the monophysites of the East—Syrian, Coptic, and Abyssinian. The later years of the sixth century, however, witnessed the rise of grave quarrels between the Syrian and Alexandrian monophysites, which were not healed until early in the seventh century, when the hostile advance of the Persians under Chosroes II. ravaged the chief seats of the monophysite Syrians in Mesopotamia and northern Syria. At that time the monophysite titular " patriarch of Antioch," Athanasius I. (Camelarius ; 595–631), whose actual residence had been at a monastery near Callinicus on the Euphrates, more than once visited Alexandria in the interest of peace ; and about 613, when the Persians were in full occupation of his own country, he came again, with five of his bishops. Welcomed by the ' Faithful ' of Alexandria, they seem to have consummated their ministry of reconciliation between the two branches of the

---

[1] Considerable fragments of a reconstruction of the ' Euthalian ' material for the Pauline epistles are found in the Peshitto manuscript, Brit. Mus. add. 7157, and are probably derived from the Philoxenian. The Harclean Codex Ridleyanus (Oxford, New College, 333), used by White, contains a ' Euthalian ' apparatus to these epistles, drawn from the same Greek text as is the Philoxenian and not independent of the latter in rendering, but brought closer to the Greek original in arrangement and expression, and supplied with an apparatus of asterisks, obeli, and marginal notes. This seems to be the revised form by Thomas of Harkel. See White, *Actuum apostolorum et epistolarum* . . . *versio Syriaca Philoxeniana*, vol. ii., 1803, pp. ix-xiv ; E. von Dobschütz, ' Euthaliusstudien,' *Zeitschrift für Kirchengeschichte*, vol. XIX., 1899, pp. 107-154.

monophysite church, and some at least of the visitors remained for several years.[1]

Among the monophysite bishops whom Athanasius brought with him, or found, as fugitives, already at Alexandria,[2] were Paul, bishop of Tella, and Thomas of Harkel,[3] bishop of Mabog, who had been expelled from that see in 602 by Domitian of Melitene. Athanasius, Paul, and Thomas lived together for a considerable period in the monastery at the nine-mile relay - station (Enaton) near Alexandria.[4] Here, at the

---

[1] A. Baumstark, *Geschichte der syrischen Literatur*, pp. 185-189 ; J. Gwynn, articles ' Paulus Tellensis ' and ' Thomas Harklensis ' in *Dictionary of Christian Biography*.

[2] That Thomas had come to Alexandria earlier is the view of Jean Maspero, *Histoire des patriarches d'Alexandrie (518-616)*, Paris, 1923, pp. 316, 322, 329-332, on the ground of positive Syriac testimony.

[3] The Greek for Harkel seems to be Heraclea ; the place may have been a town east of Antioch mentioned by Strabo xvi. p. 751 ; but see Georg Hoffmann, *Zeitschrift der Deutschen Morgenländischen Gesellschaft*, xxxii., 1878, p. 740, who thinks it was an outlying village of Mabog.

[4] The meaning of the name ' Enaton,' much discussed in the past, has now been more fully elucidated by F. M. Abel, 'TO ENNATON,' *Oriens Christianus*, vol. i., 1911, pp. 77-82. The term (or its equivalent ' *Nonum* ') is found in various parts of the world (Italy and Gaul, as well as Syria and Egypt) denoting one of the ' relay-posts ' (*mutationes*) established for remounts and changes of beasts of burden at suitable intervals on the road between two main ' stations ' (*mansiones*). The *mansiones* were usually at larger towns, and distant from one another about one day's journey. Between them relays (*mutationes*) were strung along at an average distance of twelve Roman miles, but in a number of instances, apparently as a matter of habitual regulation, the first *mutatio* is known to have been situated nine miles from the *mansio*. Around the stables and stable-men's quarters of such a relay-post would spring up a small village with taverns and shops, sometimes with barracks, and (as is known from a variety of other definite testimonies) at the Alexandrian *Nonum* a monastery was situated. It may be noted that in 613 Athanasius's host, the monophysite patriarch of Alexandria, Anastasius Apozygatius, was not allowed within the city limits, and is stated to have received his guests " in a monastery by the eastern seashore." Other views are mentioned in Gwynn's full note in art. ' Paulus Tellensis,' *Dict. of Christian Biography*, vol. iv., 1887, p. 267. For references to the *Nonum*, or *Ennaton*, of Alexandria, see H. Rosweyd, *Vitae patrum*, Antwerp, 1628, lib. V, libell. vii., par. 7 ; libell. xi., num. 11 ; libell. xii., num. 9. It was by Professor Burkitt that my attention was called to Rosweyd, who (pp. 1043 f., cf. pp. 1028 and 1055 f.) was himself in complete confusion as to the meaning of the term. See also Wright, *Catalogue of Syriac Manuscripts in the British Museum*, 1870, Part I., cols. 34, 586, 641, where will be found convincing evidence that the Syrians knew the correct vocalization and aspirate of the Greek word. J. Maspero, *op. cit.* p. 48 note 3, points

instance of Athanasius, Paul with assistance from others
translated the Old Testament from the Greek hexaplaric and
tetraplaric text of a copy made by Eusebius and Pamphilus.
Successive parts of the translation are dated in the years 616
and 617. A certain Thomas (doubtless Thomas of Harkel) was
his chief assistant in translating Kings. We may assume that
it was likewise at the instance of Athanasius, and as part of a
comprehensive plan for a new translation of the Bible, that at
the same date Thomas of Harkel with certain associates produced
his revision of the Philoxenian New Testament (including all the
twenty-seven books), which was completed in 616. The two
Testaments are translated in exactly the same manner [1]—a
painfully exact imitation of Greek idiom and order of words,
often in disregard of Syriac modes of expression, and so completely and conscientiously carried through that doubt scarcely
ever arises as to the Greek text intended by the translator.[2]
The purpose of this great undertaking must have been to
provide for Syrian monophysites a Bible agreeing with that
used and approved by their Greek fellow-believers. Made with
this intent it was a fitting part of the policy of reconciliation
which Athanasius is known to have been pursuing at this time.

out that another monastery referred to by the same term seems to have been
situated within Alexandria in the ‘Ninth Quarter’; but the famous and important monastery, so often mentioned in the sources, was the one (*El Zadjadj*)
nine miles out from the city. Hither, on a 6th of December, were transferred the venerated remains of St. Severus, patriarch of Antioch (†538), and
here dwelt the monophysite patriarch of Alexandria, Peter IV. (575–577), as
well as his vigorous successor Damian (578–604), himself a monk of the
Enaton. On the identification of the monastery and the Arabic references,
see J. Maspero, *op. cit.* pp. 158-160 note 5; cf. also ‘Enaton’ in his Index;
also Evetts and Butler, *Churches and Monasteries of Egypt*, 1895, p. 229 n. 1.

[1] Other Jacobite works, such as the Hymns of Severus, as revised in 675
by James of Edessa, are translated in much the same way. See E. W. Brooks,
James of Edessa : the Hymns of Severus of Antioch and Others (Patrologia
Orientalis, vi. 1 ; vii. 5), Paris, 1911. In this collection of hymns the text
of Acts used was not the Peshitto, and deserves investigation. This reference
is due to Professor Burkitt.

[2] For a detailed account of this peculiar Harclean style, see Gwynn, *Apocalypse*, pp. xxvii-xxxv ; *Dict. of Christian Biography*, vol. iv. p. 1016 ; Marsh’s
transl. of Michaelis’s *Introduction to the New Testament*, 1802, chap. vii. sect. xi.

The Harclean Syriac of the Gospels is found in many manuscripts, including several of great relative antiquity, at least one being ascribed to the seventh century itself, while another is dated 757. A critical examination of all these MSS. ought to be made, and White's edition (1778, based on the two New College, Oxford, MSS.) supplemented by the additional knowledge now available.

Of the Acts and Epistles (the seven Catholic as well as the Pauline) two manuscripts are known : [1]

Oxford, Library of New College, 333 (now deposited in the Bodleian Library). Eleventh century. Lacks Heb. xi. 28-xiii. 25 and the subscription to the Pauline epistles. This was the source of White's edition (1799, 1803).[2]

Cambridge, University Library, add. 1700. The "Mohl Manuscript." A.D. 1170. From this the missing close of Hebrews and the subscription to the Pauline epistles have been published by Bensly.[3]

These two copies do not appear to differ substantially in text, but the Cambridge copy lacks the diacritical signs and the marginal readings with which the Oxford copy is furnished.

In addition a twelfth-century fragment, containing Acts i. 1-10, is included in Codex canon. or. 130 of the Bodleian Library, Oxford.

For the Apocalypse several MSS. (all late) are known, from one of which (Leyden, University Library, cod. scalig. 18) the

---

[1] In addition one MS. (belonging to Dr. J. Rendel Harris) contains the four minor Catholic epistles in the Harclean, and one other (British Museum, add. 14,474 ; eleventh or twelfth century) contains 2 Peter in that version. In both cases the rest of the text is Peshitto. Gwynn, *Remnants of the Later Syriac Versions*, Part I., Appendix II. pp. 146-153. Gregory's statements about the Harclean MSS. of Acts and Epistles are beset with inextricable confusion.

[2] So far as is known, this New College, Oxford, MS. is unique for the Book of Acts, and a facsimile publication is highly desirable. A complete set of photographs of the pages containing Acts, of full size, is in the Library of Harvard University.

[3] R. L. Bensly, *The Harklean Version of the Epistle to the Hebrews, Chap. xi. 28-xiii. 25, now edited for the first time with Introduction and Notes on this Version of the Epistle*, Cambridge, 1889.

text was published by De Dieu in 1627, and has thus passed into all later editions of the Peshitto.

Subscriptions by the editor have been preserved for three of the four sections of the New Testament in one or more of the MSS., and there is convincing evidence that a similar subscription once existed for the Apocalypse.[1] To these the statements of Bar Salibi (who used the Harclean version as the basis of his commentary on the Apocalypse, Acts, and seven Catholic epistles [2]), Bar Hebraeus, and other Syriac writers add scarcely anything for our present purpose.

The subscription to Acts, substantially in the translation of White (pp. 274 f.), is as follows :

Explicit liber sanctus Actuum Apostolorum et Epistulae Catholicae septem.[3]

Descriptus est autem ex exemplari accurato eorum qui versi sunt diebus (memoriae piae) sancti Philoxeni confessoris, episcopi Mabog. Collatus est autem diligentia multa mea Thomae pauperis ad exemplar Graecum valde accuratum et probatum in Enaton Alexandriae, urbis magnae, in monasterio Antonianorum, sicut reliqui omnes libri, socii ejus.[4]

The other subscriptions are to the same purport,[5] but contain some further statements, including the date 508 for the

[1] J. Gwynn, ' On the Recovery of a Missing Syriac Manuscript of the Apocalypse,' *Hermathena*, vol. x., 1898, pp. 227-245.
[2] The commentary of Bar Salibi is edited with translation by J. Sedlacek in *Corpus scriptorum christianorum orientalium*, Series II., vol. ci., 1909, 1910. An examination of it with reference to the text of Acts might be instructive ; cf. Gwynn's observations, *Apocalypse*, pp. lxxxiv f.

[3] These last three words do not seem to be in the genitive in the Oxford MS. as published by White.

[4] The ' other associated books ' seem to be the other sections of the New Testament. A similar reference to the ' associates ' of the section in hand is found in the Harclean subscription to the Gospels in several MSS. (not, as it happens, in that followed by White in his edition, but see White, pp. 644 f., 647, 649 f.). Likewise in the subscription to the Pauline Epistles express mention is made of the work of Thomas and his associates on " the Gospel and Acts." On the interpretation of these subscriptions see J. G. Eichhorn, ' Über den Verfasser der hexaplarisch-syrischen Übersetzung,' in *Repertorium für Biblische und Morgenländische Litteratur*, Theil vii., 1780, pp. 225-250.

[5] The subscriptions to the several parts of the Syro-hexaplar Old Testament of Paul of Tella are of the same general type.

Philoxenian version and 616 for the work of Thomas. While Acts and the Catholic Epistles were compared with one accurate copy, the Gospels are stated to have been compared with three (other MSS. read ' two '), and the Pauline epistles with two. In the subscription to the Pauline epistles it is said that the present edition has been made " for the study and use . . . of those who are zealous to learn and preserve the accuracy of the apostolic (that is, the divine) words and meanings." [1]

Text.
These subscriptions make it clear that the Harclean Syriac text was a revision of the Philoxenian, and was made in 616 with the aid of ' accurate and approved ' Greek copies accessible at Alexandria. The Harclean text itself, in so far as it has been studied, does not belie this. In the Apocalypse it has been largely, though not completely, conformed to the Antiochian text (represented by Q and most minuscules) ; in the Gospels [2] and Acts, likewise, apart from certain words and phrases marked with an asterisk, it appears to give substantially the Antiochian text ; [3] and this seems to be the view of Hort with regard to the epistles also.[4] It would thus appear that the ' accurate and approved ' Greek copies (which, be it noted, are nowhere said to have been ancient) were manuscripts of the Antiochian text. Nothing in Thomas's statement implies that they were used for

[1] Similar phrases are found in the subscription to the Gospels, as given in some MSS. ; see J. G. C. Adler, *Novi Testamenti versiones Syriacae*, Copenhagen, 1789, pp. 46 f.

[2] Gwynn, *Dict. of Christian Biography*, vol. iv. p. 1018 : in the Gospels " the text represents (on the whole) a Greek basis akin in the main to the Constantinopolitan or ' Received ' Greek text, while the margin inclines strongly to the Western Greek text, as represented by D and the Old Latin, and not seldom (though less decisively) towards that of the other older uncials, mostly B and L, sometimes A, C, and others."

[3] For instance, in Acts i., of all those departures of the Antiochian text from that of Codex Vaticanus which are capable of ready expression in Syriac, only one (vs. 14, the addition of καὶ τῇ δεήσει) fails to appear in the Harclean. Moreover, in so far as I have made examination, the departures of the Harclean from the text common to the Old Uncials and the Antiochian are few and trivial, although occasionally a striking ancient reading, not marked (in our single annotated copy) by an asterisk, will stand out conspicuously against the general Antiochian background.

[4] Compare what is said by Hort, ' Introduction,' p. 156.

any other purpose than to bring the Syriac text into substantial conformity with that current and approved in the seventh century in Alexandria. No hint is given which suggests that they were made a source for marginal glosses or for the insertion of asterisks and obeli.

The evidence of the four minor Catholic epistles and the Apocalypse, where the two versions can be compared, makes it probable, as is explained below, that in the Harclean text not only turns of Syriac expression, but also renderings which imply a non-antiochian Greek text, have in some cases survived from the Philoxenian. The general style, however, of the peculiar Harclean mode of expression has been imposed by the reviser upon the whole, including asterisked phrases.

The influence of the Peshitto, clearly observable even in the extant books of the Philoxenian, where no direct dependence was possible because the Peshitto did not contain them, was undoubtedly strong in those parts where the Peshitto had preceded the Philoxenian ; and through the latter, and perhaps directly also, it reached the Harclean. But, for these books, it is impossible to say how far the Harclean version was derived from the Philoxenian.

As merely reproducing an Antiochian text, mixed with some ancient (often ' Western ') readings, the Harclean version can claim but little interest, far less than the Philoxenian (if that could be recovered). But the apparatus which was attached to it by Thomas has made it, at least for the book of Acts, one of the most important witnesses to the ' Western ' text that have come down to us. This apparatus consists of two parts. (1) In the text itself many words, parts of words (such as pronominal suffixes), and phrases, with a few longer sentences, are marked with an asterisk (⁕) or with an obelus (—), the termination of the reference being exactly indicated by a metobelus (⸌). The probable significance and origin of these will be discussed presently. (2) In the margin, with points of attachment in the text marked by various characters, are found a great number of

Asterisks and obeli; marginal notes.

notes.[1] These vary in nature. Some are variant renderings not affecting the Greek text. In the four minor epistles and the Apocalypse several cases of this kind occur, where the Harclean margin seems to give the rejected rendering of the Philoxenian (notably 2 Peter ii. 4 ; 3 John 6),[2] and that may well be the source of the marginal variant renderings in other books. In Acts i. 25 the margin renders λαβεῖν by the use, characteristic of the Philoxenian, of the future with the prefix ܕ, while the text uses the infinitive with the prefix ܠ in accordance with the regular Harclean custom.[3] In Acts i. 3 the margin gives ܐܦܠܐ for διά as a substitute for the unidiomatic and literal ܚܡܣ of the text. In other cases the margin gives explanations or statements of various kinds. Thus on Acts i. 20 the margin gives a reference to Psalm lxviii. (*i.e.* according to the Syriac enumeration) and quotes the verse in question in a text corresponding, as would be expected, not to the Peshitto but to the Syro-hexaplar of Paul of Tella, from which it differs only in a more pedantic imitation of the Greek than is exhibited by the extant Syro-hexaplaric ms. On Acts x. 1 the note gives the derivation of the name Κορνήλιος as κόρην ἡλίου. Sometimes a Greek word, rarely a Hebrew one, is written in the margin or between the lines, to justify the rendering or explain a transliteration, but these may not all be from the same source as the other notes, and are negligible for any further critical purposes.[4] Other notes are of what may be called a Masoretic character, and relate to deliberate omission of plural points, to spelling, and to pronunciation.

Longer notes.

Longer notes sometimes occur, some of which are instructive.

---

[1] The best account of these notes is that given by G. C. Storr, ' Von der philoxenianisch-syrischen Übersetzung der Evangelien,' in *Repertorium für Biblische und Morgenländische Litteratur,* Theil vii., Leipzig, 1780, pp. 15-48. On the Harclean see also G. C. Storr, ' Supplemente zu Wetsteins Varianten aus der Philoxenischen Übersetzung,' *Repertorium,* Theil x., 1782, pp. 1-58.

[2] Gwynn, *Remnants,* pp. xxxvii f., *Apocalypse,* p. lxxxiv.

[3] Gwynn, *Apocalypse,* p. xxix.

[4] G. C. Storr, in *Repertorium,* vii., 1780, pp. 15-18, gives a list of many of these, and points out that in some cases in the Gospels the Greek notes do not correspond with the actual Syriac of the text.

In quoting these and the words from the continuous text with which they are connected by the scribe, it will be convenient to use White's Latin translation (slightly corrected).

Matt. ii. 17. The text reads *per Jeremiam,* to which a note is attached : *Graecum dicit ' a Jeremia,' non ' per.'*

Matt. xxv. 1. The text reads ※ *et sponsae* ⟨. On this the note : ' *Sponsa* ' *non in omnibus exemplaribus invenitur, et nominatim* (ܐܠܟܣܢܕܪܝܐ) *in Alexandrino.*

Matt. xxvii. 35. The continuous text includes the quotation from Psalm xxii. 18, with the marginal note: *Haec periocha prophetae non inventa est in duobus exemplaribus Graecis, neque in illo antiquo Syriaco.*

Matt. xxviii. 5. The text reads *Jesum* ※ *Nazarenum* ⟨, with the note : *In tribus exemplaribus Graecis et uno Syriaco, illo antiquo, non inventum est nomen ' Nazarenum.'*

Mark viii. 17. The text reads : ※ *in cordibus vestris pusilli fide* ⟨, with the note : ' *In cordibus vestris pusilli fide* ' *non inventum est in duobus exemplaribus Graecis neque in illo antiquo Syriaco.*

Mark x. 48. To the words *fili Davidis* of the text is attached the note: *In duobus exemplaribus Graecis ' fili filii Davidis ' inventum est.*

Mark xi. 10. The text reads : *patris nostri Davidis* ※ *pax in caelo et gloria in excelsis* ⟨ *hosanna in excelsis,* with the note attached at the word *pax :* ' *Pax in caelo et gloria in excelsis* ' *non in omnibus exemplaribus Graecis invenitur neque in illo Mar Xenaiae ; in nonnullis autem accuratis, ut putamus, invenimus illud.*

Mark xii. 14. The text reads ※ *dic nobis igitur* ⟨, with the note : ' *Dic nobis igitur* ' *non invenimus in Graeco.*

Luke vi. 1. To the words *sabbatho secundo primi* of the text is attached the note : ' *Secundo primi* ' *non in omni exemplari est.*

Luke viii. 24. The text has *tranquillitas* ※ *magna* ⟨, with the note : ' *Magna* ' *non in omnibus exemplaribus invenitur.*

Luke viii. 52. The text reads *non* ※ *enim* ⟨ *mortua est*

⁘ *puella* ✓, with the note : '*Enim*,' '*puella*,' *non in omni exemplari invenitur*.

Luke ix. 23. The text reads ⁘ *quotidie* ✓, with the note : '*Quotidie* ' *non in omnibus exemplaribus invenitur*.

Luke ix. 50. The text reads ⁘ *non enim est adversus vos* ✓, with the note : '*Non enim est adversus vos* ' *non in omnibus exemplaribus invenitur*.

Luke xix. 38. The text reads ⁘ *benedictus est rex Israelis* ✓, with the note : '*Benedictus est rex Israelis* ' *non in omnibus exemplaribus invenitur*.

Luke xix. 45. The text reads ⁘ *et mensas numulariorum effudit et cathedras eorum qui vendebant columbas* ✓, with the note : '*Et mensas numulariorum effudit et cathedras eorum qui vendebant columbas* ' *non in omni exemplari est ita hîc*.

Luke xx. 34. To the word *filii* of the text is attached the note : *In exemplari antiquo est* '*gignunt et gignuntur* ' *et in Graeco non est*.

Acts iv. 30. To the words *per nomen* of the text is attached the note : *Sunt exemplaria in quibus non est* '*nomen*.'

Acts ix. 4. The text reads : ⁘ *durum est tibi calcitrare ad stimulos* ✓ with the note : '*Durum est tibi calcitrare ad stimulos* ' *non est hîc in Graeco sed ubi enarrat Paulus de se*.

Jude 12. To the words *in refectionibus* of the text is attached the note : εν ταις αγαπαις. *In Graeco* '*in dilectionibus* ' *est*.

Philippians iii. 18. The text reads — *aliter* ✓ *ambulant*, with the note : *In duobus exemplaribus accuratis Graecis non invenitur* '*aliter*.'

Colossians ii. 1. The text reads *iis qui Laodicaeae* ⁘ *et iis qui Hieropoli* ✓ with the note : εν ιεροπολει '*Qui Hieropoli* ' *non in omni exemplari invenitur*.

In these careful notes the editor calls attention to differences between the reading which he has allowed to stand in his text (usually with an asterisk) and some or all of the Greek copies which he is using for correction. In some instances he also refers to " the old Syriac," " the old copy," phrases which are to be

interpreted in the light of the note on Mark xi. 10 as referring
to the Philoxenian basis of his revision. Nothing in these notes
need suggest a direct comparison with the Peshitto ; any
agreement with the Peshitto in readings adopted or referred to
is fully accounted for by the fact that the Philoxenian must have
derived many of its renderings from that translation, and at
many points may well have coincided with it in underlying Greek
text. Every one of the notes (except those on Mark x. 48,
Luke vi. 1, and Acts iv. 30, and the exegetical note on Jude
12) relates to a reading allowed to stand (usually under
asterisk) in the Harclean text but at variance with the
Antiochian Greek text to which the great mass of the
Harclean version corresponds. In nearly all the cases the
word or phrase is found in the Harclean and absent from the
Antiochian. The very close similarity of the Greek copies
used by Thomas as a standard may be seen from the fact
that the readings in Mark x. 48 and Acts iv. 30 which he
attributes respectively to ' two copies ' and ' some copies ' are
not found in any Greek MS. known to us.

In other cases, not very numerous, the margin adds a word or **Other**
phrase, not attested in other versions or in any Greek text, such **marginal notes.**
as might naturally be supplied by a translator to complete the
sense in Syriac—a pronoun with its preposition (so Acts iii. 6 *ad
eum*), or a word amply suggested by the context (for instance,
vi. 7 *evangelii*, vii. 60 *Jesu*). These are closely similar to
the words and phrases marked in the text by obeli and to the
lesser portion of those marked by asterisks, as will presently be
explained.

But more numerous than the various types of notes hitherto
mentioned (especially in Acts) are the great number of marginal
notes which simply give without comment the Syriac rendering
of a Greek reading different from that followed in the continuous
Syriac text of the editor's version. In the Book of Acts these,
taken together with the portions of the continuous text marked
with an asterisk, constitute a delectus of ' Western ' readings of

great purity and of a value for the reconstruction of the ' Western '
recension second only (and in some respects superior) to Codex
Bezae.   The question why in a few cases the editor chose to add
a special comment to these variants cannot be answered.   Before
discussing further their significance and origin it is necessary
to speak of his use of asterisks and obeli.

Asterisks and obeli.

The meaning of these signs has been much discussed ever
since the publication of White's edition, which contains them.
The earliest assumption that the signs indicated some relation
to the Peshitto was mistaken,[1] and made satisfactory conclusions
impossible, in spite of a great amount of careful work ; and the
observation that the Peshitto should be left wholly out of account
in the study of the signs has greatly facilitated the investigation.

Difference from Hexapla.

A further embarrassment arose from the supposition that the
signs were used by Thomas in exactly the same way as by Origen
in the Hexapla.   That Thomas was familiar with the hexaplaric
signs is unquestionable, and from them he probably derived the
suggestion for his own practice ; but it is not certain that he
understood the purpose of Origen exactly as we do, and indeed
Origen's own use is not perfectly simple.[2]   In any case the
different conditions prescribed some differences of application.[3]
As his subscriptions show, the primary task of Thomas, unlike
that of Origen, was to revise the existing translation so as to
bring it into accord with the best current MSS. of the original.
The Philoxenian version can have inspired no such reverence as
Origen seems to have had for the LXX,[4] and to have followed

---

[1] A good example is Acts xxviii. 14, where Harclean reads ※ *apud eos* ✓.
The phrase is also found in the Peshitto, but that such asterisks as this were
meant to indicate cases of agreement with the Peshitto would be obviously
an absurd hypothesis.   In fact this asterisk calls attention to the retention of
the older reading (παρ αυτοις) in addition to επ αυτοις of the Antiochian text.
That Hcl. *text* has also retained επιμειναντες (614, cf. gig) for the Antiochian
επιμειναι is not brought to the reader's notice.

[2] Swete, *Introduction to the Old Testament in Greek*, p. 71.

[3] An interesting attempt by a mediaeval Latin editor to use Origen's signs
for a similar purpose in a different way is described by Rahlfs, *Der Text des
Septuaginta-Psalters*, pp. 130-134.

[4] Origen, *Ad Africanum*, 4 f.

Origen's example by trying to record all the points at which the
Syriac exemplar of Thomas had been improved would have been
a useless, as well as a desperate, undertaking. His asterisks and
obeli are to be interpreted, as well as may be, from the facts,
not from the rules followed by Origen.[1]

Such an examination of the facts shows certain general
tendencies for both margin and signs, but some confusion. The
latter, although it must probably fall in part to the account of
Thomas, is partly to be explained by our lack of a critical edition
of the Harclean Gospels, where alone the available material
makes such an edition possible. Concerning the two Oxford
MSS. of the Gospels much information is given in White's Notes,
and something is known of the Paris MS.   It appears that not
seldom text and margin have exchanged places in one or another
MS. (so Luke xviii. 9 ; John xix. 3), while in some cases the fact
that the margin offers a stricter rendering than that of the text
gives rise to the suspicion that such an exchange has taken
place. Occasionally the ' Western ' character of the reading in
the text, where the Antiochian reading is given in the margin,
suggests the same conclusion.[2]   In the Paris MS. at Matt. i. and
Luke iii. 23 ff. it is expressly stated that the grecizing readings
there found in the margin are the Harclean.[3]   It is also possible
that some inconsistencies in the use of asterisks and obeli are
due to a scribe's lack of care in a very complicated matter.[4]   It
would be almost a miracle if no signs had been omitted from the
text ; and what were originally marginal notes may now appear

[1] Storr's painstaking and instructive discussion, *Repertorium*, Theil vii.,
1780, pp. 1-77, which is still valuable, is vitiated by both the errors mentioned
above. The view of Wetstein, who supposed a comparison with the Peshitto
to be indicated, was effectively disproved by White in the Praefatio to his
edition of the Gospels, pp. xxvii ff., but White was himself led astray by his
use of Origen's practice as a guide.

[2] So, for instance, Acts xviii. 5, where the marginal reading *in spiritu* is
Antiochian.

[3] Storr, *l.c.* pp. 22-26, from J. G. C. Adler, *Novi Testamenti versiones
Syriacae*, pp. 56 f.

[4] In some MSS. of the Syro-hexaplar Old Testament asterisks have been
substituted for obeli and *vice versa* ; Gwynn, *Dictionary of Christian Biography*,
vol. iv. p. 1018.

in the text designated with an asterisk or obelus.[1] The MSS. also vary greatly in the completeness with which the apparatus is supplied. In the very carefully written Cambridge MS. of the Acts and Epistles there is no vestige of it.[2] Moreover, some of the marginal notes may be (in a few cases they certainly are) from a date later than that of Thomas.

Between the marginal notes and the words in the text distinguished by an asterisk, or even all of the words marked with an obelus, it is not possible to make a complete distinction.

Obeli in Acts. In the Book of Acts *obeli* are found in about forty-five instances in chaps. i.-xviii. (none in chaps. xix.-xxviii.), marking off a single word, or in a few cases two words. In virtually every case [3] the word or words are mere supplements required by Syriac idiom or desirable in order to complete the phrase—exactly like the italicized words of the English Bible. The obelus is, indeed, here used, as by Origen, to denote words of the version to which nothing in the original corresponds, but it is negligible for textual criticism. One half of the cases are single pronouns, and although many of these find parallels in one or other Latin or Egyptian version, only seldom does any Greek MS. show the same expansion of phrase. Three-quarters of these little supplements are found in the Peshitto also, and it may be assumed that most of them stood in the Philoxenian.

Asterisks in Acts. *Asterisks* are found in the Book of Acts in about 150 places,

---

[1] A case where this seems almost demonstrable is Acts ix. 6. Here the long gloss in the text under asterisk ends with ' *surge*,' followed by the metobelus. The continuous text then proceeds, ' *sed surge*,' etc. The gloss is plainly intended as a substitute for these following words of the text, not as a part of the same continuous text with them.

[2] For similar confusion and omission in the hexaplaric signs see Rahlfs, *Studie über den griechischen Text des Buches Ruth*, pp. 54-67.

[3] Two exceptions only appear. In Acts x. 25 we read : ÷ *et procidit* ✓ *ad pedes ejus.* This is evidently a mistake of some kind, for the words are indispensable to the sense, and no text in any language omits them. Perhaps the sign originally applied only to the conjunction *et.* In Acts xiii. 25 we read : *calceamentum* ÷ *pedum ipsius* ✓ *solvere.* For this (on which no Greek text or version throws any direct light) no explanation is forthcoming, although it is worth mentioning that the Peshitto here reads, by harmonization with Mark i. 7 and Luke iii. 16, ' the thongs of his shoes ' instead of ' the sandal of his feet.'

and are applied usually to a word or brief phrase, but sometimes to a long sentence. In all but two cases (xix. 35, where ⁛ *civitatis* ⟨ and ⁛ *ejus* ⟨ are fragments of the free rendering of the Peshitto that have survived in the Harclean) they indicate what is, or might be, a variation of underlying text, not merely of rendering. But on scrutiny it appears that about 30 of the additions thus marked are small expansions, chiefly pronouns, made incidentally to the translation for the sake of smoothness of Syriac idiom, so that in these cases the use of the asterisk is not to be distinguished from the characteristic use of the obelus just described, and is equally negligible for our purpose.[1] All but four of the cases of this type were already present in the Peshitto. This use of the asterisk does not seem to yield any parallel whatever to Origen's practice.[2] But the large bulk— about 95—of the words or phrases marked with an asterisk are substantial additions to the editor's Antiochian text, and are of ' Western ' origin.

Rarely the words under asterisk have been so introduced as to make a conflation with the neighbouring continuous text ; [3] for the most part they are sheer additions, and the glosses which are direct substitutes for words of the text are commonly relegated to the margin.

Again we see that the Harclean use of asterisks is not the same

[1] A. V. V. Richards, in a valuable review (*Journal of Theological Studies*, vol. II., 1900–1, pp. 439-447) of A. Pott, *Der abendländische Text der Apostelgeschichte und die Wir-quelle*, 1900, points out (p. 443) the suggestive fact that the obeli do not occur in our ·MS. after the close of chap. xviii., and that all but a small number of the asterisks used in the same way as obeli are found after that point.

[2] A few of these little additions are also attested in Greek or in some version, and might be regarded as the product of Greek variants. The two processes of translating and of corrupting a text work alike at this point, and either might be responsible for the result ; and translators into different languages will independently duplicate each other. It is safer to ascribe the whole of these thirty cases to a translator's activity.

[3] For instance, xiii. 19 *eorum* ⁛ *alienigenarum* ⟨ ; xvi. 39 ; also xii. 21 and xv. 11, in both which passages the repeated *autem* makes an awkward succession. In xv. 5 the difficulty created by the mention of the Pharisees in both vs. 1 and vs. 5 lies deeper, for it is present also in Codices 383 and 614. On Acts ix. 6 see above, p. clxviii note 1.

as that of the Hexapla.   The more common use of the Harclean
asterisks, as just described, is not to show the excess of the
original over a standard translation, but to preserve on the page
of the translation those readings of another (the ' Western ') type
of text side by side with those of the (Antiochian) standard
adopted by the editor.   It is also evident that the obeli and the
greater part of the asterisks pertain to two wholly distinct systems
of annotation, each having its own purpose—the obeli to exhibit
differences of the version from the original, the asterisks to record
differences between two types of the original.   This is well
illustrated by xi. 1, where, in the middle of a long passage covered
by an asterisk, a single word (*et*, evidently added in the translator's reconstruction of the sentence) is marked with an obelus.
That in thirty cases the force of the asterisks does not differ
from that of obeli is either a mark of inconsistency on the editor's
part, not surprising in so elaborate an undertaking, or the result
of the work of copyists, who through failure of understanding
confused what may originally have been an integral system.   It
is to be borne in mind that we are dependent on a single MS. of
a date more than four centuries later than that of Thomas of
Harkel.

But besides the two classes of asterisks already explained
nearly twenty cases remain which show various peculiarities.
Of these seven (ix. 37, xv. 30, xv. 36, xv. 37, xxi. 31, xxvii.
41, xxviii. 7) are glosses similar to the ' Western,' and may be
true ' Western ' additions which have survived only here.   In
eight other instances (vii. 10, xxv. 10, xxv. 16, xxvi. 30, xxvii. 7,
xxviii. 16, xxviii. 29, xxviii. 30) we find under asterisk readings
of the Antiochian text which are absent either from B and other
Old Uncials or from some of the witnesses whose peculiarities
are usually ' Western.'   This phenomenon may be due to the
fact that Thomas had a slightly different Antiochian text from
ours, or it may be that in these cases he had no other way of
indicating that his standard contained what others omit—or
some other explanation may be the true one.   The two or three

still remaining instances of peculiarity in the use of the asterisks need not be discussed.

Finally, our attention is again claimed by the marginal readings. The bulk of these, as described above (pp. clxv-vi), cannot be distinguished in character from the ninety-five asterisked phrases of the text. This conclusion is unavoidable, as is made especially clear in such a passage as Acts xviii. 26, 27, where Codex Bezae has a long expansive paraphrase. The greater part of this expansion is found in the margin of the Harclean, but the words εἰς τὴν 'Αχαίαν (in the later position, vs. 27), which plainly belong to the same paraphrastic text, are included in the Harclean continuous text under an asterisk, with the result that the same phrase occurs twice in the same verse. Similarly, in Acts xxiii. 24 a long addition in the text under an asterisk is a part of the same reading as the marginal gloss to vs. 25, which gives a brief paraphrastic substitute for the first words of that verse.

Marginal readings in Acts.

The exactness of the translation of these ' Western ' readings and their large extent make them, next to Codex Bezae, the most important single witness to the ' Western ' text of Acts. With the aid of the parallel, less complete, witnesses, chiefly Greek and Latin, it is almost always possible to make a trustworthy reconstruction of the Greek from which the Harclean asterisked and marginal readings were drawn. In many instances the Harclean evidence is better than that of Codex Bezae. Not only does it cover the whole book, including the long sections lacking in D, but it gives a text free from conflation with the Antiochian or Old Uncial text and from adjustment to a parallel Latin—those two traits which everywhere mar the text of Codex Bezae and diminish the student's confidence in its witness. Examples of ' Western ' fragments lacking in D but attested by the Harclean apparatus and confirmed by Greek mixed mss. may be found in xii. 12, xii. 25, xiii. 43, xiii. 47, xv. 23, xx. 32, and many other places. In other instances, such as xi. 17, the Harclean apparatus has preserved ' Western ' readings attested

in no Greek MS., but in the Old Latin rendering.   In such cases
as xvi. 4, xvi. 39, it gives the ' Western ' text in a form free from
the conflation found in D.   In a large number of these cases
the Greek corresponding to the Syriac of the Harclean apparatus
is found in Codex 614 or in others of the group of minuscules
which contain ' Western ' elements, and in the parts where D is
lacking nearly every gloss of the Harclean, as will be seen in
the text of the present volume, can be matched from these
codices by the corresponding Greek.   With what degree of completeness the Harclean apparatus gives the ' Western ' readings,
and what relation its selection of these readings bears to the
selection found most fully in 614 but in parallel fashion in other
minuscules, is a problem which could be worked out.   Thomas
clearly had at hand a larger body of ' Western ' readings than is
found in any one of the extant mixed MSS. so far examined.   The
study of these questions would throw light on the dissemination
and locality, and possibly on the origin, of the ' Western ' text.

In this connexion it is not to be overlooked that a number of
' Western ' readings are to be detected in the continuous text
of the Harclean unmarked by any sign.   Such cases as I have
observed will be found mentioned in the Harclean apparatus of
the present volume.   There are doubtless many others which I
have not noted.   Possibly some of these readings were once
marked by asterisks now omitted, but this can hardly be true
of all.

Source of
Harclean
' Western '
readings.

The important question which now presents itself is what
was the source from which these ' Western ' readings came into
the Harclean.   An answer commonly given is that Thomas of
Harkel found these readings in the " accurate and approved
copy " of the Greek text of Acts and the Catholic Epistles (or,
respectively, in one or more of the two or three " approved and
accurate copies " of the Gospels and the Epistles of Paul) which
he mentions in his subscriptions as having been used for his work.
But this view is forbidden by several decisive objections.   In
the first place, the language of the subscriptions does not natur-

ally suggest it. The verb used (ܐܬܦܚܡ) means 'made like,'
' compared,' ' collated,' and seems to refer to the construction of
his text,[1] not to the apparatus of variants, of which the subscription gives no definite explanation. The statement of Thomas is
fully accounted for by the observation of his procedure, demonstrable in the Apocalypse (where we have at hand for comparison the Philoxenian text which he was revising) and in the
other books made probable by the character of his continuous
text ; he was revising the older text to bring it more closely into
agreement with the Greek Antiochian text used in the seventh
century. Moreover, the ' approved ' copies are nowhere stated
to be ' old,' and it is difficult to believe that a scholar writing
in 616 in Alexandria would have described copies of the New
Testament containing a ' Western ' text as notably ' approved
and accurate.' The presumption from his language is that
these were good current MSS., such as were produced by the best
scriptoria of the period.

A further reason against the explanation mentioned is to be
drawn from the express statement of the note to Philippians iii. 18,
already cited (p. clxiv), that a certain reading (*aliter*) put under
an obelus in the text (and not, in fact, found in any other witness
known to us) was not found "in (the) two accurate Greek copies."
The two copies are therein implied to be those used for comparison
(as stated in the subscription to the Pauline Epistles), and we find
that they are expressly not used for the apparatus but that the
apparatus here represents a reading drawn from another source.
From this it may be inferred that " the Greek copies " or " the
Greek " referred to in other notes means the copies used for comparison and mentioned in the subscriptions. Of the twenty-one
notes cited above, all but two [2] refer to the absence of the reading
in question (almost always a reading under asterisk) from " the
Greek," or from some of the Greek copies. In four notes it is

---

[1] This corresponds to the regular use of ἀντεβλήθη by Greek scribes.

[2] That on Mark x. 48, which relates to a meaningless corruption of the Greek
text, and that on Jude 12, which gives a different and more exact rendering of
the same Greek word translated differently in the Syriac continuous text.

stated that the reading is also absent from the Syriac (always described as " the old Syriac " or as " the copy of Mar Xenaia "), and in one that the reading is found in "the old copy " (*i.e.* the Syriac). These notes make it practically certain that the apparatus of margin and asterisks was not constructed in order to contain the readings in which the Greek " approved copies " departed from the text adopted by Thomas, but rather to exhibit readings known to him, of which he wished to preserve some record, but which were not found in the 'approved copies,' and therefore not adopted into his continuous text. As Corssen points out, the reference in the note on Matt. xxv. 1 to " the Alexandrian copy " (and general probability as well) makes it altogether likely that these notes all proceed from Thomas himself.

If the Harclean apparatus was not drawn from the 'approved copy,' the obvious alternative suggestion is that it represents rejected readings of the Philoxenian, which Thomas was revising and to which several of the notes cited above (pp. clxiii-iv) refer, expressly or probably.[1] This view is on the whole supported by what can be observed in his treatment of the four minor Catholic Epistles and the Apocalypse, although the light they shed is less abundant than could be desired. In the four epistles the amount of text is small, and the inquiry is embarrassed by the lack of a clearly defined 'Western' text in these books for comparison, but the Harclean is clearly dependent on the Philoxenian, and seems to have been in some cases assimilated to the Antiochian text. The apparatus (including both asterisks and margin) contains several readings which seem certainly to have come from the Philoxenian, and in nearly all cases its readings (with some of the variant marginal renderings) are capable of such an explanation.[2] In the Apocalypse the text of the Philoxenian

---

[1] This is the conclusion which seems to be suggested by P. Corssen in his acute and instructive article, ' Die Recension der Philoxeniana durch Thomas von Mabug,' *Zeitschrift für die neutestamentliche Wissenschaft*, vol. II., 1901, pp. 1-12. Corssen, however, inclines to the unlikely view that the readings now found under asterisk in the text originally all stood in the margin.

[2] Gwynn, *Remnants of the Later Syriac Versions*, Part I. pp. xl-xli.

includes two elements, one, less extensive, agreeing with the
presumably Antiochian text of 046 (formerly B, or Q) and most
minuscules, the other, more pervasive, agreeing with the Old
Uncials, and in a conspicuous degree with the very ancient
African Latin ; [1] that the two elements had already been combined in the Greek copy used by Polycarp for the Philoxenian
would seem to me a likely supposition. The Harclean has
extensively revised this Philoxenian text so as to produce a
Syriac version largely agreeing with the Antiochian. In the
Apocalypse but one marginal reading of the Harclean has been
reported ; yet that gives a variant known elsewhere only in
the Philoxenian.[2] For the asterisks no full statement is available,[3] but Gwynn observes : " In much the greater part of the
places where the asterisk occurs in Σ l [i.e. the Leyden MS. of the
Harclean Apocalypse], it can be understood as referring to
something inserted in, or omitted from, the text of Σ as compared
with that of S [i.e. the Philoxenian Apocalypse of the Crawford
MS.]. In one or two of these places it cannot be accounted for
by comparison with any other known textual authority." [4]

At least once in the four epistles (2 Peter ii. 13), where the
Harclean margin seems to represent the Philoxenian, the facts
show that the later (Harclean) translator was guided in his work
by a Greek text which also contained the reading ; and in two
of the three reported cases of asterisks in the Apocalypse the
Philoxenian reading preserved under asterisk has plainly been

[1] Gwynn, *Apocalypse*, pp. lxx-lxxi.

[2] Rev. i. 10 ܝܡܝܥ ܟܚܡܟ, which seems to refer to the unique reading
of the Philoxenian ܟܚܡܟ ܝܡܝܥ ; cf. Gwynn, *Apocalypse*, p. lxxxiv, who
also points out that the comments of Bar Salibi on the Apocalypse seem
occasionally to rest on Philoxenian renderings learned from the now lost
Harclean margin. The Dublin MS. contains a few marginal notes ; a
marginal apparatus is found in the Florence MS. and in the Vatican MS. ;
see Gwynn, *Hermathena*, vol. x., 1898, p. 227.

[3] About forty asterisks are present in the Leyden MS. ; the British Museum
MS. (Nitrian) contains one asterisk.

[4] Gwynn, *Apocalypse*, p. lxxxiii. The three cases mentioned by Gwynn are as
follows : Apoc. viii. 9, ܟܚܠܘܡ, ※ (Philoxenian, ܟܚܠ) ; xix. 16, ܠܟܚ ※
(Philoxenian, ܟܟ) ; v. 5, ܚܩܦܠ ܘܩ ※ (Philoxenian, ܟܩܦܠ).

modified to conform to the grecizing manner of the Harclean. In the two cases last mentioned this can have been done without any actual reference to a Greek manuscript.

The evidence from the books in which the Philoxenian is extant is thus in accord with the supposition that the Harclean apparatus in the other epistles and in the Gospels and Acts is largely derived from the Philoxenian ; but the array of facts is too meagre to furnish convincing proof.[1] If this view be held, however, it does not follow that the ' Western ' material, liberally assembled in the Harclean margin and under the asterisks, came ultimately from the Old Syriac used by Ephrem nearly two

---

[1] The interesting view adopted by Theodor Zahn and made the basis of his treatment of the text of Acts in *Die Urausgabe der Apostelgeschichte des Lucas* (Forschungen zur Geschichte des neutestamentlichen Kanons, ix.), 1916, would accept the apparatus of the Harclean as giving direct information of the Old Syriac text which preceded the Peshitto. Zahn thinks that a copy of this lay before Thomas, and was the one referred to in his notes as " the old Syriac." This conception of the matter rests chiefly on the view that the work of Thomas was to copy exactly, and annotate, the Philoxenian Syriac text, not to revise it. This view, however, which was that of White and other older scholars, is not required by the language of the subscriptions. Especially the subscription to the Pauline Epistles shows the non-technical character of the expressions employed ; the same word (ܦ̣ܚܡ‌ܐ܇ *collatus est*) is there used to denote Thomas's use both of the Philoxenian *from which*, and of the Greek MSS. *according to which*, his text was written. Moreover, the idea that the Philoxenian and Harclean texts were substantially identical is contradicted by Bar Hebraeus, who speaks of the Harclean as the ' third ' translation, the Peshitto and Philoxenian being the first two. And, finally, the idea is made impossible for all who have been convinced by the patent evidence adduced by Gwynn that the Philoxenian is still extant for the four minor epistles and the Apocalypse, and that the Harclean was a drastic revision of it. That Zahn's discussion of the purpose and nature of the Harclean apparatus is thus at many points open to criticism does not diminish the great value of the textual discussions in connexion with which he uses it, although it often influences the form in which he couches these. Zahn's theory that the Harclean marginal and asterisked ' Western ' readings were drawn from the Old Syriac direct can, indeed, be held even on the usual view that a considerable revision of the Philoxenian was made by Thomas and appears in the Harclean text. But under such a theory it has to be assumed, as explained below, that the Old Syriac renderings were completely reconstructed and grecized by Thomas, so that the free style of the Old Syriac has disappeared. For this process it is probable that he would have required the aid of a Greek MS. containing these readings. That being so, the theory that Thomas used also an Old Syriac MS. becomes otiose, for he could equally well have drawn his ' Western ' readings from his Greek MS. alone.

centuries before the time of Philoxenus. The probability would rather be that Polycarp had made his translation from a Greek MS. either completely ' Western ' in character or else combining, as does 614, much ' Western ' matter with a text of the more usual type.[1] That such a manuscript should have been found in Mesopotamia at that period does not seem to be rendered impossible by anything that is known.

A natural interpretation, then, of the facts would be as follows : (1) The Philoxenian translation of the New Testament of 508 was made at Mabog from a Greek text containing a great number of ' Western ' readings, the question being indeterminable whether the copy from which Acts was drawn was consistently and completely ' Western ' or contained a mixed text. The translation was written in free and idiomatic Syriac. (2) Thomas of Harkel revised it in 616 by the aid of Greek MSS. of the Antiochian type, putting into his margin or marking with an asterisk some of the Syriac renderings, together with many words and sentences which were inconsistent with the Greek copies used for his revision. Although he and his associates did not succeed in making their main text (apart from the asterisked portions) in all respects a perfect equivalent of their Greek standards, yet an essential part of their aim was to make the Syriac represent in detail with slavish literalness the Greek text, including the order of words. Where Syriac idiom seemed to require an added pronoun or other word, Thomas marked these with an obelus, or sometimes (if our MS. of Acts can be

[1] That the ' Western ' readings of Acts now found in the Harclean apparatus were, if contained in the Philoxenian, drawn by the latter from the Old Syriac rather than from a Greek MS. used by Polycarp, is unlikely. For (1) the consistent Syrian tradition, beginning within a century of the date at which the Philoxenian version was made, held that Polycarp made it from the Greek. (2) In the books not previously translated, Polycarp clearly had for the Apocalypse a Greek MS. containing a strong ' Western ' element and for the four Catholic epistles a Greek text that was at any rate unusual. It is natural to suppose that the Greek text he used in the other books was of similar character. In our ignorance of the actual Philoxenian text it is impossible to say with confidence what sources besides the Peshitto (with which he was thoroughly imbued) and a Greek MS. Polycarp may have used, but nothing at present known seems to point to his use of the Old Syriac Acts.

trusted) with the same asterisk ordinarily used by him for a different purpose. Of this threefold apparatus a large part has been preserved for us in one of the two known MSS. of his Acts, how accurately and completely we cannot fully judge. The conditions in the other books show that there the apparatus was only imperfectly transmitted in the copies now known, although the oldest copies of the Gospels do not seem as yet to have been studied with reference to this question.

Such a view as this would entitle us to regard the ' Western ' readings in the margin and asterisked portions of the Harclean Acts as derived from a Greek MS. used in Mabog in 508.[1] But to this conclusion a serious objection presents itself. The ' Western ' glosses of the Harclean apparatus are written, at any rate in certain details, in the same peculiar grecizing style as the Harclean text itself. It is evident that in the form which they now wear they could not have stood in the original Philoxenian. One of the most pervasive traits of Thomas's mode of translation is the use of ﻭﺴـﻟﻮ, etc., for $a\vec{v}\tau o\hat{v}$, etc., instead of the mere pronominal suffix. This separate genitive pronoun is, indeed, found in the Philoxenian correctly enough where special emphasis is intended, and an appeal to that explanation would account for many of the cases where it appears in the Harclean margin, but it is also there found in contexts where no emphasis at all is required or permissible (e.g. Acts xii. 3). Similarly, the use of ﺴﻤﺤ for $\delta \iota \acute{a}$ in $\delta \iota \grave{a}$ $\nu \upsilon \kappa \tau \acute{o} \varsigma$, Acts xxiii. 24 margin, and in $\delta \iota \grave{a}$ $\iota \kappa \alpha \nu o \hat{v}$ $\chi \rho \acute{o} \nu o \upsilon$, Acts xi. 1 ⁂, is a glaring grecism. And the characteristic preferences of the Harclean appear in the apparatus. In Acts xvi. 39 ⁂ ﻭﻼﺴﻣ; ﺍـﻠﺴﺨﻗﻭ; ﻭ ﻭﻗﻭ all belong to the expressions which in the Apocalypse Thomas regularly substitutes for the corresponding words of the Philoxenian. In Acts xix. 1 mg ﻝ with the infinitive is used, rather than ﻭ with the finite verb, just as in the Harclean Apocalypse. So, Acts xi. 5 mg, ﻝﻮـﺴﻤ is used for $\lambda \alpha \mu \pi \rho \acute{o} \varsigma$, just as, in the Apocalypse,

---

[1] With such a view would agree the facts relating to the Syriac ' Euthalian ' apparatus to the Pauline epistles mentioned above, p. clv note 1.

Thomas has substituted it for the Philoxenian ܪܘܚܐ as the rendering of that Greek word; and likewise, Acts xiv. 1 *mg*, ܣܘܓܐܐ is used, not the Philoxenian ܟܢܫܐ. In the margin of Acts xiv. 18 εἰς τὰ ἴδια is represented by ܠܕܝܠܗܘܢ, and xiv. 19 ܠܟܢܫܐ ܕܝܢ seems intended to imitate the Greek article in τοὺς ὄχλους. In Acts xxiv. 14 the Harclean attaches a mark to the word ܕܐܡܪܝܢ, and in the margin writes ܘ, evidently with reference to a Greek reading λεγουσιν και (so the Greek codex 1611); in Syriac idiom the meaning of the Greek could not be so expressed, but ܐܦ (' also ') would be required. These are but illustrations.[1]

This evidence of grecizing, however, which has been sufficiently illustrated in the last paragraph, does not positively prove that the Harclean apparatus was merely added by Thomas from Greek sources, independently of the Philoxenian. Our best guide is to be found in the facts of the Philoxenian books which have come down to us. In the four minor epistles and the Apocalypse, although the material is meagre and the apposite cases few, yet it is clear that the Harclean margin and asterisked words in many cases certainly do, and in nearly all cases may, owe their origin to the Philoxenian text, and at the same time that some among them, whose Philoxenian origin is unmistakable, have been grecized. The grecizing process in those five books may have been applied either under the influence of a corresponding Greek MS. or, without the use of such a MS., merely by making the language conform to the general principles of Harclean grecizing style.[2] Whether the far more extensive Harclean apparatus in Acts requires the assumption that Thomas used a Greek MS. in preparing it is a question which can only be answered by Syriac scholars. There are three possibilities : Either (1) this apparatus

---

[1] Some of these illustrations I owe to Professor F. C. Burkitt and Mr. Norman McLean.

[2] In one of the cases from the Apocalypse (Rev. v. 5) the grecizing seen in the addition of ܗܘ, αὐτός, is unmistakable, but seems not to have been guided by a Greek MS., for no known Greek MS. has that reading.

consists of Philoxenian readings transformed into the Harclean
grecizing style on general principles, without the aid of a Greek
MS. ; or (2) the readings of the Philoxenian adopted for preservation in the apparatus were modified by the aid of a Greek MS. ;
or (3) the readings in question were not in the Philoxenian, and
are drawn solely from collation with a Greek MS. of utterly
different type from that " accurate and approved copy " which
Thomas adopted as a standard for his text. Whether the first
or the second of these three possibilities is to be adopted is not
certain. The third, however, I am disposed to reject, and that
for two reasons : first, because of the facts observable in the case
of the Apocalypse and the four epistles, and secondly, because it
is hard to see why Thomas in the seventh century in Alexandria,
having adopted the Antiochian text as a standard, should have
gone out of his way to preserve in Syriac a record of ' Western '
readings, unless something in the Syriac version which he was
revising suggested such a procedure and made it seem desirable.

Harclean
' Western '
readings
not Alex-
andrian.

Interesting as it would be to have this question settled, an
answer to it is not an indispensable prerequisite to the use of
this body of readings. They are certainly ' Western,' and were
certainly in existence in the early seventh century. Yet they
do not testify to a text used by Alexandrians. There is no
evidence, and it is not likely, that Polycarp's Greek MS. was
produced or preserved in Alexandria ; and, since the source of
the Harclean apparatus of Acts was not the Greek MS. referred
to in the subscription, and since thus no evidence exists that the
' Western ' readings of Thomas's apparatus were drawn from any
MS. which he obtained in Alexandria, the Harclean version
indicates nothing as to the currency of the ' Western ' Greek text
in Alexandria in the early seventh century. Thomas's ' Western '
Greek MS., if he had one, he may have brought with him from
Mesopotamia ; for aught we know, it may have been the identical
copy used a century earlier by Polycarp.

(e) PALESTINIAN

In (probably) the sixth century, pursuant to the proselytizing activities begun by the Emperor Justinian, translations from the New Testament, intended for the use of Aramaic-speaking Christians of Palestine, were made into the dialect used by Palestinian Samaritans and Jews. A few fragments of Acts in this translation, doubtless made from the current Greek text of Byzantium, have come down to us in the form of church-lessons, in MSS. of which the oldest are ascribed to the sixth century.[1] The published fragments from Acts cover i. 1-14 ; ii. 1-36 ; xiv. 5-13, 15-17 ; xvi. 16-35 ; xix. 31-xx. 14 ; xxi. 3-14, 28-30, 38-39 ; xxiv. 25-xxvi. 1 ; xxvi. 23-xxvii. 27.[2]

§ 5. OTHER VERSIONS

(a) ARMENIAN [3]

An Armenian version of the New Testament is said to have been made not later than A.D. 400. A translation of the Gospels may have been in existence in the days of St. Gregory the Illuminator († 332), but it would not follow that the Acts had been translated at that time. As might be expected, the translation of the Gospels, Pauline epistles, and Acts was made from

---

[1] F. C. Burkitt, ' Christian Palestinian Literature,' *Journal of Theological Studies*, vol. II., 1900–1, pp. 174-183 ; cf. also *ibid.* vol. VI., 1904–5, pp. 91-98.

[2] The texts are to be found in J. P. N. Land, *Anecdota Syriaca*, IV., Leyden, 1875, Syriac p. 168 ; G. Margoliouth, ' The Liturgy of the Nile,' *Journal of the Royal Asiatic Society*, London, 1896, pp. 702 f., 718-720 ; A. S. Lewis, *A Palestinian Syriac Lectionary* (Studia Sinaitica, VI.), London, 1897, pp. 131-135 ; H. Duensing, *Christlich-palästinisch-aramäische Texte und Fragmente*, Göttingen, 1906, pp. 149-151 ; A. S. Lewis, *Codex Climaci Rescriptus* (Horae Semiticae, VIII.), Cambridge, 1909, pp. 84-101.

[3] F. C. Conybeare, art. ' Armenian Version of N.T.,' in Hastings's *Dictionary of the Bible*, 1898 ; F. C. Kenyon, *Handbook to the Textual Criticism of the New Testament*, 2nd ed., 1912, pp. 172-174 ; J. A. Robinson, *Euthaliana* (Texts and Studies, iii.), 1895, pp. 72-98 ; H. Gelzer, art. ' Armenien,' in *Protestantische Realencyklopädie*, vol. ii., 1897, pp. 75-77. F. Macler, *Le Texte arménien d'après Matthieu et Marc* (Annales du Musée Guimet, Bibliothèque des études, XXVIII.), Paris, 1919, presents new materials and fresh views for the Armenian text of the Gospels ; cf. R. P. Blake, *Harvard Theol. Review*, XV., 1922, pp. 299-303.

the Syriac, which in Acts presented, at any rate largely, a form of the 'Western' text. Later, after the Council of Ephesus (431), the Armenian version was revised by the aid of Greek MSS. brought, it is said, from both Constantinople and Alexandria, and this revision is doubtless the version known to us from later copies.[1] The revision, it is clear, left unchanged a large number of ancient 'Western' readings.

The Armenian Bible was edited by Oscan, Amsterdam, 1666, and again by Zohrab, Venice, 1805. The latter edition is the source of the readings cited by Tischendorf, who obtained them from Tregelles. An edition with critical use of older MSS. than those employed by Zohrab, or at least with a critical investigation of the MSS. and a comparison with his edition, is greatly needed ; all the more because of the importance of the Armenian translation of the Commentary of Ephrem on Acts, of which a translation is printed in the present volume.

(b) GEORGIAN

Another version, neighbour to the Armenian, from which also, if it were adequately studied, profit might be derived for the textual criticism of Acts, is the Georgian, as used by the Georgians (also called Grusinians and Iberians) of the Caucasus, north-west of Armenia.[2] The Christian Church of Georgia is alleged to date from the early fourth century, the first translation of the Bible from the fifth. The translation has been subjected to later revision, and moreover the printed editions do not well

---

[1] The present Armenian text is said to show that the revision was made with the use of a Greek text resembling that of Bℵ ; F. C. Burkitt, *Encyclopaedia Biblica*, col. 5011. Compare what is said below of the Georgian version of Acts.

[2] F. C. Conybeare in *The Academy*, February 1, 1896, pp. 98 f. ; *id.*, ' The Georgian Version of the N.T.,' *Zeitschrift für die neutestamentliche Wissenschaft*, vol. XI., 1910, pp. 232-249 ; *id.*, ' The Old Georgian Version of Acts,' *ibid.* vol. XII., 1911, pp. 131-140 ; Theodor Kluge, ' Die georgischen Übersetzungen des "Neuen Testamentes,"' *ibid.* vol. XII., 1911, pp. 344-350; H. Goussen, ' Die georgische Bibelübersetzung,' *Oriens Christianus*, vol. vi., 1906, pp. 300-318 ; Harnack, *Mission und Ausbreitung des Christentums*, 4th ed., vol. ii., 1924, pp. 761 f.

represent the oldest extant MSS. Whether the version was originally made from Armenian or Syriac is disputed, but at least in certain parts of the Bible it is closely akin to the Armenian, although in its present form bearing evident traces of revision from the Greek.[1] The text of Acts in older MSS. seems to be very close to the Old Greek Uncials, with occasional Antiochian divergences. In a minute proportion of instances its departures from the Old Uncials may possibly be derived from a ' Western ' text, but the small number of these, and the intrinsic unimportance of most of them, make it impossible to draw any inference whatever from them.[2]

(c) ARABIC [3]

The Arabic versions, although found in many MSS., apparently yield but little for the purposes of textual criticism. All are comparatively late. " It was not till after the success of the Koran had made Arabic into a literary language, and the conquests of Islam had turned large portions of Christian Syria and Egypt into Arabic-speaking provinces, that the need of translations of Scripture in the Arabic vernacular was really felt." [4]

Of the Acts the following versions are known :

(1) A Sinai MS. of the ninth century contains a text which is a free translation from the Peshitto ; published in *Studia Sinaitica*, No. VII., Cambridge University Press, 1899.

(2) A version in two different recensions is found in the

---

[1] See the important article of F. C. Conybeare, 'The Growth of the Peshittâ Version of the New Testament illustrated from the Old Armenian and Georgian Versions,' *American Journal of Theology*, vol. I., 1897, pp. 883-912.

[2] The portions examined on which these statements rest are Acts v. 37-vii. 23, vii. 38-viii. 20, as rendered into Greek by Conybeare from an Athos MS. of A.D. 965 (not 13th century as Conybeare supposed), together with Acts xviii., of which Professor Robert P. Blake has furnished me with a translation from a tenth-century Tiflis MS. (Library of the Georgian Literary Society, No. 407).

[3] F. C. Burkitt, art. ' Arabic Versions,' Hastings's *Dictionary of the Bible*, vol. i. pp. 136-138 ; Gregory, *Prolegomena*, pp. 928-932.

[4] Burkitt, *op. cit.* p. 136.

Arabic New Testament of Erpenius, Leyden, 1616, and in that of Faustus Naironus, Rome, 1703. The former was chiefly drawn from an Egyptian MS. dated 1342–43 ; the latter was derived from a MS. brought from Cyprus, is in the Carshunic writing, and was intended for the use of the Maronites. This version is said to be from the Coptic, supplemented by readings drawn from the Peshitto and from the Greek.

(3) The Arabic text printed in the polyglots (Paris, 1645 ; Walton's, London, 1657) is said to be taken from a MS. brought from Aleppo, and to be a version made from a Greek text.

3. GREEK FATHERS

THE chief Latin and Syriac writers whose quotations come under consideration for the text of Acts have already been discussed in connexion with those versions. It remains to speak of the early Greek writers. For many of them no thorough investigation of their biblical text is available, and although the material to be examined is abundant, the student has at present to content himself with incomplete, merely general, or tentative, statements.

(a) EPISTLE OF BARNABAS ; POLYCRATES OF EPHESUS ; JUSTIN MARTYR ; DIDACHE

Barn. 5, 8-9 πέρας γέ τοι διδάσκων τὸν Ἰσραὴλ καὶ Barnabas.
τηλικαῦτα τέρατα καὶ σημεῖα ποιῶν ἐκήρυσσεν, καὶ ὑπερ-
ηγάπησεν αὐτόν. ὅτε δὲ τοὺς ἰδίους ἀποστόλους τοὺς
μέλλοντας κηρύσσειν τὸ εὐαγγέλιον αὐτοῦ ἐξελέξατο, ὄντας
ὑπὲρ πᾶσαν ἁμαρτίαν ἀνομωτέρους, ἵνα δείξῃ ὅτι οὐκ ἦλθεν
καλέσαι δικαίους ἀλλὰ ἁμαρτωλούς, τότε ἐφανέρωσεν ἑαυτὸν
εἶναι υἱὸν Θεοῦ.

It seems likely that this is an allusion to the ' Western ' text of Acts i. 2, which (as retranslated from Augustine's quotation in *Contra Felicem*) seems to have read : ἐν ἡμέρᾳ ᾗ τοὺς ἀποστόλους ἐξελέξατο διὰ πνεύματος ἁγίου καὶ ἐκέλευσε κηρύσσειν τὸ εὐαγγέλιον.[1]

In the letter of Polycrates of Ephesus on the paschal contro- Polycrates. versy, written in the last decade of the second century (Eusebius,

[1] This was pointed out by J. Chapman, ' Barnabas and the Western Text of Acts,' *Revue Bénédictine*, vol. xxx., 1913, pp. 219-221.

H.e. v. 24, 7), the sentence from Acts v. 29 is quoted in the usual form πειθαρχεῖν δεῖ θεῷ μᾶλλον ἢ ἀνθρώποις, not in the interrogative form of the ' Western ' text (fully attested only in Latin witnesses, see Textual Note, below, pp. 50 f.).

Justin. Justin Martyr has left no express quotations from Acts, but his references to historical events and certain apparent reminiscences of phrases confirm the presumption afforded by his abundant use of the Gospel of Luke that he was acquainted with the book. Since in the Gospels he uses the ' Western ' text,[1] the same would be expected in Acts, and some measure of evidence of this may perhaps be found in the circumstance pointed out by Zahn [2] that (*Apol.* i. 40) he treats Psalms i. and ii. as a single piece (cf. Acts xiii. 33, ' Western '), and (*Dial.* 87 fin.) cites Joel ii. 28 f. as ἐν ἑτέρᾳ προφητείᾳ, without naming the prophet, as in the ' Western ' text of Acts ii. 16.[3] Justin's well-known practice of drawing his Old Testament quotations from Paul without acknowledgment lends probability to the view that in these instances he is dependent on the ' Western ' text of Acts.

Didache. In the Didache the (negative) Golden Rule is quoted (Did. 1, 2) in a form corresponding not to Tobit iv. 15 but to the ' Western ' text of Acts xv. 20, 29 : πάντα δὲ ὅσα ἐὰν θελήσῃς μὴ γίνεσθαί σοι καὶ σὺ ἄλλῳ μὴ ποίει (cf. also Theophilus, *Ad Autol.* vi. 34, and the conflate form in *Const. Apost.* vii. 1). It is not unlikely that the Didache drew the Rule from Acts ; similarly Didache 9 corresponds with the ' Western ' (and

---

[1] E. Lippelt, *Quae fuerint Justini Martyris* Ἀπομνημονεύματα *quaque ratione cum forma evangeliorum syro-latina cohaeserint* (Dissert. philol. Halenses xv.), 1901.

[2] Zahn, *Urausgabe*, pp. 234-236. For Justin's use of Acts see Zahn, *Geschichte des neutestamentlichen Kanons*, vol. i. 2, 1889, pp. 579-581.

[3] It should, however, be noticed that our text of Justin, *Dial.* 87, has the addition to the Old Testament of the words καὶ προφητεύσουσι (as in Acts ii. 18), which are not found in D or in Old Latin witnesses, nor in the chief LXX mss., and which may be a ' Western non-interpolation ' ; see Textual Note, below, p. 17.

probably original) text of Luke xxii. 17-19 in putting the cup
before the bread at the Lord's Supper.[1]

(b) IRENAEUS (ca. 185)

The copy of Acts used by Irenaeus was, like his copies of the
Gospels and the Pauline epistles, a Greek manuscript with a
thorough-going ' Western ' text, showing but few departures
from the complete ' Western ' type. If we can trust the present
text of the Latin translation of Irenaeus, his copy occasionally
omitted a ' Western ' gloss, for instance, x. 39, ' the Jews rejected
and ' ; x. 41 καὶ συνανεστράφημεν, ἡμέρας τεσσεράκοντα ;
xv. 26 εἰς πάντα πειρασμόν ; xvii. 28 τὸ καθ' ἡμέραν ; and in
rare instances contained a reading positively of the non-western
type, as in iii. 8, where ambulans et saliens et does not belong
to the ' Western ' text, or in iii. 17, scio for ἐπιστάμεθα of D h
arm. codd.

The date of the Latin translation of Irenaeus's great work is
disputed, as between the second or early third century and the
latter half of the fourth or early fifth, but probability seems to
lie with the view that it was made between 370 and 420, in North
Africa.[2] The first writer who certainly used it is Augustine. In
the citations from the Bible the translator, as has been proved,
followed closely the Greek text as quoted by Irenaeus,
but is thought to have aided himself by the use of an
Old Latin version, which in Acts appears to have been " a copy
closely related to h, which had sustained revision and had also

---

[1] Lake, Classical Review, vol. XI., 1897, pp. 147 f.

[2] So A. Souter in Novum Testamentum Sancti Irenaei (Old-Latin Biblical
Texts, No. VII.), 1923, see esp. pp. xv-xviii, lxv-cxi. In this work will
be found full discussion from various points of view of the questions relating to
the Latin of Irenaeus. The quotations of Irenaeus from Acts are given in full
in the present volume from the text of Novum Testamentum Sancti Irenaei,
through the generous courtesy of the surviving editor, Professor C. H. Turner,
and of the publishers. See B. Kraft, Die Evangelienzitate des heiligen Irenäus
(Biblische Studien, XXI.), 1924, who is inclined to assign the translation to
about the year 300 (p. 47), and points out certain precautions which need to
be observed in the use of the biblical quotations of Irenaeus.

been later to some extent brought into line with gig." [1] It
is, however, relatively seldom that the translator is generally
believed to have been drawn away from the biblical text of
Irenaeus's Greek by that of the Latin Bible which he used.

With regard to Irenaeus's text of the Old Testament, all that
is known seems to be that in 1-4 Kingdoms, for which the evidence
is meagre but distinct, Irenaeus goes with B, the Ethiopic, and
the ancient base of the Lucianic text, against both the hexaplaric
text and the common text of the later MSS.[2]

(c) CLEMENT OF ALEXANDRIA (ca. 150–ca. 215)

The few, but distinct, direct quotations from Acts found in
the writings of Clement of Alexandria follow a text substantially
like that of Bℵ, but with occasional variations from those MSS.[3]
In several instances of divergence Clement's text had a reading
similar to, though not always quite identical with, that attested
by one or more of the extant ' Western ' witnesses. Thus, Acts
x. 11 (*Paedag.* ii. 1, Potter, p. 175), ἐκδεδεμένον (where the
' Western ' text seems to have read δεδεμένον), xvii. 23 (*Strom.*
i. 19, Potter, p. 372), ἱστορῶν for ἀναθεωρῶν (D διστορῶν);
xvii. 26 (*ibid.*), γένος (614 minn), xvii. 27 (*ibid.*) τὸ θεῖον (D gig

---

[1] Souter, *l.c.* pp. clxiii-clxv. Souter suggests (p. xcvi) that the translation
of Irenaeus is by the same hand (a Greek) from which we have the Latin of
Origen's Commentary on Matthew. J. Chapman, ' Did the Translator of St.
Irenaeus use a Latin New Testament ? ' *Revue Bénédictine*, vol. xxxvi., 1924,
pp. 34-51, holds that the translator always rendered the Greek text as quoted
by Irenaeus, and never altered the text under the influence of any Latin version,
although he knew a Latin version (but one wholly indeterminable by us), and
it " occasionally, but rarely, ran in his head " ; our MSS. of Irenaeus, according
to Chapman, have all been somewhat influenced by the Vulgate.

[2] Rahlfs, *Lucians Rezension der Königsbücher*, pp. 116-118, 138.

[3] P. M. Barnard, *The Biblical Text of Clement of Alexandria in the Four
Gospels and the Acts of the Apostles* (Texts and Studies v.), 1899, with ' Introduction ' by F. C. Burkitt (esp. p. xvii) ; the passages from Clement are given
in full, pp. 62-64. The quotations by Clement on which the statements in the
text above are founded are Acts i. 7 (*Strom.* iii. 6), ii. 26-28 (*Strom.* vi. 6), ii. 41
(*Strom.* i. 18), vi. 2 (*Paedag.* ii. 7), vii. 22 (*Strom.* i. 23), x. 10-15 (*Paedag.* ii. 1),
x. 34 f. (*Strom.* vi. 8), xv. 23 (*Paedag.* ii. 7), xv. 28 f. (*Paedag.* ii. 7 ; *Strom.* iv.
15), xvii. 22-28 (*Strom.* i. 19, v. 11-12), xxvi. 17 f. (*Strom.* i. 19).

Iren). The most noteworthy citation is that of Acts xv. 28 f.
(*Paedag.* ii. 7, Potter, p. 202 ; *Strom.* iv. 15, Potter, p. 606),
where Clement's text is closely like Bℵ and almost identical
with A. This passage is the earliest witness to the inclusion of
καὶ πνικτῶν, and seems to show that Clement did not read in
his text the (negative) Golden Rule.

In the Gospels Clement's text was predominantly, but not
completely, ' Western,' not that of Bℵ ; [1] in the Pauline epistles,
as in Acts, it corresponds in general with the type of Bℵ.[2]

For the Old Testament, in Judges Clement follows the older
text of A, not the Egyptian revision found in B ; [3] in 1-4 Kingdoms his text has close contact with B ; [4] in the Psalter his text
shows clear agreement both with that of Upper Egypt (see above,
pp. xciii-v) and with B, although, as found in our MSS. (tenth
and eleventh centuries), it seems also to have been in part
corrected to agree with the Psalter of the later minuscules.[5]
Since the text of Upper Egypt in the Psalter bears somewhat the
same relation to the text of B as does the base of the ' Western '
text in the New Testament (see above, p. xciv), the analogy
of the combination of ancient elements in Clement's Psalter with
the well-known corresponding combination in his Gospels is
striking.[6]

(d) ORIGEN (*ca.* 185–254)

Origen's text of Acts [7] was that of the Old Uncials (BℵAC 81).

[1] Burkitt, *l.c.* pp. vii-xix.
[2] Souter, *Text and Canon of the New Testament*, p. 81.
[3] G. F. Moore, *Critical and Exegetical Commentary on Judges*, p. xlvi.
[4] Rahlfs, *Lucians Rezension der Königsbücher*, pp. 118-122, 138.
[5] Rahlfs, *Der Text des Septuaginta-Psalters*, 1907, pp. 208-210.
[6] The general conclusion of Otto Stählin, *Clemens Alexandrinus und die Septuaginta*, Nürnberg, 1901, p. 77, is : " Durchweg zeigt sich eine Verschiedenheit zwischen dem Bibeltext bei Clemens und dem Codex B." Of this conclusion Rahlfs would make some qualifications for certain books of the Old Testament.
[7] The evidence as to Origen's text of Acts can be gathered by the aid of the full indexes of the Berlin edition and of De la Rue. It is carefully given by Tregelles ; Tischendorf's statements are not always correct. The observations of von Soden (*Die Schriften des Neuen Testaments*, pp. 1836 f.) are not substantially different from the judgment stated above, when translated into language not framed from his own theory. He holds that Origen in the Acts (as in the

This is clear, notwithstanding his freedom of citation [1] and the
brevity of most of his citations from Acts. Thus (*Contra Celsum*,
ii. 1) he quotes Acts x. 9-15 in a text which consistently follows
BℵAC 81 against both 'Western' and Antiochian readings,
and numerous other citations and allusions, mostly brief but
occurring through a wide range of his works, evince the same
source.

A few cases of trifling importance where his citation agrees
with the Antiochian text (for instance, *Comm. in Matt.* x. 18,
Acts i. 8 μοι for μου, πάσῃ for ἐν πάσῃ ; *De orat.* xxvii. 12, Acts
x. 12 ἑρπετὰ καὶ θηρία) are not significant exceptions; they
sometimes stand in free summaries, and may be explained on
any one of several theories. His text shows no specific 'Western'
character, although here and there it agrees with D or d against
the Old Uncials (for instance, *Contra Celsum*, i. 5, vi. 11, Acts
v. 36 μέγαν ; *Hom. in Jerem.* xiii. 3, Acts vii. 39 om αὐτῶν), but
these agreements are very few in number, and most of them are
explicable as inaccuracies of quotation or the combination in
memory of two parallel passages. Moreover, the currency of
such a reading as Acts v. 36 μέγαν was by no means limited to
the circle of 'Western' authorities (cf. A^corr minn Cyril Alex.).

As between the texts of the several Old Uncials, no close
relation of Origen to any one can be certainly shown in view of
the scantiness of the evidence. But his reading frequently
agrees with B.

Gospels, pp. 1510-1520) used the I-H-K text, that is (p. 1520), the text current
in the third century, in distinction from the special recensions which can be
recognized.

[1] The idea of differences of text in the copies of the Bible used by Origen's
several amanuenses has been shown by E. Klostermann, *Göttingische gelehrte
Anzeigen*, 1904, pp. 267-269, to lack the support which E. Preuschen, *Zeitschrift
für die neutest. Wissenschaft*, vol. iv., 1903, pp. 67-74, and *Origenes Werke*,
IV. *Der Johanneskommentar*, 1903, pp. lxxxviii-ci, thought he had found
for it; and it is in itself highly improbable that a critical student of the text
like Origen should have failed to regulate the copies provided in his own scriptorium for his assistants, or their practice in the use of them. Streeter's
discovery (see below) of the use of two distinct texts by Origen (Old Uncial
and Caesarean) has put this whole matter in a new light.

A few instances are here given, of which the most noteworthy is the first :

ii. 44 (*Comm. in Matt.* tom. xv. 15) om ἦσαν, om
    καί before εἶχον . . . . . B min
xvi. 17 (*Comm. in Joh.* tom. xxviii. 16) om τῷ
    before Παύλῳ . . . . . B
xxi. 23 (*De orat.* iii. 4) ἀφ᾽ for ἐφ᾽ . . . Bℵ
vii. 43 (*Contra Celsum*, v. 8) om ὑμῶν . . . BD
    ,,   ,,   ,,   ῥόμφα . . . BS
xii. 13 (*Comm. in Matt.* tom. xiii. 28 ; De la Rue,
    iii. p. 608) προσῆλθεν . . . . B*A 81 D
ii. 44 (*Comm. in Matt.* tom. xv. 15) πιστεύοντες . AC 81 D

In the Gospels Origen used for some purposes an Old Uncial text, but for others, after his removal from Alexandria, employed the Caesarean text (the so-called ' fam Θ ').[1] In the Old Testament, in so far as Origen does not quote his own hexaplaric text, he uses in 1-4 Kingdoms a text closely like that of B (with which agree the Ethiopic, the ancient base of the Lucianic, and in a less measure the Sahidic),[2] in the Psalter a text like that of B (and the Bohairic). On the text used by Origen as the basis for the Septuagint column of the Hexapla, see above, pp. xci-xcvii.

(e) DIDASCALIA APOSTOLORUM ; APOSTOLIC CONSTITUTIONS I.-VI.

The Didascalia Apostolorum (third century ; Syria or Palestine) is the source which has been expanded, interpolated, and corrected by a writer of *ca.* 400 (Syria) to produce Books I.-VI. of the Apostolic Constitutions.[3]

---

[1] See the highly significant investigation of B. H. Streeter, *The Four Gospels : A Study of Origins*, 1924, pp. 78-102, 585-589 ; also Souter, *Text and Canon of the New Testament*, p. 83. E. Hautsch, *Die Evangelienzitate des Origenes* (Texte und Untersuchungen, xxxiv.), 1909, p. 4, from a study of the Gospel quotations, reached the conclusion that in his several works, written under varying conditions, Origen used different copies of the New Testament.

[2] Rahlfs, *Lucians Rezension der Königsbücher*, pp. 129 f. ; *Studien zu den Königsbüchern* (Septuaginta-Studien, i.), pp. 47-87.

[3] F. X. Funk, *Didascalia et Constitutiones Apostolorum*, Paderborn, 1905, contains a full index of Scripture passages.

The Didascalia contains a number of citations from Acts, of which the most important occur in vi. 12, where the writer has curiously interwoven parts of Acts x. and xv.   His text of Acts was plainly not the Antiochian.   Thus for xv. 17 f., xv. 23, he clearly is not using that text, and he nowhere uses any reading certainly distinctive of the Antiochian text.   Of ' Western ' readings positive traces are to be observed, for instance :

Acts x. 11 the omission of καταβαῖνον from its proper place early
    in the phrase ; [1]
    xv. 1 ' except ye be circumcised and walk according to the
        law of Moses ' (D hcl.*mg* sah) ;
    xv. 10 ' the necks,' plural (d vg. *codd*) ;
    xv. 11 ' through the grace of our Lord Jesus Christ ' (CD) ;
    xv. 23 ' writing by their hands this letter ' (cf. D hcl.*mg* sah) ;
    xv. 29 πράξατε for πράξετε (CD).

It must not be overlooked that virtually all our knowledge of the Didascalia comes from a Syriac, and from a fragmentary Latin, translation of a Greek text, and that the amount of evidence is small at best.   Occasional non-western readings are found in the Syriac Didascalia, but in at least three such passages (and those the most important), Acts x. 9, 11, xv. 1-5, and xv. 20 (all found in Didascalia vi. 12, where the Latin is not available), there are reasons for suspecting that the original reading of the

---

[1] καταβαῖνον properly belongs only in the text (Old Uncial) in which the sheet-like vessel is said to be ' *lowered* by the four corners.'   In the ' Western ' text the vessel was said to be ' *tied* by the four corners and lowered (καθιέμενον).' This latter was clearly the basis of the text found in the Didascalia, but from the other text the word καταβαῖνον (with the necessary καί preceding) has been added redundantly after καθιέμενον in the Didascalia.   By the Antiochian revisers, with a similar, but different, conflation, the Old Uncial text adopted by them as their basis was modified by adding the ' Western ' δεδεμένον (with following καί) before καθιέμενον.   It would seem that the reviser of the Didascalia whose hand we detect in the Syriac version, did not venture completely to substitute the Antiochian text (with its wholly different structure) for the ' Western ' which he found in his exemplar, but tried by his addition to produce a text which should be in substantial (although not formal) agreement with the Antiochian.   The method which he employed made it impossible to complete the process by inserting the ἐπ' αὐτόν with which the Antiochian revisers had supplemented καταβαῖνον.   See below, pp. cxciii, excviii, 93.

Didascalia has been modified so as partially to accord with a non-western (probably Antiochian) text.

These reasons depend on the well-established fact that the Didascalia is the source which the author of the Apostolic Constitutions has expanded to form Books I.-VI. of his comprehensive work, and may be presented as follows :

(a) In Acts x. 11 such tampering with the text is disclosed by the fact that the present text of the Didascalia is not the true non-western, but is both defective (in omitting ὡς ὀθόνην μεγάλην) and confused (through the introduction of καταβαῖνον not in its proper place, but after καθιέμενον, as has been explained at length in the note on p. cxcii).[1]

(b) Acts xv. 1-5. The facts here can best be made clear by parallel columns.

[1] In view of the other instances it is natural to suspect that when the Syriac Didascalia reproduces Acts x. 9, ' I went up on a roof to pray,' in language closely like that of the usual text, the original form was, as in the Constitutions, ἦν ἐν τῷ ὑπερῴῳ προσευχόμενος (or something closely like it), but of this hypothesis no particular confirmation suggests itself from eithre document.

xv. 1

CODEX BEZAE.	DIDASCALIA.	ANTIOCHIAN TEXT.	APOSTOLIC CONSTITUTIONS.
ἐὰν μὴ περιτμηθῆτε καὶ τῷ ἔθει Μωϋσέως περιπατῆτε,	Except ye be circumcised and walk according to the law of Moses and be cleansed from meats and from all the other things,	ἐὰν μὴ περιτέμνησθε τῷ ἔθει Μωϋσέως,	ἐὰν μὴ περιτμηθῆτε τῷ ἔθει Μωϋσέως καὶ τοῖς ἄλλοις ἔθεσιν οἷς διετάξατο περιπατῆτε,
οὐ δύνασθε σωθῆναι.	ye cannot be saved.	οὐ δύνασθε σωθῆναι.	οὐ δύνασθε σωθῆναι.

xv. 4-5

CODEX BEZAE.	DIDASCALIA.	ANTIOCHIAN TEXT.	APOSTOLIC CONSTITUTIONS.
4. παραγενόμενοι δὲ εἰς Ἱερουσαλήμ,	And when they were come to Jerusalem,	παραγενόμενοι δὲ εἰς Ἱερουσαλήμ,	οἱ δὲ παραγενόμενοι εἰς Ἱερουσαλήμ,
ἀπήγγειλάν τε (MS. ἀπηγγειλαντες)	they told us	ἀνήγγειλάν τε	ἀνήγγειλαν ἡμῖν
. . . . .	about the dispute which they had in the church of Antioch ;	. . . . .	τὰ ζητηθέντα ἐν τῇ Ἀντιοχέων ἐκκλησίᾳ,
5. ἐξανέστησαν λέγοντές †τινες ἀπὸ τῆς αἱρέσεως τῶν Φαρισαίων πεπιστευκότες† ὅτι δεῖ περιτέμνειν αὐτοὺς παραγγέλλειν δὲ τηρεῖν τὸν νόμον Μωϋσέου.	and there arose some who believed, of the doctrine of the Pharisees, and said, It is necessary to be circumcised and to keep the law of Moses.	ἐξανέστησαν δέ τινες τῶν ἀπὸ τῆς αἱρέσεως τῶν Φαρισαίων πεπιστευκότες, λέγοντες ὅτι δεῖ περιτέμνειν αὐτοὺς παραγγέλλειν τε τηρεῖν τὸν νόμον Μωϋσέος.	καὶ ἔλεγον ὅτι δεῖ περιτέμνεσθαι καὶ τὰς ἄλλας ἁγνείας παραφυλάττειν.

Here for Acts xv. 1 the Didascalia has a free paraphrase, obviously based on the expanded 'Western' text, but still further enlarged by the noteworthy phrase ' and be cleansed from meats and from all the other things,' this being apparently the original (and not at all unsuitable) addition of the writer of the Didascalia himself. The author of the Constitutions, with his summary καὶ τοῖς ἄλλοις ἔθεσιν οἷς διετάξατο, made this more conventional and less striking, and further, in conformity to his Antiochian standard, connected τῷ ἔθει Μωυσέως with περιτμηθῆτε (notice, however, the aorist tense, as in the Old Uncials and D), but has not wholly eliminated the influence of the ' Western ' text due to the Didascalia. At the opening of verse 5 the Syriac Didascalia (like Codex Bezae) has added (doubtless from the Antiochian text) the reference to the converted Pharisees, which the Constitutions do not have and which (see below, p. 140) probably was not a part of that verse in the ' Western ' text. Further, in verse 5, where the closing phrase of the Didascalia is ' and to keep the law of Moses,' just as in the ordinary text of Acts (except for the omission of παραγγέλλειν), the Constitutions present the remarkable paraphrase τὰς ἄλλας ἁγνείας παραφυλάττειν (without παραγγέλλειν). These words are in no way derived from the Antiochian, or any other, text of Acts, and hence are unlikely to be an original alteration by the author of the Constitutions ; their obvious resemblance to the enlargement introduced at verse 1 in the Didascalia gives the key. Probably words closely like those now found in the Constitutions originally stood in the Didascalia, and were left with little or no change by the author of the Constitutions, while in the Didascalia itself the Syriac translator (or possibly a preceding Greek reviser) substituted for the original paraphrase a phrase drawn from the current biblical text of his day.

(c) In the reproduction of Acts xv. 20 in the Didascalia, ' and what is strangled ' stands in its usual (third) place among the four provisos, while the Constitutions, by the unusual position of καὶ πνικτοῦ at the end of the list, betray that these words are an addition.[1] It is impossible to suppose that the order of the Didascalia, which is in accord with the general custom, was altered by the Constitutions so as to produce a unique text. We must conclude either that the peculiar order was found in the original Didascalia and taken over by the Constitutions, or else (what is far more likely) that the Didascalia originally contained the 'Western,' text with only three provisos, and that this was modified by the author of the Constitutions, who made the sentence conform in substance, though not in order, to the Antiochian text that he was following as his standard. In either case the text of the Syriac Didascalia is seen to be an alteration of the original Greek.

Thus every one of these passages leads to the conclusion that the text of the quotations from Acts in the Didascalia was originally completely ' Western,' and has been occasionally modified in our Syriac version. The conclusion needs to be further investigated as to its applicability to quotations drawn from other books of the Bible.[2]

In the Old Testament the Didascalia in 1-4 Kingdoms likewise shows itself not under the influence of the Lucianic text, and here again the Constitutions have in one case (4 Kingdoms xxi. 13) preserved portions of the old text which are not certainly to be identified in the Syriac and Latin Didascalia.[3] The Didascalia quotes Ezek. xxxiv. 4 from Theodotion, doubtless from an hexaplaric Greek manuscript.[4] The quotation is not changed in the Constitutions (ii. 18 and 20).

[1] Later (vi. 12, 15), in quoting the words of the decree itself, Acts xv. 29, both Didascalia and Constitutions observe the usual order of the four specifications.

[2] Flemming, in H. Achelis and J. Flemming, *Die syrische Didaskalia übersetzt und erklärt* (Texte und Untersuchungen, xxv.), 1904, p. 251, expresses the conviction that in not a few cases, other than in biblical quotations, it is possible to emend the text of the Didascalia from the corresponding reading of the Constitutions. This method was employed in an exaggerated manner by Lagarde in his reconstruction of the Greek text of the Didascalia in Bunsen's *Analecta Ante-Nicaena*, vol. ii., 1854, but the validity of it within suitable limits has not been sufficiently recognized by many later scholars.

[3] Rahlfs, *Lucians Rezension der Königsbücher*, pp. 130-137, esp. pp. 136 f.

[4] E. Nestle, *Zeitschrift für die neutestamentliche Wissenschaft*, vol. i., 1900, pp. 176 f.

In the Apostolic Constitutions, Books I.-VI., evidence as to Apostolic Constitu-tions. the text of Acts employed by the interpolator and editor is to be found in some briefer citations, but especially (as in the Didascalia) in the extensive quotations from Acts x. and xv. in Const. vi. 12, where the interpolator has added much biblical matter not found in the Didascalia which he had before him. The interpolator lived in a time and country in which, we are told by St. Jerome, the Lucianic text of the LXX was dominant, and it is natural that his work should show that he had at hand an Antiochian text of Acts, for instance, in Acts xv. 18 (ἐστι τῷ θεῷ πάντα τὰ ἔργα αὐτοῦ, where the Didascalia rests on a text that lacked the sentence). But other passages of the Constitutions, probably derived from the Didascalia, show the influence of the ' Western ' text. In Acts x. 11 the Constitutions (vi. 12, 6) quote in full, and almost exactly, the ' Western ' text which, in agreement with d, must have stood on the lost page of D.[1] Other specifically ' Western ' readings (see above) are :

viii. 19 ἵνα + κἀγώ (Const. ap. vi. 7, 3 ; D perp) ;

viii. 21 τῷ λόγῳ τούτῳ] τῇ πίστει ταύτῃ (Const. ap. vi. 7, 4 ; cf. perp gig Aug pesh).

xv. 1 Μωυσέως + καὶ τοῖς ἄλλοις ἔθεσιν οἷς διετάξατο περιπατῆτε (Const. ap. vi. 12, 2 ; cf. D hcl.*mg.* sah).

xv. 20 The very unusual, and probably unique, position of καὶ πνικτοῦ (note the singular, which is Antiochian) at the end of the list in Const. ap. vi. 12, 13 suggests that it may have been added to a ' Western ' text including only the three provisos.

In its abridgment of Acts xv. 1-5 the account in the Constitutions (like the ' Western ' text) does not involve the inconsistency of the ordinary text (here by contamination found also in Codex Bezae), in which the controversy seems to be initiated first at Antioch (v. 1) and again independently at Jerusalem (v. 5).

[1] See Textual Note, below, p. 93.

The most natural explanation of all the facts is clearly that stated above, that the ' Western ' readings and allusions of the Constitutions are due to ' Western ' readings in the underlying Didascalia (of the original Greek of which we have but imperfect knowledge) which the interpolator, using for himself the Antiochian text, failed to eliminate.[1] This fully accounts for the otherwise most surprising citation of the pure ' Western ' text of Acts x. 11 by the Constitutions alone among Greek sources. But the evidence is meagre.

(f) Eusebius ; Cyril of Jerusalem ; Epiphanius

These three writers show, at least in some parts of the New Testament, a certain relation to the ' Western ' text, but evidently in a weakened form.

Eusebius (ca. 265–340), who used in the Gospels a text with distinctly ' Western ' character,[2] had a text of Acts lacking Antiochian tendency, but for the most part (so far as his quotations permit a judgment) agreeing with one or more of the Old Uncials against the ' Western '—in both these respects much like the text of Origen.

Cyril of Jerusalem (ca. 315–386) is said to show for Acts the use of a text of ' Western ' affinities.[3]

Of Epiphanius (ca. 315–403) the same can be said, but his text occasionally agrees with the Antiochian readings.[4]

(g) Athanasius ; Didymus ; Cyril of Alexandria ; Cosmas Indicopleustes

Of these writers all except Cosmas are known to have had their birth, education, and activity in Alexandria, while the merchant,

---

[1] A similar situation seems to be present in the Old Testament citations from the books of Kingdoms ; Rahlfs, *Lucians Rezension der Königsbücher*, pp. 136 f.   [2] Hort, ' Introduction,' p. 113.

[3] Von Soden, *Die Schriften des Neuen Testaments*, p. 1759.

[4] *Ibid.*   It is not impossible that a renewed study of the text of these writers would throw fresh light on the locality and history of the text contained in the various groups of manuscripts designated as I by von Soden.

and later monk, Cosmas, chiefly notable as a traveller, was
perhaps a native of that city, at any rate found in it the stable
centre of his roving earlier period, and spent his later years of
devout retirement at no very great distance from it. All four
used an Alexandrian text of the Bible similar to that of our Old
Uncials, and from their citations, if these are ever thoroughly
studied, fuller knowledge than is now at hand may be expected
with regard to the history of that text. Such knowledge would
furnish instruction for the study of the codices themselves, and
ought to throw light on the very important questions of how far
the text of the Old Uncials and their minuscule successors is to
be attributed to learned recensions, and of the significance of
Antiochian readings in the Old Uncials.

The demonstrated relation of Codex Vaticanus to Athanasius
(295-373) invites the hope that a study of his citations, made
with due regard to the problem of the text of Athanasius's own
writings, would be of value. He uses for Acts, as elsewhere, the
Old Uncial text, in clear distinction from the Antiochian and the
' Western.' Of his relation to our several extant codices nothing
appears to be known.[1] The same statement seems to be the only
one that can be made at present with regard to his contemporary
Didymus (313–398), and to Cyril of Alexandria († 444).[2]

Cosmas Indicopleustes (wrote 547) likewise uses a text of the
Old Uncial type in his extensive quotations from Acts. The copy
from which these were taken was not specially related to any
one of the group BℵAC 81, and shows nothing whatever of the
peculiarities of B, with which he never agrees except in company
with one or more of the other members of the group. Antiochian
readings seldom occur except when they are found in one or

---

[1] Von Soden, pp. 1672 f. Von Soden's mention of Migne's edition of
Athanasius seems to imply that he used that only in his study ; if so, this puts
an unfortunate limitation on the sufficiency of his results. A similar question
arises with reference to Didymus and Cyril.

[2] Von Soden, pp. 1673 f. Hort, ' Introduction,' p. 141, says : " At Alexandria
itself the Alexandrian tradition lives on through the fourth century, more or
less disguised with foreign accretions, and then in the early part of the fifth
century reappears comparatively pure in Cyril."

another of the Old Uncial group. For the Gospels Cosmas is said to have used " a late Alexandrian type of text, like L." [1]

Early in the seventh century Alexandria became the prey of the Arabs, and Greek Christian writers, who might have used the text of the Old Uncials, no longer appear.

(h) CHRYSOSTOM

The text of the Gospels and Pauline Epistles used by Chrysostom was substantially, but not exclusively, Antiochian. The other element seems to have come from the late text (the ' I-text ' of von Soden) found in mixed minuscules,[2] not from the Old Uncial text (the ' H-text '). In the Acts, Chrysostom's text is likewise mainly Antiochian,[3] but his homilies on Acts (delivered *ca.* 400) show abundant reference to characteristic ' Western ' glosses.

The homilies are found in two forms, and these may go back to distinct originals ; it is possible that we have reports written down by two different hearers. One form is found in the New College, Oxford, MS., used by Savile for his edition (1612, vol. v.) ; the other was printed by Fronto Ducaeus and his successors (Paris, 1609–1636), and reprinted by Montfaucon (Paris, 1718–1738, vol. ix.) and Migne. The excerpts from Chrysostom of the Armenian Catena on Acts (Venice, 1839) [4] represent the same text as the New College MS., possibly somewhat reinforced by ' Western ' readings drawn from Ephrem. This text contains more allusions to ' Western ' readings than does that of Fronto Ducaeus. The text used by Chrysostom as found in the homilies calls for further investigation.[5]

---

[1] Souter, *Text and Canon of the New Testament*, p. 85.

[2] Von Soden, pp. 1460 f.

[3] Hort, 'Introduction,' p. 91.

[4] The same Catena of which the sections drawn from Ephrem are printed in the present volume, pp. 381 ff.

[5] F. C. Conybeare, ' On the Western Text of the Acts as Evidenced by Chrysostom,' *American Journal of Philology*, vol. XVII., 1896, pp. 135-171. In this article (pp. 149-170) the full evidence from the Armenian Catena and from Savile's Greek is given in the case of many readings of Acts. See also

The text of Acts used by some others of the Greek fathers would doubtless, if better known, give aid in understanding the relations of our best MSS. and in determining their value. The most ancient of these MSS. are hardly, if at all, older than the works of Alexandrian, Palestinian, Antiochian, and Constantino-politan writers whose works are extant but whose evidence as to the New Testament text has been largely neglected. The Cappadocian fathers, Theodore of Mopsuestia, Theodoret, and others,[1] as well as those of whom something has been said above, need to be investigated in order that the history of the text after the rise of the Antiochian recension in the fourth century may be understood. Only through knowledge, or at least through a detailed and well-grounded theory, of that history can the wilderness of the later New Testament MSS., into which von Soden's great work has now cut some vistas, be adequately explored and mapped.

Conybeare's notes to the translation of the Commentary of Ephrem, below. It is to be observed that the views presented by Conybeare in 1896, that Chrysostom used the commentary of an older father to whom the ' Western ' readings were due, and that the Armenian rests on a fuller text than that of the New College MS. and Savile, are withdrawn in his later discussion, as now published.

    [1] Possibly Eustathius, patriarch of Antioch, *ca.* 323–330, used a ' Western ' text ; see H. C. Hoskier, *Concerning the Date of the Bohairic Version*, London, 1911, pp. 118 f.

II. THE CRITICISM AND HISTORY OF THE GREEK TEXT

1. INTRODUCTORY CONSIDERATIONS

THE witnesses to the text described above fall naturally, for Acts as for the other chief books of the New Testament, into three major groups, the members of each of which so often agree with their fellows within the group as to make it certain that the group draws its text largely from a common Greek ancestor. The three texts to which these groups point are called in this volume :

> (a) the Old Uncial text ;
> (b) the ' Western ' text ;
> (c) the Antiochian text.

The first two take their name from the most important extant representatives of the text ; the third from the place where the text was definitely formed. The term ' Old Uncial ' is used to cover what Westcott and Hort included in their " Neutral " and their " Alexandrian " text ; the term ' Antiochian ' has been preferred to their name " Syrian " as less likely to cause confusion. The unsatisfactory nature of the term ' Western ' is acknowledged, but a more convenient, and at the same time exact, name for the text in question does not present itself.

Within each of these major groups sub-groups disclose themselves, marked by participation in definite series of variant readings. To elicit these sub-groups and determine their relation to one another constitutes a large part of the work (much of it not yet performed) of preparing the material for the history of the text of the New Testament. Fortunately textual criticism properly so called, the determination of what are to be accepted as the original words of the authors, can generally be pursued with sound results by observing merely the major grouping of the witnesses. With hardly an exception the difficulty arising from the mixed character of the text in our witnesses of older and middle date is to be met, as Westcott and Hort pointed out, by dealing primarily with the common readings of notable groups, not with the evidence of single witnesses. But in order that criticism may be thoroughly convincing, it requires to be rein-forced by a well-established view of textual history, adequate for the rational explanation of the origin of the various types and of their relation to the supporting witnesses. The task will not be completely absolved until in this way the whole history of the text has been elucidated, including the later development down to the period of the printed New Testament. Only when all the late witnesses are fully understood and explained will the study of textual criticism lose its significance. The practical import-ance, however, of the study of the later forms of the text is chiefly to ensure that all out-of-the-way survivals of ancient texts which may conceivably be genuine readings, have been discovered and registered.

In the text of the Greek Bible, in both Testaments, the forces at work in producing the existing situation have been two : (1) free variation (both accidental and deliberate) and rewriting ; (2) learned recension intended to produce a definite, and in some cases an authoritative, text, together with the influence of scholars who have preferred some definite type of text and pro-moted its use. In both Testaments some of these recensions or preferred texts can be recognized and identified ; others will no doubt be determined by future inquiry. From the point of view of the study of these forces the following brief sketch of the history of the text of Acts is here outlined. The aim is to direct attention in the history to the succession of what may be called ' phases ' of the text. These are not exactly chronological stages

Phases in the history of the text.

or events, following one another (although they correspond in part to such stages), for the documents in each group in many cases had their actual origin at dates separated by long intervals of time. Many strokes in such a picture have to be guided by knowledge as yet imperfect, and in its details the sketch is presented with due reserve. Yet the general lines are, I believe, true to the history. It differs from Westcott and Hort's account chiefly in its method of grouping, rather than in the judgments of fact on which it rests.

For other books of the New Testament than Acts the sketch would require some modification. It will be observed that the classification reached in this way is different from that stated above, and it is presented as historically significant and suggestive, not as a practical classification of texts, adapted for direct use in textual criticism proper. For the latter purpose the familiar distribution into families noted by Bengel — designated by Griesbach as Alexandrian, Western, and Byzantine, and carried further by Westcott and Hort through their division of the Alexandrian family into Neutral and Alexandrian—is appropriate and, indeed, necessary.

(1) *The Primitive Phase.* In this phase the text was subject to free variation, both accidental and deliberate, and to elaborate rewriting ; many variants were present in different documents ; and the actual copying was far less subject to control than at a later time, and was often very inaccurate.[1] Here substantially belong most of the papyrus fragments, Codices BℵD, the Greek

[1] J. L. Hug, *Einleitung in die Schriften des Neuen Testaments*, 4th ed., 1847, pp. 121-127, recognized this phase of the history of the text, and applied to it the term κοινὴ ἔκδοσις, which he drew from the Alexandrian grammarians (cf. also Jerome, *Ep.* 106, *ad Sunniam et Fretelam*, 2). To it he referred Codex Bezae, but he failed to see that D represents a *rewriting* (though not in the proper sense a learned ' recension ') within this primitive phase and period. The term κοινή properly designates ' the unrevised text ' (like Westcott and Hort's name, ' neutral ') in contrast to a definite recension or recensions. The use of K(oinê) by von Soden to denote the Antiochian text was not in accord with ancient usage, although, as it happens, Jerome (*Ep.* 106) states that many applied the name ' Lucianic ' to the ' common ' text of the LXX, both terms alike serving to mark a distinction from the hexaplaric recension ; see Rahlfs, *Der Text des Septuaginta-Psalters*, pp. 170 f.

text underlying the African Latin, the text, partly conformed to a standard, from which the Sahidic was drawn, and the text used by Clement of Alexandria and (in somewhat less degree) that of Origen.[1] Attempts at recension were doubtless made within the limits of this phase ; in some centres standard copies were recognized ; and the early mixture which is unmistakable thus arose. But such early recensions have not as yet been identified by clear evidence. The ' Western text ' is included in this phase ; it was an ancient rewriting, not, like the later recognizable recensions, an attempt to select the best among extant variants, only incidentally accompanied by occasional improvement on the editor's own part. The ' Western ' text and what may for convenience be called the ' B-text ' are two divergent types of this phase, and both go back to a very remote antiquity.

This phase of the history of the text was not brought to an end by the Antiochian recension. The most valuable single representative of it is Codex Vaticanus, which, with the Bohairic version, offers in Acts a non-western text of great freedom from ' Western ' readings, and, on the other hand, shows fewer traces than any of its kin—probably, indeed, none—of influence from the Antiochian text. On these two characteristics, as has already been remarked above, not on any unique purity within its own non-western and non-antiochian field, rests, in Acts, the pre-eminence of this codex. Its relation to early, free, non-western variation, and the question whether its text was created by a recensional process in which the shorter reading was consistently preferred, have not as yet been determined. This position of Codex B both explains its superiority and accounts for its many recognizable individual faults. Many other faults, shared with other MSS. of its own type, it may also be suspected to contain, but no internal criticism enables us to detect them.

[1] Rahlfs, *Der Text des Septuaginta-Psalters*, p. 201, remarks that the evidence of Clement of Alexandria shows that in ancient times a greater number of different types of text of the Greek Psalms were current than have been preserved for us.

(2) *The Antiochian Recension and its Successive Modifications.*
The formation of the Antiochian recension in the fourth century
constituted a fateful epoch in the history of the text both of Old
and New Testaments.   Through all the centuries beginning with
the ninth the great bulk of Greek MSS. contain this text, mostly
in a fair degree of purity.   The most important question with
regard to it is how far it has preserved non-western readings
derived from the earlier stage of free variation and otherwise
unknown to us or insufficiently attested.

(3) *The Phase of Later Mixture and Supplementary Recension.*
Here belong Codices AC 81, most of the MSS. assigned by von
Soden to his H-text and I-text, and probably the Greek copies
underlying the Latin ' gigas-recension ' and the Latin Vulgate.
Whether the Greek MS. from which came the marginal and
asterisked readings of the Harclean Syriac was of this nature
or was a pure ' Western' text cannot be determined in the present
state of knowledge.   The extant Greek MSS. here mentioned show
a character of their own.   They make the impression of having
been written under definite control of various kinds ; in orthography and grammar they are more accurate by the standards of
the grammarians than those of the earliest phase ; and, apart from
mere accidents, they contain relatively few individual readings
peculiar to the several codices.

In this great and heterogeneous mass many distinct types of
mixture can be identified, and now that the fundamental spade-
work of von Soden has been done, their relations and history will
probably be more and more accurately and instructively elucidated
as the laborious research required for this study makes further
progress.   Within this phase will probably be discovered the text
of Pamphilus and Eusebius ; if so, that will form an excellent
illustration of what took place at many centres.   Some of these
texts had as one of their component elements noteworthy readings
of great antiquity in considerable abundance, and it is here that
the chief use of the minuscule codices, when fully investigated,
will lie.   Which are the useful minuscules will appear when all

those codices that are incapable of such use (constituting, in fact, the great majority) are removed from the critic's horizon.

The textual history of the New Testament and that of the Septuagint have been parallel. In both Testaments the period of Origen and that of Lucian of Antioch are the great landmarks. In both, a phase, or period, of free variation was interrupted, but not fully terminated, by the effect of great recensions ; and in both the critic's task is to determine the best extant text which preceded these recensions, and, as well, to discover and adopt any sound readings preserved in the recensions, though lacking strong, or even any, attestation outside them. In both cases the conclusion of criticism advises the adoption of Codex Vaticanus as in large measure, but only in large measure and to a degree varying greatly in different groups of books, the best single survivor of the earliest phase of textual development.

But there are important differences. Thus in the Septuagint the Lucianic text appears to contain many precious readings drawn from its ancient base and sometimes known to us from no other source, while in the New Testament it is capable of rendering a similar service, if at all, only within narrow limits.[1]

Moreover, Origen made no recension of the New Testament, and the difference between the fortunes of the Septuagint and of the New Testament in his period is the cause of a far-reaching difference in the later history of the two texts. The outcome may have been partly due to Origen in the New Testament as well as in the Old, but in the latter case his new and powerful recension entered at this time on its career as an active power, whereas in the New Testament what happened was that an ancient but neglected type of text was brought to new prominence, and the ' primitive phase ' of the text prolonged. In the Septuagint, well before the middle of the third century the recension put forth in the fifth column of the Hexapla provided a restrictive

Comparison of New and Old Testaments.

---

[1] Even von Soden's method of criticism, which allows one vote out of three to the Antiochian text, does not permit that text to outweigh the combined votes of the H-text and the I-text.

force to check free variation, although it became in itself the source of a fresh type of mixture. No similar great repressive force was at work in the New Testament at anything like so early a date. For the Book of Acts, to limit the statement to the special field of our present inquiry, what we seem to see is that not long after Origen's date a change in usage took place. In the second century the text of Acts commonly used had been the 'Western.' It penetrated to the Latin - speaking world and to the Syrian church, was long used in Palestine, and is found in Egypt at Oxyrhynchus in the third or fourth century, while the traces of it in the copy from which the Sahidic was made likewise attest its use in Egypt. But under some influence (we may guess that this was not unconnected with Origen), and before the time of Athanasius, the old B-text won the day in Alexandria over the old 'Western' text, was used as the chief basis of the recension made at Antioch, was employed by Jerome for the revision of the Latin translation, and later showed its position of full authority in Egypt, where it provided the copy from which the Bohairic version was made. One effect of this change of public favour must have been that many 'Western' copies were corrected over to a B-standard, and so gave rise, by reason of incomplete correcting, to a progeny of descendants with a mixed text. In the codex from which the Sahidic was translated many remnants of the 'Western' base survived here and there, chiefly in unimportant minor details, amid the general mass of B-readings.

Another fact of Septuagint history to which the New Testament offers no counterpart is that the influence of the Hexaplaric and of the Lucianic recensions in the Old Testament can be easily detected. Their readings stand out conspicuous against any alien background. In the New Testament the 'Western' text has something of that quality, but it belongs to the phase of primitive, free rewriting, not to that of learned recensions. Hardly any other type can be recognized by familiar features in any single sentence taken alone. The Antiochian selection of readings is, indeed, easily recognized in any considerable passage, but for a given single reading it is hardly ever possible to say whether it is Antiochian or merely a part of the older text ('Western' or, more often, Old Uncial) which the Antiochian revisers used.   No one will be able to tell what the text of the Codex of Pamphilus, followed in Eusebius's copies, was like, until by some external evidence it shall be determined what that text was.[1]

Other important differences between the two Testaments can be pointed out.   Except in the Psalms, nothing in the textual history of the Old Testament corresponding to the 'Western' text of the New Testament is known to us.   And in the later phases of the Old Testament text the most commonly adopted type was not (again with the exception of the Psalms) the Lucianic recension, but rather a modified form of the older current text.

[1] Hesychius need not be mentioned here. He is a figure shadowy enough even for the Old Testament, and for the New Testament we know nothing whatever about his work.

2. PAPYRI AND OTHER FRAGMENTS

ALTHOUGH no essential difference separates papyrus MSS. from others, yet in the present state of our knowledge of the text the papyri and certain associated fragments require separate mention. This is partly because a large proportion of them are of great antiquity, partly because their place of origin or currency is in most cases known to be Egypt.

§ 1. PAPYRI AND EGYPTIAN FRAGMENTS

In the Acts the following fragments from Egypt come in question (for fuller statements see pp. xvii-xxi). Only the four specifically so designated (Pap.) are papyri.

Pap. 29 (Oxyrhynchus 1597 ; third or fourth century).

Pap. 8 (Berlin, P 8683 ; fourth century).

057 (Berlin, P 9808 ; fourth century).

0165 (Berlin, P 271 ; fourth or fifth century).

0166 (Heidelberg 1357 ; fifth century ; bought at Akhmim, but of uncertain provenance).

0175 (Florence, Oxyrhynchus fragment, vol. ii. No. 125 ; fifth century).

076 (Amherst VIII ; fifth or sixth century).

Wess[59c] (Vienna ; Sahidic and Greek ; sixth century).

Pap. 33 (Vienna ; Pap Wess[190] ; sixth or seventh century).

Pap. Wess[237] (Vienna ; graeco-sahidic ; eleventh or twelfth century).

Of these the earliest (Pap. 29) is certainly older than our oldest codices. The text of the fragment is givĕn in full below, pp. 235, 237 ; its chief variants from B are :

xxvi. 7 ελπιζει] ελπιδι. This implies a finite verb instead of
λατρευων B ; so *deserviunt in spe pervenire* gig ; whether in Pap. 29
the noun was preceded by εν cannot be known.

8 Seems to have omitted βασιλευ τι απιστον κρινεται παρ υμιν.

20 ιεροσολυμοις] + και. The editors suggest, in view of the space,
that what followed was τη ιουδαια for πασαν τε την χωραν της
ιουδαιας B ; the reading *judaeis* of c and perp[corr] suggests also the
possibility of ιουδαιοις.

απηγγελλον] εκηρυξα (cf. *praedicavi* h, *annunciavi* gig, instead
of the usual *annuntiabam*).

These indications are meagre, but decisive ; they prove the
presence of ' Western ' readings in Oxyrhynchus as late as the
third or fourth century. The rest of the MS. would beyond reasonable doubt furnish abundant parallels to D and the Old Latin.
The fragment includes only verses which are now lacking
in D.

The other nine fragments mentioned above represent texts
current in different centuries, from the fourth to the seventh, and
in various Egyptian localities. For all except 057 the text is
known, and so far as practicable their readings are included at
the proper places in the apparatus below. In view of the broken
condition of most of them, inferences from the silence of the
apparatus in any verse need to be verified from the published
texts of the fragments (see above, pp. xvii-xx).

No one of the fragments (except the minute bit designated
1066) agrees perfectly with any known MS., but it is nevertheless
plain that all of them, except Pap. 29, represent forms of what
in this volume is called the ' Old Uncial ' text. They are conspicuously different from the Antiochian type of text, and show
hardly anything that is capable of being ascribed even to sporadic
Antiochian influence. In several cases (notably Pap. 8, 0165, 076)
their readings show special agreement with B, but none of them
shares any of the peculiar idiosyncrasies of B against all other
uncials. In Pap Wess[237] (from the Fayoum, eleventh or twelfth
century) a distinct ' Western ' element is included in the text.

The fragments are too limited in extent to justify at present any conclusions as to the history of the Old Uncial text in Egypt from the time of Athanasius to the date of the Arab conquest.

From the study of the Gospel papyrus fragments of the third and fourth centuries (mostly from Oxyrhynchus) it has been observed that, although these conform to the Old Uncial type, they never agree perfectly with any one uncial, and that in the passages (brief as those are) where the fragments overlap, they do not agree perfectly with one another.[1] It is further remarked that most of the papyri contain some unique readings, as well as not a few which elsewhere find support only in very late copies.[2] With these findings the facts of the Egyptian fragments of Acts, so far as they permit a judgment, are not out of accord.

§ 2. OTHER FRAGMENTS

Ten other fragments of varying date, origin, and character are known as follows (see pp. xvii-xxi).

At Petrograd are three palimpsests, the upper writing being Georgian :

066 (I² ; fifth century),
096 (I⁵ ; seventh century),
097 (I⁶ ; seventh century).

---

[1] Victor Martin, ' Les papyrus du Nouveau Testament et l'histoire du texte,' *Revue de Théologie et de Philosophie*, N.S., vol. VIII., 1919, pp. 43-72.

[2] A similar situation is found in papyrus MSS. of classical writers ; B. P. Grenfell, *Journal of Hellenic Studies*, vol. XXXIX., 1919, pp. 16-36 ; *The Oxyrhynchus Papyri*, vol. iii., pp. 119 f.; vol. v. pp. 243 f.; vol. xi. pp. 156-164. Grenfell says that the changes took place before the second century after Christ, and to but small extent after that. On the corrupt text of a papyrus of the Phaedo of Plato written within a century of Plato's death, as compared with the Bodleian Plato dated 895, and the causes of the superiority of the later manuscript, see H. Usener, ' Unser Platontext,' *Nachrichten*, Göttingen Academy, 1892, pp. 25-50, 181-215. For a like view for the New Testament see E. von Dobschütz, *Eberhard Nestle's Einführung in das griechische Neue Testament*, 4te Auflage, 1923, p. 8.

Also at Petrograd :

095 (G ; seventh century ; from the binding of a Syriac MS.),
0123 (Apl 70 b ; eighth century).

At Sinai are :

077 (fifth century),
0140 (tenth century).

There remain :

048 (ב ; fifth century, palimpsest, from Rossano),
093 (sixth century, from the Cairo genizah),
0120 (G^b ; ninth century, palimpsest, from Grotta Ferrata).

Of the above the text of 0140 and 048 has not been published ;
0123 and 077 are too fragmentary to be used.

The Petrograd fragments from Georgia, 066, 096, 097, come
from texts of varying type. 066 (fifth century) has an Old Uncial
text, which, so far as revealed by the fragment, is virtually
identical with that of 81 (von Soden, p. 1672) ; 096 is Old Uncial
with a slight ' Western ' trace (von Soden, p. 1672) ; 097 is from
a mixed text including a strong Antiochian element, and is
assigned by von Soden to his I - group (p. 1687). The other
Petrograd fragment 095 has an Old Uncial text, with noticeable
resemblance to AC. The most instructive observation at present
to be made on these oriental fragments is of the contrast their
variety affords to the distinctive, relatively homogeneous, Old
Uncial character of most of the fragments found in Egypt.

The two remaining fragments 093 and 0120 both give the
Antiochian text. 0120 is of the ninth century, and adds nothing
of consequence to the testimony of the other Antiochian MSS. of
the same period, although it occasionally departs from them to
agree with the Old Uncials. But 093, though but a single leaf,
is of great value, for, being of the sixth century, it is the oldest
known piece of pure Antiochian text of Acts.[1] The fragment

---

[1] Codex Laudianus (E) of about the same date is mainly Antiochian, but has
a Greek text largely conformed to its parallel Latin columns.

was found in the genizah at Cairo, but need not have been produced in Egypt.

The main use of these fragments is to enrich the background of knowledge in which the oriental non-antiochian MSS. of Acts are to be set. From the earliest of the fragments, with the similar fragments of the Gospels, we can see that in the third century the New Testament was copied with constant minor variation, so that hardly ever can two copies have been identical. The tendencies of variation perceptible are those commonly attributed to copyists, and due to carelessness in omission and alteration, and to small additions, rearrangements of order, and other changes, in accordance with personal taste. Yet in Egypt from the earliest time known to us and during the whole period of Christian domination of that country, and indeed for long after the Arab conquest, a definite but not rigidly fixed type of text was widely used by Greek-speaking Christians. Our oldest example of this text, and probably our best, is Codex Vaticanus. The type as a whole does not show signs of being a recension, although doubtless recensions were from time to time attempted within it, and from one or more of these some of our extant witnesses may come. Mingling with this text are traces of the ancient ' Western ' text, of which purer copies lingered here and there, such as Pap. 29, perhaps of the third century, from Oxyrhynchus ; and of the Antiochian recension also copies were brought to Egypt. For no other region is an equal amount of evidence available.

3. THE 'WESTERN' TEXT

§ 1. WITNESSES

OF the ' Western ' text of Acts we have no pure representative
for any large part of the book, if indeed any one of our witnesses
can be called pure. The authorities may be arranged in three
groups : 1. The chief witnesses, with a substantially ' Western '
text. 2. Mixed texts with definite and considerable ' Western '
elements. 3. Mixed texts with occasional ' Western ' survivals.

1. Codex Bezae stands alone as the only continuous Greek MS.
containing nearly the whole book in a substantially ' Western '
text ; but the defects and limitations of D have already been
sufficiently illustrated in the general description of the codex
(above, pp. lxix-lxxxiii). It is disfigured by errors ; and in using it
the possibility of conformation to the accompanying Latin and of
contamination from the non-western text must be kept in mind
at every stage. Such facts as the frequent agreement against
D of Peshitto and h, or Peshitto and gig, seem to show a greater
degree of degeneration in the ' Western ' text of D than has
usually been suspected. Next in importance to D are the readings
under asterisk and in the margin of the Harclean Syriac. These
are almost purely ' Western,' are sometimes obviously better than
the readings of D, and come in some cases from chapters where
D is defective ; but they are not continuous, although they
contain a very large proportion of the most important ' Western '
variants, especially in the way of addition. The African Latin
version, again, was almost purely ' Western,' and where we have
the evidence of Codex h, Cyprian, or Augustine, the critic is on

Codex Bezae ; Harclean apparatus African Latin ; Pap. 29.

ccxv

firm ground, but this is the case for only a small part of the book.

These three—D, Harclean apparatus, African Latin—may be called the chief witnesses to the 'Western' text, and their readings, in the absence of special indications to the contrary, are generally to be taken as representing it. With them may be put the readings implied in the Armenian version of the commentary of Ephrem Syrus, as printed below (pp. 380 ff.). The use of these is subject to some limitations because of the probability of influence from the Armenian New Testament, but they serve at least to confirm readings known from other and more trustworthy sources.

The papyrus MS. from which the fragment Pap. 29 (Oxyrh. 1597) has been preserved would probably also show itself as belonging to this group, if we had more of it.

2. Next to these chief witnesses come two groups of mixed documents, Greek and Latin, which also contain definite 'Western' elements of great importance.

I-codices. (a) A large number of Greek MSS. are included by von Soden in his I-group, and many of these, especially those of the subgroups I^{c1} and I^{c2}, contain a larger or smaller number of 'Western' readings. The codex containing the largest number appears to be 614 (formerly 137; a 364), now at Milan, which is included in the apparatus of Tischendorf, Hilgenfeld, and von Soden. Of importance is also 383 (formerly 58; a 353; Oxford, Bodleian Library, clark. 9), in which the 'Western' readings are found almost exclusively in chapters xvii.-xxii.[1] The other codices of the groups I^{c1} and I^{c2} are named above (pp. xxviif.) in the order of value assigned by von Soden. A full investigation of these mixed texts containing 'Western' readings, most of which are easily

---

[1] August Pott, *Der abendländische Text der Apostelgeschichte und die Wirquelle*, Leipzig, 1900, has tried to explain the 'Western' readings of 614 and 383 as due to the persistent influence of the 'We-source' on the text of the completed Book of Acts. For effective criticism of his theory see H. Coppieters, *De historia textus Actorum Apostolorum*, Louvain, 1902, pp. 60-68, and A. V. V. Richards, *Journal of Theological Studies*, vol. II., 1900-1, pp. 439-447.

accessible, is one of the greatest needs of the textual criticism of Acts.[1] The impression made by them, so far as they are known, is that their character is due to the introduction of striking 'Western' readings into an Antiochian text, while they also show a certain Old Uncial element of which the precise nature and channel has not been at all determined.[2] That the minutiae of the text are almost perfectly Antiochian makes it difficult to believe that we have the remains of a 'Western' base incompletely corrected to an Antiochian standard. Such a theory would imply an Antiochian corrector meticulously careful about introducing every minor detail of his new text and yet so careless as to leave standing a great number of glaring readings of a character obviously foreign to it.[3] In some cases, for instance in codex 614 in Acts xxii. 29 f., xxiii. 24 f., 34, xxiv. 27, the 'Western' reading stands by conflation side by side with the other reading for which it was intended as a substitute. In such a case as xix. 9 the 'Western' addition $\tau\omega\nu$ $\epsilon\theta\nu\omega\nu$, properly attached to $\pi\lambda\eta\theta ov$ς in D e pesh hcl ⁜, is in 614 383 misplaced and connected with the previous $\tau\iota\nu\epsilon$ς.[4] These 'Western' readings might have stood in the margin of the exemplar, which would thus have been a copy constructed somewhat after the fashion of the Oxford ms. of the Harclean Syriac.

[1] It is understood that Mr. A. V. Valentine Richards of Christ's College, Cambridge, is engaged on an edition and investigation of 614. His work will throw greatly needed light on the origin and significance of this group of Greek mss. A. Schmidtke, 'Festlegung der Evangelienausgabe Zion,' *Neue Fragmente und Untersuchungen zu den judenchristlichen Evangelien* (T.U. xxxvii.), 1911, pp. 1-21, is an instructive discussion of one group of I-codices of the Gospels. A. Vaccari, *La Grecia nell' Italia meridionale* (Orientalia Christiana, iii.), Rome, 1925, treats of the Calabrian mss. of LXX and N.T.

[2] Streeter, *The Four Gospels*, 1924, pp. 79-107, 572-584, has shown that for the Gospels Caesarea was probably the centre of diffusion of at least one type of the I-text (that chiefly used by Origen in his later period). So perhaps with Acts, for which Origen does not supply much evidence. On this text in the Gospels see also K. Lake and R. P. Blake, 'The Text of the Gospels and the Koridethi Codex,' *Harvard Theological Review*, vol. xvi., 1923, pp. 267-286.

[3] Cf. H. Coppieters, *op. cit.* pp. 60-68 ; also A. V. V. Richards, *l.c.* p. 445.

[4] What has happened is made specially evident in 614, where $\tau o\tau\epsilon$ follows $\epsilon\theta\nu\omega\nu$ in the gloss although it would be appropriate only if $\tau\omega\nu$ $\epsilon\theta\nu\omega\nu$ stood in the later position which the words actually occupy in D.

The ' Western ' fragments contained in these mixed codices represent a line of transmission of ' Western ' readings wholly distinct from that represented by D, and the I-manuscripts often agree with the Harclean apparatus against D.[1] As has been seen above, this does not imply any connexion of the I-group with the Old Syriac of the second, third, and fourth centuries, but rather that either the Philoxenian revision of the sixth century or the Harclean of the following century, or both, used a Greek MS. containing I-readings.   On the other hand, D belongs to the same line of transmission which has produced the Old Latin ' Western ' text.   Both lines, that of D and that of the Harclean apparatus and the I-group, go back to a common ' Western ' original, but the two lines show types of mixture of quite different characters, and independent the one of the other.[2]   Among the questions which cry for an answer are those as to the components of the non-western element of the text of the I-manuscripts, and as to their grouping, their centre (or centres) of dispersion, and the later history and locality of their text.   A primary question is whether they represent a single mixture, which has been disfigured and partly obliterated by later conformation to standard types, or whether they represent several similar mixtures of ' Western ' readings with a non-western text, made from similar motives but at different places and times.   This ought to be discoverable from the relations subsisting between the selection of ' Western ' readings still found in the different codices.   It would require as complete as possible an assembling of the I-texts for comparison,

---

[1] Examples of agreement of 614 or kindred texts with the Harclean apparatus against D are to be found in the following places among others: v. 33 ; vii. 43 ; xii. 11, 12, 25 ; xiii. 43, 47 ; xiv. 18, 19, 25 ; xv. 1, 23 ; xvi. 39 ; xvii. 11 ; xx. 32 ; xxii. 5, 7.   Similarly, where D is lacking, hcl.*mg* sometimes agrees with minuscules of the I-groups in ' Western ' readings for which no Latin attestation presents itself, *e.g.* Acts xxiv. 27.

[2] A certain analogy may be seen here, valuable in principle but incomplete, to Burkitt's observation of the sharp distinction between the Old Syriac and the Old Latin (and Bezan) ' Western ' text of the Gospels, as seen in the two different series of interpolations which these have received.   In Acts the salient characteristics of the ' Western ' text in the two lines of transmission go back to a single common origin more definitely and completely than in the Gospels. See Burkitt, *The Old Latin and the Itala*, pp. 17, 46-53.

but this would now present no insuperable difficulties, except for a few hardly accessible codices.

Valuable use can, even at present, be made of these ' Western ' readings, many of which will be found recorded in von Soden's apparatus. In the passages where Codex Bezae is mutilated, they are given in the pages below, and throughout the rest of Acts they can be used both to confirm and to supplement Codex Bezae. Comparison with the Harclean apparatus and with the Old Latin and the other versions throws into clear relief much of the ' Western ' element of the Greek I-codices ; in some cases, the positive character of readings serves even by itself as a criterion.[1] The ' Western ' readings of these MSS. are not infrequently better than those of D, which has suffered by scribal corruption and otherwise, and from which, in particular, ' Western ' glosses not represented by the Latin text used in constructing the MS. were likely to be omitted (for instance Acts xviii. 21, 22, and elsewhere). An apparatus showing to just what extent these Greek readings confirm, correct, or supplement the continuous text of Codex Bezae would not be difficult to print and would be highly instruct-ive. It is one of many supplements for which, it is hoped, the present volume will offer a convenient instrument and an incentive.

(b) The Old Latin and mixed Vulgate manuscripts described Old Latin. above (pp. cvi-cxii) may be classed with the Greek I-codices, for they all contain definite ' Western ' elements, and are important sources of information as to the ' Western ' text. In nearly every instance, however, they seem to have acquired their ' Western ' element by a process the opposite of that which has produced the I-codices. The latter may be thought to represent a non-western text into which ' Western ' readings of interest have been intro-duced. The Latin MSS., on the other hand, represent the remains of a sound ' Western ' base which has gradually lost by correction

---

[1] Examples of readings which look ' Western ' but have only isolated attestation, and may be merely similar expansions by a later hand, are Acts viii. 36 + συζητουντες μετ αλληλων 467 ; xxiii. 27 *clamantem et dicentem se esse civem romanum* gig. Others could easily be gathered by a little research in the apparatus of von Soden and of Wordsworth and White.

its 'Western' character, and been assimilated to the ordinary Greek text. In Spain and Languedoc and in Ireland the 'Western' readings of Acts were valued, and the sharp conflict of various types of text yielded highly composite mixtures retaining various proportions of 'Western' survivals of every sort. The daughter versions into several vernaculars preserved this character, and owe to it alone their interest for our investigation.

It thus appears that the I-codices and the Latin version have like uses. Of mixed ingredients, they are ordinarily incapable, each by itself, of furnishing any presumption in favour of the 'Western' character of readings, but their 'Western' elements can be elicited by noticing variation from the non-western text and observing the groups of witnesses which support such variants. To careful critical judgment they offer a large and trustworthy supply of knowledge of the 'Western' text.

Other 'Western' survivals.

3. In addition to these two classes of witnesses—those of tolerable purity and the mixed sources—numerous other witnesses contain occasional 'Western' elements, the channels for which sometimes can be guessed, sometimes elude our inquiry. This is true of the Old Uncial codices A and C. Thus A has the 'Western' reading in Acts viii. 39, xv. 18, xx. 4, 18, xxi. 22, to mention but a few examples. C seems to be still more tinctured with 'Western' colour both in minor details and in longer glosses ; thus Acts ix. 22, x. 32, xiv. 10, xiv. 18 f., xv. 4, 23 f., xx. 16, 24, xxi. 22, 25. In xiv. 18 f., xv. 24, C has the 'Western' reading where D has received the non-western. These illustrations can easily be supplemented from the apparatus and notes of the present volume, where further evidence as to the more restricted 'Western' elements in ‭א‬ and 81 will be found. These 'Western' readings of the Old Uncial group have as yet received no adequate study or explanation. It does not seem certain that Codex Vaticanus has any strictly 'Western' readings in Acts, but it has many in the Pauline epistles, and no one ought to be surprised if some appear elsewhere. Finally, it is not to be forgotten that the Antiochian text contains a distinct 'Western' element (see

below, pp. cclxxxv-vii) ; something of it can perhaps be elicited by the aid of the versions.

The Sahidic version contains frequent 'Western' readings, especially in minor details. The Greek MS. which it carefully followed seems to have been derived, as stated above, from a 'Western' MS. which had been corrected to the Old Uncial standard. The Peshitto exhibits many 'Western' readings in spite of its general non-western colour.[1] The Armenian also shows 'Western' readings ; and some are found unmarked by any asterisk in the continuous text of the Harclean Syriac. A systematic and judicious comparison of the Sahidic, Peshitto, and Old Latin versions with one another, with A and C, with the Antiochian text, and with the I-manuscripts, would yield evidence of many 'Western' readings hitherto unrecognized, especially in the portions of Acts where Codex Bezae is defective.[2]

In addition to these witnesses, Greek MSS. here and there contain many isolated 'Western' readings, as do the patristic writings, Greek, Latin, Syriac, and Armenian. They are of little service in constituting a text, but they indicate the range of 'Western' influence, and, meagre as they are individually, deserve close study, for they provide the means of understanding the history of the text contained in the manuscripts and versions.

§ 2. THE TEXT

A careful reading of any approximate form of the 'Western' text of Acts, such as that of Codex Bezae, or of the reconstruction by Zahn, will be likely to convince the student that on the

The 'Western' text of definite origin.

---

[1] In such a case as Acts iv. 13 f. the Peshitto has retained fragments of the 'Western' text found in full in the Latin h, while D has nothing but the non-western text. This is a good example of the kind of use to which this whole class of witnesses can be put.

[2] The evidence of Peshitto and h, of Peshitto and gigas, and perhaps of Sahidic and Latin, seems to be valuable. The agreement of Peshitto and Antiochian also may prove valuable as a guide to 'Western' readings, at least in Acts, in spite of the common assumption of a different origin of their common element. So far as I have observed, the agreements of Peshitto and Sahidic are not very fruitful of results. The other possible combinations deserve careful study.

whole, and apart from inevitable minor blemishes due to later hands, he has before him a definite integral text, not explicable as the mere accumulation of scribal errors and incidental modifications.[1] That such a text would have been modified in divers ways in its early history is to be expected, and we can assume that it varied from copy to copy, as did the rival text, but the great mass of the variations which we can identify as belonging to it show unmistakable signs of proceeding from a single hand with his own characteristic method of work.[2] Moreover, the period before *ca.* 150 is too brief to have permitted the great number of successive copyings which have to be assumed under the theory that the ' Western ' text owes its origin to the fortuitous assemblage of natural variants.   Either the ' Western ' text represents substantially the original, from which the text of BℵAC 81 as a definite recension was derived, or *vice versa* the ' Western ' is a rewriting of the original Old Uncial, or else they are both from the original writer, different stages of his own work.   To suppose that the bulk of the variations proceed not from one but from many hands is a wholly unnecessary complication and multiplication of hypotheses, and runs counter to the clear indications of unity furnished by style and method in each text.   Regarded as a paraphrastic rewriting

[1] Like others in the past (especially J. L. Hug, *Einleitung in die Schriften des Neuen Testaments*, 4th ed., 1847; B. Weiss, *Der Codex D in der Apostelgeschichte* [T. U. xvii.], 1897, pp. 2-4), E. von Dobschütz, *Literarisches Centralblatt*, 1895, col. 605, held that the ' Western ' text was an archaic text now "in einem Zustande naturwüchsiger Verwilderung," and due to mere accumulation of corruptions, not to a rewriting; and he seems to hold substantially this view in his fourth edition of *Eberhard Nestle's Einführung in das griechische Neue Testament*, 1923, p. 28.   These views receive more support in the facts of the ' Western ' text of the Gospels, for which it must at least be admitted that several types of ' Western ' text were current at a very early date.   The relation of the text used by Irenaeus in the Gospels to other ' Western ' types is here instructive; see B. Kraft, *Die Evangelienzitate des Heiligen Irenäus* (Biblische Studien, xxi.), 1924, pp. 69-112. Cf. also F. C. Burkitt, *The Old Latin and the Itala*, 1896, pp. 16 f., 46-53. For references to the views of various critics on the unity of the ' Western ' text see H. Coppieters, *op. cit.* p. 76.

[2] A good example of one sort of unity of method may be seen by comparing the ' Western ' text in Acts xiv. 7 and xv. 34.

of the original, the ' Western' text, indeed, would in kind
not be different from the free divergence of early copyists,[1]
although a highly exaggerated example of that freedom ; but
it must in the main have been due to a single editor trying to
improve the book on a large scale.

With due qualifications, then, the ' Western ' text of Acts can Date.
be treated as a real entity, which came into being at some definite
place and time, was diffused from some single centre, had its own
history, became mixed with other texts by various processes,
some easily intelligible, others more mysterious, and was finally
embodied in the many documents from which we try to recover it.
Its date of origin must have been very early. It may have been
used by the author of the Epistle of Barnabas, and so perhaps
before the middle of the second century. It certainly was the
text in the hands of Irenaeus about 185, and presumably the one
which as a young man he learned to know in Asia Minor before
150. That he had at first used a different text which at some
time he exchanged for the ' Western ' text of the later part of his
life is not intrinsically impossible, but with such a man we should
expect the change to betray itself somewhere, in his numerous
quotations or elsewhere in his voluminous work, and such a
suggestion is in fact made impossible by the emphasis with
which he expresses confidence in the unfalsified text of the
Scriptures (*Contra haer.* iv. 33. 8).[2] Before the time of Tertullian
the African Latin seems to have had a considerable history, and
already to have attained some fixity of rendering for various
Greek words in their Christian use.[3] Tertullian's intense
asseveration of the trustworthiness of the text used by the
Church (*De praescriptione haereticorum* 38) would have been
impossible if the Greek text which he used had been known
to him as a new edition introduced within his lifetime or within

---

[1] On the parallel to be seen in the highly divergent Greek text of the Psalms
current in Upper Egypt, see pp. xciii-xciv.

[2] See Zahn, *Geschichte des neutestamentlichen Kanons*, vol. i. pp. 115 note, 441 f.

[3] H. J. Vogels, *Untersuchungen zur Geschichte der lateinischen Apokalypse-
übersetzungen*, 1920, p. 130.

any period of which he had knowledge. In the Gospels the ' Western ' text, which can hardly be dissociated in origin from the corresponding text of Acts, appears about the middle of the second century in Marcion and Tatian. Thus the date of origin of the ' Western ' text of Acts must be set as early as the first half of the second century. At a very early time it was present in Egypt and was brought to Africa and to Syria. As to its place of origin there is no knowledge ; of possible conjectures something will be said below.

Inferiority of the ' Western ' text.

The differences between the ' Western ' and the Old Uncial text are so extensive and complicated that it is possible to make instructive comparison only by large sections ; the question of whether the ' Western ' form as a whole represents the original type or a rewriting of it cannot be decided by comparing single readings and summing up the results.[1] It is the general effect which counts. And here the Old Uncial seems decisively to evince itself as on the whole the original and the ' Western ' as on the whole due to recension. The ' Western ' fulness of words, the elaboration of religious expressions, such as the names for Christ and the *plus* of conventional religious phrases, the fact that the difference in language and mode of narration can often be explained as due to superficial difficulties in the other text, occasional misunderstanding, as would appear, or at least neglect, of the meaning of the other text (for instance Acts xx. 3-5), the relative colourlessness and a certain empty naïveté of the ' Western,' all contrast unfavourably with the greater conciseness, sententiousness, and vigour, and occasionally the obscurity, of the Old Uncial text.[2] And even more decisive is the fact that in all the excess of matter which the ' Western ' text shows, virtually nothing is to

---

[1] On the importance in textual criticism of considering a larger context, see the instructive observations on ' Zusammenhänge unter den Lesarten ' by H. J. Vogels, *Handbuch der neutestamentlichen Textkritik*, 1923, pp. 204-224. Vogels adduces Acts v. 22 f. and xi. 1-2 as good illustrations.

[2] An interesting contrast is offered by the abbreviation of the Syriac Didascalia in Codex h (Harris's MS. of 1036), where the abridging process results in a thinner and less clear sense ; see Flemming, *Die syrische Didaskalia* (Texte und Untersuchungen, xxv.), 1904, p. 255.

be found beyond what could be inferred from the Old Uncial text. Of the small number of substantial additions mentioned below, three may be original, lost from the other text, the rest, few as they are, are all capable of explanation under the theory that they proceed from an editor later than the author. If a reviser had had the Old Uncial text of Acts at his disposal, and had wished to rewrite it so as to make it fuller, smoother, and more emphatic, and as interesting and pictorial as he could, and if he had had no materials whatever except the text before him and the inferences he could draw from it, together with the usual religious commonplaces, it must be admitted that moderate ingenuity and much taking of pains would have enabled him to produce the ' Western ' text. On the other hand, the reverse of this process is difficult to make reasonable. We should have to suppose that a reviser, having the ' Western ' text, undertook to condense it, and in so doing was prepared to make some sacrifice of easy pictorial amplitude of expression and of the current, favourite religious names and phrases, but was determined to omit nothing that later generations were likely to value as containing substantial information, or that could not be inferred from what he left standing. In some cases, we should have to conclude, he modified the picture; often he made it less complete and superficially less consistent ; the general effect of his work was to deepen the intensity of colour by compression of style, never to heighten it by addition, and he strangely succeeded in giving a false semblance of archaic brevity and compactness.

If this account of the matter be just, it can hardly be denied that the former process supposed is one easily comprehensible under the conditions of the second century, but that the latter one is, to say the least, highly improbable. It would be tedious to try to prove by illustrations the justice of the contrast here drawn ; to reach a decision the student must make a broad comparison of the two texts as wholes ; [1] to provide the means

---

[1] As a single good illustration of some of these characteristics reference may be made to Acts xiii. 38 f., where D and the Harclean apparatus, with

for such an examination, not otherwise so easily obtainable, is the purpose for which the present volume exists. If choice has to be made between the theory that the ' Western ' text was the original, later condensed and altered so as to produce the Old Uncial text, and the theory that the Old Uncial was the original, later expanded so as to produce the ' Western,' the answer seems to me clearly in favour of the latter.

This does not exclude the occurrence of ' Western ' readings still recognizable, in spite of the rewriting, as having been part of the very ancient base on which the ' Western ' reviser worked, and which evince themselves by internal evidence as superior to those of the Old Uncial text. The surprising fact is, not that these exist, but that in Acts they are so few.[1]

Theory of A. C. Clark.

In connexion with the conclusion thus reached it may be appropriate to mention here the view of A. C. Clark, which was suggested to that scholar by certain analogies in the transmission of the Latin text of Cicero.[2] He holds that since, at one period, the Gospels appear to have been transmitted in manuscripts written in columns with very short lines of 10-12 letters each, and the Acts in columns written in irregular sense-lines, most of the cases where one form of the text has a shorter reading are to be accounted for by the accidental omission of such lines or of groups of them. Consequently the ' Western ' text, being longer than the B-text, is to be regarded as the original, which

---

fragmentary Latin support, agree in adding μετάνοια, οὖν, and παρὰ θεῷ, all part of the same process and producing a painful weakening of the sense.   Good examples of weakening of expression, and padding, are Acts xv. 38 f., xvii. 15, but these are mere random illustrations, not more worthy of note than innumerable others.   Acts ii. 37 is a good example of a ' Western ' change made in the interest of greater definiteness and clarity ; Acts x. 24-27 has been rewritten with a view to a more complete continuity of the narrative.   In both cases it would be difficult to find a motive for changing the ' Western ' to produce the usual text.   For the harmonizing with parallels characteristic of the ' Western ' text see the description of Codex Bezae, above, p. lxxi.

[1] The readings of this class which, with more or less confidence, I have thought myself able to recognize, are mentioned in the Apparatus of ' Editors ' attached to the text of Codex Vaticanus in the present volume.

[2] Albert C. Clark, *The Primitive Text of the Gospels and Acts*, Oxford, 1914.

has suffered accidental mutilation on a great scale in the texts which prevailed after the second century. But, apart from the inherent improbability of such an explanation for the complicated and various phenomena of the New Testament text, the theory, so far as Acts is concerned, does not account for the facts, as stated above, which show a rational, not merely an accidental, difference between the two types of text. The *plus* of the ' Western ' text, if due, in accordance with the view which finds it to be secondary, to addition to the original, would necessarily often consist of phrases and clauses naturally constituting single lines and groups of lines in a MS. written in sense-lines ; but, as every page of Codex Bezae shows, the vast majority of the peculiarities of the ' Western ' text are not of this nature.

But a third theory has been proposed which is not open to all of the objections which make it impossible to regard the Old Uncial text as a revision of the ' Western ' by a later hand. Since the latter part of the eighteenth century it has more than once been suggested that we have for Acts two editions, both alike from the original author of the book.[1] This view was again urged with great energy and acumen by Blass, beginning in 1894, and was adopted by Zahn and made the basis of his monumental work, *Die Urausgabe der Apostelgeschichte des Lucas*, 1916. A priori it is indeed well imaginable that the original author might have done what would be inconceivable for any one else. He might first have written the book in the ' Western ' form, and then been led to revise his work so as to give it greater conciseness

Blass's theory.

---

[1] Semler, *I. I. Wetstenii libelli ad crisin atque interpretationem Novi Testamenti*, Halle, 1766, p. 8 (cited in full by Blass, *Acta Apostolorum*, 1895, p. viii) ; J. B. Lightfoot, *On a Fresh Revision of the New Testament*, 1871, p. 29 ; Hort, ' Introduction,' 1881, p. 177 (where the idea is rejected). Blass's successive writings in advocacy of the view are named by J. Moffatt, *Introduction to the Literature of the New Testament*, 1911, p. 310, and M. Goguel, *Introduction au Nouveau Testament*, t. iii., ' Le Livre des Actes,' 1922, p. 79 (neither list is complete). For mention of many discussions of the theory see Moffatt, *l.c.*, Goguel, pp. 81 f., and Engelhard Eisentraut, *Studien zur Apostelgeschichte*, Würzburg, 1924. Eisentraut has gathered interesting facts with regard to the view of Clericus, tending to show that that scholar at any rate did not take very seriously the theory of a double edition, ascribed to him by Semler.

and vigour. Understanding, as he would have done, exactly what
it was necessary to say and what was unimportant elaboration,
he could have produced a form of the book having the general
character of the Old Uncial text. And he alone could have
done this. Instances of sections where the two forms are well
explicable by this theory are pointed out and urged with much
plausibility by Blass and others.

Nothing in this theory is inherently unreasonable. Many
cases of two differing editions of ancient works, both proceeding
from the author himself, are known to us. A writer of taste
might well have seen that compression could, with advantage, be
applied to the ' Western ' form, and might have applied it in the
partial way here supposed.   It is, to be sure, a little strange that
both editions should have circulated side by side, but it is by no
means impossible, and Blass provided an ingenious and perfectly
admissible conjecture to account for this.   Nor is it an insuperable objection that in the Gospel of Luke the critic found the
relation of the two types of text reversed, and that several
scholars who accepted the theory for Acts rejected it for the
Gospel, although Blass had been able to find an equally ingenious
and admissible conjecture to account for the facts there.   But
at least two considerations present themselves which seem to me
to be fatal to the theory.

Decisive
objections.

In the first place, a considerable number of the variants of the
' Western ' text, which are supposed to have been excised by the
author in his revised copy, fall into groups with a common
character.[1]   Thus, whereas in the non-western text the journey
of xvi. 6 is said to have been guided in its course by the Holy
Spirit, the ' Western ' text similarly mentions divine guidance for
journeys at xvii. 15, xix. 1, xx. 3.   Again the ' Western ' text
repeatedly has in excess, as compared with its rival, such phrases
as διὰ τοῦ ὀνόματος κυρίου Ἰησοῦ Χριστοῦ, ἐν τῷ ὀνόματι
Ἰησοῦ Χριστοῦ ; so vi. 8, viii. 39, xiv. 10, xvi. 4, xviii. 4, xviii. 8,

---

[1] See the brief but weighty criticism of Blass by T. E. Page, *Classical
Review*, vol. XI., 1897, pp. 317-320.

cf. also viii. 37. Likewise, the simple name 'Jesus' is found expanded into Ἰησοῦν τὸν κύριον (vii. 55), τὸν κύριον Ἰησοῦν Χριστόν (xiii. 32), Ἰησοῦ Χριστοῦ (xx. 21). And repeatedly a reference to the Holy Spirit is found which the non-western text lacks; so viii. 39, xv. 7, xv. 29 φερόμενοι ἐν τῷ ἁγίῳ πνεύματι, xv. 32 πλήρεις πνεύματος ἁγίου, xx. 3, xxvi. 1. These several groups of generally harmless variants seem to be intended to heighten, and perhaps in some cases slightly to alter, the religious colour of the narrative. That they could be added is easy to see, and this might conceivably have been done by the original author, although such a habit would be a curious trait ; but Blass's theory requires us to suppose that at these points the author was led in his revision to reduce to a lower degree the serious and religious tone which at first he had adopted. This seems so un-likely as to approach the impossible. A similar, but perhaps less convincing, argument may be found in the great number of 'Western' variants which have for their plain purpose to give a good connexion between phrases or sentences, to strengthen emphasis, to make a statement or reference quite explicit, or to provide not wholly necessary explanations. Examples of all these can easily be gathered from almost any chapter of the book. The motive for removing them would seem to imply a positive change of literary taste and preference of ear on the part of the writer, and is not easily attributable to the mere purpose of condensation.

The other, and decisive, argument against Blass is that in many passages the conception of the event described, the mental picture of what took place, is different in the two forms of the text, and that in some the 'Western' text plainly rests on a mis-understanding of the non-western.

Of this the following examples may be given.[1] On some of them the Textual Notes may be consulted.

[1] For discussion of cases where Blass's theory does not explain the variants well or at all, see M. Goguel, op. cit. pp. 85-104 ; P. Corssen, Göttingische gelehrte Anzeigen, 1896, pp. 425-448 ; and especially H. Coppieters, op. cit. pp. 125-206. Among the chief discussions of Blass's theories that of P. W. Schmiedel, art.

xi. 17. After the reference to the gift of the Holy Spirit by God to these Gentile converts as actually accomplished, the suggestion that the refusal of baptism by Peter would have prevented God ' *from giving them the Holy Spirit* ' is inappropriate.

xiv. 2-5. According to the non-western text there was one outburst of persecution, according to the ' Western ' two such.

xv. 1-5. According to the ' Western ' text not the Antiochian church, but the Jewish Christians from Jerusalem, urged Paul and Barnabas to go to Jerusalem ; and at Jerusalem it was these same persons, not a new group, who made trouble for the missionaries.

xv. 20, 29 ; xxi. 25. The two inconsistent forms of the Apostolic Decree can hardly have been transmitted by the same writer. Zahn is able to escape this consequence only by supposing the ' Western ' reading to be no part of the original ' Western ' text.

xv. 34. The ' Western ' text is more complete, but seems inconsistent with the briefer text.

xvi. 8. The ' Western ' διελθόντες, ' after going about in,' is the exact opposite of παρελθόντες, ' neglecting,' unless διελθόντες is used without understanding of the specific meaning which it commonly has in such statements in Acts, and should here be taken as meaning ' passing through.' Under either explanation Blass's theory is unacceptable, for the author is not likely to have substituted the difficult παρελθόντες for the unobjectionable διελθόντες.

xvii. 4. The non-western text speaks of two classes of persons : (1) 'godfearing Greeks ' and (2) ' leading women ' ; the ' Western ' contemplates three : (1) ' godfearing persons,' (2) ' Greeks,' and (3) ' wives of the leading men.'

xviii. 7. For ἐκεῖθεν, referring to the synagogue, the ' Western ' text, by a misunderstanding, has ἀπὸ τοῦ 'Ακύλα.

xviii. 19-22. The non - western text is unskilfully arranged

' Acts of the Apostles,' *Encyclopaedia Biblica*, vol. i., 1899, cols. 50-56, is of importance for the whole problem of the ' Western ' text.

but perfectly intelligible ; the 'Western' text (as reconstructed) is complete and regular. It cannot have been an earlier form which the same writer deliberately and without motive partly disorganized.

xviii. 18, 26. Some reason led to putting the name of Priscilla first, and the divergent practice of the two types of text in this respect is not easily explained by Blass's theory.

xix. 6. The whole conception of speaking with tongues found in Acts ii. makes it hard to think that the writer of that chapter would have introduced here the idea of the 'interpretation' of the tongues by the speakers.

xix. 9. In the non-western text τοῦ πλήθους refers to the congregation in the synagogue. In the 'Western' text, τοῦ πλήθους τῶν ἐθνῶν, the reference is to the body of heathen in the town.

xx. 3-5. The two texts give very different accounts of the motives of Paul in planning his journey, and appear to have understood in quite different senses the movements of his travelling companions ; see the Textual Note.

xxiv. 6-8. The presence of vs. 7 (' Western ') makes a difference in the antecedent of παρ' οὗ in vs. 8 ; in the 'Western' form the relative probably refers to Lysias, in the non-western definitely to Paul.

The facts thus seem to show that the 'Western' text is not from the hand of the same author as the non-western text, and that it is a rewritten text, in general inferior to the other text. If these conclusions may be taken for granted, it is possible to treat more definitely of the character of the 'Western' text, and to speak further of its origin.

The purpose of the 'Western' reviser, as shown by his work, was literary improvement and elaboration in accordance with his own taste, which was somewhat different from that of the author. He aimed at bettering the connexion, removing superficial inconsistency, filling slight gaps, and giving a more complete and

Literary traits of 'Western' rewriting.

continuous narrative.[1] Where it was possible he liked to introduce points from parallel or similar passages, or to complete an
Old Testament quotation.[2] Especially congenial to his style were
heightened emphasis and more abundant use of religious commonplaces. This effort after smoothness, fulness, and emphasis in his
expansion has usually resulted in a weaker style, sometimes showing a sort of naïve superabundance in expressly stating what
every reader could have understood without the reviser's diluting
supplement. Occasionally it relieves a genuine difficulty and is
a real improvement. In the speeches he naturally found less
scope, on the whole, for extensive addition than in the narratives.
His text is nearly one-tenth longer than that of the Old Uncials.
In his language he uses a vocabulary notably the same as that of
the original author, but with a certain number of new words—
about fifty.[3] One trick of his style is the frequent introduction of
τότε as a particle of transition—an observation which may convey
useful warning against accepting these added words as cases of
original Aramaic colour lost in the non-western text. The
debasement of the ' Western ' text in Codex Bezae, from which
our impressions of it are primarily and chiefly derived, advises
caution in judgment, but to most modern readers the Book of Acts
in its ' Western ' dress will seem inferior to the original in dignity,
force, and charm. That the rewritten form so promptly gained
popularity in the second century is perhaps not surprising for a

---

[1] For detailed description of the ' Western ' text see the instructive and
careful classification of its glosses in H. Coppieters, *op. cit.* pp. 77-92 ; also, for
the added notes of time and place, Harnack, *Die Apostelgeschichte* (Beiträge
zur Einleitung in das Neue Testament, III.), 1908, pp. 50-53, 97-100. Complete
discussion of all the readings of D will be found in B. Weiss, *Der Codex D in der
Apostelgeschichte* (Texte und Untersuchungen, XVII.), 1897. Weiss's criticism
is acute, but he does not always do justice to the great complication of the
history of the text as now found in ' Western ' witnesses.

[2] Yet the ' Western ' reviser by no means follows the principle of bringing
the text regularly into closer conformity to the LXX. He is more interested
in his own improvements, as is illustrated, for instance, in Acts ii. 17-20,
xiii. 47.

[3] On the vocabulary of the ' Western ' text see the ' Index Verborum ' in
Blass's larger edition, 1895, pp. 301-334, also his *Evangelium secundum Lucam*,
1897, pp. xxvii f., and Schmiedel, *Encyclopaedia Biblica*, vol. i. col. 55.

generation which in many regions seems to have preferred the Epistle of Barnabas to the Epistle to the Hebrews.[1]

Of any special point of view, theological or other, on the part of the 'Western' reviser it is difficult to find any trace. In one or two passages (notably xiv. 5 where for ὁρμὴ τῶν ἐθνῶν τε καὶ Ἰουδαίων is substituted οἱ Ἰουδαῖοι σὺν τοῖς ἔθνεσιν) the hostile attitude of the Jews receives special stress, and xxiv. 5, in the speech of Tertullus, the change from κινοῦντα στάσεις πᾶσιν τοῖς Ἰουδαίοις τοῖς κατὰ τὴν οἰκουμένην to concitantem seditiones non tantum generi nostro sed fere universo orbe terrarum et omnibus Judeis (gig) betrays a Gentile's feeling that any statement is inadequate which implies that Christianity in the Apostolic age was limited to Jewry.[2] This motive may also have been at work in ii. 17, where a certain emphasis attaches to the 'Western' change of ὑμῶν to αὐτῶν in two instances, and to the omission of the pronoun altogether in the other two. The reference is thus thrown back to πάσας σάρκας (D), and the universal purpose of God for all mankind, in distinction from Israel, is brought into the prophecy. Perhaps the substitution of κόσμον for λαόν, Acts ii. 47 (D d), is to be included here as a further illustration.

(margin: Emphasis on Gentile interests.)

Another trait, possibly connected with the motive just mentioned, which deserves to be broadly investigated and more fully studied, is the tendency seen, for instance, in Acts xx. 21, where πίστιν διὰ τοῦ κυρίου ἡμῶν Ἰησοῦ Χριστοῦ is substituted for πίστιν εἰς τὸν κύριον ·ἡμῶν Ἰησοῦν ; xvi. 15 πιστὴν τῷ θεῷ for πιστὴν τῷ κυρίῳ. These variants, though often small, do not all lack purpose ; they suggest a desire on the part of the editor to indicate that the 'sebomenoi' won by the apostles were converted from the status of heathen to the true God through Christ, not merely from Jewish faith to Christianity.

---

[1] J. Armitage Robinson, *Barnabas, Hermas, and the Didache*, 1920, pp. 1-5.

[2] The same motive lurks in the substitution of ἔπειθεν δὲ οὐ μόνον Ἰουδαίους ἀλλὰ καὶ"Ελληνας for ἐπειθέν τε Ἰουδαίους καὶ"Ελληνας in Acts xviii. 4. For discussion of some other possible instances (ii. 47, iv. 31, xiv. 19, xvii. 12, xviii. 4, xix. 9, xxiii. 24) see Corssen, *Göttingische gelehrte Anzeigen*, 1896, p. 444.

Not Montanistic.

That a considerable part of the variants and additions of the 'Western' text are due to a Montanist has been strongly urged, chiefly on the ground of their relation to the Acts of Perpetua and their repeated emphasis on the activity of the Holy Spirit and His presence in Christians.[1] But in fact the 'Western' text of Acts is what we should expect to find used in Africa in the year 203, and there is no reason to suppose that Perpetua's text differed from that of her Catholic contemporaries. The emphasis on the Holy Spirit (in itself wholly in accord with the ideas and habit of the author of the book) can equally well have proceeded from an early second-century reviser who was untouched by any sectarian movement.[2] And the supposed indication of Montanist tendency is more than matched, and is perhaps actually disproved, by the somewhat clearer, though slight, indication of what may fairly be called ' anti-feminist ' tendency in the variants of xvii. 12 and of chapter xviii.

Made in Greek.

The theories of a Latin and of a Syriac origin of the ' Western ' text have been discussed above, pp. lxxii-lxxx, in connexion with the description of Codex Bezae. The dependence of both the Old Latin and the Old Syriac, as well as, in part, the Sahidic, on the ' Western ' revision, and the presence of a great number of the most characteristic ' Western ' readings in Greek MSS. of all ages from the third or fourth century on (including perhaps the copy used by Philoxenus in Mesopotamia in 508) makes it impossible

---

[1] So J. R. Harris, *Codex Bezae*, 1891, pp. 148-153, 221-225. P. Corssen, *Göttingische gelehrte Anzeigen*, 1896, pp. 445 f., rests the case for a Montanistic reviser chiefly on ἦν δὲ πολλὴ ἀγαλλίασις in Acts xi. 2, 7, but is unconvincing. It may be mentioned here that J. R. Harris, ' New Points of View in Textual Criticism,' *Expositor*, 1914, vol. VII., pp. 318-320, urges that the omission by Codex Bezae of ανατεθραμμενος and αυτω in Luke iv. 16 is a Marcionite alteration.

[2] The later use by schismatics of Latin texts, and of versions dependent on the Latin, which had a definite ' Western ' character, was not due, as some might suppose, to a schismatic or heretical interest in a non-ecclesiastical text, but to the fact that the geographical relations of these movements led them to use the current Latin text of Languedoc, which by reason of its subjection to Spanish, and so to African, influence was impregnated with ' Western ' readings. These late ' Western ' texts, Latin, Romance, and Germanic, have been transmitted to us both through correct ecclesiastical and through schismatic channels. See above, pp. cxxxv-cxlii.

to accept either of these inherently improbable theories. The revision was certainly made in Greek.[1]

It has already been observed that ' Western ' readings are sometimes to be recognized as superior to their rivals. A few times it is possible to detect in ' Western ' readings words probably contained in the original which have disappeared in other witnesses, thus Acts xx. 15 καὶ μείναντες ἐν Τρωγυλίᾳ ; xxi. 1 καὶ Μύρα (of Greek mss. only in D) ; xxvii. 5 δι᾽ ἡμερῶν δεκάπεντε (614 minn hcl ※). There may be others. *Genuine readings in ' Western ' text.*

On the other hand, since the ' Western ' reviser's regular habit was to expand, and since in his expansion he usually shows himself punctilious to represent somehow every element of the text before him, any omissions in the 'Western' text of what the other text contains deserve special attention, and sometimes give evidence, more or less conclusive, that the text of B, on its side, has suffered expansion. The most widely recognized instances of this sort in the New Testament are the ' Western non-interpolations ' in the Gospels pointed out by Westcott and Hort,[2] chiefly from the last three chapters of Luke. In Acts i. 2 the ' Western ' text is plainly related to the ' non-interpolated ' text of Luke xxiv. 51. A striking example in Acts is the reading (with three instead of four " provisos ") in Acts xv. 20, 29, xxi. 25. It must

---

[1] On the basis of isolated readings, and in disregard of general probabilities, a case could perhaps be made for the origin of the ' Western ' text by retranslation from the Coptic. Thus, Acts xvi. 29 D (d) adds πρὸς τοὺς πόδας to προέπεσεν, and a similar addition is found in perp gig vg. *many codices* Lucif hcl. *with obelus* sah. Now " the Coptic word requires a preposition to follow the word meaning ' before,' and the one regularly used in this connexion means, literally, ' at the feet of.' " Again, Acts xx. 28 Iren (*sibi constituit*) vg. *one codex* boh sah add ἑαυτῷ to περιεποιήσατο, and in Coptic this addition is necessary in order that the verb (properly meaning ' produce ') may mean ' acquire.' Acts xx. 38, the change to the second person found in gig and perhaps in D is " quite in accordance with Coptic idiom." Acts xx. 13, θασον (Antiochian pesh) for ασσον might have originated from a misunderstanding of the Coptic feminine article, which is actually found prefixed here in the Sahidic. Such an asyndeton as that of D in Acts xvii. 2 agrees with Coptic idiom. Note also the frequent confusion of τε and δέ, the addition of ' said ' and of the oblique cases of αὐτός, and many small additions and omissions. These examples are mentioned as a warning, not an incentive.

[2] 'Introduction,' pp. 175-177.

never be forgotten that the basis of the ' Western ' revision was a text far more ancient than any MS. now extant or even any considerable patristic testimony still accessible to us.

In drawing inferences, however, from ' Western ' omissions caution is necessary, because occasionally the ' Western ' text omits something which can hardly have been lacking in the original ; and this uncertainty is increased by the circumstance that not infrequently, where the question arises, our knowledge of the ' Western ' text is derived from a single source, so that the omission may be due to an idiosyncrasy of the sole witness.[1] Noteworthy instances, apart from those mentioned above (pp. lxxiii f.), are the following :

Acts iii. 16, ἡ δι' αὐτοῦ, om h.

iv. 5, ἐν Ἰερουσαλήμ, om h pesh.

ix. 12, where h omits the whole verse, this page of D being no longer extant.

xvii. 18, ὅτι Ἰησοῦν καὶ τὴν ἀνάστασιν εὐηγγελίζετο, om D d gig Aug (h is lacking).

xviii. 3, ἦσαν γὰρ σκηνοποιοὶ τῇ τέχνῃ, om D d gig (h has the sentence).

xxi. 39, οὐκ ἀσήμου πόλεως πολίτης, om D (partly contained in d ; h is lacking).

xxvi. 22, ἄχρι τῆς ἡμέρας ταύτης, om h.

26, παρρησιαζόμενος, οὐ πείθομαι, οὐ γάρ ἐστιν ἐν γωνίᾳ πεπραγμένον τοῦτο, om h.

xxvii. 1, σπείρης Σεβαστῆς, om h (the words are included in the paraphrase of the hcl.mg).

2, εἰς τοὺς κατὰ τὴν Ἀσίαν τόπους, om h.

2, Θεσσαλονικέως. Nothing corresponds to this in h.

3, τῇ . . . ἑτέρᾳ, om h.

6, κἀκεῖ. ἐκεῖ is not represented in h.

6, εἰς αὐτό, om h sah.

7, μόλις, om h.

7, μὴ προσεῶντος ἡμᾶς τοῦ ἀνέμου, om h. On this and the

<hr>

[1] On these omissions see H. Coppieters, op. cit. pp. 201-205.

following reading note the words of h, *inde cum tulissemus*, which may be an undecipherable survival of the translation of some Greek words.

7, κατὰ Σαλμώνην, om h.

8, μόλις τε παραλεγόμενοι αὐτὴν ἤλθομεν, om h.

8, Λασέα, om h.

10, τοῦ φορτίου καί, om h.

12, ἀνευθέτου δὲ τοῦ λιμένος ὑπάρχοντος πρὸς παραχειμασίαν οἱ πλείονες, om h.

12, βλέποντα κατὰ λίβα καὶ κατὰ χῶρον, om h.

13, δόξαντες τῆς προθέσεως κεκρατηκέναι, om h.

Other omissions, not too numerous, can be gathered from the collation of Codex Bezae and from the apparatus of Wordsworth and White's Vulgate, and some are noticed in the Textual Notes below. On the instances given above the following comments may be made.

The omission (D d gig Aug) from xvii. 18 is probably an accident, which may be suspected to have affected the African translation, and in D may be due to the influence of the Latin side. In xviii. 3 the omission (D d gig, but not h) is probably due to an oversight in the process of combining the non-western and ' Western ' texts, a process which is here observable both in D d and gig, and may or may not have taken place independently in the two. In xxi. 39 the omission (D) is probably accidental.

For the omissions of h (which nearly all happen to lie in sections where D is defective) confirmation would seem to present itself in only two instances. The omission of the whole verse ix. 12 cannot give the original text, for προσεύχεται is almost meaningless without it.[1] On xxvi. 22 there is nothing to say. In xxvi. 26 the whole verse appears in an abridged form, and a similar abridgment seems to be the cause of most of the omissions in xxvii. 1-13. The strange text, indeed, of the latter section can be excused by the difficulty of the geographical and other

---

[1] But for a different view see P. Corssen, *Der Cyprianische Text der Acta apostolorum*, 1892, pp. 22 f.

technical expressions, which have also led to extraordinary later corruption in the Latin text itself. For the omissions by h in chapter xxvii a 'Western non-interpolation' can be seriously suspected only in the case of Θεσσαλονικέως, vs. 2, and of εἰς αὐτό, vs. 6. In vs. 2 Θεσσαλονικέως, the complicated evidence is not easy to interpret satisfactorily, and Acts xx. 4 can have served as the source for an interpolation in the B-text, as it certainly has for the longer one found in some forms of the 'Western' text. In vs. 6 sah coincides with h in omitting εἰς αὐτό. In connexion with the omissions here commented on it should be mentioned that the best text of the Vulgate omits the whole verse xviii. 4, probably through some accident in connexion with the change from the 'Western' to the very different non-western form of the verse.[1]

Substitutions in 'Western' text.

'Western' substitutions of one word or phrase for another rarely commend themselves as probably right. Yet there are a few acceptable cases. So perhaps i. 2 ἐν ἡμέρᾳ ᾗ (Augustine) for ἄχρι ἧς ἡμέρας; iv. 6 Ἰωνάθας for Ἰωάννης; xiii. 33 πρώτῳ for δευτέρῳ. The instances of all kinds where the 'Western' reading seems to me preferable to that of Codex Vaticanus are mentioned in the Apparatus to the text below.

'Western' readings with substantial content.

Emphasis has been laid above on the lack of positive substance in most of the variants of the 'Western' text. To this observation there are exceptions, mostly additions, in which a substantial statement is made, or at least the 'Western' text is characterized by greater vigour and boldness than usual, but the fewness of these cases is impressive.[2] In several instances, as we have seen, iv. 6 (Ἰωνάθας), xv. 20, 29 and xxi. 25 (the omission of 'things strangled'), xx. 15 (Trogylia) and xxi. 1 (Myra), xxvii. 5 (' for

---

[1] On the tendency of the African Latin text of k (Matthew and Mark) to omit, see Sanday, *Old-Latin Biblical Texts, No. II*. p. 121 : "There seems to be a certain impatience of anything of the nature of a repetition. Asyndeton is affected ; and there is a fondness for reducing a sentence to its simplest and barest form without any of those heightening expressions that are found in most other MSS."

[2] On some of the more substantial additions of Codex Bezae see B. Weiss, *Der Codex D in der Apostelgeschichte*, pp. 107-112.

fifteen days ') the corruption is probably on the side of the non-western text. Apart from these the following are among the most notable cases ; except where otherwise indicated they occur in D, sometimes with further Latin and Syriac attestation :

Acts xi. 28. The introduction of ἡμῶν in the expansion. For other sporadic instances of the introduction of the first person in various witnesses cf. xvi. 8 (Irenaeus), xvi. 13 (BAC 81 sah), xxi. 29 (D), xxvii. 19 (Antiochian). The converse change of the first person to the third is more common ; cf. xvi. 17 (L etc.), xx. 5 (D, cf. cod. 2147), xx. 7 (Antiochian), xxi. 1 (cod. 255), xxi. 8 (Antiochian), xxi. 10 (א), xxvii. 1 (P etc.), xxviii. 1 (Antiochian), xxviii. 16 (H).

xii. 10, τοὺς ζ βαθμούς.

xiv. 20, et [cum disce]ssisset populus vespere, h.

xv. 2, ἔλεγεν γὰρ ὁ Παῦλος μένειν οὕτως καθὼς ἐπίστευσαν διισχυριζόμενος.

xv. 20, 29. Besides the absence of ' things strangled,' the addition, in the later form of the ' Western ' text, of the (negative) Golden Rule.

xviii. 21 f., δεῖ δὲ πάντως τὴν ἑορτὴν ἡμέραν ἐρχομένην ποιῆσαι εἰς Ἱεροσόλυμα.

xix. 1, θέλοντος δὲ τοῦ Παύλου κατὰ τὴν ἰδίαν βουλὴν πορεύεσθαι εἰς Ἱεροσόλυμα εἶπεν αὐτῷ τὸ πνεῦμα ὑποστρέφειν εἰς τὴν Ἀσίαν.

xix. 9, ἀπὸ ὥρας ε ἕως δεκάτης.

xix. 28, δραμόντες εἰς τὸ ἄμφοδον.

xx. 5, προελθόντες for προσελθόντες.

xx. 18, ἢ καὶ πλεῖον.

xxiii. 23, ' they (or he) said : They are ready (or let them be ready) to go,' hcl. mg.

xxviii. 16, ὁ ἑκατόνταρχος παρέδωκε τοὺς δεσμίους τῷ στρατοπεδάρχῃ τῷ δὲ Παύλῳ ἐπετράπη 614 etc.

Others might be added to the above ; it is a question of the impression of boldness made by the variant. Comments will be found in the Textual Notes below. Nearly all of the variants just cited fall fairly within the range of the reviser's habit of work. Two only stand out from the others as perhaps implying real additional knowledge : xix. 9 (' from the fifth to the tenth hour '), which may, however, come from a knowledge of the usual custom in such a room as the School of Tyrannus, and xii. 10 (' the seven steps ') which has so far defied satisfactory explanation.

The basic text and the re-writing. The ' Western' text thus includes two elements: an ancient base, which would be of the greatest possible value if it could be recovered, and the paraphrastic rewriting of a second-century Christian. In the Acts, variants not represented in any of the Old Uncial group but probably drawn from the ancient base have so far been found in but few instances, and even in the case of variations between the Old Uncials the ' Western ' text seldom provides the clear and useful evidence which might have been expected. B. Weiss [1] finds about ten cases where D agrees with wrong readings represented otherwise by B alone, and about twenty where D and B agree, without other support, in what appear to be the right readings. It is possible that further detailed study might lead, within limited range, to valuable conclusions, but the investigation is made difficult because Codex Bezae has been so much conformed in detail to the non-western Greek and to the Latin. In the Gospels, the ' Western ' text appears to include the same two elements—an ancient base and a paraphrastic rewriting, and there it is not unlikely that the ancient base is to be detected in a larger proportion of cases than in Acts.

Date On the date of the ' Western ' rewriting of Acts the evidence which carries it back as early as the first half of the second century has already been discussed (above, pp. ccxxiii-iv). Any closer estimate does not seem possible, although an early date in the period is probable on general grounds.

Place of origin. Equally impossible to determine with certainty is its place of origin and centre of diffusion. It was brought to Northern

---

[1] B. Weiss, *Die Apostelgeschichte ; textkritische Untersuchungen und Text-herstellung* (Texte und Untersuchungen, IX.), 1893, p. 67 : *Der Codex D in der Apostelgeschichte* (Texte und Untersuchungen, XVII.), 1897, p. 107.

Africa and to Lyons in Gaul in the second century, and at least
the 'Western' Gospels came to Rome (Justin Martyr, Hippolytus) at not far from the same date. In the same century the
'Western' Gospels were used by Clement of Alexandria, and the
papyrus of Acts of the third or fourth century, as well as one of
the strands woven into the Sahidic version, indicate that in the
third century the 'Western' text of Acts was current in Egypt.
The Diatessaron in Syria, perhaps based on a Greek text brought
from Rome, and likewise the 'separate' Syriac Gospels, show
'Western' character, and the same was true of Marcion's Greek
text of Luke, perhaps brought from Pontus, perhaps acquired at
Rome. In Syria, again, the first translation of Acts into the
vernacular (of unknown, but certainly very early, date) was made
from a thorough-going 'Western' text and continued in use
beyond the fourth century. In the third century the Didascalia
evidences the use of the 'Western' text of Acts in Syria or
Palestine. It would seem probable that at the end of the
second century no region of the Christian world was unacquainted
with the 'Western' text of Acts.

For the source of this wide diffusion we should naturally look
to some central locality. For those who do not hold Blass's
theory nothing points with any decisiveness to Rome. Even if
the Carthaginians received their Christianity and their first copies
of the Greek New Testament from Rome (which is by no means
certain [1]), this would not lead to the inference that Rome was the
centre of diffusion of the 'Western' text to any other region,
least of all to the Orient.[2] The analogy of the sources of the

[1] A. von Harnack, *Die Mission und Ausbreitung des Christentums in den
ersten drei Jahrhunderten*, 4th ed., 1924, p. 891, note 2, calls attention to the
constant intercourse between Carthage and the East both through direct
channels and by way of Rome, and refers to Tertullian's excellent and detailed
knowledge of events and conditions in the Greek-speaking churches of the East,
but concludes that whether Christianity had actually been brought to North
Africa from Rome or directly from the East is wholly uncertain.

[2] Strzygowski remarks that in respect to early Christian art Rome was
a "sponge"; and it seems doubtful whether in other aspects of Christian
thought, except in administration, the early Roman Church proper, as distinct
from heretics and schismatics, showed any considerable originating capacity.

African text of the Psalter (above, p. cxxvi) is ambiguous. The source to which the Syriac-speaking Christians first looked for their Greek MSS. may have been Antioch or Caesarea or even Alexandria, although a certain presumption would hold in favour of Greek-speaking Syria or Palestine. The evidence upon which Ramsay relies for his belief that the ' Western ' reviser was peculiarly familiar with the geography and customs of Asia Minor is inconclusive.[1] No one of these lines of inquiry or general probabilities leads to any conclusion.

Knowledge of Hebrew and of Palestine.   One small group of facts, however, especially if it can be extended by further observations, is suggestive. While, as has been shown above (p. ccxxxiii), the ' Western' text seems to have come from a Gentile Christian source, yet in at least two instances it shows dependence on the Hebrew Old Testament. In the utterance of Jesus on the cross Codex Bezae reads, both Matt. xxvii. 46 and Mark xv. 34, ηλει ηλει λαμα ζαφθανει—in the first and last words, at least, showing that the writer is transliterating the Hebrew of Psalm xxii. 1, not the Aramaic equivalent to be seen in the Old Uncial ελωι ελωι λεμα σαβαχθανει. That this is not a mere peculiarity of Codex Bezae is shown by the similar reading of various Old Latin MSS., as well as by the readings of Greek MSS.[2] Again, in Matt. xiii. 15, a k Irenaeus (Latin translation

---

' *Nihil innovetur* ' was, rather, its motto. See G. La Piana, 'The Roman Church at the End of the Second Century,' *Harvard Theological Review*, 1925, vol. XVIII. pp. 201-277.

[1] W. M. Ramsay, *The Church in the Roman Empire*, 1893, chap. ii. 3, chap. viii., and elsewhere. In *St. Paul the Traveller and the Roman Citizen*, 1896, p. 27, Ramsay says of the ' Western ' text : " The home of the Revision is along the line of intercourse between Syrian Antioch and Ephesus, for the life of the early Church lay in intercommunication, but the Reviser was connected with Antioch, for he inserts ' we ' in xi. 28." A list of the passages containing the readings relied on by Ramsay is given by Coppieters, *op. cit.* pp. 216 f., classified as follows : " not significant," xi. 27-28, xvi. 7, xviii. 21, xix. 1, 28 ; " more of the nature of evidence," xix. 9, xx. 15, xxi. 1 ; " likewise noteworthy," xviii. 27, xx. 4 ; " most nearly convincing," xiii. 14, xiv. 19. The claim made by Ramsay that the ' Western ' text shows ignorance of Macedonia and Achaia is not found to be substantiated in xvi. 12, xvii. 12.

[2] From the confused mass of readings collected in the apparatus to Matt. xxvii. 46 and Mark xv. 34 it appears that (1) D is uniform in both Matthew and Mark, and has good Latin support ; (2) in Matthew, Bℵ 33 boh follow the Aram-

only) substitute imperatives for ἐπαχύνθη, ἤκουσαν, ἐκάμμυσαν, showing unmistakable dependence on the Hebrew, in distinction from the LXX, of Ps. vi. 10.[1] In the latter passage (Matt. xiii. 15) the possibility is, indeed, present that the ' Western ' text of the Old Latin and Irenaeus represents the original readings of the Greek Matthew, lost in the other witnesses, in all of which a correction from the LXX might be supposed to have been introduced. If the case stood alone, this would perhaps be the better inference. But in the words from the cross such an explanation is not admissible, for here there is no room for LXX influence. The non-western texts are probably original, for an alteration, under the influence of the Hebrew Bible, from Aramaic to Hebrew is more easily conceivable than the reverse movement; but in either case contact with Semitic centres would be indicated.[2] To

---

aizing form substantially as given above; (3) in Mark, אCLΔ boh do the same, but B shows ' Western ' traces, reading λαμα with D, and further recalling D by the ambiguous ζαβαφθανει. The later (Antiochian) uncials in Matthew follow D in reading ηλι, but approximate to the Old Uncial text in λειμα (λιμα), and agree with it in reading σαβαχθανι; in Mark they go with the Old Uncial text, except in reading λειμα (λιμα) for λεμα. Minor variations and inconsistencies in individual MSS. abound. The Hebraizing word most characteristic of the ' Western ' text and most consistently rejected by all others (except partly in the monstrosity found in B) is ζαφθανει.

[1] Hans von Soden, Das lateinische Neue Testament in Afrika (Texte und Untersuchungen XXXIII.), pp. 213 f.

[2] On certain strange readings in the Gospels, perhaps of Semitic origin, see F. H. Chase, The Syro-Latin Text of the Gospels, 1895, pp. 109-111. In John xi. 54 Σαμφουρειν D, Sapfurim d, is the name of Sepphoris, about ten miles south of which lay a Galilean town Ephraim; the closer identification of the ' town called Ephraim,' as in ' the country of Sepphoris,' though doubtless mistaken, would thus testify to the knowledge of Palestinian geography possessed by the editor of the ' Western ' text. There is no sufficient reason for suspecting here the echo of a Semitic shem. See Zahn, Neue kirchliche Zeitschrift, 1908, pp. 38 f.; Schürer, Geschichte des jüdischen Volkes im Zeitalter Jesu Christi, 2nd ed., vol. ii.,1886, p. 121,note 358; 4th ed., vol. ii.,1907, p. 210, note 490, "Hier ist, wie die Namensform zeigt, sicher Sepphoris gemeint." Of ουλαμμαους D, for εμμαους, in Luke xxiv. 13 (cf. Gen. xxviii. 19) no convincing explanation has been offered. Chase, The Old Syriac Element in the Text of Codex Bezae, 1893, pp. 138-148, quotes a large part of a review by Sanday, in The Guardian, May 18 and 25, 1892, in which the following evidence is adduced for Antioch as the birthplace of the ' Western ' text: (1) Luke iii. 1, επιτροπευοντος is correctly substituted for "the vague and general" ηγεμονευοντος; Mark xii. 14, the correct

these examples the form Βαριησοῦα, Acts xiii. 6, may be added, for the additional (fourth) syllable, attested by several witnesses, seems clearly due to an attempt to give a Greek transliteration of the Semitic 'ain by a method which implies knowledge of Semitic sounds. Similarly the second vowel of the ' Western ' form Σίλεας for Silas seems intended to represent a Semitic guttural (see below, pp. 269 f.). Knowledge of Hebrew, and of Semitic forms of names, on the part of Greek-speaking Gentile Christians, is more readily accounted for if the ' Western ' text arose in Palestine or Syria.[1] Nor is it wholly without significance that in xiii. 33 the (probably original) reading πρωτω, which accorded with Jewish usage, did not give the offence which early caused it in Alexandria to be altered to δευτερω under the influence of the LXX. In Acts iii. 11 the ' Western ' reviser seems to show independent knowledge of the plan of the temple - area at Jerusalem (see the Exegetical Note on that passage).

Conclu-
sions.
Our conclusion, then, is that the ' Western ' text was made before, and perhaps long before, the year 150, by a Greek-speaking

---

επικεφαλαιον for κηνσον. (2) Matt. xxvii. 46, Mark xv. 34 (as above); Mark v. 41, the fuller form κουμι, as written but not spoken in Aramaic (not peculiar to ' Western ' witnesses) ; Luke xvi. 20, the Semitic eleazarus (c e C T) for λαζαρος, and John xi. 14, lazar (b d) ; John v. 2, βηζαθα or the like (not peculiar to ' Western ' witnesses, but intelligently preserved by them). These readings are certainly in accord with the attribution to Antioch, but Sanday's further argument that the Latin version itself was made there does not have adequate support either from the fact that in Luke xx. 20 e (Codex Palatinus) renders ηγεμων by the appropriate Latin legatus or from the more general considerations presented (Chase, op. cit. pp. 141 f.).

[1] Several other Semitisms pointed out in the ' Western ' text have no bearing on the matter discussed in the text, and are to be ascribed to a variety of causes. The frequent use of τότε as a particle of continuation is probably not significant as indicating translation from the Aramaic ; for a list of instances see Zahn, Kommentar, p. 263, note 85. Nestle's explanation (Studien und Kritiken, vol. LXIX., 1896, pp. 102-104) of ii. 47, κοσμον for λαον, from a confusion of Aramaic 'alma and 'amma ; and of iii. 14, εβαρυνατε for ηρνησασθε, from Aramaic kebar and kebad, does not commend itself as probable. The theory of Aramaic sources of Acts does not throw light on the two forms of the Greek text, except in so far as one of these latter may have corrected awkwardness of Greek expression which had been originally occasioned by excessive literalness of translation of an Aramaic original.

Christian who knew something of Hebrew, in the East, perhaps
in Syria or Palestine.   The introduction of ' we ' in the ' Western '
text of xi. 27 possibly gives some colour to the guess that the
place was Antioch.[1] The reviser's aim was to improve the text,
not to restore it, and he lived not far from the time when the
New Testament canon in its nucleus was first definitely assembled.
It is tempting to suggest that the ' Western ' text was made
when Christian books valued for their antiquity and worth were
gathered and disseminated in a collection which afterwards
became the New Testament, and that the two processes were
parts of the same great event, perhaps at Antioch—in other
words, that the ' Western ' text was the original ' canonical ' text
(if the anachronism can be pardoned) which was later supplanted
by a ' pre-canonical ' text of superior age and merit.[2]   But such

[1] Hort, ' Introduction,' p. 108, says : " On the whole we are disposed to
suspect that the ' Western ' text took its rise in North-western Syria or Asia
Minor, and that it was soon carried to Rome, and thence spread in different
directions to North Africa and most of the countries of Europe.   From North-
western Syria it would easily pass through Palestine and Egypt to Ethiopia."

[2] Ambrosiaster (375–385), who believed the Latin Scriptures, as used by
Tertullian, Victorinus, and Cyprian, to represent the uncorrupted Greek
original, may have had some historical knowledge of the process which had
actually taken place, when he so confidently asserted that the non-western
Greek text was introduced by " *sofistae Graecorum.*" (Cf. likewise Dionysius
of Corinth ap. Eus. *h.e.* iv. 23, 12.)   The passages are as follows :
On Romans v. 14 : Et tamen sic praescribere nobis volunt de Graecis
codicibus, quasi non ipsi ab invicem discrepent ; quod fecit studium conten-
tionis.   quia enim propria quis auctoritate uti non potest ad victoriam, verba
legis adulterat, ut sensum suum quasi verbis legis adserat, uti non ratio sed
auctoritas praescribere videatur.   constat autem quosdam Latinos porro olim
de veteribus Graecis translatos codicibus, quos incorruptos simplicitas temporum
servavit et probat : postquam autem a concordia animis dissidentibus et
hereticis perturbantibus torqueri quaestiones coeperunt, multa inmutata sunt
ad sensum humanum, ut hoc contineretur litteris, quod homini videretur.
unde et ipsi Graeci diversos codices habent.   hoc autem verum arbitror,
quando et ratio et historia et auctoritas conservatur : nam hodie quae in
Latinis reprehenduntur codicibus sic inveniuntur a veteribus posita, Ter-
tulliano et Victorino et Cypriano.
On Galatians ii. 1-2 : Praeterea, cum legem dedissent non molestari eos
qui ex gentibus credebant, sed ut ab his tantum observarent, id est, a sanguine
et fornicatione et idolatria, nunc dicant sofistae Graecorum, qui sibi peritiam
vindicant, naturaliter subtilitate ingenii se vigere, quae tradita sunt gentibus
observanda.   quae ignorabant, an quae sciebant ? sed quo modo fieri potest
ut aliquis discat ea quae novit ? ergo haec inlicita esse ostensa sunt gentibus,

a theory involves many considerations, and would have grave consequences for the earliest history of the New Testament canon ; and it cannot be discussed in the present Essay.[1]

Recon-
structions
of the
'Western'
Text.

The reconstruction of the ' Western ' text of Acts in a Greek form which shall be superior to the confused and altered text of Codex Bezae is a task which is capable of only approximate execution. Blass's text (*Acta Apostolorum, sive Lucae ad Theophilum liber alter, secundum formam quae videtur Romanam*, 1896) was constructed under the influence of his theory of two editions from the same author; it suffers from the influence of that theory, from insufficient weighing of the precise character of all the heterogeneous witnesses, and from arbitrariness of judgment. Hilgenfeld's text (*Acta apostolorum graece et latine*, 1899) is founded on the editor's judgment of the superiority of the ' Western ' text, but is inadequate.[2]   Zahn agrees with Blass's theory, and his Greek text (*Die Urausgabe der Apostelgeschichte des Lucas*, 1916), with its admirable apparatus, is of great and permanent value, and approaches the ideal much more closely than either of the other reconstructions, but at many points other scholars will find occasion to reach a different conclusion as to what the original ' Western ' text probably read.

---

quae putabant licere. ac per hoc non utique ab homicidio prohibiti sunt, cum jubentur a sanguine observare; sed hoc acceperunt quod Noe a deo didicerat, ut observarent a sanguine edendo cum carne. nam quo modo fieri poterat ut Romanis legibus imbuti, quorum tanta auctoritas in servandis mandatis est, nescirent homicidium non esse faciendum, quippe cum adulteros et homicidas et falsos testes et fures et maleficos et ceterorum malorum admissores puniant leges Romanae ? denique tria haec mandata ab apostolis et senioribus data repperiuntur, quae ignorant leges Romanae, id est ut observent se ab idolatria et sanguine, sicut Noe, et a fornicatione. quae sofistae Graecorum non intellegentes, scientes tamen a sanguine abstinendum, adulterarunt scripturam, quartum mandatum addentes, ' et a suffocato ' observandum (*v.l.* abstinendum) ; quod, puto, nunc dei nutu intellecturi sunt, quia jam supra dictum erat, quod addiderunt.

[1] A certain approach to the general view here suggested is made in the important article by J. Chapman, ' The Earliest New Testament,' *Expositor*, 1905, vol. XII. pp. 119-127, the theme of which is " the contents of the Western New Testament."

[2] See Corssen's review, with much instructive discussion of the general subject, in *Göttingische gelehrte Anzeigen*, vol. 163, 1901, pp. 1-15.

NOTE ON VON SODEN'S VIEW OF HIS SUPPOSED
I-TEXT OF ACTS

Von Soden has tried to show that the witnesses to the
'Western' text owe their peculiarities to a variety of causes, at
work in various ways in the individual cases, and that the I-text
as a whole, when properly clarified and recovered, is closely akin
to the H-text and to the base of the K-text. Under his view
the ordinary conception of the 'Western' text as a strikingly
divergent text, which may have been due to a rewriting, largely
disappears. Comment on this view is in place here.

As a rule, though not quite always, the mixed character of
the witnesses to the 'Western' text of Acts, and the fragmentary
nature of many of them, make the positive fact of the *presence*
of a 'Western' reading in one or more of them much more
important than the *absence* of any given 'Western' reading
from the great mass of them. That von Soden missed this is the
great source of weakness in his treatment of the 'Western' text.
The original 'Western' text must be regarded as a paraphrastic
text which differed from the Old Uncial text more radically and
completely than any of its descendants, and which in a long
course of history in widely distant localities has been combined
by various mixtures with the competing texts, so that in the
extant Greek documents it nowhere exists in its purity, but only
in a weakened form or (in most cases) in isolated fragments.
Through the recognition and combination of these survivals,
now found in strangely scattered places, the text which once
existed in unity can be measurably recovered. Von Soden,
on the contrary, took as the primary subject of his study not
the scattered 'Western' fragments, recognizable even though
attested by only one or two of the witnesses, but the agreements
between the main types of 'Western' witnesses ; thus he hoped
to arrive at their common base. So in D he not only first purges
the text of its obvious latinizations, and of the conflations and
substitutions from the non-western text, and of its own individual

vagaries, as every student must do before using it as a ' Western '
witness, but carries this process to an unreasonable extreme, by
the use of the I-codices, so that all that is left for his I-text is
a comparatively harmless body of readings capable of serving as
a common base for all the I-codices, and from which nearly all
the readings that make the group interesting have been dropped
as later corruptions of the original I-text.   This means in practice
that the weaker representatives of the ' Western ' textual tradition are taken as the standard, and that from the more characteristic members of the group (like D) only those parts are used
which stand on this lower level.   The result is the supposed
discovery that for the most part the I-text was merely one
particular selection and combination among others, all drawn
from the variant readings which circulated in the second and
third centuries.   That may have been the case with the text of
Eusebius, with which von Soden identifies his I-text, but the
' Western ' text as found in the African Latin or, in damaged
form, in Codex Bezae is not to be explained from such an origin.
The list of readings in which von Soden finds that the I-text
differed from the H-text is a short one, covering barely a page
and a half (pp. 1756-1758), and, apparently, in not a single case
among these few is the reading ascribed to the I-text foreign to
the H-text, or at least to some one or more of the H-codices.
The I-text, as a really distinct form of text, has evaporated.   In
von Soden's apparatus (in his volume ii.), in Acts, chaps. i.-v.,
I in black-faced type occurs about thirty-eight times, indicating
cases where the editor thinks he has surely identified the I-
reading (cf. vol. ii. p. 25).   Of these, twenty-eight agree with the
black-faced **H**, two more with Codex B, four more with black-
faced **K**.   In the face of these facts there can be little confidence
that what von Soden calls the I-text in Acts represents any real
entity that ever actually existed.   At best it would seem to be
merely a mixed text of late date.   At the close of his discussion
the really interesting readings, which successively, one class after
another, have previously been thrown to one side as not a part

of the I-text, are brought to the front again, and von Soden argues (pp. 1833 f.) from the diversity and kaleidoscopic combinations of the witnesses that these have all " enriched " their text from a common source. That is perhaps true of most or all of the mixed I-codices (including Codex Laudianus) which, with Codex Bezae, make up von Soden's lists of I-groups ; but for Codex Bezae and the manuscripts containing Old Latin readings (but not for Codex Laudianus) the process seems to have been the reverse of this. Rather, by gradual stages and under the intricate working of various forces, a ' Western ' archetypal text has been *impoverished*, and the resulting text brought to correspond more and more closely to the types which became prevalent in the fourth century and thereafter. Von Soden's assemblage and grouping of the numerous I-codices was novel, and possesses great permanent value; and all who study the text of any section of the New Testament have occasion for gratitude to its author; but in his attempt to recover an I-text, his treatment, at any rate for the Book of Acts, has confused two wholly different phenomena, and has thus led him to entirely wrong conclusions.

4. THE OLD UNCIAL TEXT

Witnesses. IF we may conclude that the ' Western ' text of Acts was due to a rewriting which took place early in the second century, it follows that the original text in greater or less purity has been preserved for us by the witnesses here termed the ' Old Uncial ' group. The chief of these are BℵAC 81 and other minuscules (von Soden's H-group; see above, p. xxiv), together with many of the papyri and other ancient fragments, the Sahidic, and especially the Bohairic version.[1] Probably the oldest form of the Georgian version belongs with these, as does the Latin Vulgate. The meagre citations of Clement of Alexandria and Origen are sufficient to justify the inclusion of those fathers in the list, and here belong also the later Alexandrian writers—Athanasius, Didymus, Cyril of Alexandria, Cosmas Indicopleustes.

Alexandria. Nearly all of this evidence can be traced to Alexandria, or at least to Egypt. That country seems to have been the place of origin of codices Bℵ 81 ; and the papyri are all Egyptian, as are most of the other early fragments (fourth to seventh century) which show the characteristics of this text. The Alexandrian writers who quote this text in Acts cover the whole period from the end of the second to the middle of the sixth century, and no Alexandrian writers appear in those centuries who used any other text for our book. The two vernacular Egyptian versions speak for themselves; and Jerome was dependent on Alexandrian learning. Of the codices, however, the provenance of A and C is

---

[1] The Bohairic version is an excellent representative of the Old Uncial text, so far as the nature of the Coptic vernacular permits. Its precise relationship to the several witnesses of its group can be studied in the Appendix, below (pp. 357-371).ʼ

doubtful; as we have seen, A may have come from Constantinople.
Two fragments containing this text (fifth century and seventh
century) have come through Georgian hands,[1] one (seventh
century) through Syrian ; but these indications throw little light
on the earlier use of the Old Uncial text.   We have at present no
direct knowledge as to what type of Acts was current in the
Greek-speaking regions of Palestine and Syria in the second
century, or in Asia Minor or Greece in the second and third
centuries, before the rise of the Antiochian revision in the fourth
century and the spread of that revision and of mixed texts in the
subsequent period. As for the Latin-speaking Christianity of the
West and the Syriac-speaking Christians of the East, no evidence
has as yet been adduced to show that any other Greek text than
the ' Western' had made its way into these lands earlier than the
fourth century in the West and the fifth century in the East.

On the other hand, against the supposition that the Old
Uncial text remained through the centuries the only text known
in Alexandria, we may take warning from the fact that the " very
accurate and approved " copy from which the Harclean Syriac
was revised in Alexandria in 616 was of the Antiochian type, and
from the discovery in the Genizah at Cairo of a sixth-century
palimpsest fragment (093) with an excellent Antiochian text.   Of
the later diffusion of the Old Uncial text something could be
learned by study of the minuscules belonging to this group and
named above (p. xxiv).   Such a study might possibly throw
light on the earlier history as well.   If Hesychius prepared
a recension of the New Testament, it was before the time of
Jerome, and would have to be looked for somewhere among
the Old Uncial witnesses, but, as has already been sufficiently
emphasized, this elusive personage constitutes a problem, not a
datum, of criticism.[2]

[1] On the relation of Georgian Christianity to the monastery at Mount Sinai,
see Robert P. Blake, ' The Text of the Gospels and the Koridethi Codex,'
Harvard Theological Review, vol. xvi., 1923, pp. 277-283.

[2] See above, pp. xc, xcii, xcv note 2, ciii note 5.   Bousset, ' Die Recension
des Hesychius,' *Textkritische Studien zum Neuen Testament* (Texte und

Greek
codices.

As documents of the Old Uncial text of Acts in Greek, codices BℵAC 81 are chiefly to be considered. Next to them, but at a considerable remove, and much more mixed in character, would probably come Ψ and 33 (" the queen of the cursives "). Von Soden states (pp. 1668 f.) that 326 (Oxford, Lincoln College, E. 82 ; formerly Gregory 33[ac] ; *a* 257) is akin to 33, and that the text of their common ancestor, which can be reconstructed, would probably be found as good as that of A or C. Also the Patmos manuscript 1175 (Monastery of St. John, 16 ; formerly Gregory 389[ac] ; *a* 74) appears from von Soden's statements to be of equal excellence with 81.[1]

In the case of all these MSS. it is necessary to ask whether their text has been in any degree contaminated from the 'Western' text or from the Antiochian recension. Their dates do not in any instance exclude the possibility of Antiochian influence. But this inquiry meets grave difficulties. Not only is the 'Western' text imperfectly known to us, and its chief Greek representative positively known to be contaminated from the non-western side, but both in the 'Western' and the Antiochian text a large proportion of the readings were not newly coined and peculiar to these texts, but ancient readings derived from their bases, so that the presence of such readings in one of the Old Uncial group need not imply contamination.

Bearing these considerations in mind, we turn to the five chief MSS. of the Old Uncial group—BℵAC 81. From them in the main must be elicited by critical processes knowledge of the text of Acts as it existed apart from the 'Western' rewriting and before the Antiochian recension.

Codex
Vaticanus.

First to be considered is Codex Vaticanus. Here four questions arise :

Untersuchungen, XI.), 1894, pp. 74-110, thinks that in the Gospels B represents the text of Hesychius ; and von Soden has made the same conjecture, and used it to give the designation 'H' to what is called in the present volume the 'Old Uncial' text.

[1] The text of the Patmos codex is known only from von Soden's apparatus and from his discussion, pp. 1669 f., 1928.

1. Has the text of B been influenced by the 'Western' rewriting ?

2. Does it contain readings which have been introduced into it from the Antiochian recension ?

3. It contains a considerable number of individual, or 'singular,' readings in which it diverges from the other members of its group, and which either lack support altogether or find but little, and perhaps accidental, support in any other witnesses to the text of Acts. How far are these to be deemed corruptions introduced by the scribe of B or of one of its ancestors ?

4. When the testimony of the Old Uncial group of five is divided, can any general conclusions be drawn as to the usual value of the testimony of any of the sub-groups, and in particular of the sub-groups of which B is a member ?

If these questions could be convincingly and fully answered, the problem of the text of Codex Vaticanus would be mainly solved. One further question, however, ought to be mentioned, upon which light can perhaps sometime be thrown by renewed comprehensive palæographical study of the MS. itself, the question, namely, which of the corrections now found on its pages were added by the first hand, or the diorthotes, before the codex was issued from the scriptorium where it was executed.

1. To consider the four questions in order, in the first place it seems clear that B was not appreciably influenced by the 'Western' text of Acts. Characteristic readings betraying the recognizable 'Western' type do not appear in it ; and the impression gained from this observation is confirmed by the small number, and the character, of the cases in which, standing alone and departing from the other four of its group, it agrees with D.[1] For those portions of the book in which all five of the

Freedom from 'Western' influence in Acts.

[1] In Acts v. 32, the words εν αυτω, characteristic of the 'Western' text, seem to have been inserted into the text of an ancestor of B which lacked them ; but this may well have been a contamination from the ancient base of the 'Western' text, not from the 'Western' rewriting itself (see Textual Note). In Acts ii. 5 the introduction of ιουδαιοι seems to have been present in the 'Western' text, but this may have been a pre-western corruption (see Textual Note).

Old Uncial group, together with Codex Bezae, are extant, constituting about one-fourth of the whole book,[1] the figures, which include some cases where the agreement with D is only substantial and not complete, are as follows : [2]

AGREEMENTS WITH D

B alone	.	.	.	.	13
א ,,	.	.	.	.	9
A ,,	.	.	.	.	11
C ,,	.	.	.	.	34
81 ,,	.	.	.	.	11

Of the thirteen cases found for B all are trifling variants, not to be associated with the characteristic rewriting of the ' Western ' text ; and most of them are probably to be accepted as the original reading, probably preserved independently in the two lines of descent.   An examination of the several sub-groups made up of B and *two* of the others of the Old Uncial group shows, for the same portions of the book, even smaller totals in each case. (I have not found, as it happens, any instances where B accompanied by only *one* other of its group agrees with D).   The agreement of B with *three* others of its group and D is not significant for B, for it only means that in such a case one of the Old Uncial group has an isolated variant.   If C, 81, and D were extant for the whole book, the figures would all be larger, but there is no

---

[1] For the passages, covering nearly one-half of the Book of Acts, in which BאAC 81 are all extant, see below, p. cclvii note 1.   C contains not quite two-thirds of the book, 81 almost exactly three-quarters.   D is extant as follows : i. 1-viii. 29, x. 14-xxi. 2, xxi. 10-xxii. 10, xxii. 20-29.   The precise points of division within the verses will be found accurately noted by Gregory.

[2] Pains have been taken to make these and similar figures accurate, but absolute accuracy and completeness cannot be claimed for them, and they ought to be used only for inferences which are not invalidated by a reasonable margin of error.   In any case, questions of judgment often enter into the determination of how to count variants ; for instance, whether as one or two, or where slight minor variation is present.   The statistics have been drawn up from the apparatus made for the present volume, in which the aim has been to omit obvious blunders and variations due to spelling in all the MSS. used.   This should not be taken as implying that such errors and unusual spellings are not in themselves worthy of attention for certain critical purposes.

reason to suppose that their relation to one another would be substantially different. The portions covered come from various sections of chapters i.-xxii.

2. For Codex Vaticanus the claim is also made, and perhaps with justice, that it is substantially, and probably completely, free from Antiochian influence.[1] The evidence, however, for this is somewhat less decisive than that relating to 'Western' influence. The following approximate figures, again relating only to the portions common to all five of the Old Uncial group, are suggestive :

Freedom from Antiochian influence.

VARIANTS FROM ALL FOUR OTHERS OF THE GROUP

	Total 'singular' variants	Agreements with Antiochian	Percentages
B . . .	96	10	10 per cent
ℵ . . .	158	12	7 ,,
A . . .	120	13	11 ,,
C . . .	186	44	24 ,,
81 . . .	101	27	27 ,,

The groups of two MSS. containing B, ℵ, or A, show, with the exception of the group AC (see below, p. cclxviii), even smaller numbers (though generally larger percentages) of agreements with the Antiochian text.

For the whole book the corresponding figures for BℵA are :

B . . .	221	30	14 per cent
ℵ . . .	311	20	6 ,,
A . . .	297	46	15 ,,

But the small number of MSS. under comparison, and in each MS. the great mass of variants due to other causes than Antiochian influence, make this method of statistical inquiry tedious and unsatisfactory. The most that these and other comparative figures show seems to be that any influence of the Antiochian recension on B was very limited in scope, and that no positive

[1] Hort, 'Introduction,' p. 150: "Its [B's] text is throughout Pre-Syrian, perhaps purely Pre-Syrian, at all events with hardly any, if any, quite clear exceptions."

numerical evidence suggests that the text of B suffered such
influence at all. A conclusion must rest on the study of the
readings themselves, and this in fact does not reveal cases that
require the assumption of Antiochian influence. With extremely
few exceptions the cases of agreement of B and the Antiochian
can best be regarded as readings of the B-text which served as a
base for the Antiochian revisers.[1] This opinion is an inference
from the fact that these readings, so far as internal character
permits a judgment, almost always commend themselves as probably right. The situation is otherwise with the agreements, for
instance, of A and C with the Antiochian. The exceptions, where
B-Antiochian readings appear to be wrong, are (generally, if not
always) trifling variants, probably due to independent corruption,
so that the agreement is to be deemed accidental, not significant.

Superiority of B.

The view that B is superior to the other members of its group
rests on the internal superiority of its readings in those numerous
cases where the nature of the readings permits a judgment.
Where the five witnesses divide into opposing groups of two or
three, or where B with three others stands opposed to a single
dissentient, there are hardly any cases in Acts where "internal
evidence of readings" leads to the preference of the reading not
supported by B. This superiority of text, where internal tests
can be applied, is in accord with three observations already set
forth, namely (1) the fact that the text of B seems to belong,
with the papyri, to the period of earlier and freer variation ; (2)
the care with which it was written ; and (3) the pre-origenian
character of the text of many books in its Old Testament section.
Moreover, B contains in Acts fewer of what may be termed
idiosyncrasies than do others of the Old Uncial group.[2]

'Singular' readings.

3. In support of this last statement as to the 'singular'
readings of B, the following figures are instructive, although,
here as elsewhere, crude statistics are not demonstrative without

---

[1] The same problem arises in the LXX ; see above, pp. civ, cxxvi.

[2] It seems probable, moreover, that the corrections of many of the 'singular'
readings of B may be ascribed to the diorthotes of the scriptorium, so that in
justice the errors ought not to be attributed to the completed manuscript.

refinement by various reductions and analyses. For drawing up these and similar tables the Book of Acts has to be divided into the portions attested by all five, by four, and by three, witnesses of the Old Uncial group,[1] and the figures give the approximate number of instances in which each MS. stands alone without support from any other of the group.

'SINGULAR' READINGS OF THE OLD UNCIAL GROUP

	B	ℵ	A	C	81
I. (BℵAC 81) . .	96	158	120	186	101
II. (BℵAC) . . .	26	44	45	54	..
III. (BℵA 81) . . .	50	61	65	..	53
IV. (BℵA) . . .	51	48	67	..	..
	223	311	297		

The difference in the number of these 'singular' readings between B and ℵ, A, C is large enough to be significant. The relatively small number of such readings in 81 is also significant, and will come up for discussion below. The causes which have produced such 'singular' readings are different in the several MSS.

For another illustration the passage i. 2-iv. 3 may be taken.

'SINGULAR' READINGS IN I. 2—IV. 3

	B	ℵ	A	C	81
Total	17	27	17	25	14
Shared with Antiochian .	5	4	5	6	7
Not Antiochian but shared with others outside of group	7	7	6	9	2
Probably cases of idiosyncrasy	5	16	6	10	5

[1] The contents severally of the four Divisions is as follows :—I. (BℵAC 81) : i. 2-iv. 3, vii. 17-x. 42, xiii. 1-xvi. 36, xxiii. 9-18, xxiv. 15-xxvi. 19, xxvii. 16-xxviii. 4 ; II. (BℵAC): v. 35-vii. 17, xx. 10-xxi. 30, xxii. 21-xxiii. 9 ; III. (BℵA 81) : i. 1-2, iv. 3-8, x. 43-xiii. 1, xvi. 37-xvii. 28, xxiii. 18-xxiv. 15, xxvi. 19-xxvii. 16, xxviii. 5-31 ; IV. (BℵA) : iv. 8-v. 34, xvii. 29-xx. 10, xxi. 31-xxii. 20. For the precise points of division, within the verses, of the missing parts of C and 81, see Gregory.

Although judgments would differ in a few instances as to the readings here counted, such cases will be found too few to affect the plain force of the comparison.   It seems that B is superior to both ℵ and C in the small number of readings which it has that may be due merely to the vagary of the scribe.   But this investigation would have to be carried much farther to become more than a suggestive guide to research.

The figures, however, of the first table, p. cclv, show that although B is more free than the other four of its group from readings in which it stands alone among them, yet the number of its ' singular ' readings is so considerable as to constitute a definite problem.

The readings in which B has, so far as reported, no support from any Greek authority whatever are about 90 ; those others in which it has no support from the Old Uncial group are about 133.   Of the former class (no Greek support) only the following seven seem to call for acceptance, and four of these are supported by versions :

   vii. 49 και η.
    x. 19 om αυτω.
    x. 19 δυο.
  xiii. 42 εις το μεταξυ σαββατον ηξιουν.
   xvi. 19 και ιδοντες.
   xvi. 26 om παραχρημα.
  xxiv. 26 om αυτω.

All of these are found in parts of Acts where all five witnesses of the Old Uncial group are extant ; all of them, except x. 19 and xiii. 42, are of trifling importance, and in all a judgment is difficult.[1]   In a large proportion of the other readings of the ninety the ' singular ' reading of B is clearly either transcriptionally or intrinsically inferior to that of the other witnesses.   In more than three-quarters of the readings of the class no version adds its support to B ; of the barely twenty cases where a version

[1] Westcott and Hort accept the reading of B in the first three of the seven cases here listed ; in the last four they relegate it to second place.

agrees with B the reading is plainly wrong in at least four, and in all the agreement may be due to accidental coincidence in trifles. We may say with some positiveness that *where B is without other Greek support*, it is ordinarily to be rejected.[1] Of the ninety instances a little more than one-third are omissions. In fact, many of these completely ' singular ' readings do not differ essentially from the unquestionable blunders of the scribe of B which are corrected in any printed text. The only difference is that in the class of cases here under discussion the scribe's blunder happened to produce a tolerable sense ; so, for example, vii. 51, καρδιας B for καρδιαις ; xi. 25, αναστησαι B for αναζητησαι ; xii. 8 υποδυσαι B for υποδησαι ; xxvi. 7 καταντησειν B for καταντησαι ; also such cases of omission as x. 21 η ; xxiii. 6 εγω ; or the repetition in xix. 34 of μεγαλη η αρτεμις εφεσιων.

In the other class of about 133 readings, in which B stands without other Old Uncial support but with some (though often slight) support from other Greek witnesses, a little less than one-half seem on the whole worthy of acceptance. Care must here be exercised not to be much influenced by supporting testimony in cases of easy scribal errors which may well have arisen independently (for instance, xxvii. 34 προ B Ψ minuscules, surely an error for προς ; see Textual Note). In such readings isolated minuscule (or even uncial) support is of little consequence. The readings, not of this latter nature, which do receive substantial support apart from B, deserve careful consideration, particularly where D or the Antiochian reënforces B ; among these it is probable that many were also found in other very ancient MSS. Here the internally inferior readings are to be rejected ; the others, including those whose internal character gives no positive indication, I have counted as genuine, and they make up the proportion of a little less than one-half, as just stated.[2] Many

---

[1] Most of the cases in which Westcott and Hort depart from B are of the class discussed above. It would have been of advantage to their text if they had rejected more of these ' singular ' readings of B.

[2] The case of iv. 33 shows the kind of complication which is capable of arising, and may be instructive in this connexion. B του κυριου ιησου της αναστασεως

cases in this group must remain very uncertain; for instance, xiii. 44 τε BP minuscules for δε, xvi. 14 παυλου BD for του παυλου, both being cases in which I have ventured to reject the reading of B. In some such instances the habitual practice of the writer of Acts can be a guide; for instance, xiii. 17, where του B Ψ vg sah for τουτου before ισραηλ seems surely wrong. Sometimes the reading which produces a more forcible meaning in the sentence will on that ground be accepted as more probably the original writer's; for instance (to take two good instances where B has no Greek support at all), the omission by B alone of εγω in xxiii. 6, or of πασιν in xxiv. 14. It is to be observed that in the readings of the class under discussion the versions, as it happens, by reason of their inability to show varieties of Greek expression, usually give no aid in reaching a decision.

A fair conclusion seems to be that B, *when without support from others of its group but with some other support*, is sometimes wrong, sometimes right, and that while, here as elsewhere, on general grounds there may be some balance of presumption in favour of B, yet for this class of readings the presumption is not strong.

Sub-groups containing B.

4. The sub-groups which contain B. That the variations of single MSS., without support from any other MS. of the Old Uncial group, constitute the bulk of the variations within the group is shown by the following table for the portions in which BℵAC 81 are all extant (Division I.), comprising a little less than one-half of the entire book. The total number of *loci variationis*, each of which appears at least twice in the table, is about 780. The actual variants are attested as follows:

---

stands quite alone, but it is a variant (in order only) from της αναστασεως του κυριου ιησου, which happens to be preserved in Pap⁸, is the reading of the Antiochian text, and seems to be right. The opposing, wrong reading (της αναστασεως ιησου χριστου του κυριου) is supported by ℵA. C and 81 are both lacking for this passage. Of the three readings neither B nor ℵA is right, but B is much nearer right than ℵA. Pap⁸ shows that the reading of the Antiochian text is ancient. If the very unusual evidence of Pap⁸ were not available, we should have to say that the Antiochian text alone had preserved the true reading. But B has only just missed it. See the Textual Note on this passage.

By one MS. . .	B	96
	81	101
	A	120
	ℵ	158
	C	186
		——
Total, by one MS. .		661
By two MSS. . .		204
By three MSS. . .		214
By four MSS. . .		540

The discrepancies of the numbers are of course due to the fact that in some *loci* three variants occur, each attested respectively by three, one, and one, or by two, two, and one MS.

In the case of B, ' singular ' variants commend themselves as worthy of acceptance in about the proportion of two-sevenths only ; of the ' singular ' readings of the other four MSS. hardly any show positive marks of genuineness. The number of cases where a division in the group calls for a decision is thus reduced to a little over 200.

For this smaller body of variants attested by a group of *two* within the Old Uncial group, the attestation is distributed as follows (approximate accuracy only being claimed for the figures, as explained above, p. ccliv note 2) :

Groups of two.

GROUPS OF TWO MSS.

DIVISION I.   (BℵAC 81)

Bℵ	29		ℵA	10
BA	9		ℵC	15
BC	29		ℵ81	9
B 81	19			
AC	36		C 81	31
A 81	17			

Every possible combination is represented in these groups, and some, though limited, inferences can be drawn from them. Groups of this sort may mean either (*a*) that the two component

MSS. agree in authentic readings, from which all others have departed, or (*b*) that the two have been alike subjected to the same corrupting influence and perhaps are both derived from the same corrupt exemplar. In the former case (*a*), lines of ancestry of the two may have been entirely independent at every stage since the original autograph. In the latter (*b*), there will be a presumption, though not a certainty, that the two lines of ancestry are not independent of each other.

Of these binary groups only four—Bℵ, BC, AC, C 81—are noticeable for their size. The group Bℵ is not large enough to justify treating these two codices as a single persistent sub-group. If B and ℵ, being the oldest, independently contain an unusual number of uncorrupted readings, that would fully account for this group. As a matter of fact, most of these twenty-nine readings are probably original, but in a few cases the two codices seem to agree in error. A few of these errors are vii. 38 $υμιν$ Bℵ latt Iren for $ημιν$; vii. 46 $οικω$ BℵHSD 429 d sah (one codex) for $θεω$ (see Textual Note) ; with which may be mentioned v. 31 $του$ Bℵ, omitted (C and 81 being deficient) by A, D, and the Antiochian ; viii. 5 $την$ $πολιν$ BℵA minuscules, where C D 81 Antiochian sah boh omit $την$.[1] The group Bℵ is less out of scale in comparison with other binary groups containing B than when compared with those containing ℵ. This is probably due to the excellence both of the text of B and of that of ℵ (when the latter does not have an erratic ' singular ' reading), for in fact it means that ℵ relatively seldom goes wrong when in company with one other of the group. This is evidence that ℵ is not by ancestry specifically akin to any one of them.

---

[1] Of these instances, in vii. 38 and vii. 46, Westcott and Hort reject the reading of Bℵ, in v. 31 they bracket the word, in viii. 5 they follow BℵA. Von Soden rejects the reading of Bℵ in all four cases. Besides the errors in Bℵ noted in the text above, the following seem to the present writer cases where Bℵ agree in error against one or more of the Old Uncial group : v. 28 om $ου$; x. 17 om $και$; xi. 11 $ημεν$; xiii. 18 $ετροποφορησεν$; xiii. 33 $ημων$; xviii. 7 + $τιτιου$ ($τιτου$); xix. 27 $μελλειν$ $τε$ $και$ $καθαιρεισθαι$ $της$ $μεγαλειοτητος$; xx. 28 $θεου$; xxi. 21 + $παντας$.

The relatively large size of the group BC is probably to be accounted for by the goodness of C except when C is influenced by the ' Western ' or the Antiochian text. Conversely, note the small size of the group BA. In such low numbers accident may have played a considerable part, but in the other divisions of the book a similar relation of the groups Bℵ, BC, and BA is generally found, so far as the groups exist, thus :

	Bℵ	BC	BA
Division II. (BℵAC) . .	9	10	7
„ III. (BℵA 81) . .	19	—	8
„ IV. (BℵA) . . .	58	—	40

Of the groups AC and C 81 something will be said below in connexion with those codices.

The groups of *three* in Division I. are as follows :

Groups of three.

BℵA	33	ℵAC	16
BℵC	18	ℵA 81	33
Bℵ 81	31	ℵC 81	13
BAC	11		
BA 81	15	AC 81	29
BC 81	15		

From these sub-groups of three, taken by themselves, no valid inference suggests itself ; but although it is evident that B is not closely connected through any near ancestor with any other of the Old Uncial group, yet a study of the groups of two and the groups of three together will furnish further statistical evidence of the resemblance of B and ℵ. If we eliminate from consideration, as we ought to do, the ' singular ' readings, which appear in varying proportions in the several codices, ℵ evinces itself as decidedly nearer to B than is any one of the other three (AC 81), while the other three are about equal in the extent of their agreement with B. The process on which this conclusion rests may be illustrated by the comparison of ℵ and A, thus (Division I.) :

Bℵ	29		BA	9
BℵC	18		BAC	11
Bℵ 81	31		BA 81	15
	—			—
	78			35

From this it is clear that ℵ is decidedly nearer to B than is A. A similar process gives the same result for C and 81 also, as just stated.   If the figures for Division I. are taken as a whole, it appears that for each MS. the number of cases of divergence from B (omitting the 'singular' readings of each and including only those where a sub-group opposes B) is as follows : ℵ 170, A 205, C 214, 81 206.   A further investigation of all sub-groups, paying close regard to the individual readings in detail and their relation to other MSS., especially codex 1175 (Patmos), would be worth while, and might bring out some interesting relationships between the codices.

Rule for
use of B.   Where B is supported by at least one, but not by all, of the Old Uncial group, and where 'internal evidence of readings' is an applicable criterion, B is found to be probably right in nearly all cases, and the rule may be deduced that the reading of B is to be accepted unless positive evidence to the contrary can be brought.   This practice will doubtless lead the critic astray in some cases, but no better rule is at hand.[1]   On possible genuine readings embedded in the 'Western' rewriting, see above, pp. ccxxxv f.; on the possibility that all the Old Uncial group may be wrong, and the reading of the Antiochian text right, see below, pp. cclxxxiv f.   The grounds of this excellence of B have already been stated (p. cclvi).

Codex
Sinaiticus.   With regard to the text of Codex Sinaiticus in Acts not much is to be added to what has already been said in discussing Codex Vaticanus. The 'Western' text has exercised no observable influence on ℵ.   That the Antiochian likewise has probably not influenced ℵ can also be shown,[2] for if there had been any direct

---

[1] Cf. F. C. Burkitt, *The Book of Rules of Tyconius*, 1894, p. cxviii.

[2] In the LXX the text of ℵ in the Psalter and the Prophets is said to show some traces of Lucianic influence ; see pp. xcix, cclxxxviii.

influence from it, we should expect it to appear in the ' singular '
readings, where ℵ has no support from any other of its group.
But here, out of a total of about 311 such readings in the whole of
Acts, only 20 (that is, 6 per cent) agree with the Antiochian text.
It is convenient to give here the figures for the other MSS. of the
group. They are given first for Division I., then for the whole book
(Divisions I.-IV., without reference to the defects of C and 81).

'SINGULAR' READINGS COMPARED WITH ANTIOCHIAN TEXT.

DIVISION I.	B	ℵ	A	C	81
Total ' singular ' readings .	96	158	120	186	101
Agreements of these with } Antiochian	10	12	13	44	27
Percentages . . .	10	7	11	24	27

DIVISIONS I.-IV.	B	ℵ	A	C	81
Total ' singular ' readings	221	311	297	240	154
Agreements of these with } Antiochian	30	20	46	58	44
Percentages . . .	14	6	15	24	. 29

Again, where ℵ has the company of one other of the Old Uncial
group in departing from B, in no case does a large proportion of
agreement with the Antiochian text suggest influence from that
text on a common ancestor of the two.[1]   The agreement with the
Antiochian is more probably due to a resemblance between ℵ and
the Old Antiochian base of the Antiochian recension, if such a base
may properly be assumed to have existed.

[1] The group ℵA 81, indeed, which both subtends a larger number of readings
than any other group of three not containing B, and also seems to show a greater
proportion of Antiochian agreements (73 per cent), stands out in this latter
respect conspicuous.   But the explanation is probably to be sought in some
fact of textual history which has made a cleft between the two types represented respectively by BC and ℵA 81, and in some connexion between the
foundations of the Antiochian recension and the text of ℵA 81. A more
searching and comprehensive study might throw light here on some of the
general problems of the New Testament text. The positive, though limited,
' Western ' element in C does not seem to be connected in any way with this
other phenomenon.

'Singular'
readings.

The 'singular' readings of ℵ are numerous and peculiar. In 'singular' readings not in agreement with the Antiochian, ℵ leads over A and 81 by a large margin, and if 'Western' agreements are likewise omitted, ℵ shows a much larger number of 'singular' readings than C.[1] Some of these have been cited already (p. xlviii note 4) in treating of the general character of ℵ. Most of them are vagaries, perhaps of the scribe of this codex itself, and hardly any commend themselves as deserving acceptance, but a more thorough examination of them in their relations to other witnesses might bring out some useful observations.

That ℵ is nearer than any other MS. to B has already been shown.

Codex
Alexandrinus
and Codex
Ephraemi.

Codex Alexandrinus and Codex Ephraemi seem to have some bond of connexion ; in the table printed above (p. cclxi), AC is the largest of the binary groups.   Moreover, they show a curious resemblance in that almost always when an attempt is made to analyse and reduce to percentages the relation between ℵ, A, C, and 81, by using as a basis the readings in which these four depart from B, the result shows percentages of A and C close to each other, if not identical, ℵ and 81 often taking position the one on their right hand and the other on their left.   The student is continually reminded of the palaeographical resemblance of the two.   Nevertheless, the differences between A and C are, at any rate to a surface view, more striking ; and they are certainly more easily interpreted.

That a certain 'Western' element is to be recognised in A, and a larger one in C, has already been pointed out (p. ccxx). Longer, but not complete, lists of verses in which substantial agreements with the 'Western' text, or at least with the readings of Codex Bezae, occur, are as follows :

---

[1] For Division I. only, the figures of 'singular' readings, with omission of those agreeing with the Antiochian text, are : B 86, ℵ 146, A 107, C 142; Codex 81, 74.   That of the number mentioned (drawn from a little less than one-half of the whole book) C agrees with D in 30 instances, while ℵ so agrees in only 6, tells its own story, in harmony with what is said in the text above.

CODEX ALEXANDRINUS (UNSUPPORTED BY ANY OTHER OF THE
OLD UNCIAL GROUP)

ii. 6, 22.	xiv. 21, 24.
iii. 8, 13 (twice).	xv. 18.
viii. 39.	xvi. 16.
x. 37, 39.	xx. 4, 18.
xiii. 14.	xxi. 22.

CODEX EPHRAEMI (UNSUPPORTED BY ANY OTHER OF THE
OLD UNCIAL GROUP)

ii. 2, 17, 36.	xiii. 17, 20, 23, 25, 45.
iv. 2.	xiv. 6, 10, 12, 18f.
vii. 37, 60.	xv. 4, 7, 11, 23, 24, 28, 29, 34.
viii. 26.	xvi. 1, 3, 7, 19, 29, 31, 34.
ix. 22.	xxi. 25.
x. 17, 32.	

It is to be borne in mind that C includes but about two-thirds of the whole book.

In Division I., A unsupported is found in agreement with D 11 times, C in such agreement 30 times. With these figures may be compared those for א, 6 times ; for 81, 10 times ; and for B, 12 times. A and C in common against the others of the group agree in Division I. with D only about 11 times. Division I. includes about one-half of Acts, but in about one-half of this Division we do not have the evidence of D, so that the figures relate to only one-fourth of the whole book.

With regard to Antiochian influence on A and C, the evidence is more complicated, and an answer to the question more difficult to formulate with entire confidence. In other parts of the Bible, as is well known, the Psalter of A is largely Lucianic and the Gospels almost wholly Antiochian, while Lucianic influence is said to be found in the Prophets.[1] As to C, all that can be said is that in the Gospels kinship to the Antiochian text is plainly traceable, in the Pauline epistles less so (see above, p. lv).

[1] Procksch, *Studien zur Geschichte der Septuaginta : Die Propheten*, p. 86.

This inquiry in the text of Acts is best confined to Division I., for there alone is a satisfactory comparison possible. In this Division, Codex Alexandrinus stands alone in 120 readings, but in only 11 of these agrees with the Antiochian text. This seems to show that there has been no direct influence from the Antiochian text on A. The only groups containing A which suggest anything to the contrary are :

	Total readings	Agreements with Antiochian
AC	36	16
AC 81 . . .	29	18
אA 81 . . .	33	24

The facts of the groups AC and AC 81 might suggest that A and C had a common ancestor which had been slightly affected by the Antiochian recension, but the figures may equally well be due to a resemblance between the form of Old Uncial text represented by AC and that used as a base by the Antiochian revisers. The group אA 81 is the complement of BC, of which something has already been said (p. cclxiii). On the whole, it does not seem possible to affirm influence on A from the Antiochian recension.

The groups including A which depart from B seem to be less trustworthy than the complementary groups which include B, and the ' singular ' readings of A do not commend themselves as right. More complete investigation of the character of the latter is to be desired. Their number is distinctly less than that found in א or in C, but larger than that of B or 81, and this holds after agreements in each case with the Antiochian, or with D (so far as extant), or with both these, have been deducted. The figures follow :

' SINGULAR ' READINGS

DIVISION I.	B	א	A	C	81
Total ' singular ' readings .	96	158	120	186	101
Shared with Antiochian .	10	12	13	44	27
Shared with D . .	12	6	11	30	10

Codex Ephraemi wears a different aspect. Here a distinct strain of ' Western ' text is to be observed, as has been shown above. It is also probable that the Antiochian recension has exerted a direct influence on C, for out of 186 ' singular ' readings of C in Division I., 44 agree with the Antiochian. This fact may also lend significance to the group C 81, which, out of 31 readings, shows 17 in agreement with the Antiochian. Two interesting cases of agreement of C with the Antiochian text may be specially mentioned. In xx. 24 the addition $\mu\epsilon\tau a$ $\chi a\rho a\varsigma$ is characteristic of the Antiochian, and in spite of its ' Western ' ring is not attested as ' Western ' by any trustworthy testimony. In xxiv. 24, of the four different readings supported by the Old Uncial group, that of C ($\gamma v v a \iota \kappa \iota$ without addition) is identical with the Antiochian reading.

The remaining ' singular ' readings of C (112 in number in Division I.), in which it agrees neither with the Antiochian text nor with D, deserve investigation. The possibility of some obscure special relation of C to B, suggested by the group BC, has already been referred to.[1]

Codex 81 (formerly 61[ac] ; *a* 162 ; British Museum), written Codex 81.

---

[1] The relations of BℵAC to one another, to D, and to the Antiochian text, and the trustworthiness of these mss. severally, have been elaborately studied by Bernhard Weiss, *Die Apostelgeschichte : textkritische Untersuchungen und Textherstellung* (Texte und Untersuchungen, ix.), 1893, pp. 64-69. Weiss's investigation is carried on with constant reference to his conclusions as to the rightness and wrongness of the variants as given in the preceding part of his monograph (pp. 5-64), he takes careful account of the question whether a wrong reading is due to an old error or to a later emendation, and his results are presented in the form of careful and very valuable statistics. These results are not dissimilar in their broad outlines to those reached above, although his judgment naturally differs in single instances. Many cases of variation where he, with earlier critics, finds decisive internal evidence for one of the readings, would seem to me not so easy to decide. He holds that ℵ and A, as well as C, were influenced by the Antiochian text (ℵ in less degree than the others), while B was not led into error by the Antiochian. He emphasizes the small proportion of cases in which ' singular ' readings of B are to be accepted, and finds (p. 68) twenty cases where B, supported by one or more of the group ℵAC, is wrong. Weiss's criticism of the individual readings deserves careful attention from students in every case, although in order to be used it requires that an index of passages be constructed.

in 1044 by a monk John and for a monk James, is the most important minuscule of Acts of which full knowledge is at present available.[1] It was brought by Tischendorf from Egypt and may be presumed to have been written there. It contains Acts (with two gaps, iv. 8-vii. 17 ; xvii. 28-xxiii. 9), and the manuscript of the Catholic and Pauline epistles known as 2241 (formerly 241[ac] 285[p] ; Cairo, Patriarchal Library 59) was originally a part of the same codex.[2] Of handy size, not more than $18 \times 12 \cdot 6$ cm., without lectionary notes, and written with no special elegance, it was a copy such as a scholar would have had for daily use, not a church book nor a costly *édition de luxe*, and we may well question whether for informing us as to the text of Acts it is not, next to Codex Vaticanus, the most valuable MS. in existence.

Of ' Western ' influence this MS. shows hardly anything ; [3] but, as would be expected from its date in the eleventh century, when the Antiochian recension was nearly everywhere widely current, it probably shows some direct Antiochian influence. Of its ' singular ' readings a larger proportion than in the case of any other of the five MSS. of its group agree with the Antiochian, and these may well be derived therefrom.

' SINGULAR ' READINGS

DIVISION I. (BℵAC 81)	B	ℵ	A	C	81
' Singular ' readings . .	96	158	120	186	101
Shared with Antiochian .	10	12	13	44	27
Percentages . . .	10	7	11	24	27

[1] Hort, ' Introduction,' p. 154: " By far the most free [of the cursives] from Syrian readings is 61 of the Acts, which contains a very ancient text, often Alexandrian, rarely Western, with a trifling Syrian element, probably of late introduction."

[2] The credit for this important discovery belongs to Paul Glaue, one of von Soden's bibliographical explorers, now professor at Jena.

[3] The long ' Western ' addition found in 81 in Acts xiv. 19 is not a significant exception to this statement, for it is given not only by hcl.*mg* and C, but also by a very large number of minuscules. Zahn, however, is probably wrong in thinking it a part of the non-western text, and that it fell out by homoeoteleuton ; see Textual Note.

DIVISION III. (BℵA 81)	B	ℵ	A	C	81
' Singular ' readings . .	50	61	65	..	53
Shared with Antiochian .	5	2	11	..	17
Percentages . . .	10	3	17	..	32

It agrees with C thirty-one times in Division I. ; and seventeen
of these cases are readings also found in the Antiochian text, and
may be due to an Antiochian strain in the common ancestor of
the two.   The group AC 81 (29 readings, of which 18 are shared
with the Antiochian) is also noticeable, but represents merely
the complement of the group Bℵ, and, in view of the tentative
conclusion about A stated above (p. cclxviii), very probably
only reveals one line of cleavage between ancient types of the
Old Uncial text.

The striking characteristics of 81, in which its excellence lies,
are (1) that when its ' singular ' variants due to Antiochian
influence are omitted from the count, as being a definitely
explicable and not very large element, the body of readings that
remain presents a text somewhat nearer to that of B than is the
text of either A or C ; and (2) that the text of 81 shows the
smallest number of ' singular ' readings of any of the four ℵAC 81,
and, when the Antiochian variants are again omitted, a number
much smaller than even those of B.   The figures are shown above
(p. cclxx).   In a word, 81 evidently comes nearer than any other
known MS. to the common type of this group, in a form strongly
resembling those of B and A, though by no means identical with
either.   The figures are as follows :

DIVISION I.	B	ℵ	A	C
81 agrees with	461	409	460	383
81 departs from	307	359	308	385

DIVISION III.	B	ℵ	A	C
81 agrees with	116	104	110	..
81 departs from . . , .	120	132	126	..

If ' singular ' readings of all MSS. are omitted from the figures for variation, the results stand thus :

Division I.	B	ℵ	A	C
81 departs from	110	100	87	98
Division III.				
81 departs from	17	18	8	..

It is interesting to recall the fact (stated above, p. ccxiii) that the brief text of the fifth-century fragment 066 from Egypt agrees almost perfectly with 81.

The further study of these and the other MSS. of the Old Uncial group can only be made fully profitable as part of a study of the whole history of the text of the group, with complete use of the later (mixed) MSS. which represent it (see the list given above, p. xxiv). From such a study much would be gained in security in the use of this text, and perhaps something in actual conclusions as to the right use of the oldest witnesses.

' Alex-
andrian '
text.

An important question relates to what Westcott and Hort called the ' Alexandrian ' text, which they believed to be a skilful recension aiming at " correctness of phrase." Was there a true recension, now represented by no single extant MS., but to be identified in Acts in ℵACE 33 81 and other minuscules ? [1] Or have we to do merely with a mode of statement for the natural variation and consolidation within the Old Uncial group, whereby inferior readings appeared, and then, in a somewhat definite assortment, passed into that form of the text which was most often copied ? In other words, are we to assume the deliberate activity of one hand or was there a process, the steps of which we cannot trace, in which many hands were engaged ?

[1] Hort, ' Introduction,' p. 166; cf. pp. 130-132. The other minuscules named by Hort as witnesses to this ' Alexandrian ' text are (using Gregory's final numbers) 322, 323, 36ᵃᶜ, 181, 441, 429, 489, 206, 1518. The fact that these nine codices are distributed by von Soden among six of his classes (in every case but one in an I-group) shows the need of further study of the later text in so far as it is not Antiochian. 33 and 81 belong to von Soden's H-group.

The evidence that there was an ' Alexandrian ' recension
can lie only in a body of errors shared by a group of witnesses
in such a way as to point definitely to a common ancestor. Such
an ancestor need not have created the errors ; it may merely
have selected them and then been followed in that particular
selection by its descendants. Something like this seems, for
instance, to have taken place in the formation of the Antiochian
recension, which is now generally recognized to have been an
historical event.

Now in the case of Acts it is clear from the figures of the sub-
groups, as given in part above, that Bℵ sometimes agree against
the other three, and that Bℵ and one of the others frequently
agree against the other two. For Division I. the approximate
figures are as follows :

```
Total variants, excluding the cases where one
      MS. departs from the rest   .    .    .    .  209
Of these, Bℵ, BℵA, BℵC, Bℵ 81  .    .    .    .  111
   „    „    BA, BAℵ, BAC, BA 81 .    .    .    .   68
   „    „    BC, BCℵ, BCA, BC 81 .    .    .    .   73
   „    „    B 81, B 81ℵ, B 81 A, B 81 C .   .    .   80
```

Most of these readings are probably right as against the
groups not containing B, but in these latter groups every combination of component elements is found, and in every case
the groups represent small, usually very small, numbers of
readings. No well-massed agreement against Bℵ suggests that
an earlier recension has been at work which has determined
the selection of errors in any MS. or group. Likewise, in
the whole book, in sixty or more of the cases where B lacks
Old Uncial support, it seems to be right (though much more
often probably wrong), while other MSS. when they stand alone
are almost never right ; but this relatively small number of
cases (two-sevenths) where all the others in combination appear
to be in error is not sufficient to justify the assumption of a
recension. The papyri and very early fragments show a kaleidoscopic variation operating within rather narrow limits, and the

study of these is highly suggestive in regard to the question in hand. We may conclude, I think, that so far as Acts is concerned, the evidence does not make it necessary to suppose that a definite recension has controlled the selection of errors found in the later MSS. of the Old Uncial group. Yet as time went on, the text at Alexandria apparently tended to follow a more definite standard, and assumed a form in which ' singular ' variations were more rarely found than in earlier days.[1]

Text of B
' neutral ' ?

An ultimate question relating to this group of witnesses, and one of fundamental importance for the whole text, relates to the earlier history of the text of Codex Vaticanus. This codex, except where it shows singularities of the copyist or of an ancestor, represents the original, it is believed, better than any other MS. Is this superiority to be ascribed merely to the age of the MS. and to peculiarly favourable conditions which surrounded its ancestry, as stated above, so that it is properly called a ' neutral ' text ? Or is its superiority due, as in the case of a modern critical text, to the skilful work of an ancient editor, guided by sound principles of choice ? If the latter view were adopted, our general confidence in B would persist, for its excellence is demonstrated by internal evidence ; but that confidence would be tempered in those numerous instances where the guiding lantern of internal evidence is not at hand. The facts seem to me to favour the former hypothesis, namely, that the text of B is a ' neutral ' text, not a learned recension. The reasons are

---

[1] It thus appears that the conception of gradual and informal origin which has sometimes been used, as I think wrongly, to explain the phenomena of the ' Western ' text, seems to be the best account we can give of the facts of the later Alexandrian text. Nevertheless the facts sometimes recall the theory proposed to account for the mutual relationships of the copies of Alcuin's recension of the Vulgate : " a text prepared by Alcuin from various sources, with variants in the margins ; the descendants of this original edition [differing] in the degree to which they substitute these variants for the text " (and similarly for the recension of Theodulf) ; see E. K. Rand, *Harvard Theological Review*, vol. xxvii., 1924, p. 244. The only readings in Acts assigned by Hort to the ' Alexandrian ' text in the ' Notes on Select Readings ' of his ' Appendix,' p. 92, are vii. 43, ρεφαν (ραιφαν) ; xii. 25, εξ ; xv. 34, εδοξεν δε τω σιλα επιμειναι αυτους (also Western).

two. First, the text of B is substantially free from 'Western' and from 'Antiochian' influence. In these spacious aspects it is actually 'neutral.' They cover a good part, though not the whole, of its excellence, and the historical position thus attested for this text makes it not unlikely that in other respects also its ancestry may have been of superior quality. Secondly, the excellence of B largely resides in two classes of readings : (*a*) it is apt to have the 'shorter' reading, that is, to lack words found in other MSS. ; and (*b*) its readings, even when not shorter, are often 'harder,' that is, more likely than their rivals to have caused difficulty to the scribe and to have led him to alter. Now a recension, made by a scholar following the principles of Alexandrian grammarians, might have adopted the principle of usually selecting the shorter reading, and would so have produced the brevity of the text of B. But in the case of the 'harder' readings it is difficult to think of any principle of selection likely to have been adopted by an ancient critic which would have brought about such an accumulation of these readings as we find in B. This codex is by no means free from errors in the Book of Acts, but it appears to be 'neutral,' in the sense that its errors were not due to an observable recension.[1]

[1] C. H. Turner, 'Marcan Usage,' *Journal of Theological Studies*, vol. XXVI., 1924–25, pp. 14-20, has collected instances from Mark in which the text of B seems governed by the deliberate purpose of an editor to avoid the use of εἰς in phrases where no idea of motion is expressed.

5. THE ANTIOCHIAN TEXT

IT is no longer necessary to prove by argument that a recension of the New Testament text was made, probably early in the fourth century, at Antioch in Syria, largely by a selection of existing readings.[1] Its chief purpose seems not to have been, as in the creation of the 'Western' text two centuries earlier, to produce a rewritten and improved form of the book, but rather to bring the New Testament text out of the confusion into which it had fallen, and to provide Christians with copies of the Scriptures which should adequately represent the intention of the original writers. Unfortunately the critical principles employed were plainly not such as commend themselves to modern scholars, and consequently, from the modern critic's point of view, the result was not the improvement, but the deterioration of the New Testament text. This recension, termed by Westcott and Hort the 'Syrian' text, is in the present volume called the 'Antiochian,' in order to avoid confusion with the name applied to the versions in the 'Syriac' language. Its nature was established by Tischendorf, Tregelles, and especially Westcott and Hort, reënforced by other contemporaries and resting on the studies of various predecessors, notably Bengel and Griesbach ; and the results so reached constitute the most important abiding result of nineteenth-century textual criticism.

This Antiochian text early passed to Constantinople, later the greatest centre for the diffusion of copies of the New Testa-

---

[1] The demonstration by F. C. Burkitt, *S. Ephraem's Quotations from the Gospel* (Texts and Studies, VII.), 1901, that Ephrem did not use the Peshitto seems to render unnecessary the theory of successive steps in the revision, adopted by Hort, 'Introduction,' pp. 135-139.

ment, and so became the basis of the text generally used until the invention of printing, and of the printed text of the New Testament until it was displaced by the critical editions, beginning in 1830 with that of Lachmann.   Von Soden's wide-ranging investigations have now opened up to study the later history of this text during the whole period in which it circulated in manuscript form, while those of Reuss have adequately elucidated its history in print from 1514 to recent times.

For the Book of Acts the Antiochian text is found in some *Codices.* four hundred or more copies, among which, besides those not classified, at least two distinct types (K^c and K^r, the latter found frequently in Athos MSS.) have been discovered by von Soden. In the present volume we are not concerned with this later history, important as it is for the complete solution of the textual problem of the New Testament.   For our purpose it is necessary to select certain MSS. which may be accepted as giving approximately the Antiochian recension in its oldest attainable form, and the only practicable course is to take the oldest continuous texts containing the recension.   These are the ninth-century uncials H, L, P, and S of the eighth or ninth century.   Of these H is now at Modena, L at Rome, and of their origin nothing appears to be known.   P, now at Petrograd, belonged to Porfiri Uspenski, bishop of Kief in the nineteenth century, and was undoubtedly drawn by him from some oriental monastery.   S is in the library of the Laura on Mount Athos, and it may be added that a very large proportion of the extant MSS. of the Antiochian text for the various sections of the New Testament are preserved in the libraries of Mount Athos.   Many of them were probably written there, and have never left the Holy Mountain, while many of the Antiochian copies now in other libraries came from Mount Athos.   Codex S is probably the oldest of this group.   Of the four, S alone is complete ; P is a palimpsest.

In order to supply evidence for certain sections where the uncials are defective, the apparatus has been completed from the readings of one or both of the two minuscules 462 (formerly

101[ac]; thirteenth century) and 102 (formerly 99[ac]; 1345 [or 1445 ?] A.D.), these being Moscow MSS., adequately known from Matthäi's published collations and, as the apparatus shows, unmistakably containing excellent texts of the same recension represented by the uncials.

Codices HLP.

The three uncials HLP have been elaborately studied by Bernhard Weiss,[1] who reaches the conclusion that of their more than 630 variants upwards of 490 are due to the common underlying text, and that of the three P is the most faithful representative of the exemplar. The superiority of P is deduced from the figures for sub-groups :

$$
\begin{array}{lll}
\text{HL against P} & . & 16 \\
\left.\begin{array}{l} \text{HP} \\ \text{LP} \end{array}\right\} & . \quad . \quad 80 & \text{(in many cases due to the defect of L and H)}
\end{array}
$$

together with those for ' singular ' readings :

	P	H	L
Singular readings	53	97	95

The relative numbers of ' singular ' readings are the more convincing (as Weiss points out) because P is much more nearly complete than either H or L, so that in order to make a fair proportionate comparison its figure ought to be reduced well below the actual number (53) given above.[2]

This form of the Antiochian recension was copied through the centuries with remarkable exactness.[3] A single parchment leaf

---

[1] *Die Apostelgeschichte : textkritische Untersuchungen und Textherstellung* (Texte und Untersuchungen, IX.), 1893, pp. 1 f., 66.

[2] Closer inquiry, however, needs to be made into the question whether P in Acts shows a mixed text retaining traces of its Old Uncial base in the midst of the Antiochian improvements. Hort, ' Introduction,' pp. 153 f., describes it as " all but purely Syrian in the Acts and 1 Peter." In James, P contains a large ancient element, which bears a closer resemblance to B than to any other extant uncial ; see J. H. Ropes, ' The Text of the Epistle of James,' *Journal of Biblical Literature*, XXVIII., 1909, pp. 117 f.

[3] The question whether the oldest representatives of the Antiochian recension contain a special type of that text, slightly divergent from the original and to be corrected by observing the readings common to the great mass of the minuscules, deserves further investigation. Von Soden's method, if I mistake not, was first to detach the specific readings of K[c] and K[r], and then to treat a

(093) found in the Genizah at Cairo makes it possible to carry it back to the sixth century, and lends confidence to our use of the text of the later complete copies.

Although continuous pure texts of the Antiochian recension of Acts in Greek older than the eighth century have not been discovered, its readings appear frequently in the earlier centuries in mixture with the Old Uncial text, and, as has been shown above (pp. cclxvii-ix), if not A (sixth century ?), yet probably C (the same century) shows its influence. In apparently mixed texts, however, the difficult question always arises whether the result is due to direct influence on the mixed text or to the kinship of the latter with one of the ancient bases on which the Antiochian rests ; and to this question often only a qualified answer can be given. In view, however, of the known rapid progress of the Antiochian text after the fourth century, and of its wide extension, the possibility of direct influence can, at present at least, but seldom be excluded, and increases with every successive century of the period in question.

In no part of the Christian world is evidence found of the use of the Antiochian recension of Acts before a date well down in the fourth century, and wherever we have positive evidence before that time (as is the case for Alexandria and Egypt, Palestine or Syria, Lyons in Gaul, and Latin Africa), it is plain that the Antiochian text was not that in use by Christian writers. After the middle or latter part of the fourth century the evidence for the use of the Antiochian selection of readings becomes reasonably abundant. In the East, not far from the end of the fourth century, the Apostolic Constitutions and Chrysostom used it, although it is probably not the only text used by the latter ; and, a little earlier than they, Epiphanius may also have had it. These are all writers who proceeded from Syria or Palestine, and *Diffusion of Antiochian text.*

---

the true K-text those readings which are found in the great majority of other minuscules ; cf. p. 1762, where he refers to the departures of the special readings of HLPS and various minuscules " von dem durch die Übereinstimmung aller andern Codd als *K* gesicherten Text."

would naturally have fallen under the influence of Antioch.
In 616 Thomas of Harkel, working at Alexandria from what
he believed to be a "very accurate and approved" Greek
copy, made his Syriac revision conform to the Antiochian
text. Of other use of it at Alexandria no patristic evidence
has so far been brought to light. The Greek codex C (fifth or
sixth century) seems to have been influenced by the Antiochian
but its provenance is not certain. The Genizah fragment
(093) of the sixth century, with the Antiochian text, was
preserved at Cairo, but need not have been of Egyptian origin.
By the middle of the eleventh century codex 81, which doubtless
represents the text of Alexandria, clearly shows exposure to
Antiochian influence. Of the eighth and ninth century Antiochian uncials HLPS no statement of the locality whose text
they offer can be made. We may perhaps assume, however,
that they represent the influence of Constantinople, as do the
great mass of the Antiochian minuscules. One agency in extending this influence was the work of the monks of Mount Athos.
For further light in these matters textual criticism must in the
main wait on palaeography.

In the West, Codex Laudianus (E ; Sardinia, late sixth or
early seventh century) has a Greek text which is largely
Antiochian.[1]

For the Gospels the evidence as to the diffusion of the Antiochian recension is naturally much fuller. The earliest witnesses

[1] Whether the non-western Greek influence perceptible in the gigas-recension and that which is recognized in Codex Bezae included any Antiochian
element does not seem to have been worked out by any investigator. Hort,
' Introduction,' p. 155, states that what he called the ' Italian ' form of the Old
Latin, that is, Codices Brixianus (f) and Monacensis (q), contains a considerable
Antiochian element. In the Old Testament Books of Kingdoms the Latin
text of Lucifer (356–361) shows marked Lucianic elements mingling with a
text of a different type. The facts have not received decisive explanation, but
it is not improbable that the Latin recension used by Lucifer, and of which
fragments are found in Old Latin MSS., had been subject to Lucianic influence ; see Rahlfs, *Lucians Rezension der Königsbücher*, pp. 143-154 ; L. Dieu,
' Retouches Lucianiques sur quelques textes de la vieille version latine (I et II
Samuel),' *Revue Biblique*, vol. xxviii., 1919, pp. 372-403. The Vulgate appears
to be substantially free from Antiochian influence.

to it are the Apostolic Constitutions and the Antiochian fathers at the end of the fourth century—Diodorus, Chrysostom, Theodore of Mopsuestia, together with parts of the codices W (fourth or fifth century ; Egypt) and A (fifth or sixth century). But in the Gospels, much as in Acts, the earliest fragments (such as 069, 072) with an Antiochian text are of the fifth or sixth century, and the earliest complete codex (Ω) comes perhaps from the eighth century, followed by several from the ninth century.

The Antiochian recension is the New Testament part of the text which in the LXX is called Lucianic, and both of these appear to owe their origin to the work performed, doubtless by various hands,[1] under the supervision of Lucian of Antioch (†312). The often-quoted statement of Jerome (*Praef. in librum Paralipomenon*) about the three types of Old Testament Greek text— that of Hesychius used in Alexandria and Egypt, that of Lucian the martyr accepted from Constantinople to Antioch, and that of the codices based on Origen's Hexapla, which had been made popular by the efforts of Eusebius and Pamphilus and were read in Palestine [2]—is matched for the Gospels by the statement in his dedicatory *Epistula ad Damasum* (A.D. 384) :

Relation of Antiochian New Testament to Lucianic Old Testament.

Praetermitto eos codices quos a Luciano et Hesychio nuncupatos paucorum hominum adserit perversa contentio : quibus utique nec in veteri instrumento post septuaginta interpretes emendare quid licuit nec in novo profuit emendasse, cum multarum gentium linguis scriptura ante translata doceat falsa esse quae addita sunt.[3]

---

[1] For evidence that several persons were engaged in the recension see Rahlfs, *Lucians Rezension der Königsbücher*, pp. 294 f.

[2] Rahlfs, *Das Buch Ruth griechisch*, 1922, p. 13, believes that the Origenian MSS. of Pamphilus and Eusebius (which contained the text that Jerome did approve) represent a reaction against the influence of Antioch with the deliberate purpose of preventing the Lucianic text from coming into general use. Jerome's hostile reference to the Lucianic codices of the Gospels tends to confirm this view, which is obviously of great importance in opposition to any suggestion that the edition of Pamphilus and Eusebius was a compromise-text, partly made up from the Lucianic recension.

[3] Jerome's reference here is quite correct. Down to his time no translation of the New Testament had been made under the influence of the Antiochian recension. Even the Peshitto, the product of the following century and of

In large measure the Lucianic text of the Greek Old Testament has now been identified, and the MSS. recognized, especially by the aid of the quotations of Chrysostom and Theodoret (bishop of Cyrus in Syria ; † *ca.* 457),[1] the direct references to the Lucianic text of the Psalter made by Jerome in his letter ˙to the Goths Sunnias and Fretelas (*Ep.* 106, 2), and certain marginal readings, expressly indicated as Lucianic, in the Syro-hexaplaric version and in some Greek MSS. Various considerations prove its connexion with the Antiochian text of the New Testament.

Thus, certain illustrations have been pointed out of agreement in the form of proper names. The Lucianic text (3 Kgds. xvii. 9) has, against all others, Σάρεπτα τῆς Σιδῶνος, for the earlier Σάρεπτα (or Σάρεφθα) τῆς Σιδωνίας. This is the exact form in which the phrase appears in the Antiochian text of Luke iv. 26, the same variations occurring among the earlier types. Similarly the Lucianic and Antiochian agree (4 Kgds. v. 1 ff. ; Luke iv. 27) in the spelling Νεεμάν instead of the earlier Ναιμάν.[2] Equally characteristic of the common principles guiding the recension of the two parts of the Bible is the plain endeavour to make endings and grammatical forms correspond to the grammarians' rules, as, for instance, in the consistent use of εἶπον and the like for εἶπαν, or of ὁ ἔλεος, at least in the accusative, for τὸ ἔλεος,[3] or the strong tendency to correct ἐγενήθη to ἐγένετο.[4]

Characteristics.

But the reasons for accepting the Lucianic Old Testament

Syria, does not render, in Acts at least, a text of that type. That Jerome decisively rejects the codices of Hesychius is instructive in view of the fact that the Greek text which he himself used was one corresponding to the Old Uncials.

[1] See Rahlfs, 'Theodorets Zitate aus den Königsbüchern und dem 2. Buche der Chronik,' *Studien zu den Königsbüchern* (Septuaginta-Studien, I.), pp. 16-46.

[2] Rahlfs, *Lucians Rezension der Königsbücher*, pp. 113 f.

[3] Rahlfs, *Das Buch Ruth griechisch*, 1922, p. 13. A comparison of the details assembled for the New Testament by von Soden, pp. 1456-1459 (cf. 1361-1400), 1786, with the Lucianic text of the Old Testament would undoubtedly yield a great number of other illustrations.

[4] Rahlfs, *Lucians Rezension der Königsbücher*, pp. 294 f.

and the Antiochian New Testament as constituting one revised Greek Bible are broader than these special observations, even though the latter are no doubt capable of being multiplied indefinitely. The two recensions were made at about the same time and at the same centre, and their principles and general character are identical. For the New Testament the comprehensive and elegant summary statement of Hort (' Introduction,' § 187, pp. 134 f.) is familiar to all students; it might be expanded and elaborated, but can hardly be improved.[1] In the Old Testament for a number of books, historical, prophetic, and poetical, the Lucianic recension has now been studied and described, and the facts everywhere appear to be the same. Besides the attempt at closer approximation to the Hebrew text the chief features are conformation to the language of similar passages in nearer or remoter context, grammatical correction to a standard of forms and syntax, improvement in expression alike in order, diction, and style, with a view to greater smoothness, fulness, and intelligibility. Synonyms are substituted to suit the reviser's taste, particles changed or added ; the text is often somewhat expanded, very rarely made shorter. There is not one of the well-known characteristics of the Antiochian New Testament which cannot be illustrated from the Old Testament of Lucian.[2]

The critical principles and the aim of the Antiochian revisers Sources. are plainly discernible from the result of their labours. Less easy to form, but for the purposes of critical study indispensable, is a judgment as to the basis of their work and the sources from which they drew their selection of readings. That they made some changes of their own, without older manuscript authority,

[1] See also von Soden's account, pp. 1456-1459, of the general character of the Antiochian recension, with many illustrations.

[2] On the characteristics of the Lucianic text of Chronicles, Ezra, and Nehemiah, see C. C. Torrey, *Ezra Studies*, Chicago, 1910, pp. 106-109 ; for other books, W. O. E. Oesterley, *Studies in the Greek and Latin Versions of the Book of Amos*, 1902, pp. 61-67 ; Rahlfs, *Lucians Rezension der Königsbücher*, 1911, pp. 171-183, 239-288, 294 ; Rahlfs, *Der Text des Septuaginta-Psalters*, 1907, p. 231 ; Rahlfs, *Studie über den griechischen Text des Buches Ruth*, 1922, pp. 83-90 ; O. Procksch, *Studien zur Geschichte der Septuaginta : Die Propheten*, 1910, pp. 79-87.

is commonly assumed, and their methods in the revision of the Old Testament make this probable ; but the main substance of their text came from earlier sources.[1] The determination of these sources, and the discrimination of the inherited from the new readings, is made difficult by the almost complete lack of Greek manuscripts of unquestionably earlier date than the Antiochian recension, and by the vast influence which that recension presently came to exercise over the Greek text of the New Testament. We have already seen how hard it is to make sure whether the Greek codices ℵ and A are akin to the base of the Antiochian recension or have been influenced by the recension itself ; and even in the case of C and 81 the question admits of argument. In Codex Bezae all agreements with the Antiochian require to be closely examined to see whether they are components of the ' Western ' text or whether they owe their presence to the later chances which befell the text of that MS.

We may assume that the revisers worked, in part at least, on the basis of Greek MSS. preserved at Antioch that represented such a text as had long been used in this great, rich, and active church, but no literary monuments from Antioch earlier than the time of Lucian are capable of aiding our inquiry. It may well happen, therefore, that readings now found only in the Antiochian recension,[2] or in texts dependent upon it, had been current in Antioch from the earliest times. Any reading, however, which is to be accepted as of this sort, must

[1] E. von Dobschütz, *Eberhard Nestle's Einführung in das griechische Neue Testament*, 4th ed., 1923, p. 8, may be deemed to go too far, if he means, as he seems to do, that all variant readings except ' Mischlesarten ' must be assumed to have existed in the second century. Hort's statement, *The New Testament in the Original Greek*, smaller edition, p. 549, is duly guarded : " The Syrian text has all the marks of having been carefully constructed out of materials which are accessible to us on other authority, and apparently out of these alone. All the readings which have an exclusively Syrian attestation can be easily accounted for as parts of an editorial revision " ; this is consistent with his fuller discussion, ' Introduction,' pp. 132-135.

[2] In order to distinguish the Antiochian recension of the fourth century from the Old Antiochian text, it will be convenient sometimes from here on to designate the recension as ' Lucianic ' not merely, as hitherto, for the Old Testament but also for the New Testament.

possess very strong internal credentials of genuineness. Readings peculiar to Lucian which are inherently improbable, and even those which are merely possible with nothing that positively recommends them, will have to be referred—provisionally at least —to the later recension. One case in which I am disposed to accept the Lucianic reading, in spite of a general consensus of Old Uncial authorities against it, may serve as an illustration. In Acts xvii. 14 ἔως (ℵAC 81, omitted by D d gig) is superficially unobjectionable, but a consideration of the relation of the Lucianic ὡς to the statement of vs. 15 shows so interesting a meaning, and one so little obvious, that the argument from 'intrinsic probability' is very strong. Another case where Lucian, supported by Pap. 8 and the Sahidic, gives the right reading against both ℵA and B (which differ, C and 81 being here defective) is iv. 33 τῆς ἀναστάσεως τοῦ κυρίου Ἰησοῦ. Such cases, however, are rare in Acts. In iv. 17 the Lucianic addition of a Semitic ἀπειλῇ (cf. v. 28) appeals to the critic, but the possibility of an Old Antiochian dittography will make him hesitate to adopt it.[1]

The Antiochian recension bears a general similarity to the text of the Old Uncials. It differs from their text far less than from the ' Western,' and supports them against the ' Western ' in many noteworthy readings ; for instance xi. 20 Ἑλληνιστάς against Ἕλληνας of D (and A), or in all but a single word of the striking ' Western' rewriting of xviii. 5 f. Of this it is needless to multiply illustrations.

Relation to Old Uncial and to ' Western ' text.

But on the other hand the Antiochian recension of Acts

---

[1] In Acts xiii. 17 the omission of Ἰσραήλ by the Lucianic text in agreement with the Peshitto looks like an Old Antiochian reading, since the Lucianic rarely omits words ; but the omission can hardly give the true text. Any single agreement of the Lucianic and the Peshitto need not point to influence from the recension upon the Syriac translation, for both may go back independently to ancient texts. Thus in Luke ii. 14 εὐδοκία was the reading not only of Lucian, with some of the Alexandrian uncials, but also of the Old Syriac (as found in the Diatessaron [Ephrem], the Sinaitic Syriac, Aphraates), and seems to me to be the true reading, in spite of the support given to εὐδοκίας by ℵA, Origen, and the ' Western ' text (D and all Latin witnesses) ; see J. H. Ropes,' Good Will toward Men,' *Harvard Theological Review*, vol. x., 1917, pp. 52-56.

contains many agreements with the 'Western' text. In some instances these are found in conflate readings in which the revisers have united the Old Uncial and the 'Western.'[1] Thus, in Acts xx. 28 B ℵ and others read τοῦ θεοῦ, the 'Western' reading was τοῦ κυρίου, while HLPS have combined these into τοῦ κυρίου καὶ θεοῦ. Again, in xxviii. 14 the text of LP (but not HS) has ἐπ᾽ αὐτοῖς ἐπιμεῖναι, which looks like a combination of the modified 'Western' ἐπ᾽ αὐτοῖς ἐπιμείναντες with the Old Uncial (BℵA 066 81 boh) παρ᾽ αὐτοῖς ἐπιμεῖναι, although the case is not so clear as in xx. 28.

In many other cases the Antiochian recension either has a 'Western' gloss, or other peculiarity, or else shows a text built up by modifying the basic 'Western' reading. Some examples of this from Acts are the following :

ii. 30 + τὸ κατὰ σάρκα ἀναστήσειν τὸν Χριστόν.

ii. 43 om ἐν Ἰερουσαλὴμ φόβος τε ἦν μέγας ἐπὶ πάντας. (Here ℵAC seem to have the right reading; the Antiochian might have come from a text like B, but equally well from a 'Western' text.)

iv. 33 τῆς ἀναστάσεως τοῦ κυρίου Ἰησοῦ. (Here, as in ii. 43, the Antiochian sides with the general type of B and the 'Western,' not with the later text of ℵA.)

ix. 5 ὁ δὲ κύριος εἶπεν.

x. 32 + ὃς παραγενόμενος λαλήσει σοι.

xv. 37 ἐβουλεύσατο, for ἐβούλετο.

xviii. 5 πνεύματι, for λόγῳ. (The only reason for thinking this to be 'Western' is that it is found in the Harclean margin.)

xix. 1f. εὑρὼν . . . εἶπεν, for εὑρεῖν . . . εἶπέν τε.

xx. 24 οὐδενὸς λόγον ποιοῦμαι οὐδὲ ἔχω τὴν ψυχήν [μου]. (This is a modification of the 'Western' reading.)

xxiii. 11 + Παῦλε.

xxiii. 12 τινες τῶν Ἰουδαίων, for οἱ Ἰουδαῖοι.

xxv. 16 + εἰς ἀπώλειαν.

xxvi. 25 om Παῦλος.

---

[1] Conflations appear to be much more numerous in the Lucianic Old Testament ; see Rahlfs, *Lucians Rezension der Königsbücher*, pp. 192 ff. ; Oesterley, *Amos*, p. 112.

xxvi. 28 γενέσθαι, for ποιῆσαι.

xxvi. 30 + καὶ ταῦτα εἰπόντος αὐτοῦ.

xxvii. 2 μέλλοντες, for μέλλοντι.

xxviii. 16 ὁ ἑκατόνταρχος παρέδωκε τοὺς δεσμίους τῷ στρατοπεδάρχῳ τῷ δὲ Παύλῳ ἐπετράπη, for ἐπετράπη δὲ τῷ Παύλῳ.

xxviii. 29 + καὶ ταῦτα αὐτοῦ εἰπόντος ἀπῆλθον οἱ Ἰουδαῖοι πολλὴν ἔχοντες ἐν ἑαυτοῖς συζήτησιν.

These examples, many of which are discussed in the Textual Notes of the present volume, and to which very many more might be added, will serve to illustrate the relationship. The not infrequent occurrence of small and unimportant agreements, as in some of the cases cited, suggests that either the Lucianic text or its Old Antiochian ancestor was a ' Western ' copy imperfectly corrected to an Old Uncial standard, rather than an Old Uncial text interlarded with ' Western ' readings. It is perhaps more likely that this operation had been performed in an ancestor than by the Lucianic revisers, for their own work rested mainly on a good Old Uncial text, with which they combined many important, not insignificant, ' Western ' readings, and their resultant text includes vastly more from the Old Uncial text than from the ' Western.' They were engaged in preparing an exemplar from which copies should be made, not merely, as might have been true of more primitive hands, in bringing a valuable old copy up to date in accordance with a newly accepted standard.[1]

Apart from the ' Western ' readings found in the Antiochian recension, the Old Uncial base which the revisers used was evidently an excellent text.[2] With this conclusion correspond

[1] A. Souter, *Text and Canon of the New Testament*, 1913, p. 122, expresses the opinion that the Lucianic revisers used the ' Western ' text " for their usual base," and illustrates this (p. 120) by the readings in Luke xxiv. 53, where the ' Western ' αἰνοῦντες is expanded by addition from the Old Uncial text into αἰνοῦντες καὶ εὐλογοῦντες. Acts xx. 28 τοῦ κυρίου καὶ θεοῦ shows the same phenomenon. But in both instances a sensitive taste would in any case have preferred the order actually adopted.

[2] So B. Weiss, *Die Apostelgeschichte : textkritische Untersuchungen und Textherstellung*, p. 67.

the results of the criticism of the text of the Septuagint. In the Books of Kingdoms the Lucianic recension rested on a pre-hexaplaric text standing next to Codex Vaticanus and the Ethiopic version, and sometimes, though rarely, better than they.[1] In Ruth the same is true, and the pre-hexaplaric base was closely akin to B.[2] In the Psalter, passages are found where the Lucianic recension has a better reading than the agreeing texts of Upper Egypt, Lower Egypt (Codex B and the Bohairic), and the Old Latin. If in these cases the possibility is alleged that by their own correction the Lucianic revisers produced their superior text,[3] it is to be observed that the resemblances between the text of Lucian and the African Old Latin show that many Lucianic readings, not found in B, are in fact of ancient origin.[4] In the Prophets, the base of Lucian's text was of great antiquity, and akin to that of Codex Vaticanus, Codex Sinaiticus, and the corresponding minuscules.[5] In Chronicles, Ezra, and Nehemiah (all drawn from Theodotion) the Lucianic text contains " valuable material not found elsewhere," and depends on a different type of Greek text from that of B and A. In 1 Esdras the Old Latin (African) adds its attestation to the antiquity of the base of the Lucianic recension.[6]

The Antiochian revision of the New Testament text deserves a fresh and penetrating investigation, which should aim at discriminating the new readings introduced by the revisers from the ancient base on which they worked, should try to determine the relative significance of the older texts they used, and in particular should inquire into the character of the text current in Antioch in the second and third centuries. A complete answer to these

---

[1] Rahlfs, *Lucians Rezension der Königsbücher*, pp. 290 f., 129 f.

[2] Rahlfs, *Studie über den griechischen Text des Buches Ruth*, pp. 89 f.

[3] Rahlfs, *Der Text des Septuaginta-Psalters*, pp. 229-231 (§ 61, § 62. 1).

[4] Capelle, *Le Texte du psautier latin en Afrique*, pp. 198 f., 211.

[5] Procksch, *Studien zur Geschichte der Septuaginta : Die Propheten*, 1910, p. 79 ; F. C. Burkitt, *The Book of Rules of Tyconius*, 1894, pp. cxvi-cxvii ; W. O. E. Oesterley, *Studies in the Greek and Latin Versions of the Book of Amos*, 1902, pp. 103-105.

[6] Torrey, *Ezra Studies*, pp. 101-106, 111.

important questions is hardly attainable, but neither the utter
neglect of the Antiochian readings which has become common in
the last generation, nor the method devised by von Soden of using
it for constructing a text is a satisfactory solution of the problem
which it presents.

6. THE HISTORY OF THE TEXT

FROM the facts which have been presented and discussed it is now in place to try to sketch briefly the history of the text of Acts, as it appears to have run its course through the centuries. In such a reconstruction it will conduce to clearness if the statements are made for the most part positively, and without regard to the fact that hypotheses, not proved conclusions, sometimes underlie them. The reader who wishes to know the precise degree of probability which the statements possess, may be referred to the discussions of the preceding sections of this Essay.

The Book of Acts, written, we know not where, toward the end of the first century, was early separated from its companion volume of evangelical history, when the Gospel of Luke was united with those of Matthew, Mark, and John to form the canon of four Gospels ; but Acts was preserved by being associated with that canon as the historical section of the sacred writings relating to the Apostolic Age. The text was, from the first, subject to the inevitable alterations which copying unsupervised by authority 'Western' produced. On the basis of one of these slightly divergent copies, rewriting. before the middle of the second century, the book was drastically rewritten to suit the taste of the time, and with special reference to easy fulness of the narrative. The hypothesis has been suggested above that this rewriting proceeded from the same circle as the primitive nucleus of the New Testament canon. That at least the Gospels were combined into one corpus, and equipped with their uniform titles, at not far from the same date as that at which the ' Western ' text arose is generally admitted.[1]

[1] Harnack, ' Einige Bemerkungen zur Geschichte der Entstehung des Neuen Testaments,' in *Reden und Aufsätze*, vol. ii., 1904, p. 241, assigns the combination

Such a theory would dispel much of the mystery attending the position and influence of the 'Western' text in the second century, and against it no conclusive objection seems to present itself.[1] But it is insusceptible of direct proof, and could be taken out of the realm of the merely possible only by elaborate justification in many directions.

At any rate, the 'Western' text of Acts, whose origin, as Dr. Hort is said to have been in the habit of explaining, "is lost in the mists of a hoar antiquity," met the needs of its century, and was widely used. Carried to the East, it was the basis of the earliest Syriac translation, used in the fourth century in Mesopotamia; and probably before the end of the fourth century the Armenian version was made from a Syriac text largely or wholly 'Western' in character. Earlier, in the third century, it is found in Greek in Syria or Palestine. As late as the third or fourth century we have it in Egypt. On the other side of the world, the West received it in the second century, not many years after its creation, and the earliest Latin version, used in Africa, was made from it, while in the same period the 'Western' Greek text was used by the Greek colony of Lyons in Gaul. So far as

---

of the Four Gospels in one collection to Asia Minor in the period 120–130 ; see also his full discussion, ' Das εὐαγγέλιον τετράμορφον,' in *Die Chronologie der altchristlichen Litteratur bis Eusebius*, vol. i., 1897, pp. 681-700, especially pp. 694, 699 f. ; and *Die Mission und Ausbreitung des Christentums*, 4th ed., 1924, p. 784. He thinks that Acts was added much later, probably at Ephesus. See also J. Leipoldt, *Geschichte des neutestamentlichen Kanons*, vol. i., 1907, pp. 149 f. Zahn, *Grundriss der Geschichte des neutestamentlichen Kanons*, 1901, p. 40, holds that in the period 80–110 the canon of Four Gospels and also the collection of thirteen epistles of Paul were formed and passed into liturgical use in the Gentile churches of the whole region from Antioch to Rome. He is doubtful whether Acts was widely used in church services at so early a date. See also *Geschichte des neutestamentlichen Kanons*, vol. i., 1889, pp. 941-950, where Zahn urges that the canon of Four Gospels was created at Ephesus in consequence of the composition of the Gospel of John.

[1] The argument of Zahn, *Geschichte des neutestamentlichen Kanons*, vol. i., 1888, pp. 440-445, that the supposed formation of the New Testament canon in the years 160–180 would have required also the establishment at the same time of an authoritative Catholic recension of the text, which in fact did not then take place, is suggestive in this connexion. Zahn's polemic does not touch the question of such a relation of collection and text fifty years earlier.

our limited knowledge permits a judgment, the 'Western' text of Acts in the second century (and not much less completely in a large part of the third) swept the field—with the conspicuous exception of one locality, Alexandria.

Text used in Alex-andria. At Alexandria, at least, not all the copies of the older text of Acts (from one form of which the 'Western' text was made) disappeared from use in the days of 'Western' dominance, as is probably shown by the undoubtedly non-western quotations in Clement of Alexandria ; and we may detect a reaction at the time of Origen, and possibly under the influence of the attention given by him to Christian scholarship in that centre.   How widely the non-western copies were used is not known, but in the third century older manuscripts of the 'Western' type began to be corrected by a different standard, though not without retaining fragmentary 'Western' survivals, readings which failed to be expunged by the correctors' pens.   In the fair copies of these corrected manuscripts the resulting mixture preserved a record of what had taken place.   To one such the Sahidic translation of Upper Egypt owed its origin, somewhere about the year 300.   In the towns and villages of Egypt in the third century many copies may be supposed in use (and of this positive evidence is not wholly lacking) which conformed to Origen's text, not to the rewritten form previously so popular.   By that time the star of the 'Western' rewritten text seems to have set for the Greek-speaking section of the Christian world.[1]

With Constantine the Church entered on a new era, and from the fourth century, when the systematic destruction of Christian books ceased, the sources flow more freely and the monuments are more abundant.   Alexandria, still a great Christian centre, used a sound non-western text of Acts, but encouraged a limited modification and supposed improvement, and the copies used there showed a tendency to avoid singularities and to approach a fixed standard.   Of the history of this text

---

[1] A knowledge, if it were available, of the text of Acts used in Caesarea in Palestine would perhaps show a parallel, but different, history.

the details are obscure, but its development, which included a
disposition to adopt readings, and even to approve complete
copies, of the text of Constantinople, continued until the down-
fall of Christian civilization under the Moslems in the seventh
century, and for centuries beyond that disaster. From the fourth
century we still have Codex Vaticanus and Codex Sinaiticus,
superb copies made for great Egyptian churches, and the testimony of Athanasius ; from the fifth century comes Cyril ; from
the sixth Cosmas ; from the seventh a great monument in the
Bohairic version ; and from later ages important witnesses, not
yet fully explored.

The great rival of Alexandria in Christian learning was Antioch.
Antioch. What text of Acts had been current there in the recension.
second and third centuries is not known, but about the year 300,
under the leadership of Lucian, a text of the whole Greek Bible
was produced at Antioch which contended with that of Alexandria for supremacy, and finally—in the New Testament—won
the victory. Older copies were more or less successfully revised
to conform to it, and vast numbers of new copies made. Combining in Acts an ancient text like that of Alexandria with a
lesser proportion of ' Western ' readings and some original revision, its merit lay in its fitness for the use of educated Christians,
given through its care for grammar and style and its inclusive-
ness. An irresistible force in its behalf was the adoption of it
by the capital, Constantinople, intellectually dependent on Antioch
and increasingly for centuries the centre of the production of
Bibles. We can trace this text from the Antiochian and Syrian
Greek writings of the fourth century, from later fathers, from
one sixth-century fragment, from excellent copies of the ninth
(and perhaps the eighth) century, and from a host of copies
of the long succeeding centuries in which it was almost completely dominant. The monks of Mount Athos made many hundred
copies of it ; it pervaded Greece and Asia Minor, and at an early
date was not unknown, nor without influence, in Alexandria
itself. It suffered some changes, the locality and date of which

have not yet been fully elucidated, but the copies brought to the West when the Byzantine power collapsed in the fifteenth century were largely of this type. From them were drawn the earliest printed editions and their successors until the middle of the nineteenth century, and on the text of Antioch depend the great Protestant translations of Germany, France, and England. For the greater part of sixteen centuries it needed to fear no rival, and to-day it is read in some form by a great proportion of Christian people.

Text of Pamphilus and Eusebius.

From the time of its first circulation, however, the Antiochian text did not lack a competitor, even apart from Alexandria itself. At Caesarea in Palestine—where Origen took up his residence in 211–12—a definite tradition of the text of the New Testament had its seat, and in the early fourth century two Caesarean scholars who revered Origen—Pamphilus and Eusebius—promulgated an edition of the Bible which claimed superiority to the Antiochian recension. In the Book of Acts the nature of this Caesarean text—its relation to Origen, its component elements, and its history—is still a subject of inquiry, but in an ample body of manuscripts dating from the tenth century on there is contained a group of texts made up of excellent ancient readings, partly non-western, partly ' Western,' and mixed in various degrees with the Antiochian text of Constantinople, which may represent this attempt to counter the influence of Lucian. In its essential character the Lucianic text of Antioch may be regarded as not different from these other contemporary texts. Like them it consisted mainly of a combination of readings, drawn partly from such a text as that of Codex Vaticanus, partly from the ' Western ' text. But, as it happened, to its particular combination, rather than to any other, went the palm in the rivalry of later texts.

Syriac versions.

If we turn from the history of the Greek text to that of the versions, we find the two great churches at the two ends of the Empire each with its own translation and its own history. For the old Syriac translation of Acts made from the ' Western ' text the Syrians of Edessa in the early fifth century, as a part of their great ecclesiastical version, the Peshitto, substituted a new translation in which Old Uncial and ' Western ' readings alike are liberally represented. In the Syrian church, torn by faction and subject to a measure of alien Greek control, it is not surprising that in the sixth century a fresh effort was made to provide the great dissident Monophysite body with a different text, and again a century later to cement the union of the Monophysites of Mesopotamia with their ' faithful ' brethren of Egypt by a further revision, which in fact brought their text into close harmony with that of Constantinople. Yet the ancient tradition of the Peshitto, beloved in spite of, perhaps because of, its antiquated differences from any Greek text, survived, and has held control to the present day in all branches of Syriac-speaking Christianity. But, by a happy chance, the apparatus of variants attached to the later form of the Mono-physite revision has preserved a record of unmistakable ' Western ' readings, precious though of uncertain immediate origin.

In the Latin church of the West the text of Acts had a history   Latin versions. similar at the start to the Syrian but different in its outcome. Here likewise, in the second century and thus possibly even earlier than in Syria, a translation of Acts was made from a completely ' Western ' Greek copy, was used perhaps first, certainly longest, in Africa, and received there no considerable modification from any other type of Greek text. In (probably) Sicily the Greek text on which it was founded was known and copied as late as the fifth century. This ' African ' Latin version passed into Spain, entered into union with later Latin revisions, came to Languedoc, and affected the current text of that centre of far-reaching influences. Besides other changes it suffered an elabor-ate revision as early as the first half of the fourth century, both to improve its Latin phraseology and to bring it into accord with the non-western Greek text which increasing contact of East with West had made known to Latin-speaking scholars. This revision is well known to us from Codex Gigas and the quotations

of Lucifer of Cagliari ; its use spread rapidly over the whole
Occidental world from Toledo to Nish, and it was for many
centuries current in Italy and Gaul.   Whence was derived the
Greek non-western text by which it was made is not known,
but we may recall that for seven years, beginning about 340,
Athanasius was in exile in the West, and that he spent the first
three of these years in Rome.   With the completion about 385
of Jerome's revision of the Latin New Testament, Rome for the
first time definitely enters the history of the New Testament text

Vulgate.   of Acts.   The Vulgate Acts rested on a form of the Latin version
akin to that of Codex Gigas ; the Greek text to which it was
brought into close correspondence was that of Alexandria.   The
story has been told above of the manifold combination of Old Latin
and Vulgate, and the diffusion of these mixed texts (with readings
partly ' Western,' partly Alexandrian) from two centres, on the
one hand from Ireland, by missionaries to France, the Rhine
country, Switzerland, and North Italy, and on the other from
Spain and Languedoc, through Provençal, Italian, Old German,
and Bohemian daughter-translations, as well as in Latin texts.
Italy supplemented its own copies with texts from Spain ; in
France Alcuin's revision of the Vulgate at least put an end to the
use of the Old Latin and prepared the way for the composite
Paris text of the thirteenth century, from which sprang the
printed text, and finally, as the standard of the Roman Catholic
Church, the Clementine printed edition.

The first contest in the history of the text of Acts was between
the ' Western ' text and what I have termed the ' Old Uncial.'
Among the Greeks this struggle ended in the abandonment of
the ' Western ' text by reason of the early dominance of Alexandrian thought ; in the West the result was a combination
of the two texts, with later virtual elimination of ' Western '
elements.   The next great contest reflected the rivalry of Antioch
and Alexandria.   Antioch allied herself with Constantinople, and
her text gained supremacy over both the text of Alexandria
and the Caesarean text fathered by Eusebius.   In modern times

the efforts of critical scholars have reversed the process, and brought Alexandria to her own again. Recent attempts to go still farther back and annul the verdict of ancient Christian history by preferring the ' Western ' to the Old Uncial text seem to me to have been unsuccessful, even in the modified form of an attempt to treat both these ancient texts as coeval and as equally the work of the original author of the book.

Many defects appear in any attempt to draw up an account of this history under the present conditions of knowledge. The outlines are often too sharp, the contrasts harsh, and the definitions too narrow ; while lack of available information often requires statements to be painfully guarded, and blurred with qualifications which do injustice to the relations which fuller knowledge would elucidate. But enough is known to make it evident that a comprehensible historical process has here gone on, in which all the witnesses had their due position,[1] and which followed and reflected significant movements of Christian life and thought. The history of the text of the New Testament is the illustration in a single field of the general history of the Christian Church, to serve which the text was formed.

---

[1] A diagram intended to show the relation of the several witnesses in one case where the evidence lends itself to such presentation will be found below on p. 260.

7. THE METHOD OF CRITICISM

THE history of the New Testament text, while interesting in itself as a fragment of church history, is primarily studied in order to aid in the practice of textual criticism and the recovery of the original text from the divergent witnesses. The incidental observations already made on the use of the materials of textual criticism in Acts may here be briefly resumed.

Antiochian.   1. In the first place it may be taken as accepted that the Antiochian recension, in so far as it contained new readings of the Lucianic revisers, was wrong, and that when it agrees with older types of text it can rarely add any weight to the evidence of the latter. In a few cases it may contain ancient readings not otherwise attested, which yet commend themselves for acceptance as right; hence its readings require to be studied, but they will very seldom be adopted. When its true form has been established, the later developments of its text become of merely historical interest; but the copies containing these can be definitely and completely excluded from consideration only when their relation to one another and to the fourth-century recension itself has been fully worked out.

'Western.'   2. The 'Western' text has come down to us only in fragments, in consequence of the complete disuse into which, relatively early, it fell in every region to which it penetrated. It can be fully used only when it is reconstructed and restored, for by reason of its nature as a free recasting of the original the comparison of isolated variants without their 'Western' context often fails to reveal their true significance. In the recovery of it Codex Bezae, unsatisfactory and often misleading as is its testimony, is necessarily the starting-point; next in importance come the Harclean

Syriac apparatus and the Old Latin versions, by the aid of which the ' Western ' elements of the Greek I-codices can be identified ; in addition every scrap of scattered evidence has to be gathered and scrutinized where better lights fail.   The talk often heard of great unexplored resources for the New Testament text lying unused in the mass of Greek minuscules is justified chiefly with regard to these I-codices, which seem to rest on one or more combinations of the most ancient text with the ' Western ' text. The group, or a part of it, may owe its unity to descent from the Caesarean edition of Eusebius, and may contain genuine readings attested but slightly, or not at all, elsewhere.[1]

As has been emphasized at greater length above, the signifi- cance of the ' Western ' text lies in its antiquity.   Its confirma- tion of readings of the Old Uncial text is valuable, for, when its own readings can be certainly ascertained, they carry back the evidence to the early second century.   And it is probable that sometimes—less often, however, in Acts than in the Gospels— an ancient reading embedded in it can be recognized which on internal grounds approves itself as better than the reading of its usually more trustworthy rival.

3. For our chief source of knowledge we are thus thrown on the text of the Old Uncial group,[2] represented in greatest purity, so far as is at present known, by Codices BℵAC 81, but also found in a series of minuscules in which the mixture with Antiochian readings does not preclude the recognition of excellent

Old Uncial.

---

[1] In two of these MSS. (1852 [a 114] and 2138 [a 116]), whose eleventh- century text was not known until the publication of von Soden's apparatus, Harnack, *Sitzungsberichte*, Berlin Academy, 1915, pp. 534-542, has made the extraordinary and suggestive discovery of a reading, probably genuine, in 1 John v. 18, hitherto known in no Greek MS., but found in the Vulgate and Latin fathers, namely η γεννησις for ο γεννηθεις.   This reading makes sense in a difficult passage where no other reading is tolerable ; and the change involved only the alteration of one letter (−CЄIC, −ѲЄIC) together with the resulting adjustment of the article from η to o.   The two MSS. are at Upsala and Moscow.   This is not the only noteworthy reading contained in the Upsala MS. ; the testimony of the latter is not given in full by von Soden.

[2] Compare what is said by Rahlfs, *Studie über den griechischen Text des Buches Ruth*, pp. 149 ff., with reference to the text of the Greek Old Testament.

ancient elements as well. These latter need to be investigated, and their non-antiochian readings carefully studied, especially in order to discover evidence that apparently ' singular ' readings of the five chief MSS. do not really stand alone, and also to find out whether any groups in which the minuscules share are of signal excellence and authority. Here again something may be recovered from the unexplored resources of minuscules, but the result will make no revolution in criticism.

Rules of criticism.   In the study of the five chief members of this group, four of them (BℵAC) being the oldest representatives of it, it has appeared that Codex Vaticanus, when its readings have any other support within the group of five and when they can be tested by internal evidence, is generally right. Consequently we are left to follow it also in those non-singular variant readings where internal evidence gives little or no aid. But when B stands alone, or with very weak support, it seems to be more often wrong than right. The main labour in the actual construction of a text of Acts from the materials at present available will consist in the comparison of the readings of BℵAC 81 in the moderate number of instances in which they depart from one another, and especially in those cases in which two or three of them agree in their support of a variant. When one of the four ℵAC 81 goes its own way, its variant reading hardly ever commends itself for acceptance.

The result of such a procedure will be a text more like Codex Vaticanus than like any other single MS., but it will depart from B at many points. The preservation in this codex of a text so little retouched and representing so excellent an exemplar of the earliest period is a piece of good fortune which could not have been anticipated, but which in view of all that we know of the history is entirely comprehensible. The view that B has this superior character requires no incredible assumptions. In spite of the best critical efforts the result of the process of criticism here indicated will include erroneous readings which we have no means of detecting, but if Codex Vaticanus had not been preserved the number of these would have been still greater.

The conclusions thus arrived at are substantially those of Westcott and Hort, whose text, however, seems to the present writer to follow B too closely in readings where B stands alone, and to neglect some few indications of better readings which can be derived from ' Western ' evidence.   The method of von Soden, who tried to determine the three texts of Alexandria (Hesychius), Eusebius, and Lucian, and then treated these three as independent of one another, so that the vote of any two of them was to be taken as decisive for their underlying earlier common base, seems to me an untrustworthy guide, although it has led to a result not very different from that produced by what appears a sounder process.   The fundamental defects of von Soden's method are two : (1) He failed to treat the second-century ' Western ' text as a real thing, to be reconstructed from all the evidence, and missed the true character of the I-codices (Eusebian ?) as including a mixture of two elements (' Western ' and ' Old Uncial '), both very ancient but quite disparate.   In consequence his mode of using the I-text is misleading.   What his I-text really gives is (*a*) evidence as to the ' Western ' rewriting, often of unique value ; (*b*) evidence of ancient non-western readings which represent a lost MS. or MSS. of uncertain age, parallel to the Old Uncial codices, but not necessarily independent of their text.   (2) He aimed to treat the Antiochian text as representing an ancient type equal in weight to the old Alexandrian and the Eusebian.   But here again his authority is mixed, containing in fact not only original and authentic readings but also a ' Western ' strain and a new Lucianic element, and these untrustworthy components can be excluded from consideration chiefly by noting agreements of the Antiochian text with the Old Uncials.   Even if ancient Antiochian readings departing from all, or from one sub-group, of the Old Uncials can sometimes be identified, these merely represent a lost second-century or third-century MS. parallel to the (somewhat younger) Old Uncial codices, not necessarily independent of their text, and by no means necessarily better.   Such readings merely signify that another important Old Uncial witness has been added

Von Soden's method.

to our resources, to be treated in just the same way as the several witnesses to the Old Uncial text already at the disposal of criticism, and with no greater reverence than is accorded to these latter. The study of the extant Old Uncials shows that von Soden's assumption of a single Alexandrian recension, which we can reconstruct from divergent witnesses, is a fallacy. What we have to do is to recover as many second-century readings, not due to the 'Western' rewriting, as we can, and to compare them with one another. The double assumption underlying von Soden's system was that all the extant Old Uncials are derived from a particular form of the second-century text, and that the ancient Antiochian text rested on a MS. independent of that particular form ; and this twofold assumption cannot safely be made.

8. TASKS

In the preparation of an Essay like the present many topics arise on which the necessary information for a statement of the facts is not available, and many questions occur to which an answer would be desirable. In a large proportion of these problems a solution could be reached by sufficient expenditure of time and effort. Some of the problems are comprehensive, and require long research and all the resources of matured knowledge and judgment, others are of limited range and would form good tasks for the training of younger scholars. A service may perhaps be rendered by the following list of tasks to the performance of some of which it is hoped that this volume will prove an incentive. The list is extensive, but makes no claim to completeness. It would be gratifying if the present work could be followed by a series of studies, longer and shorter, dealing with further problems of the text of Acts, by many hands and in various languages, and it is my confident expectation that in one form or another provision could be made for the publication of such supplementary studies.

I. Greek Codices and Texts

1. A renewed and thorough general study, with the aid of modern palaeographical, and especially philological, knowledge of each of the uncials אBAC. This is peculiarly needed for Codex Alexandrinus, but equally for Codex Vaticanus.

2. The correctors of א and the aims and standards of their work.

3. The singular readings of אAC 81.

4. A more thorough investigation of the readings of the Old Uncial sub-groups, including the testimony of Cod. 1175 (Patmos), 33 (formerly 13 ; Paris), 326 (formerly 33 ; Lincoln College, Oxford).

5. The group ℵA 81 ; why does it so often oppose BC, and why is it so often in agreement with the Antiochian ?

6. In general, all the questions relating to the Old Uncial text of Acts raised and discussed in the foregoing Essay need to be more thoroughly examined, with such a fresh assemblage of the facts as can easily be made from the present volume.

7. Thorough palaeographical, and especially philological, study of Codex Bezae, and particularly a definitive examination of the corrections and notes of that codex.

8. The non-western readings now found in D ; from what type of text were these derived ?

9. How much of the text of D is probably in fact due to the influence of the Latin parallel, and how much of the supposed latinization must be regarded as doubtful ?

10. Study of the I-codices, in groups containing many or few. Photographs of most of these can easily be obtained.

11. From these I-codices, as now known in published apparatus, a full (not necessarily perfectly complete) assemblage of the Greek ' Western ' fragments that can be identified, using as criteria the approximate agreement of readings with D, with the Harclean apparatus, and with the Old Latin, Peshitto, and Sahidic, as well as their internal character. This is greatly needed as a check on the evidence of D, and for confirmation and improvement of the ' Western ' text printed by Zahn.

12. A closer detailed search in the ' Western ' text for the indication of the readings of its ancient pre-western base.

13. The exploration of the ' Western ' text for instances of knowledge of Hebrew or of Palestinian conditions.

14. The character of the Old Antiochian text used as the basis of the Lucianic recension. What were the relations of its Old Uncial element to the several extant MSS. of the Old Uncial group?

15. In general, a thorough analysis of the Antiochian recension in Acts.

16. The history of the text of Acts as found in Greek lectionaries ; and the same for Latin lectionaries.

17. A study of the forms and spelling of proper names in the various types of New Testament text, with tabulation of facts observed, and with use of recent studies of the proper names of the LXX.

18. The ever-recurring problem of Euthalius and his text.

19. The prefaces to Acts, including that published by E. von Dobschütz in the *American Journal of Theology*, vol. II., 1898, pp. 353-387.

II. VERSIONS

20. Does the African Latin in Acts show any relation to the Antiochian recension, as it does in some Old Testament books ?

21. A complete investigation of the Greek text of Acts represented by Codex Gigas.

22. Does the Greek text of the ' Western ' element in the text of Gigas differ at all from the Greek source of the African Latin ?

23. A study of the relation of the Latin translations of the Gospels to the translations of Acts, especially with relation to Codex Gigas.

24. The Armenian version and the Greek text underlying it.

25. A detailed and complete study of the Peshitto of Acts.

26. The text (in distinction from the apparatus) of the Harclean Syriac. This ought to elicit some ' Western ' readings unmarked with an asterisk and overlooked in the apparatus to the present volume.

27. The Georgian version and its underlying Greek.

28. The Ethiopic version (first of all with use of the oldest Paris MS.) and its underlying Greek.

29. The Old Bohemian version and its ' Western ' elements.

III. PATRISTIC PROBLEMS

30. The text of Chrysostom in Acts.

31. The text of other Greek fathers of the fourth and subsequent centuries.

32. Examination of the relation of the Didascalia and Apostolic Constitutions for the text of other books in the light of the observations presented above relating to the text of Acts.

33. The text of Augustine. (The index to the Vienna edition of the Epistolae now furnishes new resources.)

34. The history of the Latin text of Acts as illustrated by Latin fathers after Cyprian.

EXPLANATORY NOTE TO TEXT, APPARATUS, AND TEXTUAL NOTES

THE text of the Book of Acts is printed below from Codex Vaticanus and Codex Bezae on opposite pages. The apparatus attached to these continuous texts is not intended to provide a complete statement of all known various readings, but is rather regarded as a series of textual investigations, made on the basis of the well-known comprehensive collections of readings, together with some parts of the evidence for the ' Western ' text which can with advantage be separately exhibited in this manner. The arrangement of the whole and the judgment in details, especially in the omission of certain classes of facts, have been guided by the purpose of providing means for historical study and for criticism of the text ; purely linguistic or palaeographical ends have sometimes been disregarded. In accordance with this principle variants of spelling have in most cases been deliberately neglected in the apparatus, although the actual spelling of Codices B and D and of the Latin Codices d and h has been carefully followed in the continuous texts.

1. *Codex Vaticanus.*—The text of Codex Vaticanus has been supplied with punctuation, capitals, accents, etc., and abbreviations for *nomina sacra* and the like have been resolved, so as to form a readable text, but the spelling as printed is exactly as it comes to us from the first hand, with the exception of a few changes which are all carefully indicated. Much of the spelling of Codex B which looks strange to the modern reader, because it violates the rules of the later Greek grammarians, consists merely of irregularities common in the fourth century, which the scribe, if confronted with them, would probably have been disposed to defend. In certain instances, however, he has apparently committed indefensible blunders or omissions. These are corrected in our text (angular brackets [< >] being used to indicate omissions supplied), and a very few changes of spelling have been made (chiefly in cases of confusion of v and $oι$) where the irregular spelling is a serious obstacle to the modern reader's understanding, and would perhaps have been deemed wrong by a fourth-century corrector if he had noticed it.

Twice (xviii. 2 κλανδιον ; xxv. 24 ζην) whole words necessary to the sense were omitted. In the few cases (less than twenty-five in the whole of Acts) where blunders not by omission have been observed and are corrected in the text, the reading of the MS. is recorded in the line immediately following the text. The insignificant number of such instances will indicate the conservative practice of the editor in making corrections, as well as in adding letters in the text, and itself attests the care and intelligence with which the codex was written. About half of the blunders thus noted are actually corrected in the MS. by B¹ or B², and some of these corrections ought probably to be credited to the account of the original scribe. Readings manifestly wrong but which make sense are retained in the text, as in x. 37 κηριγμα for βαπτισμα, although in this particular instance the spelling of the printed text is corrected to read κηρυγμα. In proper names the spelling of the MS. has been given without change, even when inconsistent with the scribe's usual habit.

Where the first hand of B has corrected his own work, his corrected form has been adopted. The corrections of B are not at present satisfactorily understood, and call for a renewed study, which can only be made from the pages of the MS. itself ; even the latest facsimile does not suffice for this purpose. Corrections ascribed to B³ by the Roman editors have been neglected as too late to be significant for our purpose, but those which they assign to B² (apart from mere spelling) have been mentioned in the apparatus with the variants of the Old Uncial group. Where Tischendorf's positive judgment differed from that of the Roman editors with regard to these corrections, that fact has been noted. It is probable that in some cases a competent fresh study of the corrections would lead to different conclusions from those now current.

The division into verses has been made to correspond with that of Stephen's edition of 1551.

It should be observed that the method of printing the text of Codex Vaticanus here adopted, while deemed useful for study and well adapted to the present purpose, is not recommended as a good way to prepare a critical text for general use.

2. *Editors' Readings.*—In the first section of the apparatus are noted those readings of Westcott and Hort (' WH ') and von Soden (' Soden ') which depart from B. The former give virtually the minimum of necessary departure from B ; while the text represented by the latter was formed on a different principle from that of Westcott and Hort, and of its relation to Westcott and Hort's text no full statement is elsewhere accessible. To these has been added (with the symbol ' JHR ') mention of readings in departure from B which commend themselves to the author of the present volume (not necessarily, however, to the Editors of *The Beginnings of*

Christianity). This last series of readings is not sufficient for the formation of a critical text, for which many further questions of spelling, punctuation, etc., would have to be taken into account. The confidence with which the preferences are offered varies greatly in the different cases, as will be gathered from the Textual Notes in which many of them are discussed. Those not referred to in the Notes are usually cases where B stands alone, with little or no support from other authorities.

For a new critical text the time will not be ripe until the 'I-codices'[1] are more completely known and studied, and until the versions have been exhaustively compared and investigated.

The only other recent independent text which might have been included in this portion of the apparatus is that of Bernhard Weiss, in *Texte und Untersuchungen*, ix., 1893. But this rests on principles not essentially different from those of Westcott and Hort, and is easily accessible in the apparatus to Nestle's edition of the New Testament, so that it seemed best not to make the apparatus more complicated by adding a record of Weiss's departures from B.

3. *Old Uncial Text.*—The second section of the apparatus records the variants from B of the group of codices אAC 81, together with the corrections ascribed to B[1] and B[2] and the variants of those small fragments (see pp. ccx ff.) which clearly represent this type of text. The fragments included are Pap[8], Pap[33], 066, 076, 095, 096, 0165, 0175, Wess[59c]. The relation of these readings to Codex Bezae is added, with '(+ D)' to denote complete, and '(cf. D)' to indicate substantial, agreement. But it must be remembered that these statements of relation to D include only cases where the Old Uncial authorities are divided by a variation within the group. Agreement of D with the whole group is not recorded here. The variants of אAC 81 and of the fragments are given completely, except that manifest blunders (*e.g.* xiii. 13 υπεστρεψαν א ; xiv. 10 ορθρος A ; i. 21 ημων for ημιν C ; xi. 12 ειπον for ειπεν 81) are usually omitted and variations of mere spelling and grammatical form (*e.g.* ειπον, ειπα ; πλειονες, πλειους) consistently neglected. Thus in numerous cases the characteristic habit of the scribe of 81 of adding -ν to the accusative (*e.g.* xiv. 12 διαν for δια) is not mentioned.

In some cases it has been necessary, for the sake of simplicity and clearness, to treat a group of codices as united in the support of a variant where in fact there are among them slight differences of spelling which are not mentioned (*e.g.* xvi. 25 ' σειλας BאA 81 o σιλας C ' merely means that BאA 81 agree in lacking the article ; in fact B spells the name here σειλας, אA σιλας). In general the spelling followed in this portion of the apparatus is that of B, and

---

[1] As von Soden states (pp. 1686-1688), his collation of these codices was only partial.

cannot be relied on as indicating the spelling of the other MSS. of the group, save where for some special reason that is noted. In all these matters it has been kept in view that this is an *investigation*, not a comprehensive apparatus like that of Tischendorf, and that this aim dictates the greatest simplicity compatible with full information. I do not think that these omissions need cause the student to distrust the apparatus as an instrument for the purpose for which it is constructed.

The earliest corrections of the codices of the group are given (ℵ^a ℵ^{c}A^{2}C^2), but not the later ones ; corrections by the first hand are adopted, without special mention, as the reading of the MS. (*e.g.* xvii. 24, where A* at first omitted o before ποιησας and then supplied it). It is not impossible that ℵ^a represents corrections made by the original scribe. The complicated possibilities in the case of corrections can be but imperfectly exhibited in an apparatus like the present one.

Codex 33 (formerly 13) might have been included with the Old Uncial group, but its text is much more diluted with Antiochian readings than that of 81, and it is easily accessible in Tregelles. It has accordingly seemed best to avoid a further complication of this apparatus by an addition which would have made necessary the mention of many irrelevant readings.

The apparatus relates to the text of B as printed, without usually making reference (except in recording corrections of B^1 and B^2) to the blunders mentioned in the line below the text or to the omitted letters supplied in the text.

4. *Antiochian Text.*—The section of the apparatus giving the readings in which the Antiochian text departs from Codex Vaticanus is constructed on the same plan as the Old Uncial section, and the same warnings apply as to its limitations and its use. Here, as there, blunders are generally not mentioned, spelling is not usually recorded, and the basis of comparison is the slightly corrected form of Codex Vaticanus as printed on the page. The MSS. chosen as witnesses to the Antiochian text (see pp. xx-xxi) are SHLP. The readings of S have been drawn from a photograph,[1] those of P from Tischendorf's edition. H and L are accurately known from Tischendorf and Tregelles. The readings of the sixth-century fragment 093 (Acts xxiv. 22-26, 27) are also included. In Acts i. 1-ii. 13, where P is lacking, the readings of 102 are given ; and in i. 1-v. 28, where H is lacking, those of 462. These two minuscules are excellent copies of the same recension as SHLP, and are

---

[1] Unfortunately the MS. is mutilated in Acts i. 11-14, xii. 15-19, xiii. 1-3, and the photograph was illegible in a very few words elsewhere. In S a few corrections are to be found, which have not usually been mentioned in the apparatus. S shows a tendency to omit final -ν, writing, for instance, ημερα for ημεραν.

adequately known from the apparatus of Matthäi's New Testament
(Riga, 1782). H is also defective in various other briefer sections
(see above, pp. xx-xxi) ; as is L in i. 1-viii. 10 (as far as εστιν η).
The extraordinary uniformity, however, with which the Antiochian text
was copied for many centuries renders of little moment this variation
in the attestation used for the apparatus. In this apparatus silence
of course means agreement with my (slightly corrected) printed text
of Codex Vaticanus, in so far as the witnesses regularly adduced for
the Antiochian text are extant.

For convenience of comparison the variants from B of the Textus
Receptus are included in this section of the apparatus with the
symbol ' ς ', although they do not represent the precise type of
SHLP. The text used for collation is that of Stephanus, 1550, as
given in Scrivener's New Testament, 4th edition, London and
Cambridge, 1906.

5. *Codex Bezae (Greek).*—In printing the Greek text of Codex
Bezae the same principles have been followed as with Codex
Vaticanus. The manifest blunders, however, corrected in the text
but recorded in the lines immediately following it, are far more
numerous. As in the case of Codex Vaticanus the course pursued
has been highly, perhaps excessively, conservative. Many readings
which are undoubtedly wrong, including most of those due to the
adjustment of the Greek to the Latin side, have been permitted to
stand, on the ground that although contrary to Greek idiom they
do not produce utter nonsense. In a number of cases (some being
due to the contamination of D from a non-western text) impossible readings, mostly cases where the correction is not at first sight
evident, have been permitted to stand in the text, but with an
obelus (†). The number of such obeli might perhaps have been
made greater with advantage. The spelling of Codex Bezae has
been carefully preserved except where changes are expressly noted.
In many of his aberrations the scribe was doubtless following faithfully the archaic text of his exemplar, but in some cases, especially
in inflexional endings, his spelling is so disturbing to the modern
reader that it seemed worth while to emend it (never without due
notice). Letters which presumably once stood in the text, but are
no longer legible, either through accident or by intentional erasure,
are enclosed in square brackets [ ]. For this the statements of
Scrivener's notes have been carefully studied. These are to be
carefully distinguished from omitted necessary letters which never
stood in the text of the MS. but have been added in angular
brackets < >. Abbreviations are generally resolved without
special note. Interlinear letters apparently by the original scribe
and printed by Scrivener have been adopted as a proper part of
the text ; the corrections of later scribes are not referred to. The

peculiarities of Codex Bezae are extensively discussed in the Textual Notes.

Where Codex Bezae is defective, such Greek readings as can be shown to be probably variations of the 'Western' text from the Old Uncial text have been collected and printed. This material has been drawn mainly from minuscules, but occasionally from the Antiochian uncials, from Pap²⁹ אAC, and from Greek patristic citations. In this way, where D is lacking, an unexpectedly large part of the Greek text of specifically 'Western' readings attested by the Latin side of D, by h, by Tertullian, Cyprian, and Irenaeus, and especially by the marginal glosses and asterisked words of the Harclean Syriac, has been recovered. All discoverable Greek readings which are attested, as just stated, by these almost or quite purely 'Western' witnesses have been printed for the sections in question. In addition, for these sections, search has been made in the minuscules, as cited by von Soden, for Greek readings which the mixed texts of the Latin and the Peshitto show to be probably 'Western', and this search has not been unfruitful for these pages. Probably more remains to be gathered, especially by further elicit-ing the 'Western' element of the Antiochian text through careful comparison with the Latin, Syriac, and Sahidic versions. It is evident that a great amount of 'Western' text lurks in the minus-cules of the I-groups, now made in a large degree accessible by the apparatus of von Soden, and much of it can be securely discovered by skilful comparison of the versions named, together with the Armenian, which I have not used. The same process ought also to be applied to the Greek text of Codex Bezae itself, in order now to confirm and now to forbid the acceptance of it as giving the 'Western' text. A foundation for such study has been laid in Zahn's *Urausgabe*, and many matters of this nature will be found discussed in my Textual Notes.

In my attempt to collect 'Western' readings in the sections mentioned I have not paid attention to probable 'Western' variations in the order of words. It is possible that these can some-times be detected in the minuscules. I have also refrained from drawing inferences as to 'Western' variants in the more common conjunctions (καί, τε, δέ), since these are so frequently altered in the versions.

There is need of a fresh investigation of the extent to which the 'Western' text in these sections positively agreed with the Old Uncial text, since only variations from the latter are indicated in the readings I have given.

The lemmata used to show the points of reference of the variations are, of course, drawn from the text of Codex Vaticanus.

6. *Codex Bezae* (*Latin*).—The text of d has been printed with

division of words, but with no attempt to suggest correction of its errors, and in its native spelling, without resolution of abbreviations, and without the use of capitals or punctuation to aid the reader. For the purposes of textual criticism (as distinguished from the study of the history of the Latin version) d is, in fact, chiefly, though not quite exclusively, valuable for its aid in understanding the Greek pages of Codex Bezae. One problem in printing it with division of words is an occasional haplography, by which a letter is omitted, thus xi. 23 ad$\overline{nm}$ for ad $\overline{dnm}$; xxii. 20 *sanguistephani* for *sanguis stephani*. A few words once present but now destroyed have been supplied in square brackets [ ].

7. *' Western ' Apparatus.*—It has not been practicable to print an apparatus for the ' Western ' text similar to those presented for the Old Uncial and Antiochian texts. All the Greek MSS. which contain ' Western ' elements are highly mixed, and the same is true of nearly all the Latin texts, as well as of the other versions. The variants from Codex Vaticanus of the Peshitto and Sahidic versions have been analysed, and are exhibited in Appendices III. and IV. To try to select and print the ' Western ' readings of the Old Latin would involve a judgment, often of a doubtful nature, on every case, and the result would be misleading. The student must here have recourse for himself to the apparatus of Wordsworth and White, as he must for the Greek evidence to that of Tischendorf and of von Soden. Indeed, one object of the plan adopted for the ' Western ' page is to discourage the idea that (except h) any single Latin MS. of Acts, such as gig, can be treated as if it could give by itself, apart from comparison with other authorities, direct evidence of the ' Western ' text. The student must consider, as the ' Western ' evidence, nothing less than the *whole apparatus* of Wordsworth and White, together with the versions in other languages.

In default, therefore, of pure ' Western ' Greek and Latin MSS. (other than h) it has seemed well to bring together some of the chief evidence of other kinds which can be trusted. This is the more useful that a part of it is not elsewhere so conveniently accessible in a simple form.

8. *Codex h.*—Codex h (the Fleury palimpsest) is virtually purely ' Western ' in its fragments of Acts. First deciphered by Berger, then more fully by Buchanan with the advantage of Berger's previous reading, again examined a second time by Buchanan and inspected at doubtful points by other scholars, the text of this difficult palimpsest is even now not known with perfect certainty, although there is agreement as to most of its readings (see above, pp. cvi-viii). In every line, moreover, the trimming of the pages makes supplementary conjecture necessary. The text printed below has been formed by careful consideration of the probabilities furnished by

all the available evidence. Words and letters in square brackets [ ]
are conjectures to fill the lacunae of the MS. ; for these Buchanan's
proposals have usually, but not always, been found acceptable.
Mention should be made of Souter's happy conjecture co[nsecutus]
in xxvi. 22. Where the conjectures adopted are not obvious, the
reader must weigh them for himself. The more difficult conjectures are often mentioned in the Notes. In a few instances an
erroneous letter cancelled, probably by the first hand, in the MS.
has been omitted from a word, but otherwise the spelling of the MS.,
however strange, has been preserved. The sporadic punctuation of
the MS. has not usually been reproduced.

It is worth mention that the readings of h in Wordsworth and
White were necessarily drawn from Berger, and that von Soden
follows them in neglect of Buchanan's publication.

The following substantial differences between the readings and
conjectures of Buchanan and of Berger deserve mention. Some of
the readings here attributed to Buchanan are those of his later
correction (see above, p. cvi note 2), not of his edition. Many
differences not here noted are due to the fact that Buchanan was
able to read much more than Berger could do ; in such cases Berger's
conjectures have usually been confirmed. For the study of minor
details of spelling, where Berger and Buchanan differ in their reading,
the information given in the present volume is not sufficient and
recourse must be had to the original publications. Buchanan also
reports the corrections by various hands now found in the MS.

CODEX h

	BERGER	BUCHANAN
iii. 4	ad[stans dixit]	adspic[e inquit]
12	dixit	et dixit
14	et petistis	et vos petestis
15	[autem vitae..... lign]o [intere]m[istis]	autem vi[tae s]uspendentes occidistis
16	supe[r]	supra
22	[me ipsu]m [au]di[etis]	me eum vos audituri
24	[et per]	[et pro]
iv. 3	tenuerunt	et tenuerunt
9	[hodie] rogamus	[hodie inter]rogamus
14	agnosce[bant e]os	agnosce[bant e]is
15	[adse]cuti	[conlo]cuti
17	[dentu]r	[divulgentu]r
v. 26	n[on]	n[on vero]
29	ad il[los]	ad il[lum]
34	mi[nimum d]uci	mi[nistris d]uci
41	e [conspectu]	et conspe[ctu]
42	a[utem]	atquae

		BERGER	BUCHANAN
vi.	1	d[espicer]entur	discupierentur
	7	discentiu[m nimis]	discentiu[m valde]
	7	[f]id[ei]	fid[em]
	12	[populu]m	[plebe]m
	13	[defi]cit	[quies]cit
	15	[qui sedeb]ant	[qui er]ant
ix.	4	[..]vere	[pa]vore
	9	triduum n[o]n	tridum nihil
	10	respon[dit quis] e[s]	respon[dens ait i]ta
	18	untus	tintus
	21	ut finctos	uti victos
xiv.	6	civita[tes ...... lys]tra	civitates sicut i̅h̅s̅ dixerat eis LX[XII in lys]tra
	7	et motum	ut motum
	8	in[validus pedibus]	languid[us pedibus]
	8-9	[ti]more[m d̅i̅] hic	[ti]morem hic
	9	[paulum incipientem]	apostolos in[cipientes]
	9-10	sal[varet eu]m di[xit]	salvaretur clamans dixit ei
	10	am[bula] et con[festim]	amvula et ille infirmus
	11	[turbae autem videntes] q[uae fecit]	et turbae videntes quod fe[cit]
	12-13	[mer]curiu[m sacerdos autem jovis qui] in [p]or[ticu] ci[vitatis]	[mer]curium quoniam ipse erat princeps verborum et [ad portam]
	14	sil [.................]s	suum vestimentum accurrentes
	15	[con]vertamini	[ut con]vertamini
	17	[invi]sibilem	[int]estabilem
	19	[illos ho]mines	[illis ho]minib·
	20	[cum surre]ssisset	[cum disce]ssisset
xviii.	5	fier[ent verba]	fier[et verbum]
	6	[gentes]	[nationes]
	8	[cum multus]	[quomodo mult]a
	17	[percuss]erunt	[cecid]erunt
xxiii.	15	rogamus [uti]	rogamus vos
	19	[ante homi]nes	[apud om]nes
xxvi.	24	[et c]lamavit	exclamavit
	28	[agri]ppa	[qui] ita
xxvii.	8	lege[bamus u]nde venimus	lege̅[tes cret]en devenimus
	9	paucos	plures
	13	[cum flaret]	[dum flat]

In xxvii. 7 Buchanan, in his final judgment, reads *aliquos* [*dies*], agreeing with Berger's original reading (from which, however, at the suggestion of Corssen, Berger afterward receded). Burkitt, however, after examining the MS., is sure that it reads *aliquod* [*tempus*].

9. *Tertullian ; Irenaeus ; Cyprian ; Augustine.*—In the passages
cited from the church fathers those words which are not part of the
quoted text of Acts are enclosed in square brackets.

The text of TERTULLIAN used is that of the Vienna Corpus
so far as it is available, elsewhere that of Oehler. The mere
allusions of Tertullian have not been given ; for them recourse
must be had to Rönsch, *Das Neue Testament Tertullian's*, 1871.

For IRENAEUS the courtesy of the publishers and editor of *Novum
Testamentum Sancti Irenaei*, Oxford, 1923, has permitted the use
of the text contained in that volume. Greek fragments are quoted,
so far as extant, in addition to the Latin. For renderings of the
Armenian text of Irenaeus's quotations from Acts, see Conybeare in
Novum Testamentum Sancti Irenaei, pp. 270 f., 288. A few brief
allusions by Irenaeus (*e.g.* v. 32, 2 to Acts vii. 5), chiefly significant
for the Latin words used and not for the Greek text rendered, have
not been included in my notes. The references to chapters and
sections of Irenaeus, *Adversus haereses*, are in accord with the
editions of Massuet and of Stieren, but the enumeration of Harvey's
edition, when divergent, is added in parenthesis.

The text of the quotations from CYPRIAN is taken from Hartel's
edition in the Vienna Corpus with further correction in the *Testimonia*
from the readings of Codex L as given by Hartel. In Acts i. 1-ii. 11,
by an error of judgment on my part, the quotations made by Cyprian
are not adduced in full, but only the important variants of his text
given as footnotes to the text cited by Augustine, with which
Cyprian's quotations are nearly identical. The full passages from
Cyprian are as follows :

Acts i. 7 (*Testimonia* iii. 89) nemo potest cognoscere tempus aut
tempora quae pater posuit in sua potestate.

i. 14 (*De catholicae ecclesiae unitate* 25 ; also *De dominica oratione* 8)
et erant perseverantes omnes unanimes in oratione cum
mulieribus et Maria quae fuerat mater Jesu et fratribus ejus.

i. 15 (*Epist.* 67, 4) surrexit [inquit] Petrus in medio discentium,
fuit autem turba in uno.

ii. 2-4 (*Testimonia* iii. 101) et factus est subito de caelo sonus,
quasi ferretur flatus vehemens, et inplevit totum locum
illum in quo erant sedentes. et visae sunt illis linguae
divisae quasi ignis, qui et insedit in unumquemque illorum.
et inpleti sunt omnes spiritu sancto.

From AUGUSTINE, *De actis cum Felice Manichaeo* i. 4-5, Acts i. 1-
ii. 11 is cited, with the variants found in the corresponding quotations
from Acts in *De consensu evangelistarum* iv. 8 and *Contra epistolam
Manichaei quam vocant Fundamenti* 9, together with Acts ii. 12-13
from this last treatise. There are other passages in Augustine's

writings where the African Latin of Acts is cited (see Zahn, *Urausgabe, passim*), but no discriminating study of his quotations has ever been made which could sufficiently guide use of them in the present volume. They appear to vary in character in the different works, and sometimes to have been made from memory, sometimes perhaps from, or under the influence of, the Vulgate. The Vienna edition of Augustine has been used.

10. *Harclean Syriac.*—From the Harclean Syriac the greater part of the marginal glosses and all words under asterisk (with a few obelized words) are reproduced in the apparatus. The aim has been to record all the renderings of the Harclean apparatus which represent variant Greek readings. In addition, such renderings of 'Western' readings as have been noticed in the Harclean text, not marked by an asterisk, are given. Of this class others which have escaped observation and record here are undoubtedly to be gathered, recognizable in their Antiochian surroundings. Marginal glosses have been omitted which merely reproduce the Old Testament quotations (as in i. 20), or are of an exegetical nature, or relate only to a difference in the Syriac rendering of the same Greek word (*e.g.* viii. 40, xxiii. 7), but all these together are not numerous. Two longer notes will be found quoted in full above, p. clxiv.

The Greek lemmata to which the translations of the glosses, etc., are here attached, are drawn, so far as possible, from the text of Codex Bezae or of the Greek ' Western ' fragments printed at the top of the page ; in a few cases it has been necessary to use lemmata from the text of Codex Vaticanus. The point of attachment is not always the same as that indicated in the Harclean MS., in which some manifest errors of attachment have been committed.

The rendering of the Syriac is based on that of White, but has been carefully revised and corrected. The departures from White's Latin are intentional. It should be observed that *ipse* and *ille* are used for the Syriac pronoun which represents the Greek article.

11. *Textual Notes.*—In the Textual Notes many problems and difficulties which I should have liked to resolve will be found left without a Note because I had nothing to contribute to the illumination of them. Discussion is offered of many of the readings in which, in my judgment, Codex Vaticanus goes wrong, but usually not of those where B stands with no, or almost no, support from other witnesses. In the latter class of instances all that could be said would have amounted but to a bare statement of the fact, which will be already familiar to the student of the text for whom the Notes are designed.

In general I have tried to avoid burdening the Notes with obvious remarks leading to no conclusion. The manifest differences between the two great types of text are better studied in continuous texts than in notes ; and it is from the whole body of facts that every student must make up his mind as to the general superiority of one or the other type, or as to their equal authority. Consequently no attempt has been made to give a complete running commentary on the successive details of variation of D from B. A large proportion of the Notes, however, discuss the more difficult readings of Codex Bezae, especially where the evidence adduced from other ' Western ' witnesses furnishes a more trustworthy guide to the proper ' Western ' readings than does D. A selection of such evidence, not a complete array, especially from the Latin authorities, is often sufficient to produce conviction, and that is all that has been attempted.

In citing the testimony of the Old Uncial group, Codex 81 is often not mentioned in cases where its considerable Antiochian element renders its testimony suspect.

In the Textual Notes the term ' B-text ' has commonly been used for brevity to refer to the ' non-western text ', without prejudice to the question of whether the non - western influence upon Codex Bezae came from the Old Uncial or from the Antiochian form of that text.

Where the name of a critic is given as holding a certain view, I mean to indicate that the idea would probably not have occurred to me independently. Otherwise names are not mentioned except where a fuller published discussion has to be referred to.

Five longer Detached Notes follow the last chapter of Acts.

ABBREVIATIONS

GREEK codices are consistently referred to by Gregory's later system
(1908). The Psalms are cited by the enumeration and verses
of the Hebrew.

WH	Westcott and Hort
Soden	Hermann von Soden
JHR	James H. Ropes
+	followed by
add	adds, add
corr	corrector
corr*	corrector, identical with the first hand
def	is lacking
mg	margin
min(n)	minuscule(s)
om	omits, omit
suppl	supplies
txt	text
vid	apparently
Am. J. Philol.	American Journal of Philology
L. and S.	Liddell and Scott
St. Kr. ⎱ Stud. Krit. ⎰	Theologische Studien und Kritiken
Tdf	Tischendorf
T.U.	Texte und Untersuchungen
W.W.	Wordsworth and White
Antioch ⎱ Ant ⎰	Antiochian text
ϛ	text of Stephanus, 1550
cod. ardmach	Codex Ardmachanus (the Book of Armagh)
d	Codex Bezae (Latin)
e	Codex Laudianus (Latin)
gig	Codex Gigas
h	Fleury palimpsest
lat ⎱ latt ⎰	Latin texts

m	Speculum Pseudo-Augustini
perp ⎱ p ⎰	Perpignan MS.
r	Schlettstadt lectionary
t	Liber comicus (Toledo lectionary)
vg	Vulgate
w	Wernigerode MS.
prov	Provençal version
tepl	Codex Teplensis (German)
arm	Armenian version
boh	Bohairic version
eth	Ethiopic version
hcl	Harclean Syriac version
pesh	Peshitto
sah	Sahidic version
Ambr ⎱ Ambros ⎰	Ambrose
Ambrst	Ambrosiaster
Athanas	Athanasius
Aug	Augustine
Chrys	Chrysostom
Clem. Alex	Clement of Alexandria
Const. Apost	Constitutiones Apostolorum
Cypr	Cyprian
Ephr	Ephrem
Ephr. cat	Ephrem's Catena on Acts
Eus	Eusebius
Hil	Hilary
Iren	Irenaeus
Jer	Jerome
Lucif	Lucifer of Cagliari
Orig	Origen
Perpet	Acts of Perpetua and Felicitas
Philast	Philastrius of Brescia
Prisc ⎱ Priscill ⎰	Priscillian
Prom	Liber promissionum et praedictorum dei
Proph ⎱ De Proph ⎰	Prophetiae ex omnibus libris collectae
Rebapt	De Rebaptismate (Cyprianic Appendix)
Salvian	Salvianus
Tert	Tertullian
Vig	Ps.-Vigilius, Contra Varimadum

TEXT
APPARATUS
TEXTUAL NOTES

ΠΡΑΞΕΙΣ

Τὸν μὲν πρῶτον λόγον ἐποιησάμην περὶ πάντων, ὦ Θεόφιλε, 1
ὧν ἤρξατο Ἰησοῦς ποιεῖν τε καὶ διδάσκειν | ἄχρι ἧς ἡμέρας ἐν- 2
τειλάμενος τοῖς ἀποστόλοις διὰ πνεύματος ἁγίου οὓς ἐξελέξατο
ἀνελήμφθη· οἷς καὶ παρέστησεν ἑαυτὸν ζῶντα μετὰ τὸ παθεῖν 3
αὐτὸν ἐν πολλοῖς τεκμηρίοις, δι' ἡμερῶν τεσσεράκοντα ὀπτανόμενος αὐτοῖς καὶ λέγων τὰ περὶ τῆς βασιλείας τοῦ θεοῦ. καὶ 4
συναλιζόμενος παρήγγειλεν αὐτοῖς ἀπὸ Ἱεροσολύμων μὴ χωρίζεσθαι, ἀλλὰ περιμένειν τὴν ἐπαγγελίαν τοῦ πατρὸς ἣν ἠκούσατέ
μου· ὅτι Ἰωάνης μὲν ἐβάπτισεν ὕδατι, ὑμεῖς δὲ ἐν πνεύματι 5

2 For the conclusion, indicated above, that the original text of vs. 2 read approximately εν ημερα η εντειλαμενος τοις αποστολοις δια πνευματος αγιου εξελεξατο see Detached Note, pp. 256-261.
3 δια is represented in hcl.*text* by *bejad*, for which hcl.*mg* gives *l'appai*. White notes that the latter preposition is used in the Harclean text, Mk. xv. 1, Lk. iv. 25, Acts xix. 8, to represent ἐπί, but it seems more likely that *l'appai* was an idiomatic translation of δια given as equivalent to the literal but inappropriate *bejad*. No Greek MS. is known to read επι.
4 Aug. *quomodo*, referring back to *feci*, was perhaps added by translator (see Detached Note on vs. 2).
συναλιζομενος] συναλιζομενος many minn, including 614, and many patristic texts. To this seems to correspond the use of *conversor*, Aug perp gig e vg.*codd*. Confusion of the two words was not uncommon in Greek MSS. (cf.

L. and S., s.v. συναυλίζομαι), but the difficulty and persistent attestation of συναλιζομενος here make it more likely that συναλιζομενος was an alleviation by conjecture, perhaps regarded as a mere improvement in spelling.
μου] φησιν δια του στοματος μου D lat may be original, corrected because of Semitism ; more probably it is an expansion, ameliorating the transition to direct discourse and avoiding the awkward μου, while following the familiar style of the book (cf. i. 16, iii. 18, 21, iv. 25, xv. 7, all with perfectly stable text).
5 D και ο seems to be error for ο και gig τ Hil Aug. *contra Fel., c. ep. Fund., c. Petil.* 32, c. *Cresc.* ii. 14 (17), etc. ; for a similar misplacement in D cf. xiv. 38.
Aug. *Ep.* 265, 3 quotes this passage, from Ἰωάνης μέν to πεντηκοστῆς, substantially as in *contra Felicem* (except that he writes *baptizabimini* instead of *incipietis baptizari*), and then proceeds : *aliqui autem codices habent*

ΠΡΑΞΙΣ ΑΠΟΣΤΟΛΩΝ

1 Τὸν μὲν πρῶτον λόγον ἐποιησάμην περὶ πάντων, ὦ Θεόφιλε,
2 ὧν ἤρξατο Ἰησοῦς ποιεῖν τε καὶ διδάσκειν | ἄχρι ἧς ἡμέρας ἀν-
ελήμφθη ἐντειλάμενος τοῖς ἀποστόλοις διὰ πνεύματος ἁγίου οὓς
3 ἐξελέξατο καὶ ἐκέλευσε κηρύσσειν τὸ εὐαγγέλιον· οἷς καὶ παρέστησεν ἑαυτὸν ζῶντα μετὰ τὸ παθεῖν αὐτὸν ἐν πολλοῖς τεκμηρίοις,
τεσσεράκοντα ἡμερῶν ὀπτανόμενος αὐτοῖς καὶ λέγων τὰ περὶ
4 τῆς βασιλείας τοῦ θεοῦ. καὶ συναλιζόμενος μετ᾽ αὐτῶν παρήγγειλεν αὐτοῖς ἀπὸ Ἱεροσολύμων μὴ χωρίζεσθαι, ἀλλὰ περιμένειν τὴν ἐπαγγελείαν τοῦ πατρὸς ἣν ἠκούσα<τέ> φησιν διὰ τοῦ
5 στόματός μου· ὅτι Ἰωάνης μὲν ἐβάπτισεν ὕδατι, ὑμεῖς δὲ ἐν
πνεύματι ἁγίῳ βαπτισθήσεσθε †καὶ ὃ† μέλλετε λαμβάνειν οὐ μετὰ

   3 οπτανομενοις   τα] τας   4 συναλισκομενος
   5 βαπτισθησεσθαι   μελλεται

---

1 primum quidem sermonem feci de omnibus o theofile quae incoavit i̅h̅s̅ facere d
et docere 2 usque in eum diem quem susceptus est quo praecepit apostolis
per s̅p̅m̅ sanctum quos elegit et praecepit praedicare evangelium 3 quibus et
praesentiam se vivum postquam passus est in multis argumentis post dies quadraginta
apparens eis et narrans ea quae sunt de regno d̅i̅ 4 et simul convivens cum eis
praecepit eis ab hierosolymis non discedere sed expectare pollicitationem patris quam
audistis de ore meo 5 quia johannes quidem baptizavit aqua vos autem s̅p̅o̅ sancto
baptizamini et eum accipere habetis non potest multos hos dies usque ad pentecosten

---

1 primum quidem sermonem feci de omnibus, o Theophile, quae coepit Jesus
facere et docere 2 in die quo apostolos elegit per spiritum sanctum et praecepit
praedicare evangelium, 3 quibus praebuit se vivum post passionem in multis
argumentis dierum visus eis dies quadraginta et docens de régno dei, 4 et
quomodo conversatus est cum illis, et praecepit eis ne discederent ab Hierosolymis, sed sustinerent pollicitationem patris, quam audistis, inquit, ex ore
meo ; 5 quoniam Johannes quidem baptizavit aqua, vos autem spiritu
sancto incipietis baptizari, quem et accepturi estis non post multos istos

Augustine,
C. Felicem
i. 4 ; C. ep.
Fundam. 9 ;
De cons. evv.
iv. 8

   1 fecimus Fund (cod opt)   2 usque in diem quo Cons   et praecepit] mandans
jussit Cons   3 visus est eis per Fund   4 om et 1º Fund (codd)

[2-9 ad quadraginta dies egit docens eos quae docerent. dehinc ordinatis
eis ad officium praedicandi per orbem circumfusa nube in caelum est receptus.]

Tertullian,
Apolog. 21

---

2 ανελημφθη εντειλαμενος . . . κηρυσσειν το ευαγγελιον] mg assumptus est
quum praecepisset apostolis quos elegit per spiritum sanctum et praecepit
praedicare evangelium

Harclean

βαπτισθήσεσθε ἁγίῳ οὐ μετὰ πολλὰς ταύτας ἡμέρας. οἱ μὲν 6
οὖν συνελθόντες ἠρώτων αὐτὸν λέγοντες· Κύριε, εἰ ἐν τῷ χρόνῳ
τούτῳ ἀποκαθιστάνεις τὴν βασιλείαν τῷ Ἰσραήλ; εἶπεν πρὸς 7
αὐτούς· Οὐχ ὑμῶν ἐστιν γνῶναι χρόνους ἢ καιροὺς οὓς ὁ πατὴρ
ἔθετο ἐν τῇ ἰδίᾳ ἐξουσίᾳ, ἀλλὰ λήμψεσθε δύναμιν ἐπελθόντος 8
τοῦ ἁγίου πνεύματος ἐφ᾽ ὑμᾶς, καὶ ἔσεσθέ μου μάρτυρες ἔν τε
Ἰερουσαλὴμ καὶ ἐν πάσῃ τῇ Ἰουδαίᾳ καὶ Σαμαρείᾳ καὶ ἕως
ἐσχάτου τῆς γῆς. καὶ ταῦτα εἰπὼν αὐτῶν βλεπόντων ἐπήρθη, 9
καὶ νεφέλη ὑπέλαβεν αὐτὸν ἀπὸ τῶν ὀφθαλμῶν αὐτῶν. καὶ 10

Editors 7 ειπεν]+δε Soden JHR   8 [εν 2º] WH   9 βλεποντων αυτων WH
Soden om αυτων βλεποντων JHR

Old Uncial 6 συνελθοντες BACℵᶜ 81 (+D)   ελθοντες ℵ   ηρωτων BℵAC   επηρωτων
81 (+D)   7 ειπεν B   +ουν B² vid (B³Tdf)   +δε ℵA 81   ο δε ειπεν C
8 μου BℵAC(+D)   μοι 81   εν 2º Bℵ   om AC 81 (+D)   9 ειπων
BACℵᶜ 81   ειπ οντων ℵ   αυτων βλεποντων B   βλεποντων αυτων ℵAC 81

Antiochian 6 ηρωτων] επηρωτων S 462 102ϛ(+D)   7 ειπεν]+δε S 462 102ϛ
8 μοι S 462 102ϛ   9 βλεποντων αυτων S 462 102ϛ

'vos autem spiritu sancto incipietis baptizari'; sed sive dicatur 'baptizabimini' sive dicatur 'incipietis baptizari' ad rem nihil interest; nam in quibuscumque codicibus inveniuntur 'baptizabitis' aut 'incipietis baptizare' mendosi sunt; qui ex graecis facillime convincuntur. The difference between baptizabimini and incipietis baptizari is probably purely Latin. The active reading, however, cited by Augustine might point to a Greek text Ιωανης μεν εβαπτισεν υδατι, υμεις δε εν πνευματι αγιω, with no verb expressed. This could easily give rise to all the variants, including the addition of ο και μελλετε λαμβανειν (corrupted in D to και ο), the divergent Latin translations, and the variation in the order of words in the Greek mss.: but on the other hand the omission in the original is inherently improbable, unless the active verb is expressly intended; no Greek evidence for it exists; and the various readings are all susceptible of explanation without this supposition. It seems more likely that the active voice was an attempt of purely Latin origin to find here the commission to baptize which both Luke and Acts lack.

The addition εως της πεντηκοστης D Aug Ephr (on Eph. iv. 10) sah takes vs. 5 (οτι Ιωανης . . . ημερας) as parenthesis. The text of Ephr and sah, not seeing this, have inserted 'but' before εως.

6 For this question the translation: domine, si in hoc tempore (re)praesentaberis, et quando regnum Israel? is found with slight variation many times in Augustine (e.g. c. ep. Fund. 9, c. Gaudentium i. 20 [22], tract. in ev. Joh. 25, 3, tract. in ep. Joh. 10, 9), but not in c. Fel. 4, nor in most codices of civ. dei xviii. 53, nor in perp gig. (Re)praesentaberis ('be restored,' 'be shown'), of which d restituēre is an equivalent, refers to the Parousia. The cause of the Latin form of the text would seem to be that the Semitizing ει was misunderstood and taken to mean 'if' (so in fact Augustine, sermo 265, 2), and then an apodosis constructed out of Jesus' answer. The expansion appears only in Latin, although it is possible that in D the meaningless αποκαταστανεις εις (for αποκαταστ αθηση?—see Zahn) and the unique reading του ισραηλ are due to the modification of some different earlier text.

7 The asyndetic opening of vs. 7 in B is without other Greek support. It is probably due to an accidental omission, but the striking variations in the connexion supplied (ειπεν δε, ο δε ειπεν, ο δε αποκριθεις ειπεν, και ειπεν) may well point to the fact that the omission was not peculiar to B.

For ουχ υμων . . . καιρους Augustine in several places gives the translation: nemo potest cognoscere tempus

CODEX BEZAE 5

6 πολλὰς ταύτας ἡμέρας ἕως τῆς πεντηκοστῆς. οἱ μὲν οὖν συνελθόντες ἐπηρώτων αὐτὸν λέγοντες· Κύριε, εἰ ἐν τῷ χρόνῳ
7 τούτῳ ἀποκαταστάνεις †εἰς† τὴν βασιλείαν τοῦ Ἰσραήλ; καὶ
εἶπεν πρὸς αὐτούς· Οὐχ ὑμῶν ἐστιν γνῶναι χρόνους ἢ καιροὺς
8 οὓς ὁ πατὴρ ἔθετο ἐν τῇ ἰδίᾳ ἐξουσίᾳ, ἀλλὰ λήμψεσθε δύναμιν
ἐπελθόντος τοῦ ἁγίου πνεύματος ἐφ᾽ ὑμᾶς, καὶ ἔσεσθέ μου μάρτυρες ἔν τε Ἰερουσαλὴμ καὶ πάσῃ τῇ Ἰουδαίᾳ καὶ Σαμαρίᾳ καὶ
9 ἕως ἐσχάτου τῆς γῆς. καὐτὰ εἰπόντος αὐτοῦ νεφέλη ὑπέλαβεν
10 αὐτόν, καὶ ἀπήρθη ἀπὸ ὀφθαλμῶν αὐτῶν. καὶ ὡς ἀτενίζοντες

8 λημψεσθαι   9 υπελαβεν] υπεβαλεν

---

6 hi ergo cum convenissent interrogabant eum dicentes dn̄e si in tempore hoc d
restituere regnum istrahel   7 et dixit ad eos non est vestrum scire tempor aut
momenta quae pater posuit in sua potestate   8 sed accipietis virtutem cum super-
venerit santus sp̄s super vos et eritis mei testes ad quae hierusalem et omni judaeae
et samaria et usque ad ultimum terrae   9 et cum haec dixisset nubes suscepit eum
et levatus est ab oculis eorum   10 et ut aspicientes erant in caelo abeunte eo et ecce

---

dies usque ad pentecosten.   6 illi ergo convenientes interrogabant eum *Augustine,*
dicentes: domine, si in hoc tempore praesentabis regnum Israhel?   7 ille *C. Felicem*
autem dixit: nemo potest cognoscere tempus quod pater posuit in sua *Fundam. 9*
potestate;   8 sed accipietis virtutem spiritus sancti supervenientem in vos, et *Cyprian,*
eritis mihi testes apud Hierosolymam et in tota Judaea et Samaria et usque in
totam terram.   9 cum haec diceret, nubes suscepit eum et sublatus est ab eis.
10 et quomodo contemplantes erant cum iret in caelum, ecce duo viri astabant

6 praesentabis] representaberis et quando *Fund*   7 tempus] +aut tempora *Cypr.test*
quod] quae *Cypr. test*

---

7 quae pater posuit in sua potestate.   *Irenaeus, iii. 23, 1*

(in other instances, *tempora*). The use
of a single word for χρονους η καιρους
(attested also by Hilary *tempora*) he
explains (*Ep.* 197, 1-3), doubtless correctly, to be due to the lack of
Latin synonyms. Cyprian, *Test.* iii.
89, has *tempus aut tempora*: the
Latin ultimately adopted *tempora vel
momenta* perp gig t vg.; see ·Words-
worth and White's note. The Syriac
had the same difficulty, pesh *zabna
au zabne*.

In Augustine's correspondence with
Hesychius of Salona (*Epp.* 197, 198,
199) the reading *nemo potest cognoscere*
is discussed. This probably implies ουδεις δυναται γνωναι, and that
may be the original, corrected in the
B-text so as to avoid the inclusion
of Jesus himself in the negation
(but cf. Mk. xiii. 32); more probably, however, it was the paraphrast
who substituted the direct and plain
ουδεις δυναται, under the influence of
Mk. xiii. 32.

8 That the Antiochian μοι for μου
(BℵACD) is attested by Aug. *c. Fel.,
c. ep. Fund.* Prom sah may show that
it comes from the 'Western' text.
For μου cf. xiii. 31, xxii. 20.

9 The 'Western' text seems to have
read και ταυτα ειποντος αυτου νεφελη
υπελαβεν αυτον και επηρθη απ αυτων.
So Aug. *contra Fel.* (om και 1°) sah.
Augustine has elsewhere part of the
same, and D Prom give slightly modified forms. According to this text the
cloud enveloped Jesus, and then, while
within it, he was lifted up. The usual
text represents Jesus as rising before
the disciples' view and disappearing
from sight in a cloud in the sky. The
'Western' text is doubtless to be dis-
credited here as in other free variations.
But αυτων βλεποντων, which badly over-
loads the sentence in B, has no equivalent in Dd sah (Aug), and ought
probably to be omitted. The incon-
gruous απο οφθαλμων of D was added
by conflation from the other text.

ὡς ἀτενίζοντες ἦσαν εἰς τὸν οὐρανὸν πορευομένου αὐτοῦ, καὶ
ἰδοὺ ἄνδρες δύο παρειστήκεισαν αὐτοῖς ἐν ἐσθήσεσει λευκαῖς, οἷ 11
καὶ εἶπαν· Ἄνδρες Γαλειλαῖοι, τί ἑστήκατε βλέποντες εἰς τὸν
οὐρανόν; οὗτος ὁ Ἰησοῦς ὁ ἀναλημφθεὶς ἀφ' ὑμῶν εἰς τ<ὸν> οὐρανὸν
οὕτως ἐλεύσεται ὃν τρόπον ἐθεάσασθε αὐτὸν πορευόμενον εἰς
τὸν οὐρανόν. τότε ὑπέστρεψαν εἰς Ἰερουσαλὴμ ἀπὸ ὄρους τοῦ 12
καλουμένου Ἐλαιῶνος, ὅ ἐστιν ἐγγὺς Ἰερουσαλὴμ σαββάτου
ἔχον ὁδόν. καὶ ὅτε εἰσῆλθον, εἰς τὸ ὑπερῷον ἀνέβησαν οὗ ἦσαν 13
καταμένοντες, ὅ τε Πέτρος καὶ Ἰωάνης καὶ Ἰάκωβος καὶ Ἀν-
δρέας, Φίλιππος καὶ Θωμᾶς, Βαρθολομαῖος καὶ Μαθθαῖος,
Ἰάκωβος Ἀλφαίου καὶ Σίμων ὁ ζηλωτὴς καὶ Ἰούδας Ἰακώβου.
οὗτοι πάντες ἦσαν προσκαρτεροῦντες ὁμοθυμαδὸν τῇ προσευχῇ 14
σὺν γυναιξὶν καὶ Μαριὰμ τῇ μητρὶ Ἰησοῦ καὶ σὺν τοῖς ἀδελφοῖς
αὐτοῦ.

Καὶ ἐν ταῖς ἡμέραις ταύταις ἀναστὰς Πέτρος ἐν μέσῳ τῶν 15
ἀδελφῶν εἶπεν (ἦν τε ὄχλος ὀνομάτων ἐπὶ τὸ αὐτὸ ὡς ἑκατὸν
12 εχων

Editors			
	11 βλεποντες] εμβλεποντες Soden	om εις τον ουρανον 2° JHR	14 [του]
	ιησου WH του ιησου Soden JHR	om συν 2° Soden	15 ως] ωσει Soden

Old Uncial 11 βλεποντες ℵB 81 εμβλεποντες ACℵ°(+D) τον 2° B² 13 ανεβησαν
BAC 81 (cf. D) om ℵ (ℵ° [+D] inserts before εις) ο 2° BACℵ° 81 (+D)
om ℵ 14 προσκαρτερουντες ομοθυμαδον BAC 81 (+D) ομοθυμαδον προσκαρτερουντες ομοθυμαδον ℵ (ℵ° deletes ομοθυμαδον 2°) μαριαμ B 81 μαρια
ℵAC(+D) ιησου B του ιησου ℵAC 81 (+D) συν 2° B 81
om ℵAC(+D) 15 αδελφων BℵAC μαθητων 81 (+D) τε BℵA 81
δε C ως B 81 (+D) ωσει ℵAC

Antiochian 10 εσθητι λευκη S 462 102 ϛ(+D) 11 βλεποντες] εμβλεποντες S 462
102 ϛ(+D) ελευσεται]+παλιν 102 (S def) 12 εχων 102 (S def)
13 ανεβησαν εις το υπερωον 462 102 (S def) ϛ(+D) ιακωβος και ιωαννης
462 102 (S def) ϛ 14 προσευχη]+και τη δεησει S 462 102 ϛ μαρια
S 462 102 ϛ(+D) του ιησου S 462 102 ϛ(+D) 15 αδελφων] μαθητων
S 462 102 ϛ(+D)

11 εις τον ουρανον 2° (after αφ υμων)
is probably rightly omitted by D gig
Aug (Serm. 277, not c. Fel.) Vig.
12 For σαββατου οδον pesh reads
'about seven stadia' (shabbetha eṣṭad-
wan), sah 'a journey of seven roads'
(not 'stadia,' as commonly cited). The
very rare Sahidic word rendered
'road' is now known to mean (usually,
at least) 'high road,' i.e. ὁδός, and the
translator probably understood the
phrase to mean 'a week's (σαββάτου)
journey.' The Syriac may be somehow
due to the same exegesis, which is

expressly combated by Ammonius
(c. 398 A.D. ; in Cramer's Catena).
13 The omission in D of και before
Ιακωβος 1° and Σιμων is due to the
arrangement of the names in two
columns.
14 του ιησου. B's unique omission
of του is an error.
15 αδελφων BℵAC has been altered
in the 'Western' text (D Cypr Aug
gig p e etc.) to the more common
designation μαθητων (so also 81 and
Antiochian). The paraphrast may
have deemed αδελφων ambiguous, if

ἦσαν εἰς τὸν οὐρανὸν πορευομένου αὐτοῦ, καὶ ἰδοὺ ἄνδρες δύο
11 παρειστήκεισαν αὐτοῖς ἐν ἐσθῆτι λευκῇ, | οἳ καὶ εἶπαν· Ἄνδρες
Γαλιλαῖοι, τί ἑστήκατε ἐμβλέποντες εἰς τὸν οὐρανόν; οὗτος ὁ
Ἰησοῦς ὁ ἀναλημφθεὶς ἀφ᾽ ὑμῶν οὕτως ἐλεύσεται ὃν τρόπον
12 ἐθεάσεσθε αὐτὸν πορευόμενον εἰς τὸν οὐρανόν. τότε ὑπέστρεψαν
εἰς Εἰερουσαλὴμ ἀπὸ ὄρους τοῦ καλουμένου Ἐλεῶνος, ὅ ἐστιν
13 ἐγγὺς Ἱερουσαλὴμ σαββάτου ἔχον ὁδόν. καὶ ὅτε εἰσῆλθον,
ἀνέβησαν εἰ⟨ς⟩ τὸ ὑπερῷον οὗ ἦσαν καταμένοντες,
ὅ τε Πέτρος	καὶ Ἰωάνης,
Εἰάκωβος	καὶ Ἀνδρέας,
Φίλιππος	καὶ Θωμᾶς,
Βαρθολομαῖος	καὶ Μαθθαῖος,
Ἰάκωβος	ὁ τοῦ Ἁλφαίου,
Σίμων ὁ ζηλωτὴς	καὶ Ἰούδας Ἰακώβου.
14 οὗτοι πάντες ἦσαν προσκαρτεροῦντες ὁμοθυμαδὸν τῇ προσευχῇ
σὺν ταῖς γυναιξὶν καὶ τέκνοις καὶ Μαρίᾳ μητρὶ τοῦ Ἰησοῦ καὶ
τοῖς ἀδελφοῖς αὐτοῦ.
15 Ἐν δὲ ταῖς ἡμέραις ταύταις ἀναστὰς ὁ Πέτρος ἐν μέσῳ τῶν
μαθητῶν εἶπεν (ἦν γὰρ ὁ ὄχλος ὀνομάτων ἐπὶ τὸ αὐτὸ ὡς ρκ̄)·

13 εισηλθεν

---

viri duo adsistebant eis in veste candida   11 qui et dixerunt viri galilaei qui statis d
aspicientes in caelum iste īhs qui adsumptus est a bobis sic enim veniet quemad-
modmodum vidistis eum euntem in caelum   12 tunc reversi sunt hierusalem a monte
qui vocatur oliveti qui est juxta hierusalem sabbati habens iter   13 et cum introissent
ascenderunt in superiora ubi erant commorantes petrus et johannis jacobus et andreas
philippus et thomas bartholomeus et mattheus jacobus alphei simon zelotes et judas
jacobi   14 hi omnes erant perseberantes unanimes in oratione cum mulieribus et
filiis et maria matre īhu et fratribus ejus   15 in diebus his cum surrexisset petrus in
medio discipulorum dixit erat praeterea multitudo nonomnium quasi cxx   16 viri

---

illis in veste alba,   11 qui dixerunt ad eos : viri Galilaei, quid statis respicientes Augustine,
in caelum ?   iste Jesus qui adsumptus est in caelum a vobis sic veniet, C. Felicem
i. 4 f.
quemadmodum vidistis eum euntem in caelum.   12 tunc reversi sunt Hiero- Cyprian, De
solymam a monte qui vocatur Eleon, qui est juxta Hierosolymam sabbati unit. 25 ; De
dom. orat. 8 ;
habens iter.   13 et cum introissent, ascenderunt in superiora, ubi habitabant Ep. 67. 4
Petrus et Johannes, Jacobus et Andreas, Philippus et Thomas, Bartholomaeus
et Matthaeus, Jacobus Alphaei et Symon Zelotes et Judas Jacobi.   14 et erant
perseverantes omnes unanimes in orationibus cum mulieribus et Maria quae fuerat
mater Jesu et fratribus ejus.   15 et in diebus illis exurrexit Petrus in medio
discentium, et dixit (fuit autem turba in uno hominum quasi centum viginti) :

14 oratione *Cypr* (*bis*)   15 discentium *Cypr. ep.* 67 dicentium *Fel* (*codd*)

---

13 ιακωβος ο του αλφαιου] Jacobus ⁙ ille ⟨ Alphaei   ιουδας ιακωβου] Harclean
Judas ⁙ ille ⟨ Jacobi   15 δε] *mg* autem

---

not misleading (cf. vs. 14). The   in chaps. i.-v. makes this variant
striking avoidance of μαθηταί elsewhere   important.

εἴκοσι)· Ἄνδρες ἀδελφοί, ἔδει πληρωθῆναι τὴν γραφὴν ἣν 16
προεῖπε τὸ πνεῦμα τὸ ἅγιον διὰ στόματος Δαυεὶδ περὶ Ἰούδα
τοῦ γενομένου ὁδηγοῦ τοῖς συλλαβοῦσιν Ἰησοῦν, ὅτι κατηριθμη- 17
μένος ἦν ἐν ἡμῖν καὶ ἔλαχεν τὸν κλῆρον τῆς διακονίας ταύτης. οὗτος μὲν οὖν ἐκτήσατο χωρίον ἐκ μισθοῦ τῆς ἀδικίας, 18
καὶ πρηνὴς γενόμενος ἐλάκησεν μέσος, καὶ ἐξεχύθη πάντα τὰ
σπλάγχνα αὐτοῦ. καὶ γνωστὸν ἐγένετο πᾶσι τοῖς κατοικοῦσιν 19
Ἰερουσαλήμ, ὥστε κληθῆναι τὸ χωρίον ἐκεῖνο τῇ διαλέκτῳ
αὐτῶν Ἀκελδαμάχ, τοῦτ' ἔστιν χωρίον αἵματος. γέγραπται γὰρ 20

Ps. lxix. 25 ἐν βίβλῳ ψαλμῶν· Γενηθήτω ἡ ἔπαυλις αὐτοῦ ἔρημος καὶ μὴ
Ps. cix. 8 ἔστω ὁ κατοικῶν ἐν αὐτῇ, καί· Τὴν ἐπισκοπὴν αὐτοῦ λαβέτω
ἕτερος. δεῖ οὖν τῶν συνελθόντων ἡμῖν ἀνδρῶν ἐν παντὶ χρόνῳ ᾧ 21
εἰσῆλθεν καὶ ἐξῆλθεν ἐφ' ἡμᾶς ὁ κύριος Ἰησοῦς, ἀρξάμενος ἀπὸ 22

Editors   16 [τον] ιησουν Soden   19 τη]+ιδια Soden

Old Uncial   16 ιησουν BℵAC τον ιησουν 81(+D)   17 ην BACℵc 81(+D) om ℵ
18 παντα BℵC 81(+D) om A   19 και BACℵc 81 ο και ℵ(+D)
τη Bℵ(+D) +ιδια B²(B³Tdf)AC 81   ακελδαμαχ B (cf. D) αχελδαμαχ ℵA 81
ακελδαμα C   20 αυτου 1° BℵAC(+D) αυτων 81   ερημος BℵAC(+D)
ηρημωμενη 81   21 ω BℵAC 81 (cf. D) εν ω ℵc

Antiochian   16 γραφην]+ταυτην S 462 102ϛ(+D)   τον ιησουν S 462 102ϛ(+D)
17 εν] συν S 462 102ϛ   18 του μισθου ϛ   19 τη]+ιδια S 462 102ϛ
ακελδαμα S 462 102ϛ   19-20 om τουτ εστιν χωριον αιματος γεγραπται γαρ
εν S   20 αυτου 1°] αυτων S   λαβοι S 462 102ϛ   21 ω] εν ω S 462 102ϛ

18 For πρηνης γενομενος Aug. c. Fel. reads et collum sibi alligavit et dejectus in faciem, a combination with ἀπήγξατο (Matt. xxvii. 6); out of this Old Latin reading vg suspensus may have come. In place of πρηνής, the Armenian, followed by the Georgian, has a word which means 'swelling out,' and F. H. Chase has presented evidence to show that this meaning was proper to πρηνής (cf. πίμπρημι and πρήθω), and was intended here; see especially the Latin and Armenian versions of Wisdom iv. 19, and the mediaeval Lexicon of Zonaras. Ephrem on the Diatessaron (Matt. xxvii. 5; Latin tr., p. 240) and in the Catena on Acts i. 18 (see below, p. 391) refers to the same idea, but it is to be remembered that his Syriac comes to us through the Armenian. Euthymius Zigabenus, Comm. on Matthew (xxvii. 5), quotes in a kind of paraphrase the latter part of Acts i. 18, and uses the expression πρηνὴς εἴτουν πεπρησμένος; but this is probably an explanation, not a variant reading. Nor is Papias's πρησθείς (in Cramer's Catena on Acts i. 18), although perhaps due to Acts i. 18, to be regarded as attesting any textual variant ever actually read in Acts. See F. C. Conybeare, Classical Review, vol. ix, 1895, p. 258; Zahn, Forschungen vi, 1900, pp. 153-157, and p. 126, note 1; Urausgabe, pp. 331-332; J. R. Harris, Am. Journal of Theol. vol. iv, 1900, pp. 490-513; F. H. Chase, Journal of Theol. Studies, vol. xiii, 1912, pp. 278-285, 415; Harnack, Theol. Lit.-Zeitung, 1912, cols. 235 ff.; Torrey, Composition and Date of Acts, pp. 24 f.

19 While the Aramaic phrase would be chaqal dema, the usual reading of the Old Uncial text was probably αχελδαμαχ ℵA 81. Old Latin (and vg) sah (in all known copies) boh likewise retained a final guttural. Under varying degrees of influence from Aramaic, B reads ακελδαμαχ; D ακελδαμαχ; Antiochian, with C (cf. pesh hcl), ακελδαμα.

16 Ἄνδρες ἀδελφοί, δεῖ πληρωθῆναι τὴν γραφὴν ταύτην ἣν προεῖπεν
τὸ πνεῦμα τὸ ἅγιον διὰ στόματος Δαυεὶδ περὶ Ἰούδα τοῦ γενο-
17 μένου ὁδηγοῦ τοῖς συλλαβοῦσιν τὸν Ἰησοῦν, ὅτι κατηριθμημένος
18 ἦν ἐν ἡμῖν, ὃς ἔλαχε τὸν κλῆρον τῆς διακονίας ταύτης. οὗτος
μὲν οὖν ἐκτήσατο χωρίον ἐκ μισθοῦ τῆς ἀδικίας αὐτοῦ, καὶ
πρηνὴς γενόμενος ἐλάκησεν μέσος, καὶ ἐξεχύθη πάντα τὰ σπλάγχνα
19 αὐτοῦ. ὃ καὶ γνωστὸν ἐγένετο πᾶσιν τοῖς κατοικοῦσιν Ἱερουσαλήμ, ὥστε κληθῆναι τὸ χωρίον ἐκεῖνο τῇ διαλέκτῳ αὐτῶν
20 Ἀκελδαιμάχ, τοῦτ᾽ ἔστιν χωρίον αἵματος. γέγραπται γὰρ ἐν
βίβλῳ ψαλμῶν·
Γενηθήτω ἡ ἔπαυλις αὐτοῦ ἔρημος καὶ μὴ ᾖ ὁ κατοικῶν
ἐν αὐτῇ,
καί· Τὴν ἐπισκοπὴν αὐτοῦ λαβέτω ἕτερος.
21 δ<εῖ> οὖν τῶν συνελθόντων ἡμεῖν ἀνδρῶν ἐν παντὶ τῷ χρόνῳ ὡς
22 εἰσῆλθεν καὶ ἐξῆλθεν ἐφ᾽ ἡμᾶς ὁ κύριος Ἰησοῦς Χριστός, ἀρξά-

20 γενηθητω η] γενηθητων

---

fratres oportet inpleri scripturam hanc quam praedixit s͞p͞s sanctus per os david de d
juda qui factus est dux hiis qui adpraehenderunt i͞h͞m 17 qui adnumeratus erat inter
nos et sortitus fuit sortem ministerium hujus 18 hic ergo possidit praedium ex
mercedem injustitiae suae et pronus factus crepavit medius et effusa sunt omnia
viscera ejus 19 et notum factum est omnibus qui inhabitant hierusalem ita ut
vocetur praedium illud lingua ipsorum aceldemach hoc est praedium sanguinis
20 scriptum est enim in libro psalmorum fiat habitatio eorum deserta et non sit qui
inhabitet in ea et episcopatum illius sumat alius 21 oportet ergo eorum qui venerunt
nobiscum viroru͞ in omni tempore quoniam introibit et exivit ad nos d͞n͞s i͞h͞s x͞p͞s

---

16 viri fratres, oportet adinpleri scripturam istam, quam praedixit spiritus Augustine,
sanctus ore sancti David de Juda, qui fuit deductor illorum qui comprehenderunt C. Felicem
Jesum, 17 quoniam adnumeratus erat inter nos, qui habuit sortem hujus i. 4 f.
ministerii. 18 hic igitur possedit agrum de mercede injustitiae suae, et collum
sibi alligavit et dejectus in faciem diruptus est medius et effusa sunt omnia
viscera ejus. 19 quod et cognitum factum est omnibus qui inhabitabant
Hierosolymam, ita ut vocaretur ager ille ipsorum lingua Acheldemach, id est
ager sanguinis. 20 scriptum est enim in libro Psalmorum : fiat villa ejus
deserta, et non sit qui inhabitet in ea, et episcopatum ejus accipiat alter.
21 oportet itaque ex his viris qui convenerunt nobiscum in omni tempore quo
introivit super nos et excessit dominus Jesus Christus, 22 incipiens a baptismo

---

16 viri fratres, oportet impleri scripturam hanc quam praedixit spiritus Irenaeus,
sanctus ore David de Juda, qui factus est dux his qui apprehenderunt Jesum, iii. 12, 1;
17 quoniam adnumeratus fuit inter nos. ii. 20, 2(32, 1)
20 fiat habitatio ejus deserta, et non sit qui inhabitet in ea ; et, episcopatum
eius accipiat alter.
20 et episcopatum ejus accipiat alius.

---

18 της αδικιας αυτου] iniquitatis ⸓ suae ✓   Harclean

τοῦ βαπτίσματος Ἰωάνου ἕως τῆς ἡμέρας ἧς ἀνελήμφθη ἀφ' ἡμῶν,
μάρτυρα τῆς ἀναστάσεως αὐτοῦ σὺν ἡμῖν γενέσθαι ἕνα τούτων.
καὶ ἔστησαν δύο, Ἰωσὴφ τὸν καλούμενον Βαρσαββᾶν, ὃς ἐπ- 23
εκλήθη Ἰοῦστος, καὶ Μαθθίαν. καὶ προσευξάμενοι εἶπαν· Σὺ 24
κύριε καρδιογνῶστα πάντων, ἀνάδειξον ὃν ἐξελέξω, ἐκ τούτων
τῶν δύο ἕνα, λαβεῖν τὸν τόπον τῆς διακονίας ταύτης καὶ ἀπο- 25
στολῆς, ἀφ' ἧς παρέβη Ἰούδας πορευθῆναι εἰς τὸν τόπον τὸν
ἴδιον. καὶ ἔδωκαν κλήρους αὐτοῖς, καὶ ἔπεσεν ὁ κλῆρος ἐπὶ 26
Μαθθίαν, καὶ συνκατεψηφίσθη μετὰ τῶν ἕνδεκα ἀποστόλων.
Καὶ ἐν τῷ συνπληροῦσθαι τὴν ἡμέραν τῆς πεντηκοστῆς Η
ἦσαν πάντες ὁμοῦ ἐπὶ τὸ αὐτό, καὶ ἐγένετο ἄφνω ἐκ τοῦ οὐρανοῦ 2

Editors   25 τοπον 1°] κληρον Soden mg   26 αυτοις] αυτων JHR   ενδεκα]
δωδεκα JHR   1 ομου] ομοθυμαδον Soden mg   1-2 εν τω συνπληρουσθαι
. . . εγενετο] εγενετο εν ταις ημεραις εκειναις του συνπληρουσθαι την ημεραν
της πεντηκοστης οντων αυτων παντων επι το αυτο και ειδου εγενετο JHR

Old Uncial   22 εως BC(+D)   αχρι ℵA 81   25 τοπον 1° BAC(+D)   κληρον
ℵ 81   τοπον τον ιδιον Bℵ 81 (+D)   ιδιον τοπον C   τοπον τον δικαιον A
26 συνκατεψηφισθη BACℵ° 81   κατεψηφισθη ℵ   1 παντες BACℵ° 81
Wess⁵⁹ᶜ om ℵ

Antiochian   22 γενεσθαι συν ημιν S 462 102ϛ   24 παντων] των απαντων S   εκ
τουτων των δυο ενα ον εξελεξω ϛ   25 τοπον 1°] κληρον S 462 102ϛ   αφ]
εξ S 462 102ϛ   τοπον τον ιδιον] τοπον αυτου 462   26 αυτοις] αυτων S 462
102ϛ(+D)   1 παντες] απαντες S 462 102ϛ   ομου] ομοθυμαδον 462 102ϛ
ομοθυμαδον οι αποστολοι S

23 D εστησεν is shown by Aug. c. Fel.
and gig to be no accident of this one
MS. In vs. 24 Aug. c. Fel., precatus
dixit is unique; that the plural is
found in the better text of vs. 24 speaks
strongly for εστησαν in vs. 23.
For βαρσαββαν Bℵ A 81, C Antiochian
read βαρσαβαν. D is supported by
perp gig t vg.codd in the confused
correction βαρναβαν. On further confusions see Zahn, Urausgabe, pp.
333-335.
26 The ambiguity of κληρους αυτων
D Antiochian perp gig e t hcl.text is
shown by the Latin rendering sortes
suas in Aug. c. Fel. d vg.cod. M, which
suggests a vote rather than a drawing
of lots. Hence αυτοις BℵAC 81 may
be due to a substitution made for the
sake of clearness.
μετα των δωδεκα('among the twelve')
D Eus. demonstr. ev. x. 3, 2 hcl.text
was probably the 'Western' reading;
it may be right, as it would naturally
lead to correction, cf. ii. 14. Aug.
contra Felicem, cum undecim apostolis

duodecimus may be a secondary result
from it.
1-2 The reading of D means 'and it
came to pass in those days of the
arrival of the day of pentecost that
while they were all together behold
there came,' etc.; and this is correctly,
but freely, rendered by Augustine's
text (see apparatus) and (with the
plural 'days of pentecost,' cf. vg) by
t (in temporibus illis dum complerentur
dies pentecosten). This Greek can be
explained as a literal translation from
Aramaic (cf. ℞ ℭ-text of Ruth i. 1 και
ἐγένετο ἐν ταῖς ἡμέραις τοῦ κρίνειν τοὺς
κριτὰς καὶ ἐγένετο λιμός; see Rahlfs,
Studie über den griech. Text des Buches
Ruth, 1922, pp. 105, 115, 122), or
(as Professor J. E. Frame suggests) by
the supposition of a clumsy addition
to a text which had εκειναις but did not
mention Pentecost. The smooth text of
B seems to be due to an editor. In any
case Acts x. 25 (ἐγένετο τοῦ εἰσελθεῖν) is
a wholly different construction. Note
the omission of ειδου in the B-text.

μενος ἀπὸ τοῦ βαπτίσματος Ἰωάνου ἕως τῆς ἡμέρας ἧς ἀνελήμφθη ἀφ᾽ ἡμῶν, μάρτυρα τῆς ἀναστάσεως αὐτοῦ σὺν ἡμεῖν
23 γενέσθαι ἕνα τούτων. καὶ ἔστησεν δύο, Ἰωσὴφ τὸν καλούμενον
24 Βαρνάβαν, ὃς ἐπεκλήθη Ἰοῦστος, καὶ Μαθθίαν. καὶ προσευξάμενοι εἶπαν· Κύριε καρδιογνῶστα πάντων, ἀνάδειξον ὃν ἐξ-
25 ελέξω ἐκ τούτων τῶν δύο | ἀναλαβεῖν τόπον τὸν τῆς διακονίας
ταύτης καὶ ἀποστολῆς, ἀφ᾽ ἧς παρέβη Ἰούδας πορευθῆναι εἰς
26 τὸν τόπον τὸν ἴδιον. καὶ ἔδωκαν κλήρους αὐτῶν, καὶ ἔπεσεν
κλῆρος ἐπὶ Μαθθίαν, καὶ συνεψηφίσθη μετὰ τῶν ιβ ἀποστόλων.
II Καὶ ἐγένετο ἐν ταῖς ἡμέραις ἐκείναις τοῦ συνπληροῦσθαι τὴν
2 ἡμέραν τῆς πεντηκοστῆς ὄντων αὐτῶν πάντων ἐπὶ τὸ αὐτό, καὶ

---

22 incipiens a baptismate johannen usquae in diem quo adsumptus est a nobis d
testem resurrectionis ejus nobiscum fieri unum istorum 23 et statuit duos joseph
qui cognominatur barnabas qui vocatur justus et matthias 24 et orantes dixerunt
dne qui corda nosti omnium designa quem elegisti ex his duobus unum 25 sumere
locum ministerii hujus et apostolatus a quo transgressus judas abire in locum suum
26 et dederunt sortes suas et cecidit sors super matthian et dinumeratus est cum
xii apostolos
1 et factum est in diebus illis et cum inplerentur dies pentecostes erant simul

---

Johannis usque in illum diem quo adsumptus est a nobis, testem resurrectionis Augustine,
ejus nobiscum esse. 23 et statuit duos, Joseph qui vocabatur Barsabas qui C. Felicem
et Justus, et Matthiam, 24 et precatus dixit: tu, domine, cordis omnium Fundam. 9
intellector, ostende ex his duobus quem elegisti 25 ad suscipiendum locum
hujus ministerii et adnuntiationis, a qua excessit Judas ambulare in locum
suum. 26 et dederunt sortes suas, et cecidit sors super Matthiam, et simul
deputatus est cum undecim apostolis duodecimus.
1 in illo tempore quo subpletus est dies pentecostes fuerunt omnes simul in

1 illo] loco MSS.   simul in uno] eadem animatione simul in uno Fund

---

25-26 [Judas autem abdicatus est et ejectus, et in] locum [ejus Mathias Irenaeus,
ordinatus est].   ii. 20, 2;
                                                                              cf. ii. 20, 5

---

24 αναλαβειν τοπον τον της διακονιας ταυτης] mg unum, ut accipiat locum Harclean
ministerii hujus

The plural ' days,' representing τας
ημερας (which does not occur in any
known Greek authority), is found in
perp gig vg pesh, and is clearly
secondary, having perhaps been introduced in the two languages independently of one another. The
difficult συνπληρουσθαι την ημεραν was
altered to the plural in accordance
with the later Christian use of ἡ
πεντηκοστή to denote the fifty days

from Easter to Pentecost (cf. Origen,
contra Celsum viii. 22 ταῖς ἡμέραις τῆς
πεντηκοστῆς in this sense) ; but that
meaning seems to have been wholly
unknown to Hellenistic Jews, and is
probably impossible for a Christian
writer of the first century. See J. H.
Ropes, Harvard Theological Review,
1923, pp. 168-175, where, however,
the archaic superiority of the text of
D in Acts ii. 1-2 was not recognized.

ἦχος ὥσπερ φερομένης πνοῆς βιαίας καὶ ἐπλήρωσεν ὅλον τὸν
οἶκον οὗ ἦσαν καθήμενοι, καὶ ὤφθησαν αὐτοῖς διαμεριζόμεναι 3
γλῶσσαι ὡσεὶ πυρός, καὶ ἐκάθισεν ἐφ᾽ ἕνα ἕκαστον αὐτῶν, | καὶ 4
ἐπλήσθησαν πάντες πνεύματος ἁγίου, καὶ ἤρξαντο λαλεῖν ἑτέραις
γλώσσαις καθὼς τὸ πνεῦμα ἐδίδου ἀποφθέγγεσθαι αὐτοῖς.
ἦσαν δὲ ἐν Ἰερουσαλὴμ κατοικοῦντες Ἰουδαῖοι, ἄνδρες εὐ- 5
λαβεῖς ἀπὸ παντὸς ἔθνους τῶν ὑπὸ τὸν οὐρανόν· γενομένης δὲ 6
τῆς φωνῆς ταύτης συνῆλθε τὸ πλῆθος καὶ συνεχύθη, ὅτι ἤκουσεν
εἷς ἕκαστος τῇ ἰδίᾳ διαλέκτῳ λαλούντων αὐτῶν· ἐξίσταντο δὲ 7
καὶ ἐθαύμαζον λέγοντες· Οὐχὶ ἰδοὺ πάντες οὗτοί εἰσιν οἱ λαλοῦντες
Γαλειλαῖοι; καὶ πῶς ἡμεῖς ἀκούομεν ἕκαστος τῇ ἰδίᾳ διαλέκτῳ 8

3 εκαθισαν ℵD is supported by no
other Greek or Latin ms., but by
Greek fathers pesh hcl sah boh. Ephr.
catena, p. 397, emphasizes the singular
number of the verb.
5 The several variants (εις for εν ;
variations in order ; omission of ιουδαιοι by ℵ ; omission of ευλαβεις by
Aug. c. Fel., c. ep. Fund.) seem to
indicate a corruption deeper and more
intricate than the ordinary modifications of the authorities, and may perhaps be explained as follows :
(1) The original text read with ℵ:
ησαν δε εις ιερουσαλημ κατοικουντες
ανδρες ευλαβεις απο παντος εθνους (for
ευλαβεις cf. viii. 2, xxii. 12, Lk. ii. 25).

(2) The 'Western' text read εν
δε ιερουσαλημ ησαν κατοικουντες ιουδαιοι,
ανδρες απο παντος εθνους (so Aug).
(3) In the texts of the Old Uncials
a series of conflations and changes
ensued. The text of B inserted the
'Western' ιουδαιοι (perhaps a pre-
western variant) into the original,
and improved by the use of εν for
εις (cf. ix. 21). The text of C introduced ιουδαιοι in a different place,
between ανδρες and ευλαβεις, and
adopted the order κατοικουντες εν
ιερουσαλημ.
(4) Meantime D, following in general
the 'Western' text, altered it by inserting ευλαβεις from the B-text, but

εἰδοὺ ἐγένετο ἄφνω ἐκ τοῦ οὐρανοῦ ἦχος ὥσπερ φερομένης βιαίας
3 πνοῆς καὶ ἐπλήρωσεν πάντα τὸν οἶκον οὗ ἦσαν καθεζόμενοι, καὶ
ὤφθησαν αὐτοῖς διαμεριζόμεναι γλῶσσαι ὡσεὶ πυρός, καὶ ἑκά-
4 θισάν τε ἐφ' ἕνα ἕκαστον αὐτῶν, καὶ ἐπλήσθησαν πάντες πνεύματος ἁγίου, καὶ ἤρξα⟨ν⟩το λαλεῖν ἑτέραις γλώσσαις καθὼς
5 τὸ πνεῦμα ἐδίδου ἀποφθέγγεσθαι αὐτοῖς. ἐν Ἰερουσαλὴμ ἦσαν
κατοικοῦντες Ἰουδαῖοι, εὐλαβεῖς ἄνδρες ἀπὸ παντὸς ἔθνους τῶν
6 ὑπὸ τὸν οὐρανόν· γενομένης δὲ τῆς φωνῆς ταύτης συνῆλθε
τὸ πλῆθος καὶ συνεχύθη, καὶ ἤκουον εἶς ἕκαστος λαλοῦντας ταῖς
7 γλώσσαις αὐτῶν· ἐξείσταντο δὲ καὶ ἐθαύμαζον λέγοντες πρὸς
ἀλλήλους· Οὐχ ἰδοὺ ἅπαντες οὗτοί εἰσιν οἱ λαλοῦντες Γαλι-
8 λαῖοι; καὶ πῶς ἡμεῖς ἀκούομεν ἕκαστος τὴν διάλεκτον ἡμῶν ἐν

---

omnes in unum   2 et factum est repente caelo echo tamquam ferretur violentus d
spiritus et inplevit totam domum ubi erant sedentes   3 et visae sunt ejus dividi
linguae tamquam ignis et sedit super unum quemquem eorum   4 et inpleti sunt
universi s̄p̄ū sancto et coiperunt loqui aliis linguis sic ut s̄p̄s̄ dabat eloqui eis   5 in
ierusalem erant habitantes judaei timorati viri ab omni gente quae sub caelo sunt
6 cumquae facta esset vox haec convenit multitudo et consaesae sunt qui audiebant
unus quisque loquentes eos lingua sua   7 obstupescebant autem et admirabantur
dicentes ad alterutrum nonne ecce universi hi sunt qui locuntur galilaei   8 et
quomodo nos audimus unus quisque propria lingua nostra in qua nati sumus

---

uno.   2 et factus est subito de caelo sonus, quasi ferretur flatus vehemens, et Augustine,
inplevit totam illam domum in qua erant sedentes.   3 et visae sunt illis i. 4 f.; C. ep.
linguae divisae quasi ignis, qui et insedit super unumquemque eorum.   4 et Fundam. 9
inpleti sunt omnes spiritu sancto, et coeperunt loqui variis linguis quomodo Cyprian,
spiritus dabat eis pronuntiare.   5 Hierosolymis autem fuerunt habitatores Test. iii. 101
Judaei, homines ex omni natione quae est sub caelo.   6 et cum facta esset vox,
collecta est turba et confusa, quoniam audiebat unusquisque suo sermone et
suis linguis loquentes eos.   7 stupebant autem et admirabantur ad invicem
dicentes: nonne omnes qui loquuntur natione sunt Galilaei?   8 et quomodo
agnoscimus in illis sermonem in quo nati sumus?   9 Parthi, Medi, et Elamitae,

2 totum illum locum (locum illum *Cypr.test*) in quo *Fund Cypr.test*   4 *om* variis *Fund*
9 Parthi]+et *some MSS.*   *om* et 1° *Fund*

---

6 ταις γλωσσαις αυτων] *mg* linguis ipsorum

Harclean

---

set that word before ανδρες, instead of
after it as in the original text.
6 τη ιδια διαλεκτω λαλουντων αυτων]
λαλουντας ταις γλωσσαις αυτων D pesh.
The change in order (not found in
Latins [except d], which otherwise
support in part the 'Western' reading)
is perhaps intended to make it clear
that the speaking, not the hearing
only, took place in these languages.
The same motive seems to have been

at work in vs. 8, την διαλεκτον D Aug.
c. Fel., c. ep. Fund., unit Prom perp
gig t vg.codd pesh, for τη ιδια διαλεκτω.
Note the rendering agnoscimus in Aug.
c. Fel., c. ep. Fund. Prom.
7 παντες (απαντες) after εξισταντο is
lacking not only in B but in the
'Western' text (D Aug gig) and
perhaps in the Antiochian (yet cf. S).
It was perhaps added under the
influence of vs. 12.

ἡμῶν ἐν ᾗ ἐγεννήθημεν; Πάρθοι καὶ Μῆδοι καὶ Αἰλαμεῖται, 9
καὶ οἱ κατοικοῦντες τὴν Μεσοποταμίαν, Ἰουδαίαν τε καὶ Καππα-
δοκίαν, Πόντον καὶ τὴν Ἀσίαν, | Φρυγίαν τε καὶ Παμφυλίαν, 10
Αἴγυπτον καὶ τὰ μέρη τῆς Λιβύης τῆς κατὰ Κυρήνην, καὶ οἱ
ἐπιδημοῦντες Ῥωμαῖοι, Ἰουδαῖοί τε καὶ προσήλυτοι, | Κρῆτες 11
καὶ Ἄραβες, ἀκούομεν λαλούντων αὐτῶν ταῖς ἡμετέραις γλώσσαις τὰ μεγαλεῖα τοῦ θεοῦ. ἐξίσταντο δὲ πάντες καὶ διηποροῦντο, 12
ἄλλος πρὸς ἄλλον λέγοντες· Τί θέλει τοῦτο εἶναι; ἕτεροι 13
δὲ διαχλευάζοντες ἔλεγον ὅτι Γλεύκους μεμεστωμένοι εἰσίν.
σταθεὶς δὲ ὁ Πέτρος σὺν τοῖς ἕνδεκα ἐπῆρεν τὴν φωνὴν αὐτοῦ 14
καὶ ἀπεφθέγξατο αὐτοῖς· Ἄνδρες Ἰουδαῖοι καὶ οἱ κατοικοῦντες
Ἰερουσαλὴμ πάντες, τοῦτο ὑμῖν γνωστὸν ἔστω καὶ ἐνωτίσασθε
τὰ ῥήματά μου. οὐ γὰρ ὡς ὑμεῖς ὑπολαμβάνετε οὗτοι μεθύουσιν, 15
ἔστιν γὰρ ὥρα τρίτη τῆς ἡμέρας, ἀλλὰ τοῦτό ἐστιν τὸ εἰρημένον 16

Editors   12 διηπορουν Soden   16 om ιωηλ JHR

Old Uncial   9 και αιλαμειται BACℵᶜ 096 81 (+D)   om ℵ   12 διηπορουντο B℘A
διηπορουν C 096 81 (+D)   προς B℘AC 096 81 (+D)   +τον 076   θελει
BAC 81 (+D)   θελοι ℵ   θελει τουτο B(ℵ)C 81 (+D)   τουτο θελει A   13 δια-
χλευαζοντες ελεγον B℘AC 096ᶜᵒʳʳ 81 (cf. D)   χλευαζοντες ελεγον 096   [εχ]λευαζον
λεγοντες 076 (cf. D)   14 ο B℘A 076 096 81 (+D)   om C   απεφθεγξατο
B℘A 076 096 81   +λεγων C   υμιν γνωστον B℘AC 096 81 (cf. D)   γνωστ[ον
υμιν] 076

Antiochian   12 διηπορουν S 462 102 ς(+D)   θελει] αν θελοι S 462 102 ς
13 διαχλευαζοντες] χλευαζοντες S 462 102 ς   14 om ο PS 462 ς   παντες]
απαντες PS 462 ς

---

9 ιουδαιαν is translated *Judaei* in Aug. *unit.* Pesh has 'Jews and Cappadocians' for ιουδαιαν τε και καππαδοκιαν. Sah (in spite of Zahn's vigorous argument, *Urausgabe*, pp. 337 f.) is not to be taken as attesting ιουδαιοι. Aug. *unit* and pesh are probably attempts to escape the obvious exegetical difficulty, but the repetition here and in vs. 10 of the word 'Jews' (cf. vs. 5) puts an inappropriate emphasis on the fact that these were Jews. Aug. *c. ep. Fund.* and Tertullian *adv. Judaeos* 7 (Augustine perhaps influenced by Tert. ; note their agreement in the words *regiones* [-*em*] *Africae* and *incolae*) substitute *Armeniam.* Jerome on Is. xi. 6 ff. substitutes 'Syria,' probably in accord-

ance with the geographical intention of the word 'Judaea.' These are ancient conjectures, no more weighty than the modern suggestions of ιδουμαιαν, λυδιαν, ινδιαν, βιθυνιαν, γορδ(υ)αιαν, κιλικιαν, or the proposal to reject the word as interpolated.
11 αραβοι D is a Latinism.
13 With hcl. *mg* cf. Ephrem on 1 Cor. xiv. 23 (p. 77) *de apostolis dixerunt eos musto plenos inebriatos esse*, and pesh 'these have drunk new wine and are intoxicated.'
14 τοτε D pesh is probably the reading of the 'Western' text, which frequently introduces τοτε in what might seem an Aramaizing manner (see above, pp. ccxxxii, ccxliv, note 1). By conflation D has both τοτε and δε.

9 ἦ ἐγεννήθημεν; Πάρθοι καὶ Μῆδοι καὶ Ἐλαμεῖται, οἱ κατοικοῦντες τὴν Μεσοποταμίαν, Ἰουδαίαν καὶ Καππαδοκίαν, Πόντον
10 καὶ τὴν Ἀσίαν, | Φρυγίαν καὶ Παμφυλίαν, Αἴγυπτόν τε καὶ τὰ
μέρη τῆς Λιβούης τῆς κατὰ Κυρήνην, καὶ οἱ ἐπιδημοῦντες Ῥω-
11 μαῖοι, Ἰουδαῖοί τε καὶ προσήλυτοι, | Κρῆτες καὶ Ἄραβοι, ἀκούομεν
λαλούντων αὐτῶν ταῖς ἡμετέραις γλώσσαις τὰ μεγαλεῖα τοῦ
12 θεοῦ. ἐξείσταντο δὲ πάντες καὶ διηπόρουν ἄλλος πρὸς ἄλλον
13 ἐπὶ τῷ γεγονότι, καὶ λέγοντες· Τί θέλει τοῦτο εἶναι; ἕτεροι
δὲ διεχλεύαζον λέγοντες ὅτι Γλεύκους οὗτοι μεμεστωμένοι
14 εἰσίν. τότε σταθεὶς δὲ ὁ Πέτρος σὺν τοῖς δέκα ἀποστόλοις
ἐπῆρεν πρῶτος τὴν φωνὴν αὐτοῦ καὶ εἶπεν· Ἄνδρες Ἰουδαῖοι
καὶ πάντες οἱ κατοικοῦντες Ἱερουσαλήμ, τοῦτο ὑμεῖν γνωστὸν
15 ἔστω, ἐνωτίσατε τὰ ῥήματά μου. οὐ γὰρ ὡς ὑμεῖς ὑπο-
16 λαμβάνετε οὗτοι μεθύουσιν, οὔσης ὥρας τῆς ἡμέρας γ̄, | ἀλλὰ
τοῦτό ἐστιν τὸ εἰρημένον διὰ τοῦ προφήτου·

11 κρητης   14 υμειν] ημειν   15 υπολαμβανεται

9 parthi et medi et aelamitae et qui inhabitant mesopotamiam judaeam et cappa- d
dociam pontum et asiam   10 frygiam et pamphyliam aegyptum et partes lybiae
qui est circa cyrenen et qui hic demorantur romani judaei et proselyti   11 cretenses
et arabi audivimus loquentes eos nostris linguis magnalia d̄ī   12 obstupescebant
omnes et hesitabant alius ad alium quod factum est et dicentes quid vult esse hoc
13 alii vero deridebant dicentes quia musto isti repleti sunt   14 cum stetisset autem
petrus cum decem apostolis et elebabit primus vocem suam et dixit viri judaei et
omnes qui inhabitant hierusalem hoc vobis notum sit ausilate verbis meis   15 non
enim sicut vos suspicamini hii hebrii sunt est enim hora tertia diei   16 sed hoc est

et qui inhabitant Mesopotamiam, Judaeam et Cappadociam, Pontum, Asiam, Augustine,
10 Phrygiam et Pamphyliam, Aegyptum et partes Libyae quae est ad Cyrenem, C. Felicem
et qui aderant Romani,   11 Judaeique et proselyti, Cretenses et Arabes, audie- Fundam. 8
bant loquentes illos suis linguis magnalia dei.
    12 stupebant autem et haesitabant ob id quod factum est, dicentes : quidnam
hoc vult esse ?   13 alii autem inridebant dicentes : hi musto omnes onerati sunt.

9 Judaeam] Armeniam Fund   10 Phrygiam]+que one MS.   partes Libyae]
regiones Africae Fund   aderant] advenerant Fund   11 Judaeique et proselyti] et
Judaei incolae et Fund

9 Parthi, Medi, Elamitae, et qui habitant Mesopotamiam, Armeniam, Tertullian,
Phrygiam, Cappadociam, et incolentes Pontum et Asiam, Pamphyliam, Adv. Jud. 7
10 immorantes Aegyptum et regionem Africae quae est trans Cyrenen, in-
habitantes Romani et incolae, tunc et in Hierusalem Judaei et ceterae gentes.

15 [dixit Petrus non ebrios quidem illos esse, cum sit] hora tertia diei ; Irenaeus,
16 [esse autem] hoc, quod dictum est per prophetam :   17 erit in novissimis cf. iii. 17, 1;
iii. 11, 9

8 εγεννηθημεν] mg fuimus   12 επι τω γεγονοτι] mg de illo quod factum est Harclean
13 οτι γλευκους ουτοι μεμεστωμενοι εισιν] mg quia ebrii sunt

Joel ii. 28-32 διὰ τοῦ προφήτου Ἰωήλ· Καὶ ἔσται μετὰ ταῦτα, λέγει ὁ θεός, 17
ἐκχεῶ ἀπὸ τοῦ πνεύματός μου ἐπὶ πᾶσαν σάρκα, καὶ προφητεύσουσιν οἱ υἱοὶ ὑμῶν καὶ αἱ θυγατέρες ὑμῶν, καὶ οἱ νεανίσκοι
ὑμῶν ὁράσεις ὄψονται, καὶ οἱ πρεσβύτεροι ὑμῶν ἐνυπνίοις
ἐνυπνιασθήσονται· καί γε ἐπὶ τοὺς δούλους μου καὶ ἐπὶ τὰς 18
δούλας μου ἐν ταῖς ἡμέραις ἐκείναις ἐκχεῶ ἀπὸ τοῦ πνεύματός
μου, καὶ προφητεύσουσιν. καὶ δώσω τέρατα ἐν τῷ οὐρανῷ ἄνω 19
καὶ σημεῖα ἐπὶ τῆς γῆς κάτω, αἷμα καὶ πῦρ καὶ ἀτμεῖδα καπνοῦ·

Editors　　　17 μετα ταυτα] εν ταις εσχαταις ημεραις WH Soden　　　　18 om και
προφητευσουσιν JHR

Old Uncial　　17 μετα ταυτα B 076　εν ταις εσχαταις ημεραις ℵA 096 81 (+D)　μετα ταυτα
εν ταις εσχαταις ημεραις C　　　αι θυγατερες υμων BℵA 81　θυγατερες C
υμων 4° BℵA 076 81　om Cvid (C2 suppl) (+D)　　　ενυπνιοις BℵAC 81　ενυπνια
076vid　　　18 δουλους BAC 076 81 (+D)　δουλας ℵ　　　δουλας BAC
076 81 (+D)　δουλους ℵ　　　19 ανω BℵC 076 81 (+D)　om A

Antiochian　　17 μετα ταυτα] εν ταις εσχαταις ημεραις PS 462 ϛ(+D)　　　om οι 1° S
om νεανισκοι υμων ορασεις οψονται και οι S　　　ενυπνια P 462 ϛ

16 ιωηλ omitted by D (cf. Justin. dial
87), Iren, Aug. ep. 199. 23, Hil. trin.
viii. 25. In Ps.-Orig. Tract. 20 (ed.
Batiffol and Wilmart) it is probably a
later addition.
17 μετα ταυτα B 076 Cyr. of Jer.
catech. xvii. 19 sah (3 late codd.). D,
Tertullian, adv. Marc. v. 8, with ℵA
boh and the great body of authorities,
have εν ταις εσχαταις ημεραις. This
'Western' reading was apparently
drawn from εν ταις ημεραις εκειναις, vs.
18, which is therefore in consistency
omitted by D gig Priscill Rebapt.
Combinations of the two readings
appear in C minn, and in sah.cod.B
(cent. iv).
The 'Western' substitute in vs. 17
was thus widely adopted in non-
western texts, but the corresponding
'Western' omission in vs. 18 scarcely
at all.
17-20 The quotation from Joel is
found in two forms, that of B and
that of D. Each ms. is supported
by other witnesses, Greek, Syriac,
Sahidic, and notably Latin, which
group themselves about the two leaders
in kaleidoscopic selection. Apart from
the peculiar instance of μου 2°, vs. 18,
which may or may not belong to the
series (D here agrees with B), and
with the further exceptions of ο θεος,
vs. 17, and και προφητευσουσιν, vs. 18,

the reading of B in every case agrees
with the LXX.

B

17 και (LXX)	om D
μετα ταυτα (LXX)	εν ταις εσχα- ταις ημεραις D
ο θεος	κυριος D
υμων 1° and 2° (LXX)	αυτων D
υμων 3° and 4° (LXX)	om D
18 [μου 1° (so D) (LXX)]	[om Prisc Rebapt]
[μου 2° (so D gig Prisc Perpet)]	[om Rebapt (LXX)]
εν ταις ημεραις εκειναις (LXX)	om D
[και προφητευσου- σιν]	[om D (LXX)]
19 αιμα και πυρ και ατμειδα καπνου (LXX)	om D
20 και επιφανη (LXX)	om D

In some cases manifestly, and probably in all, the departures in D from
the LXX-text spring from one motive,
namely to adapt the quotation to the
situation to which Peter here applies
it. This adaptation may be the
work of the original author, and the
agreement of the B-text with the LXX
may have been effected by an editor.

17 Ἔσται ἐν ταῖς ἐσχάταις ἡμέραις, λέγει κύριος, ἐκχεῶ ἀπὸ
τοῦ πνεύματός μου ἐπὶ πάσας σάρκας, καὶ προφητεύσουσιν
οἱ υἱοὶ αὐτῶν καὶ θυγατέρες αὐτῶν, καὶ οἱ νεανίσκοι ὁράσει

18 ὄψονται, καὶ οἱ πρεσβύτεροι ἐνυπνιασθήσονται, | καὶ ἐγ[ὼ] ἐπὶ
τοὺς δούλους μου καὶ ἐπὶ τὰς δούλας μου ἐκχεῶ ἀπὸ τοῦ

19 πνεύματός μου. καὶ δώσω τέρατα ἐν τῷ οὐρανῷ ἄνω καὶ

20 σημεῖα ἐπὶ τῆς γῆς κάτω· ὁ ἥλιος μεταστρέφεται εἰ⟨ς⟩

---

quod dictum est per prophetam. 17 erit in novissimis diebus dicit d̄n̄s̄ effundam d
sp̄m̄ meum super omnem carnē et prophetabunt fili eorum et filias eorum et jubenes
visiones videbunt et seniores somnia somniabunt 18 et ego super servos meos et
super ancillas meas effundam spiritum meum 19 et dabo prodigia in caelo susum et
signa in terra deorsum 20 sol convertetur in tenebris et luna in sanguine prius

---

17 [illa promissio spiritus facta] per Johelem: in novissimis temporibus Tertullian,
effundam de meo spiritu in omnem carnem et prophetabunt filii filiaeque Marc. v. 8;
eorum. 18 et super servos et ancillas meas de meo spiritu effundam.   cf. v. 4, 11,
                                                                              17 ; Res.
                                                                              carn. 63

---

diebus, dicit dominus, effundam de spiritu meo in omnem carnem et Irenaeus,
prophetabunt.   iii. 12, 1

Under this view the text of D will be
preferred. Equally possible, however,
is the view that the author copied
exactly, or nearly so, from his LXX,
and that the modifications are due to
the customary freedom of the paraphrastic 'Western' reviser ; cf. vii.
18, 26, 33, 43 (om υμων ; επι τα μερη
βαβυλωνος), xiii. 47 (where D is not
conformed to LXX). For this latter
view speaks the characteristic transfer
of εν ταις ημεραις εκειναις (cf. vs. 18)
to vs. 17 in the form εν ταις εσχαταις
ημεραις, as well as the habitual
fidelity to the text of the LXX which
the author of Acts elsewhere displays
where making formal quotations.
Examples of this may be seen in vss.
25-28, 34 f., iv. 25 f., etc.
The case of the addition to the LXX
of και προφητευσουσιν in vs. 18 is
peculiar, because D perp r Prisc here
omit, with best MSS. of LXX, while
B and all others (including Justin)
have the words. These are parallel to
vs. 17, and are clearly an adaptation of
the OT passage to the present situation.
Such an adaptation does occur in
the undoubtedly original words λεγει
ο θεος (v.l. κυριος), vs. 16 ; but in the
case of και προφητευσουσιν, vs. 18, the

wiser judgement is perhaps to assume
an addition to the author's quotation
before the formation of the text of B,
i.e. a 'Western non-interpolation,'
and to reject the words. If they were
originally present, the only reason for
omitting them in D would have been
the desire to conform to the LXX, but,
as has been shown, this motive is the
opposite of that which, under any
hypothesis, governed the formation of
the D-text.
In the case of μου 1° and 2° D is on
the side of B, and the omission in Latin
witnesses may be due to the further
working at some later time of the
motive of adaptation. But possibly
D may here be conflate, and the
omission of both words in De Rebaptismate, etc., may alone represent the
original.
It is to be noted that certain
additions to the LXX text, of purely
rhetorical nature, seem to have been
made by the author himself—not
only λεγει ο θεος, vs. 17, but ανω, σημεια,
and κατω, vs. 19. He has also permitted himself ενυπνιοις, vs. 17, for
ενυπνια LXX, and perhaps dropped την
before ημεραν, vs. 20 (but LXX text is
in both cases doubtful). Among these

ὁ ἥλιος μεταστραφήσεται εἰς σκότος καὶ ἡ σελήνη εἰς αἷμα 20
πρὶν ἢ ἐλθεῖν ἡμέραν κυρίου τὴν μεγάλην καὶ ἐπιφανῆ. καὶ 21
ἔσται πᾶς ὃς ἐὰν ἐπικαλέσηται τὸ ὄνομα κυρίου σωθήσεται.
ἄνδρες Ἰστραηλεῖται, ἀκούσατε τοὺς λόγους τούτους. Ἰησοῦν 22
τὸν Ναζωραῖον, ἄνδρα ἀποδεδειγμένον ἀπὸ τοῦ θεοῦ εἰς ὑμᾶς
δυνάμεσι καὶ τέρασι καὶ σημείοις οἷς ἐποίησεν δι᾽ αὐτοῦ ὁ θεὸς
ἐν μέσῳ ὑμῶν, καθὼς αὐτοὶ οἴδατε, | τοῦτον τῇ ὡρισμένῃ βουλῇ 23
καὶ προγνώσει τοῦ θεοῦ ἔκδοτον διὰ χειρὸς ἀνόμων προσπήξαντες
ἀνείλατε, ὃν ὁ θεὸς ἀνέστησε λύσας τὰς ὠδεῖνας τοῦ θανάτου, 24
καθότι οὐκ ἦν δυνατὸν κρατεῖσθαι αὐτὸν ὑπ᾽ αὐτοῦ· Δαυεὶδ γὰρ 25
Ps. xvi. 8-11 λέγει εἰς αὐτόν· Προορώμην τὸν κύριον ἐνώπιόν μου διὰ παντός,
ὅτι ἐκ δεξιῶν μού ἐστιν ἵνα μὴ σαλευθῶ. διὰ τοῦτο ηὐφράνθη μου 26
ἡ καρδία καὶ ἠγαλλιάσατο ἡ γλῶσσά μου, ἔτι δὲ καὶ ἡ σάρξ μου
κατασκηνώσει ἐπ᾽ ἐλπίδι· ὅτι οὐκ ἐνκαταλείψεις τὴν ψυχήν μου 27
εἰς ᾄδην, οὐδὲ δώσεις τὸν ὅσιόν σου ἰδεῖν διαφθοράν. ἐγνώρισάς 28
μοι ὁδοὺς ζωῆς, πληρώσεις με εὐφροσύνης μετὰ τοῦ προσώπου

Editors   20 om η WH (but cf. mg) Soden JHR   την ημεραν Soden

---

Old Uncial   20 πριν η B 076   om η ℵAC 81 (+D)   ημεραν Bℵ 076 (+D)   την ημεραν
ACℵᶜ 81   και επιφανη BAC 076 81   om ℵ(+D)   21 om vs. 21 ℵ
(ℵᵃ suppl)   22 αποδεδειγμενον απο του θεου BℵC 81   απο του θεου αποδεδειγμενον A(cf. D)   ο BℵA 81 (+D)   om C   23 εκδοτον BℵAC 81
+λαβοντες ℵᶜ(+D)   25 αυτον BℵC 81 (+D)   αυτην A   κυριον BAC 81
+μου ℵ (+D)   26 μου η καρδια Bℵ   η καρδια μου ACℵᶜ 81 (+D)
28 ευφροσυνης BℵC 81(+D)   ευφροσυνην Aᵛⁱᵈ

Antiochian   20 την ημεραν PS 462 ϛ   22 απο του θεου αποδεδειγμενον PS 462 ϛ(cf. D)
καθως] +και PS 462 ϛ   23 εκδοτον] +λαβοντες PS 462 ϛ(+D)   χειρων
PS 462 ϛ   26 η καρδια μου PS 462 ϛ(+D)   27 αδου PS 462 ϛ

---

all but λεγει ο θεος and σημεια have been corrected to the LXX standard in some extant witness or group of witnesses.

Minor variants occur in D which have been deliberately passed by in this note, as not forming part of the main problem. See also p. ccxxxiii.

20 The unimportant addition of η in B 076 and the Antiochian text has against it not only ℵAC 81, but also D, and may best be rejected from the text.

σκότος καὶ ἡ σελήνη εἰς αἷμα πρὶν ἐλθεῖν ἡμέραν κυρίου τὴν
21 μεγάλην. καὶ ἔσται πᾶς ὃς ἂν ἐπικαλέσηται τὸ ὄνομα τοῦ
κυρίου σωθήσεται.
22 Ἄνδρες Ἰσραηλεῖται, ἀκούσατε τοὺς λόγους τούτους. Ἰησοῦν
τὸν Ναζοραῖον, ἄνδρα ἀπὸ τοῦ θεοῦ [δεδοκιμ]ασμένον εἰς ἡμᾶς
δυνάμεσει καὶ τέρασι καὶ σημίοις ὅσα ἐποίησεν δι' αὐτοῦ ὁ θεὸς
23 ἐν μέσῳ ὑμῶν, καθὼς αὐτοὶ οἴδατε, | τοῦτον τῇ ὡρισμένῃ βουλῇ
καὶ προγνώσει τοῦ θεοῦ ἔκδοτον λαβόντες διὰ χειρὸς ἀνόμων
24 προσπήξαντες ἀνείλατε, ὃν ὁ θεὸς ἀνέστησεν λύσας τὰς ὠδῖνας
τοῦ ᾅδου, καθότι οὐκ ἦν δυνατὸν κρατεῖσθαι αὐτὸν ὑπ' αὐτοῦ·
25 Δανεὶδ γὰρ λέγει εἰ<ς> αὐτόν·
Προορώμην τὸν κύριόν μου ἐνώπιόν μου διὰ παντός, ὅτι
26 ἐκ δεξιῶν μού ἐστιν ἵνα μὴ σαλευθῶ. διὰ τοῦτο ηὐφράνθη
ἡ καρδία μου καὶ ἠγαλλιάσατο ἡ γλῶσσά μου, ἔτι δὲ καὶ ἡ
27 σάρξ μου κατασκηνώσει ἐφ' ἐλπίδει· ὅτι οὐκ ἐνκαταλείψεις
τὴν ψυχήν μου εἰς ᾅδην, οὐδὲ δώσεις τὸν ὅσιόν σου ἰδεῖν
28 διαφθοράν. γνωρίσας μοι ὁδοὺς ζωῆς πληρώσεις με εὐφροσύνης μετὰ τοῦ προσώπου σου.

quam veniat dies dni magnus 21 et erit omnis quicumque invocaverit nomen dni **d**
salvus erit 22 viri istrahelitae audite sermones hos īhm nazoraeum virum a do
probatum in nobis virtutibus et prodigiis et signis quae fecit per eum ds in medio
vestrum sicut ipsi scitis 23 hunc destinato consilio et providentia di auditum
accepistis per manus iniquorum adfixum interfecistis 24 quem ds suscitavit solutis
amitibus inferiorū quoniam possibile non esset detineri eum ab ipso 25 david enim
dicit in eum providebam dnm meum in conspectu meo semper quia a dextra mea est
ut non commovear 26 propterea laetatum est cor meum et exultavit lingua mea
adhuc autem et caro mea inhabitavit in spsem 27 quia non derelinques animam
meam aput inferos nequae dabis sanctum tuum videre corruptionem 28 notas
fecisti mihi vias vitae inplevis me jucunditate cum facie tua 29 viri fratres licet

22 viri Israelitae, auribus mandate quae dico : Jesum Nazarenum, virum a Tert. *Pud.* 21;
deo vobis destinatum. cf. *Res. carn.* 15

22 viri [enim, inquit Petrus,] Israelitae, audite sermones meos : Jesum Irenaeus,
Nazareum, virum adprobatum a deo in vobis virtutibus et prodigiis et signis, iii. 12, 2
quae fecit per ipsum deus in medio vestrum, quemadmodum ipsi scitis,
23 hunc definito consilio et praescientia dei traditum per manus iniquorum
affigentes interfecistis, 24 quem deus excitavit solutis doloribus inferorum,
quoniam non erat possibile teneri eum ab eis. 25 David enim dicit in ipsum :
providebam dominum in conspectu meo semper, quoniam a dextris meis est, ut
non movear. 26 propter hoc laetatum est cor meum, et exsultavit lingua mea,
insuper et caro mea requiescet in spe ; 27 quoniam non derelinques animam
meam in inferno, neque dabis sanctum tuum videre corruptionem.

25 meo] mei *Turner*

---

23 προσπήξαντες] affigentes ⁒ in cruce ✓ Harclean

σου. ἄνδρες ἀδελφοί, ἐξὸν εἰπεῖν μετὰ παρρησίας πρὸς ὑμᾶς περὶ 29
τοῦ πατριάρχου Δαυείδ, ὅτι καὶ ἐτελεύτησεν καὶ ἐτάφη καὶ τὸ
μνῆμα αὐτοῦ ἔστιν ἐν ἡμῖν ἄχρι τῆς ἡμέρας ταύτης· προφήτης 30

Ps. cxxxii. 11 οὖν ὑπάρχων, καὶ εἰδὼς ὅτι ὅρκῳ ὤμοσεν αὐτῷ ὁ θεὸς ἐκ καρποῦ
τῆς ὀσφύος αὐτοῦ καθίσαι ἐπὶ τὸν θρόνον αὐτοῦ, προιδὼν ἐλά- 31
λησεν περὶ τῆς ἀναστάσεως τοῦ Χριστοῦ ὅτι οὔτε ἐνκατελείφθη
εἰς ᾅδην οὐδὲ ἡ σὰρξ αὐτοῦ εἶδεν διαφθοράν. τοῦτον τὸν Ἰησοῦν 32
ἀνέστησεν ὁ θεός, οὗ πάντες ἡμεῖς ἐσμὲν μάρτυρες. τῇ δεξιᾷ 33
οὖν τοῦ θεοῦ ὑψωθεὶς τήν τε ἐπαγγελίαν τοῦ πνεύματος τοῦ
ἁγίου λαβὼν παρὰ τοῦ πατρὸς ἐξέχεεν τοῦτο ὃ ὑμεῖς καὶ
βλέπετε καὶ ἀκούετε. οὐ γὰρ Δαυεὶδ ἀνέβη εἰς τοὺς οὐρανούς, 34

Ps. cx. 1 λέγει δὲ αὐτός· Εἶπεν κύριος τῷ κυρίῳ μου· Κάθου ἐκ δεξιῶν
μου | ἕως ἂν θῶ τοὺς ἐχθρούς σου ὑποπόδιον τῶν ποδῶν σου. 35
ἀσφαλῶς οὖ‹ν› γεινωσκέτω πᾶς οἶκος Ἰσραὴλ ὅτι καὶ κύριον 36
αὐτὸν καὶ Χριστὸν ἐποίησεν ὁ θεός, τοῦτον τὸν Ἰησοῦν ὃν ὑμεῖς

Editors   30 οσφυος αυτου] + [το κατα σαρκα αναστησειν τον χριστον] Soden
31 ουδε] ουτε WH Soden JHR   33 [και 1°] WH   34 ο κυριος Soden
36 ο θεος εποιησεν Soden

Old Uncial   31 ενκατελειφθη BℵAC² 81 (+D)   ενκατελημφθη C   αδην Bℵ 8] αδου
AC(+D)   ουδε B   ουτε ℵAC 81 (+D)   32 ημεις εσμεν BAC 81
(cf. D)   εσμεν ημεις ℵ   33 και 1° B(+D)   om ℵAC 81   34 κυριος
Bℵ(+D)   ο κυριος B²(B³ Tdf)ACℵ° 81   36 ουν B²   οικος BℵA 81
ο οικος C(+D)   αυτον και χριστον BℵAC   και χριστον αυτον 81
εποιησεν ο θεος Bℵ 81   ο θεος εποιησεν AC(+D)

Antiochian   30 του καρπου P   οσφυος αυτου]+το κατα σαρκα αναστησειν τον χριστον
PS 462 ϛ(cf. D)   θρονου PS   του θρονου 462 ϛ   31 ουτε] ου PS 462 ϛ
ενκατελειφθη] κατελειφθη η ψυχη αυτου PS 462 ϛ   αδου PS 462 ϛ(+D)
32 om εσμεν P   33 του πνευματος του αγιου] του αγιου πνευματος PS 462 ϛ(+D)
ο]+νυν PS 462 ϛ   υμεις] ημεις S   om και 1° PS 462 ϛ   34 ο κυριος
PS 462 ϛ   36 και χριστον αυτον PS 462 ϛ   ο θεος εποιησε PS 462 ϛ(+D)

---

30 οσφυος] ventris (i.e. κοιλιας, conformed to Ps. cxxxii. 11) perp gig Iren
pesh. καρδιας D seems based on
κοιλιας.

The awkwardness of the Semitic εκ
καρπου, treated like a noun and serving
as object of the verb, gave occasion
for the expansion κατα σαρκα αναστησαι

τον χριστον και D, which in Latin
appears only in d e (om secundum
carnem) and, with conflation, in
Vigilius, but (with somewhat varying
form) was adopted by the Antiochian
revisers. The enlargement may have
been subsequent to the formation of
the 'Western' text.

CODEX BEZAE 21

29 ἄνδρες ἀδελφοί, ἐξὸν εἰπεῖν μετὰ παρρησίας πρὸς ὑμᾶς περὶ
τοῦ πατριάρχου Δαυείδ, ὅτι καὶ ἐτελεύτησεν καὶ ἐτάφη καὶ τὸ
30 μνημῖον αὐτοῦ ἔστιν παρ' ἡμῖν ἄχρι τῆς ἡμέρας ταύτης· προφήτης οὖν ὑπάρχων, καὶ εἰδὼν ὅτι ὅρκῳ ὤμοσεν αὐτῷ ὁ θεὸς
ἐκ καρποῦ τῆς καρδίας αὐτοῦ κατὰ σάρκα ἀναστῆσαι τὸν Χρι-
31 στὸν καὶ καθίσαι ἐπὶ τὸν θρόνον αὐτοῦ, <προιδὼν ἐλάλησεν περὶ
τῆς> ἀναστάσεως τοῦ Χριστοῦ ὅτει οὔτε ἐνκατελείφθη εἰς ᾅδου
32 οὔτε ἡ σάρξ αὐτοῦ εἶδεν διαφθοράν. τοῦτον οὖν Ἰησοῦν ἀν-
33 έστησεν ὁ θεός, οὗ πάντες ἡμεῖς μάρτυρές ἐσμεν. τῇ δεξιᾷ οὖν
τοῦ θεοῦ ὑψωθεὶς καὶ τὴν ἐπαγγελίαν τοῦ ἁγίου πνεύματος λαβὼν
34 παρὰ τοῦ πατρὸς ἐξέχεεν ὑμεῖν ὃ καὶ βλέπετε καὶ ἀκούετε. οὐ
γὰρ Δαυεὶδ ἀνέβη εἰς τοὺς οὐρανούς, εἴρηκεν γὰρ αὐτός·
35 Λέγει κύριος τῷ κυρίῳ μου· Κάθου ἐκ δεξιῶν μου | ἕως θῶ
τοῦ<ς> ἐκθρούς σου ὑποπόδιον τῶν ποδῶν σου.
36 ἀσφαλῶς οὖν γεινωσκέτω πᾶς ὁ οἶκος Ἰσραὴλ ὅτι καὶ κύριον
καὶ Χριστὸν ὁ θεὸς ἐποίησεν τοῦτον Ἰησοῦν ὃν ὑμεῖς ἐσταυρώ-

30 ωμασεν   31 ενκαταλειφθη   ειδεν] ειδειν

mihi dicere cum fiducia ad vos de patriarcha david quia defunctus est et sepultus d
est et monumentum ejus est aput nos usque in hunc diem   30 cum esset autem
propheta et sciret quia jurejurando juravit in d̄s de fructum de praecordia ejus
secundum carne suscitare x̄p̄m̄ collocare super thronum ejus   31 resurrectione x̄p̄ī
quia neque derelictus est aput inferos neque caro ejus vidit corruptionem   32 hunc
ergo īh̄n resuscitavit d̄s cujus nos omnes testes sumus   33 dextera ergo d̄ī exaltatus
et pollicitationem s̄p̄s̄ sancti accepta a patre effudit vobis quod et vidistis et audistis
34 non enim david ascendit in caelos dixit enim ipse dixit d̄n̄s d̄n̄o meo sede ad
dexteram meam   35 donec ponam inimicos tuos scamillum pedum tuorum   36 pro
certo ergo sciat omnis domus istrahel quia et d̄n̄m et x̄p̄m̄ d̄s fecit hunc īh̄m̄ quem

33 dextera dei exaltatus [sicut Petrus in Actis contionatur].

Tert. Prax. 17

36 firmissime itaque cognoscat omnis domus Israhel quod et dominum et
Christum [id est unctum] fecerit eum deus, hunc Jesum quem vos crucifixistis.

Prax. 28

[29 dehinc rursum fiducialiter illis dicit de patriarcha David, quoniam
mortuus est et sepultus, et sepulchrum ejus fit apud eos usque in hunc diem.]
30 propheta autem [inquit] cum esset et sciret quoniam jurejurando ei juravit
deus de fructu ventris ejus sedere in throno ejus,   31 providens locutus est de
resurrectione Christi, quoniam neque derelictus est apud inferos, neque caro ejus
vidit corruptionem.   32 hunc Jesum [inquit] excitavit deus, cujus nos omnes
sumus testes :   33 qui dextera dei exaltatus, repromissionem spiritus sancti
accipiens a patre, effudit donationem hanc quam vos nunc videtis et auditis.
34 non enim David ascendit in caelos, dicit autem ipse : dixit dominus domino
meo, sede ad dexteram meam,   35 quoadusque ponam inimicos tuos sub-
pedaneum pedum tuorum.   36 certissime ergo sciat omnis domus Israel,
quoniam et dominum eum et Christum deus fecit, hunc Jesum, quem vos
crucifixistis.

Irenaeus,
iii. 12, 2

33 o] text hoc donum quod, mg hoc quod

Harclean

ἐσταυρώσατε. ἀκούσαντες δὲ κατενύγησαν τὴν καρδίαν, εἶπόν 37
τε πρὸς τὸν Πέτρον καὶ τοὺς λοιποὺς ἀποστόλους· Τί ποιήσω-
μεν, ἄνδρες ἀδελφοί; | Πέτρος δὲ πρὸς αὐτούς· Μετανοήσατε, 38
καὶ βαπτισθήτω ἕκαστος ὑμῶν ἐν τῷ ὀνόματι Ἰησοῦ Χριστοῦ
εἰς ἄφεσιν τῶν ἁμαρτιῶν ὑμῶν, καὶ λήμψεσθε τὴν δωρεὰν τοῦ
ἁγίου πνεύματος· ὑμῖν γάρ ἐστιν ἡ ἐπαγγελία καὶ τοῖς τέκνοις 39
ὑμῶν καὶ πᾶσι τοῖς εἰς μακρὰν ὅσους ἂν προσκαλέσηται κύριος
ὁ θεὸς ἡμῶν. ἑτέροις τε λόγοις πλείοσιν διεμαρτύρατο, καὶ 40
παρεκάλει αὐτοὺς λέγων· Σώθητε ἀπὸ τῆς γενεᾶς τῆς σκολιᾶς
ταύτης.
Οἱ μὲν οὖν ἀποδεξάμενοι τὸν λόγον αὐτοῦ ἐβαπτίσθησαν, 41
καὶ προσετέθησαν ἐν τῇ ἡμέρᾳ ἐκείνῃ ψυχαὶ ὡσεὶ τρισχείλιαι.
ἦσαν δὲ προσκαρτεροῦντες τῇ διδαχῇ τῶν ἀποστόλων καὶ τῇ 42
κοινωνίᾳ, τῇ κλάσει τοῦ ἄρτου καὶ ταῖς προσευχαῖς· ἐγείνετο 43
δὲ πάσῃ ψυχῇ φόβος. πολλὰ δὲ τέρατα καὶ σημεῖα διὰ τῶν

Editors 37 om λοιπους JHR   38 μετανοησατε]+φησιν Soden +εφη Soden mg
εν] επι Soden   43 δε 2°] τε Soden

Old Uncial 37 ειπον τε BAC   ειποντες ℵ   ειπον δε 81   38 μετανοησατε B +φησιν
ℵAC 81 (cf. D)   εν BC(+D)   επι ℵA 81   υμων 2° BℵA 81   ημων C
39 οσους Bℵ 81 (+D)   ους AC   41 ωσει BACℵᶜ 81 (+D)   ως ℵ
42 προσκαρτερουντες Bℵᶜ 81 (+D)   +εν A   κοινωνια BℵAC 81 (+D) +και
ℵᶜ   43 εγεινετο 1° BℵAC(+D)   εγενετο 81   δε 2° Bℵ 81   τε AC
δια των αποστολων εγεινετο Bℵ 81 (+D)   εγεινετο δια των αποστολων AC

Antiochian 37 τη καρδια PS 462ϛ(+D)   ειπον τε] ειποντες S   om τον 462
ποιησομεν ϛ(+D)   38 δε] +εφη PS 462ϛ   εν] επι PS 462ϛ
om των PS 462ϛ(+D)   om υμων 2° PS 462ϛ(+D)   40 διεμαρτυρετο
PS 462ϛ   om αυτους PS 462ϛ   41 ουν] +ασμενως PS 462ϛ
αποδεξαμενοι] δεξαμενοι S   om εν PS 462ϛ   42 κοινωνια] +και PS 462ϛ
43 εγεινετο 1°] εγενετο PS 462ϛ   δε 2°] τε PS 462ϛ

---

37 The omission of λοιπους D 241 gig Aug.unit is probably right.

38 For ιησου χριστου Iren reads ιησου, pesh του κυριου ιησου. The agreement in omission of χριστου is probably coincidence. The 'Western' text has an expanded phrase, cf. D Cypr. That the omission of υμων after εις αφεσιν αμαρτιων D gig perp Rebapt Iren Aug.unit, etc. pesh hcl.text and

Antiochian is conformation to the solemn formula of the Gospels, not an original shorter reading, seems clearly indicated by the complete absence of tendency to expand in Matt. xxvi. 28, Mk. i. 4, Lk. iii. 3.

42 τη κοινωνια τη κλασει] communicatione fractionis vg sah boh is due to taking τη κλασει as appositive. Pesh shows the same exegesis.

37 σατε. τότε πάντες οἱ συνελθόντες καὶ ἀκούσαντες κατενύγησαν
τῇ καρδίᾳ, καί τινες ἐξ αὐτῶν εἶπαν πρὸς τὸν Πέτρον καὶ
τοὺς ἀποστόλους· Τί οὖν ποιήσομεν, ἄνδρες ἀδελφοί; ὑποδείξατε
38 ἡμεῖν. Πέτρος δὲ πρὸς αὐτούς φησιν· Μετανοήσατε, καὶ
βαπτισθήτω ἕκαστος ὑμῶν ἐν τῷ ὀνόματι τοῦ κυρίου Ἰησοῦ
Χριστοῦ εἰς ἄφεσιν ἁμαρτιῶν, καὶ λήμψεσθε τὴν δωρεὰν τοῦ
39 ἁγίου πνεύματος· ἡμεῖν γάρ ἐστιν ἡ ἐπαγγελία καὶ τοῖς τέκνοις
ἡμῶν καὶ πᾶσι τοῖ‹ς› εἰς μακρὰν ὅσους ἂν προσκαλέσηται
40 κύριος ὁ θεὸς ἡμῶν. ἑτέροις δὲ λόγοις πλείοσιν διεμαρτύρατο,
καὶ παρεκάλει αὐτοὺς λέγων· Σώθητε ἀπὸ τῆς γενεᾶς ταύτης
τῆς σκολιᾶς.
41 Οἱ μὲν οὖν πιστεύσαντες τὸν λόγον αὐτοῦ ἐβαπτίσθησαν,
καὶ προσετέθησαν ἐν ἐκείνῃ τῇ ἡμέρᾳ ψυχαὶ ὡσεὶ τρισχείλειαι.
42 καὶ ἦσαν προσκαρτεροῦντες τῇ διδαχῇ τῶν ἀποστόλων ἐν
Ἰερουσαλὴμ καὶ τῇ κοινωνίᾳ, τῇ κλάσι τοῦ ἄρτου καὶ ταῖς
43 προσευχαῖς. ἐγείνετο δὲ πάσῃ ψυχῇ φόβος· πολλὰ τέρατα καὶ

38 λημψεσθαι   39 προσκαλεσητε

vos crucifixistis 37 tunc omnes qui convenerant exaudientes stimulati sunt corde d
et quidam ex ipsis dixerunt ad petrum et ad apostolos quid ergo faciemus viri fratres
ostendite nobis 38 petrus autrus autem ad eos ait paenitentiam agite et baptizetur
unus quisque vestrum in nomine dni ihu xpi in remissione peccatorum et accipite
gratiam sanctum spm 39 nobis enim est haec repromissio et filiis nostris et omnibus
qui in longinquo quos advocaverit dns ds noster 40 aliis quoque sermonibus
pluribus contestabatur et exortabatur eos dicens salvi estote ex progenie hanc prava
41 hi ergo credentes sermoni ejus baptizati sunt et adjectae sunt in illo die animae
quasi tria milia 42 et erant perseverantes in doctrina apostolorum in hierusalem et
in communicatione fractionis panis et orationibus 43 nascebatur quoque omni

38 paenitemini, et baptizetur unusquisque vestrum in nomine domini Jesu Cyprian,
Christi in remissionem peccatorum, et accipietis donum spiritus sancti. *Ep.* 73. 17
39 vobis enim est promissio et filiis vestris et omnibus deinceps, quoscumque
advocaverit dominus deus noster.

37 [cum dixissent igitur turbae :] quid ergo faciemus? 38 Petrus ad eos Irenaeus
ait : paenitentiam agite, et baptizetur unusquisque vestrum in nomine Jesu in iii. 12, 2
remissa peccatorum, et accipietis donum spiritus sancti.

37 τοτε . . . κατενυγησαν] *mg* tunc omnes qui congregati erant et audierant Harclean
compuncti sunt   υποδειξατε ημειν] *mg* monstrate nobis   40 διεμαρτυρατο]
testabatur ※· iis ✓   41 πιστευσαντες] *mg* et crediderunt et

ἀποστόλων ἐγείνετο. πάντες δὲ οἱ πιστεύσαντες ἐπὶ τὸ αὐτὸ 44
εἶχον ἅπαντα κοινά, καὶ τὰ κτήματα καὶ τὰς ὑπάρξεις ἐπίπρασκον 45
καὶ διεμέριζον αὐτὰ πᾶσιν καθότι ἄν τις χρείαν εἶχεν· καθ᾽ 46
ἡμέραν τε προσκαρτεροῦντες ὁμοθυμαδὸν ἐν τῷ ἱερῷ, κλῶντές
τε κατ᾽ οἶκον ἄρτον, μετελάμβανον τροφῆς ἐν ἀγαλλιάσει καὶ
ἀφελότητι καρδίας, αἰνοῦντες τὸν θεὸν καὶ ἔχοντες χάριν πρὸς 47
ὅλον τὸν λαόν. ὁ δὲ κύριος προσετίθει τοὺς σωζομένους καθ᾽
ἡμέραν | ἐπὶ τὸ αὐτό.   III

Πέτρος δὲ καὶ Ἰωάνης ἀνέβαινον εἰς τὸ ἱερὸν ἐπὶ τὴν ὥραν
τῆς προσευχῆς τὴν ἐνάτην, καί τις ἀνὴρ χωλὸς ἐκ κοιλίας μητρὸς 2

Editors   43 εγεινετο 2°] +εν ιερουσαλημ φοβος τε ην μεγας επι παντας Soden within [ ],
JHR   44 add και before παντες Soden JHR   επι το αυτο] ησαν επι το
αυτο και WHmg Soden   47 ημεραν] +[τη εκκλησια] Soden   1 δε πετρος
Soden mg   2 και] +ιδου JHR

Old Uncial   43 εγεινετο 2° B 81 (+D)   +εν ιερουσαλημ φοβος τε ην μεγας επι παντας ℵAC
44 παντες B   και παντες ℵAC 81   πιστευσαντες Bℵ   πιστευοντες AC 81 (+D)
επι το αυτο B   ησαν επι το αυτο και ℵAC 81(+D)   45 διεμεριζον BℵC 81 (+D)
εμεριζον A   46 ομοθυμαδον εν τω ιερω BℵA 81   εν τω ιερω ομοθυμαδον C
τε 2° BℵAC (+D)   om 81

Antiochian   44 πιστευοντες PS 462 ς(+D)   επι το αυτο] ησαν επι το αυτο και PS 462 ς
(+D)   47 ημεραν] +τη εκκλησια PS 462 ς   1 δε πετρος PS 462 ς

---

43 After εγεινετο 2° ℵAC read εν ιερουσαλημ φοβος τε ην μεγας επι παντας, and they are supported by some Greek minn and by vg and boh (pesh has εν ιερουσαλημ only). D perp gig e exhibit the shorter text with B 81 Antiochian. ℵAC (but not vg) begin vs. 44 και παντες δε. The text of ℵAC is probably genuine, for the additional words are not drawn from the 'Western' text, and are not to be accounted for from v. 5. Unless the words are due to mere lust of expansive paraphrase, which does not often appear outside of the 'Western' text, the argument from 'transcriptional' motives tells strongly in their favour, since they seem to repeat vs. 43a. In fact, the first clause of vs. 43 (ἐγείνετο δὲ πάσῃ ψυχῇ φόβος) belongs with the preceding sentence (vs. 42); the later part of vs. 43 was concluded by a similar statement, with an appropriate notice (μέγας) of increase of reverent feeling

by reason of the miracles. The same repetition is to be seen in almost exactly the same manner in v. 5, 11. Note εν ιερουσαλημ D, vs. 42. The authorities for the longer text in vs. 43 generally read και παντες δε in vs. 44 (but 81 has the shorter text and yet reads και). On transcriptional grounds και is to be accepted (cf. iii. 24, xxii. 29).

44 επι το αυτο ειχον is read by B 234 Orig. Salvian.*avarit.* iii. 10 perp gig (*munerum* for *in unum*) m r. The others present the expanded ησαν επι το αυτο και ειχον. Both here and in vs. 47 επι το αυτο gave trouble; cf. C. C. Torrey, *Composition and Date of Acts*, pp. 10-14.

45-46 D και οσοι κτηματα ειχον η υπαρξεις (cf. iv. 34) and pesh try to avoid the implication that all were property-owners.

After διεμεριζον αυτα D perp gig m r have καθ ημεραν, which D omits

44 σημεῖα διὰ τῶν ἀποστόλων ἐγείνετο. πάντες τε οἱ πιστεύοντες
45 ἦσαν ἐπὶ τὸ αὐτὸ καὶ εἶχον πάντα κοινά, καὶ ὅσοι κτήματα
εἶχον ἢ ὑπάρξεις ἐπίπρασκον καὶ διεμέριζον αὐτὰ καθ᾽ ἡμέραν
46 πᾶσι †τοῖς† ἄν τις χρείαν εἶχεν· πάντες τε προσεκαρτέρουν ἐν
τῷ ἱερῷ καὶ κατ᾽ οἴκους †ἂν† ἐπὶ τὸ αὐτό, κλῶντές τε ἄρτον
47 μετελάμβανον τροφῆς ἐν ἀγαλλιάσει καὶ ἀφελότητι καρδίας,
αἰνοῦντες τὸν θεὸν καὶ ἔχοντες χάριν πρὸς ὅλον τὸν κόσμον. ὁ
III δὲ κύριος προσετίθει τοὺς σωζομένους καθ᾽ ἡμέραν | ἐπὶ τὸ αὐτὸ
ἐν τῇ ἐκκλησίᾳ.

Ἐν δὲ ταῖς ἡμέραις ταύταις Πέτρος καὶ Ἰωάνης ἀνέβαινον
εἰς τὸ ἱερὸν τὸ δειλεινὸν ἐπὶ τὴν ὥραν ἐνάτη⟨ν⟩ τῆ⟨ς⟩ προσ-
2 ευχῆς, καὶ ἰδού τις ἀνὴρ χωλὸς ἐκ κοιλίας μητρὸς αὐτοῦ ἐβαστά-

---

animae timor multa etiam portenta et signa per apostolos fiebant 44 omnes etiam d
credentes erant in unum et habebant omnia communia 45 et qui possessiones
habebant et facultates distrahebant et dispartiebantur ea cottidie omnibus secundum
quod qui opus erat 46 omnes quoque perseverantes in templo et per domos id
ipsum capiebant panes accipientes cibum in exultatione et simplicitate cordis
47 laudem dicentes d̄o et habentes gratiam aput totum mundū d̄n̄s autem autem
adiciebat eos qui salvi fiebant cottie in unum in ecclesia
1 in diebus autem ipsis petrus et johanes ascendebant in templū ad vesperum ad
horam nonam orationis 2 et ecce quidam vir clodus ex utero matris suae baiolabatur

---

at beginning of vs. 46. The sense would be excellent, cf. vi. 1. The insertion by D of a meaningless, but suggestive, τοις after πασιν, and perhaps also the identity of phrase καθοτι αν τις χρειαν ειχεν with iv. 35, arouse the suspicion of a deep-seated corruption, and that the original text of the passage was something like διεμεριζον αντα πασιν τοις [ ] καθ ημεραν. The following sentence, vs. 46, might then have begun, as in D, παντες τε, but what follows in D (κατ οικους αν επι το αυτο) suggests that something is irrecoverably wrong in the text of both verses. As the text of D now stands, an attempt appears to have been made (κατ οικους, and especially επι το αυτο) to take it as referring expressly to the eucharist. The omission of εν ιερω by perp gig r (r reads orationi instantes) may have had a similar motive. Observe that no trustworthy witness to the primitive African text is here available.

1 επι το αυτο belongs with the preceding sentence acording to BℵAC 81 vg sah and the (somewhat expanded) text of D. The reading επι το αυτο δε πετρος is an Antiochian attempt at improvement of this difficult text; it seems to have affected no Latin document except, naturally, e.

In the ameliorative addition (εν) τη εκκλησια, D pesh Antiochian agree, probably through the ' Western' element in the Antiochian.

το δειλινον D alone, to be taken as an adverb, cf. Lev. vi. 20 (13), Susanna 7.

2 D perp[2] vg.one cod pesh και ιδου τις ανηρ may be original, since it is more Semitic. For use of ιδού to introduce preliminary explanation, cf. Lk. ii. 25, vii. 37, x. 25, xiii. 11, xiv. 2, xix. 2, xxiv. 13. The omission of υπαρχων in D pesh (perhaps indicated also by omission of qui erat [so vg] in perp gig e Lucif) is probably part of the same original context.

αὐτοῦ ὑπάρχων ἐβαστάζε‹το›, ὃν ἐτίθουν καθ' ἡμέραν πρὸς τὴν
θύραν τοῦ ἱεροῦ τὴν λεγομένην Ὡραίαν τοῦ αἰτεῖν ἐλεημοσύνην
παρὰ τῶν εἰσπορευομένων εἰς τὸ ἱερόν, ὃς ἰδὼν Πέτρον καὶ 3
Ἰωάνην μέλλοντας εἰσιέναι εἰς τὸ ἱερὸν ἠρώτα ἐλεημοσύνην
λαβεῖν. ἀτενίσας δὲ Πέτρος εἰς αὐτὸν σὺν τῷ Ἰωάννῃ εἶπεν· 4
Βλέψον εἰς ἡμᾶς. ὁ δὲ ἐπεῖχεν αὐτοῖς προσδοκῶν τι παρ' αὐτῶν 5
λαβεῖν. εἶπεν δὲ Πέτρος· Ἀργύριον καὶ χρυσίον οὐχ ὑπάρχει 6
μοι, ὃ δὲ ἔχω τοῦτό σοι δίδωμι· ἐν τῷ ὀνόματι Ἰησοῦ Χριστοῦ
τοῦ Ναζωραίου περιπάτει. καὶ πιάσας αὐτὸν τῆς δεξιᾶς χειρὸς 7
ἤγειρεν αὐτόν· παραχρῆμα δὲ ἐστερεώθησαν αἱ βάσεις αὐτοῦ
καὶ τὰ σφυδρά, | καὶ ἐξαλλόμενος ἔστη καὶ περιεπάτει, καὶ εἰσ- 8
ῆλθεν σὺν αὐτοῖς εἰς τὸ ἱερὸν περιπατῶν καὶ ἁλλόμενος καὶ αἰνῶν
τὸν θεόν. καὶ εἶδεν πᾶς ὁ λαὸς αὐτὸν περιπατοῦντα καὶ αἰνοῦντα 9
τὸν θεόν, ἐπεγείνωσκον δὲ αὐτὸν ὅτι οὗτος ἦν ὁ πρὸς τὴν ἐλεη- 10

Editors 2 om υπαρχων JHR 3 om λαβειν JHR 6 ναζωραιου] +[εγειρε
και] Soden 10 ουτος] αυτος Soden

Old Uncial 2 εβασταζετο B²(B³ Tdf) προς BℵAC 095΄(+D) επι 81 λεγομενην
BℵAC 81 (+D) καλουμενην 095 3 ος . . . το ιερον BℵAC (cf. D)
om 81 ηρωτα BℵA 095 81 (+D) ερωτα C 4 εις 1° BAC 095 81
(+D) προς ℵ πετρος εις αυτον BℵAC 81 (cf. D) εις αυτον πετρος 095
5 αυτων BℵA 095 81 (+D) αυτου C 6 ειπεν δε πετρος Bℵ 81 (cf. D)
πετρος δε ειπεν AC 095 ναζωραιου Bℵ(+D) +εγειρε (C εγειραι) και
AC 095 81 7 αι βασεις αυτου BℵAC 81 αυτου αι βασεις 095 (+D)
8 και αινων BℵC 095 81 om και A (cf. D) 9 θεον BℵA 81 (+D) κυριον C
10 αυτον BACℵ^a 81 (+D) om ℵ ουτος B(+D) αυτος ℵAC 81

Antiochian 3 om λαβειν PS 462 (+D) 6 ναζωραιου] +εγειρε (-αι ς) και PS
462 ς 7 om αυτον 2° PS 462 ς(+D)] αυτου αι βασεις PS 462 ς(+D)
9 αυτον πας ο λαος PS 462 ς 10 δε] τε PS 462 ς(+D) ην] εστιν 462

---

2 παρ αυτων εισπορευομενων αυτων
D, for παρα των εισπορευομενων,
is due to a scribe's blunder, which
made necessary the insertion of
the second αυτων, but which did not
affect d.

3 Omission of λαβειν (cf. vs. 5) by
D h perp gig Lucif and Antiochian is
to be followed.

6 Bℵ sah and D have the text without εγειρε(-αι) και; all others, including
h Cypr Iren, contain the addition (cf.
Lk. v. 23 f. and parallels).

8 The superfluous και εξαλλομενος
εστη in D (om h Iren) is due to conflation with the B-text.
περιπατων και αλλομενος και, omitted
in D h, is probably original, being
represented (after the habit of this
paraphrase) by g[audens] et exultans
(χαιρων και αγαλλιωμενος) h, χαιρομενος
(perhaps for χαιρω‹ν και αγαλλιω›μενος)
D, gaudens d e (χαιρων E), attached
in each case to περιπατει. The words
themselves are by no means otiose in
the context.

ζετο, ὃν ἐτίθουν καθ᾿ ἡμέραν πρὸς τὴν θύραν τοῦ ἱεροῦ τὴν λεγομένην Ὡραίαν τοῦ αἰτεῖν ἐλεημοσύνην παρ᾿ αὐτῶν εἰσπορευο-
3 μένων αὐτῶν εἰς τὸ ἱερόν. | οὗτος ἀτενίσας τοῖς ὀφθαλμοῖς αὐτοῦ
καὶ ἰδὼν Πέτρον καὶ ᾿Ιωάνην μέλλοντας εἰ<σιέ>ναι εἰς τὸ ἱερὸν
4 ἠρώτα αὐτοὺς ἐλεημοσύνην. ἐμβλέψας δὲ ὁ Πέτρος εἰς αὐτὸν
5 σὺν ᾿Ιωάνῃ καὶ εἶπεν· ᾿Ατένεισον εἰς ἡμᾶς. ὁ δὲ †ἀτενείσας†
6 αὐτοῖς προσδοκῶν τι λαβεῖν παρ᾿ αὐτῶν. εἶπεν δὲ ὁ Πέτρος·
᾿Αργύριον καὶ χρυσίον οὐχ ὑπάρχει μοι, ὃ δὲ ἔχω τοῦτό σοι
δίδωμι· ἐν τῷ ὀνόματι ᾿Ιησοῦ Χριστοῦ τοῦ Ναζοραίου περι-
7 πάτει. καὶ πιάσας αὐτὸν τῆς δεξιᾶς χειρὸς ἤγειρεν· καὶ παραχρῆμα ἐστάθη, καὶ ἐστερεώθησαν αὐτοῦ αἱ βάσεις καὶ τὰ σφυρά,
8 | καὶ ἐξαλλόμενος ἔστη καὶ περιεπάτει †χαιρόμενος†, καὶ εἰσ-
9 ῆλθεν σὺν αὐτοῖς εἰς τὸ ἱερὸν αἰνῶν τὸν θεόν. καὶ εἶδεν πᾶς ὁ
10 λαὸς αὐτὸν περιπατοῦντα καὶ αἰνοῦντα τὸν θεόν, ἐπεγείνωσκόν

4 ιωανην   7 εσταιρεωθησαν

quem ponebant cottidie ad januam templi eam quae dicitur pulchra ut peteret d
elemosynam ab his qui ingrediebantur in templum   3 hic respiciens oculis suis et
vidit petrum et johannen incipientes introire in templum rogabat eos elemosynam
4 intuitus autem petrus in eum cum johannen et dixit aspice ad nos   5 ad ille
adtendebat eos expectans aliquid accipere ab eis   6 dixit autem petrus argentum et
aurum non est mihi quod habeo hoc tibi do in nomine i̅h̅u̅ x̅p̅i̅ nazorei ambula   7 et
adpraehensum eum dextera manu suscitabit et confestim stetit et firmatae sunt ejus
vases et crura   8 et cum exsiluisset stetit et ambulabat gaudens et introibit cum
eis in templum laudem dans do   9 et vidit omnis populus eum ambulantem et

2 qui introibant templum.   3 hic contemplatus o[culis su]is, cum vidisset h
Petrum et Johannem incipien[tes in]troiret in templum, rogabat illos elemosynam.
4 [intui]tus autem eum Petrus cum Joanne, adspic[e, inquit], et contemplare
me.   5 ille autem contemplatus e[st eos,] sperans aliquid accipere ab eo.
6 dixit autem [Petrus] ad eum: argentum quidem et aurum non est [mihi:
quod] autem habeo, hoc do tibi: in nomine I̅h̅u̅ X̅p̅i̅ Na[zareni] surge et
ambula.   7 et adpraehensa manu e[jus deste]ra, excitavit eum, et continuo
stetit, confirm[atique] sunt gressus ejus et laccania,   8 et ambulabat g[audens]
et exultans.   introivit autem cum eis in tem[plum lau]dans d̅m̅.   9 et vidit
eum omnis populus ambulan[tem et] d̅m̅ laudantem.   10 agnoscebant autem

6 dixit autem Petrus ad eum: argentum quidem et aurum non est mihi; Cyprian,
quod autem habeo hóc tibi do.   in nomine Jesu Christi Nazarei surge et Test. iii. 61
ambula.   7 et adpraehensa manu ejus dextera excitavit eum.

6 argentum et aurum non est mihi; quod autem habeo, hoc do tibi: in Irenaeus,
nomine Jesu Christi Nazareni surge et ambula.   7 et statim ejus confirmati iii. 12, 3
sunt gressus et plantae,   8 et ambulabat et introivit cum ipsis in templum,
ambulans et saliens et glorificans deum.

6 πετρος] +mg ad eum   Harclean

μοσύνην καθήμενος ἐπὶ τῇ Ὡραίᾳ Πύλῃ τοῦ ἱεροῦ, καὶ ἐπλήσθησαν θάμβους καὶ ἐκστάσεως ἐπὶ τῷ συμβεβηκότι αὐτῷ.
κρατοῦντος δὲ αὐτοῦ τὸν Πέτρον καὶ τὸν Ἰωάνην συνέδραμεν 11
πᾶς ὁ λαὸς πρὸς αὐτοὺς ἐπὶ τῇ στοᾷ τῇ καλουμένῃ Σολομῶντος
ἔκθαμβοι. ἰδὼν δὲ ὁ Πέτρος ἀπεκρίνατο πρὸς τὸν λαόν· Ἄνδρες 12
Ἰστραηλεῖται, τί θαυμάζετε ἐπὶ τούτῳ, ἢ ἡμῖν τί ἀτενίζετε ὡς
ἰδίᾳ δυνάμει ἢ εὐσεβείᾳ πεποιηκόσιν τοῦ περιπατεῖν αὐτόν; ὁ 13
θεὸς Ἀβραὰμ καὶ Ἰσαὰκ καὶ Ἰακώβ, ὁ θεὸς τῶν πατέρων
ἡμῶν, ἐδόξασεν τὸν παῖδα αὐτοῦ Ἰησοῦν, ὃν ὑμεῖς μὲν παρεδώκατε καὶ ἠρνήσασθε κατὰ πρόσωπον Πειλάτου, κρείναντος
ἐκείνου ἀπολύειν· ὑμεῖς δὲ τὸν ἅγιον καὶ δίκαιον ἠρνήσασθε, 14

Editors   13 και 1°] +ο θεος Soden   και 2°] +ο θεος Soden

Old Uncial   10 τη ωραια πυλη BACℵᶜ 81 (+D)   την ωραιαν πυλην ℵ   11 δε BℵC 81
τε A   τον 2° BℵA 81   om C (cf. D)   12 τουτω BℵAC(+D)
τουτο 81   του BℵAC (+D)   om 81   13 και 1° B 81   +θεος A(+D)
+ο θεος ℵC   και 2° B 81   +θεος A(+D)   +ο θεος ℵC   παιδα
BAC 81 (+D)   πατερα ℵ   κρειναντος BℵA 81 (+D)   κρινοντος C
απολυειν BAC 81 (+D)   απολλυειν ℵ

Antiochian   11 αυτου] του ιαθεντος χωλου PS 𝕾   om τον 2° PS 462 𝕾 (cf. D)
προς αυτους πας ο λαος PS 462 𝕾   12 om ο PS 462 𝕾   13 και 1°]
+ο θεος S (cf. D)   om μεν S 𝕾(+D)   ηρνησασθε] +αυτον PS 462 𝕾(+D)

---

11 The 'Western' reviser, understanding that the Porch of Solomon
was not inside but outside of the
Beautiful Gate, has rewritten this
verse, and his paraphrase is found
substantially intact in D; while it
rests on a partial and conflate version
of it, in which the words of the B-text
from συνεδραμεν πας ο λαος to εκθαμβοι
have been substituted for οι δε θαμβηθεντες εστησαν of D. In D perhaps
και αυτος, represented in h, has been
dropped after συνεξεπορευετο, and
certainly εκθαμβοι is due to conflation
from the B-text. οι θαμβηθεντες refers
to the crowd; the awkwardness in
the B-text of the plural εκθαμβοι after
συνεδραμεν may have led to the
'Western' rewriting of the second
half of the verse.

12 ευσεβεια] εξουσια h perp² vg.codd
pesh arm. Iren omits the word
altogether.

13 D του κρειναντος is due to conflation; cf. h Iren.

14 For εβαρυνατε D Iren (adgravastis)
Aug. peccat. meritis i. 52 (inhonorastis
et negastis) no good explanation can be
given. Harvey on Iren. iii. 12, 3 points
out the resemblance of the Syriac
words kephar (ἀρνεῖσθαι) and kebad
(βαρύνειν). See also Nestle, Philologica
Sacra, 1896, pp. 40 f., who suggests
kebar. It is more probable that
εβαρυνατε is a retranslation of the
Latin gravastis d, adgravastis Iren.
But why the Latin translation took
this turn is not explained; the Greek
text of Irenaeus, if extant, would probably supply the key to the problem.
The Sahidic rendering (cod. B) would
correspond to ηρνησασθε και κατεφρονη-
σατε αυτου (or ητιμασατε αυτον), but it
throws no light on the problem, since
the second verb 'would never be used
to render βαρυνειν' (H. Thompson).

τε αὐτὸν ὅτι οὗτος ἦν ὁ πρὸς τὴν ἐλεημοσύνην καθεζόμενος ἐπὶ
τῇ 'Ωρέᾳ Πύλῃ τοῦ ἱεροῦ, καὶ ἐπλήσθησαν θάμβους καὶ ἐκ‹σ›τά-
11 σεως ἐπὶ τῷ γεγενημένῳ αὐτῷ. ἐκπορευομένου δὲ τοῦ Πέτρου
καὶ 'Ιωάνου συνεξεπορεύετο κρατῶν αὐτούς, οἱ δὲ θαμβηθέντες
ἔστησαν ἐν τῇ στοᾷ, ἡ καλουμένη Σολομῶνος, ἔκθαμβοι.
12 ἀποκριθεὶς δὲ ὁ Πέτρος εἶπεν πρὸς αὐτούς· "Ανδρες 'Ισραηλῖ-
ται, τί θαυμάζετε ἐπὶ τούτῳ, ἢ ἡμεῖν τί ἀτενίζετε ὡς ἡμῶν
τῇ ἰδίᾳ δυνάμι ἢ εὐσεβίᾳ τοῦτο πεποιηκότων τοῦ περιπατεῖν
13 αὐτόν; ὁ θεὸς 'Αβραὰμ καὶ θεὸς 'Ισὰκ καὶ θεὸς 'Ιακώβ, ὁ
θεὸς τῶν πατέρων ἡμῶν, ἐδόξασεν τὸν παῖδα αὐτοῦ 'Ιησοῦν
Χριστόν, ὃν ὑμεῖς παρεδώκατε εἰς κρίσιν καὶ ἀπηρνήσασθε αὐτὸν
κατὰ πρόσωπον Πειλάτου, τοῦ κρείναντος, ἐκείνου ἀπολύειν
14 αὐτὸν θέλοντος· ὑμεῖς δὲ τὸν ἅγιον καὶ δίκαιον ἐβαρύνατε, καὶ

| 10 τε] ται | 12 θαυμαζεται | του] τουτο |
| 13 υμεις] ημεις | απηρνησασθαι | |

---

laudantem d̄m̄ 10 cognoscebantque eum quia hic erat qui ad elemosynam sedebat d
in porta illa pulchra templi et repleti sunt terroris et stupefactionis in eo quod
contegerat ei 11 exeunte autem petrum et johannen cum eis ibat tenens eos
stupentes autem stabant in porticum qui vocatur solomonis stupebat 12 respondens
autem petrus dixit ad eos viri istrahelitae quid admiramini super hoc aut nos quid
intuemini quasi nos nostra propria virtute aut pietate hoc fecerimus ut ambulet hic
13 d̄s̄ abraham et d̄s̄ isac et d̄s̄ iacob d̄s̄ patrum nostrorum clarificavit puerum suum
īh̄m̄ x̄p̄m̄ quem tradidistis in judicio et negastis eum ante faciem pilati cum judicasset
ille dismittere eum voluit 14 vos autem ipsum sanctum et justum grabastis et

---

eum, qu[oniam] ipse fuit qui ad elemosynam sedebat ad horr[eam por]tam h
templi: et inpleti sunt omnes ammiration[e], et stupebant de eo quod illi
accidit sanitas. 11 [exeun]tibus autem Petro et Joanne simul et ipse pro[dibat]
tenens eos, et concurrit omnis populus ad eos [in porti]cu quae vocatur
Solomonis, stupentes. 12 cum v[ideret] autem Petrus, respondit ad populum
et dixit : v[iri Istra]elitae, quid ammiramini super hoc, aut nos qu[id intu]emini,
quasi nos nostra virtute aut potestate [fecerimu]s ut amvularet istae ? 13 d̄s̄
Abraham et Isac et Ja[cob, d̄s̄] patrum nostrorum clarificabit filium suum īh̄m̄
[x̄p̄m̄, qu]em vos quidem tradidisti ad judicium, et negastis [ante] faciem Pilati,
illo volente eum dimittere. 14 vos autē [sanct]um et justum negastis, et vos

---

12 viri Israelitae, quid miramini in hoc, et nos quid intuemini, quasi Irenaeus,
nostra virtute fecerimus hunc ambulare ? 13 deus Abraham, deus Isaac, iii. 12, 3
deus Jacob, deus patrum nostrorum, glorificavit filium suum, quem vos
quidem tradidistis in judicium, et negastis ante faciem Pilati, cum remittere
eum vellet. 14 vos autem sanctum et justum adgravastis, et petistis virum

---

13 εις κρισιν] mg in judicium   Harclean

καὶ ἠτήσασθε ἄνδρα φονέα χαρισθῆναι ὑμῖν, | τὸν δὲ ἀρχηγὸν 15
τῆς ζωῆς ἀπεκτείνατε, ὃν ὁ θεὸς ἤγειρεν ἐκ νεκρῶν, οὗ ἡμεῖς
μάρτυρές ἐσμεν. καὶ τῇ πίστει τοῦ ὀνόματος αὐτοῦ τοῦτον ὃν 16
θεωρεῖτε καὶ οἴδατε ἐστερέωσεν τὸ ὄνομα αὐτοῦ, καὶ ἡ πίστις
ἡ δι' αὐτοῦ ἔδωκεν αὐτῷ τὴν ὁλοκληρίαν ταύτην ἀπέναντι πάντων
ὑμῶν. καὶ νῦν, ἀδελφοί, οἶδα ὅτι κατὰ ἄγνοιαν ἐπράξατε, ὥσπερ 17
καὶ οἱ ἄρχοντες ὑμῶν· ὁ δὲ θεὸς ἃ προκατήγγειλεν διὰ στόματος 18
πάντων τῶν προφητῶν παθεῖν τὸν Χριστὸν αὐτοῦ ἐπλήρωσεν
οὕτως. μετανοήσατε οὖν καὶ ἐπιστρέψατε πρὸς τὸ ἐξαλιφθῆναι 19
ὑμῶν τὰς ἁμαρτίας, ὅπως ἂν ἔλθωσιν καιροὶ ἀναψύξεως ἀπὸ 20
προσώπου τοῦ κυρίου καὶ ἀποστείλῃ τὸν προκεχειρισμένον ὑμῖν
Χριστὸν Ἰησοῦν, ὃν δεῖ οὐρανὸν μὲν δέξασθαι ἄχρι χρόνων ἀπο- 21

Editors   16 και 1°] +επι Soden   19 προς] εις Soden

Old Uncial   16 και 1° BℵA 81   +επι ACℵ°(+D)   18 παθειν τον χριστον BℵC 81 (+D)
om A   19 επιστρεψατε BℵA 81 (+D)   επιτρεψατε C   προς Bℵ
εις AC 81 (+D)   20 χριστον ιησουν Bℵ(+D)   ιησουν χριστον AC 81

Antiochian   16 και 1°] +επι PS 462 ς(+D)   αυτου 1°] τουτου S   18 αυτου
παθειν τον χριστον PS 462 ς   19 προς] εις PS 462 ς(+D)   20 προ-
κεχειρισμενον] προκεκηρυγμενον ς   προκεχαρισμενον S   ιησουν χριστον ς

---

14 To the addition of *potius* by hcl. *mg* after ητησατε corresponds *petistis magis* e E.

16 τη πιστει Bℵ 81; επι τη πιστει ACD h (*supra*; Iren and other Latin documents read *in* and probably represent τη πιστει) Antiochian. Since the Antiochian text probably did not influence h, the reading with επι is ancient, but the shorter of the two ancient readings is to be preferred to the common phrase with επι.

19 προς Bℵ alone ; εις AC81D Antiochian. The only ground of decision is the relative value ascribed to the opposing groups.

20 For hcl ⸓ cf. the addition of *vobis* in varying positions by Iren boh ; by h Tert ; and by e vg.*codd.*

15 ἠτήσατε ἄνδρα φονέα χαρισθῆναι ὑμεῖν, τὸν δὲ ἀρχηγὸν τῆς
ζωῆς ἀπεκτείνατε, ὃν ὁ θεὸς ἤγειρεν ἐκ νεκρῶν, οὗ ἡμεῖς μάρτυρές
16 ἐσμεν. καὶ ἐπὶ τῇ πίστει τοῦ ὀνόματος αὐτοῦ τοῦτον θεωρεῖτε
καὶ οἴδατε ὅτι ἐστερέωσεν τὸ ὄνομα αὐτοῦ, καὶ ἡ πίστις ἡ δι'
αὐτοῦ ἔδωκεν αὐτῷ τὴν ὁλοκληρίαν ταύτην ἀπέναντι πάντων
17 ὑμῶν. καὶ νῦν, ἄνδρες ἀδελφοί, ἐπιστάμεθα ὅτι ὑμεῖς μὲν κατὰ
18 ἄγνοιαν ἐπράξατε πονηρόν, ὥσπερ καὶ οἱ ἄρχοντες ὑμῶν· ὁ δὲ
θεὸς ὃ προκατήγγειλεν διὰ στόματος πάντων τῶν προφητῶν
19 παθεῖν τὸν Χριστὸν αὐτοῦ ἐπλήρωσεν οὕτως. μετανοήσατε οὖν
20 καὶ ἐπιστρέψατε εἰς τὸ ἐξαλειφθῆναι τὰς ἁμαρτίας ὑμῶν, ὅπως
ἂν ἐπέλθωσιν καιροὶ ἀναψύξεως ἀπὸ προσώπου τοῦ κυρίου καὶ
21 ἀποστείλῃ τὸν προκεχιρισμένον ὑμῖν Χριστὸν Ἰησοῦν, ὃν δεῖ

14 φονεια   15 ημεις] υμεις

---

postulastis virum homicida donari vobis 15 principem vero vitae interfecistis quem d
d̄s̄ suscitavit a mortuis quibus nos testes sumus 16 et in fide nominis ejus hunc
quem vidistis et scitis consoldavit nomen ejus et fides que per ipsum est dedit ei
integritatem hanc coram omnibus vobis 17 et nunc viri fratres quia vos quidem per
ignorantiam egistis iniquitatem sicut et principes vestri 18 d̄s̄ autem quae praenuntiavit per os omnium prophetarum pati x̄p̄m̄ suum inplevit sic 19 paenitentiam
ergo agite et convertimini ad hoc ut deleantur peccata vestra 20 ut veniant tempora
refrigerii a facie d̄m̄ī et mittat praedestinatum vobis īh̄m̄ x̄p̄m̄ 21 quem oportet

---

petestis homicidam [homi]nem vivere et donari vobis : 15 principem autem h
vi[tae s]uspendentes occidistis, quem d̄s̄ excitavit a mor[tuis, cuj]us nos sumus
testes. 16 et supra fidelitate nominis [ejus h]unc quem videtis et nostis confirmavit nomen [ejus, et] fides dedit ei integritatem istam in cons[pectu
o]mnium vestrum. 17 et nunc, viri fratres, scimus quo[niam no]n quidem per
scientiam fecistis nequam, sicut [et princ]ipes vestri. 18 verum d̄s̄, quod
adnuntiabit ore ō[nium pr]ofetarum passurum x̄p̄m̄ suum, et inplebit. 19 [peni-
tea]t itaquae vos et convertimini ad perdelenda [peccata] vesta, 20 ut tempora
vobis refrigeris supraviniāt [a facie d]ni, et mittat vobis praeparatum Īh̄m̄ X̄p̄m̄:

---

19 paeniteat itaque vos et respicite ad abolenda delicta vestra, 20 uti tempora Tertullian,
vobis superveniant refrigerii ex persona dei et mittat praedesignatum nobis Res. carn. 23

---

homicidam donari vobis : 15 ducem autem vitae occidistis, quem deus Irenaeus,
excitavit a mortuis, cujus nos testes sumus. 16 et in fide nominis ejus iii. 12, 3
hunc quem videtis et scitis confirmavit nomen ejus, et fides quae est per
ipsum dedit ei incolumitatem coram vobis omnibus. 17 et nunc, fratres, scio
quoniam secundum ignorantiam fecistis nequam ; 18 deus autem quae praedixit
ore omnium prophetarum pati Christum suum adimplevit. 19 paenitentiam
igitur agite et convertimini ut deleantur peccata vestra, 20 et veniant vobis
tempora refrigerii a facie domini, et mittat praeparatum vobis Christum Jesum,

---

14 .ητησατε]+mg potius   17 πονηρον] mg malum   20 επελθωσιν] Harclean
veniant ·※· vobis ✓

καταστάσεως πάντων ὧν ἐλάλησεν ὁ θεὸς διὰ στόματος τῶν
ἁγίων ἀπ' αἰῶνος αὐτοῦ προφητῶν. Μωυσῆς μὲν εἶπεν ὅτι 22
Deut. xviii. Προφήτην ὑμῖν ἀναστήσει κύριος ὁ θεὸς ἐκ τῶν ἀδελφῶν ὑμῶν
15-19 ὡς ἐμέ· αὐτοῦ ἀκούσεσθε κατὰ πάντα ὅσα ἂν λαλήσῃ πρὸς ὑμᾶς.
ἔσται δὲ πᾶσα ψυχὴ ἥτις ἂν μὴ ἀκούσῃ τοῦ προφήτου ἐκείνου 23
Lev. xxiii. 29 ἐξολεθρευθήσεται ἐκ τοῦ λαοῦ. καὶ πάντες δὲ οἱ προφῆται 24
ἀπὸ Σαμουὴλ καὶ τῶν καθεξῆς ὅσοι ἐλάλησαν καὶ κατήγγειλαν
τὰς ἡμέρας ταύτας. ὑμεῖς ἐστὲ οἱ υἱοὶ τῶν προφητῶν καὶ 25
τῆς διαθήκης ἧς ὁ θεὸς διέθετο πρὸς τοὺς πατέρας ὑμῶν,
Gen. xxii. 18 λέγων πρὸς Ἀβραάμ· Καὶ ἐν τῷ σπέρματί σου εὐλογηθή-
σονται πᾶσαι αἱ πατριαὶ τῆς γῆς. ὑμῖν πρῶτον ἀναστήσας 26

24 προφητοι

Editors   22 θεος] +ημων Soden   25 διεθετο ο θεος Soden   υμων] ημων WHmg
ευλογηθησονται] ενευλογηθησονται Soden

Old Uncial   21 αγιων BℵAC 81   +των B² (B³ Tdf) ℵ° (cf. D)   22 θεος B +ημων ℵC
+υμων Aℵ° 81 (+D)   24 προφηται B² (?)   οσοι BAC 81   οι ℵC²
ελαλησαν BℵAC 81   επροφητευσαν C²   κατηγγειλαν BℵAC 81 (+D)
προκατηγγειλαν C²   [α]νανγγει[λαν] 0165   25 ο θεος διεθετο B 0165
(+D)   διεθετο ο θεος ℵAC 81   υμων BAℵ° 81   ημων ℵC 0165 (+D)
εν BℵAC 81 (+D)   om 0165   ευλογηθησονται B   ευλογησονται A
ενευλογηθησονται ℵA² 0165 81 (+D)   επευλογηθησονται C   26 αναστησας
ο θεος BℵC 0165   ο θεος αναστησας A 81 (+D)

Antiochian   21 των] παντων των PS 462   παντων 5   αυτου προφητων απ αιωνος PS 462 5
22 μεν] +γαρ (S om γαρ) προς τους πατερας PS 462 5(cf. D)   θεος] +ημων P
+υμων S 462 5(+D)   24 κατηγγειλαν] προκατηγγειλαν 5   25 om οι
PS 462 5(+D)   διεθετο ο θεος PS 462 5   υμων] ημων PS 462 5(+D)
om εν 5   ευλογηθησονται] ενευλογηθησονται PS 462 5(+D)   26 ο θεος
αναστησας P 5(+D)   om ο θεος S

---

24 D ο ελαλησαν (MS. -εν), for οσοι
ελαλησαν, is due to misunderstanding
of the Latin quotquot (quodquod d h),
which accurately rendered οσοι.
25 υμων BA 81 has been conformed
in ℵC 0165 D Antiochian to the
general usage of Acts in referring to
' our fathers.'

For αι πατριαι hcl.mg has 'emwatha
daberitha, perhaps meaning that
'emwatha is the word used in the
passage of Genesis (beritha) from
which the quotation is drawn (Gen.
xxii. 18). The Syro-hexaplar is lacking in this passage; pesh renders by
'amme.

οὐρανὸν μὲν δέξασθαι ἄχρι χρόνων ἀποκαταστάσεως πάντων
ὧν ἐλάλησεν ὁ θεὸς διὰ στόματος τῶν ἁγίων αὐτοῦ τῶν προφητῶν·
22 Μωυσῆς μὲν εἶπεν πρὸς τοὺς πατέρας ἡμῶν ὅτι Προφήτην ὑμεῖν
ἀναστήσει κύριος ὁ θεὸς ὑμῶν ἐκ τῶν ἀδελφῶν ἡμῶν· ὡς ἐμοῦ
23 αὐτοῦ ἀκούσεσθε κατὰ πάντα ὅσα ἂν λαλήσῃ πρὸς ὑμᾶς· ἔσται
δὲ πᾶσα ψυχὴ ἥτις ἂν μὴ ἀκούσῃ τοῦ προφήτου ἐκείνου ἐξολε-
24 θρευθήσεται ἐκ τοῦ λαοῦ. καὶ πάντες οἱ προφῆται ἀπὸ Σαμουὴλ
καὶ τῶν κατεξῆς ὃ ἐλάλησαν καὶ κατήγειλαν τὰς ἡμέρας ταύτας.
25 ὑμεῖς ἐστὲ υἱοὶ τῶν προφητῶν καὶ τῆς διαθήκης ἣν ὁ θεὸς διέθετο
πρὸς τοὺς πατέρας ἡμῶν, λέγων πρὸς Ἀβραάμ· Καὶ ἐν τῷ σπέρ-
26 ματί σου ἐνευλογηθήσονται πᾶσαι αἱ πατριαὶ τῆς γῆς. ὑμεῖν

21 χρονον   22 ακουσεσθαι   24 ελαλησεν   25 εσται

caelum quidem accipere usque ad tempora restitutionis omnium quae locutus est d̄s d
per os sanctorum suorū prophetarum 22 moyses quidem dixit ad patres nostros
quia prophetam vobis suscitavit d̄n̄s d̄s vester de fratribus vestris tamquam me ipsum
audietis secundum omnia quaecumq·locutus fuerit ad vos   23 erit autem omnis anima
quaecumq·non audierit prophetam illum disperibit de populo 24 et omnis prophetae
a samuel et eorum qui ordine fuerunt quodquod locuti sunt et adnuntiaverunt dies
hos 25 vos estis filii prophetarum et ejus dispositionis quam d̄s disputavit ad patres
nostros dicens ad abraham et in semine tuo benedicetur omnis patriae terrae

21 quē [oporte]t caelos recipere usquae ad tempora dispositi[onis om]nium h
quae locutus est d̄s ore santorum pro[fetaru]m suorum. 22 Moyses quidem
dixit ad patres [nostro]s : profetam vobis excitavit d̄n̄s d̄s de fratrib·
[vestri]s tanquam me : eum vos audituri per omnia que[cumqu]e locutus
fuerit ad vos. 23 omnis autem anima quaecumquae non audierit profetam
illum, e[xtermi]navitur de populo. 24 et omnes profetae a Samuel [et per]
ordinem quodquod locuti sunt, adnuntiaver[unt is]tos dies. 25 vos estis fili
profetorum, et testament[i quod] di disposuit ad patres nostros, dicens ad
Abra[ham : et] in semine tuo venedicetur omnes nation[es ter]rae. 26 vobis

Christum, 21 quem oportet accipere caelos ad usque tempora exhibitionis Tertullian,
omnium quae locutus est deus ore sanctorum prophetarum.   Res. carn. 23

21 quem oportet caelum quidem suscipere usque ad tempora dispositionis Irenaeus,
omnium quae locutus est deus per sanctos prophetas suos. 22 Moyses quidem iii. 12, 3
dicit ad patres nostros quoniam prophetam vobis excitabit dominus deus
vester ex fratribus vestris quemadmodum me, ipsum audietis in omnibus
quaecumque locutus fuerit ad vos : 23 erit autem omnis anima quaecumque
non audierit prophetam illum peribit de populo. 24 et omnes a Samuel et
deinceps, quotquot locuti sunt, et adnuntiaverunt dies istos. 25 vos estis
filii prophetarum et testamenti quod deus disposuit ad patres nostros, dicens
ad Abraham : et in semine tuo benedicentur omnes tribus terrae. 26 vobis

ὁ θεὸς τὸν παῖδα αὐτοῦ ἀπέστειλεν αὐτὸν εὐλογοῦντα ὑμᾶς ἐν τῷ ἀποστρέφειν ἕκαστον ἀπὸ τῶν πονηριῶν.

Λαλούντων δὲ αὐτῶν πρὸς τὸν λαὸν ἐπέστησαν αὐτοῖς οἱ IV ἀρχιερεῖς καὶ ὁ στρατηγὸς τοῦ ἱεροῦ καὶ οἱ Σαδδουκαῖοι, δια- 2 πονούμενοι διὰ τὸ διδάσκειν αὐτοὺς τὸν λαὸν καὶ καταγγέλλειν ἐν τῷ Ἰησοῦ τὴν ἀνάστασιν τὴν ἐκ νεκρῶν, καὶ ἐπέβαλον αὐτοῖς 3 τὰς χεῖρας καὶ ἔθεντο εἰς τήρησιν εἰς τὴν αὔριον, ἦν γὰρ ἑσπέρα ἤδη. πολλοὶ δὲ τῶν ἀκουσάντων τὸν λόγον ἐπίστευσαν, καὶ 4 ἐγενήθη ἀριθμὸς τῶν ἀνδρῶν ὡς χειλιάδες πέντε.

Ἐγένετο δὲ ἐπὶ τὴν αὔριον συναχθῆναι αὐτῶν τοὺς ἄρχοντας 5 καὶ τοὺς πρεσβυτέρους καὶ τοὺς γραμματεῖς ἐν Ἰερουσαλήμ | (καὶ Ἄννας ὁ ἀρχιερεὺς καὶ Καιάφας καὶ Ἰωάννης καὶ Ἀλέξ- 6

Editors   26 πονηριων] +[υμων] WH   +υμων Soden JHR   1 αρχιερεις]
ιερεις WHmg Soden JHR   4 [ο] αριθμος Soden   ως] [ωσει] Soden
5 εν] εις JHR   6 ιωαννης] ιωναθας JHR

Old Uncial   26 αυτου BℵAC 81 (+D)   αυτον 0165   πονηριων B   +υμων ℵA 0165 81
(+D)   +αυτων C   1 αρχιερεις BC   ιερεις ℵA 0165 81 (+D)   2 διαπονουμενοι
BℵA 0165 81   και διαπονουμενοι Cvid (cf. D)   τω BℵAC 81   om 0165   την εκ
BℵAC 81   των 0165 (+D)   3 εθεντο Bℵ 0165 81 (+D)   +αυτους AC
εις την αυριον (ℵ γαυριον) BℵA 81   την επαυριον 0165 (cf. D)   4 τον λογον
Bℵ 0165 81 (+D)   om A   αριθμος Bℵ 0165 (+D)   ο αριθμος A 81
των ανδρων BℵA 81 (cf. D)   ανθρωπων 0165   ως B 0165 (+D)   om ℵA 81
5 τους 3° BℵA 81   om 0165 (cf. D)   εν BA 81 (+D)   εις ℵ 0165

Antiochian   26 αυτου] +ιησουν PS 462 ϛ   πονηριων] +υμων PS 462 ϛ(+D)
1 αρχιερεις] ιερεις PS 462 ϛ(+D)   2 την εκ] των PS 462 (+D)   4 ο αριθμος
PS 462 ϛ   ως] ωσει PS 462 ϛ   5 τους 2° om PS 462 ϛ   τους 3°
om PS 462 ϛ(cf. D)   εν] εις PS 462 ϛ   6 ανναν τον αρχιερεα
και καιαφαν και ιωαννην και αλεξανδρον PS 462 ϛ

26 The omission of αυτον by D h perp gig Iren is improvement of style.

1 ιερεις ℵAD Antiochian sah is to be preferred to the more usual αρχιερεις BC.

D omits και ο στρατηγος του ιερου. The word used for στρατηγος in gig pesh hcl.text sah.cod boh is plural.

5 The agreement of h pesh in translating : (et pesh) postero die collecti sunt magistratus, etc. suggests that εγενετο (δε) in D is due to conflation with the B-text, and that the shorter text is the true 'Western,' a simplifi-

cation, at the same time providing a grammatical construction for the nominatives in vs. 6, which Antiochian has made over into the accusative. But the paraphrase might have been independent in Syriac and Latin.

εις ℵ 0165 is to be preferred to the more elegant εν ; see Note on ii. 5.

6 D perp gig prov tepl read ιωναθας for ιωαννης of all other MSS. and versions (including h). Probability seems to lie with the far less usual 'Jonathan,' for h is by no means impeccable. Ionatha is included as one of the proper names of Acts in Jerome,

πρῶτον ὁ θεὸς ἀναστήσας τὸν παῖδα αὐτοῦ ἐξαπέστειλεν εὐλογοῦντα ὑμᾶς ἐν τ<ῷ> ἀποστρέφειν ἕκαστον ἐκ τῶν πονηριῶν
ὑμῶν.

IV   Λαλούντων δὲ αὐτῶν πρὸς τὸν λαὸν τὰ ῥήματα ταῦτα ἐπ-
2 έστησαν οἱ εἱερεῖς καὶ οἱ Σαδδουκαῖοι, διαπονούμενοι διὰ τὸ
διδάσκειν αὐτοὺς τὸν λαὸν καὶ ἀναγγέλλειν τὸν Ἰησοῦν ἐν τῇ
3 ἀναστάσει τῶν νεκρῶν, καὶ ἐπειβαλόντες αὐτοῖς τὰς χεῖρας καὶ
4 ἔθεντο εἰς τήρησιν εἰς τὴν ἐπαύριον, ἦν γὰρ ἑσπέρα ἤδη. πολλοὶ
δὲ τῶν ἀκουσάντων τὸν λόγον ἐπίστευσαν, καὶ ἀριθμός τε ἐγενήθη
ἀνδρῶν ὡς χιλιάδες ε̄.

5   Ἐγένετο δὲ ἐπὶ τὴν αὔριον ἡμέραν συνήχθησαν οἱ ἄρχοντες
6 καὶ οἱ πρεσβύτεροι καὶ γραμματεῖς ἐν Ἰερουσαλήμ, | καὶ Ἅννας
ὁ ἀρχιερεὺς καὶ Καίφας καὶ Ἰωνάθας καὶ Ἀλέξανδρος καὶ ὅσοι

26 ευλογουντας   εκαστος   2 διαπονουμενοι] καιαπονουμενοι

---

26 vobis primum d̄s̄ suscitavit puerum suum misit benedicentem vos in eo cum d
abertatur unus quisque a nequitiis suis
1 loquentibus autem eis ad populum verba haec adsisterunt sacerdotes et
sadducaei   2 dolore percussi eo quod docerent ipsi populum et adnuntiarent īh̄m in
resurrectione mortuorum   3 et inmiserunt eis manus et posuerunt in adsertionem in
crastinū erant enim vespera jam   4 multi vero eorum qui audierunt verbum
crediderunt et factus est numerus virorum ad quinq· milia   5 contigit autem in
crastinum diem congregati sunt principes et seniores et scribae in hierusalem   6 et
annas pontefex et caifas et joathas et alexander et quodquod erant ex genere

---

primo d̄s̄ excitabit filium suum, et [misit] venedicentem vos, ad avertendum h
unumqu[emque] a nequitis suis.
1 loquentibus autem illis ad po[pulum] verba ista, adstiterunt sacerdotes et
praeto[r templi] et sadducei,   2 dolentes de eo quod docerent po[pulum], et
adnuntiarent in īh̄m resurrectionem mo[rtuorū].   3 et injectis manibus et
tenuerunt eos et tra[diderunt] custodie in crastinum : fuit autem jam vesper[a.
4 mul]ti tamen ex eis qui audierunt crediderunt : nu[merus] autem factus ad
quinquae milia hominum.   5 posttero die collecti sunt magistratus et prin[cipes
et] seniores et scribe   6 et pontifex Annas et Caip[has et Jo]hannes et Alexander

---

primum deus excitans filium suum misit benedicentem vos, uti convertat se Irenaeus
unusquisque a nequitiis suis.
2 in Jesu resurrectionem quae est a mortuis adnuntians.   iii. 12, 3
2 ἐν Ἰησοῦ τὴν ἀνάστασιν τῶν νεκρῶν κηρύσσων.   [catena]

---

1 τα ρηματα ταυτα] mg sermones hos   Harclean

Nom. hebr. p. 103), which probably
rests on a Greek work of the latter
half of the third century.   It does
not seem likely that the 'Western'

reviser has made a learned correction
on the basis of Josephus, Antiq. xviii.
4, 3, or from similar information of
his own.

ανδρος καὶ ὅσοι ἦσαν ἐκ γένους ἀρχιερατικοῦ), καὶ στήσαντες 7
αὐτοὺς ἐν τῷ μέσῳ ἐπυνθάνοντο· Ἐν ποίᾳ δυνάμει ἢ ἐν ποίῳ
ὀνόματι ἐποιήσατε τοῦτο ὑμεῖς; τότε Πέτρος πλησθεὶς πνεύ- 8
ματος ἁγίου εἶπεν πρὸς αὐτούς· Ἄρχοντες τοῦ λαοῦ καὶ πρεσβύτεροι, εἰ ἡμεῖς σήμερον ἀνακρεινόμεθα ἐπὶ εὐεργεσίᾳ ἀνθρώ- 9
που ἀσθενοῦς, ἐν τίνι οὗτος σέσωσται, | γνωστὸν ἔστω πᾶσιν 10
ὑμῖν καὶ παντὶ τῷ λαῷ Ἰστραὴλ ὅτι ἐν τῷ ὀνόματι Ἰησοῦ Χριστοῦ τοῦ Ναζωραίου, ὃν ὑμεῖς ἐσταυρώσατε, ὃν ὁ θεὸς ἤγειρεν
ἐκ νεκρῶν, ἐν τούτῳ οὗτος παρέστηκεν ἐνώπιον ὑμῶν ὑγιής.
Ps. cxviii. 22 οὗτός ἐστιν ὁ λίθος ὁ ἐξουθενηθεὶς ὑφ᾽ ὑμῶν τῶν οἰκοδόμων, ὁ 11
γενόμενος εἰς κεφαλὴν γωνίας. καὶ οὐκ ἔστιν ἐν ἄλλῳ οὐδενὶ 12

---

8 The addition of του ισραηλ after
πρεσβυτεροι, found in D Cypr h perp
gig Iren (perp² w prov tepl vg.codd
pesh have του οικου ισραηλ) and in
Antiochian, is a good example of the
'Western' element in the Antiochian
text.
10, 12 υγιης, vs. 10, is followed in
Cypr h hcl.mg by in alio autem nullo
(e Ē et in alio nullo). Correspondingly,
vs. 12, Cypr h Iren Aug. peccat. merit.
i. 52 omit και ουκ εστιν εν αλλω ουδενι

η σωτηρια, with non (instead of nec ;
Iren has et non) for the following
ουδε. The rearrangement, in which
η σωτηρια necessarily fell out, is
doubtless secondary, but probably
belonged to the 'Western' text. In
D conflation has reintroduced the
reading of the B-text both in vs.
10 and vs. 12, but has left traces of
the 'Western' in vs. 12 in the omission of η σωτηρια and the reading ου
for ουδε.

7 ἦσαν ἐκ γένους ἀρχιερατικοῦ, καὶ στήσαντες αὐτοὺς ἐν μέσῳ
ἐπυνθάνοντο· Ἐν ποίᾳ δυνάμι ἢ ἐν ποίῳ ὀνόματι ἐποιήσατε
8 τοῦτο ὑμεῖς; τότε Πέτρος πλησθεὶς πνεύματος ἁγίου εἶπεν πρὸς
9 αὐτούς· Ἄρχοντες τοῦ λαοῦ καὶ πρεσβύτεροι τοῦ Ἰσραήλ, | εἰ
ἡμεῖς σήμερον ἀνακρεινόμεθα ἀφ' ὑμῶν ἐπ' εὐεργεσείᾳ ἀνθρώπου
10 ἀσθενοῦς, ἐν τίνι οὗτος σέσωσται, | γνωστὸν ἔστω πᾶσιν ὑμεῖν
καὶ παντὶ τῷ λαῷ Ἰσραὴλ ὅτι ἐν τῷ ὀνόματι Ἰησοῦ Χριστοῦ
τοῦ Ναζωραίου, ὃν ὑμεῖς ἐσταυρώσατε, ὃν ὁ θεὸς ἤγειρεν ἐκ
11 νεκρῶν, ἐν τούτῳ οὗτος παρέστηκεν ἐνώπιον ὑμῶν ὑγιής. οὗτός
ἐστιν ὁ λίθος ὁ ἐξουθενηθεὶς ὑφ' ὑμῶν τῶν οἰκοδόμων, ὁ γενό-
12 μενος εἰς κεφαλὴν γωνίας. καὶ οὐκ ἔστιν ἐν ἄλλῳ οὐδενί, οὐ

---

pontificali 7 cum statuisset eos in medio interrogabant in qua virtute aut quo d
nomine fecistis hoc vos   8 tunc petrus inpletus s̄p̄o sancto dixit ad eos principes
hujus populi et seniores istrahel   9 si nos hodie interrogamur a vobis super bene-
facio hominem infirmum in quo hic salvus factus est   10 notum sit omnibus vobis
et omni populo istrahel quia in nomine x̄p̄i ih̄u nazoraei quem vos crucifixistis quem
d̄s suscitavit a mortuis in isto hic adsistit in conspectu vestro sanum   11 hic est
lapis qui praejectus est a vobis aedificatoribus qui factus est in capud anguli   12 et

---

et quodquod fuer[unt ex ge]nere pontificali ;   7 et cum statuissent [eos in h
medi]um, quaerebant in qua virtute aut in q[uo nomine] id fecissent.   8 tunc
Petrus repletus s̄p̄[u s̄c̄o̅ ait ad] eos : principes populi et seniores Istrael :   9 [si
nos hodie inter]rogamus a vobis super benefacto hominis in[firmi]s, in quo iste
salbatus est,   10 sit vobis omnibus no[tum, e]t omni populo Istrael, quoniam
in nomi d̄n̄i ih̄u [x̄p̄i N]azareni, quem vos crucifixistis, quem d̄s excita[vit a
m]ortuis, in illo iste in conspectu vestro sanus ad[stat, i]n alio autem nullo.
11 hic est lapis qui contem[tus es]t a vobis quia aedificatis, qui factus est in
caput [angu]li : 12 non est enim aliud sub caelo da[tum h]ominibus, in

---

8 principes populi et seniores Israel,   9 ecce nos hodie interrogamur a Cyprian,
vobis super benefacto hominis infirmi, in quo iste salvatus est.   10 sit *Test.* ii. 16
vobis omnibus notum et ȯmni populo Israel, quia in nomine Jesu Christi
Nazarei, quem vos crucifixistis, quem deus excitavit a mortuis, in illo iste
in conspectu vestro sanus adstat, in alio autem nullo.   11 hic est lapis
qui contemptus est a vobis qui aedificabatis, qui factus est in caput anguli.

---

8 Petrus dixit ad eos : principes populi et seniores Israelitae,   9 si nos Irenaeus,
hodie redarguimur a vobis in benefacto hominis infirmi, in quo hic sal- iii. 12, 4
vatus est,   10 cognitum sit omnibus vobis et omni populo Israel, quoniam
in nomine Jesu Christi Nazarei, quem vos crucifixistis, quem deus excitavit
a mortuis, in hoc hic adstat in conspectu vestro sanus.   11 hic est lapis
spretus a vobis aedificantibus, qui factus est in caput anguli.   12 et non

---

10 υγιης]+mg in alio autem nullo   Harclean

ἡ σωτηρία, οὐδὲ γὰρ ὄνομά ἐστιν ἕτερον ὑπὸ τὸν οὐρανὸν τὸ
δεδομένον ἐν ἀνθρώποις ἐν ᾧ δεῖ σωθῆναι ὑμᾶς. θεωροῦντες 13
δὲ τὴν τοῦ Πέτρου παρρησίαν καὶ Ἰωάννου, καὶ καταλαβόμενοι
ὅτι ἄνθρωποι ἀγράμματοί εἰσιν καὶ ἰδιῶται, ἐθαύμαζον, ἐπεγείνωσκόν τε αὐτοὺς ὅτι σὺν τῷ Ἰησοῦ ἦσαν, τόν τε ἄνθρωπον 14
βλέποντες σὺν αὐτοῖς ἑστῶτα τὸν τεθεραπευμένον οὐδὲν εἶχον
ἀντειπεῖν. κελεύσαντες δὲ αὐτοὺς ἔξω τοῦ συνεδρίου ἀπελθεῖν 15
συνέβαλλον πρὸς ἀλλήλους | λέγοντες· Τί ποιήσωμεν τοῖς ἀνθρώ- 16
ποις τούτοις; ὅτι μὲν γὰρ γνωστὸν σημεῖον γέγονεν δι᾿ αὐτῶν
πᾶσιν τοῖς κατοικοῦσιν Ἰερουσαλὴμ φανερόν, καὶ οὐ δυνάμεθα
ἀρνεῖσθαι· ἀλλ᾿ ἵνα μὴ ἐπὶ πλεῖον διανεμηθῇ εἰς τὸν λαόν, ἀπειλη- 17
σώμεθα αὐτοῖς μηκέτι λαλεῖν ἐπὶ τῷ ὀνόματι τούτῳ μηδενὶ
ἀνθρώπων. καὶ καλέσαντες αὐτοὺς παρήγγειλαν καθόλου μὴ 18

14 τεθαραπευμενον

Editors   12 υμας] ημας WH Soden JHR   18 το καθολου Soden

Old Uncial   12 ονομα εστιν ετερον B   ονομα ετερον εστιν A 0165   ετερον ονομα εστιν ℵ
(cf. D)   υμας B   ημας ℵA 0165 (+D)   13 τε BℵA 0165ᶜᵒʳʳ   δε
0165 (+D)   17 ινα BℵA(+D)   +δε A²   μηκετι Bℵ(+D)   μη A
18 καθολου Bℵ   το καθολου Aℵᶜ (cf. D)

Antiochian   12 ουδε] ουτε PS 462 𝕾   om υπο τον ουρανον PS 462   υμας] ημας
PS 462 𝕾(+D)   14 τε] δε PS 462 𝕾   15 συνεβαλον 𝕾(+D)
16 ποιησομεν PS 𝕾(+D)   αρνησασθαι PS 462 𝕾   17 λαον] +απειλη
PS 462 𝕾   απειλησομεθα P 462 (+D)   om τουτω S
ανθρωπω P   18 παρηγγειλαν] +αυτοις PS 462 𝕾   το καθολου
PS 462 𝕾 (cf. D)

13-15 The text of vss. 13-15 as found
in full in h alone doubtless represents
accurately the 'Western' rewriting.
Besides minor alterations, such as
vs. 13 ακουσαντες for θεωρουντες, etc.,
vs. 14 has been inserted after εθαυμαζον
of vs. 13, and the altered connexion
has led to various further changes, of
which the most noteworthy is the
introduction of τινες δε εξ αυτων as the
subject of επεγεινωσκον.

The only clear trace of this 'Western'
text in D consists of the addition
ποιησαι η in vs. 14. In pesh the
following fragments of the 'Western'
text have survived: vs. 13 cum
audirent; vs. 14 conversati erant (αν-
εστραφησαν for ησαν), illum infirmum;
vs. 15 tunc jusserunt. All these have
been eliminated in hcl.text.

16 The impossible γεγονεναι of D may

have come about through some adjustment between the text of h (cf. pesh)
and that of B, but the precise method
is matter for conjecture only. The
process of conflation seen in D contained the possibility of many an
accident. It is, however, also possible
that ΓΕΓΟΝΕΝΔΙ became by a corrupt dittography ΓΕΓΟΝΕΝΔΙΔΙ.

17 With hcl.mg cf. the Latin additions after populum: verba ista e E
vg.cod, verba istorum h, verba haec gig
Lucif.

Antiochian adds unaccountably απ-
ειλη before απειλησωμεθα. Possibly we
should know why, if we knew the
whole cause of the strange reading of
D επιλησομεθα ουν ουτοις.

18 παρηγγειλαν το κατα το D is
probably a mere corruption of παρηγγειλαν το καθολου of A Antiochian.

γάρ ἐστιν ἕτερον ὄνομα ὑπὸ τὸν οὐρανὸν ὃ δεδομένον ἀνθρώποις
13 ἐν ᾧ δεῖ σωθῆναι ἡμᾶς. θεωροῦντες δὲ τὴν τοῦ Πέτρου παρρησίαν καὶ Ἰωάνου, καὶ καταλαβόμενοι ὅτι ἄνθρωποι ἀγράμματοί εἰσιν, ἐθαύμαζον, ἐπεγείνωσκον δὲ αὐτοὺς ὅτι σὺν τῷ Ἰησοῦ
14 ἦσαν· τὸν ἄνθρωπον βλέποντες σὺν αὐτοῖς ἑστῶτα τὸν τεθερα-
15 πευμένον οὐδὲν εἶχον ποιῆσαι ἢ ἀντιπεῖν. κελεύσαντες αὐτοὺς
16 ἔξω τοῦ συνεδρίου ἀπαχθῆναι συνέβαλον πρὸς ἀλλήλους | λέγοντες·
Τί ποιήσομεν τοῖς ἀνθρώποις τούτοις; ὅτι μὲν γὰρ γνωστὸν
σημεῖον †γεγονέναι† δι᾽ αὐτῶν πᾶσιν τοῖς κατοικοῦσιν Ἰερουσαλὴμ
17 φανερότερόν ἐστιν, καὶ οὐ δυνάμεθα ἀρνῖσθαι· ἵνα μὴ ἐπὶ πλέον
τι διανεμηθῇ εἰς τὸν λαόν, ἀπειλησόμεθα οὖν αὐτοῖς μηκέτι
18 λαλεῖν ἐπὶ τῷ ὀνόματι τούτῳ μηδενὶ ἀνθρώπων. συνκατα-
τιθεμένων δὲ αὐτῶν τῇ γνώμῃ φωνήσαντες αὐτοὺς παρήγγει-

14 αυτοις] αυτων   καιλευσαντες   17 επιλησομεθα
αυτοις] ουτοις

non est in alio quondam nequae aliud est nomen suc caelo quod datum est hominibus d
in quo oportet salbos fieri nos   13 intuentes vero petri fiduciam et johannis et
adsecuti quia homines sine litteris sunt admirabantur cognoscebant autem eos quia
cum ihu erant   14 hominem quoque conspicientes cum ipsis stantem illum que
curatum nihil habebant contradicere   15 cum jussissent autem eos extra consilium
habire conferebant ad invicem   16 dicentes quid faciamus hominibus istis quoniam
quidem notum signum factum est per ipsos omnibus qui inhabitant hierusalem
manifestum est et non possumus negare   17 sed ut non amplius quid serpiat in
populum comminemur ergo eis jam non loqui in nomine hoc cuiquam hominum
18 consentientibus autem omnibus notitiā vocantes eos praeceperunt illis ne omnino

quo oportet salvari nos.   13 cum au[diren]t autem omnes Petri constantiam et h
Joannis, [persu]asi quoniam homines inlitterati sunt et idio[tae, am]mirati sunt :
14 videntes autem et illum infirmū [cum ei]s stantem curatum, nihil potuerunt
facere [aut co]ntradicere.   quidam autem ex ipsis agnosce[bant e]is, quoniam cum
ihu conversabantur.   15 tunc [conlo]cuti jusserunt foras extra concilium adduci
[Petru]m et Johanem : et quaerebant ab invicem,   16 dicē[tes : qui]d faciemus
istis hominib·?   nam manifestum [signum] factum ab eis omnibus habitantib·
Hierosoly[mis app]aret, et non possumus negare.   17 sed ne plus [divulgentu]r
in populum verba istorum, comminavi[mur eis ultr]a non loqui in nomine isto
ulli hominum.   18 [consentien]tib· autem ad sententiam, denuntiaverunt

12 non est enim nomen aliud sub caelo datum hominibus, in quo oportet   Cyprian,
salvari nos.   Test. ii. 16

est aliud nomen sub caelo quod datum sit hominibus in quo oporteat salvari   Irenaeus,
nos.   iii. 12, 4
    12 [And there is] none other name [of the Lord] given under heaven whereby   Dem. of Ap.
men are saved.   Preach. 96

17 εις τον λαον] +mg a sermonibus his   18 συνκατατιθεμενων δε αυτων   Harclean
τη γνωμη] mg quum consensissent autem ad sententiam

φθέγγεσθαι μηδὲ διδάσκειν ἐπὶ τῷ ὀνόματι Ἰησοῦ. ὁ δὲ Πέτρος 19
καὶ Ἰωάννης ἀποκριθέντες εἶπαν πρὸς αὐτούς· Εἰ δίκαιόν ἐστιν
ἐνώπιον τοῦ θεοῦ ὑμῶν ἀκούειν μᾶλλον ἢ τοῦ θεοῦ κρείνατε, οὐ 20
δυνόμεθα γὰρ ἡμεῖς ἃ εἴδαμεν καὶ ἠκούσαμεν μὴ λαλεῖν. οἱ δὲ 21
προσαπειλησάμενοι ἀπέλυσαν αὐτούς, μηδὲν εὑρίσκοντες τὸ πῶς
κολάσωσιν αὐτούς, διὰ τὸν λαόν, ὅτι πάντες ἐδόξαζον τὸν θεὸν
ἐπὶ τῷ γεγονότι· ἐτῶν γὰρ ἦν πλειόνων τεσσεράκοντα ὁ ἄνθρωπος 22
ἐφ᾽ ὃν γεγόνει τὸ σημεῖον τοῦτο τῆς ἰάσεως.
Ἀπολυθέντες δὲ ἦλθον πρὸς τοὺς ἰδίους καὶ ἀπήγγειλαν 23
ὅσα πρὸς αὐτοὺς οἱ ἀρχιερεῖς καὶ οἱ πρεσβύτεροι εἶπαν. οἱ δὲ 24
ἀκούσαντες ὁμοθυμαδὸν ἦραν φωνὴν πρὸς τὸν θεὸν καὶ εἶπαν·
Δέσποτα, σὺ ὁ ποιήσας τὸν οὐρανὸν καὶ τὴν γῆν καὶ τὴν θάλασσαν
καὶ πάντα τὰ ἐν αὐτοῖς, ὁ τοῦ πατρὸς ἡμῶν διὰ πνεύματος ἁγίου 25
Ps. ii. 1 f. στόματος Δαυεὶδ παιδός σου εἰπών· Ἵνα τί ἐφρύαξαν ἔθνη καὶ

Editors   18 [του] ιησου WH   του ιησου Soden JHR   21 κολασωνται WH Soden
JHR   22 om τουτο JHR   24 συ] +[ο θεος] Soden   25 †ο του
πατρος ημων δια πνευματος αγιου στοματος† WHmg

Old Uncial   18 ιησου B   του ιησου B²(B³ Tdf)ℵA 0165 (+D)   19 ο δε πετρος BℵA
πετρος δε 0165 (cf. D)   ιωαννης Bℵ 0165 (+D)   ο ιωαννης A   ειπαν
B   ειπον ℵA(+D)   ειπεν 0165   21 κολασωσιν B   κολασωνται B²(B³ Tdf)
ℵA(+D)   23 απηγγειλαν BA(+D)   ανηγγειλαν ℵ

Antiochian   18 του ιησου PS 462 𝕾(+D)   19 προς αυτους ειπον PS 462 𝕾
21 κολασονται P 462   κολασωνται S 𝕾(+D)   24 συ] +ο θεος PS 462 𝕾(+D)
25 ο του πατρος ημων δια πνευματος αγιου στοματος δαυειδ] ο δια στοματος δαβιδ
PS 462 𝕾   του παιδος 𝕾

---

21 The reading of B κολασωσιν is supported only by 61 (codex Montfortianus). The change spoils the neat sense of the middle κολασωνται, 'have them punished.'
22 The omission of τουτο D perp gig Iren Lucif may well be original.
23 With hcl·⁜· cf. αυτοις 1874 vg.
25 The consistent reading of all the Old Uncial group, BℵA (C 81 are lacking) Athanasius, ο του πατρος ημων δια πνευματος αγιου στοματος δαυειδ παιδος σου ειπων is probably to be adopted here ; see exegetical note for Torrey's explanation from Aramaic original. To assume, as the Antiochian revisers appear to have done, that both του πατρος ημων and πνευματος αγιου were

interpolated, imputes too great ineptitude to the supposed primitive interpolator, whose text was certainly widely adopted; and the hypothesis is intrinsically too easy to be safe. Iren has the full text, but with changed position of του πατρος ημων ; vg is similar.
The 'Western' text of D (no 'African' document is here extant) excised the unintelligible του πατρος ημων, and, failing to recognize the dependence of πνευματος αγιου on στοματος, created an additional member by inserting δια του. Whether D's ⟨ε⟩λαλησας, with its noteworthy but not unsuitable position, may be original instead of B's ειπων is a question impossible to answer. The

λαν †τὸ κατὰ τὸ† μὴ φθέγγεσθαι μηδὲ διδάσκειν ἐπὶ τῷ ὀνόματι
19 τοῦ Ἰησοῦ. ἀποκρειθεὶς δὲ Πέτρος καὶ Ἰωάνης εἶπον πρὸς
αὐτούς· Εἰ δίκαιόν ἐστιν ἐνώπιον τοῦ θεοῦ ὑμῶν ἀκούειν μᾶλλον
20 ἢ τοῦ θεοῦ κρείνατε, οὐ δυνάμεθα γὰρ ἡμεῖς ἃ εἴδαμεν καὶ ἠκού-
21 σαμεν λαλεῖν. οἱ δὲ προσαπειλησάμενοι ἀπέλυσαν αὐτούς, μὴ
εὑρίσκοντες αἰτίαν τὸ πῶς κολάσωνται αὐτούς, διὰ τὸν λαόν, ὅτι
22 πάντες ἐδόξαζον τὸν θεὸν ἐπὶ τῷ γεγονότι· ἐτῶν γὰρ πλειόνων
μ̄ ἦν ὁ ἄνθρωπος ἐφ' ὃν γεγόνει τὸ σημεῖον τῆς εἰάσεως.
23 Ἀπολυθέντες δὲ ἦλθον πρὸς τοὺς ἰδίους καὶ ἀπήγγειλαν
24 ὅσα πρὸς αὐτοὺς οἱ ἀρχιερεῖς καὶ οἱ πρεσβύτεροι εἶπαν. οἱ δὲ
ἀκούσαντες καὶ ἐπιγνόντες τὴν τοῦ θεοῦ ἐνέργειαν ὁμοθυμαδὸν
ἦραν φωνὴν πρὸς τὸν θεὸν καὶ εἶπαν· Δέσποτα, σὺ ὁ θεὸς ὁ
ποιήσας τὸν οὐρανὸν καὶ τὴν γῆν καὶ τὴν θάλασσαν καὶ πάντα
25 τὰ ἐν αὐτοῖς, ὃς διὰ πνεύματος ἁγίου διὰ τοῦ στόματος <ἐ>λάλησας
Δαυειδ παιδός σου·

22 γαρ] + ην

---

loquerentur neque docerent in nomine i̅h̅u̅   19 respondens autem petrus et johannes d
dixerunt ad eos si justum est in conspectu d̅i̅ vestri audire magis quam d̅m̅ judicate
20 non possumus enim nos quae vidimus et audivimus loqui   21 ad illi etiam
comminat dimiserunt eos nihil invenientes causam qua punirent eos propter populum
quoniam omnes clarificabant d̅m̅ super quod factum est   22 annorum autem erat
plurimum xl his homo super quem factum erat hoc signum sanitatis   23 dismissi
autem venerunt ad suos et renuntiaverunt quanta ad eos pontifices et seniores
dixerunt   24 ad illi cum audissent et cognovissent d̅i̅ virtute̅ unanimiter autem
vocem levaverunt ad d̅m̅ et dixerunt dne tu es d̅s̅ qui fecisti caelum et terram et
mare et omnia quae in eis sunt   25 qui per s̅p̅m̅ sanctum per os locutus est david

---

22 annorum enim [inquit scriptura] plus quadraginta erat homo in quo Irenaeus,
factum est signum curationis.   iii. 12, 5
24 [audientes, inquit, tota.ecclesia] unanimes extulerunt vocem ad deum
et dixerunt : domine, tu es deus qui fecisti caelum et terram et mare et omnia
quae in eis,   25 qui per spiritum sanctum ore David patris nostri pueri

---

23 απηγγειλαν] annunciarunt ⁙ iis ✓   Harclean

---

versions, no one of which seems to correspond exactly to the text of D although most of them have retained the device of διὰ τοῦ στόματος, have helped themselves by various re-arrangements and slight retouchings. Apparently with a conflation, sah has *qui locutus est . . . dicens,* cf. eth and arm. The investigation of the many divergent combinations is rendered unsatisfactory because the versions exercise a legitimate freedom in order of words, and are incapable of indicating exactly the minor differences of the Greek by which the influence of the two Greek texts could be traced.

λαοὶ ἐμελέτησαν κενά; παρέστησαν οἱ βασιλεῖς τῆς γῆς καὶ οἱ 26
ἄρχοντες συνήχθησαν ἐπὶ τὸ αὐτὸ κατὰ τοῦ κυρίου καὶ κατὰ
τοῦ Χριστοῦ αὐτοῦ. συνήχθησαν γὰρ ἐπ' ἀληθείας ἐν τῇ πόλει 27
ταύτῃ ἐπὶ τὸν ἅγιον παῖδά σου Ἰησοῦν, ὃν ἔχρεισας, Ἡρῴδης
τε καὶ Πόντιος Πειλᾶτος σὺν ἔθνεσιν καὶ λαοῖς Ἰσραήλ, ποιῆσαι 28
ὅσα ἡ χείρ σου καὶ ἡ βουλὴ προώρισεν γενέσθαι. καὶ τὰ νῦν, 29
κύριε, ἔπιδε ἐπὶ τὰς ἀπειλὰς αὐτῶν, καὶ δὸς τοῖς δούλοις σου
μετὰ παρρησίας πάσης λαλεῖν τὸν λόγον σου, ἐν τῷ τὴν χεῖρα 30
ἐκτείνειν σε εἰς ἴασιν καὶ σημεῖα καὶ τέρατα γείνεσθαι διὰ
τοῦ ὀνόματος τοῦ ἁγίου παιδός σου Ἰησοῦ. καὶ δεηθέντων 31
αὐτῶν ἐσαλεύθη ὁ τόπος ἐν ᾧ ἦσαν συνηγμένοι, καὶ ἐπλήσθησαν
ἅπαντες τοῦ ἁγίου πνεύματος, καὶ ἐλάλουν τὸν λόγον τοῦ θεοῦ
μετὰ παρρησίας.

Τοῦ δὲ πλήθους τῶν πιστευσάντων ἦν καρδία καὶ ψυχὴ 32

Editors   28 βουλη] +σου Soden   30 χειρα] +σου Soden JHR   32 [η] καρδια
και [η] ψυχη Soden

Old Uncial   25 κενα B   καινα ℵA(+D)   27 πολει Bℵ(+D)   +σου A   28 βουλη
BA   +σου ℵA²(+D)   30 χειρα εκτεινειν σε B   χειρα σε εκτεινειν A   χειρα σου
εκτεινειν σε (ℵᶜ om σε) ℵℵᶜ (cf. D)   31 απαντες BAℵᶜ(+D)   παντες ℵ Pap⁸

Antiochian   27 om εν τη πολει ταυτη PS 462 ⌐   28 βουλη] +σου PS 462 ⌐(+D)
29 απειλας] βουλας S   30 χειρα] +σου PS 462 ⌐(+D)   31 του αγιου
πνευματος] πνευματος αγιου PS 462 ⌐   32 η καρδια και η ψυχη PS 462 ⌐

---

25 κενα B Antiochian. Even with
the spelling καινα ℵAD, the meaning
was vana, as in all versions.
27 For λαοις BℵAD perp gig Iren
Lucif sah (cod. B), the reading λαος E
(e populo) minn Aug. praed. sanct.
Hil is probably an ancient correction,
and may give the 'Western' text; cf.
pesh (synagoga) hcl.text (populo) sah
('the people,' codd. of cent. xii-xiii).

30 Hcl.mg attaches to the word
which renders ονοματος this note:
'Copies exist in which "name" does
not occur.' This probably relates to
Greek copies, but no such variant in
Greek or in any version is otherwise
recorded.
32 Cyprian cites not only in Test.
iii. 3, but also in De unit. 25, De op.
et el. 25, Ep. 11. 3.

26 Ἵνα τί ἐφρύ⟨α⟩ξαν ἔθνη καὶ λαοὶ ἐμελέτησαν κενά; | παρ-
έστησαν οἱ βασιλεῖς τῆς γῆς καὶ οἱ ἄρχοντες συνήχθησαν
ἐπὶ τὸ αὐτὸ κατὰ τοῦ κυρίου καὶ κατὰ τοῦ Χριστοῦ αὐτοῦ.
27 συνήχθησαν γὰρ ἐπ᾽ ἀληθείας ἐν τῇ πόλει ταύτῃ ἐπὶ τὸν ἅγιόν
σου παῖδα Ἰησοῦν, ὃν ἔχρεισας, Ἡρῴδης τε καὶ Πόντιος Πιλᾶτος
28 σὺν ἔθνεσιν καὶ λαοῖς Ἰσραήλ, ποιῆσαι ὅσα ἡ χείρ σου καὶ ἡ
29 βουλή σου προώρισεν γενέσθαι. καὶ τὰ νῦν, κύριε, ἔφιδε ἐπὶ
τὰς ἀπειλὰς αὐτῶν, καὶ δὸς τοῖς δούλοις σου μετὰ πάσης παρ-
30 ρησίας λαλεῖν τὸν λόγον σου, ἐν τῷ τὴν χεῖρά σου ἐκτείνειν ⟨ε⟩ἰς
ἴασιν καὶ σημεῖα καὶ τέρατα γενέσθαι διὰ τοῦ ὀνόματος τοῦ
31 ἁγίου παιδός σου Ἰησοῦ. καὶ δεηθέντων αὐτῶν ἐσαλεύθη ὁ
τόπος ἐν ᾧ ἦσαν συνηγμένοι, καὶ ἐπλήσθησαν ἅπαντες τοῦ ἁγίου
πνεύματος, καὶ ἐλάλουν τὸν λόγον τοῦ θεοῦ μετὰ παρρησίας
παντὶ τῷ θέλοντι πιστεύειν.

32 Τοῦ δὲ πλήθους τῶν πιστευσάντων ἦν καρδία καὶ ψυχὴ μία,

25 κενα] καινα   29 απειλας] αγιας

---

puero tuo quare fremuerunt gentes et populi meditati sunt inania   26 adsisterunt d
reges terrae et principes congregati sunt in unū adversus d̄n̄m̄ et adversus x̄p̄m̄ ejus
27 collecti sunt enim revera in civitate hac super sanctum puerum tuum īh̄m̄ quem
unxist[i] herodes vero et pontius pilatus cum gentibus et populis istrahel   28 facere
quaecumq· manus tua et voluntas t[ua] praedestinavit fieri   29 et nunc sunt d̄n̄e aspice
super minacias eorū et da servis tuis cum fiducia omni loqui verbum tuum   30 in eo
cum manum extendas ad curationē et signa et portenta fiant per nomen santi pueri
tui īh̄ū   31 et cum obsecrassent ipsi commotus est locus in quo erant collecti et
inpleti sunt omnes sancto s̄p̄ō et loquebantur verbum d̄ī cum fiducia omni volenti
credere   32 multitudinis autem eorum qui crediderunt erat cor et anima una et non

---

27 convenerunt enim universi in ista civitate adversus sanctum filium tuum,
quem unxisti, Herodes et Pilatus cum nationibus.

Tertullian,
Prax. 28 ;
cf. Bapt. 7

convenerunt enim universi] collecti sunt enim vere Bapt

---

32 turba autem eorum, qui crediderant, anima ac mente una agebant, nec

Cyprian,
Test. iii. 3
etc.

---

tui dixisti : quare fremuerunt gentes, et populi meditati sunt inania?
26 adstiterunt reges terrae, et principes congregati sunt in unum adversus
dominum et adversus Christum ejus.   27 convenerunt enim vere in civitate
hac adversus sanctum filium tuum Jesum, quem unxisti, Herodes et Pontius
Pilatus, cum gentibus et populis Israel,   28 facere quaecumque manus tua et
voluntas tua praedestinaverat fieri.

Irenaeus,
iii. 12, 5

31 commotus est [enim, inquit,] locus in quo erant collecti, et repleti sunt
omnes spiritu sancto, et loquebantur verbum dei cum fiducia omni volenti
credere.

iii. 12, 5 (c)

31 ἐσαλεύθη [γάρ, φησίν,] ὁ τόπος ἐν ᾧ ἦσαν συνηγμένοι, καὶ ἐπλήσθησαν
ἅπαντες τοῦ ἁγίου πνεύματος καὶ ἐλάλουν τὸν λόγον τοῦ θεοῦ μετὰ παρρησίας
παντὶ τῷ θέλοντι πιστεύειν.

[catena]

---

30 [See note on opposite page]   32 καρδια] cor ·※· unum ✓   Harclean

44 CODEX VATICANUS

μία, καὶ οὐδὲ εἷς τι τῶν ὑπαρχόντων αὐτῷ ἔλεγον ἴδιον εἶναι, ἀλλ᾽ ἦν αὐτοῖς πάντα κοινά. καὶ δυνάμει μεγάλῃ ἀπεδίδουν τὸ 33 μαρτύριον οἱ ἀπόστολοι τοῦ κυρίου Ἰησοῦ τῆς ἀναστάσεως, χάρις τε μεγάλη ἦν ἐπὶ πάντας αὐτούς. οὐδὲ γὰρ ἐνδεὴς ἦν τις 34 ἐν αὐτοῖς· ὅσοι γὰρ κτήτορες χωρίων ἢ οἰκιῶν ὑπῆρχον, πω- λοῦντες ἔφερον τὰς τειμὰς τῶν πιπρασκομένων | καὶ ἐτίθουν 35 παρὰ τοὺς πόδας τῶν ἀποστόλων· διεδίδετο δὲ ἑκάστῳ καθότι ἄν τις χρείαν εἶχεν. Ἰωσὴφ δὲ ὁ ἐπικληθεὶς Βαρνάβας ἀπὸ 36 τῶν ἀποστόλων, ὅ ἐστιν ἑρμηνευόμενον υἱὸς παρακλήσεως, Λευείτης, Κύπριος τῷ γένει, | ὑπάρχοντος αὐτῷ ἀγροῦ πωλήσας 37 ἤνεγκεν τὸ χρῆμα καὶ ἔθηκεν παρὰ τοὺς πόδας τῶν ἀποστόλων.

Ἀνὴρ δέ τις Ἁνανίας ὀνόματι σὺν Σαπφείρῃ τῇ γυναικὶ V αὐτοῦ ἐπώλησεν κτῆμα | καὶ ἐνοσφίσατο ἀπὸ τῆς τιμῆς, συν- 2 ιδυίης καὶ τῆς γυναικός, καὶ ἐνέγκας μέρος τι παρὰ τοὺς πόδας

Editors   32 ελεγεν WH Soden JHR   παντα] απαντα Soden   33 της
αναστασεως του κυριου ιησου Soden JHR   34 τις ην WH Soden JHR
36 ερμηνευομενον] μεθερμηνευομενον WH Soden JHR

Cld Uncial   32 αυτω BℵA   αυτου Pap⁸(+D)   ελεγον B   ελεγεν ℵA Pap⁸(+D)
παντα B Pap⁸(+D)   απαντα ℵA   33 το μαρτυριον οι αποστολοι Bℵ Pap⁸(+D)
οι αποστολοι το μαρτυριον A   του κυριου ιησου της αναστασεως B   της
αναστασεως του κυριου ιησου Pap⁸ (cf. D)   της αναστασεως ιησου χριστου του κυριου
ℵA (cf. D)   34 ην τις B   τις ην ℵA   τις υπηρχεν Pap⁸(+D)   υπηρχον
BAℵᶜ Pap⁸(+D)   om ℵ   35 δε BℵA(+D)   om Pap⁸   36 ερμηνευομενον B
μεθερμηνευομενον ℵA Pap⁸ ᵛⁱᵈ(+D)   37 παρα BA(+D)   προς ℵ
1 ανανιας ονοματι Bℵ   ονοματι ανανιας A(+D)

Antiochian   32 αυτω] αυτων P 462   ελεγον] ελεγεν PS 462 ϛ(+D)   παντα]
απαντα PS 462 ϛ   33 μεγαλη δυναμει PS 462 ϛ   της αναστασεως του
κυριου ιησου PS 462 ϛ(cf. D)   34 ην τις] τις υπηρχεν PS 462 ϛ(+D)
35 καθοτι αν] καθο PS   36 ιωσης PS 462 ϛ   απο] υπο ϛ(+D)
ερμηνευομενον] μεθερμηνευομενον (-os S) PS 462 ϛ(+D)   37 αυτω] αυτου 462
2 γυναικος] +αυτου PS 462 ϛ

32 Tertullian, apol. 39, itaque qui animo animaque miscemur, nihil de rei communicatione dubitamus. omnia indiscreta sunt apud nos praeter uxores, may be a reminiscence of the 'Western' text of this verse.
33 The original reading was απεδιδουν το μαρτυριον οι αποστολοι της αναστασεως του κυριου ιησου Pap⁸ (cent. iv.) Antiochian sah, with της αναστασεως taken as dependent on μαρτυριον. This was doubtless the Greek which underlay

the 'Western' text, as in perp gig Iren (Aug. serm. 356). In B alone (the support from Chrys. Hom. xi.— note the longer phrase with χριστου— is probably a coincidence) the order of the last two phrases was reversed so as to connect του κυριου ιησου with αποστολοι. In a revised text, seen in ℵ, ιησου χριστου του κυριου was substituted for the simpler του κυριου ιησου, and in AE minn vg the text suffered further by the change of order

καὶ οὐκ ἦν διάκρισις ἐν αὐτοῖς οὐδεμία, καὶ οὐδείς ‹τι› τῶν
ὑπαρχόντων αὐτοῦ ἔλεγεν ἴδιον εἶναι, ἀλλὰ ἦν αὐτοῖς πάντα
33 κοινά. καὶ δυνάμει μεγάλῃ ἀπεδίδουν τὸ μαρτύριον οἱ ἀπόστολοι
τῆς ἀναστάσεως τοῦ κυρίου Ἰησοῦ Χριστοῦ, χάρις τε μεγάλη
34 ἦν ἐπὶ πάντας αὐτούς. οὐδὲ γὰρ ἐνδεής τις ὑπῆρχεν ἐν αὐτοῖς·
ὅσοι γὰρ κτήτορες ἦσαν χωρίων ἢ οἰκειῶν †ὑπῆρχον†, πωλοῦντες
35 [κ]αὶ φέροντες τειμὰς τῶν πιπρασκό[ντ]ων | καὶ ἐτίθουν παρὰ
τοὺς πόδας τῶν ἀποστόλων· διεδίδετο δὲ ἑνὶ ἑκάστῳ καθότι
36 ἄν τις χρείαν εἶχεν. Ἰωσὴφ δὲ ὁ ἐπικληθεὶς Βαρνάβας ὑπὸ
τῶν ἀποστόλων, ὅ ἐστιν μεθερμηνευόμενον υἱὸς παρακλήσεως,
37 Κύπριος, Λευείτης τῷ γένει, | ὑπάρχοντος αὐτῷ χωρίου πωλήσας
ἤνεγκε τὸ χρῆμα καὶ ἔθηκεν παρὰ τοὺς πόδας τῶν ἀποστόλων.
v Ἀνὴρ δέ τις ὀνόματι Ἀνανίας σὺν Σαφφύρᾳ τῇ γυναικὶ αὐτοῦ
2 ἐπώλησεν κτῆμα | καὶ ἐνοσφίσατο ἐκ τῆς τιμῆς, συνειδυίας καὶ
τῆς γυναικός, καὶ ἐνέγκας μέρος τι παρὰ τοὺς πόδας τῶν ἀπο-

37 χωριον   2 γυναικαικος

erat accusatio in eis ulla et nemo quicquam ex eo quod possidebant dicebant suum d
esse sed erant eis omnia communia   33 et virtute magna reddebant testim apostoli
resurrectionem d̄n̄i ī h̄u x̄p̄i gratia magna erat super eos omnes   34 nec enim inosp
quisquam erat in eis quodquod possessores erant praediorum aut domum vendentes
et adferebant praetia quae veniebant   35 et ponebant ad pedes apostolorum dis-
tribuebantur vero singulis secundum cuique opus erat   36 joseph autem qui
cognominatus est barnabas ab apostolis quod est interpraetatum filius exhorationis
cyprius levita genere   37 cum esset ei ager venundato eo adtulit hanc pecuniam et
posuit juxta pedes apostolorum
    1 quidam autem vir nomine ananias cum sapphira uxore sua vendidit pos-
sessione   2 et subtraxit de praetio conscia uxore sua et cum adtulissent partem

fuit inter illos discrimen ullum, nec quicquam suum judicabant ex bonis, quae Cyprian,
eis erant, sed fuerunt illis omnia communia.   Test. iii. 3;
Deop. et el.25

33 virtute [enim] magna [inquit] reddebant testimonium apostoli resurrec- Irenaeus,
tionis domini Jesu.   iii. 12, 5 (6)

απεδιδουν οι αποστολοι το μαρτυριον. D
preserves the original text, with only
the addition of χριστου at the end.
The Antiochian here followed the true
text, not the revised form.
    The difference in the form of the
name is the index of the most important bifurcation of the text. If this
guide be followed, the witnesses fall
into two groups: (1) Pap⁸ B, 'Western,'

Antiochian, sah ; (2) ℵ, AE minn vg.
Within each group subordinate modifications took place. Between the
two forms of the name the tendency
to expand is a more significant
transcriptional motive to be taken
as text-critical guide than a supposed
disposition to alter the unusual, but
wholly unexceptionable, phrase ιησου
χριστου του κυριου.

τῶν ἀποστόλων ἔθηκεν. εἶπεν δὲ ὁ Πέτρος· Ἀνανία, διὰ τί 3
ἐπλήρωσεν ὁ Σατανᾶς τὴν καρδίαν σου ψεύσασθαί σε τὸ πνεῦμα
τὸ ἅγιον καὶ νοσφίσασθαι ἀπὸ τῆς τιμῆς τοῦ χωρίου; οὐχὶ μένον 4
σοὶ ἔμενεν καὶ πραθὲν ἐν τῇ σῇ ἐξουσίᾳ ὑπῆρχεν; τί ὅτι ἔθου ἐν
τῇ καρδίᾳ σου τὸ πρᾶγμα τοῦτο; οὐκ ἐψεύσω ἀνθρώποις ἀλλὰ
τῷ θεῷ. ἀκούων δὲ ὁ Ἀνανίας τοὺς λόγους τούτους πεσὼν 5
ἐξέψυξεν· καὶ ἐγένετο φόβος μέγας ἐπὶ πάντας τοὺς ἀκούοντας.
ἀναστάντες δὲ οἱ νεώτεροι συνέστειλαν αὐτὸν καὶ ἐξενέγκαντες 6
ἔθαψαν. ἐγένετο δὲ ὡς ὡρῶν τριῶν διάστημα καὶ ἡ γυνὴ αὐτοῦ 7
μὴ εἰδυῖα τὸ γεγονὸς εἰσῆλθεν. ἀπεκρίθη δὲ πρὸς αὐτὴν Πέτρος· 8
Εἰπέ μοι, εἰ τοσούτου τὸ χωρίον ἀπέδοσθε; ἡ δὲ εἶπεν· Ναί,
τοσούτου. ὁ δὲ Πέτρος πρὸς αὐτήν· Τί ὅτι συνεφωνήθη ὑμῖν 9
πειράσαι τὸ πνεῦμα κυρίου; ἰδοὺ οἱ πόδες τῶν θαψάντων τὸν
ἄνδρα σου ἐπὶ τῇ θύρᾳ καὶ ἐξοίσουσίν σε. ἔπεσεν δὲ παραχρῆμα 10
πρὸς τοὺς πόδας αὐτοῦ καὶ ἐξέψυξεν· εἰσελθόντες δὲ οἱ νεανίσκοι
εὗρον αὐτὴν νεκράν, καὶ ἐξενέγκαντες ἔθαψαν πρὸς τὸν ἄνδρα
αὐτῆς. καὶ ἐγένετο φόβος μέγας ἐφ' ὅλην τὴν ἐκκλησίαν καὶ ἐπὶ 11
πάντας τοὺς ἀκούοντας ταῦτα.

Διά τε τῶν χειρῶν τῶν ἀποστόλων ἐγείνετο σημεῖα καὶ τέρατα 12

Editors 8 [ο] πετρος Soden 10 προς] παρα Soden mg 12 τε] δε
WH Soden JHR

Old Uncial 3 δια BℵA(+D) om Pap⁸ vid επληρωσεν BA Pap⁸ ℵᶜ(+D) επηρωσεν ℵ
5 τους 2° BℵA(+D) om Pap⁸ 7 ως BAℵᶜ(+D) εως ℵ γεγονος
BℵA(+D) γεγονοτ[ ] Pap⁸ 8 πετρος BℵA ο πετρος Pap⁸ vid (+D)
ναι Bℵ(+D) om A 9 πετρος Bℵ(+D) +ειπε A τι BAℵᶜ(+D)
+ουν ℵ τη θυρα Bℵ(+D) ταις θυραις A 11 επι Bℵ(+D) om A
12 τε B δε ℵA(+D)

Antiochian 3 om ο before πετρος PS 462 ϛ(+D) νοσφισασθαι] +σε PS 462 (+D)
4 om εν 1° P 5 om ο before ανανιας ϛ(+D) ακουοντας] +ταυτα
PS 462 ϛ 8 προς αυτην] αυτη PS 462 ϛ ο πετρος PS 462 ϛ(+D)
9 πετρος] +ειπε PS 462 ϛ 10 προς 1°] παρα PS 462 ϛ αυτου] αυτων S
νεανισκοι] νεωτεροι 462 11 ακουοντας] κατοικουντας P 12 τε] δε
PS 462 ϛ(+D) εγενετο Sϛ

3 With hcl ⁎ cf. the addition of
προς αυτον in E minn versions.
For επληρωσεν (επηρωσεν ℵ) vg reads
temtavit, and is supported (επειρασεν) by
Athanasius, Epiphanius, Didymus, but
by no Greek ms. Theodoret twice
quotes the verse with ηπατησεν for
επληρωσεν.
3, 4 Cyprian, test. iii. 30, has as

substitute for και νοσφισασθαι . . .
υπηρχεν only the words cum esset
fundus in tua potestate. No explanation of this text is forthcoming.
Valerian of Cimiez (c. 450), hom.
4, used the Testimonia, and has the
reading. Augustine, c. litt. Petil. iii.
48 (58), and Ambrosiaster, quaest. vet.
et novi test. 97, curiously agree in break-

3 στόλων ἔθετο. εἶπεν δὲ Πέτρος πρὸς Ἀνανίαν· Διὰ τί ἐπλήρωσεν
ὁ Σατανᾶς τὴν καρδίαν σου ψεύσασθαί σε τὸ ἅγιον πνεῦμα καὶ
4 νοσφίσασθαί σε ἀπὸ τῆς τειμῆς τοῦ χωρίου; οὐχὶ μένον σοὶ
ἔμενεν καὶ πραθὲν ἐν τῇ ἐξουσίᾳ ὑπῆρχεν; τί ὅτι ἔθου ἐν τῇ
καρδίᾳ σου ποιῆσαι πονηρὸν τοῦτο; οὐκ ἐψεύσω ἀνθρώποις ἀλλὰ
5 τῷ θεῷ. ἀκούσας δὲ Ἀνανίας τοὺς λόγους τούτους παραχρῆμα
πεσὼν ἐξέψυξεν· καὶ ἐγένετο φόβος μέγας ἐπὶ πάντας τοὺς ἀκούον-
6 τας. ἀναστάντες δὲ οἱ νεώτεροι συνέστιλαν αὐτὸν καὶ ἐξενέγκαντες
7 ἔθαψαν. ἐγένετο δὲ ὡς ὡρῶν γ̄ διάστημα καὶ ἡ γυνὴ αὐτοῦ
8 μὴ ἰδυῖα τὸ γεγονὸς εἰσῆλθεν. εἶπεν δὲ πρὸς αὐτὴν ὁ Πέτρος·
Ἐπερωτήσω σε εἰ ἄρα τὸ χωρίον τοσούτου ἀπέδοσθε. ἡ δὲ εἶπεν·
9 Ναί, τοσούτου. ὁ δὲ Πέτρος ⟨πρὸς⟩ αὐτήν· Τί ὅτι †συνεφώνησεν†
ὑμεῖν πειράσαι τὸ πνεῦμα τοῦ κυρίου; ἰδοὺ οἱ πόδες τῶν θαψάν-
10 των τὸν ἄνδρα σου ἐπὶ τῇ θύρᾳ καὶ ἐξοίσουσίν σε. καὶ ἔπεσεν
παραχρῆμα πρὸς τοὺς πόδας αὐτοῦ καὶ ἐξέψυξεν· εἰσελθόντες δὲ
οἱ νεανίσκοι εὗρον αὐτὴν νεκράν, καὶ συνστείλαντες ἐξήνεγκαν
11 καὶ ἔθαψαν πρὸς τὸν ἄνδρα αὐτῆς. καὶ ἐγένετο φόβος μέγας ἐφ᾽
ὅλην τὴν ἐκκλησίαν καὶ ἐπὶ πάντας τοὺς ἀκούοντας ταῦτα.
12 Διὰ δὲ τῶν χειρῶν τῶν ἀποστόλων ἐγείνετο σημεῖα καὶ τέρατα

4 μενον] μεσον	εψευσου	7 διαστεμα
8 δε 2°] δη	11 ακουοντες	

quandam juxta pedes apostolorum posuit 3 dixit autem petrus ad ananian ut quid d
adinplevit satanas cor tuum mentiri te spiritui sancto et intercipere te ex praetium
praedii 4 nonne manens tibi manebat et destractum in tua potestate erat quid
utique posuisti in corde tuo facere dolose rem istam non es mentitus hominibus sed
dō 5 audies autem ananias sermones hos subito cum cecidisset obriguit et factus
est timor magnus super omnes qui audiebant 6 cum surrexissent autem jubenes
involuerunt eū et cum extulissent sepelierunt 7 factum est quasi horarum trium
spatium et uxor ejus nesciens quod factum erat introibit 8 dixit autem ad eam
petrus dic mihi si tanti praedium vendedistis et illa dixit etiam tantum 9 petrus
vero ad eam quid utique convenit vobis teptare spm dni ecce pedes eorum qui
sepelierunt virum tuū ad ostium et efferen te 10 et ceciditque confestim ad pedes
ejus et perobriguit cumque introissent jubenes invenerunt eam mortuam et cum
extulissent sepelierunt ad virum suum 11 et factus est timor magnus super totam
ecclesiam et super omnes qui audierunt haec 12 per manus vero apostolorum

3 inplevit Satanas cor tuum mentiri te aput spiritum sanctum, 4 cum Cyprian,
esset fundus in tua potestate. non hominibus mentitus es, sed deo. *Test.* iii. 30

3 προς ανανιαν] ⁘ ad eum ✓ Anania   8 προς αυτην⌋ ⁘ ei ✓ Harclean
10 αυτου] mg ejus

ing off their quotation at just this   *Testimonia.* Moreover, Augustine may
point, and may have been using the   be dependent on Ambrosiaster.

48 CODEX VATICANUS

πολλὰ ἐν τῷ λαῷ· καὶ ἦσαν ὁμοθυμαδὸν πάντες ἐν τῇ Στοᾷ
Σολομῶνος· τῶν δὲ λοιπῶν οὐθεὶς ἐτόλμα κολλᾶσθαι αὐτοῖς· 13
ἀλλ᾽ ἐμεγάλυνεν αὐτοὺς ὁ λαός, | μᾶλλον δὲ προσετίθεντο πι- 14
στεύοντες τῷ κυρίῳ πλήθη ἀνδρῶν τε καὶ γυναικῶν· ὥστε καὶ 15
εἰς τὰς πλατείας ἐκφέρειν τοὺς ἀσθενεῖς καὶ τιθέναι ἐπὶ κλιναρίων
καὶ κραβάττων, ἵνα ἐρχομένου Πέτρου κἂν ἡ σκιὰ ἐπισκιάσει
τινὶ αὐτῶν. συνήρχετο δὲ καὶ τὸ πλῆθος τῶν πέριξ πόλεων 16
Ἰερουσαλήμ, φέροντες ἀσθενεῖς καὶ ὀχλουμένους ὑπὸ πνευμάτων
ἀκαθάρτων, οἵτινες ἐθεραπεύοντο ἅπαντες.

Ἀναστὰς δὲ ὁ ἀρχιερεὺς καὶ πάντες οἱ σὺν αὐτῷ, ἡ οὖσα 17
αἵρεσις τῶν Σαδδουκαίων, ἐπλήσθησαν ζήλους | καὶ ἐπέβαλον 18
τὰς χεῖρας ἐπὶ τοὺς ἀποστόλους καὶ ἔθεντο αὐτοὺς ἐν τηρήσει
δημοσίᾳ. ἄγγελος δὲ κυρίου διὰ νυκτὸς ἤνοιξε τὰς θύρας τῆς 19
φυλακῆς, ἐξαγαγὼν δὲ αὐτοὺς εἶπεν· Πορεύεσθε καὶ σταθέντες 20
λαλεῖτε ἐν τῷ ἱερῷ τῷ λαῷ πάντα τὰ ῥήματα τῆς ζωῆς ταύτης.
ἀκούσαντες δὲ εἰσῆλθον ὑπὸ τὸν ὄρθρον εἰς τὸ ἱερὸν καὶ ἐδίδασκον. 21
παραγενόμενοι δὲ ὁ ἀρχιερεὺς καὶ οἱ σὺν αὐτῷ συνεκάλεσαν τὸ
συνέδριον καὶ πᾶσαν τὴν γερουσίαν τῶν υἱῶν Ἰσραήλ, καὶ ἀπέστειλαν εἰς τὸ δεσμωτήριον ἀχθῆναι αὐτούς. οἱ δὲ παραγενό- 22
μενοι ὑπηρέται οὐχ εὖρον αὐτοὺς ἐν τῇ φυλακῇ, ἀναστρέψαντες
δὲ ἀπήγγειλαν | λέγοντες ὅτι Τὸ δεσμωτήριον εὕρομεν κεκλει- 23

Editors   12 παντες] απαντες Soden   16 πολεων] +[εις] Soden   17 ζηλου
WH Soden JHR   18 χειρας] +[αυτων] Soden   19 ανοιξας Soden
δε 2º] τε WH Soden JHR   21 παραγενομενος WH Soden JHR
23 το] +[μεν] Soden

Old Uncial   12 παντες ΒΑ   απαντες ℵ(+D)   14 πιστευοντες Βℵ(+D)   οι πιστευοντες Α
15 κλιναριων Βℵ(+D)   των κλιναριων Α   αυτων ΒΑℵ^c(+D)   αυτω ℵ
17 ζηλους Β   ζηλου ℵΑ(+D)   18 επεβαλον Βℵ(+D)   επεβαλλον Α
19 νυκτος ΒℵΑ(+D)   της νυκτος ℵ^c   ηνοιξε Β   ανοιξας ℵΑ   δε 2º Β
τε ℵΑ(+D)   21 παραγενομενοι Β   παραγενομενος Β²ℵΑ(+D)

Antiochian   12 εν τω λαω πολλα PS 462 𝕾   παντες] απαντες PS 462 𝕾(+D)
15 και εις] κατα PS 462 𝕾 (cf. D)   κλιναριων] κλινων PS 462 𝕾   επισκιαση
PS𝕾(+D)   16 πολεων] +εις PS 462 𝕾(+D)   17 ζηλου PS 462 𝕾(+D)
18 χειρας] +αυτων PS 462 𝕾   19 της νυκτος PS 462 𝕾   δε 2º] τε
PS 462 𝕾(+D)   21 παραγενομενος PS 462 𝕾(+D)   22 υπηρεται
παραγενομενοι PS 462 𝕾(+D)   23 το] +μεν PS 462 𝕾

---

17 For αναστας perp has 'Annas'
(cf. vg. cod. ardm.), clearly primitive,
but wrong.
21 For ακουσαντες δε the reading εξ-

ελθοντες δε εκ της φυλακης E e, and similarly pesh arm, is probably a bit of
'Western' text not elsewhere preserved.

πολλὰ ἐν τῷ λαῷ· καὶ ἦσαν ὁμοθυμαδὸν ἅπαντες ἐν τῷ ἱερῷ ἐν
13 τῇ στοᾷ τῇ Σολομῶνος· καὶ οὐδεὶς τῶν λοιπῶν ἐτόλμα κολλᾶσθαι
14 αὐτοῖς· ἀλλ' ἐμεγάλυνεν αὐτοὺς ὁ λαός, μᾶλλον δὲ προσετίθεντο
15 πιστεύοντες τῷ κυρίῳ πλήθη ἀνδρῶν τε καὶ γυναικῶν· ὥστε
κατὰ πλατείας ἐκφέρειν τοὺς ἀσθενεῖς αὐτῶν καὶ τιθέναι ἐπὶ
κλιναρίων καὶ κραβάττων, ἵνα ἐρχομένου Πέτρου κἂν ἡ σκιὰ
ἐπισκιάσῃ τινὶ αὐτῶν· ἀπηλλάσσοντο γὰρ ἀπὸ πάσης ἀσθενίας
16 ὡς εἶχεν ἕκαστος αὐτῶν. συνήρχετο δὲ πλῆθος τῶν πέρι<ξ>
πόλεων εἰς Ἰερουσαλήμ, φέροντες ἀσθενεῖς καὶ ὀχλουμένους
ἀπὸ πνευμάτων ἀκαθάρτων, καὶ εἰῶντο πάντες.
17 Ἀναστὰς δὲ ὁ ἀρχιερεὺς καὶ πάντες οἱ σὺν αὐτῷ, ἡ οὖσα
18 αἵρεσις τῶν Σαδδουκαίων, ἐπλήσθησαν ζήλου | καὶ ἐπέβαλον τὰς
χεῖρας ἐπὶ τοὺς ἀποστόλους καὶ ἔθεντο αὐτοὺς ἐν τηρήσει δημοσίᾳ·
19 καὶ ἐπορεύθη εἷς ἕκαστος εἰς τὰ ἴδια. τότε διὰ νυκτὸς ἄγγελος
κυρίου ἀνέῳξεν τὰς θύρας τῆς φυλακῆς, ἐξαγαγών τε αὐτοὺς
20 εἶπεν· Πορεύεσθε καὶ σταθέντες λαλεῖτε ἐν τῷ ἱερῷ τῷ λαῷ
21 πάντα τὰ ῥήματα τῆς ζωῆς ταύτης. ἀκούσαντες δὲ εἰσῆλθον
ὑπὸ τὸν ὄρθρον εἰς τὸ ἱερὸν καὶ ἐδίδασκον. παραγενόμενος δὲ
ὁ ἀρχιερεὺς καὶ οἱ σὺν αὐτῷ, ἐγερθέντες τὸ πρωὶ καὶ συν-
καλεσάμενοι τὸ συνέδριον καὶ πᾶσαν τὴν γερουσίαν τῶν υἱῶν
Ἰσραήλ, καὶ ἀπέστειλαν εἰς τὸ δεσμωτήριον ἀχθῆναι αὐτούς.
22 οἱ δὲ ὑπηρέται παραγενόμενοι καὶ ἀνοίξαντες τὴν φυλακὴν οὐκ
23 εὗρον αὐτοὺς ἔσω· ἀναστρέψαντες καὶ ἀπήγγειλαν | λέγοντες ὅτι

14 πληθι   18 ηθεντο   19 ανεωξαν   20 λαλειται
22 ανυξαντες

fiebant signa et portenta multa in populo et erant pariter universi in tem in porticum d
solomonis 13 nec quisquam ex ceteris curabat adherere eis sed magnificabat eos
populos 14 magisque adiciebantur credentes dnomultitudo virorumque et mulierum
15 ita ut in plateis inferrent infirmos eorum et ponerent in lectulis et grabattis ut
venientis petri vel umbra inumbraret quemcumque illorum et liverabantur ab omnem
valetudinem quem habebant unus quisque eorum 16 conveniebat vero multitudo
finium undique in hierusalem ferentes infirmos et qui vexabantur ab spiritibus in
mundis qui curabantur universi 17 cum surrexisset autem pontifex et omnes qui
cum ipso quae est secta sadducaeorum inpleti sunt aepulationem 18 et miserunt
manus in apostolos et posuerunt eos in adservatione publica et abierunt unus quisque
in domicilia 19 per nocte vero angelus dni aperuit januas carceris cumque dixisset
eos dixit 20 ite et stantes loquimini in templo populo omnia verba vitae ejus
21 cum audissent autem introierunt sub antelucē in templum et docebant cumque
venisset pontifex et qui cum ipso exurgentes ante lucem et convocaverunt concilium
et omnem senatum filiorum istrahel et miserunt ad carcerem adduci eos 22 ministri
vero cum venissent et aperuissent carcerem non invenerunt eos intus reversi sunt et

22 και ανοιξαντες την φυλακην] ⁙ aperuerunt carcerem ✓   Harclean

σμένον ἐν πάσῃ ἀσφαλείᾳ καὶ τοὺς φύλακας ἐστῶτας ἐπὶ τῶν θυρῶν, ἀνοίξαντες δὲ ἔσω οὐδένα εὔρομεν. ὡς δὲ ἤκουσαν τοὺς 24 λόγους τούτους ὅ τε στρατηγὸς τοῦ ἱεροῦ καὶ οἱ ἀρχιερεῖς, διηπόρουν περὶ αὐτῶν τί ἂν γένοιτο τοῦτο. παραγενόμενος δέ τις 25 ἀπήγγειλεν αὐτοῖς ὅτι Ἰδοὺ οἱ ἄνδρες οὓς ἔθεσθε ἐν τῇ φυλακῇ εἰσὶν ἐν τῷ ἱερῷ ἐστῶτες καὶ διδάσκοντες τὸν λαόν. τότε 26 ἀπελθὼν ὁ στρατηγὸς σὺν τοῖς ὑπηρέταις ἦγεν αὐτούς, οὐ μετὰ βίας, ἐφοβοῦντο γὰρ τὸν λαόν, μὴ λιθασθῶσιν. ἀγαγόντες δὲ 27 αὐτοὺς ἔστησαν ἐν τῷ συνεδρίῳ. καὶ ἐπηρώτησεν αὐτοὺς ὁ ἀρχιερεὺς | λέγων· Παραγγελίᾳ παρηγγείλαμεν ὑμῖν μὴ διδά- 28 σκειν ἐπὶ τῷ ὀνόματι τούτῳ, καὶ ἰδοὺ πεπληρώκατε τὴν Ἰερουσαλὴμ τῆς διδαχῆς ὑμῶν, καὶ βούλεσθε ἐπαγαγεῖν ἐφ᾽ ἡμᾶς τὸ αἷμα τοῦ ἀνθρώπου τούτου. ἀποκριθεὶς δὲ Πέτρος καὶ οἱ ἀπό- 29

25 εθεσθαι

Editors

26 ηγαγεν Soden   28 παραγγελια] ου παραγγελια Soden JHR

Old Uncial

24 τι ΒΑℵᶜ(+D)   το τι ℵ   25 οι ΒΑℵᶜ(+D)   om ℵ   εστωτες
και ΒΑℵᶜ(+D)   om ℵ (ℵᵃ suppl εστωτες)   26 ηγεν Βℵ   ηγαγεν Α (cf. D)
μη Βℵ(+D)   ινα μη Α   28 παραγγελια ΒℵΑ   ου παραγγελια ℵᶜ(+D)
διδασκειν Βℵ(+D)   λαλειν Α   πεπληρωκατε Β(+D)   επληρωσατε ℵΑ

Antiochian

23 φυλακας] +εξω ς̄   επι] προ PS 462 ς̄   24 ο τε] +ιερευς και ο
PS 462 ς̄   25 αυτοις] +λεγων ς̄   26 ηγαγεν PS 462 ς̄ (cf. D)
μη] ινα μη PS 462 ς̄   28 παραγγελια] ου παραγγελια PS 462 ς̄(+D)
ημας] υμας S   29 ο πετρος ς̄ (cf. D)

---

23 In D ενκλεκλεισμενον the first two letters are by dittography from the preceding ευρομεν.

26 D omits ου ; h probably had *non vero* (αλλ ου). Perhaps ου was omitted by oversight in the process of deleting αλλ.

φοβουμενοι γαρ D is conflation ; h *mettues* (for *metuens*) translates φοβουμενος.

27 For εν, h and pesh seem to have followed a text which read εμπροσθεν.

h *praetor* for αρχιερευς may have in mind a Roman trial, but possibly (cf. iv. 1) his text read ο στρατηγος. D ιερευς is probably due to the influence of the Latin (cf. gig Lucif), the oldest form of which often translated ἀρχιερεύς by *sacerdos* ; see Zahn, *Urausgabe*, p. 177.

28 επηρωτησεν, vs. 27, seems to imply the presence before παραγγελια of ου D h (*non*)ː perp e (*nonne*) sah Antiochian pesh. But the text of h pesh, perhaps

from the feeling that even so the utterance was not properly called a question, seems to have read ηρξατο λεγειν προς αυτους for επηρωτησεν αυτους.

D omits και before ιδου. Probably υμεις δε, represented in h pesh, has been omitted in D to conform to the ordinary text, but without restoring και.

28, 29 The rendering of vs. 29 in h Aug. *c. Crescon.* i. 8 (11) doubtless correctly represents the 'Western' text. Gig has the same, but with some conformation to the B-text : *respondens autem petrus et apostoli dixerunt : utrum oportet obaudire, deo an hominibus ? at ille dixit : deo. et petrus ait ad illos.* Of this Lucifer has *utrum* and *deo an hominibus.* Six vulgate codices have retained the sentence *at illi dixerunt : deo* ; and a single trace in e (*an* for *quam*) caught the keen eye of Bede ("interrogative legitur in Graeco ").

Τὸ δεσμωτήριον εὕρομεν ἐνκεκλεισμένον ἐν πάσῃ ἀσφαλίᾳ
καὶ τοὺς φύλακας ἑστῶτας ἐπὶ τῶν θυρῶν, ἀνοίξαντες δὲ ἔσω
24 οὐδένα εὕρομεν. ὡς δὲ ἤκουσαν τοὺς λόγους τούτους ὅ τε
στρατηγὸς τοῦ ἱεροῦ καὶ οἱ ἀρχιερεῖς, διηπόρουν περὶ αὐτῶν τί
25 ἂν γένηται τοῦτο. παραγενόμενος δέ τις ἀπήγγειλεν αὐτοῖς ὅτι
᾽Ιδοὺ οἱ ἄνδρες οὓς ἔθεσθε ἐν τῇ φυλακῇ εἰσὶν ἐν τῷ ἱερῷ ἑστῶτες
26 καὶ διδάσκοντες τὸν λαόν. τότε ἀπελθὼν ὁ στρατηγὸς σὺν τοῖς
ὑπηρέταις ἤγαγον αὐτοὺς μετὰ βίας, φοβούμενοι †γὰρ† τὸν
27 λαόν, μὴ λιθασθῶσιν· ἀγαγόντες δὲ αὐτοὺς ἔστησαν ἐν τῷ συν-
28 εδρίῳ. καὶ ἐπηρώτησεν αὐτοὺς ὁ ἱερεὺς | λέγων· Οὐ παραγγελίᾳ
παρηγγείλαμεν ὑμεῖν μὴ διδάσκειν ἐπὶ τῷ ὀνόματι τούτῳ;
ἰδοὺ πεπληρώκατε τὴν ᾽Ιερουσαλὴμ τῆς διδαχῆς ὑμῶν, καὶ βού-
29 λεσθε ἐπαγαγεῖν ἐφ᾽ ἡμᾶς τὸ αἷμα τοῦ ἀνθρώπου ἐκείνου | πειθ-
30 αρχεῖν δὲ θεῷ μᾶλλον ἢ ἀνθρώποις. ὁ δὲ Πέτρος εἶπεν πρὸς

23 ενκλεκλεισμενον   28 βουλεσθαι εφαγαγειν

---

renuntiaverunt   23 dicentes quia carcerem invenimus clusum in omni diligentia et d
ugiles stantes ad ostium aperientes intus neminem invenimus   24 ut vero audierunt
sermones hos praetorque templi et ipsi pontefices haesitabant de eis quidnam fieret
de hoc   25 cum venisset autem quidam adnuntiavit eis quia ecce viri quos posuistis
in carcerem sunt in templo stantes et docentes populum   26 tunc cum abisset ipse
praetor cum ministris deducebant eos cum vim timebant enim populum ne lapi-
darentur   27 cumque adduxissent eos statuerunt in concilio et interrogavit eos
pontefix   28 dicens denuntiatione praecepimus vobis non docere in nomine hoc ecce
inplestis hierusalem doctrine vestra et vultis adducere super nos sanguinem hominis
hujus obtemperare   29 do oportet magis quam honibus   30 petrus vero respondit

---

22 [. . . . .] verunt   23 dicentes: quoniam pignarium in[venimus] clausum h
in omni firmitate, et custodes stan[tes ante] ostia : cum aperuiesmus autem,
neminem.in[venimus].   24 et quomodo audierunt verba ista magistrat[us templi]
et pontifices, confundebantur de ipsis quidn[am illud] esset,   25 adveniens autem
quidam nuntiavit [eis, dicens] : quoniam ecce viri quos misistis in custodi[am,
in tem]plo sunt, stantes et docentes populum.   26 tu[nc abiit] magistratus cum
ministris, et abduxit eos, n[on vero] per vi, mettues ne forte lapiraretur a popul[o.
27 et quo]modo perduxerunt eos in conspectu conci[lii, incepit] ad eos praetor
dicere :   28 non praecepto prae[cepimus] vobis ne umquam in hoc nomine
doceretis ?   vos autem ecce implestis Hierosolymam do[ctrina ves]tra : et vultis
super nos adducere sanguine h[ominis] illius.   29 respondens autem Petrus dixit

---

The text of D has here again
suffered by conformation, consisting
of the excision of the words corresponding to *respondens autem petrus dixit
ad illum cui* h, for which the B-reading
ought to have been substituted, and
of the insertion of μαλλον.   δε (d
oportet) is an attempt at connexion.
In the sentence following ανθρωποις
the ' Western ' Greek reappears in D.

Second and third century witnesses
to the B-text are Polycrates' letter to
Victor, ap. Eus. *h.e.* v. 24, 7, Origen
c. Cels. viii. 26, and Hippolytus, *c.
Noët.* 6 fin. (ed. Lagarde p. 48), all
of whom quote the affirmative form
πειθαρχειν γαρ δει θεω μαλλον η ανθρωποις, and would not have found the
text available for their purpose in
its ' Western ' guise.

στολοι εἶπαν· Πειθαρχεῖν δεῖ θεῷ μᾶλλον ἢ ἀνθρώποις. ὁ θεὸς 30
τῶν πατέρων ἡμῶν ἤγειρεν Ἰησοῦν, ὃν ὑμεῖς διεχειρίσασθε
κρεμάσαντες ἐπὶ ξύλου· τοῦτον ὁ θεὸς ἀρχηγὸν καὶ σωτῆρα 31
ὕψωσεν τῇ δεξιᾷ αὐτοῦ, τοῦ δοῦναι μετάνοιαν τῷ Ἰσραὴλ
καὶ ἄφεσιν ἁμαρτιῶν· καὶ ἡμεῖς ἐν αὐτῷ μάρτυρες τῶν ῥημάτων 32
τούτων, καὶ τὸ πνεῦμα τὸ ἅγιον ἔδωκεν ὁ θεὸς τοῖς πειθαρχοῦσιν
αὐτῷ. οἱ δὲ ἀκούσαντες διεπρείοντο καὶ ἐβούλοντο ἀνελεῖν αὐτούς. 33
ἀναστὰς δέ τις ἐν τῷ συνεδρίῳ Φαρεισαῖος ὀνόματι Γαμαλιήλ, 34
νομοδιδάσκαλος τίμιος παντὶ τῷ λαῷ, ἐκέλευσεν ἔξω βραχὺ τοὺς
ἀνθρώπους ποιῆσαι, | εἶπέν τε πρὸς αὐτούς· Ἄνδρες Ἰσραηλεῖ- 35
ται, προσέχετε ἑαυτοῖς ἐπὶ τοῖς ἀνθρώποις τούτοις τί μέλλετε
πράσσειν. πρὸ γὰρ τούτων τῶν ἡμερῶν ἀνέστη Θευδᾶς, λέγων 36
εἶναί τινα ἑαυτόν, ᾧ προσεκλίθη ἀνδρῶν ἀριθμὸς ὡς τετρακοσίων·

Editors 31 [του] WH om του Soden JHR 32 εν αυτω] εσμεν WH Soden JHR
εν αυτω or εσμεν αυτω WHmg αγιον] +ο WH Soden JHR 33 εβουλοντο]
εβουλενοντο Soden 34 ανθρωπους Soden mg αποστολους Soden

Old Uncial 30 ο B(+D) +δε ℵA 31 του Bℵ om Aℵᶜ(+D) 32 εν αυτω
μαρτυρες B εσμεν μαρτυρες ℵ(+D) μαρτυρες εσμεν A αγιον B +ο ℵA
(cf. D) 33 εβουλοντο BA εβουλευοντο ℵ(+D) 35 τε BℵA(+D) δε C
36 εαυτον BℵAC +μεγαν A²(cf. D) προσεκλιθη BℵACᶜᵒʳʳ (cf. D) προσ-
εκληθησαν C ως BACℵᶜ(+D) ωσει ℵ τετρακοσιων BACℵᶜ(+D)
τετρακοσιοι ℵ

Antiochian 31 om του HPSϚ(+D) 32 εν αυτω] εσμεν αυτου HPSϚ πνευμα] +δε
HPSϚ αγιον] +ο HPSϚ (cf. D) 33 ακουοντες P εβουλοντο]
εβουλευοντο HPSϚ(+D) 34 βραχυ τους ανθρωπους] βραχυ τι τους αποστολους PϚ τους αποστολους βραχυ τι HS 36 προσεκλιθη] προσεκληθη HPS
(+D) προσεκολληθη Ϛ αριθμος ανδρων HPSϚ(+D) ως] ωσει HPSϚ

31 For δεξια the reading δοξη D
perp gig (h?) Iren Aug sah seems to
be a very ancient accidental error ; for
the same confusion cf. LXX. Is. lxii. 8,
2 Chron. xxx. 8 (Nestle, *Expositor*,
5th ser., ii., 1895, pp. 238 f.).

του Bℵ (dittography?) is probably
to be omitted with A D Antiochian.
In such cases the author of Acts sometimes uses του, as in Acts xxvi. 18
(twice), Lk. i. 74, 77, 79 ; sometimes
not, as in Lk. i. 54, 79.

32 The text of ℵ(A) gig vg pesh,
which lacks εν αυτω and reads και ημεις
εσμεν μαρτυρες, is probably right. The
'Western' text had the addition εν
αυτω at the close of vs. 31 ; so D d h
perp Aug. *peccat. merit.* i. 52 sah.
(The Greek basis of h apparently had
εσμεν mutilated into μεν.) The words
were inserted in B, but in the wrong

place, contrary to the sense, after
ημεις ; and εσμεν was extruded in
making the correction. Iren has
exactly the text of B. Several
minuscules read εν αυτω εσμεν. The
Antiochian, on the basis of the B-text,
improved εν αυτω awkwardly into αυτου.
The omission of δ by B minn sah
boh was probably an accidental error ;
the variants ου DE, ο ℵA Antiochian,
and του πνευματος του αγιου ο h perp
may possibly suggest a deeper but
hidden cause.

33 With hcl ※ cf. the added τα
ρηματα ταυτα 614 minn.

34 For the lacuna in h, Berger's conjecture *mi[nimum]* is not wholly satisfactory, and Buchanan's *mi[nistris]*
still less so. Vg. *cod. par. 11533* reads
modicum.

36 The attestation of the expanded

αὐτούς· Ὁ θεὸς τῶν πατέρων ἡμῶν ἤγειρεν Ἰησοῦν, ὃν ὑμεῖς
31 διεχειρίσασθε κρεμάσαντες ἐπὶ ξύλου· τοῦτον ὁ θεὸς ἀρχηγὸν
καὶ σωτῆρα ὕψωσεν τῇ δόξῃ αὐτοῦ, δοῦναι μετάνοιαν τῷ Ἰσραὴλ
32 καὶ ἄφεσιν ἁμαρτιῶν ἐν αὐτῷ. καὶ ἡμεῖς ἐσμὲν μάρτυρες
πάντων τῶν ῥημάτων τούτων, καὶ τὸ πνεῦμα τὸ ἅγιον ὃν ἔδωκεν
33 ὁ θεὸς τοῖς πιθαρχοῦσιν αὐτῷ. οἱ δὲ ἀκούσαντες διεπρίοντο καὶ
34 ἐβουλεύοντο ἀνελεῖν αὐτούς. ἀναστὰς δέ τις ἐκ τοῦ συνεδρίου
Φαρισαῖος ὀνόματι Γαμαλιήλ, νομοδιδάσκαλος τίμιος παντὶ τῷ
35 λαῷ, ἐκέλευσεν τοὺς ἀποστόλους ἔξω βραχὺ ποιῆσαι, | εἶπέν
τε πρὸς τοὺς ἄρχοντας καὶ τοὺς συνέδρους· Ἄνδρες Ἰσραηλεῖται, προσέχετε ἑαυτοῖς ἐπὶ τοῖς ἀνθρώποις τούτοις τί μέλλετε
36 πράσσειν. πρὸ γὰρ τούτων τῶν ἡμερῶν ἀνέστη Θευδᾶς, λέγων
εἶναί τινα μέγαν ἑαυτόν, ᾧ καὶ προσεκλίθη ἀριθμὸς ἀνδρῶν ὡς

| 30 διεχειρισασθαι | 35 συνεδριους | προσεχεται |
| εαυτους | μελλεται | 36 προσεκληθη |

ad eos d̄s̄ patrum nostrorum suscitavit ih̄m̄ quem vos interfecistis suspensum in ligno **d**
31 hunc d̄s̄ ducem et salvatorem exaltavit caritate sua dare paenitentiam istrahel et
remissionem peccatorum in ipso   32 et nos ipsi testes sumus omnium verborum
horum et s̄p̄m̄ sanctum quem dedit d̄s̄ hiis qui obtemperat ei   33 ad illi audientes
discruciabantur et cogitabant interficere eos   34 cum surrexisset autem quidam in
concilio pharisaeus nomine gamaliel legis doctor honorabiles apud omnem populum
jussit apostolos foras pusillum facere   35 dixitque ad principes et concilium viri
istrahelitae adtendite vobis super istis hominibus quidnam incipiatis agere   36 ante
hos enim dies surrexit theudas dicens esse quendam magnum ipsorum cui adsensum

ad il[lum] : cui obaudire oportet, d̄ō an hominib· ?   ille aut[em ait : d̄ō].   30 et **h**
dixit Petrus ad eum : d̄s̄ patrum nostroru[m excita]vit ih̄m̄, quos vos inter-
emistis, suspendent[es in ligno].   31 hunc principem d̄s̄ et salvatorem exalt[avit
gloria] sua, dare penitentiam Istrael et remissi[onem peccati] in se: 32 et
nos quidem testes sumus omniu[m verborum] istorum, et s̄p̄s̄ sc̄ī, quem dedit d̄s̄
eis qui[cumq· crediderint in eu]m.   33 haec cum audirent verba, dirrupie-
bantur, [et cogita]bant perdere eos.   34 exurrexit autem de cō[cilio fari]seus
quidam, nomine Gamaliel, qui erat legis [doctor e]t acceptus totae plebi : et
jussit apostolos mi[. . . d]uci interim foras: 35 et ait ad totum concilium :
[viri Istra]elite, attendite vobis quid de istis hominibus [agere i]ncipiatis.
36 nomen ante hoc tempus surrexit [Theudas] quidam, dicens se esse magnum,

30 deus patrum nostrorum excitavit Jesum, quem vos adprehendistis, et Irenaeus,
interfecistis suspendentes in ligno.   31 hunc deus principem et salvatorem iii. 12, 5 (6)
exaltavit gloria sua, dare paenitentiam Israel, et remissionem peccatorum:
32 et nos in eo testes sermonum horum, et spiritus sanctus, quem dedit deus
credentibus ei.

33 ακουσαντες] quum audivissent ⁖ sermones hos ✓   Harclean

reading τινα εαυτον μεγαν (cf. viii. 9)   presence in D (τινα μεγαν εαυτον), Old
is interesting.   Not only does its   Latin (h gig vg.codd. Jerome), pesh,

ὃς ἀνῃρέθη, καὶ πάντες ὅσοι ἐπείθοντο αὐτῷ διελύθησαν καὶ ἐγένοντο εἰς οὐδέν. μετὰ τοῦτον ἀνέστη ᾿Ιούδας ὁ Γαλειλαῖος ἐν 37
ταῖς ἡμέραις τῆς ἀπογραφῆς καὶ ἀπέστησε λαὸν ὀπίσω αὐτοῦ·
κἀκεῖνος ἀπώλετο, καὶ πάντες ὅσοι ἐπείθοντο αὐτῷ διεσκορπίσθησαν. καὶ νῦν λέγω ὑμῖν, ἀπόστητε ἀπὸ τῶν ἀνθρώπων τούτων 38
καὶ ἄφετε αὐτούς· ὅτι ἐὰν ᾖ ἐξ ἀνθρώπων ἡ βουλὴ αὕτη ἢ τὸ
ἔργον τοῦτο, καταλυθήσεται· εἰ δὲ ἐκ θεοῦ ἐστίν, οὐ δυνήσεσθε 39
καταλῦσαι αὐτούς· μή ποτε καὶ θεομάχοι εὑρεθῆτε. ἐπείσθησαν 40
δὲ αὐτῷ, καὶ προσκαλεσάμενοι τοὺς ἀποστόλους δείραντες
παρήγγειλαν μὴ λαλεῖν ἐπὶ τῷ ὀνόματι τοῦ ᾿Ιησοῦ καὶ ἀπέλυσαν.
οἱ μὲν οὖν ἐπορεύοντο χαίροντες ἀπὸ προσώπου τοῦ συνεδρίου 41

Editors 38 τα νυν Soden JHR [τα νυν] WH   αφετε Soden mg εασατε Soden
40 απελυσαν] +[αυτους] Soden

Old Uncial 37 λαον BℵA +πολυ C +πολυν C^corr (+D)   οσοι BℵAC²(+D) οι C
38 νυν B τα νυν B¹(?)B²ℵAC(+D)   υμιν Bℵ^aAC(+D) om ℵ   39 δυνη-
σεσθε BℵC(+D) δυνασθε A   αυτους BℵAC²(+D) αυτο C   40 λαλειν
BℵC(+D) +αυτους A

Antiochian 37 απεστησε] ανεστησεν H   λαον] +ικανον HPS5 (cf. D)   38 νυν]
τα νυν HPS5(+D)   αφετε] εασατε HPS5(+D)   om αυτη HPS
39 δε] +και S   δυνησεσθε] δυνασθε HPS5   αυτους] αυτο HPS5
40 απελυσαν] +αυτους HPS5(+D)

---

614 and many minuscules show it to
have been 'Western,' but it is found
in Origen c. Cels. i. 57 and in Cyril
Alex., and has been inserted by A².
    36, 37 The use, instead of ανηρεθη
in vs. 36, of διελυθη D, κατελυθη Euseb.
h.e. ii. 11, 1, dissolutus est perp, and
in vs. 37 of dissolutus est perp for
απωλετο, may be an attempt to improve
the argument of Gamaliel, under the
view that the apostles (rather than
Jesus) are here compared with Theudas
and Judas. But more probaby in vs.
36 ος διελυθη D was taken to refer to
αριθμος. και παντες will then stand in

apposition, διελυθησαν being necessarily
omitted.
    38 On the late Latin use of sic for
si, found in d, cf. vii. 1, Jn. xxi. 22,
and see J. R. Harris, Codex Bezae,
pp. 33-40.
    39 The 'Western' gloss, ουτε υμεις
ουτε βασιλεις ουτε τυραννοι· απεχεσθε
ουν απο των ανθρωπων τουτων D hcl ※
and, in part, h e E minn, may possibly
show use of Wisdom xii. 14 ουτε
βασιλευς ἢ τύραννος ἀντοφθαλμῆσαι
δυνήσεταί σοι περὶ ὧν ἀπώλεσας. See
J. R. Harris, Expositor, 6th ser., vol.
ii., 1900, pp. 394-400.

τετρακοσίων· ὃς διελύθη αὐτὸς δι' αὐτοῦ καὶ πάντες ὅσοι ἐπίθοντο
37 αὐτῷ καὶ ἐγένοντο εἰς οὐθέν. μετὰ τοῦτον ἀνέστη 'Ιούδας ὁ
Γαλιλαῖος ἐν ταῖς ἡμέραις τῆς ἀπογραφῆς καὶ ἀπέστησεν λαὸν
πολὺν ὀπίσω αὐτοῦ· κἀκεῖνος ἀπώλετο, καὶ ὅσοι ἐπίθοντο αὐτῷ
38 διεσκορπίσθησαν. καὶ τὰ νῦν †εἰσιν,† ἀδελφοί, λέγω ὑμεῖν, ἀπόστητε ἀπὸ τῶν ἀνθρώπων τούτων καὶ ἐάσατε αὐτοὺς μὴ μιάναντες
τὰς χεῖρας· ὅτι ἐὰν ᾖ ἐξ ἀνθρώπων ἡ βουλὴ αὕτη ἢ τὸ ἔργον
39 τοῦτο, καταλυθήσεται· εἰ δὲ ἐκ θεοῦ ἐστίν, οὐ δυνήσεσθε κα<τα>-
λῦσαι αὐτοὺς οὔτε ὑμεῖς οὔτε βασιλεῖς οὔτε τύραννοι. ἀπέχεσθε
οὖν ἀπὸ τῶν ἀνθρώπων τούτων μή ποτε θεομάχοι εὑρεθῆτε.
40 †[.]επειστ[. . .]εϲ† δὲ αὐτῷ, καὶ προσκαλεσάμενοι τοὺς ἀποστόλους δείραντες παρήγγειλαν μὴ λαλεῖν ἐπὶ τῷ ὀνόματι τοῦ
41 'Ιησοῦ καὶ ἀπέλυσαν αὐτούς. οἱ μὲν οὖν ἀπόστολοι ἐπορεύοντο

39 δυνησεσθαι   απεχεσθαι   40 επι] επει

est numeri virorum quasi quagringentorum qui interfectus est et omnes quodquod d
obtemperabant ei facti sunt nihil 37 post hunc surrexit judas galilaeus in diebus
professionis et alienavit populum post se et ille periit et qui credebant illi dispersi
sunt 38 et quae nunc fratres dico vobis discedite ab hominibus istis et dismittite
eos non coinquinatas manus quia sic erit ab hominibus consilium istud aut hopus hoc
destruetur 39 si autem a d̄o est non poteritis destruere eos nec vos nec imperatores
nec reges discedite ergo ab hominibus istis ne forte d̄o repugnantes inveniamini
40 consenserunt itaquae ei et et cum vocasset apostolos caesis eis praeceperunt non
ļoqui in nomine īh̄ū et dismiserunt eos 41 apostoli vero ibant gaudentes a conspectu

cui sensit [numer]us hominum non minus quadrigentorum : [qui jug]ulatus est, h
et omnes qui ei consenserant co̅[fusi sun]t et nihil sunt facti. 37 post hunc
deinde sur[rexit Ju]das Galileus in diebus census, et convertit [multa]m plebem
post se : et ille perit, quodquod ei cre[didera]nt persecutiones habuerunt.
38 nunc au[tem, frat]res, dico vobis, ab istis hominib· recedatis, et [eos
dimi]ttatis, et non maculetis manus vestras : quo[niam si] haec potestas humani
voluntatis est, dissol[vetur vir]tus ejus : 39 si autem haec potestas ex d̄ī
volu̅[tate est, no]n poteritis dissolbere illos, neque vos neq· [principes] ac
tyranni. abstinete itaquae vos ab is[tis homini]bus, ne forte et adversus
d̄m̄ inveniamini [pugnantes. 40 con]senserunt itaque illi : et vocaverunt
apos[tolos, et caeso]s dimiserunt eos, praecipientes ne umquam loquerentur
alicui in nomine īh̄u. 41 [illi] autem dimissi avierunt gaudentes et conspe[ctu

[39 non te terremus, qui nec timemus, sed velim ut omnes salvos facere Tertullian,
possimus monendo μὴ θεομαχεῖν.] Scap. 4

39 ουτε υμεις ουτε βασιλεις ουτε τυραννοι· απεχεσθε ουν απο των ανθρωπων Harclean
τωντων] ⸆ neque vos neque reges neque tyranni ; abstite ergo ab hominibus
his ⸌

ὅτι κατηξιώθησαν ὑπὲρ τοῦ ὀνόματος ἀτιμασθῆναι· πᾶσάν τε 42
ἡμέραν ἐν τῷ ἱερῷ καὶ κατ' οἶκον οὐκ ἐπαύοντο διδάσκοντες καὶ
εὐαγγελιζόμενοι τὸν Χριστὸν Ἰησοῦν.

Ἐν δὲ ταῖς ἡμέραις ταύταις πληθυνόντων τῶν μαθητῶν VI
ἐγένετο γογγυσμὸς τῶν Ἑλληνιστῶν πρὸς τοὺς Ἐβραίους ὅτι
παρεθεωροῦντο ἐν τῇ διακονίᾳ τῇ καθημερινῇ αἱ χῆραι αὐτῶν·
προσκαλεσάμενοι δὲ οἱ δώδεκα τὸ πλῆθος τῶν μαθητῶν εἶπαν· 2
Οὐκ ἀρεστόν ἐστιν ἡμᾶς καταλείψαντας τὸν λόγον τοῦ θεοῦ
διακονεῖν τραπέζαις· ἐπισκεψώμεθα δέ, ἀδελφοί, ἄνδρας ἐξ ὑμῶν 3
μαρτυρουμένους ἑπτὰ πλήρεις πνεύματος καὶ σοφίας, οὓς καταστήσομεν ἐπὶ τῆς χρείας ταύτης· ἡμεῖς δὲ τῇ προσευχῇ καὶ 4
τῇ διακονίᾳ τοῦ λόγου προσκαρτερήσομεν. καὶ ἤρεσεν ὁ λόγος ἐν- 5
ώπιον παντὸς τοῦ πλήθους, καὶ ἐξελέξαντο Στέφανον, ἄνδρα πλήρη

Editors 3 ἐπισκεψασθε WH Soden JHR δε] ουν Soden [δη] WHmg
5 πληρης Soden JHR

Old Uncial 42 χριστον BℵA κυριον C (cf. D) 1 παρεθεωρουντο BℵAC(+D)
παραθεωρουνται Pap⁸ 2 ημας BℵA ημιν C(+D) καταλειψαντας
BℵA Pap⁸(+D) καταλειψαντες C 3 επισκεψωμεθα B επισκεψασθε ℵAC
Pap⁸(+D) δε Bℵ δη A ουν C αδελφοι BℵC om A(+D)
πληρεις BℵC Pap⁸(+D) πληρης A πνευματος BℵC² vid Pap⁸(+D) +αγιου AC
και BACℵᶜ Pap⁸(+D) om ℵ 5 ενωπιον BℵA(+D) εναντιον C
εξελεξαντο BAC εξελεξαν τον ℵ πληρη BCᶜᵒʳʳ πληρης ℵAC(+D)

Antiochian 41 υπερ του ονοματος (+αυτου Ϛ) κατηξιωθησαν HPSϚ(+D) 42 ιησουν
τον χριστον HPSϚ (cf. D) 3 επισκεψασθε HPSϚ(+D) δε]
ουν HPSϚ πληρεις] πληρης HP πληρις S πνευματος] +αγιου
HPSϚ καταστησωμεν HPS 4 προσκαρτερησωμεν HS
5 πληρης HS(+D) πληρις P

---

3 ἐπισκεψώμεθα B, attested by no
other witness, seems to be due to the
desire not to exclude the apostles from
a share in the selection of the Seven.
It is clearly inconsistent with vs. 6
in the usual text. Perhaps the

'Western' ουτοι εσταθησαν in the
latter verse has arisen from the same
motive.
5 πληρη BCᶜᵒʳʳ minn is a correction
for the indeclinable πληρης ℵACD
Antiochian.

χαίροντες ἀπὸ προσώπου τοῦ συνεδρίου ὅτι ὑπὲρ τοῦ ὀνόματος
42 κατηξιώθησαν ἀτιμασθῆναι· πᾶσαν δὲ ἡμέραν ἐν τῷ ἱερῷ καὶ κατ᾽
οἶκον οὐκ ἐπαύοντο διδάσκοντες καὶ εὐαγγελιζόμενοι τὸν κύριον
Ἰησοῦν Χριστόν.

VI Ἐν δὲ ταύταις ταῖς ἡμέραις πληθυνόντων τῶν μαθητῶν
ἐγένετο γογγυσμὸς τῶν Ἑλληνιστῶν πρὸς τοὺς Ἑβραίους ὅτι
παρεθεωροῦντο ἐν τῇ διακονίᾳ καθημερινῇ αἱ χῆραι αὐτῶν ἐν τῇ
2 διακονίᾳ τῶν Ἑβραίων. προσκαλεσάμενοι οἱ ιβ τὸ πλῆθος τῶν
μαθητῶν εἶπον πρὸς αὐτούς· Οὐκ ἀρεστόν ἐστιν ἡμεῖν καταλεί-
3 ψαντας τὸν λόγον τοῦ θεοῦ διακονεῖν τραπέζαις. τί οὖν ἐστίν,
ἀδελφοί; ἐπισκέψασθε ἐξ ὑμῶν αὐτῶν ἄνδρας μαρτυρουμένους
ζ πλήρεις πνεύματος καὶ σοφίας, οὓς καταστήσομεν ἐπὶ τῆς
4 χρίας <τ>αύτης· ἡμεῖς δὲ ἐσόμεθα τῇ προσευχῇ καὶ τῇ δια-
5 κονίᾳ τοῦ λόγου προσκαρτεροῦντες. καὶ ἤρεσεν ὁ λόγος οὗτος
ἐνώπιον παντὸς τοῦ πλήθους τῶν μαθητῶν, καὶ ἐξελέξαντο
Στέφανον, ἄνδρα πλήρης πίστεως καὶ πνεύματος ἁγίου,
3 ἐπισκεψασθαι

---

concilii quia pro nomine digni habitati sunt contumeliam pati 42 omni autem die d
in templo et domi non cessabant docentes et evangelizantes dum ihm xpm
  1 in diebus autem istis multiplicantibus discipulis facta est murmuratio quae ex
grecis erant adversus aebraeos quia discupiuntur in ministerio diurno viduae ipsorum
in ministerio haebreorum 2 convocantes itaque xii multitudinem discipulorum
dixerunt ad eos non enim placet nobis derelicto verbo dī ministrare mensis 3 quid
ergo est fratres prospicite itaque ex vobis viros testimonio bono vii plenos spu et
sapientia quos constituamus in negotio hoc 4 nos autem sumus oratione et ministerio
berbi perseveramus 5 et placuit sermo hic in conspectu omni multitudini discipulorum et elegerunt stephanum virum plenum fidei et spiritu sancti et philippum et

---

con]cilii, quod digni habiti essent ignominias pati [in nomi]ne īhu. 42 omni h
atquae die in templo et in domib[us non] cessabant docentes et annuntiantes
dnm ih[m xpm].
  1 in diebus autem illis, cum abundaret turba di[scentiū], facta est contentio
Graecorum adversus Ebr[. . . .] quod in cottidiano ministerio viduae Graec[orum]
a ministris Hebraecorum discupierentur. 2 et [convo]caverunt illi xii totam
plebem discipulorum, [et dixe]runt eis: non est aecum vobis reliquisse ver[bum
dī] et ministrare mensis. 3 quid est ergo, frat[res? ex]quirite ex vobis ipsis
homines probatos sep[tem, ple]nos spu sco et sapientia dni, quos constitu[amus
in] hunc usum. 4 nos autem orationi verbi adse[rvientes] erimus. 5 et placuit
sermo iste in conspectu o[mnium] discentium: et elegerunt Stefanum, hominem

---

2 et convocaverunt [inquit] illi duodecim totam plebem discipulorum et Cyprian,
dixerunt eis. *Ep. 67, 4*

---

42 omni [quoque] die [inquit] in templo et in domo non cessabant docentes Irenaeus,
et evangelizantes Christum Jesum filium dei. iii. 12, 5 (6)
  in domo] domo *or* domi *Turner·*

---

4 εσομεθα προσκαρτερουντες] *mg* [erimus] perseverantes Harclean

πίστεως καὶ πνεύματος ἁγίου, καὶ Φίλιππον καὶ Πρόχορον καὶ Νικάνορα καὶ Τείμωνα καὶ Παρμενᾶν καὶ Νικόλαον προσ- ήλυτον Ἀντιοχέα, | οὓς ἔστησαν ἐνώπιον τῶν ἀποστόλων, καὶ 6 προσευξάμενοι ἐπέθηκαν αὐτοῖς τὰς χεῖρας.

Καὶ ὁ λόγος τοῦ θεοῦ ηὔξανεν, καὶ ἐπληθύνετο ὁ ἀριθμὸς τῶν 7 μαθητῶν ἐν Ἰερουσαλὴμ σφόδρα, πολύς τε ὄχλος τῶν ἱερέων ὑπήκουον τῇ πίστει.

Στέφανος δὲ πλήρης χάριτος καὶ δυνάμεως ἐποίει τέρατα καὶ 8 σημεῖα μεγάλα ἐν τῷ λαῷ. ἀνέστησαν δέ τινες τῶν ἐκ τῆς 9 συναγωγῆς τῆς λεγομένης Λιβερτίνων καὶ Κυρηναίων καὶ Ἀλεξανδρέων καὶ τῶν ἀπὸ Κιλικίας καὶ Ἀσίας συνζητοῦντες τῷ Στεφάνῳ, καὶ οὐκ ἴσχυον ἀντιστῆναι τῇ σοφίᾳ καὶ τῷ πνεύματι 10 ᾧ ἐλάλει. τότε ὑπέβαλον ἄνδρας λέγοντας ὅτι Ἀκηκόαμεν 11 αὐτοῦ λαλοῦντος ῥήματα βλάσφημα εἰς Μωυσῆν καὶ τὸν θεόν·

Old Uncial   5 πιστεως και πνευματος BACℵ℅Pap⁸(+D)   πνευματος και πιστεως ℵ
7 ιερεων BACℵ℅ 0175 ᵛⁱᵈ (+D) ιουδαιων ℵ   υπηκουον BℵC 0175(+D)
υπηκουεν A   9 των 1° BAC 0175(+D)   om ℵ   της λεγομενης BC(+D)
των λεγομενων ℵA 0175   αλεξανδρεων BℵAC 0175(+D)   αλεξανδρινων
Pap⁸   κιλικιας BℵAC(+D) της κιλικιας 0175   και ασιας BℵC
0175 om A(+D)   11 λεγοντας BC λεγοντες ℵA   λαλουντος
BCℵ℅A²Pap⁸(+D)   λεγοντος ℵ   om A   βλασφημα BℵᵃAC Pap⁸ βλασ-
φημιας ℵ(+D)

Antiochian   8 χαριτος] πιστεως HPSϛ

---

6 *hos statuerunt* h (cf. d *quos*) is partial conformation to the B-text, against 'Western' ουτοι εσταθησαν D perp pesh.

7 των ιερεων BACD Antiochian is to be accepted in preference to των ιουδαιων ℵ minn pesh, and to the obviously corrupt εν τω ιερω which underlies h (*in templo*). This last reading seems to be due to some confusion with εν ιερουσαλημ (just before), which h 181 omit.

9 For λιβερτινων the conjecture of λιβιστινων or λιβυστινων ('Libyans') has been much discussed ever since the mention of it by Beza, in his notes in R. Stephen's Latin New Testament, Geneva, 1556. It is attractive but unnecessary. The explanation 'Libyans' quoted from Chrysostom in the Armenian catena, and found in the Armenian vulgate text, may be an interpretation, not a variant reading; see Conybeare, *Am. J. Philol.* xvii., 1896, p. 152.

A 60ˡᵉᶜᵗ support D d in omitting και ασιας.

10 The 'Western' addition is found in vg. *codd* and in tepl and the Bohemian.

καὶ Φίλιππον
καὶ Νικ‹άν›ορα
καὶ Παρμενᾶ‹ν›
προσήλυτον

καὶ Πρόχορον
καὶ Τείμωνα
καὶ Νικόλαον
Ἀντιοχέα.

6 οὗτοι ἐστάθησαν ἐνώπιον τῶν ἀποστόλων, οἵτινες προσευξάμενοι ἐπέθηκαν αὐτοῖς τὰς χεῖρας.

7 Καὶ ὁ λόγος τοῦ κύριου ηὔξανεν, καὶ ἐπληθύνετο ὁ ἀριθμὸς τῶν μαθητῶν ἐν Ἰερουσαλὴμ σφόδρα, πολύς τε ὄχλος τῶν ἱερέων ὑπήκουον †α[.]† τῇ πίστι.

8 Στέφανος δὲ πλήρης χάριτος καὶ δυνάμεως ἐποίει τέρατα καὶ σημεῖα μεγάλα ἐν τῷ λαῷ διὰ τοῦ ὀνόματος κυρίου Ἰησοῦ Χρι-
9 στοῦ. ἀνέστησαν δέ τινες τῶν ἐκ τῆς συναγωγῆς τῆς λεγομένης Λειβερτείνων καὶ Κυρηνέων καὶ Ἀλεξανδρέων καὶ τῶν ἀπὸ
10 Κιλικίας συνζητοῦντες τῷ Στεφάνῳ, οἵτινες οὐκ ἴσχυον ἀντιστῆναι τῇ σοφίᾳ τῇ οὔσῃ ἐν αὐτῷ καὶ τῷ πνεύματι τῷ ἁγίῳ ᾧ ἐλάλει,
11 διὰ τὸ ἐλέγχεσθαι αὐτοὺς ἐπ' αὐτοῦ μετὰ πάσης παρρησίας. μὴ δυνάμενοι οὖ‹ν› ἀντοφθαλμεῖν τῇ ἀληθείᾳ, τότε ὑπέβαλον ἄνδρας λέγοντ[.]ς ὅτι Ἀκηκόαμεν αὐτοῦ λαλοῦντος ῥήματα βλασφημίας

---

prochorum et nicanorem et timonem et permenan et nicholaum proselytum antiocensem **d**
6 quos statuerunt in conspectu apostolorum cumque orassent superposuerunt eis
manus 7 et verbum d̄n̄i crescebat et multiplicabatur numerus discipulorum in
hierusalem nimis multaque turba sacerdotum oboediebant fidei 8 stephanus vero
plenus gratia et virtute faciebat portenta et signa magna in populo per nomen d̄n̄i
ih̄u x̄p̄i 9 surrexerunt autem quidam qui erant de synagoga quae dicitur livertinorum
et cyrenensium et alexandrinorum et eorum qui sunt a cilicia altercantes cum stephano
10 qui non poterant resistere sapientiae quae erat in eo et s̄p̄o sancto in quo loquebatur quoniam probatur illis ab illo cum omni fiducia 11 non potentes autem
resistere veritati tunc summiserunt viros qui dicerent quia audivimus eum loquentem

---

[plenum] fide et s̄c̄o s̄p̄u, et Filippum et Proculum et N[icanorē] et Simonem et **h**
Parmenen et Nicolaum pros[elytum] Antiocensem. 6 hos statuerunt ante
apostol[os et orā]tes inposuerunt eis manus. 7 et verbum d̄n̄i ad[cresce]bat, et
multiplicabantur numerus discentiu[m . . . .]]: magna autem turba in templo
audiebant fid[ei]. 8 [Stef]anus autem plenus gratiam et virtute faciebat
[prod]igia et signam coram plebem in nomine īh̄u x̄p̄i. 9 [exur]rexerunt autem
quidam ex synagoga quae [dicit]ur Libertinorum et alii Cyrenaei et ab
Alexan[dria e]t Cilicia et Asia, contendentes cum Stefano: 10 qui [non
v]alebant contradicere sapientiae quae erat in [eo et s̄]p̄u̅i s̄c̄o quo loquaebatur,
et quod revincebantur [ab eo c]um omni fiducia. 11 tunc itaque, non valen[tes
res]istere adversus veritatem, summiserunt ho[mines], qui dicerent: audivimus

---

7 πιστει] +*mg* evangelii   8 δια του ονοματος κυριου ιησου χριστου] ✲· per Harclean
nomen domini ✓   10-11 δια το ελεγχεσθαι αυτους επ αυτου μετα πασης
παρρησιας. μη δυναμενοι ουν αντοφθαλμειν τη αληθεια] *mg* quoniam arguerentur
ab eo cum omni libertate.   quum non possent igitur intueri contra veritatem

συνεκείνησάν τε τὸν λαὸν καὶ τοὺς πρεσβυτέρους καὶ τοὺς γραμ- 12
ματεῖς, καὶ ἐπιστάντες συνήρπασαν αὐτὸν καὶ ἤγαγον εἰς τὸ
συνέδριον, | ἔστησάν τε μάρτυρας ψευδεῖς λέγοντας· Ὁ ἄνθρωπος 13
οὗτος οὐ παύεται λαλῶν ῥήματα κατὰ τοῦ τόπου τοῦ ἁγίου
τούτου καὶ τοῦ νόμου, ἀκηκόαμεν γὰρ αὐτοῦ λέγοντος ὅτι 14
Ἰησοῦς ὁ Ναζωραῖος οὗτος καταλύσει τὸν τόπον τοῦτον καὶ
ἀλλάξει τὰ ἔθη ἃ παρέδωκεν ἡμῖν Μωυσῆς. καὶ ἀτενίσαντες εἰς 15
αὐτὸν πάντες οἱ καθεζόμενοι ἐν τῷ συνεδρίῳ εἶδαν τὸ πρόσωπον
αὐτοῦ ὡσεὶ πρόσωπον ἀγγέλου.
Εἶπεν δὲ ὁ ἀρχιερεύς· Εἰ ταῦτα οὕτως ἔχει; | ὁ δὲ ἔφη· Ἄνδρες VII 2
ἀδελφοὶ καὶ πατέρες, ἀκούσατε. ὁ θεὸς τῆς δόξης ὤφθη τῷ
πατρὶ ἡμῶν Ἀβραὰμ ὄντι ἐν τῇ Μεσοποταμίᾳ πρὶν ἢ κατοικῆσαι
Gen. xii. 1 αὐτὸν ἐν Χαρράν, | καὶ εἶπεν πρὸς αὐτόν· Ἔξελθε ἐκ τῆς γῆς 3
σου καὶ τῆς συγγενείας σου, καὶ δεῦρο εἰς τὴν γῆν ἣν ἄν σοι

14 εθη] εθνη

---

15 J. R. Harris, *Four Lectures on
the Western Text*, pp. 70-74, argues
that the rendering of d *stans in medio
eorum* points to a text in which this
phrase related to the high priest and
belonged to the following sentence (cf.
Mk. xiv. 60); in reply see Corssen,
Göttingische gelehrte Anzeigen, 1896,
pp. 434 f.

3-51 In the phrases drawn from the
O.T. in vss. 3-51 about 30 variants
between B and D occur in which one
agrees with LXX against the other.
Vs. 21, D adds παρα τον ποταμον, and
is supported for substance by E e vg.
8 codd hcl ※. Vs. 24, D with support
from w vg. *one cod* eth adds και εκρυψεν
αυτον εν τη αμμω. Since both these

readings are from LXX, a large number
of others where D agrees with LXX
may safely be ascribed to the same
tendency to conformation. In another
series of cases, such as vs. 18, εμνησθη
D E e gig perp; vs. 26, τι ποιειτε ανδρες
αδελφοι (without εστε) D; vs. 43, επι
τα μερη D gig (perp) (e) sah (see note
below), and others, the reading of D
in departure from LXX has the
appearance of 'Western' paraphrase.
Vs. 31, ο κυριος ειπεν αυτω λεγων D
eth (pesh seems to be a combination
of both readings) was probably introduced to agree with LXX, and in
compensation, vs. 33, και εγενετο φωνη
προς αυτον D (not in LXX) was substituted for the original reading. In

12 εἰς Μωυσῆν καὶ τὸν θεόν· συνεκείνησάν τε τὸν λαὸν καὶ τοὺς
πρεσβυτέρους καὶ τοὺς γραμματεῖς, καὶ ἐπιστάντες συνήρπασαν
13 αὐτὸν καὶ ἤγαγον εἰς τὸ συνέδριον, καὶ ἔστησαν μάρτυρας ψευ-
δεῖς κατὰ αὐτοῦ λέγοντας· Ὁ ἄνθρωπος οὗτος οὐ παύεται ῥήματα
14 λαλῶν κατὰ τοῦ τόπου τοῦ ἁγίου καὶ τοῦ νόμου, ἀκηκόαμεν γὰρ
αὐτοῦ λέγοντος ὅτι Ἰησοῦς ὁ Ναζοραῖος οὗτος καταλύσει τὸν
τόπον τοῦτον καὶ ἀλλάξει τὰ ἔθη ἃ παρέδωκεν ἡμῖν Μωυσῆς.
15 καὶ ἠτένιζον δὲ αὐτῷ πάντες οἱ καθήμενοι ἐν τῷ συνεδρίῳ καὶ
εἶδον τὸ πρόσωπον αὐτοῦ ὡσεὶ πρόσωπον ἀγγέλου ἑστῶτος ἐν
μέσῳ αὐτῶν.
VII Εἶπεν δὲ ὁ ἀρχιερεὺς τῷ Στεφάνῳ· Εἰ ἄρα τοῦτο οὕτως ἔχει;
2 | ὁ δὲ ἔφη· Ἄνδρες ἀδελφοὶ καὶ πατέρες, ἀκούσατε. ὁ θεὸς τῆς
δόξης ὤφθη τῷ πατρὶ ἡμῶν Ἀβραὰμ ὄντι ἐν τῇ Μεσοποταμίᾳ
3 πρὶν ἢ κατοικῆσαι αὐτὸν ἐν Χαράν, | καὶ εἶπεν πρὸς αὐτόν· Ἔξελθε
ἀπὸ τῆς γῆς σου καὶ τῆς συγγενίας σου, καὶ δεῦρο †ειτ† εἰς τὴν γῆν

2 αδελφοι] αδελφη   3 εξηλθε

---

verba blasphema in moysen et in dum   12 commoveruntque populum et seniores et d
scribas et adgressi adrripuerunt eum et adduxerunt in concilium   13 et statuerunt
testes falsos adversum eum dicentes homo hic non cessabit verba loquens adversus
locum sanctum et legem   14 audivimus enim eum dicentem quia ihs nazoraeus hic
destruet locum istum et mutavit iterum quos tradidit nobis moyses   15 et intuiti in
eum omnes qui sedebant in concilio et viderunt faciem ejus quasi faciem angeli stans
in medio eorum
1 ait autem pontifex stephano sic haec sic habent   2 ad ille dixit viri fratres et
patres audite ds claritatis visus est patri nostro abraham cum esset in mesopotamiam
postea quam mortuus esset in charris   3 et dixit ad eum exi de terra tua et a

---

eum loquentem [verba] blasphemiae in Monsen et in dm.   12 et concitaverunt h
[plebe]m et majores natu et scribas: venerunt et rapu[erunt] eum, et
perduxerunt in concilium,   13 et statue[runt a]dversus eum testes falsos, qui
dicerent: non [quies]cit homo iste verba jacere adversus legem [et adv]ersus
hunc locum scm: 14 audivimus autem eum [dicent]em quod ihs Nazarenus
dissolbet templum is[tum et] consuetudinem istam mutavit quam trade[dit
no]bis Moyses.   15 et cum ¦intueretur eum omnes [qui er]ant in concilio,
videbant vultu ejus tamquā [vultum] angeli dī stantis inter illos.
1 et interrogavit [sacer]dos Stefanum: si haec ita se haberent.   2 [ad ille
re]spondit: viri fratres et patres audite: ds clari[tatis]

---

2 deus gloriae visus est patri nostro Abrahae,   3 et dixit ad eum: exi   Irenaeus,
de terra tua et de cognatione tua, et veni in terram quam demonstrabo tibi: iii. 12, 10 (13)
3 tibi demonstrabo *Turner*

---

only one instance (vs. 18, see below)
is there reason to suspect that the
B-text has been conformed to LXX.
On the agreement of BD minn against

the other uncials in omitting υμων in
vs. 43 see note below.
3, 4, 5 With the purpose of bringing
the text into better accord with the

δείξω· | τότε ἐξελθὼν ἐκ γῆς Χαλδαίων κατῴκησεν ἐν Χαρράν. 4
κἀκεῖθεν μετὰ τὸ ἀποθανεῖν τὸν πατέρα αὐτοῦ μετῴκισεν αὐτὸν
εἰς τὴν γῆν ταύτην εἰς ἣν ὑμεῖς νῦν κατοικεῖτε, καὶ οὐκ ἔδωκεν 5
αὐτῷ κληρονομίαν ἐν αὐτῇ οὐδὲ βῆμα ποδός, καὶ ἐπηγγείλατο

Gen. xvii. 8 δοῦναι αὐτῷ εἰς κατάσχεσιν αὐτὴν καὶ τῷ σπέρματι αὐτοῦ μετ᾽
αὐτόν, οὐκ ὄντος αὐτῷ τέκνου. ἐλάλησεν δὲ οὕτως ὁ θεὸς ὅτι 6

Gen. xv. 13 f. ἔσται τὸ σπέρμα αὐτοῦ πάροικον ἐν γῇ ἀλλοτρίᾳ, καὶ δουλώσουσιν
αὐτὸ καὶ κακώσουσιν ἔτη τετρακόσια· καὶ τὸ ἔθνος ᾧ ἂν δουλεύ- 7
σωσιν κρινῶ ἐγώ, ὁ θεὸς εἶπεν, καὶ μετὰ ταῦτα ἐξελεύσονται καὶ
λατρεύσουσίν μοι ἐν τῷ τόπῳ τούτῳ. καὶ ἔδωκεν αὐτῷ διαθήκην 8
περιτομῆς· καὶ οὕτως ἐγέννησεν τὸν Ἰσὰκ καὶ περιέτεμεν
αὐτὸν τῇ ἡμέρᾳ τῇ ὀγδόῃ, καὶ Ἰσαὰκ τὸν Ἰακώβ, καὶ Ἰακὼβ
τοὺς δώδεκα πατριάρχας. καὶ οἱ πατριάρχαι ζηλώσαντες τὸν 9
Ἰωσὴφ ἀπέδοντο εἰς Αἴγυπτον· καὶ ἦν ὁ θεὸς μετ᾽ αὐτοῦ, | καὶ 10
ἐξείλατο αὐτὸν ἐκ πασῶν τῶν θλείψεων αὐτοῦ, καὶ ἔδωκεν αὐτῷ
χάριν καὶ σοφίαν ἐναντίον Φαραὼ βασιλέως Αἰγύπτου, καὶ
κατέστησεν αὐτὸν ἡγούμενον ἐπ᾽ Αἴγυπτον καὶ ὅλον τὸν οἶκον
τοῦτον. ἦλθεν δὲ λειμὸς ἐφ᾽ ὅλην τὴν Αἴγυπτον καὶ Χαναὰν καὶ 11

Editors   5 αυτην εις κατασχεσιν αυτω Soden   7 δουλευσουσιν WH Soden
ειπεν ο θεος Soden   10 add εφ before ολον WHmg Soden   τουτον]
αυτου WH Soden JHR   11 αιγυπτον] γην αιγυπτου Soden (but cf. mg)

Old Uncial   4 το BℵC(+D) om A   5 αυτω εις κατασχεσιν αυτην BC(+D)   αυτην εις
κατασχεσιν αυτω ℵA   αυτω 3° BℵA(+D)   αυτου C   6 ουτως
BAC(+D)   αυτω ℵ   αυτου BAC(+D)   σου ℵ   κακωσουσιν
BℵA(+D)   +αυτο C   7 και το BℵA(+D)   το δε C   δουλευσωσιν
Bℵ   δουλευσουσιν AC(+D)   λατρευσουσιν BℵA   λατρευσωσιν Cᵛⁱᵈ
8 ογδοη BACℵᶜ(+D)   εβδομη ℵ   10 αυτω BℵC (cf. D)   om A
εναντιον BAC(+D)   εναντι ℵ   ολον B(+D)   εφ ολον ℵAC   τουτον B
αυτου B¹ℵAC(+D)

Antiochian   4 εν] εις HS   5 αυτω δουναι ϛ   6 ουτως] αυτω H   7 ειπεν
ο θεος HPSϛ(+D)   8 om αυτον S   ισαακ 2°] ο ισαακ HPSϛ(+D)
ιακωβ 2°] ο ιακωβ HPSϛ   τουτον] αυτου HPSϛ(+D)   11 αιγυπτον]
γην αιγυπτου HPSϛ

statements of Gen. xi. and xii., perp gig
have a text which removes μετα το
αποθανειν τον πατερα αυτου from its
place in vs. 4 and inserts the words
just before vs. 3. Possibly with the
same motive, in vs. 4, D reads κακει
ην (d et ibi erat) for κακειθεν. The
quotation by Irenaeus is so greatly
abridged that its omissions ought not
to be used as evidence here.

4 With hcl ⁕ agree minn in reading
υμων in both cases.

10 It is noteworthy that φαραω,
which hcl marks with ⁕, is omitted
in Greek texts, so far as known, only
by 614 431. The ⁕ is usually employed
by the Harclean to indicate a word
added, not omitted, by the 'Western'
text ; cf. xxvii. 7 and p. clxx above.

4 ἦν ἄν σοι δείξω· τότε Ἀβραὰμ ἐξελθὼν ἐκ γῆς Χαλδαίων καὶ
κατῴκησεν ἐν Χαρράν. κἀκεῖ ἦν μετὰ τὸ ἀποθανεῖν τὸν πατέρα
αὐτοῦ· καὶ μετῴκισεν αὐτὸν εἰς τὴν γῆν ταύτην εἰς ἣν ὑμεῖς νῦν
5 κατοικεῖτε καὶ οἱ πατέρες ἡμῶν οἱ πρὸ ἡμῶν, καὶ οὐκ ἔδωκεν
αὐτῷ κληρονομίαν ἐν αὐτῇ οὐδὲ βῆμα ποδός, ἀλλ᾽ ἐπηγγείλατο
δοῦναι αὐτῷ εἰς κατάσχεσιν αὐτὴν καὶ τῷ σπέρματι αὐτοῦ μετ᾽
6 αὐτόν, οὐκ ὄντος αὐτῷ τέκνου. ἐλάλησεν δὲ οὕτως ὁ θεὸς πρὸς
αὐτὸν ὅτι ἔσται τὸ σπέρμα αὐτοῦ πάροικον ἐν γῇ ἀλλοτρίᾳ, καὶ
7 δουλώσουσιν αὐτοὺς καὶ κακώσουσιν ἔτη ῡ· καὶ τὸ ἔθνος ᾧ ἂν
δουλεύσουσιν κρινῶ ἐγώ, εἶπεν ὁ θεός, καὶ μετὰ ταῦτα ἐξελεύσον-
8 ται καὶ λατρεύσουσίν μοι ἐν τῷ τόπῳ τούτῳ. καὶ ἔδωκεν αὐτῷ
διαθήκην περιτομῆς· καὶ οὕτως ἐγέννησεν τὸν Ἰσὰκ καὶ περιέτεμεν αὐτὸν τῇ ἡμέρᾳ τῇ ὀγδόῃ, καὶ ὁ Ἰσὰκ τὸν Ἰακώβ, καὶ
9 Ἰακὼβ τοὺς ῑβ πατριάρχας. καὶ οἱ πατριάρχαι ζηλώσαντες τὸν
10 Ἰωσὴφ ἀπέδοντο εἰς Αἴγυπτον· καὶ ἦν ὁ θεὸς μετ᾽ αὐτοῦ, | καὶ
ἐξίλατο αὐτὸν ἐκ πασῶν τῶν θλείψεων αὐτοῦ, καὶ ἔδωκεν
χάριν αὐτῷ καὶ σοφίαν ἐναντίον Φαραὼ βασιλέως Αἰγύπτου, καὶ
κατέστησεν αὐτὸν ἡγούμενον ἐπ᾽ Αἴγυπτον καὶ ὅλον τὸν οἶκον
11 αὐτοῦ. ἦλθεν δὲ λειμὸς ἐφ᾽ ὅλης τῆς Αἰγύπτου καὶ Χαναὰν καὶ

4 μετωκησεν   κατοικειται

cognatione tua et veni in terra quamcumq· tibi monstravero   4 tunc abraham exibit d
de terra chaldeorum et habitavit in charra et ibi erat post mortem patris sui et
intransmigravit eum in terram hanc in qua vos nunc habitatis et patres nostri qui
ante nos   5 et non dedit ei possessionem heredetatis in ea nec quantum tenet gradus
pedis sed promisit ei dare eam in possessionem et semini ejus post ipsum quando non
esset ei filium   6 locutus est autem sic d̄s ad eum quia erit semen ejus peregrinum
in terra aliena et in servitute redigent eos et male tractabunt annis cccc   7 et gentem
cui servierint judicavo ego dicit d̄ns et postea xibunt et deservient mihi in loco hoc
8 et dedit ei dispositionem circumcisionis et sic genuit isac et circumcidit eum die
octabo et isac ipsum jacob et jacob xii patriarchas   9 et patriarchae hemulati joseph
distraxerunt in aegyptum et erat d̄s cum illo   10 et eripuit eum ex omnibus con-
flictationibus ejus et dedit ei gratiam et sapientiam coram farao regae aegypti et
constituit eum in aegyptum et omnem domum suam   11 venit autem famis super

4 et transtulit illum in terram hanc, quam nunc et vos inhabitatis,   5 et non
dedit ei hereditatem in ea, nec gressum pedis, sed promisit dare ei in possessionem
eam, et semini ejus post eum.   6 locutus est autem sic deus ad eum, quoniam
erit semen ejus peregrinans in terra aliena, et in servitutem redigentur, et
vexabuntur annis quadringentis ;   7 et gentem cui servient judicabo ego, dicit
dominus, et postea exient et servient mihi in isto loco.   8 et dedit ei testamentum circumcisionis, et sic generavit Isaac.

Irenaeus,
iii. 12, 10 (13)

4 και οι πατερες ημων οι προ ημων] ⁚ ※ et patres vestri ante vos ✓   10 φαραω] Harclean
※ Pharaone ✓

θλεῖψις μεγάλη, καὶ οὐχ ηὕρισκον χορτάσματα οἱ πατέρες ἡμῶν·
ἀκούσας δὲ Ἰακὼβ ὄντα σειτία εἰς Αἴγυπτον ἐξαπέστειλεν τοὺς 12
πατέρας ἡμῶν πρῶτον· καὶ ἐν τῷ δευτέρῳ ἐγνωρίσθη Ἰωσὴφ 13
τοῖς ἀδελφοῖς αὐτοῦ, καὶ φανερὸν ἐγένετο τῷ Φαραὼ τὸ γένος
Ἰωσήφ. ἀποστείλας δὲ Ἰωσὴφ μετεκαλέσατο Ἰακὼβ τὸν πατέρα 14
αὐτοῦ καὶ πᾶσαν τὴν συγγένειαν ἐν ψυχαῖς ἐβδομήκοντα πέντε,
| κατέβη δὲ Ἰακώβ. καὶ αὐτὸς ἐτελεύτησεν καὶ οἱ πατέρες ἡμῶν, 15
καὶ μετετέθησαν εἰς Συχὲμ καὶ ἐτέθησαν ἐν τῷ μνήματι ᾧ 16
ὠνήσατο Ἀβραὰμ τιμῆς ἀργυρίου παρὰ τῶν υἱῶν Ἐμμὼρ ἐν
Συχέμ. καθὼς δὲ ἤγγιζεν ὁ χρόνος τῆς ἐπαγγελίας ἧς ὡμο- 17
λόγησεν ὁ θεὸς τῷ Ἀβραάμ, ηὔξησεν ὁ λαὸς καὶ ἐπληθύνθη ἐν
Αἰγύπτῳ, | ἄχρι οὗ ἀνέστη βασιλεὺς ἕτερος ἐπ᾽ Αἴγυπτον, ὃς 18
οὐκ ᾔδει τὸν Ἰωσήφ. οὗτος κατασοφισάμενος τὸ γένος ἡμῶν 19
ἐκάκωσεν τοὺς πατέρας τοῦ ποιεῖν τὰ βρέφη ἔκθετα αὐτῶν εἰς
τὸ μὴ ζωογονεῖσθαι. ἐν ᾧ καιρῷ ἐγεννήθη Μωυσῆς, καὶ ἦν 20
ἀστεῖος τῷ θεῷ· ὃς ἀνετράφη μῆνας τρεῖς ἐν τῷ οἴκῳ τοῦ πατρός·

15 The omission of δε in D perp gig   into connexion with the following
brings the mention of Jacob's journey   statement of his death, but the

θλεῖψις μεγάλη, καὶ οὐχ εὕρισκον χορτάσματα οἱ πατέρες ἡμῶν·
12 ἀκούσας οὖν Ἰακὼβ ὄντα σειτία ἐν Αἰγύπτῳ ἐξαπέστειλεν τοὺς
13 πατέρας ἡμῶν πρῶτον· καὶ ἐπὶ τῷ δευτέρῳ ἀνεγνωρίσθη Ἰωσὴφ
τοῖς ἀδελφοῖς αὐτοῦ, καὶ φανερὸν ἐγενήθη τῷ Φαραὼ τὸ γένος τοῦ
14 Ἰωσήφ. ἀποστείλας δὲ Ἰωσὴφ μετεκαλέσατο Ἰακὼβ τὸν πατέρα
15 αὐτοῦ καὶ πᾶσαν τὴν συγγένειαν αὐτοῦ ἐν ο̄ καὶ ε̄ ψυχαῖς. κατέβη
Ἰακὼβ εἰς Αἴγυπτον, καὶ ἐτελεύτησεν αὐτός τε καὶ οἱ πατέρες
16 ἡμῶν, καὶ μετήχθησαν εἰς Συχὲν καὶ ἐτέθησαν ἐν τῷ μνήματι
ᾧ ὠνήσατο Ἀβραὰμ τειμῆς ἀργυρίου παρὰ τῶν υἱῶν Ἐμμὼρ
17 τοῦ Συχέμ. καθὼς δὲ ἤγγιζεν ὁ χρόνος τῆς ἐπαγγελίας ἧς ἐπηγγείλατο ὁ θεὸς τῷ Ἀβραάμ, ηὔξησεν ὁ λαὸς καὶ ἐπληθύνθη
18 ἐν Ἐγύπτῳ, ἄχρι οὗ ἀνέστη βασιλεὺς ἕτερος ὃς οὐκ ἐμνήσθη τοῦ
19 Ἰωσήφ, καὶ κατασοφισάμενος τὸ γένος ἡμῶν ἐκάκωσεν τοὺς
πατέρας τοῦ ποιεῖν ἔκθετα τὰ βρέφη αὐτῶν εἰς τὸ μὴ ζωογονεῖ-
20 σθαι. ἐν ᾧ καιρῷ ἐγεννήθη Μωυσῆς, καὶ ἦν ἀστῖος τῷ θεῷ· ὃς
21 ἀνετράφη μῆνας τρῖς ἐν τῷ οἴκῳ τοῦ πατρὸς αὐτοῦ· ἐκτεθέντος δὲ

11 θλειψεις   19 ζωογονεισθε

---

omnem terram aegypti et chanaam et conflictatio magna et non inveniebant utensilia **d**
patres nostri   12 cum audisset vero jacob esse frumenta in aegypto misit patres
nostros primum   13 et in secundo recognitus est joseph a fratribus suis et manifestum factum est ipsi pharao genus joseph   14 cum misisset autem joseph accersibit
jacob patrem suum et omnem cognationem ejus in lxx et v animabus   15 descendit
jacob in aegyptum et defuctus est ipseque et pátres nostri   16 et translati sunt in
sychem et positi sunt in sepulchro quod mercatus est abraham praetio argenti a
filiis emmor et sychem   17 ut vero adpropinquavit tempus promissionis quam
pollicitus est d̄s ipsi abraham auctus est populus et multiplicatus est in aegypto
18 donec alius exurrexerit rex qui non meminisset ipsius joseph   19 cum justitias
coepisset cum genus nostrū male tractavit patres ut faceret exponi infantes eorum ut
non educarentur   20 in quo tempore natus esset moyses et erat eligans d̄o qui
mensibus tribus educatus est in domo patris ejus   21 cum vero expositus esset secus

---

17 επηγγειλατο] *mg* pollicitus erat   18 βασιλευς ετερος] +*mg* in aegypto   Harclean

---

context speaks for the conjunction.
For δε B Antiochian the more Semitic
και ℵACP may be preferable.
16 εν συχεμ BℵC sah boh ; του εν
συχεμ AE e vg.*codd* ; του συχεμ D
Antiochian perp (*qui fuit sychem*)
vg (*filii sychem*). Cf. Josh. xxiv. 32
(Heb. and LXX differ), Gen. xxxiii.
19. The 'Western' text has taken

Sychem as a personal name but confused the relationship ; perhaps the
B-text is to be preferred, but a confident decision is not possible.
18 επ αιγυπτον BℵAC pesh is omitted
by DE e gig Antiochian, and may be
addition under influence of LXX.
With hcl.*mg* here agrees pesh, but
not the Latin 'Western' and D.

ἐκτεθέντος δὲ αὐτοῦ ἀνείλατο αὐτὸν ἡ θυγάτηρ Φαραὼ καὶ 21
ἀνεθρέψατο αὐτὸν ἑαυτῇ υἱόν. καὶ ἐπαιδεύθη Μωυσῆς πάσῃ 22
σοφίᾳ Αἰγυπτίων, ἦν δὲ δυνατὸς ἐν λόγοις καὶ ἔργοις αὐτοῦ.
ὡς δὲ ἐπληροῦτο αὐτῷ τεσσερακονταετὴς χρόνος, ἀνέβη ἐπὶ 23
τὴν καρδίαν αὐτοῦ ἐπισκέψασθαι τοὺς ἀδελφοὺς αὐτοῦ υἱοὺς
Ἰσραήλ. καὶ ἰδών τινα ἀδικούμενον ἠμύνατο καὶ ἐποίησεν 24
ἐκδίκησιν τῷ καταπονουμένῳ πατάξας τὸν Αἰγύπτιον. ἐνόμιζεν 25
δὲ συνιέναι τοὺς ἀδελφοὺς ὅτι ὁ θεὸς διὰ χειρὸς αὐτοῦ δίδωσιν
σωτηρίαν αὐτοῖς, οἱ δὲ οὐ συνῆκαν. τῇ τε ἐπιούσῃ ἡμέρᾳ ὤφθη 26
αὐτοῖς μαχομένοις καὶ συνήλλασσεν αὐτοὺς εἰς εἰρήνην εἰπών·
Ἄνδρες, ἀδελφοί ἐστε· ἵνα τί ἀδικεῖτε ἀλλήλους; | ὁ δὲ ἀδικῶν 27

Ex. ii. 14 τὸν πλησίον ἀπώσατο αὐτὸν εἰπών· Τίς σε κατέστησεν ἄρχοντα
καὶ δικαστὴν ἐφ᾽ ἡμῶν; μὴ ἀνελεῖν με σὺ θέλεις ὃν τρόπον 28
ἀνεῖλες ἐχθὲς τὸν Αἰγύπτιον; ἔφυγεν δὲ Μωυσῆς ἐν τῷ λόγῳ 29
τούτῳ, καὶ ἐγένετο πάροικος ἐν γῇ Μαδιάμ, οὗ ἐγέννησεν υἱοὺς
δύο. καὶ πληρωθέντων ἐτῶν τεσσεράκοντα ὤφθη αὐτῷ ἐν τῇ 30
ἐρήμῳ τοῦ ὄρους Σεινὰ ἄγγελος ἐν φλογὶ πυρὸς βάτου· ὁ δὲ 31
Μωυσῆς ἰδὼν ἐθαύμασεν τὸ ὅραμα· προσερχομένου δὲ αὐτοῦ

Ex. iii. 6 κατανοῆσαι ἐγένετο φωνὴ κυρίου· Ἐγὼ ὁ θεὸς τῶν πατέρων σου, 32
ὁ θεὸς Ἀβραὰμ καὶ Ἰσαὰκ καὶ Ἰακώβ. ἔντρομος δὲ γε‹νόμε›νος

25 Hcl.mg 'the children of Israel' is found also in pesh, but not in D or
Latin witnesses.

αὐτοῦ παρὰ τὸν ποταμὸν ἀνείλατο αὐτὸν ἡ θυγάτηρ Φαραώ, ἀν-
22 εθράψατο αὐτῇ εἰς υἱόν. καὶ ἐπαιδεύθη Μωυσῆς πᾶσαν τὴν σοφίαν
23 Αἰγυπτίων, ἦν τε δυνατὸς ἐν λόγοις καὶ ἔργοις αὐτοῦ. ὡς δὲ
ἐπληροῦτο τεσσαρακονταετὴς αὐτῷ χρόνος, ἀνέβη ἐπὶ τὴν καρδίαν
αὐτοῦ ἐπισκέψασθαι τοὺς ἀδελφοὺς αὐτοῦ τοὺς υἱοὺς Ἰσραήλ.
24 καὶ ἰδών τινα ἀδικούμενον ἐκ τοῦ γένους ἡμύνετο καὶ ἐποίησεν
ἐκδίκησιν τῷ καταπονουμένῳ πατάξας τὸν Αἰγύπτιον, καὶ
25 ἔκρυψεν αὐτὸν ἐν τῇ ἄμμῳ. ἐνόμιζεν δὲ συνιέναι τοὺς ἀδελφοὺς
αὐτοῦ ὅτι ὁ θεὸς διὰ χειρὸς αὐτοῦ δίδωσει σωτηρίαν αὐτοῖς,
26 οἱ δὲ συνῆκαν. τότε ἐπιούσῃ ἡμέρᾳ ὤφθη αὐτοῖς μαχομένοι⟨ι⟩ς
καὶ εἶδεν αὐτοὺς ἀδικοῦντας, καὶ συνήλλασσεν αὐτοὺς εἰς εἰρήνην
εἰπών· Τί ποιεῖτε, ἄνδρες ἀδελφοί, ἵνα τί ἀδεικεῖτε εἰς ἀλλήλους;
27 ὁ δὲ ἀδικῶν τὸν πλησίον ἀπώσατο αὐτὸν εἴπας· Τίς σὲ κατ-
28 έστησεν ἄρχοντα καὶ δικαστὴν ἐφ᾽ ἡμᾶς; μὴ ἀνελεῖν με σὺ θέλεις
29 ὃν τρόπον ἀνεῖλες ἐχθὲς τὸν Αἰγύπτιον; οὕτως καὶ ἐφυγάδευσεν
Μωυσῆς ἐν τῷ λόγῳ τούτῳ, καὶ ἐγένετο πάροικος ἐν γῇ Μαδιάμ,
30 οὗ ἐγέννησεν υἱοὺς δύο. καὶ μετὰ ταῦτα πλησθέντων αὐτῷ ἐτῶν
μ̄ ὤφθη αὐτῷ ἐν τῇ ἐρήμῳ τοῦ ὄρου Σεινὰ ἄγγελος κυρίου ἐν
31 φλογὶ πυρὸς βάτου· ὁ δὲ Μωυσῆς εἰδὼν ἐθαύμαζεν τὸ ὄραμα·
καὶ προσερχομένου αὐτοῦ [κ]αὶ κατανοῆσαι ὁ κύριος εἶπεν αὐτῷ
32 λέγων· Ἐγὼ ὁ θεὸς τῶν πατέρων σου, ὁ θεὸς Ἀβραὰμ καὶ θεὸς
Ἰσὰκ καὶ θεὸς Ἰακώβ. ἔντρομος δὲ γενόμενος Μωυσῆς οὐκ

| 22 επεδευθη | 23 τεσσαρακονταετης] ·μ̄· ετης | 25 ενομιζον |
| 26 αδεικειται | 28 αιχθες | 29 δυω | 30 ετων] ετη |

flumen sustulit eum filia pharao et vice fili educavit sibi   22 et eruditus est moyses d
omni sapientia aegyptiorū eratquae potens in sermonibus et operibus suis   23 ad
ubi inpletur ei xl annorum tempus ascendit in cor ejus visitare fratres suos filios
istrahel   24 et cum vidisset quendam injuriari de genere suo vindicavit et praestitit
vindictam ei qui vexabatur percusso aegyptio et abscondit eum in harena   25 arbi-
trabatur autem intellegere fratres suos quia d̄s per manus ejus dat salutem ipsis ad
illi non intellexerunt   26 tunc sequenti die visus est eis litigantibus et vidit eos
iniquitantes et reconciliavit eos in pacem dicens quid facitis viri fratres ut quid
injuriam facitis invicem   27 qui autem injuriam faciebat proximo repulit eum dicens
quis te constituit principem et judicem super nos   28 numquid interficere me vis
quemadmodum interfecisti externa die aegyptium   29 adque ita profugit moyses in
sermone hoc et fuit incola in terram madiam ubi genuit filios duos   30 et post haec
et inpletis annis xl visus est ei in solitudine in monte sina angelus d̄n̄i in flamma
ignis rubi   31 moyses enim cum vidisset mirabatur visum cumque ipse accederet et
consideraret d̄n̄s ait ad eum dicens   32 ego sum d̄s patrum tuorum d̄s abraham et
d̄s isac et d̄s jacob tremibundusque factus moyses non audiebat considerare   33 et

21 παρα τον ποταμον] ·⁜· in flumen √   24 εκ του γενους] ·⁜· ex genere Harclean
suo √   25 τους αδελφους αυτου] +mg filios Israelis

Μωυσῆς οὐκ ἐτόλμα κατανοῆσαι. εἶπεν δὲ αὐτῷ ὁ κύριος· 33

Ex. iii. 5 Λῦσον τὸ ὑπόδημά σου τῶν ποδῶν, ὁ γὰρ τόπος ἐφ᾽ ᾧ ἕστηκας

Ex. iii. 7 f., 10 γῆ ἁγία ἐστίν. ἰδὼν εἶδον τὴν κάκωσιν τοῦ λαοῦ μου τοῦ ἐν 34 Αἰγύπτῳ, καὶ τοῦ στεναγμοῦ αὐτοῦ ἤκουσα, καὶ κατέβην ἐξελέσθαι αὐτούς· καὶ νῦν δεῦρο ἀποστείλω σε εἰς Αἴγυπτον. τοῦτον 35 τὸν Μωυσῆν, ὃν ἠρνήσαντο εἰπόντες· Τίς σὲ κατέστησεν ἄρχοντα καὶ δικαστήν; τοῦτον ὁ θεὸς καὶ ἄρχοντα καὶ λυτρωτὴν ἀπέσταλκεν σὺν χειρὶ ἀγγέλου τοῦ ὀφθέντος αὐτῷ ἐν τῇ βάτῳ. οὗτος ἐξήγαγεν αὐτοὺς ποιήσας τέρατα καὶ σημεῖα ἐν τῇ Αἰγύπτῳ 36 καὶ ἐν Ἐρυθρᾷ Θαλάσσῃ καὶ ἐν τῇ ἐρήμῳ ἔτη τεσσεράκοντα.

Deut. xviii. 15 οὗτός ἐστιν ὁ Μωυσῆς ὁ εἴπας τοῖς υἱοῖς Ἰσραήλ· Προφήτην ὑμῖν 37 ἀναστήσει ὁ θεὸς ἐκ τῶν ἀδελφῶν ὑμῶν ὡς ἐμέ. οὗτός ἐστιν ὁ 38 γενόμενος ἐν τῇ ἐκκλησίᾳ ἐν τῇ ἐρήμῳ μετὰ τοῦ ἀγγέλου τοῦ λαλοῦντος αὐτῷ ἐν τῷ ὄρει Σινὰ καὶ τῶν πατέρων ἡμῶν, ὃς ἐξελέξατο λόγια ζῶντα δοῦναι ὑμῖν, ᾧ οὐκ ἠθέλησαν ὑπήκοοι γενέ- 39 σθαι οἱ πατέρες ἡμῶν ἀλλὰ ἀπώσαντο καὶ ἐστράφησαν ἐν ταῖς

Ex. xxxii. 1 καρδίαις αὐτῶν εἰς Αἴγυπτον, | εἰπόντες τῷ Ἀαρών· Ποίησον 40 ἡμῖν θεοὺς οἳ προπορεύσονται ἡμῶν· ὁ γὰρ Μωυσῆς οὗτος, ὃς

Editors   33 των ποδων σου WH Soden JHR   34 αυτου] αυτων Soden
36 τη 1°] γη Soden   37 ειπας] ειπων Soden   38 εξελεξατο] εδεξατο
WH Soden JHR   υμιν] ημιν WHmg Soden JHR

Old Uncial   32 ετολμα BAC 81 (+D)   ετολμησεν ℵ   33 ο 1° BℵC 81   om A
σου των ποδων B   των ποδων σου ℵA 81 (+D)   σου (C² om σου) εκ των ποδων σου C
ω BℵA 81 (+D)   +συν C (συ C²)   34 αυτου B(+D)   αυτων ℵAC 81
35 δικαστην BA   +εφ ημων ℵC 81 (+D)   και 2° Bℵª 81 (+D)   om ℵAC
λυτρωτην BACℵᶜ 81 (+D)   δικαστην ℵ   απεσταλκεν BℵA 81 (+D)   απεστειλεν C   συν BAC 81 (+D)   εν ℵ   36 τη 1° BC   γη ℵA 81 (+D)
37 αναστησει BℵA 81 (+D)   +κυριος C   υμων BACℵᶜ 81 (+D)   om ℵ
εμε BℵA 81   +αυτου ακουσεσθε C(+D)   38 ημων BAC 81 (+D)   υμων ℵ
εξελεξατο B   εδεξατο ℵAC 81 (+D)   υμιν Bℵ   ημιν AC 81 (+D)   39 ημων
BℵAC(+D)   υμων 81   εστραφησαν BACℵª 81 (cf. D)   +και ℵ   εν BℵAC
om 81 (+D)   40 ουτος BAC 81 (+D)   +ο ανθρωπος ℵ

Antiochian   33 των ποδων σου HPSϚ(+D)   εφ] εν HPSϚ   34 αυτου] αυτων
HPSϚ   αποστελω HPSϚ   35 om και 2° HPSϚ   απεστειλεν HPSϚ
συν] εν HPSϚ   36 τη 1°] γη HPSϚ(+D)   αιγυπτου Ϛ(+D)   37 om
ο before μωυσης HS(+D)   ειπας] ειπων HPSϚ   αναστησει] +κυριος
HPSϚ   θεος] +υμων PSϚ   +ημων H   εμε] +αυτου ακουσεσθε Ϛ
(cf. D)   38 αυτω] αυτου H   εξελεξατο] εδεξατο HPSϚ(+D)
υμιν] ημιν HPSϚ(+D)   39 om εν HPSϚ(+D)   τη καρδια HPS

33 ἐτόλμα κατανοῆσαι. καὶ ἐγένετο φωνὴ πρὸς αὐτόν· Λῦσ[ο]ν
τὸ ὑπόδημα τῶν ποδῶν σου, ὁ γὰρ τόπος οὗ ἕστηκας γῆ ἁγία
34 ἐστίν. καὶ ἰδὼν γὰρ ἴδον τὴν κάκωσιν τοῦ λαοῦ τοῦ ἐν Ἐγύπτῳ,
καὶ τοῦ στεναγμοῦ αὐτοῦ ἀκήκοα, καὶ κατέβην ἐξελέσθαι αὐτούς·
35 καὶ νῦν δεῦρο ἀποστείλω σε εἰς Αἴγυπτον. τοῦτον τὸν Μωυσῆν,
ὃν ἠρνήσαντο εἰπόντες· Τίς σὲ κατέστησεν ἄρχοντα καὶ δικαστὴν
ἐφ᾽ ἡμῶν, τοῦτον ὁ θεὸς καὶ ἄρχοντα καὶ λυτρωτὴν ἀπέσταλκεν
36 σὺν χειρὶ ἀγγέλου τοῦ ὀφθέντος αὐτῷ ἐν τῇ βάτῳ. οὗτος ἐξήγαγεν
αὐτούς, ὁ ποιήσας τέρατα καὶ σημεῖα ἐν γῇ Αἰγύπτου καὶ ἐν
37 Ἐρυθρᾷ Θαλάσσῃ καὶ ἐν τῇ ἐρήμῳ ἔτη μ̄. οὗτός ἐστιν Μωυσῆς
ὁ εἴπας τοῖς υἱοῖς Ἰσραήλ· Προφήτην ὑμεῖν ἀναστήσει ὁ θεὸς ἐκ
38 τῶν ἀδελφῶν ὑμῶν ὡσεὶ ἐμέ· αὐτοῦ ἀκούεσθε. οὗτός ἐστιν ὁ
γενόμενος ἐν τῇ ἐκκλησίᾳ ἐν τῇ ἐρήμῳ μετὰ τοῦ ἀγγέλου
λαλοῦντος αὐτῷ ἐν τῷ ὄρει Σεινὰ καὶ τῶν πατέρων ἡμῶν, ὃς
39 ἐδέξατο λόγια ζῶντα δοῦναι ἡμῖν, ὅτι οὐκ ἠθέλησαν ὑπήκοοι γενέσθαι οἱ πατέρες ἡμῶν ἀλλὰ ἀπώσαντο καὶ ἀπεστράφησαν ταῖς
40 καρδίαις εἰς Αἴγυπτον, | εἴπαντες τῷ Ἀαρών· Ποίησον ἡμεῖν
θεοὺς οἳ προπορεύσονται ἡμῶν. ὁ γὰρ Μωυσῆς οὗτος, ὃς

36 ερυθρα] υρεθρα   37 ακουεσθε] MS. perhaps reads ακουσεσθε
39 γενεσθε

---

facta est vox ad eum solve calciamentum pedum tuorum locus enim in quo stas terra d
santa est 34 intuitus enim vidi mulcationem populi qui est in aegypto et gemitus
ejus audivi et descendi eripere eos et nunc veni mittam te in aegyptum 35 hunc
ipsum moysen quem negaverunt dicentes quis te constituit principem et judicem
super nos hunc d̄s̄ et principem et redemptorem misit in manu angeli qui visus est ei
in rubo 36 hic eduxit eos cum fecisset portenta et signa in aegypto et in rubro mari
et in solitudine per annos xl 37 hic est moyses qui dixit filiis istrahel prophetam
vovis suscitavit d̄s̄ de fratribus vestris tamquam me ipsum audietis 38 hic est qui
fuit in ecclesia in solitudine cum angelo qui loquebatur ei in monte sina et patribus
nostris qui accipit eloquia viventium dare nobis 39 cui noluerunt oboedientes esse
patres nostri sed repulerunt et conversi sunt cordibus in aegyptum 40 dicentes ad
aaron fac nobis d̄ēo qui praecedant nos moyses enim hic qui eduxit nos de terra

---

38 [ille quidem] accepit praecepta dei vivi dare vobis, 39 cui noluerunt   Irenaeus,
oboedire patres vestri, sed abjecerunt et conversi sunt corde suo in Aegyptum,   iv. 15, 1
40 dicentes ad Aaron : fac nobis deos qui nos antecedant ; Moyses enim qui   (26, 1)

38 praecepta] 'words' (=λόγια) Armen   39 cui . . . vestri] 'and when our fathers
would not be submissive and obedient' Armen   corde suo] 'with their hearts' Armen
40 Moyses] 'this Moses' Armen

---

35 εφ ημων] ·⋇· super nos ✓   Harclean

---

38 ημιν AC 81 D Antiochian seems   accident, the intrinsic evidence of
preferable to υμιν Bℵ minn perp Iren.   fitness to the context (cf. οι πατερες
The variation being probably due to   ημων) is to be accepted.

ἐξήγαγεν ἡμᾶς ἐκ γῆς Αἰγύπτου, οὐκ οἴδαμεν τί ἐγένετο αὐτῷ. 41
καὶ ἐμοσχοποίησαν ἐν ταῖς ἡμέραις ἐκείναις καὶ ἀνήγαγον θυσίαν
τῷ εἰδώλῳ, καὶ εὐφραίνοντο ἐν τοῖς ἔργοις τῶν χειρῶν αὐτῶν.
ἔστρεψεν δὲ ὁ θεὸς καὶ παρέδωκεν αὐτοὺς λατρεύειν τῇ στρατειᾷ 42
τοῦ οὐρανοῦ, καθὼς γέγραπται ἐν βίβλῳ τῶν προφητῶν· Μὴ
σφάγια καὶ θυσίας προσηνέγκατέ μοι ἔτη τεσσεράκοντα, οἶκος
Ἰσραήλ; καὶ ἀνελάβετε τὴν σκηνὴν τοῦ Μολὸχ καὶ τὸ ἄστρον 43
τοῦ θεοῦ Ῥομφά, τοὺς τύπους οὓς ἐποιήσατε προσκυνεῖν αὐτοῖς.
καὶ μετοικιῶ ὑμᾶς ἐπέκεινα Βαβυλῶνος. | ἡ σκηνὴ τοῦ μαρτυρίου 44
ἦν τοῖς πατράσιν ἡμῶν ἐν τῇ ἐρήμῳ, καθὼς διετάξατο ὁ λαλῶν τῷ
Μωυσῇ ποιῆσαι αὐτὴν κατὰ τὸν τύπον ὃν ἑωράκει, ἣν καὶ εἰσ- 45
ήγαγον διαδεξάμενοι οἱ πατέρες ἡμῶν μετὰ Ἰησοῦ ἐν τῇ κατασχέσει τῶν ἐθνῶν ὧν ἐξῶσεν ὁ θεὸς ἀπὸ προσώπου τῶν πατέρων

Amos v. 25-27 *(margin beside lines 4–8)*

Editors   42 τεσσερακοντα] +εν τη ερημω WH Soden JHR   43 θεου] +υμων Soden
ρομφα] ρεφαν Soden JHR

Old Uncial   41 εγενετο BℵAC   γεγονεν 81 (+D)   42 δε BℵA 81 (+D)
+αυτους C   αυτους BℵAC(+D)   αυτοις 81   ετη τεσσερακοντα οικος
ισραηλ B   ετη τεσσερακοντα εν τη ερημω οικος ισραηλ B²(?)ℵC 81 (+D)   εν τη ερημω
οικος ισραηλ ετη τεσσερακοντα A   ισραηλ Bℵ(A) 81 (+D)   +λεγει κυριος C
43 θεου B(+D)   +υμων ℵAC 81   ρομφα B   ρομφαν ℵ   ρεμφα 81   ραιφαν
Aℵᶜ   ρεφαν C   44 ημων BℵC 81 (+D)   υμων A   διεταξατο BACℵᶜ
81 (+D)   εταξατο ℵ

Antiochian   40 γεγονεν HPS𝄐(+D)   42 λατρευειν] +εν S   τεσσερακοντα] +εν
τη ερημω HPS𝄐(+D)   43 θεου] +υμων HPS𝄐   ρεφα H   ρεφφαν 102
462 ᵐᵍ   ρεφφαν P   ρεμφαν 462 ᵗˣᵗ 𝄐 (cf. D)   ρομφα S   44 ην] +εν 𝄐(+D)
ημων] υμων S   εωρακεν HS(+D)

43 The omission of υμων after θεου
in BD gig Iren Philast might have
been due to a reluctance to admit that
the heathen divinity was in any sense
the Hebrews' ('your') god; but the
original writer may have been led by
the same motive to omit the word. On
the whole it is better to explain the
presence of the word in ℵAC Antiochian
as a case of conformation to the text
of the LXX, and to follow BD.

It is safest to assume that the
original spelling for the name of the
god here was ρεφαν (ραιφαν), as in
LXX. The chief spellings in the
MSS. of Acts are as follows : ρεφαν
(ραι- A) ACE e (repham) pesh hcl sah
boh (ρεφαν or ρηφαν) ; ρεφα H ; ρεφφαν
(-φρ- P) P 102 462ᵐᵍ ; ρεμφαν 1 69 minn
d h perp gig Iren vg. W. W. (in all these

Latin documents rempham); ρεμφαμ D
(Latinism?); ρεμφα 81 vg.codd.   BS
Origen (Cels. v. 8, but vv. ll.) have
ρομφα, ℵ 3 ρομφαν, but the untrust-
worthiness of B and ℵ in the spelling
of unusual proper names is notori-
ous ; cf. Torrey, Ezra Studies, pp.
94 f.

επι τα μερη D (perp) gig (e) sah
('to this side of Babylon') is probably
'Western' paraphrase, bringing the
statement into better agreement with
historical fact.   The reading επεκεινα
of all other witnesses agrees indeed
with LXX (Amos v. 27), but a corrector, conforming to LXX, would not
have left βαβυλωνος untouched.

The addition of hcl.text and ⁑
(from Amos v. 27) is found in full in
1611 λεγει κυριος ο θεος ο παντοκρατωρ

ἐξήγαγεν ἡμᾶς ἐκ γῆς Αἰγύπτου, οὐκ οἴδαμεν τί γέγονεν αὐτῷ.
41 καὶ ἐμοσχοποίησαν ἐν ταῖς ἡμέραις ἐκείναις καὶ ἀνήγαγον θυσίαν
τῷ εἰδώλῳ, καὶ ηὐφραίνοντο ἐν τοῖς ἔργοις τῶν χειρῶν αὐτῶν.
42 ἔστρεψεν δὲ ὁ θεὸς καὶ παρέδωκεν αὐτοὺς λατρεύειν τῇ στρατειᾷ
τοῦ οὐρανοῦ, καθὼς γέγραπται ἐν βίβλῳ προφητῶν· Μὴ σφάγια
καὶ θυσίας προσηνέγκατέ μοι ἔτη μ̄ ἐν τῇ ἐρήμῳ, οἶκος Ἰσραήλ;
43 καὶ ἀνελάβετε τὴν σκηνὴν τοῦ Μολὸχ καὶ τὸ ἄστρον τοῦ θεοῦ
Ῥεμφάμ, τοὺς τύπους οὓς ἐποιήσατε προσκυνεῖν αὐτοῖς. καὶ
44 μετοικιῶ ὑμᾶς ἐπὶ [τὰ μέ]ρη Βαβυλῶνος. ἡ σκηνὴ τοῦ μαρτυρίου
ἦν ἐν τοῖς πατράσιν ἡμῶν ἐν τῇ ἐρήμῳ, καθὼς διετάξατο λαλῶν
τῷ Μωυσῖ ποιῆσαι αὐτὴν κατὰ τὸ πα[ράτ]υπον ὃν ἑόρακεν,
45 ἦν καὶ εἰσήγαγον διαδεξάμενοι οἱ πατέρες ἡμῶν μετὰ Ἰησοῦ ἐν
τῇ κατασχέσει τῶν ἐθνῶν ὧν ἐξῶσεν ὁ θεὸς ἀπὸ προσώπου τῶν

41 ανηγαγον] απηγαγοντο   44 πατερεσιν   45 ιησουν

aegypti nescimus quid contegerit ei   41 et vitulum fecerunt in diebus illis et **d**
obtulerunt hostiam simulacro et jucundabantur in operibus manum suarum   42 convertit autem d̄s̄ et tradidit eos deservire exercitui caeli sicut scriptum est in libro
prophetarum numquid hostias et sacrificia obtulisti mihi annis xl in solitudine domus
istrahel   43 et adsumpsistis tabernaculnm ipsius moloch et astrum d̄ī rempham
figuras quae fecistis adorare eis et transmigravo vos in illas partes babylonis
44 tabernaculum testimonii erat penes patres nostros in solitudine sicut disposuit
qui loquebatur moysi facere illud juxta figuram quam viderat   45 quod etiam intro-
duxerant patres nostri cum jesum in possessionem gentium quas expulit d̄s̄ a facie

42 tunc itaque pervertit illos deus, et tradidit il[los ser]vire exercitui caeli, **h**
sicut scriptum est in libr[o profe]tarum : numquid hostias et immolation[es
obtu]listis mihi per annos xl in deserto, domus Is[trael]?   43 et recepistis
domum Moloc, et sidus d̄ī ve[stri Rē]pham, et effigies quas fecistis ut adoretis
ea[s : et trans]feram vos ultra Babylonem.   44 et domus te[stimonii] fuit
patribus nostris in deserto, sicut praec[epit loquens] ad Mossem, faceret eam
secundum effigie[m quam] vidit.   45 quam et induxerunt recipientes pat[res
nos]tri cum īhu in possessione nationum, ex q[uibus] salvabit d̄s̄ a conspectu

eduxit nos de terra Aegýpti, quid ei contigerit ignoramus.   41 et vitulum   Irenaeus,
fecerunt in diebus illis, et obtulerunt sacrificia idolo, et laetabantur in factis   iv. 15, 1
manuum suarum.   42 convertit autem deus, et tradidit eos servire exercitibus   (26, 1)
caeli, quemadmodum scriptum est in libro prophetarum : numquid oblationes
et sacrificia obtulistis mihi annis quadraginta in eremo, domüs Israel?   43 et
accepistis tabernaculum Moloch, et stellam dei Rempham, figuras quas fecistis
adorare eas.

40 quid ei contigerit] *after* ignoramus *Armen*   42 exercitibus] *sing. Armen*

43 βαβυλωνος] Babylonem, dicit dominus deus, omnipotens ⁛ nomen ei ✓   Harclean

ονομα αυτω ; and with varying ininor   44 In Codex Bezae for Scrivener's
omissions in several other minuscules.   πα[. . .]υπον Blass (*St. Kr.*, 1898, p. 540)
614 431 omit ονομα αυτω.   thought πα[. .]τυπον was legible.

ἡμῶν ἕως τῶν ἡμερῶν Δαυείδ· ὃς εὗρεν χάριν ἐνώπιον τοῦ θεοῦ 46
καὶ ᾐτήσατο εὑρεῖν σκήνωμα τῷ οἴκῳ Ἰακώβ. Σολομῶν δὲ 47
οἰκοδόμησεν αὐτῷ οἶκον. ἀλλ' οὐχ ὁ ὕψιστος ἐν χειροποιήτοις 48

Is. lxvi. 1 f. κατοικεῖ· καθὼς ὁ προφήτης λέγει· | Ὁ οὐρανός μοι θρόνος, 49
καὶ ἡ γῆ ὑποπόδιον τῶν ποδῶν μου· ποῖον οἶκον οἰκοδομήσατέ
μοι, λέγει κύριος, ἢ τίς τόπος τῆς καταπαύσεώς μου; οὐχὶ ἡ 50
χείρ μου ἐποίησεν ταῦτα πάντα; σκληροτράχηλοι καὶ ἀπερί- 51
τμητοι καρδίας καὶ τοῖς ὠσίν, ὑμεῖς ἀεὶ τῷ πνεύματι τῷ ἁγίῳ
ἀντιπείπτετε, ὡς οἱ πατέρες ὑμῶν καὶ ὑμεῖς. τίνα τῶν προφητῶν 52
οὐκ ἐδίωξαν οἱ πατέρες ὑμῶν; καὶ ἀπέκτειναν τοὺς προκατ-
αγγείλαντας περὶ τῆς ἐλεύσεως τοῦ δικαίου οὗ νῦν ὑμεῖς προδόται καὶ φονεῖς ἐγένεσθε, οἵτινες ἐλάβετε τὸν νόμον εἰς δια- 53
ταγὰς ἀγγέλων, καὶ οὐκ ἐφυλάξατε.

Ἀκούοντες δὲ ταῦτα διεπρίοντο ταῖς καρδίαις αὐτῶν καὶ 54

Editors   46 οικω] θεω WH Soden   κυριω JHR   †θεω† WHmg   49 και η] η δε
WHmg Soden   οικοδομησετε WH Soden JHR   51 καρδιαις
WH Soden JHR   καρδιας WHmg

Old Uncial   46 ητησατο BAℵᶜ (+D)   om ℵ   οικω Bℵ(+D)   θεω ACℵᶜ 81   47 αυτω
BℵA 81 (+D)   εαυτω C   49 και η B   η δε ℵAC 81 (+D)   οικοδομησατε
B   οικοδομησετε ℵAC 81 (+D)   50 ταυτα παντα Bℵ 81   παντα ταυτα
AC(+D)   51 καρδιας B   καρδιαις AC(+D)   ταις καρδιαις υμων ℵ   τη καρδια 81
53 εφυλαξατε BℵC 81 (+D)   εφυλαξεσθε A   54 ταυτα BACℵᶜ 81   om ℵ

Antiochian   46 οικω] θεω PϚ   47 αυτω] εαυτω H   48 χειροποιητοις] +ναοις
HPϚ   κατοικει] +ναοις S   49 και η] η δε HPϚ(+D)   om οικον H
οικοδομησετε HPϚϚ(+D)   50 παντα ταυτα P(+D)   51 καρδιας] τη
καρδια HPϚ   52 υμων] ημων S   γεγενησθε HPϚϚ

---

46 οικω BℵHS 429 D d sah (cod. B)
is generally held to be so difficult that
it must be considered a very ancient
error, for which θεω ACP minn
Latin (except d), Syriac, Bohairic, was
an early emendation, probably following Ps. cxxxii. 5. Hort conjectured
that ΚΩ was the original, and although
this does not appear among the various
Greek translations of 'the Mighty One
of Jacob' (אֲבִיר יַעֲקֹב, Ps. cxxxii. 5, cf.
Gen. xlix. 24, Ps. cxxxii. 2, Is. xlix.
26, lx. 16, see also Is. i. 24), yet that
phrase was evidently a difficult one,
and received several renderings in the
Greek Old Testament, one of which,
δυνάστης Ἰακώβ (Gen. xlix. 24, Is. i.
24 [v.l.], and Ps. cxxxii. 2 Aquila),

is not very far from κύριος Ἰακώβ.
Plainly οικω was found admissible by
many early readers of Acts, and it is
not quite impossible; but the whole
context makes it unlikely. If we
have here a translation from an Aramaic
source, it is easy to suppose that the
Aramaic equivalent of the Hebrew
phrase was first rendered by τω κυριω
ιακωβ, and then this unusual expression
corrupted to the familiar-sounding
but inappropriate phrase τω οικω ιακωβ.

51 καρδιαις ℵACD is to be preferred
to καρδιας B unsupported (cf. Jer. ix.
26). Note the readings ταις καρδιαις
υμων ℵ, τη καρδια 81 Antiochian gig g₂
h Lucif Aug (cf. Ezek. xliv. 7, 9), and
other forms of scribal modification.

46 πατέρων ὑμῶν ἕως τῶν ἡμερῶν Δαυείδ· ὃς εὗρε χάριν ἐνώπιον
47 τοῦ θεοῦ καὶ ἠτήσατο σκήνωμα εὑρεῖν τῷ οἴκῳ Ἰακώβ. Σολο-
48 μῶν δὲ οἰκοδόμησεν αὐτῷ οἶκον. ὁ δὲ ὕψιστος οὐ κατοικεῖ ἐν
χειροποιήτοις· ὡς ὁ προφήτης λέγει·
49   Ὁ οὐρανός μού ἐστιν θρόνος, ἡ δὲ γῆ ὑποπόδιον τῶν ποδῶν
μου· ποῖον οἶκον οἰκοδομήσετέ μοι, λέγει κύριος, ἢ ποῖος τόπος
50   τῆς καταπαύσεώς μου ἐστιν; οὐχὶ ἡ χείρ μου ἐποίησεν πάντα
ταῦτα;
51 σκληροτράχηλοι καὶ ἀπερίτμητοι καρδίαις καὶ τοῖς ὠσίν, ὑμεῖς
ἀεὶ τῷ πνεύματι τῷ ἁγίῳ ἀντιπίπτετε, καθὼς οἱ πατέρες καὶ
52 ὑμῶν. τίνα τῶν προφητῶν οὐκ ἐδίωξαν ἐκεῖνοι; καὶ ἀπέκτειναν
αὐτοὺς τοὺς προκαταγγέλλοντας περὶ ἐλεύσεως τοῦ δικαίου οὗ
53 νῦν ὑμεῖς προδόται καὶ φονεῖς ἐγένεσθε, οἵτινες ἐλάβετε τὸν
νόμον εἰς διαταγὰς ἀγγέλων, καὶ οὐκ ἐφυλάξατε.
54   Ἀκούσαντες δὲ αὐτοῦ διεπρίοντο ταῖς καρδίαις αὐτῶν καὶ

49 οικοδομησεται   51 αντιπιπτεται   52 εγενεσθαι

---

patrum nostrorum usque ad dies davit   46 qui referit gratiam in sconspectu d̅i̅ et d
petiit tabernaculum invenire sedes domui jacob   47 solomon autem aedificavit ei
domum   48 sed ipse altissimus inhabitavit in manufactis sicut profeta dixit
49 caelum est meus thronus terra vero scamillum pedum meorum qualem domum
aedificatis mihi dicit d̅n̅s̅ aut quis locus requens mea est   50 nonne manus mea fecit
haec omnia   51 durae cervices et incircumcisi cordibus et auribus vos semper s̅p̅o̅
sancto obstitistis sicut patres vestri et vos   52 quem prophetarum non persecuti
sunt illi et occiderunt eos qui praenuntiaverunt de adventu justi cujus nunc vos
proditores et homicidae effecti estis   53 qui accepistis legem in dispositiones
angelorum et non custoditis   54 audientes autem eum discruciabantur cordibus suis

---

patrum nostroru[m, usque] in diem David,   46 qui invenit gratiam coram [d̅o̅], h
et petit habitationem invenire in d̅o̅ Jacob.   47 [Solomō] autem aedificavit illi
domum.   48 sed altissim[us noʾn] habitat in aedificis manu factis hominu[m, sicut]
dicit profeta : 49 caelus mihi tronus est et [terra sub]pedaneum pedum meorum.
qualem do[mum ae]dificavitis mihi, vel qualis domus quietis m[eae est]?
50 nunquid non manus mea fecit omnia ista ?   51 duricordes, et incircumcisi
corde et auribus, vos semper s̅c̅o̅ s̅p̅u̅i̅ contradixisti, sicut p[atres] vestri.
52 quem non ex profetis illi persecut[i sunt ? et occideru]nt qui nuntiaverunt
de adventum justi, cu[jus vos] nunc proditores et latrones fuistis,   53 [qui
acc]epistis legem in praeceptis angelorum, nec ō[nino s]ervastis.   54 et cum

---

49 *Heaven is my throne, and earth is my footstool : what house will ye build*   Irenaeus,
me, or what is the place of my rest?   Dem. of Ap.
Preach. 45

51 σκληροτραχηλοι] ⸰※ ο ⸜ duri cervice   Harclean

ἔβρυχον τοὺς ὀδόντας ἐπ᾽ αὐτόν. ὑπάρχων δὲ πλήρης πνεύματος 55
ἁγίου ἀτενίσας εἰς τὸν οὐρανὸν εἶδεν δόξαν θεοῦ καὶ ᾽Ιησοῦν
ἑστῶτα ἐκ δεξιῶν τοῦ θεοῦ, | καὶ εἶπεν· ᾽Ιδοὺ θεωρῶ τοὺς οὐρανοὺς 56
διηνοιγμένους καὶ τὸν υἱὸν τοῦ ἀνθρώπου ἐκ δεξιῶν ἑστῶτα τοῦ
θεοῦ. κράξαντες δὲ φωνῇ μεγάλῃ συνέσχον τὰ ὦτα αὐτῶν, καὶ 57
ὥρμησαν ὁμοθυμαδὸν ἐπ᾽ αὐτόν, καὶ ἐκβαλόντες ἔξω τῆς πόλεως 58
ἐλιθοβόλουν. καὶ οἱ μάρτυρες ἀπέθεντο τὰ ἱμάτια ἑαυτῶν παρὰ
τοὺς πόδας νεανίου καλουμένου Σαύλου. καὶ ἐλιθοβόλουν τὸν 59
Στέφανον ἐπικαλούμενον καὶ λέγοντα· Κύριε ᾽Ιησοῦ, δέξαι τὸ
πνεῦμά μου· | θεὶς δὲ τὰ γόνατα ἔκραξεν φωνῇ μεγάλῃ· Κύριε, 60
μὴ στήσῃς αὐτοῖς ταύτην τὴν ἁμαρτίαν· καὶ τοῦτο εἰπὼν
ἐκοιμήθη. Σαῦλος δὲ ἦν συνευδοκῶν τῇ ἀναιρέσει αὐτοῦ. VIII
᾽Εγένετο δὲ ἐν ἐκείνῃ τῇ ἡμέρᾳ διωγμὸς μέγας ἐπὶ τὴν

56 διηνυγμενους

Editors   58 εαυτων] αυτων WH Soden JHR   60 την αμαρτιαν ταυτην Soden

---

Old Uncial   55 πληρης BAC 81 (+D) +πιστεως και ℵ   δεξιων του θεου
BℵA 81(+D)   δεξιων αυτου C   56 εκ δεξιων εστωτα Bℵᶜ 81 (+D)   εστωτα
εκ δεξιων ℵAC   57 φωνη μεγαλη BℵAC(+D)   φωνην μεγαλη 81
58 εκβαλοντες BℵC 81 (+D)   +αυτον A   εαυτων B   αυτων ℵAC 81 (+D)
59 ιησου BℵA 81 (+D)   +χριστε C   60 φωνη μεγαλη BAC²ℵᶜ 81   φωνην
μεγαλη C (cf. D)   om ℵ   ταυτην την αμαρτιαν BAC(+D)   την αμαρτιαν
ταυτην ℵ 81

Antiochian   55 δεξιων του θεου] δεξιων αυτου S   56 διηνοιγμενους] ανεωγμενους
HPSϛ(+D)   58 εαυτων] αυτων ϛ(+D)   om HPS   60 την αμαρτιαν
ταυτην HPSϛ

---

55 The reading of h [ipse aut]em cum esset in spiritu sancto (ο δε υπαρχων εν πνευματι αγιω) has a less usual expression and, in ο δε, a better connexion than the Greek text. The former consideration perhaps speaks for, the latter against, its originality. If the reading represented by h is original 'Western,' D is here conformed to the B-text.

55 ἔβρυχόν τε τοὺς ὀδόντας ἐπ᾽ αὐτόν. ὑπάρχων δὲ πλήρης πνεύματος ἁγίου ἀτενείσας εἰς τὸν οὐρανὸν εἶδε δόξαν θεοῦ καὶ
56 Ἰησοῦν τὸν κύριον ἐκ δεξιῶν τοῦ θεοῦ ἑστῶτα, | καὶ εἶπεν· Ἰδοὺ
θεωρῶ τοὺς οὐρανοὺς ἠνεῳγμένους καὶ τὸν υἱὸν τοῦ ἀνθρώπου
57 ἐκ δεξιῶν ἑστῶτα τοῦ θεοῦ. κράξαντες δὲ φωνῇ μεγάλῃ συν-
58 έσχαν τὰ ὦτα αὐτῶν, καὶ ὥρμησαν ὁμοθυμαδὸν ἐπ᾽ αὐτόν, | καὶ
ἐκβαλόντες ἔξω τῆς πόλεως ἐλιθοβόλουν αὐτόν. καὶ οἱ μάρτυρες
ἀπέθεντο τὰ εἱμάτια αὐτῶν παρὰ τοὺς πόδας νεανίου τινὸς
59 καλουμένου Σαύλου. καὶ ἐλιθοβόλουν τὸν Στέφανον ἐπικαλού-
60 μενον καὶ λέγοντα· Κύριε Ἰησοῦ, δέξαι τὸ πνεῦμά μου· | θεὶς τὰ
γόνατα ἔκραξεν φωνὴν μεγάλην λέγων· Κύριε, μὴ στήσῃς αὐτοῖς
VIII ταύτην τὴν ἁμαρτίαν· καὶ τοῦτο εἰπὼν ἐκοιμήθη. Σαῦλος δὲ
ἦν συνευδοκῶν τῇ ἀναιρέσει αὐτοῦ.

Ἐγένετο δὲ ἐν ἐκείνῃ τῇ ἡμέρᾳ διωγμὸς μέγας καὶ θλεῖψις
60 δεξε στησεις 1 ανεραισι θλειψεις

et stridebant dendibus super eum 55 cumque esset plenus s̄p̄u̅ sancto intuitus in d
caelum vidit gloriam d̄ī et īh̄m d̄n̄m ad dexteram d̄ī stantem 56 et dixit ecce video
caelos apertos et filium hominis ad dexteram d̄ī stantem 57 et cum exclamasset
voce magna conpresserunt aures eorum et inpetum unanimiter fecerunt in eū 58 et
ejectum extra civitatem lapidabant eum adque ipsi testes deposuerunt vestimenta
sua ad pedes adulescentes cujusdam nomine sauli 59 et lapidabant stephanum
invocantem et dicentem d̄n̄e īh̄u accipe s̄p̄m̄ meum 60 cumq· posuisset genua et
clamavit voce magna dicens d̄n̄e ne statuas illis peccatum hoc et cum hoc dixisset
dormibit
1 saulus vero erat consentiens interfecti ejus facta est itaque in illa die persecutio

haec illi audissent, fre[meban]t intra corda sua, et stridebant dentes in eū. h
55 [ipse aut]em cum esset in s̄p̄u̅ s̄c̄o̅, et intueretur caelū, [vidit ho]norem d̄ī, et
īh̄m d̄n̄m ad dexteram d̄ī stan[tem, 56 et d]ixit : ecce video caelos apertos, et
filium homi[nis ad d]exteram d̄ī stantem. 57 tunc populus exclama[vit voce]
magna et continuerunt aures suas, et in[rueru]nt pariter omnes in eum. 58 et
expulerunt eū [extra ci]vitate, et lapidabunt eum : et illi testes posu[erunt]
vestimenta sua ante pedes juvenis, cujus [nome]n vocatur Saulus. 59 et
lapidabunt Stefanum [invoca]ntem et dicentem : dne īh̄u recipe s̄p̄ūm̄ meū.
60 [et geni]bus positis exclamavit voce magna : d̄n̄e ne [statuas i]llis hoc
peccatum. et dum hoc dicit, obdor[mivit].
1 [Sa]ulus autem erat conprobator neci Stefani. [et in illi]s diebus facta est

[55 hunc videt Stephanus, cum lapidaretur, adhuc stantem ad dexteram dei.] Tertullian,
Prax. 30

60 domine, ne statuas illis hoc peccatum. Cyprian,
Bon. pat. 16

55 [Stephanus haec docens, adhuc cum super terram esset,] vidit gloriam dei Irenaeus,
et Jesum ad dexteram, 56 et dixit : ecce video caelos apertos et filium hominis iii. 12, 13 (16)
ad dexteram adstantem dei.

60 domine, ne statuas eis peccatum hoc. iii. 12, 13 (16)

58 ελιθοβολουν αυτον] lapidabant ⁘ eum ✓ 60 κυριε] +mg Jesu Harclean

ἐκκλησίαν τὴν ἐν Ἱεροσολύμοις· πάντες δὲ διεσπάρησαν κατὰ
τὰς χώρας τῆς Ἰουδαίας καὶ Σαμαρείας πλὴν τῶν ἀποστόλων.
συνεκόμισαν δὲ τὸν Στέφανον ἄνδρες εὐλαβεῖς καὶ ἐποίησαν 2
κοπετὸν μέγαν ἐπ' αὐτῷ. Σαῦλος δὲ ἐλυμαίνετο τὴν ἐκκλησίαν 3
κατὰ τοὺς οἴκους εἰσπορευόμενος, σύρων τε ἄνδρας καὶ γυναῖκας
παρεδίδου εἰς φυλακήν.
Οἱ μὲν οὖν διασπαρέντες διῆλθον εὐαγγελιζόμενοι τὸν λόγον. 4
Φίλιππος δὲ κατελθὼν εἰς τὴν πόλιν τῆς Σαμαρείας ἐκήρυσσεν 5
αὐτοῖς τὸν Χριστόν. προσεῖχον δὲ οἱ ὄχλοι τοῖς λεγομένοις ὑπὸ 6
τοῦ Φιλίππου ὁμοθυμαδὸν ἐν τῷ ἀκούειν αὐτοὺς καὶ βλέπειν τὰ
σημεῖα ἃ ἐποίει· πολλοὶ γὰρ τῶν ἐχόντων πνεύματα ἀκάθαρτα 7
βοῶντα φωνῇ μεγάλῃ ἐξήρχοντο, πολλοὶ δὲ παραλελυμένοι καὶ
χωλοὶ ἐθεραπεύθησαν· ἐγένετο δὲ πολλὴ χαρὰ ἐν τῇ πόλει ἐκείνῃ. 8
ἀνὴρ δέ τις ὀνόματι Σίμων προυπῆρχεν ἐν τῇ πόλει μαγεύων 9
καὶ ἐξιστάνων τὸ ἔθνος τῆς Σαμαρείας, λέγων εἶναί τινα ἑαυτὸν
μέγαν, ᾧ προσεῖχον πάντες ἀπὸ μεικροῦ ἕως μεγάλου λέγοντες· 10
Οὗτός ἐστιν ἡ δύναμις τοῦ θεοῦ ἡ καλουμένη μεγάλη. προσεῖχον 11

Editors	1 [δε 3°] WH	5 om την Soden JHR	9 εξιστανων] εξιστων Soden

Old Uncial   1 παντες δε BC 81 (+D)   παντες τε A   και παντες ℵᶜ   om δε ℵ   3 ανδρας
BACℵᶜ 81 (+D)   τους ανδρας ℵ   4 διηλθον BACℵᶜ 81 (+D)   ηλθον ℵ
5 δε BℵAC 81ᶜᵒʳʳ (+D)   τε 81   την BℵA   om C 81 (+D)   σαμαρειας
BACℵᶜ 81 (+D)   καισαριας ℵ   6 φιλιππου BℵC 81 (+D)   παυλου A
αυτους BACℵᶜ 81 (+D)   αυτου ℵᵛⁱᵈ   a BℵC 81 (+D)   om A

Antiochian   1 παντες δε] παντες τε Ϛ   2 εποιησαντο HPSϚ   μεγα H   επ
αυτον HS   5 om την HPSϚ (+D)   6 δε] τε HPSϚ   7 πολλοι 1°]
πολλων HPSϚ   μεγαλη φωνη Ϛ   εξηρχετο HPSϚ   8 εγενετο δε]
και εγενετο HPSϚ   πολλη χαρα] χαρα μεγαλη HPSϚ (+D)   9 εξιστανων]
εξιστων HSϚ   10 om παντες HPS   om καλουμενη HLPSϚ

5 εις την πολιν της σαμαρειας BA
69 181 460 1175 1898, εις την
πολιν της καισαριας ℵ, om την CD
Antiochian sah boh, *Samaria in
civitate* perp. The presence of the
article is strongly attested, but not
so decisively as to make the difficult
phrase with the article acceptable.
The meaning cannot be 'the capital
of Samaria'; while the name Samaria
for the city itself is improbable for
New Testament times, even if the
genitive in such a use were not
chiefly poetic and in the N.T. un-

exampled (except in 2 Peter ii. 6),
cf. e.g. Acts xi. 5 ἐν πόλει Ἰόππῃ.
The phrase Lk. ix. 52 (ℵΓΔ minn)
εις πολιν σαμαριτων shows a certain
similarity. See C. C. Torrey, *Composition and Date of Acts*, p. 18
note 2. The reading of ℵ is probably due to some knowledge of the
tradition connecting Simon Magus
and Philip with Caesarea.
7 In Codex Bezae Scrivener was
inclined to read π[αρ]α. Blass (*St. Kr.*,
1898, p. 540) thinks the scribe more
probably wrote π[αμ].

ἐπὶ τὴν ἐκκλησίαν τὴν ἐν Ἱεροσολύμοις· πάντες δὲ διεσπάρησαν
κατὰ τὰς χώρας Ἰουδαίας καὶ Σαμαρίας πλὴν τῶν ἀποστόλων,
2 οἳ ἔμειναν ἐν Ἱερουσαλήμ. συνκομίσαντες τὸν Στέφανον ἄνδρες
3 εὐλαβεῖς καὶ ἐποίησαν κοπετὸν μέγαν ἐπ' αὐτῷ. ὁ δὲ Σαῦλος
ἐλυμαίνετο τὴν ἐκκλησίαν κατὰ τοὺς οἴκους εἰσπορευόμενος,
σύρων τε ἄνδρας καὶ γυναῖκας παρεδίδου εἰς φυλακήν.
4 Οἱ μὲν οὖν διασπαρέντες διῆλθον εὐαγγελιζόμενοι τὸν λόγον.
5 Φίλιππος δὲ κατελθὼν εἰς πόλιν τῆς Σαμαρίας ἐκήρυσσεν
6 αὐτοῖς τὸν Χριστόν. ὡς δὲ ἤκουον πᾶν, οἱ ὄχλοι προσεῖχον
τοῖς λεγομένοις ὑπὸ Φιλίππου [. . .]οντ[.] ἐν τῷ ἀκούειν
7 αὐτοὺς καὶ βλέπειν τὰ σημεῖα ἃ ἐποίει· π[. .] πολλοῖς γὰρ
τῶν ἐχόντων πνεύματα ἀκάθαρτα βοῶντα φωνῇ μεγάλῃ ἐξ-
8 ήρχοντο, πολλοὶ δὲ παραλελυμένοι χωλοὶ ἐθεραπεύοντο· χαρά τε
9 μεγάλη ἐγένετο ἐν τῇ πόλει ἐκείνῃ. ἀνὴρ δέ τις ὀνόματι Σίμων
προυπάρχων ἐν τῇ πόλει μαγεύων ἐξε[. . .] τὸ ἔθνος τῆς
10 Σαμαρίας, λέγων εἶναί τινα ἑαυτὸν μέγαν, | ᾧ προσεῖχον πάντες
ἀπὸ μεικροῦ ἕως μεγάλου λέγοντες· Οὗτός ἐστιν ἡ δύναμις τοῦ
11 θεοῦ ἡ καλουμένη μεγάλη. προσεῖχον δὲ αὐτῷ διὰ τὸ ἱκανῷ

3 ελυμενετο   παρεδιδους   5 καλελθων

---

magna et tribulatio super ecclesiam quae est in hierosolymis omnis enim dispersi d
sunt per regiones judaeae et samariae praeter apostolos qui manserunt hierusalem
2 conportaveruntquae stephanum viri timorati et fecerunt planctum magnum super
eum 3 Saulus autem divastabat ecclesias per singulas quae domos ingrediens
trahensque viros et mulieres tradebat in carcerem 4 ad illi quidem qui dispersi
erant adnuntiabant evangelizantes verbum 5 philippus vero cum venisset in civitate
samariae praedicabat eis x͞p͞m 6 intendebant autem omnis turbae his qui dicebantur
a philippo unanimo in eo quod audierint ipsi et videbant signa quae faciebat 7 a
multis enim qui habebant spiritum in mundum clamantes voce magna exiebant multi
enim paralysin passi clodi curabantur 8 gaudium magnum factum est in civitate illa
9 viri autem quidam nomine simon jam pridem erat in ipsa civitate magika faciens et
mentem auferens gentibus samariae dicens esse quendam magnum 10 cui intendebant
omnes a pusillo usque ad magnum dicentes hic est virtus d͞i quae vocatur magna
11 intendebant autem ei propterea quod plurimo tempore magicis rebus mentem

tribulatio et persecutio [magna] ecclesiae quae est Hirosollimis. omnes autē h
[dispersi] sunt circa civitates Judeae et Samariae, [praete]r apostolos, qui
remanserant Hierosylymis. 2 [portaver]unt autem Stefanum homines pii, et
fecerunt

9 vir autem quidam nomine Simon, qui ante erat in civitate, magicam Irenaeus,
exerçens, et seducens gentem Samaritanorum, dicens se esse aliquem magnum, i. 23, 1 (16, 1)
10 quem auscultabant a pusillo usque ad magnum, dicentes: hic est virtus dei
quae vocatur magna. 11 intuebantur autem eum propter quod multo tempore
magicis suis dementasset eos.
9 magicam] magiam *Turner*

7 εξηρχοντο] egrediebantur ⁛ ꞏꙑb iis ✓   Harclean

δὲ αὐτῷ διὰ τὸ ἱκανῷ χρόνῳ ταῖς μαγείαις ἐξεστακέναι αὐτούς.
ὅτε δὲ ἐπίστευσαν τῷ Φιλίππῳ εὐαγγελιζομένῳ περὶ τῆς βασιλείας 12
τοῦ θεοῦ καὶ τοῦ ὀνόματος Ἰησοῦ Χριστοῦ, ἐβαπτίζοντο ἄνδρες
τε καὶ γυναῖκες. ὁ δὲ Σίμων καὶ αὐτὸς ἐπίστευσεν, καὶ βαπτι- 13
σθεὶς ἦν προσκαρτερῶν τῷ Φιλίππῳ· θεωρῶν τὰ σημεῖα καὶ
δυνάμεις μεγάλας γεινομένας ἐξίστατο. ἀκούσαντες δὲ οἱ ἐν 14
Ἱεροσολύμοις ἀπόστολοι ὅτι δέδεκται ἡ Σαμαρεία τὸν λόγον
τοῦ θεοῦ ἀπέστειλαν πρὸς αὐτοὺς Πέτρον καὶ Ἰωάνην, οἵτινες 15
καταβάντες προσεύξαντο περὶ αὐτῶν ὅπως λάβωσιν πνεῦμα
ἅγιον· οὐδέπω γὰρ ἦν ἐπ᾽ οὐδενὶ αὐτῶν ἐπιπεπτωκός, μόνον δὲ 16
βεβαπτισμένοι ὑπῆρχον εἰς τὸ ὄνομα τοῦ κυρίου Ἰησοῦ. τότε 17
ἐπετίθοσαν τὰς χεῖρας ἐπ᾽ αὐτούς, καὶ ἐλάμβανον πνεῦμα ἅγιον.
ἰδὼν δὲ ὁ Σίμων ὅτι διὰ τῆς ἐπιθέσεως τῶν χειρῶν τῶν ἀποστόλων 18
δίδοται τὸ πνεῦμα προσήνεγκεν αὐτοῖς χρήματα, | λέγων· Δότε 19
κἀμοὶ τὴν ἐξουσίαν ταύτην ἵνα ᾧ ἐὰν ἐπιθῶ τὰς χεῖρας λαμβάνῃ
πνεῦμα ἅγιον. Πέτρος δὲ εἶπεν πρὸς αὐτόν· Τὸ ἀργύριόν σου 20
σὺν σοὶ εἴη εἰς ἀπώλειαν, ὅτι τὴν δωρεὰν τοῦ θεοῦ ἐνόμισας διὰ
χρημάτων κτᾶσθαι. οὐκ ἔστιν σοι μερὶς οὐδὲ κλῆρος ἐν τῷ λόγῳ 21
τούτῳ, ἡ γὰρ καρδία σου οὐκ ἔστιν εὐθεῖα ἔναντι τοῦ θεοῦ. μετα- 22
νόησον οὖν ἀπὸ τῆς κακίας σου ταύτης, καὶ δεήθητι τοῦ κυρίου

Editors 13 τα] τε WH Soden JHR   18 πνευμα] +το αγιον Soden

Old Uncial 12 τω φιλιππω ευαγγελιζομενω BACℵc 81 (+D) του φιλιππου ευαγγελιζομενου ℵ
θεου BACℵc 81 (+D) κυριου ℵ   τε BℵC 81 (+D) om A   13 τα B
τε ℵAC 81 (+D)   γεινομενας BℵA 81 (+D) om C   εξιστατο
BAC²ℵc 81 εξισταντο ℵC(+D)   14 θεου BACℵc 81 (+D) χριστου ℵ
18 πνευμα Bℵ +το αγιον AC 81 (+D)   20 αυτον BACℵc 81 (+D)
αυτους ℵ   21 εναντι BℵA(+D) εναντιον C 81

Antiochian 12 περι] τα περι HLPSϛ   add του before ιησου ϛ   13 τα] τε
HLPSϛ(+D)   δυναμεις και σημεια HLPS   om μεγαλας HLPS
γινομενα HLPS   14 τον πετρον HLPSϛ   16 ουδεπω] ουπω HLPSϛ
κυριου] χριστου HLPS   18 ιδων] θεασαμενος HLPSϛ   πνευμα] +το αγιον
HLPSϛ(+D)   20 om ειη S   om του H   21 εναντι] ενωπιον
HLPSϛ   22 om ουν S   κυριου] θεου HLPSϛ

21. That the 'Western' text read   reading of perp gig pesh Aug Const.
τη πιστει ταυτη for τω λογω τουτω is   Ap. vi. 7. 2.
indicated by the agreement in that

12 χρόνῳ ταῖς μαγίαις ἐξεστακέναι αὐτούς. ὅτε δὲ ἐπίστευσαν τῷ
Φιλίππῳ εὐαγγελιζομένῳ περὶ τῆς βασιλίας τοῦ θεοῦ καὶ τοῦ
ὀνόματος Ἰησοῦ Χριστοῦ, ἐβαπτίζοντο ἄνδρες τε καὶ γυναῖκες.
13 ὁ δὲ Σίμων καὶ αὐτὸς ἐπίστευσεν, καὶ βαπτισθεὶς ἦν καὶ προσκαρτερῶν τῷ Φιλίππῳ, θεωρῶν τε σημεῖα καὶ δυνάμις μεγάλας
14 γεινομένας ἐξείστατο. ἀκούσαντες δὲ οἱ ἐν Ἰερουσαλὴμ ἀπόστολοι ὅτι δέδεκται ἡ Σαμαρία τὸν λόγον τοῦ θεοῦ ἀπέστειλαν πρὸς
15 αὐτοὺς Πέτρον καὶ Ἰωάνην, οἵτινες καταβάντες προσηύξαντο
16 περὶ αὐτῶν ὅπως λάβωσιν πνεῦμα ἅγιον· οὐδέπω γὰρ ἦν ἐπὶ
οὐδένα αὐτῶν ἐπιπεπτωκός, μόνον δὲ βεβαπτισμένοι ὑπῆρχον
17 εἰς τὸ ὄνομα τοῦ κυρίου Ἰησοῦ Χριστοῦ. τότε ἐπετίθουν τὰς
18 χεῖρας ἐπ᾽ αὐτούς, καὶ ἐλάμβανον πνεῦμα ἅγιον. ἰδὼν δὲ ὁ
Σίμων ὅτι διὰ τῆς ἐπιθέσεως τῶν χειρῶν τῶν ἀποστόλων δίδοται
19 τὸ πνεῦμα τὸ ἅγιον προσήνεγκεν αὐτοῖς χρήματα, παρακαλῶν
καὶ λέγων· Δότε κἀμοὶ τὴν ἐξουσίαν ταύτην ἵνα ᾧ ἂν ἐπιθῶ
20 κἀγὼ τὰς χεῖρας λαμβάνῃ πνεῦμα ἅγιον. Πέτρος δὲ εἶπεν πρὸς
αὐτόν· Ἀργύριον σὺν σοὶ εἴη εἰς ἀπώλειαν, ὅτι τὴν δωρεὰν τοῦ
21 θεοῦ ἐνόμισας διὰ χρημάτων κτᾶσθαι. οὐκ ἔστιν σοι μερὶς
οὐδὲ κλῆρος ἐν τῷ λόγῳ τούτῳ, ἡ καρδία σου οὐκ ἔστιν εὐθεῖα
22 ἔναντι τοῦ θεοῦ. μετανόησον οὖν ἀπὸ τῆς κακίας σου ταύτης,

13 εξεισταντο   18 προσηνεγκαν   21 μερεις

abstulisset eis   12 cum vero crederent philippo evangelizantem regnum dī et de d
nomine ihu xpi baptizabantur viri ac mulieres   13 simon quoque et ipse credidit et
baptizatus est et adherebat philippo videns signa et virtutes magnas fieri obstupiscebat
14 cum vero audissent qui in hierusalem erant apostoli quia excepit samaria verbum
dī miserunt ad eos petrum et johannen   15 qui cum descendissent oraverunt super
eos ut accipiant spm sanctum   16 nondum enim erat super quemquam eorū inlapsus
tantum autem baptizati erant in nomine dnī ihu xpi   17 tunc inponebant manus
super eos et accipiebant spm sanctum   18 cum vidisset simon quia per inpositionem
manum apostolorum datur sps sanctus obtulit eis paecunias   19 rogando et dicendo
date et mihi potestatem hanc ut cuicumque inposuero et ego manus accipiat spm
sanctum   20 petrus autem dixit ad eum

20 pecunia tua tecum sit in interitum, quoniam gratiam dei pretio conse-quendam putasti.	Tertullian, *Fug.* 12
21 non est tibi pars neque sors in ista ratione.	*Idol.* 9
20 pecunia tua tecum sit in perditione, quia existimasti gratiam dei per pecuniam possideri.	Cyprian, *Test.* iii. 100
20 pecunia tua tecum sit in perditione, quoniam donum dei existimasti pecunia possideri : 21 non est tibi pars neque sors in sermone hoc ; cor enim tuum non est rectum coram deo.	Irenaeus, i. 23, 1 (16, 1)

13 σημεια και δυναμεις μεγαλας] virtutes et signa ⁙ magna ✓	Harclean

εἰ ἄρα ἀφεθήσεταί σοι ἡ ἐπίνοια τῆς καρδίας σου· εἰς γὰρ χολὴν 23
πικρίας καὶ σύνδεσμον ἀδικίας ὁρῶ σε ὄντα. ἀποκριθεὶς δὲ ὁ 24
Σίμων εἶπεν· Δεήθητε ὑμεῖς ὑπὲρ ἐμοῦ πρὸς τὸν κύριον ὅπως
μηδὲν ἐπέλθῃ ἐπ᾽ ἐμὲ ὧν εἰρήκατε. οἱ μὲν οὖν διαμαρτυράμενοι 25
καὶ λαλήσαντες τὸν λόγον τοῦ κυρίου ὑπέστρεφον εἰς Ἱεροσόλυμα,
πολλάς τε κώμας τῶν Σαμαρειτῶν εὐηγγελίζοντο.

Ἄγγελος δὲ Κυρίου ἐλάλησεν πρὸς Φίλιππον λέγων· Ἀνά- 26
στηθι καὶ πορεύου κατὰ μεσημβρίαν ἐπὶ τὴν ὁδὸν τὴν καταβαίνουσαν ἀπὸ Ἱερουσαλὴμ εἰς Γάζαν· αὕτη ἐστὶν ἔρημος.
καὶ ἀναστὰς ἐπορεύθη, καὶ ἰδοὺ ἀνὴρ Αἰθίοψ εὐνοῦχος δυνάστης 27
Κανδάκης βασιλίσσης Αἰθιόπων, ὃς ἦν ἐπὶ πάσης τῆς γάζης
αὐτῆς, ὃς ἐληλύθει προσκυνήσων εἰς Ἱερουσαλήμ, | ἦν δὲ ὑπο- 28
στρέφων καὶ καθήμενος ἐπὶ τοῦ ἅρματος αὐτοῦ καὶ ἀνεγείνωσκεν τὸν προφήτην Ἡσαίαν. εἶπεν δὲ τὸ πνεῦμα τῷ Φιλίππῳ· 29
Πρόσελθε καὶ κολλήθητι τῷ ἅρματι τούτῳ. προσδραμὼν δὲ ὁ 30
Φίλιππος ἤκουσεν αὐτοῦ ἀναγεινώσκοντος Ἡσαίαν τὸν προφήτην,
καὶ εἶπεν· Ἆρά γε γεινώσκεις ἃ ἀναγεινώσκεις; ὁ δὲ εἶπεν· 31
Πῶς γὰρ ἂν δυναίμην ἐὰν μή τις ὁδαγήσει με; παρεκάλεσέν τε
τὸν Φίλιππον ἀναβάντα καθίσαι σὺν αὐτῷ. ἡ δὲ περιοχὴ τῆς 32

Is. liii. 7 f. γραφῆς ἣν ἀνεγείνωσκεν ἦν αὕτη· Ὡς πρόβατον ἐπὶ σφαγὴν ἤχθη,
καὶ ὡς ἀμνὸς ἐναντίον τοῦ κείροντος αὐτὸν ἄφωνος, οὕτως οὐκ

26 την οδον] +την οδον

Editors | 27 [ος 2°] WH | 28 δε] τε Soden | 32 κειραντος WHmg

---

Old Uncial | 24 επ BℵA 81 om C | 25 διαμαρτυραμενοι BAC 81 (+D) διαμαρτυ-
ρομενοι ℵ κυριου BℵC 81 (+D) θεου A υπεστρεφον BℵA 81 (+D)
υπεστρεψαν C 26 πορευου BℵA 81 πορευθητι C(+D) επι BℵAC(+D)
om 81 την 2° BACℵᶜ 81 (+D) +καλουμενην ℵ εστιν BℵAC(+D)
om 81 27 ος 2° BC²ℵᶜ 81 om ℵAC(+D) 28 δε BC τε ℵA 81
(+D) του BℵA 81 (+D) om C και ανεγεινωσκεν BCℵᶜ 81
ανεγινωσκεν τε A ανεγινωσκεν ℵ τον προφητην ησαιαν BℵA 81 (+D)
ησαιαν τον προφητην C 30 δε BℵAC τε 81 ησαιαν τον προφητην
BℵAC τον προφητην ησαιαν 81 31 αν BℵC 81 om A οδαγησει με
B(ℵA 81) με οδηγησει C 32 κειροντος B 81 κειραντος ℵAC

Antiochian | 24 om ο H ων] ως L 25 διαμαρτυρομενοι LP υπεστρεψαν
HLPSⲋ ιερουσαλημ HLPSⲋ ευηγγελισαντο HLPSⲋ
26 επι] εις H 27 της βασιλισσης HLPSⲋ εις] εν L 28 δε] τε
HLPSⲋ(+D) 30 τον προφητην ησαιαν HLPSⲋ 32 κειραντος HL
ουτως] ουτος HL

---

24 For evidence that Chrysostom verse see J. R. Harris, Four Lectures,
used the 'Western' text of this p. 94.

καὶ δεήθητι τοῦ κυρίου εἰ ἄρα ἀφηθήσεταί σου ἡ ἐπίνοια τῆς
23 καρδίας σου· ἐν γὰρ πικρίας χολῇ καὶ συνδέσμῳ ἀδικίας θεωρῶ
24 σε ὄντα. ἀποκρειθεὶς δὲ ὁ Σίμων εἶπεν πρὸς αὐτούς· Παρακαλῶ,
δεήθητε ὑμεῖς περὶ ἐμοῦ πρὸς τὸν θεὸν ὅπως μηδὲν ἐπέλθῃ μοι
τούτων τῶν κακῶν ὧν εἰρήκατέ μοι, ὃς πολλὰ κλαίων οὐ διελίμ-
25 πανεν. οἱ μὲν οὖν διαμαρτυράμενοι καὶ λαλήσαντες τὸν λόγον
τοῦ κυρίου ὑπέστρεφον εἰς Εἱεροσόλυμα, πολλὰς δὲ κώμας τῶν
Σαμαρειτῶν εὐηγγελίζοντο.
26 Ἄγγελος δὲ κυρίου ἐλάλησεν πρὸς Φίλιππον λέγων· Ἀναστὰς
πορεύθητι κατὰ μεσημβρίαν ἐπὶ τὴν ὁδὸν τὴν καταβαίνουσαν ἀπὸ
27 Ἰερουσαλὴμ εἰς Γάζαν· αὕτη ἐστὶν ἔρημος. καὶ ἀναστὰς ἐπορεύθη, καὶ ἰδοὺ ἀνὴρ Αἰθίοψ εὐνοῦχος δυνάστης Κανδάκης βασι-
λείσσης τινὸς Αἰθιόπων, ὃς ἦν ἐπὶ πάσης τῆς γάζης †αὐτοῦ,†
28 ἐληλύθει προσκυνήσων Ἰερουσαλήμ, ἦν τε ὑποστρέφων καθήμενος ἐπὶ τοῦ ἅρματος ἀναγεινώσκων τὸν προφήτην Ἰσαίαν.
29 εἶπεν δὲ τὸ πνεῦμα τῷ Φιλίππῳ·

29   τούτῳ] αὐτοῦ 614 (cf. τούτου 1518)

23 εν] ην   24 ων] ον   διελυμπανεν

[24 nam et Simon Samarites in Actis Apostolorum redemptor spiritus sancti,   Tertullian,
posteaquam damnatus ab apostolo cum pecunia sua interitum frustra flevit.]   *Anima* 34

---

23 in felle enim amaritudinis, et obligatione injustitiae video te esse.   Irenaeus,
i. 23, 1 (16, 1)
32 tamquam ovis ad victimam ductus est, quemadmodum agnus ante iii. 12, 8 (10)
tondentem se sine voce, sic non aperuit os.
32 quemadmodum ovis ad victimam ductus est, et quemadmodum agnus in iv. 23 (37), 2
conspectu tondentis sine voce, sic non aperuit os suum.

---

24 παρακαλω] ⁘ obsecro ✓   θεον] mg dominum   ος πολλα Harclean
κλαιων ου διελιμπανεν] mg flens multum et non cessans

---

27 os 2° B Antiochian sah, om אAC
D perp vg (gig r t insert *hic*). The
relative was omitted because the full
sentence-building virtue of ιδου was
not felt.
29 From viii. 29 to x. 14 the Greek
of Codex Bezae is lacking. From
various Greek sources, chiefly minuscules of the I-type, there are included
in the following pages readings (not
belonging to the text of BאAC 81)
which seem, with varying degrees of

probability, to be fragments of the
'Western' rewriting. They have been
identified by the aid of d, which is
extant for x. 4-14, together with other
Latin witnesses and the Harclean
apparatus. Such readings have not
been inserted unless they are actually
attested in Greek ; and no attempt
has been made to determine 'Western'
order of words, or to indicate the
'Western' variant in the case of the
conjunctions καί, δέ, and τε.

ἀνοίγει τὸ στόμα αὐτοῦ. ἐν τῇ ταπεινώσει ἡ κρίσις αὐτοῦ 33
ἤρθη· τὴν γενεὰν αὐτοῦ τίς διηγήσεται; ὅτι αἴρεται ἀπὸ τῆς
γῆς ἡ ζωὴ αὐτοῦ. ἀποκριθεὶς δὲ ὁ εὐνοῦχος τῷ Φιλίππῳ εἶπεν· 34
Δέομαί σου, περὶ τίνος ὁ προφήτης λέγει; περὶ ἑαυτοῦ ἢ περὶ
ἑτέρου τινός; ἀνοίξας δὲ ὁ Φίλιππος τὸ στόμα αὐτοῦ καὶ ἀρ- 35
ξάμενος ἀπὸ τῆς γραφῆς ταύτης εὐηγγελίσατο αὐτῷ τὸν Ἰησοῦν.
ὡς δὲ ἐπορεύοντο κατὰ τὴν ὁδόν, ἦλθον ἐπί τι ὕδωρ, καί φησιν ὁ 36
εὐνοῦχος· Ἰδοὺ ὕδωρ· τί κωλύει με βαπτισθῆναι; καὶ ἐκέλευσε 38
στῆναι τὸ ἅρμα, καὶ κατέβησαν ἀμφότεροι εἰς τὸ ὕδωρ ὅ τε
Φίλιππος καὶ ὁ εὐνοῦχος, καὶ ἐβάπτισεν αὐτόν. ὅτε δὲ ἀν- 39
έβησαν ἐκ τοῦ ὕδατος, πνεῦμα κυρίου ἥρπασεν τὸν Φίλιππον, καὶ
οὐκ εἶδεν αὐτὸν οὐκέτι ὁ εὐνοῦχος, ἐπορεύετο γὰρ αὐτοῦ τὴν
ὁδὸν χαίρων. Φίλιππος δὲ εὑρέθη εἰς Ἄζωτον, καὶ διερχόμενος 40
εὐηγγελίζετο τὰς πόλεις πάσας ἕως τοῦ ἐλθεῖν αὐτὸν εἰς Καισαρείαν.

Ὁ δὲ Σαῦλος, ἔτι ἐνπνέων ἀπειλῆς καὶ φόνου εἰς τοὺς μαθητὰς IX
τοῦ κυρίου, προσελθὼν τῷ ἀρχιερεῖ | ᾐτήσατο παρ' αὐτοῦ ἐπιστολὰς 2
εἰς Δαμασκὸν πρὸς τὰς συναγωγάς, ὅπως ἐάν τινας εὕρῃ τῆς
ὁδοῦ ὄντας, ἄνδρας τε καὶ γυναῖκας, δεδεμένους ἀγάγῃ εἰς Ἰερουσαλήμ. ἐν δὲ τῷ πορεύεσθαι ἐγένετο αὐτὸν ἐγγίζειν τῇ Δαμασκῷ, 3
ἐξέφνης τε αὐτὸν περιήστραψεν φῶς ἐκ τοῦ οὐρανοῦ, | καὶ πεσὼν 4

1 ετι] οτι

Editors 33 ταπεινωσει] +αυτου Soden την] + δε Soden 34 λεγει]
+τουτο WH Soden JHR 39 την οδον αυτου WH Soden JHR

Old Uncial 33 ταπεινωσει BℵA +αυτου C 81 την BℵAC +δε 81
34 λεγει B +τουτο B²ℵAC 81 35 ταυτης BACℵᶜ 81 +και ℵ
39 ανεβησαν BℵAC 81 ανεβη C² πνευμα BℵC 81 +αγιον επεπεσεν επι
τον ευνουχον αγγελος δε A αυτου την οδον B την οδον αυτου ℵAC 81
40 ευηγγελιζετο τας πολεις πασας BℵC 81 τας πολεις πασας ευηγγελιζετο A
1 ετι B²(B³ Tdf)ACℵᶜ 81 οτι B om ℵ 2 παρ αυτου επιστολας BAC 81
επιστολας παρ αυτου ℵ της οδου οντας BC οντας της οδου ℵA 81 3 εν
δε BℵAC om 81 τω BℵAC το 81 περιηστραψεν φως BℵC 81
φως περιηστραψεν A

Antiochian 33 ταπεινωσει] +αυτου HLPSϚ την] +δε HLPSϚ 34 λεγει]
+τουτο HLPSϚ εαυτου] αυτου H 35 om ο before φιλιππος H
37 add ειπε δε ο φιλιππος· ει πιστευεις εξ ολης της καρδιας, εξεστιν. αποκριθεις δε
ειπε· πιστευω τον υιον του θεου ειναι τον ιησουν χριστον Ϛ 39 την οδον
αυτου HLPSϚ 3 τω] το HL εξεφνης τε] και εξαιφνης HLPSϚ
περιηστραψεν αυτον HLPSϚ εκ] απο HPSϚ

36   εὐνοῦχος] + τῷ Φιλίππῳ 489

37   εἶπεν δὲ (+ αὐτῷ 1522) ὁ Φίλιππος (om. ὁ Φίλιππος minn)·
Εἰ πιστεύεις ἐξ ὅλης τῆς καρδίας (+ σου minn), ἔξεστιν. ἀποκριθεὶς δὲ εἶπεν· Πιστεύω τὸν υἱὸν τοῦ θεοῦ εἶναι τὸν (om. τὸν
minn) Ἰησοῦν Χριστόν 2298 minn

39   πνεῦμα κυρίου ἥρπασεν τὸν Φίλιππον] πνεῦμα ἅγιον ἐπέπεσεν
ἐπὶ τὸν εὐνοῦχον· ἄγγελος δὲ κυρίου ἥρπασεν τὸν Φίλιππον
A minn

---

36 ecce aqua, quid est quod me inpediat tingui? 37 tunc dixit Philippus : Cyprian,
si credis ex toto corde tuo, licet.   *Test.* iii. 43

---

33 nativitatem autem ejus quis enarrabit? quoniam tolletur a terra vita Irenaeus,
ejus.   iii. 12, 8 (10)

    in humilitate judicium ejus ablatum est.   iv. 23 (37), 2

    37 credo filium dei esse Jesum.   iii. 12, 8 (10)

    πιστεύω τὸν υἱὸν τοῦ θεοῦ εἶναι Ἰησοῦν Χριστόν.   [catena]

    [solum adventum ignorabat] filii dei, [quem cum breviter cognovisset] iv. 23 (37), 2
39 agebat iter gaudens.

---

37 ειπεν δε ο φιλιππος· ει πιστευεις εξ ολης της καρδιας, εξεστιν. αποκριθεις δε Harclean
ειπεν· πιστευω τον υιον του θεου ειναι τον ιησουν χριστον] ⸓ dixit autem ei¦: Si
credis ex toto corde tuo, licet. respondens autem dixit : Credo in filium dei esse
Jesum Christum   39 αγιον] *mg* sanctus   επεπεσεν επι τον ευνουχον·
αγγελος δε κυριου] ⸓ cecidit in eunuchum ; angelus autem domini ✓   τον
φιλιππον] +*mg* ab eo

---

37 Vs. 37 is a 'Western' addition, not found in BℵAC Antiochian vg. W.W. sah cop pesh, but read, with minor variants, in many minuscules. A part is quoted by Iren Cypr ; and the whole (with minor variants) is found in perp gig e E vg.*codd* hcl·⸓· arm. The most noteworthy variant is πιστευω εις τον χριστον τον υιον του θεου (without the following words) E e. The text of E is, as usual, a retranslation from e ; *suscepis* e (in place of εξεστιν) is probably rightly corrected by e^corr to *salvus eris*, to which σωθησει E corresponds. The error of e was due to an earlier scribe's confusion of ρ and p.
    39 The 'Western' addition to vs.

39 in A (written by first hand over erasure) is found also in a series of minuscules, and in perp vg.*codd* hcl·⸓· arm, and is quoted, or definitely referred to, by Ephrem, Cyril of Jerusalem, Didymus, Jerome, and Augustine. The geographical range of attestation is noteworthy. The purpose of the addition was to make explicit that the baptism was followed by the gift of the Holy Spirit.
    Ab eo hcl.*mg* is found also in perp Aug.
    2 The difficulty of τῆς ὁδοῦ was felt in ancient times, and an attempt made to relieve it by adding ταυτης ; so 104 181 1838 perp gig e vg pesh hcl.*text*.

ἐπὶ τὴν γῆν ἤκουσεν φωνὴν λέγουσαν αὐτῷ· Σαούλ, Σαούλ, τί
με διώκεις; | εἶπεν δέ· Τίς εἶ, κύριε; ὁ δέ· Ἐγώ εἰμι Ἰησοῦς 5
ὃν σὺ διώκεις· ἀλλὰ ἀνάστηθι καὶ εἴσιθι εἰς τὴν πόλιν, καὶ λαλη- 6
θήσεταί σοι ὅτι σε δεῖ ποιεῖν. οἱ δὲ ἄνδρες οἱ συνοδεύοντες αὐτῷ 7
εἰστήκεισαν ἐνεοί, ἀκούοντες μὲν τῆς φωνῆς μηδένα δὲ θεωροῦντες.
ἠγέρθη δὲ Σαῦλος ἀπὸ τῆς γῆς, ἀνεῳγμένων δὲ τῶν ὀφθαλμῶν 8
αὐτοῦ οὐδὲν ἔβλεπεν· χειραγωγοῦντες δὲ αὐτὸν εἰσήγαγον εἰς
Δαμασκόν. καὶ ἦν ἡμέρας τρεῖς μὴ βλέπων, καὶ οὐκ ἔφαγεν 9
οὐδὲ ἔπιεν.
Ἦν δέ τις μαθητὴς ἐν Δαμασκῷ ὀνόματι Ἁνανίας, καὶ 10
εἶπεν πρὸς αὐτὸν ἐν ὁράματι ὁ κύριος· Ἁνανία. ὁ δὲ εἶπεν· Ἰδοὺ
ἐγώ, κύριε. ὁ δὲ κύριος πρὸς αὐτόν· Ἀνάστα, πορεύθητι ἐπὶ 11
τὴν ῥύμην τὴν καλουμένην Εὐθεῖαν καὶ ζήτησον ἐν οἰκίᾳ Ἰούδα
Σαῦλον ὀνόματι Ταρσέα, ἰδοὺ γὰρ προσεύχεται, | καὶ εἶδεν ἄνδρα 12
ἐν ὁράματι Ἁνανίαν ὀνόματι εἰσελθόντα καὶ ἐπιθέντα αὐτῷ τὰς

Editors 6 εισιθι] εισελθε WH Soden JHR 11 αναστας WHmg Soden JHR
12 [εν οραματι] WH εν οραματι ανδρα Soden om εν οραματι JHR [τας] WH
om τας Soden

Old Uncial 5 ει BℵA 81 +συ C o δε BAC +ειπεν ℵ 81 ιησους Bℵ 81
+o ναζωραιος AC 6 εισιθι B εισελθε ℵAC 81 7 εωτηκεισαν
BℵAC ειστησαν 81 μεν BℵAC δε 81 δε 2ᵒ Bℵ AC om 81
θεωρουντες BACℵᶜ 81 ορωντες ℵ 8 ουδεν Bℵ A ουδενα A²C 81 9 ουδε
Bℵ A 81 και ουκ C 10 εν οραματι ο κυριος BℵAC ο κυριος εν οραματι 81
11 αναστα B αναστας ℵAC 81 12 εν οραματι BC om ℵA 81 τας
Bℵᶜ om ℵAC 81

Antiochian 5 o δε] +κυριος ειπεν HLPS 6 instead of αλλα insert σκληρον σοι προς
κεντρα λακτιζειν. τρεμων τε και θαμβων ειπε· κυριε, τι με θελεις ποιησαι; και ο
κυριος προς αυτον S εισιθι] εισελθε HLPSS οτι] τι HLPSS
8 o σαυλος HLPSS δε 2ᵒ] τε HLPS ουδενα HLPSS 10 o
κυριος εν οραματι HLPSS 11 αναστας HLPSS 12 εν οραματι
ανδρα ονοματι ανανιαν HLPSS om τας HLPSS

---

4 After τι με διωκεις 431 e E vg.codd
pesh hcl ⁕ add σκληρον σοι προς κεντρα
λακτιζειν. This appears to be a fragment of the larger 'Western' addition
of vss. 5, 6, transferred to this position
in order to agree with xxvi. 14.
To the sentence under asterisk in
hcl.text, hcl.mg adds the following
note: 'Durum est tibi calcitrare ad
stimulos' non est hoc loco in Graeco,
sed ubi enarrat de se Paulus. On the
series of marginal notes to which this
belongs see above, pp. clxii-clxv.
5, 6 The 'Western' addition found

in h (vanum . . . eum) appears in
vg.many codd in the following form:
durum est tibi contra stimulum calcitrare. et tremens ac stupens (+ in
eo quod fuerat [factum erat] vg.codd)
dixit: domine quid me vis facere?
et dominus ad eum (cf. xxii. 10,
xxvi. 14). With this substantially
agree perp hcl ⁕ (cf. mg, vs. 4). Gig
has durum . . . calcitrare, but no
more, and Hilary quotes (in a slightly
different text) the part et tremens . . .
facere. Aug and Ambrose refer to
the sentence: domine quid me vis

IX 4   τί με διώκεις] + σκληρόν σοι πρὸς κέντρα λακτίζειν 431

5   ὁ δέ] + κύριος εἶπεν HLPS(Ψ) minn

add πρὸς αὐτόν before Ἐγώ Ψ 323

Ἰησοῦς] + ὁ Ναζωραῖος AC minn

6   καὶ 2°] + ἐκεῖ 614 minn

11 Ταρσέα] τῷ γένει Ταρσέα 36

---

4 [in pa]vore, et audivit vocem dicentem sibi : Saule, [Saule], quid me per- **h**
sequeris ? 5 qui respondit, dicens : [quis es], d̄n̄e̅ ? et dixit d̄n̄s̄ : ego sum īh̄s̄
Nazarenus que[m tu per]sequeris : vanum autem est tibi contra stim[ulum
cal]citrare. qui tremens, timore plenus in isto sib[i facto], dixit : d̄n̄e̅, quid
me vis facere ? 6 et d̄n̄s̄ ad eum : ex[urge, et] introi in civitatem, et ibi tibi
dicetur quid te o[porteat] facere. 7 homines autem illi, qui ei comitaban[tur,
sta]bant stupefacti, et audiebant quidem vocem [sed ne]minem videbant, cum
loqueretur. sed ait ad [eos : leva]te me de terra. 8 et cum lebassent illum,
nihil [videbat] apertis oculis : et tenentes manus ejus dedux[erunt] Damascum.
9 et sic mansit per tridum nihil vid[ens, et] neque cibum neque potum accepit.

10 erat a[utem] quidam discens Damasci, nomine Annanias : [et ei in]
visionem d̄n̄s̄ ait : Annania. qui respon[dens ait : i]ta, d̄n̄e̅. 11 et d̄n̄s̄ ad
eum : surge et vade in vicum [qui voca]tur, et quaere in domum Judae nomine
Saul[um, na]tione Tarseum : ecce enim adorat ipse.

---

6 exsurge, [dicens,] et introi Damascum, illic tibi demonstrabitur quid **Tertullian,**
debeas agere.   *Bapt.* 13

---

4 Saule, Saule, quid me persequeris ? 5 ego sum Jesus Christus, quem tu **Irenaeus,**
persequeris.   **iii. 15, 1**

---

4 σκληρον σοι προς κεντρα λακτιζειν] ⁙ durum est tibi calcitrare ad stimulos ✓ **Harclean**
5 ο ναζωραιος] ⁙ Nazarenus ✓   5, 6 ον συ διωκεις] quem tu persequeris
⁙ ille autem tremens et pavens super eo quod factum fuerat ei dixit :
Domine quid vis me facere et dominus [+*mg* dixit] ad eum : Surge ✓
11 σαυλον] Saulum ⁙ quendam ✓

---

facere? The addition is found in no
Greek MS., and is lacking in many
codd of vg, including Amiatinus, as
well as in pesh sah boh. The most
important peculiarity of h, *vanum* for
durum, may represent a reading κενον
or εἰς κενον in the original ' Western ' ;
if so, in all other Latin copies the text
has been conformed to xxvi. 14.

The Greek text found in 𝕾 is due to
the hand of Erasmus, who translated
it from the Latin of vg and introduced
it in his first edition, 1516. He frankly
indicates the facts, *Annotationes*, p.
385.

7, 8 After vs. 7 θεωρουντες the additions of h are supported as follows :
cum loqueretur] *qui loqueretur* perp
w tepl gig (*cum quo*) ; *sed ait ad* [*eos
leva*]*te me de terra*] perp w vg.*codd*

(all with minor variations). In the
words *et cum lebassent illum* h stands
alone. The whole text of h here
doubtless represents the ' Western,'
elsewhere found only in fragments.

12 Vs. 12 is omitted by h, but with
no extant support ; it is in all probability an integral part of the original
text, since προσευχεται is meaningless
without it. See, however, P. Corssen,
*Der Cyprianische Text der Acta aposto-
lorum*, Berlin, 1892, pp. 21-23.

εν οραματι after ανδρα BC ; before
ανδρα Antiochian pesh hcl ; omitted
by ℵA 81 perp gig vg sah boh. The
reading which omits is probably
right.

12, 17 Vs. 12 τας χειρας BE ; χειρας
ℵAC 81, *manus* gig e vg ; χειρα
Antiochian perp r t pesh hcl. Sah is

χεῖρας ὅπως ἀναβλέψῃ· | ἀπεκρίθη δὲ Ἀνανίας· Κύριε, ἤκουσα 13
ἀπὸ πολλῶν περὶ τοῦ ἀνδρὸς τούτου, ὅσα κακὰ τοῖς ἁγίοις σου
ἐποίησεν ἐν Ἰερουσαλήμ· καὶ ὧδε ἔχει ἐξουσίαν παρὰ τῶν 14
ἀρχιερέων δῆσαι πάντας τοὺς ἐπικαλουμένους τὸ ὄνομά σου.
εἶπεν δὲ πρὸς αὐτὸν ὁ κύριος· Πορεύου, ὅτι σκεῦος ἐκλογῆς 15
ἐστίν μοι οὗτος τοῦ βαστάσαι τὸ ὄνομά μου ἐνώπιον τῶν
ἐθνῶν τε καὶ βασιλέων υἱῶν τε Ἰσραήλ, ἐγὼ γὰρ ὑποδείξω αὐτῷ 16
ὅσα δεῖ αὐτὸν ὑπὲρ τοῦ ὀνόματός μου παθεῖν. ἀπῆλθεν δὲ 17
Ἀνανίας καὶ εἰσῆλθεν εἰς τὴν οἰκίαν, καὶ ἐπιθεὶς ἐπ᾽ αὐτὸν τὰς
χεῖρας εἶπεν· Σαοὺλ ἀδελφέ, ὁ κύριος ἀπέσταλκέν με, Ἰησοῦς
ὁ ὀφθείς σοι ἐν τῇ ὁδῷ ᾗ ἤρχου, ὅπως ἀναβλέψῃς καὶ πλησθῇς
πνεύματος ἁγίου. καὶ εὐθέως ἀπέπεσαν αὐτοῦ ἀπὸ τῶν ὀφθαλ- 18
μῶν ὡς λεπίδες, ἀνέβλεψέν τε, καὶ ἀναστὰς ἐβαπτίσθη, | καὶ λαβὼν 19
τροφὴν ἐνισχύθη.

Ἐγένετο δὲ μετὰ τῶν ἐν Δαμασκῷ μαθητῶν ἡμέρας τινάς, | καὶ 20
εὐθέως ἐν ταῖς συναγωγαῖς ἐκήρυσσεν τὸν Ἰησοῦν ὅτι οὗτός
ἐστιν ὁ υἱὸς τοῦ θεοῦ. ἐξίσταντο δὲ πάντες οἱ ἀκούοντες καὶ 21
ἔλεγον· Οὐχ οὗτός ἐστιν ὁ πορθήσας ἐν Ἰερουσαλὴμ τοὺς ἐπικαλουμένους τὸ ὄνομα τοῦτο, καὶ ὧδε εἰς τοῦτο ἐληλύθει ἵνα
δεδεμένους αὐτοὺς ἀγάγῃ ἐπὶ τοὺς ἀρχιερεῖς; Σαῦλος δὲ μᾶλλον 22
ἐνεδυναμοῦτο καὶ συνέχυννεν Ἰουδαίους τοὺς κατοικοῦντας ἐν
Δαμασκῷ, συμβιβάζων ὅτι οὗτός ἐστιν ὁ Χριστός. ὡς δὲ ἐπλη- 23

21 εξισταντος

Editors 13 ακηκοα Soden 15 [των] WH om των Soden 18 απο των
οφθαλμων αυτου Soden (but cf. mg) ως] ωσει Soden 21 εν] εις
Soden JHR 22 τους ιουδαιους Soden

Old Uncial 13 σου BℵAC om 81 εποιησεν εν ιερουσαλημ BℵC 81 εν ιερουσαλημ
εποιησεν A 15 των BC om ℵACcorr 81 17 δε BℵC 81 τε A επ
αυτον τας χειρας BℵA 81 τας χειρας επ αυτον C η ηρχου Bℵ*AC 81 om ℵ
18 αυτου απο των οφθαλμων BA απο των οφθαλμων αυτου ℵC 81 ως BℵA 81
ωσει Cℵc τε BA 81 δε ℵ δε παραχρημα C2 19 ενισχυθη BC ενισχυσεν
ℵAC2 81 21 εν BC 81 εις ℵA εληλυθει BℵAC εληλυθεν 81
22 ενεδυναμουτο BℵA 81 +τω λογω C ιουδαιους Bℵ τους ιουδαιους ACℵc 81

Antiochian 12 χειρας] χειρα HLPSϛ 13 ο ανανιας ϛ ακηκοα HLPSϛ
εποιησεν τοις αγιοις σου HLPSϛ 15 μοι εστιν HLPSϛ om των
before εθνων HLPSϛ om τε 1ο HLPSϛ 16 αυτω] αυτον L
17 om ιησους HLPS 18 απο των οφθαλμων αυτου HLPSϛ ως] ωσει
HLPSϛ τε] +παραχρημα Lϛ 19 ενισχυσεν HLPSϛ 20 δε] +ο
σαυλος HLPSϛ των] +οντων HLPS ιησουν] χριστον HLPSϛ
21 om οι ακουοντες S εληλυθεν HLPS αγαγη] αναγαγη P
22 τους ιουδαιους HLPSϛ

17   ἀπῆλθεν δὲ 'Ανανίας] τότε ἐγερθεὶς 'Ανανίας ἀπῆλθε 614
      minn

18   ἀνέβλεψέν τε] + παραχρῆμα L 614 minn

20   ἐκήρυσσεν] + μετὰ πάσης παρρησίας Iren
      θεοῦ + τοῦ ζῶντος 181

21   πάντας τοὺς ἐπικαλουμένους 1898 minn

22   ἐνεδυναμοῦτο] + τῷ λόγῳ C 467

---

13 res[pondit] autem Annanias : d̄n̄e, audivi ego de isto hom[ine a] multis, h
quantas persecutiones fecerit sti[s tuis] Hierosolymam : 14 et ecce accepit a
sacerdoti[bus] potestatem in nos, uti alliget universos qu[i invocant nom]en
tuum. 15 cui dixit d̄n̄s : vade, quia vas elec[tionis e]st mihi homo iste, ut
ferat nomen meum corā [gentib]us et regib· et filiis Istrael : 16 ego enim
demons[trabo e]i quanta oporteat eum pati causa nominis mei. 17 [et sur]rexit
Annanias, et abiit ad domum : et inposuit [ei man]um in nomine īh̄u x̄p̄i,
dicens : Saule frater, [d̄n̄s me] misit, īh̄s qui tivi visus est in via per quam
ve[nisti, ut] videas, et replearis s̄p̄s s̄t̄o. 18 et estatim cecide[runt d]e oculis
ejus tamquam squamae, et continuo [vidit : et] surrexit et tintus est. 19 et
accepit civum, et con[fortatu]s est.
    dies autem plurimos et in civitate Damus[co cum] discentibus transsegit.
20 et introibit in sinago[gas Jude[orum, et praedicavit cum omni fiducia d̄n̄m
[īh̄m, qu]ia hic est x̄p̄s, filius d̄i. 21 stupebant autem omnes [qui a]udiebant,
et intra se dicebant : ita non hic est [qui per]sequitur omnes Hierosolymis
qui invocant [nomen is]tut, et nunc quoq· propterea venit uti victos [eos
addu]cat sacerdotibus ? 22 Saulus autem magis conro[borab]atur in verbo, et
perturbat Judeos qui mora[bantur] Damasci, inducens quia hic est x̄p̄s in quē
[bene se]nsit d̄s.

---

    15 vade, quoniam vas electionis est mihi iste, ut portet nomen meum in Irenaeus,
gentibus et regibus et filiis Israel ; 16 ego enim demonstrabo ei ex ipso, quanta iii. 15, 1
oporteat eum pati propter nomen meum.
    20 in synagogis [ait] in Damasco praedicabat cum omni fiducia Jesum, iii. 12, 9 (11)
quoniam hic est Christus filius dei.
    20 ἐν ταῖς συναγωγαῖς [φησίν] ἐν Δαμασκῷ ἐκήρυσσε μετὰ πάσης παρρησίας τὸν [catena]
'Ιησοῦν, ὅτι οὗτός ἐστιν ὁ υἱὸς τοῦ θεοῦ ὁ Χριστός.

---

idiomatically indeterminate. Vs. 17,
for τας χειρας of all Greek documents,
with (perp) gig vg hcl sah (cod W,
cent. xii.-xiii.), manum is read by h r
t pesh sah (codd. BV, cent. iv.).
No confident decision is possible, but
in both cases τας χειρας may perhaps
be adopted in agreement with the
uniform usage of Acts.
    21 For εν ιερουσαλημ BC Antiochian,

εις ιερουσαλημ אA minn is to be
preferred. As in ii. 5, iv. 5, xvi. 36,
εν is probably due to emendation of
what seemed unliterary use. In all
four cases א, once supported by A
and once by 0165, has preserved the
earlier text against B. For the use
of εις in this sense in Lk. and Acts see
Tischendorf's note on Acts ii. 5.

ροῦντο ἡμέραι ἱκαναί, συνεβουλεύσαντο οἱ Ἰουδαῖοι ἀνελεῖν αὐτόν·
| ἐγνώσθη δὲ τῷ Σαύλῳ ἡ ἐπιβουλὴ αὐτῶν. παρετηροῦντο δὲ 24
καὶ τὰς πύλας ἡμέρας τε καὶ νυκτὸς ὅπως αὐτὸν ἀνέλωσιν·
λαβόντες δὲ οἱ μαθηταὶ αὐτοῦ νυκτὸς διὰ τοῦ τείχους καθῆκαν 25
αὐτὸν χαλάσαντες ἐν σπυρίδι. παραγενόμενος δὲ εἰς Ἰερουσαλὴμ 26
ἐπείραζε κολλᾶσθαι τοῖς μαθηταῖς· καὶ πάντες ἐφοβοῦντο αὐτόν,
μὴ πιστεύοντες ὅτι ἐστὶν μαθητής. Βαρνάβας δὲ ἐπιλαβόμενος 27
αὐτὸν ἤγαγεν πρὸς τοὺς ἀποστόλους, καὶ διηγήσατο αὐτοῖς πῶς
ἐν τῇ ὁδῷ εἶδεν τὸν κύριον καὶ ὅτι ἐλάλησεν αὐτῷ, καὶ πῶς ἐν
Δαμασκῷ ἐπαρρησιάσατο ἐν τῷ ὀνόματι Ἰησοῦ. καὶ ἦν μετ᾽ 28
αὐτῶν εἰσπορευόμενος καὶ ἐκπορευόμενος εἰς Ἰερουσαλήμ, παρρησιαζόμενος ἐν τῷ ὀνόματι τοῦ κυρίου, ἐλάλει τε καὶ συνεζήτει 29
πρὸς τοὺς Ἑλληνιστάς· οἱ δὲ ἐπεχείρουν ἀνελεῖν αὐτόν. ἐπι- 30
γνόντες δὲ οἱ ἀδελφοὶ κατήγαγον αὐτὸν εἰς Καισαρείαν καὶ ἐξαπέστειλαν αὐτὸν εἰς Ταρσόν.

Ἡ μὲν οὖν ἐκκλησία καθ᾽ ὅλης τῆς Ἰουδαίας καὶ Γαλειλαίας 31
καὶ Σαμαρείας εἶχεν εἰρήνην οἰκοδομουμένη, καὶ πορευομένη
τῷ φόβῳ τοῦ κυρίου καὶ τῇ παρακλήσει τοῦ ἁγίου πνεύματος
ἐπληθύνετο.

Ἐγένετο δὲ Πέτρον διερχόμενον διὰ πάντων κατελθεῖν καὶ 32
πρὸς τοὺς ἁγίους τοὺς κατοικοῦντας Λύδδα. εὗρεν δὲ ἐκεῖ ἄν- 33
θρωπόν τινα ὀνόματι Αἰνέαν ἐξ ἐτῶν ὀκτὼ κατακείμενον ἐπὶ

30 εξαπεστειλεν

Editors   27 του ιησου Soden   32 λυδδα[ν] Soden

Old Uncial   24 ημερας τε και νυκτος οπως αυτον ανελωσιν BℵC 81 (ℵᶜ ανελωσιν αυτον) οπως
πιασωσιν αυτον ημερας και νυκτος A   27 τους BℵAC αντους 81   και 3°
BℵᵃAC 81   om ℵ   ιησου BC   του ιησου ℵ 81   κυριου A   28 εισπορευομενος και εκπορευομενος BℵAC   εκπορευομενος και εισπορευομενος 81   του
κυριου BℵA 81   +ιησου ℵᶜ   ιησου C   29 ελληνιστας BℵC 81   ελληνας A
30 καισαρειαν BℵC 81   ιεροσολυμα A   αυτον 2° BℵC 81   om A   31 του
1° BℵC   om A 81   32 λυδδα BℵᵃA   λυδδαν C 81   εν λυδδα ℵ

Antiochian   23 αι ημεραι H   om οι S   24 σαυλω] παυλω H
παρετηρουν HLPSϚ   δε και] δε L   τε HPSϚ   25 οι μαθηται
αυτον] αυτον οι μαθηται HLPϚ   οι μαθηται S   καθηκαν δια του τειχους HLPSϚ
26 δε] +ο σαυλος HLPSϚ   εις] εν HLPS   επειραζε] επειρατο HLPSϚ
om μη πιστευοντες S   27 του ιησου HLPSϚ   28 om και
εκπορευομενος HLPS   εις] εν HϚ   add και before παρρησιαζομενος
HLPSϚ   του κυριου] +ιησου HLSϚ   29 αυτον ανελειν HLPSϚ
30 om αυτον 1° L   31 αι μεν ουν εκκλησιαι . . . ειχον . . . οικοδομουμεναι
. . . πορευομεναι . . . επληθυνοντο HLPSϚ   32 λυδδαν HLPSϚ
33 αινεαν ονοματι HLPSϚ

27   ὀνόματι] + κυρίου 1522^corr minn
28   κυρίου] + ᾽Ιησοῦ א^cHLPS
30   Καισαρείαν] + νυκτὸς 614 minn
31   αἱ μὲν οὖν ἐκκλησίαι . . . εἶχον . . . οἰκοδομούμεναι . . .
      πορευόμεναι . . . ἐπληθύνοντο HLPS

---

23 et cum jam multi dies implerentur, con[silium] ceperunt Judaei uti eum h
interficerent : 24 notae [autem] Saulae factae sunt cogitationes eorum, quod

---

30 νυκτος] ·※· nocte ✓   Harclean

---

25 οι μαθηται αυτου Bא AC 81 (perp) vg ; αυτον οι μαθηται Antiochian gig e pesh hcl sah boh. The readings οι μαθηται αυτον and οι μαθηται are each supported by a few minuscules. The weight of the authorities and the transcriptional probability against the reading αυτον lead necessarily to the rejection of the Antiochian text. But the soundness of our text must remain doubtful unless it can be made to appear natural to describe any Christians at Damascus as 'Paul's disciples.'

29 After ελαλει τε the addition gentibus vg. codd (not perp gig) ethiopic is perhaps not part of the 'Western' text. The suggestion that it is due to a survival of the variant ελληνας from the following sentence is possible, but it is not certain that any Greek MS. except A ever contained that variant.

ελληνιστας Bא C 81 pesh Chrys (who explains as τοὺς ἑλληνιστὶ φθεγγομένους in distinction from οἱ βαθεῖς 'Εβραῖοι); ελληνας A. The word occurs elsewhere in the New Testament only in Acts vi. 1, xi. 20. In vi. 1 no Greek variant is reported ; in xi. 20 the support is : ελληνιστας B 81 (א) Antiochian ; ελληνας AD. The versions in most cases offer no evidence. In Latin graeci is the only rendering for ελληνισται in all three cases ; similarly sah and boh in all cases employ the usual native word for 'Greeks,' which sah also uses for ελληνες in four cases out of nine in Acts, and boh in all nine instances. Pesh translates by the usual word for 'Greeks' in vi. 1, xi. 20, but here in ix. 29 indicates ελληνιστας by the free rendering 'those who knew Greek' (cf. Chrys.). ελληνιστας, as both an unusual word and here better attested, is to be read here. See note on xi. 20.

30 καισαρειαν] + νυκτος 257 431 467 614 913 1518 perp gig e (per noctem, retranslated in E δια νυκτος) vg.3 codd pesh hcl ·※· sah.

31 That the 'Western' text read αι μεν ουν εκκλησιαι, with the following verbs in the plural, is indicated by the reading of perp gig Aug. unit. eccl. vg.codd.

κραββάτου, ὃς ἦν παραλελυμένος. καὶ εἶπεν αὐτῷ ὁ Πέτρος· 34
Αἰνέα, εἶαταί σε Ἰησοῦς Χριστός· ἀνάστηθι καὶ στρῶσον σεαυτῷ·
καὶ εὐθέως ἀνέστη. καὶ εἶδαν αὐτὸν πάντες οἱ κατοικοῦντες 35
Λύδδα καὶ τὸν Σαρῶνα, οἵτινες ἐπέστρεψαν ἐπὶ τὸν κύριον.
Ἐν Ἰόππῃ δέ τις ἦν μαθήτρια ὀνόματι Ταβειθά, ἣ διερμη- 36
νευομένη λέγεται Δορκάς· αὕτη ἦν πλήρης ἔργων ἀγαθῶν καὶ
ἐλεημοσυνῶν ὧν ἐποίει. ἐγένετο δὲ ἐν ταῖς ἡμέραις ἐκείναις 37
ἀσθενήσασαν αὐτὴν ἀποθανεῖν· λούσαντες δὲ ἔθηκαν ἐν ὑπερῴῳ.
ἐγγὺς δὲ οὔσης Λύδδας τῇ Ἰόππῃ οἱ μαθηταὶ ἀκούσαντες ὅτι 38
Πέτρος ἐστὶν ἐν αὐτῇ ἀπέστειλαν δύο ἄνδρας πρὸς αὐτὸν παρα-
καλοῦντες· Μὴ ὀκνήσῃς διελθεῖν ἕως ἡμῶν· | ἀναστὰς δὲ Πέτρος 39
συνῆλθεν αὐτοῖς· ὃν παραγενόμενον ἀνήγαγον εἰς τὸ ὑπερῷον,
καὶ παρέστησαν αὐτῷ πᾶσαι αἱ χῆραι κλαίουσαι καὶ ἐπιδικνύ-
μεναι χιτῶνας καὶ ἱμάτια ὅσα ἐποίει μετ᾽ αὐτῶν οὖσα ἡ Δορκάς.
ἐκβαλὼν δὲ ἔξω πάντας ὁ Πέτρος καὶ θεὶς τὰ γόνατα προσηύξατο, 40
καὶ ἐπιστρέψας πρὸς τὸ σῶμα εἶπεν· Ταβειθά, ἀνάστηθι. ἡ
δὲ ἤνοιξεν τοὺς ὀφθαλμοὺς αὐτῆς, καὶ ἰδοῦσα τὸν Πέτρον ἀν-
εκάθισεν. δοὺς δὲ αὐτῇ χεῖρα ἀνέστησεν αὐτήν, φωνήσας δὲ 41
τοὺς ἁγίους καὶ τὰς χήρας παρέστησεν αὐτὴν ζῶσαν. γνωστὸν 42
δὲ ἐγένετο καθ᾽ ὅλης Ἰόππης, καὶ ἐπίστευσαν πολλοὶ ἐπὶ τὸν
κύριον. ἐγένετο δὲ ἡμέρας ἱκανὰς μεῖναι ἐν Ἰόππῃ παρά τινι 43
Σίμωνι βυρσεῖ.
Ἀνὴρ δέ τις ἐν Καισαρείᾳ ὀνόματι Κορνήλιος, ἑκατοντάρχης Χ

Editors   34 ο χριστος Soden   35 λυδδα[ν] Soden   36 αγαθων εργων Soden
37 add αυτην before εθηκαν Soden   εθηκαν] +αυτην WHmg JHR   42 της
ιοππης Soden   43 δε] +[αυτον] Soden

Old Uncial   34 σε BℵC 81 +ο κυριος A   χριστος BℵC ο χριστος B²(?)(B³ Tdf)A 81
35 λυδδα BℵA λυδδαν C 81   τον 1º BACℵ° 81 om ℵ   σαρωνα
BℵAC σαρωναν 81   36 εργων αγαθων BC αγαθων εργων ℵA 81   37 δε
1º BℵAC om 81   εθηκαν B +αυτην ℵA 81 αυτην εθηκαν Cℵ°
υπερωω Bℵ 81 τω υπερωω AC   38 λυδδας BℵC 81 λυδδα Aℵ°
39 πετρος BℵA 81 ο πετρος C   40 εξω παντας BℵA 81 παντας εξω C
41 δε 1º BℵC 81 τε A   42 ιοππης BC της ιοππης ℵA 81   43 δε BℵC
+αυτον Aℵ° 81   ικανας BℵA 81 τινας C   μειναι BℵA 81 +αυτον C

Antiochian   33 κραβαττω HLPSϛ   34 om ιησους H   ο χριστος HLPSϛ
σεαυτον L   35 λυδδαν HLPSϛ   σαρωνα] ασσαρωνα HLS ασαρωνα P
σαρωναν ϛ   36 αγαθων εργων HLPSϛ   37 add αυτην before εθηκαν
HLPSϛ   38 οι] +δε H   om δυο ανδρας HLPS   οκνησαι HLPSϛ
ημων] αυτων HLPSϛ   40 om και before θεις LPSϛ   42 της ιοππης
PSϛ τη ιοππη L   πολλοι επιστευσαν LPSϛ   43 μειναι] +αυτον LPSϛ
om εν ιοππη L   1 τις] +ην Pϛ   εκατονταρχης] om L εκατονταρχος P

34 σε] + ὁ κύριος A minn
39 παρέστησαν αὐτῷ] περιέστησαν αὐτὸν 1518
42 γνωστὸν δὲ] + τοῦτο 467

---

40 Tabitha, exurge in nomine Jesu Christi.
 1 Cornelius centurio . . .

Cyprian,
Op. et eleem. 6

---

1 [erat enim, inquit, Cornelius hic]

Irenaeus,
iii. 12, 7 (8)

---

37 αποθανειν] mortua est ⁛ quum esset autem Petrus Lyddae ✓
40 αναστηθι] surge ⁛ in nomine domini nostri Jesu Christi ✓

Harclean

---

34 For και ειπεν αυτω ο πετρος perp reads : *intendens autem in eum petrus dixit ei*, with which sah agrees. Doubtless the true 'Western.'

35 σαρωνα BℵACE (ℵA -ρρ-); σαρωναν 81 minn. To these correspond *sarona* gig, *saronam* perp e, *saronae* vg. Antiochian read ασσαρωνα (ασαρωνα P by incomplete correction from σαρωνα in ancestor). Perhaps (Zahn) the initial *a* was prefixed in imitation of the Hebrew article, although the Aramaic article was already indicated by the final *a*. See reference to the two spellings in the anonymous onomasticon published in Tischendorf, *Anecdota sacra et profana*, p. 126.

40 αναστηθι] +*in nomine domini nostri iesu christi* hcl ⁛ sah Cypr perp gig m vg.*codd* Ambros, in slightly varying forms (cf. iv. 10).

The 'Western' addition of 'immediately' to ηνοιξεν is attested by perp gig m e (E) sah eth.

ἐκ σπείρας τῆς καλουμένης Ἰταλικῆς, εὐσεβὴς καὶ φοβούμενος 2
τὸν θεὸν σὺν παντὶ τῷ οἴκῳ αὐτοῦ, ποιῶν ἐλεημοσύνας πολλὰς τῷ
λαῷ καὶ δεόμενος τοῦ θεοῦ διὰ παντός, εἶδεν ἐν ὁράματι φανερῶς 3
ὡσεὶ περὶ ὥραν ἐνάτην τῆς ἡμέρας ἄγγελον τοῦ θεοῦ εἰσελθόντα
πρὸς αὐτὸν καὶ εἰπόντα αὐτῷ· Κορνήλιε. ὁ δὲ ἀτενίσας αὐτῷ 4
καὶ ἔμφοβος γενόμενος εἶπεν· Τί ἐστιν, κύριε; εἶπεν δὲ αὐτῷ·
Αἱ προσευχαί σου καὶ αἱ ἐλεημοσύναι σου ἀνέβησαν εἰς μνημό-
συνον ἔμπροσθεν τοῦ θεοῦ· καὶ νῦν πέμψον ἄνδρας εἰς Ἰόππην 5
καὶ μετάπεμψαι Σίμωνά τινα ὃς ἐπικαλεῖται Πέτρος· οὗτος 6
ξενίζεται παρά τινι Σίμωνι βυρσεῖ, ᾧ ἐστὶν οἰκία παρὰ θάλασσαν.
ὡς δὲ ἀπῆλθεν ὁ ἄγγελος ὁ λαλῶν αὐτῷ, φωνήσας δύο τῶν οἰκετῶν 7
καὶ στρατιώτην εὐσεβῆ τῶν προσκαρτερούντων αὐτῷ | καὶ ἐξ- 8
ηγησάμενος ἅπαντα αὐτοῖς ἀπέστειλεν αὐτοὺς εἰς τὴν Ἰόππην.
τῇ δὲ ἐπαύριον ὁδοιπορούντων ἐκείνων καὶ τῇ πόλει ἐγγιζόντων 9
ἀνέβη Πέτρος ἐπὶ τὸ δῶμα προσεύξασθαι περὶ ὥραν ἕκτην.
ἐγένετο δὲ πρόσπεινος καὶ ἤθελε γεύσασθαι· παρασκευαζόντων δὲ 10
αὐτῶν ἐγένετο ἐπ᾽ αὐτὸν ἔκστασις, καὶ θεωρεῖ τὸν οὐρανὸν ἀν- 11
εῳγμένον καὶ καταβαῖνον σκεῦός τι ὡς ὀθόνην μεγάλην τέσσαρσιν
ἀρχαῖς καθειέμενον ἐπὶ τῆς γῆς, ἐν ᾧ ὑπῆρχεν πάντα τὰ τετράποδα 12
καὶ ἑρπετὰ τῆς γῆς καὶ πετεινὰ τοῦ οὐρανοῦ. καὶ ἐγένετο 13
φωνὴ πρὸς αὐτόν· Ἀναστάς, Πέτρε, θῦσον καὶ φάγε. ὁ δὲ 14

Editors   9 εκεινων] αυτων Soden   11 αρχαις] + δεδεμενον και Soden

---

Old Uncial   2 θεον BℵAC   κυριον 81   3 ωσει BACℵ^c   ως ℵ 81   4 αι 2° BℵA
om C 81   εις μνημοσυνον BACℵ^c 81 om ℵ   εμπροσθεν BℵA 81 ενωπιον C
5 τινα BAC 81   om ℵ   6 τινι σιμωνι BℵA 81   σιμωνι τινι C   ω BℵAC
ως 81   οικια BℵA 81   η οικια C   8 απαντα αυτοις BℵA 81   αυτοις
απαντα C   9 εκεινων BC   αυτων ℵA 81   εκτην BℵC 81
εναστην ℵ^c   εκτην της ημερας A   10 επ αυτον εκστασις BℵA   εκστασις
επ αυτον C   om επ αυτον 81   11 μεγαλην BℵA 81   om C²
αρχαις BℵAC² + δεδεμενον και C^{vid} 81   της γης BℵAC   την γην 81
12 πετεινα BℵAC² 81   τα πετεινα C

Antiochian   2 ποιων] +τε LPSϚ   3 om περι LPSϚ   3-4 om κορνηλιε ο δε
ατενισας αυτω L   4 om αι 2° S   εμπροσθεν] ενωπιον LPSϚ
5 εις ιοππην ανδρας LPSϚ   om τινα LPSϚ   ος επικαλειται πετρος]
τον επικαλουμενον πετρον LPS   6 θαλασσαν] +ουτος λαλησει σοι τι σε δει
ποιειν Ϛ   7 om ο before λαλων LP   αυτω 1°] τω κορνηλιω LPSϚ
οικετων] +αυτου LPSϚ   8 αυτοις απαντα LPSϚ   9 εκεινων] αυτων L
10 ηθελε] ηλθεν S   αυτων] εκεινων LPSϚ   γενετο 2°] επεπεσεν LSϚ
11 καταβαινον] +επ αυτον LPSϚ   αρχαις] +δεδεμενον και LPSϚ
12 τα τετραποδα και ερπετα της γης] τα τετραποδα της γης και τα θηρια και τα
ερπετα LPSϚ   τα πετεινα LPSϚ

X 4 αὐτῷ 1°] εἰς αὐτὸν 88 1311
    Τί ἐστιν] Τίς εἶ 1828

5   om τινα אLPS

6   οὗτος . . . βυρσεῖ] καὶ αὐτός ἐστι ξενιζόμενος πρὸς Σίμωνά
    τινα βυρσέα 614 minn
    θάλασσαν] + ὃς λαλήσει ῥήματα πρὸς σὲ ἐν οἷς σωθήσῃ σὺ
    καὶ πᾶς οἶκός σου 466 467 (88)

9   ἕκτην] + τῆς ἡμέρας A

11 καὶ καταβαῖνον . . . γῆς] καὶ τέσσαρσιν ἀρχαῖς δεδεμένον
    σκεῦός τι ὡς ὀθόνην λαμπρὰν καὶ καθιέμενον ἐπὶ τῆς γῆς Const.
    Apost. vi. 12, 6 (cf. 33 minn)

---

4 et trepidus factus dixit quid est d̄n̄e dixit autem ei orationis tuae et aelemosynae d
ascenderunt in recordatione coram d̄ēō 5 et nunc mitte viros in joppen et accersi
simonem qui cognominatur petrus 6 hic est ospitans aput simonem pellionem
cujus est domus juxta mare 7 ut autem dissit angelus qui loquebatur ei vocatis
duobus famulorum ejus et militem fidelem ex his qui praesto erant 8 enarravit
illis visum et misit illos in joppen 9 postera autem die iter illis facientibus et
adpropiantibus civitati ascendit petrus in cenaculum et horabit circa hora sexta
10 factus est autem esuriens et bolebat gustare praeparantibus vero ipsis cecidit
super eum mentis stupor 11 et vidit caelum apertum ex quattuor principiis
ligatum vas quodam et linteum splendidum quod differebatur de caelo in terram
12 et erant omnia quadripedia et serpentia et volatilia caeli 13 et facta est vox ad
eum petre surge immola et manduca 14 ad illi dixit non d̄n̄e quoniam numquam

---

2 . . . fuit faciens multas eleemosynas in plebem et semper orans deum. Cyprian,
3 . . . huic circa horam nonam oranti adstitit angelus . . . dicens : Corneli, Dom. or. 32
4 . . . orationes tuae et eleemosynae tuae ascenderunt ad memoriam coram deo.

---

2 religiosus, et timens deum cum tota domo sua, et faciens eleemosynas Irenaeus,
multas in populo, et orans deum semper. 3 vidit ergo circa horam nonam iii. 12, 7 (8)
diei, angelum dei introeuntem ad se et dicentem : 4 eleemosynae tuae
ascenderunt in recommemorationem in conspectu dei ; 5 [propter quod] mitte
[ad Simonem,] qui vocatur Petrus. [9-15 Petrus autem cum vidisset revelationem
in qua respondit ad eum caelestis vox :]

---

5 τινα] mg quendam   11 λαμπραν] mg splendidum   Harclean

---

11 For και καταβαινον . . . επι της
γης the citation in Const. Apost. vi.
12, 6 corresponds almost exactly to
the Latin of d and doubtless gives substantially the 'Western' reading. A
form somewhat like this but nearer the
usual text is offered by minn. Cod. 33
differs from Const. Apost. only in reading μεγαλην καταβαινον και καθιεμενον
instead of λαμπραν και καθιεμενον,
while perp gig Ambr. spir. ii. 10 have
a Latin text resembling that of d.
Note also hcl. mg. The word δεδεμενον

in Antiochian pesh hcl. text seems to
be a 'Western' survival ; Clem. Alex.
reads εκδεδεμενον. The mixed form in
hcl. text is noteworthy : et vas quoddam
devinctum quatuor extremis velut linteum magnum descendens et inclinans
in terram. Apparently the 'Western'
text described the vessel as 'bound by
the four corners,' instead of 'lowered
by the four corners,' and in consequence
of this change dropped καταβαινον.
The texts with all three participles are
conflate. See above, p. cxcii, note 1.

94   CODEX VATICANUS

Πέτρος εἶπεν· Μηδαμῶς, κύριε, ὅτι οὐδέποτε ἔφαγον πᾶν
κοινὸν καὶ ἀκάθαρτον. καὶ φωνὴ πάλιν ἐκ δευτέρου πρὸς αὐτόν· 15
Ἃ ὁ θεὸς ἐκαθάρισεν σὺ μὴ κοίνου. τοῦτο δὲ ἐγένετο ἐπὶ τρίς, 16
καὶ εὐθὺς ἀνελήμφθη τὸ σκεῦος εἰς τὸν οὐρανόν. ὡς δὲ ἐν αὐτῷ 17
διηπόρει ὁ Πέτρος τί ἂν εἴη τὸ ὅραμα ὃ εἶδεν, ἰδοὺ οἱ ἄνδρες οἱ
ἀπεσταλμένοι ὑπὸ τοῦ Κορνηλίου διερωτήσαντες τὴν οἰκίαν τοῦ
Σίμωνος ἐπέστησαν ἐπὶ τὸν πυλῶνα, καὶ φωνήσαντες ἐπύθοντο 18
εἰ Σίμων ὁ ἐπικαλούμενος Πέτρος ἐνθάδε ξενίζεται. τοῦ δὲ 19
Πέτρου διενθυμουμένου περὶ τοῦ ὁράματος εἶπεν τὸ πνεῦμα·
Ἰδοὺ ἄνδρες δύο ζητοῦντές σε· | ἀλλὰ ἀναστὰς κατάβηθι καὶ 20
πορεύου σὺν αὐτοῖς μηδὲν διακρεινόμενος, ὅτι ἐγὼ ἀπέσταλκα
αὐτούς· | καταβὰς δὲ Πέτρος πρὸς τοὺς ἄνδρας εἶπεν· Ἰδοὺ 21
ἐγώ εἰμι ὃν ζητεῖτε· τίς αἰτία δι' ἣν πάρεστε; οἱ δὲ εἶπαν· 22
Κορνήλιος ἑκατοντάρχης, ἀνὴρ δίκαιος καὶ φοβούμενος τὸν
θεὸν μαρτυρούμενός τε ὑπὸ ὅλου τοῦ ἔθνους τῶν Ἰουδαίων,
ἐχρηματίσθη ὑπὸ ἀγγέλου ἁγίου μεταπέμψασθαί σε εἰς τὸν
οἶκον αὐτοῦ καὶ ἀκοῦσαι ῥήματα παρὰ σοῦ. εἰσκαλεσάμενος 23
οὖν αὐτοὺς ἐξένισεν.

Editors   17 αυτω] εαυτω WH Soden JHR   ιδου] και ιδου JHR   18 επυνθανοντο
WHmg Soden   19 πνευμα] +αυτω WHmg Soden   δυο] τρεις Soden
[τρεις] WHmg   ζητουσι Soden   21 η αιτια WH Soden JHR

Old Uncial   14 και ΒΝΑ   η C 81 (+D)   17 αυτω Β   εαυτω ΝΑC 81 (+D)
ιδου ΒΝΑ 81   και ιδου C(+D)   υπο ΒΝ 81   απο ΑC(+D)   18 επυθοντο
ΒC επυνθανοντο ΝΑ 81 (+D)   19 πνευμα Β   +αυτω ΝΑC 81 (cf. D)
δυο Β   τρεις ΝΑC 81   ζητουντες ΒΝ 81   ζητουσι ΑC(+D)
20 εγω ΒΝΑC(+D)   om 81   21 τους ανδρας ΒΝΑ 81 (+D)   αυτους C
αιτια Β   η αιτια ΝΑC 81 (+D)

Antiochian   14 και] η LPSς(+D)   16 ευθυς] παλιν LPSς(+D)   17 αυτω]
εαυτω LPSς(+D)   ιδου] και ιδου LPSς(+D)   υπο] απο LPSς(+D)
om του before σιμωνος LPSς   18 επυνθανοντο LPSς(+D)   19 διενθυμου-
μενου] ενθυμουμενου ς   ειπεν] +αυτω LPSς(+D)   δυο] om HLPS
(+D)   τρεις ς   ζητουσι HLPSς(+D)   20 οτι] διοτι LPSς
21 ο πετρος L(+D)   ανδρας] +τους απεσταλμενους απο (+του ς) κορνηλιου προς
αυτον (αυτους S) HSς   η αιτια HLPSς(+D)   22 om τε S

---

16 With omne vas hcl.mg cf. απαντα
minn for το σκευος.

17 For ιδου ΒΝΑ 81 the more difficult
και ιδου C D perp e Antiochian is to
be preferred.

19 ανδρες δυο Β without support;
ανδρες τρεις (cf. xi. 11) ΝΑC 81 E e gig
vg pesh hcl.mg sah boh ; ανδρες D perp
Aug. gen. ad litt. xii. 11, Cyr. of Jer.,

etc., Antiochian. The reading δυο Β,
whether original or not, assumes that
only the two οικεται (vs. 7) need be
mentioned as responsible messengers,
the soldier merely serving as a guard.
In spite of the narrow attestation of
Β alone, this seems more likely to
have been the view of the original
author than of a scribe. τρεις is plainly

14, 15 πᾶν κοινὸν ἢ ἀκάθαρτον. φωνήσας δὲ πάλιν ἐκ δευτέρου πρὸς
16 αὐτόν· Ἃ ὁ θεὸς ἐκαθάρισεν σὺ μὴ κοίνου. τοῦτο δὲ ἐγένετο
17 ἐπὶ τρίς, καὶ ἀνελήμφθη πάλιν τὸ σκεῦος εἰς τὸν οὐρανόν. ὡς δὲ
ἐν ἑαυτῷ ἐγένετο, διηπόρει ὁ Πέτρος τί ἂν εἴ<η> τὸ ὅραμα ὃ
εἶδεν, καὶ εἰδοὺ οἱ ἄνδρες οἱ ἀπεσταλμένοι ἀπὸ Κορνηλίου ἐπερω-
18 τήσαντες τὴν οἰκίαν τοῦ Σίμωνος ἐπέστησαν ἐπὶ τὸν πυλῶνα, καὶ
φωνήσαντες ἐπυνθάνοντο εἰ Σίμων ὁ ἐπικαλούμενος Πέτρος
19 ἐνθάδε ξενίζεται. τοῦ δὲ Πέτρου διενθυμουμένου περὶ τοῦ
ὁράματος εἶπεν αὐτῷ τὸ πνεῦμα· Ἰδοὺ ἄνδρες ζητοῦσίν σε·
20 ἀλλὰ ἀνάστα, κατάβηθι καὶ πορεύου σὺν αὐτοῖς μηδὲν διακρι-
21 νόμενος, ὅτι ἐγὼ ἀπέσταλκα αὐτούς. τότε καταβὰς ὁ Πέτρος
πρὸς τοὺς ἄνδρας εἶπεν· Ἰδοὺ ἐγώ εἰμι ὃν ζητεῖτε· τί θέλετε ἢ
22 τίς ἡ αἰτία δι᾽ ἣν πάρεστε; οἱ δὲ εἶπον πρὸς αὐτόν· Κορνήλιός
τις ἑκατοντάρχης, ἀνὴρ δίκαιος καὶ φοβούμενος τὸν θεὸν μαρτυρούμενός τε ὑφ᾽ ὅλου τοῦ ἔθνους τῶν Ἰουδαίων, ἐχρηματίσθη
ὑπὸ ἀγγέλου ἁγίου μεταπέμψασθαί σε εἰς τὸν οἶκον αὐτοῦ καὶ
23 ἀκοῦσαι ῥήματα παρὰ σοῦ. τότε εἰσαγαγὼν ὁ Πέτρος ἐξένισεν
αὐτούς.

15 συ] σοι   21 θελεται

manducavi omne commune et inmundum 15 et vox rursum iterato ad eum quae d
d̄s̄ mundavit tu noli communicare 16 hoc enim factum est per ter et adsumptum
est ipsum vas in caelum 17 et dum intra se factus est haesitabat petrus quae esset
visio quam viderat et ecce viri qui missi erant a cornelio inquirentes domum simonis
adsisterunt ad januam 18 et cum clamassent interrogabant si simon qui cognominatur petrus hic ospitatur. 19 petro autem cogitante de visione dixit ei s̄p̄s̄
ecce viri quaerunt te 20 sed surge et descende et vade cum eis nihil dubitant quia
ego misi eos 21 tunc descendens petrus ad ipsos viros dixit ecce ego sum quem
queritis quid vultis quae causa propter quam venistis 22 ad illi dixerunt ad eum
cornelius centurio vir justus et timens d̄m̄ testimonio quoque a tota gente judaeorum
responsum accepit ab angelo sancto accersire te in domum suam et audire verba abs
te 23 tunc ergo ingressus petrus hospitio excepit eos ac postera die cum surrexisset

15 quae deus emundavit, tu ne commune dixeris.   Iren. iii.12,7 (8)
ἃ ὁ θεὸς ἐκαθάρισε, σὺ μὴ κοίνου.   [catena]

16 και ανελημφθη παλιν το σκευος εις τον ουρανον] mg et statim receptum est Harclean
omne vas in coelum   17 κορνηλιου] +mg [quum] appropinquassent et
19 διενθυμουμενου] [quum] cogitaret ·※· et haesitaret ✓   ανδρες] +mg tres
22 θεον] +mg et

a deliberate transcriptional improvement (cf. xi. 11), and the same motive
would account for the 'Western'
and Antiochian omission of δυο. Cf.

ix. 38, where Antiochian lacks the
superfluous but unobjectionable δυο
ανδρας of B℣AC 81 E and all the
versions.

Τῇ δὲ ἐπαύριον ἀναστὰς ἐξῆλθεν σὺν αὐτοῖς, καί τινες τῶν
ἀδελφῶν τῶν ἀπὸ Ἰόππης συνῆλθαν αὐτῷ. τῇ δὲ ἐπαύριον 24
εἰσῆλθεν εἰς τὴν Καισαρείαν· ὁ δὲ Κορνήλιος ἦν προσδοκῶν αὐτοὺς
συγκαλεσάμενος τοὺς συγγενεῖς αὐτοὺς καὶ τοὺς ἀναγκαίους
φίλους. ὡς δὲ ἐγένετο τοῦ εἰσελθεῖν τὸν Πέτρον, συναντήσας 25
αὐτῷ ὁ Κορνήλιος πεσὼν ἐπὶ τοὺς πόδας προσεκύνησεν. ὁ δὲ 26
Πέτρος ἤγειρεν αὐτὸν λέγων· Ἀνάστηθι· καὶ ἐγὼ αὐτὸς ἄνθρωπός
εἰμι. καὶ συνομειλῶν αὐτῷ εἰσῆλθεν, καὶ εὑρίσκει συνεληλυθότας 27
πολλούς, | ἔφη τε πρὸς αὐτούς· Ὑμεῖς ἐπίστασθε ὡς ἀθέμιτόν 28
ἐστιν ἀνδρὶ Ἰουδαίῳ κολλᾶσθαι ἢ προσέρχεσθαι ἀλλοφύλῳ·
κἀμοὶ ὁ θεὸς ἔδειξεν μηδένα κοινὸν ἢ ἀκάθαρτον λέγειν ἄνθρωπον·
| διὸ καὶ ἀναντιρήτως ἦλθον μεταπεμφθείς. πυνθάνομαι οὖν 29
τίνι λόγῳ μετεπέμψασθέ με. καὶ ὁ Κορνήλιος ἔφη· Ἀπὸ 30
τετάρτης ἡμέρας μέχρι ταύτης τῆς ὥρας ἤμην τὴν ἐνάτην προσευχόμενος ἐν τῷ οἴκῳ μου, καὶ ἰδοὺ ἀνὴρ ἔστη ἐνώπιόν μου ἐν

24-27 The 'Western' text has skilfully rewritten these verses (notably
vs. 25) in order to present a completely
continuous narrative. D d is supported
by gig hcl.*mg* and in part by perp
and other Latin codices. See Corssen,
Götting. gel. Anzeigen, 1896, pp. 437 ff.
26 *αναστηθι*] τι ποιεις (cf. vii. 26,
xiv. 15) D d hcl.*mg* and, with conflation of both phrases, perp w prov
vg.*codd*. Some of the last mentioned
Latin texts, and prov, add *deum adora*
(cf. Rev. xix. 10) either before *αναστηθι*
or at the end of the verse.
27 D d omits *συνομιλων* without any
corresponding substitute, but it is
found in perp gig, and need not be
regarded as a 'Western non-interpolation.'
30 The use of ἀπό and μέχρι here
to indicate the point of time when

the angel appeared to Cornelius must
be explained on linguistic grounds,
whether vulgar Greek or Semitic (cf.
C. C. Torrey, *Composition and Date
of Acts*, pp. 34 f.), not by arbitrary
reconstruction of the text (Blass conjectures *τεταρτην ημεραν ταυτην*). The
added *νηστευων* and the following copula
(*τε* or *και*) D Antiochian gig pesh hcl sah
is a 'Western' expansion of familiar
type. *της τριτης* D d (*nustertiana*) for
τεταρτης of all other witnesses is merely
a different way of counting days (i.e.
by not including the current day).
αρτι for *ταυτης* is a matter of taste.
E e while taking ἀπό and μέχρι in their
normal sense, tried to attain a meaning
for the whole on the basis of the
Antiochian text by adding *απο εκτης
ωρας* (cf. vs. 9), altering *την εναατην* to
εως εναατης, and improving the order

Τῇ δὲ ἐπαύριον ἀναστὰς ἐξῆλθεν σὺν αὐτοῖς, καί τινες τῶν
24 ἀδελφῶν ἀπὸ Ἰόππης συνῆλθαν αὐτῷ. τῇ δὲ ἐπαύριον εἰσῆλθεν εἰς
Καισαρίαν· ὁ δὲ Κορνήλιος ἦν προσδεχόμενος αὐτούς, καὶ συνκαλεσάμενος τοὺς συνγενεῖς αὐτοῦ καὶ τοὺς ἀναγκαίους φίλους περι-
25 έμεινεν. προσεγγίζοντος δὲ τοῦ Πέτρου εἰς τὴν Καισαρίαν
προδραμὼν εἷς τῶν δούλων διεσάφησεν παραγεγονέναι αὐτόν. ὁ
δὲ Κορνήλιος ἐκπηδήσας καὶ συναντήσας αὐτῷ πεσὼν πρὸς τοὺς
26 πόδας προσεκύνησεν αὐτόν. ὁ δὲ Πέτρος ἤγειρεν αὐτὸν λέγων·
27 Τί ποιεῖς; κἀγὼ ἄνθρωπός εἰμι ὡς καὶ σύ. καὶ εἰσελθών τε
28 καὶ εὗρεν συνεληλυθότας πολλούς, | ἔφη τε πρὸς αὐτούς· Ὑμεῖς
βέλτιον ἐφίστασθε ὡς ἀθέμιστόν ἐστιν ἀνδρὶ Ἰουδαίῳ κολλᾶσθαι
ἢ προσέρχεσθαι ἀνδρὶ ἀλλοφύλῳ· κἀμοὶ ὁ θεὸς ἐπέδιξεν μη<δέ>να
29 κοινὸν ἢ ἀκάθαρτον λέγειν ἄνθρωπον· διὸ καὶ ἀναντιρήτως ἦλθον
μεταπεμφθεὶς ὑφ᾽ ὑμῶν. πυνθάνομαι οὖν τίνι λόγῳ μετεπέμ-
30 ψασθέ με. καὶ ὁ Κορνήλιος ἔφη· Ἀπὸ τῆς τρίτης ἡμέρας μέχρι
τῆς ἄρτι ὥρας ἤμην νηστεύων τὴν ἐνάτην τε προσευχόμενος ἐν
τῷ οἴκῳ μου, καὶ ἰδοὺ ἀνὴρ ἔστη ἐνώπιόν μου ἐν ἐσθῆτι λαμπρᾷ

23 ιοππην   28 εφιστασθαι   29 μετεπεμψασθαι

exibit cum eis et quidam fratrum qui ab joppen simul venerunt cum eo   24 postero d
quoque die ingressus est caesaream cornelius vero erat expectans eos et convocatis
cognatis suis et necessariis amicis sustinuit   25 cum adpropiaret autem petrus in
caesaraeam praecurrens unus ex servis nuntiavit venisse eum cornelius autem exiliens
et obvius factus est ei procidens ad pedes ejus adoravit eum.   26 vero petrus levabit
eum dicens quid facis et ego homo sum quomodo et tu   27 et introibit et invenit
convenisse multos   28 aitque ad eos vos melius scitis ut nefas sit viro judaeo
adherere aut accedere ad allophylum et mihi d̄s ostendit neminem communem aut
immundum dicere hominem   29 propter quod et sine cunctatione veni transmissus
a vobis interrogo ergo qua ratione accersisti me   30 et cornelius ait a nustertiana
die usque in hunc diem eram jajunans et nona oravam in domo mea et ecce vir

28 dominus mihi dixit neminem hominum communem dicendum et Cyprian.
inmundum.   *Ep.* 64, 5

28 ipsi scitis quoniam non est fas viro Judaeo adjungi aut convenire cum Irenaeus,
allophylo ; mihi autem deus ostendit neminem communem aut immundum iii. 12, 15 (18)
dicere hominem : 29 quapropter sine contradictione veni.

24 εισηλθεν] *mg* introierunt   24, 25 περιεμεινεν προσεκυνησεν αυτον προς Harclean
τους ποδας] *mg* sustinuit.   quum appropinquasset autem Petrus Caesaream,
praecucurrit quidam ex servis et nunciavit quod veniret.   ipse autem Cornelius
exiliit et occurrit et cecidit ad pedes ejus— et procidit ✓   26 τι ποιεις]
mg quid facis   30 ανηρ] *mg* angelus

of words, thus : απο τεταρτης ημερας   προσευχομενος απο εκτης ωρας εως ενατης
μεχρι ταυτης της ωρας ημην νηστευων και   εν τω οικω μου, και ιδου, κτλ.

ἐσθῆτι λαμπρᾷ | καί φησι· Κορνήλιε, εἰσηκούσθη σου ἡ προσευχὴ 31
καὶ αἱ ἐλεημοσύναι σου ἐμνήσθησαν ἐνώπιον τοῦ θεοῦ· πέμψον 32
οὖν εἰς Ἰόππην καὶ μετακάλεσαι Σίμωνα ὃς ἐπικαλεῖται Πέτρος·
οὗτος ξενίζεται ἐν οἰκίᾳ Σίμωνος βυρσέως παρὰ θάλασσαν.
ἐξαυτῆς οὖν ἔπεμψα πρὸς σέ, σύ τε καλῶς ἐποίησας παραγενό- 33
μενος. νῦν οὖν πάντες ἡμεῖς ἐνώπιον τοῦ θεοῦ πάρεσμεν ἀκοῦσαι
πάντα τὰ προστεταγμένα σοι ὑπὸ τοῦ κυρίου. ἀνοίξας δὲ Πέτρος 34

Deut. x. 17 τὸ στόμα εἶπεν· Ἐπ᾽ ἀληθείας καταλαμβάνομαι ὅτι οὐκ ἔστιν
προσωπολήμπτης ὁ θεός, ἀλλ᾽ ἐν παντὶ ἔθνει ὁ φοβούμενος αὐτὸν 35
καὶ ἐργαζόμενος δικαιοσύνην δεκτὸς αὐτῷ ἐστίν. τὸν λόγον 36
ἀπέστειλεν τοῖς υἱοῖς Ἰσραὴλ εὐαγγελιζόμενος εἰρ‹ήν›ην διὰ
Ἰησοῦ Χριστοῦ· οὗτός ἐστιν πάντων κύριος. οἴδατε τὸ γενόμενον 37
ῥῆμα καθ᾽ ὅλης τῆς Ἰουδαίας, ἀρξάμενος ἀπὸ τῆς Γαλειλαίας
μετὰ τὸ κήρυγμα ὃ ἐκήρυξεν Ἰωάνης, Ἰησοῦν τὸν ἀπὸ Ναζαρέθ, 38
ὡς ἔχρεισεν αὐτὸν ὁ θεὸς πνεύματι ἁγίῳ καὶ δυνάμει, ὃς διῆλθεν

30 αισθητι   37 κηριγμα

Editors   32 θαλασσαν] +ος παραγενομενος λαλησει σοι Soden   33 ουν] ιδου JHR
του θεου] σου JHR   om παρεσμεν JHR   36 λογον] +ον WHmg
Soden   37 add υμεις before οιδατε WH Soden JHR   αρξαμενον
Soden   κηρυγμα] βαπτισμα WH Soden JHR

Old Uncial   32 εν οικια σιμωνος βυρσεως B‍א‍A 81 (+D)   παρα τινι σιμωνι βυρσει C
θαλασσαν B‍א‍A 81   + ος παραγενομενος λαλησει σοι C(+D)   33 τε B‍א‍C 81
γε A   παντα τα προστεταγμενα σοι B‍א‍C 81   τα προστεταγμενα σοι παντα A
υπο B‍א 81   απο AC‍א‍c(+D)   του 2ο B‍א‍AC(+D)   om 81   34 στομα
B‍א 81 (+D)   +αυτου AC‍א‍c   35 εστιν B‍א‍C 81 (+D)   εσται A   36 τον
B‍א‍AC2vid 81   +γαρ Cvid(+D)   λογον B‍א‍aA 81   +ον א‍C(+D)
ειρηνην B2   37 οιδατε B   υμεις οιδατε א‍AC 81 (+D)   γενομενον
B‍א‍A 81 (+D)   γεγονος C   αρξαμενος B‍א‍C   +γαρ A(+D)   αρξαμενον 81
κηρυγμα (B)   βαπτισμα B2א‍AC 81 (+D)   38 ος BAC‍א‍c 81   ως א

Antiochian   32 θαλασσαν] +ος παραγενομενος λαλησει σοι HLPSϛ(+D)   33 κυριου]
θεου HLPSϛ(+D)   36 λογον] +ον HLPSϛ(+D)   ειρηνην] δικαιοσυνην S
37 add υμεις before οιδατε HLPSϛ(+D)   αρξαμενον LPSϛ   κηρυγμα]
βαπτισμα HLPSϛ(+D)   38 add εν before πνευματι L

33 ιδου, with omission of παρεσμεν,
D pesh sah may be preferable to the
reading ουν of the B-text; note the
Semitism.
σου D d vg pesh sah may be preferable to the more religious phrase
του θεου.
36 τον λογον απεστειλεν B‍א‍aA 81
vg ; verbum suum misit gig d sah ; τον
λογον ον απεστειλεν א E e Antiochian ;
τον γαρ λογον αυτου απεστειλεν 614 perp
t m vg.codd ; τον γαρ λογον ον απεστειλεν

Cvid D pesh hcl ·⁜·. γαρ and ον seem
to be different attempts at amelioration, although in the case of ον transcriptional change might perhaps
have worked in either direction.
Note that ον was probably struck
out in א before the codex was issued
from the scriptorium. 'His' with
λογον, found frequently in versions
(Latin, Sahidic), need not imply a
different Greek text (but cf. 614).
37 αρξαμενος B‍א‍ACDHE ; αρξαμενον

CODEX BEZAE

31 | καί φησιν· Κορνήλιε, εἰσηκούσθη σου ἡ προσευχὴ καὶ αἱ ἐλεη-
32 μοσύναι σου ἐμνήσθησαν ἐνώπιον τοῦ θεοῦ· πέμψον οὖν εἰς
Ἰόππην καὶ μετακάλεσαι Σίμωνα ὃς ἐπικαλεῖται Πέτρος·
οὗτος ξενίζεται ἐν οἰκίᾳ Σίμωνος βυρσέως παρὰ θάλασσαν, ὃς
33 παραγενόμενος λαλήσει σοι. ἐξαυτῆς οὖ⟨ν⟩ ἔπεμψα πρὸς σὲ
παρακαλῶν ἐλθεῖν πρὸς ἡμᾶς, σὺ δὲ καλῶς ἐποίησας ἐν τάχει
παραγενόμενος. νῦν ⟨ἰ⟩δοὺ πάντες ἡμεῖς ἐνώπιόν σου, ἀκοῦσαι
34 βουλόμενοι παρὰ σοῦ τὰ προστεταγμένα σοι ἀπὸ τοῦ θεοῦ. ἀνοίξας δὲ τὸ στόμα Πέτρος εἶπεν· Ἐπ' ἀληθείας καταλαμβανόμενος
35 ὅτι οὐκ ἔστιν προσωπολήμπτης ὁ θεός, ἀλλ' ἐν παντὶ ἔθνι ὁ
φοβούμενος αὐτὸν καὶ ἐργαζόμενος δικαιοσύνην δεκτὸς αὐτῷ
36 ἐστίν. τὸν γὰρ λόγον ὃν ἀπέστιλεν τοῖς υἱοῖς Ἰσραὴλ εὐαγγελιζόμενος εἰρήνην διὰ Ἰησοῦ Χριστοῦ (οὗτός ἐστιν πάντων
37 κύριος) | ὑμεῖς οἴδατε, τὸ γενόμενον καθ' ὅλης Ἰουδαίας, ἀρξά-
μενος γὰρ ἀπὸ τῆς Γαλιλαίας μετὰ τὸ βάπτισμα ὃ ἐκήρυξεν
38 Ἰωάνης, | Ἰησοῦν τὸν ἀπὸ Ναζαρέθ, ὃν ἔχρισεν ὁ θεὸς ἁγίῳ πνεύ-
ματι καὶ δυνάμει· οὗτος διῆλθεν εὐεργετῶν καὶ εἰώμενος πάντας

38 ειωμενας

---

stetit in conspecto meo in veste splendida   31 et ait corneli exaudita est oratio tua et d
aelemosynae tuae in mente habitae sunt in conspectu d̄ī   32 mitte ergo in joppen et
accersi simonem qui cognominatur petrus hic hospitatur in domum simonis pellionis
juxta mare qui cum venerit loquatur tibi   33 e vestigio ergo misi ad te rogando
venire te ad nos tu autem bene fecisti in brevi advenire nunc ergo nos omnes in
conspectu tuo audire volumus a te quae praecepta sunt tibi a d̄o   34 aperiens autem
os petrus dixit in veritate expedior quia non est personarum acceptor d̄s   35 sed in
omni gente qui timet eum et operatur justitiam acceptus est ei   36 verbum suum
misit filiis istrahel evangelizare pacem per ī̄h̄m x̄p̄m hic est omnium d̄n̄s   37 vos
scitis quid factum est per totam judaeā cum coepisset enim a galilaea post baptismum
quod praedicavit johannes   38 ī̄h̄m a nazareth quem unxit d̄s sancto s̄p̄o et virtute
hic pergressus est benefaciens et sanans omnes qui obtenebantur a diabolo quia d̄s

---

34 in veritate comperi quoniam non est personarum acceptor deus,   35 sed Irenaeus,
in omni gente qui timet eum et operatur justitiam acceptabilis ei est. iii. 12, 7 (8)
cf. iv. 27, 1

37 vos scitis quod factum est verbum per omnem Judaeam, incipiens enim
a Galilaea post baptismum quod praedicavit Johannes,   38 Jesum a Nazareth
quemadmodum unxit eum deus spiritu sancto et virtute: ipse circumivit
benefaciens et curans omnes qui oppressi erant a diabolo, quoniam deus erat

---

31 φησιν] dicit ⁙ mihi ✓   33 παρακαλων ελθειν προς ημας] ⁙ rogans Harclean
ut venires ad nos ✓   36 γαρ] ⁙ enim ✓

Antiochian (attempt to improve grammar). Cf. Lk. xxiii. 5, xxiv. 47 (note vv. ll.), Acts i. 22, for noteworthy instances of this Aramaism,

and see Torrey, *Composition and Date of Acts*, pp. 25-28.

D d omit ρημα ('matter'), thereby avoiding the Semitism.

εὐεργετῶν καὶ ἰώμενος πάντας τοὺς καταδυναστευομένους ὑπὸ
τοῦ διαβόλου, ὅτι ὁ θεὸς ἦν μετ' αὐτοῦ· καὶ ἡμεῖς μάρτυρες πάντων 39
ὧν ἐποίησεν ἔν τε τῇ χώρᾳ τῶν Ἰουδαίων καὶ Ἰερουσαλήμ· ὃν
καὶ ἀνεῖλαν κρεμάσαντες ἐπὶ ξύλου. τοῦτον ὁ θεὸς ἤγειρεν τῇ 40
τρίτῃ ἡμέρᾳ καὶ ἔδωκεν αὐτὸν ἐμφανῆ γενέσθαι, οὐ παντὶ τῷ 41
λαῷ ἀλλὰ μάρτυσι τοῖς προκεχειροτονημένοις ὑπὸ τοῦ θεοῦ,
ἡμῖν, οἵτινες συνεφάγομεν καὶ συνεπίομεν αὐτῷ μετὰ τὸ ἀναστῆναι αὐτὸν ἐκ νεκρῶν· καὶ παρήγγειλεν ἡμῖν κηρύξαι τῷ λαῷ καὶ 42
διαμαρτύρασθαι ὅτι οὗτός ἐστιν ὁ ὡρισμένος ὑπὸ τοῦ θεοῦ κριτὴς
ζώντων καὶ νεκρῶν. τούτῳ πάντες οἱ προφῆται μαρτυροῦσιν, 43
ἄφεσιν ἁμαρτιῶν λαβεῖν διὰ τοῦ ὀνόματος αὐτοῦ πάντα τὸν
πιστεύοντα εἰς αὐτόν. ἔτι λαλοῦντος τοῦ Πέτρου τὰ ῥήματα 44
ταῦτα ἐπέπεσε τὸ πνεῦμα τὸ ἅγιον ἐπὶ πάντας τοὺς ἀκούοντας
τὸν λόγον. καὶ ἐξέστησαν οἱ ἐκ περιτομῆς πιστοὶ οἳ συνῆλθαν 45
τῷ Πέτρῳ, ὅτι καὶ ἐπὶ τὰ ἔθνη ἡ δωρεὰ τοῦ πνεύματος τοῦ
ἁγίου ἐκκέχυται· ἤκουον γὰρ αὐτῶν λαλούντων γλώσσαις καὶ 46
μεγαλυνόντων τὸν θεόν. τότε ἀπεκρίθη Πέτρος· | Μήτι τὸ ὕδωρ 47
δύναται κωλῦσαί τις τοῦ μὴ βαπτισθῆναι τούτους οἵτινες τὸ

Editors   39 ιερουσαλημ] εν ιερουσαλημ Soden   45 οι 2°] οσοι WHmg Soden JHR
πνευματος του αγιου] αγιου πνευματος Soden   47 κωλυσαι δυναται Soden mg

---

Old Uncial   39 ημεις ΒℵC 81   υμεις Α(+D)   ιερουσαλημ Β(+D)   εν ιερουσαλημ
ℵAC 81   40 ηγειρεν ΒΑℵᶜ 81   +εν ℵC   41 υπο του θεου ημιν
ΒℵΑ 81 (+D)   ημιν υπο του θεου C   συνεφαγομεν ΒℵΑ 81 (+D)   +αυτω C
42 ουτος ΒC(+D)   αυτος ℵΑ 81   44 επεπεσε Βℵ 81   επεσε Α(+D)
45 οι 2° Β   οσοι ℵΑ 81 (+D)   πνευματος του αγιου Β (cf. D)
αγιου πνευματος ℵΑ 81

Antiochian   39 ημεις] +εσμεν HLPSϛ   ιερουσαλημ] εν ιερουσαλημ HLPSϛ
om και after ον ϛ   42 ουτος] αυτος H(L?)PSϛ   43 τουτω] τουτον HL
45 οι 2°] οσοι HLPSϛ(+D)   πνευματος του αγιου] αγιου πνευματος HLPSϛ
46 ο πετρος HLPSϛ(+D)   47 κωλυσαι δυναται τις HLPSϛ

---

40 (εν) τη τριτη ημερα] μετα την
τριτην ημεραν D d t. D d show a
similar variation of text in Matt. xvi.
21, xvii. 23, as do also the Latin
codices a k (but not D d) in Mk. viii.
31; see J. R. Harris, Codex Bezae,
1891, pp. 91 f.
41 The addition of 'forty days'
(D d hcl·※·) is found also in E e perp

gig t vg.codd sah Vigilius Const.
Apost. vi. 30.
46 To the erased words of D correspond in d: praevaricatis linguis et
magnificantes (i.e. ετεραις (?) γλωσσαις
και μεγαλυνοντων). Most Latin texts
lack praevaricatis altogether; vg.cod.
ardmach reads variis (cf. pesh),
Rebapt suis, sah 'other.'

CODEX BEZAE 101

τοὺς καταδυναστευθέντας ὑπὸ τοῦ διαβόλου, ὅτι ὁ θεὸς ἦν μετ᾽
39 αὐτοῦ· καὶ ἡμεῖς μάρτυρες αὐτοῦ ὧν ἐποίησεν ἔν τε τῇ χώρᾳ τῶν
Ἰουδαίων καὶ Ἰερουσαλήμ· ὃν καὶ ἀνεῖλαν κρεμάσαντες ἐπὶ
40 ξύλου. τοῦτον ὁ θεὸς ἤγειρεν μετὰ τὴν τρίτην ἡμέραν καὶ ἔδωκεν
41 αὐτῷ ἐνφανῆ γενέσθαι, οὐ παντὶ τῷ λαῷ ἀλλὰ μάρτυσι τοῖς
προκεχειροτονημένοις ὑπὸ τοῦ θεοῦ, ἡμεῖν, οἵτινες συνεφάγομεν
καὶ συνεπίομεν αὐτῷ καὶ συν‹αν›εστράφημεν μετὰ τὸ ἀναστῆναι
42 ἐκ νεκρῶν ἡμέρας μ̄· καὶ ἐνετείλατο ἡμεῖν κηρύξαι τῷ λαῷ καὶ
διαμαρτύρασθαι ὅτι οὗτός ἐστιν ὁ ὡρισμένος ὑπὸ τοῦ θεοῦ κριτὴς
43 ζώντων καὶ νεκρῶν. τούτῳ πάντες οἱ προφῆται μαρτυροῦσιν,
ἄφεσιν ἁμαρτιῶν λαβεῖν διὰ τοῦ ὀνόματος αὐτοῦ πάντα τὸν πι-
44 στεύοντα εἰς αὐτόν. ἔτι λαλοῦντος τοῦ Πέτρου τὰ ῥήματα ταῦτα
ἔπεσεν τὸ πνεῦμα τὸ ἅγιον ἐπὶ πάντας τοὺς ἀκούοντας τὸν λόγον.
45 καὶ ἐξέστησαν οἱ ἐκ περιτομῆς πιστοὶ ὅσοι συνῆλθον τῷ Πέτρῳ,
ὅτι καὶ ἐπὶ τὰ ἔθνη ἡ δωρεὰ τοῦ πνεύματος ἁγίου ἐκκέχυται·
46 ἤκουον γὰρ αὐτῶν λαλούντων [. . . . . καὶ
47 μεγαλυνόντω]ν τὸν θεόν. εἶπεν δὲ ὁ Πέτρος· | Μήτι τὸ ὕδωρ
κωλ‹ῦσ›αί τις δύναται τοῦ μὴ βαπτισθῆναι αὐτοὺς οἵτινες τὸ

39 ημεις] υμεις

---

erat cum illo   39 et nos testes ejus quae fecit in regione judaeorum et hierusalem d
quem etiam interfecerunt suspensum in ligno   40 hunc d̄s̄ suscitavit post tertium
dieum et dedit ei manifestum fieri   41 non omni populo sed testibus praedestinatis
a d̄ō nobis qui simul manducavimus et simul bibimus cum eo et conversi sumus
postquam surrexit a mortuis dies xl   42 et praecepit nobis praedicare populo et
protestari quia ipse est qui praestitus est a d̄ō judex vivorum et mortuorum
43 huic omnes prophetae testimonium peribent remissionem peccatorum accipere
per nomen ejus omnem qui credit in eum   44 adhuc loquente petro berba haec
cecidit s̄p̄s̄ sanctus super omnes qui audiebant verbum   45 et obstupefacti sunt qui
erant ex circumcisio fideles qui simul venerunt cum petro quia et super gentes
donum s̄p̄s̄ sancti effusum est   46 audiebant enim eos loquentes praevaricatis
linguis et magnificantes d̄m̄ dixit autem petrus   47 numquid aliquis aquam

cum eo.   39 et nos testes omnium eorum quae fecit et in regione Judaeorum et | Irenaeus,
in Hierusalem ; quem interfecerunt suspendentes in ligno.   40 hunc deus | iii. 12, 7 (8) cf. iv. 27, 1
excitavit tertia die, et dedit eum manifestum fieri,   41 non omni populo, sed
testibus nobis praedestinatis a deo, qui cum eo et manducavimus et bibimus
post resurrectionem a mortuis ;   42 et praecepit nobis adnuntiare populo et
testificari quoniam ipse est praedestinatus a deo judex vivorum et mortuorum. | cf. iv. 20, 2
43 huic omnes prophetae testimonium reddunt remissionem peccatorum accipere
per nomen ejus omnem credentem in eum.
   47 numquid aliquis aquam vetare potest ad baptizandum hos qui | iii. 12, 15 (18)
   μήτις τὸ ὕδωρ κωλῦσαι δύναται τούτους, οἵτινες

---

39 ον] quem ⸪ rejecerunt Judaei ⸜   41 και συνανεστραφημεν ημερας | Harclean
μ̄] et versati sumus ⸪ cum eo dies quadraginta ⸜   46 και μεγαλυνοντων]
text et magnificantes (?), mg et glorificantes

πνεῦμα τὸ ἅγιον ἔλαβον ὡς καὶ ἡμεῖς; προσέταξεν δὲ αὐτοὺς 48
ἐν τῷ ὀνόματι Ἰησοῦ Χριστοῦ βαπτισθῆναι. τότε ἠρώτησαν
αὐτὸν ἐπιμεῖναι ἡμέρας τινάς.

Ἤκουσαν δὲ οἱ ἀπόστολοι καὶ οἱ ἀδελφοὶ οἱ ὄντες κατὰ τὴν XI
Ἰουδαίαν ὅτι καὶ τὰ ἔθνη ἐδέξαντο τὸν λόγον τοῦ θεοῦ. ὅτε δὲ 2
ἀνέβη Πέτρος εἰς Ἰερουσαλήμ, διεκρείνοντο πρὸς αὐτὸν οἱ ἐκ
περιτομῆς | λέγοντες ὅτι εἰσῆλθεν πρὸς ἄνδρας ἀκροβυστίαν ἔχοντας 3
καὶ συνέφαγεν αὐτοῖς. ἀρξάμενος δὲ Πέτρος ἐξετίθετο αὐτοῖς 4
καθεξῆς λέγων· Ἐγὼ ἤμην ἐν πόλει Ἰόππῃ προσευχόμενος καὶ 5
εἶδον ἐν ἐκστάσει ὅραμα, καταβαῖνον σκεῦός τι ὡς ὀθόνην μεγάλην
τέσσαρσιν ἀρχαῖς καθιεμένην ἐκ τοῦ οὐρανοῦ, καὶ ἦλθεν ἄχρι ἐμοῦ·
εἰς ἣν ἀτενίσας κατενόουν καὶ εἶδον τὰ τετράποδα τῆς γῆς καὶ τὰ 6
θηρία καὶ τὰ ἑρπετὰ καὶ τὰ πετεινὰ τοῦ οὐρανοῦ· ἤκουσα δὲ καὶ 7

Editors 1 ηκουσαν δε οι αποστολοι και οι αδελφοι] ακουστον δε εγενετο τοις αποστολοις
και τοις αδελφοις JHR   2 ιεροσολυμα Soden   3 εισηλθες WHmg
Soden (but cf. mg) JHR   συνεφαγες WHmg Soden (but cf. mg) JHR

Old Uncial 48 δε B𝔁 81   τε A   αυτους B 81 (+D)   αυτοις 𝔁A   ονοματι B𝔁A
+του κυριου 81 (+D)   3 εισηλθεν B 81   εισηλθες 𝔁A(+D)   συνεφαγεν
B 81   συνεφαγες 𝔁A(+D)   5 προσευχομενος BA𝔁° 81 (+D)   om 𝔁
καταβαινον σκευος τι B𝔁A(+D)   σκευος τι καταβαινων 81

Antiochian 47 ως] καθως HLPS𝕾   48 δε] τε HLPS𝕾   εν τω ονοματι
ιησου χριστου βαπτισθηναι] βαπτισθηναι εν τω ονοματι του κυριου HLPS𝕾 (cf. D)
2 οτε δε] και οτε HLPS𝕾   ιεροσολυμα HLPS𝕾 (cf. D)   3 προς
ανδρας ακροβυστιαν εχοντας εισηλθες (-εν L) και συνεφαγες (-εν L) HLPS𝕾 (cf. D)
4 ο πετρος HLPS𝕾   om καθεξης L   6 om της γης HPS
ερπετα] +της γης H   7 om και 1° HLPS𝕾

1-2 The rewritten 'Western' text of vss. 1, 2 is transmitted on the whole more completely in D d than in any of the Latin or Syriac witnesses, which, however, are numerous and contain large parts of it. Vs. 1, for οι D should perhaps be read τοις ; for εδεξατο possibly εδεξαντο. After τον λογον του θεου the addition, not found in D d, of και εδοξαζον (εδοξασαν ?) τον θεον (cf. xi. 18, xxi. 20) is adequately attested for the 'Western' text by perpᶜᵒʳʳ vg.codd hcl·⋇·. Vs. 2, at some point after επιστηριξας an omitted verb (εξηλθεν ?) seems to be attested by perp vg.codd hcl·⋇·. For κατηντησεν αυτοις the conjecture of Zahn, κατηντησεν αυτον, commends itself, but beginning with ος και the testimony of the versions (except d) fails. A few other minor variants require no

mention. The Latin authorities for the 'Western' expansion in vs. 2 have a form abbreviated to a less degree than hcl ·⋇· but in somewhat the same way.

1 The reading of D (substantially confirmed by pesh) : ακουστον δε εγενετο τοις αποστολοις και τοις αδελφοις is more Semitic than the B-text. Cf. LXX Gen. xlv. 2, Is. xxiii. 5, xlviii. 3, 20 ; ακουστον does not occur in N.T. D may here have the original text.

2 προσφωνησας D may be an error for προσφωνησαι, cf. hcl·⋇· loqui ; but the Latin witnesses agree with D.

κατηντησεν αυτοις D is hardly tolerable ; possibly αυτοις is a mistake for αυτου (Zahn), but more probably it is due to the Latin εις of d.

3 εισηλθες, συνεφαγες 𝔁AD Antiochian perp gig vg hcl.mg sah boh ;

48 πνεῦμα τὸ ἅγιον ἔλαβον ὥσπερ καὶ ἡμεῖς; τότε προσέταξεν
αὐτοὺς βαπτισθῆναι ἐν τῷ ὀνόματι τοῦ κυρίου Ἰησοῦ Χριστοῦ.
τότε παρεκάλεσαν αὐτὸν πρὸς αὐτοὺς διαμεῖναι ἡμέρας τινάς.
XI Ἀκουστὸν δὲ ἐγένετο τοῖς ἀποστόλοις καὶ τοῖς ἀδελφοῖς οἳ
2 ἐν τῇ Ἰουδαίᾳ ὅτι καὶ τὰ ἔθνη ἐδέξατο τὸν λόγον τοῦ θεοῦ. ὁ μὲν
οὖν Πέτρος διὰ ἱκανοῦ χρόνου ἠθέλησε πορευθῆναι εἰς Ἱεροσό-
λυμα· καὶ προσφωνήσας τοὺς ἀδελφοὺς καὶ ἐπιστηρίξας αὐτούς,
πολὺν λόγον ποιούμενος, διὰ τῶν χωρῶν διδάσκων αὐτούς· ὃς
καὶ κατήντησεν αὐτοῖς καὶ ἀπήγγιλεν αὐτοῖς τὴν χάριν τοῦ
θεοῦ. οἱ δὲ ἐκ περιτομῆς ἀδελφοὶ διεκρίνοντο πρὸς αὐτὸν
3 | λέγοντες ὅτι Εἰσῆλθες πρὸς ἄνδρας ἀκροβυστίαν ἔχοντας καὶ
4 συνέφαγες σὺν αὐτοῖς. ἀρξάμενος δὲ Πέτρος ἐξετίθετο αὐτοῖς
5 τὰ κατεξῆς λέγων· Ἐγὼ ἤμην ἐν Ἰόππῃ πόλει προσευχόμενος
καὶ εἶδον ἐκστάσει ὅραμα, καταβαῖνον σκεῦός τι ὡς ὀθόνην
μεγάλην τέτρασιν ἀρχαῖς καθιεμένην ἐκ τοῦ οὐρανοῦ, καὶ ἦλθεν
6 ἕως ἐμοῦ· εἰς ἣν ἀτενίσας κατενόουν καὶ εἶδον τετράποδα τῆς
7 γῆς καὶ τὰ θηρία καὶ ἑρπετὰ καὶ πετεινὰ τοῦ οὐρανοῦ· καὶ

2 ηθελησαι   6 αθενισας

---

prohibere potest ut baptizentur isti qui s̅p̅m̅ sanctum acceperunt sicut et nos d
48 tunc praecepit eos baptizari in nomine d̅n̅i̅ i̅h̅u̅ x̅p̅i̅ tunc rogaverunt eum ad eos
demorari dies aliquos
1 audito vero apostoli et fratres qui erant in judaeam quia et gentes
exceperunt verbum d̅i̅ 2 quidem ergo petrus per multo tempore voluit proficisci in
hierosolyma et convocavit fratres et confirmavit eos multum verbum faciens per
civitates docens eos quia et obviavit eis et enuntiavit eis gratiam d̅i̅ quia erant de
circumcisione fratres judicantes ad eum 3 dicentes quia introisti ad viros praeputia
habentes et simul manducasti cum eis 4 incipiens autem petrus exponebat eis per
ordinem dicens 5 ego eram in joppen civitate orans et vidi in mentis stupore visum
descendere vas quodam velut linteum magnum quattuor principibus dimittebatur de
caelo et venit usque ad me 6 in quod intuitus considerabat et vidi quadripedes
terrae et vestias et repentia et volatilia caeli 7 et audivi vocem dicentem mihi

---

47 spiritum sanctum acceperunt quemadmodum et nos?   Irenaeus
τὸ πνεῦμα τὸ ἅγιον ἔλαβον ὡς καὶ ἡμεῖς;   [catena]

---

2 ο μεν ουν πετρος . . . διδασκων αυτους] ÷· et benedicebant deo. ipse Harclean
quidem igitur Petrus per tempus non modicum volebat abire Hierosolymam et
loqui fratribus; et quum confirmasset, profectus est — et ✓ docuit eos ✓
3 εισηλθες, και συνεφαγες] mg ingressus sis et ederis   5 μεγαλην] mg
splendidum

εισηλθεν, συνεφαγεν B 81 L minn pesh   inferior. Cf. perp gig vg and hcl. text
hcl. text. The B-text is due to the   (' propter ').
failure to recognize οτι as direct   5 With hcl. mg cf. perp splendidum
interrogative (' why ? '), hence is   magnum.

φωνῆς λεγούσης μοι· Ἀναστάς, Πέτρε, θῦσον καὶ φάγε. εἶπον 8
δέ· Μηδαμῶς, κύριε, ὅτι κοινὸν ἢ ἀκάθαρτον οὐδέποτε εἰσῆλθεν
εἰς τὸ στόμα μου. ἀπεκρίθη δὲ ἐκ δευτέρου φωνὴ ἐκ τοῦ οὐρανοῦ· 9
Ἃ ὁ θεὸς ἐκαθάρισεν σὺ μὴ κοίνου. τοῦτο δὲ ἐγένετο ἐπὶ τρίς, καὶ 10
ἀνεσπάσθη πάλιν ἅπαντα εἰς τὸν οὐρανόν. καὶ ἰδοὺ ἐξαυτῆς 11
τρεῖς ἄνδρες ἐπέστησαν ἐπὶ τὴν οἰκίαν ἐν ᾗ ἦμεν, ἀπεσταλμένοι
ἀπὸ Καισαρείας πρός με. εἶπεν δὲ τὸ πνεῦμά μοι συνελθεῖν αὐτοῖς 12
μηδὲν διακρείναντα. ἦλθον δὲ σὺν ἐμοὶ καὶ οἱ ἓξ ἀδελφοὶ οὗτοι,
καὶ εἰσήλθομεν εἰς τὸν οἶκον τοῦ ἀνδρός. ἀπήγγειλεν δὲ ἡμῖν 13
πῶς εἶδεν τὸν ἄγγελον ἐν τῷ οἴκῳ αὐτοῦ σταθέντα καὶ εἰπόντα·
Πέμψον εἰς Ἰόππην καὶ μετάπεμψαι Σίμωνα τὸν ἐπικαλούμενον
Πέτρον, ὃς λαλήσει ῥήματα πρὸς σὲ ἐν οἷς σωθήσῃ σὺ καὶ πᾶς ὁ 14
οἶκός σου. ἐν δὲ τῷ ἄρξασθαί με λαλεῖν ἐπέπεσεν τὸ πνεῦμα τὸ 15
ἅγιον ἐπ᾽ αὐτοὺς ὥσπερ καὶ ἐφ᾽ ἡμᾶς ἐν ἀρχῇ. ἐμνήσθην δὲ τοῦ 16
ῥήματος τοῦ κυρίου ὡς ἔλεγεν· Ἰωάνης μὲν ἐβάπτισεν ὕδατι
ὑμεῖς δὲ βαπτισθήσεσθε ἐν πνεύματι ἁγίῳ. εἰ οὖν τὴν ἴσην 17
δωρεὰν ἔδωκεν αὐτοῖς ὁ θεὸς ὡς καὶ ἡμῖν πιστεύσασιν ἐπὶ τὸν
κύριον Ἰησοῦν Χριστόν, ἐγὼ τίς ἤμην δυνατὸς κωλῦσαι τὸν θεόν;
ἀκούσαντες δὲ ταῦτα ἡσύχασαν καὶ ἐδόξασαν τὸν θεὸν λέγοντες· 18
Ἄρα καὶ τοῖς ἔθνεσιν ὁ θεὸς τὴν μετάνοιαν εἰς ζωὴν ἔδωκεν.

Editors   9 φωνη εκ δευτερου WHmg Soden   11 ημην WHmg Soden JHR
12 μοι το πνευμα Soden   13 ειποντα] +[αυτω] Soden   πεμψον]
αποστειλον WH Soden JHR

Old Uncial   9 εκ δευτερου φωνη B   φωνη εκ δευτερου אA 81   11 ημεν BאA(+D)
ημην 81   12 διακρειναντα BאᶜС 81   διακρινοντα א   εξ BאA(+D)
+οι 81   13 πεμψον B   αποστειλον אA 81 (+D)   14 ο BאA(+D)
om 81   16 εμνησθην Bא 81 (+D)   εμνησθημεν A   ελεγεν BאA 81
(+D)   +οτι אᶜ   17 εδωκεν BA 81 (+D)   δεδωκεν א   τις BאA(+D)
om 81   18 εδοξασαν Bא 81   εδοξαζον A

Antiochian   8 οτι] +παν HLPSς̄   9 δε] +μοι HLPSς̄ (cf. D)   φωνη εκ δευτερου
HLPSς̄   10 om δε Η   παλιν ανεσπασθη HLPSς̄   11 ημην
HLPSς̄   12 μοι το πνευμα HLPSς̄   διακρινομενον HLPSς̄
13 δε] τε HLPSς̄   ειποντα] +αυτω HLPSς̄(+D)   πεμψον] αποστειλον
HLPSς̄(+D)   ιοππην] +ανδρας HLPSς̄   16 om του 2ᵒ HLPSς̄
17 εγω] +δε HLPSς̄   18 εδοξαζον HLPSς̄   αρα] αραγε HLPSς̄
εδωκεν εις ζωην HLPSς̄

11 ημην 81 Antiochian, all versions ;
ημεν BאA D vg.2 codd. This purely
accidental change of ημην to ημεν seems
to have been an early occurrence ; the
versions point to the true reading.
12 Om μηδεν διακριναντα D d perp
hcl. For διακρινομενον א E Antiochian

e (dubitantem) vg (haesitans) cf. x. 20.
That the text of B is a conformation
to x. 20 is made less likely by the
active voice and telling force of the
participle.
17 D d vg.one cod Rebapt Aug. trin
xv. 19, 35 omit ο θεος. This may be

ἤκουσα φωνὴν λέγουσάν μοι· ᾿Ανάστα, Πέτρε, θῦσον καὶ φάγε.
8 εἶπα δέ· Μηδαμῶς, κύριε, ὅτι κοινὸν ἢ ἀκάθαρτον οὐδέποτε
9 εἰσῆλθεν εἰς τὸ στόμα μου. ἐγένετο φωνὴ ἐκ τοῦ οὐρανοῦ
10 πρός με· ῍Α ὁ θεὸς ἐκαθάρισεν σὺ μὴ κοίνου. τοῦτο δὲ
ἐγένετο ἐπὶ τρίς, καὶ ἀνεσπάσθη πάλιν ἅπαντα εἰς τὸν οὐρανόν.
11 καὶ ἰδοὺ ἐξαυτῆς γ̅ ἄνδρες ἐπέστησαν ἐπὶ τὴν οἰκίαν ἐν ᾗ ἦμεν,
12 ἀπεσταλμένοι ἀπὸ Καισαραίας πρός με. εἶπεν δὲ τὸ πνεῦμά μοι
συνελθεῖν αὐτοῖς. ἦλθον σὺν ἐμοὶ καὶ οἱ ἐξ ἀδελφοὶ οὗτοι, καὶ
13 εἰσήλθομεν εἰς τὸν οἶκον τοῦ ἀνδρός. ἀπήγγειλεν δὲ ἡμεῖν πῶς
εἶδεν ἄγγελον ἐν τῷ οἴκῳ αὐτοῦ σταθέντα καὶ εἰπόντα αὐτῷ·
᾿Απόστειλον εἰς ᾿Ιόππην καὶ μετάπεμψαι Σίμωνα τὸν ἐπικαλού-
14 μενον Πέτρον, ὃς λαλήσει ῥήματα πρὸς σὲ ἐν οἷς σωθήσῃ σὺ
15 καὶ πᾶς ὁ οἶκός σου. ἐν δὲ τῷ ἄρξασθαί με λαλεῖν αὐτοῖς ἔπεσεν
16 τὸ πνεῦμα τὸ ἅγιον ἐπ᾿ αὐτοῖς ὡς καὶ ἐφ᾿ ἡμᾶς ἐν ἀρχῇ. ἐμνήσθην δὲ τοῦ ῥήματος τοῦ κυρίου ὡς ἔλεγεν· ᾿Ιωάννης μὲν ἐβάπ-
17 τισεν ὕδατι ὑμεῖς δὲ βαπτισθήσεσθε ἐν πνεύμα‹τι› ἁγίῳ. εἰ
οὖν τὴν ἴσην δωρεὰν ἔδωκεν αὐτοῖς ὡς καὶ ἡμεῖν πιστεύσασιν ἐπὶ
τὸν κύριον ᾿Ιησοῦν Χριστόν, ἐγὼ τίς ἤμην δυνατὸς κωλῦσαι τὸν
θεὸν τοῦ μὴ δοῦναι αὐτοῖς πνεῦμα ἅγιον πιστεύσασιν ἐπ᾿ αὐτῷ;
18 ἀκούσαντες δὲ ταῦτα ἡσύχασαν καὶ ἐδόξα‹σα›ν τὸν θεὸν λέγον-
τες· ῍Αρα καὶ τοῖς ἔθνεσιν ὁ θεὸς μετάνοιαν εἰς ζωὴν ἔδωκεν.

16 βαπτισθησεσθαι

---

surgens petre immola et manduca   8 dixit autem absit d̅n̅e̅ quia commune et d
inmundum numquam introibit in os meum   9 respondit vero vox de caelo ad me
quae d̅s̅ mundavit tu noli communicare   10 hoc autem factum est per ter et sublata
sunt iterum omnia in caela   11 et ecce statim tres viri supervenerunt ad domum
in qua erant missi a caesarea ad me   12 et dixit s̅p̅s̅ mihi simul venire cum eis
veneruntque mecum etiam sex fratres isti et introibimus in domum ipsius viri
13 adnuntiavit autem nobis quomodo vidit angelum in domo sua stetisse et dixisse
ei mitte in joppen et accersi simonem qui cognominatur petrus   14 qui loquebatur
verba ad te in quibus salvus fias et omnis domus tua   15 et dum coepisset loqui eis
cecidit s̅p̅s̅ sanctus super eos sicut super nos in principium   16 recordatus sum
verbum d̅n̅i̅ sicut dicebat johannes quidem baptizavit aqua vos autem baptizamini s̅p̅o̅
sancto   17 si autem aequalem donum dedit eis sicut nobis credentibus in d̅n̅m̅ i̅h̅m̅
x̅p̅m̅ ego quis eram qui possim prohibere d̅u̅m̅ ut non daret eis s̅p̅m̅ sanctum credentibus in eum   18 cum autem audissent haec siluerunt et clarificaverunt d̅n̅m̅ dicentes

---

17 του μη δουναι αυτοις πνευμα αγιον πιστευσασιν επ αυτω] ⁙ ut non daret iis Harclean
spiritum sanctum, quum credidissent in dominum Jesum Christum ✓

---

right, but is more probably due to the
'Western' reviser's view that the Holy
Spirit was the gift of Christ.

Like hcl ⁙ vg.cod reads in dominum Jesum Christum; cf. vg.codd in
nomine Jesu Christi, and Bohemian.

Οἱ μὲν οὖν διασπαρέντες ἀπὸ τῆς θλείψεως τῆς γενομένης ἐπὶ 19
Στεφάνῳ διῆλθον ἕως Φοινείκης καὶ Κύπρου καὶ Ἀντιοχείας,
μηδενὶ λαλοῦντες τὸν λόγον εἰ μὴ μόνον Ἰουδαίοις. ἦσαν δέ 20
τινες ἐξ αὐτῶν ἄνδρες Κύπριοι καὶ Κυρηναῖοι, οἵτινες ἐλθόντες
εἰς Ἀντιόχειαν ἐλάλουν καὶ πρὸς τοὺς Ἑλληνιστάς, εὐαγγελιζόμενοι τὸν κύριον Ἰησοῦν. καὶ ἦν χεὶρ κυρίου μετ᾽ αὐτῶν, πολύς 21
τε ἀριθμὸς ὁ πιστεύσας ἐπέστρεψεν ἐπὶ τὸν κύριον. ἠκούσθη δὲ 22
ὁ λόγος εἰς τὰ ὦτα τῆς ἐκκλησίας τῆς οὔσης ἐν Ἰερουσαλὴμ περὶ
αὐτῶν, καὶ ἐξαπέστειλαν Βαρνάβαν ἕως Ἀντιοχείας· ὃς παρα- 23
γενόμενος καὶ ἰδὼν τὴν χάριν τὴν τοῦ θεοῦ ἐχάρη καὶ παρεκάλει
πάντας τῇ προθέσει τῆς καρδίας προσμένειν ἐν τῷ κυρίῳ, ὅτι 24
ἦν ἀνὴρ ἀγαθὸς καὶ πλήρης πνεύματος ἁγίου καὶ πίστεως. καὶ
προσετέθη ὄχλος ἱκανός. ἐξῆλθεν δὲ εἰς Ταρσὸν ἀναστῆσαι 25
Σαῦλον, | καὶ εὑρὼν ἤγαγεν εἰς Ἀντιόχειαν. ἐγένετο δὲ αὐτοῖς καὶ 26

Editors   21 [ο] Soden   22 βαρναβαν] +[διελθειν] Soden   23 [την 2°] Soden
[εν] WH om εν Soden JHR   24 ικανος] +τω κυριω WH Soden JHR
25 αναστησαι] αναζητησαι WH Soden JHR

Old Uncial   19 στεφανω BΝ 81   στεφανου A (cf. D)   ιουδαιοις BA 81   ιουδαιοι Ν
20 και 2° BΝA 81 om Νᶜ(+D)   ελληνιστας B 81   ευαγγελιστας Ν ελληνας
AΝᶜ(+D)   22 ουσης BΝ 81 om A(+D)   23 την 2° BΝA om 81 (+D)
εν B om ΝA 81 (+D)   24 ην ανηρ BA 81 (+D)   ανηρ ην Ν   ικανος B
+τω κυριω B²ΝA 81 (+D)   25 ταρσον BΝA +ο βαρναβας 81   αναστησαι
B αναζητησαι B²ΝA 81 (cf. D)   26 και ενιαυτον BΝA ενιαυτον 81 (cf. D)

Antiochian   20 ελθοντες] εισελθοντες HPSⳄ   om και 2° HLPSⳄ(+D)   21 om
ο HLPSⳄ(+D)   22 om ουσης HLPSⳄ(+D)   ιεροσολυμοις HLPSⳄ
βαρναβαν] +διελθειν HLPSⳄ(+D)   23 om την 2° HLPSⳄ(+D)
om εν HLPSⳄ(+D]   24 ικανος] +τω κυριω HLPSⳄ(+D)   25 ταρσον] +ο
βαρναβας HLPSⳄ   αναστησαι] αναζητησαι HLPSⳄ (cf. D)
26 ευρων] +αυτον HLPSⳄ   ηγαγεν] +αυτον HLPSⳄ   αυτους HLPSⳄ
om και before ενιαυτον HLPSⳄ (cf. D)

20 ελληνιστας B 81 Antiochian, ευαγγελιστας (error for ελληνιστας) Ν; ελληνας ADΝᶜ 1518. 'Greeks' is the rendering of all versions, but is not decisive as to the word in the Greek copies used. Eusebius and Chrysostom refer to Ἕλληνες in this connexion, but the reading of the text they used is not thereby certainly indicated (cf. vi. 1); it may have been either ελληνιστας ('Greek-speaking persons') or ελληνας. The unusual ελληνιστας is probably right; note on the part of cod. A the same tendency to alter in Acts ix. 29, where A reads ελληνας for ελληνιστας. The context in the verse

under discussion requires a contrast between Jews and non-Jews, and no reason appears why the latter should not be designated by the term 'Greek-speaking persons.' The specific meaning 'Greek-speaking Jews' belongs to the word only where that is clearly indicated by the context, as is certainly not the case here. See B. B. Warfield, *Journal of Biblical Literature and Exegesis*, Boston, 1883, pp. 113-127.

21 ο before πιστευσας BΝA 81 minn is awkward and probably to be retained. D Antiochian omit.

23 The addition of εν BΨ 181 is not to be accepted; the evidence of

19 Οἱ μὲν οὖν διασπαρέντες ἀπὸ τῆς θλείψεως τῆς γενομένης ἀπὸ
τοῦ Στεφάνου διῆλθον ἕως Φοινείκης καὶ Κύπρου καὶ Ἀντιο-
20 χείας, μηδενὶ τὸν λόγον λαλοῦντες εἰ μὴ μόνοις Ἰουδαίοις. ἦσαν
δέ τινες ἐξ αὐτῶν ἄνδρες Κύπριοι καὶ Κυρηναῖοι, οἵτινες ἐλθόντες
εἰς Ἀντιόχειαν ἐλάλουν πρὸς τοὺς Ἕλληνας, εὐαγγελιζόμενοι
21 τὸν κύριον Ἰησοῦν Χριστόν. ἦν δὲ χεὶρ κυρίου μετ' αὐτῶν,
22 πολύς τε ἀριθμὸς πιστεύσας ἐπέστρεψεν ἐπὶ τὸν κύριον. ἠκούσθη δὲ ὁ λόγος εἰς τὰ ὦτα τῆς ἐκκλησίας τῆς ἐν Ἰερουσαλὴμ
περὶ αὐτῶν, καὶ ἐξαπέστειλαν Βαρνάβαν διελθεῖν ἕως τῆς Ἀντιο-
23 χείας· ὃς καὶ παραγενόμενος καὶ ἰδὼν τὴν χάριν τοῦ θεοῦ ἐχάρη
καὶ παρεκάλει πάντας τῇ προθέσει τῆς καρδίας προσμένειν τῷ
24 κυρίῳ, ὅτι ἦν ἀνὴρ ἀγαθὸς καὶ πλήρης πνεύματος ἁγίου καὶ
25 πίστεως. καὶ προσετέθη ὄχλος ἱκανὸς τῷ κυρίῳ. | ἀκούσας δὲ
26 ὅτι Σαῦλός ἐστιν εἰς Θαρσὸν ἐξῆλθεν ἀναζητῶν αὐτόν, †καὶ ὡς†
συντυχὼν παρεκάλεσεν ἐλθεῖν εἰς Ἀντιόχειαν. οἵτινες παρα-

---

forsitam et gentibus d̄s̄ paenitentiam in vitam dedit   19 illi quidem dispersi a con- d
flictatione quae facta est sub stephano transierunt usque phoenicen et cyprum et
antiochiam nemini verbum loquentes nisi solis judaeis   20 erant autem quidam ex
ipsis viri cyprii et cyrinenses qui cum venissent antiochiam loquebantur cum craecos
evangelizare d̄n̄m̄ īh̄m̄ x̄p̄m̄   21 et erat manus d̄n̄i cum eis multisque numeris cum
credidissent reversi sunt ad d̄n̄m̄   22 auditus est vero hic sermo in auribus ecclesiae
quae erat in hierusalem de eis et miserunt barnabant ut iret usque antiocham   23 qui
cum venisset et vidisset gratiam d̄ī gavisus est et adorabantur omnes ipso proposito
cordis permanere a d̄n̄m̄   24 quia erat vir vonus et plenus s̄p̄ō sancto et fidei et
adposita est turba copiosa ad d̄n̄m̄   25 audiens autem quod saulus est tharso exiit
requirere eum   26 et cum invenissent depraecabantur venire antiochiam contigit vero

---

25-26 ακουσας δε . . . συνεχυθησαν] mg quum audivisset autem Saulum esse Harclean
Tarsi, exiit ad quaerendum eum. qui, quum collocutus esset cum eo, persuasit
eum venire Antiochiam. quum venissent autem, annum integrum congregati
sunt

---

vg (in domino), (d) perp (ad dominum), and of sah ('in') boh ('in') does not necessarily point to the presence of the preposition in the underlying Greek. With εν the phrase, if not due to translation, would probably have to be taken in the characteristic Pauline sense, nowhere else found in Acts (iv. 2, xiii. 39 are different). Cf. xiii. 43 προσμενειν τη χαριτι.

26 The 'Western' text of vs. 26 in D is corrupt, but can be restored with the help of perp gig (in part) and hcl.mg. For και ως we may substitute ω και (with support of perp vg quem cum invenisset) or, more probably, ος

και (to which hcl.mg seems to point, cf. vs. 23). Both perp and hcl.mg show by the following sentence that (unlike gig vg) they are rendering the 'Western' text. οχλον ικανον may have been clumsily introduced from the B-text, and thus have supplanted a previous appropriate τη εκκλησια (so perp vg.cod.R^mg); but it is perhaps more likely (Zahn) that in D (also d, in part) the words τη εκκλησια και εδιδασκον (cf. perp vg.cod.R^mg) have dropped out between συνεχυθησαν and οχλον ικανον. Note the different forms of the text in D and d. For εχρηματισεν D we should read -αν.

ἐνιαυτὸν ὅλον συναχθῆναι ἐν τῇ ἐκκλησίᾳ καὶ διδάξαι ὄχλον ἱκανόν, χρηματίσαι τε πρώτως ἐν Ἀντιοχείᾳ τοὺς μαθητὰς Χρειστιανούς.

Ἐν αὐταῖς δὲ ταῖς ἡμέραις κατῆλθον ἀπὸ Ἱεροσολύμων 27 προφῆται εἰς Ἀντιόχειαν· ἀναστὰς δὲ εἷς ἐξ αὐτῶν ὀνόματι 28 Ἄγαβος ἐσήμαινεν διὰ τοῦ πνεύματος λειμὸν μεγάλην μέλλειν ἔσεσθαι ἐφ᾽ ὅλην τὴν οἰκουμένην· ἥτις ἐγένετο ἐπὶ Κλαυδίου. τῶν δὲ μαθητῶν καθὼς εὐπορεῖτό τις ὥρισαν ἕκαστος αὐτῶν εἰς 29 διακονίαν πέμψαι τοῖς κατοικοῦσιν ἐν τῇ Ἰουδαίᾳ ἀδελφοῖς· ὃ καὶ ἐποίησαν ἀποστείλαντες πρὸς τοὺς πρεσβυτέρους διὰ χειρὸς 30 Βαρνάβα καὶ Σαύλου.

Κατ᾽ ἐκεῖνον δὲ τὸν καιρὸν ἐπέβαλεν Ἡρῴδης ὁ βασιλεὺς τὰς XII χεῖρας κακῶσαί τινας τῶν ἀπὸ τῆς ἐκκλησίας. ἀνεῖλεν δὲ Ἰά- 2 κωβον τὸν ἀδελφὸν Ἰωάνου μαχαίρῃ. ἰδὼν δὲ ὅτι ἀρεστόν ἐστιν 3 τοῖς Ἰουδαίοις προσέθετο συλλαβεῖν καὶ Πέτρον, ἦσαν δὲ ἡμέραι τῶν ἀζύμων, | ὃν καὶ πιάσας ἔθετο εἰς φυλακήν, παραδοὺς τέσσαρ- 4

Editors		
26 συναχθηναι] συνχυθηναι JHR		χριστιανους WH Soden
27 αυταις] ταυταις WH Soden JHR		28 εσημανεν WHmg Soden JHR
3 [αι] ημεραι Soden		

Old Uncial		
26 πρωτως Bא πρωτον A 81 (+D)		εν αντιοχεια Bא 81 (+D) εις
αντιοχειαν A χρειστιανους B (cf. D)	χρηστιανους א 81 χριστιανους A	
27 αυταις B ταυταις אA 81 (+D)		28 εσημαινεν B εσημανεν אA 81
29 ωρισαν Bא 81 (+D) ωρισεν A		30 και 1° BאᵃA 81 (+D) +ο א
1 ηρωδης ο βασιλευς BA(+D) ο βασιλευς ηρωδης א 81		3 εστιν BAאᶜ 81
(+D) om א ημεραι Bא αι ημεραι A 81 (+D)		4 παραδους Bא 81 (+D)
παραδιδους A		

Antiochian		
26 om εν before τη εκκλησια HLPS		πρωτον HLPSϛ(+D)
χριστιανους HLPSϛ 27 αυταις] ταυταις HLPSϛ(+D)		28 εσημανεν
HLPSϛ μεγαν HLPSϛ(+D)	ητις] οστις και HLPSϛ κλαυδιου]	
+καισαρος HLPSϛ 30 ο] οι L		3 ιδων δε] και ιδων HLPSϛ(+D)
αι ημεραι S(+D)		

26 The singular word συνεχυθησαν D is represented by *commisceri* gig (d), *commiscuerunt se* perp vg.*cod.R*ᵐᵍ, and perhaps by *conversati sunt* vg. May it be the original verb for which συναχθηναι has been substituted in all other texts? If a merely accidental error, so strange a variant would seem hardly likely to perpetuate itself. The omission by the Antiochian text of εν before τη εκκλησια, difficult to explain if the verb was συναχθηναι, may point to an original συνχυθηναι.

27, 28 The 'Western' text is notable for the addition, widely attested in Latin (including perp Aug. *serm. dom.*

in monte ii. 37, De prophetiis, etc.), containing the first person ημων. Otherwise the addition does not differ in character from the 'Western' expansions in general, and it has in fact no greater claim than they to acceptance. Elsewhere 'we' means 'Paul and his companions'; in this instance, 'the church at Antioch.' Apparently the reviser was aware of the tradition connecting the author of the book with Antioch. See Harnack, *Sitzungsberichte*, Berlin Academy, 1899, pp. 316-327.

28 εφη σημαινων for αναστας εσημαινεν is found in D d alone, and Zahn argues

γενόμενοι ἐνιαυτὸν ὅλον συνεχύθησαν †ὄχλον ἱκανόν†, καὶ τότε
πρῶτον ἐχρημάτισαν ἐν 'Αντιοχείᾳ οἱ μαθηταὶ Χρειστιανοί.

27 Ἐν ταύταις δὲ ταῖς ἡμέραις κατῆλθον ἀπὸ 'Ιεροσολύμων
28 προφῆται εἰς 'Αντιόχειαν, ἦν δὲ πολλὴ ἀγαλλίασις· συνεστραμ-
μένων δὲ ἡμῶν ἔφη εἰς ἐξ αὐτῶν ὀνόματι "Αγαβος σημαίνων
διὰ τοῦ πνεύματος λειμὸν μέγαν μέλλειν ἔσεσθαι ἐφ' ὅλην τὴν
29 οἰκουμένην· ἥτις ἐγένετο ἐπὶ Κλαυδίου. οἱ δὲ μαθηταὶ καθὼς
εὐπορῦντο ὥρισαν ἕκαστος αὐτῶν εἰς διακονίαν πέμψαι τοῖς
30 κατοικοῦσιν ἐν τῇ 'Ιουδαίᾳ ἀδελφοῖς· ὃ καὶ ἐποίησαν ἀποστείλαντες πρὸς τοὺς πρεσβυτέρους διὰ χειρὸς Βαρνάβα καὶ
Σαύλου.

XII Κατ' ἐκεῖνον δὲ τὸν καιρὸν ἐπέβαλεν τὰς χεῖρας 'Ηρῴδης ὁ
βασιλεὺς κακῶσαί τινας τῶν ἀπὸ τῆς ἐκκλησίας ἐν τῇ 'Ιουδαίᾳ.
2, 3 καὶ ἀνεῖλεν 'Ιάκωβον τὸν ἀδελφὸν 'Ιωάνου μαχαίρᾳ. καὶ ἰδὼν
ὅτι ἀρεστόν ἐστιν τοῖς 'Ιουδαίοις ἡ ἐπιχείρησις αὐτοῦ ἐπὶ τοὺς
πιστοὺς προσέθετο συνλαβεῖν καὶ Πέτρον, ἦσαν δὲ αἱ ἡμέραι τῶν
4 ἀζύμων· τοῦτον πιάσας ἔθετο εἰς φυλακήν, παραδοὺς τέσσαρσιν

26 εχρηματισεν   28 σημενων   30 αποστειλαστες
3 επιχειρησεις

---

eis annum totum commiscere ecclesiam et tunc primum nuncupati sunt in antiochiā d
discipulos christianos 27 in istis autem diebus advenerunt ab hierosolymis prophetae
in antiochiam erant autem magna exultatio 28 revertentibus autem nobis ait unus
ex ipsis nomine agabus significabat per spm famem magnam futuram esse in toto orbe
terrae quae fuit sub claudio 29 discipuli autem sicut prout copiam singuli autem
ipsorum in ministerium mittere hiis qui inhabitant in judaea fratribus 30 quod
etiam fecerunt cum misissent ad presbyteros per manum barnabae et sauli
1 per illum vero temporis inmisit manus suas herodes rex maletractare quosdam
qui erant ab ecclesia in judaea 2 et interfecit jacobum fratrem johannis gladio
3 et cum vidisset quod placeret hoc judaeis conpraehensio ejus super credentes
adjecit adpraehendere et petrum erant autem dies asymorum 4 hunc adprehensum
posuit in carcerem traditum quattuor quaternionibus militū custodire eum volens

---

1 εν τη ιουδαια] ⁂ quae erat in Judaea ✓   3 η επιχειρησις αυτου επι Harclean
τους πιστους] mg aggressus ejus in fideles

---

with much force and acuteness that
the 'Western' text originally read
ανεστη σημαινων (cf. vg surgens significabat). His reasoning is as follows :
(1) For σημαινων d has significabat.
Since this is incompatible with the
preceding ait of d, the latter word has
probably been introduced to conform
to the Greek side, and has taken the
place of surgens, proper to that Latin
(vulgate type) on which d was here
based. Consequently, for εφη ait

D and d constitute but one witness.
(2) εφη σημαινων is inherently difficult,
since the oratio obliqua clearly depends
on σημαινων. (John xviii. 32, xxi. 19
are different.) (3) In perp vg.cod.R
De proph. we find qui significabat, a
reading not easily explained unless a
finite verb had once preceded in place
of surgens.
μεγαν . . . ητις D is due to an incomplete correction (cf. μεγαλην . . . ητις
BℵA 81 ; μεγαν . . . οστις Antiochian).

σιν τετραδίοις στρατιωτῶν φυλάσσειν αὐτόν, βουλόμενος μετὰ τὸ
πάσχα ἀναγαγεῖν αὐτὸν τῷ λαῷ. ὁ μὲν οὖν Πέτρος ἐτηρεῖτο ἐν 5
τῇ φυλακῇ· προσευχὴ δὲ ἦν ἐκτενῶς γεινομένη ὑπὸ τῆς ἐκκλησίας
περὶ αὐτοῦ. ὅτε δὲ ἤμελλεν προσαγαγεῖν αὐτὸν ὁ Ἡρῴδης, 6
τῇ νυκτὶ ἐκείνῃ ἦν ὁ Πέτρος κοιμώμενος μεταξὺ δύο στρατιωτῶν
δεδεμένος ἁλύσεσιν δυσίν, φύλακές τε πρὸ τῆς θύρας ἐτήρουν τὴν
φυλακήν. καὶ ἰδοὺ ἄγγελος κυρίου ἐπέστη, καὶ φῶς ἔλαμψεν ἐν 7
τῷ οἰκήματι· πατάξας δὲ τὴν πλευρὰν τοῦ Πέτρου ἤγειρεν αὐτὸν
λέγων· Ἀνάστα ἐν τάχει· καὶ ἐξέπεσαν αὐτοῦ αἱ ἁλύσεις ἐκ
τῶν χειρῶν. εἶπεν δὲ ὁ ἄγγελος πρὸς αὐτόν· Ζῶσαι καὶ ὑπόδυσαι 8
τὰ σανδάλιά σου· ἐποίησεν δὲ οὕτως. καὶ λέγει αὐτῷ· Περιβαλοῦ τὸ ἱμάτιόν σου καὶ ἀκολούθει μοι· καὶ ἐξελθὼν ἠκολούθει, 9
καὶ οὐκ ᾔδει ὅτι ἀληθές ἐστιν τὸ γεινόμενον διὰ τοῦ ἀγγέλου,
ἐδόκει δὲ ὅραμα βλέπειν. διελθόντες δὲ πρώτην φυλακὴν καὶ 10
δευτέραν ἦλθαν ἐπὶ τὴν πύλην τὴν σιδηρᾶν τὴν φέρουσαν εἰς τὴν
πόλιν, ἥτις αὐτομάτη ἠνοίγη αὐτοῖς, καὶ ἐξελθόντες προῆλθον
ῥύμην μίαν, καὶ εὐθέως ἀπέστη ὁ ἄγγελος ἀπ᾽ αὐτοῦ. καὶ ὁ 11

10 ηνυγη

Editors   5 εκτενης Soden   εκκλησιας] +προς τον θεον WH Soden JHR
6 προσαγαγειν] προαγαγειν WHmg Soden JHR   8 δε 1ο] τε Soden
υποδυσαι] υποδησαι WH Soden JHR

Old Uncial   4 αναγαγειν Bℵ 81 (+D)   αγαγειν A   5 εκτενως BℵA^vid εκτενης A²81
γεινομενη BℵA   γενομενη 81   εκκλησιας B +προς τον θεον ℵA 81 (+D)
περι BℵA² 81 (+D)   υπ (?) A   6 προσαγαγειν B   προαγαγειν A 81 (cf. D)
προσαγειν ℵ (cf. D)   της θυρας Bℵ 81 (+D)   τη θυρα A   8 δε 1ο
B(+D)   τε ℵA 81   υποδυσαι B υποδησαι B²ℵA 81 (+D)   ουτως
BℵA(+D)   ουτος 81   9 ηκολουθει BℵA 81 (+D)   +αυτω ℵᶜ   γεινομενον
BℵA(+D)   γενομενον 81   δια Bℵ 81 (+D)   υπο A   δε BAℵ^c 81 om ℵ
10 δε BℵA(+D)   om 81   εις BℵA(+D)   επι 81   απεστη Bℵ 81 (+D)
απηλθεν A

Antiochian   5 εκτενης HLPSϛ   γενομενη P   εκκλησιας] +προς τον θεον
HLPSϛ(+D)   περι] υπερ HLPSϛ   6 προσαγαγειν αυτον] αυτον
προαγειν HLPSϛ(+D)   8 δε 1ο] τε LPϛ   προς αυτον ο αγγελος L
ζωσαι] περιζωσαι HLPSϛ   υποδυσαι] υποδησαι HLPSϛ(+D)   9 om
και εξελθων ηκολουθει P   ηκολουθει] +αυτω HLSϛ   γενομενον L
δια] υπο H   10 om δε S   om την φερουσαν εις την πολιν L
ηνοιχθη HLPSϛ   προηλθον] προσηλθον L(+D)

4 Hcl.mg gives *ascendere facere*
(αναγαγειν) as a substitute for
tradere of the text. Perhaps this
rendering of the text (with which
pesh agrees) rested on αγαγειν A minn.
5 φυλακη] + *a cohorte regis* perp

vg.cod hcl·⸓. The relation of this
body to the sixteen soldiers of vs. 4
is not plain.
The omission of γινομενη in D is
probably accidental. All Latin codices
except d read *fiebat*.

τετραδίοις στρατιωτῶν φυλάσσ‹ε›ιν, βουλόμενος μετὰ τὸ πάσχα
5 ἀναγαγεῖν αὐτὸν τῷ λαῷ. ὁ μὲν οὖν Πέτρος ἐτηρεῖτο ἐν τῇ
φυλακῇ· πολλὴ δὲ προσευχὴ ἦν ἐν ἐκτενείᾳ περὶ αὐτοῦ ἀπὸ τῆς
6 ἐκκλησίας πρὸς τὸν θεὸν †περὶ αὐτοῦ†. ὅτε δὲ ἔμελλεν προάγειν
αὐτὸν Ἡρῴδης, τῇ νυκτεὶ ἐκείνῃ ἦν ὁ Πέτρος κοιμώμενος
μεταξὺ δύο στρατιωτῶν δεδεμένος ἁλύσεσι δυσίν, φύλακες δὲ
7 πρὸ τῆς θύρας ἐτήρουν τὴν φυλακήν. καὶ ἰδοὺ ἄγγελος κυρίου
ἐπέστη τῷ Πέτρῳ, καὶ φῶς ἐπέλαμψεν τῷ οἰκήματι· νύξας δὲ
τὴν πλευρὰν τοῦ Πέτρου ἤγειρεν αὐτὸν λέγων· Ἀνάστα ἐν τάχει·
8 καὶ ἐξέπεσαν αἱ ἁλύσεις ἐκ τῶν χειρῶν αὐτοῦ. εἶπεν δὲ ὁ ἄγγελος
πρὸς αὐτόν· Ζῶσαι καὶ ὑπόδησαι τὰ σανδάλιά σου· ἐποίησεν δὲ
οὕτως. καὶ λέγει αὐτῷ· Περιβαλοῦ τὸ ἱμάτιόν σου καὶ ἀκολούθει
9 μοι· καὶ ἐξελθὼν ἠκολούθει, καὶ οὐκ ᾔδει ὅτι ἀληθές ἐστιν τὸ
10 γεινόμενον διὰ τοῦ ἀγγέλου, ἐδόκει γὰρ ὅραμα βλέπειν. διελθόντες δὲ πρώτην καὶ δευτέραν φυλακὴν ἦλθον ἐπὶ τὴν πύλην τὴν
σιδηρᾶν τὴν φέρουσαν εἰς τὴν πόλιν, ἥτις αὐτομάτη ἠνοίγη αὐτοῖς,
καὶ ἐξελθόντες κατέβησαν τοὺς ζ βαθμοὺς καὶ προσῆλθαν ρύμην
11 μίαν, καὶ εὐθέως ἀπέστη ὁ ἄγγελος ἀπ' αὐτοῦ. καὶ ὁ Πέτρος ἐν

6 κοιμουμενος   10 ηνυγη

post pascha producere eum populo 5 vero petrus custodiebatur in carcere multa **d**
vero oratio erat instantissime pro eo ab ecclesia ad d̄ūm super ipso 6 ad vero cum
incipiebat prodocere eum herodes nocte illa erat petrus dormiens inter duos milites
ligatus catenis duabus vigiles autem ante ostium adservabant carcerem 7 et ecce
angelus d̄n̄i adsistit petro et lux refulgens in illo loco pungens autem latus petri
suscitavit eum dicens surge cilerius et ceciderunt ejus catenae de manibus 8 dixit
autem angelus ad eum praecinge te et calciate calciamenta tua fecit autem sic et dicit
ei operi te vestimentum tuum et sequere me 9 et cum exisset sequebatur et non
sciebat quia verum est quod fiebat per angelum putabat enim visum videre 10 cum
praeterissent primam et secundam custodiam venerunt ad portam ferream quae ducit
in civitatem quae sua sponte aperta est eis et cum exissent descenderunt septem
grados et processerunt gradum unum et continuo discessit angelus ab eo 11 et

4 αναγαγειν] *mg* ascendere facere   5 φυλακη] + ⁘ a cohorte regis ✓ Harclean
7 τω πετρω] ⁘ Petro ✓   επελαμψεν] + *mg* ab eo   9 δια] *mg* ab
11 και ο πετρος] *mg* tunc Petrus

περι αυτου 2° D is conflation. Perp
has it only in the earlier position.
7 For hcl.*mg* ab eo cf. επ αυτου,
which minn substitute for εν τω
οικηματι, and ab eo perp gig Lucif,
in varying positions but in each case
in addition to the rendering of εν τω
οικηματι.

10 'The seven steps' of D d perp
(*descenderunt grades*, without *septem*)
seems to imply local knowledge not
to be drawn from the B-text. Cf.
xxi. 35, 40. Ezek. xl. 22, 26, 31
furnishes no satisfactory explanation.
11 For hcl.*mg* cf. τοτε ο πετρος
1611 perp.

Πέτρος ἐν αὐτῷ γενόμενος εἶπεν· Νῦν οἶδα ἀληθῶς ὅτι ἐξαπέστειλεν ὁ κύριος τὸν ἄγγελον αὐτοῦ καὶ ἐξείλατό με ἐκ χειρὸς Ἡρῴδου καὶ πάσης τῆς προσδοκίας τοῦ λαοῦ τῶν Ἰουδαίων. συνιδών τε ἦλθεν ἐπὶ τὴν οἰκίαν τῆς Μαρίας τῆς μητρὸς Ἰωάνου 12 τοῦ ἐπικαλουμένου Μάρκου, οὗ ἦσαν ἱκανοὶ συνηθροισμένοι καὶ προσευχόμενοι. κρούσαντος δὲ αὐτοῦ τὴν θύραν τοῦ πυλῶνος 13 προσῆλθε παιδίσκη ὑπακοῦσαι ὀνόματι Ῥόδη, καὶ ἐπιγνοῦσα τὴν 14 φωνὴν τοῦ Πέτρου ἀπὸ τῆς χαρᾶς οὐκ ἤνοιξεν τὸν πυλῶνα, εἰσδραμοῦσα δὲ ἀπήγγειλεν ἑστάναι τὸν Πέτρον πρὸ τοῦ πυλῶνος. | οἱ δὲ πρὸς αὐτὴν εἶπαν· Μαίνῃ. ἡ δὲ διισχυρίζετο οὕτως ἔχειν. 15 οἱ δὲ εἶπαν· Ὁ ἄγγελός ἐστιν αὐτοῦ. | ὁ δὲ Πέτρος ἐπέμενεν 16 κρούων· ἀνοίξαντες δὲ εἶδαν αὐτὸν καὶ ἐξέστησαν. κατασείσας 17 δὲ αὐτοῖς τῇ χειρὶ σειγᾶν διηγήσατο αὐτοῖς πῶς ὁ κύριος αὐτὸν ἐξήγαγεν ἐκ τῆς φυλακῆς, εἶπέν τε· Ἀπαγγείλατε Ἰακώβῳ καὶ τοῖς ἀδελφοῖς ταῦτα. καὶ ἐξελθὼν ἐπορεύθη εἰς ἕτερον τόπον. γενομένης δὲ ἡμέρας ἦν τάραχος οὐκ ὀλίγος ἐν τοῖς στρατιώταις, 18 τί ἄρα ὁ Πέτρος ἐγένετο. Ἡρῴδης δὲ ἐπιζητήσας αὐτὸν καὶ 19 μὴ εὑρὼν ἀνακρείνας τοὺς φύλακας ἐκέλευσεν ἀπαχθῆναι, καὶ κατελθὼν ἀπὸ τῆς Ἰουδαίας εἰς Καισαρείαν διέτρειβεν.

Ἦν δὲ θυμομαχῶν Τυρίοις καὶ Σειδωνίοις· ὁμοθυμαδὸν δὲ 20

Editors   11 αυτω] εαυτω WH Soden JHR   om ο 2° WHmg Soden   12 [της 1°]
Soden   13 προσηλθε] προηλθε WHmg   15 ειπαν 2°] ελεγον WH
Soden JHR   ειπαν WHmg   αυτου εστιν Soden

Old Uncial   11 αυτω B   εαυτω ℵA 81 (+D)   ο 2° B   om ℵA 81 (+D)   του
λαου Bℵ 81 (+D)   om A   12 τε Bℵ   δε A 81   13 κρουσαντος BℵA
κρουσαντες 81 (+D)   προσηλθε BA 81 (+D)   προηλθε B²ℵ   υπακουσαι
BℵᵃA 81 (+D)   υπακουουσα ℵ   15 ειπαν 2° B   ελεγον ℵA 81 (+D)
ο BAℵᶜ 81 (+D)   om ℵ   εστιν αυτου BℵA   αυτου εστιν ℵᶜ 81 (+D)
17 κατασεισας δε αυτοις Bℵ 81 (+D)   κατασεισαντος δε αυτου A   αυτοις 2° B(+D)
om ℵA 81   ο κυριος αυτον εξηγαγεν Bℵ (+D)   αυτον ο κυριος εξηγαγεν A
ο κυριος εξηγαγεν αυτον 81   19 δε Bℵ 81 (+D)   τε A   διετρειβεν Bℵ
81 (+D)   διετριψεν A

Antiochian   11 εν αυτω γενομενος] γενομενος εν εαυτω HLPSSʹ (cf. D)   om ο 2°
HLPSSʹ(+D)   + εκ before πασης S   12 τε]+ ο πετρος P
om της before μαριας HLPSSʹ   13 αυτου] του πετρου HSSʹ   15 ειπαν
2°] ελεγον HLPSSʹ(+D)   αυτου εστιν HLPSSʹ(+D)   17 τε] δε HLPSʹ
(S def) (+D)   19 την καισαρειαν HLPSSʹ   20 ην δε] + ο ηρωδης HLPSSʹ

---

12 For hcl ⁘ fratres cf. αδελφοι 614 minn.
13 In the rasura of Codex Bezae Blass (St.Kr. 1898, pp. 540 f.) thought

he could detect ε[ξ]ω (so also Wetstein), and that πυλωνος was too long for the space. d has foris, with no other word to represent πυλωνος.

ἑαυτῷ γενόμενος εἶπεν· Νῦν οἶδα ὅτι ἀληθῶς ἐξαπέστειλεν κύριος
τὸν ἄγγελον αὐτοῦ καὶ ἐξείλατό με ἐκ χειρὸς Ἡρῴδου καὶ πάσης
12 τῆς προσδοκείας τοῦ λαοῦ τῶν Ἰουδαίων. καὶ συνειδὼν ἦλθεν
ἐπὶ τὴν οἰκείαν τῆς Μαρίας τῆς μητρὸς Ἰωάνου τοῦ ἐπικαλουμένου
‹Μ›άρκου, οὗ ἦσαν ἱκανοὶ συνηθροισμένοι καὶ προσευχόμενοι.
13 κρούσαντος δὲ αὐτοῦ τὴν θύραν τοῦ [. . . . . .] προσῆλθεν
14 παιδίσκη ὀνόματι Ῥόδη ὑπακοῦσαι, καὶ ἐπιγνοῦσα τὴν φωνὴν
τοῦ Πέτρου ἀπὸ τῆς χαρᾶς οὐκ ἤνοιξε τὸν πυλῶνα, καὶ εἰσ-
15 δραμοῦσα δὲ ἀπήγγειλεν ἑστάναι Πέτρον πρὸ τοῦ πυλῶνος. ο‹ί›
δὲ ἔ[λε]γον αὐτῇ· Μαίνῃ. ἡ δὲ διισχυρίζετο οὕτως ἔχειν. οἱ
16 δὲ ἔλεγον πρὸς αὐτήν· Τυχὸν ὁ ἄγγελος αὐτοῦ ἐστιν. ὁ δὲ ἐπ-
έμενεν κρούων· ἐξανοίξαντες δὲ καὶ ἰδόντες αὐτὸν καὶ ἐξέστησαν.
17 κατασείσας δὲ αὐτοῖς τῇ χειρὶ ἵνα σειγά[σω]σιν εἰσῆλθεν καὶ
διηγήσατο αὐτοῖς πῶς ὁ κύριος αὐτὸν ἐξήγαγεν ἐκ τῆς φυλακῆς·
εἶπεν δέ· Ἀπανγείλατε Ἰακώβῳ καὶ τοῖς ἀδελφοῖς ταῦτα. καὶ
18 ἐξελθὼν ἐπορεύθη εἰς ἕτερον τόπον. γενομένης δὲ ἡμέρας ἦν
19 τάραχος ἐν τοῖς στρατιώταις, τί ἄρα ὁ Πέτρος ἐγένετο. Ἡρῴδης
δὲ ἐπιζητήσας αὐτὸν καὶ μὴ εὑρὼν ἀνακρείνας τοὺς φύλακας
ἐκέλευσεν ἀπ[ο]κ[τ]ανθῆναι, καὶ κατελθὼν ἀπὸ τῆς Ἰουδαίας εἰς
Καισαραίαν διέτριβεν.
20 ⸆Ην γὰρ θυμομαχῶν Τυρίοις καὶ Σιδωνίοις· οἱ δὲ ὁμοθυμαδὸν

12 μαρκου] αρκου, but possibly 1st hand added μ   13 κρουσαντες   14 ηνυξε   15 διεσχυριζετο

petrus in se conversus dixit nunc scio quia vere misit d̄n̄s angelum suum et eripuit d
me de manibus herodis et omni expectationi populi judaeorum 12 et cum con-
siderasset venit ad domum mariae matris johannis qui cognominatur marcus ubi
erant copiosi coacervati et orantes 13 cumque ipse pulsasset januam foris accessit
puella nomine rhode respondere 14 et cum cognovisset vocem petri a gaudio non
aperuit januam et adcurrens autem adnuntiavit stare petrum ante januam 15 ad
illi ad eam dixerunt insanis ad illa vero perseverabat ita esse qui autem dixerunt ad
eam forsitam angelus ejus est 16 ipse vero perseverabat pulsans et cum aperuisset
viderunt eunt et obstupuerunt 17 cumque significasset eis de manu ut silerent
introiens eterrabit eis quemadmodum d̄n̄s eum liveravit de carcere dixit autem
renuntiate jacobo et fratribus haec et egressus abiit in alium 18 facto autem die
erat turbatio in militibus quid petrus factus esset 19 herodes vero cum irequisisset
eum et non invenisse interrogatione habita vigiles jussit obduci et cum descendisset a
judaea in caesaraeam demorabatur 20 erat enim animus inpugnans tyrios et sidonios

12 ησαν] erant ※ fratres ✓   14 ηνοιξε] + ※ ei ✓   17 εισηλθεν και Harclean
διηγησατο αυτοις] ※ ingressus est et narravit iis ✓   20 οι δε] mg hi autem

14 For hcl ※ ei cf. αυτω 1518 e   perp gig Lucif, and may be an addition
(E) pesh.   to the original text.
18 ουκ ολιγος is omitted by D d 142

παρῆσαν πρὸς αὐτόν, καὶ πείσαντες Βλάστον τὸν ἐπὶ τοῦ κοιτῶνος τοῦ βασιλέως ἠτοῦντο εἰρήνην διὰ τὸ τρέφεσθαι αὐτῶν τὴν χώραν ἀπὸ τῆς βασιλικῆς. τακτῇ δὲ ἡμέρα ʻΗρώδης ἐνδυσάμενος 21 ἐσθῆτα βασιλικὴν καθίσας ἐπὶ τοῦ βήματος ἐδημηγόρει πρὸς αὐτούς· | ὁ δὲ δῆμος ἐπεφώνει· Θεοῦ φωνὴ καὶ οὐκ ἀνθρώπου. 22 παραχρῆμα δὲ ἐπάταξεν αὐτὸν ἄγγελος κυρίου ἀνθ᾽ ὧν οὐκ 23 ἔδωκεν τὴν δόξαν τῷ θεῷ, καὶ γενόμενος σκωληκόβρωτος ἐξέψυξεν.

ʻΟ δὲ λόγος τοῦ κυρίου ηὔξανεν καὶ ἐπληθύνετο. Βαρνάβας 24, 25 δὲ καὶ Σαῦλος ὑπέστρεψαν εἰς ʼΙερουσαλὴμ πληρώσαντες τὴν διακονίαν, συνπαραλαβόντες ʼΙωάννην τὸν ἐπικληθέντα Μάρκον·

ªΗσαν δὲ ἐν ʼΑντιοχείᾳ κατὰ τὴν οὖσαν ἐκκλησίαν προφῆται XIII

Editors 21 [ο] ηρωδης WH   ο ηρωδης Soden JHR   βασιλικην] +[και] Soden
24 κυριου] θεου WHmg Soden JHR   25 εις] εξ Soden   εις ιερουσαλημ
πληρωσαντες την] †εξ ιερουσαλημ πληρωσαντες την† WHmg   επικαλουμενον
Soden

Old Uncial 20 ητουντο BΝ 81 (+D)   ητησαντο A   21 ηρωδης B   ο ηρωδης ΝA 81
(+D)   βασιλικην BΝ 81   +και A(+D)   22 ανθρωπου BΝc 81 (+D)
ανθρωπων Ν   24 κυριου B   θεου ΝA 81 (+D)   ηυξανεν BΝ 81 (+D)
ηυξανετο A   25 εις BΝ (corrected, apparently by Ν*, from εξ) 81   εξ A
(cf. D)   συνπαραλαβοντες BΝA(+D)   + και 81]   επικληθεντα B(+D)
επικαλουμενον ΝA 81

Antiochian 21 ο ηρωδης HLPSϚ(+D)   βασιλικην] +και HLPSϚ(+D)   22 φωνη
θεου HLS   om φωνη P   23 om την HLPS(+D)   24 κυριου] θεου
HLPSϚ(+D)   25 εις] εξ Ϛ (cf. D)   συνπαραλαβοντες] +και HLPSϚ
1 δε] +τινες HLPSϚ

21-22 Besides various expansions in the preceding verses, the 'Western' text had between vs. 21 and vs. 22 an addition, found in an incomplete form in D d hcl·⁙· (*reconciliatus est iis autem*). Perp² and vg.*codd* add to the usual text *et regratiato eo tyriis et sidoniis*; while perp* reads *cumque reconclamasset ei*. φωναι for φωνη is attested by perp gig Lucif vg pesh. The Greek, as restored by Zahn, runs smoothly : αντιφωνησαντος δε αυτω του δημου, καταλλαγεντι τυριοις και σιδωνιοις, επιφωνουσιν αυτω· θεου φωναι και ουκ ανθρωπου, but more probably *reconclamasset* perp is merely a corruption of *reconciliatus esset*.

23 On D d cf. Ephrem, below, p. 416.

25 σαυλος] + ος επεκληθη παυλος 614 perp hcl·⁙·. Minn read παυλος ·for σαυλος ; so do 614 and two others in xi. 25, and perp, etc., in xiii. 1, 2.

εις ιερουσαλημ B (in B εις is correction by first hand over απο [εξ']) Ν 81 Antiochian hcl.*mg* ; εις αντιοχειαν minn ; εξ ιερουσαλημ A minn boh ; απο ιερουσαλημ D 614 181 minn gig vg ; εξ (απο E e 1898 ; pesh indeterminate) ιερουσαλημ εις αντιοχειαν 1898 minn perp e E pesh sah. The exegetical difficulty of the best attested reading (εις ιερουσαλημ) is not insuperable, for εις ιερουσαλημ may have been intended to mean 'at Jerusalem'; at any rate this reading was adopted in carefully written MSS. for many centuries. The conjecture of WH, την εις ιερουσαλημ πληρωσαντες διακονιαν, would solve the problem by a mere change of order, but does not account for the origin of the difficult reading of BΝ 81 etc.

The agreement in the singular number between D απεστρεψεν απο (d *reversi sunt ab*) and hcl.*mg reversus*

ἐξ ἀμφοτέρων τῶν πόλεων παρῆσαν πρὸς τὸν βασιλέα, καὶ
πείσαντες Βλάστον τὸν ἐπὶ τοῦ κοιτῶνος αὐτοῦ ἠτοῦντο εἰρήνην
21 διὰ τὸ τρέφεσθαι τὰς χώρας αὐτῶν ἐκ τῆς βασιλικῆς. τακτῇ δὲ
ἡμέρᾳ ὁ Ἡρώδης ἐνδυσάμενος ἐσθῆτα βασιλικὴν καὶ καθίσας
ἐπὶ τοῦ βήματος ἐδημηγόρει πρὸς αὐτούς· καταλλαγέντος δὲ
22 αὐτοῦ τοῖς Τυρίοις | †ὁ δὲ δῆμος ἐπεφώνει† · Θεοῦ φωναὶ καὶ οὐκ
23 ἀνθρώπου. παραχρῆμα δὲ αὐτὸν ἐπάταξεν ἄγγελος κυρίου ἀνθ'
ὧν οὐκ ἔδωκεν δόξαν τῷ θεῷ, καὶ καταβὰς ἀπὸ τοῦ βήματος,
γενόμενος ‹σ›κωληκόβρωτος ἔτι ζῶν καὶ οὕτως ἐξέψυξεν.
24, 25 Ὁ δὲ λόγος τοῦ θεοῦ ηὔξανε καὶ ἐπληθύνετο. Βαρνάβας
δὲ καὶ Σαῦλος ἀπέστρεψεν ἀπὸ Ἰερουσαλὴμ πληρώσαντες τὴν
διακονίαν, συνπαραλαβόντες τὸν Ἰωάνην τὸν ἐπικληθέντα Μάρκον.
XIII   *Ἦσαν δὲ ἐν Ἀντιοχείᾳ κατὰ τὴν οὖσαν ἐκκλησίαν προφῆται

21 αισθητα   εδημειγορει   24 ευξανε

---

unanimiter autem ab invice civitates venerunt ad regem et cum suasissent blasto qui d
a cubiculo erat postulabant pacem propter ne alienarentur regiones eorum de regno
21 constituto autem die herodes indutus habito regio et sedi pro tribunali con-
tentionabatur ad eos cum ingratiasset cum tyrios   22 populus vero adclamabant di
voces et non hominis   23 et confestim eum percussit angelus d̄n̄i pro eo quod non
dedit claritatem d̄ō et cum descendisset de tribunal sed et a bermibus comestus
adhuc vivens et sic expiravit   24 verbum autem d̄ī augebatur et multiplicabatur
25 barnabas vero et saulus reversi sunt ab hierusalem impleto ministerio adsupto
johannen qui cognominatur marcus
1 erant autem in antiochia aput quem erat ecclesiam prophetae et doctores in

---

20 εξ αμφοτερων των πολεων] ·⁑· ex ambabus civitatibus ✓   21 κατ- Harclean
αλλαγεντος δε αυτου τοις τυριοις] ·⁑· reconciliatus est iis autem ✓   25 σαυλος]
+ ·⁑· qui vocabatur Paulus ✓   απεστρεψεν απο] mg reversus est in

est in is to be noted, but no explanation
is forthcoming.
1-3 The tract *Prophetiae ex omnibus
libris collectae*, from Cod. sangallensis
133 (cent. ix.), perhaps written in
Africa between 305 and 325, sum-
marizes these verses in the following
peculiar form : *Erant etiam in eclesia
prophetae et doctores Barnabas et
Saulus, quibus inposuerunt manus
prophetae, Symeon qui appellatus est
Niger et Lucius Cyrinensis qui manet
usque adhuc et Ticius conlactaneus,
qui acceperant responsum ab spiritum
sanctum. Unde dix̄: Segregate mihi
Barnaban et Saulum in opus quo vocavi
eos, hoc est propheciae. Quibus impositis manibus dimiserunt eos et
abierunt.* See Zahn, *Urausgabe*, pp.
20-22, 145-149, 350, and in *Geschicht-*

*liche Studien Albert Hauck zum 70.
Geburtstag dargebracht*, 1916, pp. 52-63.
But it is impossible to believe that
this is anything more than a free
account of this " prophecy " composed
on the basis of Acts xiii. 1-3, probably from the African Latin. No
important light on the 'Western'
text seems to proceed from it. The
strange phrase *qui manet usque adhuc
et Ticius* is probably derived by
an obscure corruption from some form
of *manaen etiam herodis tetrarchae*
perp, or *et manaen qui erat herodis
tetrarchae* vg. Manaen accounts for
manet ; *tetrarchae* for *ticius*.
1 For ησαν . . . εκκλησιαν perp
renders *erant autem secundum unam-
quamque ecclesiam*. From this, and
from the addition after διδασκαλοι of

καὶ διδάσκαλοι ὅ τε Βαρνάβας καὶ Συμεὼν ὁ καλούμενος Νίγερ,
καὶ Λούκιος ὁ Κυρηναῖος, Μαναήν τε Ἡρῴδου τοῦ ‹τε›τράρχου
σύντροφος καὶ Σαῦλος. λειτουργούντων δὲ αὐτῶν τῷ κυρίῳ καὶ 2
νηστευόντων εἶπεν τὸ πνεῦμα τὸ ἅγιον· Ἀφορίσατε δή μοι τὸν
Βαρνάβαν καὶ Σαῦλον εἰς τὸ ἔργον ὃ προσκέκλημαι αὐτούς.
τότε νηστεύσαντες καὶ προσευξάμενοι καὶ ἐπιθέντες τὰς χεῖρας 3
αὐτοῖς ἀπέλυσαν.

Αὐτοὶ μὲν οὖν ἐκπεμφθέντες ὑπὸ τοῦ ἁγίου πνεύματος κατ- 4
ῆλθον εἰς Σελεύκειαν, ἐκεῖθέν τε ἀπέπλευσαν εἰς Κύπρον, | καὶ 5
γενόμενοι ἐν Σαλαμεῖνι κατήγγελλον τὸν λόγον τοῦ θεοῦ ἐν ταῖς
συναγωγαῖς τῶν Ἰουδαίων· εἶχον δὲ καὶ Ἰωάννην ὑπηρέτην.
διελθόντες δὲ ὅλην τὴν νῆσον ἄχρι Πάφου εὗρον ἄνδρα τινὰ 6
μάγον ψευδοπροφήτην Ἰουδαῖον ᾧ ὄνομα Βαριησοῦς, ὃς ἦν σὺν 7

Editors	6 βαριησου JHR

Old Uncial	1 τετραρχου B² 2 τον BℵAC(+D) + τε 81 σαυλον BℵᵃAC 81 (+D)
	τον σαυλον ℵ 4 ουν BℵAC(+D) om 81 κατηλθον BℵC 81 (cf. D)
	απηλθον A τε BℵAC δε 81 5 εν 1° BACℵᶜ 81 (+D) εις ℵ
	δε BℵAC(+D) τε 81 6 ευρον BℵA 81 (+D) +εκει C βαριησους BC
	βαριησου ℵ βαριησουν A 81

Antiochian	2 τον] +τε Ϛ (S def) τον σαυλον HLPϚ 4 αυτοι] ουτοι HLPSϚ
	αγιου πνευματος] πνευματος του αγιου HLPSϚ (cf. D) την σελευκειαν HLPSϚ
	εκειθεν] κακειθεν S τε] δε LPS την κυπρον HLPSϚ 6 om
	ολην HLPSϚ om ανδρα HLPSϚ βαριησουν HLPS

εν οις D (d in quo) vg, an obliterated and
unrecoverable 'Western' paraphrase,
or even a corruption of the ordinary
Greek text, may possibly be suspected.

3-4 It is a fair conjecture that the
text of D is here conflate, and that, in
vs. 3, τοτε νηστευσαντες . . . αυτοις
and in vs. 4, εκπεμφθεντες υπο του
πνευματος αγιου have been introduced
from the B-text. The noteworthy
variants, some of which suggest this,
are: Dd, vs. 3, the omission of απελυσαν,
and vs. 4, οι μεν ουν for αυτοι (ουτοι
Antiochian) μεν ουν ; perp, vs. 4 (for
αυτοι . . . κατηλθον) egressi igitur a
sanctis devenerunt ; sah 'by the saints'
for υπο του αγιου πνευματος ; and the
form in proph (above), quibus impositis
manibus dimiserunt eos et abierunt.
But of the Greek text which underlay
the Latin of perp and proph no satisfactory reconstruction has been proposed. It is possible that the phrases
omitted by D d were a very early non-

western addition to the true text, but
the absence of a sound African Latin
here leaves us helpless.

In vs. 4 υπο του αγιου πνευματος
may be secondary to υπο των αγιων
perp sah, but the latter reading,
which omits a reference to the Holy
Spirit, is strange as a part of the
'Western' text (see above, p. ccxxix).
δε, vs. 4, may be an attempt at adjustment made necessary by the conflation.

6 In Codex Bezae περιελθοντων (Blass,
St. Kr., 1898, p. 541, and Wetstein)
for [. .]ριελθοντων (Scrivener).

βαριησου ℵ gig perpᵛⁱᵈ vg boh perhaps best accounts for the variants.
βαριησους BC E e (barihesus) sah is
an attempt to improve the grammar.
The accusative βαριησουν of the Antiochian text and of A 81 would
appear due to the same motive, but,
strangely, seems to depend on the
reading ονοματι, or ονοματι καλουμενον,
found in D minn perp but not
in any of the chief Antiochian

καὶ διδάσκαλοι, ἐν οἷς Βαρνάβας καὶ Συμεὼν ὁ ἐπικαλούμενος
Νίγερ, καὶ Λούκειος Κυρηναῖος, Μαναήν τε Ἡρῴδου καὶ τε-
2 τράρχου σύντροφος καὶ Σαῦλος. λειτουργούντων δὲ αὐτῶν τῷ
κυρίῳ καὶ νηστευόντων εἶπεν τὸ πνεῦμα τὸ ἅγιον· Ἀφορίσατε δή
μοι τὸν Βαρνάβαν καὶ Σαῦλον εἰς τὸ ἔργον ὃ προσκέκλημαι
3 αὐτούς. †τότε νηστεύσαντες καὶ προσευξάμενοι πάντες καὶ ἐπιθέντες τὰς χεῖρας αὐτοῖς.†
4   Οἱ μὲν οὖν ἐκπεμφθέντες ὑπὸ τοῦ πνεύματος ἁγίου κατα-
5 βάντες δὲ εἰς Σελευκίαν, ἐκεῖθεν ἀπέπλευσαν εἰς Κύπρον, | γενό-
μενοι δὲ ἐν τῇ Σαλαμεῖνι κατήγγειλαν τὸν λό‹γο›ν τοῦ κυρίου
ἐν ταῖς συναγωγαῖς τῶν Ἰουδαίων· εἶχον δὲ καὶ Ἰωάννην ὑπηρε-
6 τοῦντα αὐτοῖς. καὶ περιελθόντων δὲ αὐτῶν ὅλην τὴν νῆσον ἄχρι
Πάφου εὗρον ἄνδρα τινὰ μάγον ψευδοπροφήτην Ἰουδαῖον ὀνόματι
7 καλούμενον Βαριησοῦα, ὃς ἦν σὺν τῷ ἀνθυπάτῳ Σεργίῳ Παύλῳ,

6 νησσον   βαριησουα] so 1st hand probably, but perhaps -αν
or -αμ

quo barnabas et symeon qui vocatur niger et lucius cyrenensis manaenque herodis d
et tetrarchi conlactaneus et saulus 2 deservientibus autem eis d̄n̄o et jejunantibus
dixit s̄p̄s sanctus secernite mihi barnaban et saulum ad opus vocavi eos 3 tunc cum
jajunassent et orassent omnes et inposuissent manus eis 4 ipsi vero dismissi ab
s̄p̄o sancto descenderunt seleuciam inde vero navigaverunt in cyprum 5 et cum
fuissent salamina adnuntiabant verbum d̄i in synagogis judaeorum habebant vero et
johannen ministrantem eis 6 cum pergressi fuissent totam insulam usquae ad
paphum invenerunt virum quendam magum pseudoprophetam judaeum nomine qui
vocatur barjesuam 7 qui erat cum proconsule sergio paulo viro prudenti hic cum

[6-8 multa utique et adversus apostolos Simon dedit et Elymas magi.]   Tertullian,
                                                                            Anima 57

4 εκειθεν] + mg autem   5 υπηρετουντα αυτοις] mg ministrantem iis   Harclean

authorities. The Latin barieu and
barihen (perp.mg : quidam barihen
alii barieu) are apparently derived
from the abbreviations βαριηυ and
barihu (so perp vg.cod.O ; cf. the
comment of Bede) ; nevertheless
Jerome (Nom. Hebr. iii. 99) prefers
berieu, which he interprets maleficum
sive in malo [i.e. רבעין], adding non-
nulli bariesu corrupte legunt. The
form βαριησονα[μ?] D d (bariesuam)
produced bariesuban (Lucif), varisuas
(Op. imperf. in Matt. xxiv. 3), and was
probably an accusative (note the construction in D) from a form βαρισονα
intended to represent more perfectly
בר ישוע. For similar indication of
Semitic knowledge in D see above,
pp. ccxlii-iv. From the substitution

bar shuma pesh (cf. Burkitt, Proc.
British Acad. v., 1912, p. 22) and
from bar ieshu' hcl.text no light is
thrown on the Greek text.
βαριησους] + quod interpraetatur paratus gig Lucif vg.codd (some reading
qui for quod), + quod interpraetatur
elymas e E (ο μεθερμηνευεται ελυμας).
This, as Zahn convincingly argues,
is a gloss, never found without the
presence of the statement in vs. 8,
from which it is derived ; it is of
Latin origin (hence, by modification
and translation, in E), not an element
of the original 'Western' text. The
'Western' reviser seems to have had
a knowledge of languages which would
have made him incapable of saying
that the name 'Barjesus' meant

τῷ ἀνθυπάτῳ Σεργίῳ Παύλῳ, ἀνδρὶ συνετῷ. οὗτος προσκαλεσάμενος Βαρνάβαν καὶ Σαῦλον ἐπεζήτησεν ἀκοῦσαι τὸν λόγον
τοῦ θεοῦ· ἀνθίστατο δὲ αὐτοῖς Ἐλύμας ὁ μάγος, οὕτως γὰρ 8
μεθερμηνεύεται τὸ ὄνομα αὐτοῦ, ζητῶν διαστρέψαι τὸν ἀνθύπατον
ἀπὸ τῆς πίστεως. Σαῦλος δέ, ὁ καὶ Παῦλος, πλησθεὶς πνεύ- 9
ματος ἁγίου ἀτενίσας εἰς αὐτὸν εἶπεν· Ὦ πλήρης παντὸς δόλου 10
καὶ πάσης ῥᾳδιουργίας, υἱὲ διαβόλου, ἐχθρὲ πάσης δικαιοσύνης,
οὐ παύσῃ διαστρέφων τὰς ὁδοὺς τοῦ κυρίου τὰς εὐθείας; καὶ 11
νῦν ἰδοὺ χεὶρ κυρίου ἐπὶ σέ, καὶ ἔσῃ τυφλὸς μὴ βλέπων τὸν
ἥλιον ἄχρι καιροῦ. παραχρῆμα δὲ ἔπεσεν ἀχλὺς καὶ σκότος,
καὶ περιάγων ἐζήτει χειραγωγούς. τότε ἰδὼν ὁ ἀνθύπατος τὸ 12
γεγονὸς ἐπίστευσεν ἐκπληττόμενος ἐπὶ τῇ διδαχῇ τοῦ κυρίου.

Ἀναχθέντες δὲ ἀπὸ τῆς Πάφου οἱ περὶ Παῦλον ἦλθον εἰς 13
Πέργην τῆς Παμφυλίας· Ἰωάνης δὲ ἀποχωρήσας ἀπ' αὐτῶν
ὑπέστρεψεν εἰς Ἱεροσόλυμα. αὐτοὶ δὲ διελθόντες ἀπὸ τῆς 14
Πέργης παρεγένοντο εἰς Ἀντιόχειαν τὴν Πισιδίαν, καὶ ἐλθόντες
13 ανεχθεντες

Editors   8 ετοιμας JHR   10 om του WHmg Soden   11 δε] τε WHmg
επεσεν] +επ αυτον WH Soden JHR   14 της πισιδιας Soden
ελθοντες] εισελθοντες Soden

Old Uncial   8 ουτως BℵAC(+D)   ουτος 81   10 του Bℵ   om ACℵᶜ 81 (+D)
11 δε BA   τε ℵC 81   επεσεν B   επεσεν επ αυτον ℵ 81 (+D)   επεσεν αυτον
Aᵛⁱᵈ   επεπεσεν επ αυτον C   12 επιστευσεν εκπληττομενος BℵC 81 (cf. D)
εκπληττομενος επιστευσεν A   κυριου BℵA 81 (+D)   θεου C   13 αν-
αχθεντες B²   14 παρεγενοντο BℵC 81 (+D)   εγενοντο A   την πισιδιαν
BℵAC   της πισιδιας 81 (+D)   ελθοντες BℵC 81   εισελθοντες Aℵᶜ(+D)

Antiochian   8 μαγος] μεγας L   9 αγιου] +και HPS5(+D)   10 om πασης 1°
P(+D)   om του HLPS5 (+D)   11 του κυριου 5   τυφλος]
+και P   επεσεν] επεπεσεν επ αυτον HLPS5 (cf. D)   13 τον παυλον
HLPS5   om δε 2° H   14 της πισιδας HLPS5(+D)   ελθοντες]
εισελθοντες HLPS5(+D)

ἕτοιμος. No text of vs. 8 makes, or
could justify, any such absurd statement as that.   Apart from E the
gloss is found only in Latin, and it is
not contained in perp (which from this
point to xxviii. 16 ceases to give an
Old Latin text) d vg.

8 For ελυμας, found in all other
Greek witnesses than in gig perp e vg
(gig vg.codd spell elimas) pesh hcl
sah boh, D reads ετ[.]ιμας, d etoemas.
To this substantially correspond
etoemus Lucif, etimas Ambrosiaster,
Quaest. 102. 2, hetymam Pacianus, Ep.

ii. 5. Tertullian, indeed, De anima 57,
De pudicitia 21, in all cited mss.
reads elimas or elymas; but the text
of Tertullian in such a matter is not
above question, and the fact, pointed
out by Zahn, that Ambrosiaster l.c.,
with etimas, seems dependent on Tert.
pudicit. 21 goes far to neutralize the
evidence of the mss. of Tertullian.
It is therefore probable (cf. gloss in
vs. 6) that the form with -i- stood
in the original Latin rendering and
in its underlying Greek. As to the
original Greek name we can only say

ἀνδρὶ συνετῷ. οὗτος συνκαλεσάμενος Βαρνάβαν καὶ Σαῦλον καὶ
8 ἐζήτησεν ἀκοῦσαι τὸν λόγον τοῦ θεοῦ· ἀνθείστατο δὲ αὐτοῖς
Ἐτ[.]ιμας ὁ μάγος, οὕτως γὰρ μεθερμηνεύεται τὸ ὄνομα αὐτοῦ,
ζητῶν διαστρέψαι τὸν ἀνθύπατον ἀπὸ τῆς πίστεως, ἐπ<ε>ιδὴ
9 ἥδιστα ἤκουεν αὐτῶν. Σαῦλος δέ, ὁ καὶ Παῦλος, πληθεὶς πνεύ-
10 ματος ἁγίου καὶ ἀτενείσας εἰς αὐτὸν | εἶπεν· Ὦ πλήρης παντὸς
δόλου καὶ ῥαδιουργίας, υἱὸς διαβόλου, ἐκθρὲ πάσης δικαιοσύνης,
11 οὐ παύσῃ διαστρέφων τὰς ὁδοὺς κυρίου τὰς οὔσας εὐθείας; καὶ
νῦν εἰδοὺ ἡ χεὶρ κυρίου ἐπὶ σέ, καὶ ἔσῃ τυφλὸς μὴ βλέπων τὸν
ἥλειον ἕως καιροῦ. καὶ εὐθέως ἔπεσεν ἐπ᾽ αὐτὸν ἀχλὺς καὶ
12 σκότος, καὶ περιάγων ἐζήτει χειραγωγούς. ἰδὼν δὲ ὁ ἀνθύπατος
τὸ γεγονὸς ἐθαύμασεν καὶ ἐπίστευσεν τῷ θεῷ ἐκπλησσόμενος ἐπὶ
τῇ διδαχῇ τοῦ κυρίου.
13 Ἀναχθέντες δὲ ἀπὸ τῆς Πάφου οἱ περὶ Παῦλον ἦλθον εἰς
Πέργην τῆς Παμφυλίας· Ἰωάνης δὲ ἀποχωρήσας ἀπ᾽ αὐτῶν ὑπ-
14 έστρεψεν εἰς Ἱεροσόλυμα. αὐτοὶ δὲ διελθόντες ἀπὸ τῆς Πέργης
παρεγένοντο εἰς Ἀντειόχειαν τῆς Πεισιδίας, καὶ εἰσελθόντες

10 υιος] υιοι   11 ἤ] point by first hand

---

vocasset barnaban et saulum et quaesire voluit audire verbum d̄ī 8 resistabat d
autem eis etoemas magus sic enim interpraetabatur nomen ejus quaerens vertere
proconsolem a fidem quoniam liventer audiebat eos   9 saulus vero qui et paulus
inpletus s̄p̄ō sancto et intuitus in eum   10 dixit o plenae omnis dolus et falsi fili
diabole inimicae omnis justitiae non cessas evertere vias domini quas sunt rectas
11 et nunc ecce manus d̄n̄ī super te et eris caecus non videns solem usq· ad tempus
et confestim caecidit super eum caligo et tenebrae et circumiens quaerebat ad manum
deductores   12 tunc cum vidisset proconsul quod factum est miratus est et credidit
in d̄ō stupens super doctrina d̄n̄ī   13 supervenientes a papho qui erant circa paulo
venerunt in pergen pamphyliae johannes vero cum discedisset ab eis reversus est
hierosolymis   14 isti autem cum transissent a pergen venerunt antiochiam pisidiae

---

8 επειδη ηδιστα ηκουεν αυτων] ⁛ quia libenter audiebat eos ✓   Harclean

---

that between υ and οι confusion is common, and that likewise either of the two letters, τ or λ, may have been an accidental substitution for the other. Greek personal names derived from ἕτοιμος and from ἕτυμος are known; while no analogy speaks for the name Elymas. See Burkitt, *J. Theol. Stud.* iv., 1902-3, pp. 127-129.

The substitution in gig Lucif of *interpretatum dicitur* for μεθερμηνευεται may possibly be intended to make explicit the idea that the name was

actually a translation of Βαριησοῦς, whereas the Greek perhaps means no more than that it was a usual substitute for it.

14 την πισιδιαν BℵAC; της πισιδιας D 81 Antiochian, all Latin texts, sah. The reading of B agrees with the correct usage of earlier times; it was probably altered in accordance with the habit of speech of a later age. Antioch was properly designated as near, not in, Pisidia. Cf. W. M. Ramsay, *The Church in the Roman Empire*, pp. 25 f.

εἰς τὴν συναγωγὴν τῇ ἡμέρᾳ τῶν σαββάτων ἐκάθισαν. μετὰ 15
δὲ τὴν ἀνάγνωσιν τοῦ νόμου καὶ τῶν προφητῶν ἀπέστειλαν οἱ
ἀρχισυνάγωγοι πρὸς αὐτοὺς λέγοντες· Ἄνδρες ἀδελφοί, εἴ τις
ἔστιν ἐν ὑμῖν λόγος παρακλήσεως πρὸς τὸν λαόν, λέγετε. ἀναστὰς 16
δὲ Παῦλος καὶ κατασείσας τῇ χειρὶ εἶπεν· Ἄνδρες Ἰσραηλεῖται
καὶ οἱ φοβούμενοι τὸν θεόν, ἀκούσατε. ὁ θεὸς τοῦ λαοῦ τοῦ 17
Ἰσραὴλ ἐξελέξατο τοὺς πατέρας ἡμῶν, καὶ τὸν λαὸν ὕψωσεν ἐν
τῇ παροικίᾳ ἐν γῇ Αἰγύπτου, καὶ μετὰ βραχείονος ὑψηλοῦ ἐξ-
ήγαγεν αὐτοὺς ἐξ αὐτῆς, | καί, ὡς τεσσερακονταετῆ χρόνον ἐτροπο- 18
φόρησεν αὐτοὺς ἐν τῇ ἐρήμῳ, καθελὼν ἔθνη ἑπτὰ ἐν γῇ Χαναὰν 19
κατεκληρονόμησεν τὴν γῆν αὐτῶν | ὡς ἔτεσι τετρακοσίοις καὶ 20
πεντήκοντα. καὶ μετὰ ταῦτα ἔδωκεν κριτὰς ἕως Σαμουὴλ προφήτου. κἀκεῖθεν ᾐτήσαντο βασιλέα, καὶ ἔδωκεν αὐτοῖς ὁ θεὸς 21
τὸν Σαοὺλ υἱὸν Κείς, ἄνδρα ἐκ φυλῆς Βενιαμείν, ἔτη τεσσερά-
κοντα· καὶ μεταστήσας αὐτὸν ἤγειρεν τὸν Δαυεὶδ αὐτοῖς εἰς 22

Editors   17 του 2°] τουτου WH Soden JHR   om ισραηλ JHR   18 ετροπο-
φορησεν] ετροφοφορησεν JHR   19 καθελων] και καθελων WHmg Soden
20 και before ως ετεσι instead of after πεντηκοντα JHR   om μετα ταυτα JHR
[του] προφητου Soden   22 αυτοις τον δαυιδ Soden (but cf. mg)

Old Uncial   17 του 2° B   τουτου ℵAC 81 (+D)   αιγυπτου BℵA 81   αιγυπτω C(+D)
18 ετροποφορησεν BℵC² 81 (+D)   ετροφοφορησεν AC   19 καθελων B 81   και
καθελων ℵAC(+D)   κατεκληρονομησεν Bℵ 81 (+D)   +αυτοις AC   20 προφητου
BℵAᵛⁱᵈ 81   του προφητου C(+D)   22 τον δανειδ αυτοις BℵA (cf. D)   αυτοις
τον δαυειδ C 81

Antiochian   15 om τις HLPSϚ   om εν H   λογος εν υμιν LPSϚ (cf. D)
16 οι] +εν υμιν H   17 του 2°] τουτου HLPSϚ(+D)   om ισραηλ
HLPS   αιγυπτω HLPSϚ(+D)   19 add και before καθελων HLPSϚ(+D)
γη] τη HS   κατεκληρονομησεν] +αυτοις HLPS   κατεκληροδοτησεν αυτοις Ϛ
20 και μετα ταυτα ως ετεσι τετρακοσιοις και πεντηκοντα HLPSϚ   του
προφητου HLPSϚ(+D)   22 αυτοις τον δανειδ HLPSϚ

17 του B, for τουτου ℵAC 81 D, is not to be adopted, although vg sah boh do not render τουτου. ο λαος του ισραηλ is an expression almost without parallel ; for the ordinary usage cf. Lk. ii. 32, Acts iv. 10. The omission of ισραηλ by the Antiochian text (with pesh) probably reproduces an ancient reading, and may point to the original reading, since improvement by omission was not the usual method of Antiochian revisers. The various isolated modifications found in minn are not significant.
δια D d gig hcl.text for και 1° was probably a very ancient accidental

error perpetuated in the ' Western ' text. The sense speaks strongly against it.
18 ετροποφορησεν BℵC² 81 D Antiochian vg, ετροφοφορησεν AC*E minn d gig e sah boh pesh hcl. In Deut. i. 31, from which the word comes, both readings are found (ετροφ- ΒΑ); the author of Acts could have known either text of the LXX, or both. The ' Western ' text of Acts perhaps read ετροφ- ; in that case D ετροπ- is contaminated, as elsewhere, from the B-text. The decision in Acts is doubtful, but ετροφοφορησεν suits the context better, and may be preferred on that ground.

15 εἰς τὴν συναγωγὴν τῇ ἡμέρᾳ τῷ σαββάτῳ ἐκάθισαν. μετὰ δὲ
τὴν ἀνάγνωσιν τοῦ νόμου καὶ τῶν προφητῶν ἀπέστειλαν οἱ ἀρχισυνάγωγοι πρὸς αὐτοὺς λέγοντες· "Ανδρες ἀδελφοί, εἴ τις ἔστιν
λόγος σοφίας ἐν ὑμεῖν †παρακλήσεως† πρὸς τὸν λαόν, λέγετε.
16 ἀναστὰς δὲ ὁ Παῦλος καὶ κατασείσας τῇ χειρὶ εἶπεν· "Ανδρες
17 Ἰστραηλῖται καὶ οἱ φοβούμενοι τὸν θεόν, ἀκούσατε. ὁ θεὸς τοῦ
λαοῦ τούτου Ἰσραὴλ ἐξελέξατο τοὺς πατέρας ἡμῶν, διὰ τὸν
λαὸν ὕψωσεν ἐν τῇ παροικίᾳ ἐν τῇ γῇ Αἰγύπτῳ, καὶ μετὰ βραχείο-
18 νος ὑψηλοῦ ἐξήγαγεν αὐτοὺς ἐξ αὐτῆς, καὶ ἔτη μ̄ ἐτροποφόρησεν
19 αὐτοὺς ἐν τῇ ἐρήμῳ, καὶ καθελὼν ἔθνη ἑπτὰ ἐν γῇ Χαναὰμ κατ-
20 εκληρονόμησεν τὴν γῆν τῶν ἀλλοφύλων | καὶ ὡς ἔτεσι ῡ καὶ ῡ
21 ἔδωκεν κριτὰς ἕως Σαμουὴλ τοῦ προφήτου. κἀκεῖθεν ἠτήσαντο
βασιλέα, καὶ ἔδωκεν αὐτοῖς ὁ θεὸς τὸν Σαοὺλ υἱὸν Κείς, ἄνδρα
22 ἐκ φυλῆς Βενιαμίν, ἔτη μ̄· | καὶ μεταστήσας αὐτὸν ἤγειρεν Δαυείδ

14 τῃ ἡμερα] την ημετερα   15 λογος] λογου   λεγεται
20 ως] εως

et cum introissent in synagogam die sabbatorum sederunt 15 post lectionem vero **d**
legis et prophetarum miserunt archisynagogi ad eos dicentes viri fratres si quis est
sermo et intellectus in vobis exhortationis ad populum dicite 16 cum surrexisset
paulus et silentium manu postulasset dixit viri instrahelitae et qui timetis d̄m̄
audite 17 d̄s̄ populi hujus istrahel elegit patres nostros propter populum exaltatum
in peregrinatione in terra aegypti et cum brachio alto eduxit eos ex ipsa 18 et
annis xl ac si nutrix aluit eos in solitudine 19 et sublatisq· gentibus septe in terra
chanaam possidere eos fecit terram allophoelorum 20 et quasi annis cccc et l dedit
judices usque ad samuel prophetam 21 et exinde petierunt regem et dedit eis d̄s̄
saul filium cis virum ex tribu benjamin annis xl 22 et remoto eo excitavit davit

19 των αλλοφυλων] eorum ⁜ alienigenarum ✓   Harclean

19 B 81 sah are right in omitting
και before καθελων. If και is read, the
preceding phrase means 'about forty
years.' But it is unlikely that this
writer should have expressly indicated
that that brief and familiar traditional
number of years was only approximate;
and equally unlikely that, if he had
done so, an editor should have removed
the indication by so subtle a process
as the omission of the subsequent και,
instead of the simple expedient (so
D sah boh) of dropping ως. και is
doubtless an early undesigned addition, by dittography.

20 BℵAC sah boh hcl vg connect the
words ως ετεσι τετρακοσιοις και πεντηκοντα with the preceding sentence,
and make the statement of time refer
to the period occupied in securing the
land for the people. D d gig e E

pesh Antiochian, putting the note of
time after και, treat it as giving the
duration of the period of the judges.
The latter representation is evidently
that of the 'Western' text, and suits
the context best, but may have offended
some student who thought (cf. 1 Kgs.
vi. 1) the Exodus the proper starting-
point for any such chronological
estimate. The 'Western' position of
the words is to be preferred.

The 'Western' text lacked μετα
ταυτα (omitted in D d gig sah pesh
hcl) and these words (found in BℵAC
81 and in Antiochian e E vg) were
perhaps introduced when the text of
B was formed. Their purpose would
then be to relieve the baldness occasioned by the withdrawal of the note
of time from the sentence relating to
the judges.

Ps.lxxxix.20 βασιλέα, ᾧ καὶ εἶπεν μαρτυρήσας· Εὗρον Δαυεὶδ τὸν τοῦ Ἰεσσαὶ
1 Sam. xiii. κατὰ τὴν καρδίαν μου, ὃς ποιήσει πάντα τὰ θελήματά μου. τού- 23
14 του ὁ θεὸς ἀπὸ τοῦ σπέρματος κατ᾽ ἐπαγγελίαν ἤγαγεν τῷ Ἰσραὴλ
σωτῆρα Ἰησοῦν, προκηρύξαντος Ἰωάνου πρὸ προσώπου τῆς εἰσ- 24
όδου αὐτοῦ βάπτισμα μετανοίας παντὶ τῷ λαῷ Ἰσραήλ. ὡς δὲ 25
ἐπλήρου Ἰωάννης τὸν δρόμον, ἔλεγεν· Τί ἐμὲ ὑπονοεῖτε εἶναι, οὐκ
εἰμὶ ἐγώ· ἀλλ᾽ ἰδοὺ ἔρχεται μετ᾽ ἐμὲ οὗ οὐκ εἰμὶ ἄξιος τὸ ὑπόδημα τῶν ποδῶν λῦσαι. ἄνδρες ἀδελφοί, υἱοὶ γένους Ἀβραάμ, 26
οἱ ἐν ὑμῖν φοβούμενοι τὸν θεόν, ἡμῖν ὁ λόγος τῆς σωτηρίας
ταύτης ἐξαπεστάλη. οἱ γὰρ κατοικοῦντες ἐν Ἰερουσαλὴμ καὶ οἱ 27
ἄρχοντες αὐτῶν τοῦτον ἀγνοήσαντες καὶ τὰς φωνὰς τῶν προφητῶν
τὰς κατὰ πᾶν σάββατον ἀναγεινωσκομένας κρείναντες ἐπλήρωσαν,
καὶ μηδεμίαν αἰτίαν θανάτου εὑρόντες ᾐτήσαντο Πειλᾶτον ἀναιρε- 28
θῆναι αὐτόν· ὡς δὲ ἐτέλεσαν πάντα τὰ γεγραμμένα περὶ αὐτοῦ, 29
καθελόντες ἀπὸ τοῦ ξύλου ἔθηκαν εἰς μνημεῖον. ὁ δὲ θεὸς 30
ἤγειρεν αὐτὸν ἐκ νεκρῶν· ὃς ὤφθη ἐπὶ ἡμέρας πλείους τοῖς συν- 31

Editors 22 ιεσσαι] +[ανδρα] WH +ανδρα Soden JHR 26 αβρααμ] +και WH
Soden JHR 27 αυτων] αυτης JHR om τουτον JHR om και 2°
JHR om κρειναντες JHR 28 ευροντες] +κρειναντες JHR
ητησαντο] ητησαν τον WHmg αναιρεθηναι] ινα αναιρωσιν JHR 29 περι
αυτου γεγραμμενα WH Soden JHR [γεγραμμενα περι αυτου] WHmg 30 om
εκ νεκρων JHR

Old Uncial 22 ιεσσαι B +ανδρα אAC 81 (+D) 23 απο του σπερματος BACאᶜ 81 (+D)
om א ηγαγεν BאA 81 ηγειρε C(+D) τω ισραηλ BאAC(+D) om 81
24 λαω BאC 81 (+D) om A (א* first omitted λαω, then included it)
25 τι εμε BאA 81 τινα με C(+D) 26 αβρααμ B +και אAC
81(+D) υμιν BאC ημιν A 81 (+D) ημιν BאA 81 (+D) υμιν C
λογος BאA 81 (+D) +ουτος C ταυτης BאA 81 (+D) om C 27 εν
BאA(+D) om C 81 28 ητησαντο BACאᶜ 81 ητησαν τον א
29 γεγραμμενα περι αυτου B περι αυτου γεγραμμενα אAC 81 (+D)

Antiochian 22 ιεσσαι] +ανδρα HLPSϚ(+D) 23 ηγαγεν] ηγειρε Ϛ(+D) σωτηρα
ιησουν] σωτηριαν HLS 24 om παντι HLPS om λαω HLPS
25 ο ιωαννης LPϚ τι εμε] τινα με HLPSϚ(+D) 26 αβρααμ] +και
HLPSϚ(+D) ημιν] υμιν HLPSϚ εξαπεσταλη] απεσταλη HLPSϚ
29 παντα] απαντα Ϛ περι αυτου γεγραμμενα HLPSϚ(+D)

---

22 ανδρα is omitted by B Athanasius. | been likely to supply ανδρα, but rather
codd Hilary.*codd*. It corresponds to | the LXX word.
ανθρωπον in the LXX text (1 Sam. xiii. | **25** τι εμε BאA 81 sah corresponds
14), and ανδρα may have caused objec- | to the Aramaic usage. τινα CD Anti-
tion because not found in that familiar | ochian gig d e vg pesh hcl boh is a
Old Testament passage. In any case | linguistic improvement. See Torrey,
a harmonizing copyist would not have | *Composition and Date of Acts*, pp. 37 f.

αὐτοῖς εἰς βασιλέα, ᾧ καὶ εἶπεν μαρτυρήσας· Εὗρον Δαυεὶδ τὸν
υἱὸν Ἰεσσαί, ἄνδρα κατὰ τὴν καρδίαν μου, ὃς ποιήσει πάντα τὰ
23 θελήματά μου. ὁ θεὸς οὖν ἀπὸ τοῦ σπέρματος αὐτοῦ κατ' ἐπ-
24 αγγελείαν ἤγειρεν τῷ Ἰσραὴλ σωτῆρα τὸν Ἰησοῦν, προκηρύξαντος
Ἰωάνου πρὸ προσώπου τῆς εἰσόδου αὐτοῦ βάπτισμα μετανοίας
25 παντὶ τῷ λαῷ Ἰσραήλ. ὡς δὲ ἐπλήρου Ἰωάνης τὸν δρόμον,
ἔλεγεν· Τίνα με ὑπονοεῖτε εἶναι, οὐκ εἰμὶ ἐγώ· ἀλλὰ ἰδοὺ ἔρχεται
μεθ' ἐμὲ οὗ οὐκ εἰμὶ ἄξιος τὸ ὑπόδημα τῶν ποδῶν λῦσαι.
26 ἄνδρες ἀδελφοί, υἱοὶ γένους Ἀβραὰμ καὶ οἱ ἐν ἡμεῖν φοβούμενοι τὸν θεόν, ἡμεῖν ὁ λόγος τῆς σωτηρείας ταύτης ἐξαπεστάλη.
27 οἱ γὰρ κατοικοῦντες ἐν Ἰερουσαλὴμ καὶ οἱ ἄρχοντες αὐτ[ῆ]ς
μ[ὴ συνιέν]τες τὰς γρ[αφ]ὰς τῶν προφητῶν τὰς κατὰ πᾶν
28 σάββατον ἀναγεινωσκομένας καὶ κρείναντες ἐπλήρωσαν, καὶ
μηδεμίαν αἰτίαν θανάτου εὑρόντες ἐν αὐτῷ, κρείναντες αὐτὸν
29 παρέδωκαν Πειλάτῳ †ἵνα† εἰς ἀναίρεσιν· ὡς δὲ ἐτέλουν πάντα τὰ
περὶ αὐτοῦ γεγραμμένα †εἰσίν†, ἠτοῦντο τὸν Πειλᾶτον τοῦτον
†μὲν σταυρῶσαι† καὶ ἐπιτυχόντες †πάλιν† καὶ καθελόντες ἀπὸ τοῦ
30, 31 ξύλου καὶ ἔθηκαν εἰς μνημεῖον. ὃν ὁ θεὸς ἤγειρεν. | οὗτος ὤφθη
τοῖς συναναβαίνουσιν αὐτῷ ἀπὸ τῆς Γαλιλαίας εἰς Ἰερουσαλὴμ

25 επληρουν   υπονοειται   27 μ[η συνιεν]ταις

---

eis in regem cui etiam dixit testimonio inveni david filium jessae virum secundum d
cor meum qui faciet omnes voluntates meas   23 d̄s̄ autem a semine hujus secundum
pollicitationem resurrexit ipsi istrahel salbatorem īh̄m̄   24 cum prius praedicasset
johannes ante faciem ingressionis ejus baptisma paenitentiae omni populo istrahel
25 et dum inpleret cursum johannes dicebat quem suspicamini me esse non sum
ego sed ecce veniet post me cujus non sum dignus calciamentum pedum solvere
26 viri fratres fili generis abraham et qui in nobis timentes d̄m̄ nobis verbum
salutis hujus missum est   27 qui enim habitabat in hierusalem et principes ejus non
intellegentes scripturas prophetarū quae per omnem sabbatum leguntur et cum
judicassent inplerunt   28 et nullam causam mortis inventa est in eo judicantes
autem eum tradiderunt pilato ut interficeretur   29 et consummaverunt omnia quae
de illo scripta sunt petierunt pilatum hunc crucifigi et inpetraverunt iterum et
deposuerunt de ligno et posuerunt in monumento   30 quem d̄s̄ vero excitavit
31 hic qui visus est his qui simul ascenderunt cum eo a galilaea in hierusalem in

---

26 ημειν] mg nobis   28 εν αυτω] ⋇ in eo ✓   29 ητουντο . . . Harclean
μνημειον] mg postquam crucifixus est, petierunt Pilatum ut de ligno detraherent
eum.   impetrarunt : et detrahentes eum posuerunt eum in sepulchro

---

27-29 The text of vss. 27-29 is dis-   30 The omission of εκ νεκρων D d
cussed in a Detached Note, pp. 261-263.   gig may be the original reading.

ἀναβᾶσιν αὐτῷ ἀπὸ τῆς Γαλειλαίας εἰς Ἰερουσαλήμ, οἵτινές εἰσι
μάρτυρες αὐτοῦ πρὸς τὸν λαόν. καὶ ἡμεῖς ὑμᾶς εὐαγγελιζόμεθα 32
τὴν πρὸς τοὺς πατέρας ἐπαγγελίαν γενομένην | ὅτι ταύτην ὁ θεὸς 33
ἐκπεπλήρωκεν τοῖς τέκνοις ἡμῶν ἀναστήσας Ἰησοῦν, ὡς καὶ ἐν
Ps. ii. 7 τῷ ψαλμῷ γέγραπται τῷ δευτέρῳ· Υἱός μου εἶ σύ, ἐγὼ σήμερον
γεγέννηκά σε. ὅτι δὲ ἀνέστησεν αὐτὸν ἐκ νεκρῶν μηκέτι μέλ- 34
Is. lv. 3 λοντα ὑποστρέφειν εἰς διαφθοράν, οὕτως εἴρηκεν ὅτι Δώσω ὑμῖν
Ps. xvi. 10 τὰ ὅσια Δαυεὶδ τὰ πιστά. διότι καὶ ἐν ἑτέρῳ λέγει· Οὐ δώσεις 35
τὸν ὅσιόν σου ἰδεῖν διαφθοράν· Δαυεὶδ μὲν γὰρ ἰδίᾳ γενεᾷ ὑπ- 36
ηρετήσας τῇ τοῦ θεοῦ βουλῇ ἐκοιμήθη καὶ προσετέθη πρὸς τοὺς
πατέρας αὐτοῦ καὶ εἶδεν διαφθοράν, ὃν δὲ ὁ θεὸς ἤγειρεν οὐκ 37
εἶδεν διαφθοράν. γνωστὸν οὖν ἔστω ὑμῖν, ἄνδρες ἀδελφοί, 38
ὅτι διὰ τοῦτο ὑμῖν ἄφεσις ἁμαρτιῶν καταγγέλλεται, | καὶ ἀπὸ 39
πάντων ὧν οὐκ ἠδυνήθητε ἐν νόμῳ Μωυσέως δικαιωθῆναι ἐν
τούτῳ πᾶς ὁ πιστεύων δικαιοῦται. βλέπετε οὖν μὴ ἐπέλθῃ 40
Hab. i. 5 τὸ εἰρημένον ἐν τοῖς προφήταις· Ἴδετε, οἱ καταφρονηταί, καὶ 41

Editors   31 εισι] [νυν] εισι WH   νυν εισι Soden JHR   33 ημων] †ημων† WHmg
αυτων ημιν Soden   ημιν JHR   ψαλμω γεγραπται τω δευτερω] πρωτω ψαλμω
γεγραπται JHR   35 διο Soden   38 τουτο] τουτου WH Soden JHR
40 επελθη] +[εφ υμας] Soden

Old Uncial   31 εισι B   εισι νυν ℵ   νυν εισι AC 81 (cf. D)   33 ημων BℵAC(+D)
αυτων ημιν 81   ιησουν BℵC 81 (cf. D)   αυτον εκ νεκρων A (but rewritten)
35 διοτι BℵA 81   διο C   37 ο θεος BℵAC(+D)   om 81   38 εστω υμιν
BC 81 (+D)   υμιν εστω ℵA   τουτο B   τουτου ℵAC 81 (+D)   39 και
B 81 (cf. D)   om ℵAC   40 επελθη (ℵ απελθη) Bℵℵc(+D)   +εφ υμας AC 81

Antiochian   31 om αυτου H   33 ημων] αυτων ημιν HLPSς   ψαλμω γεγραπται
τω δευτερω] ψαλμω τω δευτερω γεγραπται LPSς   δευτερω ψαλμω γεγραπται H
35 διοτι] διο HLPSς   37 om ον δε ο θεος ηγειρεν ουκ ειδεν διαφθοραν S
38 τουτο] τουτου LPSς(+D)   39 τω νομω LPSς   40 επελθη] +εφ
υμας LPSς

---

31 The unconventional (cf. ii. 32, iii. 15, v. 32, x. 39) and broadly attested νυν is to be retained in spite of its omission in B Antiochian.

33 For the obviously corrupt τοις τεκνοις ημων BℵACD vg, 'to their sons' (without ημιν) is the reading of gig sah boh.*codd*, while Antiochian pesh read τοις τεκνοις αυτων ημιν. Perhaps τοις τεκνοις ημιν was the original text (so WH), early corrupted to τοις τεκνοις ημων. The Antiochian may testify to such an earlier text, or may be due

to a conjectural improvement of the B-text.

For hcl ※ *dominum nostrum* cf. τον κυριον ημων 614.

For the readings πρωτω D, δευτερω BℵAC 81 Antiochian, and the grounds for preferring the former, see Detached Note, pp. 263-265.

The completion of the quotation from Ps. ii. 8 in D d hcl.*mg* is perhaps to be associated with the preceding enlargement of ιησουν to read τον κυριον ιησουν χριστον D d (614) Hilary (*dominum nostrum Jesum*) hcl.*mg* sah.

ἐφ᾽ ἡμέρας πλείονας, οἵτινες ἄχρι νῦν εἰσιν μάρτυρες αὐτοῦ πρὸς
32 τὸν λαόν. καὶ ἡμεῖς ὑμᾶς εὐαγγελιζόμεθα τὴν πρὸς τοὺς πατέρας
33 ἡμῶν γενομένην ἐπαγγελίαν | ὅτι ταύτην ὁ θεὸς ἐκπεπλήρωκεν
τοῖς τέκνοις ἡμῶν ἀναστήσας τὸν κύριον Ἰησοῦν Χριστόν· οὕτως
γὰρ ἐν τῷ πρώτῳ ψαλμῷ γέγραπται·
Υἱός μου εἶ σύ, ἐγὼ σήμερον γεγέννηκά σε· αἴτησαι παρ᾽
ἐμοῦ καὶ δώσω σοι ἔθνη τὴν κληρονομίαν σου, καὶ τὴν
κατάσχεσίν σου τὰ πέρατα τῆς γῆς.
34 ὅτε δὲ ἀνέστησεν αὐτὸν ἐκ νεκρῶν μηκέτι μέλλοντα ὑποστρέφειν
εἰς διαφθοράν, οὕτως εἴρηκεν
ὅτι Δώσω ὑμεῖν τὰ ὅσια Δαυεὶδ τὰ πιστά.
35 καὶ ἑτέρως λέγει·
Οὐ δώσεις τὸν ὅσιόν σου ἰδεῖν διαφθοράν·
36 Δαυεὶδ γὰρ ἰδίᾳ γενεᾷ ὑπηρετήσας τῇ τοῦ θεοῦ βουλῇ ἐκοιμήθη
37 καὶ προσετέθη πρὸς τοὺς πατέρας αὐτοῦ καὶ ἶδεν διαφθοράν, ὃ‹ν›
38 δὲ ὁ θεὸς ἤγειρεν οὐκ εἶδεν δειαφθοράν. γνωστὸν οὖν ἔστω
ὑμεῖν, ἄνδρες ἀδελφοί, ὅτι διὰ τούτου ὑμεῖν ἄφεσις ἁμαρτιῶν
39 καταγγέλλεται καὶ μετάνοια ἀπὸ πάντων ὧν οὐκ ἠδυνήθητε ἐν
νόμῳ Μωσέως δικαιωθῆναι, ἐν τούτῳ οὖν πᾶς ὁ πιστεύων δικαιοῦ-
40 ται παρὰ θεῷ. βλέπετε οὖν μὴ ἐπέλθῃ τὸ εἰρημένον ἐν τοῖς
41 προφήταις· Ἴδετε, οἱ καταφρονηταί, καὶ θαυμάσατε καὶ ἀφανί-

33 εμου] αιμου   38 αφεσεις   39 δικαιουτε
41 καταφρονητε

diebus pluribus qui usquae nunc sunt testes ejus ad populū   32 et nos vos d
evangelizamus eam quae patres nostros factam pollicitationem   33 quia hanc d̄s̄
adimplevit filiis nostris suscitavit d̄n̄m īh̄s̄ x̄p̄m̄ sicut enim in primo psalmo
scriptum est filius meus es tu ego hodie genui te postula a me et dabo tibi gentes
hereditatem tuam et possessionem tuam terminos terrae   34 quando suscitavit eum a
portuis jam non rediturum in interitum ita dicit quia dabo vobis sancta david fidelia
35 ideoque et alia dicit non dabis sanctum tuum videre corruptionem   36 david
enim sua progenie cum ministrasset d̄o voluntate dormivit et adpositus est ad patres
suos et vidit corruptionem   37 quem autem d̄s̄ suscitavit non vidit corruptio[nem]
38 notum ergo sit vobis viri fratres quia per hunc vobis remissio peccatorum
adnuntiatur   39 et paenitentia ab omnibus quibus non potuistis in lege moysi justi-
ficari in isto enim omnis qui credit justificatur a d[eo]   40 videte ergo ne superveniat
quod dictum est in prophetis   41 videte contemptores et admiramini et extermina-

33 τον κυριον] ·✠· dominum nostrum ✓   αιτησαι . . . γης] mg pete a Harclean
me, et dabo tibi gentes in haereditatem tuam et in possessiones tuas limites
terrae   38 και μετανοια] ·✠· et poenitentia ✓   39 ουν] mg igitur
παρα θεω] mg a deo

34 οτι 1°] οτε D 614 d (quando) gig   is preferable because of the sense (cf.
(cum) Hil (cum) is unsuited to the   vs. 39 εν τουτω) to δια τουτο B
context.   minn, in which Y slipped out by
38 δια τουτου א̇AC 81 D Antiochian   haplography.

θαυμάσατε καὶ ἀφανίσθητε, ὅτι ἔργον ἐργάζομαι ἐγὼ ἐν ταῖς
ἡμέραις ὑμῶν, ἔργον ὃ οὐ μὴ πιστεύσητε ἐάν τις ἐκδιηγῆται
ὑμῖν. ἐξιόντων δὲ αὐτῶν εἰς τὸ μεταξὺ σάββατον ἠξίουν λαλη- 42
θῆναι αὐτοῖς τὰ ῥήματα ταῦτα. λυθείσης δὲ τῆς συναγωγῆς 43
ἠκολούθησαν πολλοὶ τῶν Ἰουδαίων καὶ τῶν σεβομένων προσηλύτων τῷ Παύλῳ καὶ τῷ Βαρνάβᾳ, οἵτινες προσλαλοῦντες αὐτοῖς
ἔπειθον αὐτοὺς προσμένειν τῇ χάριτι τοῦ θεοῦ.
Τῷ τε ἐρχομένῳ σαββάτῳ σχεδὸν πᾶσα ἡ πόλις συνήχθη 44
ἀκοῦσαι τὸν λόγον τοῦ θεοῦ. ἰδόντες δὲ οἱ Ἰουδαῖοι τοὺς ὄχλους 45
ἐπλήσθησαν ζήλου καὶ ἀντέλεγον τοῖς ὑπὸ Παύλου λαλουμένοις
βλασφημοῦντες. παρρησιασάμενοί τε ὁ Παῦλος καὶ ὁ Βαρνάβας 46
εἶπαν· Ὑμῖν ἦν ἀναγκαῖον πρῶτον λαληθῆναι τὸν λόγον τοῦ θεοῦ·
ἐπειδὴ ἀπωθεῖσθε αὐτὸν καὶ οὐκ ἀξίους κρείνετε ἑαυτο‹ὺ›ς τῆς

Editors   42 †ἐξιοντων . . . ταυτα† WHmg   εις το μεταξυ σαββατον ηξιουν]
παρεκαλουν εις το μεταξυ σαββατον WH Soden   44 τε] δε WH Soden JHR
τε WHmg   ερχομενω] εχομενω WHmg   θεου] κυριου WHmg Soden JHR
45 του παυλου Soden   46 επειδη] επει δε WHmg   επειδη δε Soden

Old Uncial   41 θαυμασατε BAC 81 (+D)   θαυμασετε ℵ   εργον εργαζομαι εγω
BA 81 (+D)   εργον εγω εργαζομαι C   εργον ο (ℵᶜ om ο) εγω εργαζομαι εγω ℵ
42 εις το μεταξυ σαββατον ηξιουν B   παρεκαλουν εις το μεταξυ σαββατον ℵAC 81
(cf. D)   43 δε BACℵᶜ 81 (+D)   +αυτοις ℵ   αυτους BℵC(+D) αυτου A
αυτοις 81   44 τε B   δε ℵAC 81 (+D)   ερχομενω BℵC 81 (+D)
εχομενω AC²   θεου BC   κυριου B²(B³ Tdf)ℵA 81 (cf. D)   45 δε BℵAC
om 81   παυλου BℵA   του παυλου C 81 (+D)   λαλουμενοις BℵA 81
λεγομενοις C(+D)   46 ην BℵA 81 (cf. D)   om C   επειδη Bℵ(+D)
επει δε C 81   επειδη δε Aℵᶜ   εαυτους B²

Antiochian   41 εγω εργαζομαι LPS5⁻   om εργον 2° LPS(+D)   ο] ω 5⁻
42 εξιοντων δε αυτων] εξιοντων δε (+αυτων LS) εκ της συναγωγης των ιουδαιων LPS5⁻
εις το μεταξυ σαββατον ηξιουν] παρεκαλουν τα εθνη εις το μεταξυ σαββατον LPS5⁻
om ταυτα PS   43 om τω 2° L(+D)   om αυτους LPS
προσμενειν] επιμενειν LPS5⁻   44 τω τε] τοτε L   τω δε 5⁻(+D)   45 του
παυλου LPS5⁻ (+D)   λαλουμενοις] λεγομενοις LPS5⁻(+D)   add αντι-
λεγοντες και before βλασφημουντες PS5⁻(+D)   46 τε] δε LPS5⁻   επειδη]
+δε LPS5⁻

42 B omits παρεκαλουν and inserts
ηξιουν after σαββατον ; boh implies
ηξιουν. E e omit παρεκαλουν, perhaps
per incuriam. Possibly the expansion
αξιουντες βαπτισθηναι in vs. 43, following βαρναβα in 614 minn hcl·※·,
apparently implied by Chrysostom
(Hom. in Act. xxx. 1), and doubtless a part of the original 'Western'
text, may be regarded as supporting the reading of B boh as against
ℵAC 81.

Exegetical difficulties (found mainly
in the parallelism of vs. 42 and vs. 43),
together with some of the variants in
vs. 42 (notably ηξιουν, παρεκαλουν ;
μεταξυ, εξης), have led to a suspicion
of primitive corruption of the text
(cf. WH, 'Appendix,' pp. 95 f.). But
these difficulties (if they are deemed
significant at all) can perhaps be
better explained from some relation
of the author to his source.
44 ερχομενω BℵC 81 D Antiochian is

σθητε, ὅτι ἔργον ἐργάζομαι ἐγὼ ἐν ταῖς ἡμέραις ὑμῶν, ὃ οὐ μὴ
42 πιστεύσητε ἐάν τις ἐκδιηγήσεται ὑμεῖν. καὶ ἐσείγησαν· | ἐξιόντων
δὲ αὐτῶν παρεκάλουν εἰς τὸ ἑξῆς σάββατον λαληθῆναι αὐτοῖς
43 ῥήματα ταῦτα. λυθείσης δὲ τῆς συναγωγῆς ἠκολούθησαν πολλοὶ
τῶν Ἰουδαίων καὶ τῶν σεβομένων προσηλύτων τῷ Παύλῳ καὶ
Βαρνάβᾳ, οἵτινες προσλαλοῦντες αὐτοῖς ἔπ‹ε›ιθον τ[.] αὐτοὺς
προσμένειν τῇ χάριτι τοῦ θεοῦ. ἐγένετο δὲ καθ' ὅλης τῆς πόλεως
διελθεῖν τὸν λόγον τοῦ θεοῦ.
44 Τῷ δὲ ἐρχομένῳ σαββάτῳ σχεδὸν ὅλη ἡ πόλις συνήχθη ἀκοῦσαι Παύλου. πολύν τε λόγον ποιησαμένου περὶ τοῦ κυρίου,
45 καὶ ἰδόντες οἱ Ἰουδαῖοι τὸ πλῆθος ἐπλήσθησαν ζήλου καὶ ἀντέλεγον τοῖς λόγοις ὑπὸ τοῦ Παύλου λεγομένοις ἀντιλέγοντες καὶ
46 βλασφημοῦντες. παρρησια‹σά›μενός τε ὁ Παῦλος καὶ Βαρνάβας
εἶπαν πρὸς αὐτούς· Ὑμεῖν πρῶτον ἦν λαληθῆναι τὸν λό‹γο›ν
τοῦ θεοῦ· ἐπ‹ε›ιδὴ ἀπωθεῖσθε αὐτὸν καὶ οὐκ ἀξίους κρείνετε

46 απωθεισθαι   κρεινατε

mini quia opus operor ego in diebus vestris quod non creditis si quis exposuerit d
vobis et tacuerunt   42 progregientibus vero eis rogabant in sequente sabbato
narrari sibi haec verba   43 et dismissa synagoga saecuti sunt multi judaeorum et
colentium proselytorum paulum et barnabam qui loquentes cum illis persuadentes eis
permanere in gratia d̄ī factum est autem per omnem civitatem transire verbum d̄nī
44 sequenti autem sabbato paene tota civitas collecta est audire paulū multum
verbum faciens de d̄no   45 et cum vidissent judaei turbam repleti sunt aemulatione
et contradicebant sermonibus quae a paulo dicebantur contradicentes et blas-
phemantes   46 adhibita vero fiducia paulus et barnabas dixerunt ad eos vobis
oportebat primum loqui verbum d̄nī sed quia repulistis illud et non dignos judicastis

46 vobis oportuit in primis sermonem dei tradi, sed quoniam repulistis eum Tertullian,
nec dignos vos aeterna vita existimastis, ecce convertimus nos ad nationes.   *Fug.* 6

46 vobis primum oportuerat indicari verbum domini, sed quia expulistis Cyprian,
illud nec vos dignos vitae aeternae judicastis, ecce convertimus nos ad gentes. *Test.* i.121

41 και εσειγησαν] ·※· et tacuit ✓   43 βαρναβα] + ·※· rogantes Harclean
baptizari ✓   εγενετο δε καθ ολης της πολεως διελθειν τον λογον] *mg* factum
est autem per omnem civitatem transire verbum

so deeply rooted in the tradition of the
text, and εχομενω AC²E minn is so
easy an emendation, that the harder
reading ought to be adopted, if possible.
For the same v.l. cf. Thucyd. vi. 3.
κυριου אA 81 gig vg sah is more
significant in the context than θεου.
τον λογον του θεου BC Antiochian pesh
hcl boh is a phrase of relatively frequent occurrence; the substitution of
it may have been suggested here by

vs. 46 (where του θεου well suits the
context). κυριου is also supported by
the fact that D, in the expanded form
of this part of the sentence, reads
περι του κυριου. (τον λογον του θεου
D, earlier in the verse, stands in a
different gloss; even there it is probably due to unskilful conflation with
the B-text, since e E vg.*codd* hcl.*mg*,
which all contain the gloss, have
τον λογον only.)

αἰωνίου ζωῆς, ἰδοὺ στρεφόμεθα εἰς τὰ ἔθνη· οὕτω γὰρ ἐντέταλται 47

Is. xlix. 6 ἡμῖν ὁ κύριος· Τέθεικά σε εἰς φῶς ἐθνῶν τοῦ εἶναί σε εἰς σωτηρίαν ἕως ἐσχάτου τῆς γῆς. ἀκούοντα δὲ τὰ ἔθνη ἔχαιρον καὶ ἐδό- 48 ξαζον τὸν λόγον τοῦ θεοῦ, καὶ ἐπίστευσαν ὅσοι ἦσαν τεταγμένοι εἰς ζωὴν αἰωνίαν· διεφέρετο δὲ ὁ λόγος τοῦ κυρίου δι' ὅλης τῆς 49 χώρας. οἱ δὲ Ἰουδαῖοι παρώτρυναν τὰς σεβομένας γυναῖκας τὰς 50 εὐσχήμονας καὶ τοὺς πρώτους τῆς πόλεως καὶ ἐπήγειραν διωγμὸν ἐπὶ τὸν Παῦλον καὶ Βαρνάβαν, καὶ ἐξέβαλον αὐτοὺς ἀπὸ τῶν ὁρίων. οἱ δὲ ἐκτιναξάμενοι τὸν κονιορτὸν τῶν ποδῶν ἐπ' αὐτοὺς 51 ἦλθον εἰς Εἰκόνιον, οἵ τε μαθηταὶ ἐπληροῦντο χαρᾶς καὶ πνεύ- 52 ματος ἁγίου.

Ἐγένετο δὲ ἐν Εἰκονίῳ κατὰ τὸ αὐτὸ εἰσελθεῖν αὐτοὺς εἰς XIV τὴν συναγωγὴν τῶν Ἰουδαίων καὶ λαλῆσαι οὕτως ὥστε πιστεῦ- σαι Ἰουδαίων τε καὶ Ἑλλήνων πολὺ πλῆθος. οἱ δὲ ἀπειθήσαντες 2 Ἰουδαῖοι ἐπήγειραν καὶ ἐκάκωσαν τὰς ψυχὰς τῶν ἐθνῶν κατὰ

Editors			
48 θεου] κυριου WHmg Soden		αιωνιον WH Soden JHR	50 οριων]
+αυτων WH Soden JHR	52 τε] δε WHmg		

Old Uncial			
47 εντεταλται BℵAC (cf. D)	εντελλεται 81		ο BACℵᶜ 81 (+D) om ℵ
48 θεου B(+D)	κυριου ℵAC 81		αιωνιαν B αιωνιον ℵAC 81 (+D)
49 δι BC(+D)	καθ ℵA 81	50 παρωτρυναν BℵAC (cf. D)	παρωξυναν 81
γυναικας] BACℵᶜ 81 (+D)	+και ℵ		οριων B +αυτων ℵAC 81 (+D)
52 τε BA δε ℵC 81 (+D)		1 των ιουδαιων BACℵᶜ 81 (+D)	om ℵ

Antiochian			
48 εχαιρεν PS	εδοξαζεν P	θεου] κυριου LPS⌐	αιωνιον
LPS⌐(+D)	50 γυναικας]·+και LPS⌐		τον βαρναβαν PS⌐
οριων] +αυτων LPS⌐(+D)	51 κονιορτον] +απο S	ποδων] +αυτων LPS⌐(+D)	
52 τε] δε LPS⌐(+D)	1 ελληνων τε και ιουδαιων L	2 απειθουντες	
LPS⌐			

47 ιδου φως τεθεικα σε τοις εθνεσιν D d (super gentibus) Cypr (inter gentes) was the 'Western' reading. Also 314 1838 e E have preserved ιδου; gig vg gentibus, e super gentibus. The facts are accounted for if the B-text of Acts is a translation from the Hebrew (or an Aramaic equivalent) made probably with the aid of, but not wholly in accordance with, the LXX, which reads ιδου δεδωκα σε εις διαθηκην γενους εις φως εθνων. (The words εις διαθηκην γενους are lacking in Hebrew.) In that case the 'Western' text altered the form by adding ιδου (LXX; not Hebrew), by improving the barbarous εις φως εθνων to φως τοις εθνεσιν, and by giving φως a more prominent position.

For hcl.mg cf. σωτηριαν εν τοις εθνεσιν 6 14.

2 The words των ιουδαιων and της συναγωγης D d, which are not found in hcl.mg, may be later additions to the 'Western' gloss; they introduce a certain inaptness, from which the corresponding text of hcl.mg is wholly free. επηγαγον D for επηγειραν d hcl.mg is also doubtful. αυτοις D (om d) is superfluous in the face of κατα των δικαιων, and its origin is not easily guessed, but it ought not to be neglected (cf. vs. 27 and Note). Pesh renders: 'but the Jews who had not believed stirred up the gentiles that they should hurt the brethren,' which might represent επηγειραν τα εθνη του κακωσαι τους αδελφους, but is

47 ἑαυτοὺς τῆς αἰωνίου ζωῆς, ἰδοὺ στρεφόμεθα εἰς τὰ ἔθνη· οὕτως
γὰρ ἐντέταλκεν ὁ κύριος· Ἰδοὺ φῶς τέθεικά σε τοῖς ἔθνεσιν τοῦ
48 εἶναί σε εἰς σωτηρίαν ἕως ἐσχάτου τῆς γῆς. καὶ ἀκούοντα τὰ
ἔθνη ἔχαιρον καὶ ἐδέξαντο τὸν λόγον τοῦ θεοῦ, καὶ ἐπίστευσαν
49 ὅσοι ἦσαν τεταγμένοι εἰς ζωὴν αἰώνιον· καὶ διεφέρετο ὁ λόγος
50 τοῦ κυρίου δι' ὅλης τῆς χώρας. οἱ δὲ Ἰουδαῖοι παρώτρυνον
τὰς σεβομένας γυναῖκας τὰς εὐσχήμονας καὶ τοὺς πρώτους τῆς
πόλεως καὶ ἐπήγειραν θλεῖψειν μεγάλην καὶ διωγμὸν ἐπὶ Παῦλον
51 καὶ Βαρνάβαν, καὶ ἐξέβαλον αὐτοὺς ἀπὸ τῶν ὁρίων αὐτῶν. οἱ
δὲ ἐκτιναξάμενοι τὸν κονιορτὸν τῶν ποδῶν αὐτῶν ἐπ' αὐτοὺς
52 κατήντησαν εἰς Εἰκόνιον, οἱ δὲ μαθηταὶ ἐπληροῦντο χαρᾶς καὶ
πνεύματος ἁγίου.

XIV Ἐγένετο δὲ ἐν Ἰκονίῳ κατὰ τὸ αὐτὸ εἰσελθεῖν αὐτὸν εἰς τὴν
συναγωγὴν τῶν Ἰουδαίων καὶ λαλῆσαι οὕτως πρὸς αὐτοὺς ὥστε
2 πιστεύειν Ἰουδαίων τε καὶ Ἑλλήνων πολὺ πλῆθος. οἱ δὲ ἀρχισυνάγωγοι τῶν Ἰουδαίων καὶ οἱ ἄρχοντες τῆς συναγωγῆς ἐπήγαγον
αὐτοῖς διωγμὸν κατὰ τῶν δικαίων, καὶ ἐκάκωσαν τὰς ψυχὰς τῶν

50 επι] επει

---

eos in aeternam vitam ecce convertimur ad gentes 47 ita enim mandatum dedit d
nobis d̄n̄s ecce lumen posui te super gentibus ut sint in salutem usquae ad ultimum
terrae 48 et cum audirent gentes gavisae sunt et exceperunt verbum d̄n̄i et
crediderunt quodquod erant in vitam aeternam 49 et provulgabatur verbum d̄n̄i
per omnem regionem 50 judaei autem instigaverunt caelicolas mulieres honestas
et principes civitatis et suscitaverunt tribulationem magnam et persecutionem super
paulum et barnabā et ejecerunt eos de finibus eorum 51 ad illi excusso pulvere de
pedibus suis super eos venerunt in hiconio 52 discipuli vero inplebantur gaudio
et s̄p̄u̅ sancto
1 contigit autem ut ichonio similiter introire eos in synagoga judaeorum et loqui
sic ad eos ita ut crederent judaeorum et grecorum copiosa multitudo 2 archisynagogae judaeorum et principes synagogae incitaverunt persecutionem adversus justos

---

47 sic enim dixit per scripturam dominus : ecce lucem posui te inter gentes, Cyprian
ita ut sis in salvationem usque ad fines terrae. *Test. i.* 21

---

47 σωτηριαν] + eis ※ gentibus ✓ 2 οι δε αρχισυναγωγοι . . . Harclean
ειρηνην] *mg* illi autem archisynagogae et principes excitaverunt persecutionem,
et male affectos reddiderunt animos gentium adversus fratres. dominus autem
dedit cito pacem

---

perhaps only a free translation of the
B-text. The precise form of the
'Western' text cannot be recovered.
For an attempted different explanation

of κατα των δικαιων as meaning 'in
respect of legal proceedings,' see
W. M. Ramsay, *The Church in the
Roman Empire*, 1893, p. 46.

τῶν ἀδελφῶν. ἱκανὸν μὲν οὖν χρόνον διέτρειψαν παρρησιαζό- 3
μενοι ἐπὶ τῷ κυρίῳ τῷ μαρτυροῦντι τῷ λόγῳ τῆς χάριτος αὐτοῦ,
διδόντι σημεῖα καὶ τέρατα γείνεσθαι διὰ τῶν χειρῶν αὐτῶν.
ἐσχίσθη δὲ τὸ πλῆθος τῆς πόλεως, καὶ οἱ μὲν ἦσαν σὺν τοῖς 4
Ἰουδαίοις οἱ δὲ σὺν τοῖς ἀποστόλοις. ὡς δὲ ἐγένετο ὁρμὴ 5
τῶν ἐθνῶν τε καὶ Ἰουδαίων σὺν τοῖς ἄρχουσι αὐτῶν ὑβρίσαι καὶ
λιθοβολῆσαι αὐτούς, συνιδόντες κατέφυγον εἰς τὰς πόλεις τῆς 6
Λυκαονίας Λύστραν καὶ Δέρβην καὶ τὴν περίχωρον, κἀκεῖ εὐ- 7
αγγελιζόμενοι ἦσαν.

Καί τις ἀνὴρ ἀδύνατος ἐν Λύστροις τοῖς ποσὶν ἐκάθητο, χωλὸς 8
ἐκ κοιλίας μητρὸς αὐτοῦ, ὃς οὐδέποτε περιεπάτησεν. οὗτος 9

Editors   3 μαρτυρουντι] +επι JHR   8 εν λυστροις αδυνατος Soden

---

Old Uncial   3 διετρειψαν BℵC 81   διετριβον A   μαρτυρουντι BCℵ° 81 (+D)   +επι ℵA
διδοντι BA(+D)   διδοντος ℵ   και διδοντι C   και διδοντος 81   6 λυστραν
BℵAC² 81   εις λυστραν C(+D)   7 ευαγγελιζομενοι ησαν BℵA 81 (+D)
ησαν ευαγγελιζομενοι C   8 αδυνατος εν λυστροις Bℵ   εν λυστροις αδυνατος
ACℵ° 81

Antiochian   3 om επι S   διδοντι] και διδοντι LS   7 ησαν ευαγγελιζομενοι
HLPSS   8 εν λυστροις αδυνατος HLPSS   αυτου] +υπαρχων
HLPSS   περιπεπατηκει HLPSS(+D)

The motive of the 'Western' additions in this verse is plainly to over-
come the exegetical difficulties of vs. 3
on the assumption that two stages of
persecution, a brief lighter one and
another more violent, were separated
by a period of peace. This is made
still more explicit by the form taken
in hcl. *mg* by vs. 5, where D, perhaps
under Latin influence, conforms substantially to the B-text.

The comment of Ephrem on 2 Tim.
iii. 11 (Latin translation, Venice, 1893,
pp. 264 f.), as well as his Commentary
on Acts, *ad loc.* (see below, p. 418),
show traces of the 'Western' character
of the Old Syriac used by him in Acts
xiii. 50, xiv. 2, 5, 6 (see J. R. Harris,
Four Lectures, pp. 23 f.; Zahn, *Urausgabe*, pp. 357 f. and *Kommentar*, pp.
462 f.).

3 επι ℵA pesh boh is so unusual a
construction after μαρτυρουντι that it
is probably genuine. Its presence
may well be due to an Aramaic
original (בֿ); cf. pesh John v. 33, xviii.

37, Acts x. 22, 3 John 3; Targum of
Job xxix. 11 אסהדת עלי, representing
Heb. וַתְּעִידֵנִי; Palestinian Syriac, Lk.
iv. 22 'and all bore to (בֿ) him witness'
(C. C. Torrey). In Heb. xi. 4 επι has
a different meaning, and is, moreover,
probably drawn from the LXX of
Gen. iv. 4.

6 In h, as Zahn points out, the
pronoun *eis* before LX[. . .] translates τοις; this would prove that this
addition was found in the underlying
Greek. It should be noted that Berger was not able to decipher anything
of the words *sicut iħs dixerat eis LX*;
but Buchanan, after renewed examination of the MS., is sure of them. No
other authority seems to give any
hint of this gloss. Buchanan deems
it "almost certain from considerations
of space that our MS. read LXXII and
not LXX."

7 The rendering *omne genus* h is held
by Zahn to represent ολον το εθνος (see
xvii. 26, where all Latin texts except
d render *genus*, but cf. v.l. γενος

ἐθνῶν κατὰ τῶν ἀδελφῶν. ὁ δὲ κύριος ἔδωκεν ταχὺ εἰρήνην·
3 ἱκανὸν μὲν οὖν χρόνον διατρείψαντες παρ‹ρ›ησια‹σά›μενοι ἐπὶ
τῷ κυρίῳ τῷ μαρτυροῦντι τῷ λόγῳ τῆς χάριτος αὐτοῦ, διδόντι
4 σημεῖα καὶ τέρατα γείνεσθαι διὰ τῶν χειρῶν αὐτοῦ. ἦν δὲ ἐσχι-
σμένον τὸ πλῆθος τῆς πόλεως, καὶ οἱ μὲν ἦσαν σὺν τοῖς Ἰουδαίοις
ἄλλοι δὲ σὺν τοῖς ἀποστόλοις κολλώμενοι διὰ τὸν λόγον τοῦ
5 θεοῦ. ὡς δὲ ἐγένετο ὁρμὴ τῶν ἐθνῶν καὶ τῶν Ἰουδαίων σὺν
6 τοῖς ἄρχουσιν αὐτῶν ὑβρίσαι καὶ λιθοβολῆσαι αὐτούς, συνιδόντες καὶ κατέφυγον εἰς τὰς πόλ‹ε›ις τῆς Λυκαωνίας εἰς
7 Λύστραν καὶ Δέρβην καὶ τὴν περίχωρον ὅλην, κἀκεῖ εὐαγγελιζόμενοι ἦσαν, καὶ ἐκεινήθη ὅλον τὸ πλῆθος ἐπὶ τῇ διδαχῇ. ὁ
δὲ Παῦλος καὶ Βαρνάβας διέτριβον ἐν Λύστροις.
8 Καί τις ἀνὴρ ἐκάθητο ἀδύνατος τοῖς ποσὶν ἐκ κοιλίας τῆς
9 μητρὸς αὐτοῦ, ὃς οὐδέποτε περιπεπατήκει. οὗτος ἤκουσεν τοῦ

---

3 αυτου 2°] corrected to αυτων, perhaps by 1st hand   8 περει-
πεπατηκει

---

et maletractaverunt animas gentium adversus fratres d̅n̅s̅ autem dedit comfestim d
pacem 3 plurimo ergo tempore commorati sunt habita fiducia in d̅n̅o̅ qui testimonium perhibuit verbo gratiae ipsius dans signa et portenta fieri per manus eorum
4 divisa autem erat multitudo civitatis et alii quidem erant cum judaeis alii vero
cum apostolis adherentes propterter verbum d̅i̅ 5 ut autem factum est impetus
gentilium et judaeorum cum magistribus ipsorum et injuriaverunt et lapidaverunt
eos 6 intellexerunt et fugerunt in civitates lycaoniae in lystra et derben et circum
totam regionem 7 et illic erant evangelizantes et commota est omnis multitudo in
doctrinis paulus autem et barnabas moras faciebant in lystris 8 et quidam vir
sedebat adynatus a pedibus ab utero matris suae qui numquam ambulaverat 9 hic

---

5 runt eos et lapidaverunt,   6 intellexerunt [et fugerunt] in Lycaoniae h
civitates, sicut i̅h̅s̅ dixerat eis LX[. ., in Lys]tra et Derben et omnes confines
regionis. 7 [et bene nū]tiabant ut motum est omne genus in doctri[na eorum].
Paulus autem et Barnabas commorabantu[r in Lystris]. 8 illic fuit quidam
infirmus sedens, languid[us pedibus], qui a vente matris numquam ambulaver[at,
habens ti]morem. 9 hic libenter audivit apostolos in[cipientes] loqui. intuitus

---

8 [et iterum Lystris Lyciae cum esset Paulus cum Barnaba et a nativitate Irenaeus,
claudum]   iii. 12, 9 (12

4-6 κολλωμενοι . . . δερβην] mg adhaerentes propter verbum dei. et iterum Harclean
excitaverunt persecutionem secundo Judaei cum gentibus ; et lapidantes eos
ejecerunt eos ex civitate ; et fugientes pervenerunt in Lycaoniam in civitatem
quandam quae vocatur Lystra et Derben

---

minn), and this to be the proper
' Western ' reading, and, in the sense
of ' all the country-side,' to give a
better sense than πληθος, which regu-

larly means a definite community ;
see Zahn, Urausgabe, pp. 151 f., 175.
8 χωλος is omitted by D d gig,
probably as superfluous ; h read it.

ἤκουεν τοῦ Παύλου λαλοῦντος· ὃς ἀτενίσας αὐτῷ καὶ ἰδὼν ὅτι
ἔχει πίστιν τοῦ σωθῆναι | εἶπεν μεγάλῃ φωνῇ· Ἀνάστηθι ἐπὶ 10
τοὺς πόδας σου ὀρθός· καὶ ἥλατο, περιεπάτει. οἵ τε ὄχλοι 11
ἰδόντες ὃ ἐποίησεν Παῦλος ἐπῆραν τὴν φωνὴν αὐτῶν Λυκαονιστὶ
λέγοντες· Οἱ θεοὶ ὁμοιωθέντες ἀνθρώποις κατέβησαν πρὸς ἡμᾶς·
| ἐκάλουν τε τὸν Βαρνάβαν Δία, τὸν δὲ Παῦλον Ἑρμῆν ἐπειδὴ 12
αὐτὸς ἦν ὁ ἡγούμενος τοῦ λόγου. ὅ τε ἱερεὺς τοῦ Διὸς τοῦ ὄντος 13
πρὸ τῆς πόλεως ταύρους καὶ στέμματα ἐπὶ τοὺς πυλῶνας ἐνέγκας
σὺν τοῖς ὄχλοις ἤθελεν θύειν. ἀκούσαντες δὲ οἱ ἀπόστολοι Βαρνά- 14
βας καὶ Παῦλος, διαρρήξαντες τὰ ἱμάτια ἑαυτῶν ἐξεπήδησαν εἰς

Editors   9 ηκουσεν Soden   10 τη φωνη Soden   ηλατο] +και WH Soden
JHR   11 τε] δε Soden   14 εαυτων] αυτων WHmg   [ε]αυτων Soden

---

Old Uncial   9 ηκουεν BC   ηκουσεν A 81 (+D)   ουκ ηκουσεν ℵ   λαλουντος BACℵ°c 81 (+D)
λεγοντος ℵ   10 φωνη BℵC 81   τη φωνη A   +σοι λεγω εν τω ονοματι του
κυριου C (cf. D)   ηλατο B   +και B² vid ℵAC 81 (+D)   11 τε BℵA
δε C 81 (+D)   ιδοντες BℵA 81 (+D)   ιδοτες C   παυλος BℵAC(+D)
ο παυλος 81   αυτων BACℵ°c 81 (+D)   om ℵ   ανθρωποις BACℵ°c 81
(cf. D)   ανθρωποι ℵ   12 επειδη BACℵ°c 81 (+D)   επι ℵ   ο BℵA 81
om C(+D)   13 ο τε BℵAC²   τοτε C   τοτε ο 81   προ BℵA (cf. D)
προς C   προς των πυλων 81   ηθελεν BℵAC   ηθελον 81 (+D)
14 εαυτων BAℵc   αυτων ℵC 81 (+D)   εις BℵA 81 (+D)   επι C

Antiochian   9 ηκουσεν HL(+D)   πιστιν εχειHLPS 5   10 τη φωνη HLPS5
ορθως HP   ηλατο] ηλλετο (ηλετο H) HLPS5   add και before περιεπατει
HLPS5 (+D)   11 τε] δε HLPS5(+D)   ο παυλος HLPS5   αυτων
την φωνην S   12 του 1°] +μεν HLPS5   13 τε] δε HLPS5 (cf. D)
πολεως] +αυτων HLPS5   ηθελον HS(+D)   14 εαυτων] αυτων
HLPS5(+D)   εξεπηδησαν] εισεπηδησαν HLPS5

---

9 υπαρχων εν φοβω D, possidens in
timore d, [habens ti]morem h, is
intended to justify Paul's confidence
in the man's faith. Note that h puts
it in a different position, at the close
of vs. 8 ; that possidens d may imply
the same text as habens h ; and that
Antiochian inserts υπαρχων after αυτου,
vs. 8. The same motive here observed
has led to the text of gig: hic cum
audisset paulum loquentem, credidit.

10 The 'Western' text of Paul's
address to the lame man is plainly
assimilated to the language of Peter,
Acts iii. 6.

The peculiar reading και ευθεως συν
τω λογω αναστας ηλατο 1838 seems to
be an attempt to improve the difficult

ευθεως παραχρημα of D (supported by
hcl.mg).

13 The reading of D minn (incl.
614) του οντος διος προ της (D om της)
πολεως may be a conformation to a
current name Ζεὺς πρὸ πόλεως; see
Ramsay, The Church in the Roman
Empire, pp. 51 f., who adduces a dedi-
cation Διι προαστιω, and from an inscription of Smyrna the phrase ιερεια
προ πολεως ; cf. also Inscr. Gr. Insul.
(Thera), 522 ιερεα . . του προ πολεως
Διονυσου ; 420 η γεραιρα του προ πολεως
. . Διονυσου, cited by Blass, Stud. Krit.,
1900, p. 27. The unhellenic phrase
of the B-text του διος του οντος προ της
πολεως may well reflect a Semitic
original. It is further possible (cf.

Παύλου λαλοῦντος ὑπάρχων ἐν φόβῳ· ἀτενίσας δὲ αὐτῷ ὁ Παῦλος
10 καὶ ἰδὼν ὅτι ἔχει πίστιν τοῦ σωθῆναι | εἶπεν μεγάλῃ φωνῇ· Σοὶ
λέγω ἐν τῷ ὀνόματι τοῦ κυρίου Ἰησοῦ Χριστοῦ, ἀνάστηθι ἐπὶ
τοὺς πόδας σου ὀρθὸς καὶ περιπάτει. καὶ εὐθέως παραχρῆμα
11 ἀνήλατο καὶ περιεπάτει. οἱ δὲ ὄχλοι ἰδόντες ὃ ἐποίησεν Παῦλος
ἐπῆραν φωνὴν αὐτῶν Λυκαωνιστὶ λέγοντες· Οἱ θεοὶ ὁμοιωθέντες
12 τοῖς ἀνθρώποις κατέβησαν πρὸς ἡμᾶς· ἐκάλουν δὲ Βαρνάβαν
Δίαν, τὸν δὲ Παῦλον Ἑρμῆν ἐπ‹ε›ιδὴ αὐτὸς ἦν ἡγούμενος τοῦ
13 λογοῦ. οἱ δὲ ἱερεῖς τοῦ ὄντος Διὸς πρὸ πόλεως ταύρους αὐτοῖς
καὶ στέμματα ἐπὶ τοὺς πυλῶνας ἐνέγκαντες σὺν τοῖς ὄχλοις
14 ἤθελον ἐπιθύειν. ἀκούσας δὲ Βαρνάβας καὶ Παῦλος, διαρρήξαντες τὰ ἱμάτια αὐτῶν καὶ ἐξεπήδησαν εἰς τὸν ὄχλον, κράζοντες

audivit paulum loquentem possidens in timore intuitus autem eum paulum et videns **d**
quia habet fidem ut salvus fiat   10 dixit voce magna tibi dico in nomine d̄n̄i ī̄h̄u x̄p̄ī
surge supra pedes tuos rectus et ambula et statim subito exilivit et ambulabat
11 turba autem videns quod fecit paulus levaverunt vocem suam lycaoni dicentes
dii adsimulati hominibus descenderunt ad nos   12 vocabant barnaban jovem paulum
vero mercurium quoniam ipse erat princeps sermonum   13 sacerdotes autem qui
erant jovis ante civitate tauros eis et coronas ad januas adferentes cum turba bolentes
immolare   14 cum audisset autem barnabas et paulus consciderunt vestimenta sua

est eum et cognobit Populu[s quoniam] haberet fidem ut salvaretur.   10 clamans **h**
dixit ei [magna vo]ce: tibi dico in nomine ī̄h̄u, nostri d̄n̄i, fili d̄ī, sur[ge
supra pe]des tuos rectus, et amvula.   et ille infirmus [exilivit] et ambulabat.
11 et turbae, videntes quod fe[cit Paulus], adlevaverunt vocem Lycaonicae
dicent[es: dii simi]laverunt se hominibus et descenderun[t ad nos.   12 et]
vocaverunt Barnaban Jovem Populum a[utem Mer]curium, quoniam ipse erat
princeps verborum.   13 et [ad portam] erat sacerdos Jovis: tauros et dia-
demata e[t coronas] adduxit ad januas cum plebe, volens immo[lare].   14 et cum
audissent Paulus et Barnabas ista, con[sciderunt] suum vestimentum, accurrentes

10 in nomine domini nostri Jesu Christi [ambulare fecisset].
10 *om* nostri *Turner*

10 σοι λεγω . . . περιεπατει] *mg* tibi dico in nomine domini Jesu Christi,
surge in pedes tuos recte, et ambula.   et statim eadem hora exiliebat et
ambulabat   11 λυκαωνιστι] *mg* lingua Lycaoniae

Ramsay) that the 'Western' οι ιερεις   θυειν of all other witnesses, but since
D 460 d gig Ephr made the scene more   it does not always have any distinc-
conceivable to a Greek familiar with   tive meaning, and the context here
the customs of temples served by more   suggests none, there is no sufficient
than one priest.   But in both points   internal reason for preferring either
the variants are also susceptible of   reading.
explanation in the reverse order. The   See W. M. Calder, in *Expositor*,
decision must depend on the general   7th Series, vol. x, 1910, pp. 1 ff., 148 ff.
view taken of the two texts.   **14** The omission of οι αποστολοι in
   The conjectured reading in h [*ad*   D d h gig pesh is balanced in h, vs. 9,
portam] is by no means certain.   by the substitution of *apostolos* for
   επιθνειν D is a less common word than   *Paulum*.

τὸν ὄχλον, κράζοντες | καὶ λέγοντες· Ἄνδρες, τί ταῦτα ποιεῖτε; 15
καὶ ἡμεῖς ὁμοιοπαθεῖς ἐσμεν ὑμῖν ἄνθρωποι, εὐαγγελιζόμενοι ὑμᾶς
ἀπὸ τούτων τῶν ματαίων ἐπιστρέφειν ἐπὶ θεὸν ζῶντα ὃς ἐποίη-
Ex. xx. 11 σεν τὸν οὐρανὸν καὶ τὴν γῆν καὶ τὴν θάλασσαν καὶ πάντα τὰ ἐν
αὐτοῖς· ὃς ἐν ταῖς παρῳχημέναις γενεαῖς εἴασεν πάντα τὰ ἔθνη 16
πορεύεσθαι ταῖς ὁδοῖς αὐτῶν· καίτοι οὐκ ἀμάρτυρον αὐτὸν ἀφῆκεν 17
ἀγαθουργῶν, οὐρανόθεν ὑμῖν ὑετοὺς διδοὺς καὶ καιροὺς καρποφόρους, ἐμπιπλῶν τροφῆς καὶ εὐφροσύνης τὰς καρδίας ὑμῶν.
καὶ ταῦτα λέγοντες μόλις κατέπαυσαν τοὺς ὄχλους τοῦ μὴ θύειν 18
αὐτοῖς. ἐπῆλθαν δὲ ἀπὸ Ἀντιοχείας καὶ Εἰκονίου Ἰουδαῖοι, καὶ 19

Editors   17 αυτον] εαυτον Soden   διδους υετους Soden

Old Uncial   15 τι BℵC 81 (+D)   ει τι A   εσμεν υμιν BℵA 81 (+D)   υμιν εσμεν C
ζωντα BACℵᶜ 81 (+D)   τον ζωντα ℵ   17 καιτοι BACℵᶜ 81   καιτοιγε ℵ
(cf. D)   αυτον BℵA   εαυτον Cℵᶜ 81 (+D)   υμιν BℵC(+D)   om Aℵᶜ 81
υετους διδους BC(+D)   διδους υετους ℵA 81   υμων BℵC 81 (+D)   ημων Aℵᶜ
18 κατεπαυσαν BℵA 81 (+D)   κατεπαυσαντο C   αυτοις BℵA(+D)   +αλλα
πορευσθαι εκαστον εις τα ιδια C 81   19 επηλθαν δε BℵA   διατριβοντων δε
αυτων και (om και C) διδασκοντων επηλθον C 81 (cf. D)

Antiochian   15 om και before ημεις S(+D)   om υμιν H   τον θεον τον ζωντα
HLPSⳐ (cf. D)   17 καιτοι] καιτοιγε HLPSⳐ (cf. D)   αυτον] εαυτον
HLPSⳐ(+D)   αγαθουργων] αγαθοποιων HLPSⳐ(+D)   υμιν] ημιν Ⳑ
υμων] ημων HLPSⳐ

---

15 The conjectured d[e his vanis ut con]vertamini h is less likely than d[m ut ab his vanis con]vertamini, as in D d Ps.-Aug. spec. Iren. The rendering of h ad eum qui fecit (i.e. επι τον ποιησαντα) may correctly represent the 'Western' text, since it may be suspected that the text of D is conflate, and that τον θεον ζωντα has been supplied from the B-text. The text which seems to be represented by h corresponds well to the familiar traits of the 'Western' paraphrast, who objected to the unexampled use here of ευαγγελιζομενοι followed by an appeal instead of an announcement, and therefore introduced θεον in a different connexion.

18 For hcl.mg [quum haec] dixissent cf. ειπορτες 614 min.
The reading [persu]aserunt h is supported by επεισαν 917 1874 sah, and perhaps by suaderent vg.cod.D. It suits well the addition αλλα πορευεσθαι εκαστον εις τα ιδια C 81 614 and many minuscules (cf. v. 18 D), which, although attested as 'Western'

by hcl.mg, is not found in D. The rendering of h is in any case probably free, but the conjectural restoration di[miserun]t is doubtful. The older conjecture di[scedere] seems, however, to be forbidden by the following t, and by the fact that a transitive verb is required by the following eos.

19 The addition και διαλεγομενων αυτων . . . ψευδονται, found not in D d but in C 81 minn h hcl.mg, gives the 'Western' paraphrase; the early Latin translators in part failed to understand the Greek, taking αυτων to refer to the Jews, in part indulged in their habitual freedom. After ψευδονται (which closes the passage in C 81 minn) the 'Western' text seems to have continued with και επισεισαντες τους οχλους και λιθασαντες τον παυλον (so hcl.mg ; h substantially the same, freely rendered). επεισεισαντες D (cf. d gig e pesh) is a survival from this text, not a mere corruption of πεισαντες, as might at first be supposed.
The suggestion of Zahn that the

15 | καὶ φωνοῦντες· Ἄνδρες, τί ταῦτα ποιεῖτε; ἡμεῖς ὁμοιοπαθεῖς
ἐσμὲν ὑμεῖν ἄνθρωποι, εὐαγγελιζόμενοι ὑμεῖν τὸν θεὸν ὅπως
ἀπὸ τούτων τῶν ματαίων ἐπιστρέψητε ἐπὶ τὸν θεὸν ζῶντα τὸν
ποιήσαντα τὸν οὐρανὸν καὶ τὴν γῆν καὶ τὴν θάλασσαν καὶ πάντα
16 τὰ ἐν αὐτοῖς· ὃ‹ς› ἐν ταῖς παρῳχημέναις γενεαῖς εἴασε πάντα τὰ
17 ἔθνη πορεύεσθαι ταῖς ὁδοῖς αὐτῶν· καίγε οὐκ ἀμάρτυρον ἀφῆκεν
ἑαυτὸν ἀγαθοποιῶν, οὐρανόθεν ὑμεῖν ὑετοὺς διδοὺς καὶ καιροὺς
καρποφόρους, ἐνπιμπλῶν τροφῆς καὶ εὐφροσύνης καρδίας ὑμῶν.
18 καὶ ταῦτα λέγοντες μόγις κατέπαυσαν τοὺς ὄχλους τοῦ μὴ θύειν
19 αὐτοῖς. διατριβόντων αὐτῶν καὶ διδασκόντων ἐπῆλθόν τινες

15 ποιειται   ομοιοιπαηθεις   επιστρεψηται
16 παντα] κατα

---

et exilierunt ad turbas clamantes 15 et vociferantes viri quid haec facitis nos d
patientes sumus vobis hominibus evangelizamus vobis dm ut ab his vanis convertamini ad d̄m̄ vivum qui fecit caelum et terram et mare et omnia quae in eis sunt
16 qui in praeteritis saeculis sanavit omnes gentes ambulate vias suas 17 et quidem
non sine testimonio reliquid se ipsū benefaciens de caelo vobis imbrens dans et
tempora fructifera implens civo et jucunditate corda vestra 18 et haec dicentes et
conpescuerunt turbas ne sibi immolarent 19 moras facientes eos et docentes super-

---

ad plebem. 15 [et clamā]tes dicebant : viri, quid haec facitis ? nos ho[mines h
su]mus vestri corporis, nuntiantes vobis d[. . . . . con]vertamini ad eum
qui fecit caelum et terrā, [mare et] omnia quae in eis sunt : 16 qui praeteritis tempo[ribus di]misi omni gentis hominum ire in viam suam. 17 [et non
int]estabilem dimisit se, sed magis benefecit, dans [vobis plu]biam dae caelo et
tempora fructuosa, adimplens [cibo et ju]cunditate corda vestra. 18 et haec
dicentes, [vix persu]aserunt ne inmolarent sibi illi homines : et di[miserun]t
eos ab se. 19 et cum ibi commorarentur et doce[rent, supe]rvenerunt quidam

---

15 nos similes vobis sumus homines, evangelizantes vobis deum, uti ab eis Irenaeus,
vanis simulacris convertamini ad deum vivum, qui fecit caelum et terram, mare iii. 12, 9 (12)
et omnia quae in eis sunt : 16 qui in praeteritis temporibus permisit omnes
gentes abire vias suas, 17 quamquam non sine testimonio semetipsum reliquit
benefaciens, de caelo dans vobis pluvias et tempora fructifera, adimplens cibo et
hilaritate corda vestra.

---

18 λεγοντες] mg [quum] dixissent   του μη θνειν αυτοις] + mg sed abire Harclean
quemque ad sua   19 διατριβοντων . . . πολεως] mg quum commorarentur
autem et docerent, venerunt contra eos Judaei ab Iconio et ab Antiochia, et cum
fiducia loquentes persuaserunt turbis discedere ab iis, dicentes quod nihil veri
dicerent sed omnia falso affirmarent. quum excitassent turbas et lapidassent
Paulum, traxerunt eum extra civitatem

---

addition in C, etc., is a part of the
B-text which fell out by an early
homoeoteleuton (επεισαν τους οχλους
. . . επισεισαντες τους οχλους) is made
less probable by the inclusion in C

etc. of the preceding words διαλεγομενων αυτων παρρησια, which do not
fall within the homoeoteleuton, and
by the fact that C elsewhere contains
survivals of the 'Western' paraphrase.

πείσαντες τοὺς ὄχλους καὶ λιθάσαντες τὸν Παῦλον ἔσυρον ἔξω
τῆς πόλεως, νομίζοντες αὐτὸν τεθνηκέναι. κυκλωσάντων δὲ τῶν 20
μαθητῶν αὐτὸν ἀναστὰς εἰσῆλθεν εἰς τὴν πόλιν. καὶ τῇ ἐπαύριον
ἐξῆλθεν σὺν τῷ Βαρνάβᾳ εἰς Δέρβην. εὐαγγελισάμενοί τε τὴν 21
πόλιν ἐκείνην καὶ μαθητεύσ‹αντες› ἱκανοὺς ὑπέστρεψαν εἰς τὴν
Λύστραν καὶ εἰς Εἰκόνιον καὶ ᾽Αντιόχειαν, ἐπιστηρίζοντες τὰς 22
ψυχὰς τῶν μαθητῶν, παρακαλοῦντες ἐμμένειν τῇ πίστει καὶ ὅτι
διὰ πολλῶν θλείψεων δεῖ ἡμᾶς εἰσελθεῖν εἰς τὴν βασιλείαν τοῦ
θεοῦ. χειροτονήσαντες δὲ αὐτοῖς κατ᾽ ἐκκλησίαν πρεσβυτέρους 23
προσευξάμενοι μετὰ νηστειῶν παρέθεντο αὐτοὺς τῷ κυρίῳ εἰς
ὃν πεπιστεύκεισαν. καὶ διελθόντες τὴν Πισιδίαν ἦλθαν εἰς τὴν 24
Παμφυλίαν, καὶ λαλήσαντες ἐν Πέργῃ τὸν λόγον κατέβησαν εἰς 25
᾽Ατταλίαν, | κἀκεῖθεν εἰς ᾽Αντιόχειαν, ὅθεν ἦσαν παραδεδομένοι 26

Editors 21 αντιοχειαν] [εις] αντιοχειαν WH εις αντιοχειαν Soden JHR 25 εν περγη] εις την περγην WHmg JHR λογον] +του κυριου Soden 26 κακειθεν] +απεπλευσαν WH Soden JHR

Old Uncial 19 πεισαντες τους οχλους ΒΑ και διαλεγομενων αυτων παρρησια επεισαν (81 ανεπεισαν) τους οχλους αποστηναι απ αυτων λεγοντες οτι ουδεν αληθες λεγουσιν αλλα παντα ψευδονται C 81 λιθασαντες ΒΝC 81 (+D) λιθοβοληϲαντες A εξω ΒΑCΝ° 81 (+D) om Ν νομιζοντες ΒΝΑ 81 (+D) νομισαντες C 20–21 om και τη επαυριον . . . την πολιν Ν (Ν° suppl) 21 ευαγγελισαμενοι ΒCΝ° 81 ευαγγελιζομενοι Α(+D) μαθητευσαντες Β² αντιοχειαν Β 81 (+D) εις αντιοχειαν ΝΑC 22 παρακαλουντες ΒΝΑ 81 και παρακαλουντες C παρακαλουντες τε Ν°(+D) 24 διελθοντες ΒΑC 81 (+D) +εις Ν την 2° ΒΝC 81 om Α(+D) 25 εν περγη ΒΝ°(+D) εις περγην Α εις την περγην Ν 81 λογον Β(+D) +του κυριου ΝΑC 81 26 κακειθεν Β +απεπλευσαν Β²ΝΑC 81 (+D)

Antiochian 19 νομισαντες HLPSϛ τεθναναι HLPSϛ(+D) 20 αυτον (αυτων LS) των μαθητων HLPSϛ εξηλθεν] εισηλθεν H 21 ευαγγελιζομενοι HP(+D) om εις 2° HLPSϛ(+D) 23 πρεσβυτερους κατ εκκλησιαν HLPSϛ αυτους] αυτοις L 24 om την 2° HLPSϛ(+D) 26 κακειθεν] +απεπλευσαν LPSϛ(+D) +ανεπλευσαν H

20 In h *dicentes* is an error for *discentes*. For [*cum disce*]*ssisset* another conjectural restoration is [*cum surre*]*sisset*. With this latter, *populus* is an error for *paulus*, as in vss. 9 and 12, and the clause is repeated in *levavit se*. The clause in h is not otherwise attested. Possibly *circumdederunt* may explain the impossible κυκλωσαντες of D d, in which MS. the 'Western' text may have been badly conformed to the B-text. αυτον D d e (E αυτον των μαθητων αυτον) finds no support in h and is probably an early error for αυτον.

The addition of *vespere* h is found also in sah and, in much expanded form, in Ephrem's Commentary (below, p. 420).

In Codex Bezae Blass (*St. Kr.*, 1898, p. 541) suggests ο[υ]τω for Scrivener's [συν] τω, partly on the ground of space.

21 ευαγγελιζομενοι A D Antiochian is probably due to an incomplete conformation of a 'Western' ευηγγελιζετο [-οντο ?] (cf. h) to the text of BC 81 L ευαγγελισαμενοι (Ν is here lacking by a homoeoteleuton). As between the

Ἰουδαῖοι ἀπὸ Ἰκονίου καὶ Ἀντιοχίας, καὶ ἐπισείσαντες τοὺς
ὄχλους καὶ λιθάσαντες τὸν Παῦλον ἔσυραν ἔξω τῆς πόλεως,
20 νομίζοντες τεθνάναι αὐτόν. κυκλωσάντων δὲ τῶν μαθητῶν
αὐτοῦ ἀναστὰς εἰσῆλθεν εἰς τὴν Λύστραν πόλιν. καὶ τὴν ἐπ-
21 αύριον ἐξῆλθεν [σὺν] τῷ Βαρνάβᾳ εἰς Δέρβην. εὐαγγελιζόμενοι
δὲ τοὺς ἐν τῇ πόλει καὶ μαθητεύσαντες πολλοὺς ὑπέστρεφον
22 εἰς Λύστραν καὶ Εἰκόνιον καὶ Ἀντιόχειαν, ἐπιστηρίζοντες τὰς
ψυχὰς τῶν μαθητῶν, παρακαλοῦντές τε ἐμμένειν τῇ πίστει καὶ
ὅτι διὰ πολλῶν θλείψεων δ‹ε›ῖ ἡμᾶς ἐλθεῖν εἰς τὴν βασιλείαν
23 τοῦ θεοῦ. χειροτονήσαντες δὲ αὐτοῖς κατὰ ἐκκλησίαν πρεσβυτέρους προσευξάμενοι δὲ μετὰ νηστειῶν παρέθεντο αὐτοὺς τῷ
24 κυρίῳ εἰς ὃν πεπιστεύκασιν. διελθόντες δὲ τὴν Πισιδίαν ἦλθαν
25 εἰς Παμφυλίαν, καὶ λαλήσαντες ἐν Πέργῃ τὸν λόγον κατέβησαν
26 εἰς Ἀτταλίαν εὐαγγελιζόμενοι αὐτούς, κἀκεῖθεν ἀπέπλευσαν
εἰς Ἀντιόχειαν, ὅθεν ἦσαν παραδεδομένοι τῇ χάριτι τοῦ θεοῦ

19 επεισεισαντες   20 κυκλωσαντες

---

venerunt autem judaei ab iconio et antiochia et cum istigassent turbam et lapidassent d
paulum traxerunt extra civitatem existimantes mortuum esse eum   20 circueuntes
enim discipuli ejus cum surrexisset introibit in lystram civitate et altera die exivit
cum barnaban derben   21 evangelizantes autem in illa civitate et discipulos fecissent
plures reversi sunt lystram et iconium et antiochiam   22 confirmantes enim animas
discipulorum exhortantes ut permanerent in fidem et quia per multas conflictationes
oportet nos introire in regnum d̄ī   23 et cum ordinassent illis per ecclesias presbyteros orantes autem cum jejunationibus conmendaverunt eos d̄o in quem crediderunt
24 regressi autem pisidiam venerunt in pamphyliam   25 et locuti aput pergen
verbum descenderunt in attaliam evangelizantes eos   26 et inde enavigarunt antio-

---

Judaei ab Iconia et Antio[chia, qui] palam disputabant verbum d̄ī.   persuade- h
bant [illis ho]minib· ne crederent eis docentibus, dicentes [quia nihil] veri
dicunt sed in omnibus mentiuntur. [et concita]berunt turbam, ut lapidarent
Paulum : quē [trahente]s foras·extra civitatem, putaberunt eum esse [mortuum].
20 tunc circumdederunt eum dicentes, et [cum disce]ssisset populus vespere,
levavit se, et intro[ivit civit]atem Lystrum, et altera die exibit cum Barna[ban
in] Derben.   21 ec bene nuntiavit eis qui erant in [civita]te, et docuerunt
multos.   tunc reversi sunt [Lystra] et Iconium et Antiochiam,   22· confortantes
ani[mas disce]ntium, et rogantes eos permanere in fide, [dicentes] quia per
multas tribulationes oportebit vos [introire] regnum d̄ī.   23 et constituerunt
eis majores na[tu]

---

22 και] +mg dicentes   25 τον λογον] verbum ⁝ domini √   ευαγγελι- Harclean
ζομενοι αυτους] ⁝ evangelizantes iis √

---

two participles, the aorist alone yields   22 For hcl.mg cf. λεγοντες 1611
a possible sense.   h^vid.

τῇ χάριτι τοῦ θεοῦ εἰς τὸ ἔργον ὃ ἐπλήρωσαν. παραγενόμενοι 27
δὲ καὶ συναγαγόντες τὴν ἐκκλησίαν ἀνήγγελλον ὅσα ἐποίησεν ὁ
θεὸς μετ᾽ αὐτῶν καὶ ὅτι ἤνοιξεν τοῖς ἔθνεσιν θύραν πίστεως.
διέτρειβον δὲ χρόνον οὐκ ὀλίγον σὺν τοῖς μαθηταῖς. 28
Καί τινες κατελθόντες ἀπὸ τῆς Ἰουδαίας ἐδίδασκον τοὺς XV
ἀδελφοὺς ὅτι Ἐὰν μὴ περιτμηθῆτε τῷ ἔθει τῷ Μωυσέως, οὐ
δύνασθε σωθῆναι. γενομένης δὲ στάσεως καὶ ζητήσεως οὐκ 2
ὀλίγης τῷ Παύλῳ καὶ τῷ Βαρνάβᾳ πρὸς αὐτοὺς ἔταξαν ἀναβαίνειν
Παῦλον καὶ Βαρνάβαν καί τινας ἄλλους ἐξ αὐτῶν πρὸς τοὺς
ἀποστόλους καὶ πρεσβυτέρους εἰς Ἰερουσαλὴμ περὶ τοῦ ζητήματος

---

1 περιτμηθῆτε] περιθμητε

Editors   2 om εξ αυτων JHR

Old Uncial   27 συναγαγοντες BℵAC (cf. D)   συναγοντες 81   εποιησεν ο θεος BAC 81
     ο θεος εποιησεν ℵ(+D)   28 ουκ BℵAC(+D)   om 81   1 περιτμηθητε
     B²(B³ Tdf)   εθει BAC 81 (+D)   εθνι ℵ   δυνασθε BℵA 81 (+D)
     δυνησησθαι C   2 δε BℵC 81 (+D)   ουν A   αλλους εξ αυτων BAC 81
     εξ αυτων αλλους ℵ   πρεσβυτερους BℵA 81 (+D)   τους πρεσβυτερους C

Antiochian   27 ανηγγειλαν HLPSς(+D)   28 δε] +εκει HLPSς   1 περιτεμνησθε
     HLPSς   om τω 2° HLPSς(+D)   2 δε] ουν HPSς
     ζητησεως] συζητησεως ς

---

27 The reading μετα των ψυχων αυτων D d gig cannot be explained except from Semitic influence of some kind, which is, however, equally present in μετ αυτων of the usual text. The difficulty in the way of the simple explanation that μετα των ψυχων αυτων is the original direct translation from Aramaic, later softened to μετ αυτων, is that the corresponding Aramaic would mean, not 'with them,' but 'with *themselves*' (reflexive or emphatic), while here no such emphasis is admissible. That is, the reading of D looks like either imitation of Aramaic or the result of some still more complicated process. The preceding αυτοις (D d, not represented in gig) cannot easily be explained as due to conflation, since no other known text has αυτοις ; cf. the similar superfluous αυτοις in xiv. 2 D. Both may well be due to the Aramaic proleptic pronoun ; cf. also αυτοις xv. 2 D d, and see Torrey, *Composition and Date of Acts*, p. 38, where, however, the more difficult problem of xiv. 27 is not discussed.

1-5 The narrative of vss. 1-5 was extensively and consistently rewritten in the ' Western ' text at several points. All the more important ' Western ' readings have been preserved in hcl. *mg.* or hcl ⁜ ; all but one (vs. 1, + των πεπιστευκοτων απο της αιρεσεως των φαρισαιων) in D d. Some of these are still found in other Greek and in Latin codices and in Ephrem. The distinctive general picture of the course of events on the part of the ' Western ' reviser is noteworthy ; and seems inconsistent with any hypothesis of identity of authorship for the two forms of the text. As between the two texts the B-text is clearly the more original. Many minor variants cannot be referred to here.

One leading motive for rewriting was to obviate the strange lack of sequence by which in the B-text the controversy at Jerusalem is introduced in vs. 5 quite as if no previous controversy at Antioch had just been described. The ' Western ' text, moreover, enhances the importance of the Judaean Christians by stating that they (rather than the Antiochian church, as in the B-text) urged that

27 εἰς τὸ ἔργον ὃ ἐπλήρωσαν. παραγενόμενοι δὲ καὶ συνάξαντες τὴν ἐκκλησείαν ἀνήγγειλαν ὅσα ὁ θεὸς ἐποίησεν αὐτοῖς μετὰ τῶν ψυχῶν αὐτῶν καὶ ὅτι ἤνοιξε τοῖς ἔθνεσιν θύραν πίστεως. 28 διέτριβον δὲ χρόνον οὐκ ὀλίγον σὺν τοῖς μαθηταῖς.

XV Καί τινες κατελθόντες ἀπὸ τῆς Ἰουδαίας ἐδίδασκον τοὺς ἀδελφοὺς ὅτι Ἐὰν μὴ περιτμηθῆτε καὶ τῷ ἔθει Μωσέως περι- 2 πατῆτε, οὐ δύνασθε σωθῆναι. γενομένης δὲ στάσεως καὶ ζητή- σεως οὐκ ὀλίγης τῷ Παύλῳ καὶ Βαρνάβᾳ σὺν αὐτοῖς, ἔλεγεν γὰρ ὁ Παῦλος μένειν οὕτως καθὼς ἐπίστευσαν διισχυριζόμενος, οἱ δὲ ἐληλυθότες ἀπὸ Ἰερουσαλήμ παρήγγειλαν αὐτοῖς τῷ Παύλῳ καὶ Βαρνάβᾳ καί τισιν ἄλλοις ἀναβαίνειν πρὸς τοὺς ἀποστόλους καὶ πρεσβυτέρους εἰς Ἰερουσαλήμ ὅπως κριθῶσιν ἐπ' αὐτοῖς

27 ανηγγειλον   ηνυξε   2 στασεως] εκτασεως

chiam unde erant traditi in cratia d̄ī ad opus quod inpleverunt   27 cum advenissent d autem et collegissent ecclesiam renuntiaverunt quae d̄s fecit illis cum animabus eorum et quia aperuit gentibus osteum fidei   28 demorabantur vero tempus non modicum cum discipulis
1 et quidam cum advenissent a judaea docebant fratres quia non circumcisi fueritis et more moysi ambulaveritis non potestes salvi fieri   2 facta ergo seditione et questione non modica a paulo et barnaba ad eos dicebat autem paulus manere sic sicut crediderunt qui autem venerunt ab hierusalem statuerunt eis paulo et barnabae et quosdam alios ascendere apostolos et presbyteros in hierusalem ut judicent super

1 ιουδαιας] +mg ex illis qui crediderunt de haeresi Pharisaeorum   και 2°] Harclean mg quoque   περιπατητε] mg ambuletis   2 ελεγεν . . . αποστολους] mg dicebat enim Paulus manere ita sicut quis crediderit firmiter. illi autem qui venerant ab Hierosolyma jusserunt tunc Paulum et Barnabam et quosdam alios ascendere ad apostolos   οπως κριθωσιν επ αυτοις] ⋇· ut dijudicarentur coram iis ✓

Paul and Barnabas should go up to Jerusalem, and that the purpose was the trial of the case before (literally, ' in the presence of') the apostles and elders at Jerusalem.

1 The designation of the brethren arriving from Judaea as former Pharisees (614 minn hcl.mg) was drawn from vs. 5, and it seems to have been intended that it should there be omitted. In D d hcl.mg it was restored in vs. 5, and in D d, consistently, dropped in vs. 1. The text of D d in vs. 5 is a crude and easily recognizable conflation, and clearly reveals what has taken place. See Conybeare's note on the text of Ephrem (below, pp. 423, 425).

2 (a) The addition ελεγεν γαρ . . . διισχυριζομενος (cf. 1 Cor. vii. 8, 20, 24, 40, which is probably the source of the addition) is found with some

variation of language in D d gig w vg.codd hcl.mg, and Ephrem. Nowhere is it introduced after the genitive absolute with complete grammatical success (d vg.codd dicebat autem ; D ελεγεν γαρ ; gig hcl.mg 'for'); and a conflation (not, however, peculiar to D) may be suspected. διισχυριζομενος was nowhere adopted save in D and in hcl.mg (where it is represented by an adverb).

(b) οι δε εληλυθοτες . . . και τισιν αλλοις seems to be an integral part of this gloss, but is found only in D d hcl.mg, although it is implied in Ephrem and autem gig is perhaps a surviving trace of it. αυτοις D d (εις) is not easily explained.

(c) οπως κριθωσιν επ αυτοις D d 614 minn (επ αυτων) hcl·⋇· Ephrem.

(d) αλλους εξ αυτων] εξ αυτων αλλους

τούτου. οἱ μὲν οὖν προπεμφθέντες ὑπὸ τῆς ἐκκλησίας διήρχοντο 3 τήν τε Φοινίκην καὶ Σαμαρείαν ἐκδιηγούμενοι τὴν ἐπιστροφὴν τῶν ἐθνῶν, καὶ ἐποίουν χαρὰν μεγάλην πᾶσι τοῖς ἀδελφοῖς. παραγενόμενοι δὲ εἰς Ἱεροσόλυμα παρεδέχθησαν ἀπὸ τῆς ἐκ- 4 κλησίας καὶ τῶν ἀποστόλων καὶ τῶν πρεσβυτέρων, ἀνήγγειλάν τε ὅσα ὁ θεὸς ἐποίησεν μετ᾽ αὐτῶν. ἐξανέστησαν δέ τινες τῶν 5 ἀπὸ τῆς αἱρέσεως τῶν Φαρεισαίων πεπιστευκότες, λέγοντες ὅτι δεῖ περιτέμνειν αὐτοὺς παραγγέλλειν τε τηρεῖν τὸν νόμον Μωυσέως. Συνήχθησάν τε οἱ ἀπόστολοι καὶ οἱ πρεσβύτεροι ἰδεῖν περὶ 6 τοῦ λόγου τούτου. πολλῆς δὲ ζητήσεως γενομένης ἀναστὰς 7 Πέτρος εἶπεν πρὸς αὐτούς· Ἄνδρες ἀδελφοί, ὑμεῖς ἐπίστασθε ὅτι ἀφ᾽ ἡμερῶν ἀρχαίων ἐν ὑμῖν ἐξελέξατο ὁ θεὸς διὰ τοῦ στόματός μου ἀκοῦσαι τὰ ἔθνη τὸν λόγον τοῦ εὐαγγελίου καὶ πιστεῦσαι, καὶ ὁ 8 καρδιογνώστης θεὸς ἐμαρτύρησεν αὐτοῖς δοὺς τὸ πνεῦμα τὸ

Editors   4 απο] υπο Soden   8 δους] +[αυτοις] Soden

Old Uncial   3 τε BℵC 81 (+D) om A   εκδιηγουμενοι BACℵª 81 (+D)
διηγουμενοι ℵ   4 ιεροσολυμα BA 81   ιερουσαλημ ℵC(+D)   παρεδεχθησαν
BℵA 81 (cf. D)   απεδεχθησαν μεγαλως C(+D)   απο BC   υπο ℵA 81 (+D)
και 1º BACℵª 81 (+D)   om ℵ   τε BACℵº 81 (+D)   om ℵ   ο θεος εποιησεν
μετ αυτων BℵAC   εποιησεν μετ αυτων ο θεος 81 (cf. D)   5 τινες BℵC 81 (+D)
+ανδρες A   6 τε BC 81   δε ℵA(+D)   7 δε BℵAC(+D)   τε 81
ζητησεως BℵA 81   συνζητησεως C(+D)   οτι BACℵº 81 (+D)   om ℵ
8 εμαρτυρησεν BℵA 81 (+D)   διεμαρτυρησεν C   δους;BℵA 81   +αυτοις C
(cf. D)

Antiochian   3 om τε HLPSϚ   την σαμαριαν HS(+D)   om πασι S
4 ιερουσαλημ HLPSϚ(+D)   παρεδεχθησαν] απεδεχθησαν HLPSϚ
απο] υπο HLPSϚ(+D)   αυτων] +και οτι ηνοιξεν τοις εθνεσιν θυραν πιστεως HL
5 πεπιστευκοτων L   6 τε] δε HLPSϚ(+D)   7 ζητησεως] συνζητησεως
HLPSϚ(+D)   εν υμιν εξελεξατο ο θεος] ο θεος εν ημιν εξελεξατο HLPSϚ
om τον λογον P   8 δους] +αυτοις HLPSϚ (cf. D)

ℵ. This variation in order and the absence of anything corresponding to εξ αυτων in the ‘Western’ paraphrase lead to the suspicion that εξ αυτων did not form a part of the original text. Possibly the translation of the Peshitto, ‘with them,’ is evidence in the same direction.

5 In the face of οι δε παραγγειλαντες . . . πρεσβυτερους D d hcl.mg, the words from the B-text τινες . . . πεπιστευκοτες ought not to appear in the ‘Western’ text, which had sufficiently described these persons in vs. 1 (so 614 minn hcl.mg). In

hcl.mg the roughness of the text produced by the conflation is somewhat reduced; in D d the glaring incongruity is left unrelieved. Const. Apost. vi. 12 (see above, pp. cxciii-viii) does not refer to ‘Pharisees’ in its résumé of vs. 5, and probably follows the thoroughly ‘Western’ text of the original Didascalia (modified in the extant Syriac translation). Ephrem (Catena, see below, p. 423, with Conybeare’s note) seems to imply for vs. 1 a text like that of D, and gives no indication that his text mentioned ‘Pharisees’ in vs. 5.

3 περὶ τοῦ ζητήματος τούτου. οἱ μὲν οὖν προπεμφθέντες ὑπὸ
τῆς ἐκκλησίας διήρχοντο τήν τε Φοινίκην καὶ τὴν Σαμαρίαν
ἐκδιηγούμενοι τὴν ἐπιστροφὴν τῶν ἐθνῶν, καὶ ἐποίουν χαρὰν
4 μεγάλην πᾶσιν τοῖς ἀδελφοῖς. παραγενόμενοι δὲ εἰς Ἱερουσαλὴμ παρεδέχθησαν μεγάλως ὑπὸ τῆς ἐκκλησίας καὶ τῶν
ἀποστόλων καὶ τῶν πρεσβυτέρων, †ἀπηγγειλαντες† ὅσα ἐποίησεν
5 ὁ θεὸς μετ᾽ αὐτῶν. οἱ δὲ παραγγείλαντες αὐτοῖς ἀναβαίνειν
πρὸς τοὺς πρεσβυτέρους ἐξανέστησαν λέγοντές †τινες ἀπὸ τῆς
αἱρέσεως τῶν Φαρισαίων πεπιστευκότες† ὅτι δεῖ περιτέμνειν
αὐτοὺς παραγγέλλειν δὲ τηρεῖν τὸν νόμον Μωσέως.
6 Συνήχθησαν δὲ οἱ ἀπόστολοι καὶ πρεσβύτεροι ἰδεῖν περὶ τοῦ
7 λόγου τούτου. πολλῆς δὲ συνζητήσεως γενομένης ἀνέστ[η]σεν
ἐν πνεύματι Πέτρος καὶ εἶπεν πρὸς αὐτούς· Ἄνδρες ἀδελφοί,
ὑμεῖς ἐπίστασθε ὅτι ἀφ᾽ ἡμερῶν ἀρχαίων ἡμεῖν ὁ θεὸς ἐξελέξατο
διὰ στόματός μου ἀκοῦσαι τὰ ἔθνη τὸν λόγον τοῦ εὐαγγελίου καὶ
8 πιστεῦσαι, ὁ δὲ καρδιογνώστης ὁ θεὸς ἐμαρτύρησεν αὐτοῖς δοὐ‹ς›

4 παρεδεχθησαν] παρεδοθησαν   5 αιρεσεως] ερεσεως
7 επιστασθαι

---

eos de questione hanc 3 illi quidem praemissi ab ecclesia regrediebantur phoenicem **d**
et samariam exponentes reversionem gentium et efficiebat gaudium magnum omnibus
fratribus 4 cum pervenissent autem hierusalem excepti sunt mirae ab ecclesia et
apostolis et presbyteris renuntiaverunt quanta fecit d̄s̄ cum illis 5 qui autem praeceperunt eis ascendere ad praesbyteros surrexerunt dicentes quidam de heresim
pharisaeorum crediderunt quia oportet circumcidi eos praecipiendumquae serbari
legem moysi 6 convenerunt autem apostoli et praesbyteri videre de sermone hoc
7 et cum multa altercatio fieret surrexit in s̄p̄o petrus et dixit ad eos viri fratres vos
scitis quia a diebus antiquis in nobis d̄s̄ elegit per os meum audire gentes verbum
evangelii et credere 8 qui autem corda nobit d̄s̄ testimonium perhibuit eis dedit

---

7 Petrus dixit eis : viri fratres, vos scitis quoniam a diebus antiquis in vobis Irenaeus,
deus elegit, ut ex ore meo audirent gentes verbum evangelii et crederent : 8 et iii. 12, 14 (17)
cordis inspector deus testimonium perhibuit eis, dans eis spiritum sanctum

---

4 μεγ‹αλ›ως] ⁙ magnifice ✓   5 οι δε παραγγειλαντες . . . πεπιστευκοτες] Harclean
mg illi autem quum jussissent eos ascendere ad seniores surrexerunt adversus
apostolos, quum essent illi qui credidissent de haeresi Pharisaeorum   6 πρε-
σβυτεροι] *text* seniores cum multis   7 εν πνευματι] *mg* in spiritu sancto

---

6 πρεσβυτεροι] +συν τω πληθει 614   (Catena, below, p. 425) both had the
minₙ hcl.*text* Ephrem (Catena, below,   gloss.
p. 425) ; probably 'Western,' plainly   εν υμιν BℵAC 81 Iren vg.*cod.ard-*
suggested by vs. 22.   *mach* is probably right. The change
7 Like hcl.*mg*, 614 257 read εν   to εν ημιν Antiochian gig Rebapt vg
πνευματι αγιω, placing the words after   was easy. Pesh sah omit. Cf.
πετρος ; similarly D d have εν πνευματι   Torrey, *Composition and Date of Acts*,
before πετρος. Tertullian and Ephrem   pp. 21 f.

ἅγιον καθὼς καὶ ἡμῖν, καὶ οὐθὲν διέκρεινεν μεταξὺ ἡμῶν τε καὶ 9
αὐτῶν, τῇ πίστει καθαρίσας τὰς καρδίας αὐτῶν. νῦν οὖν τί 10
πειράζετε τὸν θεόν, ἐπιθεῖναι ζυγὸν ἐπὶ τὸν τράχηλον τῶν μαθητῶν ὃν οὔτε οἱ πατέρες ἡμῶν οὔτε ἡμεῖς ἰσχύσαμεν βαστάσαι;
ἀλλὰ διὰ τῆς χάριτος τοῦ κυρίου Ἰησοῦ πιστεύομεν σωθῆναι 11
καθ' ὃν τρόπον κἀκεῖνοι. ἐσείγησεν δὲ πᾶν τὸ πλῆθος, καὶ 12
ἤκουον Βαρνάβα καὶ Παύλου ἐξηγουμένων ὅσα ἐποίησεν ὁ θεὸς
σημεῖα καὶ τέρατα ἐν τοῖς ἔθνεσιν δι' αὐτῶν. μετὰ δὲ τὸ σειγῆσαι 13
αὐτοὺς ἀπεκρίθη Ἰάκωβος λέγων· "Ἄνδρες ἀδελφοί, ἀκούσατέ
μου. Συμεὼν ἐξηγήσατο καθὼς πρῶτον ὁ θεὸς ἐπεσκέψατο 14
λαβεῖν ἐξ ἐθνῶν λαὸν τῷ ὀνόματι αὐτοῦ. καὶ τούτῳ συμφωνοῦσιν 15
Jer. xii. 15 οἱ λόγοι τῶν προφητῶν, καθὼς γέγραπται· Μετὰ ταῦτα ἀνα- 16
Amos ix. στρέψω καὶ ἀνοικοδομήσω τὴν σκηνὴν Δαυεὶδ τὴν πεπτωκυῖαν
11 f. καὶ τὰ κατεστρεμμένα αὐτῆς ἀνοικοδομήσω καὶ ἀνορθώσω αὐτήν,

---

Editors   9 ουθεν] ουδεν WHmg Soden   11 αλλα] αλλ η JHR   15 τουτω]
            ουτως JHR   16 κατεστρεμμενα] κατεσκαμμενα Soden

Old Uncial   9 και 1° BℵC 81 (+D)   ουθεν B   ουδεν ℵAC 81 (+D)   10 ουν
            BℵA 81 (+D)   om Cᵛⁱᵈ   ζυγον Bℵ*A 81 (+D)   om ℵ   11 ιησου BℵA 81
            +χριστου C(+D)   πιστευομεν BAC 81   πιστευσομεν ℵ(+D)   12 εσειγησεν BℵA
            81 (+D)   εσιγησαν C   εξηγουμενων BℵAC   εξηγουμενου 81   14 λαβειν εξ εθνων
            BℵA 81 (+D)   εξ εθνων λαβειν C   16 κατεστρεμμενα Bℵ   κατεσκαμμενα
            AC 81 (+D)   ανοικοδομησω 2° BℵA 81 (+D)   οικοδομησω Cᵛⁱᵈ

Antiochian   9 ουθεν] ουδεν ϛ(+D)   11 om του Hϛ   ιησου] +χριστου ϛ(+D)
            14 λαον] +επι HLPSϛ   15 τουτο HL   16 κατεστρεμμενα] κατ-
            εσκαμμενα LPSϛ(+D)   σκαμμενα H

---

11 αλλ η 614 minn (i.e. ἀλλ' ἤ, 'but
in fact') appears to be represented
by sed enim Tert, and may give the
proper 'Western' text. If so, it is
perhaps to be preferred to αλλα of

the B-text; cf. Lk. xii. 51 and v.l.
there.
15 ουτως D d gig Iren sah may be
the original which has given rise to
τουτω BℵAC 81 vg, τουτο HL.

9 ἐπ' αὐτοὺς τὸ πνεῦμα τὸ ἅγιον καθὼς καὶ ἡμεῖν, καὶ οὐδὲν διέκρεινεν μεταξὺ ἡμῶν καὶ αὐτῶν, τῇ πίστει καθαρίσας τὰς καρ-
10 δίας αὐτῶν. νῦν οὖν τί π‹ε›ιράζετε τὸν θεόν, ἐπιθεῖναι ζυγὸν ἐπὶ
τὸν τράχηλον τῶν μαθητῶν ὃν οὔτε οἱ πατέρες ἡμῶν οὔτε ἡμεῖς
11 ἰσχύσαμεν βαστάσαι; ἀλλὰ διὰ τῆς χάριτος τοῦ κυρίου Ἰησοῦ
12 Χριστοῦ πιστεύσομεν σωθῆναι καθ' ὃν τρόπον κἀκεῖνοι. συν-
κατατεθεμένων δὲ τῶν πρεσβυτέρων τοῖς ὑπὸ τοῦ Πέτρου εἰρημένοις ἐσείγησεν πᾶν τὸ πλῆθος, καὶ ἤκουον Βαρνάβαν καὶ Παῦλον
ἐξηγουμένους ὅσα ἐποίησεν ὁ θεὸς σημεῖα καὶ τέρατα ἐν τοῖς
13 ἔθνεσιν δι' αὐτῶν. μετὰ δὲ τὸ σειγῆσαι αὐτοὺς ἀναστὰς Ἰάκω-
14 βος εἶπεν· Ἄνδρες ἀδελφοί, ἀκούσατέ μου. Συμεὼν ἐξηγήσατο
καθὼς πρῶτον ὁ θεὸς ἐπεσκέψατο λαβεῖν ἐξ ἐθνῶν λαὸν τῷ ὀνό-
15 ματι αὐτοῦ. καὶ οὕτως συνφωνήσουσιν οἱ λόγοι τῶν προφητῶν,
16 καθὼς γέγραπται· Μετὰ δὲ ταῦτα ἐπιστρέψω καὶ ἀνοικοδομήσω
τὴν σκηνὴν Δαυεὶδ τὴν πεπτωκυῖαν καὶ τὰ κατεσκαμμένα αὐτῆς

12 ἐξηγουμενοι

---

super eos spm sanctum sicut et nobis   9 et nihil discrevit inter nos et ipsos fidei d
emundatis cordibus eorum   10 nunc ergo quid temptatis dm inponere jugum super
cervices discipulorum quod nequae patres nostri neque nos potuimus bajolare
11 sed per gratiam dni ihu xpi credimus salbi fieri quemadmodum et illi   12 des-
ponentes autem presbyteros quae a petro dicebantur silevitque omnis multitudo et
audiebant barnabam et paulum exponentes quanta fecerit ds signa et prodigia in
gentibus per ipsos   13 postquam autem hii silerunt surgens jacobus dixit viri
fratres audite me   14 symeon exposuit quemadmodum primum ds prospexit
accipere ex gentibus populum nomini suo   15 et sic consonat sermones prophetarum
sicut scriptum est   16 post haec autem convertar et aedificabo tabernaculum david

---

10 [sed et in illa disceptatione custodiendae necne legis primus omnium Tertullian,
Petrus spiritu instinctus et de nationum vocatione praefatus,] et nunc, [inquit,] Pudic. 21
cur temptastis dominum de imponendo jugo fratribus quod neque nos neque
patres nostri sufferre valuerunt? 11 sed enim per gratiam Jesu credimus nos
salutem consecuturos sicut et illi.

---

sicut et nobis,   9 et nihil discrevit inter nos et ipsos, emundans per fidem corda Irenaeus,
illorum.   10 nunc igitur quid temptatis deum, imponere jugum super cervicem iii. 12, 14(17)
discipulorum quod neque patres nostri neque nos valuimus portare?   11 sed
per gratiam domini nostri Jesu Christi credimus nos posse salvari quomodo
et illi.

14 viri fratres, Symeon retulit quemadmodum deus excogitavit accipere ex
gentibus populum nomini suo.   15 et sic conveniunt sermones prophetarum,
sicut scriptum est: 16 post haec revertar, et reaedificabo tabernaculum David

---

10 ουν] igitur ⁒ vos √   12 συνκατατεθεμενων δε των πρεσβυτεροις τοις Harclean
υπο του πετρου ειρημενοις] ⁒ quum assensissent autem simul seniores iis quae a
Petro dicta fuerant √   οσα] ⁒ omnia √ quae

144   CODEX VATICANUS

ὅπως ἂν ἐκζητήσωσιν οἱ κατάλοιποι τῶν ἀνθρώπων τὸν κύριον, 17
καὶ πάντα τὰ ἔθνη ἐφ' οὓς ἐπικέκληται τὸ ὄνομά μου ἐπ' αὐτούς,
λέγει κύριος ποιῶν ταῦτα | γνωστὰ ἀπ' αἰῶνος. | διὸ ἐγὼ κρείνω 18, 19
μὴ παρενοχλεῖν τοῖς ἀπὸ τῶν ἐθνῶν ἐπιστρέφουσιν ἐπὶ τὸν θεόν,
ἀλλ' ἐπιστεῖλαι αὐτοῖς τοῦ ἀπέχεσθαι τῶν ἀλισγημάτων τῶν 20
εἰδώλων καὶ τῆς πορνείας καὶ πνικτοῦ καὶ τοῦ αἵματος· Μωυσῆς 21
γὰρ ἐκ γενεῶν ἀρχαίων κατὰ πόλιν τοὺς κηρύσσοντας αὐτὸν
ἔχει ἐν ταῖς συναγωγαῖς κατὰ πᾶν σάββατον ἀναγεινωσκόμενος.
τότε ἔδοξε τοῖς ἀποστόλοις καὶ τοῖς πρεσβυτέροις σὺν ὅλῃ τῇ 22
ἐκκλησίᾳ ἐκλεξαμένους ἄνδρας ἐξ αὐτῶν πέμψαι εἰς Ἀντιόχειαν
σὺν τῷ Παύλῳ καὶ Βαρνάβᾳ, Ἰούδαν τὸν καλούμενον Βαρσαβ-
βᾶν καὶ Σείλαν, ἄνδρας ἡγουμένους ἐν τοῖς ἀδελφοῖς, | γράψαντες 23

Editors   17 ο ποιων Soden   20 απεχεσθαι] +απο Soden   του πνικτου
Soden   om και πνικτου JHR

Old Uncial   17 ποιων Bℵ   ο ποιων ACℵ° 81   18 γνωστα απ αιωνος BℵC 81   γνωστον
απ αιωνος τω κυριω το εργον αυτου A (cf. D)   20 απεχεσθαι Bℵ 81 (+D)
+απο AC   πνικτου BA 81   του πνικτου ℵC   του αιματος BℵAC(+D)
αιματος 81   21 κατα πολιν τους κηρυσσοντας αυτον BℵA 81 (cf. D)   τους
κηρυσσοντας αυτον κατα πολιν C   22 εξ αυτων BℵC 81 (+D)   om A
ηγουμενους BACℵ° 81 Pap³³ (+D)   ηγουμενοις ℵ

Antiochian   17 ο ποιων HLPSϚ   ταυτα] παντα ταυτα LPS   ταυτα παντα HϚ
18 αιωνος] +εστι τω θεω παντα τα εργα αυτου HLPSϚ (cf. D)   20 om του
1° H   απεχεσθαι] +απο HLPSϚ   του πνικτου HLPSϚ   22 om
τω HLPS(+D)   καλουμενον] επικαλουμενον HPSϚ

---

18 The reading ποιων ταυτα γνωστα απ αιωνος BℵC 81 sah was altered and expanded in the 'Western' text to read γνωστον απ αιωνος εστιν (om εστιν A) τω κυριω (deo Iren ; om τω κυριω hcl.mg) το εργον αυτου A D d Iren vg hcl.mg, perhaps in order thereby to dissociate from the quotation the words γνωστα απ αιωνος, which are not found in Amos ix. 11 f. The Antiochian text seems to have combined the two variant readings, adopting from the B-text the plural (γνωστα, etc.) and making minor changes. With the Antiochian substantially agree gig e (E) pesh ('known from eternity are the works of God'). Minor variants are also found within the B-text and the Antiochian. It is noteworthy that no tendency appears to restore, either here by omission or

in vs. 16 by addition, the precise text of the LXX, from which Acts in fact departs. In vs. 17 ο ποιων ACℵ° 81 Antiochian for ποιων agrees with LXX, but is a natural independent improvement of language.

Of ποιησει D no trace appears elsewhere. It is probably a mere error, perhaps introduced in an attempt to make D conform to the B-text.

20 (a) om και πνικτου D d gig Iren.

(b) The addition of the (negative) Golden Rule in vs. 20 is found (with variations in detail) in D d minn Iren vg.cod. ardmach sah. That in both (a) and (b) the Greek text of Iren agreed with the Latin translation is made certain by a scholion in cod. 1739 ; see E. v. d. Goltz, Eine textkritische Arbeit des zehnten bezw. sechsten Jahrhunderts (T. U. xvii.), 1899,

17 ἀνοικοδομήσω καὶ ἀνορθώσω αὐτήν, ὅπως ἂν ἐκζητήσωσιν οἱ
κατάλοιποι τῶν ἀνθρώπων τὸν θεόν, καὶ πάντα τὰ ἔθνη ἐφ' οὓς
ἐπικέκληται τὸ ὄνομά μου ἐπ' αὐτούς, λέγει κύριος †ποιήσει
18 ταῦτα†. γνωστὸν ἀπ' αἰῶνός ἐστιν τῷ κυρίῳ τὸ ἔργον αὐτοῦ.
19 διὸ ἐγὼ κρείνω μὴ παρενοχλεῖν τοῖς ἀπὸ τῶν ἐθνῶν ἐπιστρέφουσιν
20 ἐπὶ τὸν θεόν, ἀλλὰ ἐπιστεῖλαι αὐτοῖς τοῦ ἀπέχεσθαι τῶν ἀλισγημάτων τῶν εἰδώλων καὶ τῆς πορνείας καὶ τοῦ αἵματος, καὶ
21 ὅσα μὴ θέλουσιν ἑαυτοῖς γείνεσθαι ἑτέροις μὴ ποιεῖτε· Μωυσῆς
γὰρ ἐκ γενεῶν ἀρχαίων κατὰ πόλιν ἔχει τοὺς κηρύσσοντας αὐτὸν
ε[. . .] ἐν ταῖς συναγωγαῖς κατὰ πᾶν σάββατον ἀναγεινωσκό-
22 μενος. τότε ἔδοξεν τοῖς ἀποστόλοις καὶ τοῖς πρεσβυτέροις
σὺν ὅλῃ τῇ ἐκκλησίᾳ ἐκλεξαμένους ἄνδρας ἐξ αὐτῶν πέμψαι εἰς
Ἀντιόχειαν σὺν Παύλῳ καὶ Βαρνάβᾳ, Ἰούδαν τὸν καλούμενον
Βαραββᾶν καὶ Σείλαν, ἄνδρας ἡγουμένους ἐν τοῖς ἀδελφοῖς,

22 εδοξεν] εδοξασεν

---

quod cecidit et quae dimolita sunt ejus raeaedificabo et erigam illud   17 et ex- d
quiram residui hominum d͞m et omnes gentes super quos invocatum est nomen meum
super ipsos dicit d͞n͞s faciens haec.   18 notum a saeculo est d͞n͞o opus ipsius
19 propter quod ego judico non sumus molesti his qui de gentibus convertuntur ad
d͞m   20 sed praecipere eis ut abstineant a contaminationibus simulacrorum et
stupris et sanguinem et quae volunt non fieri sibi aliis ne faciatis   21 moyses enim
ex progeniebus antiquis per civitates habet qui eum praedicant habent in synagogis
per omne sabbatum ut legatur   22 tunc visum est apostolis et presbyteris cum tota
ecclesia electos viros ut ex eis mitterent in antiochiam cum paulo et barnaba judas
qui vocatur barabbas et silan viros principales ad fratribus   23 scripserunt epistulam

---

quod cecidit, et disturbata ejus aedeaedificabo, et erigam illud,   17 uti requirant Irenaeus,
reliqui hominum dominum, et omnes gentes in quibus invocatum est nomen iii. 12, 14 (17)
meum super eos, dicit dominus, faciens haec.   18 cognitum a saeculo est deo
opus ejus.   19 propterea ego secundum me judico non molestari eos qui ex
gentibus convertuntur ad deum :   20 sed praecipiendum eis uti abstineant a
vanitatibus idolorum et a fornicatione et a sanguine ; et quaecumque nolunt
sibi fieri, aliis ne faciant.

20 om τοῦ πνικτοῦ.   [cod. 1739
καὶ ἂν μὴ θέλωσιν αὐτοῖς γενέσθαι ἑτέροις μὴ ποιεῖν.   ing. ad loc.]

---

18 γνωστον απ αιωνος εστιν τω κυριω το εργον αυτου] mg notum a saeculo est Harclean
opus ejus

---

pp. 41-43. See Detached Note on   vs. 20 and vs. 29 must have stood
vs. 29 (below, pp. 265-269), for which   in agreement, although that is not
verse a much larger body of evidence   the case in all extant copies. Cf. also
is available. In the original text,   xxi. 25.

διὰ χειρὸς αὐτῶν· Οἱ ἀπόστολοι καὶ οἱ πρεσβύτεροι ἀδελφοὶ τοῖς
κατὰ τὴν Ἀντιόχειαν καὶ Συρίαν καὶ Κιλικίαν ἀδελφοῖς τοῖς
ἐξ ἐθνῶν χαίρειν. ἐπειδὴ ἠκούσαμεν ὅτι τινὲς ἐξ ἡμῶν ἐτάραξαν 24
ὑμᾶς λόγοις ἀνασκευάζοντες τὰς ψυχὰς ὑμῶν, οἷς οὐ διεστειλάμεθα, ἔδοξεν ἡμῖν γενομένοις ὁμοθυμαδὸν ἐκλεξαμένοις ἄνδρας 25
πέμψαι πρὸς ὑμᾶς σὺν τοῖς ἀγαπητοῖς ἡμῶν Βαρνάβᾳ καὶ Παύλῳ,
ἀνθρώποις παραδεδωκόσι τὰς ψυχὰς αὐτῶν ὑπὲρ τοῦ ὀνόματος 26
τοῦ κυρίου ἡμῶν Ἰησοῦ Χριστοῦ. ἀπεστάλκαμεν οὖν Ἰούδαν 27
καὶ Σείλαν, καὶ αὐτοὺς διὰ λόγου ἀπαγγέλλοντας τὰ αὐτά. ἔδοξεν 28
γὰρ τῷ πνεύματι τῷ ἁγίῳ καὶ ἡμῖν μηδὲν πλέον ἐπιτίθεσθαι

Editors   23 αυτων] +ταδε Soden   πρεσβυτεροι] +[και οι] Soden   24 εταραξαν]
εξελθοντες εταραξαν Soden   25 εκλεξαμενους WHmg Soden

Old Uncial   23 αυτων BℵA   +ταδε ℵ^c 81   +επιστολην περιεχουσα ταδε C (cf. D)
πρεσβυτεροι BℵAC 81 Pap³³(+D)   +και οι ℵ^c   τοις 1° BℵAC² 81
Pap³³(+D)   om C   24 επειδη BACℵ^c 81 Pap³³ (+D)   επι δε ℵ
ημων BACℵ^c 81 Pap³³ (+D)   υμων ℵ   εταραξαν Bℵ   εξελθοντες
εταραξαν ACℵ^c 81 Pap³³ (cf. D)   ψυχας υμων BℵA 81 Pap³³ (+D)
+λεγοντες περιτεμνεσθαι και τηρειν τον νομον C   25 εκλεξαμενοις BA 81
εκλεξαμενους ℵC(+D)   28 τω πνευματι τω αγιω BℵA 81   τω αγιω πνευματι
C(+D)   [τω αγ]ιω π̅ν̅ι̅ τω αγὶω [π̅]ν̅[ι̅] Pap³³   ημιν BℵAC(+D)   υμιν 81
επιτιθεσθαι BℵAC 81 (+D)   επιθεσθαι Pap³³

Antiochian   23 αυτων] +ταδε HLPSς̅   πρεσβυτεροι] +και οι HLPSς̅   om εξ H
24 εταραξαν] ελθοντες εταραξαν HL   εξελθοντες εταραξαν PSς̅ (cf. D)   υμων]
+λεγοντες περιτεμνεσθαι και τηρειν τον νομον HLPSς̅   25 εκλεξαμενους
HPSς̅(+D)   28 τω πνευματι τω αγιω] τω αγιω πνευματι HLPSς̅(+D)

---

23 Since hcl.*text* reads *per manum eorum haec*, it is not certain from the marginal gloss that δια χειρος αυτων was lacking in the text followed in hcl.*mg*.
For hcl.*mg et mittentes* cf. και πεμψαντες 614 minn.
24 The addition, after ψυχας υμων, of λεγοντες περιτεμνεσθαι και τηρειν τον νομον in C Antiochian pesh hcl.*text* is found also in e (E) and for substance, in a slightly different position, in Iren gig vg. *one cod.* Although absent in D, it is probably a part of the 'Western' text.

28 By the omission of των before επαναγκες ℵ D 33 (and perhaps Pacian, cf. Tert), επαναγκες would become part of a new sentence, and the construction would be better suited to an Aramaic original. Sah (cod. B) also is so punctuated. But in the lack of competent Latin evidence it is perhaps better to suppose an accidental omission.
29 For the reasons which advise the rejection from the text of the words και πνικτων, as well as of the (negative) Golden Rule found in D d and many authorities, see Detached Note, pp. 265-269.

23 | γράψαντες ἐπιστολὴν διὰ χειρὸς αὐτῶν περιέχουσαν τάδε· Οἱ
ἀπόστολοι καὶ οἱ πρεσβύτεροι ἀδελφοὶ τοῖς κα‹τὰ› τὴν Ἀντιόχειαν καὶ Συρείαν καὶ Κιλ‹ικ›είαν τοῖς ἐξ ἐθνῶν ἀδελφοῖς
24 χαίρειν. ἐπ‹ε›ιδὴ ἠκούσαμεν ὅτι τινὲς ἐξ ἡμῶν ἐξελθόντες
ἐξετάραξαν ὑμᾶς λόγοις ἀνασκευάζοντες τὰς ψυχὰς ὑμῶν, οἷς οὐ
25 διεστειλάμεθα, ἔδοξεν ἡμεῖν γενομένοις ὁμοθυμαδὸν ἐκλεξαμένους ἄνδρας πέμψαι πρὸς ὑμᾶς σὺν τοῖς ἀγαπητοῖς ὑμῶν Βαρνάβᾳ
26 καὶ Παύλῳ, ἀνθρώποις παραδεδωκόσιν τὴν ψυχὴν αὐτῶν ὑπὲρ
τοῦ ὀνόματος τοῦ κυρίου ἡμῶν Ἰησοῦ Χριστοῦ εἰς πάντα πει-
27 ρασμόν. ἀπεστάλκαμεν οὖν Ἰούδαν καὶ Σίλαν, καὶ αὐτοὺς διὰ
28 λόγου ἀπαγγελοῦντας ταῦτα. ἔδοξεν γὰρ τῷ ἁγίῳ πνεύματι
καὶ ἡμεῖν μηδὲν πλεῖον ἐπιτίθεσθαι ὑμεῖν βάρος πλὴν τούτων

24 διεστειλομεθα   26 παραδεδωκασιν   28 υμειν] ημειν

per manus suas continentem haec apostoli et presbyteri fratres hiis qui sunt per d
antiochiam et syriam et ciliciam qui sunt ex gentibus fratribus salutem   24 quoniam
audivimus quod quidam ex nobis exeuntes perturbaberunt vos verbis destruentes animas
vestras quibus non injunximus   25 visum est nobis constitutis pariter electos viros
mittere ad vos cum dilectissimis nostris barnaba et paulo   26 hominibus qui tradiderunt anim suam propter nomen d̄n̄i nostri ih̄u x̄p̄i in omni temptationi   27 misimus
ergo judam et silan et ipsos verbo adnuntiantes haec   28 visum est enim sancto
spui et nobis nihil amplius ponere vobis honeris praeter haec quae necesse est

28 visum est [inquiunt] spiritui sancto et nobis nullum amplius vobis Tertullian,
Pud. 12
adicere pondus, quam eorum

28 visum est sancto spiritui et nobis nullam vobis inponere sarcinam quam Cyprian,
Test. iii. 11ᴐ
ista,

23 apostoli et presbyteri fratres his qui sunt in Antiochia et Syria et Cilicia Irenaeus,
fratribus ex gentibus salutem.   24 quoniam audivimus quia ex nobis quidam iii. 12, 14(17)
exeuntes turbaverunt vos sermonibus, destruentes animas vestras, quibus non
praecepimus, dicentes, circumcidimini et servate legem,   25 placuit nobis con-
venientibus in unum electos viros mittere ad vos cum dilectissimis nostris
Barnaba et Paulo,   26 hominibus qui tradiderunt animam suam pro nomine cf. iii. 12, 13
domini nostri Jesu Christi.   27 misimus igitur Judam et Sileam et ipsos per
sermonem adnuntiantes nostram sententiam.   28 placuit enim sancto spiritui
et nobis nullum amplius vobis pondus imponere quam haec

23 επιστολην δια χειρος αυτων περιεχουσαν ταδε] mg epistolam, et mittentes, Harclean
in qua erant haec   24 εξελθοντες] mg profecti sunt ad vos et   26 εις
παντα πειρασμον] mg in omnem tentationem

ὑμῖν βάρος πλὴν τούτων τῶν ἐπάναγκες, ἀπέχεσθαι εἰδωλοθύτων 29 καὶ αἵματος καὶ πνικτῶν καὶ πορνείας· ἐξ ὧν διατηροῦντες ἑαυτοὺς εὖ πράξετε. ἔρρωσθε.

Οἱ μὲν οὖν ἀπολυθέντες κατῆλθον εἰς Ἀντιόχειαν, καὶ 30 συναγαγόντες τὸ πλῆθος ἐπέδωκαν τὴν ἐπιστολήν· ἀναγνόντες 31 δὲ ἐχάρησαν ἐπὶ τῇ παρακλήσει. Ἰούδας τε καὶ Σείλας, καὶ 32 αὐτοὶ προφῆται ὄντες, διὰ λόγου πολλοῦ παρεκάλεσαν τοὺς ἀδελφοὺς καὶ ἐπεστήριξαν· ποιήσαντες δὲ χρόνον ἀπελύθησαν 33 μετ' εἰρήνης ἀπὸ τῶν ἀδελφῶν πρὸς τοὺς ἀποστείλαντας αὐτούς. Παῦλος δὲ καὶ Βαρνάβας διέτρειβον ἐν Ἀντιοχείᾳ διδάσκοντες 35 καὶ εὐαγγελιζόμενοι μετὰ καὶ ἑτέρων πολλῶν τὸν λόγον τοῦ κυρίου.

Μετὰ δέ τινας ἡμέρας εἶπεν πρὸς Βαρνάβαν Παῦλος· Ἐπι- 36 στρέψαντες δὴ ἐπισκεψώμεθα τοὺς ἀδελφοὺς κατὰ πόλιν πᾶσαν ἐν αἷς κατηγγείλαμεν τὸν λόγον τοῦ κυρίου, πῶς ἔχουσιν. Βαρ- 37

Editors   29 om και πνικτων JHR

Old Uncial   28 τουτων των BCℵ° 81   om τουτων A   om των ℵ(+D)   29 πνικτων
BℵAC 81   πνικτου ℵ°A²   πραξετε BℵA 81 Pap³³   πραξατε C(+D)
32 και επεστηριξαν BℵᵃAC 81(+D)   om ℵ   33 αυτους BAC 81 (+D)
εαυτους ℵ   34 om vs. 34 BℵA 81   εδοξε δε τω σιλα επιμειναι αυτους C(+D)
36 δη BACℵ° 81 (+D)   δε ℵ   πολιν πασαν BℵAC   πασαν πολιν 81 (+D)
κατηγγειλαμεν BℵA 81 (+D)   εκηρυξαμεν C

Antiochian   28 των επαναγκες τουτων LP5   29 πνικτου HLPSS   πραξατε
HL(+D)   30 κατηλθον] ηλθον HLPSS   επεδωκαν] εδωκαν S
33 αποστειλαντας αυτους] αποστολους HLPSS   34 εδοξε δε τω σιλα επιμειναι
αυτου 5 (cf. D)   36 παυλος προς βαρναβαν HLPSS (cf. D)   επισκεψο-
μεθα Η   αδελφους] +ημων HLPSS   πασαν πολιν HLPSS(+D)

---

29 φερομενοι εν τω (om τω Iren) αγιω πνευματι D d Iren(Gk. and Lat.) Tert Ephr appears to be a part of the earliest 'Western' text.
34 εδοξε δε τω σιλα (σειλεα D latt) επιμειναι αυτου (αυτους C D d, αυτοθι minn) C D 614 minn gig d vg.codd hcl ·※· sah boh.codd ; +μονος δε ιουδας επορευθη D d gig vg.codd Ephrem. Probably both parts of the verse were contained in the 'Western' text. The reading αυτου suits the context better than αυτους, and is to be

preferred ; cf. the same variation Mk. vi. 33.
To the dative form σειλεα (d sileae) corresponds xvii. 4 the dative σιλαια D. For the name Silas the Latin codices which contain considerable Old Latin elements have, with marked individual consistency, forms from nom. sileas, syleas, silias. Gig follows in every one of the thirteen cases the form syleas. Cf. Ency. Bibl., 'Silas,' cols. 4519 f. ; Zahn, Einleitung, vol. i. § 1, Anm. 16. See Detached Note.

29 ἐπάναγκες, ἀπέχεσθαι εἰδωλοθύτων καὶ αἵματος καὶ πορνίας,
καὶ ὅσα μὴ θέλετε ἑαυτοῖς γείνεσθαι ἑτέρῳ μὴ ποιεῖν· ἀφ' ὧν διατηροῦντες ἑαυτοὺς εὖ πράξατε φερόμενοι ἐν τῷ ἁγίῳ πνεύματι.
ἔρρωσθε.

30 Οἱ μὲν οὖν ἀπολυθέντες ἐν ἡμέραις ὀλίγαις κατῆλθον εἰς
Ἀντιόχειαν, καὶ συνάγοντες τὸ πλῆθος ἐπέδωκαν τὴν ἐπιστολήν·
31,32 ἀναγνόντες δὲ ἐχάρησαν ἐπὶ τῇ παρακλήσει. Ἰούδας δὲ καὶ
Σείλας, καὶ αὐτοὶ προφῆται ὄντες πλήρεις πνεύματος ἁγίου, διὰ
33 λόγου παρεκάλεσαν τοὺς ἀδελφοὺς καὶ ἐπεστήριξαν· ποιήσαντες
δὲ χρόνον ἀπελύθησαν μετ' εἰρήνης ἀπὸ τῶν ἀδελφῶν πρὸς τοὺς
34 ἀποστείλαντας αὐτούς. ἔδοξε δὲ τῷ Σειλέᾳ ἐπιμεῖναι αὐτούς,
35 μόνος δὲ Ἰούδας ἐπορεύθη. ὁ δὲ Παῦλος καὶ Βαρνάβας διέτρειβον ἐν Ἀντιοχείᾳ διδάσκοντες καὶ εὐαγγελιζόμενοι καὶ
μετὰ ἑτέρων πολλῶν τὸν λόγον τοῦ <κυρίου>.

36 Μετὰ δέ τινας ἡμέρας εἶπεν ὁ Παῦλος πρὸς Βαρνάβαν· Ἐπι-
στρέψαντες δὴ ἐπισκεψώμεθα τοὺς ἀδελφοὺς τοὺς κατὰ πᾶσαν
πόλιν ἐν οἷς κατηνγείλαμεν τὸν λόγον τοῦ κυρίου, πῶς ἔχουσιν.

29 abstinere sacrificatis et sanguine et stupris et quaecumque non vultis vobis fieri d
alii ne feceritis a quibus conversantes vos ipsos bene agitis ferentes in santo s͞p͞o
valete 30 illi quidem dismissi in diebus paucis pervenerunt antiochiam et cum
collegissent multitudinem tradiderunt epistulam 31 et cum legissent gavisi sunt
super hanc oration͞e 32 judas quoque et silas etiam ipsi prophetae cum essent pleni
s͞p͞o sancto sermoni exhortati sunt fratres et perconfirmati sunt 33 cum fecissent
autem tempus dismissi sunt cum pace a fratribus ad ipsos qui miserant eos
34 placuit autem sileae sustinere eos solus autem judas profectus est 35 paulus
vero et barnabas demorabantur antiochia docentes et evangelizantes et cum aliis
multis verbum d͞n͞i 36 et post aliquos dies ait paulus ad barnaban reversique
visitemus fratres per omnem civitatem penes quos adnuntiabimus verbum dni

29 a quibus necesse est abstineri, a sacrificiis et a fornicationibus et sanguine, | Tertullian,
a quibus observando vos recte agetis, vectante spiritu sancto. | Pud. 12

29 quae ex necessitate sunt : abstinere vos ab idololatriis et sanguine et | Cyprian,
fornicatione, et quaecumque vobis fieri non vultis, alii ne feceritis. | Test. iii. 119

29 quae sunt necessaria, ut abstineatis ab idolothytis et sanguine et fornicatione, | Irenaeus,
et quaecumque non vultis fieri vobis, alii ne faciatis : a quibus custodientes vos | iii. 12, 14 (17)
ipsos bene agetis, ambulantes in spiritu sancto.

29 om τοῦ πνικτοῦ. | [cod. 1739
ἐξ ὧν διατηροῦντες ἑαυτοὺς εὖ πράξετε φερόμενοι ἐν ἁγίῳ πνεύματι. | mg. ad loc.

29 και οσα μη θελετε . . . μη ποιειν] ⋇ et [ut] omnia quae nolitis vobis fieri Harclean
aliis ne faciatis ⋋ 30 την επιστολην] epistolam ⋇ Judas et Silas ⋋ 34 εδοξε
δε τω σειλεα επιμειναι αυτους] ⋇ Silae autem visum est manere ibi ⋋
36 τους 2°] ⋇ illos ⋋ του κυριου] domini ⋇ et videamus ⋋ πως εχουσιν]
quomodo se habeant ⋇ placuit autem cogitatio Barnabae ⋋

νάβας δὲ ἐβούλετο συνπαραλαβεῖν καὶ τὸν Ἰωάννην τὸν καλούμενον Μάρκον· Παῦλος δὲ ἠξίου, τὸν ἀποστάντα ἀπ' αὐτῶν 38 ἀπὸ Παμφυλίας καὶ μὴ συνελθό‹ν›τα αὐτοῖς εἰς τὸ ἔργον, μὴ συνπαραλαμβάνειν τοῦτον. ἐγένετο δὲ παροξυσμὸς ὥστε ἀπο- 39 χωρισθῆναι αὐτοὺς ἀπ' ἀλλήλων, τόν τε Βαρνάβαν παραλαβόντα τὸν Μάρκον ἐκπλεῦσαι εἰς Κύπρον. Παῦλος δὲ ἐπιλεξάμενος 40 Σείλαν ἐξῆλθεν παραδοθεὶς τῇ χάριτι τοῦ κυρίου ὑπὸ τῶν ἀδελφῶν, διήρχετο δὲ τὴν Συρίαν καὶ τὴν Κιλικίαν ἐπι- 41 στηρίζων τὰς ἐκκλησίας. κατήντησεν δὲ καὶ εἰς Δέρβην καὶ εἰς XVI Λύστραν. καὶ ἰδοὺ μαθητής τις ἦν ἐκεῖ ὀνόματι Τιμόθεος, υἱὸς γυναικὸς Ἰουδαίας πιστῆς πατρὸς δὲ Ἕλληνος, ὃς ἐμαρτυρεῖτο 2 ὑπὸ τῶν ἐν Λύστροις καὶ Εἰκονίῳ ἀδελφῶν· τοῦτον ἠθέλησεν ὁ 3 Παῦλος σὺν αὐτῷ ἐξελθεῖν, καὶ λαβὼν περιέτεμεν αὐτὸν διὰ τοὺς Ἰουδαίους τοὺς ὄντας ἐν τοῖς τόποις ἐκείνοις, ᾔδεισαν γὰρ ἅπαντες ὅτι Ἕλλην ὁ πατὴρ αὐτοῦ ὑπῆρχεν. ὡς δὲ δι- 4 επορεύοντο τὰς πόλεις, παρεδίδοσαν αὐτοῖς φυλάσσειν τὰ δόγματα τὰ κεκριμένα ὑπὸ τῶν ἀποστόλων καὶ πρεσβυτέρων τῶν ἐν

Editors   41 [την 2°] WH   om Soden

Old Uncial   37 συνπαραλαβειν BℵC 81 (+D)   συνπαραλαμβανειν A   τον 1° Bℵ 81   om AC(+D)   καλουμενον BℵA   επικαλουμενον Cℵᶜ 81 (+D)   38 αποσταντα BℵC 81 αποστατησαντα A (cf. D)   απο παμφυλιας BℵA 81(+D)   om C² (C uncertain)   συνελθοντα B²   39 δε BℵA 81 (+D)   ουν C τον 2° BℵC 81 (+D)   om A   40 κυριου BℵA 81 (cf. D)   θεου C   41 την 2° B(+D)   om ℵAC 81   1 και 1° BA   om ℵC 81 (+D)   εις 2° BℵA 81   om C(+D)   2 εικονιω BAC 81 (+D)   ικονιω ℵ   3 απαντες BℵA 81   παντες C(+D)   4 κεκριμενα BℵAC   κεκρυμμενα 81

Antiochian   37 εβουλετο] εβουλευσατο HLPSϛ (cf. D)   om και HLPSϛ(+D) 38 συμπαραλαβειν HLPSϛ   39 δε] ουν HLPSϛ   αυτοις L τε] δε HS   40 κυριου] θεου HLPSϛ   41 om δε S   om την 2° HLPSϛ   1 om και 1° HLPSϛ(+D)   om εις 2° HLPSϛ(+D) γυναικος] +τινος HLPSϛ   3 om λαβων περιετεμεν αυτον δια τους L   οτι ελλην ο πατηρ αυτου] τον πατερα αυτου οτι ελλην HLPSϛ(+D)   4 διεπορευοντο] επορευοντο H   των πρεσβυτερων HLPSϛ

41 The 'Western' addition is given by gig vg.codd in a form somewhat nearer to hcl.mg than is that of D. The Latin authorities read praecipiens custodire praecepta apostolorum et seniorum.

3 τον πατερα αυτου οτι ελλην υπηρχεν D Antiochian gig d pesh hcl may have been the original, ruder expression, for which has been substituted

οτι ελλην ο πατηρ αυτου υπηρχεν BℵAC 81 minn vg sah boh; but it is also possible that the 'Western' glossator wished to put the word 'father' into a more prominent position than it occupied in the B-text. The decision must turn on the general estimate of the two types of text.

4 D d και παρεδιδοσαν αυτοις is not

37 Βαρνάβας δὲ ἐβουλεύετο συνπαραλαβεῖν Ἰωάνην τὸν ἐπι-
38 καλούμενον Μάρκον· Παῦλος δὲ οὐκ ἐβούλετο, λέγων τὸν ἀπο-
στ‹ατ›ήσαντα ἀπ᾿ αὐτῶν ἀπὸ Παμφυλίας καὶ μὴ συνελθόντα εἰς
39 τὸ ἔργον εἰς ὃ ἐπέμφθησαν τοῦτον μὴ εἶναι σὺν αὐτοῖς. ἐγένετο
δὲ παροξυσμὸς ὥστε ἀποχωρισθῆναι αὐτοὺς ἀπ᾿ ἀλλήλων.
τότε Βαρνάβας παραλαβὼν τὸν Μάρκον ἔπλευσεν εἰς Κύπρον.
40 Παῦλος δὲ ἐπιδεξάμενος Σείλαν ἐξῆλθεν παραδοθεὶς τῇ χάριτι
41 κυρίου ἀπὸ τῶν ἀδελφῶν, διήρχετο δὲ τὴν Συρίαν καὶ τὴν Κιλικίαν ἐπιστηρίζων τὰς ἐκκλησίας παραδιδοὺς τὰς ἐντολὰς τῶν
XVI πρεσβυτέρων. διελθὼν δὲ τὰ ἔθνη ταῦτα κατήντησεν εἰς Δέρβην
καὶ Λύστραν. καὶ ἰδοὺ μαθητής τις ἐκεῖ ἦν ὀνόματι Τιμόθεος,
2 υἱὸς γυναικὸς Ἰουδαίας πιστῆς πατρὸς δὲ Ἕλληνος, | ὃς ἐμαρτυ-
3 ρεῖτο ὑπὸ τῶν ἐν Λύστροις καὶ Εἰκονίῳ ἀδελφῶν· τοῦτον
ἠθέλησεν ὁ Παῦλος σὺν αὐτῷ ἐξελθεῖν, καὶ λαβὼν περιέτεμεν
αὐτὸν διὰ τοὺς Ἰουδαίους τοὺς ὄντας ἐν τοῖς τόποις ἐκείνοις,
ᾔδεισαν γὰρ πάντες τὸν πατέρα αὐτοῦ ὅτι Ἕλλην ὑπῆρχεν.
4 διερχόμενοι δὲ τὰς πόλεις ἐκήρυσσον †καὶ παρεδίδοσαν αὐτοῖς†
μετὰ πάσης παρρησίας τὸν κύριον Ἰησοῦν Χριστὸν ἅμα παρα-
διδόντες καὶ τὰς ἐντολὰς ἀποστόλων καὶ πρεσβυτέρων τῶν ἐν

quomodo habeat   37 barnabas vero volebat adsumere johannen qui cognominatur d
marcus   38 paulus autem nolebat dicens hiis qui discesserunt ab eis a pamphylia
et nec simul venerunt ad opus in quo missi erant hunc non adsumerent secum
39 facta est autem discertatio ita ut separarentur ab invicem barnabas vero
adsumpto marco navigaverunt in cyprum   40 paulus autem suscepit silan exibit
traditus gratia d̄n̄ī a fratribus   41 pergrediebatur autem syriam et ciliciā confirmans
ecclesias tradens autem mandatum presbyterorū
1 pertransiens gentes istas debenit derben et lystram ecce discipulus quidam erat
ibi nomine timotheus filius mulieris judeae fidelis patre autem graeco   2 cui testimonium perhibuit ab hiis qui lystrae et•iconio fratribus   3 hunc voluit paulus
secum exire et accipiens circumcidit eum propter judaeos qui erant in locis suis
sciebant enim omnes patrem ejus quod crecus esset   4 circumeuntes autem civitates
praedicabant et tradebant eis cum omnem fiduciam d̄n̄m̄ īh̄m̄ x̄p̄m̄ simul tradentes
et mandata apostolorum et presbyterorū his qui erant hierosolymis   5 ecclesiae

39–xvi. 7 [quoniam autem is Lucas inseparabilis fuit a Paulo et cooperarius Irenaeus
ejus in evangelio, ipse facit manifestum, non glorians, sed ab ipsa productus iii. 14, 1ː
veritate.   separatus enim, inquit, a Paulo et Barnaba et Johanne qui vocabatur
Marcus, et cum navigassent Cyprus,]

41–xvi. 1 παραδιδους . . . λυστραν] mg et tradebant iis custodire mandata Harclean
apostolorum et seniorum.   quum pertransivissent autem gentes has, pervenerunt
in Derben et in Lystram   4 εκηρυσσον . . . χριστον] mg praedicantes cum
omni fiducia dominum Jesum Christum

found in hcl. mg, and is plainly a case   since it breaks the connexion and is
of contamination from the B-text,   covered by αμα παραδιδοντες just below.

Ἱεροσολύμοις. αἱ μὲν οὖν ἐκκλησίαι ἐστερεοῦντο τῇ πίστει καὶ 5
ἐπερίσσευον τῷ ἀριθμῷ καθ᾽ ἡμέραν.

Διῆλθον δὲ τὴν Φρυγίαν καὶ Γαλατικὴν χώραν, κωλυθέντες 6
ὑπὸ τοῦ ἁγίου πνεύματος λαλῆσαι τὸν λόγον ἐν τῇ Ἀσίᾳ, ἐλθόντες 7
δὲ κατὰ τὴν Μυσίαν ἐπείραζον εἰς τὴν Βειθυνίαν πορευθῆναι καὶ
οὐκ εἴασεν αὐτοὺς τὸ πνεῦμα Ἰησοῦ· παρελθόντες δὲ τὴν Μυσίαν 8
κατέβησαν εἰς Τρῳάδα. καὶ ὅραμα διὰ νυκτὸς τῷ Παύλῳ 9
ὤφθη· ἀνὴρ Μακεδών τις ἦν ἑστὼς καὶ παρακαλῶν αὐτὸν καὶ
λέγων· Διαβὰς εἰς Μακεδονίαν βοήθησον ἡμῖν. ὡς δὲ τὸ ὅραμα 10
εἶδεν, εὐθέως ἐζητήσαμεν ἐξελθεῖν εἰς Μακεδονίαν, συνβιβάζοντες
ὅτι προσκέκληται ἡμᾶς ὁ θεὸς εὐαγγελίσασθαι αὐτούς. ἀν- 11
αχθέντες οὖν ἀπὸ Τρῳάδος εὐθυδρομήσαμεν εἰς Σαμοθρᾴκην,
τῇ δ᾽ ἐπιούσῃ εἰς Νέαν Πόλιν, | κἀκεῖθεν εἰς Φιλίππους, ἥτις 12
ἐστὶν πρώτη μερίδος τῆς Μακεδονίας πόλις, κολωνία.

Editors	9 της νυκτος Soden	11 νεα[ν] πολιν Soden	12 πρωτη της μεριδος
	WH Soden JHR †πρωτη της μεριδος† WHmg		om της before μακεδονιας
	WH Soden		

Old Uncial	5 εκκλησιαι BℵAC(+D)	αι εκκλησιαι 81	7 πορευθηναι BℵA 81
	πορευεσθαι C(+D)	ιησου BℵAC² 81 (+D) κυριου C	9 δια BℵA 81 (+D)
	om C	νυκτος BA(?)(+D) της νυκτος ℵC 81	τω παυλω ωφθη Bℵ 81
	ωφθη τω παυλω AC(+D)	10 εζητησαμεν BAC 81 εξητησαμεν ℵ	ημας
	BACℵᶜ 81 (+D) om ℵ	αυτους BℵC 81 (cf. D) αυτοις A	11 ουν BC
	δε ℵA 81 (cf. D)	νεαν πολιν BℵA νεαπολιν C 81 (+D)	12 μεριδος B
	της μεριδος ℵAC 81	της μακεδονιας B(+D) om της ℵAC 81	

Antiochian	4 ιερουσαλημ HLPSS͞	6 διελθοντες HLPSS͞	την γαλατικην
	HLPSS͞ 7 om δε HLPSS͞	εις] κατα HLPSS͞	πορευεσθαι
	HLPSS͞(+D)	αυτοις S om ιησου HLPSS͞	9 της νυκτος
	HLPSS͞	ωφθη τω παυλω HLPSS͞(+D)	τις ην μακεδων HLPSS͞
	om και 2° HLPSS͞(+D)	10 την μακεδονιαν HSS͞	θεος] κυριος
	HLPSS͞(+D)	11 της τρωαδος˙HLPᵛⁱᵈSS͞	ευθυδρομησαντες S
	δ᾽] τε HSS͞ (P illegible)	νεαπολιν HLPSS͞(+D)	12 κακειθεν] εκειθεν τε
	HPSS͞ εκειθεν δε L	της μεριδος HLPSS͞	

6 It is more likely that the Antiochian reading διελθοντες was substituted for διηλθον because of the difficulty of understanding the force of κωλυθεντες, when attached to διηλθον, than that the reverse change took place as a means of obviating an awkward accumulation of three participles (for the latter explanation, J. B. Lightfoot, *Biblical Essays*, p. 237 note).
The omission by BℵAC 81 D of την (Antiochian) before γαλατικην must be adopted on both external and in-ternal grounds, and is important for the interpretation of the phrase.

8 διελθοντες D is a correction to avoid the ambiguity of παρελθοντες, which seems intended to mean that the missionaries passed through Mysia without stopping to preach in any of the towns ; the same improvement is found, perhaps due to the translators, in gig d vg hcl.*text.*

Nos venimus of Irenaeus, for κατεβησαν, is subject to suspicion because it occurs in so free a summary ;

5 Ἱεροσολύμοις. αἱ μὲν οὖν ἐκκλησίαι ἐστερεοῦντο καὶ ἐπερίσσευον τῷ ἀριθμῷ καθ᾽ ἡμέραν.

6 Διῆλθον δὲ τὴν Φρυγίαν καὶ Γαλατικὴν χώραν, κωλυθέντες ὑπὸ τοῦ ἁγίου πνεύματος μηδενὶ λαλῆσαι τὸν λόγον τοῦ θεοῦ ἐν 7 τῇ Ἀσίᾳ, γενόμενοι δὲ κατὰ τὴν Μυσίαν ἤθελον εἰς Βιθυνίαν 8 πορεύεσθαι καὶ οὐκ εἴασεν αὐτοὺς τὸ πνεῦμα Ἰησοῦ· διελθόντες 9 δὲ τὴν Μυσίαν κατήντησαν εἰς Τρῳάδα. καὶ ἐν ὁράματι διὰ νυκτὸς ὤφθη τῷ Παύλῳ ὡσεὶ ἀνὴρ Μακεδών τις ἑστὼς κατὰ πρόσωπον αὐτοῦ παρακαλῶν καὶ λέγων· Διαβὰς εἰς Μακεδονίαν 10 βοήθησον ἡμεῖν. διεγερθεὶς οὖν διηγήσατο τὸ ὅραμα ἡμῖν, καὶ ἐνοήσαμεν ὅτι προσκέκληται ἡμᾶς ὁ κύριος εὐαγγελίσασθαι τοὺς 11 ἐν τῇ Μακεδονίᾳ. τῇ δὲ ἐπαύριον ἀχθέντες ἀπὸ Τρῳάδος εὐθυδρομήσαμεν εἰς Σαμοθράκην, καὶ τῇ ἐπιούσῃ ἡμέρᾳ εἰς Νεάπολιν, 12 | κἀκεῖθεν εἰς Φιλίππους, ἥτις ἐστὶν κεφαλὴ τῆς Μακεδονίας, πόλις κολωνία.

7 γενομενοι] γενομενην	ηθελαν	βυθυνιαν

ergo consolidabantur et abundabant numero cottidie 6 pertransiebant autem d phygiam et galatiam regionem prohibiti a sancto s͞p͞o nemini loqui verbum d͞i in asia 7 cum venissent autem circa mysiam volebant bithyniam abire et vetuit illos s͞p͞s i͞h͞u 8 cum transissent autem mysiam descenderunt troada 9 et visum per noctem apparuit paulo quasi vir macedo quidam stans anti faciem ejus et rogans dicens transi in macedonia auxiliari nobis 10 exurgens ergo enarrabit visum nobis et intellegimus quoniam provocavít nos d͞n͞s evangelizare qui in macedonia sunt 11 alia die perducti a troadae cursum direximus in samotrachiam et sequenti die neapolim 12 indie autem philippis quae est capud macedoniae civitas colonia

8 nos venimus in Troadem: 9 [et cum vidisset Paulus per somnium virum Irenaeus, Macedonem dicentem :] veniens in Macedoniam opitulare nobis Paule, 10 statim, iii. 14, 1 [ait,] quaesivimus proficisci in Macedoniam, intelligentes quoniam provocavit nos dominus evangelizare eis. 11 navigantes igitur a Troade, direximus navigium in Samothracen.

8 Troadem *Turner*

9 κατα προσωπον αυτου] ⸆ coram facie ejus ✓ 11 τη δε επαυριον] *mg* Harclean crastino autem

but his argument is scarcely sound unless he thought he had a Greek text with the first person. It is not unlikely that he misquoted this verse through a confusion with Acts xx. 6, from which he quotes in this same paragraph (iii. 14, 1) the sentence, "*et venimus Troadem.*" This latter quotation also, it will be noticed, Irenaeus has given in a form abridged from the Greek.

10 From the 'Western' text sah has preserved : 'and having arisen he

told us the vision' (for ως δε το οραμα ειδεν), in substantial agreement with D d, which are not supported by any other Latin witness. Cf. the 'Western' form of ix. 17.

12 For πρωτη της (om της B) μεριδος BאAC 81 Antiochian vg, the (wrong) interpretation κεφαλη D d is supported by pesh ('head '). κεφαλη itself is not used in this sense in Greek and must be accounted a Latinism, but the adoption of the reading in pesh makes difficult the suggestion that the text

Ἦμεν δὲ ἐν ταύτῃ τῇ πόλει διατρείβοντες ἡμέρας τινάς. | τῇ 13
τε ἡμέρᾳ τῶν σαββάτων ἐξήλθομεν ἔξω τῆς πύλης παρὰ ποταμὸν
οὗ † ἐνομίζομεν προσευχὴ † εἶναι, καὶ καθίσαντες ἐλαλοῦμεν ταῖς
συνελθούσαις γυναιξίν. καί τις γυνὴ ὀνόματι Λυδία, πορφυρό- 14
πωλις πόλεως Θυατείρων σεβομένη τὸν θεόν, ἤκουεν, ἧς ὁ κύριος
διήνοιξεν τὴν καρδίαν προσέχειν τοῖς λαλουμένοις ὑπὸ Παύλου.
ὡς δὲ ἐβαπτίσθη καὶ ὁ οἶκος αὐτῆς, παρεκάλεσεν λέγουσα· Εἰ 15
κεκρίκατέ με πιστὴν τῷ κυρίῳ εἶναι, εἰσελθόντες εἰς τὸν οἶκόν
μου μένετε· καὶ παρεβιάσατο ἡμᾶς. ἐγένετο δὲ πορευομένων 16
ἡμῶν εἰς τὴν προσευχὴν παιδίσκην τινὰ ἔχουσαν πνεῦμα πύθωνα
ὑπαντῆσαι ἡμῖν, ἥτις ἐργασίαν πολλὴν παρεῖχεν τοῖς κυρίοις
αὐτῆς μαντευομένη· αὕτη κατακολουθοῦσα Παύλῳ καὶ ἡμῖν 17
ἔκραζεν λέγουσα· Οὗτοι οἱ ἄνθρωποι δοῦλοι τοῦ θεοῦ τοῦ ὑψίστου
εἰσίν, οἵτινες καταγγέλλουσιν ὑμῖν ὁδὸν σωτηρίας. τοῦτο δὲ 18
ἐποίει ἐπὶ πολλὰς ἡμέρας. διαπονηθεὶς δὲ Παῦλος καὶ ἐπιστρέψας
τῷ πνεύματι εἶπεν· Παραγγέλλω σοι ἐν ὀνόματι Ἰησοῦ Χριστοῦ

Editors   13 ενομιζομεν προσευχην WH   ενομιζετο προσευχη Soden JHR   14 του
παυλου Soden JHR   15 μεινατε Soden   16 πυθωνος Soden (but cf. mg)
υπαντησαι] απαντησαι Soden (but cf. mg)   17 κατακολουθησασα Soden
[τω] παυλου WH   τω παυλω Soden JHR   υμιν] ημιν Soden mg
18 ο παυλος Soden

Old Uncial   13 ου BאAC(+D)   om 81   ενομιζομεν BA(rewritten) C(-ζαμεν) 81
ενομιζεν א   προσευχη BA (cf. D)   προσευχην אC 81   συνελθουσαις
BאC 81 (cf. D)   +ημιν אC   14 παυλου B(+D)   του παυλου אAC 81
15 εβαπτισθη BאAC 81 (+D)   +αυτη אᶜ   μενετε BאA 81 (+D)   μεινατε C
16 παιδισκην BאAC(+D)   παιδισκη 81   εχουσαν BACאᶜ 81 (+D)   οχουσαν א
υπαντησαι BאC 81   απαντησαι A(+D)   παρειχεν BאA 81 (+D)   παρειχετο C
17 κατακολουθουσα Bא(+D)   κατακολουθησασα AC   παρακολουθησασα 81
παυλω B   τω παυλω אAC 81 (+D)   υμιν Bא(+D)   ημιν AC² 81
18 παυλος BאA   ο παυλος C 81 (+D)   παραγγελλω BאA(+D)   παραγγελω C 81

Antiochian   12 ταυτη] αυτη HLPS   13 πυλης] πολεως HLPSϚ   ενομιζετο
προσευχη (ευχη S) HLPSϚ (cf. D)   14 ηκουσεν LS(+D)   του
παυλου HLPSϚ   15 μεινατε HLPSϚ   16 om την HLPSϚ(+D)
πυθωνος HLPSϚ   υπαντησαι] απαντησαι HLPSϚ(+D)   17 κατακολουθησασα HLPSϚ   τω παυλω HLPSϚ(+D)   ημιν] τω σιλα L
υμιν] ημιν HLPSϚ   18 om δε 1° H   ο παυλος HLPSϚ(+D)
τω ονοματι HLPSϚ(+D)

of D is derived by retranslation from d (or its Latin exemplar). For πρωτη μερις E (e reads *prima partis* with vg) cf. sah.*codd*. *W and Wess*[11] ('prima pars'). πρωτη μεριδος (without της) B could be accepted only on the supposition that it was a current technical phrase, not otherwise known to us, and is probably an error (haplography) due to the collocation of letters ΤΗΤΗΣ. The rendering *primae partis* is found in the vg codices Θ c Par.11505[2], and doubtless comes from Languedoc, but in the

13 *Ημεν δὲ ἐν ταύτῃ τῇ πόλει διατρείβοντες ἡμέρας τινάς. | τῇ
δὲ ἡμέρᾳ τῶν σαββάτων ἐξήλθομεν ἔξω τῆς πύλης παρὰ τὸν
ποταμὸν οὗ ἐδόκει προσευχὴ εἶναι, καὶ καθίσαντες ἐλαλοῦμεν
14 ταῖς συνεληλυθυίαις γυναιξίν. καί τις γυνὴ ὀνόματι Λυδία,
πορφυρόπωλις τῆς πόλεως Θυατείρων σεβομένη τὸν θεόν, ἤκουσεν,
ἧς ὁ κύριος διήνοιξεν τὴν καρδίαν προσέχειν τοῖς λαλουμένοις ὑπὸ
15 Παύλου. ὡς δὲ ἐβαπτίσθη καὶ πᾶς ὁ οἶκος αὐτῆς, παρεκάλεσε
λέγουσα· Εἰ κεκρίκατέ με πιστὴν τῷ θεῷ εἶναι, εἰσελ‹θ›όντες εἰς
16 τὸν οἶκόν μου μένετε· καὶ παρεβειάσατο ἡμᾶς. ἐγένετο δὲ πορευομένων ἡμῶν εἰς προσευχὴν παιδίσκην τινὰ ἔχουσαν πνεῦμα
πύθωνα ἀπαντῆσαι ἡμεῖν, ἥτις ἐργασίαν πολλὴν παρεῖχε τοῖς
17 κυρίοις διὰ τούτου μαντευομένη· αὕτη κατακολουθοῦσα τῷ Παύλῳ
καὶ ἡμεῖν καὶ ἔκραζεν λέγουσα· Οὗτοι οἱ δοῦλοι τοῦ θεοῦ τοῦ
ὑψίστου εἰσίν, οἵτινες εὐαγγελίζοντες ὑμεῖν ὁδὸν σωτηρίας.
18 | τοῦτο δὲ ἐποίει ἐπὶ πολλὰς ἡμέρας. ἐπιστρέψας δὲ ὁ Παῦλος τῷ
πνεύματι καὶ διαπονηθεὶς εἶπεν· Παραγγέλλω σοι ἐν τῷ ὀνόματι

13 ημεν] ημην   14 διηννξεν   17 εκραζον

---

fuimus in ista civitate demorantes dies aliquos   13 die autem sabbati exibimus d
extra portam secundum flumen ubi oratio esset bidebatur et cum sedissemus
loquebatur quae cum venerant mulieres   14 et quaedam mulier nomine lydia
purpuraria thyatirum civivitatis colens d̄m audiebat cujus d̄n̄s aperuit cor intendere
eis quae dicebantur a paulo   15 ut autem baptizata est et omnis domus ejus rogavit
dicens si judicastis me fidelem d̄n̄o esse ingressi in domum meam manete et extorsuit
nobis   16 contigitquae euntibus nobis ad orationem puella quendam habentem s̄p̄m
phytonem obviam fieri nobis quae reditum multum praestabat dominis suis per hoc
divinando   17 haec persecuta est paulum et nos et clamabat dicens hi servi d̄i
excelsi sunt qui evangelizant vobis viam salutis   18 hoc autem faciebat per multos
dies conversus autem paulus in s̄p̄u et cum indoluisset dixit praecipio tibi in nomine

---

13 sedentes [enim, inquit,] locuti sumus mulieribus quae convenerant.   Irenaeus,
iii. 14, 1

---

13 συνεληλυθυιαις] quae congregatae erant ⁕ ibi ✓   Harclean

---

absence of any corresponding Greek
reading we may best regard it as of
strictly Latin origin. Other readings
which occur are negligible.

13 ενομιζετο ('it was customary')
προσευχη ειναι, as in the Antiochian,
is probably the 'Western' reading,
and the true text. 'Seemed,' or the
like, was a wrong translation of
ενομιζετο in gig d vg pesh hcl.text
(εδοκει D is a retranslation from videbatur). ενομιζομεν (-αμεν C) προσευχην
ειναι ('we thought,' etc.) C 81 boh
was probably a substitute to avoid
ενομιζετο in its less usual sense.

ενομιζεν προσευχην ειναι ℵ is an error,
either for ενομιζομεν or for a parallel
substitution with ενομιζον ('they
thought,' etc.). ενομιζομεν προσευχη
ειναι BA sah ('to a place wherein we
are accustomed to pray') combines
the Antiochian ('Western') reading
with that of C 81 boh, προσευχῇ being
taken (so sah) as dative ('in prayer').
Blass's conjecture ενομιζον ('they were
accustomed') εν προσευχη ειναι (cf.
Lk. vi. 12) would also provide a
common source (note the indefinite
subject) for both the text of BA sah
and the Antiochian, and is attractive.

ἐξελθεῖν ἀπ' αὐτῆς· καὶ ἐξῆλθεν αὐτῇ τῇ ὥρᾳ. καὶ ἰδόντες οἱ 19
κύριοι αὐτῆς ὅτι ἐξῆλθεν ἡ ἐλπὶς τῆς ἐργασίας αὐτῶν ἐπιλαβόμενοι
τὸν Παῦλον καὶ τὸν Σείλαν εἵλκυσαν εἰς τὴν ἀγορὰν ἐπὶ τοὺς
ἄρχοντας, καὶ προσαγαγόντες αὐτοὺς τοῖς στρατηγοῖς εἶπαν· 20
Οὗτοι οἱ ἄνθρωποι ἐκταράσσουσιν ἡμῶν τὴν πόλιν Ἰουδαῖοι
ὑπάρχοντες, καὶ καταγγέλλουσιν ἔθη ἃ οὐκ ἔξεστιν ἡμῖν παρα- 21
δέχεσθαι οὐδὲ ποιεῖν Ῥωμαίοις οὖσιν. καὶ συνεπέστη ὁ ὄχλος 22
κατ' αὐτῶν, καὶ οἱ στρατηγοὶ περιρήξαντες αὐτῶν τὰ ἱμάτια
ἐκέλευον ῥαβδίζειν, πολλὰς δὲ ἐπιθέντες αὐτοῖς πληγὰς ἔβαλον 23
εἰς φυλακήν, παραγγείλαντες τῷ δεσμοφύλακι ἀσφαλῶς τηρεῖν
αὐτούς· ὃς παραγγελίαν τοιαύτην λαβὼν ἔβαλεν αὐτοὺς εἰς τὴν 24
ἐσωτέραν φυλακὴν καὶ τοὺς πόδας ἠσφαλίσατο αὐτῶν εἰς τὸ
ξύλον. κατὰ δὲ τὸ μεσονύκτιον Παῦλος καὶ Σείλας προσευχό- 25
μενοι ὕμνουν τὸν θεόν, ἐπηκροῶντο δὲ αὐτῶν οἱ δέσμιοι· ἄφνω 26
δὲ σεισμὸς ἐγένετο μέγας ὥστε σαλευθῆναι τὰ θεμέλια τοῦ δεσμωτηρίου, ἠνεῴχθησαν δὲ αἱ θύραι πᾶσαι, καὶ πάντων τὰ δεσμὰ
ἀνέθη. ἔξυπνος δὲ γενόμενος ὁ δεσμοφύλαξ καὶ ἰδὼν ἀνεῳγμένας 27
τὰς θύρας τῆς φυλακῆς σπασάμενος τὴν μάχαιραν ἤμελλεν ἑαυτὸν
ἀναιρεῖν, νομίζων ἐκπεφευγέναι τοὺς δεσμίους. ἐφώνησεν δὲ 28
Παῦλος μεγάλῃ φωνῇ λέγων· Μηδὲν πράξῃς σεαυτῷ κακόν,
ἅπαντες γάρ ἐσμεν ἐνθάδε. αἰτήσας δὲ φῶτα εἰσεπήδησεν, καὶ 29

Editors 19 και ιδοντες] ιδοντες δε WH Soden και ιδοντες WHmg 23 δε] τε
WHmg 24 αυτων ησφαλισατο Soden (but cf. mg) 26 δε 2°]
+παραχρημα WH Soden 27 om την Soden 28 φωνη μεγαλη ο παυλος
Soden

Old Uncial 19 και ιδοντες B om και A^vid ιδοντες δε ℵC 81 (cf. D) τον 2° BℵA 81
om C(+D) 23 δε B 81 τε ℵAC(+D) παραγγειλαντες BACℵᶜ 81
(+D) παραγγιλας τε ℵ 24 εβαλεν BℵC 81 (+D) ελαβεν A
ησφαλισατο αυτων BℵAC 81 αυτων ησφαλισατο C²(+D) 25 το BAC 81
om ℵ σειλας BℵA 81 (+D) ο σιλας C αυτων BℵA 81 (+D)
+και C 26 δε 2° B δε (C τε) παραχρημα ℵAC 81 (+D) ανεθη
BACℵᶜ 81 ανελυθη ℵ(+D) 27 ανεωγμενας τας θυρας BℵA 81 (+D) τας
θυρας ανεωγμενας C την BC 81 (+D) om ℵA αναιρειν BℵA 81 (+D)
ανελειν C 28 παυλος μεγαλη φωνη B μεγαλη φωνη ο παυλος A φωνη
μεγαλη (+ ο 81 [+D]) παυλος ℵC 81 (cf. D) σεαυτω BℵAC (+D) σεαυτον 81

Antiochian 19 και ιδοντες] ιδοντες δε HLPSς(cf. D) 21 εθη] ηθη L εξεστιν]
εστιν S 23 δε] τε HLPSς(+D) 24 λαβων] ειληφως HLPSς
αυτων ησφαλισατο HLPSς(+D) 26 δε 2°] τε παραχρημα HLPSς
27 om την HLPSς 28 φωνη μεγαλη ο παυλος HLPSς(+D)

27 The reading ο δεσμοφυλαξ ο πιστος στεφανας 614 2147 is noteworthy.

Ἰησοῦ Χριστοῦ ἵνα ἐξέλθῃς ἀπ᾽ αὐτῆς· καὶ εὐθέως ἐξῆλθεν.

19 ὡς δὲ εἶδαν οἱ κύριοι τῆς παιδίσκης ὅτι ἀπεστέρηνται τῆς ἐργασίας
αὐτῶν ἧς εἶχαν δι᾽ αὐτῆς, ἐπιλαβόμενοι τὸν Παῦλον καὶ Σίλαν
20 εἵλκυσαν εἰς τὴν ἀγορὰν ἐπὶ τοὺς ἄρχοντας, καὶ προσαγαγόντες
αὐτοὺς τοῖ‹ς› στρατηγοῖς εἶπον· Οὗτοι οἱ ἄνθρωποι ἐκταράσ-
21 σουσιν ἡμῶν τὴν πόλιν Ἰουδαῖοι ὑπάρχοντες, καὶ καταγγέλλουσιν τὰ ἔθη ἃ οὐκ ἔξεστιν ἡμᾶς παραδέξασθαι οὔτε ποιεῖν Ῥω-
22 μαίοις ὑπάρχουσιν. καὶ πολὺς ὄχλος συνεπέστησαν κατ᾽ αὐτῶν
κράζοντες. τότε οἱ στρατηγοὶ περιρήξαντες αὐτῶν τὰ ἱμάτεια
23 ἐκέλευον ῥαβδείζειν, πολλάς τε ἐπιθέντες αὐτοῖς πληγὰς ἔβαλον
εἰς φυλακήν, παραγγείλαντες τῷ δεσμοφύλακει ἀσφαλῶς τηρεῖ-
24 σθαι αὐτούς· ὁ δὲ παραγγελείαν τοιαύτην λαβὼν ἔβαλεν αὐτοὺς
εἰς τὴν ἐσωτέραν φυλακὴν καὶ τοὺς πόδας αὐτῶν ἠσφαλίσατο ἐν
25 τῷ ξύλῳ. κατὰ δὲ μέσον τῆς νυκτὸς ὁ Παῦλος καὶ Σίλας προσευχόμενοι ὕμνουν τὸν θεόν, ἐπηκροῶντο δὲ αὐτῶν οἱ δέσμ‹ι›οι·
26 ἄφνω δὲ σεισμὸς ἐγένετο μέγας ὥστε σαλευθῆναι τὰ θεμέλια τοῦ
δεσμωτηρίου, ἠνεῴχθησαν δὲ παραχρῆμα αἱ θύραι πᾶσαι, καὶ
27 πάντων τὰ δεσμὰ ἀνελύθη. καὶ ἔξυπνος γενόμενος ὁ δεσμοφύλαξ
καὶ ἰδὼν ἀνεῳγμένας τὰς θύρας τῆς φυλακῆς καὶ σπασάμενος τὴν
μάχαιραν ἔμελλεν ἑαυτὸν ἀναιρεῖν, νομίζων ἐκπεφευγέναι τοὺς
28 δεσμίους. ἐφώνησεν δὲ φωνῇ μεγάλῃ ὁ Παῦλος λέγων· Μηδὲν
29 πράξῃς σεαυτῷ τι κακόν, ἅπαντες γάρ ἐσμεν ἐνθάδε. φῶτα δὲ

| 19 πεδισκης | απεστερησθαι | 20 προσαγαγοντας |
| 21 εθη] εθνη | 24 ησφαλισαντο | |

25 circa mediam autem noctem Paulus et Sileas orantes gratias agebant deo,
audiebant autem eos vincti.

Cyprian,
Test. iii. 14

28 ἐφώνησεν] clamavit ·⁙· ei ✓

Harclean

ἔντρομος γενόμενος προσέπεσεν τῷ Παύλῳ καὶ Σείλᾳ, καὶ προ- 30
αγαγὼν αὐτοὺς ἔξω ἔφη· Κύριοι, τί με δεῖ ποιεῖν ἵνα σωθῶ; | οἱ 31
δὲ εἶπαν· Πίστευσον ἐπὶ τὸν κύριον Ἰησοῦν, καὶ σωθήσῃ σὺ καὶ
ὁ οἶκός σου. καὶ ἐλάλησαν αὐτῷ τὸν λόγον τοῦ θεοῦ σὺν πᾶσιν 32
τοῖς ἐν τῇ οἰκίᾳ αὐτοῦ. καὶ παραλαβὼν αὐτοὺς ἐν ἐκείνῃ τῇ ὥρᾳ 33
τῆς νυκτὸς ἔλουσεν ἀπὸ τῶν πληγῶν, καὶ ἐβαπτίσθη αὐτὸς καὶ οἱ
αὐτοῦ ἅπαντες παραχρῆμα, ἀναγαγών τε αὐτοὺς εἰς τὸν οἶκον 34
παρέθηκεν τράπεζαν, καὶ ἠγαλλιάσατο πανοικεὶ πεπιστευκὼς τῷ
θεῷ. ἡμέρας δὲ γενομένης ἀπέστειλαν οἱ στρατηγοὶ τοὺς ῥαβ- 35
δούχους λέγοντες· Ἀπόλυσον τοὺς ἀνθρώπους ἐκείνους. ἀπ- 36
ήγγειλεν δὲ ὁ δεσμοφύλαξ τοὺς λόγους πρὸς τὸν Παῦλον, ὅτι
Ἀπέσταλκαν οἱ στρατηγοὶ ἵνα ἀπολυθῆτε· νῦν οὖν ἐξελθόντες
πορεύεσθε ἐν εἰρήνῃ. ὁ δὲ Παῦλος ἔφη πρὸς αὐτούς· Δείραντες 37
ἡμᾶς δημοσίᾳ ἀκατακρίτους, ἀνθρώπους Ῥωμαίους ὑπάρχοντας,
ἔβαλαν εἰς φυλακήν· καὶ νῦν λάθρᾳ ἡμᾶς ἐκβάλλουσιν; οὐ γάρ,
ἀλλὰ ἐλθόντες αὐτοὶ ἡμᾶς ἐξαγαγέτωσαν. ἀπήγγειλαν δὲ τοῖς 38

Editors 29 *τω σιλα* Soden 31 *ιησουν*] +*χριστον* Soden 32 *θεου*] *κυριου* WHmg Soden 33 *απαντες*] *παντες* Soden 36 *λογους*] +*τουτους* Soden om *εν ειρηνη* JHR

Old Uncial 29 *γενομενος* BℵA 81 *υπαρχων* C(+D) *σειλα* BC(+D) *τω σιλα* ℵA 81 30 *προαγαγων* BACℵ^c (cf. D) *προαγων* ℵ *προσαγαγων* 81 31 *ιησουν* BℵA 81 +*χριστον* C(+D) 32 *θεου* Bℵ *κυριου* ACℵ^c 81 (cf. D) 33 *οι* BℵC 81 (+D) +*οικιοι* A *απαντες* Bℵ *παντες* AC 81 (+D) 34 *τε* BℵA 81 (+D) *δε* C *οικον* BC 81 +*αυτου* ℵA(+D) *ηγαλλιασατο* BℵAC^2 81 *ηγαλλιατο* C^{vid}(+D) 36 *λογους* BC(+D) +*τουτους* ℵA 81 *απεσταλκαν* BℵA (cf. D) *απεστειλαν* C 81 *εν ειρηνη* BAC 81 *εις ειρηνην* ℵ 37 *εφη* BℵA(+D) om 81 38 *δε* 1° BA 81 (+D) *τε* ℵ

Antiochian 29 *τω σιλα* HLPSϚ 31 *ιησουν*] +*χριστον* HLPSϚ(+D) 32 *θεου*] *κυριου* HLPSϚ(+D) *συν*] *και* HLSϚ 33 *απαντες*] *παντες* HLPSϚ(+D) 34 *οικον*] +*αυτου* HLSϚ(+D) *ηγαλλιατο* P(+D) *θεω*] *κυριω* S 36 *λογους*] +*τουτους* HLPSϚ 37 om *ημας* 3° HPS 38 *απηγγειλαν*] *ανηγγειλαν* HLPSϚ

---

30 Hcl. ·※· *appropinquavit* represents, apparently with a change of order, *προσαγαγων*, which is found for *προαγαγων* in 614 minn.

32 Tischendorf *ad loc.* argues, with full references, that *του κυριου* AC ℵ^c 81 (D), Antiochian, versions, should be accepted rather than *του θεου* Bℵ. His ground is that *λογος του κυριου* is elsewhere often altered to *λογος του θεου*, but that the reverse process does not usually take place, though it sometimes occurs. But it is safer to follow Bℵ here, as usual; especially since a special force resides in *θεου*, which calls attention to the divine truth of the answer of vs. 31. In vs. 15, on the other hand, *θεω* D is inappropriate and reflects later and less precise ideas, while *κυριω* of nearly every other witness alone suits the situation.

36 *εν ειρηνη* (ℵ *εις ειρηνην*), omitted by D d gig, is inappropriate in the mouth of a Greek jailer; it may have been an early addition in 'biblical' style, for its inaptness would not be

αἰτήσας εἰσεπήδησεν, καὶ ἔντρομος ὑπάρχων προσέπεσεν πρὸς
30 τοὺς πόδας τῷ Παύλῳ καὶ Σίλᾳ, καὶ προήγαγεν αὐτοὺς ἔξω
τοὺς λοιποὺς ἀσφαλισάμενος, καὶ εἶπεν αὐτοῖς· Κύριοι, τί με δεῖ
31 ποιεῖν ἵνα σωθῶ; οἱ δὲ εἶπαν· Πίστευσον ἐπὶ τὸν κύριον Ἰησοῦν
32 Χριστόν, καὶ σωθήσῃ σὺ καὶ ὁ οἶκός σου. καὶ ἐλάλησαν αὐτῷ
33 τὸν λόγον κυρίου σὺν πᾶσιν τοῖς ἐν τῇ οἰκίᾳ αὐτοῦ. καὶ παραλαβὼν αὐτοὺς ἐν ἐκείνῃ τῇ ὥρᾳ τῆς νυκτὸς ἔλυσεν ἀπὸ τῶν
πληγῶν, καὶ αὐτὸς ἐβαπτίσθη καὶ οἱ αὐτοῦ πάντες παραχρῆμα,
34 [καὶ] ἀναγαγών τε αὐτοὺς εἰς τὸν οἶκον αὐτοῦ [καὶ] παρέθηκεν
τράπεζαν, καὶ ἠγαλλιᾶτο σὺν τῷ οἴκῳ αὐτοῦ πεπιστευκὼς ἐπὶ
35 τὸν θεόν. ἡμέρας δὲ γενομένης συνῆλθον οἱ στρατηγοὶ ἐπὶ τὸ
αὐτὸ εἰς τὴν ἀγορὰν καὶ ἀναμνησθέντες τὸν σεισμὸν τὸν γεγονότα
ἐφοβήθησαν, καὶ ἀπέστειλαν τοὺς ῥαβδούχους λέγοντας· Ἀπόλυσον
36 τοὺς ἀνθρώπους ἐκείνους οὓς ἐχθὲς παρέλαβες. καὶ εἰσελθὼν
ὁ δεσμοφύλαξ ἀπήγγειλεν τοὺς λόγους πρὸς τὸν Παῦλον, ὅτι
Ἀπεστάλκασιν οἱ στρατηγοὶ ἵνα ἀπολυθῆτε· νῦν οὖν ἐξελθόντες
37 πορεύεσθε. ὁ δὲ Παῦλος ἔφη πρὸς αὐτούς· Ἀναιτείους δείραντες
ἡμᾶς δημοσίᾳ ἀκατακρίτους, ἀνθρώπους Ῥωμαίους ὑπάρχοντας, ἔβαλαν εἰς φυλακήν· καὶ νῦν λάθρα ἡμᾶς ἐκβάλλουσιν;
38 οὐ γάρ, ἀλλὰ ἐλθόντες αὐτοὶ ἡμᾶς ἐξαγαγέτωσαν. ἀπήγγειλαν

29 αιτησας] ετησας   35 οι] οις   36 πορευεσθαι

---

vero petens accucurrit et tremibundus factus procidit ad pedes paulo et silae   30 et **d**
cum produxisset eos foras ceteros custodivit et dixit illis domini quid me oportet
facere ut salvus fiam   31 ad illi dixerunt crede in d̄n̄o ī̄h̄ū x̄p̄o et salvus fies tu et
domus tua   32 et locuti sunt ei verbum d̄n̄ī cum omnibus qui erant in domum ejus
33 et adpraehendit eos in illa hora noctis solvit plagas et ipse baptizatus est et ejus
omnes confestim   34 et perduxit eos in domum suam et posuit mensam et exultabat
cum tota domu sua credens in d̄n̄o   35 die autem facta convenerunt magistrati id
ipsud in foro et rememorati sunt terrae motum qui factus est timuerunt et trans-
miserunt lectores dicentes dimitte homines illos quos externa die suscepisti   36 et
ingressus optio carceris renuntiavit hos sermones ad paulum quoniam miserunt
praetores ut dimittamini nunc ergo exeuntes ambulate   37 paulus autem ait ad
ipsos anetios caesos nos publice indemnatos homines romanos cives miserunt in
carcerem et nunc occultae nos eiciunt non ita sed veniant ipsi nos producant

---

30 και προηγαγεν αυτους εξω τους λοιπους ασφαλισαμενος και] et quum eduxisset **Harclean**
eos foras ·※· et reliquos astrinxisset tuto, appropinquavit et ✓   35 συνηλθον
. . . εφοβηθησαν] mg congregati sunt praefecti una in foro et recordati terrae-
motus qui factus erat timuerunt

---

likely to cause offence to an ancient
copyist or editor.
37 αναιτειους D d pesh is the
'Western' substitute, in changed

position, for ακατακριτους of the B-text.
The latter is omitted by pesh, and
probably was brought into the text of
D d by conflation.

στρατηγοῖς οἱ ῥαβδοῦχοι τὰ ῥήματα ταῦτα· ἐφοβήθησαν δὲ
ἀκούσαντες ὅτι Ῥωμαῖοί εἰσιν, καὶ ἐλθόντες παρεκάλεσαν αὐτούς, 39
καὶ ἐξαγαγόντες ἠρώτων ἀπελθεῖν ἀπὸ τῆς πόλεως. ἐξελθόντες 40
δὲ ἀπὸ τῆς φυλακῆς εἰσῆλθον πρὸς τὴν Λυδίαν, καὶ ἰδόντες
παρεκάλεσαν τοὺς ἀδελφοὺς καὶ ἐξῆλθαν.

Διοδεύσαντες δὲ τὴν Ἀμφίπολιν καὶ τὴν Ἀπολλωνίαν ἦλθον XVII
εἰς τὴν Θεσσαλονείκην, ὅπου ἦν συναγωγὴ τῶν Ἰουδαίων. κατὰ δὲ 2
τὸ εἰωθὸς τῷ Παύλῳ εἰσῆλθεν πρὸς αὐτοὺς καὶ ἐπὶ σάββατα τρία
διελέξατο αὐτοῖς ἀπὸ τῶν γραφῶν, διανοίγων καὶ παρατιθέμενος 3
ὅτι τὸν Χριστὸν ἔδει παθεῖν καὶ ἀναστῆναι ἐκ νεκρῶν, καὶ ὅτι
οὗτός ἐστιν ὁ Χριστός, ὁ Ἰησοῦς ὃν ἐγὼ καταγγέλλω ὑμῖν. καί 4

Editors   39 om και εξαγαγοντες ηρωτων JHR   1 om την 3° WH Soden JHR
             3 om ο before χριστος WHmg   om ο before ιησους WHmg Soden JHR

Old Uncial   38 εφοβηθησαν BℵA(+D)   φοβηθησαντες 81   40 απο Bℵ   εκ A 81 (+D)
             1 αμφιπολιν BAℵcorr 81 (+D)   πολιν ℵ   την 3° B om ℵA 81 (+D)
             2 εισηλθεν BℵA(+D)   εισηλθον 81   3 ο χριστος ο ιησους B   χριστος
             ιησους A 81 (+D)   ιησους χριστος ℵ   καταγγελλω BℵA(+D)   καταγγελω 81

Antiochian   38 εφοβηθησαν δε] και εφοβηθησαν HLPSϚ   39 απελθειν] εξελθειν
             HLPSϚ(+D)   om απο HLPSϚ(+D)   40 απο] εκ HLPSϚ(+D)
             προς] εις Ϛ   παρεκαλεσαν τους αδελφους] τους αδελφους παρεκαλεσαν αυτους
             HLPSϚ (cf. D)   1 om την 2° HLPSϚ(+D)   om την 3° HLPSϚ(+D)
             η συναγωγη HLPSϚ   2 διελεγετο HLPSϚ   3 om ο before ιησους HLPSϚ(+D)

---

38 (αυ)τοις(οι) στρατηγοις D d is
otiose, in view of the following προς
τους στρατηγους, and is probably due
to contamination from the B-text.
The omission of τοις στρατηγοις in 383
may be a genuine 'Western' survival,
but is more likely to be an emendation.
Probably the 'Western' text had
αυτοι, the combination of which with
an interlinear τοις would produce the
monstrum αυτοισοι. In pesh a modified
fragment of the 'Western' text survives in a rendering equivalent to τα
ρηματα ταυτα τα ρηθεντα αυτοις. τα
ρηματα ταυτα seems to owe its place
in D to contamination.

39 In the 'Western' addition to
vs. 39 the words εξαγαγοντες παρεκαλεσαν αυτους λεγοντες D d are not found
in 614 and other minn, and are not
represented in hcl ※ nor in the free
quotation by Ephrem in the Armenian
commentary (below, pp. 430 ff.). Since
with this exception (apart from unimportant minor variants) the whole
gloss (εξελθειν . . . καθ υμων) is found

in these witnesses, it is probable that
these words, originally absent from
the 'Western' text, have been introduced into the text of D d by conflation from the B-text (which, however,
reads ηρωτων, not παρεκαλεσαν). One
element of the narrative in the B-text
would thus wholly disappear in the
'Western.' Since omission of this kind
is contrary to the usual practice of the
'Western' glossator, it seems not
improbable that the original text read
παρεκαλεσαν αυτους απελθειν, and that
και εξαγαγοντες ηρωτων in the B-text
is a very early gloss suggested by
εξαγαγετωσαν of vs. 37. This would
account for the present text of BℵA
81, in which both the absence of an
infinitive after παρεκαλεσαν and the
presence of εξαγαγοντες (vs. 39) side
by side with εξελθοντες (vs. 40) are
harsh.

Hcl also shows a conflation, since
the words covered by ※ are properly
a substitute for the sentence which
follows. This may indicate that

δὲ τοῖς στρατηγοῖς οἱ ῥαβδοῦχοι τὰ ῥήματα ταῦτα τὰ
ῥηθέντα πρὸς τοὺς στρατηγούς· οἱ δὲ ἀκούσαντες ὅτι Ῥωμαῖοί
39 εἰσιν ἐφοβήθησαν, καὶ παραγενόμενοι μετὰ φίλων πολλῶν εἰς
τὴν φυλακὴν παρεκάλεσαν αὐτοὺς ἐξελθεῖν εἰπόντες· Ἠγνοήσαμεν τὰ καθ᾽ ὑμᾶς ὅτι ἐστὲ ἄνδρες δίκαιοι. καὶ ἐξαγαγόντες
παρεκάλεσαν αὐτοὺς λέγοντες· Ἐκ τῆς πόλεως ταύτης ἐξέλθατε μήποτε πάλιν συνστραφῶσιν ἡμεῖν ἐπικράζοντες καθ᾽
40 ὑμῶν. ἐξελθόντες δὲ ἐκ τῆς φυλακῆς ἦλθον πρὸς τὴν Λυδίαν,
καὶ ἰδόντες τοὺς ἀδελφοὺς διηγήσαντο ὅσα ἐποίησεν κύριος
αὐτοῖς παρακαλέσαντες αὐτούς, καὶ ἐξῆλθαν.
XVII Διοδεύσαντες δὲ τὴν Ἀμφίπολιν καὶ κατῆλθον εἰς Ἀπολ-
λωνίδα κἀκεῖθεν εἰς Θεσσαλονίκην, ὅπου ἦν συναγωγὴ τῶν Ἰου-
2 δαίων. καὶ κατὰ τὸ εἰωθὸς ὁ Παῦλος εἰσῆλθεν πρὸς αὐτούς, ἐπὶ
3 σάββατα τρία διελέχθη αὐτοῖς ἐκ τῶν γραφῶν, διανοίγων καὶ
παρατιθέμενος ὅτι Χριστὸν ἔδει παθεῖν καὶ ἀναστῆναι ἐκ νεκρῶν,
καὶ ὅτι οὗτός ἐστιν Χριστός, Ἰησοῦς ὃν ἐγὼ καταγγέλλω ὑμεῖν.

38 τοις] αυτοισοι   39 εστε] εσται   2 ειωθος] εισωθος

---

38 renuntiaverunt autem praetoribus lectores verba haec quae dicta sunt a praetores d
cum autem audierunt quia romani sunt timuerunt 39 et cum venissent cum amicis
multis in carcerem rogaverunt eos exire dicentes ignoramus adversum uos quoniam
estis viri justi et cum produxissent rogaverunt eos dicentes de civitate ista exite ne
forte iterum convertantur ad nos clamantes adversum vos 40 et cum exissent de
carcere venerunt ad lydiam et cum vidissent fratres narraverunt quanta fecit d̄n̄s
cum eis exhorti sunt eos et exierunt
  1 cum ambulassent autem amphipolim et descenderunt apolloniam et inde
thessalonicam ubi erat synagoga judaeorum 2 et secundum consuetudinem paulus
introibit ad eos per sabbata tria disputabit eis de scripturis 3 adaperiens et confirmans quia x̄p̄m̄ oportet pati et resurgere a mortuis et quia hic est x̄p̄s̄ īh̄s̄ quem

---

39 εις την φυλακην] ⁙ in carcerem √   εξελθειν ειποντες . . . επικραζοντες Harclean
καθ υμων] ⁙ exire dicentes : Nesciebamus ea quae de vobis quod essetis viri
justi ; et ex hac civitate exite, ne forte convertantur rursus illi qui clamaverunt contra vos √ et quum eduxissent eos persuadebant ut egrederentur ex
civitate

---

what was originally a marginal note
has come to be wrongly inserted with
⁙ in the text.
For the order of words *convertantur rursus* hcl.*mg* cf. επιστραφωσι
παλιν 614 minn ; likewise for *illi qui
clamaverunt* cf. οι επικραξαντες 614
minn.
40 From a Bohemian MS. of 1429 a

'Western' reading is cited as follows :
"Und als sie die Brüder gesehen,
erzählten sie ihnen, was ihnen aus
Gnade der Herr gethan, ermunterten
dieselben, und reisten ab" ; see
Oesterreichisches Litteraturblatt, vol.
vi, 1897, cols. 163 f. For Latin
evidence to the gloss see Wordsworth
and White.

τινες ἐξ αὐτῶν ἐπείσθησαν καὶ προσεκληρώθησαν τῷ Παύλῳ
καὶ Σείλᾳ, τῶν τε σεβομένων Ἑλλήνων πλῆθος πολὺ γυναικῶν
τε τῶν πρώτων οὐχ ὀλίγαι. ζηλώσαντες δὲ οἱ Ἰουδαῖοι καὶ 5
προσλαβόμενοι τῶν ἀγοραίων ἄνδρας τινὰς πονηροὺς καὶ ὀχλο-
ποιήσαντες ἐθορύβουν τὴν πόλιν, καὶ ἐπιστάντες τῇ οἰκίᾳ Ἰάσονος
ἐζήτουν αὐτοὺς προαγαγεῖν εἰς τὸν δῆμον· μὴ εὑρόντες δὲ αὐτοὺς 6
ἔσυρον Ἰάσονα καί τινας ἀδελφοὺς ἐπὶ τοὺς πολιτάρχας, βοῶντες
ὅτι Οἱ τὴν οἰκουμένην ἀναστατώσαντες οὗτοι καὶ ἐνθάδε πάρεισιν,
| οὓς ὑποδέδεκται Ἰάσων· καὶ οὗτοι πάντες ἀπέναντι τῶν δογμάτων 7
Καίσαρος πράσσουσιν, βασιλέα ἕτερον λέγοντες εἶναι Ἰησοῦν.
ἐτάραξαν δὲ τὸν ὄχλον καὶ τοὺς πολιτάρχας ἀκούοντας ταῦτα, 8
καὶ λαβόντες τὸ ἱκανὸν παρὰ τοῦ Ἰάσονος καὶ τῶν λοιπῶν ἀπ- 9

Editors   4 [τω] σιλα WH   τω σιλα Soden JHR   γυναικες JHR

Old Uncial   4 σειλα B   τω σιλα אA 81 (+D)   τε 1° BאA   δε 81   σεβομενων
     Bא +και A 81 (+D)   5 ανδρας τινας BA 81   τινας ανδρας א(+D)
     αυτους Bא 81 (+D)   αυτον Aᵛⁱᵈ   6 εσυρον BAא° 81 (cf. D)   ευρον א
     βοωντες Bא 81 (+D)   βοωντας A

Antiochian   4 τω σιλα HLPSϚ(+D)   τε 1°] δε H   om ελληνων S   πολυ
πληθος HLPSϚ   5 ζηλωσαντες δε οι ιουδαιοι και προσλαβομενοι] προσλαβομενοι
δε οι ιουδαιοι οι απειθουντες HLPS (cf. D)   ζηλωσαντες δε οι απειθουντες ιουδαιοι και
προσλαβομενοι Ϛ   τινας ανδρας HLPSϚ(+D)   και επισταντες]
επισταντες τε (δε S) HLPSϚ   προαγαγειν] αγαγειν HPSϚ   αναγαγειν L
6 τον ιασονα HLPSϚ   om τινας αδελφους επι S   7 πρασσουσιν]
ταρασσουσιν S   λεγοντες ετερον HLPSϚ(+D)   om ιησουν S

4 In the text of D two matters are
to be noted :

(a) τη διδαχη probably shows that
τω παυλω και τω σιλαια was introduced
by conflation.

(b) πληθος πολυ D is redundant after
πολλοι, and is probably due to conflation from the B-text. Observe
that the Antiochian text reads πολυ
πληθος, with change in the order of
the words. Pesh reads: 'and many
(cf. πολλοι D) of the Greeks who feared
God and also noble women not a few.'

Thus emended, D appears to offer
the 'Western' text, of which the
following account can be given : (1) in
order to avoid the awkwardness in the
B-text of the loosely appended additional subject πληθος, the paraphrast
substituted for it πολλοι, in a different
position, and dropped τε before σεβομενων, thus making πολλοι the subject
of προσεκληρωθησαν.

(2) Because of the unusual character

of the expression των σεβομενων
ελληνων of the B-text, και was inserted after σεβομενων so as to indicate
two classes instead of one.

As to (1) and (2), πολλοι has survived
in pesh, while the omission of τε and
the insertion of και are both found
in gig; the insertion of και is still
seen in A 81 minn vg boh. In both
these points the text of BאC seems
clearly more original.

(3) The 'Western' και γυναικες των
πρωτων D d hcl, in the sense 'wives
of the leading men,' seems a better
reading than γυναικων τε των πρωτων
of the B-text, to which, under a desire
for grammatical uniformity, it could
easily be altered. Vg pesh have
preserved the nominative in their
free rendering (cf. vs. 12), 'noble
women.'

For a different view of the verse
see Ramsay, *St. Paul the Traveller*,
pp. 226 f., 235 f., who thinks the

CODEX BEZAE 163

4 καί τινες ἐξ αὐτῶν ἐπίσθησαν, καὶ προσεκληρώθησαν †τῷ Παύλῳ
καὶ τῷ Σιλαίᾳ† τῇ διδαχῇ πολλοὶ τῶν σεβομένων καὶ Ἑλλήνων
5 πλῆθος πολὺ καὶ γυναῖκες τῶν πρώτων οὐκ ὀλίγαι. οἱ δὲ
ἀπειθοῦντες Ἰουδαῖοι συνστρέψαντές τινας ἄνδρας τῶν ἀγοραίων
πονηροὺς ἐθορυβοῦσαν τὴν πόλιν, καὶ ἐπιστάντες τῇ οἰκίᾳ Ἰά-
6 σωνος ἐζήτουν αὐτοὺς ἐξαγαγεῖν εἰς τὸν δῆμον· μὴ εὑρόντες δὲ
αὐτοὺς ἔσυραν Ἰάσωναν καί τινας ἀδελφοὺς ἐπὶ τοὺς πολειτ-
άρχας, βοῶντες καὶ λέγοντες ὅτι Οἱ τὴν οἰκουμένην ἀνα-
7 στατώσαντες οὗτοί εἰσιν καὶ ἐνθάδε πάρεισιν, οὓς ὑποδέδεκται
Ἰάσων· καὶ οὗτοι πάντες ἀπέναντι τῶν δογμάτων Καίσαρος πράσ-
8 σουσιν, βασιλέα λέγοντες ἕτερον εἶναι Ἰησοῦν. καὶ ἐτάραξαν
9 τοὺς πολιτάρχας καὶ τὸν ὄχλον. ἀκούσαντες ταῦτα | καὶ λαβόντες
τὸ ἱκανὸν παρὰ τοῦ Ἰάσωνος καὶ τῶν λοιπῶν ἀπέλυσαν αὐτούς.

6 τινας] τινες   8 εταραξεν

ego adnuntio vobis 4 et quidam ex eis persuasum est et consortes facti sunt paulo d
et silae doctrinae multi caelicolarum et graecorum multitudo magna et mulieres quae
morum non pauce 5 adsuptis vero judaeis convertentes quosdam viros forenses
subdoles turbabant civitatem et circumstantes ad domum jasonis quaerebant eos
producere ad populum 6 cum vero non invenissent eos traxerunt jasonē et quosdam
fratres ad principes civitatis clamantes et dicentes quia qui orbem terrae inqui-
taverunt hi sunt et hoc venerunt 7 quos suscepit jason et isti omnes contra
consulta caesaris agunt regem dicentes alium esse īhm 8 et concitaverunt principes
et turbam audientes haec 9 et accipientes satis ab jasonem et ceteris dismiserunt

8 ακουσαντες] mg [quum] dicerent   9 και λαβοντες το ικανον] mg ipsi Harclean
quidem primores civitatis, quum accepissent sponsores

author intended to distinguish between 'sebomenoi' and heathen
'Greeks,' and who therefore prefers
the 'Western' addition of και after
σεβομενων. Cf. above, p. ccxxxiii.
8 The nominative ακουσαντες D (ακουοντες 614) belongs to the 'Western'
text. Pesh renders freely, with the
main verb ('were disturbed') in the
passive, and so retains the participle
in the nominative. In hcl.mg the
participle rendered seems to have
been λεγοντες, a substitution otherwise

unattested but still nominative. The
nominative was probably an early
accidental variant. The sense of the
B-text is superior, both as to the
order of τον οχλον και τους πολιταρχας
and as to the bearing of ακουοντας.
Pesh and hcl.mg both render το
ικανον with the same word (a different
one from that used in hcl.text), while
otherwise their renderings are not
identical. The word had perhaps
been taken over by the Philoxenian
from the Peshitto.

ἔλυσαν αὐτούς. οἱ δὲ ἀδελφοὶ εὐθέως διὰ νυκτὸς ἐξέπεμψαν τόν 10
τε Παῦλον καὶ τὸν Σείλαν εἰς Βέροιαν, οἵτινες παραγενόμενοι
εἰς τὴν συναγωγὴν τῶν Ἰουδαίων ἀπῄεσαν· οὗτοι δὲ ἦσαν εὐγενέ- 11
στεροι τῶν ἐν Θεσσαλονείκῃ, οἵτινες ἐδέξαντο τὸν λόγον μετὰ
πάσης προθυμίας, τὸ καθ᾽ ἡμέραν ἀνακρείνοντες τὰς γραφὰς
εἰ ἔχοι ταῦτα οὕτως. πολλοὶ μὲν οὖν ἐξ αὐτῶν ἐπίστευσαν, 12
καὶ τῶν Ἑλληνίδων γυναικῶν τῶν εὐσχημόνων καὶ ἀνδρῶν οὐκ
ὀλίγοι. ὡς δὲ ἔγνωσαν οἱ ἀπὸ τῆς Θεσσαλονείκης Ἰουδαῖοι ὅτι 13
καὶ ἐν τῇ Βεροίᾳ κατηγγέλη ὑπὸ τοῦ Παύλου ὁ λόγος τοῦ θεοῦ,
ἦλθον κἀκεῖ σαλεύοντες καὶ ταράσσοντες τοὺς ὄχλους. εὐθέως 14
δὲ τότε τὸν Παῦλον ἐξαπέστειλαν οἱ ἀδελφοὶ πορεύεσθαι ἕως ἐπὶ
τὴν θάλασσαν· ὑπέμεινάν τε ὅ τε Σείλας καὶ ὁ Τιμόθεος ἐκεῖ.
οἱ δὲ καθιστάνοντες τὸν Παῦλον ἤγαγον ἕως Ἀθηνῶν, καὶ 15
λαβόντες ἐντολὴν πρὸς τὸν Σείλαν καὶ τὸν Τιμόθεον ἵνα ὡς
τάχιστα ἔλθωσιν πρὸς αὐτὸν ἐξῄεσαν.

Ἐν δὲ ταῖς Ἀθήναις ἐκδεχομένου αὐτοὺς τοῦ Παύλου, παρ- 16

Editors   11 [το] WH Soden   14 εως] ως JHR   15 καθιστανοντες] καθιστωντες
Soden

Old Uncial   10 ευθεως δια νυκτος εξεπεμψαν B(+D)   ευθεως εξεπεμψαν δια νυκτος ℵ   εξεπεμψαν A   ευθεως εξεπεμψαν 81   τε BℵA   δε 81   11 το B
om ℵA 81 (+D)   12 ελληνιδων BℵA   ελληδων 81 (cf. D)   14 δε BℵA
om 81   υπεμειναν Bℵ 81   υπεμεινεν A(+D)   15 καθιστανοντες BA
(cf. D)   καθισπαντες ℵ   καθιστωντες ℵᶜ   αποκαθιστανοντες 81   τον 3° Bℵ 81
om A(+D)   16 αυτους BAℵᶜ 81   αυτου ℵ(+D)   του παυλου BAℵᶜ 81
(+D)   om ℵ

Antiochian   10 της νυκτος HLPSꞅ   απηεσαν των ιουδαιων HLPS   13 om
και ταρασσοντες HLPSꞅ   τον οχλον H   14 εως] ως HLPꞅ
om S(+D)   υπεμεινον (-εν S) HLPSꞅ   τε 1°] δε HLPSꞅ(+D)   εκει ο τε
σιλας και ο τιμοθεος H   15 καθιστανοντες] καθιστωντες HLPSꞅ
ηγαγον] +αυτον HLPSꞅ   om τον 3° HLPSꞅ(+D)

---

11 For hcl.*mg* cf. καθως παυλος
απαγγελλει 614 minn gig vg.*cod.*
ardmach.
14-15 For εως the reading ως HLP
hcl.*text* (S minn D gig omit altogether;
d *ad mare versus*) yields an attractive
sense in view of vs. 15 (which does not
suggest a sea voyage), and is perhaps to
be preferred, in spite of the lack of
ancient attestation.
The gloss, παρηλθεν δε . . . τον
λογον, in vs. 15, found in D d and
supported in part by Ephrem (below,
p. 432) and by the Armenian catena-
fragment (Chrysostom?) cited in

the following paragraph, creates the
suspicion that the 'Western' text of
vs. 14 was based on a corrupt variant,
θεσσαλιαν (Ephr 'Thessalonica')
for θαλασσαν. The words επι την θαλασσαν
(without ως or εως) would thus owe
their presence in D d to a later
restoration from the usual text.
This corruption would have made
natural the 'Western' explanation
offered in vs. 15 to show why Paul
did not preach in Thessaly after all.
That the supposed variant θεσσαλιαν
is the true reading is rendered unlikely
by the word εξαπεστειλαν, to which it

10 οἱ δὲ ἀδελφοὶ εὐθέως διὰ νυκτὸς ἐξέπεμψαν τὸν Παῦλον καὶ τὸν
Σείλαν εἰ‹ς› Βέροιαν, οἵτινες παραγενόμενοι εἰς τὴν συναγωγὴν
11 τῶν Ἰουδαίων ἀπῄεσαν· οὗτοι δὲ ἦσαν εὐγενεῖς τῶν ἐν τῇ Θεσ-
σαλονίκῃ, οἵτινες ἐδέξαντο τὸν λόγον μετὰ πάσης προθυμίας,
καθ᾽ ἡμέραν ἀνακρείνοντες τὰς γραφὰς εἰ ἔχει ταῦτα οὕτως.
12 τινὲς μὲν οὖν αὐτῶν ἐπίστευσαν, τινὲς δὲ ἠπίστησαν, καὶ τῶν
Ἑλλήνων καὶ τῶν εὐσχημόνων ἄνδρες καὶ γυναῖκες ἱκανοὶ ἐπί-
13 στευσαν. ὡς δὲ ἔγνωσαν οἱ ἀπὸ Θεσσαλονίκης Ἰουδαῖοι ὅτι λόγος
θεοῦ κατήγγελη εἰς Βέροιαν καὶ ἐπίστευσαν, καὶ ἦλθον εἰς αὐτὴν
κἀκεῖ σαλεύοντες καὶ τα‹ρά›σσοντες τοὺς ὄχλους οὐ διελίμπανον.
14 τὸν μὲν οὖν Παῦλον οἱ ἀδελφοὶ ἐξαπέστειλαν ἀπελθεῖν ἐπὶ τὴν
15 θάλασσαν· ὑπέμεινεν δὲ ὁ Σείλας καὶ ὁ Τιμόθεος ἐκεῖ. οἱ δὲ
καταστάνοντες τὸν Παῦλον ἤγαγον ἕως Ἀθηνῶν, παρῆλθεν δὲ
τὴν Θεσσαλίαν, ἐκωλύθη γὰρ εἰς αὐτοὺς κηρύξαι τὸν λόγον,
λαβόντες δὲ ἐντολὴν παρὰ Παύλου πρὸς τὸν Σείλαν καὶ Τιμόθεον
ὅπως ἐν τάχει ἔλθωσιν πρὸς αὐτὸν ἐξῄεσαν.
16 Ἐν δὲ ταῖς Ἀθήναις ἐκδεχομένου αὐτοῦ τοῦ Παύλου, παρ-

eos   10 vero fratres statim per noctem dismiserunt paulum et silan beroean qui d
cum advenissent in synagogam judaeorum ibant   11 hi autem sunt nobiliores qui
thessalonicae sunt qui exceperunt verbum cum omni animatione cottidiae exani-
mantes scripturas si habeant haec ita   12 multi ergo ex his crediderunt quidam vero
credere noluerunt et grecorum et non placentium et viri et mulieris pleres crediderunt
13 ut autem cognoverunt qui a thessalonica judaei quia verbum d̄ī adnuntiatum est
in beroean et credederunt et venerunt in eam et illic commoventes et turbantes
multitudinem non cessabant   14 statimquae paulum fratres dismiserunt abire ad
mare versus substinuit autem silas et timotheus ibi   15 qui autem ducebant paulum
perduxerunt usque athenis transiit vero thessaliam vetatus est enim super eos
praedicare sermonem ut accepissent mandatum a paulo ad silam et timotheum ut
quam cileriter veniant ad eum proficiscebantur   16 vero athenis expectante eo

---

11 ουτως] + ⁙ sicut Paulus evangelizabat ✓   Harclean

---

is not natural to join a destination at
which Paul did not stop. And with
the readings ως and θεσσαλιαν combined, the sentence would lose all
meaning, for Paul's route lay not only
ostensibly but actually through
Thessaly.

A passage in the Armenian catena,
there ascribed to Ephrem but only
in part included in the Ephrem-
extracts printed in this volume because for the most part not confirmed
by Ephrem's continuous text, reads:
"He came then as far as the shore,
receding (ὑποχωρῶν ?). But the Holy
Spirit prevented him from preaching,

lest perhaps they should slay him.
And those who conducted Paul led
him as far as Athens." This may be
Chrysostom. With it compare Chrysostom (ed. Savile, p. 816, line 4)
ὅρα αὐτὸν καὶ ὑποχωροῦντα καὶ ἐνιστά-
μενον καὶ πολλὰ ἀνθρωπίνως ποιοῦντα,
also p. 817, lines 31 ff., and p. 817,
lines 2 ff.   It has been sought to
bring the reading of d abire ad mare
versus into relation with these
passages, but with no clear result.
See J. R. Harris, Four Lectures, pp.
47, 93 f., Conybeare, American
Journal of Philology, xvii, 1896,
pp. 164 f.

ωξύνετο τὸ πνεῦμα αὐτοῦ ἐν αὐτῷ θεωροῦντος κατείδωλον οὖσαν
τὴν πόλιν. διελέγετο μὲν οὖν ἐν τῇ συναγωγῇ τοῖς Ἰουδαίοις 17
καὶ τοῖς σεβομένοις καὶ ἐν τῇ ἀγορᾷ κατὰ πᾶσαν ἡμέραν πρὸς
τοὺς παρατυγχάνοντας. τινὲς δὲ καὶ τῶν Ἐπικουρίων καὶ 18
Στωικῶν φιλοσόφων συνέβαλλον αὐτῷ, καί τινες ἔλεγον· Τί ἂν
θέλοι ὁ σπερμολόγος οὗτος λέγειν; οἱ δέ· Ξένων δαιμονίων
δοκεῖ καταγγελεὺς εἶναι· ὅτι τὸν Ἰησοῦν καὶ τὴν ἀνάστασιν
εὐηγγελίζετο. ἐπιλαβόμενοι δὲ αὐτοῦ ἐπὶ τὸν Ἄρειον Πάγον 19
ἤγαγον, λέγοντες· Δυνάμεθα γνῶναι τίς ἡ καινὴ αὕτη ὑπὸ σοῦ
λαλουμένη διδαχή; ξενίζοντα γάρ τινα εἰσφέρεις εἰς τὰς ἀκοὰς 20
ἡμῶν· βουλόμεθα οὖν γνῶναι τίνα θέλει ταῦτα εἶναι. Ἀθηναῖοι 21
δὲ πάντες καὶ οἱ ἐπιδημοῦντες ξένοι εἰς οὐδὲν ἕτερον ηὐκαίρουν
ἢ λέγειν τι ἢ ἀκούειν τι καινότερον. σταθεὶς δὲ Παῦλος ἐν μέσῳ 22
τοῦ Ἀρείου Πάγου ἔφη· Ἄνδρες Ἀθηναῖοι, κατὰ πάντα ὡς
δεισιδαιμονεστέρους ὑμᾶς θεωρῶ· διερχόμενος γὰρ καὶ ἀναθεωρῶν 23
τὰ σεβάσματα ὑμῶν εὗρον καὶ βωμὸν ἐν ᾧ ἐπεγέγραπτο· Ἀγνώστῳ
Θεῷ. ὃ οὖν ἀγνοοῦντες εὐσεβεῖτε, τοῦτο ἐγὼ καταγγέλλω ὑμῖν.
ὁ θεὸς ὁ ποιήσας τὸν κόσμον καὶ πάντα τὰ ἐν αὐτῷ, οὗτος οὐρανοῦ 24

23 υμιν] υμων

Editors			
19 δε] τε Soden	αυτη] +[η] WH	+η Soden JHR	21 η 2°] και
Soden mg	[τι 2°] Soden	22 ο παυλος Soden	23 ον Soden mg
τουτον Soden mg			

Old Uncial			
18 ευηγγελιζετο BΝ	+αυτοις AΝᶜ 81	19 δε B 81 (cf. D)	τε ΝA
ηγαγον BΝ 81 (+D)	ηγον A	αυτη B(+D) +η ΝA 81	λαλουμενη
BΝA λεγομενη 81	20 εισφερεις BAΝᶜ 81 (cf. D)	εισφερει Ν	21 η 2°
BΝA(+D) και 81	τι 2° BΝA om 81 (+D)		22 παυλος BΝA
ο παυλος 81 (+D)	εφη BA 81 (+D) ειπεν Ν		23 σεβασματα BA 81 (+D)
σεβαστα Ν	ο BΝA 81 (+D) ον A² Νᶜ		τουτο BΝA(+D) τουτον
A² Νᶜ 81	καταγγελλω BΝA(+D) καταγγελω 81		υμιν B²(B³ Tdf)

Antiochian			
16 θεωρουντι HLPSS⸌(+D)	18 om και 1° S⸌	των στωικων
HLPSS⸌(+D)	συνεβαλον L (cf. D)	αναστασιν] +αυτοις S⸌	ευηγγε-
λιζετο] +αυτοις H	19 δε] τε HLPSS⸌	αυτου] αυτους S	αυτη]
+η HLPSS⸌	20 τινα θελει] τι αν θελοι (θελει P) HLPSS⸌(+D)	21 η 2°]
και HLPSS⸌	om τι 2° HLPSS⸌(+D)	22 ο παυλος HLPSS⸌(+D)
om ανδρες αθηναιοι κατα παντα S	23 ο] ον HLPSS⸌	ευσεβειτε] σεβητε L
τουτον HLPSS⸌	καταγγελω HS	

17 τοις before εν τη αγορα D d hcl.mg
sah makes προς τους παρατυγχανοντας
(D παρατυχοντας) superfluous. The
fact that d (unlike D) inserts et his
qui forte aderant before et hiis qui in
foro, together with the varying form

of the pronoun (his, not hiis), suggests that the insertion of τοις in the
'Western' text was balanced by the
omission of προς τους παρατυγχανοντας,
and that these latter words have been
reintroduced in D d sah from the

ωξύνετο πνεῦμα αὐτοῦ ἐν αὐτῷ θεωροῦντι κατείδωλον οὖσαν τὴν
17 πόλιν. διελέγετο μὲν οὖν ἐν τῇ συναγωγῇ τοῖς Ἰουδαίοις καὶ
τοῖς σεβομένοις καὶ τοῖς ἐν τῇ ἀγορᾷ κατὰ πᾶσαν ἡμέραν πρὸς
18 τοὺς παρατυχόντας. τινὲς δὲ καὶ τῶν Ἐπικουρίων καὶ τῶν Στοι-
κῶν φιλοσόφων συνέβαλον αὐτῷ, καί τινες ἔλεγον· Τί ἂν θέλῃ
ὁ σπερμολόγος οὗτος λέγειν; οἱ δέ· Ξένων δαιμονίων δοκεῖ
19 καταγγελεὺς εἶναι. μετὰ δὲ ἡμέρας τινὰς ἐπιλαβόμενοι αὐτοῦ
ἤγαγον αὐτὸν ἐπὶ Ἄριον Πάγον, πυνθανόμενοι καὶ λέγοντες·
Δυνάμεθα γνῶναι τίς ἡ καινὴ αὕτη ὑπὸ σοῦ καταγγελλομένη
20 διδαχή; ξενίζοντα γάρ τινα φέρεις ῥήματα εἰς τὰς ἀκοὰς ἡμῶν·
21 βουλόμεθα οὖν γνῶναι τί ἂν θέλοι ταῦτα εἶναι. Ἀθηναῖοι δὲ
πάντες καὶ οἱ ἐπιδημοῦντες εἰς αὐτοὺς ξένοι εἰς οὐδὲν ἕτερον
22 ηὐκαίρουν ἢ λέγειν τι ἢ ἀκούειν καινότερον. σταθεὶς δὲ ὁ Παῦλος
ἐν μέσῳ τοῦ Ἀρίου Πάγου ἔφη· Ἄνδρες Ἀθηναῖοι, κατὰ πάντα
23 ὡς δεισιδαιμονεστέρους ὑμᾶς θεωρῶ· διερχόμενος γὰρ καὶ δι-
ιστορῶν τὰ σεβάσματα ὑμῶν εὗρον καὶ βωμὸν ἐν ᾧ ἦ‹ν› γε-
γραμμένον· Ἀγνώστῳ Θεῷ. ὃ οὖν ἀγνοοῦντες εὐσεβεῖτε, τοῦτο
24 ἐγὼ καταγγέλλω ὑμεῖν. ὁ θεὸς ὁ ποιήσας τὸν κόσμον καὶ

18 συνεβαλον] συνελαβον   οι δε] οιδεν   20 ξηνιζοντα

paulum incitabatur sps ejus in eo videnti simulacris esse civitatem 17 disputabat d
ergo in synagoga judaeis et hiis qui colunt et his qui forte aderant et hiis qui in foro
per omnem diem 18 quidam autem et epicuriorum et stoicorum philosoporum
conferebant cum eo et quidam dicebant quid nunc vellit spermologus hic dicere alii
noborum daemoniorum videtur adnuntiator esse 19 post dies aliquos adpraehensum-
que eum adduxerunt ad arium pagum cogitantes et dicentes possumus scire que
est novitas haec a te narratio doctrinae 20 nova enim quaedam adferens inter
locutiones adversus nostras volumus ergo scire quid nunc sibi vellint haec esse
21 athenenses vero omnes et qui advenerant hospitiis ad nihil aliut vacabant quam
dicere aliquid aut audire novius 22 cum stetisset autem paulus in medio arii pagi
ait viri athenenses per omnia superstitiosos vos video esse 23 circumambulans enim
et perspiciens ea quae colitis inveni etiam et aram in qua scriptum erat ignoto do
quod ergo ignorantes colitis hoc ego adnuntio vobis 24 ds qui fecit mundum et

24 deus qui fecit mundum et omnia quae in eo, hic caeli et terrae dominus Irenaeus,
iii. 12, 9 (11)

17 και τοις 3°] mg et illis   19 μετα δε ημερας τινας] ⸓ post autem dies Harclean
aliquot ✓

B-text. But no 'Western' authority
omits them.
18 D d gig omit οτι τον ιησουν και την
αναστασιν ευηγγελιζετο, and thus throw
some doubt on the genuineness of

the sentence. In Aug. C. Cresc. i. 12
(15) the omission is not certainly
attested. Cf., however, the omission
of similar sentences by h and D d gig,
mentioned above, pp. ccxxxvi-viii.

168 CODEX VATICANUS

καὶ γῆς ὑπάρχων κύριος οὐκ ἐν χειροποιήτοις ναοῖς κατοικεῖ
| οὐδὲ ὑπὸ χειρῶν ἀνθρωπίνων θεραπεύεται προσδεόμενός τινος, 25
αὐτὸς διδοὺς πᾶσι ζωὴν καὶ πνοὴν καὶ τὰ πάντα· ἐποίησέν τε 26
ἐξ ἑνὸς πᾶν ἔθνος ἀνθρώπων κατοικεῖν ἐπὶ παντὸς προσώπου τῆς
γῆς, ὁρίσας προστεταγμένους καιροὺς καὶ τὰς ὁροθεσίας τῆς
κατοικίας αὐτῶν, ζητεῖν τὸν θεὸν εἰ ἄρα γε ψηλαφήσ<ε>ιαν αὐτὸν 27
καὶ εὕροιεν, καί γε οὐ μακρὰν ἀπὸ ἑνὸς ἑκάστου ἡμῶν ὑπάρχοντα.
ἐν αὐτῷ γὰρ ζῶμεν καὶ κεινούμεθα καὶ ἐσμέν, ὡς καί τινες 28
τῶν καθ᾽ ἡμᾶς ποιητῶν εἰρήκασιν· Τοῦ γὰρ καὶ γένος ἐσμέν.
γένος οὖν ὑπάρχοντες τοῦ θεοῦ οὐκ ὀφείλομεν νομίζειν χρυσῷ ἢ 29
ἀργύρῳ ἢ λίθῳ, χαράγματι τέχνης καὶ ἐνθυμήσεως ἀνθρώπου, τὸ
θεῖον εἶναι ὅμοιον. τοὺς μὲν οὖν χρόνους τῆς ἀγνοίας ὑπεριδὼν 30
ὁ θεὸς τὰ νῦν ἀπαγγέλλει τοῖς ἀνθρώποις πάντας πανταχοῦ
μετανοεῖν, καθότι ἔστησεν ἡμέραν ἐν ᾗ μέλλει κρείνειν τὴν 31

Editors   26 παντος προσωπου] παν το προσωπον Soden   28 ημας] υμας WH Soden
JHR   ημας WHmg   om ποιητων JHR   30 απαγγελλει] παραγγελλει
Soden

Old Uncial   25 χειρων ανθρωπινων BA 81 (+D)   ανθρωπινων χειρων ℵ   θεραπευεται
BAℵᶜ 81 (+D)   +ως ℵ   προσδεομενος BAℵᶜ 81 (+D)   ως προσδεομενος ℵ   τα
BAℵᶜ(+D)   om ℵ 81   27 ψηλαφησειαν BA 81   ψηλαφησειεν ℵ   και
1° Bℵ 81   η A(+D)   και γε B 81 (+D)   καιτοι A   καιτοιγε ℵ   ου BℵA(+D)
ουκ αμαρτυρον 81   ημων BℵAᶜᵒʳʳ* 81 (+D)   υμων A   28 ημας B   υμας
ℵA 81 (+D)   29 χρυσω B(+D)   χρυσιω ℵA   αργυρω Bℵ(+D)   αργυριω A
30 απαγγελλει Bℵ   παραγγελλει Aℵᶜ(+D)

Antiochian   24 κυριος υπαρχων HLPSⲊ(+D)   25 ανθρωπινων] ανθρωπων HLPSⲊ
om προσδεομενος τινος S (cf. D)   om αυτος HS(+D)   δους HS(+D)
και τα] κατα HLPSⲊ   26 ενος] +αιματος HLPSⲊ(+D)   παντος
προσωπου] παν το προσωπον HLPSⲊ   προστεταγμενους] προτεταγμενους Ⲋ
(+D)   27 θεον] κυριον PⲊ   ψηλαφησαιεν S   και γε] καιτοιγε Ⲋ
ημων] υμων L   28 ημας] υμας HLPⲊ(+D)   30 απαγγελλει] παραγγελλει HLPSⲊ(+D)   πασι HLPSⲊ   31 καθοτι] διοτι HLSⲊ

27 Can the superfluous εστιν D be a survival, in a changed position, of the reading in the later part of the sentence ευροισαν (-οιεν) τις εστιν implied by hcl.mg? But cf. the similar case in xxi. 21 τους κατα εθνη εισιν ιουδαιους D, where εισιν seems introduced in order to complete the parallelism with the Latin.

28 The omission of ποιητων in D d gig Iren, Pacianus, Ambrose, Ambrosiaster, Augustine, Pelagius (on 1 Cor. ix. 21) is sufficient to raise doubts as to the true text. Pesh has 'wise men.' ποιητων is attested by Clem. Alex., Origen, Didymus.

πάντα τὰ ἐν αὐτῷ, οὗτος οὐρανοῦ καὶ γῆς κύριος ὑπά₁ʿχων οὐκ ἐν
25 χειροποιήτοις ναοῖς κατοικεῖ | ο‹ὐ›δὲ ὑπὸ χειρῶν ἀνθρωπίνων
θεραπεύεται προσδεόμενος, ὅτι οὗτος ὁ δοὺς πᾶσι ζωὴν καὶ πνοὴν
26 καὶ τὰ πάντα | ἐποίησεν ἐξ ἑνὸς αἵματος πᾶν ἔθνος ἀνθρώπου κατ-
οικεῖν ἐπὶ παντὸς προσώπου τῆς γῆς, ὁρίσας προτεταγμένους
27 καιροὺς κατὰ ὁροθεσίαν τῆς κατοικίας αὐτῶν, μάλιστα ζητεῖν τὸ
θεῖόν †ἐστιν† εἰ ἄρα γε ψηλαφήσαισαν αὐτὸ ἢ εὕροισαν, καί γε
28 οὐ μακρὰν ὂν ἀφ' ἑνὸς ἑκάστου ἡμῶν. ἐν αὐτῷ γὰρ ζῶμεν καὶ
κεινούμεθα καὶ ἐσμὲν τὸ καθ' ἡμέραν, ὥσπερ καὶ τῶν καθ' ὑμᾶς
29 τινες εἰρήκασιν· Τούτου γὰρ καὶ γ‹έν›ος ἐσμέν. γένος οὖν
ὑπάρχοντες τοῦ θεοῦ οὐκ ὀφίλομεν νομίζειν οὔτε χρυσῷ ἢ ἀργύρῳ
ἢ λίθῳ, χαράγματι τέχνης ἢ ἐνθυμήσεως ἀνθρώπου, τὸ θεῖον
30 εἶναι ὅμοιον. τοὺς μὲν οὖν χρόνους τῆς ἀγνοίας ταύτης παριδὼν
ὁ θεὸς τὰ νῦν παραγγέλλει τοῖς ἀνθρώποις ἵνα πάντες πανταχοῦ
31 †μετανοεῖν†, καθότι ἔστησεν ἡμέραν κρεῖναι τὴν οἰκουμένην ἐν

24 κατοικοι   27 και γε] και τε   28 αυτω] αυτη
31 εστησαν

---

omnia quae in eo sunt hic cum sit caeli et terrae d̄n̄s qui est non in manufactis d
templis inhabitat   25 neque manibus humanis curatur tamquam egeat quod ipse
dederit omnia vitam et spiramentū et omnia   26 fecit ex uno sanguine omnem
nationem hominum inhabitare super omnem faciem terrae cum definisset imperata
tempora et determinationes inhabitationes eorum   27 quaerere quod divinum est
si forte tractent illud inveniant quidem non longe ab uno quoque nostrorum   28 in
ipso enim vivimus et movemur et simus in diurnum sicut qui secundum vos sunt
quidam dixerunt hujus enim et genus sumus   29 genus ergo cum simus d̄ī non
debemus existimare neque auro aut argento aut lapidi sculptioni artis et cupiditatis
humanae quod divinum est esse simile   30 itaquae temporibus ignorantiae hujus
despiciens d̄s jam nunc adnuntiat hominibus ut omnes ubique paenitentiam agant
31 quoniam statuit diem judicare orbem terrae in justitia in viro ī̄h̄u cujus constituit

---

24 non habitat in manufactis.

Tertullian,
Prax. 16

existens non in manufactis templis inhabitat,   25 nec a manibus humanis Irenaeus,
tractatur, tamquam alicujus indigens, cum ipse omnibus dederit vitam et iii. 12, 9 (11)
spiritum et omnia,   26 feceritque ex uno sanguine omne genus hominum inhabitare super faciem totius terrae, praefiniens tempora secundum determina-
tionem inhabitationis eorum,   27 quaerere illud quod est divinum, si quo
modo tractare possint illud aut invenire, quamvis etiam non longe sit ab
unoquoque nostrum ;   28 in ipso enim vivimus et movemur et sumus ; et
quemadmodum quidam secundum vos dixerunt : hujus enim et genus sumus.
29 genus igitur cum simus dei, non oportet nos putare id quod est divinum
simile esse auro vel argento vel lapidi per artem vel concupiscentiam hominis
deformato.   30 tempora igitur ignorantiae despiciens deus nunc praecepit hominibus omnibus ubique paeniteri in ipsum,   31 quoniam constituit diem judicari

---

26 εθνος] mg genera   27 ευροισαν] mg et invenirent quis esset   Harclean

οἰκουμένην ἐν δικαιοσύνῃ ἐν ἀνδρὶ ᾧ ὥρισεν, πίστιν παρασχὼν πᾶσι ἀναστήσας αὐτὸν ἐκ νεκρῶν. ἀκούσαντες δὲ ἀνάστασιν 32 νεκρῶν οἱ μὲν ἐχλεύαζον οἱ δὲ εἶπαν· Ἀκουσόμεθά σου περὶ τούτου καὶ πάλιν. οὕτως ὁ Παῦλος ἐξῆλθεν ἐκ μέσου αὐτῶν· 33 τινὲς δὲ ἄνδρες κολληθέντες αὐτῷ ἐπίστευσαν, ἐν οἷς καὶ Διο- 34 νύσιος Ἀρεοπαγείτης καὶ γυνὴ ὀνόματι Δάμαρις καὶ ἕτεροι σὺν αὐτοῖς.

Με⟨τὰ⟩ ταῦτα χωρισθεὶς ἐκ τῶν Ἀθηνῶν ἦλθεν εἰς Κόρινθον. XVIII καὶ εὑρών τινα Ἰουδαῖον ὀνόματι Ἀκύλαν, Ποντικὸν τῷ γένει, 2 προσφάτως ἐληλυθότα ἀπὸ τῆς Ἰταλίας καὶ Πρίσκιλλαν γυναῖκα αὐτοῦ διὰ τὸ διατεταχέναι ⟨Κλαύδιον⟩ χωρίζεσθαι πάντας τοὺς Ἰουδαίους ἀπὸ τῆς Ῥώμης, προσῆλθεν αὐτοῖς, | καὶ διὰ τὸ ὁμό- 3 τεχνον εἶναι ἔμενεν παρ' αὐτοῖς καὶ ἠργάζοντο, ἦσαν γὰρ σκηνο-

Editors			
	34 [ο] αρεοπαγιτης WH ο αρεοπαγιτης Soden JHR		1 χωρισθεις] +[ο
	παυλος] Soden	3 ηργαζετο WHmg ειργαζετο Soden	

Old Uncial			
	34 αρεοπαγειτης B (cf. D) ο αρεοπαγιτης ℵA	1 μετα B²	χωρισθεις
	Bℵ (cf. D) +ο παυλος A	2 διατεταχεναι BAℵᶜ τε⟨τα⟩χεναι ℵ(+D)	
	κλαυδιον ℵA(+D) om B	3 ηργαζοντο Bℵ ηργαζετο A(+D)	ειργαζετο ℵᶜ

Antiochian			
	32 περι τουτου και παλιν] παλιν περι τουτου HLPS𝕊 (cf. D)		33 add και
	before ουτως HLPS𝕊	34 ο αρεοπαγιτης HLPS𝕊	1 μετα] +δε HLPS𝕊
	χωρισθεις] + ο παυλος HLPS𝕊	2 διατεταχεναι] τεταχεναι LPS(+D)	
	απο 2°] εκ HPS𝕊	3 εμεινεν HLS ειργαζετο HLPS𝕊 (cf. D)	

34 For γυνη e reads *mulier honesta* (translated into Greek in E as γυνη τιμια). D ευσχημων is plainly a survival of this gloss, and the omission in D of the name Damaris is probably somehow due to an attempt to excise the gloss, in which the wrong word got omitted. Ramsay, *The Church in the Roman Empire*, chap. viii. 5.

2–3 In D the 'Western' additions attested by h hcl.*mg* have been omitted, and other changes have been made, all doubtless by conformation to the B-text. The 'Western' Greek seems to have read approximately as follows (the reconstruction is chiefly from h and hcl.*mg*; some details are uncertain): 2 και ευρεν ακυλαν, ποντικον τω γενει, ιουδαιον, προσφατως εληλυθοτα απο της ιταλιας συν πρισκιλλη γυναικι αυτου, και προσηλθεν αυτοις· ουτοι δε εξηλθον απο της ρωμης δια το τεταχεναι κλαυδιον καισαρα χωριζεσθαι παντας ιουδαιους απο της ρωμης· οι και κατωκησαν εις την αχαιαν. ο δε παυλος εγνωρισθη τω ακυλα 3 δια το ομοφυλον και ομοτεχνον ειναι, και εμενεν προς αυτους και ηργαζετο· ησαν

γαρ σκηνοποιοι τη τεχνη. For προσηλθεν αυτοις the Greek may have read ησπασατο αυτους, but *salutavit eos* h is explicable as a free rendering of the former phrase.

Interesting survivals of this 'Western' text are found. (1) Vg.*cod*.*R*² has, in substantial agreement with h, *et salutavit eos. hii autem egressi fuerant a roma*, but does not follow h thereafter ; (2) m, closely like h, reads *paulus autem agnitus erat aquilae* at the close of vs. 2 ; (3) gig vg.*codd* have *et salutavit eos*, but in a different position from h, appending it by conflation to *accessit ad eos* of the B-text; (4) pesh reads 'Claudius Caesar' (cf. also *Doct. of Addai*, ed. Phillips, p. 16), and thus gives support to the conjectural reading for the lacuna of h.

It is not clear that the 'Western' changes were meant to imply that Paul had known Aquila previously.

2 That the use of *urbs* for Rome in h implies nothing as to the place of origin of the Latin version, may be seen from the passages assembled by Zahn, *Geschichte des neutestamentlichen Ka-*

δικαιοσύνῃ ἀνδρὶ Ἰησοῦ ᾧ ὥρισεν, πίστιν παρασχεῖν πᾶσιν
32 ἀναστήσας αὐτὸν ἐκ νεκρῶν. ἀκούσαντες δὲ ἀνάστασιν νεκρῶν
οἱ μὲν ἐχλεύαζον οἱ δὲ εἶπον· Ἀκουσόμεθά σου περὶ τούτου
33, 34 πάλιν. οὕτως ὁ Παῦλος ἐξῆλθεν ἐκ μέσου αὐτῶν· τινὲς δὲ ἄνδρες
ἐκολλήθησαν αὐτῷ, ἐπίστευσαν, ἐν οἷς καὶ Διονύσιός τις Ἀρεοπαγείτης εὐσχήμων καὶ ἕτεροι σὺν αὐτοῖς.
XVIII Ἀναχωρήσας δὲ ἀπὸ τῶν Ἀθηνῶν ἦλθεν εἰς Κόρινθον.
2 καὶ εὑρών τινα Ἰουδαῖον ὀνόματι Ἀκύλαν, Ποντικὸν τῷ γένει,
προσφάτως ἐληλυθ<ότ>α ἀπὸ τῆς Ἰταλίας καὶ Πρίσκιλλαν
γυναῖκα αὐτοῦ διὰ τὸ τεταχέναι Κλαύδιον χωρίζεσθαι πάντας
Ἰουδαίους ἀπὸ τῆς Ῥώμης, οἳ καὶ κατῴκησαν εἰς τὴν Ἀχαίαν,
3 προσῆλθεν αὐτῷ ὁ Παῦλος, | καὶ διὰ τὸ ὁμότεχνον ἔμενεν πρὸς
4 αὐτοὺς καὶ ἠργάζετο. εἰσπορευόμενος δὲ εἰς τὴν συναγωγὴν

31 παρεσχειν   2 κλανδιος   οι και] οι κε   κατωκησεν

fidem exibere omnibus resuscitavit eum a mortuis   32 audientes autem resurrectione d
mortuorum aliquid eridebant alii vero dixerunt audimus te de hoc iterum   33 sic
paulus exibit de medio illorum   34 quidam autem viri cum esitassent ei crediderunt
in quibus et dionysius quis areopagita conplacens et alii cum eis
   1 regressus vero ab athenis venit in corinthum   2 et cum invenissent quemdam
judaeum nomine acylam pontium nomine recens venisse ab italia et priscillam
uxorem ejus eo quod praecepisset claudius discedere omnes judaeos ex urbem qui et
demorati sunt in achaiam accessit ad eos paulus   3 et propter artificium manebat
apud eos et operabatur   4 ingressus autem synagogam per omne sabbatum dis-

   34 quidam autem crediderunt : in quibus Dion[ysius qui]dam Areopagites, h
et mulier nomine Damalis, e[t multi ce]teris cum eis.
   1 et cum recessisset Paulus ab At[henis, venit] Corinthum :   2 et invenit
Aquilam, natione Pon[ticum, Ju]daeum, qui in recenti verant ab Italia, cum
[Pris]cilla uxore sua, et salutavit eos.   hii aute[m propte]rea exsierunt ab urbe,
quod dixisset Claud[ius Caesar] uti omnes Judaei exirent ab urbe : qui vene[r . . .
in Acha]iam.   Paulus autem agnitus est Aquilae, 3 [quoniam] esset ejusdem
artis, et mansit apud eum : e[rant eni] arteiicio lectari.   4 et cum introiret in

orbem terrae in justitia in viro Jesu, in quo statuit fidem, excitans eum a   Irenaeus,
mortuis.   iii. 12, 9 (11)

   2–3 και πρισκιλλαν . . . προς αυτους] mg cum Priscilla uxore ejus.   hi autem   Harclean
exierant a Roma quod praecepisset Claudius ut discederent omnes Judaei ab
Italia.   hi <. . . .> Achaiam.   ipse autem Paulus agnovit Aquilam, et propter
paritatem gentis et paritatem opificii <. . . .> apud eos

nons, vol. ii. p. 132, note 1. The usage | omitted by D d gig, possibly by an
was current in all parts of the empire. | error incident to the conflation of
   3 The omission by h of και ηργαζοντο | 'Western' and B-texts, which charac-
(-ετο) might be a 'Western non-inter- | terizes both mss. in the following
polation,' but m Aug have it in the | verses. The presence of the sentence
noteworthy form opus faciens. | in h speaks strongly against the theory
   ησαν γαρ σκηνοποιοι τη τεχνη is | of a 'Western non-interpolation.'

ποιοὶ τῇ τέχνῃ. διελέγετο δὲ ἐν τῇ συναγωγῇ κατὰ πᾶν σάββατον, 4
ἔπειθέν τε Ἰουδαίους καὶ Ἕλληνας. ὡς δὲ κατῆλθον ἀπὸ τῆς 5
Μακεδονίας ὅ τε Σείλας καὶ ὁ Τιμόθεος, συνείχετο τῷ λόγῳ
ὁ Παῦλος, διαμαρτυρόμενος τοῖς Ἰουδαίοις εἶναι τὸν Χριστὸν
Ἰησοῦν. ἀντιτασσομένων δὲ αὐτῶν καὶ βλασφημούντων ἐκτιναξά- 6
μενος τὰ ἱμάτια εἶπεν πρὸς αὐτούς· Τὸ αἷμα ὑμῶν ἐπὶ τὴν κεφαλὴν
ὑμῶν· καθαρὸς ἐγώ· ἀπὸ τοῦ νῦν εἰς τὰ ἔθνη πορεύσομαι. καὶ 7
μεταβὰς ἐκεῖθεν ἦλθεν εἰς οἰκίαν τινὸς ὀνόματι Τιτίου Ἰούστου
σεβομένου τὸν θεόν, οὗ ἡ οἰκία ἦν συνομοροῦσα τῇ συναγωγῇ.
Κρεῖσπος δὲ ὁ ἀρχισυνάγωγος ἐπίστευσεν τῷ κυρίῳ σὺν ὅλῳ 8

Editors	7 ηλθεν] εισηλθεν Soden	τιτιου] τιτου Soden om τιτιου JHR
Old Uncial	5 τοις ιουδαιοις Bℵ(+D) om A	7 ηλθεν B εισηλθεν ℵA (cf. D)
	ονοματι Bℵ (cf. D) om A	τιτιου B τιτου ℵ om A(+D)
Antiochian	3 την τεχνην HSſ 4 παν] μιαν H	5 om της L λογω]
	πνευματι HLPSſ om τοις ιουδαιοις H	om ειναι HLPSſ om
	ιησουν P 6 πορευομαι HL(+D)	7 om τιτιου HLSſ(+D) τιτου P
	8 συν] εν H	

4 Gig agrees with the B-text except in the retention after σαββατον of *interponens nomen domini jesu*, which is also found in vg.*codd* prov tepl. Vg omits vs. 4 altogether; probably the 'Western' form of the underlying Old Latin was dropped, and by some accident the proper substitute from the B-text failed to get introduced.

5–6 In vs. 5 D is plainly conflate, the words συνειχετο . . . ιησουν belonging to the B-text. These being omitted, D substantially agrees in vss. 5-6a with h hcl.*mg*. Yet the text of D is left in some disorder, for αυτων, vs. 6, can hardly have been intended to refer to Timothy and Silas, but rather (cf. h) to the Jews. The text of d in this verse is not without interest. A few details require mention in vs. 5. *Supervenerunt* h may imply (so Zahn) Greek επηλθον instead of παρεγενοντο; τοτε D (not d) before σιλας may be due to corruption of o τε of the B-text, but cf. (in earlier position) *tunc* h. *Iterum* h has no other support; *multis* seems to be an error for *multum* (cf. hcl.*mg*). One form of the 'Western' text perhaps read πολλων δε λογων, cf. hcl.*mg*.

The two rival forms of vss. 1-6 must be taken each as a whole. In the 'Western' text the passage has apparently been rewritten, and the difficult συνειχετο τω λογω (Antiochian and hcl.*mg* πνευματι) made over into πολλου δε λογου γεινομενου. (Pesh has tried to relieve the difficulty of the B-text in its own way by treating αντιτασσομενων δε αυτων και βλασφημουντων as if these words stood before διαμαρτυρομενος.) On the other hand the 'Western' εντιθεις το ονομα του κυριου ιησου is a striking expression and without parallel, and if it were not associated with the other 'Western' readings it would probably seem original as compared with the more conventional διαμαρτυρομενος τοις ιουδαιοις ειναι τον χριστον ιησουν of the B-text, for which it is the substitute. The available explanations of the text of these verses do not solve the whole problem.

7 In Codex Bezae, for Scrivener's [. . .]λα, Blass was able to read ακυλα (*Stud. Krit.*, 1898, p. 541). For [δε απο], [απο του] is equally possible. For the following [εισ]ηλθεν Blass thought he read ε[ισ]ηλθεν, while J. R. Harris believed that he could detect traces of και ηλθεν (*ib.* p. 541). απο ακυλα for εκειθεν D d h (εκειθεν απο του ακυλα 614) is probably a misinterpretation; the divergence is wholly inconsistent with the idea of a common authorship for the two forms of the text.

κατὰ πᾶν σάββατον διελέγετο, καὶ ἐντιθεὶς τὸ ὄνομα τοῦ κυρίου
Ἰησοῦ, καὶ ἔπιθεν δὲ οὐ μόνον Ἰουδαίους ἀλλὰ καὶ Ἕλληνας.
5 παρεγένοντο δὲ ἀπὸ τῆς Μακεδονίας τότε Σίλας καὶ Τιμόθεος.
συνείχετο τῷ λόγῳ Παῦλος, διαμαρτυρόμενος τοῖς Ἰουδαίοις
εἶναι τὸν Χριστὸν κύριον Ἰησοῦν. πολλοῦ δὲ λόγου γεινομένου
6 καὶ γραφῶν διερμηνευομένων | ἀντιτασσομένων δὲ αὐτῶν καὶ
βλασφημούντων ἐκτιναξάμενος ὁ Παῦλος τὰ εἱμάτια αὐτοῦ
εἶπεν πρὸς αὐτούς· Τὸ αἷμα ὑμῶν ἐπὶ τὴν κεφαλὴν ὑμῶν· καθαρὸς
7 ἐγώ· ἀ[φ᾽ ὑμῶ]ν νῦν εἰς τὰ ἔθνη πορεύομαι. μεταβὰς [δὲ ἀπὸ
Ἀκύ]λα [εἰσ]ῆλθεν εἰς τὸν [ο]ἶ[κό]ν τινος ὀνόματι Ἰούστου
σεβομένου τὸν θεόν, οὗ ἡ οἰκία ἦν συνομοροῦσα τῇ συναγωγῇ.
8 ὁ δὲ ἀρχισυνάγωγος Κρίσπος ἐπίστευσεν εἰς τὸν κύριον σὺν ὅλῳ

5 διαμαρτυρουμενος   6 αντιτασσομενων] [ε]τι τασσομενων
7 ονοματ[ο]ς   συνομοροουσα

---

putabat et interponens nomen d̅n̅i̅ i̅h̅u̅ et persuadebat non solos judaeos sed et d
graecos 5 ut vero advenerunt in macedonia silas et timotheus instabant sermoni
paulus testificabatur judaeis esse xpm dnm ihm 6 multoque verbo facto et scripturis
disputantibus resistentibus autem eis et blasphemantibus excutiens paulus vestimenta
sua dixit ad eos sanguinem vestrum super caput vestrum mundus ego a bobis nunc
ad gentes vado 7 et cum recessisset ab acyla introibit in domum cujusdam nomine
justi colentis d̅m̅ cujus domus erat confinis synagoga 8 vero archisynagogus crispus

---

syna[gogam, per] omnem sabbatum disputabat, interponen[s nomen] d̅n̅i̅ i̅h̅u̅ : h
suadebat autem non tantum Judae[is sed et Gre]cis. 5 tunc supervenerunt a
Macedonia [Sileas et] Timotheus. atque iterum, cum multis fier[et verbum], et
scripturae interpraetarentur, 6 contr[adicebant] Judaei quidam, et maledice-
bant. tunc exc[ussit ves]tem suam Paulus, et dixit ad eos : sanguis ves[ter
super] caput vestrum : mundus ego : nunc vado ad [gentes] ab vobis. 7 et
recessit ab Aquila, et abiit in do[mum Justi], metuentis d̅m̅ : erat autem domus
ejus co[nfinis sy]nagogae. 8 arcihisynagogus autem quida[m, nomine] Crispus,

---

4 εντιθεις το ονομα του κυριου ιησου] mg interponens nomen domini Jesu Harclean
5 τω λογω] mg in spiritu   ειναι τον χριστον κυριον ιησουν] quod Jesus ⁛
esset ✓ Christus   πολλου δε λογου γεινομενου και γραφων διερμηνευομενων]
mg quum verba autem multa facta fuissent et scripturae explicatae essent
7 [εισ]ηλθεν] mg introivit

For τιτιου ιουστου the reading with
a single name ιουστου A D d h^vid
Antiochian, Jerome (?), is probably
original. By dittography ΤΙΙΟΤ gave
rise to τιτιου B D^corr (corrector B,
cent. vii.) hcl.*text*, and that to the
more familiar τιτου ℵ E minn boh
('Titus of Justus'). The Latin *titi
iusti* gig vg is indeterminate as between *titius* and *titus*. The reading
τιτου (without ιουστου) pesh sah vg.*codd*

tepl has nothing to commend it.
8 επιστευον και is superfluous in
view of the following πιστευοντες κτλ.
of D. It is omitted by h and clearly
stands in D d by conflation with the
B-text. Hcl ⁛ has preserved most
of the 'Western' gloss, as have 614
minn ; pesh has τω θεω from the
same source. The 'Western' reviser
expressly indicates these converts as
gentiles, not Jews.

τῷ οἴκῳ αὐτοῦ, καὶ πολλοὶ τῶν Κορινθίων ἀκούοντες ἐπίστευον
καὶ ἐβαπτίζοντο. εἶπεν δὲ ὁ κύριος ἐν νυκτὶ δι' ὁράματος τῷ 9
Παύλῳ· Μὴ φοβοῦ, ἀλλὰ λάλει καὶ μὴ σιωπήσῃς, | διότι ἐγώ 10
εἰμι μετὰ σοῦ καὶ οὐδεὶς ἐπιθήσεταί σοι τοῦ κακῶσαί σε, διότι
λαός ἐστί μοι πολὺς ἐν τῇ πόλει ταύτῃ. ἐκάθισεν δὲ ἐνιαυτὸν 11
καὶ μῆνας ἓξ διδάσκων ἐν αὐτοῖς τὸν λόγον τοῦ θεοῦ. Γαλλίωνος 12
δὲ ἀνθυπάτου ὄντος τῆς Ἀχαίας κατεπέστησαν οἱ Ἰουδαῖοι
ὁμοθυμαδὸν τῷ Παύλῳ καὶ ἤγαγον αὐτὸν ἐπὶ τὸ βῆμα, λέγοντες 13
ὅτι Παρὰ τὸν νόμον ἀναπείθει οὗτος τοὺς ἀνθρώπους σέβεσθαι
τὸν θεόν. μέλλοντος δὲ τοῦ Παύλου ἀνοίγειν τὸ στόμα εἶπεν ὁ 14
Γαλλίων πρὸς τοὺς Ἰουδαίους· Εἰ μὲν ἦν ἀδίκημά τι ἢ ῥᾳδιούργημα πονηρόν, ὦ Ἰουδαῖοι, κατὰ λόγον ἂν ἀνεσχόμην ὑμῶν·
εἰ δὲ ζητήματά ἐστιν περὶ λόγου καὶ ὀνομάτων καὶ νόμου τοῦ 15
καθ' ὑμᾶς, ὄψεσθε αὐτοί· κριτὴς ἐγὼ τούτων οὐ βούλομαι εἶναι.

Editors   12 ομοθυμαδον οι ιουδαιοι WHmg Soden JHR   15 κριτης] +[γαρ] Soden

---

Old Uncial   9 εν νυκτι Bℵ(+D)   om A   δι οραματος Bℵ (cf. D)   εν οραματι A
             11 ενιαυτον BA(+D)   +ενα ℵ   12 οι ιουδαιοι ομοθυμαδον B   ομοθυμαδον οι
             ιουδαιοι ℵA(+D)   επι BA(+D)   παρα ℵ   14 αν Bℵ(+D)   om A

Antiochian   8 ακουσαντες HLS   9 δι οραματος εν νυκτι (της νυκτος H) HLPSϚ (cf. D)
            10 μοι εστιν L   11 δε] τε HLPSϚ   12 ανθυπατου οντος] ανθυπατευοντος
            HLPSϚ   ομοθυμαδον οι ιουδαιοι HLPSϚ(+D)   13 ουτος αναπειθει
            (πειθει H) HLPSϚ(+D)   14 μεν] +ουν HLPSϚ   om ην L
            15 ζητημα HLPSϚ(+D)   κριτης] +γαρ HLPSϚ

---

12 The text of h points to the
assumption that in the 'Western'
text προς τον ανθυπατον stood in place
of επι το βημα ; cf. hcl ※. D has probably suffered here from correction to
the B-text. There is no convincing
evidence of any Greek text in which

both phrases were found side by side.

14 For κατα λογον at least one form
of the 'Western' text seems to have
read ευλογως, which is preserved (the
Greek word being used) in sah. Cf. e
(rationaliter), gig (merito), vg (recte),
boh (καλως).

τῷ οἴκῳ αὐτοῦ, καὶ πολλοὶ τῶν Κορινθίων ἀκούοντες ἐπίστευον
καὶ ἐβαπτίζοντο πιστεύοντες τῷ θεῷ διὰ τοῦ ὀνόματος τοῦ
9 κυρίου ἡμῶν Ἰησοῦ Χριστοῦ. εἶπεν δὲ κύριος δι᾽ ὁράματος
τῷ Παύλῳ ἐν νυκτί· Μὴ φοβοῦ, ἀλλὰ λάλει καὶ μὴ σειω<πή>σῃς,
10 διότι ἐγώ εἰμι μετὰ σοῦ καὶ οὐδεὶς ἐπιθήσεται τοῦ κακῶσαί σε,
11 διότι λαός ἐστί μοι πολὺς ἐν τῇ πόλι ταύτῃ. καὶ ἐκάθισεν ἐν
Κορίνθῳ ἐνιαυτὸν καὶ μῆνας ἓξ διδάσκων αὐτοὺς τὸν λόγον
12 τοῦ θεοῦ. Γαλλίωνός τε ἀνθυπάτου ὄντος τῆς Ἀχαίας κατεπέστησαν ὁμοθυμαδὸν οἱ Ἰουδαῖοι συνλαλήσαντες μεθ᾽ ἑαυτῶν ἐπὶ
τὸν Παῦλον, καὶ ἐπιθέντες τὰς χεῖρας ἤγαγον αὐτὸν ἐπὶ τὸ βῆμα,
13 καταβοῶντες καὶ λέγοντες ὅτι Παρὰ τὸν νόμον οὗτος ἀναπείθει
14 τοὺς ἀνθρώπους σέβεσθαι τὸν θεόν. μέλλοντος δὲ τοῦ Παύλου
ἀνοίγειν τὸ στόμα εἶπεν ὁ Γαλλίων πρὸς τοὺς Ἰουδαίους· Εἰ μὲν
ἦν ἀδίκημά τι ἢ ῥᾳδιούργημα πονηρόν, ὦ ἄνδρες Ἰουδαῖοι, κατὰ
15 λόγον ἂν ἠνεσχόμην ὑμῶν· εἰ δὲ ζήτημα ἔχετε περὶ λόγου καὶ
ὀνομάτων καὶ νόμου τοῦ καθ᾽ ὑμᾶς, ὄψεσθε αὐτοί· κριτὴς ἐγὼ
15 οψεσθαι

credidit in d̅n̅o̅ cum tota domo sua et multi corinthiorum audientes credebant et d
baptizabantur credentes in d̅o̅ per nomen d̅n̅i̅ nostri i̅h̅u̅ x̅p̅i̅ 9 dixit antem d̅n̅s̅ per
visum paulo per noctem ne timeas sed loquere et ne tacueris 10 quoniam ego sum
tecum et nemo adgreditur te ut malefaciat tibi quoniam populus est mihi multus in
civitate hac 11 et consedit in corintho anno et mensibus sex docens penes ipsos
vervum d̅i̅ 12 cumque gallio proconsol essed achaie inruerunt unanimiter judaei
conloquentes inter semetipsos de paulo et inponentes manum adduxerunt eum ad
tribunal 13 clamantes et dicentes quia contra legem hic persuadet hominibus
colere d̅m̅ 14 incipiente autem paulo aperire os dixit gallio ad judaeos si quidem
esset injuria aut falsum subdolum o viri judaei cum ratione forsitam paterer vos
15 si autem questio est de verbo et nominibus et legem quae secundum vos est

credidit in d̅n̅m̅ cum tota domo sua : et [quomodo mult]a plebs Corinthiorum h
audierant verbum d̅n̅i̅, [tinti sun]t, credentes d̅o̅ in nomine i̅h̅u̅ x̅p̅i̅. 9 tunc
dixit [d̅n̅s̅ ad Pa]ulum in visum : ne timeas, sed loquaere, et vi[de ne tac]eas :
10 quoniam ego sum tecum : et nemo cona[bitur m]ale facere tibi, propterea
quod plebs est mihi [multa i]n ista civitate. 11 et sedit Corinthi per annu et
[sex men]ses, docens apud eos verbum d̅i̅. 12 Gallio autē [cum ess]et pro
consule Achaiae, exurreserunt cō[sentient]es Jubaei, et conlocuti secum de
Paulo. inje[cerunt ei] manus, et perduxerunt ad proconsulem, 13 cla[mantes]
et dicentes quia adversus legem suadet homi[nibus d]m colere. 14 et cum vellet
Paulus os aperire, dixit [Gallio a]d Judeos : si esset aliqua iniquitas in eo vel
fa[cinus neq]uam, o viri Judei, recte vos sustinerem. 15 sed [si quaes]tiones
aliquae sunt inter vos vel de verbo [vel de no]minib· vel de lege vestra, ipsi

8 ακουοντες . . . χριστου] quum aŭdivissent credebant ⁘ per nomen domini Harclean
Jesu Christi ✓ et baptizabantur 11 εν κορινθω] ⁘ in Corintho ✓
12 και επιθεντες τας χειρας] ⁘ et injecerunt manus in eum ✓ et αυτον]
eum ⁘ ad proconsulem ✓

καὶ ἀπήλασεν αὐτοὺς ἀπὸ τοῦ βήματος. ἐπιλαβόμενοι δὲ πάντες 16, 17
Σωσθένην τὸν ἀρχισυνάγωγον ἔτυπτον ἔμπροσθεν τοῦ βήματος·
καὶ οὐδὲν τούτων τῷ Γαλλίωνι ἔμελεν.

Ὁ δὲ Παῦλος ἔτι προσμείνας ἡμέρας ἱκανὰς τοῖς ἀδελφοῖς 18
ἀποταξάμενος ἐξέπλει εἰς τὴν Συρίαν, καὶ σὺν αὐτῷ Πρείσκιλλα
καὶ Ἀκύλας, κειράμενος ἐν Κενχρεαῖς τὴν κεφαλήν, εἶχεν γὰρ
εὐχήν. κατήντησαν δὲ εἰς Ἔφεσον, κἀκείνους κατέλιπεν αὐτοῦ, 19
αὐτὸς δὲ εἰσελθὼν εἰς τὴν συναγωγὴν διελέξατο τοῖς Ἰουδαίοις.
ἐρωτώντων δὲ αὐτῶν ἐπὶ πλείονα χρόνον μεῖναι οὐκ ἐπένευσεν, 20
| ἀλλὰ ἀποταξάμενος καὶ εἰπών· Πάλιν ἀνακάμψω πρὸς ὑμᾶς τοῦ 21

| Editors | 17 παντες] + [οι ελληνες] Soden | 19 αυτου] εκει JHR | διελεχθη Soden |

Old Uncial

18 παυλος ΒΑℵᶜ(+D)   +εφη ℵ   19 κατελιπεν Βℵ(+D)   κατελειπεν Α
αυτου Β   εκει ℵΑ(+D)   20 μειναι Βℵ𝐀(+D)   επιμειναι ℵᶜ

Antiochian

17 παντες] + οι ελληνες HLPSꟅ(+D)   18 την κεφαλην εν κεγχρεαις
HLPSꟅ(+D)   19 κατηντησε HLPSꟅ   κατελειπεν HLPS
διελεχθη HLPSꟅ   20 αυτον L   μειναι] + παρ αυτοις HLPSꟅ(+D)
21 αποταξαμενος και] απεταξατο αυτοις HLPSꟅ   ειπων] + δει με παντως την
εορτην την ερχομενην ποιησαι εις ιεροσολυμα HLPSꟅ (cf. D)   παλιν] +δε
HLPSꟅ

---

17 Before σωσθενην in D about four
letters were erased, and Blass (Stud.
Krit., 1898, p. 541) thinks that he
finds traces of [μετ]α, which he explains as the remains of μετα ταυτα.
The last sentence in D is unknown,
the whole line containing the words
after βηματος having been erased and
rewritten. d reads (cf. h and Ephr.cat)
tunc gallio fingebat eum non videre,
and it is fair to assume that the text
of D corresponded to this. Scrivener
thinks an initial τ can be made out;
the other letters which he prints seem
wholly uncertain. See Scrivener's note,
p. 445, and the not wholly convincing
remarks of Blass, Stud. Krit., 1898,
pp. 541 f.
18 For κειραμενος the best codices
of vg read totonderant (cod. A -erunt),
and for ειχεν habebant. The plural in
the former case is supported by eth.
two codd.
19, 21-22 Vs. 19, τω επιοντι σαββατω
D 614 minn d h sah hcl ⁘ clearly
belongs with εισελθων εις την συναγωγην, but in all witnesses (except
sah and perhaps h, which is defective)
it is separated from its verb by the
phrase, 'he left them there but
he himself' (with slightly varying

language). The resulting text is
impossible, whether τω επιοντι σαββατω be connected with κατηντησαν
(-σε) (614, hcl) or with κατελιπεν (D
d). Probably (so Zahn) the proper
'Western' text read καταντησας δε εις
εφεσον, τω επιοντι σαββατω εισελθων
εις την συναγωγην, while, in all extant
copies in which the note of time
appears at all, conflation with the
B-text has taken place, with resulting
disaster to the sense.
The statement 'he left them there'
the 'Western' reviser, according to his
habit, has introduced later in vss. 21,
22, where 614 and, in part, other minn
(pesh) hcl.mg read τον δε ακυλαν ειασεν
εν εφεσω, αυτος δε αναχθεις (ανεχθεις 614)
ηλθεν εις καισαρειαν. In 614 minn the
gloss is inserted at the close of vs. 21
after εφεσου; in pesh it appears, correctly, as a substitute for ανηχθη . . .
κατελθων εις καισαρειαν. In hcl.mg the
same may be intended; the mark in
the text is written after the word for
εφεσον. D d do not have it, probably
under the influence of the Latin, in
no form of which is any trace preserved of this gloss in vs. 21.
Pesh lacks the 'Western' addition
in vs. 19, but has preserved the

16 τούτων οὐ θέλω εἶναι. καὶ ἀπέλυσεν αὐτοὺς ἀπὸ τοῦ βήματος.
17 [ἀ]πολαβόμενοι δὲ πάντες οἱ ˝Ελληνες [. . .] Σωσθένην τὸν
ἀρχεισυνάγωγον ἔτυπτον ἔνπροσθεν τοῦ βήματος · τ[. . . . . .
. . . .].
18 ῾Ο δὲ Παῦλος ἔτι προσμίνας ἡμέρας εἰκανὰς τοῖς ἀδελφοῖς
ἀποταξάμενος ἔπλευσεν εἰς τὴν Συρίαν, καὶ σὺν αὐτῷ Πρίσκιλλα καὶ ᾿Ακύλας, κειράμενος τὴν κεφαλὴν ἐν Κενχρειαῖς,
19 εἶχεν γὰρ πρ[ο]σευχήν. καταντήσας δὲ εἰς ˝Εφεσον καὶ τῷ
ἐπιόντι σαββάτῳ ἐκείνους κατέλιπεν ἐκεῖ, αὐτὸς δὲ εἰσελθὼν
20 εἰς τὴν συναγωγὴν διελέγετο τοῖς ᾿Ιουδαίοις. ἐρωτώντων τε
αὐτῶν ἐπὶ πλ[ε]ίον ‹α› χρόνον μεῖναι παρ᾿ αὐτοῖς οὐκ ἐπένευσεν,
21 | ἀλλὰ ἀποταξάμενος καὶ εἰπών· Δεῖ δὲ πάντως τὴν ἑορτὴν ἡμέραν
ἐρχομένην ποιῆσαι εἰς ᾿Ιεροσόλυμα ἀνα[. . .]ω πρὸς ὑμᾶς

17 τ[. . . . .]ω γαλλιω [. . . .]εν (Scrivener)

videritis ipsi judex horum ego nolo esse   16 et abjecit eos a tribunal   17 adprae- **d**
hendentes eum omnes graeci cum sosthenen archisynagogum caedebant ante tribunal
tunc gallio fingebat eum non videre   18 vero paulus adhuc memoratus dies plurimos
fratribus valefecit navigavit in syriam et cum ipso priscilla et aquila tonso capite in
cenchris habebebat enim orationem   19 devenerunt ephesum et sequenti sabbato
illos reliquerunt ibi ipse vero ingressus in synagogam disputabat judaeis   20 roganti-
busque eis longiore tempore manere cum eis non adnuit   21 sed cum salutasset eos
et dixit oportet me sollemnem diem advenientem facere hierosolymis iter et reverti

videritis : judex [horum n]olo esse.   16 et dimisit eos a tribunali suo.   17 et **h**
cō[prehen]derunt Graeci Sostenen archisynagogū, [et cecid]erunt ante tribunal :
et Gallio simulabat [se non vi]dere.   18 Paus autem, commoratus illic con-
plu[ribus die]bus, valefecit fratrib., navigans in Syriam, [et cum e]o Priscilla et
Aquila, qui votum cum fecisset [Cenchris], capud tondit.   19 et cum venisset
Ephesum in se[quenti]

19 και τω επιοντι σαββατω] ⁓ sabbato sequenti ✓   Harclean

'Western' transference of κακεινους
κατελιπεν αυτου αυτος δε to vs. 21,
where it appears in the form : 'and
Aquila and Priscilla he left at Ephesus,
and he journeyed by sea and came to
Caesarea.'
Sah also omits κακεινους κατελιπεν
εκει in vs. 19, but inserts it later, in
vs. 21 after αλλα.
The motive of the 'Western' reviser
is obvious ; he wished to avoid the
infelicity of the B-text, which mentioned the departure from Ephesus
before telling of the visit to the
synagogue which in fact preceded it.
Cf. the 'Western' reconstruction of
xiv. 1-3.

19 The harsh sound of κακεινους
κατελιπεν εκει א A(D) may have given
rise to the improvement αυτου for εκει
in B Antiochian.

21 The long addition (δει δε παντως,
κτλ.) near the beginning of this verse
(cf. xx. 16), found in both 'Western'
witnesses (cf. Ephr.cat) and Antiochian
(hence hcl.text), would correspond to
the understanding of αναβας, vs. 22, as
meaning a journey to Jerusalem, but
such an understanding on the part of
the 'Western' paraphrast seems unlikely (though not impossible) in view
of the 'Western' form of xix. 1 (D d
hcl.mg Ephr.cat).

θεοῦ θέλοντος, ἀνήχθη ἀπὸ τῆς Ἐφέσου, | καὶ κατελθὼν εἰς Και- 22
σαρείαν, ἀναβὰς καὶ ἀσπασάμενος τὴν ἐκκλησίαν, κατέβη εἰς
Ἀντιόχειαν, | καὶ ποιήσας χρόνον τινὰ ἐξῆλθεν, διερχόμενος 23
καθεξῆς τὴν Γαλατικὴν χώραν καὶ Φρυγίαν, στηρίζων πάντας
τοὺς μαθητάς.

Ἰουδαῖος δέ τις Ἀπολλὼς ὀνόματι, Ἀλεξανδρεὺς τῷ γένει, 24
ἀνὴρ λόγιος, κατήντησεν εἰς Ἔφεσον, δυνατὸς ὢν ἐν ταῖς γραφαῖς.
οὗτος ἦν κατηχημένος τὴν ὁδὸν κυρίου καὶ ζέων τῷ πνεύματι, 25
ἐλάλει δὲ καὶ ἐδίδασκεν ἀκριβῶς τὰ περὶ τοῦ Ἰησοῦ, ἐπιστάμενος
μόνον τὸ βάπτισμα Ἰωάνου. οὗτός τε ἤρξατο παρρησιάζεσθαι 26
ἐν τῇ συναγωγῇ· ἀκούσαντες δὲ αὐτοῦ Πρίσκιλλα καὶ Ἀκύλας
προσελάβοντο αὐτὸν καὶ ἀκριβέστερον αὐτῷ ἐξέθεντο τὴν ὁδὸν
τοῦ θεοῦ. βουλομένου δὲ αὐτοῦ διελθεῖν εἰς τὴν Ἀχαίαν προ- 27
τρεψάμενοι οἱ ἀδελφοὶ ἔγραψαν τοῖς μαθηταῖς ἀποδέξασθαι
αὐτόν· ὃς παραγενόμενος συνεβάλετο πολὺ τοῖς πεπιστευκόσιν

Editors	23 στηριζων] επιστηριζων Soden (but cf. mg) 25 του κυριου WH Soden
	JHR κυριου WHmg om δε WH Soden JHR 26 ακυλας και
	πρισκιλλα Soden om του θεου JHR

Old Uncial	21 ανηχθη BAℵ°(+D) +δε ℵ 23 διερχομενος BAℵ°(+D) +και ℵ
	24 απολλως BAℵ° (cf. D) απελλης ℵ 25 κυριου B του κυριου ℵA(+D)
	ελαλει δε B ελαλει Aℵ° (cf. D) ω ελαλει ℵ 27 προτρεψαμενοι Bℵ
	προπεμψαμενοι A συνεβαλετο Bℵ συνεβαλλετο A(+D)

Antiochian	21 θελοντος] +και HLPSϛ 23 στηριζων] επιστηριζων HLPSϛ(+D)
	25 του κυριου HLPSϛ(+D) om δε HLPSϛ(+D) ιησου] κυριου HPSϛ
	26 om τε H(+D) ακυλας και πρισκιλλα HLPSϛ(+D) εξεθετο H
	την του θεου οδον HLPSϛ

26 την οδον (without qualifying genitive) D d is probably to be accepted, in agreement with the usage of ix. 2, xix. 9, 23, xxii. 4, xxiv. 14, 22. The variation in the genitive employed, and in its position, tends to confirm this view ; and the preservation in all texts of the unusual την οδον [του] κυριου in vs. 25 makes improbable the opposite theory that the genitive was omitted with a view to agreement with the other passages in Acts.

The reading τον λογον for την οδον, supported here by minn, and in vs. 25 by D d min sah.cod, is clearly an attempt to make a hard word easier.

For πρισκιλλα και ακυλας ℵABE 33 boh sah.cod vg, ακυλας και πρισκιλλα is read in D d gig Aug and in the Antiochian recension. The desire to reduce the prominence of Priscilla

seems to have been at work in a number of places in this chapter. The original writer appears never to have mentioned Aquila without Priscilla, and always (except at the first introduction, vs. 2) put Priscilla's name first ; the glossator departs from him in both respects. Only in vs. 18, where κειραμενος was interpreted of Aquila (cf. h) does the 'Western' reviser fail to put the husband first. It is hardly conceivable that the opposite change (i.e. from D to B) could have taken place, or that the two forms of text can have proceeded from the same hand. Cf. the 'Western' text of vs. 2 ('with Priscilla' ; αυτω for αυτοις D), vs. 3 ('Aquila'), vs. 7 (απο ακυλα), vs. 21 (τον δε ακυλαν, instead of κακεινους, vs. 19), vs. 26 (ακυλας και πρισκιλλα).

22 τοῦ θεοῦ θέλοντος, ἀνήχθη ἀπὸ τοῦ Ἐφέσου, | καὶ κατελθὼν εἰς
Καισαρίαν, καὶ ἀναβὰς καὶ ἀσπασάμενος τὴν ἐκκλησίαν, κατέβη
23 εἰς Ἀντιόχειαν, | καὶ ποιήσας χρόνον τινὰ ἐξῆλθεν, διερχόμενος
κατεξῆς τὴν Γαλατικὴν χώραν καὶ Φρυγίαν, καὶ ἐπιστηρίζων
πάντας τοὺς μαθητάς.

24 Ἰουδαῖος δέ τις ὀνόματι Ἀπολλώνιος, γένει Ἀλεξανδρεύς,
ἀνὴρ λόγιος, κατήντησεν εἰς Ἔφεσον, δυνατὸς ὢν ἐν ταῖς γραφαῖς,
25 | ὃς ἦν κατηχημένος ἐν τῇ πατρίδι τὸν λόγον τοῦ κυρίου, καὶ ζέων
τῷ πνεύματι ἀπελάλει καὶ ἐδίδασκεν ἀκριβῶς τὰ περὶ Ἰησοῦ,
26 ἐπιστάμενος μόνον τὸ βάπτισμα Ἰωάνου. οὗτος ἤρξατο παρ-
‹ρ›ησιάζεσθαι ἐν συναγωγῇ· καὶ ἀκούσαντες αὐτοῦ Ἀκύλας καὶ
Πρίσκιλλα προσελάβοντο αὐτὸν καὶ ἀκριβέστερον αὐτῷ ἐξέθεντο
27 τὴν ὁδόν. ἐν δὲ τῇ Ἐφέσῳ ἐπιδημοῦντές τινες Κορίνθιοι καὶ
ἀκούσαντες αὐτοῦ παρεκάλουν διελθεῖν σὺν αὐτοῖς εἰς τὴν πατρίδα
αὐτῶν. συνκατανεύσαντος δὲ αὐτοῦ οἱ Ἐφέσιοι ἔγραψαν τοῖς
ἐν Κορίνθῳ μαθηταῖς ὅπως ἀποδέξωνται τὸν ἄνδρα· ὃς ἐπιδημήσας εἰς τὴν Ἀχαίαν πολὺ συνεβάλλετο ἐν ταῖς ἐκκλησίαις·

26 ουτος] ητος   ακουσαντες] ακουσαντος   εξεθοντο
27 πολυν

---

ad vos d͞o volente redie ab epheso   22 et descendit caesaream et cum ascedisset et **d**
salutasset ecclesiam descendit in antiochiam   23 et cum fecissent tempus quodam
pexivit pergrediens ex ordine galatiam regionem et phrygiam confirmans omnes
discipulos   24 judaeus autem quidam nomine apollonius natione alexandrinus vir
disertus devenit ephesum potens in scripturis   25 hic erat doctus in patria verbum
d͞ni et ferbens s͞pu eloquebatur et docebat diligenter de i͞hu sciens solum baptisma
johannis   26 adque hic coepit cum fiducia loqui in synagoga et cum audissent eum
aquilas et priscilla adprehenderunt eum et diligentius ei exposuerunt viam   27 in
aephesum autem exeuntes quidam corinthii et audierunt eum hortantes transire
cum ipsis in patria ipsorum redeunte autem eo ephesi scripserunt qui sunt in
corintho discipulis quomodo exciperent hunc virum qui cum exibit in achaiam

---

21-22 ανηχθη . . . ασπασαμενος] *mg* Aquilam autem reliquit Ephesi ; ipse Harclean
autem quum navem conscendisset, venit in Caesaream. quum ascendisset
autem et salutasset   27 εν δε τη εφεσω . . . τον ανδρα] *mg* quum autem
venissent in Ephesum quidam Corinthii, et audivissent eum, rogaverunt
eum transire cum ipsis in patriam suam. quum autem consensisset iis, fratres
scripserunt discipulis qui erant Corinthi ut exciperent virum   os
επιδημησας εις την αχαιαν] qui quum profectus est et ⁘ in Achaiam ✓

Note also the placing of Priscilla first in the greetings sent to the couple, Rom. xvi. 3, 2 Tim. iv. 19 ; and the greeting from them, with Aquila first, 1 Cor. xvi. 19.

A similar change is found in Acts xvii. 12 ανδρες και γυναικες D d (pesh).

See Harnack, ' Über die beiden Re-

censionen der Geschichte der Prisca und des Aquila in Act. Apost. 18, 1-27,' *Sitzungsberichte*, Berlin Academy, 1900, pp. 2-13.

27 The bold paraphrase of vs. 27 found in D d and (with little variation) in hcl.*mg* (cf. Ephr.*cat*) vg.*cod*.*R*² was probably written because the glossator

διὰ τῆς χάριτος· εὐτόνως γὰρ τοῖς Ἰουδαίοις διακατηλέγχετο 28
δημοσίᾳ ἐπιδικνὺς διὰ τῶν γραφῶν εἶναι τὸν Χριστὸν Ἰησοῦν.

Ἐγένετο δὲ ἐν τῷ τὸν Ἀπολλὼ εἶναι ἐν Κορίνθῳ Παῦλον XIX
διελθόντα τὰ ἀνωτερικὰ μέρη ἐλθεῖν εἰς Ἔφεσον καὶ εὑρεῖν τινὰς
μαθητάς, | εἶπέν τε πρὸς αὐτούς· Εἰ πνεῦμα ἅγιον ἐλάβετε πιστεύ- 2
σαντες; οἱ δὲ πρὸς αὐτόν· Ἀλλ' οὐδ' εἰ πνεῦμα ἅγιον ἔστιν
ἠκούσαμεν. | εἶπέν τε· Εἰς τί οὖν ἐβαπτίσθητε; οἱ δὲ εἶπαν· 3
Εἰς τὸ Ἰωάνου βάπτισμα. εἶπεν δὲ Παῦλος· Ἰωάνης ἐβάπτισεν 4
βάπτισμα μετανοίας, τῷ λαῷ λέγων εἰς τὸν ἐρχόμενον μετ'
αὐτὸν ἵνα πιστεύσωσιν, τοῦτ' ἔστιν εἰς τὸν Ἰησοῦν. ἀκούσαντες 5
δὲ ἐβαπτίσθησαν εἰς τὸ ὄνομα τοῦ κυρίου Ἰησοῦ· καὶ ἐπιθέντος 6
αὐτοῖς τοῦ Παύλου χεῖρας ἦλθε τὸ πνεῦμα τὸ ἅγιον ἐπ' αὐτούς,
ἐλάλουν τε γλώσσαις καὶ ἐπροφήτευον. ἦσαν δὲ οἱ πάντες ἄνδρες 7
ὡσεὶ δώδεκα.

Εἰσελθὼν δὲ εἰς τὴν συναγωγὴν ἐπαρρησιάζετο ἐπὶ μῆνας 8
τρεῖς διαλεγόμενος καὶ πείθων περὶ τῆς βασιλείας τοῦ θεοῦ. ὡς 9

Editors   1 ελθειν] κατελθειν Soden   3 ειπεν τε] ο δε ειπεν WHmg   6 [τας]
χειρας Soden   8 πειθων]+τα Soden

Old Uncial   1 απολλω BAℵᶜ   απολλων A²   απελλην ℵ   ελθειν B (cf. D)   κατελθειν
ℵA   3 ειπεν τε B   ο δε ειπεν ℵA   8 πειθων B(+D)   +τα ℵA

Antiochian   1 ελθειν] διελθειν P   ευρων HLPSϚ(+D)   2 ειπαν S om τε
HLPSϚ(+D)   οι δε]+ειπον HLPSϚ   3 ειπεν τε]+προς αυτους HLPSϚ
4 δε] τε HS   ιωανης]+μεν HLPSϚ   om μετ S   add χριστον before
ιησουν HLPSϚ (cf. D)   6 τας χειρας LSϚ   7 δωδεκα] δεκαδυο HLPSϚ
8 πειθων]+τα HLPSϚ

understood βουλομενου to find its
explanatory reason in προτρεψαμενοι,
which was hence an act earlier in
time. It was then not unnatural
(although wrong) to take οι αδελφοι
of the Corinthians (so hcl.*mg* 'the
brethren'; D d have obscured this by
substituting εφεσιοι for αδελφοι), and
to supply further in a few words an
explanation of how they came to invite
Apollos to come to their country.

614, exactly like hcl ⋇, adds εις
την αχαιαν to παραγενομενος of the
B-text, and agrees with hcl.*text* in
omitting δια της χαριτος. Both these
variants came from the 'Western'
rewriting.

1 The addition in vs. 1, found in D
d vg.*cod.R²* hcl.*mg*, Ado. *martyrol*
(see above, pp. lx-lxii; cf. Ephr.
cat, also Pionius [ca. 350 A.D.], *vita
Polycarpi* 2, see Zahn, *Urausgabe*, p.

370) would seem more appropriate to
a position immediately after xviii. 22.
The addition is not fully explained.
Why is so much said about a purpose
which failed of fulfilment?

6 The addition in hcl.*mg*, vs. 6, is
also attested by Ephr.*cat*, and in part
by p vg. *five codd from southern France
mentioned by Berger*, which add, after
επροφητευον, *ita ut ipsi sibi interpretarentur*.

8 επαρρησιαζετο D seems to be
drawn from the B-text. The original
'Western' text may have read ελαλει,
although this has not been preserved
in Greek; cf. gig *confidentes loquebantur* (where plural is by error), vg
cum fiducia loquebatur. Pesh hcl.*text*
have 'he spoke,' with no indication of the specific force of επαρρησιαζετο. See J. R. Harris, *Codex
Bezae*, pp. 86 f.

28 εὐτόνως γὰρ τοῖς Ἰουδαίοις διακατηλέγχετο δημοσίᾳ διαλεγόμενος καὶ ἐπιδικνὺς διὰ τῶν γραφῶν τὸν Ἰησοῦν εἶναι
Χριστόν.

XIX Θέλοντος δὲ τοῦ Παύλου κατὰ τὴν ἰδίαν βουλὴν πορεύεσθαι
εἰς Ἱεροσόλυμα εἶπεν αὐτῷ τὸ πνεῦμα ὑποστρέφειν εἰς τὴν
Ἀσίαν, διελθὼν δὲ τὰ ἀνωτερικὰ μέρη ἔρχεται εἰς Ἔφεσον, καὶ
2 εὑρών τινας μαθητὰς | εἶπεν πρὸς αὐτούς· Εἰ πνεῦμα ἅγιον ἐλά-
βετε πιστεύσαντες; οἱ δὲ πρὸς αὐτόν· Ἀλλ' †οὐδὲ† πνεῦμα
3 ἅγιον λαμβάνουσίν τινες ἠκούσαμεν. εἶπεν δέ· Εἰς τί οὖν ἐβαπ-
4 τίσθητε; οἱ δὲ ἔλεγον· Εἰς τὸ Ἰωάνου βάπτισμα. | εἶπεν δὲ ὁ
Παῦλος· Ἰωάνης ἐβάπτισεν βάπτισμα μετανοίας, τῷ λαῷ λέγων
εἰς τὸν ἐρχόμενον μετ' αὐτὸν ἵνα πιστεύσωσιν, τοῦτ' ἔστιν εἰς
5 Χριστόν. ἀκούσαντες δὲ τοῦτο ἐβαπτίσθησαν εἰς τὸ ὄνομα
6 κυρίου Ἰησοῦ Χριστοῦ εἰς ἄφεσιν ἁμαρτιῶν· καὶ ἐπιθέντο<ς>
αὐτοῖς χεῖρα τοῦ Παύλου εὐθέως ἐπέπεσεν τὸ πνεῦμα τὸ ἅγιον
7 ἐπ' αὐτοῖς, <ἐ>λάλουν δὲ γλώσσαις καὶ ἐπροφήτευον. ἦσαν δὲ
οἱ πάντες ἄνδρες ὡσεὶ δώδεκα.

8 Εἰσελθὼν δὲ ὁ Παῦλος εἰς τὴν συναγωγὴν ἐν δυνάμει μεγάλῃ
ἐπαρρησιάζετο ἐπὶ μῆνας ·γ̅ διαλεγόμενος καὶ πείθων περὶ τῆς

---

multum contulit in ecclesias 28 fortiter enim judaeos convincebat publicae dis- **d**
putante et ostendens per scripturas i̅h̅m̅ esse x̅p̅m̅
  1 volente vero paulo secundum suum consilium exire in hierosolyma dixit ei s̅p̅s̅
revertere in asiam perambulantes superioris partibus venit in ephesum et cum
invenisset quosdam discipulos 2 dixit ad eos si s̅p̅m̅ sanctum accepistis cum credi-
dissetis illi vero ad eum sed neque s̅p̅m̅ sanctum accipiunt quidam audivimus
3 dixitque quid ergo baptizati estis ad illi dixerunt in johannis baptisma 4 dixit
autem paulus johannes baptizavit baptisma paenitentiae populo dicens in eum qui
venerit post ipsum ut crederent hoc est in x̅p̅m̅ 5 cum audissent hoc baptizati sunt
in nomine d̅n̅i̅ i̅h̅u̅ x̅p̅i̅ in remissione peccatorum 6 et cum inposuisset eis manum
paulus statim cecidit s̅p̅s̅ sanctus super eos loquebatur linguis et profetabant
7 erant autem universi viri quasi duodecim 8 cum introisset autem paulus in
synagogā cum fiducia magna palam loquebatur per trens menses disputans et

---

1 θελοντος δε . . . εφεσον] *mg* quum autem vellet Paulus cogitatione sua ire Harclean
Hierosolymam, dixit ei spiritus : Revertere in Asiam. quum peragrasset
autem partes superiores, venit in Ephesum   2 λαμβανουσιν τινες] *mg*
accipiant aliqui   5 χριστου εις αφεσιν αμαρτιων] ⸓ Christi in remissione
peccatorum ✓ 6 <ε>λαλουν δε γλωσσαις και επροφητευον] *mg* et loquebantur
linguis aliis et cognoscebant ipsi eas, quas et interpretabantur ipsi sibi ;
quidam autem etiam prophetabant   8 εν δυναμει μεγαλη] *mg* in virtute
magna

δέ τινες ἐσκληρύνοντο καὶ ἠπείθουν κακολογοῦντες τὴν ὁδὸν
ἐνώπιον τοῦ πλήθους, ἀποστὰς ἀπ᾽ αὐτῶν ἀφώρισεν τοὺς μαθητάς,
καθ᾽ ἡμέραν διαλεγόμενος ἐν τῇ σχολῇ Τυράννου. τοῦτο δὲ 10
ἐγένετο ἐπὶ ἔτη δύο, ὥστε πάντας τοὺς κατοικοῦντας τὴν ᾽Ασίαν
ἀκοῦσαι τὸν λόγον τοῦ κυρίου, ᾽Ιουδαίους τε καὶ ῞Ελληνας.
δυνάμεις τε οὐ τὰς τυχούσας ὁ θεὸς ἐποίει διὰ τῶν χειρῶν Παύλου, 11
ὥστε καὶ ἐπὶ τοὺς ἀσθενοῦντας ἀποφέρεσθαι ἀπὸ τοῦ χρωτὸς 12
αὐτοῦ σουδάρια ἢ σιμικίνθια καὶ ἀπαλλάσ‹σ›εσθαι ἀπ᾽ αὐτῶν
τὰς νόσους, τά τε πνεύματα τὰ πονηρὰ ἐκπορεύεσθαι. ἐπεχείρησαν 13
δέ τινες καὶ τῶν περιερχομένων ᾽Ιουδαίων ἐξορκιστῶν ὀνομάζειν
ἐπὶ τοὺς ἔχοντας τὰ πνεύματα τὰ πονηρὰ τὸ ὄνομα τοῦ κυρίου
᾽Ιησοῦ λέγοντες· ῾Ορκίζω ὑμᾶς τὸν ᾽Ιησοῦν ὃν Παῦλος κηρύσσει.
ἦσαν δέ τινος Σκευᾶ ᾽Ιουδαίου ἀρχιερέως ἑπτὰ υἱοὶ τοῦτο ποιοῦντες. 14
ἀποκριθὲν δὲ τὸ πνεῦμα τὸ πονηρὸν εἶπεν αὐτοῖς· Τὸν μὲν 15

Editors   9 τυραννου] +τινος Soden   14 τινες Soden JHR   15 [μεν] WH
om μεν Soden

Old Uncial   12 απαλλασσεσθαι B²   13 τον ΒΑℵᶜ(+D) +κυριον ℵ   14 τινος
B(+D)   τινες ℵA   σκευα Βℵ(+D)   σκευια A   15 μεν Βℵᶜ   om ℵA(+D)

Antiochian   9 τυραννου] +τινος HLPSϚ(+D)   10 δυο ετη L   κυριου] +ιησου
HLPϚ   11 εποιει ο θεος HLPSϚ   12 αποφερεσθαι] επιφερεσθαι
HLPSϚ(+D)   αυτου] +επιφερεσθαι L   εκπορευεσθαι] εξερχεσθαι
απ αυτων HLPSϚ   13 om και LϚ(+D)   add απο before των
περιερχομενων HLPSϚ (cf. D)   ορκιζομεν HLPSϚ   ο παυλος LϚ
14 τινες HLPSϚ   υιοι σκευα ιουδαιου (ιουδαιοι L) αρχιερεως επτα HLPSϚ
(cf. D)   add οι before τουτο HLPSϚ   15 om αυτοις HLPSϚ
om μεν HLPSϚ(+D)

---

9 των εθνων D d E e pesh hcl ⁜,
populi r, seems to be due to a misunderstanding of του πληθους (which
really refers to the synagogue). The
glossator has overlooked the clear
implication of the following αποστας
απ αυτων. 383 614 add των εθνων to
τινες at the opening of the verse ; the
fact that 614 reads τινες των εθνων
τοτε confirms the suspicion that this
is merely a misplacement of the gloss,
which belonged after πληθους.
απο ωρας πεμπτης εως δεκατης D d
383 614 gig vg.*codd* (cf. Ambrst on
2 Cor. xi. 23), hcl.⁜; cf. Wendt *ad loc.*
14 In the long addition D d hcl.*mg*
and Ephr.*cat.* (in part) agree almost
verbatim ; w tepl have the same
without the sentence (οι) εθος . . .
εξορκιζειν. The need of accounting

for εκ του οικου εκεινου, vs. 16, was a
part of the glossator's motive.
τινες ℵA Antiochian vg hcl.*text* is
to be preferred to τινος BDE minn
vg.*codd* pesh hcl.*mg*. The sons, not
the father, are the persons introduced
to the reader. The omission of
ιουδαιου seems to have characterized
the ᾽Western᾽ paraphrase (so not
only D d hcl.*mg* but also gig r) ;
whether ιουδαιων, vs. 13, caused its
addition or omission is hard to say.
αρχιερεως is probably original, since
sacerdos is a not unusual rendering of
the word (cf. Zahn, *Urausgabe*, pp.
168, 177 f.), and pesh in Acts xxiii.
4, 5, 14 shows that the same possibility existed in Syriac ; ιερεως D
stands alone in Greek, and is probably
due to influence from d.

9 βασιλείας τοῦ θεοῦ. τινὲς μὲν οὖν αὐτῶν ἐσκληρύνοντο καὶ
ἠπίθουν κακολογοῦντες τὴν ὁδὸν ἐνώπιον τοῦ πλήθους τῶν ἐθνῶν.
τότε ἀποστὰς ὁ Παῦλος ἀπ' αὐτῶν ἀφώρισεν τοὺς μαθητάς, τὸ
καθ' ἡμέραν διαλεγόμενος ἐν τῇ σχολῇ Τυραννίου τινὸς ἀπὸ ὥρας
10 ε̄ ἕως δεκάτης. τοῦτο δὲ ἐγένετο ἐπὶ ἔτη δύο, ἔ[ω]ς πάντες
οἱ κατοικοῦντες τὴν Ἀσίαν [ἤ]κουσαν τοὺς λόγους τοῦ κυρίου,
11 Ἰουδαῖοι καὶ Ἕλληνες. δυνάμεις δὲ οὐ τὰς τυχούσας ὁ θεὸς
12 ἐποίει διὰ τῶν χειρῶν Παύλου, ὥστε καὶ ἐπὶ τοὺς ἀσθενοῦντας
ἐπιφέρεσθαι ἀπὸ τοῦ χρωτὸς αὐτοῦ σουδάρια ἢ καὶ σιμικίνθια καὶ
ἀπαλλάσσεσθαι ἀπ' αὐτῶν τὰς νόσους τά τε πνεύματα πονηρὰ
13 ἐκπορεύεσθαι. ἐπεχείρησαν δέ τινες ἐκ τῶν περιερχομένω<ν>
Ἰουδαίων ἐξορκιστῶν ὀνομάζειν ἐπὶ τοὺς ἔχοντας τὰ πνεύματα
πονηρὰ τὸ ὄνομα κυρίου Ἰησοῦ λέγοντες· Ὁρκίζω ὑμᾶς τὸν
14 Ἰησοῦν ὃν Παῦλος κηρύσσει. ἐν οἷς καὶ υἱοὶ Σκευᾶ τινος ἱερέως
ἠθέλησαν τὸ αὐτὸ ποιῆσαι (ἔθος εἶχαν τοὺς τοιούτους ἐξορκίζειν),
καὶ εἰσελθόντες πρὸς τὸν δαιμονιζόμενον ἤρξαντο ἐπικαλεῖσθαι
τὸ ὄνομα λέγοντες· Παραγγέλλομέν σοι ἐν Ἰησοῦ ὃν Παῦλος
15 †ἐξελθεῖν† κηρύσσει. τότε ἀπεκρίθη τὸ πνεῦμα τὸ πονηρόν, εἶπεν

persuadens de regno d̄i̅ 9 ut vero quidam eorum cum indurarent et non crederent d
maledicentes viam in conspectu multitudinis gentiū tunc recessit paulus ab eis
segregavit discipulos cottidie disputans in scola tyranni cujusdam ab hora v̄ usque
decima 10 hoc autem factum est in annos duos ita ut omnes qui habitant asiam
audirent verba d̄n̅i̅ judaeique et craeci 11 virtutes etiam non quasilibet d̄s̅ faciebat
per manus pauli 12 ita ut et super infirmantes inferentur a corpore ejus sudaria
aut simicintia et recedent ab eis infirmitatis ut s̅p̅s̅ malignus exiret 13 adgressi
sunt quidam ex circumvenientibus judaeis exorcistarum nominare super eos qui
haberent s̅p̅s̅ malignos nomen d̄n̅i̅ i̅h̅u̅ dicentes adjuro vos per i̅h̅m̅ quem paulus
praedicat 14 in quo et fili scevae cujusdam sacerdotis voluerunt similiter facere
consuetudinem habebant apud eos exorcizare et introierunt adimplentes coeperunt
invocare nomen dicentes praecipimus tibi i̅h̅u̅ quem paulus praedicat exire 15 tunc

9 των εθνων τοτε] ⁘ gentis tunc ✓   απο ωρας ε̄ εως δεκατης] ⁘ ab Harclean
hora quinta usque ad horam decimam ✓   14–15 εν οις . . . ειπεν] mg in
quibus erant filii septem Scevae cujusdam sacerdotis qui voluerunt id ipsum
facere ; qui soliti erant adjurare super eos qui ita erant. et quum ingressi
essent ad daemoniacum, coeperunt invocare nomen dicentes: Praecipimus tibi
per Jesum quem Paulus praedicat ut exeas. respondens autem spiritus ille
malus dixit

On the difficult επτα (cf. vs. 16 αμφοτερων) textual conditions throw no light. Notwithstanding hcl.mg it was probably lacking in the 'Western' text (D d r); duo gig is emendation, hardly supposable to have arisen out of an omitted ιουδαιου. That επτα should have been added in the face of αμφοτερων vs. 16 is incredible, even if αμφοτερων be explained as here used in the sense of 'all'; hence επτα is to be retained.

Ἰησοῦν γεινώσκω καὶ τὸν Παῦλον ἐπίσταμαι, ὑμεῖς δὲ τίνες
ἐστέ; καὶ ἐφαλόμενος ὁ ἄνθρωπος ἐπ' αὐτοὺς ἐν ᾧ ἦν τὸ πνεῦμα 16
τὸ πονηρὸν κατακυριεύσας ἀμφοτέρων ἴσχυσεν κατ' αὐτῶν,
ὥστε γυμνοὺς καὶ τετραυματισμένους ἐκφυγεῖν ἐκ τοῦ οἴκου
ἐκείνου. τοῦτο δὲ ἐγένετο γνωστὸν πᾶσιν Ἰουδαίοις τε καὶ 17
Ἕλλησι τοῖς κατοικοῦσιν τὴν Ἔφεσον, καὶ ἐπέπεσεν φόβος ἐπὶ
πάντας αὐτούς, καὶ ἐμεγαλύνετο τὸ ὄνομα τοῦ κυρίου Ἰησοῦ.
πολλοί τε τῶν πεπιστευκότων ἤρχοντο ἐξομολογούμενοι καὶ 18
ἀναγγέλλοντες τὰς πράξεις αὐτῶν. ἱκανοὶ δὲ τῶν τὰ περίεργα 19
πραξάντων συνενέγκαντες τὰς βίβλους κατέκαιον ἐνώπιον πάντων·
καὶ συνεψήφισαν τὰς τειμὰς αὐτῶν καὶ εὗρον ἀργυρίου μυριάδας
πέντε. οὕτως κατὰ κράτος τοῦ κυρίου ὁ λόγος ηὔξανεν καὶ 20
ἴσχυεν.

Ὡς δὲ ἐπληρώθη ταῦτα, ἔθετο ὁ Παῦλος ἐν τῷ πνεύματι 21
διελθὼν τὴν Μακεδονίαν καὶ Ἀχαίαν πορεύεσθαι εἰς Ἰεροσόλυμα,
εἰπὼν ὅτι Μετὰ τὸ γενέσθαι με ἐκεῖ δεῖ με καὶ Ῥώμην ἰδεῖν.
ἀποστείλας δὲ εἰς τὴν Μακεδονίαν δύο τῶν διακονούντων αὐτῷ, 22
Τιμόθεον καὶ Ἔραστον, αὐτὸς ἐπέσχεν χρόνον εἰς τὴν Ἀσίαν.
ἐγένετο δὲ κατὰ τὸν καιρὸν ἐκεῖνον τάραχος οὐκ ὀλίγος περὶ τῆς 23
ὁδοῦ. Δημήτριος γάρ τις ὀνόματι, ἀργυροκόπος, ποιῶν ναοὺς 24
Ἀρτέμιδος παρείχετο τοῖς τεχνείταις οὐκ ὀλίγην ἐργασίαν, οὓς 25

Editors   20 ο λογος του κυριου Soden   24 ναους] +[αργυρους] WH   +αργυρους
Soden JHR

Old Uncial   16 εφαλομενος BℵA   εφαλλομενος ℵ^c (cf.D)   κατακυριευσας Bℵ^c(+D)
κατακυριευσαν A   και κατακυριευσας ℵ   ισχυσεν BAℵ^c(+D)   ενισχυσεν ℵ
εκφυγειν Bℵ(+D)   +αυτους A   17 την Bℵ(+D)   om A   επεπεσεν
Bℵ   επεσεν A(+D)   φοβος BAℵ^c(+D)   ο φοβος Bℵ   20 του
κυριου ο λογος BAℵ   ο λογος του κυριου ℵ^c   21 διελθων Bℵ   διελθειν A(+D)
αχαιαν Bℵ   την αχαιαν A(+D)   22 την 1° BA(+D)   om ℵ   διακονουντων
αυτω Bℵ(+D)   διακονουν αυτων A   24 ναους B   +αργυρους Aℵ^c(+D)
ναον αργυρουν ℵ   παρειχετο BℵA²   παρειχε A(+D)

Antiochian   16 εφαλλομενος HLPSϚ (cf. D)   επ αυτους ο ανθρωπος HLPSϚ (cf. D)
πονηρον] +και HLPSϚ   κατακυριευσαν HLPS   αμφοτερων] αυτων
HLPSϚ   17 τοις ιουδαιοις P   om του P(+D)   18 ηρχοντο]
ηρξαντο S   20 ο λογος του κυριου HLPSϚ   21 διελθειν P(+D)
ιερουσαλημ HLPSϚ   22 αυτω] αυτων H   24 ναους] +αργυρους
HLPSϚ(+D)   εργασιαν ουκ ολιγην HLPSϚ

---

16 The singular paraphrase of the
whole verse in Ephr : *et stridit dentibus daemonium illud ad rectam et
sinistram et expulit eos a domo*, suggests (so Conybeare) the conjectural

Greek ακρωτηριασας απ' αμφοτερων for
κατακυριευσας αμφοτερων, and this
would relieve the difficulty about επτα,
vs. 14. But if the paraphrase is
significant at all, it seems more prob-

αὐτοῖς· Τὸν Ἰησοῦν γεινώσκω καὶ τὸν Παῦλον ἐπίσταμαι,
16 ὑμεῖς δὲ τίνες ἐστέ; καὶ ἐναλλόμενος εἰς αὐτοὺς ὁ ἄνθρωπος ἐν
ᾧ ἦν τὸ πνεῦμα τὸ πονηρὸν κυριεύσας ἀμφοτέρων εἴσχυσεν κατ'
αὐτῶν, ὥστε γυμνοὺς καὶ τετραυματισμένους ἐκφυγεῖν ἐκ τοῦ
17 οἴκου ἐκείνου. τοῦτο δὲ ἐγένετο γνωστὸν πᾶσι Ἰουδαίοις καὶ
Ἕλλησιν τοῖς κατοικοῦσιν τὴν Ἔφεσον, καὶ φόβος ἔπεσεν ἐπὶ
18 πάντας αὐτούς, καὶ ἐμεγαλύνετο τὸ ὄνομα κυρίου Ἰησοῦ. πολλοὶ
δὲ τῶν πιστευόντων ἤρχοντο ἐξομολογούμενοι καὶ ἀναγγέλλοντες
19 τὰς πράξεις αὐτῶν. ἱκανοὶ τῶν τὰ περίεργα πραξάντων συνενέγκαντες καὶ τὰς βίβλους κατέκαιον ἐνώπιον πάντων· καὶ συνεψήφισαν τὰς τιμὰς αὐτῶν· εὗρον ἀργυρίου μυρι‹ά›δας πέντε.
20 οὕτως κατὰ κράτος †ἐνίσχυσεν καὶ ἡ πίστις τοῦ θεοῦ ηὔξανε καὶ
ἐπλήθυνε†.

21 Τότε Παῦλος ἔθετο ἐν τῷ πνεύματι διελθεῖν τὴν Μακεδονίαν
καὶ τὴν Ἀχαίαν καὶ πορεύεσθαι εἰς Ἱεροσόλυμα, εἰπὼν ὅτι
22 Μετὰ τὸ γενέσθαι με ἐκεῖ δεῖ με καὶ Ῥώμην ἰδεῖν. καὶ ἀποστείλας εἰς τὴν Μακεδονίαν δύο τῶν διακονούντων αὐτῷ, Τιμόθεον
23 καὶ Ἔραστον, αὐτὸς ἐπέσχεν χρόνον ὀλίγον ἐν τῇ Ἀσίᾳ. ἐγένετο
δὲ κατὰ τὸν καιρὸν ἐκεῖνον τάραχος οὐχ ὀλίγος περὶ τῆς ὁδοῦ.
24 Δημήτριος γάρ τις ἦν ἀργυροκόπος, ποιῶν ναοὺς ἀργυροῦς Ἀρτέ-
25 μιδος, ὃς παρεῖχε τοῖς τεχνείταις οὐκ ὀλίγην ἐργασίαν, οὗτος

15 εστε] εσται   19 τα περιεργα] περι τα εργα   κατεκαιον]
καταικεον   συνεψηφισον   21 ιεροσολυσολυμα   με] μαι

respondens sp̄s malignus dixit ad eos īhm adgnosco et paulum scio vos autem qui d
estis 16 et insilien in eos homo in quo erat sp̄s nequa dominatus utrisque valuit
adversus eos ita ut nudi et vulnerati effugerent de domo illa 17 hoc autem factum
est notum omnibus judaeis et grecis his qui habitant in ephesum et incidit timor
super omnes eos et magnificabatur nomen dn̄i īhu 18 multique credentium veniebant
confitentes et nuntiantes actos suos 19 multi autem ex his qui curiosa gesserunt
adtulerunt et libros commurebant coram omnibus et conputatis praetiis illorum
invenerunt denariorum sestertia docenta 20 sic potens convalescebat et fides dī
crescebat et convalescebat 21 tunc paulus adposuit in sp̄o transire per macedoniam
et achaiam et sic ire in hierosolyma dicens quia cum fuero ibi necesse est me roma
videre 22 et misit in macedoniam duos qui sibi ministrabant timotheum et erastum
ipse vero substitit tempus in asiàm 23 factum est autem in illo tempore tumultus
non modicus de hac via dn̄i 24 demetrius enim quidam argentarius faciens tempula
argentea dianae qui prestabat artificibus non modicam adquisitionem 25 hic con-

18 ηρχοντο] mg coeperunt—ηρξαντο   23 οδου] via ⁖ dei ✓   Harclean

ably due to a misinterpretation of
the usual text, perhaps made with
επτα, vs. 14, in mind.

20 D d is somehow conflate. The

proper ' Western' text may have lacked
ηυξανε. Cf. sah ('grew and was established and prevailed'); and pesh
('there was established and multiplied
the faith of God ').

συναθροίσας καὶ τοὺς περὶ τὰ τοιαῦτα ἐργάτας εἶπεν· Ἄνδρες, ἐπίστασθε ὅτι ἐκ ταύτης τῆς ἐργασίας ἡ εὐπορία ἡμῖν ἐστίν, | καὶ 26 θεωρεῖτε καὶ ἀκούετε ὅτι οὐ μόνον Ἐφέσου ἀλλὰ σχεδὸν πάσης τῆς Ἀσίας ὁ Παῦλος οὗτος πείσας μετέστησεν ἱκανὸν ὄχλον, λέγων ὅτι οὐκ εἰσὶν θεοὶ οἱ διὰ χειρῶν γεινόμενοι. οὐ μόνον δὲ 27 τοῦτο κινδυνεύει ἡμῖν τὸ μέρος εἰς ἀπελεγμὸν ἐλθεῖν, ἀλλὰ καὶ τὸ τῆς μεγάλης θεᾶς Ἀρτέμιδος ἱερὸν εἰς οὐθὲν λογισθῆναι, †μέλλειν τε καὶ καθαιρεῖσθαι τῆς μεγαλειότητος† αὐτῆς, ἣν ὅλη Ἀσία καὶ οἰκουμένη σέβεται. ἀκούσαντες δὲ καὶ γενόμενοι 28 πλήρεις θυμοῦ ἔκραζον λέγοντες· Μεγάλη ἡ Ἄρτεμις Ἐφεσίων. καὶ ἐπλήσθη ἡ πόλις τῆς συγχύσεως, ὥρμησάν τε ὁμοθυμαδὸν 29 εἰς τὸ θέατρον συναρπάσαντες Γαῖον καὶ Ἀρίσταρχον Μακεδόνας, συνεκδήμους Παύλου. Παύλου δὲ βουλομένου εἰσελθεῖν εἰς τὸν 30 δῆμον οὐκ εἴων αὐτὸν οἱ μαθηταί· τινὲς δὲ καὶ τῶν Ἀσιαρχῶν, 31 ὄντες αὐτῷ φίλοι, πέμψαντες πρὸς αὐτὸν παρεκάλουν μὴ δοῦναι ἑαυτὸν εἰς τὸ θέατρον. ἄλλοι μὲν οὖν ἄλλο τι ἔκραζον, ἦν γὰρ 32

Editors　27 [η] ασια και [η] οικουμενη WH　η ασια και η οικουμενη Soden JHR 30 παυλου δε] του δε παυλου Soden

Old Uncial　26 αλλα B‭ℵ‬　+και A(+D)　πεισας B(+D)　πεισαν A　om ‭ℵ‬　οι BA‭ℵ‬ᶜ(+D)　om ‭ℵ‬　27 κινδυνευει (κινδυνευσι ‭ℵ‬) ημιν το μερος B‭ℵ‬ (cf. D)　το μερος κινδυνευει ημιν A　αλλα BA‭ℵ‬ᶜ(+D) om ‭ℵ‬　λογισθηναι B‭ℵ‬　λογισθησεται A(+D)　μελλειν B‭ℵ‬A²　μελλει A (cf. D)　ασια B　η ασια ‭ℵ‬A (cf. D)　οικουμενη B　η οικουμενη ‭ℵ‬A(+D)　28 πληρεις B‭ℵ‬(+D) πληρης A　29 της B‭ℵ‬A　om ‭ℵ‬ᶜ　30 παυλου B‭ℵ‬A　του παυλου ‭ℵ‬ᶜ (cf. D)　31 εαυτον BA‭ℵ‬ᶜ(+D)　αυτον ‭ℵ‬

Antiochian　25 ημων HLPS‭ϛ‬　26 αλλα] +και L(+D)　γενομενοι L(+D) 27 ιερον αρτεμιδος HPS(+D)　τε] δε HLS‭ϛ‬　την μεγαλειοτητα HLPS‭ϛ‬　η ασια HLPS‭ϛ‬ (cf. D)　η οικουμενη HLPS‭ϛ‬(+D) 29 πολις] +ολη HLPS‭ϛ‬ (cf. D)　om της ‭ϛ‬　του παυλου ‭ϛ‬ 30 παυλου δε] του δε παυλου HLPS‭ϛ‬ (cf. D)

26 That τις τοτε D d is a mistake for τις ποτε is indicated by gig *hic paulus nescio quem* (cf. xvii. 7).

27 The text of D d, in which after μελλει several words have probably fallen out, may be completed by the aid of gig vg, *sed et destrui incipiet majestas ejus quam*, to read αλλα καθαιρ⟨ε⟩ισθαι μελλει ⟨η μεγαλειοτης αυτης ην⟩. This is probably nearer the original than the monstrous sentence of the B-text, of which the Antiochian την μεγαλειοτητα is a well-meant but only partial amelioration. The B-text probably owes its form to the slight

difficulty in the second αλλα ('nay'). Not only, however, is the B-text monstrous, but it has completely destroyed the highly effective rhetorical climax —one quite beyond the range of the 'Western' glossator's usual power. The retention in vg of the Old Latin, without alteration to conform it to Greek standards, is significant.

28 (και) δραμοντες εις το αμφοδον (εδφοδον 614) D d 383 614 minn hcl.*mg* is one of the few intrinsically interesting 'Western' additions.

The omission, vss. 28 and 34, of η before αρτεμις in D (supported by

συναθροίσας τοὺς περὶ τὰ τοιαῦτα τεχνείτας ἔφη πρὸς αὐτούς·
Ἄνδρες συντεχνεῖται, ἐπίστασθε ὅτι ἐκ ταύτης τῆς ἐργασίας ἡ
26 εὐπορία ἡμεῖν ἐστιν, καὶ ἀκούετε καὶ θεωρεῖτε ⟨ὅτι⟩ οὐ μόνον
ἕως Ἐφέσου ἀλλὰ καὶ σχεδὸν πάσης Ἀσίας ὁ Παῦλος οὗτος τίς
ποτε πίσας μετέστησεν ἱκανὸν ὄχλον, λέγων ὅτι οὗτοι οὐκ εἰσὶν
27 θεοὶ οἱ διὰ χειρῶν γενόμενοι. οὐ μόνον δὲ τοῦτο ἡμεῖν κινδυνεύει
τὸ μέρος εἰς ἀπελεγμὸν ἐλθεῖν, ἀλλὰ καὶ τὸ τῆς μεγάλης θεᾶς
ἱερὸν Ἀρτέμιδος εἰς οὐδὲν λογισθήσεται· ἀλλὰ καθαιρῖσθαι μέλλει
⟨.................⟩ ἡ ὅλη Ἀσία καὶ ἡ οἰκουμένη
28 σέβεται. ταῦτα δὲ ἀκούσαντες καὶ γενόμενοι πλήρεις θυμοῦ
δραμόντες εἰς τὸ ἄμφοδον ἔκραζον λέγοντες· Μεγάλη Ἄρτεμις
29 Ἐφεσίων. καὶ συνεχύθη ὅλη ἡ πόλις †αἰσχύνης†, ὥρμησαν δὲ
ὁμοθυμαδὸν εἰς τὸ θέατρον καὶ συναρπάσαντες Γαῖον καὶ
30 Ἀρίσταρχον Μακεδόνας, συνεκδήμους Παύλου. βουλομένου δὲ
31 τοῦ Παύλου εἰσελθεῖν εἰς τὸν δῆμον οἱ μαθηταὶ ἐκώλυον· τινὲς
δὲ καὶ τῶν Ἀσιαρχῶν, ὑπάρχοντες αὐτῷ φίλοι, πέμψαντες πρὸς
32 αὐτὸν παρεκάλουν μὴ δοῦναι ἑαυτὸν εἰς τὸ θέατρον. ἄλλοι

25 τεχνειτας] τεχνεταις	επιστασται	26 ακουεται
θεωρειται εφεσιου	ποτε] τοτε	27 καθερισθαι
29 μακεδονες		

vocavit eos qui circa haec operabantur ait ad eos viri artifices scitis quia ex hac d
operationem adquisitio est nobis 26 et audistis et videtis quia non solum ipsius
ephesi sed paenae omnis asiae paulus hic quidam tunc suadens eduxit plurimam
turbam dicens quoniam non sunt dii qui fiunt manibus 27 non solum autem nobis
periclitatur pars in redargutionem venire sed etiam magnae deae templum dianae
in nihilum deputabitur sed destrui incipiet tota asia et orbis terrarum colitur
28 haec autem cum audissent et fuissent pleni indignatione currentes in campo
clamaverunt dicentes magna est diana ephesiorum 29 et repleta est tota civitas
confusionem impetumque fecerunt unanimiter in theatru et rapuerunt gaium et
aristarchum macedonibus comitibus pauli 30 ipso autem volente paulo introire in
turbam discipuli non sinebant 31 quidam vero asiarcharum qui erant amici ejus
cum mississent ad eum rogabant eum ne darent se in theatrum 32 alii autem vero

25 συντεχνειται] ⋇ cooperarii ✓   28 δραμοντες εις το αμφοδον] mg et Harclean
currebant in foro

minn in vs. 28) is probably, but not
certainly, accidental. See W. M.
Ramsay, *The Church in the Roman
Empire*, pp. 137-142.
29 αισχυνης D is superfluous, and is
absent in gig sah. It is to be explained as retranslation from *confusionem* in d, which here follows not
the 'Western' but the B-text. For
the equivalence of the two terms cf.
the Latin vulgate rendering of Lk. ix.

26, xiv. 9, xvi. 3; Jude 13; Phil. iii.
19; Heb. xii. 2; Rev. iii. 18.
The accusative *confusionem* (as in
vg.cod. *I*) is probably an instance of
the common corruption of terminations in early Latin MSS. αισχυνης
may have been translated from a
Latin ablative; that it is in the
genitive may be due to subsequent
conformation to the B-text. But see
J. R. Harris, *Codex Bezae*, pp. 106 f.

ἡ ἐκκλησία συγκεχυμένη, καὶ οἱ πλείους οὐκ ᾔδεισαν τίνος ἕνεκα
συνεληλύθεισαν. ἐκ δὲ τοῦ ὄχλου συνεβίβασαν Ἀλέξανδρον προ- 33
βαλόντων αὐτὸν τῶν Ἰουδαίων, ὁ δὲ Ἀλέξανδρος κατασείσας
τὴν χεῖρα ἤθελεν ἀπολογεῖσθαι τῷ δήμῳ. ἐπιγνόντες δὲ ὅτι 34
Ἰουδαῖός ἐστιν φωνὴ ἐγένετο μία ἐκ πάντων ὡσεὶ ἐπὶ ὥρας δύο
κραζόντων· Μεγάλη ἡ Ἄρτεμις Ἐφεσίων, μεγάλη ἡ Ἄρτεμις
Ἐφεσίων. καταστείλας δὲ τὸν ὄχλον ὁ γραμματεύς φησιν· 35
Ἄνδρες Ἐφέσιοι, τίς γάρ ἐστιν ἀνθρώπων ὃς οὐ γεινώσκει τὴν
Ἐφεσίων πόλιν νεωκόρον οὖσαν τῆς μεγάλης Ἀρτέμιδος καὶ
τοῦ διοπετοῦς; ἀναντιρήτων οὖν ὄντων τούτων δέον ἐστὶν ὑμᾶς 36
κατεσταλμένους ὑπάρχειν καὶ μηδὲν προπετὲς πράσσειν. ἠγάγετε 37
γὰρ τοὺς ἄνδρας τούτους οὔτε ἱεροσύλους οὔτε βλασφημοῦντας
τὴν θεὸν ἡμῶν. εἰ μὲν οὖν Δημήτριος καὶ οἱ σὺν αὐτῷ τεχνεῖται 38
ἔχουσι πρός τινα λόγον, ἀγοραῖοι ἄγονται καὶ ἀνθύπατοί εἰσιν,
ἐγκαλείτωσαν ἀλλήλοις. εἰ δέ τι περαιτέρω ἐπιζητεῖτε, ἐν τῇ 39
ἐννόμῳ ἐκκλησίᾳ ἐπιλυθήσεται. καὶ γὰρ κινδυνεύομεν ἐγκαλεῖσθαι 40
στάσεως περὶ τῆς σήμερον μηδενὸς αἰτίου ὑπάρχοντος, περὶ οὗ οὐ

Editors | 34 ωσει] ως WHmg Soden JHR   κραζοντες WHmg   om μεγαλη η
αρτεμις εφεσιων 2° WH (but cf. mg) Soden JHR   35 ο γραμματευς τον
οχλον Soden JHR   39 περαιτερω] περι ετερων Soden mg   40 †περι
της σημερον . . . ταυτης† WHmg

Old Uncial | 33 ο δε Bℵᶜ(+D)   ο ουν A   ο δ᾽ ουν ℵ   την χειρα BℵA   τη χειρι ℵᶜ(+D)
ηθελεν BAℵᶜ(+D)   ηλθεν ℵ   34 ωσει B   ως ℵA(+D)   κραζοντων
B(+D)   κραζοντες ℵA   μεγαλη η αρτεμις εφεσιων twice B, once only ℵA
(cf. D)   35 τον οχλον ο γραμματευς B   ο γραμματευς τον οχλον ℵA(+D)
εφεσιοι BAℵᶜ(+D)   αδελφοι ℵ   της BAℵᶜ(+D)   και της ℵ   36 οντων
τουτων Bℵᶜ(+D)   οντων ℵ   τουτων οντων A   προπετες BℵA(+D)
+τι ℵᶜ   39 περαιτερω B   περι ετερων ℵA(+D)

Antiochian | 32 συνεληλυθασιν H   33 συνεβιβασαν] προεβιβασαν HLPSꟅ
προβαλλοντων LP(+D)   αυτων L   34 επιγνοντων Ʂ   ωσει] ως
HLPSꟅ(+D)   om μεγαλη η αρτεμις εφεσιων 2° HLPSꟅ(+D)   35 ο
γραμματευς τον οχλον HLPSꟅ(+D)   ανθρωπος HLPSꟅ (cf. D)   μεγαλης]
+θεας HLPSꟅ   37 om ηγαγετε γαρ τους ανδρας τουτους P   θεον]
θεαν PꟅ(+D)   ημων] υμων HLPSꟅ   38 προς τινα λογον εχουσιν Ʂ
39 περαιτερω] περι ετερων (+ετι S) HLPSꟅ(+D)   40 ου 1°] ουν L
om ου 2° Ʂ(+D)

33 συνεβιβασαν BℵA E ; προεβιβασαν
Antiochian ; κατεβιβασαν D, to which
detraxerunt gig vg (distrax- d, destrax-
p) seems to correspond. The strange-
ness of συνεβιβασαν ('instructed'?)
seems to have given rise to the
variants.
34 κραζοντες ℵA is probably derived

from κραζοντων B D Antiochian by
assimilation to επιγνοντες.
The repetition of μεγαλη η αρτεμις
εφεσιων is peculiar to B, and is to be
rejected.
35 διοσπετους D. Wordsworth and
White suggest that vg jovisque prolis
is derived from a corrupt form του διος

μὲν οὖν ἄλλο ἔκραζον, ἡ γὰρ ἐκκλησία ἦν συνκεχυμένη, καὶ
33 οἱ πλεῖστοι οὐκ ᾔδεισαν τίνος ἕνεκεν συνεληλύθεισαν. ἐκ δὲ
τοῦ ὄχλου κατεβίβασαν Ἀλέξανδρον προβαλλόντων αὐτὸν τῶν
Ἰουδαίων, ὁ δὲ Ἀλέξανδρος κατασείσας τῇ χειρὶ ἤθελεν
34 ἀπολογεῖσθαι τῷ δήμῳ. ἐπιγνόντες δὲ ὅτι Ἰουδαῖός ἐστιν
φωνὴ ἐγένετο μία πάντων ὡς ἐπὶ ὥρας δύο κραζόντων· Μεγάλη
35 Ἄρτεμις Ἐφεσίων. κατασείσας δὲ ὁ γραμματεὺς τὸν ὄχλον
φησίν· Ἄνδρες Ἐφέσιοι, τίς γάρ ἐστιν ὁ ἄνθρωπος ὃς οὐ γεινώσκει τὴν ἡμετέραν πόλιν ναοκόρον εἶναι τῆς μεγάλης Ἀρτέμι-
36 δος καὶ τοῦ διοσπετοῦς; ἀναντιρρήτων οὖν ὄντων τούτων δέον
ἐστὶν ὑμᾶς κατεσταλμένους ὑπάρχειν καὶ μηδὲν προπετὲς πράσ-
37 σειν. ἠγάγετε γὰρ τοὺς ἄνδρας τούτους ἐνθάδε μήτε ἱεροσύλους
38 μήτε βλασφημοῦντας τὴν θεὰν ἡμῶν. εἰ μὲν οὖν Δημήτριος
οὗτος καὶ οἱ σὺν αὐτῷ τεχνεῖται ἔχουσι πρὸς αὐτούς τινα λόγον,
ἀγοραῖοι ἄγονται καὶ ἀνθύπατοί εἰσιν, ἐνκαλίτωσαν ἀλλήλοις.
39 εἰ δέ τι περὶ ἑτέρων ἐπιζητεῖτε, ἐν †τῷ νόμῳ† ἐκκλησίᾳ ἐπι-
40 λυθήσεται. καὶ γὰρ κινδυνεύομεν σήμερον ἐνκαλεῖσθαι στάσεως

35 γεινωσγει   38 και οι] οι και   τεχνειτε

---

aliut clamabant erat enim ecclesia confusa et plures nesciebant cujus rei causa d
convenerint 33 de ipsa turba distraxerunt alexandrum propellentibus eum judaeis
alexander autem innuens manu volebat rationem reddere populo 34 cognito autem
eo quod judaeus esset vox facta est una omnium quasi horis duabus clamantium
magna est diana ephesiorum 35 cum conpescuisset scriba turba ait viri ephesi quis
enim est homo qui ignorat vestram civitatem aedituam esse magnae dianae et hujus
jovis 36 contradictione itaque non capientibus his oportet vos questos esse et nihil
temere agere 37 adduxistis enim viros istos hoc neque sacrilegos neque blasphe-
mantes deam nostram 38 si quidem ergo demetrius hic et qui cum eo sunt artefices
habent cum aliquos quendam verbum conventus aguntur et proconsoles sunt accusent
se invicem 39 si quid autem ulterius requiritis in legem ecclesiae discutietur
40 nam etiam periclitamur hodie accusari seditionis nullius causa esse cujus

---

34 μια] ⁘ una ✓   35 γραμματευς] scriba ⁘ civitatis ✓ Harclean
διοσπετους] et diopetous ⁘ ejus [i.e. 'her'] ✓   37 ενθαδε] mg huc

---

παιδος. With the rendering of d hujus
jovis is to be compared hcl ⁘.
39 περαιτερω B minn, ulterius gig d,
seems to be the true reading. περι
ετερων ℵA D Antiochian is due to an
error ; it does not suit the context.
Vg alterius rei is an attempt to represent περι ετερων without departing
too far from the Old Latin rendering.

τω νομω D can, with existing evidence, be explained only as an error
for τη εννομω.
40 The omission of οὐ by DE minn
gig vg sah boh seems an unsuccessful
emendation of a difficult, and perhaps
corrupt, text. The reading of Bℵא
Antiochian pesh hcl may contain some
very ancient error.

δυνησόμεθα ἀποδοῦναι λόγον περὶ τῆς συστροφῆς ταύτης. καὶ 41
ταῦτα εἰπὼν ἀπέλυσεν τὴν ἐκκλησίαν.

Μετὰ δὲ τὸ παύσασθαι τὸν θόρυβον μεταπεμψάμενος ὁ Παῦλος ΧΧ
τοὺς μαθητὰς καὶ παρακαλέσας ἀσπασάμενος ἐξῆλθεν πορεύεσθαι
εἰς Μακεδονίαν. διελθὼν δὲ τὰ μέρη ἐκεῖνα καὶ παρακαλέσας 2
αὐτοὺς λόγῳ πολλῷ ἦλθεν εἰς τὴν Ἑλλάδα, ποιήσας τε μῆνας 3
τρεῖς γενομένης ἐπιβουλῆς αὐτῷ ὑπὸ τῶν Ἰουδαίων μέλλοντι
ἀνάγεσθαι εἰς τὴν Συρίαν ἐγένετο γνώμης τοῦ ὑποστρέφειν διὰ
Μακεδονίας. συνείπετο δὲ αὐτῷ Σώπατρος Πύρρου Βεροιαῖος, 4
Θεσσαλονεικέων δὲ Ἀρίσταρχος καὶ Σέκουνδος, καὶ Γάιος
Δερβαῖος καὶ Τιμόθεος, Ἀσιανοὶ δὲ Τύχικος καὶ Τρόφιμος·
οὗτοι δὲ προσελθόντες ἔμενον ἡμᾶς ἐν Τρῳάδι· ἡμεῖς δὲ ἐξεπλεύσα- 5, 6

Editors 4 αυτω] +αχρι της ασιας Soden   om πυρρου JHR   5 προσελθοντες]
προελθοντες WHmg

Old Uncial 1 μεταπεμψαμενος Bℵ   προσκαλεσαμενος A(+D)   παρακαλεσας BA
+και ℵ   μακεδονιαν Bℵ(+D)   την μακεδονιαν A   4 αυτω Bℵ +αχρι της
ασιας A (cf. D)   δερβαιος Bℵ (cf. D)   ο δερβαιος A   5 προσελθοντες
BℵA   προελθοντες B²(B³ Tdf)(+D)   εμενον BA(+D)   εμεινον ℵ

Antiochian 40 αποδουναι] δουναι HLPS   om περι 3° HLPSϚ(+D)   1 μετα-
πεμψαμενος] προσκαλεσαμενος HLPSϚ(+D)   om παρακαλεσας HLPSϚ
πορευθηναι HLPSϚ   την μακεδονιαν H(Lsil)PSϚ   3 γενομενης] +δε L
αυτω επιβουλης HLPSϚ(+D)   γνωμη HLPSϚ   4 αυτω] +αχρι της
ασιας HLPSϚ (cf. D)   om πυρρου HLPSϚ   5 om δε HLPSϚ(+D)
προσελθοντες] προελθοντες Ϛ(+D)

3–5 The text of Bℵ 33 is right in vs. 4 in reading συνειπετο δε αυτω and omitting μεχρι της ασιας, and in vs. 5 in reading προσελθοντες (not προελθοντες). Although the statement is very condensed, the author clearly meant to say (1) that when Paul had made up his mind to sail (ἀνάγεσθαι) from Corinth for Syria, the Jews' plot made a sea voyage dangerous and led him to change his plans so as first to 'return' via Macedonia (i.e. to Asia, for υποστρεφειν vs. 3 does not mean 'return to Syria,' but is directly opposed to 'sail for Syria'); (2) that the persons named in vs. 4 were 'associated with Paul' (συνειπετο δε αυτω is to be thus translated; the reference is to a general 'association' for the journey to Syria); and (3) that they assembled (from their several places of residence in Greece and Asia Minor) at Troas (vs. 5), where Paul, who sailed from Philippi instead of Corinth, joined them (vs. 6). The account is consistent and intelligible; but the 'Western' glossator partly misunderstood it. The Jews' plot he understood to have been the occasion of Paul's purpose to sail for Syria, not of his subsequent change of plan from a sea-voyage to a land-journey; the latter change was attributed by the glossator to an intimation of the Spirit. In taking this view the glossator perhaps followed the suggestion of xix. 21, xx. 22. By υποστρεφειν he correctly understood a return to Asia (whence Paul had started in vs. 1), and he has shown this by adding μεχρι της ασιας in vs. 4. In D συνειπετο αυτω dropped out (but note comitari d), and the

μηδενὸς αἰτίου ὄντος περὶ οὗ δυνησόμεθα ἀποδοῦναι λόγον τῆς
41 συστροφῆς ταύτης. κạὶ ταῦτα εἰπὼν ἀπέλυσε τὴν ἐκκλησίαν.
XX Μετὰ δὲ τὸ παύσασθαι τὸν θόρυβον προσκαλεσάμενος Παῦλος
τοὺς μαθητὰς καὶ πολλὰ παρακελε[ύ]σας ἀποσπασάμενος ἐξ-
2 ῆλθεν εἰς Μακεδονίαν. διελθὼν δὲ πάντα τὰ μέρη ἐκεῖνα καὶ
3 χρησ[άμενο]ς λόγῳ πολλῷ ῆλθεν εἰς τὴν Ἑλλάδα, ποιήσας δὲ
μῆνας γ̄ καὶ γενηθείσ⟨ης⟩ αὐτῷ ἐπιβουλῆς ὑπὸ τῶν Ἰουδαίων
ἠθέλησεν ἀναχθῆναι εἰς Συρίαν, εἶπεν δὲ τὸ πνεῦμα αὐτῷ
4 ὑποστρέφειν διὰ τῆς Μακεδονίας. μέλλοντος οὖν ἐξειέναι αὐτοῦ
μέχρι τῆς Ἀσίας Σώπατρος Πύρρου Βεροιαῖος, Θεσσαλονικέων δὲ
Ἀρίσταρχος καὶ Σέκουνδος, καὶ Γαῖος Δουβ[έ]ριος καὶ Τιμόθεος,
5 Ἐφέσιοι δὲ Εὔτυχος καὶ Τρόφιμος, | οὗτοι προελθόντες ἔμενον

2 εκεινα] εκεινη   4 βεροιαος] βερνιαος

---

possumuε reddere rationem de hoc concurso 41 et haec cum dixisset dissoluit **d**
ecclesiam

1 posquam autem cessavit tumultus convocavit paulus discipulos et multo
exhortatus salutans exiit in macedoniam 2 cum perambulasset omnes partes illas
et exortatus sermone multo venit in ellada 3 fecit autem menses tres et cum
fierent ei insidiae a judaeis voluit in syriam perduci dixitque s̄p̄s̄ ei revertere per
macedoniam 4 volente autem comitari eum usquae ad asīā sopater virri beryensis
thessalonicensium vero aristarchus et secundus et gaius doverius et timotheus ephesii
autem eutychus et trophimus 5 hic cum praecessissent expectabant nos troade

---

3–4 ηθελησεν . . . βεροιαος] *mg* volebat ire in Syriam ; dixit ei autem Harclean
spiritus reverti per Macedoniam. quum futurus esset autem exire, comitati
sunt eum autem usque in Asiam Sopater Barpurus Beroeensis   4 εφεσιοι] *mg*
ex Asia Ephesii

---

purpose of the assembly of friends at
Troas is left unexplained, while the
resulting connexion of μεχρι της ασιας
with μελλοντος εξιεναι yields but in-
different sense. In the text underlying hcl.*mg*, however, συνειποντο αυτω
was read, with the result that the
persons named are represented as
associated with Paul from Corinth all
the way to (μεχρι) Asia ; but nevertheless it is implied that they leave
him somewhere, for they go to Troas
by themselves. This, rather than the
defective text of D, is to be taken as
the proper 'Western.' The glossator
wrongly took συνειπετο (-οντο) to refer,
not, as intended in the B-text, to a
general companionship on the journey

to Syria, but to the first event in a
series (συνείποντο : προελθόντες : ἔμενον :
ἐξεπλεύσαμεν). προελθοντες D minn vg
pesh hcl sah may have originated in
an accidental error, but its persistence was due to the mistaken notion
of the glossator that the whole party
assembled at Corinth. The self-contra-
diction of the 'Western' text and the
historical superiority of the account
given by the B-text are plain.
  4 The omission of πυρρου in Antiochian pesh hcl.*text* arouses suspicion that
in the case of Sopater there was originally no exception to the simplicity of
form found in the other names, and
that ΠΤΡΡΟΤ has somehow arisen out
of the preceding ΠΑΤΡΟΣ.

μεν μετὰ τὰς ἡμέρας τῶν ἀζύμων ἀπὸ Φιλίππων, καὶ ἤλθομεν
πρὸς αὐτοὺς εἰς τὴν Τρῳάδα ἄχρι ἡμερῶν πέντε, οὗ διετρείψαμεν
ἡμέρας ἑπτά. ἐν δὲ τῇ μιᾷ τῶν σαββάτων συνηγμένων ἡμῶν 7
κλάσαι ἄρτον ὁ Παῦλος διελέγετο αὐτοῖς, μέλλων ἐξιέναι τῇ
ἐπαύριον, παρέτεινέν τε τὸν λόγον μέχρι μεσονυκτίου. ἦσαν δὲ 8
λαμπάδες ἱκαναὶ ἐν τῷ ὑπερῴῳ οὗ ἦμεν συνηγμένοι· καθεζόμενος 9
δέ τις νεανίας ὀνόματι Εὔτυχος ἐπὶ τῆς θυρίδος, καταφερόμενος
ὕπνῳ βαθεῖ διαλεγομένου τοῦ Παύλου ἐπὶ πλεῖον, κατενεχθεὶς
ἀπὸ τοῦ ὕπνου ἔπεσεν ἀπὸ τοῦ τριστέγου κάτω καὶ ἤρθη νεκρός.
καταβὰς δὲ ὁ Παῦλος ἐπέπεσεν αὐτῷ καὶ συνπεριλαβὼν εἶπεν 10
μὴ θορυβεῖσθαι, ἡ γὰρ ψυχὴ αὐτοῦ ἐν αὐτῷ ἐστίν. ἀναβὰς δὲ 11
κλάσας τὸν ἄρτον καὶ γευσάμενος ἐφ’ ἱκανόν τε ὁμειλήσας ἄχρι
αὐγῆς οὕτως ἐξῆλθεν. ἤγαγον δὲ τὸν παῖδα ζῶντα, καὶ παρ- 12
εκλήθησαν οὐ μετρίως. ἡμεῖς δὲ προσελθόντες ἐπὶ τὸ πλοῖον 13
ἀνήχθημεν ἐπὶ τὴν Ἄσσον, ἐκεῖθεν μέλλοντες ἀναλαμβάνειν τὸν
Παῦλον, οὕτως γὰρ διατεταγμένος ἦν μέλλων αὐτὸς πεζεύειν.

13 διατεταγμενον

Editors   6 ου][οπ]ου Soden   10 θορυβεισθε WH Soden JHR   θορυβεισθαι
WHmg   11 δε]+[και] WH   +και Soden JHR   13 προσελθοντες]
προελθοντες WH (but cf. mg) JHR

Old Uncial   6 αχρι ΒΑ   απο ℵ   ου Β   οπου ℵΑ   10 συνπεριλαβων ΒℵℵΑ(+D)
συνπεριβαλων αυτου C   θορυβεισθαι ΒC   θορυβεισθε ℵΑ   11 δε Β
+και ℵΑC(+D)   τον ΒℵℵΑC(+D)   om ℵᶜ   αυγης ΒΑCℵᶜ(+D)   αυτης ℵ
13 προσελθοντες ΒΑ   προελθοντες ℵC   διατεταγμενος Β²   εντεταλμενος C

Antiochian   7 ημων] των μαθητων HLPSϛ   add του before κλασαι ϛ(+D)
8 ημεν] ησαν Sϛ   9 καθεζομενος] καθημενος HLPSϛ   απο 1°] υπο
HS(+D)   10 θορυβεισθε P (HL not known) ϛ   αυτω] εαυτω L
11 δε]+και HLPSϛ(+D)   om τον HLPSϛ   13 προσελθοντες]
προελθοντες Lϛ   επι 2°] εις HLPSϛ(+D)   ασσον] θασον LP
ουτως] ουτος S   ην διατεταγμενος HLPSϛ(+D)

7 μια D has come in by conflation.
8 The word υπολαμπαδες D is found
elsewhere only in Athenaeus xii. 9,
p. 536 E, from Phylarchus, and in
a Delian inscription (Dittenberger,
Sylloge inscriptionum graecarum², ii,
1900, p. 344, No. 588, line 219, το
κλειθρον της υπολαμπαδος). In both
cases it seems to mean ‘window,’ or
‘look-out hole.’ If that is the sense
here, the word has been adopted by
D with θυρίς, vs. 9, in mind. The
rendering of d is *faculae.*
13 προελθοντες ℵCL minn e (*provecti*)

suits the context perfectly, and is
to be preferred to προσελθοντες ΒΑ
Antiochian, which may have been
originally due to accidental error.
Confusion of these compounds in
transcription frequently occurs. For
the ‘Western’ κατελθοντες D gig
pesh it can be urged that a scribe,
missing the point, might have observed that embarkation is by ascent
into a ship, not by descent, and
therefore substituted a different verb.
But the peculiar aptness of προελθοντες does not fit the case of so

6 αὐτὸν ἐν Τρῳάδι· ἡμεῖς δὲ ἐξεπλεύσαμεν μετὰ τὰς ἡμέρας τῶν
ἀζύμων ἀπὸ Φιλίππων, καὶ ἤλθομεν πρὸς αὐτοὺς εἰς Τρῳάδα
7 πεμπταῖοι, ἐν ᾗ καὶ διετρίψαμεν ἡμέρας ἑπτά. ἔν τε τῇ †μιᾷ†
πρώτῃ τῶν σαββάτων συνηγμένων ἡμῶν τοῦ κλάσαι ἄρτον ὁ
Παῦλος διελέγετο αὐτοῖς, μέλλων ἐξιέναι τῇ ἐπαύριον, παρέτινε
8 τὸν λόγον μέχρι μεσονυκτίου. ἦσαν δὲ ὑπολαμπάδες ἱκαναὶ ἐν
9 τῷ ὑπερῴῳ οὗ ἦμεν συνηγμένοι· καθεζόμενος δέ τις νεανίας
ὀνόματι Εὔτυχος ἐπὶ τῇ θυρίδι, κατεχόμενος ὕπνῳ βαρεῖ διαλεγομένου Παύλου ἐπὶ πλεῖον, κατενεχθεὶς ὑπὸ τοῦ ὕπνου ἔπεσεν
10 ἀπὸ τοῦ τριστέγου κάτω †καὶ† ὃς ἤρθη νεκρός. καταβὰς δὲ ὁ
Παῦλος ἔπεσεν ἐπ' αὐτῷ καὶ συνπεριλαβὼν καὶ εἶπεν μὴ θορυ-
11 βῖσθαι, ἡ γὰρ ψυχὴ αὐτοῦ ἐν αὐτῷ ἐστίν. ἀναβὰς δὲ καὶ κλάσας
τὸν ἄρτον καὶ γευσάμενος ἐφ' ἱκανὸν δὲ ὁμειλήσας ἄχρις αὐγῆς
12 οὕτως ἐξῆλθεν. ἀσπαζομένων δὲ αὐτῶν ἤγαγεν τὸν νεανίσκον
13 ζῶντα, καὶ παρεκλήθησαν οὐ μετρίως. ἡμεῖς δὲ κατελθόντες
εἰς τὸ πλοῖον ἀνήχθημεν εἰς τὴν Ἄσσον, ἐκεῖθεν μέλλοντες
ἀναλαμβάνειν τὸν Παῦλον, οὕτως γὰρ ἦν διατεταγμένος ὡς

---

6 nos vero enavigavimus post dies azymorum a philippis et venimus ad eos troadam **d**
quintani iu qua demorati sumus dies septem   7 in una autem sabbati collectis nobis
frangere panem paulus disputabat eis incipiens exire post alia die extenditque
sermonem usque in media nocte   8 et erant faculae copiosae in superioribus ubi
eramus collecti   9 sedens autem quidam jubenis nomine eutychus super fenestram
demersu somno gravi disputante paulo prolixius praeceps datus est a somno cecidit
de tristego zosum et sublatus est mortuus   10 cum descendisset autem paulus
cecidit super eū et circumplexit et dixit nolite turbari anima enim ejus in ipso est
11 cum ascendisset et fregisset panem et gustasset satisque fabulatus esset usquae
ad lucem sic profectus est   12 salutantes aut eos adduxerunt jubenem viventem et
consolati sunt non mediocriter   13 nos vero ascendimus in navem devenimus assum
inde mox recepturi paulum sic enim disposuerat incipiens ipse iter facere   14 ut

---

6 nos autem navigavimus post dies azimorum a Philippis, et venimus Irenaeus,
Troadem, ubi et commorati sumus diebus septem.   iii. 14, 1

dull a scribe, and seems equally unlikely to be due to a subsequent happy
accident.
13, 14 For ασσον, vs. 13, Pap. Wess.
237, some Antiochian codices (LP
minn), pesh hcl.*text* read θασον. Sah
reads in one cod. θαρσος, in the other
θασος ; but "T is the feminine article
in Coptic, and before Greek words
commencing with a vowel it united
with the aspirate of the vowel to
form an initial sound which is very
frequently written Θ. Thus θαρσος,

θασος may be taken to represent Greek
αρσος, ασος" (H. Thompson).
In vs. 14, θασον (θασσον) P minn
pesh hcl.*text* sah (only one cod.
extant).
The wide extension and firm hold
of this impossible reading with θ is
notable. We can hardly refer to a
Sahidic scribe's blunder the form in the
Antiochian codices and in the Syriac,
but a form corrupted under Coptic
influence may have been current in
Egypt. The conjunction, however,

ὡς δὲ συνέβαλλεν ἡμῖν εἰς τὴν Ἄσσον, ἀναλαβόντες αὐτὸν ἤλθομεν 14
εἰς Μιτυλήνην, κἀκεῖθεν ἀποπλεύσαντες τῇ ἐπιούσῃ κατηντή- 15
σαμεν ἄντικρυς Χίου, τῇ δὲ ἑσπέρᾳ παρεβάλομεν εἰς Σάμον, τῇ
δὲ ἐχομένῃ ἤλθομεν εἰς Μείλητον· κεκρ‹ίκ›ει γὰρ ὁ Παῦλος 16
παραπλεῦσαι τὴν Ἔφεσον, ὅπως μὴ γένηται αὐτῷ χρονοτριβῆσαι
ἐν τῇ Ἀσίᾳ, ἔσπευδεν γὰρ εἰ δυνατὸν εἴη αὐτῷ τὴν ἡμέραν τῆς
πεντηκοστῆς γενέσθαι εἰς Ἱεροσόλυμα.
Ἀπὸ δὲ τῆς Μειλήτου πέμψας εἰς Ἔφεσον μετεκαλέσατο 17
τοὺς πρεσβυτέρους τῆς ἐκκλησίας. ὡς δὲ παρεγένοντο πρὸς 18
αὐτὸν εἶπεν αὐτοῖς· Ὑμεῖς ἐπίστασθε ἀπὸ πρώτης ἡμέρας ἀφ᾽
ἧς ἐπέβην εἰς τὴν Ἀσίαν πῶς μεθ᾽ ὑμῶν τὸν πάντα χρόνον
ἐγενόμην, δουλεύων τῷ κυρίῳ μετὰ πάσης ταπεινοφροσύνης καὶ 19
δακρύων καὶ πειρασμῶν τῶν συμβάντων μοι ἐν ταῖς ἐπιβουλαῖς
τῶν Ἰουδαίων· ὡς οὐδὲν ὑπεστειλάμην τῶν συμφερόντων τοῦ 20
μὴ ἀναγγεῖλαι ὑμῖν καὶ διδάξαι ὑμᾶς δημοσίᾳ καὶ κατ᾽ οἴκους,
διαμαρτυρόμενος Ἰουδαίοις τε καὶ Ἕλλησιν τὴν εἰς θεὸν μετά- 21
νοιαν καὶ πίστιν εἰς τὸν κύριον ἡμῶν Ἰησοῦν. καὶ νῦν ἰδοὺ δεδε- 22

Editors   14 συνεβαλεν Soden   15 εσπερα] ετερα WH Soden JHR   εσπερα WHmg
σαμον] + [και μειναντες εν τρωγυλλιω] Soden + και μειναντες εν τρωγυλλιω JHR
[δε 2°] Soden   om JHR   16 ιερουσαλημ Soden   21 ιησουν] +χριστον
WHmg Soden

Old Uncial   14 δε BℵA(+D)   om C^{vid}   συνεβαλλεν BAℵᶜ   συνεβαλεν C(+D)
συνεβαλλον ℵ   εις 1° BACℵᶜ(+D)   επι ℵ   15 εσπερα B   ετερα
ℵAC(+D)   16 κεκρικει B²   εσπευδεν BℵAC²(+D)   εδει C perhaps
ιεροσολυμα BC(+D)   ιερουσαλημ ℵA   18 αυτον BℵC   +ομου οντων αυτων A
(cf. D)   19 κυριω BℵA(+D)   +μεθ υμων C   και 1° BℵA(+D)
+πολλων C   συμβαντων BℵA(+D)   συμβαινοντων C   20 υπεστειλαμην
των συμφεροντων BℵA(+D)   των συμφεροντων υπεστειλαμην C   21 θεον BℵC
τον θεον A(+D)   ιησουν B   +χριστον ℵAC (cf. D)

Antiochian   14 συνεβαλεν HLSς(+D)   ασσον] θασον P   ηλθομεν] ανηλθομεν L
15 αντικρυς] αντικρυ HPς   εσπερα] ετερα HLPSς(+D)   σαμον] +και
μειναντες εν τρωγυλλιω HLPSς (cf. D)   om δε 2° HLPSς(+D)   16 κεκρικει]
εκρινε HLPSς   αυτω 1°] αυτον H   om ει δυνατον ειη αυτω H(+D)
ειη] η LPSς   τη ημερα H   19 και 1°] +πολλων HLPSς
20 om και 2° S   21 διαμαρτυραμενος H   τον θεον HLPSς(+D)
πιστιν] +την HLPSς   ιησουν]+χριστον ς (cf. D)   22 εγω δεδεμενος
HLPSς(+D)

of Antiochian text and Syriac versions is noteworthy, and not without significant parallels (cf. e.g. Lk. ii. 14). In xxvii. 13 the adverb ᾶσσον is rendered *celerius* in h ; this may point to a variant θασσον ; cf. vg *thalassa* for αλασσα in xxvii. 8.

15 εσπερα B minn for ετερα is inconsistent with the sentence immediately preceding, for that seems intended to cover the whole of the distance traversed on the second day ; and it is also geographically improbable. It is doubtless a scribal error.

14 μέλλων αὐτὸς πεζεύειν. ὡς δὲ συνέβαλεν ἡμεῖν εἰς τὴν Ἄσσον,
15 ἀναλαβόντες αὐτὸν ἤλθομεν εἰς Μιτυλήνην, | κἀκεῖθεν ἀπο-
πλεύσαντες τῇ ἐπιούσῃ κατηντήσαμεν ἄντικρυς Χείου, τῇ δὲ
ἑτέρᾳ παρεβάλομεν εἰς Σάμον, καὶ μείναντες ἐν Τρωγυλίᾳ τῇ
16 ἐρχομένῃ ἤλθομεν εἰς Μείλητον· κεκρίκει γὰρ ὁ Παῦλος παραπλεῦσαι τὴν Ἔφεσον, μήποτε γενηθῇ αὐτῷ κατάσχεσίς τις ἐν τῇ
Ἀσίᾳ, ἔσπευδε γὰρ εἰς τὴν ἡμέραν τῆς πεντηκοστῆς γενέσθαι
†ἐν Ἱεροσόλυμα†.
17 Ἀπὸ δὲ τῆς Μειλήτου πέμψας εἰς Ἔφεσον μετεπέμψατο
18 τοὺς πρεσβυτέρους τῆς ἐκκλησίας. ὡς δὲ παρεγένοντο πρὸς
αὐτὸν ὁμόσε ὄντων αὐτῶν εἶπεν πρὸς αὐτούς· Ὑμεῖς ἐπίστασθε,
ἀδελφοί, ἀπὸ πρώτης ἡμέρας ἐφ᾽ ἧς ἐπέβην εἰς τὴν Ἀσίαν ὡς
τριετίαν ἢ καὶ πλεῖον ποταπῶς μεθ᾽ ὑμῶν ἦν παντὸς χρόνου,
19 δουλεύων τῷ κυρίῳ μετὰ πάσης ταπεινοφροσύνης καὶ δακρύων
καὶ πειρασμῶν τῶν συνβάντων μοι ἐν ταῖς ἐπιβουλαῖς τῶν Ἰου-
20 δαίων· ὡς οὐδὲν ὑπεστειλάμην τῶν συνφερόντων τοῦ ἀναγγεῖλαι
21 ὑμεῖν καὶ διδάξαι κατ᾽ οἴκους καὶ δημοσίᾳ, διαμαρτυρόμενος
Ἰουδαίοις τέ καὶ Ἕλλησιν τὴν εἰς τὸν θεὸν μετάνοιαν καὶ πίστιν
22 διὰ τοῦ κυρίου ἡμῶν Ἰησοῦ Χριστοῦ. καὶ νῦν εἰδοὺ ἐγὼ δεδεμένος

15 παρεβαλομεν] παρελαβομεν	16 κεκρικει] καικρικι
18 ομωσε επιστασθαι	21 διαμαρτυρουμενος

autem convenit nos in assum adsupto eo venimus mitylenen   15 et inde cum d
enavigassemus pridie pervenimus contra chium et alia die applicavimus samum et
manentes in trogylio sequenti venimus in miletum   16 judicaverat enim paulus
praeternavigare ephesum ut non contingeret ei morandi quis in asia festinabat enim
in die pentecostes adesse in hierosolymis   17 a mileto autem cum misisset in
ephesum transmisit presbyteros de ecclesiam   18 ad ubi venerunt ad eum simulque
cum esset ait ad eos vos scitis fratres a prima die in qua ingressus sum asiam quasi
triennium et amplius quemadmodum vobiscum fui per omne tempore   19 serviens
dno cum omni humilitati sensui et lacrimis et temptationibus quae evenerunt mihi
ex insidiis a diudaeis   20 quam nihil substraxerimque utilia essent ut adnuntiarem
vobis et docerem per domos et publice   21 testificando judaeisquae et graecis quae
in do paenitentiam agent et fidem in dnm nostrum ihm xpm   22 et nunc ecce ego

Probably the words και μειναντες εν
τρωγυλια (-λιω, -λλιω) D, Pap. Wess.
237, Antiochian gig pesh hcl.*text* (sah)
are genuine, and fell out by accident
at some very early stage of the text.
If added, that could have been only
with purpose, and it is as difficult to
suggest a motive for adding as for
deliberately omitting. The omission

of δε before εχομενη (ερχομενη) is a part
of the reading.

16 The omission of ει δυνατον ειη
αυτω in D d H is probably due to
accident (16 letters).

18 ως δε παρεγενοντο προς αυτον may
have come in by conflation, but cf.
gig vg.

μένος ἐγὼ τῷ πνεύματι πορεύομαι εἰς Ἰερουσαλήμ, τὰ ἐν αὐτῇ
συναντήσοντα ἐμοὶ μὴ εἰδώς, πλὴν ὅτι τὸ πνεῦμα τὸ ἅγιον κατὰ 23
πόλιν διαμαρτύρεταί μοι λέγον ὅτι δεσμὰ καὶ θλείψεις με μένουσιν·
ἀλλ' οὐδενὸς λόγου ποιοῦμαι τὴν ψυχὴν τιμίαν ἐμαυτῷ ὡς τελειώσω 24
τὸν δρόμον μου καὶ τὴν διακονίαν ἣν ἔλαβον παρὰ τοῦ κυρίου
Ἰησοῦ, διαμαρτύρασθαι τὸ εὐαγγέλιον τῆς χάριτος τοῦ θεοῦ.
καὶ νῦν ἰδοὺ ἐγὼ οἶδα ὅτι οὐκέτι ὄψεσθε τὸ πρόσωπόν μου ὑμεῖς 25
πάντες ἐν οἷς διῆλθον κηρύσσων τὴν βασιλείαν· διότι μαρτύρομαι 26
ὑμῖν ἐν τῇ σήμερον ἡμέρᾳ ὅτι καθαρός εἰμι ἀπὸ τοῦ αἵματος
πάντων, οὐ γὰρ ὑπεστειλάμην τοῦ μὴ ἀναγγεῖλαι πᾶσαν τὴν 27
βουλὴν τοῦ θεοῦ ὑμῖν. προσέχετε ἑαυτοῖς καὶ παντὶ τῷ ποιμνίῳ, 28
ἐν ᾧ ὑμᾶς τὸ πνεῦμα τὸ ἅγιον ἔθετο ἐπισκόπους, ποιμαίνειν τὴν
ἐκκλησίαν τοῦ θεοῦ, ἣν περιεποιήσατο διὰ τοῦ αἵματος τοῦ ἰδίου.

Editors   24 τελειωσαι WHmg Soden   μου] +[μετα χαρας] Soden   28 θεου]
κυριου Soden JHR   †ιδιου† WHmg

Old Uncial   22 συναντησοντα B‭‮   συναντησαντα A(+D)   συμβησομενα C   23 δια-
μαρτυρεται B‭‮C(+D)   διεμαρτυρατο A‭‮c   24 λογου B‭‮C   λογον εχω ουδε
A‭‮c (cf. D)   ως B‭‮A   εως ‭‮c   ως το C   τελειωσω B‭‮   τελειωσαι AC
(cf. D)   μου B‭‮A(+D)   +μετα χαρας C   25 εγω οιδα B‭‮A(+D)
οιδα εγω C   ουκετι BAC(+D)   ουκ ‭‮   26 διοτι B‭‮A   διο C
ειμι B‭‮C(+D)   εγω A   27 πασαν την βουλην του θεου υμιν B‭‮C(+D)
υμιν πασαν την βουλην του θεου A‭‮c   28 προσεχετε B‭‮A(+D)   +ουν C
θεου B‭‮   κυριου AC(+D)

Antiochian   22 συναντησαντα H(+D)   23 om μοι HLPSϛ   λεγων HLP(+D)
με και θλιψεις LPSϛ   24 λογου ποιουμαι την ψυχην] λογον ποιουμαι ουδε
εχω την ψυχην μου (om μου LP) HLPSϛ (cf. D)   τελειωσαι HLPSϛ (cf. D)
δρομον μου] +μετα χαρας HLPSϛ   25 βασιλειαν] +του θεου HLPSϛ (cf. D)
26 διοτι] διο HLSϛ   ειμι] εγω HLPSϛ   27 πασαν την βουλην του
θεου υμιν] υμιν πασαν την βουλην του θεου HLPSϛ   28 προσεχετε] +ουν
HLPϛ   θεου] κυριου και θεου HLPS (cf. D)   του αιματος του ιδιου]
του ιδιου αιματος HLPSϛ

---

22 συναντησαντα ADEH minn,
although strangely persistent, is probably only a careless spelling for
-οντα, which alone makes sense. Cf.
Thackeray, *Grammar of the Old Testament in Greek*, i. p. 77.
24 In the first clause of this verse,
(1) the reading of B‭‮C sah (ουδενος
λογου ποιουμαι την ψυχην τιμιαν εμαυτω)
is idiomatic, and is to be followed,
with the meaning 'I make of no
account my life, as precious to myself'
(similarly English R.V.). To avoid
the difficulty of the superfluous ουδενος
λογου, gig Lucif render these words
by *pro nihilo*, apparently without

warrant. (2) In the 'Western' text
(shown in D) the awkwardness of the
phrase was avoided by introducing
εχω μοι ουδε, in connexion with which
λογου was necessarily changed to λογον.
εμαυτου D may at first have been an
error for εμαυτω, but vg *quam me*
seems to rest on it, and in the unusually
free rendering of vg, τιμιαν is taken
as equivalent to a comparative,
'*pretiosiorem*'; similarly Orig.*interpr.*
Ambrose Aug[?]. (3) A‭‮c agree substantially with D; while Antiochian
has made a fresh combination of the
'Western' addition with the original
text.

τῷ πνεύματι πορεύομαι εἰς Ἱεροσόλυμα, τὰ ἐν αὐτῇ συναντήσαντά
23 μοι μὴ γεινώσκων, πλὴν ὅτι τὸ ἅγιον πνεῦμα κατὰ πᾶσαν πόλιν
διαμαρτύρεταί μοι λέγων ὅτι δεσμὰ καὶ θλείψεις μένουσίν μοι
24 ἐν Ἱεροσολύμοις· ἀλλ' οὐδενὸς λόγον ἔχω μοι οὐδὲ ποιοῦμαι τὴν
ψυχήν μου τιμίαν †ἐμαυτοῦ† τοῦ τελιῶσαι τὸν δρόμον μου καὶ
τὴν διακονίαν τοῦ λόγου ὃν παρέλαβον παρὰ τοῦ κυρίου Ἰησοῦ,
διαμαρτύρασθαι Ἰουδαίοις καὶ Ἕλλησιν τὸ εὐαγγέλιον τῆς
25 χάριτος θεοῦ. καὶ νῦν εἰδοὺ ἐγὼ οἶδα ὅτι οὐκέτι ὄψεσθε τὸ
πρόσωπόν μου ὑμεῖς πάντες ἐν οἷς διῆλθον κηρύσσων τὴν βασι-
26 λείαν τοῦ Ἰησοῦ· ἄχρι οὖν τῆς σήμερον ἡμέρας καθαρός εἰμι
27 ἀπὸ τοῦ αἵματος πάντων, οὐ γὰρ ὑπεστειλάμην τοῦ ἀναγγεῖλαι
28 πᾶσαν τὴν βουλὴν τοῦ θεοῦ ὑμῖν. προσέχετε ἑαυτοῖς καὶ παντὶ
τῷ ποιμνίῳ, ἐν ᾧ ὑμᾶς τὸ ἅγιον πνεῦμα ἔθετο ἐπισκόπους,
ποιμαίνειν τὴν ἐκκλησίαν τοῦ κυρίου, ἣν περιεποιήσατο ἑαυτῷ

25 οψεσθαι   27 υμιν] ημιν   28 προσεχεται
ποιμενειν

---

ligatus spo vado in hierosolyma quae in ea mihi ventura sunt nesciens   23 tamquam d
spm sanctum per singulas civitates protestatur mihi dicens quia vincula et tribulationes manen mi in hierosolymis   24 sed nihil horum cura est mihi neque habeo
ipsam animam caram mihi quam consummare cursum meum et ministerium verbi
quod accepi a dno ihu testificari judaeis et crecis evangelium gratiae di   25 et nunc
ecce ego scio quia non videbis faciem meam vos omnis inter quos perambulavi
praedicans illud regnum ihu   26 propter quod hodierno die mundus sum a sanguine
omnium   27 non enim substraxi ut non adnuntiem omnem volumptatem di vobis
28 attendite vos et omni gregi in vobis sps sanctus posuit episcopos regere ecclesiam

---

25 scio quoniam jam non videbitis faciem meam :   26 testificor igitur vobis Irenaeus,
hac die quoniam mundus sum a sanguine omnium.   27 non enim subtraxi uti iii. 14, 2
non adnuntiarem vobis omnem sententiam dei.   28 adtendite igitur et vobis
et omni gregi in quo vos spiritus sanctus praeposuit episcopos, regere ecclesiam

---

23 εν ιεροσολυμοις] ⁙ in Hierosolymis ✓   26 ουν] ⁙ quapropter ✓ Harclean
28 κυριου] mg domini

The addition μετα χαρας after τον
δρομον μου, supported by C Antiochian
e, sounds like a fragment of the
'Western' paraphrase, but it is not
found in D, nor in any convincing
'Western' authority (yet cf. e), and
its origin and claim to acceptance
must remain doubtful.

26 Hcl ⁙ quapropter represents a
Syriac phrase used to translate διο (C
Antiochian).

28 (1) του θεου BΝ minn vg pesh.codd
hcl.text boh.one cod, Greek fathers from
4th cent. (incl. Cyril Alex.), Latin
fathers later than vg, is shown by the

agreement of BΝ to be ancient, and
through its adoption by vg Cyril to
have been highly regarded in and after
the 4th century. (2) του κυριου D d
ACE minn gig e hcl.mg boh sah
Irenlat Greek fathers (incl. Athanas[?]
Didymus Chrysvid), Latin fathers (incl.
Proph Lucif Jerome Quaest.vet.et
nov.test. [domini jesu], Ambrosecodd)
appears to have been the 'Western'
reading (Greek, Latin, Syriac), and to
have been current as early as the 4th
century in circles whose text was
in general not 'Western.' It is also
indirectly attested by the variants

ὅτι ἐγὼ οἶδα ὅτι εἰσελεύσονται μετὰ τὴν ἄφειξίν μου λύκοι βαρεῖς 29
εἰς ὑμᾶς μὴ φειδόμενοι τοῦ ποιμνίου, καὶ ἐξ ὑμῶν ἀναστήσονται 30
ἄνδρες λαλοῦντες διεστραμμένα τοῦ ἀποσπᾶν τοὺς μαθητὰς
ὀπίσω ἑαυτῶν· διὸ γρηγορεῖτε, μνημονεύοντες ὅτι τριετίαν νύκτα 31
καὶ ἡμέραν οὐκ ἐπαυσάμην μετὰ δακρύων νουθετῶν ἕνα ἕκαστον.
καὶ τὰ νῦν παρατίθεμαι ὑμᾶς τῷ κυρίῳ καὶ τῷ λόγῳ τῆς χάριτος 32
αὐτοῦ τῷ δυναμένῳ οἰκοδομῆσαι καὶ δοῦναι τὴν κληρονομίαν
ἐν τοῖς ἡγιασμένοις πᾶσιν. ἀργυρίου ἢ χρυσίου ἢ ἱματισμοῦ 33
οὐδενὸς ἐπεθύμησα. αὐτοὶ γεινώσκετε ὅτι ταῖς χρείαις μου καὶ 34
τοῖς οὖσι μετ' ἐμοῦ ὑπηρέτησαν αἱ χεῖρες αὗται. πάντα ὑπέδειξα 35
ὑμῖν ὅτι οὕτως κοπιῶντας δεῖ ἀντιλαμβάνεσθαι τῶν ἀσθενούντων,
μνημονεύειν τε τῶν λόγων τοῦ κυρίου Ἰησοῦ ὅτι αὐτὸς εἶπεν·
Μακάριόν ἐστιν μᾶλλον διδόναι ἢ λαμβάνειν. καὶ ταῦτα εἰπὼν 36
θεὶς τὰ γόνατα αὐτοῦ σὺν πᾶσιν αὐτοῖς προσεύξατο. ἱκανὸς δὲ 37
κλαυθμὸς ἐγένετο πάντων, καὶ ἐπιπεσόντες ἐπὶ τὸν τράχηλον

Editors   29 om οτι 1° WH Soden JHR   εγω] +[γαρ] Soden   οιδα] +[τουτο]
Soden   30 υμων] +[αυτων] WH   +αυτων Soden JHR   εαυτων]
αυτων Soden   32 κυριω] θεω WHmg Soden JHR

Old Uncial   29 οτι εγω B   εγω ℵAC(+D)   εγω δε ℵc   30 υμων B   +αυτων
ℵAC(+D)   εαυτων BℵA   αυτων C(+D)   32 υμας BA(+D)   υμιν ℵ
υμας αδελφοι C   κυριω B   θεω ℵAC(+D)   δουναι BℵA(+D)   +υμιν C
κληρονομιαν BℵC(+D)   +αυτου A   34 γεινωσκετε BℵC(+D)   οιδατε A
35 παντα BℵA (cf. D)   και παντα C   αντιλαμβανεσθαι των ασθενουντων
BℵC(+D)   των ασθενουντων αντιλαμβανεσθαι A   τε BℵC   om Avid(+D)
ιησου BℵAC(+D)   om A²   36 αυτοις BℵA(+D)   om C   37 δε BAC(+D)
τε ℵ

Antiochian   29 οτι εγω] εγω γαρ HLPSϛ   οιδα] +τουτο HLPSϛ   30 υμων]
+αυτων HLPSϛ(+D)   εαυτων] αυτων HLPSϛ(+D)   32 υμας] υμιν H
+αδελφοι HLPSϛ   κυριω] θεω HLPSϛ(+D)   οικοδομησαι] εποικο-
δομησαι HLPSϛ   δουναι] +υμιν HLPSϛ   om την HLPSϛ(+D)
34 αυτοι] +δε ϛ   35 των λογων] τον λογον LP   ˋδιδοναι μαλλον ϛ
37 εγενετο κλαυθμος HLPSϛ

του χριστου pesh.codd Const. Apost.
Athanas. codd; jesu christi m. (3)
του κυριου και θεου HLPS is plainly
conflate.

From the external evidence it is
impossible to affirm of either θεου or
κυριου that it was the earlier reading.
The unusual nature of the expression
'church of the Lord' (paralleled only
in Rom. xvi. 16) speaks strongly for
the authenticity of κυριου on transcriptional grounds. (With regard to
the interchange of κυριος and θεος see
Tischendorf on Acts xvi. 32; B. Weiss,

Die Apostelgeschichte, 1893, pp. 5-7.)
On the other hand it is possible,
though less likely, that a second-
century scribe might have felt the
difficulty of the implied idea 'God's
own blood' so strongly that he would
have deliberately altered θεου into
κυριου.

It must be observed, however, that
the peculiar expression του αιματος του
ιδιου, instead of του ιδιου αιματος
(Antiochian has actually improved the
text by substituting the latter reading),
raises a doubt as to the soundness of

29 διὰ τοῦ αἵματος τοῦ ἰδίου. ἐγὼ οἶδα ὅτι εἰσελεύσονται μετὰ τὴν
   ἄφιξίν μου λύκοι βαρεῖς εἰς ὑμᾶς μὴ φειδόμενοι τοῦ ποιμνείου,
30 καὶ ἐξ ὑμῶν αὐτῶν ἀναστήσονται ἄνδρες λαλοῦντες διεστραμ-
31 μένα τοῦ ἀποστρέφειν τοὺς μαθητὰς ὀπίσω αὐτῶν· διὸ γρηγορεῖτε, μνημονεύοντες ὅτι τριετίαν νύκτα †δὲ† ἡμέραν οὐκ ἐπαυ-
32 σάμην μετὰ δακρύων νουθετῶν ἕνα ἕκαστον ὑμῶν. καὶ τὰ νῦν
   παρατίθεμαι ὑμᾶς τῷ θεῷ καὶ τῷ λόγῳ τῆς χάριτος αὐτοῦ τῷ
   δυναμένῳ οἰκοδομῆσαι ὑμᾶς καὶ δοῦναι κληρονομίαν ἐν αὐ[τοῖ]ς
33 τοῖς ἡγιασμένοις †τῶν πάντων†. ἀργυρίου καὶ χρυσίου ἢ εἱματισμοῦ
34 οὐδενὸς ὑμῶν ἐπεθύμησα· αὐτοὶ γεινώσκετε ὅτι †τὰς χρείας μου†
35 πᾶσιν καὶ τοῖς οὖσιν μετ᾽ ἐμοῦ ὑπηρέτησαν αἱ χεῖρές μου. πᾶ[σ]ι
   ὑπέδειξα ὑμεῖν ὅτι οὕτως κοπιῶντας δεῖ ἀντιλαμβάνεσθαι τῶν
   ἀσθενούντων, μνημονεύειν τῶν λόγων τοῦ κυρίου Ἰησοῦ ὅτι
36 οὗτος εἶπεν· †Μακάριός† ἐστιν μᾶλλον διδόναι ἢ λαμβάνειν. καὶ
37 ταῦτα εἴπας θεὶς τὰ γόνατα σὺν πᾶσιν αὐτοῖς προσεύξατο. ἱκανὸς
   δὲ κλαυθμὸς ἐγένετο πάντων, καὶ ἐπιπεσόντες ἐπὶ τὸν τράχηλον

29 αφεξιν   πυμνειου   34 γεινωσκεται

---

dni quam adquisibit sibi per sanguinem suum   29 ego scio quia introibunt pos d
diescessum meum lupi graves in vos non parcentes gregi   30 et ex vobis ipsis
exurgent viri loquentes perversa ut abstrahant discipulos post seipsos   31 propter
quod vigilate memores estote quia triennio nocte ac die

domini, quam sibi constituit per sanguinem suum. . . .   29 ego scio quoniam Irenaeus,
advenient post discessum meum lupi graves ad vos non parcentes gregi,   30 et iii. 14, 2
ex vobis ipsis exsurgent viri loquentes perversa, uti convertant discipulos
post se.

32 των παντων] ⋮ cui gloria in saecula, amen ✓   Harclean

---

the text at that point. Hort conjectured του ιδιου ‹υιου›. If some such
conjecture could in any way be made
probable, the reading of ℵ would
stand. On the possibility of reaching
the same result by taking του ιδιου to
mean 'his dear one,' or the like, see
J. H. Moulton, *Prolegomena*, pp. 90 f.
See Hort, 'Appendix,' pp. 98-100,
Tischendorf *ad loc.*, and especially the
exhaustive investigation by Ezra
Abbot in *The Authorship of the
Fourth Gospel and other Critical
Essays*, Boston, 1888, pp. 294-331 (also
published in *Bibliotheca Sacra*, vol.
xxxiii, 1876, pp. 313-352).

29 οτι εγω B without other support.
οτι is probably an alleviating addition.
Antiochian, some Latin texts (*enim*),
and pesh hcl sah add γαρ.

32 After τοις ηγιασμενοις πασιν, 614
minn hcl ⋮ add (minor variants) αυτω
η δοξα εις τους αιωνας των αιωνων αμην.
D των παντων seems to be a survival
of των αιωνων from this reading.

34 The text of D is confused, and
perhaps conflate, but the means at
hand do not suggest a probable explanation of it.

35 On μακαριος D (cf. *beatus* gig
vg.*codd* for *beatius* vg) see Harnack,
Sitzungsberichte, Berlin Academy,
1904, pp. 170 f. Pesh and Const.
Apost. iv. 3, 1 (from some other source
than Didascalia) agree in implying
the form, 'Blessed is the giver rather
than the receiver,' but no clear connexion can be made out between this
and the reading of D gig.

τοῦ Παύλου κατεφίλουν αὐτόν, ὀδυνώμενοι μάλιστα ἐπὶ τῷ λόγῳ 38
ᾧ εἰρήκει ὅτι οὐκέτι μέλλουσιν τὸ πρόσωπον αὐτοῦ θεωρεῖν.
προέπεμπον δὲ αὐτὸν εἰς τὸ πλοῖον.

Ὡς δὲ ἐγένετο ἀναχθῆναι ἡμᾶς, ἀποσπασθέντες ἀπ' αὐτῶν, XXI
εὐθυδρομήσαντες ἤλθομεν εἰς τὴν Κῶ, τῇ δὲ ἑξῆς εἰς τὴν Ῥόδον,
κἀκεῖθεν εἰς Πάταρα· καὶ εὑρόντες πλοῖον διαπερῶν εἰς Φοινείκην 2
ἐπιβάντες ἀνήχθημεν. ἀναφάναντες δὲ τὴν Κύπρον καὶ κατα- 3
λιπόντες αὐτὴν εὐώνυμον ἐπλέομεν εἰς Συρίαν, καὶ κατήλθομεν
εἰς Τύρον, ἐκεῖσε γὰρ τὸ πλοῖον ἦν ἀποφορτιζόμενον τὸν γόμον.
ἀνευρόντες δὲ τοὺς μαθητὰς ἐπεμείναμεν αὐτοῦ ἡμέρας ἑπτά, 4
οἵτινες τῷ Παύλῳ ἔλεγαν διὰ τοῦ πνεύματος μὴ ἐπιβαίνειν εἰς
Ἰεροσόλυμα. ὅτε δὲ ἐγένετο ἐξαρτίσαι ἡμᾶς τὰς ἡμέρας, ἐξ- 5
ελθόντες ἐπορευόμεθα προπεμπόντων ἡμᾶς πάντων σὺν γυναιξὶ
καὶ τέκνοις ἕως ἔξω τῆς πόλεως, καὶ θέντες τὰ γόνατα ἐπὶ τὸν
αἰγιαλὸν προσευξάμενοι | ἀπησπασάμεθα ἀλλήλους, καὶ ἐνέβημεν 6
εἰς τὸ πλοῖον, ἐκεῖνοι δὲ ὑπέστρεψαν εἰς τὰ ἴδια. ἡμεῖς δὲ τὸν 7
πλοῦν διανύσαντες ἀπὸ Τύρου κατηντήσαμεν εἰς Πτολεμαΐδα, καὶ
ἀσπασάμενοι τοὺς ἀδελφοὺς ἐμείναμεν ἡμέραν μίαν παρ' αὐτοῖς.
τῇ δὲ ἐπαύριον ἐξελθόντες ἤλθαμεν εἰς Καισαρείαν, καὶ εἰσ- 8
ελθόντες εἰς τὸν οἶκον Φιλίππου τοῦ εὐαγγελιστοῦ ὄντος ἐκ τῶν

4 after πνευματος MS. repeats ελεγαν

Editors 1 αποσπασθεντας WH Soden   αποσπασθεντες WHmg   παταρα] +και
μυρα JHR   3 αναφανεντες Soden   5 ημας εξαρτισαι WHmg Soden
6 ενεβημεν] ανεβημεν Soden JHR

Old Uncial 1 αναχθηναι BCℵc   om Avid (A² suppl after ημας)   αναχθεντας ℵ   αποσπασθεντες B   αποσπασθεντας ℵAC   την 2° BℵA om C(+D)   2 δια-
περων BℵAC(+D)   διαπερον ℵc   3 αναφαναντες Bvidℵ αναφανεντες B²AC
και 1° BℵC   om A   καταλιποντες BℵC   καταλειποντες A   επλεομεν
BℵC   om A   κατηλθομεν BℵA   κατηχθημεν C   4 αυτου BℵC
αυτοις A   5 εξαρτισαι ημας BA   ημας εξαρτισαι B²ℵC   εξελθοντες
BℵC   om A   εως BAC om ℵ   6 απησπασαμεθα BℵC
απησπασμεθα A   ενεβημεν Bℵc ανεβημεν ℵAC   7 κατηντη-
σαμεν BℵC   κατεβημεν Aℵc   εμειναμεν BℵC   επεμειναμεν A

Antiochian 38 om το before πλοιον P   1 αναχθηναι] αχθηναι P   αποσπασθεντας
HPSϛ   3 αναφανεντες HLPS   δε] +εις P   καταλειποντες
HLS   κατηλθομεν] κατηχθημεν HLPSϛ   εκε.σε] εκει H   ην το
πλοιον HLPSϛ   4 ανευροντες δε] και ανευροντες HLPSϛ   om τους HLPS
αυτου] αυτοις L   επιβαινειν] αναβαινειν HLPSϛ   ιερουσαλημ HLPSϛ
5 ημας εξαρτισαι HLPSϛ   προσηυξαμεθα HLPSϛ   6 απησπασαμεθα
αλληλους και] και ασπασαμενοι αλληλους HLPSϛ   ενεβημεν] επεβημεν HLPSϛ
8 εξελθοντες] +οι περι τον παυλον HLPSϛ   ηλθον HLPSϛ   ευαγγελιστου]
+του ϛ

38 τοῦ Παύλου κατεφίλουν αὐτόν, μάλιστα ἐπὶ τῷ λόγῳ ὀδυνώμενοι ὅτι εἶπεν οὐκέτι μέλλει [. .]ι τὸ πρόσωπον θεωρεῖν. προέπεμπον δὲ αὐτὸν ἐπὶ τὸ πλοῖον.

XXI [Κα]ὶ ἐπι[β]άντ[ε]ς ἀνήχθημεν, ἀποσπασθέντων δὲ [ἡμῶ]ν ἀπ' αὐτῶν εὐθυδρομήσαντες ἤκομεν εἰς Κῶ, τῇ δὲ ἐπιούσῃ εἰς 2 Ῥόδον, κἀκεῖθεν εἰς Πάταρα καὶ Μύρα· καὶ εὑρόντες πλοῖον διαπερῶν εἰς Φ[.]νείκην

3 εὐώνυμα 337 242
4 αὐτοῦ] αὐτοῖς A L minn

ascendentes navigavimus 3 videntes autem cyprum et relinquentes eas a sinistro d collavimus in syriam enavigavimus in tyro ibi erat enim navis expostura onus 4 et inventis discipulis mansimus apud eos dies septem quidam autem paulo dicebant per spm non ingredi hierosolyma 5 sequenti autem die exeuntes ambulamus viam nostram deducentibus omnibus nos cum uxoribus et filiis extra civitatem et positis genibus in litore oravimus 6 et cum salutassemus invicem reversi vero quisque ad sua 7 nos autem navigatione expedita a tyro venimus ptolemaidem et salutavimus fratres [et mansimus diem u]num aput eos 8 [sequenti cum exissemus venimus caesaream et cum introissemus in domum philippi evangelistae qui erat de VII

---

38 επι 2°] ⋇ usque ad ✓   Harclean

38 In Codex Bezae Blass (*St. Kr.*, 1898, p. 542) reads μελλε[τ]αι for μελλει[..]ι. This recalls *videbitis faciem meam* gig sah, and the omission of αυτου in D leaves the way open for this restoration. Scrivener's conjecture was μελλει [σο]ι.

1 The addition και μυρα D, Pap. Wess. 237 ([. . . .] μυρα), similarly gig vg.*codd* sah, is significant because it involves a different point of transhipment (cf. xxvii. 5 μυρα της λυκιας) ; either port would be suitable. The reference to a residence of Paul in Myra in the Acts of Paul and Thecla (C. Schmidt, *Acta Pauli*, pp. 50, 52, 55, 58, 212) ought not to be used as evidence for this reading. The words are probably original, and omitted by accident, perhaps by a simple homoeoteleuton (**ΠΑΤΑΡΑ ΚΑΙΜΤΡΑ**). It is more difficult to suppose them added (by dittography) ; for then we should have to assume a very active-minded scribe acquainted with the geography of south-west Asia Minor. For deliberate change, either by omission or addition, no sufficient motive is easy to assign.

3 αναφαναντες Bᵛⁱᵈ ℵ minn 'having brought into sight,' although lacking complete parallel, is intelligible and

probably right, as against αναφανεντες AC Antiochian, which seems to be a correction to a more familiar participle, but yields no good natural sense.

With regard to the reading of B, the note of Fabiani-Cozza is : "B² in fine . . ΦΑΝΑ, B³ . . ΦΑΝΕ . . alia manus superp. A fecitque ΦΑΝᴬ." To judge by the photographic facsimile, the reading of B* was probably -φανα.

The reading *a sinistro* d may represent ευωνυμα 337 242, intended as an adverb belonging to επλεομεν ; hence ευωνυμα was perhaps the reading of D.

6 ανεβημεν ℵAC, the less usual word, seems to have been corrected in Bℵᶜ minn to ενεβημεν, and in Antiochian to επεβημεν.

In d words between *invicem* and *reversi*, doubtless constituting one line of the archetype, have been accidentally omitted. This is noted in the margin of the ms. by a small uncial α and γ.

7-10 The restoration of the Latin text of d is derived from the statements of Dickinson, with some confirmation from Ussher, Mill, and Wetstein (see note on vss. 15-18). For *eam*, vs. 10 (Dickinson), no explanation is forthcoming.

ἑπτὰ ἐμείναμεν παρ' αὐτῷ. τούτῳ δὲ ἦσαν θυγατέρες τέσσαρες 9
παρθένοι προφητεύουσαι. ἐπιμενόντων δὲ ἡμέρας πλείους κατ- 10
ῆλθέν τις ἀπὸ τῆς Ἰουδαίας προφήτης ὀνόματι Ἅγαβος, καὶ 11
ἐλθὼν πρὸς ἡμᾶς καὶ ἄρας τὴν ζώνην τοῦ Παύλου δήσας ἑαυτοῦ
τοὺς πόδας καὶ τὰς χεῖρας εἶπεν· Τάδε λέγει τὸ πνεῦμα τὸ ἅγιον·
Τὸν ἄνδρα οὗ ἐστὶν ἡ ζώνη αὕτη οὕτως δήσουσιν ἐν Ἰερουσαλὴμ
οἱ Ἰουδαῖοι καὶ παραδώσουσιν εἰς χεῖρας ἐθνῶν. ὡς δὲ ἠκού- 12
σαμεν ταῦτα, παρεκαλοῦμεν ἡμεῖς τε καὶ οἱ ἐντόπιοι τοῦ μὴ ἀναβαίνειν αὐτὸν εἰς Ἰερουσαλήμ. τότε ἀπεκρίθη Παῦλος· Τί ποιεῖτε 13
κλαίοντες καὶ συνθρύπτοντές μου τὴν καρδίαν; ἐγὼ γὰρ οὐ
μόνον δεθῆναι ἀλλὰ καὶ ἀποθανεῖν εἰς Ἰερουσαλὴμ ἑτοίμως ἔχω
ὑπὲρ τοῦ ὀνόματος τοῦ κυρίου Ἰησοῦ. μὴ πειθομένου δὲ αὐτοῦ 14
ἡσυχάσαμεν εἰπόντες· Τοῦ κυρίου τὸ θέλημα γεινέσθω.

Μετὰ δὲ τὰς ἡμέρας ταύτας ἐπισκευασάμενοι ἀνεβαίνομεν 15
εἰς Ἰεροσόλυμα· συνῆλθον δὲ καὶ τῶν μαθητῶν ἀπὸ Καισαρείας 16

Editors   10 δε] +ημων Soden   13 [o] παυλος WH   ο παυλος Soden JHR
παυλος] +[και ειπεν] Soden

Old Uncial   9 θυγατερες τεσσαρες παρθενοι BℵA   παρθενοι θυγατερες τεσσαρες C   10 δε
BAC   +αυτων ℵ   +ημων ℵᶜ   11 τους ποδας και τας χειρας BℵC(+D)   τας
χειρας και τους ποδας A   εις BACℵᶜᵒʳʳ(+D)   +τας ℵ   13 απεκριθη BℵA
+δε C (cf. D)   παυλος B   ο παυλος B²(B³Tdf)C (cf. D)   ο παυλος και ειπεν
ℵA (cf. D)   κλαιοντες και BACℵᶜ(+D)   om ℵ   εις ιερουσαλημ
ετοιμως εχω BℵC(+D)   ετοιμως εχω εις ιερουσαλημ A   ιησου BℵA   +χριστου
C(+D)   15 επισκευασαμενοι BAℵᶜ   επισκευασαμενον ℵ   παρασκευασαμενοι C
ανεβαινομεν BACℵᶜ (cf. D)   om ℵ

Antiochian   9 παρθενοι τεσσαρες HLPSϚ   10 δε] +ημων LPϚ   προφητης απο
της ιουδαιας L   11 εαυτου] τε αυτου HLPSϚ   τας χειρας και τους
ποδας Ϛ   13 τοτε απεκριθη] απεκριθη τε HLPS   απεκριθη δε Ϛ (cf. D)
ο παυλος HLPSϚ(+D)   14 το θελημα του κυριου HLPSϚ (cf. D)   γενεσθω
HLPϚ   15 επισκευασαμενοι] επισκεψαμενοι H   αποσκευασαμενοι Ϛ
αναβαινομεν L(+D)   ιερουσαλημ HLPSϚ

---

9 Prophetiae, which uses an ancient African text, reads *cui erant etiam filiae quinque virgines prophetantes.*

11 For hcl ⁘ cf. δησουσιν αυτον minn ; παραδωσουσιν αυτον 431.

15-18 The text of D in this passage has been destroyed by three successive mutilations of the folio, the first before the collation made for Ussher (not later than 1650), the second before

that of Mill (published 1707), and the last after the copies made by Wetstein (1716) and Dickinson (about 1733), and before the edition of Kipling (1793) ; but by the aid of the statements of these scholars, and with the use of the untrustworthy transcript made for Whitgift (1583), the text can be restored with almost complete certainty, and is printed above between brackets. See Scrivener, *Bezae Codex*

10 ἐπιμενόντων δὲ] +ἡμῶν ℵ^c LP

11 προφήτης ὀνόματι Ἄγαβος, ἀνελθὼν δὲ πρὸς ἡμᾶς καὶ ἄρας τὴν
ζώνην τοῦ Παύλου δήσας ἑαυτοῦ τοὺς πόδας καὶ τὰς χεῖρας
εἶπεν· Τάδε λέγει τὸ πνεῦμα τὸ ἅγιον· Τὸν ἄνδρα οὗ ἐστὶν ἡ ζώνη
αὕτη οὕτως δήσουσιν εἰς Ἱερουσαλὴμ Ἰουδαῖοι καὶ παραδώσου-
12 σιν εἰς χεῖρας ἐθνῶν. ὡς δὲ ἠκούσαμεν ταῦτα, παρακαλοῦμεν
ἡμεῖς καὶ οἱ ἐντόπιοι τὸν Παῦλον τοῦ μὴ ἐπιβαίνειν αὐτὸν εἰς
13 Ἱερουσαλήμ. εἶπεν δὲ πρὸς ἡμᾶς ὁ Παῦλος· Τί ποιεῖτε κλαίοντες
καὶ θορυβοῦντές μου τὴν καρδίαν; ἐγὼ γὰρ οὐ μόνον δεθῆναι
βούλομαι ἀλλὰ καὶ ἀποθανεῖν εἰς Ἱερουσαλὴμ ἑτοίμως ἔχω
14 ὑπὲρ τοῦ ὀνόματος τοῦ κυρίου Ἰησοῦ Χριστοῦ. μὴ πειθομένου δὲ
αὐτοῦ ἡσυχάσαμεν †οἳ† εἰπόντες πρὸς ἀλλήλους· Τὸ θέλημα τοῦ
θεοῦ γεινέσθω.
15 Μετὰ δέ τινας ἡμέρας ἀποταξάμενοι ἀναβαίνομεν εἰς Ἱερ[ο-
16 σόλυμα]· <   .   .   .   .   .   > ἐκ Κεσα[ραίας σὺν

13 ποιειται

---

mansimus ad eum   9 cui erant filiae ΙΙΙΙ virgines profetantes   10 et mansimus aput d
eam.   .   .   .   .]
profeta nomine agabus   11 cum venisset ad nos et tulisset zonam pauli ligavit suos
pedes et manus et dixit haec dicit s̄p̄s̄ sanctus eum virum cus est zona haec sic
ligabunt hierusalem judaei et tradent in manus gentium   12 et vero audivimus haec
depraecabamur nos et incolae loci illius paulum ut non ascenderet hierusalem
13 respondit autem ad nos paulus quid facitis plorantes et conturbantes meum cor
ego enim non solum ligari volo sed et mori in hierusalem propositum habeo propter
nomen d̄n̄ī x̄p̄ī ī̄h̄ū   14 cum non suaderetur ei quievimus dicentes ad invicem
voluntas d̄n̄ī fiat   15 post hos autem dies refecimus nos et ascendimus hierosolyma

---

13 quid [inquit] facitis lacrimantes et conturbantes cor meum? ego enim Tertullian,
non modo vincula pati optaverim, sed etiam mori Hierosolymis pro nomine ^{Fug. 6}
domini mei Jesu Christi.   14 [atque ita omnes aierunt :] fiat voluntas domini.
13 quid fletis [inquit] et contristatis cor meum? at ego non modo vincula Scorp. 15
Hierosolymis pati optaverim, verum etiam mori pro nomine domini mei Jesu
Christi.   14 [atque ita cesserunt dicendo :] fiat voluntas domini.

---

10 ημων] mg [quum autem] nos [maneremus]   11 δησουσιν] vincient Harclean
⁂ eum ✓   παραδωσουσιν] tradent ⁂ eum ✓

Cantabrigiensis, 1864, pp. x ff.,
446 f. From the collation made for
Ussher (which is more full than
Scrivener was aware) I have been able
to correct and complete Scrivener's
data ; see J. H. Ropes, 'The Reconstruction of the Torn Leaf of Codex
Bezae,' Harvard Theological Review,
xvi, 1923, pp. 162-168, and R. P.
Casey, ibid. pp. 392-394. The omission in vs. 15 (both D and d) of συνηλθον δε και των μαθητων is due to an
oversight of the scribe, not to mutilation of the codex.

σὺν ἡμῖν, ἄγοντες παρ᾽ ᾧ ξενισθῶμεν Μνάσω‹νί› τινι Κυπρίῳ,
ἀρχαίῳ μαθητῇ. γενομένων δὲ ἡμῶν εἰς Ἱεροσόλυμα ἀσμένως 17
ἀπεδέξαντο ἡμᾶς οἱ ἀδελφοί. τῇ δὲ ἐπιούσῃ εἰσῄει ὁ Παῦλος 18
σὺν ἡμῖν πρὸς Ἰάκωβον, πάντες τε παρεγένοντο οἱ πρεσβύτεροι.
καὶ ἀσπασάμενος αὐτοὺς ἐξηγεῖτο καθ᾽ ἓν ἕκαστον ὧν ἐποίησεν 19
ὁ θεὸς ἐν τοῖς ἔθνεσιν διὰ τῆς διακονίας αὐτοῦ. οἱ δὲ ἀκούσαντες 20
ἐδόξαζον τὸν θεόν, εἶπόν τε αὐτῷ· Θεωρεῖς, ἀδελφέ, πόσαι
μυριάδες εἰσὶν ἐν τοῖς Ἰουδαίοις τῶν πεπιστευκότων, καὶ πάντες
ζηλωταὶ τοῦ νόμου ὑπάρχουσιν· κατηχήθησαν δὲ περὶ σοῦ ὅτι 21
ἀποστασίαν διδάσκεις ἀπὸ Μωυσέως τοὺς κατὰ τὰ ἔθνη πάντας
Ἰουδαίους, λέγων μὴ περιτέμνειν αὐτοὺς τὰ τέκνα μηδὲ τοῖς
ἔθεσιν περιπατεῖν. | τί οὖν ἐστίν; πάντως ἀκούσονται ὅτι ἐλή- 22

Editors　　21 om παντας JHR　　　22 παντως] + [δει συνελθειν πληθος] Soden　+[δει
πληθος συνελθειν] Soden mg　　　　　ακουσονται] +[γαρ] Soden

Old Uncial　16 μνασωνι AC (cf. D)　μνασω B　ιασονι ℵ　　　　　τινι BℵC　om A
18 δε BC(+D)　τε ℵA　　19 αυτους BℵA　αυτου C　　　　δια BAC(+D)
om ℵ　　　　　20 εδοξαζον BAC　εδοξασαν ℵ(+D)　　　　ειπον τε BℵA
ειποντες C(+D)　　εν τοις ιουδαιοις BAC (cf. D)　om ℵ　　21 δε BACℵᶜ(+D)
om ℵ　　　　παντας BℵC　om A(+D)　　　　λεγων BACℵᶜ　λεγω ℵ
22 παντως BC　+δει συνελθειν πληθος ℵAC² (cf. D)　　　ακουσονται BℵC
+γαρ Aℵᶜ(+D)　　οτι BACℵᶜ(+D)　om ℵ

Antiochian　17 απεδεξαντο] εδεξαντο HLPSS͂　　　18 τε] γαρ S　　　19 αυτους]
αυτοις L　　εν εκαστον] ενα εκαστον H (cf. D)　　　20 ακουοντες HL
θεον] κυριον HPSS͂(+D)　　εν τοις ιουδαιοις] ιουδαιων HLPSS͂　　22 παντως]
+δει πληθος συνελθειν HLPSS͂(+D)　　ακουσονται] +γαρ HLPSS͂(+D)

16 Hcl.mg, as far as it goes, is here
in substantial agreement with D d,
for an inspection of the Syriac MS.
shows (as Zahn had conjectured) that
the gloss is marked to be attached
after αγοντες, not at the point wrongly
indicated in White's edition. The
chief matter of interest in this
'Western' paraphrase is the transfer
of Mnason's residence from Jerusalem
to "a certain village." The 'Western'
text is inherently highly improbable.
Its indefinite reference to the 'village'
is futile and over-emphasized, especially in view of the extreme interest
and importance of the goal of their
journey. As their village-host, Mnason
is wholly without significance; whereas
as a resident of Jerusalem this 'old
disciple' was of real consequence to
the narrative. Moreover, the travellers
would probably spend as much as
two nights on the way (not less than

sixty miles) before reaching Jerusalem.
That the party had to stop somewhere
over night between Caesarea and
Jerusalem is well within the range of
the glossator's possible knowledge.

D d have omitted a line, of which
simul d seems to be a survival,
representing the συν- of συνηλθον.

20 The omission of εν τοις ιουδαιοις
by ℵ is probably an accident. That
the omission occurs also in the otherwise unimportant minn 3 4 97 209
is probably due to homoeoteleuton in
the Antiochian text (ιουδαιων, πεπιστευκοτων). The reading εν τοις ιουδαιοις
of BACE e vg Ambrst is to be preferred
to the 'Western' εν τη ιουδαια D d gig
perp pesh sah Jerome (once only;
twice judaeorum) Aug. Ep. 82, 9, in
which the awkwardness of the B-text
has been avoided. The Antiochian
revisers made the sentence run more
smoothly by altering to ιουδαιων.

ἡμεῖν· οὗτοι δὲ ἤγαγον ἡμᾶς πρὸς οὓς ξενισθῶμεν. καὶ παραγενόμενοι εἴς τινα κώμην ἐγενόμεθα παρὰ Νάσωνί τινι Κυπρίῳ
17 μαθητῇ ἀρχαίῳ. κἀκεῖθεν ἐξιόντες ἤλθομεν εἰς Ἱεροσόλυμα·
18 ὑπεδέξαντο δὲ ἡμᾶς ἀσμένως οἱ ἀδελφοί. τῇ δὲ ἐπιούσῃ εἰσῄει
ὁ Παῦλος σὺν ἡμῖν πρὸς Ἰάκωβον·] ἦσαν δὲ παρ' αὐτῷ οἱ πρε-
19 σβύτεροι συνηγμένοι. οὓς ἀσπα⟨σά⟩μενος διηγεῖτο ἐν ἕκαστον
20 ὡς ἐποίησεν ὁ θεὸς τοῖς ἔθνεσιν διὰ τῆς διακονίας αὐτοῦ. οἱ
δὲ ἀκούσαντες ἐδόξασαν τὸν κύριον εἰπόντες· Θεωρεῖς, ἀδελφέ,
πόσαι μυριάδες εἰσὶν ἐν τῇ Ἰουδαίᾳ τῶν πεπιστευκότων, καὶ
21 πάντες οὗτοι ζηλωταὶ τοῦ νόμου ὑπάρχουσιν· κατήχησαν δὲ
περὶ σοῦ ὅτι ἀποστασίαν διδάσκεις ἀπὸ Μωσέως τοὺς κατὰ
ἔθνη †εἰσὶν† Ἰουδαίους μὴ περιτέμνειν αὐτοὺς τὰ τέκνα μήτε
22 ἐν τοῖς ἔθεσιν αὐτοῦ περιπατεῖν. | τί οὖν ἐστίν; πάντως δεῖ
23 πλῆθος συνελθεῖν, ἀκούσονται γὰρ ὅτι ἐλήλυθας. τοῦτο οὖν

19 εν] ενα   20 εισιν] ειεισιν   ουτοι] τουτοι
21 κατηχησαν] κατηκησαν   περι] περει   ιουδαιοις
εθεσιν] εθνεσιν

16 de caesarea nobiscum simul quae adduxerunt nos apud quem ospitaremur et d
cum venerunt in quendam civitatem fuimus ad nasonem quendam cyprium discipulum
antiquum   17 et inde exeuntes venimus hierosolyma susceperunt autem nos cum
laetitia fratres   18 sequenti autem die introibit paulus nobiscum ad jacobum erant
autem cum eo praesbyteri conventi   19 cum salutasset eos narrabat per singula quae
fecit d̄s in gentibus per ministerium ejus   20 ad illi cum audissent clarificaverunt
d̄n̄m dicentes vides frater quanta milia sint in judaea qui crediderunt et omnes isti
hemulatores legis sunt   21 diffamaverunt autem de te quia abscensionem docens a
moysen qui in gentibus sunt judaeos ne circumcidat filios neque gentes ejus ambulant
22 quid ergo est utique oportet multitudinem convenire audient enim quia venisti

16–17 προς ους ξενισθωμεν . . . εις ιεροσολυμα] mg apud quem hospitaremur. Harclean
et quum venissemus in pagum, fuimus apud Mnasonem quendam, Cyprium,
ex discipulis primis.   et inde exeuntes fuimus in Hierosolymis   19 δι-
ηγειτο] narrabat ⁜ iis ✓   ·   21 αυτου] mg ejus

21 εισιν D is explicable only as imi-
tated from d *sunt*.
In omitting παντας D d are supported by A 33 boh e (E) vg and
all other Latin witnesses, and it
may be inferred that in the Greek
text on which the 'Western' paraphrase was based the word was lacking.
The word is so awkwardly placed that
it is hard to believe it original;
especially since the improving touch
of a copyist would have been more
likely to remove it to its appropriate
position before τους than to delete it
altogether.

On the other hand λεγων, itself not
superfluous, is omitted by D d only,
without other support, and is to be
accepted as genuine.

22 The additional sentence δει πληθος συνελθειν, with the consequent
insertion of γαρ in the following
sentence, is probably a 'Western'
expansion (D d e gig vg). It
must, however, have gained wide
acceptance, for it has found its way
into ℵA and was adopted by the
Antiochian revisers. It is not found
in BC 614 pesh hcl.*text* sah boh.

λυθες. τοῦτο οὖν ποίησον ὅ σοι λέγομεν· εἰσὶν ἡμῖν ἄνδρες 23
τέσσαρες εὐχὴν ἔχοντες ἀφ' ἑαυτῶν. τούτους παραλαβὼν 24
ἁγνίσθητι σὺν αὐτοῖς καὶ δαπάνησον ἐπ' αὐτοῖς ἵνα ξυρήσονται
τὴν κεφαλήν, καὶ γνώσονται πάντες ὅτι ὧν κατήχηνται περὶ
σοῦ οὐδέν ἔστιν, ἀλλὰ στοιχεῖς καὶ αὐτὸς φυλάσσων τὸν νόμον.
περὶ δὲ τῶν πεπιστευκότων ἐθνῶν ἡμεῖς ἀπεστείλαμεν κρείναντες 25
φυλάσσεσθαι αὐτοὺς τό τε εἰδωλόθυτον καὶ αἷμα καὶ πνικτὸν
καὶ πορνείαν. τότε ὁ Παῦλος παραλαβὼν τοὺς ἄνδρας τῇ ἐχομένῃ 26
ἡμέρᾳ σὺν αὐτοῖς ἁγνισθεὶς εἰσήει εἰς τὸ ἱερόν, διαγγέλλων τὴν
ἐκπλήρωσιν τῶν ἡμερῶν τοῦ ἁγνισμοῦ ἕως οὗ προσηνέχθη ὑπὲρ
ἑνὸς ἑκάστου αὐτῶν ἡ προσφορά.
Ὡς δὲ ἔμελλον αἱ ἑπτὰ ἡμέραι συντελεῖσθαι, οἱ ἀπὸ τῆς 27
Ἀσίας Ἰουδαῖοι θεασάμενοι αὐτὸν ἐν τῷ ἱερῷ συνέχεον πάντα
τὸν ὄχλον καὶ ἐπέβαλαν ἐπ' αὐτὸν τὰς χεῖρας, | κράζοντες· Ἄνδρες 28
Ἰσραηλεῖται, βοηθεῖτε· οὗτός ἐστιν ὁ ἄνθρωπος ὁ κατὰ τοῦ
λαοῦ καὶ τοῦ νόμου καὶ τοῦ τόπου τούτου πάντας πανταχῇ
διδάσκων, ἔτι τε καὶ Ἕλληνας εἰσήγαγεν εἰς τὸ ἱερὸν καὶ κεκοί-
νωκεν τὸν ἅγιον τόπον τοῦτον. ἦσαν γὰρ προεωρακότες Τρό- 29
φιμον τὸν Ἐφέσιον ἐν τῇ πόλει σὺν αὐτῷ, ὃν ἐνόμιζον ὅτι εἰς

28 βοηθειται

Editors   23 αφ] εφ WHmg Soden   24 ξυρησωνται Soden   25 απεστειλαμεν]
επεστειλαμεν WHmg Soden

Old Uncial   23 αφ Bℵ   εφ AC(+D)   24 αυτοις 2° BℵAcorrC   αυτους A (cf. D)
ξυρησονται Bℵ   ξυρησωνται AC   ων BℵA(+D)   περι ων C   αλλα
BℵC (cf. D)   +και A   25 απεστειλαμεν B(+D)   επεστειλαμεν ℵAC
κρειναντες BℵA   +μηδεν τοιουτο τηρειν αυτους ει μη C(+D)   27 οι απο της
ασιας ιουδαιοι before θεασαμενοι BℵA (cf. D)   after ιερω C   συνεχεον BℵA
(+D)   συνεχεαν C   28 τοπου BℵC(+D)   +του αγιου AC²   κεκοινωκεν
BℵAC   κεκοινωνηκεν B²(B³ Tdf) (cf. D)   29 τον BAC(+D)   om ℵ   κεκοινωκεν

Antiochian   23 αφ] εφ HLPSϛ(+D)   24 om και δαπανησον επ αυτοις S   ξυρησωνται HLϛ   γνωσι HLPSϛ   τον νομον φυλασσων HLPSϛ
25 απεστειλαμεν] επεστειλαμεν HLPϛ   κρειναντες] +μηδεν τοιουτον τηρειν
αυτους ει μη HLPSϛ(+D)   το αιμα HLPSϛ   26 παραλαβων ο παυλος S
27 τας χειρας επ αυτον HLPSϛ   28 πανταχη] πανταχου HLPSϛ
29 προεωρακοτες] εορακοτες HLP

23 αφ Bℵ three minn Origen (Orat.
iii. 4) sah boh yields good sense ('of
their own act,' in contrast to Paul's
intervention ; for εὐχὴν ἔχοντες, in
the sense of 'under a vow,' cf.
xviii. 18). Especially in view of
the infrequency of agreement between
B and ℵ in errors peculiar to them,

αφ is to be accepted against the testimony of other witnesses to the reading
εφ. The latter makes a weak phrase,
which, however it originated, would
commend itself to the mind of tran-
scribers. On the testimony of sah and
boh see H. Thompson's note, below,
p. 349.

ποίησον ὃ σοι λέγομεν· εἰσὶν ἡμεῖν ἄνδρες τέσσαρες εὐχὴν
24 ἔχοντες ἐφ᾽ ἑαυτῶν. τούτους παραλαβὼν ἁγνίσθητι σὺν αὐτοῖς
καὶ δαπάνησον εἰς αὐτοὺς ἵνα ξυρῶνται τὴν κεφαλήν, καὶ
γνώσονται πάντες ὅτι ὧν κατήχηνται περὶ <σ>οῦ οὐδὲν ἔστιν,
25 ἀλλ᾽ ὅτι πορεύῃ αὐτὸς φυλάσσων τὸν νόμον. περὶ δὲ τῶν
πεπιστευκότων ἐθνῶν οὐδὲν ἔχουσι λέγειν πρὸς σέ, ἡμεῖς γὰρ
ἀπεστείλαμεν κρείνοντες μηδὲν τοιοῦτον τηρεῖν αὐτοὺς εἰ μὴ
φυλάσσεσθαι αὐτοὺς τὸ ἐ<ι>δωλόθυτον καὶ αἷμα καὶ πορνείαν.
26 τότε Παῦλος παραλαβὼν τοὺς ἄνδρας τῇ ἐπιούσῃ ἡμέρᾳ σὺν
αὐτοῖς ἁγνεισθεὶς εἰσῆλθεν εἰς τὸ ἱερόν, διαγγέλλων τὴν ἐκπλήρωσιν τῶν ἡμερῶν τοῦ ἁγνισμοῦ †ὅπως† προσηνέχθη ὑπὲρ
ἑνὸς ἑκάστου αὐτῶν προσφορά.
27 Συντελουμένης δὲ τῆς ἑβδόμης ἡμέρας, οἱ δὲ ἀ<πὸ> τῆς
Ἀσίας Ἰουδαῖοι ἐληλυθότες θεασάμενοι αὐτὸν ἐν τῷ ἱερῷ συνέχεον πάντα τὸν ὄχλον καὶ ἐπιβάλλουσιν ἐπ᾽ αὐτὸν τὰς χεῖρας,
28 | κράζοντες· Ἄνδρες Ἰστραηλεῖται, βοηθεῖτε· οὗτός ἐστιν ὁ
ἄνθρωπος ὁ κατὰ τοῦ λαοῦ καὶ τοῦ νόμου καὶ τοῦ τόπου τούτου
πάντας πανταχῇ διδάσκων, ἔτι καὶ Ἕλληνας εἰσῆγεν <ε>ἰς ἱερὸν
29 καὶ ἐκοίνωσεν τὸν ἅγιον τόπον τοῦτον. ἦσαν γὰρ προεωρακότες Τρόφιμον τὸν Ἐφέσιον ἐν τῇ πόλει σὺν αὐτῷ, ὃν ἐνόμισαν

24 πορευη] πορευου   28 βοηθειται   εκοινωσεν]
εκοινωνησεν   29 ενομισαμεν

23 hoc ergo fac quod tibi digimus sunt nobis viri quattuor votum habentes super se d
24 hos adsume purificate cum illis et eroga in eos ut radant caput et cognoscant
omnes quia quae audierunt de te nihil est sed ambulans ipse custodiens legem
25 de illis vero qui crediderunt gentibus nihil habent quod dicere in te nos enim
scripsimus judicantes nihil tale observare eos nisi custodirent se a sacrificato et
sanguine et fornicatione 26 tunc paulus adsumpsit viros sequenti die cum ipsis
purificatus introibit in templum adnuntians expeditionem dierum purificationis
donec oblata est pro uno quoque eorum oblatio 27 cum repletur autem eis
septimus dies qui ab asia erant judaei venerant videntes eum in templo confuderunt
omnem turbam et miserunt super eum manus 28 clamantes viri istrahelitae adjuvate
hic est homo qui adversus populum et legem et locum hunt omnes ubique docet
insuper et grecos introduxit in templum et communicavit sanctum locum hunc
29 erant autem providentes trophimum et ephesium in civitate cum eo quem

25 απεστειλαμεν BD minn boh hcl.
text, used absolutely, without an
object, is common in LXX, but has
been altered to the more elegant
Greek επεστειλαμεν in the other witnesses here ; cf. also επιστειλαι, Acts
xv. 20.
The 'Western' explanatory expansion of this verse is given with

substantial completeness by D d, and
much of it has survived in various
other documents. It was founded on
a text in which και πνικτον was lacking
(so D d gig Aug. Ep. 82, 9) ; but no
witness to this verse introduces the
(negative) Golden Rule. The variants
of E are due, as usual, to reaction
from e.

τὸ ἱερὸν εἰσήγαγεν ὁ Παῦλος. ἐκεινήθη τε ἡ πόλις ὅλη καὶ 30
ἐγένετο συνδρομὴ τοῦ λαοῦ, καὶ ἐπιλαβόμενοι τοῦ Παύλου εἷλκον
αὐτὸν ἔξω τοῦ ἱεροῦ, καὶ εὐθέως ἐκλείσθησαν αἱ θύραι. ζητούν- 31
των τε αὐτὸν ἀποκτεῖναι ἀνέβη φάσις τῷ χειλιάρχῳ τῆς σπείρης
ὅτι ὅλη συγχύννεται Ἰερουσαλήμ, ὃς ἐξαυτῆς λαβὼν στρατιώτας 32
καὶ ἑκατοντάρχας κατέδραμεν ἐπ᾽ αὐτούς, οἱ δὲ ἰδόντες τὸν
χειλίαρχον καὶ τοὺς στρατιώτας ἐπαύσαντο τύπτοντες τὸν
Παῦλον. τότε ἐγγίσας ὁ χιλίαρχος ἐπελάβετο αὐτοῦ καὶ ἐκέλευσε 33
δεθῆναι ἁλύσεσι δυσί, καὶ ἐπυνθάνετο τίς εἴη καὶ τί ἐστιν πεποιη-
κώς· | ἄλλοι δὲ ἄλλο τι ἐπεφώνουν ἐν τῷ ὄχλῳ· μὴ δυναμένου δὲ 34
αὐτοῦ γνῶναι τὸ ἀσφαλὲς διὰ τὸν θόρυβον ἐκέλευσεν ἄγεσθαι
αὐτὸν εἰς τὴν παρεμβολήν. ὅτε δὲ ἐγένετο ἐπὶ τοὺς ἀναβαθμούς, 35
συνέβη βαστάζεσθαι αὐτὸν ὑπὸ τῶν στρατιωτῶν διὰ τὴν βίαν
τοῦ ὄχλου, | ἠκολούθει γὰρ τὸ πλῆθος τοῦ λαοῦ κράζοντες· Αἶρε 36
αὐτόν. μέλλων τε εἰσάγεσθαι εἰς τὴν παρεμβολὴν ὁ Παῦλος 37
λέγει τῷ χειλιάρχῳ· Εἰ ἔξεστίν μοι εἰπεῖν τι πρὸς σέ; ὁ δὲ ἔφη·
Ἑλληνιστὶ γεινώσκεις; οὐκ ἄρα σὺ εἶ ὁ Αἰγύπτιος ὁ πρὸ τούτων 38
τῶν ἡμερῶν ἀναστατώσας καὶ ἐξαγαγὼν εἰς τὴν ἔρημον τοὺς
τετρακισχειλίους ἄνδρας τῶν σεικαρίων; εἶπεν δὲ ὁ Παῦλος· 39
Ἐγὼ ἄνθρωπος μέν εἰμι Ἰουδαῖος, Ταρσεὺς τῆς Κιλικίας, οὐκ
ἀσήμου πόλεως πολίτης· δέομαι δέ σου, ἐπίτρεψόν μοι λαλῆσαι
πρὸς τὸν λαόν. ἐπιτρέψαντος δὲ αὐτοῦ ὁ Παῦλος ἑστὼς ἐπὶ 40

Editors   31 συγκεχυται Soden mg   32 λαβων] παραλαβων WH Soden JHR
λαβων WHmg   εκατονταρχους Soden

Old Uncial   30 και ευθεως εκλεισθησαν αι θυραι BACℵᶜ(+D)   εκλισθη (εκλισθησαν ℵᶜᵒʳʳ)
ευθεως ℵ   31 συγχυννεται BℵA(+D)   συνκεχυται ℵᶜ   32 λαβων B
παραλαβων ℵA(+D)   39 ειμι BAℵᶜ(+D)   om ℵ   μοι BAℵᶜ(+D)
+λογον ℵ

Antiochian   31 τε] δε HLPS⳽   αυτον] αυτων S   συγχυννεται] συγκεχυται
HLPS⳽   32 λαβων] παραλαβων HLPS⳽(+D)   εκατονταρχους HLPS⳽
33 τοτε εγγισας] εγγισας δε HLPS   αυτου] αυτον L   τις] +αν HLPS⳽
34 επεφωνουν] εβοων HLPS⳽   δυναμενου δε αυτου] δυναμενος δε HLPS⳽
36 κραζον HLPS⳽(+D)   37 om τι HLPS(+D)   39 om δε 2° L

---

36 αιρε αυτον is intensified in gig
(tolle inimicum nostrum) and sah ('take
our enemy from the midst'); cf.
xxiv. 18 vg.codd.
39 The omission in D of ουκ ασημου
πολεως πολιτης is probably due to the

accidental omission of a line in the
archetype; cf. d, which has the Latin
corresponding to these words, and in
which it has consequently been necessary to protract the line to an unusual
length.

30 ὅτι εἰς τὸ ἱερὸν εἰσήγαγεν Παῦλος. ἐκεινήθη τε ἡ πόλις ὅλη
καὶ ἐγένετο συνδρομὴ τοῦ λαοῦ, καὶ ἐπιλαβόμενοι τοῦ Παύλου
31 εἷλκον ἔξω τοῦ ἱεροῦ, καὶ εὐθέως ἐκλείσθησαν αἱ θύραι. [καὶ]
ζητούντων αὐτὸν ἀποκτεῖναι ἀνέβη φάσις τῷ χιλιάρχῳ τῆς
32 σπείρης ὅτι ὅλη συνχύννεται Ἰερουσαλήμ, ὃς ἐξαυτῆς παραλαβὼν
στρατιώτας καὶ ἑκατοντάρχας κατέδραμεν ἐπ᾽ αὐτούς, οἱ δὲ
εἰδόντες τὸν χειλίαρχον καὶ τοὺ⟨ς⟩ στρατιώτας ἐπαύσαντο τύ-
33 πτοντες τὸν Παῦλον. τότε ἐγγίσας ὁ χιλίαρχος ἐπελάβετο αὐτοῦ
καὶ ἐκέλευσεν δεθῆναι ἁλύσεσιν δυσίν, καὶ ἐπυνθάνετο τίς εἴη
34 καὶ τί ἐστιν πεποι⟨η⟩κώς· ἄλλοι δὲ ἄλλα ἐπεφώνουν ἐν τῷ ὄχλῳ·
καὶ μὴ δυναμένου αὐτοῦ γνῶναι τὸ ἀσφαλὲς διὰ τὸν θόρυβον
35 ἐκέλευσε ἄγεσθαι αὐτὸν εἰς τὴν παρεμβολήν. ὅτε δὲ ἐγένετο εἰς
τοὺς ἀναβαθμούς, συνέβη τὸν Παῦλον βαστάζεσθαι ὑπὸ τῶν
36 στρατιωτῶν διὰ τὴν βίαν τοῦ λαοῦ, ἠκολούθ⟨ε⟩ι γὰρ τὸ πλῆθος
37 κρᾶζον ἀναιρεῖσθαι αὐτόν. μέλλων τε εἰσάγεσθαι εἰς τὴν παρεμβολὴν τῷ χειλιάρχῳ ἀποκρειθεὶς εἶπεν· Εἰ ἔξεστίν μοι λαλῆσαι
38 πρὸς σέ; ὁ δὲ ἔφη· Ἑλληνιστὶ γεινώσκεις; | οὐ σὺ εἶ ὁ Ἐγύ-
πτιος ὁ πρὸ τούτων τῶν ἡμερῶν ἀναστατώσας καὶ ἐξαγαγὼν εἰς
39 τὴν ἔρημον τοὺς τετρακισχειλίους ἄνδρας τῶν σικαρίων; εἶπεν
δὲ ὁ Παῦλος· Ἐγὼ ἄνθρωπος μέν εἰμι Ἰουδαῖος ἐν Ταρσῷ δὲ
τῆς Κιλικίας γεγεννημένος· δέομαι δέ σου, συνχωρῆσαί μοι λαλῆ-
40 σαι πρὸς τὸν λαόν. καὶ ἐπιτρέψαντος δὲ τοῦ χιλιάρχου ἑστὼς

30 ειλκων   33 τι] τις   34 εκευλευσε   39 δεομαι]
δαιομε

---

putaverunt quia in templum induxit paulus 30 et commota est civitas tota et d
facta est concursio populi et cum adprehendissent paulum trahebant extra templum
et continuo clusae sunt januae 31 et cum quererent eum occidere nuntiatum est
tribuno cohortis quia tota confusa est in hierusalem 32 qui statim sumptis militibus
et centurionibus procucurrit ad eos ad illi cum vidissent tribunum et milites cessa-
verunt percutientes paulum 33 tunc cum adpropinquasset tribunus conpraehendit
eum et jussit ligari catenis duabus et interrogabat quis sit et quid fecisset 34 alii
autem aliud clamabant in turba et cum non possit scire quod certum est propter
tumultum jussit adduci eum in castra 35 cum autem adhuc esset in gradus obtigit
paulum bajulari a militibus propter vim populi 36 sequebatur enim multitudo
clamans tollite eum 37 et cum jam induceretur in castris tribuno respondens dixit
si licet mihi loqui at te ad ille ait grece nosti 38 nonne tu es ille aegyptius qui
anti hos dies sollicitasti et eduxisti in eremum quattuor milia virorum sicariorum
39 dixit autem paulus ego homo quidem sum judaeus tarsensis ex ciliciae non
ignotae civitatis cujus rogo obsegro autem mihi loqui ad populum 40 et cum

---

29 εισηγαγεν] introduxit ·※· eum ✓   31 ιερουσαλημ] + ·※· vide Harclean
igitur ne faciant insurrectionem ✓   36 το πληθος] mg populus

τῶν ἀναβαθμῶν κατέσεισε τῇ χειρὶ τῷ λαῷ, πολλῆς δὲ γενομένης
σειγῆς προσεφώνησεν τῇ Ἑβραΐδι διαλέκτῳ λέγων· Ἄνδρες XXII
ἀδελφοὶ καὶ πατέρες, ἀκούσατέ μου τῆς πρὸς ὑμᾶς νυνὶ ἀπολογίας. ἀκούσαντες δὲ ὅτι τῇ Ἑβραΐδι διαλέκτῳ προσεφώνει ²
αὐτοῖς μᾶλλον παρέσχον ἡσυχίαν. καί φησιν· | Ἐγώ εἰμι ἀνὴρ ³
Ἰουδαῖος, γεγεννημένος ἐν Ταρσῷ τῆς Κιλικίας, ἀνατεθραμμένος
δὲ ἐν τῇ πόλει ταύτῃ παρὰ τοὺς πόδας Γαμαλιήλου, πεπαιδευ-
μένος κατ᾽ ἀκρείβειαν τοῦ πατρῴου νόμου, ζηλωτὴς ὑπάρχων
τοῦ θεοῦ καθὼς πάντες ὑμεῖς ἐστὲ σήμερον, ὃς ταύτην τὴν ὁδὸν ⁴
ἐδίωξα ἄχρι θανάτου, δεσμεύων καὶ παραδιδοὺς εἰς φυλακὰς
ἄνδρας τε καὶ γυναῖκας, ὡς καὶ ὁ ἀρχιερεὺς ἐμαρτύρει μοι καὶ ⁵
πᾶν τὸ πρεσβυτέρειον· παρ᾽ ὧν καὶ ἐπιστολὰς δεξάμενος πρὸς
τοὺς ἀδελφοὺς εἰς Δαμασκὸν ἐπορευόμην ἄξων καὶ τοὺς ἐκεῖσε
ὄντας δεδεμένους εἰς Ἰερουσαλὴμ ἵνα τιμωρηθῶσιν. ἐγένετο δέ ⁶
μοι πορευομένῳ καὶ ἐγγίζοντι τῇ Δαμασκῷ περὶ μεσημβρίαν
ἐξαίφνης ἐκ τοῦ οὐρανοῦ περιαστράψαι φῶς ἱκανὸν περὶ ἐμέ,
| ἔπεσά τε εἰς τὸ ἔδαφος καὶ ἤκουσα φωνῆς λεγούσης μοι· Σαούλ, ⁷
Σαούλ, τί με διώκεις; | ἐγὼ δὲ ἀπεκρίθην· Τίς εἶ, κύριε; εἶπέν ⁸
τε πρὸς ἐμέ. Ἐγώ εἰμι Ἰησοῦς ὁ Ναζωραῖος ὃν σὺ διώκεις. οἱ ⁹
δὲ σὺν ἐμοὶ ὄντες τὸ μὲν φῶς ἐθεάσαντο τὴν δὲ φωνὴν οὐκ ἤκουσαν
τοῦ λαλοῦντός μοι. | εἶπον δέ· Τί ποιήσω, κύριε; ὁ δὲ κύριος ¹⁰
εἶπεν πρός με· Ἀναστὰς πορεύου εἰς Δαμασκόν, κἀκεῖ σοι

Editors   40 σιγης γενομενης WH Soden JHR   γενομενης σιγης WHmg   3 εγω]
+[μεν] Soden   γαμαλιηλ WH Soden JHR   5 μαρτυρει WH Soden
JHR

Old Uncial   40 γενομενης σειγης B   σιγης γενομενης ℵA (cf. D)   εβραιδι Bℵ(+D)
ιδια A   2 αυτοις Bℵ   αυτων Avid   3 ειμι ανηρ BA (cf. D)   ανηρ
ειμι ℵ   γεγεννημενος Bℵ(+D) γεγενημενος A   5 εμαρτυρει B
μαρτυρει ℵA   8 απεκριθην BA(+D)   +και ειπα ℵ   9 εθεασαντο
BAℵc(+D)   εθεατο ℵ   ηκουσαν BℵA(+D)   ηκουον ℵc

Antiochian   40 τον λαον H   σιγης γενομενης HLPS⳽ (cf. D)   1 υμας] ημας L
νυνι] νυν ⳽   2 προσφωνει HS(+D)   προσεφωνησεν L   3 εγω] +μεν
HLPS⳽   πεπαιδευμενος] +δε HS   5 μαρτυρει HLPS⳽   om αξων
και τους εκεισε οντας δεδεμενους H   6 περιαστραψαν P   9 εθεασαντο]
+ και εμφοβοι εγενοντο LPS⳽(+D)

3 The inflected proper name γαμα-
λιηλου is supported by BΨ 614 minn,
a noteworthy array, but is probably an
isolated scribal attempt at hellenization, such as is found, applied consistently, in 1 Esdras and in Josephus;

see Thackeray, Grammar of O.T. in
Greek, i, pp. 160 ff.
For hcl ※: traditionum paternarum
mearum cf. legis vg.
5 For hcl.mg cf. αρχιερευς ανανιας
614 minn.

ὁ Παῦλος ἐπὶ τῶν ἀναβαθμῶν καὶ σείσας τῇ χειρὶ πρὸς αὐτούς,
πολλῆς τε ἡσυχίας γενομένης, προσεφώνησεν τῇ Ἑβραΐδι
XXII διαλέκτῳ λέγων· Ἄνδρες ἀδελφοὶ καὶ πατέρες, ἀκούσατέ μου
2 τῆς πρὸς ὑμᾶς νυνεὶ ἀπολογίας. ἀκούσαντες δὲ ὅτι τῇ Ἑβραΐδι
3 διαλέκτῳ προσφωνεῖ μᾶλλον ἡσύχασαν. καί φησιν· | Ἐγώ εἰμι
Ἰουδαῖος ἀνήρ, ἐν Ταρσῷ τῆς Κιλικίας γεγεννημένος, ἀνατεθραμμένος δὲ ἐν τῇ πόλει ταύτῃ παρὰ τοὺς πόδας Γαμαλιήλ,
παιδευόμενος κατὰ ἀκρίβιαν τοῦ πατρῴου νόμου, ζηλωτὴς τοῦ
4 θεοῦ καθὼς ἐστὲ ὑμεῖς πάντες σήμερον, καὶ ταύτην τὴν ὁδὸν
ἐδίωξα μέχρι θανάτου, δεσμεύων καὶ παραδιδοὺς εἰς φυλακὴν ἄν-
5 δρας τε καὶ γυναῖκας, ὡς καὶ ἀρχιερεὺς μαρτυρήσει μοι καὶ ὅλον
τὸ πρεσβυτέριον· παρ᾽ ὧν ἐπιστολὰς δεξάμενος παρὰ τῶν ἀδελφῶν εἰς Δαμασκὸν ἐπορευόμην ἄξων καὶ τοὺς ἐκεῖ ὄντας δεδεμέ-
6 νους ἐν Ἰερουσαλὴμ ἵνα τειμωρηθῶσιν. ἐνγίζοντι δ[έ μ]οι μεσ-
ημβρίας Δαμασκῷ ἐξέφνης ἀ[πὸ] τοῦ οὐρανοῦ περιήστραψέ μ[ε]
7 φῶς ἱκανὸν †περὶ ἐμέ†, καὶ ἔπεσον εἰς τὸ ἔδαφος καὶ ἤκουσα
8 φωνῆς λεγούσης μοι· Σαῦλε, Σαῦλε, τί με διώκεις; | ἐγὼ δὲ ἀπ-
εκρίθην· Τίς εἶ, κύριε; εἶπεν δὲ πρός με· Ἐγώ εἰ‹μι› Ἰησοῦς
9 ὁ Ναζοραῖος ὃν σὺ δειώκεις. οἱ δὲ σὺν ἐμοὶ ὄντες τὸ μὲν φῶς
ἐθεάσαντο καὶ ἔνφοβοι ἐγένοντο τὴν δὲ φωνὴν οὐκ ἤκουσαν τοῦ
10 λαλοῦντός μοι. | εἶπα δέ· Τί ποιήσω, κύριε; ὁ δὲ εἶπεν πρός
με· Ἀναστὰς πορεύου εἰς Δαμασκόν, κἀκεῖ σοι λαληθήσεται
περὶ πάντων

3 εστε] εσται   6 περιεστραψα

permisisset ei tribunus stans paulus in gradibus et movit manum ad eos magnoque d
silentio facto adlocutus est hebreica lingua dicens
   1 viri fratres et patres audite me nunc aput vos reddo rationem   2 cum audissent
autem quia hebreica lingua adloquitur

3 του θεου] ⋇ traditionum paternarum mearum ✓   5 αρχιερευς] Harclean
princeps sacerdotum ⋇ Ananias ✓   7 λεγουσης μοι σαυλε σαυλε
τι με διωκεις] mg dialecto Hebraea loquentem mihi: Saule, Saule, quid me
persequeris? durum est tibi contra stimulos calcitrare

εμαρτυρει B has only the support of
reddidit vg.*two codices*, and is not to
be accepted. Zahn suggests as a
cause for it the variant επιμαρτυρει
614 383 2147.
  6 In D περι εμε is superfluous after
μ[ε], and may well be due to contamination from the B-text. A text
(in several respects similar to D) with
με but without περι εμε is actually
found in Athanasius, *Serm. maj. de*

fide 30, and is implied by gig vg
circumfulsit me.
  7 For hcl.*mg* cf. *lingua hebraica* gig
(from xxvi. 14). The further addition
from xxvi. 14 of σκληρον σοι προς
κεντρα λακτιζειν is found with minor
variation in 255 gig e E vg.*codd*
hcl.*mg* Athanasius (*ut supra*).
  10 From vs. 10 to vs. 20 one leaf
of D is lacking. In d the lacuna runs
from vs. 2 to vs. 10.

λαληθήσεται περὶ πάντων ὧν ἐντέτακταί σοι ποιῆσαι. ὡς δὲ 11
οὐδὲν ἔβλεπον ἀπὸ τῆς δόξης τοῦ φωτὸς ἐκείνου, χειραγωγού-
μενος ὑπὸ τῶν συνόντων μοι ἦλθον εἰς Δαμασκόν. Ἀνανίας 12
δέ τις ἀνὴρ εὐλαβὴς κατὰ τὸν νόμον, μαρτυρούμενος ὑπὸ πάντων
τῶν κατοικούντων Ἰουδαίων, ἐλθὼν πρὸς ἐμὲ καὶ ἐπιστὰς εἶπέν 13
μοι· Σαοὺλ ἀδελφέ, ἀνάβλεψον· κἀγὼ αὐτῇ τῇ ὥρᾳ ἀνέβλεψα
εἰς αὐτόν. ὁ δὲ εἶπεν· Ὁ θεὸς τῶν πατέρων ἡμῶν προεχειρίσατό 14
σε γνῶναι τὸ θέλημα αὐτοῦ καὶ ἰδεῖν τὸν δίκαιον καὶ ἀκοῦσαι
φωνὴν ἐκ τοῦ στόματος αὐτοῦ, ὅτι μάρτυς αὐτῷ πρὸς πάντας 15
ἀνθρώπους ἔσῃ ὧν ἑώρακας καὶ ἤκουσας. καὶ νῦν τί μέλλεις; 16
ἀναστὰς βάπτισαι καὶ ἀπόλουσαι τὰς ἁμαρτίας σου ἐπικαλεσά-
μενος τὸ ὄνομα αὐτοῦ. ἐγένετο δέ μοι ὑποστρέψαντι εἰς Ἰερου- 17
σαλὴμ καὶ προσευχομένου μου ἐν τῷ ἱερῷ γενέσθαι με ἐν ἐκστάσει
| καὶ ἰδεῖν αὐτὸν λέγοντά μοι· Σπεῦσον καὶ ἔξελθε ἐν τάχει ἐξ 18
Ἰερουσαλήμ, διότι οὐ παραδέξονταί σου μαρτυρίαν περὶ ἐμοῦ.
κἀγὼ εἶπον· Κύριε, αὐτοὶ ἐπίστανται ὅτι ἐγὼ ἤμην φυλακίζων 19
καὶ δέρων κατὰ τὰς συναγωγὰς τοὺς πιστεύοντας ἐπὶ σέ· καὶ 20
ὅτε ἐξεχύννετο τὸ αἷμα Στεφάνου τοῦ μάρτυρός του, καὶ αὐτὸς
ἤμην ἐφεστὼς καὶ συνευδοκῶν καὶ φυλάσσων τὰ ἱμάτια τῶν
ἀναιρούντων αὐτόν. καὶ εἶπεν πρός με· Πορεύου, ὅτι ἐγὼ εἰς 21
ἔθνη μακρὰν ἀποστελῶ σε. ἤκουον δὲ αὐτοῦ ἄχρι τούτου τοῦ 22
λόγου καὶ ἐπῆραν τὴν φωνὴν αὐτῶν λέγοντες· Αἶρε ἀπὸ τῆς γῆς
τὸν τοιοῦτον, οὐ γὰρ καθῆκεν αὐτὸν ζῆν. κραυγαζόντων τε 23

Editors   10 εντετακται] τετακται WH Soden JHR   11 ουδεν εβλεπον] ουκ ενεβλεπον
WH Soden JHR   ουδεν εβλεπον WHmg   15 εση before μαρτυς instead of after
ανθρωπους WH Soden JHR   20 εξεχυννετο] εξεχειτο Soden   21 απο-
στελω] εξαποστελω WH Soden JHR   αποστελω WHmg   23 τε] δε Soden

Old Uncial   10 εντετακται B   τετακται ℵA   εντεταλται B⁴   11 ουδεν εβλεπον B
ουκ ενεβλεπον ℵA   υπο Bℵ απο A   12 ευλαβης Bℵ   om A
μαρτυρουμενος Bℵ   μαρτυρομενος A   13 ανεβλεψα Bℵ   εβλεψα A
14 και 1° Bℵ   om A   του Bℵ   om A   15 εση after ανθρωπους B
before μαρτυς ℵA   18 ιδειν BA   ιδον ℵ   20 στεφανου Bℵ   om A
εφεστως Bℵ   εστως A   21 αποστελω B   εξαποστελω ℵAC (cf. D)
23 κραυγαζοντων BℵA(+D)   κραζοντων C   τε BAC   δε ℵ(+D)

Antiochian   10 περι παντων ων εντετακται σοι] τι σε δει HS   εντετακται] τετακται
LPS⸓   11 ουδεν εβλεπον] ουκ ενεβλεπον HLPSS⸓   12 ευλαβης]
ευσεβης S⸓   κατοικουντων] +εν δαμασκω HLS   15 εση before μαρτυς
instead of after ανθρωπους HLPSS⸓   16 αυτου] του κυριου HLSS⸓
17 μου] μοι S   με] μοι L   18 την μαρτυριαν HLPSS⸓   20 εξεχυν-
νετο] εξεχειτο HLPSS⸓   μαρτυρος] πρωτομαρτυρος L   συνευδοκων] +τη
αναιρεσει αυτου HLPSS⸓   om και before φυλασσων HLPS   21 αποστελω]
εξαποστελω HLPSS⸓ (cf. D)   22 καθηκεν] καθηκον S⸓   23 τε] δε
HLPSS⸓(+D)

περὶ πάντων ὧν ἐντέτακταί σοι ποιῆσαι] τί σε δεῖ ποιῆσαι
(or ποιεῖν) 1765 minn

11 ὡς δὲ] ἀναστὰς δὲ οὐκ ἐνέβλεπον· ὡς δὲ 1611

13 om εἰς αὐτόν 5

18 ἰδεῖν] ‹ε›ῖδον ℵ minn

20 μάρτυρος] πρωτομάρτυρος L 614 minn

21 καὶ φυλάσσων τὰ εἱμάτια τῶν ἀναιρούντων αὐτόν. καὶ εἶπεν
   πρός με· Πορεύου, ὅτι ἐγὼ εἰς ἔθνη μακρὰν ἐξαποστέλλω σε.
22 ἤκουσαν δὲ αὐτοῦ ἄχρι τούτου τοῦ λόγου καὶ ἐπῆραν τὴν φωνὴν
   αὐτ[ῶ]ν λέγοντες· Αἶρε ἀπὸ τῆς γῆς τὸν τοιοῦτ[ο]ν, οὐ γὰρ
23 καθῆκεν αὐτὸν ζῆν. κραυγαζόντω‹ν› δὲ καὶ ῥειπτόντω‹ν› τὰ

quae te oportet facere   11 ut autem surrexit non videbam a claritate lucis illius et **d**
ad manum deductus qui mecum erant veni in damascum   12 ananias quidam vir
timoratus secundum legem et testimonio ab omnibus judaeis   13 cum venisset ad me
dix[it] mihi saule saule frater aspi[c]e et ego ipsa hora aspexi   14 et dixit mihi d̄s
patrum nostrorum praeordinavit te ut cognosceris voluntatem ejus et videre justum
et audire vocem ex ore ejus   15 qui eris testis ejus aput omnes homines eorum quae
vidisti et audisti   16 et nunc quid expectas surge baptizare et ablue peccata tua
invocans nomen ejus   17 factum est autem mihi reverso hierusalem orante me in
templo fieri me in soporem   18 et vidi eum dicentem mihi festina et exi cito de
hierusalem quia non recipient testimonium meum   19 et dixi d̄ne ipsi sciunt quia
ego eram in carcere includens et caedens per synagogas eos qui credebant in te
20 et cum effunderetur sangui stephani martyris ego eram adsistans et consentiens

11 αναστας] *mg* [quum] surrexissem   Harclean

11 ουδεν εβλεπον B (cf. ουκ εβλεπον   For the 'Western' text with αναστας
E minn) seems to be a skilful correc- 1611 d gig hcl.*mg*, cf. Ephrem,
tion for ουκ ενεβλεπον, which is strange *Hymni et sermones*, ed. Lamy, i.
in the sense of 'was without sight.'   p. 203.

αὐτῶν καὶ ῥειπτούντων τὰ ἱμάτια καὶ κονιορτὸν βαλλόντων εἰς
τὸν ἀέρα | ἐκέλευσεν ὁ χειλίαρχος εἰσάγεσθαι αὐτὸν εἰς τὴν παρεμ- 24
βολήν, εἴπας μάστιξιν ἀνετάζεσθαι αὐτὸν ἵνα ἐπιγνῷ δι᾽ ἣν αἰτίαν
οὕτως ἐπεφώνουν αὐτῷ. ὡς δὲ προέτειναν αὐτὸν τοῖς ἱμᾶσιν 25
εἶπεν πρὸς τὸν ἑστῶτα ἑκατόνταρχον ὁ Παῦλος· Εἰ ἄνθρωπον
Ῥωμαῖον καὶ ἀκατάκριτον ἔξεστιν ὑμῖν μαστίζειν; ἀκούσας δὲ 26
ὁ ἑκατόνταρχος προσελθὼν· τῷ χειλιάρχῳ ἀπήγγειλεν λέγων·
Τί μέλλεις ποιεῖν; ὁ γὰρ ἄνθρωπος οὗτος Ῥωμαῖός ἐστιν. | προσ- 27
ελθὼν δὲ ὁ χειλίαρχος εἶπεν αὐτῷ· Λέγε μοι, σὺ Ῥωμαῖος εἶ;
ὁ δὲ ἔφη· Ναεί. | ἀπεκρίθη δὲ ὁ χειλίαρχος· Ἐγὼ πολλοῦ κε- 28
φαλαίου τὴν πολειτείαν ταύτην ἐκτησάμην. ὁ δὲ Παῦλος ἔφη·
Ἐγὼ δὲ καὶ γεγέννημαι. εὐθέως οὖν ἀπέστησαν ἀπ᾽ αὐτοῦ οἱ 29
μέλλοντες αὐτὸν ἀνετάζειν· καὶ ὁ χειλίαρχος δὲ ἐφοβήθη ἐπιγνοὺς
ὅτι Ῥωμαῖός ἐστιν καὶ ὅτι αὐτὸν ἦν δεδεκώς.

Τῇ δὲ ἐπαύριον βουλόμενος γνῶναι τὸ ἀσφαλὲς τὸ τί κατηγο- 30
ρεῖται ὑπὸ τῶν Ἰουδαίων ἔλυσεν αὐτόν, καὶ ἐκέλευσεν συνελθεῖν
τοὺς ἀρχιερεῖς καὶ πᾶν τὸ συνέδριον, καὶ καταγαγὼν τὸν Παῦλον
ἔστησεν εἰς αὐτούς. ἀτενίσας δὲ Παῦλος τῷ συνεδρίῳ εἶπεν· XXIII
Ἄνδρες ἀδελφοί, ἐγὼ πάσῃ συνειδήσει ἀγαθῇ πεπολίτευμαι τῷ
θεῷ ἄχρι ταύτης τῆς ἡμέρας. ὁ δὲ ἀρχιερεὺς Ἀνανίας ἐπέταξεν 2
τοῖς παρεστῶσιν αὐτῷ τύπτειν αὐτοῦ τὸ στόμα. τότε ὁ Παῦλος 3
πρὸς αὐτὸν εἶπεν· Τύπτειν σε μέλλει ὁ θεός, τοῖχε κεκονιαμένε·
καὶ σὺ κάθη κρείνων με κατὰ τὸν νόμον, καὶ παρανομῶν κελεύεις
με τύπτεσθαι; | οἱ δὲ παρεστῶτες εἶπαν· Τὸν ἀρχιερέα τοῦ θεοῦ 4

Editors   26 εκατονταρχης WH JHR   1 τω συνεδριω ο παυλος WHmg Soden

Old Uncial   24 επιγνω BℵC(+D)   γνω A   25 εξεστιν BACℵᶜ(+D)   εστιν ℵ
26 εκατονταρχος Bℵᶜ   εκατονταρχης ℵAC(+D)   27 μοι BACℵᶜ(+D)   om ℵ
28 δε 1° BℵC   om A   την BℵA(+D)   om C   δε 3° BAℵᶜ(+D)   om ℵC
γεγεννημαι BℵC(+D)   γεγενημαι A   29 δε BACℵᶜ   om ℵ   1 παυλος
τω συνεδριω B   τω συνεδριω ο παυλος ℵAC   2 επεταξεν BℵA   εκελευσεν C
αυτω BACℵᶜ   om ℵ   3 προς αυτον before ειπεν BA   after ειπεν C
before ο παυλος ℵ

Antiochian   23 ρειπτουντων] ριπτοντων HLS(+D)   24 ο χειλιαρχος εισαγεσθαι αυτον]
αυτον ο χιλιαρχος αγεσθαι HLPSϚ   25 προετειναν] προετεινεν PϚ   προσετεινεν
HS   μαστιζειν υμιν H   26 απηγγειλεν τω χιλιαρχω HLPSϚ
λεγων] +ορα HLPSϚ(+D)   27 αυτω] τω παυλω L   μοι] +ει LPϚ
28 δε 1°] τε HPSϚ   om L   om ο δε παυλος εφη H   29 ην αυτον HLPSϚ
30 υπο] παρα HLPSϚ   αυτον] +απο των δεσμων HLPSϚ   συνελθειν]
ελθειν HPLSϚ   παν] ολον HLPSϚ   συνεδριον] +αυτων HLPSϚ
1 ο παυλος HLPSϚ

CODEX BEZAE 215

24 εἰμάτια καὶ κονιορτὸν βαλλόντων εἰς τὸν οὐρανὸν | ἐκέλευσεν ὁ
χειλίαρχος εἰσάγεσθαι αὐτὸν εἰς τὴν παρεμβολήν, εἴπας μάστιξιν
ἀνετάζειν αὐτὸν ἵνα ἐπιγνῷ δι' ἣν αἰτίαν οὕτως κατεφώνουν περὶ
25 αὐτοῦ. ὡς δὲ προσέτιναν αὐτὸν τοῖς εἵμασιν εἶπεν πρὸς τὸν
ἑστῶτα ἑκατοντάρχην· Εἰ ἔξεστιν ὑμεῖν ἄνθρωπον 'Ρωμαῖον
26 καὶ ἀκατάκριτον μαστίζειν; τοῦτο ἀκούσας ὁ ἑκατονάρχης ὅτι
'Ρωμαῖον ἑαυτὸν λέγει προσελθὼν τῷ χειλειάρχῳ [.]πήγγειλεν
αὐτῷ· Ὅρα τί μέλλεις ποιεῖν· [ὁ] ἄνθρωπος οὗτος 'Ρωμαῖός
27 ἐστιν. τότε προσελθὼν ὁ χειλίαρχος ἐπηρώτησεν αὐτόν· Λέγε
28 μοι, σὺ 'Ρωμαῖος εἶ; ὁ δὲ εἶπεν· Εἰμί. | καὶ ἀποκριθεὶς ὁ
χειλίαρχος [καὶ] εἶπεν· Ἐγὼ οἶδα πόσου κεφαλαίου τὴν
πολειτείαν ταύτην ἐκτησάμην. Παῦλος δὲ ἔφη· Ἐγὼ δὲ καὶ
29 γεγέννημαι. τότε ἀπέστησαν ἀπ' αὐτοῦ

δεδεκώς] + καὶ παραχρῆμα ἔλυσεν αὐτόν 614 1611
30 τῇ δὲ ἐπαύριον] τῇ τε ἐπιούσῃ 1518 2138 (614)
'Ιουδαίων] + πέμψας 614 1611 minn

26 επηγγειλεν Wetstein, Kipling

4 sic insilis in sacerdotem dei maledicendo ?	Cyprian, Ep. 3, 2 ; 59, 4 ; 66, 3
4 dei] om Ep. 66, most codices	

26 αυτω] ⁎ ei ✓   28 δε και] autem etiam ⁎ in ea ✓   29 και Harclean
παραχρημα ελυσεν αυτον] ⁎ et statim solvit eum ✓   30 πεμψας] ⁎ misit ✓

26 εκατονταρχος ΒℵᶜΕ Antiochian. The value of the confirmation of B by the Antiochian text is here diminished by the fact that the latter shows in Acts a certain tendency to adopt the second-declension form of this word.

The reading επηγγειλεν in D is attested by Wetstein (1716) and Kipling (before 1793). These collators may have been able to read more than is possible to-day ; in any case επηγγειλεν is out of the question for the text of Acts.

28 Bede, *Expositio*, supported in part and with minor variation by vg. *codd* and Bohemian version, knew the following text of the first half of this verse : *dixit tribunus, tam facile dicis civem romanum esse? ego enim scio quanto pretio civilitatem istam possedi.* This may be a 'Western' survival,

otherwise unattested (except for οιδα ποσου D), or may be a Latin expansion. For hcl.*mg* cf. *in ea* vg.cod.*R.*

29 From this point on, to the end of Acts, Codex Bezae is lacking. The Latin side stops in the middle of vs. 20.

29, 30 The 'Western' addition in vs. 29 of και παραχρημα ελυσεν αυτον makes ελυσεν αυτον και in vs. 30 otiose, and that phrase is omitted by sah. The insertion before ελυσεν, vs. 30, of πεμψας 614 1611 minn, 'misit' hcl ⁎, suggests that the 'Western' text here substituted επεμψεν for ελυσεν.

4 The translation used by Cyprian, *sic insilis in sacerdotem dei maledicendo*, perhaps shows that the 'Western' text offered here some kind of intensifying expansion, but Zahn's rendering ουτως εισπηδας εις τον ιερεα του θεου λοιδορων is not convincing.

λοιδορεῖς; | ἔφη τε ὁ Παῦλος· Οὐκ ᾔδειν, ἀδελφοί, ὅτι ἐστὶν 5

Ex. xxii. 28 ἀρχιερεύς· γέγραπται γὰρ ὅτι "Αρχοντα τοῦ λαοῦ σου οὐκ ἐρεῖς

κακῶς. γνοὺς δὲ ὁ Παῦλος ὅτι τὸ ἓν μέρος ἐστὶν Σαδδουκαίων 6

τὸ δὲ ἕτερον Φαρεισαίων ἔκραζεν ἐν τῷ συνεδρίῳ· "Ανδρες ἀδελφοί,

ἐγὼ Φαρεισαῖός εἰμι, υἱὸς Φαρεισαίων· περὶ ἐλπίδος καὶ ἀνα-

στάσεως νεκρῶν κρείνομαι. τοῦτο δὲ αὐτοῦ λαλοῦντος ἐπέπεσε 7

στάσις τῶν Φαρεισαίων καὶ Σαδδουκαίων, καὶ ἐσχίσθη τὸ πλῆθος.

Σαδδουκαῖοι γὰρ λέγουσιν μὴ εἶναι ἀνάστασιν μήτε ἄγγελον μήτε 8

πνεῦμα, Φαρεισαῖοι δὲ ὁμολογοῦσιν τὰ ἀμφότερα. ἐγένετο δὲ 9

κραυγὴ μεγάλη, καὶ ἀναστάντες τινὲς τῶν γραμματέων τοῦ

μέρους τῶν Φαρεισαίων διεμάχοντο λέγοντες· Οὐδὲν κακὸν εὑρί-

σκομεν ἐν τῷ ἀνθρώπῳ τούτῳ· εἰ δὲ πνεῦμα ἐλάλησεν αὐτῷ ἢ

ἄγγελος; πολλῆς δὲ γεινομένης στάσεως φοβηθεὶς ὁ χειλίαρχος 10

μὴ διασπασθῇ ὁ Παῦλος ὑπ' αὐτῶν ἐκέλευσεν τὸ στράτευμα

καταβὰν ἁρπάσαι αὐτὸν ἐκ μέσου αὐτῶν, ἄγειν εἰς τὴν παρεμβο-

λήν. τῇ δὲ ἐπιούσῃ νυκτὶ ἐπιστὰς αὐτῷ ὁ κύριος εἶπεν· Θάρσει, 11

ὡς γὰρ διεμαρτύρω τὰ περὶ ἐμοῦ εἰς Ἰερουσαλὴμ οὕτω σε δεῖ

καὶ εἰς Ῥώμην μαρτυρῆσαι. γενομένης τε ἡμέρας ποιήσαντες 12

συστροφὴν οἱ Ἰουδαῖοι ἀνεθεμάτισαν ἑαυτοὺς λέγοντες μήτε

Editors

6 νεκρων] +εγω WHmg JHR   7 λαλουντος] ειποντος WHmg Soden
επεπεσε] εγενετο WH Soden JHR   επεπεσεν WHmg   8 σαδδουκαιοι]
+μεν WHmg Soden JHR   10 γενομενης Soden   αγειν] +τε WHmg
Soden JHR   12 τε] δε WH Soden JHR   τε WHmg

Old Uncial

5 οτι 2° BℵA   om C   6 εκραζεν BℵC εκραξεν A   νεκρων B
+εγω ℵAC(?)C²   7 λαλουντος B λαλησαντος C ειπαντος ℵ ειποντος Aℵᶜ
επεπεσε B επεσε B² vid εγενετο ℵAC   φαρισαιων και σαδδουκαιων BAC
σαδδουκαιων και φαρισαιων ℵ   8 σαδδουκαιοι B   +μεν ℵAC
9 τινες των γραμματεων Bℵ   τινες εκ των γραμματεων C   τινες A   του
μερους BℵC   om A   διεμαχοντο BAC +προς αλληλους ℵ   εν BACℵᶜ 81
om ℵ   10 γεινομενης στασεως Bℵ στασεως γενομενης AC 81   υπ
BℵA 81 απ C   εκ μεσου αυτων BACℵᶜ 81 om ℵ   αγειν B αγειν τε
ℵC αγειν δε 81 απαγειν τε A   11 θαρσει BℵAC +παυλε 81   διεμαρτυρω
BℵA 81 διεμαρτυρου C   12 τε B δε ℵAC 81   λεγοντες BℵA 81 om
Cℵᶜ

Antiochian

5 om οτι 2° HLPSS͞   6 ετερον] +των L   εκραξεν HLPSS͞
φαρισαιων 2°] φαρισαιου HLPSS͞   νεκρων] +εγω HLPSS͞   7 λαλησαντος
HLPSS͞   επεπεσε] εγενετο HLPSS͞   των σαδδουκαιων HLSS͞
om και σαδδουκαιων P   8 σαδδουκαιοι] +μεν HLPSS͞   μητε 1°] μηδε
HLPSS͞   9 τινες των γραμματεων] γραμματεις HLP   οι γραμματεις SS͞
αγγελος] +μη θεομαχωμεν HLPSS͞   10 γενομενης HLPSS͞   φοβηθεις]
ευλαβηθεις HLPSS͞   καταβαν] καταβηναι και HLPS   αγειν] +τε HLPSS͞
11 θαρσει] +παυλε HLPSS͞   12 τε] δε HLPSS͞   συστροφην οι ιουδαιοι]
τινες των ιουδαιων συστροφην HPSS͞   συστροφην τινες των ιουδαιων L

XXIII 6   om νεκρῶν 1898 minn

10   ἄγειν] + τε אAC HLPS

11   θάρσει] + Παῦλε HLPS

12   οἱ Ἰουδαῖοι] τινες τῶν Ἰουδαίων HLPS

---

8 confitentur esse resurrectionem et ang[elum et] s͞p͞m. 9 et cum clamor ortus h esset inter eos, divi[debantur]: et quidam de scribis et parte Phariseorum co[ntradice]bant, dicentes: quid autem mali in hoc homine [inveni]mus? ssip͞s͞p͞u͞s locutus est ad eum vel angelus? 10 [et cū] e[s]set inter illos magna dissensio, timens tr[ibunus] ne carperetur ab eis Paulus, jussit numerum [militū] venire, et rapere eum de medio ipsorum, et ad[ducere] in castra. 11 sequenti autem nocte adstitit ei d͞[ns, et ait]: bono animo esto, Paule: quomodo enim testi[monium] perhibebas Hierosolymis, ita oportet et Rom[ae testi]monium dicere. 12 et cum dies factus est, cong[regave]runt se quidam ex Judeis, et devoverunt se, di[centes] neque edere nequae vivere donec occi-

---

6 viri [inquit] fratres, ego Pharisaeus sum, filius Pharisaeorum, de spe nunc et de resurrectione judicor apud vos.   Tertullian, *Res. carn.* 39

9 [non te terremus, qui nec timemus, sed velim ut omnes salvos facere possimus monendo μὴ θεομαχεῖν.]   *Scap.* 4

---

5 nesciebam, fratres, quia pontifex est.   scriptum est enim: principem tuae plebis non maledices.   Cyprian, *Ep.* 3, 2; 59, 4; 66, 3

5 principi *Ep.* 59   plebis tuae *Ep.* 3

---

6 περι ελπιδος] ※ et ✓ de spe   12 λεγοντες] *mg* dicentes   Harclean

---

6 The omission of εγω before κρεινομαι by B is supported only by gig (and the free rendering of Tert, cf. Acts xxiv. 21), and is not to be accepted. 10 The omission of τε B 69 is probably an accidental error.

φαγεῖν μήτε πεῖν ἕως οὗ ἀποκτείνωσιν τὸν Παῦλον. ἦσαν δὲ 13
πλείους τεσσεράκοντα οἱ ταύτην τὴν συνωμοσίαν ποιησάμενοι·
οἵτινες προσελθόντες τοῖς ἀρχιερεῦσιν καὶ τοῖς πρεσβυτέροις 14
εἶπαν· Ἀναθέματι ἀνεθεματίσαμεν ἑαυτοὺς μηδενὸς γεύσασθαι
ἕως οὗ ἀποκτείνωμεν τὸν Παῦλον. νῦν οὖν ὑμεῖς ἐμφανίσατε 15
τῷ χειλιάρχῳ σὺν τῷ συνεδρίῳ ὅπως καταγάγῃ αὐτὸν εἰς ὑμᾶς
ὡς μέλλοντας διαγεινώσκειν ἀκριβέστερον τὰ περὶ αὐτοῦ· ἡμεῖς
δὲ πρὸ τοῦ ἐγγίσαι αὐτὸν ἕτοιμοί ἐσμεν τοῦ ἀνελεῖν αὐτόν. ἀκού- 16
σας δὲ ὁ υἱὸς τῆς ἀδελφῆς Παύλου τὴν ἐνέδραν παραγενάμενος
καὶ εἰσελθὼν εἰς τὴν παρεμβολὴν ἀπήγγειλεν τῷ Παύλῳ. προσ- 17
καλεσάμενος δὲ ὁ Παῦλος ἕνα τῶν ἑκατονταρχῶν ἔφη· Τὸν νεανίαν τοῦτον ἄπαγε πρὸς τὸν χειλίαρχον, ἔχει γὰρ ἀπαγγεῖλαί τι
αὐτῷ. ὁ μὲν οὖν παραλαβὼν αὐτὸν ἤγαγεν πρὸς τὸν χειλίαρχον 18
καί φησιν· Ὁ δέσμιος Παῦλος προσκαλεσάμενός με ἠρώτησεν
τοῦτον τὸν νεανίαν ἀγαγεῖν πρὸς σέ, ἔχοντά τι λαλῆσαι. ἐπι- 19
λαβόμενος δὲ τῆς χειρὸς αὐτοῦ ὁ χειλίαρχος καὶ ἀναχωρήσας
κατ' ἰδίαν ἐπυνθάνετο· Τί ἐστιν ὃ ἔχεις ἀπαγγεῖλαί μοι; | εἶπεν 20
δὲ ὅτι Οἱ Ἰουδαῖοι συνέθεντο τοῦ ἐρωτῆσαί σε ὅπως αὔριον
τὸν Παῦλον καταγάγῃς εἰς τὸ συνέδριον ὡς μέλλων τι ἀκρειβέστερον πυνθάνεσθαι περὶ αὐτοῦ· σὺ οὖν μὴ πεισθῇς αὐτοῖς, 21

Editors   15 εις] προς Soden   17 απαγαγε Soden   18 νεανιαν] νεανισκον
WHmg Soden   λαλησαι] +σοι WH Soden JHR   20 μελλον JHR

Old Uncial   12 αποκτεινωσιν BℵC 81   ανελωσιν A   15 εις BℵA 81   προς C
διαγεινωσκειν ακριβεστερον BℵA 81   ακριβεστερον γινωσκειν C   του 2° BACℵc 81
om ℵ   16 ⸀παρεμβολην BℵC 81   συναγωγην A   17 εφη BℵA   ειπεν C 81
απαγε Bℵ 81   απαγαγε AC   απαγγειλαι τι BA 81   τι απαγγειλαι ℵC
18 νεανιαν B   νεανισκον ℵA 81   λαλησαι B   +σοι B² vidℵA 81   19 επι-
λαβομενος BAℵc 81   επιλαβομενου ℵ   κατ ιδιαν επυνθανετο Bℵ 81   επυνθανετο κατ ιδιαν A   20 μελλων BA 81   μελλον ℵ   μελλοντων ℵc

Antiochian   13 πεποιηκοτες HPSꙅ   ποιησαντες L   15 οπως] +αυριον HLPSꙅ
αυτον καταγαγη HPSꙅ   εις] προς HLPSꙅ   16 την ενεδραν] το ενεδρον
HLPSꙅ   17 απαγαγε HLPSꙅ   τι απαγγειλαι HLPSꙅ
18 λαλησαι] +σοι HLPSꙅ   20 εις το συνεδριον καταγαγης τον παυλον HPSꙅ
καταγαγης τον παυλον εις το συνεδριον L   μελλοντα HLPS   μελλοντες ꙅ
ακριβεστερον] +τι S   πυνθανεσθαι] +τι H

15 Comparison of h gig Lucifer hcl. *mg* sah points to a Greek 'Western' text approximately as follows (partly taken from Zahn): *νυν ουν ερωτωμεν υμας τουτο ημιν παρεχειν· συναγογοντες το συνεδριον εμφανισατε τω χιλιαρχω οπως καταγαγη αυτον εις υμας.* The substitution here of *συναγογοντες το συνεδριον* for *συν τω συνεδριω* is a distinct improvement on the part of the 'Western' paraphrast, and probably does justice to the meaning of the somewhat obscure original. Other details require mention as follows: (1) *petite a* [*tribuno*] h is probably only a free translation of the usual

15 om σὺν τῷ συνεδρίῳ (1829)
    om τὰ 614 2138
    ἀνελεῖν αὐτόν] + ἐὰν δέη καὶ ἀποθανεῖν 614 2147
19 ἐπυνθάνετο] + παρ' αὐτοῦ 1838
20 μέλλων] μέλλοντες minn
    περὶ] παρ' 1838

---

der[ent Paulū]. 13 erat autem plus XL qui se devoverant : 14 acces[serunt] h
itaque ad sacerdotes et majores natu, et dix[erunt] : devobimus nos ne quid
gustemus in totum, d[onec occi]damus Paulum. 15 nunc itaque rogamus vos
ho[c : nobis] praestetis ; congraegate concilium, et petite a [tribuno] uti
deducant eum ad vos, tamquam certius al[iquid in]quisituri de eo. nos autem
parati erimus ad ne[candum] eum, licet oporteat ad nos mori. 16 sed cum
aud[ivisset] juvenis filius sororis Pauli conventionem eo[rum, venit in cas]tra,
et intravit ad Paulum, et indicavit ei. 17 [et vocav]it Paulus unum ex cen-
turionib·, et dixit ei : juve[nem ist]um duc ad tribunum : habet enim quod illi
in[dicet. 18 qu]i confestim adduxit juvenem ad tribunum, †[habet e]nim quod
illi indicet qui confestim adduxit ju[venem] ad tribunum† dicens : victus me
Paulus vocavit [ad se, rog]ans uti istum perducerem ad te : quia habet quod
[indicet] tibi. 19 adpraehensa autem manu ejus, tribunus [. . . .]nes et secessit
cum eo et inquirebat ab eo, quid [esset q]uod haberet illi dicere. 20 qui ait :
Judaeis conven[it roga]ret te crastina die, ut deducas Laulum in conci[lium,
ta]mquam volentes certius ab eo aliquid inquire[re] : 21 ergo tu ne suadaris :

---

13 τεσσερακοντα] quadraginta ·✕· viri ✓   15 υμεις . . . εις υμας] mg Harclean
rogamus vos ut hoc nobis faciatis, ut quum congregaveritis congregationem,
indicetis tribuno ut producat eum ad nos   εαν δεη και αποθανειν] mg etiamsi
necesse sit mori   εγγισαι αυτον] appropinquet ·✕· ad vos ✓   16 την
ενεδραν] insidias ·✕· has ✓   17 εφη] dixit ·✕· ei ✓   18 ηρωτησεν]
petiit ·✕· a me ✓

Greek text ; (2) deducant h is an
error ; (3) εις (or προς) ημας minn
hcl.mg sah.best codd is due to accidental or thoughtless error ; (4) [in]-
quisituri h perhaps points to a Greek
reading μελλοντες, which may be
intended by the contraction in 81
(cf. Tregelles, Greek New Testament
ad loc.) ; but the variation does not
affect the sense.
The point of attachment for the
addition etiamsi necesse sit mori hcl.mg
is wrongly stated in White's edition.
In the MS. the indication follows
the words which represent τον ανελειν
αυτον.
19 The reconstruction of h proposed
by Buchanan [apud om]nes is very
doubtful. Berger proposed [ante homi-]
nes ; Zahn suggests [ejecit om]nes,
recommended by the following et.
20 μελλον ℵ 33 is probably the

original reading here, as the sense
requires that the ostensible motive
be ascribed to the sanhedrim or to
the Jews ; μελλων BA 81 minn is a
not unusual error of spelling ; the
Antiochian μελλοντα is peculiarly unfortunate. μελλοντες minn h pesh
hcl.text sah, and μελλοντων ℵ° minn,
one or the other of which underlies
gig vg, are secondary, but yield the
correct meaning. e has volens, which
is ambiguous ; E, interpreting this
as nominative masculine, has derived
therefrom the reading μελλων, and
must not be taken as supporting
BA 81, although it happens to agree
with them. It is barely possible that
h e pesh point to a 'Western' reading
with some form of θελω.
The reading of h was conver[it], a
blunder for convenit, to which the
diorthotes corrected it.

ἐνεδρεύουσιν γὰρ αὐτὸν ἐξ αὐτῶν ἄνδρες πλείους τεσσεράκοντα,
οἵτινες ἀνεθεμάτισαν ἑαυτοὺς μήτε φαγεῖν μήτε πεῖν ἕως οὗ
ἀνέλωσιν αὐτόν, καὶ νῦν ε<ἰ>σὶν ἕτοιμοι προσδεχόμενοι τὴν ἀπὸ
σοῦ ἐπαγγελίαν. ὁ μὲν οὖν χειλίαρχος ἀπέλυσε τὸν νεανίσκον 22
παραγγείλας μηδενὶ ἐκλαλῆσαι ὅτι ταῦτα ἐνεφάνισας πρὸς ἐμέ.
καὶ προσκαλεσάμενός τινας δύο τῶν ἑκατονταρχῶν εἶπεν· Ἑτοι- 23
μάσατε στρατιώτας διακοσίους ὅπως πορευθῶσιν ἕως Καισαρείας, καὶ ἱππεῖς ἑβδομήκοντα καὶ δεξιολάβους διακοσίους, ἀπὸ
τρίτης ὥρας τῆς νυκτός, κτήνη τε παραστῆσαι ἵνα ἐπιβιβάσαν- 24
τες τὸν Παῦλον διασῶσι πρὸς Φήλικα τὸν ἡγεμόνα, γράψας 25
ἐπιστολὴν ἔχουσαν τὸν τύπον τοῦτον· Κλαύδιος Λυσίας τῷ 26
κρατίστῳ ἡγεμόνι Φήλικι χαίρειν.   τὸν ἄνδρα τοῦτον συλλημ- 27
φθέντα ὑπὸ τῶν Ἰουδαίων καὶ μέλλοντα ἀναιρεῖσθαι ὑπ' αὐτῶν
ἐπιστὰς σὺν τῷ στρατεύματι ἐξειλάμην, μαθὼν ὅτι Ῥωμαῖός
ἐστιν, βουλόμενός τε ἐπιγνῶναι τὴν αἰτίαν δι' ἣν ἐνεκάλουν αὐτῷ· 28
| ὃν εὗρον ἐνκαλούμενον περὶ ζητημάτων τοῦ νόμου αὐτῶν, μηδὲν 29

    27 ανερεισθαι

Editors   23 δυο τινας Soden mg   24 διασωσι] διασωσωσι WH Soden JHR
28 τε] δε Soden mg   αυτω]+ [κατηγαγον εις το συνεδριον αυτων] WH
+ κατηγαγον αυτον εις το συνεδριον αυτων Soden   + κατηγαγον εις το συνεδριον αυτων
JHR

Old Uncial   21 εισιν B² vid   22 νεανισκον BℵA   νεανιαν 81   παραγγειλας BℵA
+αυτον 81   23 τινας δυο Bℵ 81   δυο τινας A   δεξιολαβους Bℵ 81
δεξιοβολους A   24 διασωσι B   διασωσωσι B²(?)(B³ Tdf)ℵA 81   25 εχουσαν
Bℵ 81   περιεχουσαν A   28 τε BℵA   δε 81   αυτω B 81   +κατηγαγον
(+αυτον B²) εις το συνεδριον αυτων B²ℵA

Antiochian   21 om πλειους S   ετοιμοι εισι HLPSϛ   22 νεανισκον] νεανιαν
HLPSϛ   23 δυο τινας HLPSϛ   24 om τε H   διασωσι] διασωσωσι
LPSϛ   25 εχουσαν] περιεχουσαν HLPSϛ   26 om φηλικι H (bu
supplied in mg, apparently by H*)   27 εξειλαμην] +αυτον HLPSϛ
28 τε] δε HLPSϛ   επιγνωναι] γνωναι HLPSϛ   αυτω] +κατηγαγον
αυτον εις το συνεδριον αυτων HLPSϛ

23 (1) The reconstruction [armati] h
is supported by seven minuscules (von
Soden) and possibly by the language of
Cassiodorus, Complexiones ad loc.

(2) Corresponding to the closing
words of vs. 23 and the opening words
of vs. 24 in h, we read in vg.codex
colbertinus (after απο τριτης ωρας της
νυκτος): sint parati exire et centurionibus praecepit stare, and in cod.
wernigerod.: et parati sint exire. The
reading of hcl.mg is wrongly attached

and is mistranslated by White. It
is also wrongly attached (after ειπεν
[αυτοις]) in the Harclean ms. itself, for
it plainly belongs at the close of the
verse, the main body of which is shown
by neighbouring marginal notes to
have been present in the text from
which these notes are taken. The
meaning of hcl.mg is probably, as
given above, dixerunt: parati erunt
exire; although the copula may in
itself be rendered equally well sint

22 om ταῦτα 88 915
23 om τινας 1831 1838
om διακοσίους 1° 920
στρατιώτας] + ἐνόπλους 88 915 minn
ἑβδομήκοντα] ἑκατὸν 614 1611
24 Παῦλον] + νυκτὸς 614 1611
διασῶσι] + εἰς Καισαρείαν 614 1611 2147
25 γράψας . . . τοῦτον] ἐφοβήθη γὰρ μήποτε ἁρπάσαντες αὐτὸν
οἱ Ἰουδαῖοι ἀποκτένωσι, καὶ αὐτὸς μεταξὺ ἔγκλησιν ἔχῃ ὡς
ἀργύριον εἰληφώς· ἔγραψε δὲ ἐπιστολὴν περιέχουσαν τάδε 614
(2147)
29 εὗρον] εὑρὼν 614
αὐτῶν] + Μωυσέως καὶ Ἰησοῦ τινος 614 2147

---

sunt enim ex eis plus homi[nib· xl] parati qui eum interficiant : qui et devo- h
verunt [se null]am rem gustaturos, quoadusq· hoc agant : [et nunc] parati sunt,
sperantes pollicitationem tuam.   22 et [tribun]us quidem juvenem illum dimisit, praecipiens [ne quis] sciret quod sibi nuntiasset.   23 et vocavit duos [ex
cent]urionibus, et dixit : praeparate milites qui eant [armati] usq· in Caesarea,
equites centum et pedites du[centos.   e]t ad hora noctis tertiam imperat ut
parati [essent ad] eundum : 24 et centurionib· praecepit uti jumenta [praepara-
r]ent et inponerent Paulum, et deducerent per noc[tem]

---

23 ειπεν] dixit ※ iis ✓   εκατον] mg centum   24 κτηνη τε Harclean
παραστησαι] mg dixerunt : Parati erunt exire. et centurionibus jussit ut etiam
jumentum pararent   νυκτος] mg per noctem   εις καισαρειαν] ※ in
Caesaream ✓   25 εφοβηθη γαρ . . . αργυριον ειληφως] ※ timebat enim
ne forte raperent eum Judaei, occiderent eum, et ipse postea calumnias sustineret
tanquam qui pecuniam accepisset ✓   εγραψε δε επιστολην περιεχουσαν ταδε]
mg scripsit autem epistolam in qua erant haec   29 μωυσεως και ιησου τινος]
mg Mosis et Jesu cujusdam

---

or *sunt* or *estote*. In any case hcl. *mg*
attests a genuine 'Western' expansion, which also underlies the Latin
of h.
(3) εβδομηκοντα B‡A 81 Antiochian,
εκατον 614 1611 h hcl. *mg* sah.
(4) The internal difficulty of the
verse is avoided by h, which, if a
literal rendering, implies, as the
Greek original, στρατιωτας without διακοσιους and the omission of και before
ιππεις. But whether this thoroughly
intelligible text, which treats στρατιώτας as including the ἱππεῖς and δεξιο-
λάβοι, is really due to the Greek or to
improvement by a translator remains
hard to say. The apparently isolated

reading of 920, which omits διακοσιους
after δεξιολαβους, is not of sufficient
weight to give any help.
25 The additional sentences of the
'Western' text constitute a substitute
for γραψας επιστολην εχουσαν τον τυπον
τουτον, and should follow ηγεμονα,
vs. 24, as they do in 2147 perp gig hcl.
※ and *mg*, vg.*codd* ; cf. Cassiodorus.
In the conflate text of 614 the gloss
is inserted inappropriately after τουτον,
vs. 25.
28 The omission of κατηγαγον εις
το συνεδριον αυτων B 81 is by homoeoteleuton. Were the words written
in the margin of B before the ms.
was issued from the scriptorium ?

δὲ ἄξιον θανάτου ἢ δεσμῶν ἔχοντα ἔγκλημα. μηνυθείσης δέ 30
μοι ἐπιβουλῆς εἰς τὸν ἄνδρα ἔσεσθαι ἐξαυτῆς ἔπεμψα πρὸς σέ,
παραγγείλας καὶ τοῖς κατηγόροις λέγειν πρὸς αὐτὸν ἐπὶ σοῦ.
οἱ μὲν οὖν στρατιῶται κατὰ τὸ διατεταγμένον αὐτοῖς ἀναλαβόντες 31
τὸν Παῦλον ἤγαγον διὰ νυκτὸς εἰς τὴν Ἀντιπατρίδα· τῇ δὲ 32
ἐπαύριον ἐάσαντες τοὺς ἱππεῖς ἀπέρχεσθαι σὺν αὐτῷ ὑπέστρεψαν
εἰς τὴν παρεμβολήν· οἵτινες εἰσελθόντες εἰς τὴν Καισαρείαν καὶ 33
ἀναδόντες τὴν ἐπιστολὴν τῷ ἡγεμόνι παρέστησαν καὶ τὸν Παῦλον
αὐτῷ. ἀναγνοὺς δὲ καὶ ἐπερωτήσας ἐκ ποίας ἐπαρχείας ἐστὶν 34
καὶ πυθόμενος ὅτι ἀπὸ Κιλικίας, | Διακούσομαί σου, ἔφη, ὅταν 35
καὶ οἱ κατήγοροί σου παραγένωνται· κελεύσας ἐν τῷ πραιτωρίῳ
τῷ Ἡρῴδου φυλάσσεσθαι αὐτόν.
    Μετὰ δὲ πέντε ἡμέρας κατέβη ὁ ἀρχιερεὺς Ἀνανίας μετὰ XXIV
πρεσβυτέρων τινῶν καὶ ῥήτορος Τερτύλλου τινός, οἵτινες ἐνεφάνισαν τῷ ἡγεμόνι κατὰ τοῦ Παύλου. κληθέντος δὲ ἤρξατο 2
κατηγορεῖν ὁ Τέρτυλλος λέγων· Πολλῆς εἰρήνης τυγχάνοντες
διὰ σοῦ καὶ διορθωμάτων γεινομένων τῷ ἔθνει τούτῳ διὰ τῆς
σῆς προνοίας | πάντῃ τε καὶ πανταχοῦ ἀποδεχόμεθα, κράτιστε 3
Φῆλιξ, μετὰ πάσης εὐχαριστίας. ἵνα δὲ μὴ ἐπὶ πλεῖόν σε ἐν- 4
κόπτω, παρακαλῶ ἀκοῦσαί σε ἡμῶν συντόμως τῇ σῇ ἐπιεικείᾳ.
εὑρόντες γὰρ τὸν ἄνδρα τοῦτον λοιμὸν καὶ κεινοῦντα στάσεις 5
πᾶσι τοῖς Ἰουδαίοις τοῖς κατὰ τὴν οἰκουμένην πρωτοστάτην τε

ἔχοντα ἔγκλημα] + ἐξήγαγον αὐτὸν μόλις τῇ βίᾳ 614 2147

30   om εἰς τὸν ἄνδρα 36ᵃ 431

34, 35   ἀναγνοὺς δὲ . . . Διακούσομαί σου] ἀναγνοὺς δὲ τὴν ἐπιστολὴν ἐπηρώτησε τὸν Παῦλον· Ἐκ ποίας ἐπαρχίας εἶ; ἔφη·
Κίλιξ. καὶ πυθόμενος ἔφη· Ἀκούσομαί σου 614 2147

35   om καὶ 614 2138 minn

---

29 εξηγαγον αυτον μολις τη βια] ※ abduxi eum vix violentia √   34–35 την Harclean
επιστολην . . . παραγενωνται] mg epistolam, interrogavit Paulum : Ex quali
provincia es ? et dixit : Cilicia. et quum cognovisset, dixit : Audiam quum
accusatores tui venerint

---

30 The omission by B of τα before
προς αυτον is an accidental corruption.
προς αυτον B 81 Antiochian sah is to
be preferred to the weaker phrase
with αυτους אA.

2 B unsupported omits αυτου after
κληθεντος δε ; for grammatical parallels
cf. Moulton, *Prolegomena*, p. 74, Blass-
Debrunner, *Grammatik*, § 423. 6.
Doubtless an accidental error.

5 For πασι τοις ιουδαιοις τοις κατα
την οικουμενην, gig reads *non tantum
generi nostro sed fere universo orbe
terrarum et omnibus judeis,* doubtless
the ' Western ' rewriting, and wholly
in accord with the glossator's method
elsewhere.

τῆς τῶν Ναζωραίων αἱρέσεως, ὃς καὶ τὸ ἱερὸν ἐπείρασεν βεβη- 6
λῶσαι, ὃν καὶ ἐκρατήσαμεν, | παρ᾽ οὗ δυνήσῃ αὐτὸς ἀνακρείνας 8
περὶ πάντων τούτων ἐπιγνῶναι ὧν ἡμεῖς κατηγοροῦμεν αὐτοῦ.
συνεπέθεντο δὲ καὶ οἱ Ἰουδαῖοι φάσκοντες ταῦτα οὕτως ἔχειν. 9
ἀπεκρίθη τε ὁ Παῦλος νεύσαντος αὐτῷ τοῦ ἡγεμόνος λέγειν· 10
Ἐκ πολλῶν ἐτῶν ὄντα σε κριτὴν τῷ ἔθνει τούτῳ ἐπιστάμενος
εὐθύμως τὰ περὶ ἐμαυτοῦ ἀπολογοῦμαι, δυναμένου σου ἐπιγνῶναι, 11
ὅτι οὐ πλείους εἰσίν μοι ἡμέραι δώδεκα ἀφ᾽ ἧς ἀνέβην προσκυνήσων εἰς Ἰερουσαλήμ, καὶ οὔτε ἐν τῷ ἱερῷ εὗρόν με πρός 12
τινα διαλεγόμενον ἢ ἐπίστασιν ποιοῦντα ὄχλου οὔτε ἐν ταῖς συναγωγαῖς οὔτε κατὰ τὴν πόλιν, οὐδὲ παραστῆσαι δύνανταί σοι περὶ 13
ὧν νυνεὶ κατηγοροῦσίν μου. ὁμολογῶ δὲ τοῦτό σοι ὅτι κατὰ 14
τὴν ὁδὸν ἣν λέγουσιν αἵρεσιν οὕτως λατρεύω τῷ πατρῴῳ θεῷ,
πιστεύων τοῖς κατὰ νόμον καὶ τοῖς ἐν τοῖς προφήταις γεγραμ-
μένοις, | ἐλπίδα ἔχων εἰς τὸν θεόν, ἣν καὶ αὐτοὶ οὗτοι προσ- 15
δέχονται, ἀνάστασιν μέλλειν ἔσεσθαι δικαίων τε καὶ ἀδίκων· ἐν 16
τούτῳ καὶ αὐτὸς ἀσκῶ ἀπρόσκοπον συνείδησιν ἔχειν πρὸς τὸν
θεὸν καὶ τοὺς ἀνθρώπους διὰ παντός. δι᾽ ἐτῶν δὲ πλειόνων 17
ἐλεημοσύνας ποιήσων εἰς τὸ ἔθνος μου παρεγενόμην καὶ προσ-
φοράς, | ἐν αἷς εὗρόν με ἡγνισμένον ἐν τῷ ἱερῷ, οὐ μετὰ ὄχλου 18
οὐδὲ μετὰ θορύβου, τινὲς δὲ ἀπὸ τῆς Ἀσίας Ἰουδαῖοι, | οὓς ἔδει 19
ἐπὶ σοῦ παρεῖναι καὶ κατηγορεῖν εἴ τι ἔχοιεν πρὸς ἐμέ,—ἢ αὐτοὶ 20

Editors   14 πιστευων] +πασι WH Soden JHR   τον νομον WH Soden JHR

Old Uncial   8 αυτος Bﬡ 81   om A   11 σου Bﬡ 81   om A   προσκυνησων BﬡA
προσκυνησω 81   12 επιστασιν BﬡA   εποστασιαν 81   ουτε 3° BﬡA
ουδε 81   13 ουδε Bﬡ 81   ουτε A   σοι Bﬡ 81   σου A
14 πιστευων B   +πασι ﬡA 81   νομον B   τον νομον ﬡA 81   τοις εν Bﬡ 81
om Aﬡᶜ   15 εις τον BA 81   προς τον ﬡ   προς C   ουτοι BAC 81   om ﬡ
17 παρεγενομην και προσφορας BﬡC 81   και προσφορας παρεγενομην ﬡᶜ   om παρεγενομην A   18 δε BﬡA 81   +των C

Antiochian   6-8 εκρατησαμεν] +και κατα τον ημετερον νομον ηθελησαμεν κρινειν.   παρελθων
δε λυσιας ο χιλιαρχος μετα πολλης βιας εκ των χειρων ημων απηγαγε, κελευσας τους
κατηγορους αυτου ερχεσθαι επι σε ϛ   9 συνεπεθεντο] συνεθεντο ϛ   om οι
before ιουδαιοι L   10 τε] δε HLPSϛ   ευθυμως] ευθυμοτερον HLPSϛ
11 επιγνωναι] γνωναι HLPSϛ   ημεραι] +η ϛ   δωδεκα] δεκαδυο HLPSϛ
ανεβη L   εις] εν LPSϛ   12 επιστασιν] επισυστασιν HLPSϛ
om την S   13 ουδε] ουτε HLPSϛ   παραστησαι] +με ϛ   +με νυν HPS
om σοι HLPSϛ   νυνι] νυν HLPSϛ   14 πιστευων] πιστευ εν (πιστευω S)
πασι HLPSϛ   τον νομον HLPSϛ   om τοις εν HLPSϛ   15 εχω S
εσεσθαι] +νεκρων HLPSϛ   16 και 1°] δε HPSϛ   εχειν] εχων HLPS
προς] +τε LS   17 παρεγενομην ελεημοσυνας ποιησων εις το εθνος μου HLPSϛ
18 αις] οις HLPSϛ   om δε HLPS   19 δει HLSϛ

XXIV 6 ἐκρατήσαμεν] + καὶ κατὰ τὸν ἡμέτερον νόμον ἠθελήσαμεν
   7 κρίνειν. παρελθὼν δὲ Λυσίας ὁ χιλίαρχος μετὰ πολλῆς βίας
   8 ἐκ τῶν χειρῶν ἡμῶν ἀπήγαγε, κελεύσας τοὺς κατηγόρους αὐτοῦ
     ἔρχεσθαι ἐπὶ σοῦ (with minor variants) Ψ 614 minn
   9 συνεπέθεντο δὲ] εἰπόντος δὲ αὐτοῦ ταῦτα συνεπέθεντο 614
     (2147)
  10 κριτήν] + δίκαιον 614 minn
  11 προσκυνῆσαι Ψ 614

14 λέγουσιν] + καὶ 1611
    πατρῴῳ] + μου 614

---

    9 ειποντος δε αυτου ταυτα] ※ quum dixisset autem ille haec ✓   10 λεγειν] Harclean
mg defensionem habere pro se, statum autem assumens divinum dixit: Ex
multis annis es judex   12 κατα την πολιν] mg in foro   14 λεγουσιν]
+ mg et   17 δι] mg per

6-8 The long 'Western' expansion
is preserved in Ψ 614, many minn
(hence in ς), and passed into e (E) gig
many codd. of vg, pesh hcl.*text*, but is
omitted in older uncials, and in sah
boh. Note Lysias's μολις τη βια xxiii.
29 and Tertullus's μετα πολλης βιας
xxiv. 7, both 'Western.' Minn show
variants in minor details.
    The chief effect of the addition is
to cause παρ ου, vs. 8, to refer
apparently to Lysias, cf. vs. 22,
instead of Paul.
    10 To the strange gloss of hcl.*mg*
no other known text contains any
parallel. The last words of the gloss
(*es judex*) seem to show that επιστα-
μενος was omitted in this text. For
a similar gloss cf. xxvi. 1 hcl.*mg*.
    14 Gig *secundum sectam quam di-
cunt isti* and pesh ' in that doctrine (*or

heresy) in which they say' suggest
that the 'Western' text had a variant
in which την οδον did not appear.
From the text of gig the rendering
of vg *secundum sectam quam dicunt
heresim* is somehow to be explained.
See Wordsworth and White's note.
    18 The reading εν αις BℵAC 81 might
seem a correction of εν οις Antiochian,
but the latter is not attested earlier
than the 8th-9th century uncials, and
the reading of the older and usually
better witnesses is to be retained,
although with some hesitation.
    The addition following θορυβου
found in perp² vg.*codd* (with slight
minor variation), *et apprehenderunt me
clamantes et dicentes, tolle inimicum
nostrum*, seems to be proved ancient
by the reference in Ephrem's commentary ; cf. also xxi. 36 gig sah.

οὗτοι εἰπάτωσαν τί εὗρον ἀδίκημα στάντος μου ἐπὶ τοῦ συνεδρίου
| ἢ περὶ μιᾶς ταύτης φωνῆς ἧς ἐκέκραξα ἐν αὐτοῖς ἑστὼς ὅτι Περὶ 21
ἀναστάσεως νεκρῶν ἐγὼ κρείνομαι σήμερον ἐφ᾿ ὑμῶν. ἀν- 22
εβάλετο δὲ αὐτοὺς ὁ Φῆλιξ, ἀκρειβέστερον εἰδὼς τὰ περὶ τῆς
ὁδοῦ, εἴπας· "Οταν Λυσίας ὁ χειλίαρχος καταβῇ διαγνώσομαι
τὰ καθ᾿ ὑμᾶς· διαταξάμενος τῷ ἑκατοντάρχῃ τηρεῖσθαι αὐτὸν 23
ἔχειν τε ἄνεσιν καὶ μηδένα κωλύειν τῶν ἰδίων αὐτοῦ ὑπηρετεῖν
αὐτῷ. μετὰ δὲ ἡμέρας τινὰς παραγενόμενος ὁ Φῆλιξ σὺν Δρου- 24
σίλλῃ τῇ ἰδίᾳ γυναικὶ οὔσῃ Ἰουδαίᾳ μετεπέμψατο τὸν Παῦλον
καὶ ἤκουσεν αὐτοῦ περὶ τῆς εἰς Χριστὸν Ἰησοῦ⟨ν⟩ πίστεως.
διαλεγομένου δὲ αὐτοῦ περὶ δικαιοσύνης καὶ ἐγκρατείας καὶ τοῦ 25
κρίματος τοῦ μέλλοντος ἔμφοβος γενόμενος ὁ Φῆλιξ ἀπεκρίθη·
Τὸ νῦν ἔχον πορεύου, καιρὸν δὲ μεταλαβὼν μετακαλέσομαί σε·
ἅμα καὶ ἐλπίζων ὅτι χρήματα δοθήσετα⟨ι⟩ ὑπὸ τοῦ Παύλου· 26
διὸ καὶ πυκνότερον αὐτὸν μεταπεμπόμενος ὡμείλει αὐτῷ. διετίας 27
δὲ πληρωθείσης ἔλαβεν διάδοχον ὁ Φῆλιξ Πόρκιον Φῆστον·
θέλων τε χάριτα καταθέσθαι τοῖς Ἰουδαίοις ὁ Φῆλιξ κατέλιπε
τὸν Παῦλον δεδεμένον.

Φῆστος οὖν ἐπιβὰς τῇ ἐπαρχείᾳ μετὰ τρεῖς ἡμέρας ἀνέβη εἰς XXV

---

27   Φῆστον] + τὸν δὲ Παῦλον εἴασεν ἐν τηρήσει διὰ Δρούσιλλαν
614 2147

---

24 συν δρουσιλλη . . . παυλον] *mg* cum Drusilla uxore ejus quae erat Judaea,   Harclean
quae rogabat ut videret Paulum et audiret verbum.   volens igitur satisfacere ei
accersivit Paulum   27 τον δε παυλον ειασεν εν τηρησει δια δρουσιλλαν] *mg*
Paulum autem reliquit in carcere propter Drusillam

---

24 The gloss of hcl.*mg* implies a text in which a finite verb took the place of παραγενομενος. The language of Cassiodorus, *Post aliquot autem dies Drusilla uxor Felicis, quae erat Judaea. Post aliquot dies rogatus Felix a Drusilla conjuge sua coram ea Paulum fecit adduci,* seems to show acquaintance with a text like hcl.*mg.* The Bohemian version (Tischendorf) gives in part this 'Western' text. Pesh renders: 'And after a few days Felix sent, and Drusilla his wife, who was a Jewess, and summoned Paul, and they heard from him concerning faith in Christ.' The purpose of the expansion is to justify the mention of Drusilla by ascribing to her a part in the action. Note the corresponding paraphrase of the 'Western' text of vs. 27b in 614 hcl.*mg.*

1 Against the evidence of ℵA for επαρχειω, the reading επαρχεια B (and all others) is to be retained. The same variation is found in MSS. of Josephus and Eusebius ; we do not know what habits and tendencies, perhaps changing with succeeding centuries, may have led to the preference in a given case for the one or the other declension of this adjective. Cf. G. Kaibel, *Inscriptiones Graecae Italiae et Siciliae* (Inscr. Graecae xiv), No. 911, επιτροπευσαντι επαρχειου βριταννειας (third century after Christ, sarcophagus from Velletri).

For μετα τρεις ημερας gig has *post biduum*, s *post duos dies* ; Lucifer omits.

Ἰεροσόλυμα ἀπὸ Καισαρείας, ἐνεφάνισάν τε αὐτῷ οἱ ἀρχιερεῖς 2
καὶ οἱ πρῶτοι τῶν Ἰουδαίων κατὰ τοῦ Παύλου, καὶ παρεκάλουν
αὐτὸν | αἰτούμενοι χάριν κατ᾽ αὐτοῦ ὅπως μεταπέμψηται αὐτὸν 3
εἰς Ἰερουσαλήμ, ἐνέδραν ποιοῦντες ἀνελεῖν αὐτὸν κατὰ τὴν ὁδόν.
ὁ μὲν οὖν Φῆστος ἀπεκρίθη τηρεῖσθαι τὸν Παῦλον εἰς Καισαρείαν, 4
ἑαυτὸν δὲ μέλλειν ἐν τάχει ἐκπορεύεσθαι· Οἱ οὖν ἐν ὑμῖν, φησίν, 5
δυνατοὶ συνκαταβάντες εἴ τί ἐστιν ἐν τῷ ἀνδρὶ ἄτοπον κατηγο-
ρείτωσαν αὐτοῦ. διατρείψας δὲ ἐν αὐτοῖς ἡμέρας οὐ πλείονας 6
ὀκτὼ ἢ δέκα, καταβὰς εἰς Καισαρείαν, τῇ ἐπαύριον καθίσας ἐπὶ
τοῦ βήματος ἐκέλευσεν τὸν Παῦλον ἀχθῆναι. παραγενομένου δὲ 7
αὐτοῦ περιέστησαν αὐτὸν οἱ ἀπὸ Ἰεροσολύμων καταβεβηκότες
Ἰουδαῖοι, πολλὰ καὶ βαρέα αἰτιώματα καταφέροντες ἃ οὐκ
ἴσχυον ἀποδεῖξαι, τοῦ Παύλου ἀπολογουμένου ὅτι Οὔτε εἰς τὸν 8
νόμον τῶν Ἰουδαίων οὔτε εἰς τὸ ἱερὸν οὔτε εἰς Καίσαρά τι ἥμαρτον.
ὁ Φῆστος δὲ θέλων τοῖς Ἰουδαίοις χάριν καταθέσθαι ἀποκριθεὶς 9
τῷ Παύλῳ εἶπεν· Θέλεις εἰς Ἰεροσόλυμα ἀναβὰς ἐκεῖ περὶ
τούτων κριθῆναι ἐπ᾽ ἐμοῦ; εἶπεν δὲ ὁ Παῦλος· Ἑστὼς ἐπὶ τοῦ 10
βήματος Καίσαρος, ἑστώς εἰμι οὗ με δεῖ κρίνεσθαι. Ἰουδαίους
οὐδὲν ἠδίκηκα, ὡς καὶ σὺ κάλλιον ἐπιγεινώσκεις. εἰ μὲν οὖν 11
ἀδικῶ καὶ ἄξιον θανάτου πέπραχά τι, οὐ παραιτοῦμαι τὸ ἀπο-
θανεῖν· εἰ δὲ οὐδὲν ἔστιν ὧν οὗτοι κατηγοροῦσίν μου, οὐδείς με

11 παραιτουμε

Editors				
	6 πλειονας] πλειους WH Soden JHR		10 om εστως 1ο Soden	om
	εστως 2ο WH JHR	ηδικησα Soden		

Old Uncial				
	2 των ιουδαιων BℵAC της πολεως 81		3 κατ αυτου BℵA 81 παρ	
	αυτου C	αυτον 1ο BℵA 81 αυτον C	4 εν ταχει εκπορευεσθαι	
	BℵAC 81 εκπορευεσθαι εν ταχει ℵᶜ		5 υμιν BAC 81 ημιν ℵ	
	συνκαταβαντες BAC 81 καταβαντες ℵ		6 ημερας ου πλειονας (πλειους AC)	
	BAC 81 ου πλειους ημερας ℵ	καισαρειαν BℵC 81 +και A	αχθηναι	
	BACℵᶜ 81 προαχθηναι ℵ	7 αυτον BℵAC αυτω 81	ισχυον	
	BACℵᶜ 81 ισχυσαν ℵ	9 δε BℵC 81 ουν A	χαριν BℵC 81	
	χαριτα A 10 ο BℵC 81 om A		εστως twice B om 1ο ACℵᶜ 81	
	om 2ο ℵ ηδικηκα Bℵ 81 ηδικησα AC		επιγεινωσκεις BℵA 81	
	γινωσκεις C			

Antiochian				
	2 τε] δε HLPSϛ	ο αρχιερευς HPSϛ	3 ενεδρα S	4 εν
	καισαρεια HLPSϛ	5 οι] ει L	δυνατοι εν υμιν φησιν HLPSϛ	
	ατοπον] τουτω HLPSϛ	6 om ου HLPSϛ	om οκτω HLPSϛ	
	αχθηναι τον παυλον L	7 om αυτον HPSϛ	αιτιωματα] αιτιαματα ϛ	
	καταφεροντες] φεροντες κατα του παυλου HPSϛ		φεροντες κατ αυτου L	
	8 τον παυλου απολογουμενου] απολογουμενου αυτου HPSϛ		του παυλου	
	απολογουμενου αυτου L	9 τοις ιουδαιοις θελων HLPSϛ		κρινεσθαι
	HLPSϛ	10 om εστως 1ο HLPSϛ	ηδικησα HLPSϛ	11 ουν]
	γαρ HLPSϛ	του H	μου] μοι L	

XXV 3   κατ' αὐτοῦ] παρ' αὐτοῦ C 431 minn

11   καὶ[ἣ 323

---

3 ενεδραν . . . οδον] *mg* illi qui votum fecerant quomodo obtinerent ut in Harclean
manibus suis esset   6 εν αυτοις] *mg* in iis. apud eos   10 ουδεν]
⁜ aliquid ✓ non

---

3 The Greek translated in the gloss of hcl.*mg* may have run somewhat as follows : οι ευχην ποιησαμενοι οπως επιτυχωσι του γενεσθαι αυτον εν ταις χερσιν αυτων. But the paraphrase probably involved other changes, no longer recoverable, from the B-text, and the Syriac is perhaps not a perfectly literal rendering. No other trace of the gloss is known. The paraphrast seems to have overlooked the lapse of two years since xxiv. 12.

δύναται αὐτοῖς χαρίσασθαι· Καίσαρα ἐπικαλοῦμαι. τότε ὁ Φῆστος 12
συνλαλήσας μετὰ τοῦ συμβουλίου ἀπεκρίθη· Καίσαρα ἐπικέκλησαι,
ἐπὶ Καίσαρα πορεύσῃ.

Ἡμερῶν δὲ διαγενομένων τινῶν Ἀγρίππας ὁ βασιλεὺς καὶ 13
Βερνίκη κατήντησαν εἰς Καισαρείαν ἀσπασάμενοι τὸν Φῆστον.
ὡς δὲ πλείους ἡμέρας διέτρειβον ἐκεῖ, ὁ Φῆστος τῷ βασιλεῖ 14
ἀνέθετο τὰ κατὰ τὸν Παῦλον λέγων· Ἀνήρ τίς ἐστιν καταλελιμ-
μένος ὑπὸ Φήλικος δέσμιος, περὶ οὗ γενομένου μου εἰς Ἱερο- 15
σόλυμα ἐνεφάνισαν οἱ ἀρχιερεῖς καὶ οἱ πρεσβύτεροι τῶν Ἰουδαίων,
αἰτούμενοι κατ' αὐτοῦ καταδίκην· πρὸς οὓς ἀπεκρίθην ὅτι οὐκ 16
ἔστιν ἔθος Ῥωμαίοις χαρίζεσθαί τινα ἄνθρωπον πρὶν ἢ ὁ κατ-
ηγορούμενος κατὰ πρόσωπον ἔχοι τοὺς κατηγόρους τόπον δὲ
ἀπολογίας λάβοι περὶ τοῦ ἐγκλήματος. συνελθόντων οὖν ἐνθάδε 17
ἀναβολὴν μηδεμίαν ποιησάμενος τῇ ἑξῆς καθίσας ἐπὶ τοῦ βήματος
ἐκέλευσα ἀχθῆναι τὸν ἄνδρα· περὶ οὗ σταθέντες οἱ κατήγοροι 18
οὐδεμίαν αἰτίαν ἔφερον ὧν ἐγὼ ὑπενόουν ·πονηρῶν, ζητήματα 19
δέ τινα περὶ τῆς ἰδίας δισιδαιμονίας εἶχον πρὸς αὐτὸν καὶ περί
τινος Ἰησοῦ τεθνηκότος, ὃν ἔφασκεν ὁ Παῦλος ζῆν. ἀπορούμε- 20
νος δὲ ἐγὼ τὴν περὶ τούτων ζήτησιν ἔλεγον εἰ βούλοιτο πορεύεσθαι εἰς Ἱεροσόλυμα κἀκεῖ κρίνεσθαι περὶ τούτων. τοῦ δὲ Παύλου 21
ἐπικαλεσαμένου τηρηθῆναι αὐτὸν εἰς τὴν τοῦ Σεβαστοῦ διάγνωσιν,
ἐκέλευσα τηρεῖσθαι αὐτὸν ἕως οὗ ἀναπέμψω αὐτὸν πρὸς Καίσαρα.

15 ενεφανισθησαν

Editors   13 †ασπασαμενοι† WHmg   16 δε] τε WH Soden JHR   δε WHmg
          17 ενθαδε] αυτων ενθαδε Soden   18 πονηραν WHmg Soden

Old Uncial   11 αυτοις BℵA 81   τουτοις C   12 συμβουλιου BℵA 81   συνεδριου C
             13 κατηντησαν BℵA 81   κατηντησεν C   ασπασαμενοι BℵA   ασπασομενοι 81
             14 τα BℵC 81   om A   15 ενεφανισαν B²   κατα-
             δικην BℵAC   δικην 81   16 τινα BℵA 81   τινι C   κατα προσ-
             ωπον εχοι BAC 81   εχοι κατα προσωπον ℵ   δε B   τε ℵAC 81
             17 ενθαδε B   αυτων ενθαδε ℵA 81   ενθαδε αυτων C   ποιησαμενος BACℵᶜ 81
             ποιησαμενοι ℵ   18 ου BℵAC   ουν 81   πονηρων BℵᶜC 81   πονηραν AC
             πονηρα ℵC²   19 αυτον BℵC 81   αυτους A   20 εγω BℵA 81   +εις C
             πορευεσθαι BACℵᶜ 81   κρινεσθαι ℵ   21 τηρηθηναι BℵA 81   τηρεισθαι C

Antiochian   11 αυτοις] τουτοις L   12 συμβουλιου] συμβουλου L   13 ασπασαμενοι]
             ασπασομενοι ϛ   14 διετριβεν HPS   15 καταδικην] δικην HLPSϛ
             16 ρωμαιους P   ανθρωπον] + εις απωλειαν HLPSϛ   δε] τε HLPSϛ
             17 add αυτων before ενθαδε HLPSϛ   18 εφερον] επεφερον HPSϛ
             υπενοουν εγω HLPSϛ   om πονηρων HLPSϛ   20 εγω] +εις Lϛ
             τουτων 1°] τουτου HPSϛ   ιερουσαλημ LPSϛ   κριθηναι L
             21 αναπεμψω] πεμψω HLPSϛ

16   ἄνθρωπον] + εἰς ἀπώλειαν HLPS

19   ἔφασκεν] ἔλεγεν 614 1518 minn

---

16 εις απωλειαν] ·✕· in perditionem ✓   ο κατηγορουμενος] mg judicatus   Harclean

---

13 ασπασομενοι Ψ 81 minn seems clearly a correction of ασπασαμενοι. The agreement of BℵA minn Antiochian in support of the aorist is in itself strong proof that the latter does nớt make nonsense, although many modern critics have thought otherwise.

18 πονηρων Bℵc 81 minn (and, still more, πονηραν AC, πονηρα ℵ) is not necessary for the sense; but the omission in the Antiochian text, supported by no version, is probably not a case of ' non-interpolation.'

21 The rendering found in gig may well represent with fair accuracy the ' Western ' paraphrase : *tunc paulus appellavit cesarem et petiit ut reservaretur ad augusti cognitionem ; cumque eum non possem judicare jussi eum reservari ut remittam eum cesari.*

Ἀγρίππας δὲ πρὸς τὸν Φῆστον· Ἐβουλόμην καὶ αὐτὸς τοῦ 22
ἀνθρώπου ἀκοῦσαι. Αὔριον, φησίν, ἀκούσῃ αὐτοῦ. | τῇ οὖν 23
ἐπαύριον ἐλθόντος τοῦ Ἀγρίππα καὶ τῆς Βερνίκης μετὰ πολλῆς
φαντασίας καὶ εἰσελθόντων εἰς τὸ ἀκροατήριον σύν τε χειλιάρχοις
καὶ ἀνδράσιν τοῖς κατ᾽ ἐξοχὴν τῆς πόλεως καὶ κελεύσαντος τοῦ
Φήστου ἤχθη ὁ Παῦλος. καί φησιν ὁ Φῆστος· Ἀγρίππα βασιλεῦ 24
καὶ πάντες οἱ συνπαρόντες ἡμῖν ἄνδρες, θεωρεῖτε τοῦτον περὶ
οὗ ἅπαν τὸ πλῆθος τῶν Ἰουδαίων ἐνέτυχέν μοι ἔν τε Ἱεροσολύμοις καὶ ἐνθάδε, βοῶντες μὴ δεῖν αὐτὸν <ζῆν> μηκέτι. ἐγὼ δὲ 25
κατελαβόμην μηδὲν ἄξιον αὐτὸν θανάτου πεπραχέναι, αὐτοῦ δὲ
τοῦ Παύλου ἐπικαλεσαμένου τὸν Σεβαστὸν ἔκρεινα πέμπειν. περὶ 26
οὗ ἀσφαλές τι γράψαι τῷ κυρίῳ οὐκ ἔχω· διὸ προήγαγον αὐτὸν
ἐφ᾽ ὑμῶν καὶ μάλιστα ἐπὶ σοῦ, βασιλεῦ Ἀγρίππα, ὅπως τῆς
ἀνακρίσεως γενομένης σχῶ τί γράψω· ἄλογον γάρ μοι δοκεῖ 27
πέμποντα δέσμιον μὴ καὶ τὰς κατ᾽ αὐτοῦ αἰτίας σημᾶναι.
Ἀγρίππας δὲ πρὸς τὸν Παῦλον ἔφη· Ἐπιτρέπεταί σοι ὑπὲρ XXVI
σεαυτοῦ λέγειν. τότε ὁ Παῦλος ἐκτείνας τὴν χεῖρα ἀπελογεῖτο·
Περὶ πάντων ὧν ἐγκαλοῦμαι ὑπὸ Ἰουδαίων, βασιλεῦ Ἀγρίππα, 2
ἥγημαι ἐμαυτὸν μακάριον ἐπὶ σοῦ μέλλων σήμερον ἀπολογεῖσθαι,
μάλιστα γνώστην ὄντα σε πάντων τῶν κατὰ Ἰουδαίους ἐθῶν τε 3

---

26   τῷ κυρίῳ] + μου 431 minn

---

23 τοις κατ εξοχην . . . παυλος] *mg* qui descendissent de provincia, praecepit Harclean
Festus ut adduceretur Paulus   24-26 εν τε ιεροσολυμοις . . . ουκ εχω] *mg*
et in Hierosolymis et hic, ut traderem eum iis ad tormentum sine defensione.
non potui autem tradere eum, propter mandata quae habemus ab Augusto.
si autem quis eum accusaturus esset, dicebam ut sequeretur me in Caesaream,
ubi custodiebatur : qui quum venissent, clamaverunt ut tolleretur e vita.
quum autem hanc et alteram partem audivissem, comperi quod in nullo reus
esset mortis.   quum autem dicerem : Vis judicari cum iis in Hierosolyma ?
Caesarem appellavit.   de quo aliquid certum scribere domino meo non habeo
26 τω κυριω μου] domino ⁛ meo ✓
1 τοτε ο παυλος εκτεινας την χειρα] *mg* tunc ipse Paulus, confidens et in spiritu
sancto consolatus, extendit manum

---

23 The gloss of hcl.*mg*, otherwise unattested, seems to represent τοις κατελθουσιν απο της επαρχειας, and probably took the place of τοις κατ εξοχην της πολεως. The usual diacritical mark indicating point of attachment has been omitted in hcl.*text*. To the latter part of the gloss corresponds *jussit festus adduci paulum* gig s.

24-26 Of the ' Western ' paraphrase preserved in full in hcl.*mg*, the earlier part, ending with the words corresponding to *tolleretur e vita* of the Latin translation of hcl.*mg*, is contained also in vg. *cod. ardmach* and the Bohemian version (Tischendorf). Apart from minor variants in these two witnesses the following points deserve mention. At the opening of the gloss in hcl.*mg* the words *et* (before *in Hierosolymis*) and *et hic* (following) are plainly part of hcl.*text* carried into the marginal gloss for purposes of identification. They are impossible in view of what follows, and are lacking in *cod. ardmach*. In the gloss to vs. 24, both *cod. ardmach.* and Bohemian have ' Caesar' instead of ' Augustus ' (hcl.*mg*). In vs. 25 hcl.*mg* alone gives the ' Western ' paraphrase, and reads therein ' Caesar' (cf. vs. 11) instead of ' Augustus' of the usual text.

1-2 In addition to hcl.*mg* the readings *permittitur enim rationem reddere* (απολογεισθαι) *de te* gig and *coepit rationem reddere* (ηρξατο απολογεισθαι) *dicens* gig (vg) may represent fragments of the ' Western ' text.

καὶ ζητημάτων· διὸ δέομαι μακροθύμως ἀκοῦσαί μου. τὴν μὲν 4
οὖν βίωσίν μου ἐκ νεότητος τὴν ἀπ᾽ ἀρχῆς γενομένην ἐν τῷ ἔθνει
μου ἔν τε Ἱεροσολύμοις ἴσασι πάντες Ἰουδαῖοι, προγεινώσκοντές 5
με ἄνωθεν, ἐὰν θέλωσιν μαρτυρεῖν, ὅτι κατὰ τὴν ἀκρειβεστάτην
αἵρεσιν τῆς ἡμετέρας θρησκείας ἔζησα Φαρεισαῖος. καὶ νῦν ἐπ᾽ 6
ἐλπίδι τῆς εἰς τοὺς πατέρας ἡμῶν ἐπαγγελίας γενομένης ὑπὸ τοῦ
θεοῦ ἕστηκα κρεινόμενος, εἰς ἣν τὸ δωδεκάφυλον ἡμῶν ἐν ἐκτενείᾳ 7
νύκτα καὶ ἡμέραν λατρεῦον ἐλπίζει καταντήσειν· περὶ ἧς ἐλπίδος
ἐγκαλοῦμαι ὑπὸ Ἰουδαίων, βασιλεῦ· τί ἄπιστον κρείνεται παρ᾽ 8
ὑμῖν εἰ ὁ θεὸς νεκροὺς ἐγείρει; ἐγὼ οὖν ἔδοξα ἐμαυτῷ πρὸς τὸ 9
ὄνομα Ἰησοῦ τοῦ Ναζωραίου δεῖν πολλὰ ἐναντία πρᾶξαι· διὸ καὶ 10
ἐποίησα ἐν Ἱεροσολύμοις, καὶ πολλοὺς τῶν ἁγίων ἐγὼ ἐν φυλα-
καῖς κατέκλεισα τὴν παρὰ τῶν ἀρχιερέων ἐξουσίαν λαβών, ἀν-
αιρουμένων τε αὐτῶν κατήνεγκα ψῆφον, καὶ κατὰ πάσας τὰς 11
συναγωγὰς πολλάκις τειμωρῶν αὐτοὺς ἠνάγκαζον βλασφημεῖν·
περισσῶς ἐμμαινόμενος αὐτοῖς ἐδίωκον ἕως καὶ εἰς τὰς ἔξω
πόλεις. ἐν οἷς πορευόμενος εἰς τὴν Δαμασκὸν μετ᾽ ἐξουσίας 12
καὶ ἐπιτροπῆς τῆς τῶν ἀρχιερέων | ἡμέρας μέσης κατὰ τὴν ὁδὸν 13
εἶδον, βασιλεύς, οὐρανόθεν ὑπὲρ τὴν λαμπρότητα τοῦ ἡλίου
περιλάμψαν με φῶς καὶ τοὺς σὺν ἐμοὶ πορευομένους· πάντων 14

Editors   4 μου 1°] +[την] Soden   7 καταντησαι WHSoden JHR   καταντησειν
WHmg   9 εγω] +μεν WH (but cf. mg) Soden JHR   10 διο]
o WH Soden JHR   πολλους] +τε WH Soden   11 περισσως]
+τε WH Soden JHR   13 βασιλευ WH Soden JHR

Old Uncial   3 ζητηματων Bℵ 81   +επισταμενος ACℵᶜ   δεομαι BℵA 81   +σου C
4 μου 1° BC   +την ℵAC² 81   τε BℵA   om C 81(?)   ιουδαιοι
BC 81   οι ιουδαιοι ℵAC²   προγεινωσκοντες BℵA 81   προσγινωσκοντες C
6 εις BℵA 81   προς C   7 καταντησειν B   καταντησαι ℵAC 81   βασιλευ
BℵC 096 81   om A   9 εγω B   +μεν ℵAC 096 81   ιησου BACℵᶜ 096 81
του ιησου ℵ   10 διο B   o ℵAC 096 81   εποιησα BACℵᶜᵒʳʳ 096 81
εποιησαν ℵ   πολλους B   +τε ℵAC 096ᵛⁱᵈ 81   κατηνεγκα BAC 096 81
κατηνεγκαν ℵ   11 περισσως B   +τε ℵAC 096 81   αυτοις BℵAC 81
αυτους 096   12 την 1° BℵC 096 81   om A   της BℵC 81   om A 096
των BℵA 096 81   παρα των C   13 ημερας BACℵᶜ 81   om ℵ   βασιλευς B
βασιλευ B²ℵAC 81   περιλαμψαν BℵAC 096   περιλαμψαντα 81

Antiochian   3 δεομαι] +σου HLPSϚ   4 μου 1°] +την LPϚ   om τε HLPSϚ
οι ιουδαιοι HLPSϚ   6 εις] προς HLPSϚ   om ημων HLPSϚ   om του L
7 καταντησαι HLPSϚ   υπο ιουδαιων βασιλευ] βασιλευ αγριππα υπο [+των Ϛ]
ιουδαιων HLPSϚ   9 εγω] +μεν HLPSϚ   10 διο] o HLPSϚ
om εν before φυλακαις HPSϚ   τε 2°] δε H   11 περισσως] +τε HLPSϚ
12 οις] +και HLPSϚ   των] παρα των HLPSϚ   13 βασιλευ HLPSϚ
με] μοι L

XXVI, 7 τὸ δωδεκ[άφυλον ἡμῶν ἐν ἐκτε]νίᾳ νύκτ[α καὶ ἡμέραν λα-
τρεύει ἐν (?)] ἐλπίδι ϗ[αταντῆσαι· περὶ ἧς νῦν (?)] ἐνκαλοῦ[μαι
8 ὑπὸ .'Ιουδαίων· εἰ (?)] ὁ θεὸς νεκρ[οὺς ἐγείρει] Pap.29

9 πραξαι] ·⁛· me ✓ facere   11 εδιωκον] persequebar ·⁛· eos ✓ Harclean
13 βασιλευς] ·⁛· o ✓ rex

7–8, 20 The fragment Pap. 29 (Oxyrhynchus Papyrus 1597), third or fourth century, here printed with Grenfell's conjectural reconstruction of the lacunae, can fairly be regarded as a piece of 'Western' text. In vs. 7 ελπιδι (which may or may not have been preceded by εν) in any case implies λατρευει, not λατρευον. This corresponds to gig deserviunt in spe. Instead of νυν (gig nunc) there is perhaps space in the lacuna for ελπιδος. In vs. 8, instead of ει, it is barely possible to find space for βασιλευ, as in the usual text. Gig, however, omits rex, in agreement with A minn.

In vs. 20, instead of the restoration τε και (BℵΤ 81), και εν (cf. A) is equally possible. και τοις εν (614 minn) would correspond to gig et his qui in, but seems to be too long for the space. The reading of h civitatibus for εθνεσιν, together with the obviously short text of the papyrus in the lacuna, leads to the suspicion that a 'Western' paraphrase, beyond the reach of our conjecture, was found here. εκηρυξα corresponds to h prae dicavi.

τε καταπεσόντων εἰς τὴν γῆν ἤκουσα φωνὴν λέγουσαν πρός με
τῇ Ἑβραΐδι διαλέκτῳ· Σαούλ, Σαούλ, τί με διώκεις; σκληρόν
σοι πρὸς κέντρα λακτίζειν. | ἐγὼ δὲ εἶπα· Τίς εἶ, κύριε; ὁ δὲ 15
κύριος εἶπεν· Ἐγώ εἰμι Ἰησοῦς ὃν σὺ διώκεις· | ἀλλὰ ἀνάστηθι 16
ἐπὶ τοὺς πόδας σου· εἰς τοῦτο γὰρ ὤφθην σοι, προχειρίσασθαί
σε ὑπηρέτην καὶ μάρτυρα ὧν τε εἶδές με ὧν τε ὀφθήσομαί σοι,
| ἐξαιρούμενός σε ἐκ τοῦ λαοῦ καὶ ἐκ τῶν ἐθνῶν, εἰς οὓς ἐγὼ 17
ἀποστέλλω σε | ἀνοῖξαι ὀφθαλμοὺς αὐτῶν, τοῦ ἐπιστρέψαι ἀπὸ 18
σκότους εἰς φῶς καὶ τῆς ἐξουσίας τοῦ Σατανᾶ ἐπὶ τὸν θεόν, τοῦ
λαβεῖν αὐτοὺς ἄφεσιν ἁμαρτιῶν καὶ κλῆρον ἐν τοῖς ἡγιασμένοις
πίστει τῇ εἰς ἐμέ. ὅθεν, βασιλεῦ Ἀγρίππα, οὐκ ἐγενόμην 19
ἀπειθὴς τῇ οὐρανίῳ ὀπτασίᾳ, ἀλλὰ τοῖς ἐν Δαμασκῷ πρῶτόν 20
τε καὶ Ἱεροσολύμοις, πᾶσάν τε τὴν χώραν τῆς Ἰουδαίας, καὶ
τοῖς ἔθνεσιν ἀπήγγελλον μετανοεῖν καὶ ἐπιστρέφειν ἐπὶ τὸν θεόν,
ἄξια τῆς μετανοίας ἔργα πράσσοντας. ἕνεκα τούτων με Ἰουδαῖοι 21
συλλαβόμενοι ἐν τῷ ἱερῷ ἐπειρῶντο διαχειρίσασθαι. ἐπικουρίας 22
οὖν τυχὼν τῆς ἀπὸ τοῦ θεοῦ ἄχρι τῆς ἡμέρας ταύτης ἕστηκα
μαρτυρόμενος μεικρῷ τε καὶ μεγάλῳ, οὐδὲν ἐκτὸς λέγων ὧν τε
οἱ προφῆται ἐλάλησαν μελλόντων γείνεσθαι καὶ Μωσῆς, εἰ παθη- 23
τὸς ὁ Χριστός, εἰ πρῶτος ἐξ ἀναστάσεως νεκρῶν φῶς μέλλει

Editors   14 καταπεσοντων] +ημων WH Soden JHR   λεγουσαν] λαλουσαν Soden
με 1°] +και λεγουσαν Soden   16 αναστηθι] +και στηθι WH Soden JHR
om με Soden   20 ιεροσολυμοις] +εις Soden   21 συλλαβομενοι] +οντα
Soden

Old Uncial   14 τε BℵA 096 81   δε C   καταπεσοντων B   +ημων ℵAC 096 81
εις BℵAC επι 81   15 δε 1° BℵAC 81   om 096 (?)   16 αναστηθι B
+ και στηθι B²ℵAC 096 81   σε BACℵᶜ 096 81   σοι ℵ   με BCᵛⁱᵈ
om ℵAC² 096 81   17 εκ 2° BℵA 096 81   om C   αποστελλω BℵA
αποστελω 096   εξαποστελλω C   εξαποστελω 81   18 αυτων BℵAC 81   τυφλων
096   επιστρεψαι BℵC 096   αποστρεψαι A 81   και 1° BℵA 81   +απο C
20 και 1° Bℵ 81   +εν A   ιεροσολυμοις BℵA   +εις 81   21 με (+οι ℵᶜ)
ιουδαιοι συλλαβομενοι Bℵ   οι ιουδαιοι συλλαβομενοι με A   ιουδαιοι με συλλαβομενοι 81
εν BA   οντα με εν ℵ   οντα εν ℵᶜ 81   διαχειρισασθαι BAℵᶜ 81   διαχιρωσα-
σθαι ℵ   23 μελλει BAℵᶜ ᵛⁱᵈ   μελλειν ℵ 81

Antiochian   14 τε] δε HLPSϚ   καταπεσοντων] +ημων HLPSϚ   λεγουσαν]
λαλουσαν HLPSϚ   με 1°] +και λεγουσαν LPϚ   15 om κυριος HPSϚ
16 αναστηθι] +και στηθι HLPSϚ   om με HLPSϚ   17 om εκ 2°
HLPSϚ   εγω] νυν Ϛ   αποστελλω σε] σε αποστελλω LϚ   σε αποστελω
HPS   18 επιστρεψαι] αποστρεψαι H   υποστρεψαι PS   και 1°] +απο L
20 om τε 1° HLPSϚ   ιεροσολυμοις] +εις HLPSϚ   om τε 2° L
om την H   απαγγελλων HLPSϚ   21 οι ιουδαιοι HPSϚ   ιουδαιοι
με L   συλλαμβανομενοι P   22 απο] παρα HLPSϚ   μαρτυρομενος]
μαρτυρουμενος Ϛ   23 μελλειν HP

14   γῆν] + διὰ τὸν φόβον ἐγὼ μόνος 614 1611 2147
15   Ἰησοῦς] + ὁ Ναζωραῖος 614 minn
19, 20 [ἀπειθὴς τῇ οὐρανίῳ ὀπτασίᾳ, ἀ]λλὰ τοῖς ἐ[ν Δαμασκῷ
      πρῶτόν τε καὶ Ἱερο]σολόμοις κα[ὶ τῇ Ἰουδαίᾳ καὶ τοῖς ἔθνεσιν]
      ἐκήρυξα [. . . μετανοεῖν καὶ ἐπιστρέφειν ἐ]πὶ τὸν θεόν, [. . .
      ἄξια τῆς μετανοίας ἔργα πρ]άσσοντας Pap. 29
      τοῖς ἐν Ἱεροσολύμοις 614 1518 minn
      θεόν] + ζῶντα 431 minn
21   με Ἰουδαῖοι συλλαβόμενοι] Ἰουδαῖοι συλλαβόμενοί με ὄντα
      614 (ℵ) (81) minn
22   om τε after ὧν 337 460

20 civitatibus praedicabi peniteri et reverti [ad d̄m̄], digna opera penitentiae h
agentes. 21 horum cau[sa me] Judaei, cum essem in templo, conpraehenderu[nt,
et ne]gare conati sunt. 22 cum ergo auxilium d̄ī sim co[nsecutus], esto indicans
majori ac minori, nihil amplius d[icens quā] quae profetae dixerunt futura esse.
scriptum [est enim] in Moysen : 23 si passivilis x̄p̄s, ex resurrexione mo[rtuorum]

22 [proinde et apud Agrippam nihil se ait proferre citra quam prophetae Tertullian,
annuntiassent . . . . . . nam et de resurrectione mortuorum apud Moysen *Res. carn.* 3ɔ
scriptum commemorans corporalem eam norat, in qua scilicet sanguis hominis
exquiri habebit.]

14 εις την γην δια τον φοβον εγω μονος ηκουσα] *mg* prae timore in terram, ego Harclean
tantum audivi   15 ο ναζωραιος] ⋇· Nazarenus ✓

16 The evidence for με from BC^vid
614 minn pesh hcl.*text* Ambrose
Augustine must be taken as decisive
in support of this perplexing 'lectio
ardua.'
20 Before πασαν τε την χωραν the
Antiochian text adds εις, which is
lacking in Bℵ︎A vg. *codd.* As Greek,
the text without εις is hardly tolerable.
The omission may be a very ancient
accidental error (-OICEIC), but with
so firmly attested a text the theory
of a Semitism suggests itself, in view
of the strikingly Semitic cast and
grammatical difficulties of vss. 16–18.
Cf. Deut. i. 19 ἐπορεύθημεν πᾶσαν τὴν
ἔρημον τὴν μεγάλην καὶ τὴν φοβεράν.
On the text of Pap. 29 see Textual
Note on p. 235, above.
22 In the text of h Souter's conjecture (*Journal of Theol. Studies*, xi,
1909–10, pp. 563 f.) co[nsecutus] (for
τυχων) has been adopted, instead of
Buchanan's co[nfisus].

The words αχρι της ημερας ταυτης
are not represented in h.
Buchanan's conjecture in h d[icens
quā] quae gives the reading of gig.
The 'Western' paraphrase of e,
scriptum est enim in Moyse, coincides
exactly (except for one letter) with
the text of h. Probably the paraphrast explained the difficulty of ει,
vs. 23, by assuming the verse to be
a quotation; cf. Ambrosiaster on
1 Cor. xv. 23, *sicut in Actibus Apostolorum testatur scriptum esse in Moyse :
Si passibilis Christus, si prior surgens
ex mortuis* ; vg.cod.ardmach, *quae
profetae sunt locuti futura esse. Et
Moisses dixit : Si passibilis*, etc.
Corssen (*Göttingische gelehrte Anzeigen*, 1896, pp. 429 f.) points out
that Tertullian, *De resurr. carnis* 39,
used the 'Western' text here, and
understood the O.T. reference to
allude to Gen. ix. 5.

238 CODEX VATICANUS

καταγγέλλειν τῷ τε λαῷ καὶ τοῖς ἔθνεσιν. ταῦτα δὲ αὐτοῦ 24
ἀπολογουμένου ὁ Φῆστος μεγάλῃ τῇ φωνῇ φησίν· Μαίνῃ, Παῦλε·
τὰ πολλά σε γράμματα εἰς μανίαν περιτρέπει. ὁ δὲ Παῦλος· 25
Οὐ μαίνομαι, φησί, κράτιστε Φῆστε, ἀλλὰ ἀληθείας καὶ σωφρο-
σύνης ῥήματα ἀποφθέγγομαι. ἐπίσταται γὰρ περὶ τούτων ὁ 26
βασιλεύς, πρὸς ὃν παρρησιαζόμενος λαλῶ· λανθάνειν γὰρ αὐτὸν
τούτων οὐ πείθομαι οὐθέν, οὐ γάρ ἐστιν ἐν γωνίᾳ πεπραγμένον
τοῦτο. | πιστεύεις, βασιλεῦ Ἀγρίππα, τοῖς προφήταις; οἶδα ὅτι 27
πιστεύεις. ὁ δὲ Ἀγρίππας πρὸς τὸν Παῦλον· Ἐν ὀλίγῳ με 28
πείθεις Χρειστιανὸν ποιῆσαι. ὁ δὲ Παῦλος· Εὐξαίμην ἂν τῷ 29
θεῷ καὶ ἐν ὀλίγῳ καὶ ἐν μεγάλῳ οὐ μόνον σὲ ἀλλὰ καὶ πάντας
τοὺς ἀκούοντάς μου σήμερον γενέσθαι τοιούτους ὁποῖος καὶ ἐγώ
εἰμι παρεκτὸς τῶν δεσμῶν τούτων. ἀνέστη τε ὁ βασιλεὺς καὶ 30
ὁ ἡγεμὼν ἥ τε Βερνίκη καὶ οἱ συνκαθήμενοι αὐτοῖς, καὶ ἀνα- 31
χωρήσαντες ἐλάλουν πρὸς ἀλλήλους λέγοντες ὅτι Οὐδὲν θανάτου
ἢ δεσμῶν ἄξιον πράσσει ὁ ἄνθρωπος οὗτος. Ἀγρίππας δὲ τῷ 32
Φήστῳ ἔφη· Ἀπολελύσθαι ἐδύνατο ὁ ἄνθρωπος οὗτος εἰ μὴ
ἐπεκέκλητο Καίσαρα.

Editors   25 om παυλος JHR   26 ον] +και WHmg Soden JHR   αυτον] +τι
WHmg Soden   27 βασιλευ WH Soden JHR   28 †με πειθεις χρειστιανον
ποιησαι† WHmg   31 αξιον] +τι WHmg Soden

Old Uncial   23 καταγγελλειν BℵA καταγγελειν 81   24 γραμματα Bℵ 81 +επι-
στασθε A   26 ον B +και ℵA 81   αυτον B +τι ℵA 81
ου πειθομαι ουθεν Bℵ ου πειθομαι Aℵᶜ ουθεν πειθομαι 81   27 βασιλευς B
βασιλευ ℵA 81   28 πειθεις Bℵ 81 πειθη A   χρειστιανον B
χρηστιανον ℵ χριστιανον A 81   29 ευξαιμην BAℵᶜ ευξαμην ℵ 81
31 θανατου η δεσμων αξιον Bℵ 81 αξιον θανατου η δεσμων A   πρασσει B
τι πρασσει ℵA 81

Antiochian   23 καταγγελειν H   om τε LPS⁵   24 απολογουμενου αυτου H
εφη HLPS⁵   25 om παυλος HLPS⁵   26 ον] +και HLPS⁵
αυτον] +τι HLPS⁵   om εστιν HLPS   27 βασιλευ HLPS⁵
28 παυλον] +εφη HLPS⁵   χριστιανον HLPS⁵   ποιησαι] γενεσθαι
HLPS⁵   29 παυλος] +ειπεν HLPS⁵   ευξαμην HLPS⁵
μεγαλω] πολλω HLPS⁵   30 ανεστη τε] και ταυτα ειποντος αυτου ανεστη
HLPS⁵   31 αξιον η δεσμων HLPS⁵

24 For the Greek rendered by oravit
h, 'asked' pesh, no satisfactory suggestion can be made. Possibly oravit
exclamavit . . . et dixit merely represents μεγαλη τη φωνη with a single
verb. On the use of two words in
the African Latin for one Greek word
see J. R. Harris, Codex Bezae, pp. 254-
258 ; cf. h in Acts iii. 4.

In the preceding clause, vg haec
loquente eo et rationem reddente (nearly
so, gig) is a conflation of a text like
that of h et cum haec loqueretur with a
rendering of the Greek ταυτα δε αυτου
απολογουμενον. E has this conflation
by reaction from the Latin.
There seems to be no reason for
assuming in h any form longer than

25   om Παῦλος HLPS
26   οὐ γάρ] οὐδὲ γάρ 431 minn
28   Παῦλον] + ἔφη HLPS
29   Παῦλος] + εἶπεν HLPS + ἔφη Ψ minn
       om σήμερον 323
       om καὶ before ἐγώ 808
30   ἀνέστη τε] καὶ ταῦτα εἰπόντος αὐτοῦ ἀνέστη HLPS
       οἱ συνκαθήμενοι] πάντες οἱ συνκαθήμενοι minn
31   om ὅτι 69 328

---

lux annuntiabit plebi et gentib·. 24 et cum haec lo[quere]tur oravit exclamavit h
Festus, et dixit : insanis[ti, Paule], insanisti : multe te littere in insaniam
conv[ertunt]. 25 qui respondit ei : non insanio, optime legate, s[ed] veri-
tatis et sapientiae verba emitto : 26 scit aute[m] de istis rex, apud quem
loquor : nihil enim hor[um eum] latet. 27 credis, rex Agrippa, profetis ? scio
quia cr[edis. 28 qui] ita ad eum ait : modico suades mihi, Paule, x̄pian[um
. . .]. 29 ad quem sic ait : orarem d̄m̄ et in modico et in m[agno non] solum
te sed et istos qui me audiunt omnes fi[eri tales] qualis ego sum, exceptis vinculis
istis. 30 et cum [haec dixis]set, exurrexit rex et legatus, et omnes assen[. . . .],
31 et secesserunt, praefantes inter se de eo, dic[entes : nihil] mortem
dignum vel vinculorum homo iste [. . . 32 respon]dit autem rex Agrippa :
dimitti poterat hom[o iste, si non] appellavit Caesarem.

---

28 ποιησαι] mg facere   30 και ταυτα ειποντος αυτου] ⁂· et quum haec Harclean
ipse dixisset ✓

---

conv[ertunt], although Berger and
Buchanan both give conv[erterunt].

25 The 'Western' text (h gig)
probably lacked παυλος, as does the
Antiochian ; and the presence of the
word in the B-text is perhaps due to
interpolation.

25, 26 In h, vs. 25, after s[ed]
Buchanan conjectures [magis] ; and
vs. 26, after aute[m] similarly
[omnibus]. But these words are unsupported by any other witness, and
are introduced solely to fill up a space
which may have been left vacant in
the MS.

26 Whether the abbreviated form
in which h gives this verse (especially
in the second half) was found in any
Greek text or is due to the translator
must remain uncertain. Cf. the
abridgements of chap. xxvii in h.

The omission of και before παρρησιαζομενος, although found in B minn boh,
as well as in h perp vg.codd, is
probably not to be followed, since it is

the 'easier' reading, and diminishes
the vigour of the phrase.

28 The reading με πειθεις χρ(ει)-
στιανον ποιησαι of Bℵ 81 minn boh
hcl.mg and apparently Cassiodorus
(Migne, vol. lxx. 1403 respondit quod
eum sub celeritate vellet facere christianum), although difficult, yields an
intelligible sense ('play the Christian')
and must be accepted. The variants
of A (πειθη) and of the Antiochian and
vg (γενεσθαι) are two different attempts
to improve the meaning. The reading of h may have been either fieri or
facere ; that of sah is not known.

30 In h, although Buchanan reads
assen and hence conjectures assen-
[tiebant eis], the earlier conjecture,
[assedentes eis], of Berger (who was
not able to make out so many letters)
is commended by vg qui adsidebant
eis. Even with Buchanan's reading,
assen[tientes eis] is at least equally
possible, and would have to be taken
(so Zahn) as a copyist's corruption of
assedentes eis. In h, then, we find
merely the omission of η τε βερνικη.

Ὡς δὲ ἐκρίθη τοῦ ἀποπλεῖν ἡμᾶς εἰς τὴν Ἰταλίαν, παρεδίδουν XXVII
τόν τε Παῦλον καί τινας ἑτέρους δεσμώτας ἑκατοντάρχῃ ὀνόματι
Ἰουλίῳ σπείρης Σεβαστῆς. ἐπιβάντες δὲ πλοίῳ Ἀδραμυντηνῷ 2
μέλλοντι πλεῖν εἰς τοὺς κατὰ τὴν Ἀσίαν τόπους ἀνήχθημεν,
ὄντος σὺν ἡμῖν Ἀριστάρχου Μακεδόνος Θεσσαλονεικέως· τῇ τε 3
ἑτέρᾳ κατήχθημεν εἰς Σειδῶνα, φιλανθρώπως τε ὁ Ἰούλιος τῷ
Παύλῳ χρησάμενος ἐπέτρεψεν πρὸς τοὺς φίλους πορευθέντι ἐπι-
μελείας τυχεῖν. κἀκεῖθεν ἀναχθέντες ὑπεπλεύσαμεν τὴν Κύπρον 4
διὰ τὸ τοὺς ἀνέμους εἶναι ἐναντίους, τό τε πέλαγος τὸ κατὰ τὴν 5
Κιλικίαν καὶ Παμφυλίαν διαπλεύσαντες κατήλθαμεν εἰς Μύρρα
τῆς Λυκίας. κἀκεῖ εὑρὼν ὁ ἑκατοντάρχης πλοῖον Ἀλεξανδρεινὸν 6

Editors   2 αδραμυντηνω Soden   5 διαπλευσαντες] +δι ημερων δεκαπεντε JHR
μυρα Soden JHR

Old Uncial   1 παρεδιδουν Bℵ 81   παρεδιδου A   ετερους BℵA   om 81   εκατοντ-
αρχη BAℵᶜ 81   +ιουλιω ℵ   2 αρισταρχου BAℵᶜ 81   αρισταρχος ℵ
3 τε 1º BℵA   δε ℵᶜ 81   ιουλιος Bℵ 81   ιουλιανος A   5 μυρρα B
μυραν 81   λυστραν ℵ   λυστρα A   6 κακει Bℵ 81   κακειθεν A

Antiochian   1 ημας] τους περι τον παυλον P   δεσμωτας ετερους L   2 μελλοντες
HLPSς̅   om εις HLPSς̅   3 τε 1º] δε L   om τους ς̅
πορευθεντα HLPSς̅   5 μυρα LPς̅   μυραν S   6 εκατονταρχης]
εκατονταρχος LPSς̅

1–13 The text of h in vss. 1–13 shows a considerable number of omissions as compared with the B-text. Of these two only (vs. 2 θεσσαλονεικεως ; vs. 7 κατα σαλμωνην) appear to be supported by other extant witnesses, and in view of the general character of h elsewhere it must be concluded that, as in chap. xxvi., either the underlying Greek text or this Latin translation has been abridged in all or nearly all of these omissions. See above, pp. ccxxxvi-ccxxxviii.

1 Partly guided by the wish to relieve the abruptness of the B-text, the 'Western' text substituted a paraphrase which is preserved with substantial completeness and correctness in hcl.*mg* and h. The Greek text of the earlier part survives in και ουτως εκρινεν αυτον (om αυτον 421) ο ηγεμων αναπεμπεσθαι (αναπεμψαι 421) καισαρι 97 421, and this fragment is rendered in pesh and, in whole or in part, in several Latin and Provençal MSS. Apart from hcl.*mg* and h, all these witnesses present combinations with the B-text, hardly any two ex-

hibiting the same combination. The omission in h of *ex cohorte augusta* (found in hcl.*mg*) is probably an accident.

2 *Cum coepissemus navigare* h (cf. pesh), *incipientes autem navigare in Italiam* gig, imply a paraphrastic ' Western' Greek text with μελλοντες. This may underlie the (differently placed) Antiochian μελλοντες for μελλοντι.

Conscendissent hcl.*mg* seems to point to a following text different from that of B, but no further indication of it is provided in the Harclean MS.

In h nothing corresponds to εις τους κατα την ασιαν τοπους, but the Greek text with the words is probably sound. It is to be further noted that the omission of εις from this phrase belongs to the Antiochian recension, and must have been deemed good Greek in the fourth and following centuries, although only in Greek poetry are parallels found to this usage. It seems unlikely that the omission was made by the Antiochian revisers. Cf. vg *circa*.

Likewise the word θεσσαλονεικεως

XXVII 'Ως δὲ ἐκρίθη τοῦ ἀποπλεῖν ἡμᾶς εἰς τὴν Ἰταλίαν] καὶ οὕτως
ἔκρινεν αὐτὸν (om αὐτὸν 421) ὁ ἡγεμὼν ἀναπέμπεσθαι (ἀνα-
πέμψαι 421) Καίσαρι 97 421
παρεδίδουν] παρέδωκεν 1175
2 μέλλοντι] μέλλοντες HLPS
Θεσσαλονεικέως] Θεσσαλονικέων δὲ Ἀρίσταρχος καὶ Σέκουνδος 614 minn
5 διαπλεύσαντες] + δι' ἡμερῶν δεκάπεντε 614 2147 (minn)
Μύρρα] Λύστραν אA
6 κἀκεῖ] καὶ 255

---

et ita legatus mitti eum Ca[esari judicavit]. 1 [et in] crastinum vocabit **h**
centurionem quendā, [nomi]ne Julium, et tradidit ei Paulum cum ceteris
cus[todiis]. 2 cum coepissemus navigare, ascendimus in navē [Adru]metinam :
ascendit autem noviscum et Aristar[chus Ma]cedo. 3 venimus autem Sidonae :
et humanae attrac[tans Pa]julum, illē centurio permisit amicis, qui veniebant
[ad eum], uti curam ejus agerent. 4 inde autem navigantes [legimu]s Cyprum,
eo quod contrari erant venti : 5 et post [haec, na]vigantes sinum Cilium et
Pamphilium pelagū, [diebus] xv devenimus Myra Lyciae, 6 et invenit navē
[Alexan]drinam centurio ille navigantem in Italiā.

1–2 ως δε εκριθη . . . πλοιω] *mg* sic igitur judicavit praeses mittere eum ad Harclean
Caesarem.   quum die postero vocasset centurionem quendam cujus nomen
Julianus ex cohorte Augusta, tradidit ei Paulum cum et ceteris vinctis.   quum
conscendissent autem navem   1 τινι] ⋇ cuidam ✓   2 θεσσαλονικεων δε
αρισταρχος και σεκουνδος] *text* ex Thessalonicensibus autem Aristarchus et Secundus
5 δι ημερων δεκαπεντε] ⋇ per dies quindecim ✓

---

fails to appear in any form in h, probably by abridgement, while in 614
minn hcl.*text* θεσσαλονικεων δε αρισταρχος και σεκουνδος is substituted for
it, always in addition to the preceding αρισταρχου μακεδονος. The
addition is plainly derived from xx. 4,
and may have belonged to the original
'Western' text, at least in the form
current in the East.   This may be (so
White) a case where our Harclean MS.
has neglected to insert the due ⋇.
The nominative αρισταρχος in א* is
noteworthy ; pesh reads 'and there
went on board the ship with us Aristarchus a Macedonian who was from
the city of Thessalonica.'

5 *Et post* [*haec*] h, 'then' hcl.*text*,
are perhaps due to το τε of the Greek
text (misunderstood as τότε).
Sinum h is doubtless (so Wordsworth
and White) a corruption of *secundum*
(gig s for κατα).
Unless in the 'Western' text the

additional words δι ημερων δεκαπεντε
614 minn h vg.*cod ardmach* hcl⋇ are
regarded as genuine and accidentally
omitted from the B-text, no explanation is at hand.
μυρρα B minn hcl. *Greek marginal
note* [εις μυρραν] (cf. also Jer. *Nom.
hebr.* p. 102 ; sah) is not attested as
a possible spelling for μυρα (so, correctly, Antiochian and h ; S 81 μυραν),
and is to be rejected, with other strange
spellings of Codex Vaticanus for proper
names in both O.T. and N.T. ; see
C. C. Torrey, *Ezra Studies*, Chicago,
1910, pp. 93–95.   The substitution of
σμυρναν 69 E (by testimony of Bede ;
the reading of e is not known), Ps.-Jer.
(ed. Migne, vol. xxiii. 1364) is easily
accounted for from the equivalence of
meaning (remarked by Bede) between
μύρρα and σμύρνα (see Stephanus,
Thesaurus s. vv. ; cf. Rev. xviii. 13 v.l.)
λυστρα(ν) אA vg boh is a mere corruption. See Wordsworth and White's
full note.

πλέον εἰς τὴν Ἰταλίαν ἐνεβίβασεν ἡμᾶς εἰς αὐτό. ἐν ἱκαναῖς δὲ 7
ἡμέραις βραδυπλοοῦντες καὶ μόλις γενόμενοι κατὰ τὴν Κνίδον,
μὴ προσεῶντος ἡμᾶς τοῦ ἀνέμου, ὑπεπλεύσαμεν τὴν Κρήτην
κατὰ Σαλμώνην, μόλις τε παραλεγόμενοι αὐτὴν ἤλθομεν εἰς 8
τόπον τινὰ καλούμενον Καλοὺς Λιμένας, ᾧ ἐγγὺς ἦν πόλις Λασέα.
ἱκανοῦ δὲ χρόνου διαγενομένου καὶ ὄντος ἤδη ἐπισφαλοῦς τοῦ 9
πλοὸς διὰ τὸ καὶ τὴν νηστείαν ἤδη παρεληλυθέναι, παρῄνει ὁ
Παῦλος | λέγων αὐτοῖς· Ἄνδρες, θεωρῶ ὅτι μετὰ ὕβρεως καὶ 10
πολλῆς ζημίας οὐ μόνον τοῦ φορτίου καὶ τοῦ πλοίου ἀλλὰ καὶ
τῶν ψυχῶν ἡμῶν μέλλειν ἔσεσθαι τὸν πλοῦν. ὁ δὲ ἑκατοντάρχης 11
τῷ κυβερνήτῃ καὶ τῷ ναυκλήρῳ μᾶλλον ἐπείθετο ἢ τοῖς ὑπὸ
Παύλου λεγομένοις. ἀνευθέτου δὲ τοῦ λιμένος ὑπάρχοντος πρὸς 12
παραχειμασίαν οἱ πλείονες ἔθεντο βουλὴν ἀναχθῆναι ἐκεῖθεν, εἴ
πως δύναιντο καταντήσαντες εἰς Φοίνεικα παραχειμάσαι, λιμένα
τῆς Κρήτης βλέποντα κατὰ λίβα καὶ κατὰ χῶρον. ὑποπνεύ- 13
σαντος δὲ νότου δόξαντες τῆς προθέσεως κεκρατηκέναι ἄραντες
ἆσσον παρελέγοντο τὴν Κρήτην. μετ᾽ οὐ πολὺ δὲ ἔβαλεν κατ᾽ 14
αὐτῆς ἄνεμος τυφωνικὸς ὁ καλούμενος Εὐρακύλων· συναρπα- 15
σθέντος δὲ τοῦ πλοίου καὶ μὴ δυνομένου ἀντοφθαλμεῖν τῷ ἀνέμῳ
ἐπιδόντες ἐφερόμεθα. νησίον δέ τι ὑποδραμόντες καλούμενον 16
Καῦδα ἰσχύσαμεν μόλις περικρατεῖς γενέσθαι τῆς σκάφης, ἣν 17
ἄραντες βοηθείαις ἐχρῶντο ὑποζωννύντες τὸ πλοῖον· φοβούμενοί
τε μὴ εἰς τὴν Σύρτιν ἐκπέσωσιν, χαλάσαντες τὸ σκεῦος, οὕτως

16 υποδραμουντες

7 The omission of κατα σαλμωνην in   ÷ of hcl (cf. note on vii. 10 and p.
614 1765 2138 h is supported by the   clxx above); it must be regarded as

7   om κατὰ Σαλμώνην 614 minn
8   om τινὰ A 611
    Λασέα] Ἄλασσα A minn
9   om ἤδη 2° 489 920
10 om φορτίου καὶ τοῦ 255
12 καταντήσαντες] καταντῆσαι 2147
15 ἐπιδόντες] + τῷ πλέοντι καὶ συστείλαντες τὰ ἱστία 614 1518

[imposu]it nos, 7 et cum tarde navigaremus per aliquod [tempus, v]enimus **h** Gnidum : 8 et inde cum tulissemus, legē[tes Cret]en, devenimus in portum bonum, ubi Anchis ci[vitas er]at: 9 et cum plures dies illic fecissemus, et jam es[set peri]culosa navigatio, eo quod et jejunium trans[sisset], accesit Paulus, 10 dicens: viri, video nos cum injuria [multa e]t jactura, non tantum navis, sed et animarū [nostrar]um navigare incipere.   11 gubernator autem [et magis]ter navis cogitabant navigare,   12 si forte possent [venire P]hoenicem in portum, qui est Cretae.   consē[tiebat i]llis magis centurio quam Paulis verbis : 13 et [dum flat] auster, tulimus celerius et sublegebamus

---

7 κατα σαλμωνην] ⁙ contra Salmonem ✓   8 αλασσα] *mg* Alasa Harclean
15 τω πλεοντι και συστειλαντες τα ιστια] ⁙ flanti et collegimus artemonem ✓ et juxta id quod contingebat

---

a case of abridgement in the Greek 'Western' text.

7-8 μη προσεωντος ημας του ανεμου is omitted in the present text of h, but the Latin text is plainly an abridgement, as well as in disorder, and it is impossible to say what Greek h originally translated. The words *inde cum tulissemus* (cf. vs. 4 *inde cum sustulissemus* vg) show that the editor who formed this text thought that Paul's ship put in at Cnidos.

8 *Anchis* h as the name of the town is commonly supposed to be due to a misunderstanding of αγχι, which might have stood in the 'Western' text for εγγυς. Cf. vs. 13 *de Asson* vg for ἄσσον, the comparative of this same word.

For λασεα (λασαια) the vg rendering *thalassa* is a corruption which seems near to αλασσα A minn hcl.*mg*, but the precise origin of which cannot be traced.

9 The rendering *illic fecissemus* h is in some measure supported by pesh 'and we were there,' but the following sentence in pesh is a very free translation.

13 *Celerius* h represents ασσον, and may be due to a variant θασσον, which Vg took as the name of a place and

renders *de asson* (cod. D *de assole*) ; so sah 'from Alasos,' boh 'from Assos.'

The first person, *tulimus, sublegebamus* h, is supported by pesh 'we sailed.'

14 ευρακυλων BℵA is supported (with minor variations of spelling) by vg (no substantial variant known) sah boh ; the Antiochian ευροκλυδων (ευρυκλυδων) by pesh hcl.*text*.

15 The 'Western' expansion seems to be given in full by hcl·⁙ (note that ✓ is misplaced in the MS. ; it should come after *contingebat*). In 614 1528 πλεοντι is a mistake for πνεοντι (sc. ανεμω). Cassiodorus and Bede, but no other known Latin witnesses, clearly refer to that part of the 'Western' text found in 614.

17 Like the Greek MSS., the versions are divided as to the name of the island; καυδα (mod. Gozzo, i.e. Gavdhonisi) vg pesh, κλαυδα vg.*codd* hcl.*text* sah boh.

For χαλασαντες το σκευος, vg *summisso vase*, various interpretative substitutes are found : χαλασαντες τα ιστια (το ιστιον) minn pesh ; *depositis velis* s ; for the whole phrase χαλασαντες το σκευος ουτως εφεροντο, gig has *vas quoddam dimiserunt quod traheret*.

ἐφέροντο. σφοδρῶς δὲ χειμαζομένων ἡμῶν τῇ ἑξῆς ἐκβολὴν 18
ἐποιοῦντο, καὶ τῇ τρίτῃ αὐτόχειρες τὴν σκευὴν τοῦ πλοίου ἔρειψαν. 19
μήτε δὲ ἡλίου μήτε ἄστρων ἐπιφαινόντων ἐπὶ πλείονας ἡμέρας, 20
χειμῶνός τε οὐκ ὀλίγου ἐπικειμένου, περιῃρεῖτο ἐλπὶς πᾶσα τοῦ
σώζεσθαι ἡμᾶς. πολλῆς τε ἀσιτίας ὑπαρχούσης τότε σταθεὶς 21
ὁ Παῦλος ἐν μέσῳ αὐτῶν εἶπεν· Ἔδει μέν, ὦ ἄνδρες, πειθ-
αρχήσαντάς μοι μὴ ἀνάγεσθαι ἀπὸ τῆς Κρήτης κερδῆσαί τε τὴν
ὕβριν ταύτην καὶ τὴν ζημίαν. καὶ τὰ νῦν παραινῶ ὑμᾶς εὐθυμεῖν, 22
ἀποβολὴ γὰρ ψυχῆς οὐδεμία ἔσται ἐξ ὑμῶν πλὴν τοῦ πλοίου·
παρέστη γάρ μοι ταύτῃ τῇ νυκτὶ τοῦ θεοῦ οὗ εἰμί, ᾧ καὶ λατρεύω, 23
ἄγγελος | λέγων· Μὴ φοβοῦ, Παῦλε· Καίσαρί σε δεῖ παραστῆναι, 24
καὶ ἰδοὺ κεχάρισταί σοι ὁ θεὸς πάντας τοὺς πλέοντας μετὰ σοῦ.
διὸ εὐθυμεῖτε, ἄνδρες· πιστεύω γὰρ τῷ θεῷ ὅτι οὕτως ἔσται 25
καθ᾽ ὃν τρόπον λελάληταί μοι. εἰς νῆσον δέ τινα ἡμᾶς δεῖ ἐκπεσεῖν. 26
ὡς δὲ τεσσαρεσκαιδεκάτη νὺξ ἐγένετο διαφερομένων ἡμῶν ἐν 27
τῷ Ἀδρίᾳ, κατὰ μέσον τῆς νυκτὸς ὑπενόουν οἱ ναῦται προσάγειν
τινὰ αὐτοῖς χώραν. καὶ βολίσαντες εὗρον ὀργυιὰς εἴκοσι, βραχὺ 28
δὲ διαστήσαντες καὶ πάλιν βολίσαντες εὗρον ὀργυιὰς δεκαπέντε·
φοβούμενοί τε μή που κατὰ τραχεῖς τόπους ἐκπέσωμεν ἐκ πρύμνης 29
ῥείψαντες ἀγκύρας τέσσαρας εὔχοντο ἡμέραν γενέσθαι. τῶν δὲ 30
ναυτῶν ζητούντων φυγεῖν ἐκ τοῦ πλοίου καὶ χαλασάντων τὴν
σκάφην εἰς τὴν θάλασσαν προφάσει ὡς ἐκ πρῴρας ἀγκύρας μελ-

19   ἔρειψαν] + εἰς τὴν (some codd. om τὴν) θάλασσαν 614
      minn

22   οὐδεμιᾶς 1518 minn

28   καὶ 1°] οἵτινες ℵ
      om καὶ πάλιν βολίσαντες 1898 minn

---

19 εις την θαλασσαν] ⁕ in mare ✓   Harclean

---

19 + εις την θαλασσαν 614 minn hcl ⁕ gig vg.*codd* sah.

27 προσαχειν B (which might be Doric for προσηχειν) is supported by gig s *resonare sibi aliquam (quandam* s) *regionem,* but the use is strange and the form unattested elsewhere. προσαγειν, although itself difficult, is to be preferred. Vg *apparere* is a substitute, not a translation.

29 At the close of this verse gig vg. *codd* add *ut sciremus an salvi esse possimus (possemus* vg.*codd*).

λόντων ἐκτείνειν, εἶπεν ὁ Παῦλος τῷ ἑκατοντάρχῃ καὶ τοῖς 31
στρατιώταις· Ἐὰν μὴ οὗτοι μείνωσιν ἐν τῷ πλοίῳ, ὑμεῖς σωθῆναι
οὐ δύνασθε. τότε ἀπέκοψαν οἱ στρατιῶται τὰ σχοινία τῆς σκάφης 32
καὶ εἴασαν αὐτὴν ἐκπεσεῖν. ἄχρι δὲ οὗ ἡμέρα ἤμελλεν γείνεσθαι 33
παρεκάλει ὁ Παῦλος ἅπαντας μεταλαβεῖν τροφῆς λέγων· Τεσ-
σαρεσκαιδεκάτην σήμερον ἡμέραν προσδοκῶντες ἄσειτοι δια-
τελεῖτε, μηθὲν προσλαβόμενοι· διὸ καὶ παρακαλῶ ὑμᾶς μεταλαβεῖν 34
τροφῆς, τοῦτο γὰρ πρὸ τῆς ὑμετέρας σωτηρίας ὑπάρχει· οὐδενὸς
γὰρ ὑμῶν θρὶξ ἀπὸ τῆς κεφαλῆς ἀπολεῖται. εἴπας δὲ ταῦτα καὶ 35
λαβὼν ἄρτον εὐχαρίστησεν τῷ θεῷ ἐνώπιον πάντων καὶ κλάσας
ἤρξατο ἐσθείειν. εὔθυμοι δὲ γενόμενοι πάντες καὶ αὐτοὶ προσ- 36
ελάβοντο τροφῆς. ἤμεθα δὲ αἱ πᾶσαι ψυχαὶ ἐν τῷ πλοίῳ ὡς 37
ἑβδομήκοντα ἕξ. κορεσθέντες δὲ τροφῆς ἐκούφιζον τὸ πλοῖον 38
ἐκβαλλόμενοι τὸν σεῖτον εἰς τὴν θάλασσαν. ὅτε δὲ ἡμέρα ἐγένετο, 39
τὴν γῆν οὐκ ἐγείνωσκον, κόλπον δέ τινα κατενόουν ἔχοντα αἰγιαλὸν
εἰς ὃν ἐβουλεύοντο εἰ δύναιντο ἐκσῶσαι τὸ πλοῖον. καὶ τὰς 40
ἀγκύρας περιελόντες εἴων εἰς τὴν θάλασσαν, ἅμα ἀνέντες τὰς
ζευκτηρίας τῶν πηδαλίων, καὶ ἐπάραντες τὸν ἀρτέμωνα τῇ

40 αρτομωνα

Editors   34 om και WH Soden JHR   προ] προς WH Soden JHR   35 ειπας]
ειπων Soden   37 ημεν Soden   ως] διακοσιαι WHmg Soden JHR
39 εγεινωσκον] επεγινωσκον WH Soden JHR   εκσωσαι] εξωσαι WHmg
Soden JHR

Old Uncial   31 ειπεν BℵAC   +δε 81   μεινωσιν εν τω πλοιω BACℵ° 81   εν τω
πλοιω μινωσιν ℵ   32 οι στρατιωται BℵAC   om 81   33 προσλαβομενοι
BℵC 81   προσλαμβανομενοι A   34 και B   om ℵAC 81   μεταλαβειν
BACℵ° 81   +τι ℵ   προ B   προς ℵAC 81   υμετερας BℵC 81
ημετερας A   απο BAC 81   εκ ℵ   35 ειπας] BℵAC   ειπων 81
ευχαριστησεν BAC 81   ευχαριστησας ℵ   36 παντες BACℵ° vid 81   απαντες ℵ
προσελαβοντο BC 81   προσελαβον A   μεταλαβαν ℵ   37 ημεθα BℵA 81
ημεν C   αι BℵC   om A 81   ως εβδομηκοντα εξ B   διακοσιαι
εβδομηκοντα εξ ℵC 81   διακοσιαι εβδομηκοντα πεντε A   38 την BACℵ° 81
om ℵ   39 εγεινωσκον B   επεγινωσκον ℵAC 81   εις BℵC 81   προς A
εβουλευοντο BℵC   εβουλοντο A 81   δυναιντο BℵA 81   δυνατον C   εκσωσαι BC
εξωσαι B²ℵA 81   40 περιελοντες BACℵ° 81   προελοντες ℵ   αρτεμωνα B²

Antiochian   32 οι στρατιωται απεκοψαν LPSϚ   33 εμελλεν ημερα LPSϚ   γενεσθαι
S   προσλαμβομενοι (sic) P   34 om και LPSϚ   μεταλαβειν]
προσλαβειν LPSϚ   προ] προς LPSϚ   υμετερας] ημετερας LP
απο] εκ LPSϚ   απολειται] πεσειται LPSϚ   35 ειπας] ειπων LPSϚ
37 ημεν LPSϚ   εν τω πλοιω αι πασαι ψυχαι LPSϚ   ως] διακοσιαι
LPSϚ   38 της τροφης LPS   εκβαλομενοι L   39 εγεινωσκον]
επεγινωσκον LPSϚ   εβουλευσαντο LPSϚ   δυναιντο] δυνατον LPS
εκσωσαι] εξωσαι LPϚ   εξεωσαι S

31   δυνάμεθα 467 1838

35   ἐσθείειν] + ἐπιδιδοὺς καὶ ἡμῖν 614 1611 2147

39   ἐβουλεύοντο] + οἱ ναῦται 920

---

35 επιδιδους και ημιν] ※ et dedit etiam nobis ✓   Harclean

---

30 At the end of this verse gig vg.*codd* add *ut tutius navis staret*.

33 μηθεν προσλαβομενοι om gig.

34 προ B Ψ minn is to be deemed an error, which may have arisen independently in more than one MS. προ does not seem to have been commonly used in Greek in quite this sense.

ουδενος γαρ] *spero enim in deo meo quia nullius* gig.

36 προσελαβοντο] μετελαμβανον 614 minn (-οντο, προσ-), *percipiebant* gig.

37 Against διακοσιαι εβδομηκοντα εξ (πεντε A) אAC 81 Antiochian gig vg pesh hcl boh stands ως εβδομηκοντα εξ B sah. 522 omits διακοσιαι but does not insert ως ; Epiphanius (ως ἐβδο-μήκοντα) seems to be using the text of B. B is probably in error, for ΠΛΟΙΩΩΣΟΣ̄ could easily have arisen out of ΠΛΟΙΩΣΟΣ̄, and ως is inappropriate with an exact statement of number. πεντε A seems a mere mistake. 69 Ephr.*cat* read 270.

39 The gloss οι ναυται, which in 920 is attached to εβουλευοντο, appears in gig vg.*codd* sah.*cod.* P pesh as subject of 'knew not.'

In view of its regular use in the sense of 'drive ashore,' εξωσαι B²אA 81 gig vg is to be preferred to the plausible, but less apt, reading εκσωσαι BC minn sah boh.

πνεούσῃ κατεῖχον εἰς τὸν αἰγιαλόν. περιπεσόντες δὲ εἰς τόπον 41
διθάλασσον ἐπέκειλαν τὴν ναῦν, καὶ ἡ μὲν πρῷρα ἐρείσασα
ἔμεινεν ἀσάλευτος, ἡ δὲ πρύμνα ἐλύετο ὑπὸ τῆς βίας. τῶν δὲ 42
στρατιωτῶν βουλὴ ἐγένετο ἵνα τοὺς δεσμώτας ἀποκτείνωσιν, μή
τις ἐκκολυμβήσας διαφύγῃ· ὁ δὲ ἑκατοντάρχης βουλόμενος δια- 43
σῶσαι τὸν Παῦλον ἐκώλυσεν αὐτοὺς τοῦ βουλήματος, ἐκέλευσέν
τε τοὺς δυναμένους ἐκκολυμβᾶν ἀπορείψαντας πρώτους ἐπὶ τὴν
γῆν ἐξειέναι, καὶ τοὺς λοιποὺς οὓς μὲν ἐπὶ σανίσιν οὓς δὲ ἐπί 44
τινων τῶν ἀπὸ τοῦ πλοίου· καὶ οὕτως ἐγένετο πάντας διασωθῆναι
ἐπὶ τὴν γῆν.

Καὶ διασωθέντες τότε ἐπέγνωμεν ὅτι Μελιτήνη ἡ νῆσος XXVII
καλεῖται. οἵ τε βάρβαροι παρεῖχαν οὐ τὴν τυχοῦσαν φιλαν- 2
θρωπίαν ἡμῖν, ἅψαντες γὰρ πυρὰν προσελάβοντο πάντας ἡμᾶς
διὰ τὸν ὑετὸν τὸν ἐφεστῶτα καὶ διὰ τὸ ψύχος. συστρέψαντος δὲ 3
τοῦ Παύλου φρυγάνων τι πλῆθος καὶ ἐπιθέντος ἐπὶ τὴν πυράν,
ἔχιδνα ἀπὸ τῆς θέρμης ἐξελθοῦσα καθῆψε τῆς χειρὸς αὐτοῦ. ὡς 4
δὲ εἶδαν οἱ βάρβαροι κρεμάμενον τὸ θηρίον ἐκ τῆς χειρὸς αὐτοῦ,
πρὸς ἀλλήλους ἔλεγον· Πάντως φονεύς ἐστιν ὁ ἄνθρωπος οὗτος
ὃν διασωθέντα ἐκ τῆς θαλάσσης ἡ δίκη ζῆν οὐκ εἴασεν. ὁ μὲν 5
οὖν ἀποτινάξας τὸ θηρίον εἰς τὸ πῦρ ἔπαθεν οὐδὲν κακόν· οἱ δὲ 6

Editors   41 βιας] +των κυματων Soden   43 εκκολυμβαν] κολυμβαν WH Soden JHR
1 μελιτη Soden   2 προσελαβοντο] προσανελαμβανον JHR

Old Uncial   41 επεκειλαν] επωκειλαν B²(B³ Tdf)   πρωρα BNC 81   πρωτη A
εμεινεν BNC 81   εμενεν A   υπο BACNᶜᵒʳʳ 81   απο N   βιας BNA
+των κυματων CNᶜ 81   42 δε BNAC² 81   om C   αποκτεινωσιν
BNAC 81   +ινα Nᶜ   43 διασωσαι τον παυλον BNC 81   τον παυλον διασωσαι A
βουληματος BACNᶜ 81   βηματος N   τε BNA   δε C 81   εκκολυμβαν B
κολυμβαν NAC 81   την γην BAC 81   της γης N   1 μελιτηνη B
μελιτη B²NAC 81   2 τε BAC 81   δε N   προσελαβοντο BACNᶜ 81
προσανελαμβανον N   παντας BNC 81   om A   δια 2° BACNᶜ 81
om N   3 επιθεντος BNC 81   +του παυλου A   καθηψε BNA 81
καθηψατο C   4 κρεμαμενον το θηριον BNAC   το θηριον κρεμαμενον 81
της 2° BACNᶜ 81   om N   5 αποτιναξας BN   αποτιναξαμενος A 81
κακον BANᶜ 81   om N

Antiochian   41 επεκειλαν] επωκειλαν LPSς   ελυετο] διελυετο L   βιας] +των
κυματων LPSς   42 διαφυγοι ς   43 εκατονταρχης] εκατονταρχος
LPSς   εκκολυμβαν] κολυμβαν LPSς   1 διασωθεντες] +οι περι τον
παυλον εκ του πλοος L   επεγνωμεν] επεγνωσαν LPSς   μελιτηνη]
μελιτη LPSς   2 τε] δε LPSς   αψαντες] αναψαντες LPSς
εφεστωτα] υφεστωτα L   3 om τι LPSς   απο] εκ ς   εξελθουσα]
διεξελθουσα LPSς   4 ελεγον προς αλληλους LPSς   5 αποτιναξαμενος L

VIII 2   προσελάβοντο] προσανελάμβανον אΨ' 614 1518 minn

---

41 την ναυν] navem ⋇ eo ubi erat syrtis √   42 μη τις] + mg ex iis   Harclean

---

41 The curtness of υπο της βιας led to various expansions: των κυματων Cא° 81 Antiochian boh, maris gig vg, 'of the wind' sah.

43-44 The rendering of gig may give a fair idea of the 'Western' paraphrase: centurio autem prohibuit hoc fieri praecipue propter paulum ut salvum illum faceret. et jussit illos qui possent enatare primos exire ad terram et reliquos quosdam in tabulis salvos fieri. et sic omnes animae salvae ad terram venerunt. Sah translates απεριψαντας εξιεναι by 'to leap,' but perhaps does not represent a different Greek text from B. Pesh seems to retain some traces of the 'Western' text.

1 μελιτηνη B min (1 lectionary) gig vg hcl. Greek mg boh, μελιτη B²אAC 81

Antiochian vg.codd pesh sah. The collocation of letters THNHHNHCOC has played some part here.

2 For προσελαβοντο BACא° 81 Antiochian the reading προσανελαμβανον אΨ 614 1518 minn is to be preferred. Vg renders reficiebant, gig refecerunt, in the sense 'refreshed,' which is proper to προσανελαμβανον. The word προσελαβοντο, in the sense 'received,' is colourless, not likely to have been altered to a more vigorous term ; and this weak sense is the only one that can be given it here, for its more specific connotations, 'take in addition,' 'take as a helper,' 'take hold of,' or 'fasten,' are all foreign to this context. See Wordsworth and White's note.

προσεδόκων αὐτὸν μέλλειν πίμπρασθαι ἢ καταπείπτειν ἄφνω
νεκρόν. ἐπὶ πολὺ δὲ αὐτῶν προσδοκώντων καὶ θεωρούντων
μηθὲν ἄτοπον εἰς αὐτὸν γεινόμενον, μεταβαλόμενοι ἔλεγαν αὐτὸν
εἶναι θεόν. ἐν δὲ τοῖς περὶ τὸν τόπον ἐκεῖνον ὑπῆρχεν χωρία 7
τῷ πρώτῳ τῆς νήσου ὀνόματι Ποπλίῳ, ὃς ἀναδεξάμενος ἡμᾶς
ἡμέρας τρεῖς φιλοφρόνως ἐξένισεν. ἐγένετο δὲ τὸν πατέρα τοῦ 8
Ποπλίου πυρετοῖς καὶ δυσεντερίῳ συνεχόμενον κατακεῖσθαι,
πρὸς ὃν ὁ Παῦλος εἰσελθὼν καὶ προσευξάμενος ἐπιθεὶς τὰς
χεῖρας αὐτῷ ἰάσατο αὐτόν. τούτου δὲ γενομένου οἱ λοιποὶ οἱ 9
ἐν τῇ νήσῳ ἔχοντες ἀσθενείας προσήρχον⟨το⟩ καὶ ἐθεραπεύοντο,
οἳ καὶ πολλαῖς τειμαῖς ἐτείμησαν ἡμᾶς καὶ ἀναγομένοις ἐπέθεντο 10
τὰ πρὸς τὰς χρείας.

Μετὰ δὲ τρεῖς μῆνας ἀνήχθημεν ἐν πλοίῳ παρακεχειμακότι 11
ἐν τῇ νήσῳ Ἀλεξανδρινῷ, παρασήμῳ Διοσκούροις. καὶ κατ- 12
αχθέντες εἰς Συρακούσας ἐπεμείναμεν ἡμέραις τρισίν, ὅθεν περι- 13
ελόντες κατηντήσαμεν εἰς Ῥήγειον. καὶ μετὰ μίαν ἡμέραν ἐπι-
γενομένου νότου δευτεραῖοι ἤλθομεν εἰς Ποτιόλους, οὗ εὑρόντες 14
ἀδελφοὺς παρεκλήθημεν παρ' αὐτοῖς ἐπιμεῖναι ἡμέρας ἑπτά· καὶ
οὕτως εἰς τὴν Ῥώμην ἤλθαμεν. κἀκεῖθεν ἀδελφοὶ ἀκούσαντες 15

8 after προσευξαμενος MS. seems to add ευξαμενος
12 συρακουσσας

Editors 7 τρεις ημερας WHmg Soden 9 γενομενου] +[και] WH +και Soden
JHR 11 ανηχθημεν] ηχθημεν Soden mg 12 ημερας τρεις WH
Soden JHR 13 περιελοντες] περιελθοντες Soden 14 επιμειναι]
επιμειναντες JHR 15 οι αδελφοι WH Soden JHR

Old Uncial 6 μελλειν BΝ 81 μελλων A πιμπρασθαι BΝᶜ 81 πιπρασθαι A
εμπιπρασθαι Ν μεταβαλομενοι BA 81 μεταβαλλομενοι Ν αυτον
ειναι BΝ 81 ειναι αυτον A 7 ημερας τρεις B τρεις ημερας ΝA 81
8 δυσεντεριω BΝA δυσεντερια 81 om ευξαμενος 2ᵒ B² 9 γενομενου B
+και ΝA 066 81 10 τα BΝᶜ 066 81 τας A om Ν τας χρειας
BΝA 066 την χρειαν 81 12 ημεραις τρισιν B ημερας τρεις ΝA 066 81
13 περιελοντες BΝ περιελθοντες AΝᶜ 066 81 14 εις την Ρωμην ηλθαμεν
BΝ ηλθαμεν εις (+την 81) Ρωμην A 066 81 15 αδελφοι B οι αδελφοι ΝA
066 81

Antiochian 6 om αφνω S μεταβαλλομενοι LPSϚ θεον αυτον ειναι LPSϚ
7 τρεις ημερας LPSϚ 8 δυσεντερια Ϛ εισελθων] προσελθων P
9 δε] ουν LPSϚ γινομενου L add και before οι λοιποι LPSϚ
εχοντες ασθενειας εν τη νησω LPSϚ 10 om οι P την χρειαν LPSϚ
11 ανηχθημεν] ηχθημεν S 12 ημερας τρεις LPSϚ περιελοντες] περιελθοντες
LPϚ προσελθοντες S 14 παρ] επ LPSϚ επιμειναι] επιμειναντες S
ηλθαμεν] εισηλθομεν L 15 οι αδελφοι LPSϚ

6 θεωρούντων] θεωρησάντων Ψ 1518 2138

10 ἡμᾶς] + ὅσον χρόνον ἐπεδημοῦμεν minn

---

6 και θεωρησαντων] *mg* et [quum] intuiti essent   7 ημερας τρεις] tres dies ⁙· Harclean domi suae √   9 γενομενου] *mg* [quum] auditum [esset]   10 αναγομενοις] egrederemur ⁙· inde √   επεθεντο] posuerunt ⁙· in navi √   12 επεμειναμεν] mansimus ⁙· ibi √   14 επιμειναι] manentes ⁙· apud eos √

---

11 The (Ionic and late) spelling διοσκουροις is that of BℵAC and of the Antiochian text, but ΨP (corrected to -ου- by the first hand), 81* and many minuscules, sah boh gig (cf. vg.*codd.* C^mg D), have the old Attic form διοσκορ-. The minuscules that have this latter form are mainly of the I-groups, and it may well have stood in the 'Western' text.

12 ημεραις τρισιν B is not effectively supported by *triduo* vg, since vg shows a tendency elsewhere (e.g. Acts xxviii. 30 *biennio*) to substitute ablative for accusative in such an expression of time.

13 Neither περιελοντες Bℵ (*et inde tulimus et* gig; cf. h xxvii. 8 *cum tulissemus*, xxvii. 13 *tulimus* [αραντες]) nor περιελθοντες of most other witnesses yields a satisfactory sense, unless περιαιρεῖν had a technical seafaring meaning otherwise unattested (cf. xxvii. 40 τὰς ἀγκύρας περιελόντες.) περιελθοντες looks like the last resort of an editor unable to cope with the obscure περιελοντες. See Hort, 'Introduction,' pp. 226 f.

14 The textual problem in this verse is made unusually difficult by uncertainty as to the precise form of the 'Western' reading and by the superficial aptness but intrinsic inferiority of the text of Bℵ. A possible theory of the history of the passage is as follows:—

(1) παρεκληθημεν παρ αυτοις επιμειναντες gig (*consolati sumus et mansimus apud eos* ; cf. hcl 'we were consoled among them, staying ⁙· with them √'), was probably the 'Western' reading, and is to be accepted as original.

(2) In S 614 minn, επ αυτοις ('by reason of them') was substituted for παρ αυτοις, because the phrase was associated with παρεκληθημεν instead of (cf. gig pesh) επιμειναντες ; this gave the reading παρεκληθημεν επ αυτοις επιμειναντες.

(3) In the B-text (BℵA 066 81 vg pesh boh) no change was made in παρ αυτοις, but επιμειναντες was changed to επιμειναι either by accident or on purpose, and in connexion with this παρεκληθημεν was taken in the sense *rogati sumus*, as in pesh : 'they begged of us and we stayed with them.'

(4) Later, the Antiochian revisers (LP minn) accepted both these modifications, producing the text παρεκληθημεν επ αυτοις επιμειναι.

But (apart from doubts arising from the general reputation of the several witnesses) the readings themselves would also permit of other interpretations of their genetic relations.

τὰ περὶ ἡμῶν ἦλθαν εἰς ἀπάντησιν ἡμῖν ἄχρι Ἀππίου Φόρου καὶ
Τριῶν Ταβερνῶν, οὓς ἰδὼν ὁ Παῦλος εὐχαριστήσας τῷ θεῷ ἔλαβε
θάρσος. ὅτε δὲ εἰσήλθαμεν εἰς Ῥώμην, ἐπετράπη τῷ Παύλῳ 16
μένειν καθ᾽ αὑτὸν σὺν τῷ φυλάσσοντι αὐτὸν στρατιώτῃ.
Ἐγένετο δὲ μετὰ ἡμέρας τρεῖς συνκαλέσασθαι αὐτὸν τοὺς 17
ὄντας τῶν Ἰουδαίων πρώτους· συνελθόντων δὲ αὐτῶν ἔλεγεν
πρὸς αὐτούς· Ἐγώ, ἄνδρες ἀδελφοί, οὐδὲν ἐναντίον ποιήσας τῷ
λαῷ ἢ τοῖς ἔθεσι τοῖς πατρῴοις δέσμιος ἐξ Ἱεροσολύμων παρ-
εδόθην εἰς τὰς χεῖρας τῶν Ῥωμαίων, οἵτινες ἀνακρείναντές με 18
ἐβούλοντο ἀπολῦσαι διὰ τὸ μηδεμίαν αἰτίαν θανάτου ὑπάρχειν
ἐν ἐμοί· ἀντιλεγόντων δὲ τῶν Ἰουδαίων ἠναγκάσθην ἐπικαλέ- 19
σασθαι Καίσαρα, οὐχ ὡς τοῦ ἔθνους μου ἔχων τι κατηγορεῖν.
διὰ ταύτην οὖν τὴν αἰτίαν παρεκάλεσα ὑμᾶς ἰδεῖν καὶ προσ- 20
λαλῆσαι, εἵνεκεν γὰρ τῆς ἐλπίδος τοῦ Ἰσραὴλ τὴν ἅλυσιν ταύτην
περίκειμαι. οἱ δὲ πρὸς αὐτὸν εἶπαν· Ἡμεῖς οὔτε γράμματα περὶ 21
σοῦ ἐδεξάμεθα ἀπὸ τῆς Ἰουδαίας, οὔτε παραγενόμενός τις τῶν
ἀδελφῶν ἀπήγγειλεν ἢ ἐλάλησέν τι περὶ σοῦ πονηρόν. ἀξιοῦμεν 22
δὲ παρὰ σοῦ ἀκοῦσαι ἃ φρονεῖς, περὶ μὲν γὰρ τῆς αἱρέσεως ταύτης
γνωστὸν ἡμῖν ἐστὶν ὅτι πανταχοῦ ἀντιλέγεται. ταξάμενοι δὲ 23
αὐτῷ ἡμέραν ἦλθον πρὸς αὐτὸν εἰς τὴν ξενίαν πλείονες, οἷς
ἐξετίθετο διαμαρτυρόμενος τὴν βασιλείαν τοῦ θεοῦ πείθων τε

16 ἐπετράπη δὲ τῷ Παύλῳ] ὁ ἑκατόνταρχος παρέδωκε τοὺς δεσμίους τῷ στρατοπεδάρχῳ τῷ δὲ Παύλῳ ἐπετράπη LPS αὐτὸν] + ἔξω τῆς παρεμβολῆς 614 1611 2147

18 οἵτινες] + πολλὰ 614 2147 minn

19 Ἰουδαίων] + καὶ ἐπικραζόντων· Αἶρε τὸν ἐχθρὸν ἡμῶν 614 minn
κατηγορεῖν] + ἀλλ' ἵνα λυτρώσωμαι τὴν ψυχήν μου ἐκ θανάτου 614 1518 minn

22 παρὰ] περὶ 915

---

16 ο εκατονταρχος παρεδωκε τους δεσμιους τω στρατοπεδαρχω] ⸓ centurio Harclean tradidit vinctos praefecto exercitus ✓   εξω της παρεμβολης] ⸓ extra castra ✓   18 πολλα] ⸓ multa ✓   19 και επικραζοντων αιρε τον εχθρον ημων] ⸓ et [quum] clamarent: Tolle inimicum nostrum ✓   αλλ ινα λυτρωσωμαι την ψυχην μου εκ θανατου] ⸓ sed ut servarem animam meam a morte ✓   21 ελαλησεν] locutus est ⸓ nobis ✓

---

15 The omission of τα περι ημων by gig vg pesh deserves mention.

16 The expansion of επετραπη τω παυλω B𝕬 81 minn vg pesh boh into ο εκατονταρχος παρεδωκε τους δεσμιους τω στρατοπεδαρχω, τω δε παυλω επετραπη is found (with trifling variation) in 614 perp gig vg.codd hcl·⸓· sah, and was adopted by the Antiochian revisers. It was doubtless a part of the 'Western' text. Since ὁ στρατοπεδάρχος is not the title of any specific official, but seems to be a general word for 'superior officer,' 'commandant,' this longer text contains nothing beyond the capacity of the 'Western' reviser, and has no greater claim to acceptance as original than any other 'Western' paraphrastic expansion.

The addition εξω της παρεμβολης 614 perp gig vg.codd Ambrosiaster (prologue to Ephesians) hcl.mg appears in gig as a substitute for καθ εαυτον; in most of the other witnesses as an addition to these words. It is doubtless from the same source as the longer expansion. For the same phrase cf. Lev. xvi. 27, Heb. xiii. 11.

The translations of (or substitutes for) τω στρατοπεδαρχω are the following : principi peregrinorum gig, prefecto perp vg.codd ; 'the αρχων of the soldiers' sah ; 'head of the army' hcl·⸓·. See Mommsen and Harnack, in Sitzungsberichte, Berlin Academy, 1895, pp. 491–503, Zahn, Einleitung in d. N.T., vol. i, § 31, note 2.

17 Vg pesh sah render 'called together' for εγενετο . . . συνκαλεσασθαι of the B-text, and this may be a fragment of the 'Western' text. The noteworthy, and at first sight seemingly Semitic, factum est . . . convocauit of gig s hcl.text is perhaps really due to conflation of the two readings. In perp the rendering is factum est . . . ut convocaret.

ελεγεν προς αυτους] conferebat cum eis dicens gig s.

19 The 'Western' addition αλλ ινα λυτρωσωμαι κτλ. is supported by perp gig vg.codd.

αὐτοὺς περὶ τοῦ Ἰησοῦ ἀπό τε τοῦ νόμου Μωυσέως καὶ τῶν προφητῶν ἀπὸ πρωὶ ἕως ἑσπέρας. καὶ οἱ μὲν ἐπείθοντο τοῖς 24 λεγομένοις οἱ δὲ ἠπίστουν, ἀσύμφωνοι δὲ ὄντες πρὸς ἀλλήλους 25 ἀπελύοντο, εἰπόντος τοῦ Παύλου ῥῆμα ἓν ὅτι Καλῶς τὸ πνεῦμα τὸ ἅγιον ἐλάλησεν διὰ Ἠσαίου τοῦ προφήτου πρὸς τοὺς πατέρας

Ia. vi. 9 f. ὑμῶν | λέγων· Πορεύθητι πρὸς τὸν λαὸν τοῦτον καὶ εἰπόν· Ἀκοῇ 26 ἀκούσετε καὶ οὐ μὴ συνῆτε, καὶ βλέποντες βλέψετε καὶ οὐ μὴ ἴδητε· ἐπαχύνθη γὰρ ἡ καρδία τοῦ λαοῦ τούτου, καὶ τοῖς ὠσὶν 27 βαρέως ἤκουσαν, καὶ τοὺς ὀφθαλμοὺς αὐτῶν ἐκάμμυσαν· μή ποτε ἴδωσιν τοῖς ὀφθαλμοῖς καὶ τοῖς ὠσὶν ἀκούσωσιν καὶ τῇ καρδίᾳ συνῶσιν καὶ ἐπιστρέψωσιν, καὶ ἰάσομαι αὐτούς. γνωστὸν 28 οὖν ὑμῖν ἔστω ὅτι τοῖς ἔθνεσιν ἀπεστάλη τοῦτο τὸ σωτήριον τοῦ θεοῦ· αὐτοὶ καὶ ἀκούσονται.

Ἐνέμεινεν δὲ διετίαν ὅλην ἐν ἰδίῳ μισθώματι, καὶ ἀπεδέχετο 30 πάντας τοὺς εἰσπορευομένους πρὸς αὐτόν, κηρύσσων τὴν βασι- 31 λείαν τοῦ θεοῦ καὶ διδάσκων τὰ περὶ τοῦ κυρίου Ἰησοῦ Χριστοῦ μετὰ πάσης παρρησίας ἀκωλύτως.

Editors   28 εστω υμιν Soden   ακουσονται] +και ταυτα αυτου ειποντος απηλθον οι ιουδαιοι πολλην εχοντες εν εαυτοις συζητησιν Soden mg.

Old Uncial   24 μεν ΒΑℵᶜ 81   +ουν ℵ   25 δε ΒΑℵᶜ 81   τε ℵ   δια (περι ℵ) ησαιου του προφητου προς τους πατερας υμων Βℵℵᶜ 81   προς τους πατερας υμων δια ησαιου του προφητου Α   26 λεγων Βℵ   λεγον Α 81   ακουσετε Βℵ ακουσητε Α 81   και βλεποντες βλεψετε Βℵ   και βλεποντες βλεψητε Αℵᶜ   om 81 27 επαχυνθη ΒΑℵ 81   εβαρυνθη ℵ   ωσιν Β 81   +αυτων ℵΑ   και τη καρδια συνωσιν ΒΑℵᶜ 81   om ℵ   επιστρεψωσιν Βℵ   επιστρεψουσιν Α 81 ιασομαι ΒℵΑ   ιασωμαι 81   28 υμιν εστω Β 81   εστω υμιν ℵΑ   τουτο Βℵ Α 81   om ℵᶜ   30 ενεμεινεν Βℵ 81   εμεινεν Αℵᶜ   31 χριστου ΒΑℵᶜ 81 om ℵ

Antiochian   23 add τα before περι LSⸯ   25 υμων] ημων LPⸯ   26 λεγον (S uncertain)ⸯ   27 ιασωμαι Sⸯ   28 εστω υμιν LPSSⸯ   om τουτο LPSSⸯ   29 +και ταυτα αυτου ειποντος απηλθον οι ιουδαιοι πολλην εχοντες εν εαυτοις συζητησιν LPSSⸯ   30 ενεμεινεν] εμεινεν LPSSⸯ   δε] + ο παυλος LPSSⸯ

24   λεγομένοις] + ὑπὸ τοῦ Παύλου Ψ

29   + καὶ ταῦτα αὐτοῦ εἰπόντος ἀπῆλθον οἱ Ἰουδαῖοι πολλὴν
     ἔχοντες ἐν ἑαυτοῖς συζήτησιν LPS

30   δὲ] + ὁ Παῦλος LPS
     αὐτόν] + Ἰουδαίους τε καὶ Ἕλληνας 614 minn

---

28 αυτοι] ipsi ·✕· enim ✓   29 και ταυτα αυτου ειποντος απηλθον Harclean
οι ιουδαιοι πολλην εχοντες εν εαυτοις συζητησιν] ·✕· et quum haec ipse dixisset,
exierunt Judaei habentes disputationem multam invicem ✓   30 δε] mg
autem   ο παυλος] ·✕· Paulus ✓   ιουδαιους τε και ελληνας] ·✕· Judaeos
et gentiles ✓   31 ακωλυτως] + text dicens quia hic est Christus Jesus
filius dei per quem incipiet totus mundus judicari. amen.

---

29 Vs. 29, doubtless a part of the 'Western' text, and found in hcl·✕· perp gig vg.codd, cf. Cassiod., was adopted by the Antiochian revisers.

30 The addition ιουδαιους τε και ελληνας found in 614 hcl·✕· occurs also in other Greek minn and in vg.codd and Ephr. In its place perp gig vg.codd read et disputabat cum judeis et grecis, and a trace of this is preserved by the addition of disputans in vg.codd after μισθωματι in the first part of the sentence. These readings indicate a 'Western' expansion, the precise form of which cannot be determined. In perp s ενεμεινεν is represented by a participle, and the subsequent et is omitted.

31 The addition in hcl.text is not supported by any Greek witness, but is found, for substance and with variation of form and position, in perp vg.many codd, but not in gig; see D. De Bruyne, Revue Bénédictine, vol. xxiv, 1907, pp. 403 f. The name 'Jesus' seems inappropriate, and is not found in a large proportion of the Latin witnesses. The gloss is plainly of Greek origin (note incipiet judicari in many Latin codd), and is evidently ancient. It may well have been part of the 'Western' text, and the Latin witnesses seem to show that it was originally a substitute for τα περι . . . εκωλυτως, not a mere addition.

DETACHED NOTES

i. 2.

Amid the complicated divergence of texts in this verse two forms stand out as representing the sources from which the others have been derived :

(1) αχρι ης ημερας εντειλαμενος τοις αποστολοις δια πνευματος αγιου ους εξελεξατο ανελημφθη BℵAC 81 Antiochian.

(2) The Greek which can be reconstructed (with the aid of Codex Bezae) from the African Latin translation used by Augustine, *Contra Felicem* i. 4 ; *Contra epistolam Fundamenti* 9 :

> in die quo (*v.l.* qua) apostolos elegit per spiritum sanctum et praecepit praedicare evangelium,[1]
>
> εν ημερα η τους αποστολους εξελεξατο δια πνευματος αγιου και εκελευσε κηρυσσειν το ευαγγελιον.

In this reconstructed 'Western' form [2] it is plain that, in harmony with the 'Western' glossator's well-known method, και εκελευσε κηρυσσειν το ευαγγελιον has been substituted for εντειλαμενος. Jesus' choice of his apostles necessarily preceded his instruction of them, and accordingly the statement of the instruction, in expanded form, was removed to a position at the end of the sentence, after εξελεξατο. Bearing this in mind, we can reconstruct the earlier text on which the 'Western' reviser may have worked, as follows :

> εν ημερα η εντειλαμενος τοις αποστολοις δια πνευματος αγιου εξελεξατο.

This would have differed from the text of B in three respects : (1) εν ημερα η for αχρι ης ημερας B ; (2) the absence of ους, as read in B ; (3) the absence of any reference to the Ascension (ανελημφθη B). For the omission of the object of εξελεξατο cf. Acts xiii. 3. The critic's choice must lie between something like this reconstructed text, used as a basis (and modified) by the 'Western' reviser, and the text of B.

[1] The tract *Contra Varimadum* (perhaps by the anti-priscillianist Itacius Clarus, bishop of Ossonuba in Spain ; late 4th century ; wrongly attributed to Vigilius of Thapsus) twice (i. 31 and iii. 71) quotes the verse in a text closely like that of Augustine : *in die qua apostolos elegit per spiritum sanctum quibus constituit* (om *quibus constituit* iii. 71) *praedicare evangelium*. Tertullian, *Apologeticus* 21 (cited above, p. 3), seems to show (*ad officium praedicandi*) that he knew the gloss εκελευσε κηρυσσειν το ευαγγελιον ; see J. R. Harris, *Four Lectures on the Western Text of the New Testament*, 1894, pp. 55 f.

[2] Important contributions to the understanding of the evidence as to the 'Western' text of Acts i. 2 were made by P. Corssen, *Der Cyprianische Text der Acta apostolorum*, 1892, and by F. C. Burkitt, *The Old Latin and the Itala*, 1896, pp. 57 f., 66-71.

With regard to this text and Augustine's Latin a few comments may be added.

(1) The reading *in die quo (qua)* seems assured for Augustine in *Contra Felicem* and *Contra ep. Fundamenti*.[1] The reference in the form under consideration seems to be to Lk. vi. 13 ff.[2] The chief (but of course not the complete) contents of the former 'treatise' are stated to be Jesus' words and deeds from his first choice and instruction of the apostles. His instruction was completed (καὶ λέγων τὰ περὶ τῆς βασιλείας τοῦ θεοῦ Acts i. 3) during the resurrection appearances, and the present 'treatise' goes on to narrate how it was carried out by his apostles.

(2) The rendering of καὶ συναλιζομενος by *et quomodo conversatus est* may mean 'and how he associated.' In that case it shows that the translator took vss. 2-4, which repeat matters presented more at length in the Gospel of Luke, as a succession of statements describing the contents of the 'former treatise': (a) *elegit*, (b) *et precepit*, (c) *quibus praebuit se*, (d) *et quomodo conversatus est*, (e) *et precepit eis ne discederent*. This accorded with the intent of the original author (cf. the similar summary, Acts x. 40-42), and *quomodo* may represent a 'Western' ὡς, otherwise lost. Yet the addition of the word in translation would hardly be beyond the degree of freedom which the translator permits himself, and it is probably better to ascribe the addition to him.[3]

(3) The absence of any reference to the Ascension in this text is surely to be associated with the similar absence of mention of that event in the 'Western' text of Lk. xxiv. 51. The change, whether by addition or subtraction, must be ascribed to the same motive in both cases, and was part of the same reworking of the New Testament text.[4]

---

[1] On the other text used by Augustine see below, p. 258.

[2] It may be objected that no Greek text, and no other version than the Latin, has the reading 'on the day when,' and consequently the theory may be proposed that the Greek text lying before the 'Western' reviser read, like B, αχρι ης ημερας (but without ανελημφθη), and was changed, either by the reviser or the Latin translator, to 'on the day when.' On this supposition the 'day' referred to by the Greek text would have to be taken as that of the final instruction to the apostles (Lk. xxiv. 47 ff.), which included a kind of choice (cf. Acts xv. 7 and x. 41). But the lack of Greek attestation does not outweigh the positive evidence of Augustine's citations, and the reference to Lk. xxiv. 47 ff. is attended with difficulties. The suggestion that in ἐν ἡμέρᾳ ῇ the word ἡμέρα means 'period' (cf. Jer. vii. 22 ἐν ἡμέρᾳ ῇ ἀνήγαγον αὐτοὺς ἐκ γῆς Αἰγύπτου ; John xiv. 20, xvi. 23, 26, etc.) is admissible ; cf. Blass, *Philology of the Gospels*, 1898, pp. 132-137, *Evangelium secundum Lucam*, 1897, p. xxxii.

[3] Zahn argues in a valuable note (*Urausgabe*, pp. 130 f.) that *quomodo* merely means 'when,' used in translating the Greek participle by a Latin temporal clause (cf. h in Acts v. 24, 27) ; see J. Pirson, 'Quomodo en latin vulgaire' in *Philologische und volkskundliche Arbeiten Karl Vollmöller dargebracht*, Erlangen, 1908, pp. 72 f. ; and this is wholly possible. Either explanation leaves it unnecessary to suppose that the Greek text read ὡς.

[4] This point has been justly and acutely urged by F. Graefe, 'Der Schluss des Lukasevangeliums und der Anfang der Apostelgeschichte,' *Theologische Studien und Kritiken*, vol. lxi., 1888, pp. 522-541, who adopts the view that the 'Western' text of both passages excised the reference to the Ascension ; see also F. Graefe, *ibid.*, vol. lxxi., 1898, pp. 136 f. On the text of Lk. xxiv. 51 see Hort, 'Appendix,' p. 73. The other phrases and sentences in Lk. xxiv., with incomplete attestation and held by Hort to be instances of 'Western non-interpolation,' must be included in considering the problem.

Old Latin   The several forms of the Old Latin in vs. 2 are to be explained as modifications of the 'Western' text of Augustine and conflations of it with the fuller B-text. The most interesting is that of gig t :

> usque in diem quo precepit apostolis per spiritum sanctum praedicare evangelium quos elegerat (elegit *t*).

Here the Ascension has not been introduced, although in other respects (notably *usque in diem* and *quos elegerat*) the influence of the B-text is plain.

Augustine, *De consensu evangelistarum* iv. 8, offers a different Latin text from that quoted above (p. 257) from other works of his, and the same text is found in the Augustinian work of doubtful origin, *De unitate ecclesiae* (*Epistola ad Catholicos de secta Donatistarum*) 11 (27).

> usque in diem quo apostolos elegit per spiritum sanctum mandans jussit (eis *for* jussit, *De unitate*) praedicare evangelium.

This is probably a revision under the influence of the B-text through the Vulgate, which, as is well known, Augustine employed in the Gospel citations of the *De consensu*.[1] But equally with the other text of Augustine, this form lacks any reference to the Ascension.

Codex Bezae   The text of D is also conflate. It retained καὶ ἐκέλευσε κηρύσσειν τὸ εὐαγγέλιον, but nevertheless restored from the B-text ἐντειλάμενος, thus producing a doublet, and from the same source it introduced ἀνελήμφθη (necessarily in an altered position). The confused awkwardness of the resulting sentence in D proves that here, as in so many other cases, its text is conflate. The Latin d agrees substantially with D, but by the curious phrase *quem susceptus est*, which breaks an otherwise perfect connexion, d betrays even more clearly that the reference to the Ascension is an intrusion into a previously formed Latin version. Further evidence that d is a rendering not all from one hand is to be seen in the repetition of *praecepit*, where a single translator would have been almost certain to use different Latin words for ἐντειλάμενος and ἐκέλευσε. The earliest rendering, however, had adopted (so Augustine) *praecepit*, instead of *jussit*, for ἐκέλευσε, and when ἐντειλάμενος came later to be injected into this Latin translation, no other word seemed so apt as *praecipere*, in spite of the infelicitous repetition.[2]

Vulgate   Vg has conformed its rendering completely to the B-text :

> usque in diem qua praecipiens apostolis per spiritum sanctum quos elegit adsumtus est,

and this rendering is followed by perp and (with *quo* for *qua*) by e.

The Luxeuil lectionary gives substantially the Vulgate text, but with *praedicare evangelium* inserted, as in gig t, after *per spiritum sanctum*.

Sahidic   The Sahidic version seems to represent a Greek text as follows :

---

[1] Burkitt, *The Old Latin and the Itala*, pp. 58 f., 72-78.

[2] J. R. Harris, *Codex Bezae*, pp. 154 f., has tried to show that this double employment of *praecepit* indicates that the 'Western' text here was first formed in Latin, and then taken over into Greek. But all that it actually proves is that, as stated above, the Latin text of d did not reach its present form at one casting.

αχρι ης ημερας ανελημφθη εντειλαμενος τοις αποστολοις δια
πνευματος αγιου κηρυσσειν το ευαγγελιον ους εξελεξατο.

The conflation here pursues something of the same general method as
that found in D.

The Bohairic, as would be expected, follows the B-text. **Bohairic**

We may now turn to the Syriac versions. (a) Ephrem (see below, **Syriac**
p. 384) would seem to have used an Old Syriac 'Western' text
similar to that of gig ; for he states that the close of Jesus' activity was
'the day when he instructed the apostles in Galilee to preach the Gospel.'
This at any rate implies the Greek εκελευσε κηρυσσειν το ευαγγελιον,
and with almost equal certainty shows that Ephrem's text did not include
a reference to the Ascension. But Ephrem's text seems to have read
'until the day when.' (b) The Peshitto renders : 'until the day on which
he ascended, after he had instructed the apostles whom he chose by the
Holy Spirit.' This is the B-text, except that ανελημφθη is introduced,
as in D, immediately after ημερας, and δια πνευματος αγιου put after
εξελεξατο. This order may be due merely to the freedom of the translator. (c) The Harclean text is a revision according to the Antiochian
Greek standard, although, as in the Peshitto, the mention of the Holy
Spirit is put after 'whom he chose' : 'until the day when, after he had
instructed the apostles whom he chose through the Holy Spirit, he
ascended.' The Harclean margin, however, communicates a form in
which, after the same series of phrases found in pesh, there is added at
the close : 'and he commanded to preach the gospel.' The result is a
text identical with D except for the position of δια πνευματος αγιου, but
which may have arisen by a process independent of, and somewhat
different from, that which produced the text of D.

The matter of the position of δια πνευματος αγιου in the B-text has
always given trouble to the interpreter. In the versions it was not
difficult so to change it as to improve the sense, and (unless it be in the
Harclean text and margin) they can hardly be relied on for evidence as to
the order of their underlying Greek in this respect. Cyril of Alexandria
(Adv. Nestorii blasphemias iv. 3) expressly connects δια πνευματος αγιου
with the choice of the apostles, but it is more than doubtful whether this
implies any peculiarity in the form of the B-text with which he was
familiar.

From this survey of the development and influence of the 'Western' **Codex**
form we return to the B-text. It is evident that three small changes in **Vaticanus**
the text which we have reconstructed as probably lying beneath the
'Western' text (above, p. 256) would have produced the B-text, namely :
(1) εν ημερα η changed to αχρι ης ημερας (cf. Acts i. 22 εως της ημερας
ης ανελημφθη) ; (2) ους inserted before εξελεξατο ; (3) ανελημφθη added
at the close. To one who accepts the view that we have in Luke xxiv. **Conclusion**
51 an interpolation of the words και ανεφερετο εις τον ουρανον not
found in ℵD and the Old Latin [cf. also Sinaitic Syriac], but contained
in B and all other witnesses), it may well seem probable that in the
B-text of Acts i. 2 we have before us a similar expansion due to the
innocent desire of a very early editor to introduce here a mention of the

Ascension ; and this is the conclusion of the present writer. Such a view is confirmed by the fact that in Acts this reference to the Ascension is premature, since it is introduced before the mention of the preceding resurrection appearances. Without an express statement of the Ascension in Luke xxiv. 51 the reference of Acts i. 2 is positively unsuitable, and in any case the natural place for any mention of it in Acts is not reached until verse 9, where the full account of the event is given as an integral part of the narrative reserved for the present 'treatise.'

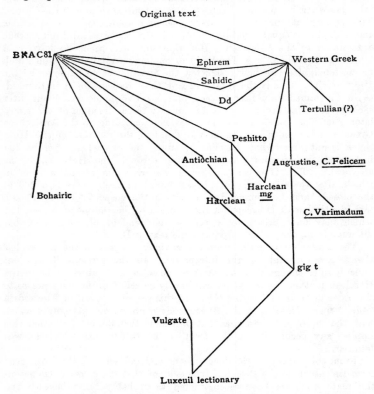

The alternative to this view is the supposition that the B-text was original, and was deliberately mutilated so as to make it omit the references to the Ascension in both Luke xxiv. 51 and Acts i. 2. A sufficient motive for this is hard to see in either passage. The considerations, just mentioned, of literary appropriateness in Acts i. 1-9 which commend the 'Western' text 'intrinsically' to our critical judgment, are not such as would have led the 'Western' reviser to abbreviate a previously existent longer text, while the idea that he noticed a contradiction between the apparent date of the event in Luke xxiv. 51

and that of the Ascension, forty days later (Acts i. 3), and therefore removed the reference to the Ascension from Luke xxiv. 51, not only is in itself highly improbable but entirely fails to explain the excision of ανελημφθη from Acts i. 2. If it be suggested that the Latin tradition rests on an abbreviation made by the African translator (see above, pp. ccxxxvi-viii), the reply is conclusive that the Old Syriac (Ephrem) had a text at least partly, and perhaps almost wholly, similar, and that the Greek text of D by its present confusion betrays its origin from a text in which ανελημφθη was lacking.

The preceding diagram exhibits, as nearly as such a method permits, Diagram the relation of the several witnesses here. The abundance of the material makes the graphic presentation unusually instructive with respect to the text of Acts in general ; but it is offered with some hesitation, because in fact the several witnesses are not, for the most part, actual members of the genealogy, but merely represent approximately types of text through which the descent has taken place. The diagram, however, displays to the eye how the original text suffered two distinct modifications, in the Old Uncial and in the ' Western ' texts, and how from these by mainly independent mixtures the successive forms were produced. It will be observed that the pure descendants of the two forms are, on the one side, the Antiochian Greek, the Bohairic, the Vulgate, and probably the Peshitto, on the other the text of Augustine, *Contra Felicem*, and of *Contra Varimadum*. The mixture found in Augustine, *De consensu*, has been omitted in order not to confuse the lines too much. The dependence of the Vulgate on the Old Latin pertains to phraseology, not to text, and is not indicated by a line. The relations of date, as between the several mixtures, have had to be partly neglected in the diagram.

xiii. 27-29.

From the conflate and corrupt text of D, with the aid of hcl.*mg* and hcl ⁘, the 'Western' text of these verses can be made out to have read approximately as follows : (27) οι γαρ κατοικουντες εν ιερουσαλημ και οι αρχοντες αυτης, μη συνιεντες τας γραφας των προφητων τας κατα παν σαββατον αναγεινωσκομενας επληρωσαν, (28) και μηδεμιαν αιτιαν θανατου ευροντες εν αυτω, κρειναντες αυτον, παρεδωκαν πειλατω εις αναιρεσιν · (29) ως δε ετελουν παντα τα περι αυτου γεγραμμενα, ητουντο τον πειλατον μετα το σταυρωθηναι αυτον απο του ξυλου καθαιρεθηναι, και επιτυχοντες καθειλον και εθηκαν εις μνημειον.

Vs. 27. αυτης (D d) was also preserved in gig vg ; likewise γραφας (D d) in e (hence in E).

That the presence in D of κρειναντες (with the requisite και prefixed) is due to contamination from the B-text is probable, since in the Bezan form of vs. 28 the same word is found just below and apparently in its right place. This probability is in some measure confirmed by the fact that d in vs. 28 renders κρειναντες by *judicantes*, but in vs. 27 has *cum judicassent* ; in vs. 27 a later translator was probably at work, following the conflate text of D. In the later position κρειναντες perfectly suits the context and carries distinct emphasis (well brought out by *autem* d).

Vs. 28. εν αυτω appears in D 614 1611 d gig vg hcl ⁓ sah ('against him') boh ('in him'). This addition might have been made in order to obviate the awkwardness of the collocation of participles (ευροντες κρειναντες) in the original text (see below). εις αναιρεσιν was the 'Western' reading. The otiose ινα D is due either to reaction from d or (more probably) to contamination from the original reading of the B-text ινα αναιρωσιν discussed below.

Vs. 29. ετελουν D may be used in the sense of 'had completed' (as in vii. 23 επληρουτο, and many other cases ; see J. H. Ropes, *Harvard Theological Review*, 1923, pp. 168-170), or may be due to the observation that the burial also was in fulfilment of prophecy (cf. πλουσιος Matt. xxvii. 57, Is. liii. 9, Hebrew). εισιν D is probably a mechanical imitation of d. The 'Western' μετα το σταυρωθηναι (or σταυρωσαι?) αυτον ητουντο τον πειλατον καθαιρεθηναι hcl.*mg* was altered in D d into ητουντο τον πειλατον τουτον μεν σταυρωσαι in order to restore the substance of ητησαντο πειλατον αναιρεθηναι αυτον, as found in the B-text of vs. 28, but with the result of wholly destroying the sequence of thought. μεν D is a curious survival from μετα (hcl.*mg*).

παλιν D d (omitted by hcl.*mg*) was added in connexion with the conflation ; it is inappropriate to επιτυχοντες, which originally referred, not to the crucified body, but to the request. και καθελοντες D probably represents a 'Western' καθειλον (cf. d *deposuerunt*) altered to agree with the B-text ; the και, which has now passed into d also, was necessarily prefixed in making the correction. These suppositions permit a smoother Greek, and serve to explain the presence of και before εθηκαν.

απο του ξυλου is in its true 'Western' position in hcl.*mg* ; the process of conformation to the B-text necessitated the change of position now seen in D d.

The original 'Western' reviser seems to have been chiefly guided by the desire to recite the events more completely. In the following details the text underlying the 'Western' revision was probably superior to that preserved in B :

(1) Vs. 27, αυτης (D d gig vg) for αυτων (cf. Lam. i. 6, ii. 2 ; Is. i. 21, lx. 17) is unconventional and appropriate.

(2) Vs. 27, for τουτον αγνοησαντες B, the shorter reading αγνοησαντες (cf. D d) is to be preferred. This verb, more commonly meaning 'be ignorant of,' 'fail to recognize,' was here used in the sense of 'not understand,' and caused difficulty (note how Lk. ix. 45 ηγνόουν τὸ ῥῆμα τοῦτο was furnished with a following explanatory sentence not found in Mk. ix. 32). The 'Western' reviser substituted μη συνιεντες ; the B-text supplied a new object τουτον.

(3) As between the position of κρειναντες in vs. 27 in the B-text and its position in vs. 28 in the 'Western' text (D d, cf. note above), every consideration of intrinsic fitness speaks for the later position. The difficulty caused by κρειναντες in vs. 27 (fully brought out in the commentaries) even led Blass to propose a conjectural emendation so that

participle and principal verb might have the same (understood) object.
To the emender who produced the B-text the transference of κρειναντες
from vs. 28 to vs. 27 may have seemed to relieve a certain baldness and
obscurity in vs. 27 ; at the same time it obviated the unpleasant collocation ευροντες κρειναντες in vs. 28. That such a collocation was possible
is shown by Acts xii. 19 ; many other cases are but little less harsh.
As a part of this operation και was inserted before τας φωνας in vs. 27.
The procedure bears a striking analogy to the anticipatory insertion of
ανελημφθη in the B-text of Acts i. 2.

(4) Vs. 28, for αναιρεθηναι B the versions attest an early ινα αναιρωσιν
(ut interficerent vg pesh, cf. boh ; improved to read ut interficeretur gig d).
This imitation of the Semitic plural (cf. Wellhausen, Einleitung in die drei
ersten Evangelien, pp. 25 f.) to denote an indefinite subject (cf. Acts iii. 2
and elsewhere) was early modified in the 'Western' text (cf. D
παρεδωκαν πειλατω . . εις αναιρεσιν), and is to be accepted, on transcriptional grounds, instead of the more sophisticated substitutes of both B
and D. Since αναιρεθηναι and εις αναιρεσιν are alike easily capable of
literal translation into both Latin and Syriac (cf. Acts viii. 1 [vg vii. 60,
pesh vii. 61]), it may be confidently assumed that these versions offer a
literal, not a free, translation of the Greek which they had before them.

xiii. 33.

πρωτω D d gig, codd. known to Bede.
δευτερω BℵAC 81 Antiochian vg pesh hcl. text sah boh.
There are minor variations of position and phrasing.
πρωτω is also expressly attested for Acts xiii. 33 in the following
passages of Origen and Hilary :

Origen, Selecta in psalmos, ψαλμὸς δεύτερος (ed. Lommatsch, vol. xi.
pp. 393 f.).

δυσὶν ἐντυχόντες ἑβραικοῖς ἀντιγράφοις, ἐν μὲν τῷ ἑτέρῳ
εὕρομεν ἀρχὴν δευτέρου ψαλμοῦ ταῦτα · ἐν δὲ τῷ ἑτέρῳ συνήπτετο
τῷ πρώτῳ. καὶ ἐν ταῖς πράξεσι δὲ τῶν ἀποστόλων τό · Υἱός μου
εἶ σύ, ἐγὼ σήμερον. γεγέννηκά σε, ἐλέγετο εἶναι τοῦ πρώτου
ψαλμοῦ · Ὡς γὰρ γέγραπται, φησίν, ἐν πρώτῳ ψαλμῷ, Υἱός μου εἶ
σύ, ἐγὼ σήμερον γεγέννηκά σε. τὰ ἑλληνικὰ μέντοι ἀντίγραφα
δεύτερον εἶναι τοῦτον μηνύει. τοῦτο δὲ οὐκ ἀγνοητέον, ὅτι ἐν τῷ
ἑβραικῷ οὐδενὶ τῶν ψαλμῶν ἀριθμὸς παράκειται, πρῶτος εἰ τύχοι,
ἢ δεύτερος, ἢ τρίτος.

Hilary, Tract. in psalm. ii.

1. Plures nostrum ambiguos facit apostolica auctoritas, utrum
psalmum hunc cohaerentem primo et veluti primi extimum putent
esse, an vero subjacentem et secundum potius connumerent. namque
in Actibus Apostolorum primum hunc haberi atque esse sub
oratione beati Pauli ita docemur : Nosque vobis evangelizamus eam
quae ad patres facta est promissio, hanc deus explevit filiis nostris,

suscitans dominum nostrum Jesum, sicut et in psalmo scriptum
est primo : Filius meus es tu, ego hodie genui te ; cum suscitavit
eum a mortuis amplius non regressurum in interitum. ob hanc
ergo apostolicam auctoritatem errore scribentium fieri creditur, ut
in ordine secundus psalmus iste numeretur, cum primus esse ipso
doctore gentium testante noscatur, cognoscenda itaque ea ratio est,
cur et a nobis secundus esse intellegendus sit, et ab apostolo esse
primus ostensus sit.

3. . . . Hi [sc. LXX interpretes] ergo psalmos inter ceteros libros
transferentes et in numerum redegerunt et in ordinem conlocaverunt
et diapsalmis distinxerunt, qui omnes secundum Hebraeos confusi
et habebantur et habentur. horum igitur translationes Hebraeis
tum lingua tantum sua utentibus non erant necessariae. . . .

4. Beatus ergo apostolus Paulus, secundum professionem suam
Hebraeus ex Hebraeis, etiam secundum hebraicam cognitionem et
fidem psalmum hunc primum esse dixit, translatorum distinctione
non usus : cui maximum hoc praedicandi ad synagogae principes
studium erat, ut dominum nostrum Jesum Christum dei filium,
natum, passum, resurgentem regnare in aeternum ex doctrina legis
ostenderet. tenuit itaque hunc modum, ut Hebraeis praedicans
Hebraeorum consuetudine uteretur. sed nobis translatorum uten-
dum auctoritate est, legem non ambiguitate litterae sed doctrinae
scientia transferentium.

The quotation comes from Ps. ii. 7, and the reading πρωτω implies
the ancient combination of Psalms i. and ii. in Hebrew MSS., which is
mentioned in rabbinical sources (early third century, Palestinian) as well
as by Origen (as above). Justin Martyr (Apol. i. 40) quotes the two
psalms as one, while Eusebius, Apollinarius, and Euthymius Zigabenus
(all perhaps in dependence on Origen) refer to this Hebrew practice.

On the Latin side, likewise, Tertullian, Adv. Marcionem, iv. 22, quotes
Ps. ii. 7 as in primo psalmo, and Cyprian, Testimonia i. 13 (codd. LV), iii.
112 (codd. LM), adduces two other passages from Ps. ii. in the same way,
although in five further cases all codices of Testimonia cite verses from
Ps. ii. as in psalmo secundo, probably by an emendation of primo origin-
ally written by Cyprian. For patristic and rabbinical references see
Tischendorf, ad loc. ; Lagarde, Novae psalterii graeci editionis specimen
(Abhandlungen, Göttingen Academy, xxxiii.), 1887, pp. 16-18 ; and
Zahn, Urausgabe, pp. 83, 234 f., with the works there cited.

On the other hand, no extant copy of the Greek Psalter combines the
two psalms in one, and neither Origen nor Hilary seems to have known
of any that did so. Justin may have learned from the Jews the practice
which he, like Origen, followed; in the case, however, of Cyprian (and
perhaps Tertullian) we must infer the actual use of copies of the
Psalter in Latin in which the two psalms were combined. This continued as the practice of African Bibles until after the middle of the
fourth century ; see G. Mercati, D' alcuni nuovi sussidi per la critica del
testo di S. Cipriano, Rome, 1899, pp. 18-25.

Acts xiii. 33 is probably the earliest known citation of a psalm by number, and no other instance is found in the New Testament. The date at which numbers began to be assigned to the several psalms is not known. Origen seems to have known no Hebrew MS. containing them, and the citation of the *first* psalm by number need not imply that the MSS. known to the writer of Acts contained numbers for other psalms. Origen himself, however, and the *Testimonia* of Cyprian, regularly cite the Greek and Latin psalms by number.

πρωτω (altogether natural if this chapter of Acts was originally written in Aramaic, and not inconceivable if the original was in Greek) probably gives the true text. In that case δευτερω was substituted for πρωτω by early editors acquainted only with the LXX, in which the two psalms were more commonly separated. This is more probable than the alternative supposition that δευτερω is original, and was emended in the 'Western' text, before the time of Origen, to conform to the Hebrew practice and to copies of the Latin (and Greek ?) Psalter like those used by Tertullian and Cyprian.

As to the other variant words in the sentence, and their order, no certain conclusion is possible.

In view of all the facts, the suggestion that the original text lacked any mention of number, and has been completed in accordance with two different methods of counting, is to be rejected. It gains no sufficient weight from the fact that a number of Greek codices of Acts omit any mention of number.

xv. 29.

The omission of και πνικτων and the addition of the (negative) Golden Rule in vs. 29 must be discussed together. Three types of text present themselves : (1) that of Tertullian without και πνικτων and without the Golden Rule ; (2) that of Irenaeus (expressly attested for the original Greek by cod. 1739 both in this verse and in vs. 20) without και πνικτων but with the Golden Rule ; (3) the B-text, with και πνικτων but without the Golden Rule. In xxi. 25 the Golden Rule does not seem to find a place in any known text.

I.

The text of Tertullian (which departs from the B text in omitting και πνικτων) adequately accounts for the others, and is to be accepted. See Tertullian *De pudicitia* 12, with which may be compared *Apologet.* 9,[1] *De monogamia* 5, *Adversus Marcionem* iv. 16. In addition to the evidence of Tertullian, this text is supported by Pacian of Barcelona († between 379 and 392), *Paraenesis* 4, in a full quotation of the decree, and probably by Ambrosiaster and Augustine. It is the text of Ephrem in vs. 20, although that father has the Golden Rule in vs. 29. Moreover, traces of the same text still survive in gig and D d.

---

[1] In *Apologet.* 9 Tertullian speaks of the actual practice of Christians in not eating 'things strangled,' but makes no reference to Acts xv. 29, which in *De pudicitia* 12 he interprets as relating to morals, not to food. It is wrong to take *Apologet.* 9 as evidence that at any period Tertullian was acquainted with a text of Acts xv. 20, 29 containing four provisos.

These statements require fuller explanation :

(a) Ambrosiaster (on Gal. ii. 1-2, quoted above, p. ccxlv, note 2), while acquainted with the reading *et a suffocato,* expressly rejects it. In the passage named he makes no mention of the Golden Rule, and it is clear that his text of the Decree did not contain it, since in *Quaest. vet. et novi testamenti,* iv. 1, he refers to the Rule as a part of '*naturalis lex,*' known to all mankind.[1]

(b) Augustine shows striking points of agreement with Ambrosiaster, and may well have been influenced by him here as elsewhere ; see *Speculum* 28 (ed. Weihrich, p. 199), *Contra Faustum* 32, 13 ; *Enarr. in Ps.* 57, 1 ; *Enarr. in Ps.* 118, cited by G. Resch (see below), p. 137. Augustine reads the text without καὶ πνικτων, and does not intimate that the decree of Acts xv. included the (negative) Golden Rule, which, on the contrary, in the comments on the Psalms named he quotes as written in our hearts and as '*naturae legem.*'

(c) Ps.-Eucherius, *Comm. in Gen. ix. 1* cannot be adduced as an independent witness to this text, since its citation of Acts xv. 29 occurs in a passage taken over bodily from Augustine, *Contra Faustum,* xxxii. 13.

(d) That the text found in gig is derived from that attested by Tertullian is shown by the following reasoning. (a) In no one of the three passages in question (xv. 20, xv. 29, xxi. 25) does gig contain the Golden Rule. (b) In xv. 20 and xxi. 25 gig omits καὶ πνικτου (καὶ πνικτον), although in xv. 29 it reads *et suffocato.* (c) But in the original text underlying gig, xv. 20 and xv. 29 must have been in agreement. Consequently it appears that the text of gig for the Decree in vs. 29 is due to alteration to make it conform to vg, with which it is almost identical in language, while in the parallel speech of James (and in xxi. 25) it has remained without retouching. The Decree would have been the most obvious point for the attention of an editor interested in conforming to vg, and hence vs. 29 would have been the passage most likely to suffer alteration. The inference from this reasoning is that gig really attests the same text as Tertullian.

A parallel to this situation is found in Ephrem (below, p. 426), who repeats James's speech without either καὶ πνικτου or the Golden Rule, but shortly after, in referring to the Decree, mentions the Golden Rule. Ephrem's *Comm. in epp. D. Pauli,* Lat. transl., Venice, 1893, p. ·243 (introduction to commentary on 1 Timothy), confirms this evidence that Ephrem's text of the Decree omitted καὶ πνικτων, but gives no indication as to the Golden Rule.

(e) D d testify in a somewhat similar way to the text of Tertullian. In all three passages both D and d omit the reference to things strangled, and in xv. 29 they add the Golden Rule in general agreement with the text of Irenaeus. But in xv. 20, although they add the Golden Rule, they have preserved in the main verb the second person (ποιειτε, *faciatis*).

---

[1] Ambrosiaster (Pseudo-Augustine), *Quaest.* iv. 1 : Primum lex formata in litteris dari non debuit, quia in natura ipsa inserta quodam modo est et creatoris notitia ex traduce non latebat. nam quis nesciat quid bonae vitae conveniat aut ignoret quia quod sibi fieri non vult alii minime debeat fieri ?

This second person is appropriate to vs. 29, but not to the immediate context in vs. 20.   The Golden Rule, therefore, in this text must first have been inserted in due form in vs. 29, and thence, in a later stage of the development of the text, have been introduced into vs. 20.[1]   This complicated process seems a necessary assumption in order to explain the present complicated state of the text of D d, and suffices to give a clear account of the latter.   It thus appears that in the stage of the text of D d immediately preceding the text of the existing MS., the Golden Rule was lacking in vs. 20 but was present in vs. 29, so that the situation was the same as that still found in gig and Ephrem.   We may therefore safely draw the same conclusion about the still earlier text on which D is ultimately based as in the case of gig, and regard D d as likewise really testifying to the same text as that used by Tertullian.

II.

The text of Irenaeus (with both the omission of καὶ πνικτῶν and the addition of the Golden Rule) is supported by Cyprian, *Testimonia*, by D d (in the present form of their text : for the earlier form, see above), and possibly by codex 1739 (in vs. 20 ; although the suspicion of accidental error is aroused by the further omission in that codex in vs. 20 of τῶν εἰδώλων and by the inclusion in vs. 29 of καὶ πνικτοῦ).

Other certain examples of the text of Irenaeus and Cyprian are not forthcoming.   The letter of a Pelagian (ed. Caspari, *Briefe, Abhandlungen und Predigten*, Christiania, 1890, p. 18), of date between 413 and 430, quotes expressly from the Decree the Golden Rule ; whether, as would seem not unlikely, the writer had a text without καὶ πνικτῶν must remain uncertain.   Conversely, Jerome, *Comm. in Gal. v. 2* (see below) quotes the Decree without καὶ πνικτῶν, but does not indicate whether or not his text included the Golden Rule.   The same is true of Fulgentius (†533), *Pro fide catholica* 9.   According to the scholion of cod. 1739, Eusebius in his work against Porphyry stated that Porphyry (third century) referred to the (negative) Golden Rule in a way damaging to the Christians, apparently drawing it from the Decree, but whether Porphyry made any further reference to the provisos is not indicated. For evidence that the original (Greek) form of the Didascalia (third century) did not mention 'things strangled' in vs. 29, see above, pp. cxcv-cxcvii.

III.

This is the point at which may most conveniently be mentioned certain mixed forms of the text.

One of these is the important form with both the four provisos and the Golden Rule.   It evidently exerted a far-reaching influence, discernible in witnesses which in other respects follow the B-text.   Such are

---

[1] In vs. 29, d reads *ne feceritis*, but D, whose text in an earlier stage probably had the corresponding Greek μὴ ποιεῖτε, has μὴ ποιεῖν.   Those minuscules (614, etc.) which here contain the Golden Rule are divided between ποιεῖτε and ποιεῖν.

numerous Greek minuscules (all of them classed by von Soden in the groups designated by I and K^c), vg.*codd* hcl ⁜ sah ; all these have both καὶ πνικτῶν (or some modification of the phrase) and the (negative) Golden Rule.

Among Latin fathers Jerome, *Comm. in Gal. v. 2*, quotes the text without καὶ πνικτῶν and adds *sive, ut in nonnullis exemplaribus scriptum est, ' et a suffocatis.'* He may here be dependent on Origen, and in any case does not indicate whether the copies referred to were Latin or Greek. So Ambrosiaster (on Gal. ii. 1-2), while using the text without καὶ πνικτῶν, refers to the Greek text that did contain the words, which he believed that ' *sofistae Graecorum* ' had interpolated. In Augustine, *Speculum* 29, the text of all three passages which mention the provisos is quoted from the Vulgate, with the four items, but Augustine's comment in his epilogue clearly follows the text with three only.

The strange translation of vg. *best codd.* in vs. 29 (not vs. 20 nor xxi. 25) *et sanguine suffocato* is supported by the reading αἱματος πνικτου in some codices of Cyril of Jerusalem, *Catech.* xvii. 29, and in Amphilochius of Iconium (fl. 370), ed. Ficker, p. 59. 14 (but cf. p. 61. 3 and 13). This may somehow point to the fact that πνικτου is an intrusion into the text.

Gaudentius of Brescia (†410 or 427 ; Migne, vol. xx. col. 954) has the form *a sanguine id est suffocatis,* and A[p]ponius (fifth century ; perhaps a Syrian, resident in Rome), *Comm. in cantic.* iii., ed. Rom. 1843, p. 178, the somewhat similar *a sanguine vel suffocato* (but *a suffocato et sanguine* in *Bibl. vet. patr.*, vol. xiv., p. 112). Probably both these expansions of the Vulgate rendering were intended to indicate that, in the view of these writers, the word *suffocato* of that version merely defined *sanguine*, without adding a fourth prohibition.[1]

The omission (vs. 29 only) of καὶ αἱματος from the B-text in sah (cod. Hunt 3 only), Origen, *Commentariorum series in Matt. xxiii.* (Latin transl., ed. Lommatzsch, vol. iv. p. 198), and Methodius, ' On the Distinction of Foods,' ed. Bonwetsch, Erlangen, 1891, p. 297, may be merely a coincidence, or may be somehow connected with the complicated history of the text. The omission of καὶ πορνειας by Origen, *Contra Celsum* viii. 29 can hardly be significant for his text.

IV.

The B-text (with καὶ πνικτῶν but without the Golden Rule) is attested not only by all Greek uncials except D and by nearly all minuscules, but by Clement of Alexandria, Origen (in all probability, although express evidence that he did not include the Golden Rule is lacking), and other Greek writers, as well as by boh pesh hcl.*text*. As is pointed out above, the (negative) Golden Rule was taken over into this text in a number of instances.

[1] So Burkitt, *Journal of Theological Studies*, vol. XI., 1909-10, pp. 267-268. Burkitt holds that this was a correct understanding of the purpose of the Vulgate rendering without *et*.

V.

The history of the text seems to have been as follows. In the East the Decree was correctly understood in the second century and later to relate to food, and under the influence of current custom the text was at first expanded by the addition of καὶ πνικτῶν. This application of the ancient prohibition of blood, so as to include all flesh improperly slaughtered, is known to have been an early Christian usage (Tertullian, *Apolog.* 9 ; cf. Justin, *Dial.* 20), as well as current with the Jews, and in the second century the introduction of an express mention of it into the text would not have seemed a substantial alteration. To Africa, however, the Decree came (in the 'Western' Greek text of Acts) in its original form, without this addition, and there it commonly received (so already Tertullian, *De pudicitia,* 12) a moral interpretation (αἵματος being taken as referring to murder). No Latin text seems to have contained the addition of 'things strangled' before the time of Jerome.

The addition of the (negative) Golden Rule, which sprang from this moral interpretation and made over the Decree fully into a brief summary of fundamental Christian morals, was effected in Greek copies of the second century (Irenaeus), and so passed into the Latin version as early as the time of Cyprian's *Testimonia* in the third century. Whether the Golden Rule was first added in East or West is uncertain. In any case the addition ultimately made its way not only into the briefer 'Western' text but also, not later than the third or fourth century (cf. sah), into some forms of the expanded B-text.

If our choice lay between the B-text and that of Irenaeus, the former would have to be preferred, since the text of Irenaeus implies the (secondary) moral interpretation of the Decree, but the text of Tertullian, simpler than either of the other two, suits all requirements for a text underlying both of them. In a word, any text of which the Golden Rule was *an integral part,* would have to be rejected as a later modification of the original.

The crucial significance of these conclusions for the theory that both the B-text and the 'Western' text came from the author of the book of Acts seems to have been apparent to every one except Blass.

See Zahn, *Urausgabe,* pp. 90-92, 154-166, 296-299, 358-365 ; G. Resch, *Das Aposteldecret nach seiner ausserkanonischen Textgestalt* (T. U. xxviii.), 1905 (where most of the material is conveniently presented) ; D. Böckenhoff, *Das apostolische Speisegesetz in den ersten fünf Jahrhunderten,* 1903 ; A. v. Harnack, *Das Aposteldecret (Act. xv. 29), und die Blass'sche Hypothese* (Sitzungsberichte, Berlin Academy), 1899, pp. 150-176, *Die Apostelgeschichte* (Beiträge zur Einleitung in das Neue Testament, iii.), 1908, pp. 188-198.

xv. 34.

For the name σειλας the 'Western' text seems to have had σειλεας. The name occurs in the following passages : Acts xv. 22, 27, 32, 34, 40 ; xvi. 19, 25, 29 ; xvii. 4, 10, 14, 15 ; xviii. 5 ; cf. hcl ※ for xv. 30.

The form with three syllables is found in Greek in Codex Bezae only, Acts xv. 34 (σειλεα, accusative) and xvii. 4 (σιλαια, dative). In the former instance, xv. 34, the whole verse is a 'Western' addition, and it may be supposed that the non-western text, by the aid of which the text of Codex Bezae has elsewhere been corrected, did not here provide the means of correction. The Latin side in xv. 34 reads *sileae*. In xvii. 4 (where d reads *silae*) no reason suggests itself for this exceptional retention in D of the 'Western' form, elsewhere supplanted by the form with two syllables, σειλας or σιλας in D, *silas* in d.

In the early Latin authorities the trisyllabic form is much more frequent. It is used by Irenaeus (xv. 27) and Cyprian (xvi. 25); gigas has consistently *syleas*, and Lucifer and Ambrosiaster likewise follow the form with three syllables, which must therefore have belonged to the gigas-recension. It is also cited from the *Itinerarium Burdigalense* (before A.D. 333; *Itinera Hierosolymitana*, vol. i., Geneva, 1879, p. 21), the anonymous *Prophetiae*, Cassiodorus, Ado of Lyons.[1] Jerome, *Comm. in Gal. i. 1*, probably refers to it. Vulgate codices containing Old Latin elements, especially manuscripts of Spanish and Irish origin, frequently show the trisyllabic form, in some cases evidently adopted deliberately and used consistently. Codex Cavensis (C) and the Book of Armagh (D) will serve as examples.

On the other hand, of the Old Uncials, B consistently gives σειλας, while אAC always have σιλας, as does the Antiochian text. To this the Vulgate form *Silas* was made to correspond.[2] The Egyptian versions read σιλας, the Peshitto and Harclean *shila*.

It would be natural to suppose 'Sileas' due to an adaptation to the form of a Semitic name containing a guttural (cf. Σίμων, Συμεών), but the names שׁילא (Talmudic), שׁאילא (Palmyrene), do not exactly correspond to the variation in the Greek and Latin texts of Acts; see Nöldeke, *Zeitschrift der Deutschen Morgenländischen Gesellschaft*, vol. xxiv., 1870, p. 97; Dalman, *Grammatik des jüdisch-palästinischen Aramäisch*, § 28, d. 4.

---

[1] A. Souter, *A Study of Ambrosiaster* (Texts and Studies, vii.), 1905, p. 208; Zahn, *Urausgabe*, pp. 90, 178.

[2] Jerome, *Nom. hebr.* p. 71 : '*Silam, missus.*'

APPENDIX I

PAPYRUS WESS[237]

Vienna, K 7541-7548. Bilingual papyrus fragments, uncial, parallel columns, Greek and Sahidic. Probably 12th-13th century. C. Wessely, *Griechische und koptische Texte theologischen Inhalts IV.* (Studien zur Paläographie und Papyruskunde, xv.), Leipzig, 1914, pp. 107-118.

K 7541a

Acts

xvii.

28 [. .] του γαρ [και γ]ε
[νος] εσμεν
29 [γε]νος ουν υπαρ
χοντες του θῡ ου
κ οφειλομεν
χρυσιω η αργυ
ριω η λ[ι]θω
χαραγματι τε
χνης και ενθυ
μιασεως ανου το
θ[ει]ον ειναι ομοιον
30 του[ς] μεν ουν χρο
[νους] τους αγνοιας
[υπεριδων ο θς̄]
[τα ν]υν παραγγε
[λλει το]ịς ανοις παν
[τας π]ανταχου με
31 [ταν]οειν καθοτι
εστησεν ημερα
εν η μελλει κρι
νειν την οικου
μενην εν δικαι
οσυνη εν αν
δρι ω

K 7541b

xvii.

32 [ακουσ]ạ[ντες δε α]
[ναστασιν νεκρ]ῷ
[. .]ν
[ακουσομεθα σ]ου
[. . . . . .]
33 [. . . ουτως ο]
[παυλος εξηλθ]ε̄
[εκ μεσου αυτω]ν
34 [τινες δε ανδρες]
[κολληθεντες α]υ
[τω επιστευσα]ν
[εν οις και διο]νυ
[σιος ο αρεοπ]α
[γιτης και γυν]η
[ονοματι δα]μạ
[ρις και ετ]ερο[ι]
[συν αυ]τοις
xviii.
1 [μετα] δε ταυτα
[χω]ρισθεις εκ
[τ]ων αθηνων
ηλθεν εις κο[ριν]
2 θον κ[αι] ευρω[ν]

271

K 7542a

xviii.

24 [. . αλεξαν]
   [δρευ]ς τω γενε[ι]
   [αν]ηρ λογιος κα
   [τηντ]ησεν εις ε
   φεσο[ν δυνατος]
   ων εν ταις γρ[αφ]αις
25 ουτος ην κ[ατ]η
   χημενος [την ο]
   δον κυ και ζε
   ων [τω] π̄ν̄[ι ε]λ[α]
   λει και εδ[ιδ]ασ
   κεν ακρ[ι]βως τα
   [περ]ι του χ̄[υ επ]ι

K 7543a

xix.

1 [. .] α [. . .]
2 [. .] προς
   [αυτους ει π̄]να
   [αγιον ελαβ]ε
   [τε πιστευσ]αντ[ες]
   [οι δε ειπο]ν πρ[ος] αυ[το]ν
   [αλλ ο]υδε η[κου]
   [σαμεν ε]ι πνα αγιο̄
   [λα]μβανουσι τινες
3 [ο δε] ειπεν εις τι
   [ο]υν εβαπτισθητε
   [οι] δε ειπον
   [εις τ]ο ιωαννου
   [β]απτισμα
4 ειπεν δε ιω
   αννης εβαπτι
   σεν βαπτισμα

K 7542b

xviii.

. . . . .
27 [πεπιστευκ]οσιν
   [δια της χαρι]τος
28 . . . . . .

K 7543b

xix.

6 . . . . . .
   [π̄να το αγιο]ν
   [επ αυτο . . ε]λα
   [λουν . . γλ]ωσ
   [σαις και επροφ]η
7 [τευον ησαν] δε
   [οι παντες αν]δρες
   [ωσει δωδεκα]
8 [εισελθων δ]ε
   [εις την συναγ]ω
   [γην επαρρησι]α
   [ζετο επι μηνα]ς
   [τρεις . . . . .]

K 7544a

xix.

13, 14 [κ]ηρυσσει ησαν
δε τινος σκευα
ιουδαιου αρχιερε
ως επτα υιοι τουτο
15 ποιουντες απο
κριθεν δε το π̅ν̅α
το πονηρον ειπε̅
αυτοις τον μεν ι̅ν̅
γινωσκω και τὸ
παυλον επισταμαι
υμεις δε τινες ε̣σ[τε]
16 [κ]αι εφαλλομε
[νος ο] α̅ν̅ο̅ς̅ επ αυτους
[εν ω] ην το π̅ν̅α το [πο]
[νηρον] κατα

K 7545a

xx.

9 [κατω κ]αι̣ ηρθη
10 [νεκρος] κ[α]τ̣α̣βα̣ς̣
[δε ο παυ]λος επε
[πεσεν] αυτω και
[συ]μπεριλαβων
[ειπ]ε[ν] μη θορυβεισ
[. . η] γ[αρ] ψυχη α̣υ̣
[το]υ εν αυτω ε[σ]
11 [τιν α]ναβας δ[ε] κ̣α̣ι̣ [κ]λ̣α̣
[σα]ς τ[ο]ν αρ[τον κ]α[ι]
[γευσα]μ[εν]ος εφ ει
[κανον τε] ομειλη
[σας αχρι α]υγης
[ουτως ε]ξ[ηλθε]ν
12 [ηγαγο]ν δε και τον
[π]αιδα [ζ]ωντά
[και πα]ρεκληθη
[σαν ο]υ μετριως
13 [ημει]ς δε προηλ
[θομε]ν εις το πλοι
[ον και α]νηχθημεν
[. .] τ̣ην̣ θασο[ν]
[εκειθ]εν μελλον
[τες αναλ]αμβανειν
τον παυ[λο]ν

K 7544b

xix.

18 . . . . . .
[πεπιστευκοτω]ν
[ηρχοντο εξομολ]ο
[γουμενοι αναγγελλοντ]ες
. . . . . .

K 7545b

xx.

15 . . . . . .
[μεινα]ντε̣ς̣
[εν τρωγυλλ]ι̣[ω]
τη δ[ε εχ]ομε̣ν̣[η]
ηλθομεν εις μ[ι]
16 λητον κεκρ[ικει]
γαρ ο παυλος π[α]
ραπλευσαι τη[ν]
εφεσον οπως
μη γενηται
αυτον χρονο
[τ]ριβη[σα]ι
. . . . . .

19 [. . . . .] κ̣α̣ι̣

K 7546a

xx.

22 [. . . . . πο]

[ρενο]μαι ε[ις] ιλη[μ τα]

[συ]μβησομεν[α]

[μοι] εν αυτη μη

23 [γι]νωσκων [π]λ[ην]

[οτι] το πν[α το α]γιο[ν]

δι[α]μα[ρτυ]ρ[ε]ται

[μοι] κατα πολιν

[λε]γο[ν οτι δεσμα]

[κ]αι θλειψις σε μ[ε]

[ν]ουσιν εν ιλημ

24 αλλ ουδενος λο

[γο]υ ποιουμαι την

[ψ]υχην τιμιαν

[εμα]υτω ως τελει

[. . . τ]ον δρομō

[μου] και τ[ην] δια

[κο]νιαν ην [παρ]

[ελαβ]α π[αρ]α τ[ου]

[κυ ι]υ διαμαρτ[υ]

[ρ]ασθαι ιουδαι

[οις] και ελλη

[σιν το ευαγγε]λ[ιον]

K 7547a

xx.

35 [. .] μ[νημο]νευε[ιν]

[τ]ε [των λο]γων [του]

[κυ ι]υ οτι αυτος ε[ι]

[πε]ν μ[α]καριον

[εστι] μα[λλ]ον δι

[δο]ναι η [λα]μβανεῖ

36 [κα]ι ταυτα ειπων

[ο] π[αυ]λος θεις τα

[γ]ον[ατα σ]υν πασιν

[α]υτοις προσηυξατο

37 [ι]κανος δε κλαυ

[θ]μ[ο]ς εγενετο παν

των [κ]αι επιπε

σοντες επι τον

τ[ρ]αχηλον αυτου

[κα]τεφιλουν

38 [αυ]τον οδυνωμε

[νο]ι μαλιστα επι

[τω λογ]ῳ ῳ ει

[ρηκ]ει οτι

[ου]κετι μελ

[λουσι] το προ

[σωπο]ν

[αυτου] θε

[ωρει]ν

K 7546b

xx.

26 . . . . . .

[. . . . το]υ

[αιματος πα]ντῶ

27 [ου γαρ υπεσ]τει

[λαμην του μ]η

[αναγγειλαι υμι]ν

[την βουλην το]υ

28 [θū π]ρ[οσ]

[εχετε]εαυ

[τοις και πα]ντι

[τω ποιμνι]ω

[εν ω υμας το π]να το

[αγιον εθετ]ο

K 7547b

xxi.

1 [. . . εις] πα

[ταρα και] μυρα

2 [και ευρον]τες

[πλοιον δ]ιαπε

[ρων εις τ]ην φοι

[νικην ε]πιβαν

[τες ανηχ]θημεν

3 [αναφαν . . .]ες δε

[την κυπρον] και

[καταλιποντ]ες

[αυτην ευωνυ]μō

4   [κ]αι

K 7548a

xxii.

11 [. . ει]ς δαμασ

12 [κον α]νανιας δε
[τις αν]ηρ ευ[. .]βης
[κατα τ]ον νομον
[μαρ]τυ[ρο]υμενος
[υ]π[ο πα]ντων των
[κατοικουντω]ν
[ε]ν τ[η] δαμασκω

13 [ιου]δαιων ελθω
προς με κ[αι ε]
πιστας ειπεν μοι
σαουλ αδελφε
αναβλεψον
[κα]γω αυτη τη
ωρα ανεβλεψα]

14 ο δε ειπεν μοι ο θ̅ς̅
των

K 7548b

xxii.

15 . . . . . .

16 [. . . . . μελλ]εις α
[ναστας βαπτι]σαι
[και απολο]υσαι τας
[αμαρτιας] σου επι
[καλεσα]μενος
[το ονομα τ]ου

17 [κυ̅ εγενετο δ]ε
[μοι υποστρ]ε
[ψαντι εις ι]λη̅μ̅
[και προσ]ε[υ]χο
[μενου μου εν] τω ιερω
[γενεσθ]αι με

APPENDIX II

THE VULGATE LATIN VERSION

THE following Tables, exhibiting the variants of the Vulgate from the Greek of Codex Vaticanus, are drawn from a collation made by Professor Henry J. Cadbury. The Latin text collated is that of Wordsworth and White (1905), and account is not taken of variants in Vulgate MSS. adduced in their apparatus. Since one of the canons of criticism followed by these editors is to adopt the Latin reading which agrees with the oldest Greek MSS., it is possible that the impression given by the Tables of agreement between the Vulgate and Codex Vaticanus is slightly in excess of the actual fact. Further, since the Tables include only *departures* from Codex B, it must not be assumed that in other cases, where the Greek witnesses are divided, the Vulgate *positively attests* the reading of that codex. All that the Tables imply by 'silence' in such instances is that the Latin rendering *can have come* from the Greek of B. It is not to be overlooked that C and 81 are defective in considerable sections, and that D fails after xxii. 10 and in some earlier passages.

The Tables are not designed to furnish material for a comparison of the Vulgate and the Old Latin, nor will they facilitate a study of the relation of the free translation of the Latin to the corresponding freedom of versions into other languages. Of Latin freedom only a few examples are given; but those passages have been included which Wordsworth and White ascribe to the probable influence of a Greek variant attested by no extant Greek manuscript.

The variation of 'and' and 'but' has usually not been mentioned except where positive Greek evidence for a variant δε or τε is at hand; similarly mention is not made of such variants as *ergo* for τε, the omission of the first τε in τε . . . τε, and of variations, unattested in Greek, in the order of words. This last type of variation is especially frequent in the use of the demonstratives attached to nouns.

The Greek of Codex Laudianus (E) has been advisedly omitted from consideration, since it is so largely conformed to the Latin

276

parallel columns of that manuscript. The miscellaneous references in the last column are not intended to be complete, but call attention to instructive attestation.

The method of constructing the Tables has perhaps caused some 'Western' readings of the Vulgate, attested only in Greek minuscules, to be overlooked.

	Vulgate	ℵAC 81	Antiochian	D	
I					
4	μου] per os meum			D	
5	εν πνευματι βαπτισθησεσθε αγιω] baptizabimini spiritu sancto	AC	Ant		
7	ειπεν] +autem	ℵAC 81	Ant		
8	μου] mihi		Ant		
	αυτων βλεποντων] videntibus illis	ℵAC 81	Ant		
10	πορευομενου αυτου] euntem illum				sah
	ανδρες δυο] duo viri				614
14	om συν 2°	ℵAC		D	
15	τε] autem	C			
	ονοματων] hominum				
16	εδει] oportet			D	
20	αυτου 1°] eorum	81			
25	αφ] de		cf. Ant		
II					
1	την ημεραν] dies (*plural*)				pesh
3	και 2°] -que	A	Ant		
4	το πνευμα] spiritus sanctus				Ψ
6	ηκουσεν] audiebat	C 81	cf. Ant		
7	δε] +omnes	ℵAC 81			S
	ουτοι εισιν οι λαλουντες γαλειλαιοι] isti qui loquuntur galilaei sunt	cf. C			
10	τε και 1°] et			D	
12	θελει τουτο ειναι] hoc vult esse	A			
13	εισιν] +isti			D	
15	ωρα τριτη της ημερας] hora diei tertia			cf. D	
17	μετα ταυτα] in novissimis diebus	ℵA 81 cf. C	Ant	D	
22	αποδεδειγμενον]adprobatum			D	
23	δια χειρος] per manus		Ant		
24	του θανατου] inferni			D	
33	om και 1°	ℵAC 81	Ant		
38	μετανοησατε] +inquit	ℵAC 81	Ant	cf. D	
40	της σκολιας ταυτης] ista prava			D	
42	τη διδαχη] in doctrina	A			
	τη κοινωνια τη κλασει] communicatione fractionis				sah boh
43	δε 2°] quoque	AC	Ant		
	εγεινετο 2°] +in hierusalem et metus erat magnus in universis	ℵAC			

	Vulgate	ℵAC 81	Antiochian	D	
44	δε] etiam	cf. ℵAC 81		D	
46	κατ οικον] circa domos			D	
III					
3	os] is			D	
4	πετρος εις αυτον] in eum petrus				095
5	παρ αυτου λαβειν] accepturum ab eis			D	
6	ειπεν δε πετρος] petrus autem dixit	AC			
	ναζωραιου] +surge et	AC 81	Ant		
7	παραχρημα δε] et protinus			D	
10	ουτος] ipse	ℵAC 81			
13	ισαακ, ιακωβ] deus isaac, deus jacob	ℵAC		D	
16	τη πιστει] in fide	cf. AC		cf. D	
20	προκεχειρισμενον] qui praedicatus est				minn
	χριστον ιησουν] jesum christum	AC 81			
21	απ αιωνος αυτου προφητων] suorum a saeculo prophetarum		cf. Ant		
22	θεος] +vester	A 81 (cf. ℵC)	Ant	D	
24	οσοι] qui	ℵ			
25	ο θεος διεθετο] disposuit deus	ℵAC 81	Ant		
26	αναστησας ο θεος] deus suscitans	A 81		D	
	των πονηριων] nequitia sua	cf. C			
IV					
1	om αυτοις			D	
	οι αρχιερεις] sacerdotes [1]	ℵA 81	Ant	D	
3	εθεντο] +eos	AC			
4	om ως	ℵA 81			
6	αρχιερατικου] sacerdotali				minn
11	οικοδομων] aedificantibus		Ant		
12	εστιν ετερον] aliud est	A			
	εν ανθρωποις] hominibus			D	
	υμας] nos	ℵA	Ant	D	
16	φανερον] +est			D	
19	υμων ακουειν μαλλον] vos potius audire				minn
21	μηδεν] non			D	
23	απηγγειλαν] +eis				1874
25	του πατρος ημων δια πνευματος αγιου στοματος] spiritu sancto per os patris nostri			cf. D	cf. minn
29	μετα παρρησιας πασης] cum omni fiducia			D	
30	χειρα] +tuam	ℵ	Ant	D	
31	του αγιου πνευματος] spiritu sancto		Ant		
32	ελεγον] dicebat	ℵA	Ant	D	

[1] On this word see Zahn, *Urausgabe*, pp. 177 f.

	Vulgate	אAC 81	Antiochian	D	
33	το μαρτυριον οι αποστολοι] apostoli testimonium	A			
	του κυριου ιησου της αναστασεως] resurrectionis jesu christi domini	אA	cf. Ant	cf. D	
34	ενδεης ην τις] quisquam egens erat	cf. אA	cf. Ant	cf. D	
V					
1	ανανιας ονοματι] nomine ananias	A		D	
2	τιμης]+agri				915
	γυναικος]+sua		Ant		
3	επληρωσεν] temtavit				{ Athan. Epiph. Did.
8	προς αυτην] ei		Ant		
12	τε] autem	אA	Ant	D	
14	προσετιθεντο πιστευοντες τω κυριω πληθη] augebatur credentium in domino multitudo			cf. D	
	om τε				1319
15	σκια]+illius				33 1891
19	ηνοιξε] aperiens	אA			
	δε 2°] et	אA	Ant	D	
21	παραγενομενοι] adveniens	B²אA	Ant	D	
22	οι δε παραγενομενοι υπηρεται ουχ ευρον αυτους εν τη φυλακη, αναστρεψαντες δε απηγγειλαν] cum venissent autem ministri et aperto carcere non invenissent illos, reversi nuntiaverunt			cf. D	
23	om οτι				913
	δεσμωτηριον]+quidem		Ant		
	εσω ουδενα] neminem intus				minn
32	εν αυτω μαρτυρες] sumus testes	א cf. A	cf. Ant	D	
	αγιον]+quem	אA	Ant	D	
33	ακουσαντες]+haec		Ant		cf. minn
	εβουλοντο] cogitabant	א	Ant	D	
38	om τουτο		cf. Ant		
40	απελυσαν]+eos		Ant	D	
41	ονοματος]+jesu				minn
42	τε] autem			D	
VI					
1	ταυταις] illis				minn
3	επισκεψωμεθα] considerate	אAC	Ant	D	
	δε] ergo	C	Ant		
	καταστησομεν] constituamus		Ant		
7	υπηκουον] oboediebat	A			
9	om των 1°	א			
11	βλασφημα] blasphemiae	א		D	
13	om τουτου	אA	Ant	D	
15	om εις	א			

	Vulgate	ℵAC 81	Antiochian	D	
VII					
5	αυτω εις κατασχεσιν αυτην] illi eam in possessionem	cf. ℵA			255
7	ο θεος ειπεν] dixit deus		Ant	D	
10	ολον] super omnem	ℵAC			
	τουτον] suam	B¹ℵAC	Ant	D	
12	εις αιγυπτον] in aegypto		Ant	D	
13	ιωσηφ 2°] ejus	ℵA			
15	ιακωβ] +in aegyptum	ℵAC	Ant	D	
	αυτος ετελευτησεν] defunctus est ipse	ℵAC	Ant	D	
16	εν συχεμ] filii sychem		Ant	D	
20	του πατρος] patris sui			D	
21	υιον] in filium	ℵAC 81	Ant	D	
26	τε] vero				P
30	εν φλογι πυρος] in igne flammae	AC			
32	ισαακ και ιακωβ] deus isaac et deus jacob		Ant	D	
33	το υποδημα σου των ποδων] calciamentum pedum tuorum	ℵA 81 cf. C	Ant	D	
34	αυτου] eorum	ℵAC 81	Ant		
35	om και 2°	ℵAC	Ant		
36	εν τη] in terra	ℵA 81	Ant	D	
	αιγυπτω] aegypti			D	
37	εμε] +ipsum audietis	C		cf. D	
38	εξελεξατο] accepit	ℵAC 81	Ant	D	
	υμιν] nobis	AC 81	Ant	D	
39	om εν	81		D	
42	τεσσερακοντα] +in deserto	B²ℵC 81 cf. A	Ant	D	
43	θεου] +vestri	ℵAC 81	Ant		
	ρομφα] rempham			D	
46	οικω] deo	AC 81			
49	θρονος] +est			D	
	και η γη] terra autem	ℵAC 81	Ant	D	
	οικοδομησατε] aedificabitis	ℵAC 81	Ant	D	
51	καρδιας] cordibus	AC cf. ℵ		D	
60	μεγαλη] +dicens			D	
VIII					
9	προυπηρχεν] qui ante fuerat			D	
	μαγευων και εξιστανων] magus seducens			D	
	ειναι τινα εαυτον] se esse aliquem				cf. minn
13	θεωρων τα] videns etiam	ℵAC 81	Ant	D	
16	ουδεπω] nondum		Ant		
18	πνευμα] spiritus sanctus	AC 81	Ant	D	
22	του κυριου] deum		Ant		
25	κωμας] regionibus				1874
27	om ος 2°	ℵAC			
28	ην δε υποστρεφων] et revertebatur	ℵA 81	Ant	D	
	om και 1°			D	
34	λεγει] +hoc	B²ℵAC 81	Ant		
39	ουκ ειδον αυτον ουκετι] amplius non vidit eum				cf. 489

	Vulgate	ℵAC 81	Antiochian	D	
39	αυτου την οδον] per viam suam	ℵAC 81	Ant		
IX					
2	om οντας				minn
3	αυτον περιηστραψεν] circumfulsit eum		Ant		
8	δε 2°] -que		Ant		cf. h
12	om εν οραματι	ℵA 81			
18	αυτου απο των οφθαλμων] ab oculis ejus	ℵC 81	Ant		cf. h
21	εληλυθει] venit	81	Ant		h
30	om αυτον 2°	A			
37	εθηκαν] +eam	ℵAC 81	Ant		
39	παρεστησαν] circumsteterunt εποιει μετ αυτων ουσα] faciebat illis				1518
40	εξω παντας] omnibus foras	C			
X					
1	τις] +erat				P
3	περι ωραν] hora		cf. Ant		
4	om και 1°				1522
6	τινι σιμωνι] simonem quendam	C			
7	των οικετων] +suos		Ant		h
11	καθιεμενον] +de caelo			d	
19	πνευμα] +ei	ℵAC 81	Ant	cf. D	
	δυο] tres	ℵAC 81			
20	αλλα αναστας] surge itaque et			cf. D	
24	αυτους 2°] suis	ℵAC	Ant	D	
28	ο θεος εδειξεν] ostendit deus	ℵA			
29	om και				2179
31	σου η προσευχη] oratio tua				minn
33	ενωπιον του θεου] in conspectu tuo			D	
37	οιδατε] vos scitis	ℵAC 81	Ant	D	
	αρξαμενος] +enim	A		D	
	κηρυγμα] baptismum	B²ℵAC 81	Ant	D	
XI					
3	εισηλθεν, συνεφαγεν] introisti, manducasti	ℵA	Ant	D	
4	καθεξης] ordinem			cf. D	
9	εκ δευτερου φωνη] vox secundo	ℵA81	Ant		
11	ημεν] eram	81			
13	ειποντα] +sibi		Ant	D	
14	ρηματα προς σε] tibi verba				minn
19	μονον ιουδαιοις] solis judaeis			D	
20	ελθοντες] cum introissent		Ant		
22	ιερουσαλημ] hierosolymis		Ant		
24	ικανος] +domino	B²ℵA 81	Ant	D	
25	αναστησαι] ut quaereret	B²ℵA 81	Ant	cf. D	
26	εγενετο δε αυτοις και ενιαυτον ολον συναχθηναι] et annum totum conversati sunt			cf. D	
	χρηματισαι τε] ita ut cognominarentur			cf. D	

	Vulgate	ℵAC 81	Antiochian	D	
27	αυταις] his	ℵA 81	Ant	D	
29	ευπορειτο] habebat				
	om εκαστος αυτων				
XII					
5	εκκλησιας]+ad deum	ℵA 81	Ant	D	
6	ημελλεν προσαγαγειν αυτον]				
	producturus eum esset	A 81	Ant	D	
7	αυτου αι αλυσεις εκ των				
	χειρων] catenae de mani-				
	bus ejus			D	
9	ηκολουθει]+eum		Ant		
10	πρωτην φυλακην και δευτε-				
	ραν] primam et secundam				
	custodiam			D	
13	προσηλθε] processit	B²ℵ			
15	εστιν αυτου] ejus est	81	Ant	D	
17	om αυτοις 2°	ℵA 81			
	αυτον εξηγαγεν] eduxisset				
	eum	81			
20	ομοθυμαδον δε] at illi un-				
	animes			D	
	αυτων την χωραν] regiones				
	eorum			D	
22	φωνη] voces			D	
25	εις] ab	cf. A		D	
XIII					
1	εν αντιοχεια κατα την ουσαν				
	εκκλησιαν] in ecclesia				
	quae erat antiochiae				
	διδασκαλοι]+in quibus			D	
	om τε 1°			D	
2	om δη				2147
3	επιθεντες]+eis			D	
	απελυσαν]+illos				255
4	του αγιου πνευματος] spiritu				
	sancto		Ant	D	
6	ανδρα τινα] quendam virum				minn
11	παραχρημα δε].et confestim	ℵC 81		D	
	επεσεν]+in eum	ℵC 81 cf. A	Ant	D	
14	την πισιδιαν] pisidiae	81	Ant	D	
18	om ως			D	
19	καθελων] et destruens	ℵAC	Ant	D	
22	τον δαυειδ αυτοις] illis david	C 81	Ant		
	ιεσσαι]+virum	ℵAC 81	Ant	D	
25	τι] quem	C	Ant	D	
26	αβρααμ]+et	ℵAC 81	Ant	D	
	ημιν] vobis	C	Ant		
27	om εν	C 81			
	αυτων] ejus			D	
28	ευροντες]+in eum			cf. D	
29	τα γεγραμμενα περι αυτου]				
	quae de eo scripta erant	ℵAC 81	Ant	D	
30	νεκρων]+tertia die				
31	οιτινες]+usque nunc	cf. ℵAC 81		D	
33	γεγραπται τω δευτερω] se-				
	cundo scriptum est		Ant		
35	εν ετερω] alias			D	

	Vulgate	אAC 81	Antiochian	D	
36	om μεν			D	
38	δια τουτο] per hunc	אAC 81	Ant	D	
39	om και	אAC			
40	επελθη]+vobis	AC81	Ant		
42	εις το μεταξυ σαββατον ηξιουν λαληθηναι] rogabant ut sequenti sabbato loquerentur	אAC 81	cf. Ant	D	
43	om αυτοις		Ant		
44	τε] vero	אAC 81		D	
	θεου] domini	B²אA 81		cf. D	
46	επειδη] sed quoniam	AC 81	Ant		
47	εθνων] gentibus			D	
48	του θεου] domini	אAC 81	Ant		
50	γυναικας]+et	א	Ant		
	οριων]+suis	אAC 81	Ant		
XIV					
5	om τε			D	
6	την περιχωρον] universam in circuitu regionem			D	
8	αδυνατος εν λυστροις] in lystris infirmus	AC 81	Ant		
	περιεπατησεν] ambulaverat		Ant	D	
10	ηλατο]+et	B²vid אAC 81	Ant	D	
11	οι τε οχλοι] turbae autem	C 81	Ant	D	
17	om υμιν	A 81			
19	δε]+quidam			D	
20	των μαθητων αυτον] eum discipulis		Ant		
22	παρακαλουντες]+ -que	cf. C			
25	εν περγη] in pergen	אA 81			
	λογον]+domini	אAC 81			
26	κακειθεν]+navigaverunt	B²אAC 81	Ant		
XV					
2	δε] ergo	A	Ant		
	om και ζητησεως				minn
3	om τε	A	Ant		
4	ανηγγειλαν τε]adnuntiantes			cf. D	
5	περιτεμνειν] circumcidi				489
7	εν υμιν] in nobis		Ant	cf. D	
8	αυτοις δους] dans illis	cf. C	cf. Ant	cf. D	
18	γνωστα απ αιωνος] notum a saeculo est domino opus suum	A	cf. Ant		
20	απεχεσθαι]+a	AC	Ant		
	πνικτου] suffocatis				
21	κατα πολιν τους κηρυσσοντας αυτον εχει] habet in singulis civitatibus qui eum praedicent			cf. D	
24	ημων]+exeuntes	AC 81	cf. Ant	D	
28	τουτων των επαναγκες] haec necessario	א		D	
29	και αιματος και πνικτων] et sanguine [suffocato]			D	
32	τε] autem			D	

		Vulgate	אAC 81	Antiochian	D	
XVI						
	1	om και 1°	אC 81	Ant	D	
	3	ελλην ο πατηρ αυτου] pater ejus gentilis		cf. Ant	cf. D	
	6	διηλθον] transeuntes		Ant		
	11	ουν] autem	אA 81		cf. D	
		δ'] et		Ant	D	
	13	τε] autem			D	
		ενομιζομεν προσευχη ειναι] videbatur oratio esse		cf. Ant	D	
	19	και ιδοντες] videntes autem	אC 81	Ant	D	
	23	δε] et	אAC	Ant	D	
	24	τους ποδας ησφαλισατο αυτων] pedes eorum strinxit		Ant	D	
	26	ηνεωχθησαν δε] et aperta sunt statim	C cf. אA 81	Ant	cf. D	
	32	του θεου] domini	AC 81	Ant	D	
	34	οικον]+suam	אA	Ant	D	
	35	απολυσον] dimittite				
	36	λογους]+haec	אA 81	Ant		
	38	δε 2°]-que		Ant		
	40	ιδοντες παρεκαλεσαν τους αδελφους] visis fratribus consolati sunt eos		Ant	cf. D	
XVII						
	2	τω παυλω] paulus				
		διεξελεξατο] disserebat		Ant		
	4	ελληνων] gentilibusque	A 81		D	
	10	om τε			D	
	11	ει εχοι ταυτα ουτως] si haec ita se haberent				minn
	12	εξ αυτων επιστευσαν] crediderunt ex eis				minn
		ανδρων] viri			cf. D	383
	13	τους οχλους] multitudinem				H
	14	τε 1°] autem		Ant	D	
		om τε 2°			D	
	15	εντολην]+ab eo			cf. D	
	18	om και 1°				minn
		ευηγγελιζετο]+eis	A 81			H
	21	om τι 1°	cf. 81	cf. Ant	cf. D	
	27	και 1°] aut	A		D	
	28	καθ ημας] vestrum	אA 81	Ant	D	
	30	αγνοιας]+hujus			D	
	32	om και		cf. Ant	D	
XVIII						
	3	ηργαζοντο] operabatur	A	Ant	D	
		ησαν] erat				
	4	om verse 4				
	5	om τε			cf. D	
	7	ηλθεν] intravit	אA		Dvid	
	12	οι ιουδαιοι ομοθυμαδον] uno animo judaei	אA	Ant	D	
	13	αναπειθει ουτος] hic persuadet		Ant	D	
	14	ω]+viri			D	

		Vulgate	אAC81	Antiochian	D	
16	απηλασεν]	minavit (for ηπειλησεν ?)				
17	ετυπτον]+eum					547
18	κειραμενos] qui sibi toton- derant					
	ειχεν] habebant					
19	κατηντησαν] devenit			Ant	D	
25	om δε		A cf. א	Ant	D	
XIX						
3	ειπεν τε] ille vero ait		אA		cf. D	
4	τω λαω] populum					
6	του παυλου χειρας] manus paulus					
13	των περιερχομενων] de cir- cumeuntibus			Ant	D	
14	τινos] quidam		אA	Ant		
16	πονηρον]+et		א	Ant		
17	εγενετο γνωστον] notum factum est					minn
24	ναous]+argenteas		A cf. א	Ant	D	
27	κινδυνευει] periclitabitur		א			
	om θεας					
	λογισθηναι] reputabitur		A		D	
	μελλειν τε και καθαιρεισθαι] sed et destrui incipiet				cf. D	
	μελλειν] incipiet		A		D	
	τε] sed			Ant		
	της μεγαλειοτητος] majestas			Ant		
30	om αυτον				D	
33	συνεβιβασαν] detraxerunt				D	
34	om εκ				D	
	om μεγαλη η αρτεμις εφεσιων 2°		אA	Ant	D	
35	τον οχλον ο γραμματευs] scriba turbas		cf. אA	cf. Ant	cf. D	
	του διοπετous] jovis prolis					
37	ημων] vestram			Ant		
39	περαιτερω] alterius rei		cf. אA	cf. Ant	cf. D	
40	στασεως περι της σημερον] seditionis hodiernae				cf. D	cf. minn
	om ου 2°				D	
	om περι 3°			Ant	D	
XX						
1	μεταπεμψαμενos] vocatis		cf. A	cf. Ant	cf. D	
3	επιβουλης αυτω] illi insidiae			Ant	D	
5	om δε			Ant	D	
	προσελθοντες] cum praeces- sissent		B²		D	
10	θορυβεισθαι] nolite turbari		אA	Ant(?)	D	
11	κλασαs] frangensque		אAC	Ant	D	
13	προσελθοντες επι το πλοιον] ascendentes navem			cf. Ant	cf. D	
14	συνεβαλλεν] convenisset		C	Ant	D	
15	δε 1°] et					623
	τη εσπερα] sequenti die		אAC	Ant	D	
18	αυτον]+et simul essent		A		D	

	Vulgate	ℵAC 81	Antiochian	D	
21	ιησουν] +christum	ℵAC		cf. D	
24	ουδενος λογου ποιουμαι την ψυχην τιμιαν εμαυτω] nihil horum vereor nec facio animam meam pretiosiorem quam me	cf. A	cf. Ant	cf. D	
25	βασιλειαν] +dei		Ant		
29	om οτι 1°	ℵAC	cf. Ant	D	
30	υμων] +ipsis	ℵAC	Ant	D	
31	εκαστον] +vestrum			D	
32	τω κυριω] deo	ℵAC	Ant	D	
35	των λογων] verbi				minn cf. LP
XXI					
3	την κυπρον] cypro				61 cf. P
	επλεομεν] navigavimus				
5	οτε δε εγενετο εξαρτισαι ημας τας ημερας] et explicitis diebus				
	προσευξαμενοι] oravimus		Ant		
6	απησπασαμεθα αλληλους και] et cum vale fecissemus invicem		Ant		
11	παυλου] +et		Ant		
12	om τε			D	
13	απεκριθη] +et dixit	ℵA			
21	om παντας	A		D	
22	παντως ακουσονται] utique oportet convenire multitudinem, audient enim	ℵA	Ant	D	
23	αφ] super	AC	Ant	D	
24	κεφαλην] capita				minn
25	απεστειλαμεν] scripsimus	ℵAC	Ant		
27	ως δε εμελλον αι επτα ημεραι συντελεισθαι] dum autem septem dies consummarentur			cf. D	
	συνεχεον] concitaverunt	C			
	οχλον] populum				minn
28	om τε			D	
29	ησαν γαρ προεωρακοτες] viderant enim		Ant		
31	τε] autem		Ant		
32	λαβων] adsumtis	ℵA	Ant	D	
35	του οχλου] populi			D	
36	κραζοντες] clamans		Ant	D	
39	ειπεν δε] et dixit ad eum				cf. minn
40	γενομενης σειγης] silentio facto	ℵA	Ant	cf. D	
XXII					
3	om υπαρχων			D	
	του θεου] legis				88
	παντες υμεις] vos omnes			D	
5	εμαρτυρει μοι] testimonium mihi reddit	ℵA	Ant		
	και τους εκεισε οντας] inde				cf. H

	Vulgate	ℵAC 81	Antiochian	D	
6	φως ικανον περι εμε] me lux copiosa			D	
10	ων εντετακται σοι ποιησαι] quae te oporteat facere			d	minn
11	ουδεν] non	ℵA	Ant	d	
12	om ευλαβης	A			
15	μαρτυς αυτω προς παντας ανθρωπους εση] eris testis illius ad omnes homines	cf. ℵA	cf. Ant		
20	και αυτος] ego			d	
23	τε] autem	ℵ	Ant	D	
24	ανεταζεσθαι] caedi et torqueri				
25	εστωτα] adstanti sibi				cf. minn
28	δε 1°] et		Ant	D	
29	και ο χειλιαρχος δε] tribunus quoque	cf. ℵ			
XXIII					
1	παυλος τω συνεδριω] concilium paulus	ℵAC			
2	αυτου το στομα] os ejus				Ψ
3	παρανομων] contra legem				1898
5	τε] autem				614 2147
	om οτι	C	Ant		
6	εκραξεν] exclamavit	A	Ant		
	νεκρων]+ego	ℵA	Ant		
7	λαλουντος] cum dixisset	ℵA cf. C	cf. Ant		
	επεπεσε] facta est	ℵAC	Ant		
9	om των γραμματεων του μερους	A			
10	πολλης δε γεινομενης στασεως] et cum magna dissensio esset	AC 81	cf. Ant		
	αγειν] ac deducere	ℵAC cf. 81	Ant		
12	τε] autem	ℵAC 81	Ant		
	οι ιουδαιοι] quidam ex judaeis		Ant		
15	μελλοντας διαγεινωσκειν ακρειβεστερον] certius cognituri	C			
17	απαγγειλαι τι] aliquid indicare	ℵC	Ant		
18	λαλησαι]+tibi	B² vid ℵA 81	Ant		
19	της χειρος αυτου ο χειλιαρχος] tribunus manum illius				1838
	επυνθανετο]+illum				cf. 1838
20	μελλων τι ακρειβεστερον πυνθανεσθαι] aliquid certius inquisituri				minn
21	μητε 1°] non				69
	εισιν ετοιμοι] parati sunt		Ant		
23	om τινας				minn
	ειπεν]+illis				hcl⋇
24	παραστησαι] praeparate				cf. hcl.mg
25	εχουσαν] continentem	A	Ant		
	τον τυπον τουτον] haec				614 / cf. 2147

		Vulgate	אAC 81	Antiochian	D
28		αυτω] +deduxi eum in concilium eorum	B² cf. אA	Ant	
30		επιβουλης εις τον ανδρα εσεσθαι εξαυτης] de insidiis quas paraverunt ei	cf. אA 81	cf. Ant	
		om προς αυτον	אA		
33		και τον παυλον αυτω] ante illum et paulum			cf. 255
35		κελευσας] jussitque		Ant	
XXIV					
2		κληθεντος δε] et citato paulo			
		om τω εθνει τουτω			
3		παντη τε] semper (=παντοτε)			minn
4		ακουσαι σε ημων συντομως] breviter audias nos			minn
10		τε] autem		Ant	
11		ημεραι] +quam			minn
14		θεω] +meo			614
		πιστευων] +omnibus	אA 81	Ant	
		om τοις 2°	cf. A	cf. Ant	
17		προσφορας] oblationes et vota			
20		τι] si quid			minn
		ευρον] +in me	C	Ant	
21		εφ] a	א	Ant	
22		λυσιας ο χειλιαρχος] tribunus lysias			minn
23		διαταξαμενος] jussitque			cf. HS cf. L
24		μετα δε ημερας τινας] post aliquot autem dies	A		
		τη ιδια γυναικι] uxore sua	א	cf. Ant	
		χριστον ιησουν] jesum christum			2138
26		αυτον μεταπεμπομενος] accersiens eum			808
27		τε] autem			minn
XXV					
4		εις καισαρειαν] in caesarea		Ant	
8		παυλου] +autem			cf. Ψ
10		om εστως 1°	AC 81	Ant	
11		μεν ουν] enim		Ant	
13		ασπασαμενοι] ad salutandum	81		
16		δε] -que	אAC 81	Ant	
18		πονηρων] malam	AC		
20		περι τουτων] hujusmodi		cf. Ant	
21		αναπεμψω] mittam		Ant	
25		του παυλου] hoc	B²אAC 81	Ant	
26		ασφαλες τι] quid certum			minn
XXVI					
7		om εν εκτενεια			
9		εγω] et ego			919
		ουν] quidem	אAC 81	Ant	
10		διο] quod	אAC 81	Ant	
11		βλασφημειν] +et	אAC 81	Ant	

	Vulgate	אAC 81	Antiochian	D
13	τους συν εμοι πορευομενους] eos qui mecum simul erant			
14	καταπεσοντων] nos cum decidissemus	אAC 81	Ant	
16	αναστηθι]+et sta	B²אAC 81	Ant	
	om με	אA 81	Ant	
17	om εκ 2°	C	Ant	
	ους]+nunc			minn
18	και 1°]+de	C		L
20	om τε 1°		Ant	
	πασαν] in omnem	81	Ant	
21	συλλαβομενοι εν τω ιερω] cum essem in templo comprehensum	א 81		
23	om τε			LP
24	αυτου απολογουμενου] loquente eo et rationem reddente			
	φησιν] dixit		Ant	
26	ον]+et	אA 81	Ant	
	om ου 1°			minn
	ου 2°] neque			minn
28	χρειστιανον ποιησαι] christianum fieri		Ant	
29	ο δε παυλος] et paulus			Ψ
31	αξιον]+quid	אA 81		
XXVII				
1	ημας] eum			cf. minn
	παρεδιδουν] et tradi			
	και τινας ετερους δεσμωτας] cum reliquis custodiis			hcl. mg
2	εις τους κατα την ασιαν τοπους] circa asiae loca		cf. Ant	
	οντος] perseverante [1]			cf. 33
3	τε 1°] autem	81		L
	τε 2°] autem			minn
	ο ιουλιος τω παυλω χρησαμενος] tractans julius paulum			cf. minn
4	τους ανεμους ειναι] essent venti			minn
5	μυρρα] lystram	אA		
8	λασεα] thalassa			
13	ασσον] de asson			cf. sah boh
20	επικειμενου]+jam	אAC 81	Ant	
22	ουδεμια] nullius			minn
23	αγγελος after λατρευω] angelus before του θεου	81	Ant	
	ειμι]+ego	אA		
26	ημας δει] oportet nos	אAC 81	Ant	
27	εγενετο] supervenit	A 81		
	προσαχειν] apparere			

[1] This seems to rest on a Greek corruption by dittography, ανηχθημεν μενοντος for ανηχθημεν οντος. See Peshitto, below, p. 315, note 1.

	Vulgate	אAC 81	Antiochian	D	
27	τινα αυτοις] sibi aliquam				minn
28	και] qui	א			
	om και παλιν βολισαντες				minn
29	τε] autem	אC 81			
30	αγκυρας μελλοντων] incipe-rent anchoras	א	Ant		
31	μεινωσιν εν τω πλοιω] in navi manserint	א			
34	τουτο γαρ προ της υμετερας σωτηριας υπαρχει] pro salute vestra				
37	αι πασαι] universae				cf. 69
	ως εβδομηκοντα εξ] ducentae septuaginta sex	אC 81 cf. A	Ant		
39	εκσωσαι] eicere	B²אA 81	Ant.		
40	ειων] committebant se				
41	περιπεσοντες] cum incidisse-mus				
	υπο της βιας]+maris	cf. C 81	cf. Ant		
43	εκκολυμβαν] natare	אAC 81	Ant		
	πρωτους]+evadere et				
XXVIII					
2	τε] vero	א	Ant		
	παντας ημας] nos omnes				minn
	om δια 2º	א			
6	μεταβαλομενοι] convertentes se	א	Ant		
7	εξενισεν] exhibuit				
9	γενομενου]+et	אA 81	Ant		
14	εις την ρωμην ηλθαμεν] veni-mus romam	A 81			
15	om τα περι ημων				pesh
	αχρι αππιου φορου και τριων ταβερνων] usque ad appii forum et tribus tabernis				
21	προς αυτον ειπαν] dixerunt ad eum				minn
	περι σου εδεξαμεθα] accepi-mus de te	A			Pvid
22	γνωστον ημιν εστιν] notum est nobis		Ant		
23	om τε 2º				minn
25	δε] -que	א	Ant		
	υμων] nostros				
27	ιασομαι] sanem	81			S
28	υμιν εστω] sit vobis	אA	Ant		
31	ακωλυτως]+amen				Ψ

APPENDIX III

THE PESHITTO SYRIAC VERSION

THE following Tables, exhibiting the variants of the Peshitto from the Greek of Codex Vaticanus, are drawn from a collation made by Professor Henry J. Cadbury, who has used the British and Foreign Bible Society's edition of 1905–1920. For chapters i-iii the aim is to give all variants of Syriac rendering, indicating in the column headed 'Translation' those which most clearly appear to be due merely to the translator, not to an underlying Greek variant reading. Thus a fair idea can be gained of the great freedom of the Syriac version, a freedom in part made necessary by the peculiar structure of the Syriac language as compared with Greek.

In the succeeding chapters (iv-xxviii) only those renderings are mentioned (with a few exceptions, chiefly in chapter xxiv) to which at least one Greek witness or a rendering in another version corresponds. Here, likewise, many of the minor variants will be recognized as probably to be charged to the account of the translator. Doubtless the form of the Syriac rendering is often merely parallel to the Greek variant, the two having been produced by similar motives working independently. This is especially likely to be the case when the Greek variant is attested by a single minuscule (other than Codex 614). Between versions into different languages the same coincidence is observable. Whether any given variant is due to the Greek text used or to the freedom of the translator is a matter of opinion and is often hard to determine, especially in small additions and in variations of order. It has seemed advisable to be liberal in adducing here such doubtful cases.

The Syriac variants are usually given in English, but occasionally for greater clearness and compactness Greek is used (usually so in matters of mere order of words), and once Latin. Occasionally it has proved impracticable to indicate the position in the sentence, or the order, of the corresponding Greek word or words.

In adducing miscellaneous witnesses in the last column no attempt at completeness has been made. The references are intended only to be suggestive, showing that testimony to the variant exists in Greek or Latin, occasionally in Sahidic. The Sahidic has not been systematically introduced into the comparison; possibly some additional scraps of 'Western' text could be discovered by a more complete study. Where Codex Bezae is defective, the Latin witnesses have been adduced in somewhat fuller measure. The Vulgate readings referred to are usually common to the Vulgate and the Old Latin texts.

The Tables show only *departures* from the Greek text of Codex B; how far in other cases, where the Tables are silent but where the Greek MSS. show variants, the Syriac not merely accords with but *positively attests* the reading of Codex B can only be learned by an examination of the Syriac text itself.

The reader is warned not to overlook the existence of lacunae in several of the Greek MSS. cited.

		Peshitto	Trans-lation	ℵAC 81	Antioch.	D	
I							
	1	ιησους] 'our Lord Christ'	×				
		om τε	×				
	2	ανελημφθη after ημερας (*order*)				D	
	3	ους εξελεξατο δια πνευμα-τος αγιου (*order*)	×				
		om τα	×				vg
	4	συναλιζομενος] + 'with them'				D	
	8	μου] μοι		81	Ant		
	9	υπελαβεν αυτον] + 'and he was hidden'				cf. D	
	10	και ιδου ανδρες δυο παρ-ειστηκεισαν] 'there were found two men standing'	×				
	12	σαββατου εχον οδον] 'and distant from it about seven stadia'	×				cf. sah
	13	ανεβησαν εις το υπερωον (*order*)			Ant	D	
		ησαν καταμενοντες] 'were'	×				
		ανδρεας] + 'and'	×				minn
		'and Matthew and Bartholomew and'	×				
	14	παντες] + 'together'		ℵ			
	15	πετρος] Symeon Cephas	×				
		αδελφων] 'disciples'		81	Ant	D	
		ην τε] 'but there was there'		C			
		ονοματων] 'of men'					vg
		om επι το αυτο					perp gig Aug
	17	εν ημιν] 'with us'			Ant		
		ελαχεν] 'he had'					Aug
	19	αυτων] 'of the country'	×				

	Peshitto	Transl.	אAC 81	Antioch.	D	
21	συνελθοντων ημιν] 'who were with us'	×				
	ο κυριος] 'our Lord'	×				1827
25	τοπον 1°] κληρον		א 81	Ant		
26	om αυτοις					
	επεσεν] 'rose'	×				
II						
1	την ημεραν] 'the days'					vg
	ησαν] 'when they were'				D	
2	om και 1°	×				
	om φερομενης	×				
	πνοης βιαιας] nominative	×				
	επληρωσεν . . . οικον] 'there was filled with it all that house'	×				
	τον οικον] 'that house'	×				Aug
3	πυρος] nominative	×				
	εκαθισεν] εκαθισαν		א		D	
4	ετεραις γλωσσαις] 'with various tongues'					cf. Aug
	αυτοις αποφθεγγεσθαι (order)	×		Ant		
5	ανδρες κατοικουντες εν ιερουσαλημ ευλαβεις ιουδαιοι (order)	×				
6	τη ιδια διαλεκτω λαλουντων] 'that they spoke in their tongues'				cf. D	
7	δε] +παντες		אAC 81			S
	λεγοντες] +προς αλληλους ουτοι παντες οι λαλουντες ουχι ιδου γαλιλαιοι εισιν (order)	×		Ant	D	
8	om και	×				
	om ημων	×				
9	ιουδαιαν τε και καππαδοκιαν] 'Jews and Cappadocians'	×				
	om τε	×.			D	
10	om τε 1°	×			D	
	παμφυλιαν] +'and' ·				D	
	om τε 2°	×				
11	αραβες] +'lo'	×				
12	τι θελει τουτο ειναι] 'of what is this will'	×				
13	διαχλευαζοντες ελεγον] διεχλευαζον αυτους λεγοντες				cf. D	
	om οτι	×				Aug
	γλευκους μεμεστωμενοι εισιν] 'these have drunk new wine and are intoxicated'					cf. hcl.mg
14	σταθεις δε] 'and afterward arose'				cf. D	
	ο πετρος] Symeon Cephas	×				

	Peshitto	Transl.	ℵAC 81	Antioch.	D	
14	παντες οι κατοικουντες (order)				D	
15	εστιν γαρ ωρα τριτη της ημερας] 'for lo until now it is three hours'	×				
16	ιωηλ του προφητου (order)	×				
17	om και 1°				D	
	μετα ταυτα] 'in the last days'		ℵA 81	Ant	D	
18	εν ταις ημεραις ταυταις after 'spirit' (order)	×				
	απο του πνευματος μου] 'my spirit' (accusative)	×				
19	om ανω		A			
	om κατω	×				
20	επιφανη] 'terrible'	×				
22	αποδεδειγμενον απο του θεου] 'of God seen' (order)		A	Ant	D	
23	τουτον] 'him who was set apart for this'	×				
	προγνωσει και βουλη (order)	×				
	εκδοτον δια χειρος] 'you delivered into the hands'	×				
24	ον ο θεος ανεστησε] 'but God raised him'	×				
	θανατου] 'sheol'				D	
	υπ αυτου] 'in sheol'	×				
25	τον κυριον] 'my Lord'		ℵ		D	
	om ενωπιον μου	×				
26	γλωσσα] 'glory'	×				
	σαρξ] 'body'	×				
30	οσφυος] 'womb'					1311
31	ουτε] 'not'			Ant		
	σαρξ] 'body'	×				
32	ου] 'and . . . of him'	×				
	ημεις παντες (order)					perp gig
33	ουν] 'and'	×				
	τουτο]+'gift'					h hcl.text
	ο]+'lo'			cf. Ant		
	om και 1°		ℵAC 81	Ant		
34	λεγει δε] 'because he said'				D	
36	om και 1°	×				minn
37	ακουσαντες]+'these'	×				
	την καρδιαν] 'their heart'	×				
	πετρον] Symeon	×				
	om ανδρες	×				
38	πετρος δε] 'Symeon'	×				cf. 522
	πετρος]+'said'			Ant		
	ιησου χριστου] 'of the Lord Jesus'				cf. D	cf. Iren
	om υμων 2°			Ant	D	
39	κυριος ο θεος ημων] 'God'	×				
40	διεμαρτυρατο] διεμαρτυρετο			Ant		

	Peshitto	Transl.	ℵAC 81	Antioch.	D	
40	ταυτης της σκολιας (*order*)				D	
41	οι μεν ουν] 'and some of them'	×				
	+'readily' *before* αποδεξαμενοι			Ant		
	αποδεξαμενοι] +'and believed'				cf. D	
	ωσει τρισχειλιαι ψυχαι (*order*)	×				
42	δε] 'and'				D	
	και τη κοινωνια] 'and were sharing in'	×				cf. vg
	τη κλασει του αρτου και ταις προσευχαις] 'in prayer and in the breaking of the eucharist'	×				
43	παση ψυχη φοβος] 'fear in every soul'	×				
	εγεινετο δια των αποστολων (*order*)		AC			
	at close, +'in Jerusalem'		ℵAC			
44	επι το αυτο] ησαν επι το αυτο και		ℵAC 81	Ant	D	
45	τα κτηματα και τας υπαρξεις] 'those who had property'				cf. D	
	om αυτα	×				
	πασιν] 'to each'	×				
46	εν τω ιερω ομοθυμαδον (*order*)		C			
	κατ οικον κλωντες (*order*)				cf. D	
	εν αγαλλιασει] 'rejoicing'	×				
	καρδιας] 'their heart'	×				
47	ο κυριος] 'our Lord'	×				
	καθ ημεραν τους σωζομενους (*order*)	×				minn
	for επι το αυτο *substitutes* 'in the church'			cf. Ant	cf. D	cf. 218
III						
1	πετρος δε] 'and it came to pass that when Symeon Cephas'	×				
2	και] +ιδου				D	
	ανηρ τις (*order*)	×			D	
	om υπαρχων				D	
	εβασταζετο . . . θυραν] 'was carried by [*lit.* there carried] men who were accustomed to bring and put him at the gate'	×				
3	ος] 'he'				D	
	πετρον] 'Symeon'	×				
	ηρωτα] +'from them'				cf. D	
	λαβειν] 'that they should give him'	×				

	Peshitto	Transl.	אAC 81	Antioch.	D	
4	ατενισας δε πετρος εις αυτον συν τω ιωαννη] 'and there looked at him Symeon and John'	×				cf. 095
	ειπεν] 'and they said'	×				cf. 1522
5	λαβειν παρ αυτων (order)				D	
6	om δε 1°					
	χρυσιον και αργυριον (order)	×				
	ναζωραιου] + 'rise'		cf. AC 81	cf. Ant		
7	της δεξιας χειρος] 'his right hand'	×				
	δε] 'and'				D	
10	ο προς την ελεημοσυνην καθημενος] 'the beggar who sat daily and asked alms'					cf. 1311
	τη ωραια πυλη] 'the gate called beautiful'	×				
	τω συμβεβηκοτι αυτω] 'that thing'	×				
11	εκθαμβοι after λαος (order)				cf. D	
12	απεκρινατο] + 'and said'				D	
	προς τον λαον] 'to them'				D	
	ευσεβεια] 'might'					h Chrys
	πεποιηκοσι] + 'this'				D	
13	απολυειν] + 'him'				D	
15	ηγειρεν ο θεος (order)	×				
	ου ημεις μαρτυρες εσμεν] 'and we all are his witnesses'	×				
16	εστερεωσεν] + 'and cured'	×				
	om το ονομα αυτου	×				
	δι αυτου] 'in him'	×				
17	αδελφοι] 'my brethren'	×				
	ωσπερ και] 'as did'	×				
20	οπως αν ελθωσιν] 'and there may come'	×				
	ελθωσιν] + 'to you'					h
	ιησουν χριστον (order)		AC 81			
21	χρονων αποκαταστασεως] 'the completion of the times'					cf. perp gig
	των αγιων απ αιωνος αυτου προφητων] 'of his prophets holy who are of old' (order)					cf. minn
22	μεν] 'for'			cf. Ant		
	αναστησαι υμιν (order)	×				
	κυριος ο θεος] 'the Lord'	×				
23	δε] 'and'	×				
	εξολοθρευσεται] + 'that soul'	×				
	του λαου] 'his people'					614
24	και παντες δε οι προφηται] 'and the prophets all'				cf. D	
	om οσοι				cf. D	

	Peshitto	Transl.	ℵAC 81	Antioch.	D	
25	διεθετο ο θεος (*order*)		ℵAC 81	Ant		
	υμων] 'our'		ℵC	Ant	D	
26	εν τω αποστρεφειν εκαστον]					
	'if you turn and are converted'	×				
	των πονηριων] 'your sins'		ℵA 81	Ant	D	
IV						
1	λαλουντων δε αυτων] 'and as they were speaking these words'				D	
	αρχιερεις] 'priests'		ℵA 81	Ant	D	
	στρατηγος] 'rulers'					gig
3	εθεντο] +'them'		AC			
5	εγενετο δε επι την αυριον συναχθηναι] 'and on the next day there were gathered'				cf. D	h
	om εν ιερουσαλημ					h
8	πρεσβυτεροι] +'of the house of Israel'			cf. Ant	cf. D	vg. *codd*
	at close, +'hear'					minn
9	ανακρεινομεθα] +'by you'				D	
12	ουδε γαρ] ου γαρ				D	
	εν ανθρωποις] 'to men'				D	
	om υμας					boh
13	θεωρουντες] 'when they heard'					h
	ησαν] 'had associated with'					cf. h
14	εστωτα συν αυτοις (*order*)					vg
	τον τεθεραπευμενον] 'the lame man who had been healed'					h
15	δε] 'then'					h
	απελθειν] 'that they should lead'				cf. D	
16	οτι μεν γαρ . . . φανερον] 'for lo a manifest sign which has been done by them to all the inhabitants of Jerusalem is known'					cf. h
17	διανεμηθη] 'this report go out'					cf. h
18	παρηγγειλαν] +'to them'			Ant		
21	μηδεν] 'not'				D	
	ευρισκοντες] +'a cause'				D	
	οτι] 'for'					gig e
23	προς αυτους οσα (*order*)					33
24	συ] +'art God'			Ant	D	
25	ο του πατρος ημων δια πνευματος αγιου στοματος δαυειδ παιδος σου ειπων] 'and thou art he who spoke through the Holy Spirit by the mouth of David thy servant'				cf. D	cf. Iren
26	συνηχθησαν] 'took counsel'					cf. minn
27	λαοις] 'assembly'				D	
28	η βουλη] 'thy counsel'		ℵ	Ant	D	440
29	και τα νυν] 'and also now'					minn
	om πασης					
30	την χειρα] 'thy hand'		ℵ	Ant	D	
32	ελεγον] ελεγεν		ℵA	Ant	D	

	Peshitto	אAC 81	Antioch.	D	
33	του κυριου ιησου της αναστασεως] 'concerning the resurrection of Jesus Christ'	cf. אA	cf. Ant	cf. D	cf. 1522
V					
2	γυναικος] 'his wife'		Ant		
3	ειπεν δε] +'to him'			cf. D	minn
8	om δε 1º				minn
9	ο δε πετρος] +'said'	A	Ant		
10	αυτου] 'their'				S
	νεκραν] + 'and they wrapped her round'			D	
16	om και 1º			D	
17	om αναστας				perp
	'and there was filled with anger' before ο αρχιερευς				
19	δε 1º] 'then'			D	
	δια νυκτος αγγελος κυριου (order)			D	
	τας θυρας] 'the door'				perp
21	ακουσαντες δε εισηλθον υπο τον ορθρον] 'and they went out at the time of dawn and entered'				cf. e (E)
	πασαν την γερουσιαν] 'the elders'				cf. vg
24	διηπορουν περι αυτων] 'were amazed and thought'				cf. e (E)
26	τον λαον μη λιθασθωσιν] 'lest the people should stone (singular) them'				cf. h
27	εν τω συνεδριω] 'before all the assembly'				cf. h
	επηρωτησεν] 'began to say'				h
28	λεγων] +'not'		Ant	D	
29	ειπαν] +'to them'			D	
	θεω δει πειθαρχειν (order)				cf. 69
32	εν αυτω μαρτυρες] 'are witnesses'	אA	cf. Ant	D	
	αγιον] +'which'	אA	Ant	D	
33	εβουλοντο] 'thought'	א	Ant	D	
34	om εν τω συνεδριω				
	νομοδιδασκαλος] +'and'				h
	ανθρωπους] 'apostles'		Ant	D	
36	ημερων] 'time'				h
	τινα] 'something great'			cf. D	
37	λαον] +'much'	C	Ant	D	
39	αυτους] 'it'	C	Ant		
	om και			D	
40	απελυσαν] +'them'		Ant	D	
42	τον χριστον ιησουν] 'our Lord Jesus Christ'	cf. C		D	
VI					
3	επισκεψωμεθα] επισκεψασθε	אAC	Ant	D	
	δε] 'therefore'	C	Ant	cf. D	
	πνευματος] +'of the Lord'				cf. h
5	ο λογος] 'this word'			D	
6	ους εστησαν] 'these stood'			D	
7	ιερεων] 'Jews'	א			
	υπηκουον] υπηκουεν	A			

	Peshitto	ℵAC 81	Antioch.	D	
8	om μεγαλα				1765
14	ημιν] 'you'				S
VII					
1	ειπεν] 'asked'				h
4	τοτε]+'Abraham'			D	
	αυτον]+'God' (nominative)				e
5	om μετ αυτον				
6	ουτως] 'with him'	ℵ			H
	αυτου] 'thy'	ℵ			
	κακωσουσιν]+'it'	C			
7	ειπεν ο θεος (order)		Ant	D	
8	ισαακ 2°]+'begat'				perp e
	ιακωβ 2°]+'begat'				perp
10	+'over' before ολον	ℵAC			
	τουτον] 'his'	B¹ℵAC	Ant	D	
12	εις αιγυπτον] 'in Egypt'		Ant	D	
14	τον πατερα αυτου ιακωβ (order)		Ant		
	την συγγενειαν] 'his kindred'			D	
15	ιακωβ]+'to Egypt'	ℵAC	Ant	D	
	ετελευτησεν]+'there'				2125
16	om εν συχεμ				
17	ης ωμολογησεν] 'which God promised by an oath'	81	Ant		gig
19	τους πατερας] 'our fathers'	AC 81	Ant		
20	αστειος] 'beloved'				cf. perp
					gig
	του πατρος] 'his father'			D	
21	εαυτη]+εις	ℵAC 81	Ant	D	
22	δυνατος] 'ready'				
24	τινα] 'from the sons of his race'			cf. D	
25	τους αδελφους] 'his brethren the sons of Israel'	cf. A 81	cf. Ant	cf. D	
	αυτοις σωτηριαν (order)		Ant		
26	μαχομενοις]+'with one another'				gig
30	πληρωθεντων]+'to him there'			cf. D	cf. Aug
	αγγελος]+'of the Lord'		Ant	D	
	φλογι πυρος βατου] 'fire which burned in a bush'	cf. AC			
31	εγενετο φωνη κυριου] 'there said to him the Lord in a voice'	cf. C	cf. Ant	cf. D	
33	των ποδων] 'from thy feet'	C			
35	κατεστησεν]+'over us'	ℵC 81		D	
	συν χειρι] 'by the hand'	ℵ	Ant		
36	τη 1°] γη	ℵA 81	Ant	D	
	αιγυπτω] 'of Egypt'			D	
37	ο θεος] 'the Lord God'	C	Ant		
	εμε]+'him shall ye hear'	C		D	
38	εξελεξατο] εδεξατο	ℵAC 81	Ant	D	
	υμιν] 'us'	AC 81	Ant	D	
42	τεσσερακοντα]+'in the wilderness'	B²ℵC 81 cf. A	Ant	D	
43	ρομφα] 'rephān'	AC			
45	om διαδεξαμενοι				d
46	οικω] 'the God'	AC 81			P
48	αλλ] 'and'			D	
49	μοι θρονος] 'my throne'			D	
51	καρδιας] 'in your heart'	cf. ℵ cf. 81	cf. Ant		

	Peshitto	אAC 81	Antioch.	D	
52	om νυν				e
54	οδοντας] 'their teeth'				minn
55	πληρης] +' of faith and'	א			
56	εστωτα εκ δεξιων (order)	אAC			
58	εκβαλοντες] 'and they seized, they cast him out'	cf. A			
	ελιθοβολουν] +' him'			D	
	νεανιου] ' of a certain youth'			D	
60	μεγαλη] +' and said'			cf. D	
VIII					
4	λογον] +' of God'				Aug
6	'And when the men there heard his words, they gave heed to him and were obedient to all that he said, because they saw the signs which he did'			cf. D	cf. 915 perp
8	πολλη] 'great'		Ant	D	
9	προυπηρχεν] 'who had lived . . . a long time'			D	
	μαγευων και εξιστανων] 'and by his magic arts he had led astray'			cf. D	cf. gig
10	om καλουμενη		Ant		
12	και του ονοματος] 'in the name'				cf. vg.codd 1547
17	επ αυτους τας χειρας (order)				
18	πνευμα] +' holy'	AC 81	Ant	D	
21	λογω] 'faith'				perp gig
22	του κυριου] 'God'		Ant		
24	τον κυριον] ' God'			D	
25	του κυριου] 'God'	A			
	ευηγγελιζοντο] ευηγγελισαντο		Ant		
26	οδον] +την ερημον				sah
	om αυτη εστιν ερημος				sah
28	om αυτου			D	
	ησαιαν τον προφητην (order)	C			
	ειπεν] +' to him'				vg.codd
31	om γαρ				minn
	δυναιμην] +' to understand'				vg.codd
33	τη ταπεινωσει] 'his humiliation'	C 81	Ant		
	+' and' before την γενεαν	81	Ant		
34	λεγει] +' this'	B²אAC 81	Ant		
35	ιησουν] +' our Lord' before 'Jesus'				Orig.
39	γαρ] 'but'				perp
40	και] +' from there'				cf. Aug.
IX					
2	της οδου] 'that way'				minn vg
3	περιηστραψεν αυτον φως (order)		Ant		vg
4	διωκεις] +' it is hard for thee to kick against the pricks'				431 h hcl·※·
5	ο δε] 'and our Lord'		Ant		h
	+ειπεν before εγω	א 81	Ant		h
	ιησους] +' the Nazarene'	AC			h hcl·※·
6	και 2°] +' there'				614 h
10	εν δαμασκω μαθητης τις (order)				perp

	Peshitto	ℵAC 81	Antioch.	D	
10	ο κυριος ειπεν προς αυτον εν οραματι (*order*)	cf. 81	cf. Ant		t
11	κυριος] +' said '				cf. 1522
12	εν οραματι ανδρα ονοματι ανανιαν (*order*)		Ant		
	χειρας] ' hand '		Ant		
13	απεκριθη] +' and said '				2085
	εποιησεν τοις αγιοις σου (*order*)		Ant		h
14	ωδε] ' lo here also '				cf. h
15	om ουτος				33
17	δε] ' then '				614
	om και εισηλθεν				h
	χειρας] ' hand '				h
19	ημερας τινας μετα των εν δαμασκω μαθητων (*order*)				cf. h
21	ακουοντες] +' him '				440
25	αυτου οι μαθηται] αυτον οι μαθηται		Ant		gig
28	εις ιερουσαλημ] ' in Jerusalem '				H
	ιερουσαλημ] +' and '		Ant		gig
29	του κυριου] ' Jesus '	C	Ant		
	ελληνιστας] ' the Jews who knew Greek '		Ant		
30	αυτον 1°] +' by night '				614
	και] +' from there '				perp gig
31	του κυριου] ' God '				Ψ minn
32	δια παντων] ' in the cities '				cf. perp
37	λουσαντες δε εθηκαν] +' her ' (*position varies*)	ℵAC 81	Ant		
38	εγγυς . . . εν αυτη] ' and the disciples heard that Symeon was in the city of Lydda, which is near Joppa '				cf. hcl·※·
	μη οκνησης] ' that he would not delay '		Ant		
	ημων] ' them '		Ant		
39	παρεστησαν] ' gathered, stood round '				cf. 1518
	εποιει μετ αυτων] ' gave to them '				cf. vg
40	παντας εξω (*order*)	C			
42	γνωστον δε εγενετο] +' this '				467
	πολλοι επιστευσαν (*order*)		Ant		
X					
4	αυτω 2°] +' the angel '				vg. *codd*
5	om τινα	ℵ	Ant	d	
6	om τινι			d	
7	των προσκαρτερουντων ' the one who waited on him '				minn
8	αυτοις απαντα (*order*)	C	Ant	d	
9	εγγιζοντων τη πολει (*order*)			d	
10	εγενετο 2°] ' fell '		Ant	d	
11	θεωρει] ' saw '			d	
	και καταβαινον σκευος τι ως οθονην μεγαλην τεσσαρσιν αρχαις] ' and a certain vessel, fastened by four corners, and it was like a great cloth '	cf. C 81	cf. Ant	cf. d	cf. 33 minn

		Peshitto	ℵAC 81	Antioch.	D	
11		καθειεμενον επι της γης] 'and it descended from heaven upon earth'			d	
13		om πετρε				gig
16		om ευθυs		cf. Ant	cf. D	minn
17		ιδου] 'there arrived'				cf. perp hcl. *mg*
19		ειπεν]+'to him'	ℵAC 81	Ant	D	
		δυο] 'three'	ℵAC 81			
20		αναστας] αναστα			D	
21		δε] 'then'			D	
		ειπεν]+'to them'				minn
22		κορνηλιος εκατονταρχης ανηρ] 'a certain man whose name is Cornelius, a centurion'			cf. D	
23		εισκαλεσαμενος ουν αυτους] 'and there brought them in Symeon'			D	
24		εισηλθεν] εισηλθον	ℵAC	Ant		gig
		αυτους 2°] αυτου	ℵAC	Ant	D	
28		αλλοφυλω] ανδρι αλλοφυλω			D	
29		om και				2180
		μεταπεμφθεις] 'when you sent for me'			cf. D	
30		ταυτης της ωρας] 'now'			cf. D	
		ημην] 'I was fasting and'			D	
		φησι]+'to me'				hcl·⁜·
32		θαλασσαν]+'he will come, will speak with thee'	C		D	
33		νυν ουν] 'and lo'			cf. D	
		ενωπιον του θεου] 'in thy presence'			D	
		om παρεσμεν			D	
		ακουσαι] 'and we desire to hear'			D	
		του κυριου] 'God'		Ant	D	
34		το στομα] 'his mouth'	AC		D	
36		τον]+γαρ	Cᵛⁱᵈ		D	
		λογον]+ον	ℵC	Ant	D	
37		+'and also you' *before* οιδατε	cf. ℵAC 81	Ant	D	
		κηρυγμα] 'baptism'	B²ℵAC 81	Ant	D	
38		ως] 'whom'			D	
		ος] 'and he it is who'			cf. D	
39		om τε				minn
		ιουδαιων] 'Judaea'				sah
		ον]+'the Jews'				cf. hcl·⁜·
41		ημιν *before* μαρτυσι (*order*)	cf. C			
		αυτω *after* συνεφαγομεν (*order*)	cf. C			
46		γλωσσαις] 'with various tongues'			cf. d	cf. vg.*cod*
		τοτε απεκριθη] 'and said'			D	
47		δυναται τις κωλυσαι (*order*)				minn
48		δε] 'then'			D	
		βαπτισθηναι εν τω ονοματι (*order*)			D	
		+'our Lord' *before* ιησου χριστου		cf. Ant	D	
		τοτε] 'and'			D	gig
		επιμειναι]+'with them'			D	

	Peshitto	ℵAC 81	Antioch.	D	
XI					
1	ηκουσαν δε οι αποστολοι] ακουστον δε εγενετο τοις αποστολοις			D	
3	προς ανδρας ακροβυστιαν εχοντας εισηλθεν (order)		Ant		
5	τεσσαρσιν αρχαις καθιεμενην] 'and it was fastened by its four corners and descended'				minn
6	της γης after ερπετα (order)				H
7	δε και] 'and'		Ant	D	
8	η] 'and'				minn
9	απεκριθη] +'to me'		Ant	D	
10	om παλιν				1874
	ημεν] 'I was lodging'	cf. 81	cf. Ant		
12	μοι το πνευμα (order)		Ant		
13	ειποντα] +'to him'		Ant	D	
18	εδωκεν την μετανοιαν εις ζωην (order)				minn
20	ελθοντες] εισελθοντες		Ant		
	om και 2°		Ant	D	
	ελληνιστας] 'Greeks'	A		D	
24	ανηρ ην (order)	ℵ			
	ικανος] +'to our Lord'	B²ℵA 81	Ant	D	
25	αναστησαι] αναζητησαι	B²ℵA 81	Ant	D	
26	ευρων] +'him'		Ant		
	ηγαγεν] +'him'		Ant		
	εγενετο δε αυτοις και ενιαυτον ολον συναχθηναι] 'and for a whole year together were they gathered'			cf. D	
	om και before ενιαυτον	81	Ant	D	
	+'from then' before πρωτως			cf. D	
27	αυταις] ταυταις	ℵA 81	Ant	D	
28	εσημαινεν] εσημανεν	ℵA 81	Ant		
	κλαυδιου] +'Caesar'		Ant		
29	πεμψαι εις διακονιαν (order)				1311
XII					
1	βασιλευς] +'he who was surnamed Agrippa'				cf. sah
4	τεσσαρσιν τετραδιοις στρατιωτων] 'sixteen soldiers'				sah
5	εκτενως] εκτενης	81	Ant		
	εκκλησιας] +'to God'	ℵA 81	Ant	D	
7	αυτου after χειρων (order)			D	
8	προς αυτον ο αγγελος (order)				L
9	ηκολουθει] +'him'		Ant		
	δε] 'for'			D	
10	om την φερουσαν εις την πολιν				L
	απ αυτου ο αγγελος (order)				1838
11	om του λαου	A			
12	ικανοι] 'many brethren'				minn
13	υπακουσαι παιδισκη (order)				minn
15	ειπαν 2°] ελεγον	ℵA 81	Ant	D	
	ειπαν 2°] +'to her'			D	
	+'perhaps' before ο αγγελος			D	
17	διηγησατο] 'he went in and told'			D	

	Peshitto	ℵAC 81	Antioch.	D	
17	ειπεν τε] +'to them'				minn
21	ενδυσαμενος ηρωδης (order)				minn
	και before καθισας	A	Ant	D	
22	θεου φωνη] 'these are daughters of the voices of God'			cf. D	
24	του κυριου] 'God'	ℵA 81	Ant	D	
	ο δε λογος του θεου ηυξανεν] 'and the gospel of God was preached'				
25	εις] 'from'	A		D	
	ιερουσαλημ] +'to Antioch'				minn
XIII					
1	μαναην] 'Manahel'				
2	σαυλον και βαρναβαν (order)				460
3	απελυσαν] +'them'				255
5	του θεου] 'our Lord'			D	
6	βαριησους] 'Barshuma'				
9	+και before ατενισας			D	
11	επεσεν] +'upon him'	ℵC 81 cf. A	Ant	D	
12	τοτε] 'and'			D	
	εκπληττομενος επιστευσεν (order)	A			
14	ελθοντες] εισελθοντες	A	Ant	D	
15	εν υμιν] 'to you'				H
17	του 2⁰] τουτου	ℵAC 81	Ant	D	
	om ισραηλ		Ant		
18	om ως			D	
	τεσσερακονταετη χρονον] 'forty years'			D	
	ετροποφορησεν] ετροφοφορησεν	AC			
19	κατεκληρονομησεν] +'to them'	AC	Ant		
20	om ως				614
	+και before ετεσι			D	
	om και μετα ταυτα			D	
22	αυτοις τον δαυειδ (order)	C 81	Ant		
	ιεσσαι] +'a man'	ℵAC 81	Ant	D	
23	ηγαγεν] ηγειρεν	C		D	
25	τι] τινα	C	Ant	D	
26	αβρααμ] +'and'	ℵAC 81	Ant	D	
	ημιν] 'you'	C	Ant		
27	εν ιερουσαλημ] 'of Jerusalem'	C 81			
28	αναιρεθηναι] 'that they kill'				vg
31	ος ωφθη] 'and he was seen'			cf. D	
	εισι] +'now'	ℵAC 81		cf. D	
32	τους πατερας] 'our fathers'			D	
33	τοις τεκνοις ημων] 'us their children'	81	Ant		
34	ανεστησεν αυτον] +'God'				Ψ
35	om διοτι			D	
38	om ανδρες				minn
	τουτο] τουτου	ℵAC 81	Ant	D	
40	επελθη] +'upon you'	AC 81	Ant		
41	om εργον 2⁰		Ant	D	
42	αυτων] +'from among them'		cf. Ant		
45	τους οχλους] 'turbam magnam'			cf. D	
	τοις] +λογοις			D	
46	τε] δε		Ant		
	επειδη] 'but because'	AC 81	Ant		

	Peshitto	אAC 81	Antioch.	D	
47	om εις 1°			D	
	τον λογον του θεου] 'God'				minn
50	των οριων] 'their borders'	אAC 81	Ant	D	
51	των ποδων] 'their feet'		Ant	D	
XIV					
1	om εν ικονιω				vg.*cod. R*
	λαλησαι]+'with them'			D	
4	+'all' *before* το πληθος				cf. gig
	συν τοις αποστολοις] 'clave to the apostles'			D	
8	εκαθητο εν λυστροις αδυνατος τοις ποσιν (*order*)			cf. D	
9	ηκουεν] ηκουσεν	אA 81		D	HL
	ος ατενισας αυτω] 'and when there had seen him Paul'			D	
	και ιδων] 'and had recognized'				h
10	φωνη]+'to thee I say in the name of our Lord Jesus Christ'	cf. C		D	
	+'and' *before* περιεπατει	B²אAC 81	Ant	D	
13	πυλωνας] 'door of the house where they dwelt'				
	om συν τοις οχλοις				917
14	om οι αποστολοι			D	
17	υμιν] 'them'	cf. A 81			
19	'from Iconium and from Antioch' (*order*)			D	
	πεισαντες] 'roused'			D	
21	την πολιν εκεινην] 'the sons of that city'			D	
	+'to' *before* αντιοχειαν	אAC			
22	+'and' *before* παρακαλουντες	C		D	
	και]+'they said to them'				cf. 1611
25	λογον]+'of the Lord'	אAC 81			
26	κακειθεν]+απεπλευσαν	B²אAC 81	Ant		
27	μετ αυτων ο θεος (*order*)				915
28	διετρειβον]+'there'		Ant		
XV					
5	παραγγελλειν τε]+'them'				minn
6	τε] δε	אA	Ant	D	
7	om εν υμιν				69
8	δους]+'to them'	C	Ant	cf. D	
11	ιησου]+'Christ'	C		D	
17	ταυτα]+παντα		Ant		
18	αιωνος]+'are the works of God'	cf. A	cf. Ant	cf. D	cf. gig
19	κρινω] 'I say'				vg.*codd*
20	επιστειλαι] 'that it be sent'				gig
23	γραψαντες]+'a letter'	C			
	χειρος] 'hands'				minn vg
	+'as follows' *before* οι αποστολοι	81 cf. C	Ant	cf. D	
	πρεσβυτεροι]+'and'		Ant		
24	om επειδη				gig
	ημων]+'have gone out and'	AC 81	Ant	D	
	υμων]+'telling you to be circumcised and keep the law'	C	Ant		cf. Iren. gig
25	+'therefore' *before* εδοξεν				cf. 88 200 perp²

	Peshitto	ℵAC 81	Antioch.	D	
29	ειδωλοθυτων] ειδωλοθυτου				minn
	πνικτων] πνικτου		Ant		vg
30	κατηλθον] 'came'		Ant		gig
33	τους αποστειλαντας αυτους] 'the apostles'		Ant		
35	του κυριου] 'God'				minn
36	παυλος προς βαρναβαν (order)		Ant	D	
	om δη				1518
	πασαν πολιν (order)	81	Ant	D	
	πως εχουσιν] 'and let us see what they do'				hcl·※
37	om και		Ant	D	
38	'But Paul did not wish to take him with them, because he left them when they were in Pamphylia and did not go with them.'				
	ηξιου . . . μη] 'did not wish'			D	
40	του κυριου] 'God'	C	Ant		gig
XVI					
1	ιουδαιας]+τινος		Ant		
3	εν τοις τοποις εκεινοις] 'in the region'				cf. 69 1175
	οτι ελλην ο πατηρ αυτου υπηρχεν] 'his father, that he was a gentile'		Ant	D	
4	παρεδιδοσαν] 'they preached and taught'			cf. D	
6	λογον] +'of God'			D	
7	επειραζον] 'they wished'			D	
9	οραμα] 'in a vision'			D	
	δια νυκτος] 'of the night'	ℵC 81	Ant		
	ωφθη τω παυλω (order)	AC	Ant	D	
	+'as' before ανηρ			D	
	ην εστως] 'who stood'			D	
	om και 3°				minn 467
10	ειδεν] +'Paul'				
	ο θεος] 'our Lord'		Ant	D	
11	ουν] 'and'	ℵA 81		D	
12	πρωτη μεριδος] 'head'			D	
13	ενομιζομεν προσευχη ειναι] 'there seemed to be a place of prayer'		Ant	D	
	συνελθουσαις] +'there'				hcl·※ minn
15	εβαπτισθη] +'she'				
18	αυτη τη ωρα εξηλθεν (order)			d cf. D	
21	καταγγελλουσιν] +'to us'				1518
22	συνεπεστη ο οχλος] 'a large crowd was assembled'			D	
	και 2°] 'then'			D	
24	ος] 'but he'			D	
	την εσωτεραν φυλακην] 'the interior of the prison'				gig
26	ηνεωχθησαν δε] +'immediately'	ℵAC 81	Ant	D	
29	προσεπεσεν] +'at the feet of'			D	
30	εφη] +'to them'			D	
31	ιησουν] +'Christ'	C	Ant	D	

	Peshitto	ℵAC 81	Antioch.	D	
32	του θεου] 'the Lord'	AC 81	Ant	D	
	συν] 'and'		Ant		
33	οι αυτου] 'those of his house'	A			vg.*codd*
34	τον οικον] 'his house'	ℵA	Ant	D	
	ηγαλλιασατο] ηγαλλιατο	C*vid*		D	P
	πανοικει] 'he and all his house'			cf. D	cf. vg
36	απηγγειλεν] 'entered and said'			D	
	τους λογους] 'this word'	cf ℵA 81	Ant		
	ουν] 'and'				cf. minn
37	δειραντες ημας δημοσια ακατακριτους] 'innocent they flogged us before the whole world'			cf. D	
38	τα ρηματα ταυτα]+'that had been spoken to them'			cf. D	
	εφοβηθησαν *after* εισιν (*order*)			D	
39	ηρωτων] 'asked' (*not* 'were asking')			cf. D	
40	ιδοντες τους αδελφους παρεκαλεσαν αυτους (*order*)		Ant	cf. D	
XVII					
3	εδει τον χριστον (*order*)				minn
4	πληθος] 'many'			cf. D	
	γυναικων τε των πρωτων] 'and noble women' (*nominative*)			cf. D	vg
5	αυτους προαγαγειν] 'bring them out thence and hand them over'			cf. D	
6	ουτοι]+'are'			D	
	+'all' *before* την οικουμενην				431
8	εταραξαν δε τον οχλον και τους πολιταρχας ακουοντας] 'but there were troubled the heads of the city and the whole people, when they heard'			cf. D	
10	απηεσαν *before* εις 2° (*order*)				gig
11	των]+'Jews'				perp
12	μεν ουν] 'and'				cf. 614 206
	και των ελληνιδων γυναικων των ευσχημονων και ανδρων ουκ ολιγοι] 'and so also of the Greeks many men and noble women'			cf. D	cf. perp gig
13	om και 1°			D	
	ο λογος του θεου κατηγγελη υπο του παυλου εν τη βεροια (*order*)			cf. D	
	σαλευοντες και ταρασσοντες] 'they ceased not to shake and trouble'			D	
14	ευθεως δε τοτε] 'and'			cf. D	
15	ηγαγον] 'came with him'				minn
	λαβοντες] 'when they went out from him, they received'			cf. D	vg E
	εντολην] επιστολην				
	om εξηεσαν				(cf. minn

	Peshitto	ℵAC 81	Antioch.	D	
16	εν δε . . . το πνευμα αυτου] 'but Paul himself, while he waited at Athens, was vexed in his spirit'				cf. Aug cf. vg
	αυτους] αυτου	ℵ		D	
17	μεν ουν] 'and'				cf. 614 226
18	οι δε] +'said'				gig
	ευηγγελιζετο] +'to them'	A 81			H
21	η 2°] 'and'		Ant		
23	om και 2°				vg.codd
	ο] 'whom'		Ant		Aug
	τουτον] 'him'	81	Ant		Aug
25	om και τα παντα				33
26	ενος] +'blood'		Ant	D	
	επι παντος προσωπου της γης] 'over the face of the whole earth'				Iren cf. 915
28	ημας] υμας	ℵA 81	Ant	D	
30	μεν ουν] 'for'				gig
	απαγγελλει] 'commands'	A	Ant	D	
	ειπαν] 'were saying'				1758
33	εξηλθεν ο παυλος (order)				minn
XVIII					
1	μετα ταυτα] 'and'			D	
	χωρισθεις] +'Paul'	A	Ant	D	
3	ηργαζοντο] ηργαζετο	A	Ant	D	
	γαρ] 'but'				vg
5	κατηλθον] 'came'			cf. D	vg
	ιησουν ειναι τον χριστον (order)				614 209
6	αυτων] 'the Jews'				cf. h
	τα ιματια] 'his raiment'			D	
7	ηλθεν] 'entered'	ℵA		D	
	τιτιου ιουστου] 'Titus'	cf. ℵ			cod.tepl.
9	om εν νυκτι	A			h
10	επιθησεται σοι] 'can'				gig
11	εξ] +'in Corinth'			D	
	εν αυτοις] 'them'			D	
15	κριτης] +γαρ		Ant		
16	του βηματος] 'his judgment seat'				h
17	παντες] +'the pagans'		Ant	D	
18	αποταξαμενος τοις αδελφοις (order)		Ant	D	h gig
	την κεφαλην εν κενχρεαις (order)		Ant	D	
19	om κακεινους κατελιπεν αυτου				1827
	διελεξατο] διελεγετο			D	
20	μειναι] +'with them'		Ant	D	
21	ειπων] +'it is necessary for me by all means to keep the coming feast in Jerusalem and'		Ant	cf. D	
22	ανηχθη απο της εφεσου] 'and Aquila and Priscilla he left in Ephesus and he went by sea'				cf. 614 minn
	κατελθων] 'came'				gig
	καισαρειαν] +'and'			D	

	Peshitto	ℵAC81	Antioch.	D
22	την εκκλησιαν] 'the sons of the church'			cf. minn
26	ακυλας και πρισκιλλα (order)		Ant	D
	του θεου] 'the Lord'			minn Aug
28	δια] 'from'			36ᵃ
	ειναι τον χριστον ιησουν] 'concerning Jesus that he was Christ'			cf. D
XIX				
3	ειπεν τε]+'to them'		Ant	
4	om εις 2°			cf. perp
	ιησουν]+'Christ'		cf. Ant	cf. D minn gig
5	ιησου]+'Christ'			D
6	χειρας του παυλου (order)			cf. D
8	εισελθων δε]+'Paul'			D
9	ως δε] 'and'			cf. D
	οδον]+'of God'			minn cf. gig
	πληθους]+'of the nations'			D
	+'then' before αποστας			D
	διαλεγομενος]+'with them'			minn
10	ωστε] 'until'			D
11	εποιει ο θεος (order)		Ant	
13	ορκιζω ορκιζομεν		Ant	vg.cod. D
	τον ιησουν] 'in the name of Jesus'			cf. 1765
16	επ αυτους ο ανθρωπος (order)		Ant	cf. D
	αμφοτερων] 'them'		Ant	
17	γνωστον εγενετο (order)			minn vg
18	εξομολογουμενοι]+'their sins'			vg. cod
20	του κυριου ο λογος] 'faith of God' (after verbs)			D
	ισχυεν και ηυξανεν (order)			cf. D
22	εις την ασιαν] 'in Asia'			D
23	οδον]+'of God'			cf. perp gig
24	γαρ] 'but'			perp gig
	+'there was' at beginning of verse			D
	ναους]+'of silver'	A cf. ℵ	Ant	D
	παρειχετο] 'who furnished'			D
25	+'he' before συναθροισας			D
	ημιν] 'our'		Ant	
26	ακουετε και θεωρειτε (order)			D
	εφεσου] 'the people of Ephesus'			gig
	αλλα]+'also'	A		gig
	om σχεδον			gig
	+'the multitude' before πασης της ασιας			cf. vg cod. R² e minn
	χειρων]+'of men'			cf. gig
27	της αρτεμιδος θεας μεγαλης (order)			
	λογισθηναι] 'will be reckoned'	A		
	εις ουδεν after 'be reckoned'			minn
28	ακουσαντες]+ταυτα			D
29	επλησθη . . . της συγχυσεως] 'was stirred'			D

	Peshitto	ℵAC 81	Antioch.	D	
29	η πολις] 'the whole city'		Ant	D	
30	ουκ ειων] 'prevented'			D	
31	om προς αυτον				1831
34	om μεγαλη η αρτεμις εφεσιων 2°	ℵ A	Ant	D	
38	μεν ουν] 'but'				cf. vg
	+'this' before δημητριος			D	
XX					
1	μεταπεμψαμενος] 'called'	A	Ant	D	
4	αυτω]+'as far as Asia'	A	Ant	D	
	om πυρρου		Ant		
5	om δε		Ant	D	
	προσελθοντες] 'went before us'	B²		cf. D	
7	τη επαυριον μελλων εξιεναι (order)				gig
10	συνπεριλαβων]+'him'	C			
	θορυβεισθαι] θορυβεισθε	ℵ A	Ant ?	D	
13	προσελθοντες] 'went down'			D	
	ασσον] 'Thasos'				LP 614 minn
14	ασσον] 'Thasos'				P 614 minn
15	εσπερα] ετερα	ℵAC	Ant	D	
	σαμον]+'and we stopped at Trogylium'		Ant	D	
16	γενεσθαι εις ιεροσολυμα] 'at Jerusalem keep'				cf. vg
17	μετεκαλεσατο] 'sent and brought'			cf. D	
19	τω κυριω] 'God'				vg. codd
21	ιησουν]+'Christ'	ℵAC		D	
22	om ιδου				perp
	εγω δεδεμενος (order)		Ant	D	
24	ψυχην] 'my life'			D	HS
25	om ιδου				minn gig
26	διοτι] 'because of this'	C	Ant		vg
	παντων] 'you all'				minn e
28	προσεχετε]+'therefore'	C	Ant		
	του ιδιου] 'his'				1874
29	μετα την αφιξιν μου εισελευσονται (order)				minn
30	υμων]+αυτων	ℵAC	Ant	D	
	αποσπαν] 'turn away'			D	
31	εκαστον]+'of you'			D	
32	τω κυριω] 'God'	ℵAC	Ant	D	
	οικοδομησαι]+'you'			D	
	δουναι]+'to you'	C	Ant		
34	αι χειρες] 'my hands'			cf. D	
35	+'and' before παντα	C			
	'Happy is he who gives rather than he who receives'			cf. D	Const. Ap.
38	μαλιστα οδυνωμενοι (order)			D	
XXI					
1	ως δε εγενετο αναχθηναι ημας αποσπασθεντες] 'and we separated'				gig
3	αναφαναντες] 'arrived'				perp
	ην το πλοιον (order)		Ant		
4	αυτου] αυτοις	A		d	L

	Peshitto	אAC 81	Antioch.	D	
5	οτε δε εγενετο εξαρτισαι ημας τας ημερας] 'and after those days'			cf. d	
	επορευομεθα] 'go on the way'			d	
6	υπεστρεψαν εκεινοι (order)			d	
7	παρ αυτοις ημεραν μιαν (order)				minn gig
9	παρθενοι τεσσαρες (order)		Ant		
10	επιμενοντων] 'and while we were there'				L P vg
11	οι ιουδαιοι εν ιερουσαλημ (order)				2147 gig
13	απεκριθη]+'and said'	אA			
	ετοιμως εχω before αλλα (order)			cf. D	
17	ασμενως after αδελφοι (order)			cf. D	gig
18	εισηει ο παυλος συν ημιν] 'we went in with Paul'				gig
	παρεγενοντο]+'with him'			cf. D	minn
19	ασπασαμενος] 'we greeted'				gig
	εξηγειτο]+'Paul'				gig
20	εν τοις ιουδαιοις] 'in Judaea'			D	
	παντες]+'these'			D	
22	τι ουν εστιν ; παντως ακουσονται] 'since therefore it has been heard by them'				cf. Jerome
					cf. Aug
	εληλυθας]+'hither'				gig
24	ουδεν εστιν] 'is false'				vg
25	απεστειλαμεν] 'we wrote'	אAC	Ant		
	om κρειναντες				1311
	το τε ειδωλοθυτον και πορνειαν και πνικτον και αιμα (order)				
27	ως δε εμελλον αι επτα ημεραι συντελεισθαι] 'and when the seventh day arrived'			D	
28	κραξοντες]+'and saying'				minn gig
31	ιερουσαλημ] 'the city'				gig
32	στρατιωτας και εκατονταρχας] 'centurion and soldiers'				cf. 614
33	τοτε] 'and'		Ant		gig
	δεθηναι] 'bind him'				e
36	om του λαου			D	
37	λεγει] 'said'			cf. D	minn
	om τι		Ant	D	
39	πολεως]+'where I was born'			D	
	om δε 2°			D	L
40	εστως ο παυλος (order)			D	
	τη χειρι] 'his hand'				minn
	τω λαω] 'to them'			D	
XXII					
1	om νυνι				gig
2	παρεσχον ησυχιαν] 'were silent'			D	
3	καθως]+'also'				vg
	υμεις παντες (order)			D	
4	ος] 'and'			D	
5	om και 3°			D	
6	εγενετο δε μοι πορευομενω και εγγιζοντι] 'and as I was going and was about to arrive'				
	περι εμε φως ικανον (order)			cf. D	
8	απεκριθην]+'and said'	א		cf. D	

	Peshitto	ℵAC 81	Antioch.	D	
10	λαληθησεται σοι (order)				minn
11	ηλθον] 'entered'				614 minn e
	ουδεν εβλεπον] 'it was not seen by me'	cf. ℵA	cf. Ant	d	
13	om και επιστας			d	
14	ειπεν]+'to me'			d	1518
15	εση before μαρτυς (order)	ℵA	Ant	d	
17	om γενεσθαι με εν εκστασει				cf. 1829
20	συνευδοκων] 'fulfilling the will of those who killed him'		cf. Ant		
21	εις εθνη] 'to preach to the nations'				cf. vg. cod. R²
23	αερα] 'heaven'			D	
25	εξεστιν υμιν ανθρωπον ρωμαιον και ακατακριτον (order)			D	
26	απηγγειλεν λεγων] 'said to him'			cf. D	
28	χειλιαρχος]+'and said'			D	
	+'in it' before γεγεννημαι				hcl·※·
29	ουν] 'and'				minn
30	συνελθειν] 'come'		Ant		
	συνεδριον] 'assembly of their leaders'		Ant		
XXIII					
2	αυτου το στομα] 'Paul on his mouth'				cf. gig
5	om τε				minn
6	+'and' before περι				hcl·※·
7	λαλουντος] 'when he had said'	ℵAC	Ant		
9	τινες των γραμματεων] 'some scribes'		Ant		
	αγγελος]+'what is there in that'				cf. h / cf. gig
10	στασεως]+'among them'				h gig
	καταβαν] 'come'				h
11	ειπεν]+'to him'				minn
12	ποιησαντες συστροφην] 'were assembled'				h
	οι ιουδαιοι] 'some of the Jews'		Ant		h
	om λεγοντες	C			
14	οιτινες] 'and they'				cf. h
15	εμφανισατε] 'ask'				cf. h / cf. hcl. mg
	ετοιμοι εσμεν του ανελειν αυτον προ του εγγισαι αυτον (order)				cf. 1522
	εγγισαι]+'to you'				hcl·※·
16	την ενεδραν] 'this plot'				hcl·※·
17	εφη]+'to him'				h
	τι απαγγειλαι (order)	ℵC	Ant		cf. h
18	ηρωτησεν]+'of me'				hcl·※·
	λαλησαι]+'to thee'	B²vidℵA 81	Ant		h
19	επυνθανετο]+'of him'				1838 h
20	το συνεδριον] 'their assembly'				483
	μελλων] μελλοντες				minn h
	περι αυτου] 'from him'				1838 h
22	παραγγειλας]+'him'				81
23	om τινας				1831 1838 h
	ειπεν]+'to them'				hcl·※·

	Peshitto	אAC 81	Antioch.	D	
23	δεξιολαβους] 'throwers with the right hand'	A			
	διακοσιους 2°] +' who should depart'				cf. hcl.*mg* cf. h cf. c
24	+' also' *before* κτηνη				e
	κτηνη] +' an animal'				hcl.*mg*
28	αυτω] +' I brought him to their assembly'	B²אA	Ant		
29	ον ευρον] 'and I found'				1522
30	εις τον ανδρα] 'against him'				gig cf. 36ª 431
	εσεσθαι] 'which . . . the Jews made'		cf. Ant		gig
	επεμψα] +' him'				1758
	τοις κατηγοροις] 'his accusers'				1838
	επι σου] +' farewell'	א81	Ant		e
35	κελευσας] 'and he ordered'		Ant		
	φυλασσεσθαι] 'keep'				gig
XXIV					
1	om τινων		Ant		
	om τινος				Ψ 614 minn
2	πολλης ειρηνης τυγχανοντες] 'in much peace we dwell'				vg
	διορθωματων] +' many'				431 cf. vg
3	παντη τε και πανταχου] 'and we all in every place'				
	αποδεχομεθα . . . μετα πασης ευχαριστιας] 'accept thy favour'				
4	ενκοπτω] 'we hinder'				vg.*codd*
	ακουσαι σε ημων συντομως τη ση επιεικεια] 'that thou hear our humility briefly'				
5	στασεις] 'sedition'		Ant		
6-8	ον και εκρατησαμεν] 'and having seized him we wished to judge him according to our law, but Lysias the chiliarch came and with much violence took him from our hands, and sent him to thee, and commanded his accusers to come before thee'				Ψ 614 minn
11	δωδεκα ημεραι (*order*)				808
14	πιστευων] +' all'	אA 81	Ant		vg
	om τοις 2°	A	Ant		cf. vg
15	αναστασιν] +' from the dead'		cf. Ant		cf. e
17	παρεγενομην *after* πλειονων (*order*)		Ant		gig
18	εν τω ιερω ηγνισμενον (*order*)				642
19	παρειναι] παραστηναι				minn
	ει τι] οτι				614
20	ευρον] +' in me'	C	Ant		vg
21	εστως εν αυτοις (*order*)		Ant		
22	ο δε φηλιξ ειδως τα περι της οδου ακριβεστερον ανεβαλετο αυτους (*order*)		cf. Ant		
	om λυσιας				cf. vg (W.andW.)
23	αυτον] 'Paul'		Ant		

	Peshitto	ℵAC 81	Antioch.	D
24	τινας ημερας (*order*)	A		
	om ιησουν	ℵA[a vid] AC[vid]		HP
26	δοθησεται] +'to him'	ℵAC 81	Ant	vg.*codd*
27	'to make favour' (*order*)			minn
XXV				
1	ουν] 'and'			1829 gig
	τη επαρχεια] 'Caesarea'			
3	κατ αυτου] 'from him'	C		vg.*codd*
5	om φησιν			102 gig
6	εν αυτοις] 'there'			cf. 1838
	om ου πλειους		cf. Ant	
	παυλον αχθηναι] 'that they bring Paul'			gig
7	καταφεροντες] +'against him'		cf. Ant	L
9	om αποκριθεις			gig
10	ειπεν] 'answered and said'			cf. 1898
	om εστως 1°	AC 81	Ant	vg
	ου] 'here'			gig
11	αδικω] αδικον			minn
	και] 'or'			323 vg
	om ουτοι			minn
				vg.*codd*
12	απεκριθη] 'said'			gig
13	κατηντησαν] κατηντησεν	C		
	om τινων			614 minn
	ασπασαμενοι] 'that they might greet'	81		minn vg
16	χαριζεσθαι] 'to grant'			vg
	ανθρωπον] +'for slaying'		Ant	hcl·※·gig
17	συνελθοντων] 'when I came'			gig
18	πονηρων] πονηραν	AC		gig
	ων] 'as'			gig
22	αγριππας δε προς τον φηστον] 'and Agrippa said'	cf. C 81	cf. Ant	cf.
				vg.*codd*
	φησιν] +'Festus'			vg.*codd*
23	ουν] 'and'			minn
				cf. vg
24	θεωρειτε τουτον περι ου] 'concerning this man whom you see'			cf. Ψ
				minn
25	του παυλου] 'he'	B²ℵAC 81	Ant	vg
27	τας κατ αυτου αιτιας] 'his fault'			cf. gig
XXVI				
1	'to speak for thyself' (*order*)			H minn
	απελογειτο] +'and said'			cf. gig
3	μαλιστα] +'because I know'	cf. AC		
	δεομαι] +'of thee'	C	Ant	vg.*codd*
7	βασιλευ] +'Agrippa'		Ant	
10	διο] 'which'	ℵAC 81	Ant	vg
11	βλασφημειν] +'the name of Jesus'			cf.
				vg.*codd*
	περισσως] +τε	ℵAC 81	Ant	vg
13	om πορευομενους			vg
14	καταπεσοντων] +ημων	ℵAC 81	Ant	vg
17	λαου] +'of the Jews'			minn
20	ιεροσολυμοις] 'those who were in Jerusalem'			614 minn

	Peshitto	ℵAC 81	Antioch.	D	
22	ουν] 'but'				vg
24	αυτου] 'Paul'				cf. gig
	φησι] 'cried'				cf. h
28	αγριππας]+'said'		cf. Ant		
	χρειστιανον ποιησαι] 'that I should be a Christian'		Ant		vg
29	παυλος]+'said'		Ant		cf. h
31	πρασσει] 'did'				vg
XXVII					
1	ως δε εκριθη του αποπλειν ημας] 'and Festus gave order concerning him that he should be sent to Caesar'				cf. 97 421 hcl.*mg* h
	παρεδιδουν] 'he committed'	A			h
	εκατονταρχη] 'a certain man, a centurion'				minn hcl·※·
2	+'and when we were about to sail' *before* επιβαντες		cf. Ant		h gig
	επιβαντες] 'we descended'				cf. gig h
	ανηχθημεν οντος συν ημιν αρισταρχου] 'and there went¹ with us on board the ship Aristarchus'	cf. ℵ			h gig
3	ο ιουλιος] 'the centurion'				h cf. gig
8	om τινα	A			gig
9	νηστειαν]+'of the Jews'				minn
10	om και 2°				323
11	επειθετο μαλλον (order)		Ant		cf. h
14	ευρακυλων] 'Euroclydon'	81	Ant		
16	μολις ισχυσαμεν (order)		Ant		gig
17	εφεροντο] 'we sailed'				minn
19	ερειψαν] 'we threw'		Ant		
20	χειμωνος τε ουκ ολιγου επικειμενου επι πλειονας ημερας μητε δε ηλιου (order)				gig
	+'nor the moon' *before* μητε αστρων				vg.*cod.D*
27	προσαχειν] 'were approaching'	cf. ℵAC 81	cf. Ant		cf. 614 minn
28	om παλιν βολισαντες				minn vg
31	εν τω πλοιω μεινωσι (order)	ℵ			
34	om και	ℵAC 81	Ant		vg
37	ως εβδομηκοντα εξ] 'two hundred and seventy and six'	ℵC 81 cf. A	Ant		
39	+'the sailors' *before* την γην				gig cf.920
	δυναιντο] 'it were possible'	C	Ant		
	εκσωσαι εξωσαι	B²ℵA 81	Ant		vg
41	βιας]+'of the waves'	C 81	Ant		cf. vg
43	'hindered them from this because he wished to save Paul'				gig
	του βουλευματος] 'this'				gig
44	εγενετο παντας διασωθηναι] 'all were brought safe'				gig

¹ The Syriac and Latin translators seem to have divided the word ανηχθημεν into ανηχθη μεν. See Vulgate, above, p. 289, note 1.

	Peshitto	ℵAC 81	Antioch.	D	
XXVIII					
1	om διασωθεντες				gig
3	om τι		Ant		gig
4	ο ανθρωπος ουτος φονευς εστι (order)				minn cf. gig
5	ο μεν ουν] 'but Paul'				gig
8	χειρας] 'hand'				gig
9	+και before οι λοιποι	ℵA 81	Ant		vg
	εχοντες ασθενειας] 'sick'				gig
12	επεμειναμεν]+'there'				vg hcl·※·
14	επιμειναι] 'and we were with them'				gig cf. hcl·※· S 614
	ηλθαμεν εις την ρωμην (order)	A 81			perp
15	om τα περι ημων				perp gig
16	επετραπη] 'the centurion permitted'		cf. Ant		cf. perp
17	εγενετο . . . συνκαλεσασθαι] 'Paul sent, called'				cf. vg
	ανδρες αδελφοι εγω (order)		Ant		
18	απολυσαι]+'me'	ℵ			
21	παραγενομενος] + 'from Jerusalem'				gig
	om απηγγειλεν η				2147
22	om μεν γαρ				cf. L 206
23	πλειονες εις την ξενιαν (order)				gig
	om τε 2º	ℵ			
24	οι μεν]+'of them'				431
28	αυτοι]+γαρ				hcl·※·

APPENDIX IV

THE SAHIDIC VERSION

THE following Tables and footnotes, together with the introductory
paragraphs on the use of the Sahidic and Boharic versions, are
drawn from collations with notes generously made for the use of
the author of the present volume by Sir Herbert Thompson.

In the Tables for chapters i-iii the Sahidic variant renderings
(Codex Vaticanus being adopted as a standard) are noted with great
fullness, even where they cannot be supposed to represent a Greek
variant and are themselves of no intrinsic interest.   In the succeeding chapters, beginning with chapter iv, all variant renderings which
correspond to known Greek variants are given, but of the rest only
such as possess special interest, either as possibly representing
Greek variants otherwise unknown, or as illustrating the habit of the
Sahidic translators and the freedom with which they worked.   Only
such renderings as depart from the text of Codex Vaticanus are
included (except in parts of chapters xxv and xxvi, where the
Sahidic evidence is of the most meagre) ; and in using the Tables it
must be remembered that Sahidic readings which do not disagree
with Codex Vaticanus may yet, by reason of the difference between
Greek and Sahidic, be equally explicable from the Greek variants
of rival codices.   In other words, the 'silence' of these Tables
must not be taken, without examination of the passage, for positive
evidence that the Sahidic was actually drawn from the Greek of
Codex Vaticanus.

The witness of אAC 81, of the Antiochian text, and of D is
always given when any of these support the variant implied by the
Sahidic rendering.   The references in the last column to other
Greek MSS. and to versions are meant to show only that the
Sahidic variant is not isolated.   They are intentionally incomplete,
and merely furnish sign-posts to further examination of the
evidence to be found in Tischendorf, von Soden, and Wordsworth
and White.   The reader is also reminded that there are lacunae in
several of the Greek MSS. cited.

In the first column ('Sahidic' MSS.) witnesses are named only
where the Sahidic is divided (except in chapters xxv and xxvi).

If no MS. is named in this column, it may be assumed that there is no known variation within the Sahidic version. But the number of Sahidic witnesses varies from verse to verse, and is often not more than two, seldom more than three.

In the second column a cross is set against those readings which are susceptible of explanation as due merely to the idiom of the language or the freedom of the translator. In many cases one or more witnesses from the Greek or from a Syriac or Latin version will also show the same variant. A large proportion of these are probably independent coincidences of variation, although sometimes an actual Greek variant seems to be the source in Sahidic. In very many cases a confident decision is impossible. These cases are all instructive, for they show the similarity in the mental processes of the Greek copyist and of the translator and constitute a warning applicable to the use of all versions. The marks in this column necessarily represent subjective judgments of probability, and are set with widely varying degrees of confidence.

The discovery in recent years of many Sahidic MSS. (largely, however, fragmentary) renders antiquated Woide's well-known translation, made from the nearly complete Oxford MS. Woide's translation itself requires some correction, and, moreover, has not always been used by Tischendorf with discretion, particularly in drawing inferences from the order of words in Sahidic. The collations of Sir Herbert Thompson were made prior to the publication of Horner's edition of the Sahidic version of Acts (1922), but to Mr. Horner's kindness is due the communication of the readings of the unpublished fragments of a lectionary designated P. In the preparation of the Tables themselves the author of the present volume has been able to avail himself of Horner's edition, and would gratefully express his indebtedness to it.

The known MSS. and fragments of the Sahidic version of Acts, with the exception of two or three unpublished Paris fragments collated by Horner, are enumerated in the list on pp. 322-324, and all have been used by Sir Herbert Thompson. Four cover all parts of Acts, namely B and V (both of the fourth century), W and H³ (both of the twelfth-thirteenth century). But V and H³ are fragmentary, V being so defective that it proves disappointing in use ; while B (papyrus), although evidently containing an extremely ancient text, is unfortunately very carelessly written and full of blunders. For the present use the original papyrus of B in the British Museum has been freshly collated by Sir Herbert Thompson. Woide's translation was founded on W, with use of H³. From Bty (recently acquired) some readings from Acts xx ff. are given.

The following paragraphs on Sahidic idiom are drawn from Thompson's notes to his collation, and present matters which require attention in any use of the Sahidic for textual criticism of the New Testament.[1] See also the corresponding notes on Bohairic idiom, below, pp. 357-360.

(a) The order of words in Sahidic is much more rigid than in Greek, especially in requiring that an adverb or adverbial phrase stand after the verb, so that in the case of Greek variants the inferences from the Sahidic order made by Tischendorf on the basis of Woide's translation are often unjustifiable ; e.g. Acts i. 5, i. 13, ii. 22, ix. 10, etc. In some cases the other order could be used in Sahidic, but only if the translator felt strongly the necessity of emphasizing the adverbial expression.

(b) The pervading practice of asyndeton in Coptic makes it in many cases unlikely that the omission of a conjunction implies any Greek variant whatever.

(c) Δ is not a letter of the Coptic alphabet, except for transcription of foreign words, and the Copt does not distinguish between T and Δ, but uses the latter quite capriciously (thus σαδανας and διμωθευς are as common as the forms with T). In consequence τε almost invariably becomes δε in Sahidic. For instance, in Acts vii. 26 τε, W reads δε, using the Greek word, but nevertheless must not be quoted in favour of an original Greek δέ. In this instance B omits δε, but has a particle meaning 'again,' which probably implies τε, certainly not δέ. Another good example out of many is Acts xxvii. 8, where Sahidic (B) has δε for the Greek τε, where the Greek text seems assured. Similarly the substitution of ουτε for ουδε in such a passage as iv. 12 means nothing for textual criticism ; in this instance W has ουδε, the Greek word being used in both cases. Conversely ουδε represents a Greek ούτε in v. 39, and elsewhere.

(d) T is the feminine article in Coptic, and before Greek words commencing with a vowel it united with the aspirate of the vowel (in some cases, such as ἐλπίς, ἔθνος, εἰκών, εἰρήνη, an unaspirated Greek word regularly receives aspiration when borrowed by Sahidic) to form an initial sound which is very frequently written Θ. Thus θαρσος, θασος, Acts xx. 13, may be taken to represent Greek αρσος, ασος.

(e) When a Greek substantive or a proper name is taken over into Coptic, it is preserved in the nominative singular, without modifying the ending for the plural or for oblique cases. The number is determined by a Coptic article, etc. Hence such a phrase as κατα πολις (Acts viii. 4) does not enable us to say whether the original had πόλιν or πόλεις.

(f) The Coptic does not admit of the definite article before

[1] See also N. Peters, *Die sahidisch-koptische Übersetzung des Buches Ecclesiasticus* (Biblische Studien iii.), Freiburg, 1898, pp. 5-30.

a personal proper name; but it always has the article before the *titles* χριστος and κυριος. The name Egypt never has an article in Sahidic.

(*g*) Sahidic does not distinguish between ἕλληνες and ἑλληνισταί, but uses for both the same Coptic word (a modification of 'Ionians'). Sahidic also adopts the Greek word ελλην, as in Acts xiv. 1, xvii. 4, xviii. 4, xix. 17, xx. 21. Bohairic always uses the native word.

(*h*) *Prepositions.*—In such a case as the Greek τῇ πίστει, with or without a preceding ἐπί (Acts iii. 16), which the Sahidic renders *in fide*, it is impossible to say which Greek reading the translator was following. These distinctions are too fine for the rather concrete Coptic mind.

Between the variants ἐπί and πρό (τῶν θυρῶν), Acts v. 23, the Sahidic preposition used, though nearer in sense to ἐπί than to πρό, gives no decision.

Either πρὸς αὐτούς or σὺν αὐτοῖς, Acts xv. 2, could hardly be rendered in Sahidic otherwise than by 'with them.'

(*i*) Like the Semitic languages, Coptic has a preposition which can mean either 'place in which' or 'instrument.' This is important in such variants as those found in i. 5.

(*j*) There is no Sahidic word for μέν, and it is rarely adopted in its Greek form; δε is often used to represent it.

(*k*) δε is constantly used in Coptic for καί, and does not necessarily imply anything as to the Greek conjunction employed.

(*l*) *Questions.*—Where the Greek introduces a question with μή or οὐ, Coptic uses the Greek μη indifferently for both.

(*m*) The Sahidic indefinite article is sometimes used, for want of an indefinite pronominal adjective, where the Greek has τις.

(*n*) The addition of 'his,' 'their' is often due solely to Coptic idiom, which almost invariably uses a possessive pronoun (as does English), for instance with the names of parts of the body (*e.g.* 'his hands'), and in many phrases where other languages omit it as superfluous.

(*o*) *Object of verb supplied.*—Coptic has a great reluctance to use a transitive verb without supplying an object; *e.g.* Acts vii. 53, 'ye kept it not' for οὐκ ἐφυλάξατε, or vii. 58, 'they stoned him' for ἐλιθοβόλουν. In such cases the object does not imply a Greek αὐτόν. Not infrequently Greek copyists have done the same, and it is often impossible to tell on what text the Sahidic rests. Similarly with the Greek dative after intransitive verbs. With the verb 'to follow' the object seems indispensable; for example, in the following passages the Coptic has it, although in some of them it is not reported from a single Greek manuscript: Matt. viii. 10, xxi. 9, Mark x. 32, xi. 9, xvi. 20, Luke xxii. 54, Acts xxi.

36, Rev. xiv. 8. For another example, in Acts xvii. 3, διανοίγων and παρατιθέμενος are both supplemented by a Sahidic rendering of αὐτοῖς, but in neither case does this necessarily point to a Greek original, although in the latter of the two cases some Greek minuscules have made the same addition.

(*p*) Between the relative pronouns οἵ and ὅσοι Coptic does not easily distinguish, having no proper word for ὅσοι. When the latter must be represented, it is done by a periphrasis.

(*q*) *Past tenses.*—The imperfect is relatively little used in Sahidic except to express continuous action, and the natural tendency is to put everything into the preterite. The Copt, who was a peasant, was quite wanting in the Greek's delicate sense for shades of meaning in the verb. The Greek imperfect is often rendered by the preterite, so that the latter cannot be taken as necessarily implying a Greek aorist; on the other hand, when the Coptic uses an imperfect in narrative, it may be taken with practical certainty to be rendering a Greek imperfect.

(*r*) *Greek aorist participle and verb.*—Coptic, having, strictly speaking, no past participle, renders the common Greek construction of participle and verb by two verbs in the preterite, either used asyndetically or joined by 'and.' But one of the two verbs may be in a certain verbal form which was formerly regarded as a participle, but is now treated as a tense (past 'circumstantial'), though usually best translated as a participle. This form differs from the ordinary preterite only by having prefixed to it an ε, which is frequently lost; hence in the MSS. there is much confusion in the use of the two forms, and no inference can usually be drawn from the form actually found as to whether the underlying Greek had two finite verbs, or a participle with a finite verb. This applies to the Sahidic variants in Acts i. 2. Another good example is ἀνάστα or ἀναστάς, Acts ix. 11, where the Sahidic is incapable of giving any aid.

The reversing of participle and verb into verb and participle is quite in accordance with Coptic idiom, and does not necessarily imply any Greek variant.

(*s*) The Sahidic use of tenses often makes it impossible to say whether the translator had a future indicative (-σο-) or an aorist subjunctive (-σω-) before him.

(*t*) *Passive.*—Coptic, having no passive voice, usually expresses the passive by an impersonal 3rd plural of the active verb; thus in Acts vi. 1, for παρεθεωροῦντο αἱ χῆραι the Sahidic rendering is literally *negligebant viduas* (cf. Woide), but the Greek original shows that the Sahidic is more correctly represented in Latin by *negligebantur viduae.*

(*u*) Sahidic often idiomatically substitutes direct discourse for *oratio obliqua,* e.g. Acts v. 36.

Symbol	MS.	Date
B	Brit. Mus. or. 7594, papyrus	*ca.* 350
V	Vienna (no number given)	*ca.* 400
Bty	Chester Beatty, London	cent. vi
W	Bodleian, hunt. 394, paper	cent. xii-xiii
Wfr	„ vellum, fragments	cent. x
H3	„ hunt. 3, paper, lectionary	cent. xii-xiii
Bodl	„ copt. d4, paper, fragments	probably cent. xii
R1	Vatican, copt. xcv	cent. xi-xii
R2	„ „ lxxviii	cent. ix
R3	„ „ lxxix	cent. xi
Wess 1-18	Vienna fragments (details below)	
Brit 116	Brit. Mus. or. 3579B, paper	cent. xi-xii
Brit 117	„ „ „	cent. xii-xiii
Brit 118	„ „ „	cent. ix
Brit 119	„ „ „ paper	cent. xii-xiii
Brit 121	„ „ „	cent. xii
Bdg 1	„ „ 7029, paper	cent. x
Bdg 2	„ „ 7021, paper	cent. x
Leid 21	Leiden, Insinger 21	?
Leid 22	„ „ 22	late
Leid 23	„ „ 23	?
Lemm	Berlin, or. 409, paper, lectionary	late
Mun	Munich, Royal Library, fragment	cent. xi
Cai	Cairo, fragment, lectionary	cent. xi
Bour	fragments from Asfûn (?)	late
Masp	fragment from Asfûn	late
P	Paris, Bibl. Nat., fragment, lectionary	late
Pet	W. M. Flinders Petrie, fragment	late
T	H. Thompson, fragment, paper	late
Ost	Cairo, Ostraca No. 8137, limestone	cent. vii (?)

AHIDIC COLLATION

ellum where not otherwise stated)

Contents	
xxiv; also xxvii-xxviii, fragmentary	Budge, Coptic Biblical Texts, 1912. (The account of this text given below rests on a fresh collation of the original papyrus.)
-xxvi, very fragmentary	Wessely, Wiener Hdschr. sah. Acta Apost. (Sitz.-ber., Vienna Academy, clxxii), 1913.
-xxviii	Unpublished.
-xxiv. 19	Woide, Appendix, 1799.
19-ii. 34	„ „ Cf. Dissert. p. 25 (nonum).
-xxvii, fragmentary	„ „ „ p. 19 and Wessely, ut supra, p. 4.
. 12-21	Winstedt, PSBA, xxvii, pp. 60-63.
vi. 26-xvii. 16, xxvii. 11-27	Balestri, Sacr. bibl. fragmenta copto-sah., iii, 1904.
xiii. 17-xxvi. 10	„ „ „ „
ii. 4-11	„ „ „ „
vi. 14-35, xx. 31-xxi. 12	Wessely, Griech. u. Kopt. Texte Theol. Inhalts II, III.
xi. 35-xxiii. 15	Unpublished.
xii. 10-20	„
xviii. 15-17, 23-25	„
ii. 34-43	„
. 1-13	Budge, Misc. Coptic Texts, 1915, p. 498.
. 43-47, iii. 1-12	„ „ „ „ p. 428.
. 16-34	Pleyte-Boeser, MSS. Coptes à Leide, 1897, pp. 90 ff.
ix. 29-xx. 2	„ „ „ „ pp. 93 ff.
.i. 1-8	„ „ „ „ pp. 96 ff.
xiii. 17-34	Lemm, Bibel-fragmenta iii.
vii. 15-21	Reich in W.Z.K.M., xxvi, p. 337.
iii. 26-40, xiii. 17-25	Munier in Bull. Inst. fr., xii, p. 256.
x. 36-x. 10	Bouriant, Miss. arch. fr., i, p. 400.
xvi. 16-19, xxvii. 35-44, xxviii. 2-3, 8-13, 20-23	Maspero, Rec. trav., vi, p. 36.
	Unpublished.
iii. 43-47	„
. 9-21	„
xvii. 9-11	Crum, Ostraca, no. 3.

DETAILS OF VIENNA FRAGMENTS
PUBLISHED BY WESSELY

(mentioned above)

Symbol	Museum Number	Century	Contents	Reference to Wessely
Wess 1	Litt. Theol. No. 16	*ca.* viii	i. 6-20	Texte II, p. 14 (No. 59).
,, 2	9714	xi-xii	i. 1-6, lectionary	,, III, p. 206 (No. 170).
,, 3	9710	xi-xii	ii. 1-19 ,,	,, ,, p. 207 (No. 171).
,, 4	9339	ix-x	ii. 12-25	,, ,, p. 108 (No. 147).
,, 5	9123	xii-xiii	iv. 14-33	,, ,, p. 110 (No. 148).
,, 6	9708	*ca.* xii	v. 12-18, lectionary	,, ,, p. 209 (No. 172).
,, 7	9723	x-xi	vii. 44-50 ,,	,, ,, p. 187 (No. 164).
,, 8	9098	viii-ix	ix. 35-x. 3	,, ,, p. 112 (No. 149).
,, 9	9117	xii-xiii	ix. 39-x. 6	,, ,, p. 115 (No. 150).
,, 10	9723	x-xi	xiii. 17-22, lectionary	,, ,, p. 187 (No. 164).
,, 11	9008-12	xii-xiii	xiii. 29-xvi. 16	,, ,, p. 121 (No. 153).
,, 12	9720	*ca.* xi	xiii. 44-50, lectionary	,, ,, p. 221 (No. 177).
,, 13	9061	*ca.* ix	xvi. 15-31	,, ,, p. 117 (No. 151).
,, 14	9049	*ca.* xii	xviii. 26-xix. 9	,, ,, p. 119 (No. 152).
,, 15	9694	xi-xii	xxi. 5-10, lectionary	,, ,, p. 214 (No. 174).
,, 16	9008-12	xii-xiii	xxii. 25-xxiii. 18	,, ,, p. 129 (No. 153).
,, 17	9152	*ca.* xii	xxvii. 9-21	,, ,, p. 132 (No. 154).
,, 18	9110	xii-xiii	xxvii. 27-34, lectionary	,, ,, p. 198 (No. 168).

	Sahidic	Sah. MSS	Tr.	אAC 81	Antioch.	D	
I							
2	αχρι ης ημερας ανελημ- φθη εντειλαμενος [a] τοις αποστολοις] +αυ- του	B	×			D	vg. cod. D
	πνευματος αγιου] του πνευματος αγιου κη- ρυσσειν το ευαγγε- λιον					cf. D	
3	om και 1°	B	×				Aug
	λεγων] +αυτοις	W	×				vg. cod
	om τα		×				
4	om μου	B	×				
	μου] +ειπεν		×				perp
5	om δε	B	×				
	ημερας] +αλλα εως της πεντηκοστης					cf. D	
6	om μεν	B	×				
	μεν ουν] δε	W Wess²	×				
	ηρωτων] ηρωτησαν	BW Wess²	×				
	ει] +ουν	B					
7	χρονους η καιρους] τους καιρους και τους χρονους		×				
8	μου] μοι			81	Ant		
	om τε		×				vg
	om εν 2°			AC 81		D	
9	om και 1°		×				Aug
	om αυτων βλεποντων απηρθη . . . αυτων] νεφελη υπελαβεν αυτον και επηρθη απ αυτων					D cf. D	
10	om και 1°	B	×				perp
	και ως] ως δε	W Wess¹					
	εις τον ουρανον πορευο- μενου αυτου] αυτω πορευομενω εις τον ουρανον						vg
	om και 2°		×				vg
11	om οι		×				Ψ minn
	ουτος] +εστιν	Wess¹	×				
	om ουτος . . . ουρανον (homoeotel.)	W	×				
12	'a journey of seven roads' [b]		×				
13	εισηλθον] κατηλθον	B	×				
14	om ησαν	B	×				
	om ομοθυμαδον	BW	×				
	om συν 2°			אAC		D	
	αυτου] +πασιν	B	×				

[a] On the relation of verb and participle here see above, p. 321.

[b] See Textual Note, above, p. 6.

	Sahidic	Sah. MSS	Tr.	ℵAC 81	Antioch.	D	
15	και εν] εν δε		×			D	
	om τε		×				
	ειπεν at close of verse		×				
	ονοματων after εικοσι		×				
	om ως						
	(Wess¹ defective)	W	×				
16	'the scripture which he foretold in the Holy Spirit'ᵃ	B					
17	ημιν] αυτοις ᵇ	Bvid	×				
18	om μεν		×				
	εκ μισθου] εν τω μισθω	W	×				
	εκ μισθου] εκ του μισθου	B Wess¹	×				minn
	αδικιας] +αυτου		×			D	
	om και 1°	B	×				
	om μεσος	B	×				
	om και 2°		×				
19	εγενετο]+'haec res'		×	cf. ℵ			
20	εν αυτη] εν τοις σκηνωμασιν αυτου (cf. Ps. lxviii. 26)		×				
21	εισηλθεν] +αυτοις	W	×				
	εφ ημας] αφ ημων		×				
22	συν ημιν] ημιν	B	×				
23	ιωσηφ] ιωσης						minn
24	om και	W	×				
	και προσευξαμενοι] προσευξαμενοι δε	BWfr	×				
	αναδειξον ενα εκ τουτων των δυο ον εξελεξω ᶜ						minn
	om εκ	BW	×				
26	κληρους] τον κληρον	B	×				
	om και 2° and και 3°	BW	×				
II							
1	om επι το αυτο		×				429
2	om και 1°	Wfr Wess³	×				minn
	βιαιας] βιαιως		×				
	om καθημενοι	B	×				
3	om και 1°	Wfr Wess³	×				
	πυρος] 'ex igne'		×				
	εκαθισεν] εκαθισαν			ℵD			
4	om και 1°	BWfr Wess³	×				
	και επλησθησαν] επλησθησαν δε	W	×				
	εδιδου] +αυτοις		×		cf. Ant		
5	om κατοικουντες	B	×				

ᵃ This is no doubt a blunder, as the verbal change involved is slight.
ᵇ Apparently, but the MS. (B) is imperfect here.
ᶜ In this passage the Sahidic was capable of preserving the order of the Greek uncials.

	Sahidic	Sah. mss	Tr.	ℵAC 81	Antioch.	D
6	γενομενης δε] και γενο- μενης	B	×			perp
	γενομενης . . . συν- εχυθη] 'and when this voice came together, the mul- titude was con- founded' [a]	B	×			
	om και	Wfr	×			
7	εξισταντο δε] +παντες			ℵAC 81		S
	εθαυμαζον] +παντες	W	×			
8	om και	B	×			
	om εκαστος	B	×			1872
	τη ιδια . . . εγεννη- θημεν] τη διαλεκτω αυτου εν η εγεννηθη		×			
9	om και 2°	B	×			Aug
11	ταις ημετεραις γλωσ- σαις] ταις γλωσσαις	B	×			
	ταις ημετεραις γλωσ- σαις] γλωσσαις	W	×			
	ταις ημετεραις γλωσ- σαις] ταις γλωσσαις αυτων	Wess[3]	×			Aug
	+ 'annuntiantes' be- fore τα μεγαλεια		×			
12	τι θελει τουτο ειναι] 'quid est haec res'		×			
13	γλευκους] + γαστερες αυτων		×			
14	ενδεκα]+αποστολοις	B				D
	απεφθεγξατο] απεκριθη	W Wess[3,4]	×			
	απεφθεγξατο] λεγων	B		C		
17	om και 1°					D
	μετα ταυτα] μετα εκει- νας τας ημερας	B		cf. C, cf.ℵA 81	cf. Ant	cf. D
	οψονται] 'shall utter'	Wess[3]	×			
20	om και 2°		×			
22	απο] υπο		×			
	εις υμας] +εν παση υποταγη [b]	B	×			
23 f.	om εκδοτον . . . ο θεος (homoeotel.)	B	×			
24	ανεστησε λυσας τας ωδεινας] ανεστησεν εκ νεκρων και των ωδεινων	B				cf. minn
26	om και 1°	B	×			
27	ψυχην μου] +εν ταις ψυχαις μου του (?) αδου [c]	B	×			

[a] B has blundered here in a manner which cannot be accounted for.

[b] For υποταγη the Greek word itself is used ; cf. 2 Cor. xii. 12 (υπομονη).

[c] This has neither sense nor (Coptic) grammar.

	Sahidic	Sah. mss	Tr.	אAC 81	Antioch.	D
28	οδους ζωης] τας οδους της ζωης ᵃ		×			
	ευφροσυνης μετα του προσωπου σου] της (om της W) ευφρο-συνης του προσωπου σου	BW	×			
33	om ουν	B	×			
	πατρος] +αυτου	B	×			
	τουτο] +το δωρον					Iren. perp pesh
	om και 1°		×	אAC 81	Ant	
34	om δε	B	{×			
36	om ουν	B	×			vg.codd minn
	om και 1°		×			
	τουτον τον ιησουν] ουτος ο ιησους		×			
37	om δε	B	×			vg
	καρδιαν] +αυτων		×			
	τι] +ουν	B				D
38	+'said' before προς αυτον	BW	×	cf. אAC 81	Ant	cf. D
	βαπτισθητω εκαστος υμων] βαπτισθητε	B	×			
	εν τω ονοματι] επι τω ονοματι ᵇ			אA 81		
	ιησου χριστου] του κυριου ιησου χριστου	W				D
	ιησου χριστου] ιησου χριστου του κυριου	B				cf. D
	δωρεαν] +τουτου	B	×			
39	οσους] ους			AC		
40	τε] δε		?			D
	ετεροις . . . παρεκαλει] εν δε ταις ημεραις εκατον λογους ελε-γεν και παρεκαλει ᶜ	B	×			
41	om ουν	B	×			perp
	προσετεθησαν]+αυτοις		×			
	ψυχαι] ανθρωποι	V				
42	τη κοινωνια της κλασεως					vg

ᵃ The Coptic article before ζωης is idiomatic, but not so that before οδους. The latter word standing without the article should be rendered in Coptic with the indefinite article, not with the definite article as here. But in Ps. xv. 11 (Sahidic) the definite article is also used to render the Greek οδους without the article.

ᵇ Sahidic reads literally εις το ονομα, which, as between επι and εν, seems to represent the former, although both επι and εν are susceptible of being rendered by their appropriate Coptic prepositions respectively.

ᶜ The text of B is strangely corrupt, but nevertheless translatable. The intrusive εκατον is merely a fragment of the lost word for πλειοσιν, but it is impossible to account for the complete disappearance of the Coptic word for διεμαρτυρατο.

	Sahidic	Sah. MSS	Tr.	אAC 81	Antioch.	D	
43	om δε 1°		×				
	φοβος] +μεγας						1518
	παση ψυχη] 'upon every one, upon every soul'	W					
	δε 2°] γαρ		×				
44	επι το αυτο] ησαν επι το αυτο και			אAC 81	Ant	D	
45	κτηματα] 'orchards'		×				
	τα κτηματα αυτων και τας υπαρξεις αυτων		×				
	om και 3°	B	×				
	διεμεριζον] διεμερισαν	B	×				
46	τε] δε		×				minn
	μετα αγαλλιασεως α-φελοτητος της καρ-διας αυτων	B	×				
	καρδιας] +αυτων		×				
47	om ολον	W					minn
III							
1	om την ενατην	Lemm	×				
	επι την ωραν την ενατην επι την ωραν της προσευχης	B				cf. D	
2	om καθ ημεραν	B Lemm	×				
3	ος] ουτος	BH³ Lemm				D	
	ος] ουτος δε	W	×				
3 f.	om μελλοντας . . . ιωανη (homoeotel.)	B	×				
3	ηρωτα αυτους διδοναι αυτω ελεημοσυνην		×				
4	om δε	W	×				
5	om ο δε επειχεν αυτοις (homoeotel.)	B	×				
6	πετρος] +αυτω		×				h
	διδωμι] δωσω		×				vg.codd
	om χριστου	B	×				Prisc
7	παραχρημα δε] και παραχρημα	B				D	
8	om και 2°	WH³ Lemm	×				
	om και 5°	WH³ Lemm		A			
9	om και 1°	BW	×				
	και ειδεν] ειδεν δε	H³	×				
10	om δε		×				pesh
	om και 1°	BW	×				
	και επλησθησαν] ε-πλησθησαν δε	H³	×				
12	απεκρινατο] ειπεν					cf. D	
	προς τον λαον] αυτοις	VWH³				cf. D	
	om προς τον λαον	B					
	ιδια δυναμει η ευσε-βεια] δυναμει ημων η ευσεβεια ημων		×			cf. D	

	Sahidic	Sah. mss	Tr.	ℵAC 81	Antioch.	D	
12	του περιπατειν αυτον] τουτο					cf. D	
13	ο θεος αβρααμ, ο θεος ισακ, ο θεος ιακωβ] +και	B B	×	ℵAC		D	
	παιδα] υιον		×				vg
	om μεν					D	
	ηρνησασθε[a]]+και κατ-εφρονησατε αυτου	B	×				
14	ηρνησασθε]+κατα προ-σωπον πιλατου	B	×				
16	om θεωρειτε και	B	×				
17	και νυν] νυν ουν		×				
18	om αυτου	WH³	×				minn
19	επιστρεψατε]+επι τον θεον	H³					
20	αν ελθωσιν] εαν ελθωσιν		×				cf. vg
	om και before απο-στειλη		×				
	υμιν] ημιν		×				
21	om στοματος	W	×				
22	μεν] γαρ	B			cf. Ant		
	ειπεν]+κατεναντι των πατερων ημων					cf. D	
	θεος]+ημων	BH³		ℵC cf. A 81	cf. Ant	cf. D	
	om ως εμε	W	×				
24	om ταυτας	BH³	×				
25	υμων] ημων	BH³		ℵC	Ant	D	
	om και 2°		×				
26	παιδα] υιον		×				vg
	πονηριων]+αυτου		×	cf. C			minn
IV[b]							
1	αρχιερεις] ιερεις			ℵA 81	Ant	D	
	ο στρατηγος] οι στρα-τηγοι	W					pesh
2	την εκ νεκρων] των νεκρων				Ant	D	
7	om υμεις		×				perp
10	om χριστου	B	×				383
12	υμας] ημας			ℵA	Ant	D	
13	ιδιωται εισιν και α-γραμματοι		×				gig
15	om δε	B	×				
16	τοις ανθρωποις τουτοις] ω ανδρες αδελφοι	B					vg.codd
18	παρηγγειλαν]+αυτοις		×		Ant		

[a] The Sahidic word does not represent a Greek εβαρυνατε, but is the usual word for 'despise,' employed to render καταφρονειν and sometimes ατιμαζειν. It has no nuance of 'weighing down,' 'oppressing,' or 'treating hardly,' and would never be used to render βαρυνειν.

[b] Beginning at this point most of the minor variants which do not correspond to known Greek readings are omitted. Some such, however, have been mentioned because of their relation to the Latin or Syriac version or as illustrations of the freedom of the Sahidic translation.

	Sahidic	Sah. mss	Tr.	ℵAC 81	Antioch.	D
24	οι δε] +παντες	B				
	συ] +ει ο θεος				Ant	D
25	' qui locutus est per spiritum sanctum in ore patris nostri David servi tui dicens ' ᵃ					
						D
27	om γαρ	W	×			minn
	ιησουν] +χριστον	B	×			
	om πειλατος	B	×			
	εθνεσιν, λαοις] τοις εθνεσιν, τοις λαοις	B etc.				
	λαοις] τω λαω	W Wessᵇ				cf. minn
28	βουλη] +σου		×	ℵ	Ant	D
30	ιασιν] ιασεις					vg
31	παρρησιας] +πασης					gig
32	καρδια] +μια					Aug
	ελεγον] ελεγεν			ℵA	Ant	D
34	των πιπρασκομενων] αυτων					Aug
36	ιωσηφ] ιωσης				Ant	
V						
2	γυναικος] +αυτου		×		Ant	
4	om μενον		×			
	εθου] +τουτο		×			
	δια τι εθου τουτο εν τη καρδια σου ποιησαι το πονηρον τουτο					cf. D
8	απεκριθη] ειπεν					D
	om δε		×			minn
9	πετρος] +ειπεν			A	Ant	
	+ισταντι before επι τη θυρα	B				θ
12	+εν τω ιερω before εν τη στοα					D
14	τω κυριω] +ιησου	R¹	×			D
16	οιτινες ' and they '					D
18	χειρας] +αυτων		×		Ant	
21	παραγενομενοι] παραγενομενος					
22	om δε 2°	B	×	B²ℵA	Ant	D
23	insert μεν in το δεσμωτηριον ευρομεν	WH³ Leid²²			Ant	D
25	om τον λαον	W				
28	+ου before παραγγελια				Ant	D
29	ειπαν] +αυτοις	H³ Leid²²	×			cf. D
	ανθρωποις] + εν αυτωᵇ	B				
31	δεξια] δοξη					D

ᵃ This seems to correspond to Codex Bezae about as exactly as Sahidic idiom permits, in both words and order. *In ore* is of course a natural rendering of δια του στοματος.

ᵇ Is this possibly a survival of the ' Western ' Greek which underlies the Latin *at ille dixit: deo* (gig) ?

	Sahidic	Sah. mss	Tr.	א AC 81	Antioch.	D	
31	αμαρτιων] +εν αυτω					D	
32	om εν αυτω			אA	Ant	D	
33	ακουσαντες] ακουοντες	W					P
	+ταυτα *before* δι-επρειοντο	W	×				minn
34	ανθρωπους]αποστολους				Ant	D	
35	προς αυτους] προς τους συναχθεντας	B				cf. D	
	προς αυτους] προς τους αρχοντας και τους συναχθεντας	W				D	
36	om τινα		×				h
37	λαον]+πολυν οτ ικανον	W		C	Ant	D	
39	αυτους] αυτο	W		C	Ant		
	+ουτε οι τυραννοι υμων *before* μηποτε	B				D	
40	παρηγγειλαν] +αυτοις	BW	×	cf. A			
	απελυσαν] +αυτους	BW	×		Ant		
41	του ονοματος] +τουτου	VW	×				cf. minn
42	τον χριστον ιησουν] τον κυριον ιησουν (τον ?) χριστον	BW		cf. C	cf. Ant	D	
VI							
1	ταυταις] εκειναις		×				minn
	πληθυνοντος του αριθμου των μαθητων	W					h
2	om δε	W	×			D	
	ειπαν]+αυτοις		×			cf. D	
3	επισκεψωμεθα] επισκεψασθε			אAC	Ant	D	
	om δε	W	×			D	
	πνευματος αγιου	W		AC	Ant		
	του πνευματος αγιου	B		cf. AC	cf. Ant		
5	om και	B	×				minn
	ο λογος] +ουτος					D	
8	λαω]+δια του ονοματος του κυριου ιησου χριστου					D	
9	της λεγομενης] των λεγομενων			אA			
12	ηγαγον]+αυτον		×	A			
14	ημιν] υμιν						S minn
15	αγγελου]+του θεου	W					h
VII							
2	+αποκριθεις *before* εφη		×				
	ακουσατε]+μου		×				minn
	της δοξης]των πατερων ημων	B	×				
5	και 2ο] αλλα					D	
6	δε]+αυτω		×	cf. א		cf. D	
	αυτου] σου		×	א			
	αυτο] αυτους		×			D	
7	και το] το δε		×	C			
10	τουτον] αυτου			B¹אAC	Ant	D	
12	εις αιγυπτον] εν αιγυπτω				Ant	D	

	Sahidic	Sah. mss	Tr.	אAC 81	Antioch.	D	
15	ιακωβ] +εις αιγυπτον			אΑC	Ant	D	
17	ηυξησεν ο λαος] ηυξη-σεν ο θεος τον λαον						
19	om εκακωσεν τους πατερας	B					
20	πατρος] +αυτου		×			D	
21	+εις before υιον			אΑC 81	Ant	D	
22	ην δε] και ην					cf. D	
23	+τους before υιους			אΑC 81	Ant	D	
25	αδελφους] +αυτου			A 81	Ant	D	
31	κυριου] +προς αυτον	W		C	Ant	cf. D	
32	ο θεος ισαακ, ο θεος ιακωβ	B			Ant	D	
34	αυτου] αυτων			אΑC 81	Ant		
35	και 1°] η	B	×				gig
	δικαστην] +εφ ημων			אC 81		D	
	συν χειρι] εν χειρι	Bdg¹		א	Ant		
37	om ο μωυσης		×				
38	om εν τη ερημω	Bdg¹	×				
	om του αγγελου		×				
	εξελεξατο] εδεξατο			אΑC 81	Ant	D	
39	ημων] υμων	W		81			minn
42	om και παρεδωκεν		×				
	τεσσερακοντα]+εν τη ερημω			B²א(Α)C 81	Ant	D	
43	ρεφαν			(A)C			
	επεκεινα] 'to this side of Babylon'					cf. D	
46	οικω] θεω	W Wess⁷		ΑC 81			P
49	μοι θρονος]ο θρονος μου					cf. D	
	οικοδομησατε] οικοδο-μησετε			אΑC 81	Ant	D	
51	καρδιας] τη καρδια			81	Ant		
57	κραξαντες δε] ο δε λαος ακουσας ταυτα εκραξε		×				
	om φωνη μεγαλη	B	×				
58	εκβαλοντες] +αυτον		×	A			
	ελιθοβολουν] +αυτον		×			D	
59	om ιησου	W	×				
60	+επεκαλεσατο λεγων before κυριε	B	×			cf. D	
VIII							
1	ημερα] + θλιψις (+ μεγαλη W) και ᵃ					cf. D	
	αποστολων] +μονων οι εμειναν εν ιερου-σαλημ					cf. D	
4	λογον] +κατα πολεις (or πολιν)						perp
5	om την			C 81	Ant	D	
6	αυτους] αυτου			אᵛⁱᵈ			
7	δε] τε (?) ᵇ						61

ᵃ There is no doubt as to the words of the original, since the Greek words (θλιψις, διωγμος) are retained in the Coptic.

ᵇ The Sahidic particle here used strongly suggests τε as its original.

	Sahidic	Sah. mss	Tr.	ℵAC 81	Antioch.	D	
9	om μεγαν						
10	om καλουμενη				Ant		
12	περι της βασιλειας] την βασιλειαν και το ονομα					cf. D	
13	τα] τε ^a			ℵAC 81	Ant	D	
16	μονον] πρωτον	B	×			D	
21	om γαρ	B				D	
24	μηδεν] μη	W	×				1838
25	διαμαρτυραμενοι]+τω πληθει (or οχλω) υπεστρεφον] υπε-στρεψαν		×	C	Ant		
	τε] δε	W				D	
	om τε	B	×				
	ευηγγελιζοντο] ευηγγελισαντο		×		Ant		
26	οδον]+την ερημον						pesh
	om αυτη εστιν ερημος						pesh
27	om και	B	×				69
	+της before βασιλισσης		×		Ant		
	om ος 2°			ℵAC		D	
28	ησαιαν τον προφητην			C			
30	εν ησαια τω προφητη ^b	W	×				
33	ταπεινωσει]+αυτου		×	C 81	Ant		
34	λεγει]+τουτο			B²ℵAC 81	Ant		
35	τον ιησουν] τον κυριον ιησουν χριστον						cf. pesh
IX							
1	om ετι	BW		ℵ			
2	om της οδου οντας	B					minn
4	σαουλ σαουλ] σαυλε σαυλε ^c						minn
5	ο δε]+κυριος ειπεν			cf. ℵ 81	Ant		
	+αυτω before εγω ειμι	W	×				minn
7	'they were hearing indeed the voice, they not understanding it; for they were not seeing anyone (or anything)'	W					
8	om δε 2°		×				minn
	om εισηγαγον	B	×				
11	κυριος]+ειπεν		×				1522
	σαυλον] ταρσεα ονοματι σαυλον						
12	om εν οραματι			ℵA 81			

^a Sahidic renders δε, and this is the reading of 242, 467 ; but τε, found in all other Greek MSS., would also be rendered by δε in Sahidic.

^b This is probably an error for the literal rendering of the Greek found in B Bour ; only the addition of a single letter is involved.

^c This vocative form is not Coptic at all, and must have been copied direct from the Greek original.

	Sahidic	Sah. MSS	Tr.	ℵAC 81	Antioch.	D	
13	απεκριθη] αποκριθεις ειπεν (or the like)		×				460
15	των βασιλεων τε και των εθνων	B	×				
17	om δε	B	×				522
	σαουλ] σαυλε a						minn
	ο κυριος] +ιησους	BV					pesh
	om ιησους				Ant		
18	om και		×				minn
	+παραχρημα before αναστας b			cf. C²			cf. L
20	συναγωγαις] +των ιου-δαιων						perp
	τον ιησουν] τον κυριον ιησουν						m
	+ο χριστος before ο υιος	B					441 Iren
	+ιησους ο χριστος be-fore ο υιος	W	×				
21	ακουοντες] +αυτου	W	×				440
	om εν ιερουσαλημ	W					
	+παντας before τους επικαλουμενους	W	×				minn
	και... εληλυθει] 'and who was sent be-cause of this hither'		×				
22	+τους before ιουδαιους	BV	AC 81	Ant			
	+παντας τους before ιουδαιους	W					
	ουτος] ιησους	V	×				
24	σαυλω] παυλω	W					H
	om και 1°		×		cf. Ant		L
25	αυτου] αυτον				Ant		
	om καθηκαν		×				
28	εις] εν		×				H
29	+και before παρρησια-ζομενος				Ant		
30	καισαρειαν] +νυκτος						minn
31	om και 3°	B	×				323
34	ειπεν αυτω ο πετρος] ο πετρος ατενισας αυτω ειπεν αυτω (om αυτω B)						perp
	om αινεα	B	×				
	+ο κυριος before ιησους			A			
35	οιτινες] και πολλοι		×				
	κυριον] θεον	BVH³	×				
36	μαθητρια] αδελφη		×				

a See note c, p. 334.

b The word for 'immediately' is clearly taken by the Sahidic translator with αναστας, and not with the preceding clause. In W it is followed by δε ; in V a stop is put after the rendering of αναβλεψας τε. In B there is neither δε nor stop ; but since Coptic idiom puts temporal adverbs at the head of their sentence, the adverb here would naturally be understood as attached to αναστας ; and this is made decisive by W and V.

	Sahidic	Sah. MSS	Tr.	ℵAC 81	Antioch.	D
37	om δε	B	×	81		
38	om οι μαθηται		×			
	παρακαλουντες] + λε-γοντες	B	×			m
39	ιματια και χιτωνας	BW	×			
	om μετ αυτων ουσα	B	×			
40	om και 1°	WH³	×		Ant	
	αναστηθι]+εν ονοματι		×			
	του κυριου ημων ιησου χριστου	WH³V Wess⁸,⁹				gig
	αναστηθι]+εν ονοματι ιησου χριστου	B Masp				vg.cod
	αυτης]+'immediately'					perp
42	κυριον] θεον	H³	×			
X						
5	om τινα		×	ℵ	Ant	
7	οικετων]+αυτου		×		Ant	
11	om καταβαινον					d
	+ιδου before σκευος	W Bdg² T²				
12	om της γης	W	×		cf. Ant	
	τα ερπετα, τα πετεινα			cf. C	Ant	
16	ευθυς] παλιν	BVT²			Ant	D
	om ευθυς		×			minn
19	ειπεν]+αυτω	BWT²		cf. ℵAC 81	Ant	D
	δυο] τρεις			ℵAC 81		
21	+η before αιτια			ℵAC 81	Ant	D
22	ειπαν]+προς αυτον					D
23	αυτους]+(ο) πετρος					D
24	εισηλθεν] εισηλθον(-αν)	W		ℵAC	Ant	D
	αυτους 2°] αυτου			ℵAC	Ant	D
25	om επι τους ποδας	H³				vg.cod C
27	αυτω] σοι^a	BV				cf. D
30	+νηστευων και before προσευχομενος				Ant	D
	ανηρ] αγγελος του κυριου	H³				
31	η προσευχη] αι προσευχαι	H³				1518
32	θαλασσαν]+ος παραγενομενος λαλησει σοι λογους οις σωθηση			cf. C	cf. Ant	cf. D
33	προς σε] προς ημας	V				cf. D
	τε] δε		×			D
	του θεου] σου					D
	om παρεσμεν					D
	om παντα					D
	κυριου] θεον				Ant	D
34	επ αληθειας] ιδου	B	×			
36	λογον]+αυτου		×			614
37	+υμεις before οιδατε			ℵAC 81	Ant	D

^a Apparently B, which omits και before συνομιλων, attaches συνομιλων σοι to the preceding ανθρωπος ειμι; in V the insertion of δε after the word for συνομιλων cuts off this latter from the preceding.

	Sahidic	Sah. MSS	Tr.	ℵAC 81	Antioch.	D	
37	κηρυγμα] βαπτισμα			B²ℵAC 81	Ant	D	
39	ημεις]+εσμεν		×		Ant		
	των ιουδαιων] της ιουδαιας						pesh
	om και 2°		×				minn
41	' nobis praedestinatis a deo' (order)			cf. C			
	νεκρων]+ημερας τεσσερακοντα					D	
44	ετι]+δε						minn
46	γλωσσαις] 'aliis linguis'					cf. d	
	πετρος]+ειπεν	B	×			cf. D	
48	αυτους] αυτοις			ℵA			
	τοτε . . . επιμειναι] επεμεινεν δε (om δε W) παρ αυτοις					cf. D	
XI							
1	οι αδελφοι και οι αποστολοι	B	×				
	κατα]+ιερουσαλημ και	B	×				
3	εισηλθεν, συνεφαγεν] εισηλθες, συνεφαγες			ℵA	Ant	D	
5	om καταβαινον						
6	ειδον]+παντα	B					cf. 1873
7	om πετρε θυσον και	B	×				
10	παλιν placed after εγενετο	W	×				
11	ημεν] ημην			81	Ant		
13	ειποντα]+αυτω	W Bodl	×		Ant	D	
15	om το αγιον	B	×				
17	ουν] δε	BV	×			d	
	εγω]+δε	W Bodl			Ant		
20	om και 2°		×		Ant	D	
22	ηκουσθη] ηλθεν		×				vg
	απεστειλαν] απεστειλεν	B	×			D	460
	βαρναβαν]+διελθειν				Ant	D	
23	om τη προθεσει της καρδιας						
24	ικανος]+τω κυριω			B²ℵA 81	Ant	D	
25	αναστησαι]αναζητησαι	BVH³ Bodl (2 mss.)		B²ℵA 81	Ant		
	αναστησαι] αναζητων	W				D	
26	om ολον						e
	χριστιανους (χρεστ- H³)						
27	αυταις] εκειναις			cf. ℵA 81	cf. Ant	cf. D	
28	εσημαινεν] εσημανεν			ℵA 81	Ant		
29	οι δε μαθηται ωρισαν καθως ευπορειτο εκαστος αυτων δουναι εις διακονιαν και πεμψαι		×			cf. D	
XII							
1	ηρωδης] αγριππας		×				cf. pesh
2	om δε	W	×				1838

	Sahidic	Sah. mss	Tr.	ℵAC 81	Antioch.	D	
3	+αι *before* ημεραι			A 81		D	
4	τεσσαρσιν τετραδιοις] 'sixteen soldiers'		×				pesh
5	ετηρειτο] +'strictly'ᵃ		×				
	προσευχη] +πολλη					D	
	om εκτενως		×				
	εκκλησιας] +προς τον θεον			ℵA 81	Ant	D	
6	ηρωδης] αγριππας		×				
7	επεστη +(τω) πετρω					D	
	χειρων] +αυτου		×			D	
8	om αυτω	BV	×				
9	ηκολουθει] +αυτω		×		Ant		
	δε] γαρ					D	
10	φυλακην] θυραν		×				
11	ηρωδου] αγριππας		×				
12	τε] δε		×	A 81			
13	προσηλθε] εξηλθεν		×				
17	ειπεν τε] +αυτοις		×				minn
	ετερον] ερημον		×				
18	+'immediately' before ην	B	×				
	ουκ ολιγος] μεγας		×				minn
19	ηρωδης] αγριππας		×				
	απαχθηναι] +'to destroy them'		×			cf. D	
	απο της ιουδαιας] εις την ιουδαιαν	B	×				
	διετριβεν] διετριψεν		×	A			
	+ εκει *at close of verse*		×	A			vg
20	ητουντο] ητησαντο		×	A			
21	+και *before* καθισας			A	Ant	D	
23	θεω] κυριω	W	×				
24	κυριου] θεου			ℵA 81	Ant	D	
25	εις ιερουσαλημ] 'from Jerusalem'	VW		A		D	minn
XIII							
1	εν . . . εκκλησιαν] εν τη εκκλησια τη εν αντιοχεια		×				vg
2	ειπεν] +αυτοις	BVH³	×				cf. minn
3	απελυσαν] +αυτους		×				255
4	του αγιου πνευματος] των αγιων						perp
5	κατηγγελλον] κατηγγειλαν		×			D	
	υπηρετην] υπηρετουντα αυτοις					D	
6	om ολην	W			Ant		
	αχρι] +'a place called'	B	×				
10	παυση] παυεις	B					minn
11	επεσεν] +επ αυτον			ℵ(A)C 81	Ant	D	

ᵃ This adverb seems to represent εκτενως (or εν εκτενεια; for the Sahidic rendering is in fact indeterminate as between these, although it is in form exactly εν εκτενεια), and to have been transferred from the later to the earlier half of the verse.

	Sahidic	Sah. MSS	Tr.	אAC 81	Antioch.	D	
14	την πισιδιαν] της πισιδιας			81	Ant	D	
	την συναγωγην] τας συναγωγας	BV	×				
	των σαββατων] του σαββατου	B	×			cf. D	917
	om εκαθισαν	W	×				
15	om τις		×		Ant		
17	om του λαου		×				1838
	εξ αυτης] εκ του τοπου εκεινου		×				
18	om ως					D	
	ετροποφορησεν] ετροφοφορησεν			AC			
19	κατεκληρονομησεν] +αυτοις	BV Wess10 Bour	×	AC	Ant		
20	om ως	B	×				614
	om ως . . . πεντηκοντα	Bour			cf. Ant	cf. D	
	om μετα ταυτα					D	
	εδωκεν] +αυτοις						minn
	κριτας] +ως ετεσι τετρακοσιοις και πεντηκοντα	Bour			Ant	D	
	+του before προφητου			C	Ant	D	
22	κατα την καρδιαν μου] 'venientem in corde meo'		×				
23	γαρ] ουν	W Bour				D	
	ηγαγεν] ηγειρεν			C		D	
24	om ισραηλ		×				minn
25	ελεγεν] + 'to the multitude ('multitudes' W)'	most codd.	×				
	μετ εμε] +ισχυροτερος μου	Bour	×				
26	αβρααμ] +και			אAC81	Ant	D	
28	ευροντες] +κατ αυτου					cf. D	
29	καθελοντες] +αυτον		×				vg
	εθηκαν] +αυτον		×				
31	οιτινες] +νυν			אAC81		cf. D	
	αυτου] αυτω	W Wess11	×				
	αυτου] συν αυτω	B	×			D	
32	πατερας] +ημων					D	
33	ημων] αυτων ημιν a			81	Ant		
	ιησουν] τον κυριον ιησουν χριστον					D	
36	om μεν	B Wess11	×			D	
38	τουτο] τουτου του ιησου		×	cf. אAC 81	cf. Ant	cf. D	gig

a Sahidic connects ημιν with αναστησας, 'having raised up to us.' See the Textual Note, above, p. 124.

	Sahidic	Sah. mss	Tr.	אAC 81	Antioch.	D	
39	ηδυνηθητε] ηδυνηθημεν	B	×			D^corr	
	εν τουτω πας ο πιστευων] πας ο πιστευων εν τουτω		×				cf. 097 minn
40	ουν] δε	Wess^11	×				
	om ουν	BW	×				
	τοις προφηταις] τω προφητη	W Wess^11	×				
	επελθη] +εφ υμας			AC 81	Ant		
42	ηξιουν] παρεκαλουν			אAC 81	Ant	D	
44	θεου] κυριου			B²אA 81		cf. D	
45	τους οχλους] 'the multitude'					cf. D	
	βλασφημουντες] 'they said, They are blaspheming'	B	×				
46	τε] δε	BV Wess^11, 12 Pet	×		Ant		
	ειπαν] +'to them'		×			D	
	om αιωνιου		×				
47	εντεταλται] ειπεν		×				
	ο κυριος] η γραφη		×				cf. Cypr
48	θεου] κυριου	W Wess^11, 12		אAC 81	Ant		
51	ποδων] +αυτων		×		Ant	D	
XIV 1	κατα το αυτο] 'according to their custom'		×				
5	των ιουδαιων τε και των εθνων	Wess^11					cf. hcl.*mg*
8	om εν λυστροις	B				D	
	om χωλος εκ κοιλιας μητρος αυτου	B				cf. D	
10	φωνη] +λεγω σοι εν τω ονοματι του κυριου ημων (om του κυριου ημων B) ιησου χριστου			cf. C		D	
	+εγειρε και *before* αναστηθι		×				
11	λυκαονιστι] 'in their tongue'		×				
14	εαυτων] αυτων		×	אC 81	Ant	D	
15	'that ye should withdraw yourselves from these vanities to turn'		×				
	+τον *before* θεον				Ant	D	
	αυτοις] αυτη	V	×				minn
17	αμαρτυρον] +αυτοις		×				
	αγαθουργων] +αυτοις		×				
	om υμιν		×	A 81			
	υμων] αυτων		×				pesh
	τροφης] +πασης	B	×				

		Sah. мss	Tr.	אAC 81	Antioch.	D	
18	κατεπαυσαν] 'they persuaded'ᵃ		×				minn
20	αυτον]+και(om και B) οψιας γενομενης						cf. h Ephr
21	ευαγγελισαμενοι] 'preached the word of the Lord'	B	×				
	om εις 2°ᵇ		×		Ant	D	
24	εις την παμφυλιαν] εις την περγην της παμφυλιας		×				
25	om εν περγη		×				
	τον λογον]+'in that place'		×				
	ατταλιαν] γαλιλεα	B	×				cf. latt
26	κακειθεν] + απεπλευ-σαν			B²אAC 81			
27	ανηγγελλον] ανηγ-γειλαν		×		Ant	D	
	+εν before τοις εθνεσιν	B	×		Ant	D	
28	διετρειβον]+εκει				Ant		
XV							
1	om κατελθοντες	most codd.	×				
	περιτμηθητε] +και περιπατητε εν					D	
2	αλλους]+αδελφους	BW	×				
	εις] εν		×				minn
3	om πασιν	W	×				minn
4	ιεροσολυμα] ιερου-σαλημ	BW		אC	Ant	D	
	αυτων]+εν τοις εθνεσιν		×				cf. HL
5	πεπιστευκοτες] πεπι-στευκοτων	VW Wess¹¹	×				L
	om πεπιστευκοτες	B	×				
7	om εν υμιν	W	×				minn
	δια] εκ	W					Iren
11	του κυριου]+ημων	all codd. exc. B	×				gig
14	εξηγησατο] ειπεν ημιν		×·				
	+παν before καθως	Wess¹¹	×				
15	τουτω] ουτως					D	
17	+αναστρεψαντες be-fore εκζητησωσιν	W	×				
20	πνικτου] 'anything dead'		×				

ᵃ This Sahidic reading, in which the Greek verb πειθειν is used, may represent no Greek variant, for the Copts were very fond of that word and not infrequently used it where there is no reason to suspect a Greek original; it was completely adopted into the Coptic language. It may here have been suggested by vs. 19.

ᵇ The omission of εις before both 'Iconium' and 'Antioch' is idiomatic in Sahidic. By using another conjunction, however, the translator could have repeated the preposition, if he had wished to do so.

	Sahidic	Sah. MSS	Tr.	ℵAC 81	Antioch.	D	
20	αιματος] + και ο μη θελωσιν αυτοις γινεσθαι ετεροις μη ποιειν (γενεσθαι for ποιειν W)					D	
23	αυτων] + επιστολην ουτως			cf. C		cf. D	
	om αδελφοι		?				61
24	+ελθοντες προς υμας before εταραξαν			cf. AC 81	cf. HL cf. PS	cf. D	
25	om συν τοις αγαπητοις ημων	B	×				
27	απαγγελλοντας] απαγγελουντας					D	
28	om και ημιν	W	×			D	
	om των a			ℵ		D	
29	om και αιματος	H³	×				
	και πνικτων] 'and the things which die'	VWH³ Wess¹¹	×				
	πορνειας]+α μη θελετε υμιν γινεσθαι (om υμιν γινεσθαι H³) μη ποιειτε ετερω (or ετεροις)					cf. D	
32	τε] δε	B Wess¹¹	×			D	
33	αδελφων] +εις ιερουσαλημ		×				
	om προς τους αποστειλαντας αυτους	B	×				
34	εδοξεν δε τω σιλα επιμειναι αυτου			cf. C		cf. D	minn
35	διετρειβον] +εν τη εκκλησια	W	×				
	κυριου] θεου		×				minn
37	om και		×		Ant	D	
39	τον τε βαρναβαν ... κυπρον] βαρναβας μεν λαβων μαρκον επλευσεν εις κυπρον					cf. D	
XVI							
6	+την before γαλατικην		×				
7	om ιησου				Ant		
9	+ωσει before ανηρ					D	
	εστως] +'before him'	W Wess¹¹				D	
10	ως δε το οραμα ειδεν] 'but when he had arisen he said unto us the vision'					cf. D	
12	πρωτη μεριδος] η πρωτη μερις	W Wess¹¹					cf. E

a B has a stop after τουτων, so as to read τουτων· επαναγκες απεχεσθαι κτλ.

	Sahidic	Sah. mss	Tr.	ℵAC 81	Antioch.	D	
12	om διατρειβοντες		×				
13	+τον before ποταμον					D	
	ου ενομιζομεν προσ-ευχη ειναι] 'to a place wherein we are accustomed to pray'						
	συνελθουσαις] 'who had come out to us'			cf. ℵC			
14	add της before πολεως					D	
	θεον] κυριον	Brit¹¹⁷	×			cf. D*	
15	εβαπτισθη]+αυτη	W	×				minn
	ει κεκρικατε με πιστην τω κυριω ποιειν	Wess¹¹ Brit¹¹⁷	×				
	ει κεκρικατε με χριστιανην ποιειν και πιστην τω κυριω	B	×				
17	υμιν] ημιν			A 81	Ant		
18	om δε 1°	W	×				H
	om και επιστρεψας	B	×				
	om χριστου	B	×				vg. cod. R
22	ο οχλος] 'a considerable multitude'	Wess¹³				D	
23	δε] 'and'			ℵAC	Ant	D	D
24	εις το ξυλον] εν ξυλω					D	D
26	ηνεωχθησαν]+παρα-χρημα			ℵAC 81	Ant	D	
29	προσεπεσεν]+'at the feet of'ᵃ		×			D	
30	εφη]+αυτοις		×			D	D
31	ιησουν]+χριστον			C	Ant	D	D
32	θεον] κυριου			AC	Ant	D	D
34	τε] δε		×	C			
	οικον]+αυτου	VWR²	×	ℵA	Ant	D	
	ηγαλλιασατο] imperfect			Cᵛⁱᵈ		D	P
	θεω] κυριω		?				minn
35	οι στρατηγοι] ο στρατηγος	B	×				
36	τους λογους]+τουτους			ℵA 81	Ant		
	οι στρατηγοι] ο στρατηγος	B					
37	ακατακριτους] 'there being no offence in us' (=αναιτειους, placed after ρωμαιους υπαρχοντας)		×			cf. D	
	om γαρ						33
38	οι ραβδουχοι] οι φυλακες	WR²	×				

ᵃ The preposition following the verb means literally 'at the feet of'; but this does not *necessarily* imply here προς τους ποδας in the original.

	Sahidic	Sah. MSS	Tr.	ℵ AC 81	Antioch.	D	
38	οι ραβδουχοι] οι δια-κονοι και οι φυλακες^a	B	×				
	εφοβηθησαν δε] και εφοβηθησαν	BWR²			Ant		
	om ακουσαντες	B	×				
40	ιδοντες τους αδελφους παρεκαλεσαν αυτους				Ant	cf. D	
XVII							
2	om και	W	×			D	
3	παρατιθεμενος] + αυ-τοις		×				minn
5	om εθορυβουν την πολιν	B	×				
6	τινας αδελφους] +αλ-λους	W	×				e
8	δε] 'and'		×			D	
11	λογον] +του κυριου	B	×				e
12	και των ελληνιδων . . . ολιγοι] 'and rich Greek women and many men' (*as part of subject*)					cf. D	
13	τους οχλους] τον οχλον	W					H
14	om τοτε					cf. D	minn
	om εως	W				D	S
15	εντολην] +παρ αυτου					cf. D	vg
17	+τοις *before* εν τη αγορα					D	
18	om και 1°	VW Cai	×				minn
	δε και] μεν	B	×				
19	δυναμεθα] 'we wish'		×				
20	θελει ταυτα ειναι] 'are these'		×				
23	om και 2°		×				1898
25	και τα παντα] 'to everything'	B			cf. Ant		
	και τα παντα] 'to the world'	W			cf. Ant		
	και τα παντα] 'in everything'	H³			Ant		
27	και 1°] η			A	Ant	D	
28	ημας] υμας			ℵA 81	Ant	D	
30	απαγγελλει] παραγ-γελλει^b			A	Ant	D	
32	om και παλιν				Ant		
33	+και *before* ουτως				Ant		
34	+ο *before* αρεοπαγειτης			ℵA	Ant		
XVIII							
1	μετα] +δε	W	×		Ant		
3	ηργαζοντο] ηργαζετο	W		A	Ant		
6	την κεφαλην] τας κεφαλας	B					minn

^a ^a B uses the Greek word διακονοι and a Coptic word for φυλακες. The Sahidic does not use in this verse the same word for ραβδουχοι as in vs. 35. V is defective here, as usually happens at points of critical interest.

^b The Greek word is used.

	Sahidic	Sah. MSS	Tr.	אAC 81	Antioch.	D	
7	οικιαν] +αδελφου		×				
	τιτιου ιουστου] τιτου			cf. א			pesh
9	δι οραματος εν νυκτι				Ant	cf. D	
11	om δε	B	×			cf. D	522
	+εκει before ενιαυτον					cf. D	
12	και] +επιθεντες τας					cf. D	
	χειρας αυτων αυτω						
14	κατα λογον] ευλογως [a]						cf. vg.
15	δε] νυν ουν		×				
	περι λογου και ονοματων						
	και νομου] περι ονο-						
	ματος η περι λογων	B					
	του νομου	cf. W	×				
	εγω] +γαρ		×		Ant		
17	παντες] +οι ελληνες				Ant	D	
18	αποταξαμενοις]+αυτοις		×				minn
	και συν αυτω πρει-						
	σκιλλα και ακυλας]						
	συν πρισκιλλα και						
	ακυλα		×				
19	εφεσον] +τω επιοντι						
	σαββατω					D	
	om κακεινους κατ-						
	ελιπεν αυτου (cf.						
	vs. 21)						pesh
	αυτος δε] παυλος		×				
20	επενευσεν] 'he re-		×				
	mained '						
21	αλλα] + κατελιπεν						cf. minn
	εκεινους (τουτους V)						pesh
	αυτου						
	αποταξαμενος] +αυτοις		×		cf. Ant		
	om παλιν					D	
23	om και φρυγιαν	B	×				
25	την οδον] την διδαχην	W				cf. D	
	κυριου] του κυριου		×	א A	Ant	D	
	om δε			A cf. א	Ant	D	
26	om αυτου	H³	×				255
	πρισκιλλα και ακυλας]						
	ακυλας και πρι-						
	σκιλλα [b]	WH³			Ant	D	

[a] The Greek adverb ευλογως, here used in the Sahidic text, is otherwise practically unknown in Coptic literature (it occurs once in a theological tract), and is not found in the Greek O.T. or N.T., except once in Maccabees (of which we have no Coptic version). In view of this it is almost certain that it was taken over from the translator's Greek original. Compare the Latin renderings, *rationaliter* e, *merito* gig, *recte* vg. It is worth noting that the Bohairic version here renders κατα λογον by the Greek adverb καλως. Now καλως is very common in Coptic literature, and was fully adopted into the language. As the Copts often substituted a familiar Greek word for an unfamiliar one, it seems likely that in the Bohairic, again, it is ευλογως or some other adverb, rather than κατα λογον, which is represented by καλως.

[b] V here follows the Greek order. B has the names in the order ' Aquila and Priscilla,' but it looks as if the order had originally been different ; for when

	Sahidic	Sah. MSS	Tr.	ℵAC 81	Antioch.	D	
28	δια] εκ						
	των γραφων] αγιας γραφης	W	×				
XIX							
2	πιστευσαντες] + και βαπτισθεντες	W	?				
	οι δε] +'said'		×		Ant		
	αλλ ουδ ... ηκουσαμεν] 'we have not even heard that such a one receives a Holy Spirit'		×				
3	ειπεν τε] ειπεν αυτοις		×		cf. Ant		
4	ιησουν]+χριστον	W			cf. Ant	cf. D	
5	ιησου]+χριστου					D	
6	om το αγιον	Wess¹⁴	?				vg.
	γλωσσαις] 'other tongues'						hcl.*mg*
12	'so that they took napkins and aprons, having applied them unto his body, and put them upon those who are sick'				cf. Ant	cf. D	
	εκπορευεσθαι]+απ αυτων		×		Ant		
13	πονηρα] ακαθαρτα	B	×		Ant		vg. *codd*
	ορκιζω] ορκιζομεν	W			Ant		
15	om μεν			ℵA	Ant	D	
16	αμφοτερων] 'them seven'		×		cf. Ant		
19	τα περιεργα] 'vainglorious things'[a]		×				
	μυριαδας πεντε]μυριαδα	B	×				
20	του κυριου] του θεου[b]	W					minn
	'thus the word of the Lord grew and was established and prevailed'					cf. D	

(as here) the subject follows the verb, a particle (similar to English 'namely') is required before it. Thus W has 'when they heard him *namely* Aquila and Priscilla,' and V has likewise '*namely* Priscilla and Aquila'; but B reads 'when they heard him and Aquila *namely* Priscilla.' This is ungrammatical nonsense, but it strongly suggests that the Coptic scribe of B had in his Coptic original the same reading as that of V, with the names perhaps marked to be reversed.

[a] The Sahidic MSS. (BW), and a citation of this verse in a Coptic version of the legend of Cyprian of Antioch, have here an abstract word formed from the Greek word πέρπερος. Such an out-of-the-way word suggests a corruption in the translator's Greek original.

[b] W reads του θεου, but has του κυριου against it in the margin. B and V read του κυριου in the text.

	Sahidic	Sah. MSS	Tr.	ℵAC 81	Antioch.	D	
21	διελθων] 'go out of' 'to go out of Macedonia and Achaia and proceed to Jerusalem'			cf. A		D	vg. codd
						D	cf. P
22	εις την ασιαν]in 'Asia'					D	
24	'for a silversmith called Demetrius'		×				
	ναους]+αργυρους			A cf. ℵ	Ant	D	
25	ους συναθροισας και] ουτος συναθροισας					D	
	ειπεν]+προς αυτους		×			D	
	ανδρες]+συντεχνιται					D	
27	'but not only this profession is in danger of being dispersed from us'		×				
	om θεας		?				vg
28	εφεσιων](της) εφεσου[a]		×				
29	πολις]+ολη				Ant	D	
	επλησθη η πολις της συγχυσεως] η πολις ολη συνεχυθη	B				D	
33	om συνεβιβασαν (προβαλοντων being made principal verb)		×				
	αλεξανδρον] τινα ονοματι αλεξανδρον	W Leid[23]	×				cf. vg. cod. D
34	εφεσιων](της) εφεσου[a]		×				
	μεγαλη . . . εφεσιων] once only			ℵA	Ant	D	
35	την εφεσιων πολιν] την πολιν εφεσον		×				
	νεωκορον...διοπετους] 'worships the great Artemis and Zeus'		×				cf. gig
37	τουτους]+ενθαδε					D	
40	om ου 2°					D	
	στασεως περι της σημερον] 'concerning the ("this" B) tumult of to-day'		×				
	om περι της συστροφης ταυτης		×				
XX							
1	παρακαλεσας]+και	W		ℵ			
3	μηνας τρεις] ημερας ικανας (or πλειους)	B	×				
	δια μακεδονιας] 'to Macedonia'		×				
4	σωπατρος]σωσιπατρος						minn
	ασιανοι]+εξ εφεσου					cf. D	
5	προσελθοντες] προελθοντες			B[2]		D	

[a] B has the article with 'Ephesus,' W omits it.

	Sahidic	Sah.MSS	Tr.	ℵAC 81	Antioch.	D	
8	ησαν] 'were lighted'		×				
13	προσελθοντες] προελθοντες			ℵC			L
	τον ασσον] θαρσος	Bty	×				LP
	τον ασσον] θασος[a]	W	×				
14	τον ασσον] θαρσος	Bty	×				
	τον ασσον] θασος	W	×				P
15	τη δε εσπερα] 'on the morrow'[b]			ℵAC	Ant	D	
	σαμον] +και μεινας εν τρωγυλιω				cf. Ant	cf. D	
18	+αδελφοι after υμεις	W					
	+αδελφοι after επιστασθε	B				D	
22	εγω δεδεμενος				Ant	D	
23	μενουσιν] +εν ιερουσαλημ					D	
24	om ιησου	W	?				gig
	διαμαρτυρασθαι]+τοις ιουδαιοις και τοις ελλησιν					D	
25	βασιλειαν]+(του)ιησου					D	
28	προσεχετε]+δε	W	×				
	το πνευμα το αγιον] ο θεος	W	×				
	θεου] κυριου			AC	cf. Ant	D	
29	οτι εγω] εγω γαρ				Ant		
31	εκαστον]+υμων					D	
32	κυριω] θεω	B Brit[117]		ℵAC	Ant	D	
	οικοδομησαι]+υμας		×			D	
	δουναι]+υμιν		×	C	Ant		
	εν τοις ηγιασμενοις] των ηγιασμενων	BW	×				
34	αυται] μου	W				D	
35	των λογων] του λογου						LP
36	ειπων]+ο παυλος	W Vprob					
	om πασιν	W	×				431 (?)
	προσευξατο] προσευξαντο	BW	×				
38	'ye will not again see my face'[c]		×			cf. D	gig
XXI							
1	παταρα]+μετα ταυτα εις μυρρα					cf. D	gig
4	ανευροντες δε] και ανευροντες				Ant		
	αυτου] 'apud eos'			A		d	L
11	τας χειρας και τους ποδας		×	A			
	εις]+τας		×	ℵ			

[a] See above, p. 319 (d).

[b] The same word is used to render τη επιουσῃ and τη ερχομενη.

[c] The conversion here of oratio obliqua into recta is quite in accordance with Coptic idiom.

	Sahidic	Sah. MSS	Tr.	אAC 81	Antioch.	D	
13	παυλος] +'saying'		×	cf. אA			
	εις] +εν		×				minn
16	+τινες before των	Vvid	×				623
	μαθητων	W					
18	παντες (τε παρεγε-						
	νοντο) πρεσβυτεροι]						
	'some elders'	BW	×				
19	om εν before τοις						
	εθνεσιν	B				D	
20	εν τοις ιουδαιοις] εν					D	
	τη ιουδαια					D	
	+ουτοι before παντες					D	
23	αφ εαυτων (as in Bא						
	Bohairic)ᵃ						
25	εθνων] +ουδεν εχουσι						
	λεγειν προς σε					D	
	ημεις] +γαρ					D	
	απεστειλαμεν] επε-						
	στειλαμεν			אAC	Ant		
	αιμα και πνικτον						
	'blood and ('of,'						
	B) dead things'		×				
27	ως δε εμελλον αι επτα						
	ημεραι συντελεισθαι]						
	'but when the						
	seven days were						
	completed'					D	
28	του νομου και του τοπου						
	τουτου] 'the law of						
	this temple'ᵇ	W	×				
	του νομου και του τοπου						
	τουτου] 'the law						
	and the 'this'						
	temple'	Bty	×				

ᵃ The Coptic preposition used here, though capable of a great variety of meanings, cannot mean to take a vow 'on one,' *i.e.* be responsible for it, which would appear to be the meaning of εφ εαυτων (AC, Antiochian, D). The primary meaning which the Coptic preposition suggests is to make a vow 'for,' or 'on behalf of,' oneself; and perhaps it might be stretched so as to mean 'of oneself,' 'of one's own accord.' It is so used in John xii. 49 (ἐξ ἐμαυτοῦ), and hence probably stands here in Acts for αφ εαυτων. Some confirmation of this may be found in the Bohairic version, where another preposition is used which makes no sense in Coptic, but is a literal translation of απο.

ᵇ The word 'temple' also stood in V, which is defective. What Greek word is rendered by the native word 'temple' is difficult to say. It might even be τοπος; for though that would normally be rendered by the native word for 'place,' yet in later Coptic, at any rate, the Greek word was adopted into the language with the technical sense of 'shrine,' usually the burial-place of a saint, and that association (supposing it to have existed so early as this Coptic version, as to which it would be rash to hazard an opinion) may have suggested the rendering 'temple' for τοπος. But of course the same native word is used to render ιερον in the present passage; while at the close of the verse τοπον is rendered by the Coptic word for 'place.'

	Sahidic	Sah. MSS	Tr.	ℵAC 81	Antioch.	D	
30	om και ευθεως εκλει-σθησαν αι θυραι	B		cf. ℵ			
31	τε] δε	W	×		Ant		
32	χιλιαρχον]+και τους εκατονταρχας						cf. 257
39	ταρσευς]+δε					cf. D	
40	αυτου] του χιλιαρχου		?			D	
XXII							
1	om μου	B	×				2147
5	εμαρτυρει] μαρτυρει			ℵA	Ant	cf. D	
	om και *before* επι-στολας		×			D	
	om προς τους αδελφους		×				
7	σαουλ σαουλ] σαυλε σαυλε^a					D	
8	απεκριθην]+λεγων	B	×	cf. ℵ			
9	εθεασαντο] + και εμ-φοβοι εγενοντο					D	LP
10	om κυριος					D	
11	ως δε]+ανεστην					d	cf. 1611
	ουδεν εβλεπον] ουκ ενεβλεπον			ℵA	Ant	d	
	του φωτος της δοξης	B Brit^119	×				gig
12	κατοικουντων] + εν δαμασκω				Ant		
13	σαουλ] σαυλε					d	614
	om εις αυτον					d	5
14	ειπεν]+μοι		×				minn
18	om εν ταχει		×				
22	αυτου]+'the multi-tude('multitudes' W Brit^118)'		×				
29	ουν] δε^b		×				minn
	om δε		×	ℵ			
	δεδεκως]+και παρα-χρημα ελυσεν αυτον						614 1611
30	om ελυσεν αυτον και						See Textual Note
	εις αυτους] 'in their midst'		×				
XXIII							
6	και αναστασεως] της αναστασεως	B Wess^16	×				
7	επεπεσε] εγενετο			ℵAC	Ant		
8	τα αμφοτερα] 'that there is resurrec-tion and there is angel and there is spirit'						
9	αγγελος]+μη θεομαχω-μεν (θεομαχειτε B)				Ant		
10	αγειν]+τε			ℵAC	Ant		h

^a So also Bty in xxvi 14.
^b Beginning at this point D is lacking for the rest of the book.

	Sahidic	Sah. MSS	Tr.	אAC 81	Antioch.	D
11	ειπεν] +αυτω	W Brit¹¹⁹ Wess¹⁶				minn
12	οι ιουδαιοι] τινες των ιουδαιων				Ant	
	om ποιησαντες συστροφην	W	×			
14	τοις πρεσβυτεροις και τοις αρχιερευσιν	BVvid Brit¹¹⁸ Wess¹⁶	×			
15	υμεις εμφανισατε τω χειλιαρχω] 'we beg you to do this for us : collect the council and tell the chiliarch'					h
	εις υμας] 'into our midst'	W				minn hcl. *mg*
	ως μελλοντας] 'as if ye would'			81 (?)		h
16	om παραγενομενος και		×			
17	'he hath something to say unto him'			אC	Ant	
18	αυτον] τον νεανιαν		×			h
	νεανιαν] νεανισκον ᵃ			אA 81		
	λαλησαι] +σοι			B²אA 81	Ant	
20	μελλων] μελλοντες					minn h
23	om τινας		×			minn
	εβδομηκοντα] εκατον ᵇ					minn h
28	τε] δε	BR³ W Mun	×	81	Ant	
	τε] ουν					
	αυτω]+κατηγαγον αυτον εις το συνεδριον αυτων			B²אA	Ant	
29	om δε	B	×	81	Ant	
30	εσεσθαι] + υπο των ιουδαιων				Ant	
	επεμψα] +αυτον		×			1758

ᵃ Coptic has two words for 'boy' or 'youth,' both native. One of these was used in vs. 17, and in the Coptic variant from the Greek at the beginning of vs. 18. For the Greek νεανιαν here (later, in vs. 18) the other Coptic word is used, as if to denote the change from νεανιας to νεανισκος (אA81), although this motive is by no means certain, as both the words are very common in Coptic. The second word often (but not necessarily) implies a more advanced age ; the first may be used even of a small child, the second never of anything less than a youth. The Bohairic uses in both places the same word (the 'second' one mentioned above). In vs. 22, for νεανισκον, the Sahidic translator uses the 'second' word again, thus confirming the inference that in vs. 18b he read νεανισκον.

ᵇ In Sahidic še=100, šfe=70, with a difference of only one letter. In B there is a small space left between š and e, but probably no letter lost, although there is a bare possibility of šfe having been corrupted into še. In W there is presumably no doubt of the reading 100 ; V is defective.

	Sahidic	Sah. mss	Tr.	אAC 81	Antioch.	D
30	τοις κατηγοροις] + αυτου		×			1838
	λεγειν προς αυτον] 'to try their cause against him' (=τα προς αυτον)			81	Ant	
31	δια νυκτος ηγαγον		?			
33	om και 2⁰					minn
34	δε] +ο ηγεμων				Ant	
35	om και	B	×			minn
	κελευσας] εκελευσε δε (or τε)		×		Ant	460
XXIV						
2	δε] +αυτου			אA 81	Ant	
3	αποδεχομεθα] 'we are honoured with much favour'		×			
4	ενκοπτω] ενκοπτωμεν		×			
5	στασεις] στασιν ᵃ	B			Ant	
8	δυνηση] +δε και	W				cf. minn
	ανακρινας] ανακρινειν	W				cf. 181
						cf. gig
	om επιγνωναι	W				cf. gig
10	ετων] ημερων	R³				cf. gig
13	om σοι				Ant	
14	τω πατρωω θεω] 'the god of my fathers'					cf. 614
	πιστευων] +πασι			אA 81	Ant	
	+τον before νομον			אA 81	Ant	
	om τοις 2⁰			A	Ant	
15	om και 1⁰ ᵇ	BW	×			
18	om δε	WR³			Ant	
19	ους] 'but these'		×			
	εδει] δει				Ant	
22	+ακουσας ταυτα at opening of verse				Ant	
	τα περι της οδου] την οδον		×			
	διαγνωσομαι τα καθ υμας] 'I will listen to you'					vg
23	αυτον] (τον) παυλον				Ant	
	αυτω] +η προσερχεσθαι αυτω				Ant	
24	τη ιδια γυναικι] τη γυναικι αυτου ᶜ			א cf. C	cf. Ant	

ᵃ The Sahidic here uses the Greek word; but, as always, in the nominative treated as indeclinable. B prefixes the indefinite article, which shows that his original was στασιν. W and R³ have no article at all, so that for them it is impossible to say whether the original was singular or plural. The Bohairic has the plural.

ᵇ B has a lacuna from xxiv. 16 to xxvi. 32; W is lacking from xxiv. 20 to the end.

ᶜ With χριστον, vs. 24, both V and R³ fail us; but R³ resumes at vs. 25 εγκρατειας.

	Sahidic	Sah. MSS	Tr.	ℵAC 81	Antioch.	D
26	χρηματα δοθησεται υπο του παυλου] 'that Paul will give him money'		×			
	δοθησεται] +αυτω παυλου] +οπως λυση αυτον			ℵAC 81	Ant	
					Ant	
27	'but when the two years of Felix were completed, there came in his place Porcius Festus'		×			
XXVᵃ						
1	επαρχεια] επαρχια (*Greek word used*)	R³		BC (81)	Ant	
2	οι αρχιερεις	R³		BℵAC 81		
6	'but when he had spent [eight] or t[en days] there (*or* with them ?)'ᵇ	R³				pesh
9	δε	V		BℵC 81	Ant	
	δε] ουν	R³		A		
	επ εμου	R³		BℵAC 81	Ant	
10	εστως *once only*			ℵAC 81	Ant	
	+τους *before* ιουδαιους		×			
13	ασπασαμενοι] ασπασομενοι		?	81		
15	ανεφανισαν] +μοι		×			E
	αιτουμενοι κατ αυτου καταδικην] 'demanding him to put him to death'		×			
16	χαριζεσθαι τινα ανθρωπον] 'to give (up) a man to slay him'					
18	ουδεμιαν . . . πονηρων] 'they set up no evil thing against him such as I thought (*or* think) it so'			AC	Ant	
22	δε] +εφη		×	C 81	Ant	
25	αυτου δε του παυλου] τουτου δε			cf. B²ℵAC 81	Ant	

ᵃ For chapter xxv we use only two fragmentary MSS., namely R³ and V. In vss. 1-12 all Sahidic readings which relate to any disputed point are cited, including those which agree with the Greek of Codex Vaticanus, and from the *silence* of the tables for these verses nothing can be inferred as to the Sahidic. From vs. 13 to the end of the chapter, R³ is nearly complete, and, in accordance with the general plan of the tables, may be taken, wherever its reading is not here noted, as not disagreeing with the Greek of Codex Vaticanus (except, as usual, in points probably referable purely to the translator).

ᵇ The words supplied fill the lacunae exactly, and can hardly be doubted.

	Sahidic	Sah. MSS	Tr.	אAC 81	Antioch.	D	
XXVI *a*							
3	δεομαι] +σου		×	C	Ant		
4	+οι *before* ιουδαιοι		×	אA	Ant		
5	μαρτυρειν] + τη αλη-θεια		×				
	ημετερας] εμης		×				
7	το δωδεκαφυλον ημων] 'the twelve tribes of our γενος'	R³	×				
10	διο] 'but this'			cf. אAC 81	cf. Ant		
11	+'against his name'	Bty					vg.*codd*
17	αποστελλω] αποστελω	P		cf. 81	Ant		096
18	επιστρεψαι]+αυτους	P	.				
	+ απο *before* της εξουσιας	P	×	C			ΨL
	αφεσιν αμαρτιων] την αφεσιν των αμαρ-τιων αυτων	P	×				
19	οθεν] +ουν	P	×				
XXVII *b*							
6	om εις αυτο	B	?				h
13	αραντες ασσον] 'having put forth (*lit.* arisen) from Alasos'						vg. esp. cod. D
14	κατ αυτης) 'against us'		×				
16	καυδα] κλαυδα (-τα)			אA 81	Ant		
19	om αυτοχειρες		×				
	την σκευην] +πασαν	Wess¹⁷	×				
	πλοιου] + εις την θα-λασσαν	Wess¹⁷					minn
20	add λοιπον *before* περιηρειτο			אAC 81	Ant		
21	την ζημιαν ταυτην και την υβριν	B	×				
23	του θεου ου ειμι] του θεου μου						cf.gig 2147
	om και		×				
27	προσαχειν τινα αυτοις χωραν] '*quod appropinquaverimus alicui regioni*'			cf. אAC	cf. Ant		
29	μη που] μηπως	Wess¹⁸		cf. A	Ant		
	μη που] μηποτε *c*	H³					

a In chapter xxvi we have vss. 1-10 in R³, and unfruitful fragments in V as far as vs. 8, and in Horner's Cod. 20 to vs. 7. For the remainder P has vss. 16 ειδες με to vs. 19 οπτασια ; B reappears in the last four words of vs. 32 ; otherwise the only Sahidic authority for xxvi. 11-32 is Bty (uncollated).

b For chapters xxvii and xxviii a nearly continuous text has been preserved, and the method ordinarily employed in constructing these tables is followed. But the very free renderings of the Sahidic, where no Greek variant is implied, are adduced somewhat more sparingly than hitherto.

c Both μηπως and μηποτε are common in Coptic, and often interchanged, so that the Coptic evidence for differences in the original is not strong.

	Sahidic	Sah. MSS	Tr.	ℵAC 81	Antioch.	D
29	εκπεσωμεν] εκπεσωσι		?	81		minn
33	+ιδου before τεσσα-ρεσκαιδεκατην		×			
34	om διο	H³	×			
	om και			ℵAC81	Ant	
	απο] εκ (probably)			ℵ	Ant	
	απολειται] πεσειται				Ant	
35	εσθιειν]+επιδιδους και ημιν	H³P				minn
36	ευθυμοι δε γενομενοι] 'gavisi sumus'	H³	×			
37	ως εβδομηκοντα εξ a					
39	ουκ εγεινωσκον] 'the sailors did not know'	P				gig
	εγεινωσκον] επεγινω-σκομεν	B	×			
40	om εις την θαλασσαν	B	×			
41	om ερεισασα	B	×			gig
	βιας]+του ανεμου	BP	×	cf. C 81	cf. Ant	cf. vg
	+τη πνεουση εις τον αιγιαλον at close of verse	B	×			
43	'he commanded those who could swim to leap the first ashore'					cf. gig
XXVIII b						
1	μελιτηνη] μελιτη			B²ℵAC 81	Ant	
2	om παντας		×	A		
	δια το ψυχος το εφ-εστος και τον υετον		×			
	om δια 2º		×	ℵ		
3	απο] εκ (probably)		×			minn
4	om προς αλληλους c		×			pesh
7, 8	ποπλιω] πουπλιος d			81		
8	τας χειρας] την χειρα	B	×			gig
9	+και before οι λοιποι			ℵA 81	Ant	
11	διοσκουροις] διοσκορος e					cf. minn
15	ηλθαν ... ταβερνων] 'came out from Thr[ee ...] to Appios Phor[os] to meet us'					cf. vg

a H³ Bty P Brit[120] have the reading of Cod. Vaticanus; B has '[. . . . se]venty-five', which leaves indeterminate the number, as well as the presence or absence of ως.

b In chapter xxviii we have B with lacunae (vss. 21, 22, 28, 29, and part of vs. 30 are missing); together with P for vss. 2-3, 8-13, 20-23; and Brit[121] for vss. 15-17, 23-25.

c After μεταβαλομενοι, vs. 6, there is a gap in B till ονοματι, vs. 7.

d The spelling που- (so Bty, vss. 7 and 8) is definitely attested for vs. 8 in B, and no doubt was also found in the same name (now mutilated) in vs. 7.

e After παρεκληθημεν, vs. 14, there is a gap in B till εις απαντησιν, vs. 15.

356

THE TEXT OF ACTS

	Sahidic	Sah. mss	Tr.	אAC 81	Antioch.	D	
16	ρωμην] +ο εκατονταρ-χος παρεδωκε τους δεσμιους τω αρχοντι των στρατιωτων (or τω στρατοπεδαρχη) επετραπη] +δε	Brit[121]			Ant Ant		
17	τους οντας των ιουδαιων πρωτους] ' the αρχοντες of the Jews '	B	?				
	om συνελθοντων δε αυτων	B	×				
20	προσλαλησαι] ' to speak with you '		×				cf. perp
23	om μωυσεως και	B					
27	ωσιν] +αυτων [a]	B	×	אA			
31	om τα	B	×				1319
	om πασης	B	×				Ψ minn

[a] We have no Sahidic text from ηκουσαν, vs. 27, to απεδεχετο, vs. 30, except Bty, which came to light too late to be fully included in these Tables.

APPENDIX V

THE BOHAIRIC VERSION

THESE paragraphs and Tables are due to Sir. H. Thompson.

Eleven MSS. of the Bohairic version of Acts were collated by Horner for his edition (1905); he has given them the following symbols :

A. Brit. Mus. or. 424. A.D. 1307. Said to be copied from a text written A.D. 1250.

B. Milan, Ambrosiana. 14th century. An oriental polyglot.

Γ. Dayr el Muharrak, Egypt, 12th century.

F. Paris, Bibl. Nat. copt. 21. A.D. 1338.

G. Rome, Vat. copt. 14. A.D. 1357.

K. Rome, Vat. copt. 12. 14th century.

N. Oxford, Bodleian, hunt. 43. A.D. 1683.

O. Rome, Vat. borg. copt. 51. A.D. 1740.

P. Brit. Mus. or. 8786 (formerly Curzon). A.D. 1797.

S. Paris, Bibl. Nat. copt. 66. A.D. 1609.

T. Paris, Bibl. Nat. copt. 65. A.D. 1660.

These MSS. fall by date into two groups :

    (1) A B Γ F G K   12th to 14th century.

    (2) N O P S T   17th to 18th century.

None, therefore, is very early.

As regards their text they fall even more distinctly into two main groups :

    (1) A B P + F S.

    (2) Γ N O T.

G K lie between these two groups.

The group Γ N O T present virtually a single text, Γ being the oldest extant MS. of any type. The text of this group seems to be somewhat influenced by the Sahidic.

A B P are closely associated ; but B is a very close follower of the Greek Codex Vaticanus, while A is an eccentric MS. with many peculiar, and often corrupt, readings. A was unfortunately adopted by Horner for his text and translation (*The Coptic Version of the New Testament in the Northern Dialect,* vol. IV, 1905), which therefore do not correspond to the average Bohairic version.

Practically A, B, and Γ are the only MSS. of any importance. In the following tables the minor MSS. are often indicated by a figure; thus 'A + 4' means A and four later MSS., not including B or Γ. Where only some of the MSS. are referred to, it may be taken for granted that other MSS. offer the competing reading. The MSS. referred to in the column giving the readings are Bohairic MSS. in every case. Greek words used in the Bohairic text are usually represented in Greek letters.

For chapters i-iii the Bohairic variants from the Greek of Codex Vaticanus are given fully, although most of them are due only to the necessity of Bohairic idiom or the freedom of the translator. Beginning with chapter iv, as a rule only those Bohairic readings are mentioned which show with more or less probability that a variant from Codex Vaticanus was present in the Greek text used by one or more of the Bohairic MSS.; minor variants, for which no Greek evidence is found in the apparatus of Tischendorf and von Soden, and which are not attested by the Latin or Syriac version, are usually omitted. No comparison with the Sahidic is here attempted; that would involve much greater complication than the purpose of the tables permits, although such a study, with adequate knowledge of the Egyptian vernacular, would be interesting and fruitful. Where no Greek evidence is at hand for a Bohairic variant, Syriac or Latin evidence is sometimes adduced; these statements, however, have not been made complete; they merely call attention to the fact that such evidence exists, and give one or two specimens of it.

The lacunae of the Greek MSS. C 81 D must not be overlooked. As in the Tables for the other versions, only departures from Codex Vaticanus are noted; 'silence' does not indicate that the Bohairic positively attests the reading of Codex Vaticanus as against a variant of other Greek MSS.

The close agreement of the Bohairic with the Old Uncial text will be observed. A large proportion of the variants included in the Bohairic Tables (in so far as they represent Greek variants at all) are cases where Codex Vaticanus stands alone among Greek MSS., or has but very slight support, perhaps due to independent coincidence with it in error on the part of one or more minuscules.

Tischendorf's statements about the Bohairic version require some revision in the light of present knowledge of the Bohairic MSS.

The following are some of the points which need to be borne in mind in seeking the Greek text implied by the Bohairic translation. It must, however, be remembered that a translator will sometimes force his native tongue to abnormal constructions which he would not use in original composition.

(*a*) Owing to frequent confusion of Δ and T in the transliteration of Greek words in Coptic, δε may represent τε as well as δέ, and not necessarily imply a variant reading; cf. Acts i. 15, ii. 40, xiii. 52.

(*b*) Asyndeton, such as the Greek does not permit, is normal in Coptic.

(*c*) Coptic has no vocative, so that, for instance, for σὺ ὁ εἰπών (Acts iv. 25) the idiomatic Coptic rendering is 'he who spoke.'

(*d*) Coptic does not distinguish between χριστός and ὁ χριστός (the article being always used); nor between κύριος and ὁ κύριος (always 'the Lord,' when used of God or Christ). Before the proper name of a person (e.g. ὁ Ἰησοῦς) Coptic does not admit of the definite article. Before the name of a city the article was sometimes used, sometimes omitted; it was never used before such a name beginning with Θ (cf. θεσσαλονεικην, Acts xvii. 1), which was regarded as already containing the feminine article (T in Coptic).

(*e*) In such a case as τοὺς ἀδελφούς (Acts vii. 25) Bohairic idiom requires the rendering 'his brethren.'

(*f*) The Coptic so-called 'future in NA' is habitually used to render the Greek aorist subjunctive, and therefore may represent either -σομεν or -σωμεν; cf. Acts ii. 37, iv. 16.

(*g*) Two indicatives (without a connecting 'and') form the idiomatic Coptic rendering of a Greek aorist participle and indicative (similarly with aorist participle and infinitive).

(*h*) The Bohairic can give a quotation only in *oratio recta*, having no construction of accusative with infinitive after a verb of saying.

(*i*) τὸ εἰρημένον and τὸ ῥηθέν are often rendered in the Bohairic version by a relative sentence with the verb in the 3rd sing. active, 'the Lord' being understood as subject; cf. Acts ii. 16.

(*j*) Coptic does not put the adverb before the verb.

(*k*) Coptic is often incapable of reproducing the artificial order of Greek, e.g. Acts xxvii. 23, xxviii. 7.

(*l*) In such an expression as Πέτρος δὲ πρὸς αὐτούς, Acts ii. 38, the addition of the verb 'said' is required by Coptic idiom.

(*m*) In such a case as Acts ix. 37, λούσαντες δὲ ἔθηκαν, 'but having washed her, they placed her' (Boh), the Coptic cannot omit the object after the transitive verb.

(*n*) In such a case as καὶ εἰς Λύστραν, Acts xvi. 1, the preposition could be repeated in Coptic, though it is more idiomatic not to do so.

(*o*) The following are some instances in which Coptic does not indicate a distinction proper to Greek :

between 'in' (local) and 'by' (instrumental);

,, ἀπό and ἐκ;

,, 'only,' adverb and adjective (e.g. Acts xi. 19);

,, λεγόμενος and καλούμενος (e.g. Acts iii. 2);

,, ἕλληνες and ἑλληνισταί (Acts ix. 29, xi. 20);

,, πρὸς αὐτούς and σὺν αὐτοῖς (Acts xv. 2).

(*p*) 'From the beginning' is the usual phrase employed to render προ- ('fore-') in compounds, as προτεταγμένους, Acts xvii. 26 (Codex Bezae).

(*q*) The Copts frequently rendered an unfamiliar Greek word by a familiar one, also Greek; thus Acts xviii. 14, for κατὰ λόγον Bohairic reads καλῶς, not the uncommon εὐλόγως (so Sahidic); Acts xix. 39, Bohairic has νόμιμος for the unfamiliar ἔννομος.

		Bohairic	Transl.	ℵAC 81	Antioch.	D	
I							
2		ανεληµφθη +'to heaven'[a]	×				
3		om τα	×				
5		ου . . . ηµερας 'after not many days these (things) happened'	×				
6		'wilt thou restore'				d	
7		ειπεν (cod. A+2)] ειπεν δε (codd. BΓ etc.)		ℵA 81	Ant		Aug
				B[corr]			
		ειπεν ουν (cod. K)					
8		om εν 2°		AC 81		D	
10		και ως] ως δε (except codd. FS, *which lack both words*)	×				
		om και 2° (cod. A)	×				
11		om εις τον ουρανον 2° (codd. A+2)				D	
13		και οτε (codd. Γ etc.)] τοτε (cod. A); 'and τοτε' (codd. BG)	×				
		και ιακωβος (codd. BG+4)]					
		om και (codd. A+4)				D	
14		ουτοι] +δε (codd. A+1)	×				
15		'but (δε) there was a multitude gathered together making about 120 names'	×				
17		'the reckoning came to him of the κληρος of this διακονια'	×				
19		'and he was manifest'[b]	×				

[a] The usual Coptic rendering of the Greek word is 'taken upward'; here the adverb is replaced by 'to heaven.' Probably, however, this merely represents ἀνα-, and not a reading εἰς τὸν οὐρανόν in the original.

[b] Elsewhere in Acts, where this phrase occurs, the Coptic (which has no neuter) inserts 'the thing' as subject. Here this is not done, and the strict translation is 'and he was manifest.'

	Bohairic	Transl.	ℵAC 81	Antioch.	D	
20	om και 2° (except cod. F)	×				
25	πορευθηναι]'having gone' (cod. A)					minn
II						
2	om και 1° (cod. A)					minn
3	'and they appeared to them as tongues of fire divided' *a*	×				
	'they sat'		ℵ		D	
4	πνευματος αγιου (codd. AB etc.)] 'the Holy Spirit' (codd. Γ+3)	×				
	'according as the Spirit gave to them to make answer'	×				
5	'but there were some dwelling in Jerusalem, Jewish men, having fear'	×	cf. C			
6	το πληθος (codd. FS)] 'the multitudes'	×				
7	εξισταντο δε]+'all'		ℵAC 81			
	και εθαυμαζον] 'wondering'	×				
8	om και (codd. A+2)	×				
	ημεις]+'all' (codd. BΓ+3)	×				
11	om ταις ημετεραις (except codd. FSK)	×				
12	τι θελει τουτο ειναι] 'what is this that hath happened'				cf. D	
13	'these have filled their bellies with new wine'	×				
	μεμεστωμενοι εισιν]+'but (δε) others were saying, These are drunk' (cod. A)					cf. pesh
14	αυτοις]+'saying' (codd. FS)		C			cf. lat
16	το ειρημενον] 'that which he said'	×			D	
17	om και 1°	?				
	μετα ταυτα] 'in the last days'		ℵA(C) 81	Ant	D	
19	om και 1°	×				
22	τους λογους τουτους (codd. Γ etc.)] 'these my words' (codd. AK); 'my words' (cod. B)	×				
23	'(ye) having delivered him into the hands of the lawless (men), ye crucified him and ye slew him'	×				
24	του θανατου] 'of Amenti' (*Hades*)				D	

a The position of 'divided' at the end is necessary idiomatically.

	Bohairic	Transl.	ℵAC 81	Antioch.	D	
25	om οτι	×				
28	οδους] 'the ways'	×				
29	του πατριαρχου] 'our patriarch'	×				
33	om ουν (codd. AB+3 ; not codd. Γ+5)	×				
34	τους ουρανους]'the heaven' (cod. A)	×				
	om δε	×				
36	'made him Lord and made him Christ'	×				
37	om λοιπους (codd. FS)				D	
	ποιησωμεν] 'shall do'	×				
38	πετρος δε] + 'said'	×				
	εν τω ονοματι] 'to the name' (= επι τω ονοματι) [a]		ℵA 81	Ant		
39	τεκνοις]'fathers' (cod. A)	×				
40	τε] δε	×				
41	om ωσει (except codd. BG)	×				
42	'and the fellowship of the breaking of the bread'	?				d vg
	προσευχαις (codd. Γ+5)] προσευχη (codd. AB+3)	×				
43	φοβος] 'a great fear' (cod. F)					1518
	εγενετο 2°] + 'in Jerusalem, but (δε) a (+ 'great,' cod. F) fear was on them all'		ℵAC			
44 f.	'but all those who believed were together and they had everything in common'		ℵAC 81	Ant	D	
46	αφελοτητι καρδιας] 'a pure heart'	×				
III						
2	και] δε	×				
	'he used to be lifted up daily and placed at the door'	×				
	αιτειν] 'receive'	×				
3	ηρωτα] 'was praying them'	×				
	ελεημοσυνην λαβειν 'wishing to receive an alms from them'	×				
5	'but he looked at them, thinking that he would receive an alms from them' (except cod. A,					

[a] The Bohairic rendering suggests an original εις το ονομα ; but if this is unlikely, the rendering probably represents επι, since Coptic cannot say 'on (επι) the name,' and εν is made unlikely by the fact that elsewhere for εν in similar phrases another preposition ('in') is used.

	Bohairic	Transl.	ℵAC 81	Antioch.	D	
	which renders 'but he was thinking that,' etc.)	×				
6	πετρος]+'to him'	×				
	περιπατει] 'rise, walk'		AC 81	Ant		
7	om δεξιας (cod. A)					1522
10	om αυτω (codd. AFS)	×				
12	η 2° (codd. AB+4)] 'and' (codd. Γ+4)	×				
13	'the God of Abraham and the God of Isaac and the God of Jacob'		ℵAC		D	
16	τη πιστει] 'in the faith'		AC	Ant	D	
	εστερεωσεν 'hath made strong' (codd. Γ+6)] 'hath healed' (codd. AB+2)	×				
18	των προφητων] 'his prophets'	?		Ant		
20	ελθωσιν] 'come to you'					{ hcl·⁙ Iren
	αποστειλη υμιν τον προκεχειρισμενον	×				
	χριστον ιησουν] 'Jesus Christ'		AC 81			
21	ουρανον] 'the heavens'	×				
	χρονων] 'the time'	×				
	'by the mouth of his holy (om'holy,' cod. A) prophets from eternity'	×				
22	αυτου ακουσεσθε] 'listen (*imperative*) to him'					minn
23	του λαου] 'her people'					614 minn
24	και παντες δε] 'and all'	×				
	om οσοι			cf. D		perp
25	υμεις]+δε (codd. A+2)	×				1872
	υμων] 'our' (except codd. Γ+3)		ℵC	Ant	D	
26	'sent him to bless you so that'	×				
	εκαστον]'each one of you'					minn
IV 1	λαλουντων δε αυτων] +'these things' (codd. Γ+4)				D	
	αρχιερεις] 'priests'		ℵA 81	Ant	D	
	ο στρατηγος]'the strategi'				D	pesh
12	εν ανθρωποις] 'to men'				D	
	σωθηναι υμας] 'that they should be saved'					pesh
21	μηδεν . . . λαον] 'not having found any pretext against them with regard to the mode of punishing them on account of the people'				D	
28	η βουλη] 'thy counsel'		ℵ	Ant	D	
32	ελεγον] ελεγεν		ℵA	Ant	D	

	Bohairic	Transl.	אAC 81	Antioch.	D	
33	του κυριου ιησου] 'Jesus Christ' (codd. FS); 'Jesus Christ the Lord' (codd. GKP); 'Christ Jesus the Lord' (codd. BΓO); 'Jesus Christ our Lord' (cod. A); 'Christ Jesus our Lord' (codd. NT)	?				minn
36	'Barsabas' (except cod. B)	?	אA			
V						
3	ειπεν δε] +'to him' (except cod. B)	?			cf. D	
8	απεκριθη] 'said'				D	
9	τη θυρα 'the doors'		A			
21	παραγενομενοι] παραγενομενος		B²אA	Ant	D	
26	ηγεν] 'they brought them'				D	
32	om εν αυτω (except cod. A)		אA		D	
36	λεγων ειναι τινα εαυτον] 'saying, I am he'					h
42	τον χριστον ιησουν] 'Jesus Christ' (except cod. B) (order)			Ant		
VI						
3	επισκεψωμεθα] επισκεψασθε		אAC	Ant	D	
	δε] ουν		C	Ant		
13	om τουτου (two late codd.)		אA	Ant	D	
VII						
6	το σπερμα αυτου] 'thy seed'		א			
8	ισαακ τον ιακωβ και ιακωβ] 'Isaac begat Jacob and Jacob begat'	?				pesh
10	+'over' before ολον		אAC			
	τον οικον τουτον] 'his house'		B¹אAC	Ant	D	
12	οντα σειτια] 'that wheat is sold'					
15	'but Jacob came down to Egypt'		אAC	Ant	D	
26	ωφθη αυτοις] 'he appeared to others'					
30	αγγελος] 'an angel of the Lord' (cod. B)			Ant	D	
31	ιδων εθαυμασεν το οραμα] 'having seen the vision wondered' (order)					minn
32	'and the God of Isaac and the God of Jacob'			Ant	D	
33	το υποδημα σου των ποδων] 'the shoe from thy feet' (order)		אAC 81	Ant	D	
35	αρχοντα και δικαστην] 'over us'		אC 81		D	

	Bohairic	Transl.	ℵAC 81	Antioch.	D	
36	τη αιγυπτω] 'the land of Egypt'		ℵA 81	Ant	D	
37	ως εμε] +' listen to him '		C		D	
38	εξελεξατο] 'received'		ℵAC 81	Ant	D	
42	'sacrifices on (the) desert forty years'		B²ℵAC 81	Ant	D	
43	του θεου] 'your god'		ℵAC 81	Ant		
	ρομφα]ρεφαν (codd. B+5); ρηφαν (codd. ΑΓ+3)		AC			
46	τω οικω] 'the God '		AC 81			
49	και η γη] 'but (δε) the earth' (codd. AB+4)		ℵAC 81	Ant	D	
	οικοδομησατε] ' ye will build'		ℵAC 81	Ant	D	
51	καρδιας] 'in their heart'		81	Ant		
55	πνευματος αγιου] 'of faith and the Holy Spirit'		ℵ			
VIII						
5	την πολιν] 'a city '		C 81	Ant	D	
14	η σαμαρεια] +' also '					minn
25	του κυριου] 'God '		A			
28	om και before καθημενος	?			D	
34	λεγει] +' this '		B²ℵAC 81	Ant		
IX						
5	ιησους] +' the ναζωρεος' (codd. B+2)		AC			minn
12	om εν οραματι (except cod. A)		ℵA 81			
17	ιησους placed after κυριος (order)	?				perp H
24	σαυλω] 'Paul' (cod. B+3)	?				
25	om αυτου			Ant		
28	του κυριου] +' Jesus ' (cod. A)			Ant		
X						
3	om ωσει					minn
6	θαλασσαν] + ' this one who if he shall come will speak to thee words in which thou wilt be saved, thou (om 'thou,' one cod.) with all thy house' (codd. GK)					minn
7	δυο των οικετων] 'two servants of his'			Ant		
11	om καταβαινον				d	
	om επι της γης	?				
18	επυθοντο] 'they were asking' (impf.)		ℵA	Ant	D	
19	το πνευμα] +' to him '		ℵAC 81	Ant	D	
	δυο] 'three'		ℵAC 81			
21	αιτια δι ην] ' the thing concerning which'		ℵAC 81	Ant		
24	τους συγγενεις αυτους] 'his kinsfolk '		ℵAC 81	Ant	D	

		Bohairic	Transl.	אAC 81	Antioch.	D	
	26	ανθρωπος ειμι] + 'like thee' (codd. KS)				D	
	37	οιδατε] 'ye (pronoun) know'		אAC 81	Ant	D	
		κηρυγμα] 'baptism'		B²אAC 81	Ant	D	
XI							
	3	εισηλθεν, συνεφαγεν] 'thou wentest,' 'didst eat'		אA	Ant	D	
	4	om καθεξης			Ant		L
	11	ημεν] 'I was'			Ant		
	24	προσετεθη οχλος ικανος] 'a great multitude followed the Lord'		B²אA 81	Ant	D	
	25	αναστησαι] 'seeking for'		B²אAC 81	Ant	D	
	26	χριστιαν- (codd. B+4)		A (cf. BD)	Ant		
		χρηστιαν- (codd. AΓ+5)		א81			
	27	αυταις] 'those'		אA 81	Ant	D	
	28	εσημαινεν] 'signified' (preterite)		אA 81	Ant		
XII							
	5	εκκλησιας] +'to God'		אA 81	Ant	D	
	13	προσηλθε] 'came forth'		B²א			
	24	του κυριου] 'God' (codd. AΓ+5)		.אA 81	Ant	D	
	25	εις ιερουσαλημ] 'from Jerusalem'		A		D	
XIII							
	6	βαριησους] βαριησου		א			vg
	9	om ατενισας εις αυτον					
	13	οι περι παυλον] +'and Barnabas' (codd. AB+1)					cf. pesh
	14	την πισιδιαν] 'of Pisidia'		81	Ant	D	
	18	om ως				D	
		ετροποφορησεν] 'he nourished them'		AC			
	20	om και πεντηκοντα [a]	×				
	22	ιεσσαι] +'a man'		אAC 81	Ant	D	
	25	τι] 'who'		C	Ant	D	
	26	αβρααμ] +'and'		אAC 81	Ant	D	
	28	αιτιαν θανατου] +'in him'				D	cf. pesh
		αναιρεθηναι αυτον] 'to kill him'					vg
	31	εισι] +'now'		אAC 81		cf. D	
	33	τοις τεκνοις ημων] 'the sons' (codd. ΑB+4); 'their sons' (codd. Γ+4)					minn
	38	τουτο] 'this (man)'		אAC 81	Ant	D	
	39	εν τουτω] 'but in this one'	?				
	40	επελθη] +'on you'		AC 81	Ant		
	46	λαληθηναι] 'to speak'	?				vg

[a] This omission was a very easy error in Bohairic, as the reading is N̄T̄N̄POMΙΙ instead of N̄T̄N̄N̄POMΙΙ.

	Bohairic	Transl.	אAC 81	Antioch.	D	
46	επειδη] +δε (codd. ΒΓ+2)		A(C) 81	Ant		
49	om δε (codd. Γ+6)	?				minn
50	γυναικας] +'and'		א	Ant		
XIV						
3	τω λογω] 'on the word'		אA			
10	φωνη] +'I say unto thee in the name of Jesus Christ'(four late codd.)		C		D	
	ηλατο] +'and'		B²אAC 81	Ant	D	
12	'they were calling μεν Barnabas Zeus'			Ant		
15	'preaching to you to withdraw yourselves from the vanities and (om 'and' Γ+5) to turn yourselves to the living God'	?				
23	προσευξαμενοι] 'and having prayed'	?			D	
26	κακειθεν] +'they sailed'		B²אAC 81	Ant	D	
XV						
2	στασεως και ζητησεως] 'disturbance' (except codd. FSᵐᵍ)					minn
	προς αυτους] +'with some others of them,' *placed here instead of after* παυλον και βαρναβαν	?				
11	ιησου] +'Christ' (7 later codd.; not ΑΒΓ+2)		C		D	
23	πρεσβυτεροι] +'and' (codd. NT)			Ant		
	συριαν και κιλικιαν] 'Cilicia and Syria'	×				
24	εξ ημων] 'from you' (codd. ΒΓ+5)		א			
	+'having come forth' *before* εταραξαν (*order*)		AC 81	Ant	D	
27	τα αυτα] 'these things'				D	
33	τους αποστειλαντας αυτους] 'the apostles' (cod. K)			Ant		
34	'but Silas wished to abide in that place' (codd. ΓΚ)		C		D	
35	του κυριου] 'God' (codd. ΑΒΓ+2)					minn
XVI						
1	om εις before λυστραν		C	Ant	D	
6	τον λογον] 'the word of God'				D	
7	το πνευμα ιησου] 'the spirit of the Lord' (codd. Γ+2)		C			
13	πυλης]'city (πολις)'(codd. ΑΒ+3)			Ant		
	ποταμον] 'the river'				D	
19	και 1°] δε		אC 81	Ant	D	

	Bohairic	Transl.	ℵAC81	Antioch.	D	
26	'but immediately all the doors were opened'		ℵAC81	Ant	D	
30	εφη] +'to them' (except ΒΓ+1)				D	
32	του θεου] 'the Lord'		AC81	Ant	D	
34	τον οικον] 'his house'	?	ℵA	Ant	D	
	τραπεζαν]+'before them'	?				pesh vg
37	om νυν (codd. ΑΓ)	?				
XVII						
3	παρατιθεμενος] +'before them'					minn
	ο χριστος ο ιησους] 'Jesus Christ' (order)		ℵ			
4	om τε 1°				D	
18	την αναστασιν] 'his resurrection'	?				minn
25	om και τα παντα (except Γ+5)					33
	και τα παντα] 'in all places' (three later codd.)			Ant		
26	προστεταγμενους] 'appointed from the beginning'				D	
28	ημας] 'you'		ℵA81	Ant	D	
29	και ενθυμησεως] 'or thought'				D	
34	αρεοπαγειτης] 'the αριοπαγιτης (or -γητης)'		ℵA	Ant		
XVIII						
7	τιτιου] 'Titus'		ℵ			
9	εν νυκτι δι οραματος] 'by means of a vision in the night' (order)			Ant	cf. D	
19	κατηντησαν] 'he went'			Ant		
21	om παλιν (codd. ΑΒ+4)				D	
22	om αναβας και					
24	απολλως] απελλης					
25	om δε after ελαλει		A cf. ℵ	Ant	D	
XIX						
2	om προς αυτον (codd. ΑΚ)	?				
4	ιωαννης] +μεν			Ant		
7	om ωσει					
12	η] 'and'					minn
	αποφερεσθαι απο του χρωτος αυτου] 'were taken from his body and placed'			cf. Ant	cf. D	
24	ναους] 'silver temples'		(ℵ)A	Ant	D	
26	θεωρειτε και ακουετε] 'hear and see' (codd. FS)				D	
	om πεισας		ℵ			
27	οικουμενη] 'the οικουμενη'		ℵA	Ant	D	
28	ακουσαντες δε] +'these (things)'				D	
34	om μεγαλη η αρτεμις εφεσιων 2°		ℵA	Ant	D	

	Bohairic	Transl.	אAC 81	Antioch.	D	
37	την θεον] 'gods'	×				
	ημων] 'your'			Ant		
40	om ου 2°				D	
XX						
5	προσελθοντες] 'having been before us'		B²		D	
11	κλασας] 'and having broken'		אAC	Ant	D	
13	προσελθοντες] 'having gone before'		אC			L
15	εσπερα] 'on the following day' (codd. FGKS)		אAC	Ant	D	
21	om ημων (codd. Γ+5)	?				minn
	ιησουν]+'Christ'		אAC		(D)	
23	με μενουσιν] 'await thee'					pesh
24	ως] 'until'					c
25	την βασιλειαν]+'of God' (codd. AB+3)			Ant		
26	παντων] 'you all'					minn
28	του θεου] 'the Lord' (except cod. G)		AC		D	
29	om οτι 1°		אAC	Ant	D	
XXI						
4	αυτου] 'with them' (codd. Γ+3)		A		d	L
	'there with them' (codd. AB+2); 'having found the disciples there, we abode with them' (codd. FGS)	?				
16	μνασωνι] νασων or νασσων (codd. AB+3); ιασσων (codd. Γ+4); ασσων (cod. S)		א		D	
18	παρεγενοντο] 'came to him'	?			cf. D	
20	εδοξαζον] 'glorified' (preterite) (codd. AB+4)		א		D	
34	om εν τω οχλω (except codd. AN)					920
XXII						
3	εγω]+μεν			Ant		
	'of Gamaliel, he who trained me in the strength of the law of our ('the,' some codd.) fathers'	×				
5	εμαρτυρει] 'witnesseth'		אA	Ant		
XXIII						
6	κρεινομαι] 'I (pronoun) am judged'		אA	Ant		
7	επεπεσε) 'happened'		אAC	Ant		
8	γαρ] μεν γαρ		אAC	Ant		
9	om των γραμματεων του μερους		A			
18	λαλησαι]+'to thee'		B²אA 81	Ant		

	Bohairic	Transl.	ℵAC 81	Antioch.	D
28	αυτω]+'I brought him to their council'		(ℵA)	Ant	
XXIV					
14	πιστευων]+'all'		ℵA 81	Ant	
	om εν τοις 2°	?	A	Ant	
26	δοθησεται]+'to him'		ℵAC 81	Ant	
	παυλου]+'and thus that he might release him'			Ant	
XXV					
10	om εστως 2°		ℵ(cf. AC 81)	cf. Ant	
25	του παυλου] 'he'		B²ℵAC 81	Ant	
XXVI					
3	om παντων		A		
9	ουν] μεν ουν		ℵAC 81	Ant	
	om δειν	?			
10	διο] 'this which'		ℵAC 81	Ant	
11	περισσως]+δε		cf. ℵAC 81	cf. Ant	
14	παντων δε καταπεσοντων] 'but we all having fallen'		ℵAC 81	Ant	
15	ειπεν]+'to me'				pesh e
16	αναστηθι]+'stand'		B²ℵAC 81	Ant	
28	ποιησαι] 'to make myself'	?		cf. Ant	
	χριστιαν- (codd. BNS)		A 81	Ant	
	χρηστιαν- (codd. ΑΓ+6)		ℵ		
XXVII					
1	'but it came to pass when he ('they,' codd. ΑΓΚ) had decided that we should sail'	?			
	παρεδιδουν] 'he delivered'		A		
5	κιλικιαν] 'Cyprus' (codd. AB)	?			
	μυρρα] 'Lystra'		ℵA		vg perp vg.*codd.*
	λυκιας 'of Cilicia'				
13	αραντες ασσον] 'they put to sea from Assos'	×			vg
	παρελεγοντο] 'they left'	×			
16	καυδα] 'Clauda'		ℵA 81	Ant	
17	εφεροντο] 'we floated along'				minn
20	επικειμενου]+λοιπον		ℵAC 81	Ant	
27	αδρια] ανδριας				minn
	προσαχειν] 'that they approached'		AC 81	Ant	
34	προ] '(the) first (thing) unto'		ℵAC 81	Ant	
37	'two hundred seventy six' (codd. ABFGKPS)		ℵ(A)C 81		
	'one hundred seventy six' (codd. ΓΝΟΤ)	×			
38	τροφης] 'the food'			Ant	

		Bohairic	Transl.	אAC 81	Antioch.	D	
41		βιας] + ' of the waves '		C 81	Ant		
44		παντας] ' us all ' [a]	?				
XXVIII							
7		ποπλιω] πουπλιος (except cod. P)		81			
8		ποπλιου] πουπλιος (except cod. T)		81			
15		αδελφοι] ' the brethren '		אA 81	Ant		
21		περι σου] ' against thee '		א			Ψ

[a] Codd. Γ + 4, while reading ' us,' have ' all ' in the 3rd person plural (declined, with pronominal suffix) instead of the 1st person. This indicates some confusion of text.

THE COMMENTARY OF EPHREM ON ACTS

By FREDERICK C. CONYBEARE

[THE translation here published of the Armenian version of Ephrem's commentary on Acts and of the sections drawn from it in the ancient Armenian catena, and most of the accompanying footnotes, were prepared for this volume by Dr. Frederick C. Conybeare, Honorary Fellow of University College, Oxford, who died January 9, 1924.

The editors of *The Beginnings of Christianity* would here express their gratitude to their friend Dr. Conybeare, and their honour for his memory. His extraordinary learning in fields explored by but few scholars, his conscientious sense of obligation for making his great acquisitions useful to the world of learning, his unremitting diligence in labour, and the fruitful activity of his distinguished and ingenious mind, are known to a wide circle of students of the subjects which touched his own. With these high qualities was associated a singular generosity in contributing assistance (not to be secured easily, if at all, from other sources) to the work of his acquaintances and friends. Those who knew him intimately not only received liberal aid from his far-ranging and freely imparted information, and from his kindly but penetrating criticism, but learned to value still more the sincerity, the single-minded fidelity to truth, the firm purpose, and the lovable nature of their friend.]

INTRODUCTORY NOTE

An Armenian catena on Acts was published in 1839 by the Mechitarist fathers of San Lazzaro in Venice [1] from two codices in their library, one written in the year 1049 of their era, that is, A.D. 1600, the other old but undated. The MSS. supply two notes, one a colophon by the Armenian translator of Chrysostom's commentary on Acts, the other a preface by the catenist George of Skevrha, who

---

[1] Meknut'iun Gorcoç Aṛak'eloç khmbagir arareal nakhneaç Yoskeberanē ev Yep'remē, i Venetik, i tparan srboyn Ghazaru, 1839 (Commentary on the Acts of the Apostles excerpted by the ancients from Chrysostom and Ephrem, Venice, Press of St. Lazarus, 1839).

adapted and abridged that translation, and interwove it, as he says, with the Armenian version of Ephrem's commentary on Acts.

The earlier note begins thus : " In the year 6501 of creation, and in 1077 of our Saviour's advent, and 525 of the Armenian era of Khosrov, in the reign of Michael, son of Ducas, and in the patriarchate of Kosmas, I, Gregory son of Gregory the Parthian (Palhavuni) . . . having been found worthy of the throne of my ancestor St. Gregory, was in accordance with the vision of the seer St. Isaac driven out by the violence of the Scythians' sword and made my way to the gleaming abode of St. Constantine [*i.e.* Constantinople]. And I discovered there the interpretation, sought for by many, of Acts by the great John Chrysostom. . . . And meeting with the wise rhetor Kirakos, who was equipped with Greek and Armenian culture, I gave the treasure of my soul to be with abundant grace translated. And having received it with sincere joy, as if it were the tablets of the first prophet, I traversed with much fatigue the expanse of the Libyan and Asiatic Sea, and providentially reached the portion of Shem on the slopes of Taurus, the angelic abode of saints, and there found my son, the gifted Kirakos, my spiritual son, and pupil of the learned George my vicegerent [*or* successor]. He gladly undertook to repair the rude text of the rhetor, remoulding it in our idiom so as to be easy to listen to and harmonious."

The above is an account of the version of Chrysostom's commentary used for this catena. If, as the Armenian editors allege, an old fifth-century translation of that father's commentary once existed, we have not got it here.[1]

In the other note the catenist dedicates his work to the Lord Johannes, Brother of the King, Bishop of Dlek Maulevon, and Overseer of the holy clergy of Grner. He declares that he has been requested by that prelate to compose this catena, asks his readers to pardon his shortcomings, and recommends them to read for themselves the full commentaries, which he has abridged and woven together.

The bulk of the catena contained in the two codices consists of extracts from Chrysostom. Next in amount to this father comes Ephrem. The catena also contains matter attributed in the lemmata to Gregory of Nyssa, Gregory of Nazianz, David the Philosopher, Dionysius [of Alexandria ?], Cyril of Jerusalem, Cyril [of

---

[1] The text of Chrysostom's commentary from which this eleventh-century version was made was almost identical with that of the tenth-century Greek MS. of the commentary in the library of New College, Oxford, which was used by Savile for his edition, but too much neglected by the Benedictine editor Montfaucon. The monastic library at Valarshapat contains a copy of the same Greek text, dated A.D. 1077, according to the catalogue of Kareneantz, but really written two centuries later.

Alexandria ?], Kirakos, and Nerses Catholicos, patriarch of Sis in Armenian Cilicia. This last father died about 1167, so that the catena may have been made soon after that date.[1]

The sections of this catena headed ' Ephrem ' were translated by me for Dr. Rendel Harris, who printed the chief part of them in his *Four Lectures on the Western Text of the New Testament*, 1894. I subsequently contributed a fuller study of it to the *American Journal of Philology*, vol. xvii., 1896, pp. 135-171.

It has been supposed by scholars that Chrysostom's commentary, which contains many Bezan readings, rests on the work of an older commentator, who used a Bezan text. I suggested in the *American Journal of Philology* that the Armenian catenist might have had in his hands not Chrysostom's commentary at all, but this assumed earlier work, perhaps written by Chrysostom's master Diodorus of Tarsus. Such an hypothesis seemed to explain several characteristics of the Armenian. *First*, the fact that its text follows the order of the verses, whereas Chrysostom, after running over a long section of the text in its proper sequence, then, after the stereotyped remark : ἀλλ' ἴδωμεν ἄνωθεν τὰ εἰρημένα, proceeds to pick out a verse or verses here and there, in any sort of order, and to append detached comments which cohere with, and sometimes even repeat, the comments made in his first and more orderly review. Not seldom, too, his commentary cites the same verse in several forms. *Secondly*, the catena, in sections ascribed in the lemmata to Chrysostom, has many Bezan readings. Were not these drawn from the older commentary used by him, from which were derived other Bezan readings of the Greek text which he was translating ? *Thirdly*, the catena constantly presents a text of Chrysostom widely different from Montfaucon's. Were not these variations of text such as might be expected, if the Armenian document said to be a version of Chrysostom really preserved the work of another older author whom Chrysostom had exploited ?

This hypothesis broke down when in 1919 I collated the New College MS. of Chrysostom on Acts, for there I found a text of Chrysostom identical with that of the catena, and so greatly different from Montfaucon's that it must represent another edition of his homilies. A comparison of the two texts suggests indeed that he

---

[1] [The Armenian historian Kirakos of Gandzak (thirteenth century) states in his History of Armenia (Tiflis edition, 1910, p. 104) that the Vardapet Ananias of Sanatin (in the Borchalo district near Tiflis) " made into a commentary on the Apostle the words of Ephrem and John Chrysostom and Cyril and other saints." Conybeare, however, to whose attention this was brought, became convinced after investigation that Kirakos was in error. Ananias, as the leading exegete of the period in the Caucasian district, was a natural subject for a compliment of Cilician origin.—R. P. B.]

delivered the homilies twice over, and that Montfaucon's text and the New College codex rest upon the shorthand notes of two different deliveries. The catenist certainly had the genuine Chrysostom in his hands, and it was he who skilfully rearranged the *disiecta membra* of the Greek original to form an orderly whole. Further, since the catenist combined Chrysostom and Ephrem, the explanation suggests itself that Bezan variants in the catena not found in the Greek texts of Chrysostom are due to the catenist's use of the only Bezan text he possessed, namely that of Ephrem.

This last surmise has been justified by a further discovery. Father Joseph Dashean's catalogue of the Armenian MSS. in the Mechitarist convent at Vienna prints from Cod. 571 the beginning and end of a long fragment, and the closing paragraph resembles the last citation from Ephrem given in the catena. By the kindness of Father Akinean, librarian of the convent, a copy of the codex was procured, and it proved to contain an almost complete text of the lost commentary of Ephrem on Acts, amply revealing the character of the earliest Syriac version used by that writer. The Mechitarist Fathers of Vienna published in 1921 the Armenian text, which is a translation made in the fifth century.[1]

This commentary of Ephrem is brief and cursory ; the author only touches on the text here and there, passing over large tracts of it without remark, and summarising only the portions which interested him, especially the speeches, in which, unfortunately, are found fewest peculiarities of the Bezan text.[2] Ephrem seldom quotes the text verbatim ; and perhaps it is well for us that he does not,

---

[1] K'nnakan Hratarakut'iun Matenagrut'ean ev T'argmanut'ean Nakhneaç Hayoç. Hator B., Prak I., Surb Ep'rem : Meknut'iun Gorcoç Aṛak'eloç, hratakeç H. Nersēs V. Akinean mkhit'i ukhtē. Vienna, Mkhit'arean Tparon, 1921 (Critical Editions of the Literature and Translations of the Ancient Armenians. Section II., Part 1. Saint Ephrem : Commentary on the Acts of the Apostles, edited by Father Nerses Akinean of the Mechitarist Brethren. Vienna, Mechitarist Press, 1921).

[2] See the careful study of August Merk, ' Der neuentdeckte Kommentar des hl. Ephraem zur Apostelgeschichte,' *Zeitschrift für katholische Theologie*, vol. xlviii., 1924, pp. 37-58, 226-260. Merk's conclusion (p. 227) as to the relation of Ephrem's Commentary to the renderings of the Armenian New Testament is as follows : " Die Untersuchung sämtlicher Schriftstellen in Kommentar wir in Scholien hat zu dem Ergebnis geführt, dass häufig der Wortlaut der armenischen Bibel bis in alle Einzelheiten übernommen ist, dass jedoch eben so oft Unterschiede sowohl in der Wortwahl wie in der Wortfolge zutage treten. Bisweilen sind die Verschiedenheiten sehr gering, in andern Fällen machen sie sich stark geltend." Merk's observations on the readings in detail include valuable comparison with the quotations from Acts in other works of Ephrem. In a number of cases his contributions have made it possible to add something to Conybeare's footnotes.

since Armenian translators regularly reproduced texts from Scripture in the current form familiar to them after the year 430. In its meagre brevity, and in the way in which it leaps from chapter to chapter, omitting entire episodes, the work resembles Ephrem's commentary on the Diatessaron, or Cassiodorus on Acts.

Between the catena and the full commentary there is a marked difference in Armenian style. The commentary is no more than a Syriac treatise written with Armenian words ; Syriac idioms and syntax colour every sentence, and the result is often a chaos which I have not tried to set in order. The split relative is everywhere, for example (chap. v. 1), *illos ' quod '* [indefinite case] *spiritus sanctus omnia explorans habitabat in illis.* The personal endings or references of the Syriac verb are regularly reproduced, although the Armenian inflexions render them superfluous ; thus, *implebant illi, dicit ille,* where *implebant* and *dicit* alone would suffice. The Semitism ' added and ' before verbs is frequent. It is the most Syriacising version of a Syriac original I have ever met with in Armenian litera- ture. It is dated by Father Akinean in the fifth century, a period in which the Armenians rendered many books from Syriac, even such, like the works of Eusebius, as they afterwards had in Greek.

The catenist, on the other hand, tried to eliminate such peculiari- ties, and to turn the text into good Armenian. Although he largely removed uncouth Syriac idioms, he was otherwise accurate in his excerpts.[1]

In the Venice codices of the catena not a little Ephremic matter is labelled ' Chrysostom ' in the lemmata ; and not a little of it is embedded in sections drawn from Chrysostom. The whole catena, like the work of Chrysostom on which it rests, is divided into fifty- five homilies, headed: " I. That it is not right to defer baptism ; II. Against the Hellenes," etc. At the beginning of each homily the name of the author cited is omitted, but the matter is in such cases Chrysostom. I have often, following Akinean, headed it ' *Anon.*' The Chrysostom matter is rearranged to suit the order of chapter and verse, as in the Greek catenae.

In the midst of his Chrysostom the catenist often introduces a single sentence of Ephrem, so that only since the recovery of Ephrem's integral text has it been possible to disentangle so confused a skein. Not so often he slips sentences of Chrysostom into sections mainly taken from Ephrem. We see here how ancient texts came to be conflated.

As to Ephrem's text of Acts, the evidence is not so ample as could be desired, but it is decisive. *First,* Ephrem knew nothing of the Peshitto text. *Secondly,* he used a primitive Syriac version

---

[1] On the date of the catena see below, p. 391, note 3.

of a Greek text almost identical with that of Codex Bezae. *Thirdly*, whenever he does vary from the Bezan text, it is never to agree with the great Greek uncials, but with the scholia of Thomas of Heracleia, or with the Fleury palimpsest of the Old Latin, or with Gigas or some other of the Old Latin texts, or with Irenaeus, Tertullian, or those parts of Augustine which preserve what I believe to have been the primitive text of Acts.

The bulk of the text of the commentary is only contained in Codex 571, f.1a-22a of the Mechitarist convent in Vienna, written A.D. 1284. In this the beginning as far as chap. ii. 14 is lost. The first part of the lost passage is found in two manuscripts of the same library, Cod. 47, f.143a-145b, and Cod. 305, f.74b-76a. Variants of Cod. 305 rarely affect the sense, and almost wholly concern the spelling.

Codex 571, besides the long lacuna Acts i. 1-ii. 14, has others, viz. : vii. 43-viii. 28 (one folio lost), xv. 3-12 (one folio), xvii. 29-xix. 9 (one folio). It is also much lacerated, so that in folios 10, 12, 13, 14, 15, 17, 18, 19, 20, 21, numerous lines or parts of lines are lost or illegible.

I have rendered the text of the three codices of the commentary into Latin, my only care being to make my version quite literal and to retain the *ordo verborum* of the original. I have added in English (with references to the pages and lines of the Venice edition, 1839) the Ephremic sections of the catena, which possesses the value of a second manuscript of the text and must be consulted, not only to fill up lacunae big or little, but also for the restoration[1] of many passages of the unmutilated text. Citations of the Armenian vulgate in the catena are rendered into Latin.

Most of the shorter lacunae of Codex 571 admit of being filled up from the catena with absolute certainty, and these supplements are added in square brackets.

Where the catena does not help us, Father Akinean has conjecturally restored the lost text, and this conjectural matter I have enclosed in round brackets.

In footnotes I have drawn attention to Bezan or primitive readings found in Ephrem. Careful scrutiny may reveal more of these.

I have excluded from my version of the catena a few sections labelled ' of Ephrem,' but really derived from Chrysostom, as a comparison of them with the original Greek, especially with the New College codex, suffices to prove. On the other hand, the catena contains, as stated above, under the heading ' of Chrysostom,' much which is really Ephrem. Where the latter's text is preserved it was a simple matter to detect these elements ; but in the long lacunae it needed much weighing of evidence to do so, and

I was guided by two considerations : first, that certain passages are in the style of Ephrem and marked by Syriac idiom ; secondly, that the Greek sources altogether lack them. It is to be hoped that a second copy of the integral text may be found in some collection of Armenian MSS. In Valarshapat, according to Kareneantz's catalogue, there are seven copies of Chrysostom's commentary and eight of a commentary on Acts by Matthew Vardapet. In some of these the work of Ephrem may easily be lurking.[1]

F. C. C.

[1] Before the late war the Valarshapat codices were removed to the Lazarevski Institute in Moscow, and are for the present inaccessible.

COMMENTARY

1. LIBER Actuum (*praks*) Apostolorum Lucae Evangelistae est sicut didicimus. Is autem quamvis unus ex discipulis est, minime sodalis fuit domini nostri. Apostolorum vero ab initio socius erat. Qui quamvis evangelium, sicut audivit a discipulis, conscripsit, Actus Apostolorum tamen scribendo personaliter fuit oculatus testis. Is igitur quum videret insidias, quia post evangelium [1] quod scripsit sumpserunt fecerunt [2] evangelium, cuius titulus Pueritia [3] Domini Nostri, sodales vero eorundem Librum Quaestionum in nomine Mariae Discipulorumque scripserunt, qui dicunt quod XVIIIesimo mense ascendit Primogenitus, de quo Apostoli eius post XL dies scribunt quod ascendit—ergo ut frustraret insidiosos libros heterodoxorum de evangelio domini nostri, iuventutis, dico, et senectutis, posuit in initio libri quem scripsit, scilicet Actuum (*praks*) Apostolorum, initium evangelii domini nostri atque finem ; ut demonstraret omnem actum, quacunque inveniatur scriptus in nomen domini nostri, qui senior est quam baptisma Iohannis, et iunior est et posterior quam dies ascensionis eius post XL dies, alienum et superfluum esse quoad verum evangelismum. Quoniam igitur dixit, Nisi ego discedam, paracletus non veniet ad vos, ergo paracletus ad finem pentecostes venit, et manifestum fuit quod ad finem XL dierum, sicut dixit apostolis, ascendit ille ; falsiloquusque fuit insidiosus sermo heterodoxorum qui dicunt quod post XVIII menses ascendit.

2. Scripsit etiam de resurrectione domini nostri et de adscensione eius et de adventu spiritus ad exitum pentecostes.

3. Scripsit etiam de paucitate discipulorum et de incremento quod quibusdam diebus lapsis factum est illorum.

4. Scripsit etiam de curatione claudi de utero matris eius, etiam quod per curationem in quadragesimo anno duo millia additi sunt ecclesiae.

5. Scripsit etiam de adventu Sauli ad Damascum et de visione quae evenit in via, de caecatis et apertis oculis eius, et de persecutione eius in Iudaea, et quod dimiserunt eum in sporta de muro, ille autem profectus est Ierusalem.

6. Scripsit etiam de descensu Shmavonis ad Lidiam urbem, et de curatione eius qui per octo annos paralyticus fuerat.

7. Scripsit etiam de muliere beata, quae experta est curationem

---

[1] Catena adds *post* which codices omit. They had the genitive-dative case and added *in* before it so as to yield the sense *in evangelio* and make grammar of their text.   [2] Sumpserunt fecerunt—a Syriasm.

[3] Cuius titulus pueritia ; literally, in nomine pueritiae—a Syriasm.

380

CATENA

Of the Acts (*gorts*) of the Apostles the author is Luke the gospeller, p. 13. 12-14. 22. who though from the beginning of Christ our Lord's preaching he was not with him, yet joined the apostles of the Lord Christ from the beginning forth of the descent of the Spirit and earlier. And although the gospel which he wrote, as he heard from Christ's disciples, he did write, yet of the Acts of the Apostles which he wrote he was with his own eyes an eyewitness sure. This then is later than his gospel which he wrote, for he saw that certain impostors wrote out of their heads a gospel, in name, ' Of the Childhood of Christ our Lord,' and others, a book of ' Questions ' in the name of Mary and of the disciples of Christ, in which they say that after the resurrection it was after eighteen months he ascended, the Firstborn, of whom his apostles write that it was after forty days exactly that he ascended into heaven,—so then Luke, in order to frustrate the false books of the heterodox from the gospel of Christ our Lord, who invent an older and younger series of works about the Lord Jesus, some of them prior to his baptism and others subsequent to his ascension after forty days, lays down in the book of Acts of the Apostles a beginning and end of our Lord's deeds, in the same way as do the other gospellers, beginning from the Lord's baptism by John until his ascension on the fortieth day, in order to show that any deed, wherever it be found written, in the name of the Lord Christ, prior to his baptism or later than the fortieth day of his ascension, is a deed foreign to Christ our Lord. And it is clear thence that Christ himself said to his disciples : Unless I go, the Comforter will not come. And the Comforter at the close of Pentecost came on the fiftieth day after his resurrection. It was clear then that at the fulfilment of the quadragesima, as the apostles said, Jesus ascended, and false are the impostors who say his ascension was after eighteen months. So then Luke wrote about the resurrection of our Lord, about his ascension, and about the coming of the Spirit, and the increase of the disciples, and of whatever followed.

per Shmavonem; et de revelatione; factum enim est super eum
venire Caesaream, ut per Cornelium incircumcisum proveheretur
novo modo evangelismus domini inter ethnicos.

8. Scripsit de discipulatu qui factus est Antiochiae per Paulum
et Barnabam, et quod appellati sunt ibi novo modo Christiani.

9. Scripsit etiam de Agabo qui prophetavit de fame quae evenit,
cuius in tempore famis dederunt portari discipuli evangelii de quovis
quodcunque eorum fuit ad ministerium sanctorum in Ierusalem.

10. Scripsit etiam de Agrippa, quod occidit Iacobum fratrem
Ioannis gladio.   Voluit occidere etiam Petrum; in eadem vero nocte
solvit vincula angelus et egressus est, liberatus est usque Caesaream.
Etiam quod propter eum accepit Agrippas retributionem peccatorum
suorum, et mortuus est de vermibus quum degrederetur de bemate[1] suo.

11. Scripsit etiam quod segregati sunt Paulus et Barnabas per
manuum impositionem apostolorum ad docendos gentiles.

12. Scripsit quod perculsus est oculos suos Barshuma magus et
admiratio [2] occupavit hegemona.

13. Scripsit curationem quae fuit per Paulum claudi ab utero
matris eius, ita ut propter curationem eius deos nuncuparent Paulum
et Barnaban.

14. Scripsit de disputatione eorum quae facta est Antiochiae,
contra Iudaeos, discipuli evangelii, qui volebant subiicere ethnicos,
qua causa a Shmavone et Iacobo.[3]

15. Scripsit quod separati sunt invicem Paulus et Barnabas, et
quod circumcidit Timotheum Paulus ipse qui impeditor erat circumcisionis.

16. Scripsit quod praepediti sunt quin loquerentur in Asia, et
quod properarunt abire et intrare Macedoniam.

17. Scripsit de puella incantatrice quae divinationibus suis
quaestum praestabat dominis suis, sed curatio eius auxit tribulationem
apostolorum.

18. Scripsit etiam de motu terrae qui factus est in carcere et de
fide facta apud custodem carceris.

19. Scripsit etiam de profectu eius usque Thessalonicam,[4] et quod
praepeditus est a spiritu quin loqueretur illic, quia persequebantur
illum ab initio quum veniret evangelizaturus eos.

20. Scripsit etiam de adventu eius ad Athenas et de circuitione
inter idola et controversione eius contra philosophos.

21. Scripsit et de adventu eius ad Corinthum et doctrinam quae
aucta est et de Apolos (sic).

22. Scripsit de Ephesiorum iterato baptismo, quia in baptisma

---

[1] xii. 23 καταβὰς ἀπὸ τοῦ βήματος D.   [2] xiii. 12 ἐθαύμασεν καὶ ἐπίστευσεν D.
[3] This paragraph lacks grammatical sequence.
[4] xvii. 15 παρῆλθεν δὲ τὴν Θεσσαλίαν· ἐκωλύθη γὰρ εἰς αὐτοὺς κηρύξαι τὸν
λόγον D.   Is Θεσσαλίαν an error for Θεσσαλονίκην ?

Ioannis baptizati erant, et acceperunt per manuum impositionem eius spiritum in omnibus linguis loquendi.

23. Scripsit de virtutibus quae per Paulum factae sunt et de Iudaeis idolorum filiis, qui dolo exorcizabant daemonia in nomine Iesu quem Paulus praedicabat.

24. Scripsit etiam de persecutione quae exorta est contra eos Ephesi per Demetrium auri opificem.

25. Scripsit etiam de congregatione suorum noctu in coenaculo, et quod obdormivit homo ceciditque, mortuus est, et suscitavit eum Paulus.

26. Scripsit de vinculis quae manebant illum in Ierusalem et de ingressu eius, et quod purificatus est et intravit templum, et quod conturbaverunt urbem contra eum Iudaei Asiani.

27. Scripsit de centurione qui dimisit eum ad proconsulem, ne putaret quod per phantasiam tradiderit eum morti.

28. Scripsit de iudicio eius coram proconsule, et quod detentus est ille in carcere biennium donec advenit alius hegemon.

29. Scripsit de Paulo, quod proconsul volebat dare eum munus Iudaeis, et quod appellavit Caesarem, ut praetextu Caesaris ante mortem suam praedicaret in Roma urbe.

30. Scripsit de descensu eius ad mare et de fluctibus tumefacti maris qui oborti sunt contra eum, quod vero dixit illi angelus in visione quod nemo eorum qui tecum sunt in nave periturus sit.

31. Scripsit de vipera quae circumvolvit sese brachio eius, et quod excussit proiecitque eam, neque nocuit illi.

32. Scripsit de ingressu illius Romam, et quod dedit mercedem biennio aedis de labore manuum suarum, dum opitulabatur cotidie hominibus qui ingrediebantur ad eum.

Codices 47 and 305. i. 1-3.

Haec omnia scripsit Lucas evangelista, sicut initio sermonis sui dixit: Primum sermonem de quo[1] incepi dicere, O Theophile, quod delectabilis est deo, neque actus apostolorum sunt quos narrare paratus sum, sed quodcunque coepit dominus noster facere. Quae ergo sint ea quae fecit, nisi quae evangelizabant, fecit scripta Lucas ? Et quando coepit facere ? A baptismo Ioannis. Et quando iterum finivit? In qua die iussit apostolos in Galilaea annuntiare evangelium.[2] Quos elegit :—id est inter omnes gentiles quos vocaverat ille.[3] Monstravit sese quia mansit post crucem non sine signis sed cum multis signis et prodigiis, quae fecit quadraginta dies, quo tempore apparebat illis in omnibus similitudinibus et loquebatur de regno quod annuntiabat ante mortem suam, una[4] cum ceteris. Cui gloria in saecula, amen.

[1] Armenian vulgate has λόγον ὅν. This may explain the addition *de quo*. Chrysostom adds ὅν, showing that it is no *proprius error* of the Armenian.

[2] See note on i. 2 *supra*, pp. 256-261. Ephrem's text plainly lacked ἀνελήμφθη and had κηρύσσειν τὸ εὐαγγέλιον. Did it read ἄχρι ἧς ἡμέρας ?

[3] Perhaps render : qui appellarunt eum ; but the grammar is defective.

[4] Una, etc., is an addition by the scribe.

Ephrem : Usque in diem praecipiendi apostolis per spiritum p. 19.
sanctum. As beforehand we said at the beginning of the acts of i. 2.
the Lord, and he fixes the end, saying : usque ad diem praecipiendi,
which is the day of his ascension, in order to dumbfound the utterers
of lies.

Ephrem : He showed then that he remained after the cross p. 20.
not without signs, but in many signs and in many prodigies, which i. 3.
he wrought in the forty days, the while (*or* how) he appeared to
them in all similitudes, sometimes among those who knew him,
sometimes among those who knew him not, as he elsewhere says :
oculi eorum tenebantur, that they should not know him. And Lk. xxiv. 16
subsequently : cognoverunt eum.[1]   Lk. xxiv. 35

Ephrem : Not as having any wants of nature thenceforth, of p. 21.
food, but condescending to a certain demonstration of the resur- i. 4.
rection.[2]

Ephrem : And this with such firmness, because he willed not p. 28.
to reveal to them this day of his ascension, which they saw with i. 7.
their own eyes.

---

[1] Arm. vlg, here cited, literally rendered means 'he gave clues to them.'
[2] The paragraph, Catena, p. 22. 3-31, though headed 'Of Ephrem,' is
Chrys. 7 D E.

LACUNA, ACTS I. 4-II. 14

Ephrem : Nam accipietis virtutem and encouragement super- p. 30.
veniente spiritu in vos. And ye shall go forth from the upper room i. 8.
and shall be manifest to the world, witnesses of my resurrection,
and of what ye heard and saw from me, not only in Jerusalem, the
city of crucifiers where ye were terrified, but also among Samaritans
and all races.

Ephrem : But as Elias ascended in sight of Elisha, lest they p. 31.
should say : Jezebel slew him. For as the signs wrought by Elisha i. 9.
make credible his ascension, so too the miracles wrought by the
apostles make credible the Lord's ascension. Lest they should
say : they stole him. Et nubes concealed eum ab oculis eorum,
clearly by his passing within, lest the apostles should over-weary
themselves by gazing after him.

Shmavon then the Zealot is by Matthew and Mark called Simon p. 35.
the Cananean. Perhaps in Hebrew he was called literally zealot, i. 13.
and it is affirmed by many that he was son of Joseph, father of
God, and brother of the Lord. Furthermore Juda son of Jacob
was a brother of the same Simon and son of Joseph, and he also
was the Lord's brother. It was he who wrote the Catholic epistle,
called after his name the Epistle of Juda, at the beginning of which,
instead of terming himself brother of the Lord, he humbly writes,
Brother of Jacobus. Whence it is clear that he is the very person
named Lebeos and Thadeos by Matthew and Mark. Nor is it true
that they refer to one person and Luke to another ; they only call
one and the same person by different names ; nor need we be surprised, for in Hebrew a man often had two names or more. Hence
the discrepancy of the evangelists in respect of Thadeos and of
Juda son of Jacobus is one of names only and not of persons,
for of the first ones chosen by Christ not one was lost save Juda
the traitor. It is certain, then, the other Thadeos who was with
Abgar was one of the LXX, as their tombs bear witness. For the
Thadeos who was of the LXX died in Armenia in the Canton of
Artaz ; but Juda son of Jacobus, the one who according to Matthew
and Mark was Thadeos one of the XII, died in Ormi of Armenia.
Thus is confirmed the harmony of the evangelists as regards the
names of the apostles.[1]

[1] That all the above, except the last two sentences, is Ephrem, is shown
by its recurrence in Isho'dad's commentary on Acts, *Horae Semiticae*, Cambridge, 1913, p. 5. Here the order of the apostles is enumerated from the
Diatessaron, and the text proceeds thus : " From which it is evident that
Simeon the Canaanite, whom Matthew and Mark mention, and the Diatessaron, is Simeon Zelotes, whom Luke mentions in his two books, and Judah
bar Jacob, whom Luke mentions in his two books, is Lebbaeus, who was called
Thaddai by Matthew and Mark, whence the one of the evangelists who mentions him does not mention the other ; and the one who mentions Simeon the
Canaanite does not mention Simeon Zelotes. Now Lebbaeus is not the name

LACUNA, ACTS I. 4-II. 14

of a man, but the name of his village, to say that he is a Lebbaean, and from this it is evident that Thaddai and James were Lebbaeans, that is, from Lebbi ; and the father of James was Halfai. But the name of Thaddai was once Judah, and, at the last, in his discipleship, his name was changed and he was called Thaddai ; as also Simeon was called Peter, and the sons of Zebedee Benai Ragshi, and Levi Matthew."

[To the above note by Conybeare, Professor Burkitt adds the following :

There are grave reasons for doubting whether any of the section attributed to Ephrem on i. 13 (the names of the apostles) really comes from him or from any of his contemporaries.

1. The Catena (on Acts i. 13) speaks (end of col. 17) of ' Jude son of James,' i.e. 'Ιούδας 'Ιακώβου, and says that this Jude was son of Joseph, therefore brother of James, and adds : " It was he who wrote the Catholic epistle." The writer of this sentence knew the Epistle of Jude and accepted it as canonical. Therefore he was no Syrian, for the Peshitta only includes James, 1 Peter, and 1 John, out of the seven Catholic Epistles. And further, even this reduced canon of the Peshitta seems to have been one of Rabbula's innovations, for there is no certain trace of any of these Epistles in Syriac before 411. Ephrem himself never refers to them in any of his voluminous genuine works. The most that can be alleged is a quotation of 1 Peter and a quotation of 1 John in the ' Severus-Catena ' (see the beginning of Samuel), itself a suspect source. When, therefore, we find Armenian compilations of a later age contradicting the testimony of the ancient Syriac evidence, it seems pretty certain that the compiler has affixed a wrong label, or has derived his material from a tainted source.

2. The compiler goes on to tell us about Lebeos and Thadeos. ' Thaddaeus,' of course, is the true reading of Mark iii. 18, including syr.sin, while the Westerns have ' Lebbaeus ' (D lat.eur), or ' Judas ' (e and virtually c), or omit altogether (W). In Matt. x. 3 the ' true ' text again has ' Thaddaeus,' but D lat.afr have ' Lebbaeus ' and lat.eur has ' Judas Zelotes.' Here syr.sin (*hiat* cur) has ' Jude son of James,' in which it is supported by the *Acts of Thomas*, and virtually by Isho'dad's Diatessaron-list (see my Note, *Evangelion da-Mepharreshē*, ii. 270 f.). The later Greek MSS. and the Peshitta have ' Lebbaeus surnamed Thaddaeus,' but there is no trace of this name in Syriac before Rabbula (411–435).

All therefore that the Armenian catenist and Isho'dad put in about ' Lebbaeus who was called Thaddaeus by Matthew and Mark ' can hardly come from Ephrem or from a Diatessaron source. It must be later, something written after the Peshitta had supplanted both the Diatessaron and the Evangelion da-Mepharreshē. Isho'dad's express quotation of the Diatessaron-list is all right ; no doubt his source knew the Diatessaron-text as well as that of the Peshitta of Matthew. That is to say, it was probably a Syriac-speaking scholar writing about the middle of the fifth century, not earlier. Or was it possibly the learned Jacob of Edessa ?

3. The Christian missionary who ' was with Abgar ' and evangelized Edessa was called ' Addai,' according to the unanimous testimony of the Syriac-speaking Church. Eusebius identified Addai (which in Greek would be Addaeus) with Thaddaeus, but this identification had no influence in Syriac-speaking lands (in Eus. *H.E.* i. 13 [Syriac] ' Thaddaeus ' is called not Thaddai but Haddai in one of the two Syriac MSS.). Therefore ' Thadeos who was with Abgar ' is not likely to be Ephrem's remark.

LACUNA, ACTS I. 4-II. 14

[1] But that he fell to earth and burst asunder and his bowels were poured out, comes to the same thing. For he shut the door against himself before he strangled himself, and remained on the gibbet there during Paraskeve Sabbath. When he swelled up and became heavy, was cut the cord by which he hung, he fell, burst asunder and was poured out. But the stench of corruption of the heap and of his guts brought together the sons of Israel to come and see his infamy and the awful sign which heralded for him hell-fire.[2]   *p. 38. i. 18.*

Ephrem : De quo excessit Iudas ambulare in locum suum. Not into that which is luminous which the Lord promised him, but into the dark.   *p. 42. i. 25.*

[Dion(ysius) : For the lot so called manifests a sort of divine gift of the holy rank of that divine election, whence also (it shows) how they received into the apostolic number of the holy Twelve the one divinely manifested by the divine lot. For he was numbered and called cum undecim apostolis twelve.[3]]   *p. 43. i. 26.*

---

4. It is true that neither the extant part of the Commentary nor the Catena mentions Matthias by that or any other name. At the same time a genuine Old Syriac Commentary on Acts might be expected to exhibit the most remarkable known peculiarity of that text, viz. the substitution of the name 'Tholomaeus' for 'Matthias': so Aphraates 4, 6 (Parisot 149. 22), and the Syriac Eusebius, *H.E.* i. 12 (ed. McLean, p. 49) and iii. 29 (ed. McLean, p. 161).

I feel pretty sure that Isho'dad and the Armenian translator of the Catena must have taken their information from something labelled Ephrem that had very little claim to be his. Possibly it is all connected with the 'Severus-Catena,' a great mass of material compiled in A.D. 861, some of it genuine Ephrem, some of it not. It seems to me to show that we should be very cautious in taking any statement in the Armenian Catena as good evidence for Ephrem's opinions or for the lost Old Syriac text of Acts.—F. C. B.]

[1] The section, Catena, p. 38. 8 ff., labelled 'Ephrem,' is from Chrys. 26 E.

[2] This passage, though coming in the middle of a section of Chrysostom, is almost certainly Ephrem. Chrysostom contains nothing of the kind. It may be taken by the catenist from the old Armenian version of Ephrem's comment on the Diatessaron, but Ephrem may equally well have repeated his story in commenting on Acts. In any case it corresponds to the reading of Augustine, *Contra Felicem*, 'collum sibi alligavit,' and of vg.*codd* 'suspensus.'

In rendering Chrysostom on this verse, the catenist cites the Armenian vulgate : 'and having swollen up he burst asunder.' The old Georgian had the same reading, equivalent to πρησθείς or πεπρησμένος found in Euthymius. The Armenian and Georgian must have preserved it from the older Syriac, and Ephrem must have read it in his text of Acts.

[3] This (not from Ephrem) involves συνκατεψηφίσθη μετὰ τῶν ἔνδεκα ἀποστόλων δωδέκατος, or some similar conflate text ; cf. Aug. *C. Felicem.* D hcl.*text* have 'twelve.' I record the passage because of the coincidence with D etc. The ordinal number was signified by the cardinal.

The first, and longer, sentence of the extract is from Dionysius Areopagita, *Eccl. hier.* v. 5 (p. 238 ; Migne, col. 513): περὶ δὲ τοῦ θείου κλήρου τοῦ τῷ Ματθίᾳ θειωδῶς ἐπιπεσόντος ἕτεροι μὲν ἄλλα εἰρήκασιν οὐκ εὐαγῶς, ὡς οἶμαι, τὴν ἐμὴν δὲ καὶ

LACUNA, ACTS I. 4-II. 14

Chrys : He shows also the prediction of Christ to have been
in part fulfilled in regard to the traitor : Vae homini illi, bonum
erat ei si natus non fuisset, which might be said in regard to the
Jews, to wit, Wretched are ye, for if your guide Judas suffered thus,
much more yourselves. But he did not say anything of the kind,
but seeing that what they bought for the Tombs of the Strangers
is aptly called the place Akeldama after the issue in chief, that is,
through the desolation which Jerusalem suffered at the hands of
Titus and his. Wherefore, setting forth next the suitable award
of the field, he adduces the prophet : It is written, he says, in the
Book of Psalms, that is in the hymns of David : Fiat commoratio
eius deserta, et in his abode (or roof) let no one dwell. This he said
about the city and house. Very aptly, for what is more waste than
a tomb. But the desolating of the house in which the traitor
strangled himself harbingered the last desolation of the Jews. For
the men of Vespasian and Titus wasting them with the sword and
hunger, the city became according to the Jews' decision a grave of
strangers, that is, of the besieging soldiers.[1]

p. 39. 22-
40. 2.
i. 19-20.

αὐτὸς ἔννοιαν ἐρῶ. δοκεῖ γάρ μοι τὰ λόγια κλῆρον ὀνομάσαι θεαρχικόν τι δῶρον,
ὑποδηλοῦν ἐκείνῳ τῷ ἱεραρχικῷ χορῷ τὸν ὑπὸ τῆς θείας ἐκλογῆς ἀναδεδειγμένον.
The identification is due to Professor Burkitt, who remarks that the Syriac
translation of Dionysius was made by Sergius of Ras 'Ain, who died in 536,
a fact which gives us a measure of the date of the catena. Isho'dad also
(Comm. on Acts i. 26, *Horae Semiticae* x. p. 7) quotes Dionysius on Acts i. 26 :
" Dionysius says that they received a revelation about this." The second,
shorter, sentence, referring to the ' eleven,' is not taken from the passage in
Dionysius Areopagita.

[1] Here as usual the catenist weaves into one connected whole the disjecta
membra of Chrysostom, 24 E and 27 B C, thus :

24 E : γενηθήτω ἡ ἔπαυλις αὐτῶν ἔρημος καὶ μὴ ἔστω ὁ κατοικῶν ἐν αὐτῇ·
τοῦτο περὶ τοῦ χωρίου καὶ τῆς οἰκίας.

27 A B : ὁ θεὸς αὐτοὺς ἠνάγκασεν οὕτω καλέσαι Ἑβραιστὶ Ἀκελδαμά· ἀπὸ
τούτου καὶ τὰ Ἰουδαίοις ἐπιέναι μέλλοντα κακὰ δῆλα ἦν· καὶ δείκνυσι τέως τὴν
πρόρρησιν ἐξελθοῦσαν ἐκ μέρους, τὴν λέγουσαν· Καλὸν ἦν αὐτῷ εἰ οὐκ (New Coll.
MS. μὴ) ἐγεννήθη ὁ ἄνθρωπος ἐκεῖνος. καὶ περὶ τῶν Ἰουδαίων τὰ αὐτὰ ἁρμόζει
λέγειν. εἰ γὰρ ὁ γενόμενος ὁδηγός, πολλῷ μᾶλλον καὶ οὗτοι· ἀλλ' οὐδὲν τούτων
λέγει τέως. εἶτα δεικνὺς ὅτι περὶ αὐτοῦ εἰκότως ἂν λέγοιτο Ἀκελδαμά, ἐπάγει τὸν
προφήτην λέγοντα· Γενηθήτω ἡ ἔπαυλις αὐτοῦ ἔρημος. τί γὰρ ἐρημότερον τοῦ
τάφου γενέσθαι ; ὥστε καὶ εἰκότως ἂν αὐτοῦ κληθείη τὸ χωρίον. ὁ γὰρ τὸ τίμημα
καταβαλών, εἰ καὶ ἕτεροι οἱ ἠγορακότες εἶεν, αὐτὸς ἂν εἴη δίκαιος λογίζεσθαι κύριος
ἐρημώσεως μεγάλης. αὕτη ἡ ἐρήμωσις προοίμιον τῆς Ἰουδαικῆς, εἴ γέ τις ἀκριβῶς
ἐξετάσεις. καὶ γὰρ ἐκεῖνοι ἑαυτοὺς ἀνεῖλον λιμῷ, καὶ πολλοὺς ἀπέκτειναν, καὶ τάφος
γέγονεν ἡ πόλις τῶν στρατιωτῶν.

The form of citation of Ps. lxix. 25 (lxviii. 26) in the catena is noteworthy.
The first part agrees with the Armenian vulgate (while Chrysostom 24 E,
but not 27, reads αὐτῶν for αὐτοῦ). The second part is given in a unique
form, not found in Chrysostom's citation (24 E) nor anywhere else, but apparently
implied in the following sentence, τοῦτο περὶ τοῦ χωρίου καὶ τῆς οἰκίας.

LACUNA, ACTS I. 4-II. 14

Ephrem (?) : Et cum complerentur dies pentecostes, erant omnes p. 44. ii. 1. concorditer in uno loco. Pentecost with the Greeks is called fifty, and it was one of the great and notable feasts of the Jews, appointed seven times seven days after Zatik on the 50th, and at the same time the beginning of harvest, on which day also took place the giving of the law in Sinai. Moreover the 50th year was at that time honoured in Israel by remission of debts and a return afresh of patrimony.[1]

Ephrem : A voice of violent wind was in the house where the p. 45. ii. 2.

The catenist goes further, and refers to ' the house in which the traitor strangled himself,' a description to which nothing in Chrysostom's text corresponds. I believe this touch must be from Ephrem, and that the catenist also derived his citation of Ps. lxix. 25 from Ephrem's commentary. We may conclude: (1) that the older commentary on Acts used by Chrysostom had the reading of Thomas of Harkel ; (2) that Ephrem had the same. The only alternative supposition is that the text of Chrysostom used by the Armenian translator of A.D. 1077 contained καὶ ἐν τῇ οἰκίᾳ, so that the catenist took it from the Armenian version of Chrysostom. Unfortunately, of this version a few pages only have been printed in Venice, so that we cannot test the hypothesis ; but it is improbable, because the New College text of Chrysostom, which otherwise perfectly fits the catena, shows no departure from the Greek text of Acts in the second part of the citation. The form of citation in the catenist does not exactly correspond to the Armenian version of the Psalms, and in any case the catenist would have had no reason to turn away from the Armenian vulgate text of Acts i. 20. The T.R. reads :

> γέγραπται γὰρ ἐν βίβλῳ ψαλμῶν,
> γενηθήτω ἡ ἔπαυλις αὐτοῦ ἔρημος,
> καὶ μὴ ἔστω ὁ κατοικῶν ἐν αὐτῇ.

This is also the reading of D. Professor A. C. Clark notes that αὐτῶν is read for αὐτοῦ probably in Thomas of Harkel's scholion, which agrees substantially with the Syro-hexaplar (see above, p. clxii), and certainly in d t, while for καὶ μὴ . . . αὐτῇ Thomas has 'et in tabernaculo eorum non sit qui habitet,' equivalent to καὶ ἐν τῷ σκηνώματι αὐτῶν μὴ ἔστω ὁ κατοικῶν.

The first αὐτῶν is found in MSS. of the Armenian lectionary, and is due to the influence of codices like C 81 from which the earlier Armenian text of Acts was revised about the year 430. The longer variant of Thomas is not recorded by Zahn or Blass, yet it stands en toutes lettres in the catena.

[1] One of the two Venice MSS. of the catena adds this note from the catenist's hand :

" Mark this passage. Pentecost is in his own commentary called by John ' the beginning of harvest,' but he means the Levitical zatik by ' beginning of harvest,' for it was at zatik they dedicated on the altar, and so far forth pentecost appears to be the end of harvest. Choose as you please. Moreover it was the 50th year in which the Lord was crucified and the Spirit descended. It is not clear. This last information we derive from Philo and the Chronicon and were perplexed."

I can find no similar passage in the Greek texts of Chrysostom. In the catena it begins the fourth homily and is acephalous, as the first section of a homily always is ; yet I doubt if Ephrem wrote it.

Codex 571.
ii. 15-22.
. . . stabant circa illos. Coepit annuntiare evangelium ad exitum pentecostes. Non dicit, Musto ebrii sumus, sed Spiritu sancto impleti sumus. Ergo considerate et mementote propheticum spiritum de ore Ioel prophetae et videte quae in illo tempore locutus est et in diebus salutis patrum nostrorum, quae facta sunt a Sninakerim rege Assyriae, mysteriose consummata sunt, en, hodie per salutem gentilium. Coram vobis actibus et re vera consummantur. Id enim quod dixit deus : In diebus novissimis emittam spiritum meum super omnem carnem, et prophetabunt filii vestri et filiae vestrae, et iuvenes vestri visiones videbunt, en hodie consummatum est re vera et actibus, sicut vox superna et odor internus et linguae, quae inter nos omnes loquuntur, testificantur nobis. Audite abhinc non verba Galilaeorum, sed verba apostolorum qui spiritu sancto digni facti sunt. Iesus igitur ille qui educatus est in Nazareth, vir ille qui apparuit in signis et prodigiis, quaecunque fecit deus per illum. Praedicabant eum illis virum, ut tanquam lac darent illis evangelium, ut postquam perfecti forent et fierent confirmati, praedicarent illis iudicem et creatorem et deum tanquam verum cibum.

ii. 23.
Hunc ait qui definitus separatus fuit consiliis dei, ad haec omnia quae fecistis apud illum, quia eum suscitavit deus, iuxta quod non decebat neque commodum erat quod maneret in inferno,[1] id quod

ii. 25-34.
David cecinit de eodem : Dixit dominus domino meo, sede ad dextram meam. Iterumque dixit : Non dereliquisti animam meam in inferno neque dedisti sancto tuo videre corruptionem.

ii. 29.
Quod minime de David implentur ista, manifestum est, quia sepulchrum Davidis usque in hodiernum diem apud nos est. Iesum autem deus suscitavit, nosque sumus testes eius, nobisque testificantur, ecce, vox et odor, omnesque linguae quibus iam ante vos loquimur. Non igitur David, qui sepultus est inter vos, ascendit in coelos, sed filius Davidis cui promissus est per Davidem thronus dei. Scripsit enim : Dixit dominus domino meo, sede ad dextram meam. Ergo e testimonio prophetarum et Davidis quod adducitur vobis, et e voce quam audistis, et odore fragrantiae quem accipitis, et omnibus linguis quas loquimur et auditis, vos, omnis domus Israelis, qui congregati estis hodie hic, sciverunt (*sic*) et cognoverunt quod fecit Christum et sedere fecit eum ad dextram, hunc Iesum quem vos crucifixistis.

[1] ii. 24 τοῦ ᾅδου D Iren.

disciples of Jesus were assembled, and a sweet smell exhaled from the violence of the wind and filled all the house.

Nyss. Eph. : Et replevit totam domum ubi erant sedentes. And how did the wind fill the house ? Evidently with a sweet odour and brilliant light.[1] p. 45. ii. 2.

Ephrem : Seditque supra singulos eorum. That is, the tongues appearing sat upon them individually. It is clear they severally sat on each, all the portions sitting down on them one by one. This is why, resuming the whole of the portions in one because of their identity of nature, he uses the singular and says, It sat upon each.[2] p. 47. ii. 3.

Ephrem : Facta autem hac voce, convenit multitudo et congregata est. The voice which came from heaven was audible to all citizens, and the smell which exhaled from the violence of the wind collected the many together. This is the sound which there was. p. 49. ii. 6-8.

Ephrem : These same people whom the dread sound stirred and the fragrant smell led gathered together, when they saw the Galileans talking in all tongues, wondered, as he says : Quoniam audiebat uniuscuiusque linguis loqui eorum. But let no one imagine the Apostles were speaking in their native tongue, while their hearers heard (them speak) in their own several tongues. p. 49. ii. 6.

And showed their good will, for, amazed at what had happened, they said, What is the meaning of this ? [3] p. 50. ii. 12.

Ephrem : For as the dawn is sign of sunrise, so the signs on the day of the cross of Christ harbingered the outpouring of the Spirit of God. p. 55. ii. 17.

Ephrem: Whose light he vouchsafed to the Gentiles, and the vapour of smoke to the crucifiers for the exacting from them of requital for the blood of Christ and of the just. And there is darkened upon them the sun before they be caught in the lake of fire, of which he says : Antequam venerit dies domini magnus et manifestus. p. 56. ii. 20.

Ephrem : He proclaims him man human, that as with milk he may feed them with the gospel, but, when they be made perfect, they shall proclaim him judge, creator, and God. p. 58. ii. 22-36.

---

[1] The above is headed Nyss-Ephrem, but it can hardly be from Gregory of Nyssa. But compare a paragraph in a later paragraph of the catena (p. 46) headed Nazianzen : " Therefore in various forms it appears, for not a wind and smell and light only, but tongues visible they saw, and these like fire, to indicate many persons through fire." But Nazianzen is no more likely than the other Gregory to have had a reference to the odour of sanctity in his text of Acts, and we may suspect here the influence of Ephrem.

[2] Chrysostom 33 B D is a little similar, but there is no reason to regard the ascription to Ephrem as wrong.

[3] The catenist injects into the middle of a passage from Chrysostom the words ἐπὶ τῷ γεγονότι (so D Aug. Contra ep. Fund). His source must have been Ephrem, for Chrysostom lacks the words, and the catenist hardly added them de suo.

ii. 37-41.   Quidam vero ex iis,[1] postquam viderunt verba prophetarum, nam
iterabat Shmavon re vera, sed et linguae quidem testificabantur de
eodem, exterriti sunt, et incipiebant dicere illi : Quid autem faciemus
et vivamus ? Ait illis : Postquam confessi eritis eum quem negastis
et poenitentiam egeritis, et baptizati eritis in nomen. illud quem
crucifixistis, remissio quae latet in baptismo eius expiat vos ab
iniquitate quam patrastis, quum crucifixistis eum. Postquam autem
expiati estis et purificati, tum denique muneribus spiritus quem
vidistis apud nos digni fietis vos. Admiserunt multi, baptizati sunt,
et appositae sunt illis animae fere tria millia.

iii. 1-16.   Iterum quum accedebant ad ecclesiam, curaverunt ibi claudum ex
utero matris eius, et quoniam non sciebat ambulatio quid esset,
exsiliens exsiliebat, et ingressus est ecclesiam. Incepit dicere congrega-
tioni quae congregabatur illic videre claudum : Deus, ait, glorificavit
filium suum variis miraculis quae fecit inter vos. Sed vos sprevistis
et negastis eum coram Pilato, qui volebat liberare eum,[2] quia scivit
propter odium eos tradidisse sibi eum ; et petivistis Baraban et
trucidastis caput repromissum vitae. Eum enim suscitavit deus,
nosque testes eius sumus, nobisque testis curatio quam vobis
omnibus coram dedimus illi.

iii. 17-26.   Ne igitur profligaret spem eorum quia crucifixerant, et omnino
prorsus perderentur, allevavit ex illis Shmavon dicens ipse : Scimus,[3]
ait, quia per ignorantiam fecistis hoc, ipsissima verba quibus usus
est dominus, Non sciunt quod faciunt. Iteravit ea etiam Paulus,
Si scivissent, non crucifixissent dominum gloriae. Deus, ait,
quod praenuntiavit[4] per os prophetarum, quod crucietur Christus,
eodem modo implevit ; neque : Vos fecistis, quamvis per invidiam
vestram fecistis. Si enim prophetae, utique non volentes, imple-
verunt apud eos, non ait : Poenitemini quia obliterabuntur peccata
vestra. Et advenient vobis[5] tempora refrigerii pro iudiciali ira quae
per Danielem imposita est vobis. Moses ergo dixit quod prophetam
suscitabit vobis dominus deus e fratribus vestris sicut me, illum
audiatis quodcunque locuturus dicturusque sit, quia filius dei est,
et quia etiam prophetae qui post Samuelem locuti sunt de his diebus.
Ne fraudemini benedictione quam benedixit deus Abraham dicens :
In semine tuo benedicentur omnes populi terrae. Propter hoc enim
ad vos missus est, non ut trucidaretis eum, sed ut benedicamini
per eum.

---

[1] ii. 37 καί τινες ἐξ αὐτῶν εἶπαν D.
[2] iii. 13 ἀπολύειν αὐτὸν θέλοντος D. Chrysostom knew of this reading. Just
before in the same verse the text warrants more than the single word ἠρνήσασθε ;
in vs. 14, Aug. *De pecc. mer.* reads 'inhonorastis et negastis.'
[3] iii. 17 ἐπιστάμεθα D h; cf. Ephrem on 1 Cor. ii. 8.
[4] Literally, praevenit praedicavit—a Syriasm.
[5] iii. 20 vobis h Iren. hcl ⁜, see Textual Note, p. 30.

Ephrem : Cui omnes nos sumus testes. And to us is witness the violent sound which resounded, and the sweet odour which exhaled, and the strange tongues we speak. p. 62.
ii. 32.

Ephrem : For the remission which lies hidden in his baptism is absolver of you from iniquity, for that ye crucified him. And when ye are absolved and sanctified, then of the gifts of the spirit ye behold in us ye become worthy, ye also. And he confirms his utterance and says : Vobis enim est repromissio et filiis vestris. Clearly it is from Joel, this thing gospelled : Effundam de spiritu meo. p. 66.
ii. 38-39.

Ephrem (?) : Quidam vero dicunt, quia imperitus erat neque scibat ambulare, nunquam enim ambulaverat. p. 73.
iii. 2.

For on the wishing of Pilate to liberate him, you did not wish. p. 78. 8.
iii. 13.

And here, that a witness for you the healing which we gave him before you all. p. 79. 15 f.
iii. 16.

Lest he should cut off their hope who crucified him, and they should be utterly lost, he returned, let them off, giving faculty of repentance.[1] p. 79. 29 f.
iii. 17.
p. 80. 29 f.
iii. 18.

Who forestalled preached by the mouth of all the prophets. p. 83. 37 ff.
iii. 18.

---

[1] This as usual amidst matter from Chrysostom.

iv. 1-4. Quia ergo exspectabant sacerdotes alteram diem ut tormentarent apostolos, sed propter curationem claudi quae facta erat appositi iv. 5-21. sunt illis, et erant quinque millia numero. Adduxerunt ergo apostolos crastina die, et quia non admisit tormentari eos curatio claudi, qui stabat ante eos, minati sunt illis et dimiserunt. Apostoli tamen resurrectionem domini coram omnibus sine timore annuntiaverunt. Et appositi denuo et dicebant : Nos quae audivimus ab illo et virtutem miraculorum quam vidimus ab illo, celare utique possumus ?

iv. 23-31. Postquam autem advenerunt apostoli narraveruntque sociis suis quae evenerant, coeperunt precari, dicendo : Tu es qui locutus es per Davidem : Quare tremuerunt [1] gentes et populi meditati sunt inania ? Contra erant reges, Herodes, et principes, Pilatus, et meditati sunt simul de uncto eius. Christum igitur quem spreverunt, patrem quem non spreverunt, spreverunt per eum. Congregati sunt reges Hebraeorum, Herodes, et principes ethnicorum, Pilatus, facere omnia quae decrevisti, id est, omne quod scripsisti in prophetis de Christo. Nisi accipiant illum, immo voluntas tua utique voluit, fiat hoc omne quod scriptum est de ingressu gentilium, quia non acceperunt illum Judaei. Si enim accepissent eum, tanquam prophetavit Zacharias, laetitia fuisset illis ingressus eius ad eos ; sed quia contristaverunt et trucidarunt eum, extirpatio et indignatio facta est illis, quomodo posuit super illos Daniel iudicium. Conturbatus est mundus omnis ad vocem petitionum et supplicationum eorum, et impleti sunt spiritu et sine metu loquebantur cum omni homine qui voluit audire verbum eorum.[2]

iv. 32-35. Et erat unanimitas inter eos : potentes qui erant inter eos possessiones suas vendebant et afferebant in medium, causa ornandi vestitu pauperes qui discipuli sunt facti, et discipulabant. Ea omnia facta sunt, ut perficerent verbum domini nostri : Egrediantur in omnes regiones ad evangelismum sine scrupulo ullo et sine praepedimento.

v. 1-10. Occiderunt domum Ananiae et suorum, non solum quia furtum fecerunt et celaverunt, sed quia non timuerunt, et voluerunt decipere eos in quibus spiritus sanctus omnia investigans habitabat.

v. 11-37. Rursus denuo apprehenderunt vinxerunt propter curationes quas faciebant, et liberati sunt ab angelo, ut advenirent loquerentur de Christo in templo. Sacerdotes destiterunt ire stare in templo in precibus mane,[3] sed adsederunt iudicandi causa apostolos, non enim magis putabantur tormenta apostolos quam preces ? Incedebant primo in ecclesiam et valuerunt, ut quum docerent, non sit opus iis mittere quaerere eos, sed actu et operibus impletum est in illis verbum

---

[1] (?) tremuerunt for fremuerunt.
[2] iv. 31 παντι τῷ θέλοντι πιστεύειν D e, omni volenti Aug.
[3] v. 21 ἐγερθέντες τὸ πρωί D.

And whereas the healing of him did not allow of torturing them. p. 90. 23.
iv. 21.

Ephrem : Adversus dominum et adversus unctum. For in p. 94.
rejecting Christ they withal rejected the Father, whom they rejected iv. 26 f.
not. Convenerunt enim, etc.

Ephrem : Thus were slain the house of Ananias, not only because p. 102.
they thieved and hid, but because they feared not, and desired to v. 1-10.
deceive them in whom the all-searching Holy Spirit dwelt.

domini nostri dicendo : Qui occidat vos, aestimabitur fidelis minister esse dei. Postquam igitur comminati sunt occidere apostolos, liberavit eos Gamaliel, qui veluti timore affecit et assentiri compulit [1] sacerdotes istis verbis : Ante, ait, quam tempus hoc, id est ante natum domini nostri, exstitit, ait, Thaude unctus magia, et aberraverunt post eum quadringenti viri, qui facti sunt in morte eius nihil. Exstitit denuo Iuda Galilaeus, in diebus quum censebant [2] homines in terrae censu, quo tempore natus est dominus noster. Hoc igitur fecit Satanas ante natum domini nostri et in hora natali, quia audivit de natu eius per annunciationem angeli, qui annunciavit Zachariae et Mariae et de eo quod impeditus est Shmavon senex quin gustaret mortem antequam videret [3] dominum Christum.

v. 40-42.   Quamvis ergo non mortui sunt apostoli propter consilium Gamalielis, minando tamen minati sunt illis ne loquerentur in nomine illo. Sed apostoli unus ab altero audiebant hoc, ita ut in templo et in domo assidue et indesinenter praedicarent dominum nostrum.

vi. 8, 10, 12.   Postea deprehenderunt Stephanum propter signa eius et prodigiosam sapientiam, et quia omni tempore roboroso argumento e
iv. 13.   prophetis desumpto circumibat eos et conturbabat,[4] quia dicebant apostolos esse ignaros et imbecillos et litterarum inscios.

vii. 2-43.   Coepit Stephanus repetere illis ab Abrahamo cum ceteris patriarchis [5] qui erant circa eum, et descendit usque ad Mosem. Itaque ostendebat quomodo contumelia affecerunt patres eorum Mosem, qui a deo missus est ad illos salvator, ita stant oppositi illi Christo. De quo Moses dixit, Prophetam suscitabit vobis dominus tanquam

---

[1] *Lit.* dabat—a Syriasm.
[2] *Lit.* scribebant.
[3] μέχρι τοῦ ὁρᾶν.
[4] vi. 10 (?) διὰ τὸ ἐλέγχεσθαι αὐτοὺς ἐπ' αὐτοῦ μετὰ πάσης παρρησίας D h.
[5] vii. 4 (?) καὶ οἱ πατέρες ἡμῶν οἱ πρὸ ἡμῶν, D hcl. ⁜ e (et patres vestri).

Ephrem : Post hunc, he says, exstitit Iudas Galilaeus in diebus p. 115.
facti census et rebellem fecit populum multum post se. Satan then v. 37.
raised them up before the birth and at the birth of our Lord. For he
heard about his birth from the words of the angel that was with
Zachariah and Mariam ; nay, and beheld that Shmavon, the old
man, was prevented from tasting death until he should behold our
Lord Jesus Christ ; he was eager by means of these revolts to
damage the economy of Christ. But in his haste, as he, so also this
one perished, and those who obeyed him were scattered.

Not only were they worsted, but they could not contest any- p. 124, 16 f.
thing against (him). For with powerful argument from the prophets vi. 10.
he turned them round and routed (them).

Ephrem : But since they taunted the apostles with being silly p. 127. 35 ff.
and ignorant, he began to repeat to them the scripture ; beginning vii. 2.
from Abraham he sums up as far as Christ and their shamelessness.

Ephrem (?) : Qui nutritus est tribus mensibus in domo patris p. 134. 39-
sui. Whom, says Paul, they hid in faith ; for the beauty of his 135. 19.
mien gave hope of God's grace to rescue him. But being no longer vii. 20.
able to hide him, though they wished to, they cast him into the
river . . . when they despaired of human aid and exposed him,
then the benevolence of God was resplendently shown . . . him
who ought to have died and was nigh unto death, having been
thrown into the river, the king himself brought up.[1]

Numquid interficere me tu vis, quemadmodum interfecisti heri p. 136. 34 ff.
Aegyptium ? Thus did they instantly forget the good service and vii. 28.
pay back with hatred his benefit. For, behold, he published abroad
what had been done in secret for his safety.[2]

Ephrem : And in order to demonstrate that it was not now p. 144.
only that their sin had begun, but from the very beginning when vii. 41-43.
they were chosen. For, lo, they worshipped idols, which thing also
God suffered, and they abandoned the service wondrous of God's

---

[1] The above is mainly from Chrysostom who wrote : ὅτε τοίνυν τὰ ἀνθρώπινα
ἀπηλπίσθη καὶ ἔρριψαν αὐτόν, τότε τοῦ θεοῦ ἡ οἰκονομία (New College MS.
εὐεργεσία) ἐδείχθη διαλάμπουσα. ἐκτεθέντα δὲ αὐτὸν ἀνείλετο ἡ θυγάτηρ Φαραώ
κτλ.
Whence does the catena add (p. 135. 17) 'into the river' ? D e vg.*codd* hcl ※·
have (ἐκτεθέντος δὲ αὐτοῦ) παρὰ τὸν ποταμόν. It is probable that the catenist
introduced the words from Ephrem ; but not certain, because Ephrem glances
already at vs. 43 where the lacuna in his text begins. It is possible, however,
that he went back on his tracks. The Armenian vulgate omits παρὰ τὸν ποταμόν.

[2] In Chrysostom we have nothing similar, and the question arises whether
the last sentence is not an echo of the words added in D after Αἰγύπτιον at
the end of vs. 24, καὶ ἔκρυψεν αὐτὸν ἐν τῇ ἄμμῳ, which Blass omits as due to
Exod. ii. 12. The catenist is unlikely to have been influenced here except
by Ephrem, who therefore must have had the addition in vs. 24 in his version
of Acts.

me, ipsum audietis. Demonstravitque iterum quod derelinquerunt tabernaculum horae et fecerunt tabernaculum Mo[loch].

LACUNA, ACTS VII. 43-VIII. 28

tabernacle, and chose the tabernacle of Moloch, the dead rot of idols. Wherefore, because of the dead image they worshipped, he reproaches their folly and impiety. Suscepistis tabernaculum Moloch. This is the excuse of sacrifices.[1]

Ephrem : Wherefore after showing how they exchanged the tabernacle of glory for the tabernacle of Moloch, and how the highest set at naught the temple of their boast, that they might make a temple for him through fear of God. But as he knew they would not profit thereby, but sought to slay him, he rejoicing in spirit turned his discourse against them and rebuked their hardness of heart in the words of the prophets, and not in his own : O duri cervice et incircumcisi cordibus, wherewith Jeremiah reproached them. He also set at naught the circumcision of the flesh and extolled that of the heart, which God seeks, God from whom they revolted. Wherefore to the accusations of the prophet he adds his own. p. 146.
vii. 43-53.

Ephrem (?) : Et ille plenus erat spiritu sancto, intendit in coelum et vidit gloriam dei et Iesum stantem a dextra dei. It is clear, lo, that the sufferers for Christ enjoy the glory of the entire Trinity. He saw the Father and Jesus on his right hand ; for Jesus only appears to his own, as after the resurrection to the Apostles. And as the champion stood in the midst of the mad slayers of the Lord without a helper, and as it was the hour of the crowning of the first martyr, he saw the Lord with a crown who stood on his right hand as one encouraging victory over death, to show that in the same way he secretly aids those who for his sake are given over to death. Therefore he reveals what he saw, the heavens opened, which since they were shut to Adam were first opened to Christ alone in the Jordan, but after the cross were opened also to the sharers of Christ's cross, and first to this man, as he says : Ecce video coelos apertos et filium hominis stantem a dextra dei. See you not, that he revealed the cause of the lightening of his countenance, for he was about to behold this marvellous vision. That is why he was changed into the likeness of an angel, that his testimony might be trustworthy.[2] p. 149. 27-
150. 14.
vii. 55-56. Cf. vi. 15. vi. 15.

Ephrem (?) : Wherefore the saint, desiring to frighten them, p. 151. 5 ff.
vii. 57.

---

[1] The above is labelled Ephrem, and it agrees with the last words before the lacuna begins ; but the paragraphs which follow it in the catena without change of ascription, and which fill most of pages 144-145, are Chrysostom.

[2] The above is not Chrysostom, though it comes amidst matter taken from him. The style resembles Ephrem. The words ' the champion stood in the midst ' seem to echo the addition of D in chap. vi. 15 ἑστῶτος ἐν μέσῳ αὐτῶν D, ' stantis inter illos ' h vg.codd. A rhapsody of Ephrem on St. Stephen, read in the Armenian menologion, rather implies the same addition. The catena-extract refers back in its context to vi. 15. The menologion runs : " The power of Christ was dwelling in him, and thereby his countenance was made resplendent in the midst of his slayers."

LACUNA, ACTS VII. 43-VIII. 28

cried out with a loud voice.[1] With high-pitched voice he pealed
into their ears what he saw, in order to quell their frenzy. But
they what ? They stopped their ears like serpents.

Ephrem : And forasmuch as it seemed a small thing in his eyes p. 152.
to cast a stone at him, he became a guardian of chattels for his vii. 58-59.
slayers, in order that the lot might be divided among all of them.[2]
Et lapidabant Stephanum. Not idly does he repeat the story of
the stoning, but in order to show that it was the false witnesses [3]
who first began to stone the Lord, so as to give the impression that
they were keeping the precept of the law which says that the hands
of the witnesses shall cast the first stones at the blasphemer. They
were craftily striving to establish such an opinion by means of false
witnesses against the saint, et lapidabant Stephanum, who cried
aloud and said : Lord Jesus, receive my spirit.

Chrysostom : But see how providentially arranged was their p. 153. 13 ff.
flight for the salvation of others, lest henceforth they should all viii. 1.
settle down in Jerusalem only, but that the word might be spread
in remote regions. . . . The apostles however because they desired
thus to draw the Jews to themselves, did not quit the city, but in
other cities also furnished cause for being bold enough to preach
the word of life.[4]

Ephrem : And it is similar that in that day they took their p. 153. 7 ff.
possessions as spoil, whom the Apostle praises, saying : Ye accepted viii. 1.
with joy the plundering of your goods. Et omnes dispersi sunt per
vicos Iudaeae et in Samariam praeter apostolos. It is clear they
were in full flight from the presence of the persecutors.

Ephrem : Saulus autem devastabat ecclesiam, per domos in- p. 154.
trans trahebat viros ac mulieres, tradebat in carcerem. For in this viii. 3.
persecution which was to scatter and pursue the disciples from

---

[1] Here d has ' et cum exclamasset.'

The catenist himself adds the remark that some (so Armenian vulgate)
read thus : ' They cried out with a loud voice and stopped their ears.' He
clearly had a text which implied not κράξαντες, but κράξαντος (so one
Greek minuscule). The passage is embedded in Chrysostom matter, but
Chrysostom has the usual Greek text. It is clearly a bit of Ephrem worked
into Chrysostom.

[2] Either read αὐτοῦ for αὐτῶν, or else (with HP many minn.) omit αὐτῶν
altogether, it being of course Stephen's clothes which were to be divided
among the slayers. The text of D at xxii. 20 has already been adapted to
the corruption (or interpretation ?) αὐτῶν, and the Peshitto shows signs of
botching in the later passage.

[3] This implies ' falsi testes ' gig perp.

[4] The first sentence is in New College MS. : τοῦτο δὲ οἰκονομία ἦν ὡς μηκέτι
λοιπὸν ἐν Ἱεροσολύμοις πάντας καθῆσθαι. The rest is not from Chrysostom,
and echoes the reading of D d. Sah : πλὴν τῶν ἀποστόλων οἳ ἔμειναν ἐν
Ἱερουσαλήμ. The catenist must have got it from Ephrem.

viii. 28-39.   . . . in currum eius et adveniens evangelizabat de Christo de lectione Isaiae, et baptizavit eum. Statim habitavit [1] super eum ascendentem e lavacro baptismi spiritus virtutis operum, ut operibus

---

[1] viii. 39 πνεῦμα ἅγιον ἐπέπεσεν ἐπὶ τὸν εὐνοῦχον A minn perp vg.*codd* hcl ※ Jerome.

Jerusalem, it seemed to the priests, the judges, and to Saul that the gospel was already paralysed at the very start; and therefore Saul roamed around from house to house to search and see if he could still find any one.

Ephrem : So Philip went down thence and in the power of his signs filled the land of the Samaritans with his teaching, so much so that even Shmavon the magus, who through his wizardry astounded the Samaritans, undertook to go down with the Samaritans unto the baptism of the font, which in due sequence the evangelist relates. p. 155.
viii. 5-13.

Ephrem : And this is why they sent Peter and John, that by their imposition of hands the Shamartatzi might receive the spirit of signs and astonish the children of Jerusalem by works of the spirit which the Shamartatzi wrought. Tunc imponebant manus super illos et accipiebant spiritum sanctum. It is clear that making prayer, as he said, they laid on hands. For not merely had the Holy Spirit been given, or they could give it, but there was need of many petitions ; for it is not the same thing to meet with healing and to receive the power of healing.[1] p. 158.
viii. 14-17.

Ephrem (?) : It was much that he even of himself confessed that he was overtaken by punishment, and that his soul was guilty. For the magus said, Precamini vos, etc. These words are of one confessing his faults, and this he said toward his purification as being repentant. But it was necessary he should from the depths of his heart weep and lament, that perchance he might be reconciled. But see him to be polluted with all wizardry, and bound with in-dissoluble knots in the cords of evil. For when he was reproved, he believed ; and when again he was reproved, he humbled himself, imagining he could hide. But affrighted at their multitude he feared to deny his revealed sins; and though he might have said : I knew not but acted out of simplicity, he dreaded to do so, for he was convicted previously by his signs, and again because he openly mocked his evil designs. Therefore in the long he fled a fugitive to Rome, thinking the Apostles would not arrive there.[2] p. 161. 9 ff.
viii. 24.

Ephrem : But it is in keeping that he came because of this, for he received it in succession from the tradition of the Queen of the South who came to worship in the temple in the days of Solomon. p. 163.
viii. 27.

Ephrem : Wherefore as he went up from the font of baptism, there dwelt forthwith upon him the spirit of might of works, that p. 166.
viii. 38-39.

---

[1] The rest of the passage is from Chrysostom 146 E f.

[2] The first part of the above is from Chrysostom 147 B as far as 'cords of evil.' The rest has nothing to correspond in the Greek and is by its style shown to be Ephrem. The phrase ' his revealed sins ' implies (viii. 24) τούτων τῶν κακῶν ὧν εἰρήκατέ μοι D. Chrysostom implies that Simon did not do what is stated in the Bezan addition, ὃς πολλὰ κλαίων οὐ διελίμπανεν, and so reveals that it stood in his text.

spiritus qui inter Indos operabatur, credibilis fiat crux pudefacta quam praedicabat.

Shavul autem minis suis quibus persequebatur omnes de Ierusalem, epistolam accepit et decretum petiit, cum nemo mandaret eum, ipse obstinatus sponte in omnes civitates, ubicunque manerent, ubicunque invocarent nomen illud, discessit persecuturus eos ; quoniam plus quam sacerdotes nimis asper erat contra ecclesiam. Non erat ei longanimitas ; si adderet persequeretur, atque deinde vocaret eam, ut antequam persequeretur quantum studuit, ecclesiae enim discipulum reddidit eum.[1] Luce ergo quia caecavit eum, metu affecit eum,[2] et leni voce persuasit eum. Is consensit assentiri, quia metuit contemnere humilitatem domini nostri qui voce apparebat, et contremuit denuo spernere violentiam eius qui per lucem praevenit eum et circumdabat. Cecidit Shavul dum stupefactus stabat, non post vocem sed ante vocem, in haesitationem et in admirationem percussus stabat, quis e coelo caecaverit eum, quia ecce Iesus neque e mortuis, uti putabat, resurrexerat. Postquam vero dixit : Shavul, cur persequeris me ? immo defecit mente sua, quod ego propter caelos persequor, neque quod eum cuius habitatio in caelis est persequor. Ait illi : Quis es tu, domine meus, qui in caelis persecutionem pateris ? Quoniam ego Iesum qui inter mortuos est, una cum discipulis Iesu, persequor. Dicit illi dominus : Ego sum Iesus quem tu persequeris. Tunc dum stabat in tremore propter ea quae evenerant illi, et quia conterritus metuebat[3] ut forsan surgeret de terra ubi coniectus erat, utque lux amota ab illo rediret ad illum, dentiumque crepitu in trepidatione erat, ne forte haberet poenam maiorem quam eam

---

[1] The meaning of this sentence is obscure, but in the catena it becomes clear.

[2] ix. 4 cum magna mentis alienatione perp; [in‾pa]vore h.

[3] ix. 5 qui tremens timore plenus in isto sib[i facto] h, and similarly vg.*codd* hcl ⁕ etc.

by the works of the spirit which he wrought in the Indies might
become worthy of credence the cross disdained, which he preached.
Et angelus domini rapuit Philippum et amplius non vidit eum
eunuchus.[1]

Ephrem : But he—for no one sent him—himself obstinate of p. 168. 18 f.
will, accessit ad principem sacerdotum etc. (to the end of the verse). ix. 1.

Ephrem : And forasmuch as he was much harsher toward the p. 169. 10 ff.
churches than the priests and others, God was not so longsuffering ix. 1.
toward him as that he should abound (or continue) in persecutions,
and he should later on call him ; but before he should persecute the
Church as much as he wished, he made of him a disciple.

Ephrem : So then in that with light he blinded, he appalled p. 169. 31-
him, and with fear of the dread glory he quenched his wrath and 170. 11.
with soft voice softened him. Wherewith even he was induced to ix. 4-5.
submit ; for he feared to despise the humility of our Lord who
with gentlest voice appeared, and he was terrified to contemn his
violence who by dint of violent light dazzled him. And while he
was flung to earth, reft of sense he lay, not after the voice but
before the voice, lost in wonder as to who from heaven had blinded
him, for lo, Jesus had then not in any wise risen from the dead according to his opinion. But when he said to him in reproach : Saul,
Saul, why persecutest thou me ? In what by me wronged doest
thou this to me, he fainted in his mind and thought : I for sake
of the Lord of heaven do persecute, can it be that I persecute him
who dwells in heaven ? Next he asks : Who art thou, Lord ?
Forthwith he owns himself a servant. Who art thou, Lord, who
in the heavens art persecuted, for I do persecute that Jesus who is
among the dead, along with his disciples.[2]

Ephrem : And whilst he still was all a-tremble because of the p. 170. 19 ff.
events which had happened to him, and, awestruck, he feared lest ix. 6, 8.
perhaps he should not rise from the ground where he was thrown,
and lest the light which was reft from him would never more return
to him, and his teeth were chattering with excitement, lest haply

[1] The catenist adds this note (p. 166. 39-167. 7) :
" But in old copies of the commentary, ' the Spirit of the Lord snatched away,'
he says, Philip.' And often he doubles the Spirit. Methinks because he wants
to establish that the rape of Philip by the angel was unseen by the eunuch,
lest the eunuch should mistake for a man an angel appearing in gross form, as to
many in human form."

[2] Here as often the catenist has woven into Ephrem's text phrases out of
Chrysostom, e.g. ' softened ' ($\mu a \lambda \acute{a} \tau \tau \epsilon \iota$) for ' stimulavit,' and the words (156 B)
$\acute{\epsilon}\sigma\beta\epsilon\sigma\epsilon\nu$ $a\grave{v}\tauo\hat{v}$ $\tau\grave{o}\nu$ $\theta\nu\mu\grave{o}\nu$ $\tau\hat{\omega}$ $\phi\acute{o}\beta\omega$, then $\grave{a}\lambda\lambda'$ $\acute{\epsilon}\gamma\kappa a\lambda\epsilon\hat{\iota}$, $\mu o\nu o\nu o\nu\chi\grave{\iota}$ $\lambda\acute{\epsilon}\gamma\omega\nu\cdot$ $\tau\acute{\iota}$ $\pi a\rho'$
$\grave{\epsilon}\mu o\hat{v}$ $\mu\acute{\epsilon}\gamma a$ $\mathring{\eta}$ $\mu\iota\kappa\rho\grave{o}\nu$ $\mathring{\eta}\delta\iota\kappa\eta\mu\acute{\epsilon}\nu o s$ $\tau a\hat{v}\tau a$ $\pi o\iota\epsilon\hat{\iota}s$; $\epsilon\hat{\iota}\pi\epsilon$ $\delta\grave{\epsilon}$ $\tau\acute{\iota}s$ $\epsilon\hat{\iota}$, $\kappa\acute{v}\rho\iota\epsilon$; $\tau\acute{\epsilon}\omega s$ $\mathring{\omega}\mu o\lambda\acute{o}\gamma\eta\sigma\epsilon\nu$
$\grave{\epsilon}a\nu\tau\grave{o}\nu$ $\deltao\hat{v}\lambda o\nu$. This passage illustrates how hard it was before the discovery
of the full text of Ephrem to separate the Ephrem and Chrysostom elements
in the catena.

quam acceperat; propterea ait illi: Quid vis, domine meus, ut faciam? nam quaecunque adhuc feci, ignarus feci; quandoquidem accepi praeconium tuum una cum praeconiatione, ut poenas rependam mea persecutione, quam cumulavit mihi persecutio mea. Attamen non curavit eum in loco ubi caecavit eum, ut Damasci cuncti advenirent et viderent eum, minitabundo signo quod impositum est illi.

Viros autem qui cum illo erant, quamvis stupefecit eos vox quae e caelo evenit, sed effusionem lucis non viderunt, ne obcaecarentur etiam illi, forentque in confusione. Caecavit Shavul re vera, sed misertus est eos per gratiam, et quia epistolam a sacerdotibus ille quaesiverat, non autem illi, et quia etiam in praedicationem et in apostolatum ille rursus selectus erat, non autem illi. Verbera hausit duobus oculis, quia ausus est persequi integrum et immaculatum corpus ecclesiae.

Amoverunt elevarunt eum de terra, et in magna ignominia, postquam levatum habebant illum, trahebant ducebant Damascum, ubi profectus incedebat magna insolentia, ducebant, introduxerunt eum illic. Sed postquam manserat ille triduum, ut agnoscerent eum Damascus et omnes qui circa eam (urbem) quod verbera adbibit, et postea consensit, neque dono corruptus persuasus est ut taceret et quiesceret.

ix. 10-19.   Apparuit dominus in visione noctis Ananiae, ut sine metu adiret curaret persecutorem. Et apparuit iterum Shavulo, ut sine scrupulo illuminaretur coram curatore suo. Ingressus est et curavit et baptizavit eum, et accepit gaudium de cibo, quia per dies non gustaverat.

ix. 20-25.   Shavul igitur qui profectus incedebat conturbare discipulos evangelii, inventus est conturbator persecutorum evangelii, et aiebat filium dei esse Iesum hunc quem vos putatis in inferno esse, duas naturas illius praedicavit, deitatis et humanitatis, audientibus et infidelibus praedicabat. Quia vero conturbavit urbem tali evangelizatione, turbata est cuncta civitas Damascenorum contra illum. Atque ne praepediretur is morte sua praedicatione cuius desiderans egebat, consilium inivit descendere per murum, non ut accederet ad civitatem ethnicorum, ubi accepti erant eum, sed

ix. 26-30.   Ierusalem, ubi plus quam Damasci comminabantur illi. Quando

penalties of punishment greater than what he had received should over-
take him, he gives him hope of clemency and of seeing once more.

But he did not heal him there on the spot, but blinded him.[1]   p. 170. 27 f.

Ephrem : In order that all Damascus might come, might see ix. 8.
him, for the awful sign which was wrought in him.   p. 170. 29 f.
ix. 6.

Ephrem : But also the strong effulgence of light they saw not, p. 171. 2 ff.
lest they too should be blinded and confusion result. But he ix. 7-8.
blinded Saul in very truth and took pity on him by grace.

And because it was he, and not they, who asked for the letter p. 171. 6 ff.
of the priests, and because it was he that was chosen for the ix. 7.
apostolate of preaching and not they.[2]

Ephrem : Therefore it was then that he both raised him aloft p. 171. 9 ff.
inscrutably into the third heaven and taught him ineffable things ix. 8.
transcendently, that he should not prove in any way inferior to
the pillars of the church and short of equality of highest honour of
apostolate.[3] But in that moment surrexit, ait, Saulus de terra,
apertisque oculis nihil videbat. He was smitten in his two eyes,
because he presumed to persecute the whole and spotless body of
the church. Ad manus illum sumentes introduxerunt Damascum.
In great ignominy they drew and brought him to Damascus, whither
setting out he was proceeding in great pride. They drew and
brought him, him who had expected to draw others by force, as if
bound they brought him within, who was about to bind others.

Ephrem : Et erat ibi tribus diebus neque videbat. In order p. 171. 30 ff.
that Damascus and all around it might know him, that he was ix. 9.
smitten and then had come to himself, and that he was not seduced
by any bribe to be silent and be quiet.

Apparuit dominus . . . curatori (lit. ' physician ') suo.   p. 172.

Ephrem : And he who set forth to go and molest the disciples ix. 10.
of the gospel, proved to be a molester of persecutors of the gospel, p. 177. 17 ff.
for he said : Jesus is the Son of God whom ye imagine to be in hell. ix. 20.
And he proclaimed his godhead and his becoming man alike to
those who listened or who believed not.

Ephrem : So then when he stirred up Damascus with the gospel p. 180. 14 ff.
which he began to preach there, all Damascus was stirred up against ix. 22-23.
him.

Ephrem : But lest he should be prevented by his death from p. 180. 35-
preaching there, which he wanted to do, he planned to descend 181. 2.
by the wall ; not in order to proceed to cities of the gentiles, where ix. 25.
they received him, but to Jerusalem, which more than Damascus

---

[1] This is wrongly assigned to Chrysostom.

[2] This is wrongly labelled Chrysostom.

[3] This section is headed Ephrem, but this first sentence is not found in the
commentary, nor yet in Chrysostom's. Perhaps the catenist put it in, unless
indeed the commentary has a lacuna in it.

igitur a Iudaeis qui ibi erant insectabatur, discipulis vero qui in Ierusalem erant non erat credibilis, tunc Barnabas ex omnibus sociis suis accessit, manu[1] prehendit eum et duxit ad apostolos. Postquam vero consederat, narravit Paulus visionem, et turbavit Iudaeos, qui studebant occidere eum, transportaverunt illum Caesaream et ab inde Tarsum, civitatem eius, miserunt eum.

ix. 33-43.   Shmavon vero postquam curaverat Anes qui erat paralyticus, etiam vivificavit Ioppae mulierem beatam, itaque resurrectione eius plurimos convertit.

x. 1-44.   Arcessivit illum Cornelius ex ethnicis per visionem quae facta est super eum. Ne autem sperneret Shmavon neque accederet, apparuit illi in visione vas veluti lintei magni, quatuor caudis suspensum de coelo, et erant in eo animalia omnia munda et immunda, et dixit illi in hora esuriendi eius : Occide et manduca. Quum non consentisset voci, addidit et dixit illi : Quod Deus purificavit, tu ne immundum fac. Atque dum admirabatur propter visionem, en, viri advenerunt propter eum. Ait illi spiritus : Ortus incede, neque haesites cum viris qui venerunt inquirere te, quia ego mittam eos. Ergo advenienti Shmavoni obviam ivit illi Cornelius, prostravit sese illi et conduxit eum in domum suam. Invenit viros multos, quia praeparati erant audiendi eum causa. Postquam vero rogavit eos quae causa fuerat arcessendi ipsum, narravit ei Cornelius visionem suam. Respondit Shmavon et ait : Certe sine personarum acceptione est deus, etenim inter ethnicos qui visi sunt nobis contemptibiles, si inveniatur aliquis qui adorat eum in veritate, acceptabilis est coram illo. Dumque ipse adveniens narrabat de praedicatione domini, unde et ubi incepit et ubi finivit per crucem, et de resurrectione eius et de XL diebus,[2] quia mansit ille et deinde ascendit,[3] et quod testificabant de eo omnes prophetae, et quod purgetur omnis quicunque baptizatur creditque in nomen eius, et ecce, spiritus sanctus per linguas advenit et habitavit super cunctos **x. 45-xi. 3.** audientes verbum, et inceperunt loqui linguis linguis. Cecidit stupor super circumcisos qui cum Shmavone erant, quod ethnicis etiam effusa diffusa sunt dona spiritus, et manifeste omnibus linguis iam stabant loquebantur veluti apostoli. Conversus est Shmavon ad circumcisos qui cum illo erant, et ait illis : Quid potest impedire baptismum in illis qui antequam baptizari acceperunt spiritum sanctum tanquam nos ? Baptizavit eos in redemptionem qui acceperant spiritum, non propter linguas tantum, sed per spiritum qui, antequam baptismum acceperunt, certiorem fecit populum quod a deo esset vocatio eorum.

---

[1] ix. 27 τῆς χειρός 1522.

[2] x. 41 ἡμέρας τεσσαράκοντα D perp hcl ✳, cf. Commentary on Diatessaron, p. 222.

[3] x. 41 ascendit in caelum perp.

threatened him.   Accipientes autem eum discipuli noctu per murum dimiserunt suspendentes dimiserunt in sporta, in order that without suspicion the matter might be.

Ephrem : So when he became a victim of persecution by the Jews who were there, and was not trusted by the disciples who were there, for, he says, non credebant quod esset discipulus, then Barnabas of all his companions who were in Jerusalem took him by his hand and led him to the apostles. p. 184. 17 ff. ix. 26-27.

And whereas he sent to Peter Cornelius of the gentiles, by mean of a dream which came upon him, he urged that Shmavon might not despise and not come.[1] p. 195. 19 f. x. 1-23.

Ephrem : That also among the heathen who to us seemed despicable, if there be found one who in truth worships him, he is acceptable before him. p. 202. 3 ff. x. 34-35.

Ephrem : While then Peter, having entered, recounted our Lord's preaching, whence and where he began, and where he ended on the cross, and about his resurrection, and about the forty days he remained and afterwards ascended, and that all the prophets witness unto him, and that every one is forgiven whosoever believes and is baptized in his name—then forthwith the Holy Spirit came by way of tongues and settled on all the hearers of the word, and they began to speak with divers tongues, as the sequel of the history shows. p. 205. 33-206. 3. x. 36-44.

Chrysostom : Wherefore too Peter taking occasion turned to the circumcised who were there with him.   He made answer and said to them : Surely water could not hinder for the not baptizing of those who too have received the Holy Spirit even as we have. . . . Therefore he first made answer, and when more particularly the facts cried out, not by the tongues alone which they spoke, but also before baptism they received the Spirit, which intimated to the congregation of Jews that of God was the calling of the gentiles. Tunc rogaverunt eum ut maneret apud eos aliquot diebus.   Because thenceforth they settled down in intimate relations with him ; p. 208. 7 ff. x. 47-xi. 2.

[1] The section, p. 195. 19 f., headed Ephrem, is from Chrysostom, 179 c.

Ergo quamvis apparebat testis et intermedia visio Cornelii et Shmavonis et adventus spiritus ad illos ante baptismum, et quod omnes linguas veluti apostoli loquebantur, tamen reprehendebant circumcisi [Shmavona quando] venit Ierusalem, et dicebant quod viros infideles introduxerat, manducavit et bibit cum illis.

xi. 19.   Persecutio vero [quae facta est] propter Stephanum dimisit eos quos persecuti erant docere et discipulos facere in Phoenice et Cypro.

xi. 22-26.   Barnabas vero accessit adduxit Paulum a Tarso Antiochiam, et per doctrinam eorum quae fuit ibi, novum nomen Christianorum in omni terra.

xii. 1-19.   Facta est denuo persecutio ab Agrippa[1] rege Iudaeorum, sumens enim habebat unam partem e quatuor regionibus Palestinorum ; occidit Iacobum filium Zebedaei.   Postquam vidit quod ad mentem inivit hoc modo Iudaeorum, deprehendit inclusit Shmavona in vinculis, ita ut mane occideret.   Apparuit angelus in luce magna, et soluta sunt vincula de manibus eius et eduxit illum.   Uti videbatur Shmavoni, visionem videbat.   Quando autem ad sese reversus est, et intellexit et gratias egit.   Accessit ubi congregati sunt omnes discipuli, et postquam agnovit puella vocem eius, minime aperuit illi ianuam, sed propter gaudium suum cucurrit adnuntiatura sociis eius.   Sed non crediderunt illi.   Dixerunt quod angelus eius sit, id est quod angelus apparuisset puellae, [quia non exspectabant] Shmavona.   Quando autem viderunt illum, [narr]avit illis quaecunque fecerat angelus.   Discedit ille in aliam regionem evangelizaturus.   Agrippa moeruit magna in ira et occidit custodes, quos enim laetos reddidit occiso Iacobo, eosdem maestos reddidit occisio custo-

xii. 21-23.   dum qui occiderant apostolum.   Ad calcem eius quoniam praestiterunt audientes Agrippae sapientiam dei neque novit sese neque glorificavit deum, subito quum descenderet de bemate suo[2] consumptus est a vermibus et mortuus est in loco.

xii.25-xiii.3.   Shavul autem et Barnabas qui tulerunt cibaria sanctorum in Ierusalem, reversi sunt cum Iohanne qui vocatus est Marcus, et Lucas Cyrenaicus (sic).   Hi autem ambo evangelistae sunt, et ante discipulatum Pauli scripserunt, et idcirco iterabat ex evangelio eorum ubique.

Dixit enim illis spiritus sanctus segregandos illos esse, Paulum et Barnaban, ad opus ad quod electi sunt, et posuerunt manus super eos, sive ut acciperent sacerdotium sive ut acciperent inde linguas et opera.   Hoc utique est quod ' dextram communionis dederunt mihi et Barnabae, ut sacerdotio fungamur et doceamus inter ethnicos, illi vero inter circumcisionem.'

xiii. 4-12.   (Et missi a spiritu descenderunt) Seleuciam et Salmenam, dum

---

[1] xii. 1 ' Herod the king who was called Agrippa ' pesh.
[2] xii. 23 καταβὰς ἀπὸ τοῦ βήματος D.

wherefore he too, suitably confident, remained with them. Now although there was as witness and intermediary of these facts the vision of Cornelius and Shmavon and the advent of the Spirit on them before their being baptized, and the fact that in all tongues like the apostles they also spake, yet not because of that were the Jews friendly disposed toward him, but the circumcised blamed Shmavon when he reached Jerusalem, as he says, Audierunt Apostoli etc.

For when she recognised his voice, far from opening the door to him, from her very joy she hastened to make the announcement to the companions.[1] . . . But they not expecting the facts, did not admit this, but said to her, Thou art mad. . . .

p. 227. 4 ff.
and 16 f.
xii. 14.

Ephrem : In order whom he rejoiced by the death of Jacob, them to sadden by the death of the slayers of the apostle.

p. 230. 11 f.
xii. 19.

For they carried the rations for the needs of the saints in Jerusalem.[2]

p. 233. 33 f.
xii. 25.

---

[1] This is embedded in matter taken from Chrysostom.
[2] Embedded in Chrysostom.

minist(rum habebant Io)annem quem Marcum vocant. Voluit disci-
pul(us fieri eo)rum hegemon terrae, sed differebat eos Barshoma
magus. Dicit illi Paulus : O plene omni malo et dolo, fiat super te
manus domini, et fias caecus a luce hac diei neque videas solem. Et
caecatus est ille in illa hora, et credidit hegemon ob signum irae quod
factum est in illo qui praepedibat eum ne crederet.

xiii. 14-   Postea venerunt Antiochiam in regione Phiposi (*sic*), et iussum
xiv. 1.   est Paulo loqui in synagoga ibi. Quum vero loqueretur e prophetis
de adventu domini nostri, de morte et resurrectione eius, et discipuli
facti sunt eorum plures de circumcisione et de acrobustia, Iudaei
autem dederunt consilium principibus et feminis nobilibus et
magnatibus urbis, et fecerunt tribulationem[1] Paulo et Barnabae, et
expulerunt eos e limitibus suis.

Profectique venerunt Iconium et converterunt plures ex Iudaeis
et Graecis.

xiv. 2-18.   Seniores vero exorti persequebantur iustos[2] et lapidaverunt et
expulerunt eos e civitate sua.[3]

Venerunt autem illi Lystram [ubi curavit Paulu]s claudum qui
nunquam ambulav(erat. Id)circoque deos nominarunt eos, et sa(cer-
dot)es[4] idolorum una cum plebe adduxerunt taurum ad sacrificium
usque ad portas domi eorum ubi ingressi erant. Consciderunt
apostoli tunicas suas, ut ostenderent et cognitum facerent quantum
conscissa essent corda sua, et coeperunt clamare et dicere : Homines
sumus quia annuntiamus vobis de deo, et ista cuncta prodigia quae
cernitis eius sunt qui permisit filiis hominum[5] ambulare in viis
idolorum. Id est, qui neglexit, ne censerent egestatem eius refugium
esse apud illos, coegit eum ut confirmaret eos et ut ostenderet et mani-
festaret. Quamvis enim neglexit eos usque ad adventum, tamen
adorare idola, id non voluit. Non reliquit semet ipsum sine cogni-
tione, quia fecit illis bona ; etenim per bona quae de caelo erant,
cognoscere et laudare dominum coelorum debebant, eo quod quam
idola magis valebant, per eadem potuerunt cognoscere creatorem.
Et quamvis non misit prophetas inter gentiles, famuli eius indesinenter locum prophetiae, quae non erat indesinens, explebant. Eo
igitur quod praedicarunt de uno deo, frustraverunt (ministerium
idol)orum ab hominibus dereli(nquentibus veritatem) et consentiverunt ci(ves ne) sacrificarent Paulian(is propter prodigia quae) per
curationem claud[i, adeo ut sacrificiis obla]tis deos facerent illos,
xiv. 19-22.   [per calumni]as hominum Iudaeorum qui adven(erant de Iconio

---

[1] xiii. 50 θλῖψιν μεγάλην καὶ διωγμόν D e.

[2] xiv. 2 οἱ δὲ ἀρχισυνάγωγοι τῶν 'Ιουδαίων καὶ οἱ ἄρχοντες τῆς συναγωγῆς
ἐπήγαγον αὐτοῖς διωγμὸν κατὰ τῶν δικαίων D, similarly hcl.*mg.*

[3] xiv. 5 et lapidantes eos eiecerunt eos ex civitate hcl.*mg*; [. . .]runt eos
et lapidaverunt h.

[4] xiv. 13 οἱ δὲ ἱερεῖς D 460 gig.   [5] xiv. 16 omni gentis hominum h.

Chrysostom : Iudaei autem concitaverunt religiosas mulieres honestas et primos civitatis, et excitaverunt persecutionem in Paulum et Barnaban et eiecerunt eos de finibus suis.[1] Do thou see how many things were done by the opponents of the preaching, and to what insolence and wickedness, of which in themselves they were not capable, they gave counsel to the head men and to women honest, noble, and the great ones of the city, and having aroused them to strife wrought also tribulation for Paul and Barnabas, and drave them out of their boundaries. p. 248.10 ff.
xiii. 50.

Ephrem : Qui in . . . vias suas. This means, as they abandoned the worship of him, he abandoned, that is neglected, that they might not suppose his need, who was a refuge unto them, constrained him from the beginning to establish them. p. 253. 23 ff.
xiv. 16.

Ephrem : That is, though he neglected them, yet he did not wish them to worship idols. Wherefore he left himself not without clear witness, out of his benevolence giving rain from heaven ; for through the blessings which were from heaven were they bound to know him and to bless the Lord from heaven. Thus in that they were very much greater than the idols, they were able by means of the same to know the Lord. For though he sent not prophets among the gentiles, yet his servants, which are the elements, continually filled the place of prophecy. p. 253. 36-
254. 7.
xiv. 16-17.

So much so that the city which, by means of the healing of the lame man, with sacrifices called them gods, by means of the evil p. 255. 27 ff.
xiv. 19.

---

[1] The difference in citing xiii. 50 between the catena and Ephrem's text is not considerable. It consists merely in the addition after ' women ' of the epithet *zgast*, which answers to ' honest, sober, prudent,' or ' self-respecting,' and in Armenian vulgate in this passage renders εὐσχήμονας. The other epithet *tikin* is one applied only to women, and answers to ' domina, matrona clarissima, lady.' The commentary of Ephrem on Acts in this passage should be confronted with his commentary on 2 Tim. iii. 11 (pp. 264 f.):

' Antiochia autem non ista Syriae, sed illa Phrygiae, ubi excitarunt Iudaei rectores civitatis et mulieres divites et fecerunt tribulationem magnam super eos, expulsis eis extra fines suos (Acts xiii. 50). Iconii autem post anteriorem tribulationem suscitarunt persecutionem Iudaei et gentiles et lapidantes eum ac Barnabam eiecerunt illos a civitate (Acts xiv. 5 f.). Porro Lystris per accusationem Iudaeorum illuc venientium ab Antiochia et Iconio lapidibus percusserunt Paulum et eduxerunt eum extra civitatem distrahendo, ita ut putarent eum mortuum esse (Acts xiv. 19). Quod autem haec ita facta fuerint, ecce in Actis duodecim apostolorum scriptum est.'

Here the usual order of τοὺς πρώτους τῆς πόλεως and γυναῖκας τὰς εὐσχήμονας in Ephrem's commentary on vs. 50, seems to be reversed, while it looks as if we had a conflation of that order with the usual one, which places the women first ; ' principibus ' looks like a doublet of ' magnatibus urbis.' There remains a doubt, however, for *metsamets*, which literally means ' very great,' ' magnas,' may render the Syriac word for ' rich,' and answer to πλούσιος. But the addition ' of the city ' makes this doubtful. I would see in it a rendering of

et Anti)ochia,[1] lapidibus lapidar[unt Paulum et trahentes] eiecerunt eum extra [civitatem. Et postquam] dies inclinavit et ten[ebrae factae sunt,[2] clam] introduxerunt eum discipuli in [civitatem. Ergo ipsis] plagis veluti lorica ingredi[ebantur adversus] persecutores suos ; sed ut confirmarent discipulos evangelii qui ibi tribulati erant. In tribulatione, ait, in qua vos estis, nosque in eadem sumus, oportet vos ingredi regnum dei, quod per nos praedicatur vobis.

xi̇v. 23. Apostoli autem qui in alia civitate erant, Iconienses et Antiochenses persecuti sunt illos, in illis civitatibus una cum evangelismo quem praedicabant, presbyteros et diaconos in fiducia intrepidos xiv. 24-28. faciebant in illis. Postquam vero transiverant regiones omnes, et venerunt Antiochiam Assyriorum unde missi sunt (et advenerunt et narraverunt) qualem ianuam (aperuisset doc)trina evan(gelii gentilibus).

xv. 1-2. Et ecce quidam Iudaei qui adven(erunt de Iudaea tur)baverunt mentem eorum qui dis(cipuli facti erant; illi vero e Shmavonis) discipulis erant, [et quamvis in Christum credi]derant,[3] circumcisionem [et legem Mosis ob]servabant ; at postquam viderunt qu[od gentiles si]ne his crediderunt, [inceperunt dicere:] Nisi iuxta praedicationem Petri et [sociorum eius cre]datis, non potestis vivere. [Quod etiam consti]tuit seditionem contra eos, et dicit, [non destruere] circumcisionem et legem, quia adhuc [apud] apostolos observabant illi. Sed quia oportet, ait, omnis homo [in quo]vis crediderit in eodem maneat,[4] id est quod incolae Iudaeae stent maneant in circumcisione et socii eorum tanquam apostoli praedicabant, gentiles vero stent maneant sine circumcisione, tanquam a nobis decretum datum est illis. Postquam viderunt illi qui e Iudaea Paulianos, quod in magna molestia

---

[1] The order ' de Iconio et Antiochia ' is proved by the survival in Codex 571 of the last syllables of Antiochia. In the order of the cities it agrees with D h hcl.*mg.* This coincidence with the Bezan text encourages the adoption of Akinean's restoration of the last preceding lacuna : ' et docentibus illis ' ; the more so because Armenian vulgate here retains from the early Syriac, from which the first Armenian text was translated, the reading διατριβόντων δὲ αὐτῶν καὶ διδασκόντων. Nevertheless this restoration does not explain the oblique case ' multitudinis ' or ' multitudini ' (the gen. and dat. cases of the Armenian word *bazmuthean* here used are the same). I am therefore inclined to see here a rendering of ὄχλους, which is found in all forms of the Greek text, and to complete the lacuna thus : ' et consilium dantibus multitudini hominibus Iudaeis qui,' as if the original had been ἐπισείσαντες τοὺς ὄχλους, as in D.

[2] xiv. 20 vespere h, cf. sah.

[3] xv. 1. 383 614 minn. hcl.*mg.* read τῶν πεπιστευκότων ἀπὸ τῆς αἱρέσεως τῶν Φαρισαίων. Ephrem omitted ἀπὸ τῆς αἱρ. τ. Φ., for he names the party of Peter (provided the conjectural restoration of the lacuna is right) and not the Pharisees ; but he perhaps implies τῶν πεπιστευκότων.

[4] xv. 2 ἔλεγεν γὰρ ὁ Παῦλος μένειν οὕτως καθὼς ἐπίστευσαν διισχυριζόμενος D gig hcl.*mg.* The words ' quia oportet ' may imply διισχυριζόμενος.

speaking of men, of Jews, with stones stoned Paul and dragged
cast (him) out of the city.[1]

Ephrem : Circumdantibus autem eum discipulis surgens intravit
civitatem. When the day grew late and darkness came on, the
disciples secretly introduced him into the city. p. 256. 4 ff.
xiv. 20.

Ephrem : Et postera die . . . in regnum dei. With the same
tribulation then as armour they took the field against the persecutors
in Lystra and Iconium and Antioch, where they persecuted them ;
not indeed to inflict wounds upon the persecutors, but to confirm
the disciples of the gospel who were there oppressed, saying : In the
tribulation in which ye are, we also are in the same, whereby ye
must needs enter the kingdom of God which is preached to you by us. p. 256. 23 ff.
xiv. 20-22.

Ephrem : Cum constituissent . . . crediderunt. Do you see
the power of the Gospel ? For in those cities whence they expelled
them along with the gospel they preached, lo, they with fearless
confidence appointed elders and deacons among them. p. 257. 25 ff.
xiv. 23.

Et quidam descendentes de Iudaea docebant fratres. Quia nisi
circumcidamini secundum morem Mosis non potestis salvari.
These men were of the Jews, men made disciples of by Peter and
his. But although they had believed in Christ they kept up circumcision and the law of Moses ; and as they saw that the gentiles
believed in Christ without this, they went down from Jerusalem
to Antioch, still having the disease of avarice. They desired to
alter from one thing to another those who were of the gentiles.
They began to say, Unless according to the teaching of Peter and
of his companions you believe, you cannot be saved. And lo,
Paul was a better expert in the law than they, but did not suffer
this in himself.[2] p. 260. 4 ff.
xv. 1.

Ephrem : Which thing indeed established a dissension against
them. And he denied abrogating the law and circumcision among
the Jews ; for until now they still among the apostles observed the
law and circumcision. But it is right, he says, that every man in
what he was when he believed, in the same shall abide. That is,
that Jews should abide in the circumcision, which Peter and his
preached, but the gentiles remain without circumcision, as was by
us decreed. But as they would not break the law, and Paul's p. 261. 1 ff.
xv. 2.

τοὺς πρώτους τῆς πόλεως. Ephrem certainly had a similar text. We note
also that neither in the commentary on Timothy nor in that on Acts is there
any trace of σεβομένας, rendered literally in Armenian vulgate by *pashtoneay*.

[1] Amid matter from Chrysostom.

[2] This acephalous section, with which Homily 32 begins, serves in part to
fill up the lacunae in the commentary. In it paragraphs from Ephrem and
Chrysostom alternate, and are mixed up together. The catenist has interpolated in Ephrem's text from Chrysostom 250 c the phrases ἔτι νοσοῦντες τὴν
φιλαργυρίαν (read φιλαρχίαν), and καίτοι καὶ Παῦλος νομομαθὴς ἦν, ἀλλ' οὐκ
ἔπασχε τοῦτο.

erant, neque observare consentiebant legem, neque absolvere, saevibant et contra stabant et volebant pronuntiari iudicium coram apostolis et presbyteris in Iudaea.

LACUNA, ACTS XV. 3-11

party did not consent to observe it, they became like wild beasts, they opposed those (*nominative*) who had come down from Jerusalem, and wished to pronounce a verdict before the apostles and the elders in Judaea.[1]

Ephrem [2] : But Paul and his, lest they should abrogate without the apostles anything which the apostles because of the weakness of the Jews observed, pass, set off to Jerusalem, that there before the disciples they may abrogate the law and circumcision, which without them they did not wish to abrogate. Which also he makes clear by saying : Facta ergo non minima seditione, etc. [3] p. 261.14 ff.
xv. 2.

Ephrem : But on their own arrival Paul and his related to the circumcised all that God had wrought through them the uncircumcised. As he says : Illi ergo deducti ab ecclesia, etc. p. 261. 39-
262, 3.
xv. 4.

Ephrem : [4] Surrexerunt quidam de haeresi Pharisaeorum, etc. Note that those who brought Paul and his to judgment, although Paul and his desired whatsoever they narrated to be approved true by means of the elders, yet of themselves they were not disposed to be silent in respect of whatever they wished. Wherefore in presence of the very elders they said : Oportet, and it is fitting for you, circumcidere the gentiles and servare legem Mosis.[5] p. 261.16 ff.
xv. 5.

---

[1] xv. 2. From this and the full commentary it is clear that Ephrem's text read : οἱ δὲ ἐληλυθότες ἀπὸ Ἰερουσαλὴμ παρήγγειλαν αὐτοῖς . . . ὅπως κριθῶσιν ἐπ' αὐτοῖς with D d.

[2] This paragraph comes under the heading ' Ephrem,' but only the initial words are his.

[3] After the citation of Acts xv. 2 in this catena-passage, a clause from Chrysostom 248 c is interpolated, and then follows another paragraph, relating to xv. 4, of which the opening part is given above. The whole of this latter paragraph is ascribed to Ephrem, but only the opening part, here quoted, can be his. Note the syriacizing style, especially the expression, ' Paul and his.' The rest of this paragraph can be identified in Chrysostom, 248 c, 250 E, 251 D. It runs :

"This narration was not greed of honour, nor for again displaying themselves or a satisfaction of any deficiency, for they were not greedy of honour, nor deficient either in anything. But it was an apology for the preaching to the gentiles, whereby they rejoiced in the conversion of the gentiles."

[4] This paragraph is still included under the ascription to Ephrem; the 'Western' readings embedded in it prove it to be his, for Chrysostom has nothing to correspond.

[5] Here the clause ' those who brought Paul and his to judgment,' besides involving once more ὅπως κριθῶσιν in vs. 2, also implies οἱ δὲ παραγγείλαντες αὐτοῖς ἀναβαίνειν πρὸς τοὺς πρεσβυτέρους D hcl.*mg* in vs. 5, and excludes the Pharisees, who figure in the Greek texts but are here mentioned only in a citation of the Armenian vulgate due, not to Ephrem, but to the catenist. Here then in vs. 5, as little as in vs. 1, does Ephrem involve τινες ἀπὸ τῆς αἱρέσεως τῶν Φαρισαίων. His text of Acts only revealed to him a Petrine faction that insisted on circumcision and the full observance

xv. 12-21.   . . . ut vivamus in illo (. . . et post sermonem il)lum appro-
barunt [1] [presbyteri verba Shmavonis et si]ne dissensione de[structa
est dissensio per ob]edientiam erga spiritu[m] : (postea locutus est
Iacobus frater domini n)ostri, et appo(suit et ait : Viri fratres, audite
me,   Shm)avon dixit   quod   certu(m   est   vobis),   [non   quod   de
intellectu s]uo, sed tanquam deus admon(uit) [significavit, id est quia
eth]nici in nomen Iesu [parati erant, quod confiter]entur, ut im-
ple[rentur verba prophetarum qui prae]venerunt praedi[caverunt]

---

[1] xv. 12 συνκατατεθειμένων δὲ τῶν πρεσβυτέρων τοῖς ὑπὸ τοῦ Πέτρου εἰρημένοις
D hcl ※.

Ephrem : And inasmuch as the adjudication was weighty with the people and with the gentiles, and with the apostles and with their companions, there came, were mustered together the apostles and priests along with the multitude,[1] in order to see what verdict would come forth about this matter. Et post multam conquisitionem surgens Petrus dixit ad eos. Because Paul stood forth in Jerusalem to speak in the presence of Shmavon and his companions against the law, as also he spoke in Antioch in his presence against keeping the law. But Shmavon, who in Antioch kept silence, when Paul stepping forth spoke against the law in Jerusalem, there dwelt in him the Holy Spirit,[2] and he began to speak against the upholders of the law thus.[3]

p. 262. 30-263, 4. xv. 6-7.

Gal. ii. 11.

Ephrem : Why then do ye judge the thoughts of God, for that is to tempt God ; for whatever God has given us through faith and through the law, he has given the same also to the gentiles through faith without observance of the law.

p. 264. 39-265, 3. xv. 10-11.

Wherefore on a sudden they reached conviction and ceased the enquiry. For the elders acquiesced in the words of Shmavon, and without dissension was annulled the dissension through the counsel of the Spirit.[4]

p. 265. 37 ff. xv. 12.

And well did he say that Shmavon has set forth, in order to show that he himself desires to be in harmony with his wishes ; for Shmavon did not presage out of his own mind, but by dint of prophetic vision, according as God by the Spirit showed to him, that primum deus visitavit in the beginning sumere populum. Nay he showeth of old that the matter is to be, that is, that the gentiles in the name of Jesus were in the future to confess, in order that there should be fulfilled the words of the prophets, who anticipated, proclaimed he would take a people from among the gentiles, that is choose, not idly, but of his name, which is to his glory.[5] And not only is he not ashamed in his name to choose the gentiles, but even accounts it greater glory.

p. 268. 3 ff. xv. 14-15.

---

of the law. Perhaps the earlier commentary used by Chrysostom did the same, for on vss. 5-7 he writes : ὅρα τὸν Πέτρον ἄνωθεν κεχωρισμένον τοῦ πράγματος καὶ μέχρι τοῦ νῦν ἰουδαΐζοντα. Of Pharisees in this connexion Ephrem knew nothing. In hcl.*mg* the gloss importing the participation of Pharisees has barely rooted itself in the text. In a later age Jerome could pretend that the battle between Peter and Paul was no more than a stage quarrel, and the Pharisee gloss was probably coined in order to veil it.

[1] xv. 6 σὺν τῷ πλήθει 383 614 hcl.*text*.

[2] xv. 7 ἐν πνεύματι D and substantially 383 614 Tert hcl.*mg*.

[3] This section is wholly from Ephrem.

[4] The above is embedded in matter from Chrysostom.

[5] This stands under the title 'Chrysostom' and is embedded in matter from him. The last sentence is not Ephrem's.

. . . (sicut ait pro)pheta : Erig(am de novo tabernaculum Davidis quod destruc)tum erat, id est [filium eius qui erexit filios homin]um, ut fiant mul(ti . . . ut) [requir]ant dominum filii [hominum, id est Iudaei et omnes] ethnici qui per prop(hetam meminerint), [invocabitur nomen meum super] illos, ait dominus. Manifestum est [semper deo opus quod impletum est] in diebus nostris, et de hoc [quantum stat in potentia [1]] mea confirmo verba Shmavonis quod (persuasimus) *non* [2] cogere gentiles ad observationem legum, sed ista omnia fiant, caveant et observent sollicito mandato, abstinere a sacrificato idolis, a fornicatione, et a sanguine,[3] id est, ne manducent super sanguinem. Imprimis Moses quidem in primis seculis in om-(nibus civitatibus habebat viros, qui ubi synagog)ae erant, stabant il(lis praedicatores quomodo legitur omni sabbato).

xv. 22-29.   Ergo elegerunt (apostoli et presbyteri Iudam et Shilan), et expediverunt il(los Antiochiam ad fideles, ut essent tes)tes cum Pau(lo et Barnaba, scribentes per manum eor)um epistolam. Nam scrip(serant id sicut pri)us dictum est. Ideo (ut dicant quodcunque proficit) tibi, malum est socio tuo.[4] (Illa vero . . . in admo)-nitionem dederunt, quia (dicunt : De quibus custodientes vos, re-pl)eti eritis spiritu sanc(to)[5] [Tanquam enim, ait, obser]vabitis ista et si[ne circumcisione et observa]tione legum, ac[cipietis spiritum sanctum loqui om]nes linguas, sicut [acceperunt socii vestri Cornel]i-

xv. 30-35.   ani qui elec[ti priusquam vos. (Et descen)derunt illi Antiochiam et . . . (tradiderunt epistolam)] ecclesiae et caute(la magna unanime stare in mandato) petiverunt fratres et con(firmaverunt eos . . .) Iudaiani et Silvanenses per pro(phetiam. Et) reversus est Iudas post dies in Ierusalem [6] et Silas remansit apud Paulum.

xv. 36-41.   Post paucas dies quando docuerant in Antiochia civitate, coepit dicere Paulus Barnabae, ut redeant visuri in omnes civitates illas ubi in omnibus civitatibus docuerant illi. Bene visum est consilium hoc [7] in oculis Barna(bae. Et voluit Barnabas ducere se)cum Marcum, quem (Paulus orabat ne sumerent eum se)cum, quia separa(verat sese ab illis dum erant in) Pamphylia, et i(bi mansit neque voluit ire) cum illis ad opus (apostolatus. Propter il)lud

[1] xv. 19 propterea ego secundum me Iren. In Rom. i. 15 Armenian vulgate renders τὸ κατ' ἐμέ somewhat similarly.

[2] The word ' non ' is necessary to the sense, but the negative is not found in the Armenian text as printed.

[3] The text here used, xv. 20, lacks καὶ τοῦ πνικτοῦ, see note *supra*, pp. 265 ff.

[4] xv. 29. On the Golden Rule here see note *supra*, pp. 265 ff. The words which remain in Ephrem's text, ' tibi malum est socio,' are a gloss on the precept. The precise nature of the words to be supplied in the lacuna, within the paren-thesis, seems doubtful ; cf. A. Merk, *op. cit.* pp. 236 f.

[5] xv. 29 φερόμενοι ἐν τῷ ἁγίῳ πνεύματι, see note *supra*, p. 148.

[6] xv. 34. So D gig vg.*codd* and in part hcl ※ etc.

[7] xv. 36. So hcl ※.

Anon. : When being born his son reigns over all, who raised up the sons of men, who were wallowing in sin, for they became a dwelling of the Son of David. p. 268. 32 ff. xv. 16.

But thus verily was raised up this city by David's begotten, through whom the remnants of men sought the Lord, that is those of the Jews who believed. And all the gentiles over whom has been called my name, saith the Lord.[1] p. 269. 6 ff. xv. 16-18.

Anon. : That is to say, clear and knowable was ever the work which through the prophets has been fulfilled in our days.[2] p. 269. 19 ff. xv. 18.

Well saith he, with authority, I esteem it right, that is : Thus do I say it to be good, and so far as it lies in my power, I confirm the words of Shmavon. And as the gentiles had never heard of the law, he profitably enacts this from out of the law, lest he should seem to have slighted that.[3] p. 269. 33 ff. xv. 19.

What Paul openly says to the Galatians : But not to straiten. That is, not to molest and constrain them to the observance of the law. . . . p. 270. 10 ff. xv. 19.

Ephrem : For, says he, as ye shall observe all this without circumcision and keeping of the law, ye shall receive the Holy Spirit to speak all tongues, as did your companions receive, Cornelius and his, who were chosen before you.[4] p. 277. xv. 29.

Well seemed this advice in the ears of Barnabas.[5] p. 280. 18. xv. 37.

---

[1] This restores the words 'invocabitur nomen meum super eos.'
[2] This supplies the words 'semper deo opus quod impletum est.'
[3] The above is embedded in matter from Chrysostom.
[4] This is a scrap of Ephrem woven into matter from Chrysostom.
[5] The above is embedded in matter from Chrysostom.

discessit (Barnabas a Paulo et assumens se)cum duxit Mar(cum, appellatum Iohannem, navigarunt) in Cyprum. At Paulu(s Silasque ab ecclesia dis)cedentes transiverunt evangeli(zare in finibus Assyriae et Ciliciae), apud quos et litteras ab [apostol]is [habebant, ut portarent ad] illos, ne venir[ent in par]tes am[bo] (et circum)irent in una regione. Est causa quare [separab]antur ire et praedicare in regiones regi[ones iuxta exem]plum quo separavit sese Abraam [a Loto, ut Ab]raam fieret doctor inter Chanan[itas, et Lot] inveniretur iuxta exemplum Sodomi[tarum].

xvi. 1-5.

Sed (Paul)iani venerunt attinuerunt Lystros ; assumpsit Tim(otheum filium) mulieris cuiusdam credentis in dominum nostrum, et vol(uit Paul)us ducere eum secum. Isque quem mater sua non circ(umcid)it, Paulus postquam accepit mandatum ab apo(sto)lis destruere circumcisionem, assumpsit circumcidit eum ; sed non sine discretione fecit hoc, is qui omnia quae operabatur seli[gens sapienter operabatur ; sed quoniam] paratus erat [evangelizare Timotheus evangel]ismum Iud[aeis ubique], ne propter perit[omen contemnerent] praedicationem eius, [consilium inivit meditatus est circum]cidere, contemptor circ(umcisionis. Ergo assumens circumc)idit Timotheum, [non ut circumcisionem con]firmaret per id des[tructor circumcisionis, sed ne ev]angelismis [causa incircumcisionis illius] distractus inven[iretur per id]. (Idcirco) assumpsit circumcidit eum (apud fratre)s qui erant in ter(ra ib)i, qui cognoscebant pa(trem. N)am quamvis dives erat, tamen gentilis erat. (Dum) transibant civitates et manifestum (faciebant et ap)ostolatu intrepido praedicabant il(li verbum spiritus sanc)ti,[1] et donec ecclesiae confirmaban(tur inter filios) virorum per signa quae facta sunt (cotidie in) illis.

xvi. 6-10.

Impedivit illos spiritus sanctus quin loquer(entur) ulli [2] verbum dei in regione ibi Asianorum, quia dignum et fas erat illos properare ire in Macedoniam. Ne igitur frustrarentur inter illos quin [3] audirent eos, revelatum est illis procedere in Macedoniam, nam exspecta-bant illos etiam Bithyni prout impediti sunt illi ab Asianis, ut properarent venire [in Macedoniam, ubi praeparatum] est illis. Ap[paruit Paulo tanquam [4] vir Macedo], adveniens enim o[rabat et impetrabat illum ut ven[iret opitularetur il[li in Macedoniam].

xvi. 16-21.

(Ibi obviam ivit) illis verna (quam habebat spiritus pytho, quae in furorem ac)ta quaestum permag(num praestabat dominis suis. Ea cum videret Paulianos clam)abat post eos (et dicebat : Homines

---

[1] xvi. 4 ἐκήρυσσον . . . μετὰ πάσης παρρησίας τὸν κύριον Ἰησοῦν χριστόν, D hcl.mg. For the lacuna Merk, p. 238, suggests rather ' (domini nost)ri ' or ' (Iesu Christi domini nost)ri.'

[2] xvi. 6 μηδενὶ λαλῆσαι D.   [3] quin or qui non.

[4] xvi. 9 ὡσεί D pesh sah.

Perambulabat, ait, regiones Syrorum et Ciliciorum, confirmabat p. 285. 11 ff.
ecclesias.   Behold unto whom they had the letter from the apostles xv. 41.
that they should carry unto them, first unto them he circulates,
because he did not regard as a work of wisdom the traversing un-
profitable courses through the same.[1]

Ephrem : Yea and otherwise. For they did not frivolously p. 283. 15 ...
abandon each other according as it was thus providentially arranged xv. 41.
that they should not proceed, both parties, in one region ; there is
a reason why they should separate severally to go and preach in
different regions (lit. in regions regions), in like manner as Abraham
parted from Lot, in order that Abraham should become teacher
among the Canaanites and Lot among the Sodomites.

Ephrem : So then taking he circumcised him. Not without p. 286. 19 ff.
discrimination doing this, he who selecting everything wisely acted ; xvi. 3.
but in that Timothy was about to preach the gospel to Jews everywhere, lest because of his uncircumcision they should set at naught
his preaching, he planned, he purposed to circumcise him—not in
order that thereby he might confirm circumcision, he the undoer
of circumcision, but that his gospelling might not by reason of his
uncircumcision be found riven asunder by the same.   Therefore
because of the gentiles he set no store by these things.

[The catenist cites the Armenian vulgate of these verses, but in p. 287. 26.
verse 5 after τῇ πίστει adds the words : ' and by means of signs xvi. 4-5.
which took place,' equivalent to καὶ τοῖς σημείοις γενομένοις, which
are wanting in the Armenian vulgate, D, etc.   It is clear that
Ephrem read them in his version.]

Cum venissent autem in Mysiam, tentabant ire in Bithyniam, p. 287. 38-
et non permisit eos spiritus. So then they were prevented, that 288, 3.
they might utter to nobody the word of God in the region of Asia, xvi. 6-7.
he tells us ; but why they were prevented he did not add.[2]

Ephrem : But lest they should be brought to nought amidst p. 289. 10 ff.
those who did not listen to them, it was revealed to them to proceed xvi. 9.
to Macedonia ; for the Bithynians also were on the look-out for
them, so that they were kept away from the Asiatics.   So then,
that they might hasten to proceed to Macedonia, where he was
prepared for them, there appeared to Paul as it were [3] a man of
Macedonia, for he came and prayed and besought of him to come
help in Macedonia.

Ut autem visum vidit . . . diebus aliquot, etc. [but reading
' Philippopolis ' for ' Philippi '].

---

[1] The above is embedded in Chrysostom.
[2] The above is embedded in matter from Chrysostom.

isti sunt) filii dei qui (annuntiant vobis viam salutis). [Ergo quomodo haec daemon loquebatur ? Clarum est quod aut] ne expellerent [illum de verna, aut sicut] decipiebat divinatione su[a et dabat opinionem quod ve]rum diceret, voluit decipere etiam in hoc [quod ver]um erat, quia testis pro veritate apud [filios veri]tatis factus est. Sed nihil erat accept[abilis apud] apostolos laudator et impeditor apostolorum, [quomo]do non fuit acceptabilis apud dominum eorum [daemon qui de domino] eorum inter Iudaeos praedicabat. Dedit illi (iussum) Paulus et exiit e verna et loc[o merced]is curationis quam debebant Paulo dom[ini pu]ellae turbaverunt civitatem contra, et apud Iudaeos quibus non praedicavit calumniabantur eum.

xvi. 22-40.　　Strategi civitatis principes scindentes tunicas suas ne foret impediebant, [et ad placitum voluntatis pop]uli qui con[gregatus est devinxerunt Pauli]anos, et egerunt pos[uerunt eos in aede carceris. Ergo facta est] commotio in urbe [ibi, et ianuae carceris apertae sunt], et vincula inclu[sorum soluta sunt ab illis, et] ne esset moeror [custodi carceris qui credi]turus erat, nemo ex [illis evasit ; [1] ergo propter hoc] dignus factus est bap[tismo lavacri) (ipse cum mulieribus et) [fi]liis suis. [Exterriti sunt et pavuerunt astratigi] optimates civ[itatis ob mo]tum, [sed nacti veri]tate sci[verunt quod re vera causa] eorum factus est motus [ille.[2] Sed] confiteri illud non admiserunt. Et mis[erunt] clam dimitti eos. Sed Pauliani, [quoniam apud le]gem Iudaicam calumniabantur ab illis in di[e [3] an]te, dixerunt quod Romani sumus, procul [et absque le]ge Iudaica et a tormentis civitatis principum, ne dimittant quidem nos clam sicut satis[facientes], sed ut illi adveniant dimittant nos. [Ergo]

---

[1] xvi. 30 (?) τοὺς λοιποὺς ἀσφαλισάμενος D hcl ⁕.

[2] xvi. 35 ἀναμνησθέντες τὸν σεισμὸν τὸν γεγονότα ἐφοβήθησαν D hcl.*mg.*

[3] xvi. 35 (?) οὓς ἐχθὲς παρέλαβες D 383, 614, hcl.*text.*

Ephrem : And why or how did the demon speak in this way ? Clearly he either considered it a bribe for the apostles, so that they should not expel him from the maiden, or else, as she deceived by dint of her divinations, and was giving the idea of speaking the truth, because also by reason of the doubtfulness of the oracles he gave, they were calling him perverse and an impostor. He desired to deceive by the very fact that he was truthful, for a witness to the truth among the sons of truth he falsely feigned to be.[1] *p. 293. 21 ff. xvi. 17.*

But it was not welcome for the apostles to be honoured and praised of him, in the same way as was not for their Lord the devil who proclaimed about their Lord among the Jews. In the same way Paul too restrains him, because out of craft and malice of speech he did this.[2] *p. 293. 30 ff. xvi. 18.*

Ephrem : And instead of a reward for the cure which was due to Paul from the owners of the girl, they stirred up the city against him, and calumniated him over the law of the Jews which he did not preach to them. *p. 294. 38- 295. 2. xvi. 19-21.*

Chrysostom-Ephrem : The head men then of the city rending their garments, wished to allay the riot of the crowd. That it should not be, they obstructed. And since they saw the mob enraged attacking, they wanted by blows to quiet down their wrath. And to gratify the will of the crowd which had collected, they pinioned Paul and his, and led off, placed them in the house of the prison ; and gave orders carefully to guard them, desiring presently to hear about their case.[3] *p. 296. 17 ff. xvi. 22-23.*

Ephrem : There was then a quaking in the city, and the gates of the prison opened and the fetters of the confined fell off them. And lest there should be distress on the part of the jailer, who was about to believe, not one of them escaped. For because of this the jailer became worthy of baptism of the font along with his intimates as he says : (xvi. 27-30). *p. 299. 24 ff. xvi. 26-34.*

Ephrem : The astaritae the optimates of the city were appalled and terrified by the earthquake, and learning the truth knew that this earthquake was really on their account, but they did not choose to admit it. They sent secretly to liberate them. . . . Because then it was as to the law of Jewry they had been traduced by them on the day before, they say : We are Romans, far away and exempt from the law of the Jews and from the tortures of the chiefs of the city. Far from their letting us out privily, as if they were in any way beholden to us for favours, let them come themselves and let us out. *p. 301. 25- 302. 6. xvi. 35-37.*

---

[1] The first sentence of the above is from Chrysostom 269 D τί δήποτε καὶ ὁ δαίμων ταῦτα ἐφθέγγετο ; But the title is ' Ephrem,' and the text of Ephrem is continued, though under the title ' Chrysostom,' into the next paragraph.

[2] Here the catenist digresses into matter taken from Chrysostom 269 D.

[3] Here the catenist diverges into Chrysostom 270 α

ut fiat erga illos gratia haec, advenerunt petiverunt illos : Non scivimus iustos esse vos,[1] veluti motus utique certiores fecit de vobis. Discedite ergo, proficiamini ab urbe, ne forte post motum congregentur contra vos iidem viri qui ante mo[tum congregati erant].[2]

xvii. 1-4.

(Et profecti sunt ex ur)be et ambu(labant circumeuntes per Amphipolim et per Apoloniam) usque ad Thes[salonicam], (ubi erat synagoga Iudaeorum, et) accedit (Paulus ad Iudaeos et quando prae)paraverat praed(icare, quidam) [ex Iudaeis] (persuasi sunt et portio facti) sunt eorum. Si(militer plures gentilium) [una cum] maximis dominabus.

xvii. 5-11.

(Zelaverunt Iudaei et) conturbaverunt urbem, (et congregati adstiterunt palatio) Iasonis. Deprehenderunt Iasonem (et fratr)es et (egerunt illos) ad principes civitatis et dicunt : Hi sunt [contra] Caesarem, quia novum principem iuxta Caesarem praedicant. Exte[rri]ti sunt et pavuerunt militum principes in eo rumore, petiverunt satisfactionem ab Iasone et a fratribus, uti m(iti)garent congregationem quae congregata est contra eos. Paulianos autem fugaverunt ad Khalaf[3] civitatem. Et docebant in synagoga Iudaeorum, et interpretabantur scripturas in aures audientium suorum, ut certiores faciant tanquam e scripturis verum esse quod docuit Paulus.[4]

xvii. 12-28.

At postquam crediderunt etiam in Khalaf et e Graecis et e feminis maximis, venerunt denuo etiam a Thessalonica, et turbaverunt urbem contra Paulum. Et praeteriit exiit Khalabean Thessalonicensium. Et abiit ille a Thessalonica,[5] unde expulsus est a persecutione. Sed impedivit [illum spiritus sanctus a praedicando[6] ne for]te occiderent [illum] . . . revert . . . (cun)ctos (venit Athenas et loquebatur in synagoga apud Iud)aeos et apud (liturgos, et adduxerunt eum in locum qui nom)ine vocatus (est Arispagos) . . . stetit (?) . . . su(o) novum aliquid (docet nos) . . . (res)ponsum dedit et ait illis (Paulus : Ministrare) et metuere scitis idolorum imagines, sed (nomen omnipotentis) dei cognoscitis, quomodo testificatur unum ex altar[ibus] vestris, illum veneramini.

---

[1] xvi. 39 ἠγνοήσαμεν τὰ καθ' ὑμᾶς ὅτι ἐστὲ ἄνδρες δίκαιοι D 383 614 minn hcl ⁕.

[2] xvi. 39 ἐκ τῆς πόλεως ταύτης ἐξέλθατε, μήποτε πάλιν συνστραφῶσιν ἡμῖν ἐπικράζοντες καθ' ὑμῶν D 383 614 minn hcl·⁕. Observe that the second invitation to depart, mentioned in the text of D, is not found in Ephrem ; see note supra, p. 160.

[3] Khalaf, i.e. Haleb, Beroea of the Thessalonians ; see Merk, op. cit. p. 47.

[4] xvii. 11 καθὼς Παῦλος ἀπαγγέλλει 383 614 gig Priscillian hcl ·⁕.

[5] See Merk, op. cit. pp. 239 f., and cf. supra, p. 382, No. 19. The Armenian is ' c̦ogav na i Tessalonikē.'

[6] xvii. 15 παρῆλθεν δὲ τὴν Θεσσαλίαν (Thessalonica ?), ἐκωλύθη γὰρ εἰς αὐτοὺς κηρύξαι τὸν λόγον D.

Ephrem : Et venientes deprecati sunt eos, et educentes rogabant ut egrederentur de urbe. So then that this act of grace might be unto them, they came and besought them saying : We knew not that ye were just, as the earthquake indeed has warned us about you. So we ask a grace of you, this, go up, depart from this city, lest perhaps after the earthquake there be gathered against you the same men who before the earthquake had been gathered. p. 302. 29 ff.
xvi. 39.

Et quidam ex eis crediderunt et adiuncti sunt Paulo et Silae. Clearly from among the Jews. . . . p. 306. 20.
xvii. 4.

Against the Caesar they say, because they proclaim a new ruler alongside of the Caesar. . . . Concitaverunt autem plebem et principes civitatis qui audiebant hoc, for the strategi were appalled and terrified at this report, et accepta satisfactione ab Iasone et a ceteris dimiserunt eos. This the magnates of the city did in order to appease the mob which surged against them.[1] p. 307. 9 ff.
xvii. 7-9.

But the Holy Spirit prevented him from preaching, lest perhaps they should slay him. p. 310. 38-
311. 1.
xvii. 15.

Paul saith, It must verily be of Jesus, and more especially of the Almighty God of all things. Him I announce to you, he says. p. 314. 32 f.
xvii. 23.

---

[1] The above is embedded in matter taken from Chrysostom.

Hunc exinde volo ostendere vobis, quod ipse est qui fecit mundum et omne quod in illo est, et non hebdomades,[1] neque habitat ille in templo sicut idola conflata vestra ; atque sacrificiis quibus daemones colebant, is non colitur, neque ullius eget omnium donator ; et ex uno sanguine,[2] id est, ex uno viro, factus est mundus hic filiorum hominum. Et divisit tempora aestatis et hiemis, et ordinavit terminos maris et siccae, et filiorum Noes. Et ut conquirant per manifesta absconditum, qui principium omnium ipse est, et ab eo stabiliuntur cuncta, et procul in abscondito suo. Quoniam per eum viximus in utero et per eundem apparemus.

[1] Perhaps a reference to Gnostic doctrine.
[2] xvii. 26 αἵματος D Iren Antiochian.

LACUNA, ACTS XVII. 29-XIX. 10

Ephrem : Non in manufactis templis habitat, he says, like your idols smelted. And with sacrifices with which demons are worshipped, he is not worshipped, and of nothing is he in need, the giver of all things.   *p. 315. 37-316. 3. xvii. 24-25.*

Ephrem : For these indeed especially communicated unto men knowledge, in every place the existence of heaven with its adornment, in every time the firm standing of earth. And he divided the seasons of summer and winter, and appointed limits of sea and dry land, even for the sons of Noe, in order that they might seek through things visible the hidden one, him that is himself cause of all.   *p. 318. 3 ff. xvii. 26-27.*

Ephrem : Rightly so, for the Athenians, who up to this passage had listened to him, had not patience to hear him about the resurrection, but they were vexed, and said : About this at another time let us hear you.   *p. 323. 15 ff. xvii. 32.*

Chrysostom : For he had to work, inasmuch as there in Corinth it was specially needful for him to take nothing because of false apostles, as he said in his letter to them : In quo gloriantur, et inveniantur sicut nos ; and non impediatur gloriatio mea in regionibus Achaiae ; and never for any act have we used this authority. Wherefore it was providentially arranged that there he should cling to them.[1]   *p. 325. 4 ff. xviii. 3.*

Ephrem : So then, on their turning against him, when he saw that the Jews outrageously outrage him, he shook out his garments, as he had learned from his Lord, and said : Let not your blood come after the preachers, who ever day by day in tribulation with divers afflictions gospel unto you the gospel of your Lord ; but let there come after you the voice which said : They would not harken unto me, as neither have ye, for ye refused to harken to me. So then I go unto the gentiles, who are prepared not to die through us like yourselves, but to live through us, which ye have not willed to do.   *p. 326. 1 ff. xviii. 6.*

Ephrem : So then, although also of the Jews one man only of the elders of the synagogue believed, yet the gentile Corinthians all together a big crowd [2] were baptized.   *p. 327. 12 ff.*

Chrysostom : . . . Sedit autem ibi annum unum et menses sex, et docebat illis verbum of the Lord. But when he continued to be there, the Jews bore it not, when they saw him making disciples of the gentiles. (vss. 12 and 13) . . . The Jews, in every way opposing the truth, after a year and six months were with one   *p. 328. 11 ff. xviii. 11-16.*

---

[1] The above is all from Chrysostom 295 c and 297 a, except the citation of 2 Cor. xi. 10 and xiii. 10, both loosely quoted from Armenian vulgate. Why does the catenist add the text of 2 Cor. xi. 10, containing the reference to Achaia ? Was it because he knew of the addition (xviii. 2) in D h hcl.*mg.* of the words οἱ καὶ κατῴκησαν εἰς τὴν ᾿Αχαίαν ? If so, was it from Ephrem that he knew of the addition ?

[2] xviii. 8 et [quomodo mult]a plebs Corinthiorum audierant verbum domini, [tinti sun]t credentes h.

LACUNA, ACTS XVII. 29-XIX. 10

accord come against him, and as they were not able to employ a
law of justice, they employed violence ; and because he continually
day by day taught them out of the law, they calumniated him before
the hegemon, and say : This man is teaching the sons of men to fear
God contra legem.   But he no ways complied with them, wherefore
Paul was in no way in need to make answer about this.[1]

Ephrem : If however he has done any wrong according to your
laws, or if unworthy statements should stand in his teaching, or
if whatever you say he rejects you, or if you should have [2] any flaw
in connection with his teaching or over your names and law, that
is, about the ruler Christ who is written of in the law, this do you
know, whatever among yourselves is your own in particular.   But
I was not sent to judge of those things, which infringe the keeping
of the law.

p. 329. 1 ff.
xviii. 14-15.

Ephrem : The Greeks who believed were beating Sosthenes
head of the synagogue.[3]

p. 329. 23 f.
xviii. 17.

Ephrem : And in order not as it were to see, the hegemon, (nor)
demand requital for the affront put on him, I mean on Sosthenes,
he became as one not seeing, so that his stripes might be all the
more.[4]

p. 329. 30 ff.
xviii. 17.

[1] Here the Syriasm ' the sons of men,' for τοὺς ἀνθρώπους betrays a Syriac
original, which can only be Ephrem, as does also the idiom *zayn or*, ' that
which,' which I render ' because.'   In Chrysostom, moreover, there is nothing
to correspond with the entire passage.   The comment fits the text of D h.
I confront it with the latter :

' were with one accord come against him, and as they were not able to employ a law of justice,	12 exurreserunt consentientes . . . et conlocuti secum de Paulo.
they employed violence ' . . .	inie[cerunt ei] manus,
' they calumniated him	et perduxerunt
before the hegemon	ad proconsulem,
and say '	13 cla[mantes] et dicentes

D reads, vs. 12. κατεπέστησαν ὁμοθυμαδὸν οἱ 'Ιουδαῖοι συνλαλήσαντες μεθ'
ἑαυτῶν ἐπὶ τὸν Παῦλον καὶ ἐπιθέντες τὰς χεῖρας ἤγαγον αὐτὸν ἐπὶ τὸ βῆμα καταβοῶντες καὶ λέγοντες.   Note that the catena, with hcl ⁎ and h, substitutes πρὸς
τὸν ἀνθύπατον for ἐπὶ τὸ βῆμα of the Greek MSS.   The word I render ' calumniated ' answers to καταβοῶντες, which has been found in no Greek MS. but D.

[2] xviii. 15 ἔχετε D, cf. gig (habetis).

[3] The Greek texts with unimportant exceptions read πάντες or πάντες οἱ
"Ελληνες, but h omits πάντες.   Ephrem in describing the Greeks who committed the outrage as those ' who believed ' at least implies the omission of
πάντες, even if his text did not contain οἱ πεπιστευκότες "Ελληνες.   Just
before, at the end of a section of Chrysostom, the catena has : ' By Greeks
here he means those Jews who spoke in the Greek language.'   This is not in
Chrysostom, and may well be Ephrem's.

[4] Et Gallio simulabat [se non vi]dere h ; tunc Gallio fingebat eum non
videre d ; D is illegible.

LACUNA, ACTS XVII. 29-XIX. 10

Anon. : He came then with Paul to Cenchron to the harbour p. 331. 18 ff.
of Corinth, for there Aquila had made a vow to shave his hair. xviii. 18 ff.
It was necessary also to offer a sacrifice by the hand of the priest,
in whatever he had been in transgression, to expiate by hand of him.
Ephrem : But when he reached Ephesus he left them (vss.
19 and 20) . . . So Paul came, reached Ephesus and with him
Aquila's party, and he spoke in the synagogue there ; and they
prayed him to remain with thém, but he consented not to tarry
with them, because it was necessary to set off to where he had
hurried himself to go.[1] But he did not simply leave them.[2]

Profectus ab Epheso et descendens Caesaream ascendit et salu- p. 332. 20 ff.
tavit ecclesiam in Jerusalem. Not for nothing had he hastened xviii. 21-22.
his journey to Caesarea, and afresh also to other regions, but in
order by his coming to confirm them. Descendit Antiochiam,
etc.[3]

Cum vellet, he says, ire in Achaiam, which is Hellada, the mother- p. 333. 28 ff.
land of the Corinthians, exhortati fratres scripserunt ad discipulos xviii. 27-28.
accipere eum ; qui cum venisset ibi, multum contulit iis qui crediderant. Vehementer enim Iudaeos revincebat publice, ostendens
per scripturas esse Christum Iesum. Aquila then and his accurately
narrated to Paulus [Apollos ?]. Nay, they urged him also to go
to Achaia, which he was himself anxious to do. And they gave
him a letter of testimony, because the man was unknown. But
he having gone, wrought much advantage, because he was very
expert in knowledge of the Scriptures, as he bore witness. And
because he was firm in the faith, he in that way accomplished his
course, preaching.[4]

[1] This seems to imply the ' Western ' addition found in D Antiochian.
[2] The rest of the paragraph is Chrys. 301 E οὐ μὴν ἁπλῶς αὐτοὺς εἴασεν . . .
[3] The above is embedded in matter from Chrysostom. Can we not trace
in the addition ' in Jerusalem' a reference to the Bezan addition (D HLP,
etc.) in vs. 21 δεῖ δὲ πάντως τὴν ἑορτὴν ἡμέραν ἐρχομένην ποιῆσαι εἰς Ἱεροσόλυμα ? The same addition underlies the passage, Catena, p. 331. 18-32, already
cited.
[4] In the above, which comes amid matter from Chrysostom, though his
Greek text has nothing similar, we have the following traces of D :
(1) The phrase ' Hellada the motherland of the Corinthians ' echoes (vs.
27) Κορίνθιοι . . . εἰς τὴν πατρίδα αὐτῶν.
(2) In the catena it is Aquila and his wife at Ephesus who exhort Apollonius (i.e. Apollos) to go to Corinth ; in D the Corinthians there ; the other
Greek texts write οἱ ἀδελφοί. Again, the catena says, ' urged him also to
go to Achaia,' and forthwith adds that he himself wanted to do so ; in D the
same sequence, παρεκάλουν . . . συνκατανεύσαντος δὲ αὐτοῦ. In the other Greek
texts βουλομένου δὲ αὐτοῦ begins the story.
(3) The catena, like D, omits διὰ τῆς χάριτος.
(4) The catena, ' But he having gone,' like the rendering in pesh hcl. text,
does not naturally suggest παραγενόμενος of the usual Greek text, nor ἐπιδημήσας

xix. 10-19.

. . . facta, don[ec omnibus audibilis factus est sermo quicunque habit]abant Asiam. Mul(ta signa fecit Paulus, et afferebant ad infirmos sudor)es eius, nam er(ant qui) [ponebant sudaria vel zon]am vel cing[ulum super] (ipsos), [et sta]tim curaban[tur a languoribus et mala daemonia discedebant]. (Imprimis filii sacerdotis idolorum) [1] super il(los qui habebant daemonia mala nomen Iesu nomi)nabant et dice(bant: [Adiuramus et iubemus te] (in no)men Christi de quo Paulus praedic[at]. (Et quando manifest)arunt dolum, quod exorciz(abant, tan)quam super illos qui daemoniaci erant. Illi (exorc)izabant super unum, et aiunt: Manda(mus tibi) in nomine Iesu, quem Paulus praedicat, ut exeas ab is(to ; [2] et) daemon conversus est ad cultorem daemonum et ait illis: Iesum cognosco Paulumque ipse de meo scio, vos autem confracti, dorsum contriti a daemonibus, vos qui estis, qui daemoniis exire mandatis ? Et stridit dentibus daemonium illud ad rectam et sinistram,[3] et expulit eos a domo. Manifestumque fuit illud cunctis, quodcunque factum est apud filios sacerdotis idolatri. Et incidit metus et pavor super Iudaeos et gentiles, quin hoc iterum facerent. Quidam vero magorum qui crediderunt libros suos magni pretii combusserunt igne.

xix. 21.

Paulus denuo posuit in mente sua per spiritum quomodo videret Macedoniam et [Achaiam, deinde rediret et veniret] Ierusalem ; quoniam non [sinebant videre eum regiones h]as Iudaei [qui in Iudaea habitabant]. (Sed etiam) [gestiebat postea et Romam urbem i]re et docere.

xix. 23-40.

(Et facta est in tempore eo) [perse]cutio magna propter it(er), [quae fuit per Demetrium au]ri opificem, nam opus ar(genti habebat, et congregans artifices artis su)ae turbabat [urbem omnem] eam universe ; cum diceret : Abhinc non nobis merces negotii, nam invenie-[bamus] e conchis quas operabamur ; qui[a] docuit et dis[ci]pulavit Paulus Asiam, ut credant non esse deos, si a filiis hominum fabricentur. Deprenderunt itineris socios Pauli, et introduxerunt eos in theatrum, et quia voluit Paulus ingredi theatrum, impediverunt eum discipuli eius propter multitudinosam congregationem. Sed quare utique congregati essent, non scibant. Postea dederunt consilium principes urbis civibus et aiunt : Quis est qui non scit civitatem nostram [4] cultricem esse Artemidos, cui obstare et frustrare mani-

---

[1] xix. 14. The space of the lacuna seems to make it probable that the MS. read ' priest,' not ' high-priest,' and (cf. D gig hcl.*mg*) did not render Ἰουδαίου (cf. Merk, *op. cit.* p. 242) ; see Textual Note *ad loc.* Ephrem makes no reference to the number of the sons (so D, but hcl.*mg* has ' seven ').

[2] xix. 14 παραγγέλλομέν σοι ἐν Ἰησοῦ ὃν Παῦλος ἐξελθεῖν κηρύσσει D w tepl hcl.*mg*.

[3] xix. 16. Cf. the catena, which suggests an original ἀκρωτηριάσας ἀπ' ἀμφοτέρων.

[4] xix. 35 τὴν ἡμετέραν πόλιν D.

Ephrem : Paul wished of his own will to go to Jerusalem, but the Spirit turned him back again to Asia, as he tells us : Factum est cum Apollo esset Corinthi, etc. (vss. 1-12).[1] *p. 334. 17 ff. xix. 1.*

And when Paul laid on them his hand, they received the Holy Spirit, spake with tongues, and interpreted themselves.[2] *p. 335. 36 ff. xix. 6. p. 338. 28 f.*

For the preaching was prolonged until the word was heard by all whoever were domiciled in Asia. *xix. 10. p. 338. 38-339. 1.*

Having taken upon themselves [3] they laid the napkin, the *zonarion* or girdle, and forthwith were healed of diseases, and the evil demons went out. *xix. 12. p. 339. 35 f. xix. 14. p. 340. 27 ff.*

But we adjure and command you in the name of Jesus, Go out of him. *xix. 13-16.*

Ephrem : Respondit spiritus nequam et dicit illis : Iesum novi et Paulum scio : vos autem qui estis ? You, he says, shattered, broken-backed by demons, who are you who order demons to go forth ? And the demon mutilated them on the right and on the left, and drove them forth from the house.

Ephrem : Dicebat : Post adventum meum illuc, oportet me et Romam videre. That is, that when he shall have seen Macedonia and Achaia, which is Hellada, then he will return and go to Jerusalem, because the Jews who lived in Judaea would not let him see these regions. *p. 345. 9 ff. xix. 21.*

Facta est autem illo tempore turbatio non minima de via. By the Way he means the course of the gospel, but by the disturbance the great persecution which befell by the hand of Demetrius the goldsmith. For it was about this he wrote to the Corinthians.[4] *p. 346. 15 ff. xix. 23.*

Chrys. (?) : Then he set forth the pains of indigence, and disturbs the whole city.

Ephrem : When he said : Henceforth we have no profit of our trade, for we obtained it out of the shrines we made. For Paul has taught and instructed Asia to believe there are not gods which may be fabricated with art by the sons of men, and since it was by this art we had to live, without it, lo, we risk falling into hunger. *p. 347. 17 ff. xix. 25-26.*

---

of D. Can the latter be a corruption of ἀποδημήσας, the ἐπι- being due to the preceding ἐπιδημοῦντες?

(5) In the catena πολύ comes before συνεβάλετο as in D gig Aug, not after it as in the other Greek mss.

[1] θέλοντος δὲ τοῦ Παύλου κατὰ τὴν ἰδίαν βουλὴν πορεύεσθαι εἰς Ἱεροσόλυμα, εἶπεν αὐτῷ τὸ πνεῦμα ὑποστρέφειν εἰς τὴν Ἀσίαν, D vg.cod. R[2] hcl.mg.

[2] Here perp adds 'ita ut ipsi sibi interpretarentur'; cf. hcl.mg. The catenist closes a section of Chrysostom with the above, but it is certainly Ephrem.

[3] xix. 12. This seems to imply ἐπιφέρεσθαι D Antiochian.

[4] Here a scrap of Ephrem is set in an alien context.

festum est neminem posse ?   Hic [1] ergo Demetrius ignobilis et turpis, immo pueri artis eius, si iudicium (δίκην) habeant inter sese, proveniant et ostendant hegemoni. Etenim [si petitio aliqua [2] sit adversus ali]quem agenda, di[iudicetur in legitima congregatione, quia in magno tumu]ltu sumus [et in grave discrimen incidimus].

xx. 1-3.   [Quia] (habebant Iudaei) odium magnum contra e[um, voluit abire Syriam.   At fecit reverti [3] eum spiritus, atque ab]iit in Macedoniam.

xx. 6-12.   Et (venit in Troada, et quum) [loqueretur] ibi a mane usque [in mediam noctem (Paulus), So]pitus adolescens cec[idit de tertio coenac]ulo, nam sedebat ibi, et tradidit animam. [Et descendit] Paulus et illapsus est super eum et vivificavit e[um].

xx. 13-16.   Ego Lucas et qui mecum intravimus navem et profecti sumus (Ass)um venturi ad Paulum, quomodo et mandavit (ille nobis.   Et tra)nsivimus cum illo oppida multa, quia fe(sti)nans properabat venire facere pentecostem in Ierusalem.

---

[1] xix. 38 Δημήτριος οὗτος D pesh.

[2] xix. 39.   Ephrem seems to have read περὶ ἑτέρων with D and most uncials (but not B).

[3] xx. 3 εἶπεν δὲ τὸ πνεῦμα αὐτῷ ὑποστρέφειν D gig hcl.*mg.*

Ephrem : This Demetrius, disreputable and infamous, he says, yea and the children of his craft, if they have any suit with other, let them stand forth and show it before the hegemon ; and if there be any other dispute, let it be settled in the legal assembly. p. 352. 3 ff.
xix. 38-39.

Ephrem : Cum fecisset ibi menses tres, factae sunt illi insidiae a Iudaeis, quum vellet exire in Syriam. Consilium habuit reverti in Macedoniam. Since the Jews plotted against him, he desired to depart to Syria, but the Spirit turned him back to Macedonia. p. 354. 11 ff.
xx. 3.

Ephrem : For as Paul talked from dawn until midnight, a youth went to sleep and fell from the third story—for he was sitting there —and gave up the ghost. And Paul went down, fell upon him, and raised, quickened him as he relates : Erant autem lampades, etc. (vss. 8-11). p. 356. 7 ff.
xx. 7-10.

Now in many places Paul was separated from his disciples, and here again he has gone by land on foot. But Luke and those (or he) with me, having entered a ship, we bore up to Ason, and there we expected again to pick up Paul ; for so he had instructed, until he was about to proceed by land ; but when he met us in Ason, having picked him up we came to Mytilene. Thus to lighter purposes urging them, but the harder toil taking on himself, he had gone off on foot, at the same time planning to discipline the disciples and instruct them by detaching themselves from him.[1] p. 357. 21 ff.
xx. 13-14.

[1] The question arises whether in vs. 13 Ephrem's Syriac text of Acts read : ' But I, Luke, and those with me.' This we we cannot say for certain, but that the Armenian translator found the words in Ephrem's Syriac commentary is certain ; otherwise, why should he render them ? Everywhere else in the we-passages the bare ἡμεῖς is reflected in the version unaltered.

Comparing the catena here with Codex 571 we note : (1) The catena reproduces verses 13 and 14 exactly as they stand in the Armenian vulgate except for the initial words. It omits, however, ' I ' before ' Luke,' and has mteal i navn, ' having entered the ship,' where Codex 571 has mtav i nav yev, ' he entered a ship and.' Here mtav, the third person singular, is an obvious scribe's error for mtaq, ' we entered,' or for mteal, ' having entered.'

(2) The catenist was so struck by the variant that he kept it and transferred it into the heart of matter from Chrysostom, in whose text, as given in the New College MS., the passage runs thus : πολλαχοῦ τῶν μαθητῶν ὁ Παῦλος χωρίζεται. ἰδοὺ γὰρ πάλιν, αὐτὸς μὲν πεζεύει, ἡμεῖς δέ φησιν ἐμβάντες ἐπὶ τὸ πλοῖον ἀνήχθημεν εἰς τὴν Θάσσον, ἐκεῖθεν (κτλ. as far as Μυτιλήνην, but reading Θάσσον a second time). κουφότερον ἐκείνοις ἐπιτρέπων, τὸ δὲ ἐπιπονώτερον αὐτὸς αἱρούμενος. ἐπέξευεν, ἄμα καὶ πολλὰ οἰκονομῶν, παιδεύων τε αὐτοὺς χωρίζεσθαι αὐτοῦ. ἀνήχθημέν φησιν εἰς τὴν Θάσσον. εἶτα παρέρχονται τὴν νῆσον. κἀκεῖθέν φησιν ἀποπλεύσαντες τῇ ἐπιούσῃ κατηντήσαμεν ἄντικρυς Χίου. This was also the text which the Armenian translator of Chrysostom had before him. The Benedictine text makes nonsense by reading παιδεύων μηδὲ αὐτοὺς χωρίζεσθαι αὐτοῦ.

(3) In the catena and in Chrysostom stress is laid on the fact that Paul often separated himself from his companions, and the passage to Assos is selected as an example. It is natural for a commentator who takes such a line to explain that here ἡμεῖς in the Greek signifies, not (as generally) ' Paul

xx. 22-34.

Et aiebat: Incedo vinctus spiritu Ierusalem. Incepit igitur narrare vere quaecunque eventura erant sibi per sacerdotes et scribas. Sed propter sanctos qui erant in Ierusalem veniebat consolari eos, iterumque ut ostenderet tormenta non metum incutere sibi. Immo ut ostendat quomodo sine scrupulo, sine metu, sine ignavia obviam tribulationi festinans iret contra. Aiebat autem eiusmodi: Nihil aestimavit anima mea aliquid pretiosius quam cursum meum. Id est, non pretii facio animam meam quam [1] labores it[ineris et quam ministeri]um evan[gelii sermonis [2] quod a domino nostro accep]eram, ut testi[ficer Iudaeis et gentilibus.[3] Et dicebat quod us]que hodie [4] purus sum [a sanguine omnium vestrum, n]am omnes tribulationes (sustinui)[pro ev]angelismo quem evangel[izo vobis; quia non missus] sum turbare vos [neque veni alio con]silio, sed ob hoc solum, ut in morte [et in vi]ta viam commodi vestri indic(ans prae)dicarem vobis. Prophetavit iterum de [apost]olorum falsitate, qui erant confus[uri] vitae viam. Et dixit quod argentum et a[ur]um et vestem non concupivi, sed laboravi et vivere de manibus meis non piger eram.

xxi. 1-3.
xxi. 15.
xxiii. 8-10.

Profecti sumus et venimus usque ad Tzor, et quando intravimus Ierusalem, Sadducaeis negantibus resurrectionem praedicavit; iudicium quod dignum iudicabat frustratum est.

xxii. 30.

Iterum conduxit eum centurio ut ante eosdem iudicaretur.

xxiii. 1-10.

Ait illis Paulus: Ego in omnibus bonis consiliis ambulavi coram deo usque hodie. Postquam vero propter hoc iussit sacerdos percutere os eius, quomodo Vae! dedit doctor eius sacerdotibus et Pharisaeis in die crucifixionis suae, eodem modo imprecatus est etiam ille diras sacerdoti, aitque illi: Quoniam ius(sisti percutere os meum in)iuste, percus(surus est etiam te deus . . .) quoniam paries es dealbatus, (quod et Christus prius dix)it eis: Quod similes estis (vos sepulchris dealbatis), intra vero pleni estis om(ni malitia. Et ille) castigatus est quia spre(vit sacerdotem quem non) agnoscebat. Quando agnovit, dixit: (Scriptum est . . . quod) ne dicant quod per vision(em . . . didicit) dum incedebat cum occisor(ibus Damascum, de pla)gis suis fiduciam suam (coram omnibus) accedebat ostendebat. Atque ut dic[ant: Verum est] quod audiverant de eo quoad legem, quia [ecce et sac]erdotem plus quam legem spre[vit, accu]rrit ad legem in verbo quod dixit et de lege quod iteravit. Et ut ostenderet iis qui sedentes iudicabant eum tanquam transgressorem, quod observabat legem et diligebat eam; quamvis enim pauculum pauculum quicquam frustraret, circumcisionem enim et sabbata dissolvebat, illi vero in maximis etiam dissolvebant eam, quia angelos et spiritum et resurrectionem quam praedicabat lex, ii non confitebantur. Illos igitur, quia omnes contra eum erant, inter sese, quia

---

[1] xx. 24 τοῦ τελειῶσαι D, cf. vg.　[2] xx. 24 τὴν διακονίαν τοῦ λόγου D gig.
[3] xx. 24 Ἰουδαίοις καὶ Ἕλλησιν D gig sah.
[4] xx. 26 ἄχρι οὖν τῆς σήμερον ἡμέρας D.

Ephrem: For as he began to tell truly what events were to happen to him in Jerusalem at the hands of priests and scribes; but he, because of the saints who were in Jerusalem, was coming to comfort them, and further in order to show that sufferings had no terror for him; for, lo, without a qualm of a fear, without flinching, he hastened on to confront tribulation. However he adds and says: I have not esteemed my soul more valuable than the labours of the gospel of life and than the service of the gospel's word, which from our Lord I received; that is, in order that I may bear witness to Jews and gentiles.

p. 363. 33-364. 5.
xx. 23-24.

Ephrem: For indeed he was about to say something heavier, namely: Mundus sum a sanguine vestrum omnium, for in nothing have I fallen short of my precepts, and all tribulations have I borne for the sake of the gospel which I gospel unto you. For I came not with any other design, but with this alone, that combating with death and with life I might indicate to you your advantage.[1]

p. 364. 10 ff.
xx. 26-27.

Ephrem: And in that he called them shepherds ordained by the Spirit, like the lord Peter, about whom although he prophesies the truth of the apostles who were in the future to deflect from the straight the path of life, yet keeping the order of his theme he opportunely adds: Ego enim scio, etc.[2]

p. 366. 7 ff.
xx. 28-29.

p. 398. 25 ff.
xxiii. 1-10.

So then that they might not say that, It is true whatever they heard about him as to the law being contemned, for, lo, it was even the priests more than the law he set at naught, he proceeded to the law.[3]

---

and I Luke,' but ' I Luke and those with me, *minus* Paul.' As long therefore as I had only the catena before me, I assumed that we were in presence of a mere gloss of Ephrem's. But with the full commentary of Ephrem as a check I do not feel so sure, for in it the text comes like a bolt from the blue, with no comment to explain it. Perhaps the older commentator used by Chrysostom also read, like Ephrem, ἐγὼ δὲ Λουκᾶς καὶ οἱ σὺν ἐμοί, and it was this in his text of Acts which excited his comment, and not *vice versa*.

[1] The first words of the above are from Chrysostom 332 D μέλλει τι φορτικώτερον λέγειν, ὅτι καθαρός εἰμι ἐγὼ ἀπὸ τοῦ αἵματος πάντων ὑμῶν, ὅτι οὐδὲν ἐλλείπεται. But the entire paragraph is labelled ' Ephrem.'

[2] Here a scrap of Ephrem is imported into matter from Chrysostom, and the whole is labelled 'Ephrem.' ' Truth,' Arm. *stugnuthiun*, is an error for *stuthiun* ' falsity,' read in the full text, and is a variant in some MSS.

[3] This is embedded in Chrysostom.

ad causam resurrectionis, quod dignum erat, assenti[ebant. Denuo] cohors Romanorum [rapuerunt eum et in aede car]ceris propter Iudaeos [et occisores suos celaverunt eum, itaque cus]toditus est.

Audibiles (erant) [insidiae] (apud Lysiam), is enim erat caput mil(lium). [Quum audisset iuramentum XL] virorum qui iuraverant occi[dere Paulum, furavit] eum nocte et per Rom[anos dedit conduci eum] ad Felicem hegemona in Caesar[eam].

xxiii. 12-
xxiv. 10.

(Et post quinque dies descendit) Ananias sacerdotum princeps (cum senioribus quibusdam ut) per Tertelium rheto(rem accusatores fi)ant contra Paulum. Postquam vero ad(venit et) [locutus est rhe]tor de pace populi· eorum et de tumultu quem in omnibus locis incitabat contra eos Paulus, deinde mandatum factum est Paulo dare responsum pro se ipso.[1]

[1] xxiv. 10 defensionem habere pro se, hcl.*mg.*

So in the matter of the resurrection which is certain, some agreed, but half of them did not believe, and they, though they were all against him, were against each other mightily in dispute.[1] p. 400. 30 ff. xxiii. 7-9.

Ephrem : Again the cohort of Romans snatched him away, and hid him in the prison because of the Jews and their assassins. And since they were about to slay him eagerly, from such a risk he was rescued. p. 401. 31 ff. xxiii. 10.

But it was providentially arranged that he should comprehend their craftiness. . . . For when the tribune heard the oath of the forty men, which they swore to slay Paul, he stole him by night and gave him to be conducted by Romans to Felix the hegemon in Caesarea.[2] p. 404. 32 ff. 36 ff. xxiii. 12-24.

Ephrem : For when the rhetor talked about the peace of their synagogue (or people) and about the disturbance which everywhere Paul stirred up against them, forthwith an order was made to Paul to make answer for himself. p. 410. 5 ff xxiv. 2-10.

Ephrem : But he stood forward and said : They have dubbed me a lunatic and madman and disturber of the people. Be sure, hegemon, that in their city I have been a few days and not many. And in the temple there when I was worshipping, they came, found me, and it is not the case that I had gathered a concourse of my own and was teaching it. If then in their population (or concourse) outside the city or right there within their city they failed to catch or detect me collecting a concourse to teach, how do they come and accuse me as a chicaner, in whom none of these transgressions were found ? p. 410. 28 ff. xxiv. 12-13.

Ephrem : However, although I am a Christian, as they allege, yet I too worship the God of our fathers, of Abraham and of his, who without the law worshipped God. As in the law and prophets whatever is written do I believe. p. 411. 18 ff. xxiv. 14.

Now how or why did I raise a tumult among them, he says, for the conferring of alms on whom I have come so long a journey ? For such is not the work of a raiser of tumults.[3] p. 412. 27 ff. xxiv. 17.

Ephrem : Iussit centurioni custodire eum et habere in requie, nec quemquam de suis prohibere ministrare ei. The hegemon then though in sentencing unjustly he did not sentence him, yet neither justifying did he justify him ; he placed him in custody. He did not want to let him go because of them, and he was unable to torture him, because it seemed shameful without crime to do this.[4] p. 415. 20 ff. xxiv. 23.

[1] This is worked into matter from Chrysostom. It seems to restore the text of Ephrem's commentary, in which after ' inter sese ' some word like ' scinde-bat ' has dropped out, and the text must also have read ' quidam assentiebant, quidam vero non credebant.' Ephrem read something similar to ' inter eos dividebantur,' as in h. [2] The above embedded in Chrysostom.

[3] The above is embedded in Chrysostom matter.

[4] The last sentence of the above is from Chrysostom 379 B.

Is ante stetit incepit loqui : Aestimaverunt me dementem et insanum et agitatorem populi. Sed hoc scito, hegemon, quod in civitate eorum paucae dies sunt meae, neque multum quid, in templo quando adorabam, invenerunt me, neque congregationem separatim congregaveram et docebam. Si igitur in congregatione [1] extra civitatem sive hic in civitate nequiverunt captare et invenire me, quod congregaverim [congregationem, quia docebam, quo]modo igitur in [quo haec omnia delicta non inven]erunt, adeuntes accu[sant me tanquam dol]osum ; nihilominus, [quamvis et Christianus et]iam sim, veluti et aiunt, [tamen deum patrum] nostrum Abrahamaeorum qui [sine lege venerati sunt deum] veneror ego ; [sicut in lege et prophetis in quibus] credunt isti, credo ego. Si ergo tan[quam] . . . (pu)eros congregationis meae (adveni tantam viam ob)laturus sacri- ficia in temp[lo], (ibique accusat)ores meos, quando purificabar, invenerunt quod (non cum multis) sive in turba multorum, sed solum (separatim). Ergo dicant accusatores et adversarii mei quare clamaverint de me, ut amoveatur inter nos,[2] aiunt, nequam et turpis. Sed hegemon quamvis inculpans in iniquitate non inculpavit eum, utique neque iustificans iustificavit illum. Apprehendit posuit illum in custodia, quia pecuniae spem habebat.

Venit ergo Festus alius hegemon Ierusalem. Adeunt sacer- dotes et dicunt illi de Paulo. Dedit mandatum et ait, Caesareae audiant iudicium. Quumque plurimis verbis iterum calumnia- rentur illum, at nihil huiusmodi potuerunt demonstrare, quia ante horam illam proposuerat in mente Paul[us ire Romam urbem et] impeditus est, et propos[uit et meditatus est ap]pellare Caesarem, ut [donec adveniens attin]gat Romam apud Caesarem, do[ceat et discipulos reddat] creaturas in do[ctrina Christi ; advenit descendit] rex Agrippas qui stetit [in loco principatus] Herodis ad salutandum hegemon[a. Is stetit indica]vit illi causam Pauli, et quod [peti- verant Paulum Iu]daei ab ipso. Sed timuit propter l[egem Romano- rum dare eum in ma]nus eorum, quoniam non inventum est in illo de[lictum, nisi] detractio legis Iudaeorum.

[Voluit] ipse Agrippas videre Paulum, quomodo Herodes, quia voluit videre dominum nostrum. Iussit agi eum Festus coram eo.[3] Quando vero dedit illi mandatum loqui Agrippas, dedit responsum et ait illi : Fiducialiter aliquatenus speraveram, quia beatum aestimo me, quod sine scrupulo interritus ingressus coram legis filio, quia legis gnarus et peritus es, do apologiam. Stetit coram iis et adiit

---

[1] Throughout this passage the word used may mean *populus* or *congregatio* equally.

[2] Ephrem's text seems to have contained an addition at the close of vs. 18 similar to that of vg.*codd* et apprehenderunt me clamantes et dicentes : Tolle inimicum nostrum.

[3] xxv. 23 iussit Festus adduci Paulum, gig s

Ephrem : For as Festus wished to make of him a present to their designs, and as before that hour Paul had settled it in his mind to go to the city of Rome and was prevented, he bethought him and purposed to appeal to Caesar, that until he going should reach Rome, unto the Caesar, he might teach and school the world in the doctrine of Christ. p. 419. 32 ff. xxv. 11.

King Agrippas came, descended, who stood in the place of the principality of Herod to salute the hegemon. He stood related before him the suit of Paul, and that the Jews asked of him Paul, but he feared for the law of the Romans to give him into their hands. For he found not about him any transgression, except that he defamed the law of the Jews.[1] p. 421. 18 ff. xxv. 13-19.

[1] The above under title of 'Chrysostom.'

repetivit de prima habitatione iuventutis suae in Ierusalem, quibusque casibus submisit ab initio eos qui invocarunt nomen Iesu. Narravit illi etiam de visione quam vidit in via Damasci, et in Ierusalem et apud gentiles, quomodo dat[um est illi mandatum, praedicavit], quia propter hoc deprehenderunt (eum in templo occisuri). Neque denique dixit illi prae(terquam quae scrip)ta sunt in libris prophetar(um, sed . . . haec) e lege et e prophe(tis stabilivit exem)plis, prae lege fili(i . . .) legem ipsius tanquam stren(uos testes verborum) suorum faciebat.

xxvi. 26-32.   Rex aut[em qui in prophetis] credebat, sed assentiri proph[etiae eorum no]lebat, respondit et ait: (In modico pu)to hodie persuades me (fieri Ch)ristianum. Ait illi Paulus : In modico (et) in magno, id est, sive parvi sive magnates, seu quando fit in me virtus, et implentur in me tribulationes, ego hoc modo in precibus sto, ut auditores mei ad instar ipsius fiant, exceptis vinculis his quibus ante vos vinctus adsto. Inceperunt illi dicere inter sese duo duobus, quod fas et possibile esset dimitti Paulum, accurate aiebat, appellabat Caesarem, nisi vultum Caesaris quaesivisset videre.

xxvii. 1-24.   Sedere fecerunt eum cum Luca et cum Aristarcho Macedone. Et advenerunt Tsadan et Cyprum et mare Ciliciae, (et inde navigarunt descenderunt Lici)am usque Nimer[1] urbem et (ibi intraverunt navem quae por)tabat in Italiam. Et praeven[it eis tempestas aspere] flans glaci[alis, et contorsum est mare] undis suis, et exorta [super illos distrac]tio cumulatarum undarum [spumantium, et proiecerunt] armamenta navis in mare. (Tunc) [revelavit] Paulus de angelo qui ap[paruit illi et dixit]: Coram Caesare adstiturus [es tu, et navis] ista frangitur, sed vir unus ex ducentis et sept[uaginta[2]] non perdetur.

xxviii. 1-10.   Ergo ascendentibus [illis] e mari apportaverunt barbari et rudes homines ignigena minuta sarmenta ponere ignem et calefacere eos. Advenit congregavit de eodem etiam Paulus. At exivit vipera et involvit sese circum manum eius. Et videbatur incolis regionis quod occisura sit eum. Ille vibravit manum suam et proiecit eam in ignem, non nocuit illi. Illi vero, quando viderunt in manu eius occisorem, reum sanguinis appellarunt eum ; quando autem proiecit eam neque illi nocuit, deum appellarunt eum, quia misericordias multas fecit apud nos, occisorem enim vastatorem incolarum regionis consumpsit in igni coram nobis. Operatus est etiam alias virtutes in insula, patrem enim hospitis sui curavit a difficili afflictione, pluribusque languentium qui ibi erant data est per manum eius curatio. Ergo honoraverunt, dederunt opsonia.

---

[1] Nimer, i.e. Μύρα. The n belongs to a preceding word and the first i signifies 'to.' Akinean regards it as a corruption of Smyrna.

[2] xxvii. 37. Merk, op. cit. p. 244, observes that the lacuna has space for '276,' but that in the catena the reading '270' (so Greek codex 69) is secure.

But when he repeated his first dwelling of his childhood in Jerusalem and what he inflicted on those who called on the name of Jesus, he also told of the dream he saw on the road of Damascus, and that in Jerusalem and to the gentiles, as was given him the command to convert, he preached. p. 430. 30 ff. xxvi. 4-20.

Ephrem : But the king, who believed in the prophets but did not wish to agree with their prophecies, forestalled him and said : In modico suades me fieri Christianum. That is, it is a skimpy and small sort of thing you are trying to persuade me of. p. 432. 23 ff. xxvi. 28.

Ephrem : I would that they who to-day hear me might become like me, small ones or great. I would that while there be in me powers, there be fulfilled in me tribulations. That is, I deem little the fulfilment of powers unto the great longing for tribulations. But so do I pray that my hearers should become like myself apart from the fetters in which I stand bound in tribulation. p. 433. 4 ff. xxvi. 29.

Anon. : And here after its being said : Thou art mad, they began to say to each other, two to two : It was possible he should be set free. And they not only let him off death, but he would have been altogether set free from his bonds, had he not appealed to Caesar. p. 435. 8 ff. xxvi. 32.

Ephrem : But when a storm caught them of bitter blast, and the sea became tempestuous with its billows, and there arose against them torrential piles of frothing waves, they cast off the movables into the sea. p. 438. 18 ff. xxvii. 14-18

Ephrem : Paul revealed about the angel which appeared to him and said to him, Before Caesar art thou to stand, and your ship is shattered, and not a man of the 270 men in it shall be lost. Sed posteaquam, etc. (vss. 27-32). p. 439. 31-440. 9. xxvii. 22-24. (xxvii. 37).

Ephrem : Because when they went up from the sea the rude barbarians brought firewood broken up small to lay a fire and warm them. Paul came and gathered, and out of it issued a viper and wound itself round his hand. As it seemed to the natives it would kill him, they called him guilty of blood. But when they beheld him shake his hand and toss the slayer into the fire and that it nowise had hurt him, they dubbed him a god, for that he wrought a great mercy upon them, in burning before our eyes in the fire the deadly slayer of the inhabitants of those regions. p. 444. 15 ff. xxviii. 3-6.

Behold again some other than that one, wonders and powers which he wrought in the island, for he healed the father of their host, and to many sick who were there was given by means of him healing.[1] p. 446. 4 ff. xxviii. 7-9.

---

[1] This stands at the end of a paragraph marked ' Chrysostom.'

Et ingressi sunt Romam. Convocavit Paulus principes Iudaeorum et manifestavit illis quod propter Christianitatem traditus erat in vincula gentilium per Iudaeos, et: Quia voluerunt Iudaei occidere me, necesse fuit mihi appellare Caesarem. At vocavi vos, non tantum ut viderem vos, sed etiam ut enarrarem vobis haec omnia. Et locutus est cum iis a mane usque ad vesperam de Christo e lege et e prophetis. Iteravit de infidelibus qui non consentiverunt verbo Isaiae quod dixit: Quod audiant non intelligant. Quando vero tentavit eos, iterum memoravit etiam de operibus manuum suarum,[1] quod dedit mercedem domus biennio uno ; loqui cum Iudaeis et cum gentilibus[2] qui ascendebant ad eum de Christo non cessabat, et aiebat quod Iesus est filius dei,[3] quod pro eo laboramus et attinemus coronas, per dominum nostrum Iesum Christum, cui cum patre, simul et spiritui sancto, gloria potestas et honor in secula ; amen.

[1] xxviii. 30. Merk, pp. 244 f., would translate ' eius,' taking the subject of ' memoravit ' to be ' the author of Acts.' ' Iterum ' will then refer to Acts xviii. 3, xx. 34.

[2] xxviii. 30 Ἰουδαίους τε καὶ Ἕλληνας, 614 minn gig p vg.*codd* hcl ⁙.

[3] xxviii. 31 quia hic est Iesus filius dei p, cf. vg.*codd* hcl.*text*.

Ephrem: Mansit autem biennio toto in suo conducto et suscipiebat omnes qui ingrediebantur ad eum. As then he conversed with Jews from morning till eve about Christ out of the law and the prophets, and repeated about the unbelievers who accepted not the word of Isaiah ; Luke in turn recorded also about the works and labour of his hands,[1] which he gave as the hire of his house for a two years' space ; and how he ceased not to converse about Christ with Jews and gentiles, who came out from and went in to him, and he alleged that Jesus Christ is the Son of God, because for his sake we toil and win crowns through Christ.

p. 454. 35-
455. 7.
xxviii. 30-
31.
xxviii. 23.

[1] See J. R. Harris, *Four Lectures on the Western Text of the New Testament,* 1894, pp. 50 f. Cf. Ephrem, *Commentarii in epistolas D. Pauli,* p. 256, prologue to 2 Timothy : ' Penulam autem et libros jussit afferre, aut ut venditis illis penderet pro domo conducta aut ut haereditare faceret cui justum esset,' and the very peculiar statement of the Preface to Acts, above, p. 384, No. 32.

INDEX

Incidental allusions in Part II. of the Introductory Essay ("The Criticism and History of the Text") are not all mentioned in this Index. For the Textual Notes the Index gives only references to modern writers there named.